A Global History of Architecture

Second Edition

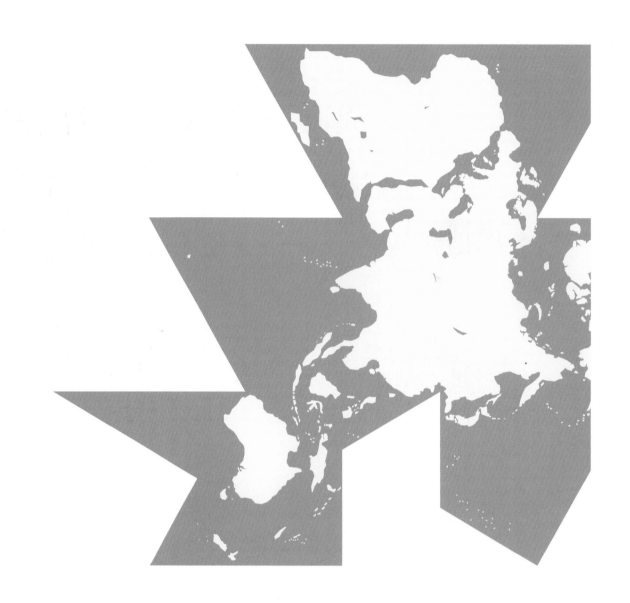

A Global History of Architecture

Second Edition

Francis D. K. Ching

Mark Jarzombek

Vikramaditya Prakash

John Wiley & Sons, Inc.

This book is printed on acid-free paper.

Published by John Wiley & Sons, Inc., Hoboken, New Jersey
Published simultaneously in Canada

For general information about our other products and services, please contact our
Customer Care Department within the United States at (800) 762-2974, outside the
United States at (317) 572-3993 or fax (317) 572-4002.

Wiley also publishes its books in a variety of electronic formats. Some content that
appears in print may not be available in electronic books. For more information about
Wiley products, visit our web site at www.wiley.com.

Library of Congress Cataloging-in-Publication Data

Ching, Frank, 1943-
 A global history of architecture / Francis D.K. Ching, Mark M. Jarzombek, Vikramaditya Prakash. -- 2nd ed.
    p. cm.
 Includes index.
  ISBN 978-0-470-40257-3 (hardback)
 1. Architecture--History. I. Jarzombek, Mark. II. Prakash, Vikramaditya. III. Title.
 NA200.C493 2010
 720.9--dc22

                        2010040984

Printed in the United States of America

10 9 8 7 6 5 4

Contents

CONTENTS

CONTENTS

CONTENTS

Preface

What is a global history of architecture? There is, of course, no single answer, just as there is no single way to define words like *global*, *history*, and *architecture*. Nonetheless, these words are not completely open-ended, and they serve here as the vectors that have helped us construct the narratives of this volume. With this book, we hope to provoke discussion about these terms, and at the same time furnish a framework students can use to begin discussion in the classroom.

This book is global in that it aspires to represent the history of the whole world. Whereas any such book must inevitably be selective about what it can and cannot include, we have attempted to represent a wide swath of the globe, in all its diversity. At the same time, for us, the global is not just a geographic construct that can be simply contrasted with the regional or local: the global is also a function of the human imagination, and one of the things we are very interested in is the manner in which local histories imagine the world. This book, however, is not about the sum of all local histories. Its mission is bound to the discipline of architecture, which requires us to see connections, tensions, and associations that transcend so-called local perspectives. In that respect, our narrative is only one of many possible narratives.

Synchrony has served as a powerful frame for our discussion. For instance, as much as Seoul's Gyeongbok Palace is today heralded in Korea as an example of traditional Korean architecture, we note that it also belongs to a Eurasian building campaign that stretched from Japan (the Katsura Imperial Villa), through China (Beijing and the Ming Tombs), to Persia (Isfahan), India (the Taj Mahal), Turkey (the Suleymaniye Complex), Italy (St. Peter's Basilica and the Villa Rotonda), Spain (El Escorial), France (Chambord), and Russia (Cathedral of the Assumption). The synchrony of these buildings opens up for us questions such as, What did one person know about the other? How did information travel? How did architectural culture move or become "translated"? Some of these questions we have addressed directly; others we have raised and left unanswered. But to call Gyeongbok Palace traditional is to overlook the extraordinary modernity of all the buildings listed above.

This is not to say that our story is only the story of influence and connection. There are numerous examples of architectural production where the specific circumstances of their making were unique to their own immediate context. Indeed, we have tried to be faithful to the specificities of each individual building while acknowledging that every specific architectural project is always embedded in a larger world that affects it directly or indirectly. These effects could be a consequence of the forces of economy, trade, and syncretism; of war, conquest, and colonization; or the exchange of knowledge, whether forced, borrowed, or bought.

Our post–19th century penchant to see history through the lens of the nation-state often makes it difficult to decipher such global pictures. Furthermore, in the face of today's increasingly hegemonic global economy, the tendency by historians, and often enough by architects, to nationalize, localize, regionalize, and even microregionalize history—perhaps as meaningful acts of resistance—can blind us to the historical interconnectivity of global realities. What would the Turks be today had they stayed in East Asia? The movement of people, ideas, and wealth has bound us to each other since the beginning of history. And so without denying the reality of nation-states and their claims to unique histories and identities, we have resisted the temptation to streamline our narratives to fit nationalistic guidelines. Indian architecture, for instance, may have some consistent traits from its beginnings to the present day, but there is less certainty about what those traits might be than one may think. The flow of Indian Buddhism to China, the settling of Mongolians in the north, the influx of Islam from the east, and the colonization by the English from the coast—not to mention India's then-current economic expansion—are just some of the more obvious links that bind India, for better or worse, to global events. It is as much these links, and the resultant architecture, as the "Indianness" of Indian architecture, that interests us. Furthermore, India has historically been divided into numerous kingdoms that, like Europe, could easily have evolved (and in some cases did evolve) into their own nations. The 10th-century Chola dynasty of peninsular India, for example, was not only an empire but possessed a unique world view of its own. In writing its history, we have attempted to preserve its distinct identity while marking the ways in which it maps its own global imagination.

Broadly speaking, our historiographic goal is to help students of architecture develop an understanding of the manner in which architectural production is always triangulated by the exigencies of time and location. More specifically, we have narrated these interdependencies to underscore what we consider to be the inevitable modernity of each period. We often think of the distant past as moving slowly from age to age, dynasty to dynasty, or king to king, and only of our recent history as moving at a faster pace. In such a teleological view, the modern present is at the apex of civilization, and history becomes a narrative of progress

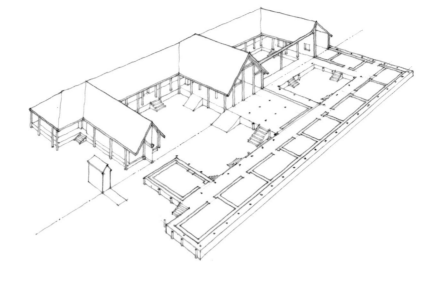

that is measured against the values of the present. By contrast, we have tried to present every period in history in terms of its own challenges and the history of architecture as the history of successive and often dramatic changes spurred on by new materials, new technologies, changing political situations, and changing aesthetic and religious ideals. These changes, spelled out differently in different times, have always challenged the norm in a way that we, in our age, would call modernity.

The Sumerian urbanization of the Euphrates Delta made the earlier village-centered economy of the Zagros Mountains obsolete. The introduction of iron in the 9th century BCE spelled the demise of the Egyptians and allowed societies such as the Dorians, Etruscans, and Nubians, who were once relatively marginal in the global perspective, to suddenly dominate the cultural and architectural landscape. The Mongolian invasion of the 13th century may have destroyed much, but in its wake came unprecedented developments. By concentrating on the modernity of each historical example, we have used the global perspective to highlight the drama of historical change, rather than viewing architecture as driven by traditions and essences.

Turning now to the term *architecture*, few would have any difficulty in differentiating it from the other arts, like painting and sculpture. But what architecture itself constitutes is always the subject of great debate, particularly among architects, architectural historians, and critics. Some have argued that architecture arises out of an urge to protect oneself from the elements, others that it is an expression of symbolic desires, or that it is at its best only when it is embedded in local traditions. In this book, without foreclosing the discussion, we hope that the reader begins to see architecture as a type of cultural production.

We have emphasized issues of patronage, use, meaning, and symbolism, where appropriate, and have attempted to paint a broad civilizational picture of time and context while, at the same time, making sure we have covered the salient formal features of a structure. Of course, words like *culture* and *civilization* are, like the word *architecture*, open to contestation and will have different meanings in different contexts. Yet despite these ambiguities, we believe that civilization is unthinkable without those buildings that are given special status, whether for purposes of religion, governance, industry, or living. Just like the processes of agricultural and animal domestication, architecture emerged in our prehistory and will remain an integral part of human expression to the very end.

By and large, we have only dealt with large or significant symbolic monuments: the traditional objects of academic scrutiny.

We have not painted a picture of the historical development of vernacular and other nonmonumental architecture, such as the domestic space. This is not because we do not recognize the importance of the latter but simply because we have used the category of monumental architecture as one of the constraints by which we have delimited the boundaries of this book. That said, our emphasis is not only on a building's monumentality. We see history as dynamic. Ideas, technologies, theories, religions, and politics are all continuing to play a role in building the history of architecture. Each chapter introduces the set of terms that shape the architectural production and meaning of that age. Changes in some places are perhaps more dramatic than in others, but in all cases we try to explain the causes. The ancient Egyptian pharaohs during a period of time commissioned pyramids; but then they stopped and built huge temples. The reader needs to come to understand the political reasoning that necessitated this. Not only did Buddhism, as it filtered its way into East Asia and Southeast Asia, morph as it went; so too did Buddhist architecture. The rock-cut temples of Ellora did not appear out of a vacuum, but the technology of rock-cutting had never been attempted at that scale and would die out by the 13th century. In that sense we ask readers to not only compare architecture across space, but also across time.

3500 BCE	
2500 BCE	
1500 BCE	
800 BCE	
400 BCE	
0	
200 CE	
400 CE	
600 CE	
800 CE	
1000 CE	
1200 CE	
1400 CE	
1600 CE	
1700 CE	
1800 CE	
1900 CE	
1950 CE	

Organization of the Book

Rather than preparing chapters on individual countries or regions, such as India, Japan, or France, we have organized the book by "time-cuts." Eighteen chronological slices of time, beginning with 3500 BCE and ending with 1950 CE, comprise the armature of the book. Each time-cut marks not the beginning of a time period, but roughly the middle of the period with which each chapter is concerned. The 800 CE time-cut, for instance, covers the period from 700 to 900 CE. Yet we have not been strict about the scope of a particular time-cut. Whenever necessary, for purposes of coherence, we have not hesitated to include material from before and after its prescribed limits. Each time-cut should, therefore, be seen more as a marker amid the complexity of the flowing river of history rather than a strict chronological measuring rod.

We have begun each time-cut with a one-page summary of the historical forces graphing that period of time, followed by a map and a timeline locating all of the major buildings we discuss. After that, the discussions of individual buildings and groups of buildings are in a series of small subsections marked by relevant subcontinental location—East Asia, Southeast Asia, South Asia, West Asia, Europe, Africa, North America, Central America, or South America.

PREFACE

Introduction Page

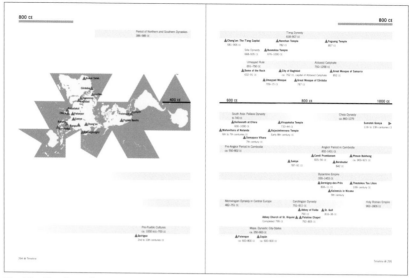

Map/Timeline Spread

Rather than arrange all the subsections in the same order, every time-cut is arranged according to its own internal logic. Despite the difficulties that this may pose, we have chosen this strategy to remind readers that the globe does not really begin in the East or the West but can indeed start and end anywhere. On the other hand, we have arranged the sequence of the subsubsections, as it makes sense to maintain continuity in the narrative of a particular chapter. Often this continuity is provided simply by geographical adjacency; in other cases, we have linked subsections to make a point about historiographical issues, such as the influence and movement of ideas or contrasts between kingdoms.

The individual subsections, which may be just a single page or up to four or five pages in length, are conceived as mini case studies, coherent in themselves. These can be prescribed as independent readings. Besides ensuring that the relevant facts and descriptions of each significant project we address are adequately covered, we have emphasized the cultural and global investments of their creators. For instance, a discussion of the Italian High Renaissance consists of pages on the Piazza del Campidoglio, il Gesù, the Villa Farnese, il Redentore, Palladian villas, and the Uffizi. The number of case studies accompanying each civilizational discussion is not uniform. Sometimes there are six—at other times, just one or two. The differences are largely a measure of our judgment of the importance of the material and the availability of literature on a topic. Indeed, there exists a great disparity in the availability of information. While we know much about the early civilizations of Mesopotamia, we know startlingly little about pre-Columbian civilization. An archaeologist we spoke with estimated that only 15 percent of such sites have been excavated. And if we look around the world, we find that there are many potential archaeological gold mines in war-torn countries, and even sites that cannot be excavated because they are seen as irrelevant to national interests. A global picture is, therefore, still a dream that we can aspire to, but are far from possessing.

The book's drawings are intended to be integral to the narrative. They are there not only to illustrate the text but also to tell a story of their own. Not everything in the text is illustrated by drawings, just as the drawings can be used to communicate things that are not referenced in the text. We have tried to make a virtue out of this fact by sharing the physical and epistemological space on each page as evenly as we could between text and image. The drawings also speak to the diminishing art of drawing in an age of photography and computer-enhanced plans.

This book's format suggests that a lecture course using this volume be organized according to the time-cuts. Since most survey courses are usually taught chronologically, this format should not pose many difficulties. Individual faculty, however, may want to emphasize certain case studies more and others less. Since all the case studies are complete mini-essays, they can be assigned as readings by themselves.

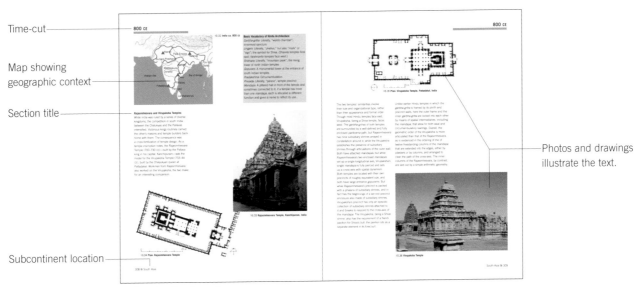

Time-cut

Map showing geographic context

Section title

Subcontinent location

Photos and drawings illustrate the text.

Typical Section Spread

Other faculty may not want to organize their syllabi by the time-cuts, in which case they may find it useful to cut and paste selectively chosen subsections together to suit their own historical narrative. Such selections could be made geographically or by other means. Once again, the fact that the subsections are conceived as individual case studies allow them to be read coherently even out of sequence.

A book like this faces almost insurmountable problems in trying to establish a single standard for use of terms and spellings, particularly those of non-Western origin. Sometimes a particular mosque, for instance, can have different English, Arabic, Persian, and Hindu names. Which does one pick? Should one say Nijo-jo or Nijo Castle (the suffix –jo in Japanese means castle)? Should one call a pagoda a *ta*, as it is called in Chinese, or should we persist with its conventional English name? Generally speaking, we have tried to use the names that are most commonly used in current scholarship in English.

It would be foolish to dispense with the Greek word for those Egyptian buildings that we call pyramids, named after the Greek bread called *pyramidos*, but we would like to suggest that Angkor Wat be called by its real name, Vrah Vishnulok, to cite one example. Once we have made a choice regarding the spelling of a particular proper noun, we have tried to remain consistent in our use of it. However, at several places, we have intentionally used non-English terms, even when the word is in common English usage. This we have done whenever we have felt that the English translation is misleading (the English *pagoda*, for instance, has nothing to do with the *ta*) or when a local linguistic discussion helps make an illuminating etymological explanation. Our aspiration is to make some small beginning toward forming a more diverse and appropriate vocabulary for the world's architecture. Language, like architecture, is a living thing with distinct yet blurry edges. It is, as such, a fascinating but somewhat messy and open-ended reminder of architecture's status as a multifaceted cultural signifier. We hope that the reader will get a sense of, and enjoy, the complex multilingual reality of architecture.

In conclusion, we would like to admit that in preparing and writing this book, a process that we have enjoyed at every turn, we were continually reminded of our ignorance on many matters. Conversations with colleagues were particularly valuable, as were the trips to some of the sites we covered. But in the end, a work like this can only be the beginning of a long process of refinement. So we ask all readers who wish to do so to contact us, to point out inaccuracies, to tell us about things that should be included in subsequent editions, or to open a conversation, even at the most fundamental level, about history, the world, and our place within it.

ACKNOWLEDGEMENTS

A work on this scale could not have been finished without the help, support, and goodwill of a very large number of people. Many students and colleagues worked on elements of the text and are to be especially noted: Jeremy Gates and Tim Morshead (1200); Fabia Cigni, Tom Dietz, and Svea Heinemann (1950); Nikki Moore (Buckminster Fuller); Mechtild Widrich (Gothic architecture); Tijana Vujosevic (Russian architecture); Luis Berrios-Negron (Caribbean modernism); Shuishan Yu and Ying Zhou (Chinese architecture); Diana Kurkovsky and Ashish Nangia (Le Corbusier); Michelangelo Sabatino (Italian Fascism); Alexander Tulinsky (Japanese architecture); M. Ijlal Muzaffar (modernism); Robert Cowherd (colonial Indonesia); Lenore Hietkamp (Khmer architecture); Kokila Lochan (Indian architecture); Alona Nitzan-Shiftan (Israeli modernism); Cynthia Bogel (Japanese architecture); and Kang Young Hwan (Korean architecture). Additionally, Alexander Tulinsky, Kokila Lochan, Jan Haag, Ashish Nangia, Kim Bahnsen, and Paula Patterson helped with the research and editing of various sections of the text. Innumerable students at MIT and the University of Washington suffered through lectures and seminars on topics in global history and offered their sage advice and student papers in assistance.

Profound gratitude is due to our friends and colleagues who gave us valuable advice and wise counsel and corrected many of our mistakes. Many prompted us to rethink our positions. These include: Nasser Rabbat, Erika Naginski, Stanford Anderson, Danilo Udovicki-Selb, Arindam Dutta, David Friedman, Anthony Vidler, Arindam Dutta, Gail Fenske, Maha Yahya, Sibel Bozdogan, Alfred B. Hwangbo, Jonghun Kim, Hadas Steiner, Annie Pedret, Jorge Otero-Pailos, Reinhold Martin, Franz Oswald, Brian McLaren, Kyoko Tokuno, Patricia Ebrey, Vince Rafael, Kent Guy, Clark Sorensen, Rick Meyer, Michael Duckworth, Jeffrey Ochsner, Trina Deines, Ken Tadashi Oshima, Kathryn Merlino, Sergio Palleroni, and Alex Anderson.

A long list of colleagues who contributed images to this text and are acknowledged on pages 819–23. Of these, some were generous enough to contribute multiple images: Stanford Anderson, David Friedman, Maha Yaha, John Lopez, Larry Vail, Nasser Rabbat, Eric Jenkins, Sibel Bozdogan, Walter Denny, David Aasen Sandved, Kang Young Hwan, Jerry Finrow, Bonnie MacDougall, Norman Johnston, Jeff Cohen, and Mark Brack. Plenteous image contributions to the text were made by the College of Architecture and Urban Planning's Visual Resources Collection at the University of Washington, the Rotch Slide Library and the Aga Khan Program for Islamic Architecture at MIT, and the R. D. MacDougall Collection in the Knight Visual Resources Facility at Cornell University.

Special thanks are due to Tunney Lee, who planted the idea for a slice in time, and to Anne Deveau and Melissa Bachman, who served as administrative assistants in the History, Theory and Criticism section at MIT, as well as librarians Merrill Smith and Michael Leininger at MIT's Rotch Library of Architecture and Planning. At the University of Washington, Y. Nancy Shoji, Karen Helland, Diane Stuart, Caroline Orr, Rachel Ward, Eric Gould, and Shanna Sukol provided excellent staff support, and Heather Seneff, Director of the College of Architecture and Urban Planning's Visual Resources Collection at the University of Washington, made available the slides in her collection. Support of various kinds was kindly provided by Dean Adèle Naudé Santos at MIT; Stanford Anderson, former chair of the Department of Architecture at MIT; and Dean Robert Mugerauer and Associate Dean Doug Zuberbuhler at the University of Washington.

We would like to especially extend our appreciation to the Graham Foundation for Advanced Studies in the Fine Arts for their financial support of this project.

For their review of early drafts of the text, we would like to thank: Richard Cleary, University of Texas at Austin; Dr. Roger T. Dunn, Bridgewater State College; Clifton Ellis, Texas Tech University; Mark Gelernter, University of Colorado at Denver; William J. Glover, University of Michigan; Kathleen James-Chakraborty, University of California at Berkeley; Edward D. Levinson, Miami-Dade Community College; Taisto Makela, University of Colorado at Denver; Anne Marshall, University of Idaho; Gerald Walker, Clemson University; and Janet White, University of Nevada at Las Vegas.

We would like to thank our publisher, John Wiley & Sons, and in particular, Amanda Miller, Paul Drougas, Lauren Olesky, and David Sassian, who worked tirelessly with the itinerant authors.

Finally, we would like to thank our families, Nancy, Andreas, and Elias, and Henry and Marianne Jarzombek; Leah, Saher, and Savitri and Aditya Prakash; and Debra, Emily, and Andrew Ching, for simply bearing with us.

Early Cultures

By 12,000 BCE humans had proliferated across much of the globe. Starting in Africa, they moved into West Asia, Europe, South and East Asia, Australia, North America, and, finally, along the west coast of the Americas to the southern tip of South America. They eventually created societies of villages and hamlets near caves or along shores and streams that allowed for a combination of farming and hunting. The domestication of animals and plants followed suit; this required not only an understanding of the seasons but also of ways to hand down that knowledge from generation to generation. The building arts, and their specialized uses for religious and communal purposes, began to develop as well—and to play an increasingly important role. Whether it was using mud for bricks or mortar, reeds for thatch, bitumen as a coating, stone as foundations, or wood as posts and beams, specialized tools and social specialization were essential. The results were by no means uniform. Some societies were more pragmatic than others, some more symbolic. Some emphasized granaries, others temples. In some places, the crafts associated with building were controlled by the elite. In other places, the building arts found more common expression. Architecture, like civilization itself, was born in our prehistory, and much as the other arts was plural from the beginning.

Paleolithic humans create animal paintings on the walls and ceilings of numerous cave sites, such as at Lascaux and Chauvet, in present-day southwestern France and northern Spain. 30,000–10,000 BCE

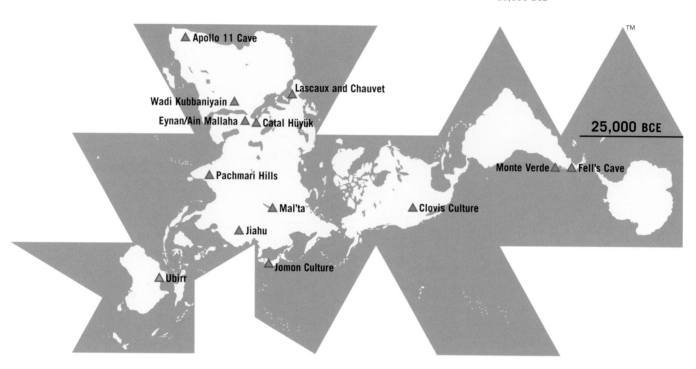

Apollo 11 Cave

Lascaux and Chauvet

Wadi Kubbaniyain

Eynan/Ain Mallaha ▲ ▲ Catal Hüyük

25,000 BCE

Pachmari Hills

Monte Verde ▲ ▲ Fell's Cave

Mal'ta

Clovis Culture

Jiahu

Jomon Culture

Ubirr

Aboriginal rock painting represents the longest continuously practiced artistic tradition in the world. The rock faces at Ubirr have been painted and repainted for millennia. ca. 40,000 BCE–present

Apollo 11 cavestones are among the oldest known artwork on the African continent. 25,500–23,500 BCE

Mal'ta cultural tradition thrives in north and central Asia. Sites consist of a series of subterranean houses containing carved bone, ivory, and antler objects. ca. 20,000 BCE

Late Paleolithic camps are established at Wadi Kubbaniyain, in what is now upper Egypt. Sites show evidence of tools for hunting, fishing, and collecting and processing plants. ca. 17,000–15,000 BCE

First permanent settlements in the Near East cultivate cereals. Rich artistic tradition exists in Eynan and Ain Mallaha in the Levant. ca. 10,000–8200 BCE

▲ Walled town of Jericho is founded. ca. 8300 BCE

Pottery and woolen textiles are made in Catal Hüyük. ca. 6000 BCE

Experimentation with copper ores begins in Anatolia. ca. 7000 BCE

15,000 BCE

5000 BCE

Peak of last Ice Age
ca. 22,000 BCE

Ice Age declines
ca. 14,000 BCE

Early Neolithic Period
ca. 10,000–5000 BCE

Farming occurs in Greece and the Aegean ca. 7000 BCE, reaching Iberia and Britain ca. 5000 BCE and Scandinavia ca. 4000 BCE.

Jomon Culture in Japan produces examples of the earliest known pottery. ca. 10,500–8000 BCE

Sandstone rock shelters are decorated with ceiling and wall paintings in the Pachmari Hills in present-day central India. ca. 9000–3000 BCE

Jiahu is a flourishing and complex society in central China, where the earliest examples of flutes have been found. Evidence of rice cultivation also exists. ca. 7000–5700 BCE

First humans migrate to the Americas. ca. 13,000 BCE

The Clovis Culture are Paleo-Indians in Central and North America who use flint spearpoints to hunt big game. ca. 10,000–9000 BCE

Corn (maize) is cultivated in Central America. ca. 5000 BCE

The lower Pacific coast region of South America evidences human inhabitation at Monte Verde and Fell's Cave, a rock shelter in Patagonia occupied by hunters who used stone tools and spearpoints. ca. 10,500–9500 BCE

1.2 Göbekli Tepe

1.1 Göbekli Tepe, Turkey

Ritual Centers

Before the development of urban civilizations along the various great rivers of Eurasia, hunter-gatherers created ritual centers to which they would travel from far away. One of these sites—Nabta Playa—was in what is today southern Egypt, some 80 kilometers west of Abu Simbel. It is now an inhospitable desert, but in 9000 BCE it was next to a large lake with pastured shores. This was not a standard Stone Age site, since it contained a circle of slender upright stones, the main stones being four pairs set close together. Compared to Stonehenge, built 4,500 years later, the circle is small, measuring roughly 4 meters in diameter, but its purpose was similar: to organize time according to the seasons. Two of the stone pairs are aligned true north-south; the other two pairs, northeast-southwest. They aided in the observation of the motion of the sun and the constellation Orion. A stone-covered tumulus 300 meters north of the calendar circle

contains the remains of cattle, indicative of the importance of cattle-raising to the local economy. Traces of habitation date to about 6000 BCE. Priests and their associated clans probably came to live there permanently, with the population swelling periodically with the seasonal arrival of nomadic tribes who would have come from far afield. Remains of goats and sheep were also found, along with large hearths. At the time, the Nile river was still a marshy valley; without large populations, its unruly floods made it difficult to master. By 3500 BCE, however, Nabta Playa became increasingly arid: the lake dried up and the villages had to be abandoned. It has thus been suggested that the exodus from the Nubian Desert played a large role in the development of social differentiation in the pre-dynastic cultures of the Nile Valley. One link may be the cattle cult that developed at Nabta Playa, which seems to be a predecessor of the Hathor cult in dynastic Egypt.

A similar ritual site has recently been found on top of a hill near the village of Urfa in southeastern Turkey. Here, too, the now arid site was once a lush forest. The oldest layer of the site appears to date back to around 9000 BCE. The temple, called Göbekli Tepe, consists of several circular dry stone walls, each of which contains monolithic pillars of limestone up to 3 meters tall. Since there appears to be no indications of any roof covering, it seems that the circles were open-air temples. The floors consisted of a concrete-like substance made of burnished lime. A low bench runs around the inside of the circle walls. The pillars show detailed reliefs of foxes, lions, cattle, wild boars, herons, ducks, scorpions, ants, and snakes, all executed with great skill, demonstrating that precision work—even without metalworking tools—was possible. Göbekli Tepe was abandoned around 4000 BCE; its last inhabitants carefully filled the site with earth, burying the great temples. No one knows why.

If we add to these two sites the Niuheliang Ritual Center (ca. 3500–3000 BCE) in northern China, with its numerous temples, and, of course, Stonehenge (2600 BCE), we have four ritual centers that served as gathering places and eventually as religious centers for settled communities—especially Niuheliang and Stonehenge. Niuheliang will be discussed in this chapter; Stonehenge, perhaps the last of the great ritual centers, will be discussed in the next.

3500 BCE

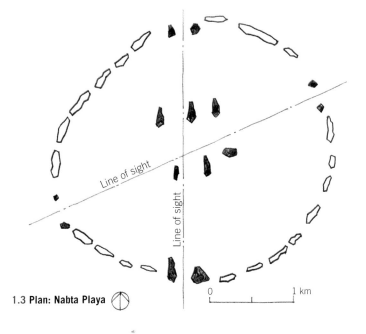

1.3 Plan: Nabta Playa

Line of sight

Line of sight

0   1 km

No single narrative fits over the whole age. In some societies, especially around the Mediterranean, the Stone Age mother goddess, a fertility cult, still reigned supreme; in others, like Mesopotamia, she was beginning to be replaced by complex pantheons. In Egypt, which had to accommodate itself to rapid growth from the beginning, the mother goddess never developed as an autonomous entity at all. In China, with its vast network of villages, religion was largely shamanistic. Similarly, architecture was not a univalent force. Though clearly within the purview of the governing elites, some buildings were built for the dead, others for the living; some were temples, others granaries. While there are many parallels among the different regions, in actuality each developed along its own pathways, with different environmental and social factors determining growth and development. This section discusses the primary sites in the world where, around 3500 BCE, these developments began to take place.

Egyptian culture, unified around 3200 BCE and densely centered along the Nile River, developed a highly vertical social structure very early on, with the ruling elites expanding their control while defining religious practices around the theme of the ruler's afterlife. The Mesopotamian highlands, which allowed for agriculture in the valleys and hunting and grazing in the hills and mountains, became

the site of a vast network of interconnected villages and social groups that traded with each other over large stretches of territory. Tombs and palaces were still quite rare. Instead, the villages in the Zagros Mountains, in the Anatolian highlands, and in Lebanon became part of an interconnected society oriented to the great Euphrates and Tigris rivers as well as to the metal-producing regions in the mountains. Grain increasingly became the principal commodity, bringing with it stability and population growth. The situation in South Asia was similar. A series of settlements developed in the hills of Baluchistan, west of the Indus River, the largest of which were located around Mehrgarh, which, quite remarkably, possessed no major religious sites, at least in its cities. China, despite the presence of equally imposing river valleys, was the least dense of these early civilizations. Its rivers did not become flashpoints for urban civilizations until the first millennium BCE. Instead, villages, spread across a vast tract of land, were connected by shared mortuary and goddess ritual centers. The Yangshao and Hongshan cultures in the north, Dawenkou and Longshan on the east coast, and Liangzhu in the south were all disaggregated but shared temples and altars.

In the Americas, the Asian people who crossed the Bering Strait into the Americas sometime around 11,000 BCE had found shelter in caves or temporary structures

made of wood. Initially, they were largely hunters, but with the warming of the climate and the expansion of forests we see the emergence of extensive river- and shore-oriented cultures. The population groups along the Peruvian Pacific coast in South America were particularly successful in drawing their sustenance from the sea. In the past this has been used to explain the slower development of South American cultures, but it has recently been proven that along the coast of Peru the shift to agricultural production—and to sociopolitical complexity and architectural monumentality—took place roughly on par with that in Eurasia, around 2500 BCE.

Europe was still a loose fabric of villages and clan-dominated areas. Grain, which had been domesticated and harvested in great quantities in Mesopotamia and Egypt, did not make it to England until about 3500 BCE. European cultures had to pay careful attention to the planting seasons, which were much shorter than in Mesopotamia. Nonetheless, the relatively warmer weather that then prevailed facilitated the development of village life. Though most housing structures in Europe were of wood, the coastal areas along the Atlantic belonged to a megalithic culture that, as in most parts of Asia, built large stone tombs. In Britain members of these cultures built thousands of stone circles that were used as religious sites and as place markers for trading.

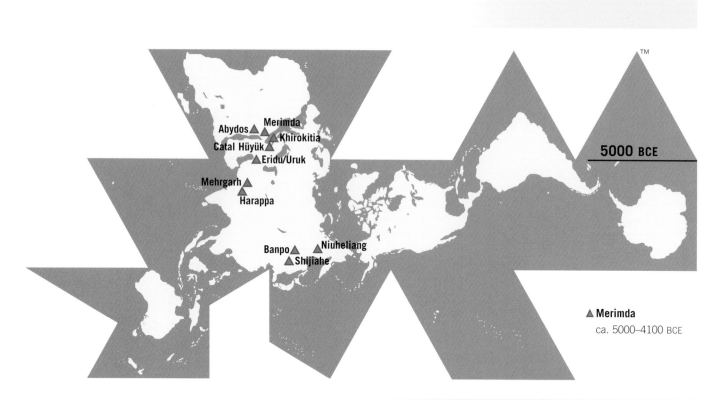

Abydos ▲ Merimda
Khirokitia ▲
Catal Hüyük ▲
▲ Eridu/Uruk
Mehrgarh ▲
Harappa
Banpo ▲ ▲ Niuheliang
▲ Shijiahe

5000 BCE

▲ Merimda
ca. 5000–4100 BCE

Mesopotamia: Ubaid Period
ca. 5500–4000 BCE

▲ Eridu settled
ca. 5000 BCE

▲ Neolithic Village of Catal Hüyük
flourishes ca. 6900–5400 BCE

China: Yangshao Culture
ca. 5000–1500 BCE

▲ Banpo
ca. 4500–3750 BCE

▲ Niuheliang Ritual Center
ca. 3500 BCE

▲ Shijiahe
ca. 2800–2000 BCE

▲ Yaoshan Ritual Altar
ca. 3300–2000 BCE

Indus Valley: Early Harappan Period
ca. 5000–2600 BCE

▲ Mehrgarh
ca. 6500–2800 BCE

▲ Harappa
ca. 3300–1300 BCE

4500 BCE	3500 BCE	2500 BCE

Late Neolithic Period
ca. 5000–2000 BCE

Early Bronze Age
ca. 3000–2000 BCE

▲ Khirokitia
ca. 4000–2500 BCE

Egypt: Pre-Dynastic Period
ca. 4500–3100 BCE

Early Dynastic Period
ca. 3100–2649 BCE

▲ Abydos
ca. 4000 BCE–641 CE

▲ Tomb of Hor Aba
ca. 3100 BCE

▲ Mastaba K1 at Bet Challaf
ca. 2600 BCE

Uruk Period
ca. 4000–3100 BCE

▲ Uruk settled
ca. 4000 BCE

▲ Tell es-Sawwan
ca. 3500 BCE

▲ Temple at Uruk
ca. 3000 BCE

▲ Temple at Eridu
ca. 3000 BCE

◉ Invention of the wheel
ca. 3600 BCE

◉ Earliest readable documents in Mesopotamia
ca. 3200 BCE

◉ Bronze casting begins in the Near East.
ca. 3600 BCE

Europe: Passage Tombs and Dolmens of Megaliths
ca. 3500–2500 BCE

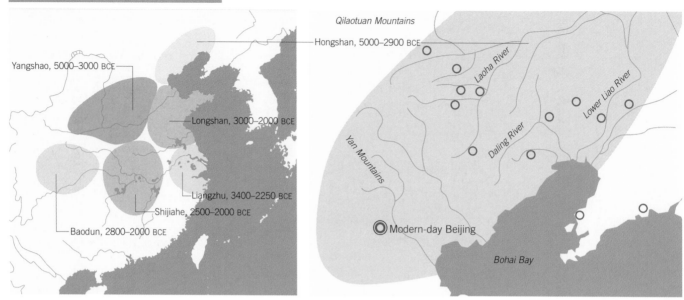

1.4 Early Chinese cultures from 5000 to 2000 BCE

1.5 Hongshan Culture sites

Beginnings of China's Civilizations

Chinese civilizational cultures developed in the plains along the numerous rivers that emptied into the Bohai and Hongzhou bays. The most prominent of these rivers, the Yellow and the Yangtze, hosted a complex fabric of villages. The climate was warmer and more humid than today, allowing for millet to be grown in the north and rice in the south. There was, however, no single "origin" of Chinese civilization. Instead, there was a gradual multinucleated development between the years 4000 and 2000 BCE—from village communities to what anthropologists call cultures to small but well-organized states. Two of the more important cultures were the Hongshan Culture (4700–2900 BCE) to the north of Bohai Bay in Inner Mongolia and Hebai Province and the contemporaneous Yangshao Culture (5000–3000 BCE) in Henan Province. Between the two, and developing later, was the Longshan Culture (3000–2000 BCE) in the central and lower Yellow River valley. These combined areas gave rise to thousands of small states and proto-states by 3000 BCE. Some continued to share a common ritual center that linked the communities to a single symbolic order, but others developed along more independent lines. All was not peaceful, and the emergence of walled cities during this time is a clear indication that the political landscape was very much in flux.

Niuheliang Ritual Center

The Hongshan Culture of Inner Mongolia (located along the Laoha, Yingjin, and Daling rivers that empty into Bohai Bay) was scattered over a large area but had a single, common ritual center that consisted of at least fourteen burial mounds and altars over several hill ridges. It dates from around 3500 BCE but could have been founded even earlier. Although there is no evidence of village settlements nearby, its size is much larger than one clan or village could support. In other words, though rituals would have been performed here for the elites, the large area implies that audiences for the ritual would have encompassed all the villages of the Hongshan Culture. As a sacred landscape, the center might also have attracted supplicants from even further afield. A north-south axis connects the ritual center with the central peak of Zhushan, or Pig Mountain, to the south. A key building is a 40-by-60-meter loam platform on which rested a structure that is presumed to have been a goddess temple. Its footings contain

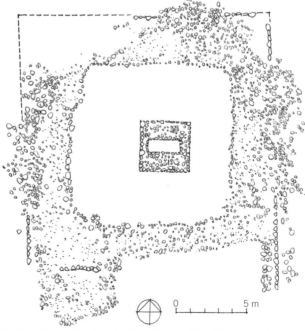

1.6 Plan: Cairn with stone tomb, Niuheliang Ritual Center, tomb site II

elaborate geometric designs made with clay in high relief and painted yellow, red, and white. On its northern end is a single detached room where excavations have uncovered clay body parts, including a head, a torso, and arms, perhaps belonging to a goddess (from which the site got its name). The platform also contains eight interconnected subterranean chambers constructed in an asymmetrical lobed shape, 25 meters from south to north and 2 to 9 meters wide. One of the tombs contained high-quality jade objects and is surrounded by smaller graves that are differentiated—so it seems—by rank.

A structure of interest to archaeologists is an artificial hill at the entrance to the valley. On the ground level, the mound is encircled by a ring of squared, white stones. Another ring of white stones is embedded in the middle of the height of the mound; a third was placed near the top. Artifacts found near the top of the mound include crude clay crucibles used for smelting copper. Since the top of a hill is a surprising place to melt copper, the structure seems to have been meant for ritual events. Burials on hills marked the north and south extremes of the moonrise in the east. All in all, this center contains the essential elements of Chinese ancestor worship—burial cairns, platforms, and a ritual temple—as evidenced, for example, by the Ming tombs built five thousand years later.

Banpo, located in the Yellow River valley (near the modern-day city of Xi'an) and dating from about 4500 BCE, was one of several large, well-organized settlements belonging to the Yangshao Culture, which developed to the south of Niuheliang along the Yellow River. It was surrounded by a

ditch or moat 5 to 6 meters wide, probably for drainage and defense. The homes were circular mud and wood structures with overhanging thatched roofs, all raised on shallow foundations with fire pits at the center. Entrance ramps sloped down into the dwelling. The dead were buried either in the back of nearby caves or in simple pits outside the village in a communal burial area. Children, it seems, were interred in urns, just outside their homes. Within the town are structures with large open plazas and storage holes, which are indicative of civic hierarchy and organization. At the center of the town was a large house, presumed to be a community center, which was built of a heavy timber construction of a type that was to become traditional in Chinese architecture. One area of the village was dedicated to the production of pottery, indicating the emergence of proto-industrial specialization. One of the oldest kilns in the world can be found here. Pottery was used not only in daily life but in mortuary rituals. The principal crop was millet.

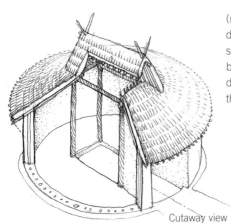

Cutaway view

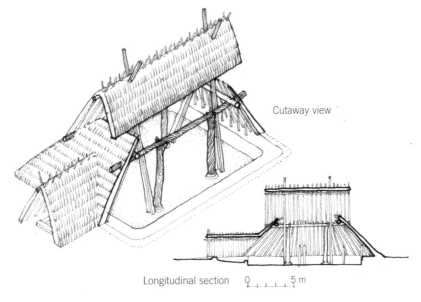

Cutaway view

Longitudinal section

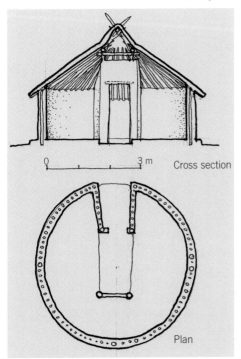

Cross section

Plan

1.7 Reconstruction of circular dwelling at Banpo

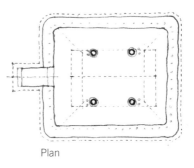

Plan

1.8 Reconstruction of meeting hall at Banpo

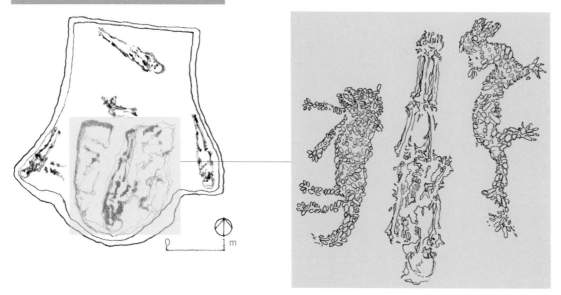

1.9 **Dragon, human, and tiger figures found in tomb at Xishuipo, Henan Province, China**

In terms of religion, the Hongshan and Yangshao cultures were shamanistic. A shaman is an intermediary between the natural and the spiritual world who travels between these worlds in a trance. A tomb at Xishuipo dating from about 4000 BCE, possibly of a shaman priest, was found in the shape of a single, squarish room with a lobed space at the rear. Under the pounded earth floor is the grave of a man flanked by the outline of a dragon on one side and a tiger on the other, both painstakingly and beautifully made of hundreds of shells. Dragons and tigers, still central to Chinese Confucian symbolism, are considered to be prospectors, both in life and death. Hill ranges, especially those with prominent peaks, are considered to be dragons.

By the time of the Liangzhu Culture (3400–2250 BCE), located in the Yangtze River delta, we see the emergence of numerous cities and mini-states. Some had walls, others had none; some were regional centers with villages around them, others were more autonomous. Generally, the Liangzhu emphasized the secular authority of the king over the priests. A city near Yuhang, south of modern Shanghai, shows that these cities were becoming quite large—in this case up to 3 million square meters. Agriculture was highly organized, as has been proven by the discovery of a Liangzhu-age plough, the earliest to be found in China. A roughly rectangular city, about 0.5 kilometers long, located a few kilometers east of the modern

town of Pingyao, is believed to have been the capital of the kingdom. It had a fortification wall and a planned irrigation system.

Rammed earth platforms on which palaces and temples were built were now a common feature of Chinese architecture. These platforms (known as *hang-t'u*) were created by pounding layers of 12 to 14 centimeters of earth onto each other with wooden or stone mallets, creating a very hard and long-lasting material. Since what was built on top was made of wood, nothing of this superstructure remains. A Liangzhu Culture ritual altar at Yaoshan, located to

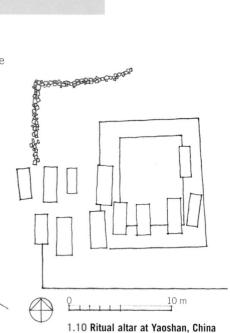

1.10 **Ritual altar at Yaoshan, China**

the west of Tai Lake, gives some indication of the religious edifices of the time. A ditch defines a sacred precinct 25 meters square, at the center of which is a platform measuring 6 by 7 meters constructed of rammed red earth. Archaeologists found twelve graves, presumed to have belonged to priests, arranged in two rows under the floor of the altar. We are still unsure how this platform was used, though it most probably involved ancestor worship. The use of jade for religious and devotional objects was by this time common to all of the Chinese cultures; the quality of Liangzhu jade was, however, quite remarkable.

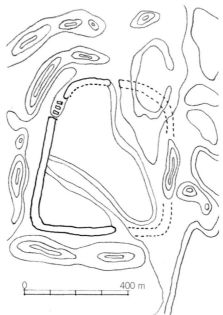

1.11 **Walled city of Shijiahe, China**

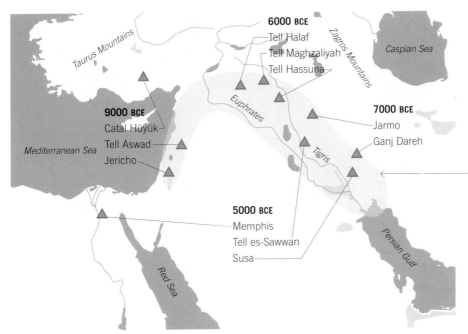

6000 BCE
Tell Halaf
Tell Maghzaliyah
Tell Hassuna

9000 BCE
Catal Hüyük
Tell Aswad
Jericho

7000 BCE
Jarmo
Ganj Dareh

5000 BCE
Memphis
Tell es-Sawwan
Susa

Mesopotamia comes from the Greek words *mesos* and *potamas*, meaning "middle river," and refers to the fertile plain between the Tigris and Euphrates rivers.

The Fertile Crescent is an agricultural region that runs along the foot of the Taurus and Zagros mountains in a broad arc from the eastern shores of the Mediterranean to present-day Iraq.

1.12 Fertile Crescent: An early, dense network of cities and villages

Mesopotamia

The Chinese cultures had geographies large enough to satisfy the diverse needs of civilizational progress. A different situation developed in the areas of the Tigris and Euphrates rivers, where, by 4000 BCE, a vast network of villages had formed in the highlands. The inhabitants had already spent several millennia transforming the valleys into one of the most productive grain-bearing regions in the world. (These areas are now divided by the borders of Iran, Iraq, Syria, Turkey, Lebanon, and Jordan.) The climate was cooler, meaning that the verdant valleys of the Tigris and Euphrates rivers were far different from the deserts of today; in the highlands, forests were interspersed with steppes and savannas rich in flora and abounding with goats, boars, deer, and foxes. Farmers worked in the valley, but the community lived in the more easily fortifiable hills. Unlike those in China, these villagers had two economic orientations: downhill to the fields of grain and uphill into the mountains with their mines of gold and copper. Mesopotamian cultures were thus continually in a state of flux, which had its own advantages and difficulties.

The urbanization of this area went through several stages:

9000 BCE. Hilltop cities evolved, like Jericho (in Israel) and Tell Aswad (in Syria, 30 kilometers east by southeast of Damascus).

7000 BCE. The Zagros Mountains became settled from Jarmo (in Iarq) to Ganj Dareh (in Iran). Then, between the Levant and the Zagros Mountains, in the flat lands of the Tigris and Euphrates, a network of smaller cities and villages developed.

6000 BCE. A dense network of villages and small cities, such as Tell Hassuna, reached to the south along the Euphrates.

5000 BCE. The Mesopotamian area became the largest network of villages and cities in the world, with the exception, perhaps, of the Indus River valley system. Khirokitia in Cyprus and settlements along the Nile completed the picture.

1.13 Tell Megiddo. *Tell*, an Arabic word for a hillock, is often used to describe the enormous mounds accumulated from the remains of mud-brick houses and generations of rubbish, such as this site of Tell Megiddo.

One of the most important groupings of villages dating from this period (6000–2500 BCE) were located just to the east of a rain-fed agricultural zone that arches northeastward from the northern tip of the Persian Gulf along the flanks of the Zagros Mountains. Among these settlements were Tell Hassuna, in western Iraq south of Mosul, in the hills above the Tigris River; Tell Maghzaliyah, 150 kilometers to the northwest; Tell es-Sawwan, on the left bank of the Tigris near Samarra; Jarmo, in northern Iraq, in the foothills of the Zagros Mountains; and Ganj Dareh in Iran. These settlements initially started as fortified villages of about two hundred people, growing over time into substantial communities. The basic building material was mud and timber; the mud was mixed with reeds and applied in horizontal courses to form walls of various heights. The walls of the houses were laid out in a honeycomb pattern to add to their durability; they were composed of rectilinear rooms measuring, on average, about 1.5 by 2 meters. At Ganj Dareh, archaeologists found house shrines with wild sheep skulls attached to the plastered walls of niches, recalling similar shrines at Catal Hüyük in Anatolia. The horizontal roofs consisted of adjoining beams of oak on which were placed a layer of branches and reeds sealed with mud, bitumen, and gypsum.

These houses were more than mere shelters. Some of the interior wall surfaces were decorated with gypsum plaster, which had been developed as early as 7000 BCE and which was to remain a central part of building construction in the entire area. From the extensive outcrops of rock gypsum in northern Iraq and Syria, stone blocks were mined, stacked, and burnt to form an easily transportable white powder. This building material was not only used locally but also was exported as a trade commodity. The development of trade in craft goods, pottery, building materials, and metal objects stimulated the economies of the region and played a central part in its drift toward craft specialization and urbanization. The Hassuna Culture produced abundant grain, which was then exported to surrounding regions. The plan of Tell es-Sawwan shows a clear hierarchy, with the important buildings in the southern half. The central building is symmetrical and has a hall or corridor down the center; it was built at a later stage in the development of the village. Its purpose is unknown, but it was possibly a granary.

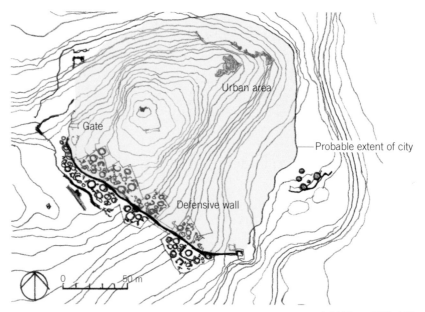

1.14 **Plan of Khirokitia**

Khirokitia

On the island of Cyprus, a large Neolithic village dating from between 4000 and 2500 BCE exhibited a well-organized architectural tradition. Spread in a semicircle on the flanks of a steep hill, Khirokitia had a population of about five hundred people and was protected by a massive stone wall almost 3 meters thick. A gate provided access through the wall into the village. Over time the village grew, and a new wall running roughly parallel to the old one was added. Houses, built in limestone, had a circular plan, the exterior diameter of which varied from about 2 to 9 meters.

1.15 **Housing pattern at Tell es-Sawwan, Iraq**

1.16 Metal-producing areas in Mesopotamia

The stones were bonded with mud. Both the inside and outside were covered with a whitish, earthen gypsum. The walls of some of the houses were decorated with paintings, but not enough have been preserved to ascertain what was represented. Roofs were flat and made of timbers surmounted by reeds and mud.

A family unit consisted of several circular structures combined around a small open space that was used for communal activities. The compounds were crowded next to each other, but with enough room between them to serve as passageways through the village. Though the mother goddess was a preeminent religious theme, there appears to be no central village religious site. Instead, burials took place within the space of a family unit's house. A pit was dug in which the dead were placed, along with various ritual objects; this was then covered with dirt and plaster. Since the village was some distance from the sea, the main economy was farming and hunting. Fish were brought up from the sea or traded in exchange for agricultural products. For reasons unknown, the site, and indeed all of Cyprus, was abandoned at some time and only reoccupied much later.

Grain and Metal

Though we often think of the Tigris and Euphrates region as the birthplace of urban civilization, the truth is that civilization—if we can use that complex and awkward word, at least in this area—was the product of a combined culture in which some raised grain while others built mines. The raising of grain and the production of metals were mutually reinforcing activities. The principal copper-producing areas stretched from the Caspian Sea through Anatolia and around the Black Sea into the Balkans. An important early Copper Age society, known as the Vinca Culture, flourished from 5500 to 4000 BCE in an area that stretches from present-day Bosnia to Romania. There one finds some of Europe's oldest mines. Another export commodity from the north was salt, which was mined early on in Austria. The Taurus Mountains in eastern Anatolia, known for their tin mines, played an important part in the West Asian economy, since tin was needed, along with copper, to make bronze. Though there were many copper-producing areas, tin was more rare. An ancient tin mine was discovered at a site named Göltepe, which was a large village from around 3290 to 1840 BCE. The miners, using narrow shafts, brought cassiterite ore to the surface, where it was crushed, washed, and smelted with charcoal in small crucibles rather than in the large furnaces characteristic of copper-smelting sites. By measuring the enormous deposits of slag (600,000 tons in one pile), researchers have ascertained that this was a major site during much of the early and middle Bronze Age.

Metal began to play an important part in international relations in the third millennium BCE. Around 2350 BCE, Sargon of Akkad invaded Anatolia from his lowland base to secure trade routes. In records that have been found, he boasts that a single caravan carried about 12 tons of tin, which can make 125 tons of bronze—enough to equip a large army. Today it is widely accepted that mining was responsible for vast deforestation and played an important part in the desertification of western Asia.

1.17 Partial modern-day reconstruction of Khirokitia, Cyprus

Catal Hüyük

Catal Hüyük in central Anatolia (near the modern city of Konya) lay at the center of the metal trade. The city dates back as far as 7400 BCE; by the third millennium BCE it had a population of about eight thousand. Metal objects found there are among the oldest known examples in the Near East. Other local commodities were traded—in particular volcanic glass, known as obsidian, which was used for decoration and as barter. The city was located in the center of a large, well-watered valley and next to a river that fed into a nearby lake. The lake and river have long since dried up. What has been recovered archaeologically is but a small part of the city that followed the slopes of the hill.

The city consisted of rectangular flat-roofed houses packed together into a single architectural mass with no streets or passageways. Inhabitants moved across rooftops and descended into their homes through the roofs via ladders. Walls were made of mud bricks reinforced by massive oak posts. Light came through small windows high in the walls. If a family died out, its house was abandoned for a period of time, leaving gaps in the urban fabric, until eventually the space was reclaimed. The typical residence contained one large room connected to smaller storage rooms. The main room was equipped with benches, ovens, and bins. The average size of the room was a generous 5 by 6 meters. Walls were plastered, and many were decorated with spectacular hunting scenes, textile patterns, or landscapes. There were raised benches on three sides of the room for sleeping and other activities. The horns of animals, especially cattle, were mounted on walls. When a house was unoccupied, it was used as a place to throw garbage, until it was reoccupied.

As at Khirokitia in Cyprus, there was no central communal sacred space. Each house had its own shrine consisting of a wall decorated with bulls or horns. In some cases pairs of horns were set in clay at the edge of platforms or embedded in benches. The dead of the family were buried in this room and their bones incorporated into the shrine. (Bodies were left outside until only the bones remained.) The principal deity was the mother goddess. Figurine representations of her, made of a variety of materials, have been found throughout the village. One statue, remarkable for its bold three-dimensional design, is of a voluminous seated woman giving birth. The chair on which she sits has armrests in the shape of lions. The figurine represented fecundity and regeneration and was part of the widespread mother-goddess worship typical of European and Mediterranean late Stone Age and early Bronze Age societies. Walls, both inside and outside, were decorated with murals—some composed of abstract shapes, others showing animals and hunting scenes.

1.18 **Terra-cotta figurine of seated woman from Catal Hüyük, near Konya, Turkey**

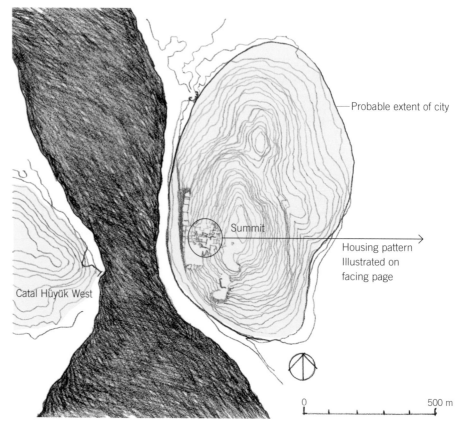

Probable extent of city

Summit

Catal Hüyük West

Housing pattern Illustrated on facing page

0   500 m

1.19 **Site plan of Catal Hüyük**

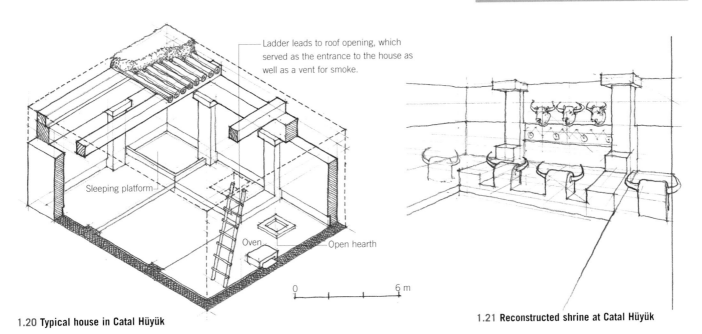

Ladder leads to roof opening, which served as the entrance to the house as well as a vent for smoke.

Sleeping platform

Oven

Open hearth

0   6 m

1.20 Typical house in Catal Hüyük

1.21 Reconstructed shrine at Catal Hüyük

1.22 Bull design on a shrine wall at Catal Hüyük

Catal Hüyük is at the northern end of a zone of developing urbanization that reach from Jericho (in Israel) to Tell Aswad (in Syria) and Susa (in Iran). Jericho was a major city—probably the largest in the whole area. Like Catal Hüyük, it had the benefit of local mines. Susa had the benefit of a well-established network of nearby villages in the Zagros Mountains, which constituted a close supply of metals. The Karun River, a river no less important than the Tigris and Euphrates, connected the city to the world at large; grains, figs, and lemons were raised in the river's broad valley.

0   15 m

1.23 Housing pattern at Catal Hüyük

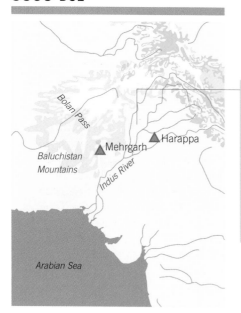

1.24 Location of the Indus civilizations of Mehrgarh and Harappa

This period is characterized by the elaboration of ceramics, the beginning of copper metallurgy, stone-bead making, and seal-bone carving. The beginning of writing is seen in the form of graffiti on pottery from ca. 3500 BCE.

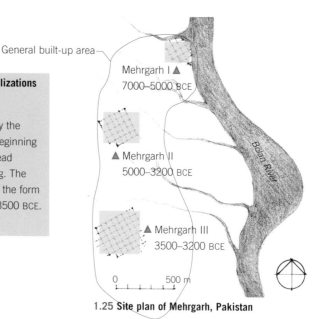

1.25 Site plan of Mehrgarh, Pakistan

Early Indus Settlements

Though evidence of the Neolithic occupation of India dates back to 10,000 BCE, settled cultures began to emerge around 7000 BCE in the eastern hills of the Baluchistan Mountains in today's Pakistan. It was a agro-pastoral environment typical for the age, allowing farming in the flat lands of the Indus River valley and herding and hunting in the hills and mountains. Though such a topography was similar to that in China and Mesopotamia, the differences in architectural response were pronounced. The Baluchistan cultures did not develop ritual sites, nor did they practice ancestral burial cults. This is perhaps because the people of the Indus River valley were among the first to develop concentrated proto-urban environments in which one's identity derived more from social structure and craft and less from family lineage or affiliation with a particular god or deity.

Mehrgarh

Of the numerous sites still being excavated, the ones around contemporary Mehrgarh have emerged as the most important. This area was strategically located overlooking the Kachi Plain southeast of modern Quetta near the Bolan Pass, an important gateway connecting South Asia to the rest of the continent. One can trace its five-thousand-year history from a village to a regional trading center, covering, at the peak of its development, an area of 200 hectares.

By 3500 BCE, its occupants had not only mastered extensive grain cultivation, but they had made it the center of their culture. Dominating the urban landscape were square mud-brick buildings, presumed to be granaries designed as multiroomed, rectangular structures with a long narrow corridor running more or less down the center. The absence of doors suggests that grain was fed from the top, as it would be into a silo. Though the presence of these granaries connotes a centralized social organization, there is no evidence of dominant temples or ritual structures. Nor are the granaries aligned with adjoining structures. And yet it is clear that the granaries were the center of social life. Outside one such granary, along its western wall, a large hearth has been found, complete with several hundred charred grains. Along the southern wall, archaeologists found the remains of the stone tools and drills of a steatite- or soapstone-cutter's workshop. On the eastern side, there were heaps of animal bones mixed with ashes, indicating the presence of intense butchering activity. Life, in other words, was organized around the granaries. The granaries were also the center of ritual mortuary practices: human bones, presumably those of priests, were found buried in its corridors and intermediary spaces.

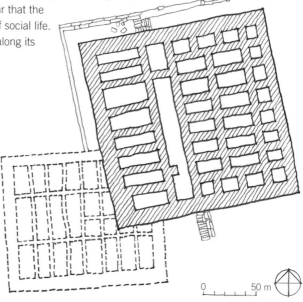

1.26 Plan: Mud-brick granaries, Mehrgarh II

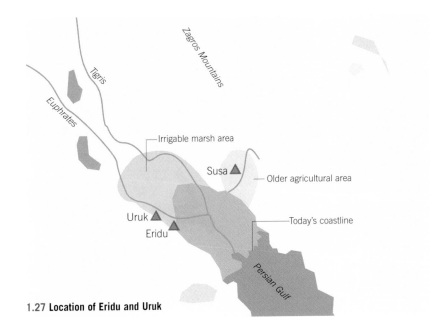

1.27 Location of Eridu and Uruk

Eridu and Uruk

The identifying elements of the proto-civilizations discussed so far are the presence of ritual centers, agro-industrial specialization, a military or religious elite, and urban density. These elements did not develop simultaneously. In China, we find ritual centers and agro-industrial production. But life still went on at the scale of the village. In the Indus River valley and at Catal Hüyük, cities emerged as sites where production could be centralized and coordinated, but we do not find large-scale ritual centers. In South Asia, the absence of communal religious sites, despite agricultural specialization, is particularly intriguing and was to remain a characteristic of its urban culture through the following millennium. The confluence of communal ritual centers, urban density, and agro-industrial production is first found in the lower Mesopotamian region of present-day southern Iraq and Iran. It has been suggested that the move into the marshes was predicated by the same changes in global climate that created the Sahara Desert. As the mountains became drier, tribes had to move to the plains in search of better soil. But whether by necessity or desire, the system of mountain villages that had given Eurasia its bounty of domesticated animals and grain was now being replaced by a more thoroughly industrialized, river-based culture.

There might have been other factors. But the change was—in the time frame of these early cultures—quite sudden. Societies gave up their partial dependency on an integrated farming-hunting lifestyle and concentrated on farming alone, making them vulnerable to the uncertainties associated with weather, rivers, and trade. The move into the marshes of the river delta went hand in hand with improved technical advances. The Tigris and Euphrates, unlike the Nile, flooded before the harvest, in April and May; this had made lower-lying reaches unusable for agriculture. But sedimentation brought by the rivers tended to build up natural levees that farmers could reinforce, allowing the riverbed to become somewhat higher than the surrounding countryside. Farmers could then make openings in the levees to feed water into the irrigation channels. Aerial photography has recently proven the extensive nature of these ancient canals and dikes, some of them more than 100 kilometers in length.

This relationship with the rivers was a delicate and dangerous one. The system was vulnerable to flood, war, and neglect. Records from Ur deal repeatedly with repair work. But the investment was worth the effort. In a few centuries the area became an economic engine unparalleled anywhere in the world

except in Egypt. It remained so until about 800 CE. Then the development of iron tools made growing and harvesting grain easier. As it became more widespread, Mesopotamia lost this economic advantage.

The need for accurate record keeping among merchants led to another civilizational achievement: writing, which was put to practical use to record trade transactions and keep up with inventory. Concomitant with this was the development of a legal and archival system. Evidence of the impact this made can be found even today in vestigial remnants of words deeply embedded in our present-day language. In Ur, the ancient title designating "king" is *lugal*, which is probably the origin of the Latin word *lex* ("law") and the English word *legal*. And another ancient Mesopotamian word, *pala*, referring to the garment of kingship, constitutes the root of our word *palace*.

We see the emergence not only of elaborate urban defensive wall systems but also of a complex religious world in tune with the equally complex life of urban civilization. The mother goddess, who had ruled in many places throughout Eurasia, now had to compete with an expanding list of divine presences—including powerful male gods who tied society firmly into a network of obligations. Concurrent with the shift was the emergence of a priestly class responsible for all aspects of society, from religion to administration to technology. Significantly, the mother goddess Apsu, who controlled the oceans, was "killed" by her son Ea, earth, who divided her unruly waters into chambers.

The culture that first began to master the Tigris and Euphrates rivers as early as 5000 BCE was known as the Ubaid. Around 3000 BCE, they were superseded by the Sumerians, who were to no small degree the first modernizers, replacing old and well-established traditions with new ones. In comparison to their new cities of Uruk, Eridu, and the Elamite city of Susa, Hassuna was now a backward village. Eridu was located on the banks of the Euphrates in the delta, which has since silted up so that its ancient site is now located 90 kilometers inland.

1.28 Temple atop the stone-faced platform at Eridu, near Abu Shahrain, Iran

1.29 Plan: Temple at Eridu

There are seventeen layers of temples at Uruk, which show the constant expansion and elaboration of the temple form. The earliest were simple boxes with an altar at the back and an oven outside in the front, where offerings were prepared. Over the centuries, the temple became larger, and at one point, the walls of the older temples were all filled in to create a mound on which a new generation of temples were built. The last temple was positioned on an enormous plinth of clay bricks and was visible for miles. It had a form defined by rhythmically spaced buttresses, and though roughly rectangular in shape, it had an irregular perimeter. A flight of steps at the center of the broader side led up to the entrance, where a shallow vestibule gave access to a large lengthwise-placed central room. Ancillary spaces, probably used as reliquaries, were located at the corners.

Unlike the older city of Susa, with its hinterland of villages with which it was networked, Eridu and Uruk were, in a sense, modern cities dependent on a single economy of grain, requiring organization and the movement of goods. It thus stands to reason

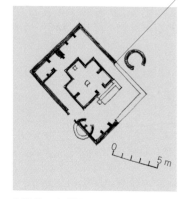

1.30 Temple XVI–XVIII at Eridu

that it was here that the wheel came into its full use to haul loads, and that standardized weights were invented.

The chief deity of the city was Ea, son of the mother goddess Apsu; he was not only an earth god but also manifest in "sweet waters." He was seen as crafty, for he "avoids rather than surmounts obstacles, goes round and yet gets to his goal." Ea, who in some accounts made human beings by mixing his own essence with that of his brother, Enlil (the earth and storm god), was also worshipped as the god of wisdom and as a friend to humankind. Images of Ea show him wearing a cloak of fish scales, and fish bones have been discovered near the offering table at Eridu. A text written somewhat later states that:

> When Ea rose, the fishes rose and adored him,
> He stood, a marvel unto the deep…
> To the sea it seemed that awe was upon him;
> To the Great River terror seemed to hover around him
> While the south wind stirred the depth of the Euphrates.*

*Thorkild Jacobsen. "Sumerian Mythology, a Review Article." *Journal of Near Eastern Studies* 5. (1946), 140.

The Temple at Eridu came to be viewed by later Mesopotamians as an important prototype: a statue made about a thousand years later, in 2150 BCE, shows the plan of a temple with similar attributes. It is placed on the lap of King Gudea of Lagash and, in its accuracy and precision, leaves no doubt as to the planning that went into these early temple designs. Its position on the king's lap also proves that the plan was more than just a convenience of the builders: it was an expression of the claim to legitimacy of

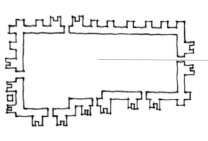

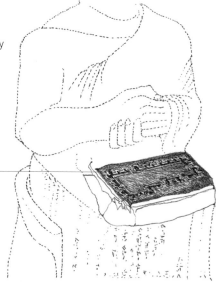

1.31 Statue of King Gudea with a temple plan carved on a lap tablet

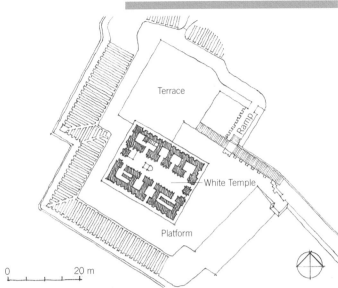

1.32 Mosaics from the Stone-Cone Temple in the Eanna District of Uruk

1.33 Plan: White Temple at Uruk, near Samawa, Iraq

the monarch and his sacrosanct function. Uruk developed into a significantly larger city than Susa or Ur, with a possible population of fifty thousand. It was in that sense a major world metropolis. The city was dedicated to the god Anu, a sky god, and an important and newly emerging deity linked to the number one, and thus to mathematics and trade. His temple, the so-called White Temple, rested on a broad terrace on top of a tall artificial mountain, irregular in outline and rising 13 meters above the plain, with its vast expanse of fields and marshes. Access was by a stairway on the northeastern face. Its overall shape was much simpler than

Eridu's, but as at Eridu, one passed through a shallow vestibule into a great hall. In Uruk, however, there was in one corner a platform or altar with a flight of narrow steps leading up to it. Toward the middle of the space was an offering table with a low semicircular hearth built up against it.

During this time, Mesopotamian builders discovered how to use the kiln to harden bricks, roof tiles, and drainage tubes. The Mesopotamians may have acquired this skill on their own but more likely learned it from the Indus Valley civilization, with which they most certainly were in contact and which had developed brick very early on. As wood

for kilns was scarce in the Mesopotamian marshes, bricks were a luxury item and were mainly used for palaces, temples, and gates; the Gate of Ishtar at Babylon is the most famous. The kilns devoured enormous amounts of wood, depleting wood resources and contributing, so it is now thought, to the growth of the desert that is now pervasive in these parts. The use of brick in the foundation of Uruk was an indication of a building's status. It was seen even by Mesopotamians as one of its wondrous aspects. Near the beginning of the epic of Gilgamesh, composed in the later third millennium BCE, we read:

> Look at its wall which gleams like copper,
> inspect its inner wall, the likes of which no one can equal!
> Take hold of the threshold stone—it dates from ancient times!
> Go close to the Eanna Temple, the residence of Ishtar,
> such as no later king or man ever equaled!
> Go up on the wall of Uruk and walk around,
> examine its foundation, inspect its brickwork thoroughly.
> Is not (even the core of) the brick structure made of kiln-fired brick,
> and did not the Seven Sages themselves lay out its plans?*

* Maureen Gallery Kovacs, trans. *The Epic of Gilgamesh.* (Stanford, CA: Stanford University Press, 1985), 3.

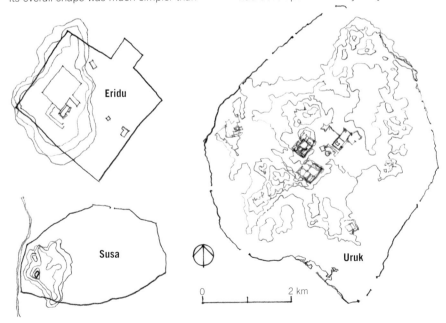

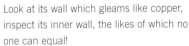

1.34 A size comparison of Eridu, Susa, and Uruk

1.35 Egypt, ca. 6th century BCE

1.36 Site of royal tombs at Umm el-Qaab, Abydos, Egypt

Pre- and Early Dynastic Egypt

North Africa was once a vast, fertile area of forests and pasturelands that was populated by humans early on. But in the sixth millennium BCE, a dramatic warming affecting the whole globe changed North Africa bit by bit into the endless stretches of sand that we now call the Sahara Desert. The populations moved either westward to Morocco, Spain, and beyond, or eastward to the banks of the Nile. The results were astonishingly quick. By the fourth millennium BCE, Egyptian villages had grown to towns, and trade was being pursued along the Nile and throughout the Aegean Islands.

The density of the Nile River population was unlike anything one would have seen anywhere else in the world at that time; that it did not overwhelm the social system was predicated on several conditions, one being that the local elites quickly learned to define themselves as divine, assuring the mechanism by which to protect and isolate their power. This meant that Egyptian religion never went through a chthonic phase based on the mother goddesses and caves that were common in many places in Eurasia and the Mediterranean. Egyptian religion was from the start a religion for the elite alone. There were no epic tales of communal destiny but rather myths of heroic actions of kings who passed the torch of succession to the next generation. This explains why a complex pantheon of gods, stretching from the bovine Hathor to the more abstract Ptah

and Amun, could develop so quickly. It was only during the New Kingdom (1540–1069 BCE) that the features of this religion began to have a broader role in society. Another factor that stabilized Egypt's existing social order was that the Nile flooded after the harvest in the middle of October; more people working the fields therefore resulted in the production of more food. But in contrast to the celebration of water and food, there was, for the Egyptians, the fearsome entombing power of the earth. Life and death, the river, and the mountains of sand became intimately and naturally connected to each other around the all-encompassing mythology of divine rulership.

One of the oldest Egyptian sites, belonging to the pre-dynastic period, is Merimda, 50 kilometers northwest of Cairo at the western base of the Nile Delta. It dates back to the sixth millennium BCE and consists of a collection of oval huts with grain silos sunk into the ground. The dead lay in shallow pits in burial grounds outside of the town. They were wrapped in matting and accompanied by goods such as clay vessels and shells. Idols, vessels (some used for the preparation of cosmetics), and wall paintings all point to an aesthetic that was to become characteristically Egyptian: smooth surfaces, abstract forms, and heroic actions.

The tombs of the First Dynasty (3100–2890 BCE) are located at Abydos, an important early city about 100 kilometers

downstream from Thebes. The tombs are outside of town under the face of an imposing cliff. A gorge opens out dramatically through the cliff at that spot and, according to some scholars, this opening was regarded as the entrance to the netherworld. The oldest tombs, of Narmer and Aha, are rather simple brick-lined rooms placed in the ground and covered with a wooden roof at ground level. Aha's tomb consisted of three chambers stockpiled with provisions for a lavish life in eternity. There were most likely large cuts of ox meat, as well as freshly killed waterbirds, loaves of bread, dried figs, and jars of beer or wine, each bearing Aha's official seal. Beside his tomb more than thirty ancillary graves for servants and animals were laid out in three neat rows. Later tombs evidence a developing conception of death. The tomb of Queen Merneith (ca. 2900 BCE), for example, is, like its predecessors, largely sunken underground, except that now the storage rooms are part of the main structure, in the from of long, thin rooms.

The ancillary tombs are also integrated into the design as a type of frame set at a respectful distance from the tomb's body. This framing is open on its southwestern side, presumably so that the spirit of the dead can exit through the gap toward a gorge that cuts through the cliffs. The tomb of the next ruler, Den, makes this connection to the cliff even more explicit. Though the main entrance is from the east, there is a special chamber

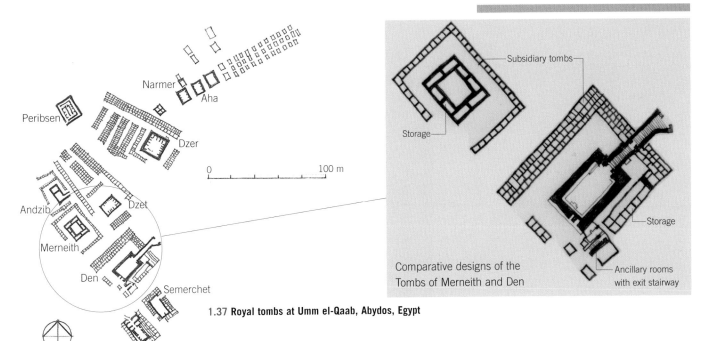

Subsidiary tombs

Storage

Storage

Ancillary rooms
with exit stairway

Comparative designs of the
Tombs of Merneith and Den

Narmer
Aha
Peribsen
Dzer
Andzib
Dzet
Merneith
Den
Semerchet
Kaa

0   100 m

1.37 Royal tombs at Umm el-Qaab, Abydos, Egypt

next to the tomb with a separate staircase leading back up to the surface and to the west.

The design and the decoration of these tombs clearly anticipates the development of the mastaba (from the Arabic word for "bank"). The grandest was the Tomb of Hor Aba at Saqqâra (ca. 3100 BCE), just outside of Memphis. Some argue that the complex niche pattern in the walls represented wooden or reed construction; others have suggested an influence from Mesopotamia or the Near East. Only the five central chambers, dug into the earth, constitute the tomb.

In this early stage of Egyptian culture, there was no temple architecture such as one might find in China, where religious practices unified broad swaths of society. Instead, architecture played the role of defining the interface between life and death for the members of the elite. Its place in society was

thus more limited than in China and India—but its purpose could not be more dramatic. Death for the Chinese involved the handing down of family memories and could be articulated spatially with house shrines and fragile wooden temples on earthen mounds. In Egypt, death—in religious terms—was only a dramatic event for the ruler, with his (and sometimes her) spirit rising majestically over the trivialities of domesticity and family in a specially constructed, simulated house with all the accoutrements of a comfortable life. What went on in that house, and how the spirit moved about, ate, and drank, was a matter of great concern, since it was thought to determine the flow of history in the present time and beyond. But the "house" was only half of the equation. Death in Egypt had an inside and an outside shape. Entombing the "house" at the scale of the landscape was the structure's outside shape. Eighty percent of Queen Merneith's mastaba was nothing more than a dark mass of walls and spaces linking these two scales. The architect's job, in essence, was to bring the inner and outer manifestations of the ruler's death into unity.

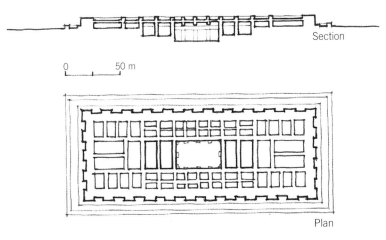

Section

0   50 m

Plan

1.38 Tomb Y (Queen Merneith) at Abydos

3500 BCE

1.39 Megalithic cultures, 4800–1200 BCE

1.40 Skara Brae, a Stone Age village in the Orkney Islands, Scotland

European Developments

Europe's complex geography of shorelines, rivers, and mountain ranges made it unlikely that it would arrange itself into a single civilizational unit like those in Egypt, China, and India. Furthermore, because of the difficulties of transplanting grain northward into different climatic regions, Europe was only fully settled around 3500 BCE. Because European cultures developed without the history of agricultural domestication, their focus was not on family matriarchal histories through which such knowledge was, by necessity, handed down, but on the clans that could pull communities together for defense or war to overcome obstacles and define their relationships to the outside world. This explains why the Europeans did not develop a temple culture or, for that matter, a more complex priestly culture until much later.

Barrow Tombs

The first architectural expressions were tombs, which preserved the memories of clan lineages and served as places for gathering, trade, and ritual. Examples can be found throughout Europe—in Portugal, Sardinia, France, and England, and as far north as Norway—as well as in Morocco. The Portuguese tombs, which are among the oldest, consist of a chamber built of stone slabs approached through a narrow passageway. These tombs are therefore often referred to as either chamber tombs or passage graves. They were covered by an artificial mound of earth or stone called a barrow—thus also the name barrow tomb—and were sometimes fortified by retaining walls.

The ceilings of some of the chambers were corbelled with stones placed farther and farther toward the center of the space till they meet at the top. An example of this can be found in the passage grave on Île Longue, South Brittany, France. At Quanterness, in Great Britain's Orkney Islands, the central chamber is surrounded by six side chambers, all with corbelled roofs. Used for over five hundred years, it accumulated the remains of about four hundred people.

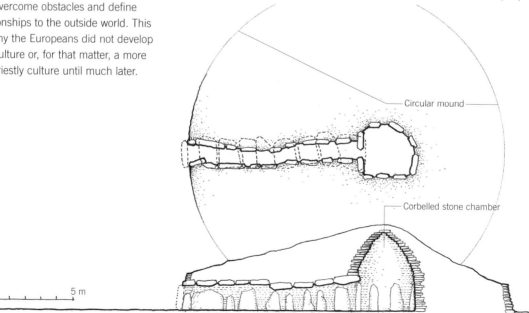

1.41 Passage grave on Île Longue, South Brittany, France, ca. 4100 BCE

1.42 **Locations of stone circles discovered in England**

Stone Circles

In England, toward the end of the fourth millennium BCE, land overuse, famine, or plague put a dent in the development of more complex social organizations. Tombs were blocked up and abandoned. A natural disaster may have been at the heart of this calamity. In Greenland there is evidence that acid rain from volcanic eruptions in Iceland, dating from 3250 BCE, created clouds so dense that they blocked the sunlight. Vast tracks of land were rendered uninhabitable. The effects were disastrous but short-lived. The weather rebounded and so too, according to Burl Aubrey, one of the leading researchers of English stone circles, did the human spirit. In fact, during the late Stone Age and early Bronze Age, the climate in England would have been warmer than it is today; farming was therefore possible in more places in 2000 BCE than in 2000 CE. A new generation of tomb structures, called coves, appeared. They consisted of three upright slabs set in the configuration of a U facing east, open to the sky, and often surrounded by circular embankments and stone circles.

The most important expression of that time, was, however, not tombs but stone circles. How widespread they were has only been understood since the second half of the 20th century, when aerial photography revealed additional locations. It is estimated that at one time there might have been as many as four thousand of them, of which two-thirds were erected in the major building phase between 3000 and 1300 BCE. The earliest circles ranged in size from 18 to 30 meters in diameter, with the stones standing shoulder to shoulder. For the most part they were near a village or clan compound and were built with local stones. The architectural expression of the circles is, however, not uniform. They could be round or oval, they could have concentric embankments of stone circles, and many had approach avenues. Some were associated with burials, others with cremation. In some locations, such as Loanhead of Daviot, the stones were not upright but lay flat on the ground, distinguished by glittering bright quartz fragments and concentrated in positions associated with the setting moon. At the center of that site, archaeologists found the remnants of a fire pit with cremated human bones. Other structures had burrows. Many had a central stone.

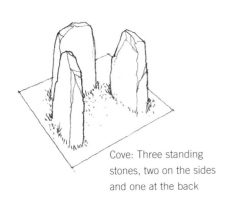

Cove: Three standing stones, two on the sides and one at the back

Trilithon: A structure consisting of two upright stones supporting a horizontal lintel

Dolmen: A burial tomb consisting of three or more upright stones and one or more capstones

1.43 **Types of early megalithic tomb structures**

1.44 **A dolmen in southern France**

1.45 **Stone circle at Avebury, England**

A cluster of early Bronze Age sites exists across the English Channel, on the southern coast of Brittany at the base of the peninsula, but circular structures, though not unknown in Europe, were uncommon. At the village of Ménec, north of the town of Carnac, is a large cromlech of closely placed stones. Leading to this stone circle is an impressive ritual road, 100 meters wide and 1,165 meters long, running southwest to northeast and formed of almost 1,100 standing stones, or menhirs, in eleven rows. How these stone circles worked as celestial observatories is much debated, but there is agreement that they were meant to follow the movements of the moon and stars (and not the sun), as would have been typical for early agrarian-based societies.

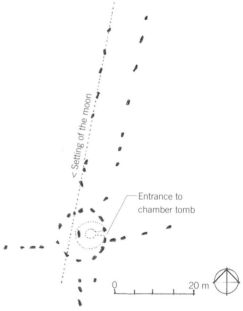

1.46 **Main circle and alignments at Callanish, Scotland**

Cromlech: A circular arrangement of monoliths enclosing a dolmen or burial mound.

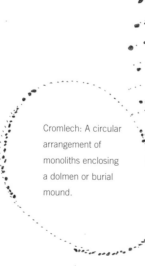

1.47 **Cromlech and alignments of standing stones near Carnac, France**

2500 BCE

By the beginning of the third millennium BCE, the various river-oriented civilizations were primed for rapid cultural development. There were at the time five principal cultural hubs: China, Egypt, Mesopotamia, Margiana, and the Indus. When taken together, they can be understood as a supraregional civilizational entity. Egypt was less prone to invasions by well-armed enemies and thus developed a consistent set of religious traditions. Furthermore, due to the seasonality of its agriculture, farm workers could be summoned by the pharaohs to perform forced labor on building projects. Zoser's temple complex, built on an unprecedented scale, was one of the first monumental stone buildings in the world. It was also a building of great complexity, answering to the intricate cosmology used by its Egyptian builders. (The Egyptians were the first to modernize their cosmology to fit the needs of their culture and economy.) In Mesopotamia, the divergent cultural elements and far-flung trade networks made it difficult for one stable, central power to emerge. Cities, dedicated to various deities, were political entities in their own right. Irrigation canals placed a great deal of wealth in the hands of the new generation of rulers, who operated in close alliance with a priestly class ruling out of temples that were built as artificial mountains rising in colorful terraces above the plains from the center of cities. Unlike in Egypt, the Mesopotamian irrigation system was more difficult to maintain and required greater coordination.

The trend toward urbanization also took place along the shores of the Indus and the Ghaggar-Hakra rivers. The cities built there were particularly sophisticated in terms of planning and water drainage. Instead of a ziggurat or pyramid at the center of the town, there were huge public baths, such as the one at Mohenjo-Daro. There was extensive trade with Mesopotamia, up the Persian Gulf, and with Margiana. Indeed, the entire area from Mesopotamia to the Indus, and from the Caspian Sea to Arabia, was what archaeologists call a zone of interconnection. This zone went up to Derbent on the Caspian

Sea, where granaries and a fortified city from the third millennium BCE have recently been uncovered.

The fourth civilizational zone developed around the Oxus River and is known as the Adronovo Culture. It was based at first around small villages, but here two large cities eventually developed (in today's Turkmenistan and Uzbekistan) that were much more urban and socially organized than previously thought. The cities were not only of great size but were designed with great geometrical precision. In China, the first recorded dynasty, the Xia dynasty, emerged around 2100 BCE. Nonetheless, we still find a horizontal civilization of villages and towns unified around common ritual centers.

In Europe we see the impact of the Beaker People, whose origins are still debated, but who most likely came from either Spain or the Balkans. Known for their advanced metalworking skill, they left their traces in various locations. They arrived in England, where they encountered such sites as Stonehenge, which they took over and redesigned, orienting it to the sun rather than to the moon. While physically this was largely a matter of "fine-tuning," the cultural implications this reorientation presupposes are imponderable.

In the Americas, the Andean population inhabited a thin sliver of coastline between the Pacific Ocean and a desert. Though these communities could easily have become a forgotten niche culture, the currents of the Pacific Ocean, with their rich bounty of marine life, helped sustain settled life until the inhabitants learned to tame the rivers descending from the Andes mountains by canalization and terracing. Very recently, archaeologists have dated a large ceremonial complex above the Supe Valley in the Peruvian Andes to about 2750 BCE. This discovery has overturned Andean chronology and required the dating of large-scale ceremonial architecture to a much earlier time period than it had been previously thought to belong to. Large tracts of Andean sites have still not been explored and carbon-dated, and their stories remain to be told.

Indus Valley: Early Harappan Period
5000–2600 BCE

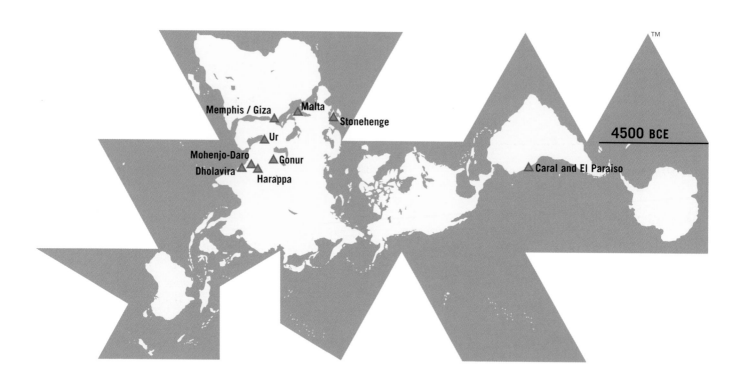

4500 BCE

Memphis / Giza
Malta
Stonehenge
Ur
Mohenjo-Daro
Gonur
Dholavira
Harappa
Caral and El Paraiso

Human settlement of Malta
ca. 5000 BCE

Ghaggar-Hakra Civilization
2600–1800 BCE

▲ **Dholavira**
ca. 3000–2000 BCE

▲ **Mohenjo-Daro and Harappa prosper.**
ca. 2600–1900 BCE

Mesopotamia: Early Dynastic Period
ca. 2900–2350 BCE

Akkadian Dynasty
ca. 2350–2150 BCE

Old Assyrian Period in the north;
Old Babylonian Period in the south
ca. 2000–1600 BCE

Palace of Naram-Sin ▲
ca. 2170 BCE

Third Dynasty of Ur
ca. 2100–2000 BCE

▲ **Ziggurat at Ur**
ca. 2100 BCE

Margiana
ca. 2200–1700 BCE

▲ **Gonur**
ca. 2200 BCE

3500 BCE   **2500 BCE**   **1500 BCE**

Late Neolithic Period
ca. 5000–2500 BCE

Early Bronze Age
ca. 3000–2000 BCE

Egypt: First Intermediate Period
ca. 2150–2030 BCE

Egypt: Old Kingdom
ca. 2649–2150 BCE

Middle Kingdom
ca. 2030–1640 BCE

▲ **Step Pyramid of Zoser**
ca. 2750 BCE

Second Intermediate Period
ca. 1640–1550 BCE

▲ **Bent Pyramid**
ca. 2600 BCE

▲ **Great Pyramid of Khufu**
ca. 2590 BCE

Building of megalithic temples
ca. 3500–2500 BCE

Brittany and British Isles: Megalithic building cultures
ca. 4200–2000 BCE

Beaker Culture
ca. 2800–1800 BCE

▲ **Stonehenge**
Begun ca. 3000 BCE

◉ 3100 BCE
Mythic base date of the
Maya long-count calendar

North and Central Andes: Early Ceramic Cultures
ca. 4000–1800 BCE

▲ **Caral**
ca. 2627–2000 BCE

▲ **El Paraiso**
ca. 1800 BCE

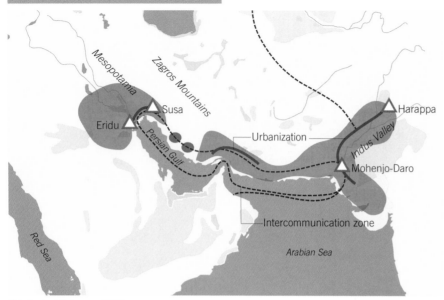

2.1 Central Asia, ca. 2500 BCE

The Indus Ghaggar-Hakra Civilization

Around 2500 BCE, the Mehrgarh people moved down from the Baluchistan Hills and settled in the river valleys that define the eastern edge of the South Asian subcontinent—those of the Indus and the now dried-up Ghaggar-Hakra rivers. The Indus/Ghaggar-Hakra region was the first urban civilization in the true sense of the word. Over a thousand cities and towns have been discovered spread over a quarter of a million square miles, an area roughly equivalent to modern-day France. Though these cities were distant from each other, they shared a common language and a standardized system of weights and measures. Although thousands of terra-cotta seals depicting a wide range of human, animal, and mythical forms, each with distinctive markings that are presumably letters of an alphabet, have been found, the Indus script has not been deciphered. The inhabitants seemed to have called themselves something akin to Meluhha. That, at least, is what the contemporaneous Mesopotamians, with whom they traded extensively both by northern land routes and by ship through the Arabian Gulf, called them. From the Indus comes the name India. In ancient Sanskrit, the Indus was called the Sindhu. In Central Asian languages, *Sindhu* became *Hindhu*, which then became *Indus* in Greek.

The Indus civilization was part of an interconnected zone that extended across western Asia and even into Egypt. Ships carried bricks, beads, lumber, metals, and lapis lazuli up the Persian Gulf to the cities of Mesopotamia. We are not sure of the nature of the return freight since few Mesopotamian objects have been found at the Indus. The area between Mesopotamia and the Indus was also urbanized with cities such as Tepe Yaha and Jiroft, in the once fertile and expansive Soghun Valley. Tepe Yaha specialized in mining a highly desired stone used to make bowls, an export item that matched those found in Mesopotamia and Indus. Not far away was an even larger city, Jiroft, which specialized in the production of golden lapis lazuli. Initially, most of the trade across this zone was by land routes. But around 2700 BCE, the exploitation of the coastal routes of the Persian Gulf multiplied the wealth of the entire zone.

The Indus Ghaggar-Hakra civilization went through roughly four phases of development.
1. The urbanization of the Ghaggar-Hakra River valley, ca. 2800 BCE
2. The rising dominance of the four cities— Harappa, Mohenjo-Daro, Rakhigarhi, and Ganweriwala—ca. 2500 BCE
3. The new urbanization of areas south and east, ca. 2200 BCE
4. The postdecline reurbanization of the Ghaggar-Hakra River, ca. 1700 BCE

Whereas the first two are part of the development and rise of the Ghaggar-Hakra civilization, the last two are part of the story of its decline, which was due primarily to the Ghaggar-Hakra River drying up. While moving close to the rivers enabled the Indus people to expand their agricultural production, they had to cope with the challenge of building near rivers consistently prone to flash flooding and sudden route changes. Bricks were used to construct huge platforms over existing mounds to make the bases for the cities. Large-scale standardized burnt-brick production was key. Walls were erected in part for defensive reasons but also to keep out floodwaters. And most importantly, elaborate interconnected drainage systems were designed to disperse storm waters. A central drain under the main gate of Harappa still stands in place. Nonetheless, the Indus flooded many times, each flood burying the city under a thick layer of silt. Harappa was rebuilt at the same spot more than seven times. It is thought to have had a population of about fifty thousand.

The largest cities were affiliated with outlying smaller cities. There were also specialized cities, such a ports and mining towns. Dholavira, located on an island in the Rann of Kutch, had to solve the opposite hydroengineering problem as Harappa's. Because the city sits in the middle of a vast delta in a very dry area, the issue was not keeping floodwater out, but ensuring that enough water could be harvested for the dry season. The solution was a series of strategically located dams and holding tanks that allowed excess water to escape during a flood. Once the tanks were full, additional water was held in huge rectangular, shallow man-made lakes that surrounded the city. In Lothal, a port city, water was let through a sluice into a vast rectangular tank that some speculate functioned as a dry dock for seafaring vessels.

The largest cities were divided into an upper town, which was on the highest ground and had large palaces, exclusive walls, and ceremonial spaces, and a lower town, which had most of the housing. The upper town usually had its own wall within the general wall that surrounded the whole city. At Dholavira the boundary wall was over 30 feet thick. Burials were often under mounds just outside the city. Road networks were rectilinear. Though these cities clearly had a social hierarchy with a strong ruling class (confirmed by the fact that they were divided

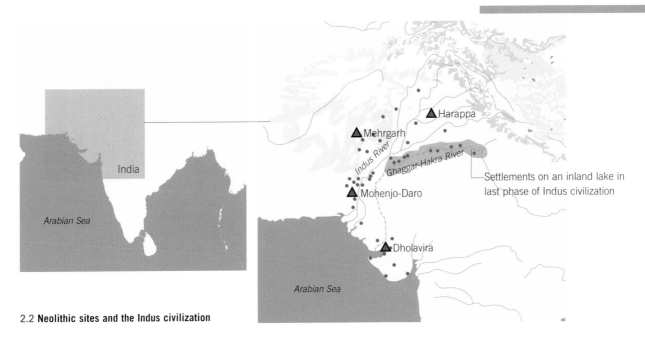

2.2 Neolithic sites and the Indus civilization

into sections with larger and smaller houses), there is little evidence of a centralized kingship, as there was in contemporaneous Egypt, Mesopotamia, and China. In the same vein, there are no large temples, castles, or palaces. As to their religious system, terra-cotta seals show a plethora of supernatural animals—in particular unicorns. There is also the depiction of a proto-Shiva-like divinity sometimes shown sitting in the lotus position. He wears bull horns on his head and seems to be worshipped by animals of all sorts. There is also a proliferation of sculptural

figures dedicated to fertility and procreation. But there are no centralized religious structures. How the Indus people managed to build a hugely successful polity without a central authority legitimized by overarching religious ideology remains an open question.

Early in the second millennium BCE, the Ghaggar-Hakra begun to dry up. The reasons are debated, but it seems an earthquake in the Himalayas caused one of its major tributaries to change course and drain into the Indus, depleting the Ghaggar-Hakra. Its waters collected in an inland

lake that spawned a successful maritime community around its shores. Subsequently, the lake, too, dried up, bringing about the final phase: the abandonment of the entire Indus Ghaggar-Hakra region. Where the people went is still debated, but the majority probably dispersed eastward to the plains of the Ganges River. Some, however, may have gone westward and relocated as far away as Assyria, causing a ripple effect of disruptions that were felt all the way to Egypt.

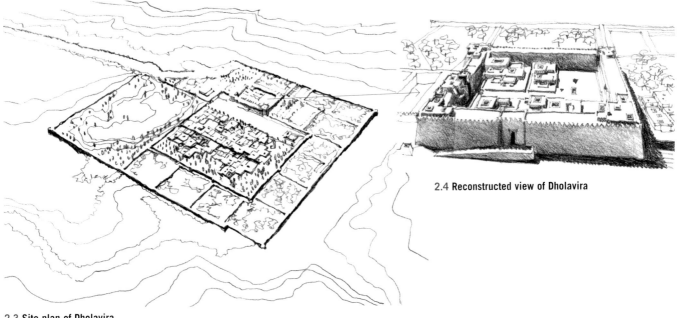

2.4 Reconstructed view of Dholavira

2.3 Site plan of Dholavira

2.5 Example of the intricately carved seals of the Indus civilization that were probably used in trade

Mohenjo-Daro

Mohenjo-Daro was the dominant city of the southern Indus. The Indus, which originates in the high Himalayas, is frequently subject to ice floes and landslides that can hold back its waters for a while but that eventually give way, resulting in huge flash floods. To guard against these, the two largest building areas of Mohenjo-Daro were raised high on a platform of bricks designed to disperse the floodwaters through a series of culverts. (The site of Mohenjo-Daro itself receives very little rain.) Under the main streets were drains running to settling tanks, which could be accessed and cleaned.

Mohenjo-Daro's neighborhoods were inward looking. The main streets were lined with the largely blank walls of houses, and even the secondary streets usually did not have any major houses opening directly onto them. Accessible by alleys only, the houses were most often faced into open courtyards, with the larger ones often having two stories, the upper level built of wood. The number of rooms in houses varied from two to more than twenty. A good number of the rooms contained wells, and the larger ones had bathrooms and toilets.

Located at the intersection of the major north-south and east-west streets, the Great Bath of Mohenjo-Daro was the social center of the city. Its 12-by-7-meter pool, which was 3 meters deep, was accessed by means of symmetrical stairs on the north and south. The bath is surrounded by a narrow deep-water channel, and an outlet from one corner of the bath leads to a high-corbelled

2.6 An entrance gate to Harappa

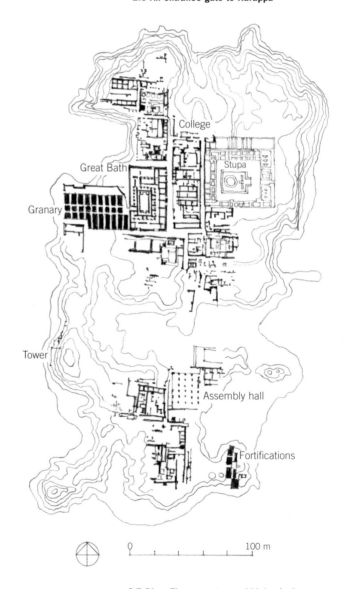

2.7 Plan: The upper town of Mohenjo-Daro

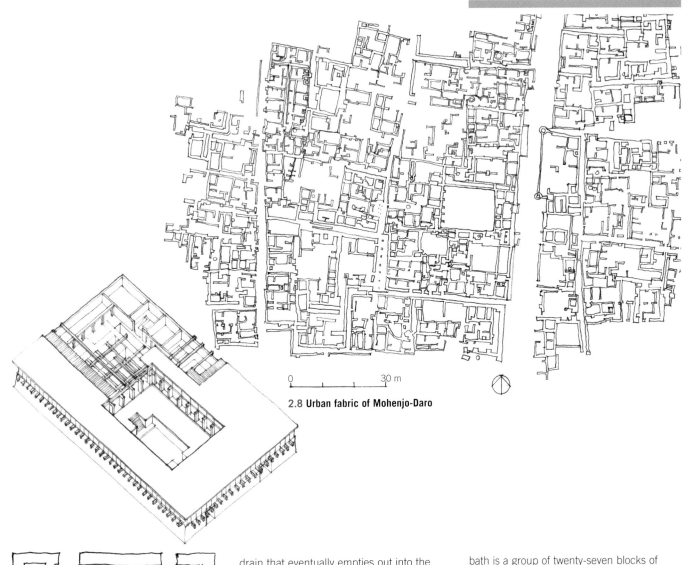

2.8 Urban fabric of Mohenjo-Daro

0   30 m

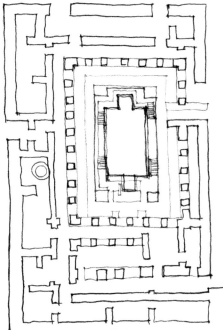

drain that eventually empties out into the surrounding lowlands. Burnt bricks lined the pool, while a layer of bitumen waterproofed it. It was surrounded by a brick colonnade, behind which were a series of rooms of various sizes (one of these with a well). The whole structure had a wooden second story, although the central pool courtyard was probably open to the sky. Access was carefully controlled, with only one opening from the south. Ritual urns with ashes—presumably of important people—were found close to the entrance.

One can only guess at the social practices that led to such an institution, but the very presence of the Great Bath indicates the dominance of water and bathing in the inhabitants' ideology. To the west of the bath is a group of twenty-seven blocks of brickwork crisscrossed by narrow ventilation channels, all of which come together to form a large, high platform. Archaeologists originally assumed this was a granary, but more recent evidence suggests that it may have been a general-purpose warehouse. As the rivers dried up, the cities were abandoned, but the process was gradual. The Great Bath, for instance, was temporarily converted into a workshop. The smaller cities in the south, around Kutch, actually grew as the big cities of the Indus decayed, but these, too, were eventually abandoned. The research work of establishing what really happened to the Indus people, what caused them to abandon their cities, still remains to be done.

2.9 **Plan and axonometric: The Great Bath of Mohenjo-Daro**

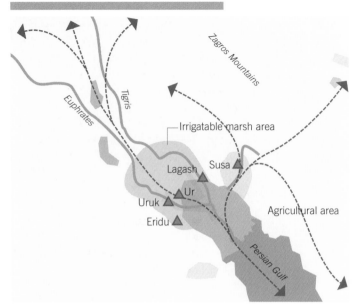

2.10 Early lower Mesopotamia

Eridu, Ur, Uruk, Lagash, and, farther to the east, Susa, which lay on the Karun River, formed a larger economic environment, with trade developing toward India to the south; toward Sialk, a metal-producing city on the other side of the Zagros Mountains; as well as, of course, toward points northward. In Lagash, archaeologists discovered the remains of a storehouse which contained not only supplies of grain and figs but also vessels, weapons, sculptures, and numerous other objects connected with the use and administration of palace and temple. Though these cities seem small by today's standards, at the time they would have been the largest in the world, along with Memphis in Egypt. The economy of the Sumerians was thus twofold: a northward-looking Mesopotamian-based one, and a southward-looking trade economy with the proto-Persians and Indus River cities.

Early Empires of Mesopotamia

Though settlements in the upper reaches of the Euphrates region date from very early on, large-scale urbanization of the lower Euphrates would have been impossible without a social system sufficiently complex and centralized to produce an economic surplus large enough to develop and pay for the technology of irrigation. The Ubaids and Sumerians were the first to make that leap, but they were soon joined in their efforts, and then rivaled, by the Akkadians to the north. No one knows when the Akkadians first began to infiltrate into central Mesopotamia, nor what their origins were, but by 2300 BCE they were predominant in the vicinity of modern Baghdad and farther north along the rivers. Akkadians came to dominate Mesopotamia with the ascendancy of Sargon, the ruler of Umma, who reigned from around 2334 to 2279 BCE. His was the first known successful centralization of power in the Mesopotamian region. His capital city, Agade, was located on the Euphrates about 30 kilometers south of modern Baghdad.

Sargon's notions of kingship had a lasting impact on Mesopotamian culture. The idea of village-based civic loyalty, so important to early Sumerians, was replaced by the concept of loyalty to a ruler, with Sargon taking measures that deliberately diminished the power of local chieftains. This new concept of kingship is expressed in the statue of a head representing an Akkadian ruler, found in the city of Nineveh. It is notable for its bold features, artfully braided beard, and majesty of bearing. The mouth, from which the pronouncements of law and rule issued forth, is as expressive as the eyes, which were once inlaid with stone, resulting in an active image in marked contrast to the quiet, open-eyed, and contemplative stare of the Sumerian figures. The new idea of an administrative center was also expressed architecturally in a vast palace with numerous offices, libraries, and storage facilities, not to mention an enormous throne room. The city of Akkad has not yet been archaeologically located, so to get a sense of Akkadian architecture we have to turn to other sites, such as Tell Brak, the ancient city of Nagar. There one finds a giant, heavily fortified building with a series of very large courts, located so as to control the southern entrance to the city. Only its foundation level has been preserved, but even the plan itself is impressive. Perhaps it was a combination of palace, garrison, and storehouse. This is the first generation of increasingly large administrative buildings in Mesopotamia. It was designed for Naram-Sin, Sargon's successor and grandson.

2.11 Statue of the head of an Akkadian ruler

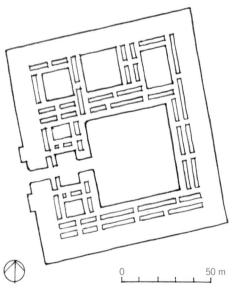

2.12 Plan: The Palace of Naram-Sin

2.13 **Group of statues from the Abu Temple, Tell Asmar**

The political structure was thus a type of theocratic socialism in which all the citizens worked in their various capacities in the service of the city-state. The chief god was Anu. Below him was Enlil, the earth or storm god, and Ea, the water god whom we encountered in Eridu. Nanna, the moon god who ruled in Ur, was among a group of gods at a slightly lower level. He measured time and provided fertility. Senior members of the pantheon served as patron deities of individual cities, while deities of lesser rank were associated with smaller urban centers. Scientific and religious texts reveal that there were over three thousand other gods and demons that governed even inanimate objects like pickaxes and brick molds. The flexibility with which the minor gods and goddesses came and went and syncretically changed their names makes it difficult to be specific about a Mesopotamian pantheon. Some of these deities were shared across various regions; some were part of local cults. This divine population was thought to meet regularly in an assembly and to arrive at agreements that bound all deities to the more senior deities. The temple was the actual domicile of the god rather than merely a place that permitted contact between the ruled and the divine powers, although one of the priests' principal jobs was the interpretation of omens, which had a powerful influence on every sphere of activity in Sumerian society.

Around 2150 BCE, the Akkadian dynasty was overthrown by tribes from the mountainous northeast who descended to the plains, contributing nothing to the civilization they ransacked. The survival of Mesopotamia was now suddenly dependent on kingdoms in the Sumerian south. They took up the challenge, drove the mountain people back, and reunited the realm under the kings of Ur. These kings, part of the Third Dynasty (2112–2004 BCE), accepted many of the innovations that had been created under Sargon. To the east, around the bend of the Persian Gulf, there was the parallel kingdom of the Elamites, who worked the fertile lowlands of the rivers descending from the Zagros Mountains. Known for their metalworking skills, they developed urban and religious practices similar to those of the Sumerians. These Sumerian cities were not only in communication with cities along the Persian Gulf but also with perhaps the hundreds of cities in the upper Euphrates region. At first the lower Euphrates and Elamite regions were more or less equal, but the Sumerians had a huge and simple advantage: the river wetlands between the Tigris and Euphrates.

The rulers of Ur defined kingship as a privilege that descended from heaven and was bestowed upon one city at a time, but only for a limited period. There was no notion of a single political entity comprising a nation in the modern sense. Rulers were, in essence, stewards of the gods who gave them protection and guidance. The temples, however, were the principal landowners, which, to all practical effects, meant that the priests controlled and organized the labor needed to build and maintain the irrigation canals and ditches. Priests were, in essence, the managers of the city's economy and infrastructure.

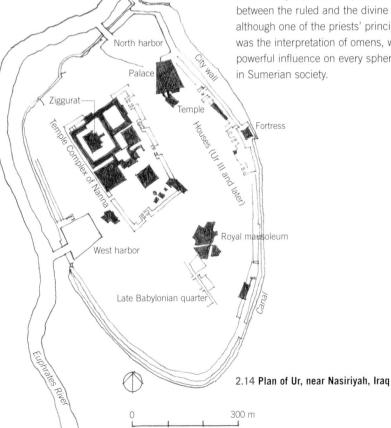

North harbor

Palace

City wall

Ziggurat

Temple

Temple Complex of Nanna

Houses (Ur III and later)

Fortress

West harbor

Royal mausoleum

Late Babylonian quarter

Canal

Euphrates River

2.14 **Plan of Ur, near Nasiriyah, Iraq**

0   300 m

Ziggurat at Ur

Mesopotamian religion was heavy in superstitions and subscriptive behavior. Life after death was portrayed as a sad and pitiable state, and the dead as potentially hostile toward the living. Thus, apart from rituals to appease the dead, burial architecture was rare. A person's association with the gods was based very much on the fulfillment of his or her duties in the here and now and on the principle of constant vigilance. For the manufacture of cult statues, for example, a text, slightly modified here, reads:

When you make the statues of cornel wood in the morning at sunrise you shall go to the wood. You shall take a golden axe and a silver saw, and with censor, torch and holy water you shall consecrate the tree.... You shall sweep the ground, sprinkle clear water, set up a folding table, sacrifice a sheep and offer the shoulder and fatty tissue and the roast, scatter dates and fine meal, set out a cake made with syrup and butter, pour out beer, kneel down, and stand up in front of the cornel tree and recite the incantation: "Evil is the broad steppe." With golden axe and the silver saw you shall touch the cornel tree and cut it down with a hatchet; you shall damp it with water, then remove the set-out material, kneel down and break the cornel tree into pieces.*

*Frans A. M. Wiggermann, *Mesopotamian Protective Spirits: The Ritual Texts* (Groningen, Netherlands: Styx, 1992), condensed from pp. 7–9.

The person then carves the statues as if "clad in their own garment, holding in their right hand a cornel-stick charred at both ends and with their left clasping their breasts." After writing his name on the statues, the person was asked to bring the statues he had made to his house for the purification ritual, placing them "on a pedestal in a walking pose so as to repel the evil ones." He was then asked to touch various parts of the house while reciting incantations and performing other prescribed rituals. Statues such as these were set up in temples, creating a charged ocular environment, with the eyes of the supplicant seeking to establish an unblinking connection between the profane and the sacred. Coming

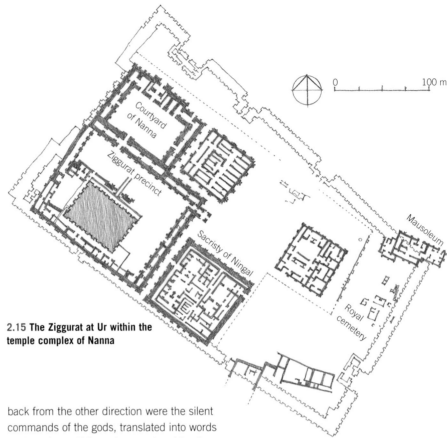

2.15 The Ziggurat at Ur within the temple complex of Nanna

back from the other direction were the silent commands of the gods, translated into words by the priests. This exchange played itself out most grandly in the ziggurats.

That ziggurats also served as conjugal sites is proven at Ur, where the ziggurat was linked by a watercourse to a small temple 4 miles west of the city dedicated to the mother goddess Ninkhursag. She was represented by the cow, whereas Nanna, the moon god who ruled over Ur, was sometimes referred to as a bull. Once a year, Ninkhursag, who was referred to as the Lady of the Mountain, whether embodied in statues or by a priestess, would have been brought to the city in a procession and led up to the shrine on top of the ziggurat to consummate her marriage while sacrifices and chants proceeded outside. Similar notions existed in Hinduism and in ancient Greece, with the celebration of the mystic marriage, the Hierogamos (from *hiero*, "sacred," and *gamos*, "marriage"). Ninkhursag thus represented the older goddess tradition that had been preserved and incorporated into the more complex mythologies needed after the move into the Mesopotamian marshes.

The Ziggurat at Ur was one of the most impressive structures of the time, and remains of it are still extant at Tall al Muqayyar in Iraq, about 42 kilometers south of Babylon. Some reconstruction drawings show it as a freestanding object similar to an Egyptian pyramid; it was in actuality surrounded by precinct walls to the east within which was a large square-shaped sanctuary dedicated to Nanna's divine wife, Ningal. A law court was close by. The whole was eventually enclosed by its own set of defensive walls.

The ziggurat measured 65 meters by 100 meters at its base, was 21 meters high, and consisted of three terraces with the sacred shrine on the highest one. Though the ornamentation of the ziggurat cannot be confirmed, the building was not the volumetric heap of bricks that we see today in the 20th-century reconstruction.

Three monumental staircases rose up the northeast flank of the ziggurat, converging at a canopied vestibule at the top of the first platform, 20 meters up from the ground. From there, the central stair continued on to the next stage and then to the third. Though highly axial, the axis did not carry through to the surrounding architecture. Access to the court was not from the front but

2.16 **Massing of the Ziggurat at Ur**

diagonally from a gate at one of its corners. The sides would have been plastered smooth and painted to serve as a visual key to a cosmological narrative, the principal character of which was Apsu, the god of the primeval waters who fathered heaven and earth. Despite his importance, he was defeated and killed by Ea, who transformed Apsu into still or stagnant subterranean waters. The lowest terrace of the ziggurat, representing Apsu, was painted white. The next terrace, probably black, represented Ea floating on and dominating the water. The top level would have been red, representing the sun-kindled air. The blue tiles that were found on the site are thought to have come from the temple at the top, which would have represented the blue heaven above the earth. What made this structure so innovative is that the elements—the stairs, the platforms, and the temple itself—were no longer arranged as a geographical mass, as at Uruk, but brought into the embrace of a unified and dramatic design. Geographical simulation had been replaced by an architectural abstraction.

The start of a construction of such a scale was initiated by elaborate rituals in which the king fashioned the first brick and carried up the first basket of earth. This act of dedication was commemorated by the burial of peg-shaped copper figurines in the foundation. The hard work was done by slaves taken from conquered lands, a common practice of the time. The structure was made of square flat bricks mortared with bitumen. Reed matting soaked with bitumen was inserted

horizontally at various layers to add cohesion and protect against vertical shear forces. The bricks were stamped with an inscription reading "Ur-Nammu, king of Ur, who built the temple of Nanna."

The city of Ur was almost oval in shape, with the Euphrates River coursing around its sides. There were harbors on its north and west sides, with the temple complex clamped between them. The surrounding walls, as is the case in all Mesopotamian cities, were intended just as much to impress as to protect. From their ramparts one would have seen the vast stretches of cultivated fields in all directions, as well as the villages of farm laborers tending them. The presence of gardens and orchards near the walls was also common. Much effort was made in the

design and outfitting of the gates, which were flanked by towers whose tops were decorated with bands of shields. The visitor, upon entering through the gates, would immediately confront the densely built-up jumble of the city. There was, however, little evidence of organized city planning. Royal roads would be designed only later. Streets varied from narrow lanes to routes 2 to 3 meters wide and served not only as passageways but also as a convenient place in which to dump garbage, a practice that one encountered even in medieval Europe. Because windows were rare, the narrow lanes formed curving chutes punctuated only by doors or enlivened by lean-tos where goods or food was sold.

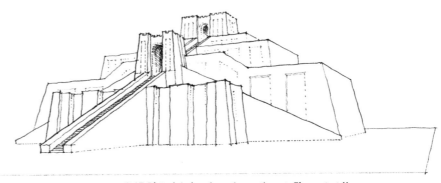

2.17 **Pictorial view from the northwest: Ziggurat at Ur**

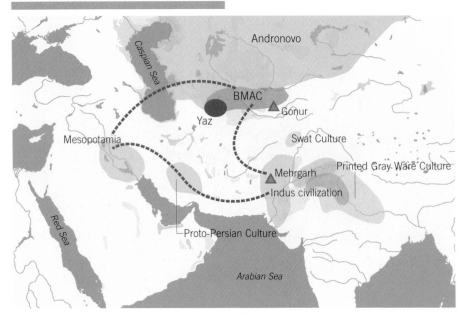

2.18 Emerging contacts: The Andronovo, BMAC, and Yaz cultures

Margiana

Archaeology has proven that by 2000 BCE in Asia, there were already many more connections across the vast expanses of the continent than had been anticipated even twenty years ago. If we look at the map of Asia, it is clear that, though the principal civilizations are far-flung, trade was already linking the entire continent into a composite whole, stretching from Egypt and Mesopotamia to the Indies and China. At the center of this vast territorial system was a region dominated by the Andronovo Culture, which includes the related Sintashta Culture, and to its south, the Margiana civilization, also known as the Bactrian-Margiana Archaeological Complex (BMAC). The original name of the Andronovo and Sintashta cultures are not known. The current names derive from villages near archaeological sites. The name Margiana is derived from the Persian word *margush*; the area is also sometimes called the Oxus civilization. Presently, most of Andronovo lies in Russia, whereas Margiana lies in modern-day Turkmenistan. Though today all we see in these areas is desert and empty tundra, at the time the areas were fertile and populated. Changes in climate as well as man-made deforestation lead to desertification—and as a consequence, depopulation—probably beginning in the early first millennium CE. The people of the Andronovo Culture (2500–

1600 BCE) were pastoralists whose principal economy included animal husbandry, agriculture, hunting, and fishing; the mining of bronze and other metals gave them further regional significance. Recently rediscovered tin mines containing pottery from both the Andronovo Culture and Margiana suggest that trade in ores or metal ingots was wide-ranging. The numerous animal sacrifices—as well as the evidence of horse-harnessing and the use of lightweight, spoke-wheeled chariots and an impressive array of metal weapons—all demonstrate a high level of cultural achievement.

Over time the settlements grew larger and developed into a series of towns, some circular and some square. Arkaim, for example, had two protective circular walls, 160 meters in diameter and 4 meters wide, built with soil that had been packed into timber frames before being faced with adobe bricks. On the interior, houses abutted the wall and were situated radially, with their doors exiting to the circular internal street. There have been many interpretations of this place's function. Most archaeologists believe that it was an administrative or ceremonial center with a set of core inhabitants—perhaps priests—and that people would have gathered there for special occasions. This place could therefore be compared with Stonehenge and, later, Persepolis.

Gonur

Margiana, which took on coherency around 2000 BCE, if not earlier, consisted of more than three hundred settlements in the valleys that form the headlands of the Oxus River before it flows northward into the Aral Sea. Gonur, along the Murghab River, seems to have been its capital. It consisted of a temple/citadel and a palace compound separated by about 300 meters. The palace was almost square (measuring 120 by 125 meters) and was surrounded by a defensive wall with towers at regular intervals. Outside were several temple areas. All of the altars were low to the ground and open to the elements, suggesting that they were used for fire rituals. There is no evidence of any statuettes of deities. To get to the throne room, one traversed two long audience halls and made two left turns. The residential part of the palace was at the center and had to its west two courtyards. There was also a chapel and a mortuary complex. Oddly, there was a suite of rooms with no access doors that was completely filled with clean river sand. The symbolic purpose of these spaces has not been ascertained. A long stairway led to the roof over these rooms, an indication that the roof was used for ritual purposes. In the wall decoration of the palace, archaeologists have noticed strong similarities to West Asian, Anatolian, and even Minoan art. Clearly these were people with strong ties to West and Central Asia. Did they emigrate from there, as some believe? Or were they a part of a larger civilization development? The parallelogram-shaped temple district went through several stages of development, the fort at the center belonging to the last stage.

To the west of the site was a large burial ground of about five thousand graves. It seems that bodies were not buried immediately after death, but were first purified by fire. This startling discovery has led archaeologists to surmise connections to the later development of Zoroastrianism, which also emphasized the purification of the body before interment. The fate of Andronovo is much debated. Some hold that with the deteriorating ecology, the inhabitants of this area migrated to Mesopotamia and India, contributing to the general upheavals that these places experienced between 1600 and 1200 BCE.

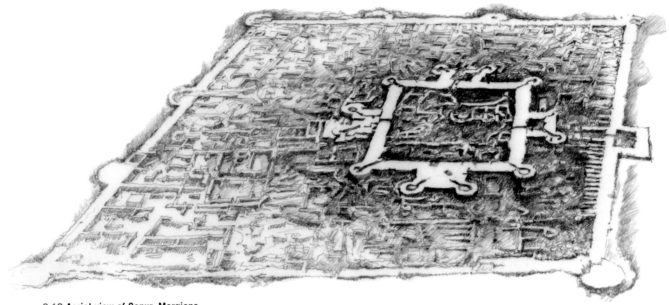

2.19 **Aerial view of Gonur, Margiana**

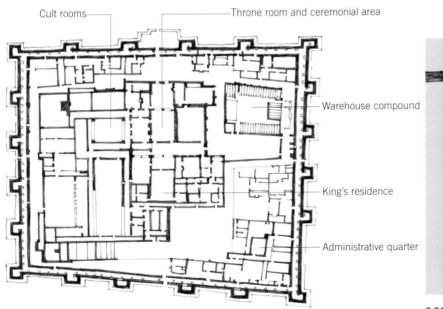

Cult rooms

Throne room and ceremonial area

Warehouse compound

King's residence

Administrative quarter

0   50 m

2.20 **Plan: The Citadel at Gonur**

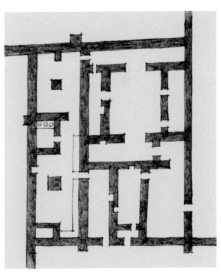

2.21 **Plan: *Temenos* No. 3 at Gonur**

2.22 **Portion of a residential quarter of Ur**

Domestic Architecture

Much of the city of Ur was built of sun-baked mud brick, making destruction by acts of war easy and common. Sargon, in a text repeated again and again by later rulers, writes: "Their twelve strong and walled cities … I captured. I destroyed their walls, I set fire to the houses inside them, I destroyed them like a flood, I turned them into mounds of ruins." Such destructions helped empty the countryside while consolidating the power of the victorious. Cities were, however, also relatively easily rebuilt. Though Ur was destroyed in several battles around 2000 BCE, it was rebuilt and remained important, mainly on account of its religious shrines. Life continued, though at a slower pace, under the tutelage of several rulers, until the city was abandoned around 400 BCE, by which time the Persian Gulf was many kilometers away due to the silting of the delta. A sacred way, used for the processions that dominated the religious calendar, led to the ziggurat precinct. But apart from this, there was little planning with respect to the residential parts. The blocks enclosed by the street system were quite large, with alleys and narrow passageways giving access to houses in the center.

Wheeled traffic would have been impossible in the narrow roads. Garbage was dumped into the streets, where it washed away with the rains. Nonetheless, the accumulation of garbage led to an increase in the elevation of the street, forcing residents to raise the thresholds of their doors. Roofs were of mud layered onto matting that was placed on a framework of wooden rafters. The houses of Ur, of varying quality depending on the wealth of the occupant, were organized around small courtyards. Some of the better ones had baked-brick foundation walls. The side opposite the entrance was generally the location of the principal room. Long and shallow, it was used for meals and receptions. At Ur, masks of the demon-god Pazzu were sometimes hung on the door jambs to protect the house against the southwest wind, which was thought to bring pestilence.

2.24 **Clay model of Mesopotamian house**

2.23 **Partial plan: A residential quarter of Ur**

0   20 m

2.25 **Egypt, ca. 3rd century BCE**

2.26 **Mortuary Complex of Zoser, Saqqâra, Egypt**

Egypt: The Old Kingdom

Though later Egyptians described their early history as emerging after the unification of Upper and Lower Egypt, archaeological evidence suggests that unification was a protracted process that took place over several centuries. Out of this unification emerged what later Egyptians would themselves call the Old Kingdom, with its capital at Memphis. This new political unity, combined with the rapid development of a hieroglyphic script and a powerful bureaucracy, was the final stage of Egypt's transformation into a complex and vertically structured society with a population of several million. Unlike Mesopotamia and China, Egypt was organized around an efficient and vast workforce that had little contact with the religious practices of the ruling elite. It has been estimated that by the third millennium BCE, the Nile Valley produced three times its own domestic requirements. From very early on, plenty of labor was available—above and beyond the stage of self-sufficiency. Soon, huge workforces of slaves, laborers, technicians, bureaucrats, and cooks were employed solely for royal projects. And there was no shortage of building material. Stone was abundant up and down the Nile: the colorful red granite of Aswan, the white marble of Gebel Rokham, and the black basalt of Faiyum—not to mention the various types of soft sandstone brought downriver from Nubia. One tremendous obelisk of red granite 41 meters long still lies on its side in the quarry near Aswan.

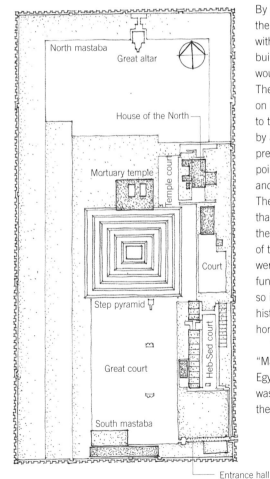

2.27 **Plan: Mortuary Complex of Zoser**

By the Third Dynasty of the Old Kingdom, the political stability of Egypt was secure, with Zoser (2686–2613 BCE) creating building projects against which later rulers would measure their accomplishments. The Mortuary Complex of Zoser, located on a slight hill west of Memphis and just to the north of Saqqâra, was enclosed by a 277-by-544 meter wall laid out in precise orientation to the four cardinal points. The walls were of white stone and an impressive 10.5 meters high. They served more symbolic purposes than defensive ones, meant to protect the mortuary complex from the chaos of the unordered world outside. There were fifteen gateways, yet only one was a functioning entrance. The structure was so impressive that for centuries, Egyptian historians would continue to praise and honor it.

The Ptah Temple in that city was called "Mansion of the Ptah," which in ancient Egyptian was pronounced *haykuptah*; it was from this that the Greeks later derived the word *Aiguptos*, or Egypt.

One entered the complex from the southern end of the eastern wall. The visitor passed through a 1-meter-wide hallway into a narrow corridor defined by two rows of columns attached to wall fins that projected into the space and supported a massive stone ceiling. These columns are probably the earliest monumental stone columns in the history of architecture. They are fluted and simulate a bundle of reeds. It was an ancient practice in Egypt to decorate wooden columns with a skirt of reeds as a representation of the mother goddess. But these columns were gigantic and meant to impose on the visitor the difference of scale that separates the divine from the mortal world. The shadowy entranceway led to the south court in front of the step pyramid. This was the Sed festival court, where ceremonial races were enacted. In the centuries before the Old Kingdom, the king had to prove that he was strong and capable of ruling by running a course for each of the provinces he governed. If he failed, he would be sacrificed in a religious ritual. From this derives the name Sed, or "slaughter festival." By the time of the Old Kingdom this practice had died out, but it remained an important element in the symbolic attributes of kingship and

in architecture itself. Zoser conceived the complex as a review stand for this event, which lasted five days, ending with a final ceremonial sprint. Originally it was to be held for every king in the thirtieth year of his reign, but that was not always the case. Ramesses II celebrated his Sed in grand style by inviting foreign dignitaries.

Since Zoser did not live long enough to perform this ritual, the court was designed so that he could perform it in death. This is confirmed by the complex's two mastabas: one on the south side, next to the wall—a type of fake mastaba—and the other, belonging to Zoser, to the north. The two structures have almost identical tomb designs, a room at the bottom of a 28-meter-deep shaft sealed by a 3-ton granite plug. In the southern mastaba, archaeologists found the wall decorated with small blue tiles with a glaze just as brilliant today as it was four thousand years ago. They represent a reed matting set in stone posts designed to imitate the appearance of wood, the whole thing creating the illusion of an outdoor canopied room. Between the tile sections is a large stone relief of Zoser "running" the ceremonial race.

Originally, the northern mastaba was similar to the southern one; both were low, flat-topped structures. But that design was changed in a dramatic way during construction, when the northern mastaba was covered with a stone superstructure with four gently sloping steps. No sooner was that built than it was decided to expand yet again. It was transformed into a 60-meter-high, six-tiered structure by adding material in the northerly direction. The first mortuary temple behind this step pyramid was also rebuilt and expanded. To the east there was another court lined on both sides with chapels, one for each of the Egyptian provinces. Behind them rose the facades of ten tall dummy buildings, replicating government buildings or, more likely, granaries. Slender columns, drawing on the imagery of reed bundles, ornamented their surfaces. On their other side are engaged columns with smooth-angled shafts holding bell-shaped capitals modeled on the shape of the papyrus flower. Like the reed-shaped columns, the papyrus also had symbolic value. It was used to decorate the Djed pillar that was thought to represent Hathor pregnant with Osiris in the Egyptian mystery play of the death and

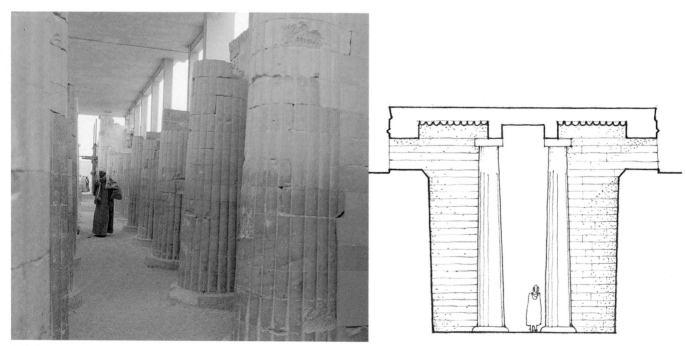

2.28 Entrance hall to the Mortuary Complex of Zoser

2.29 Section through entrance hall, Mortuary Complex of Zoser

2.30 Ka statue of Zoser

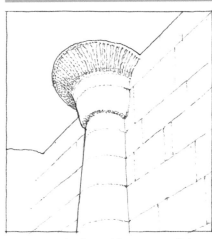

2.31 Engaged column with papyrus capital

resurrection of the god. The raising of the pillar represented the resurrection of the dead pharaoh. As part of the temple's stone architecture, they guaranteed his eternal life.

The north part of the complex was dominated by a monumental altar to which offerings were brought each day, a metaphor for the offering place of the northern heaven. In a small chapel positioned against the north side of the pyramid was a life-size statue of Zoser, showing him wearing a priest's Sed festival cloak, a ceremonial beard, and a ritual headdress. Sitting in the dark chamber, he could gaze through two small holes in the wall placed at the statue's eye level, through which he could watch the ceremonies taking place in the court.

This building represents a shift in the idea of death, and its associated religious practices began to change. The low-lying mastabas of the pharaohs were no longer considered worthy of rulers, who now ranked among the gods. In classical Egyptian, the word for *tomb* actually meant a "house of eternity" or, more precisely, a "house for eternity." The pyramids (that word was a much later Greek term) were certainly built for eternity, but they were now defined differently, as "the place where one ascends." And this might explain the steps, since that was a literal form of the Egyptian glyph, namely a set of steps. This new form was thus meant to serve two purposes: providing the king with an impregnable refuge while also assisting him in the first steps of his ascension toward the hereafter.

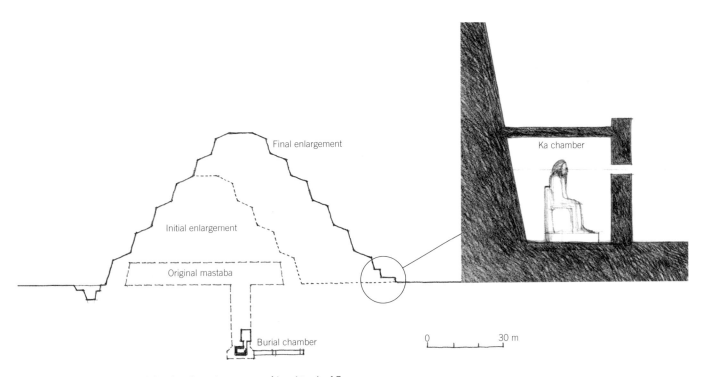

2.32 Section through step pyramid and tomb of Zoser

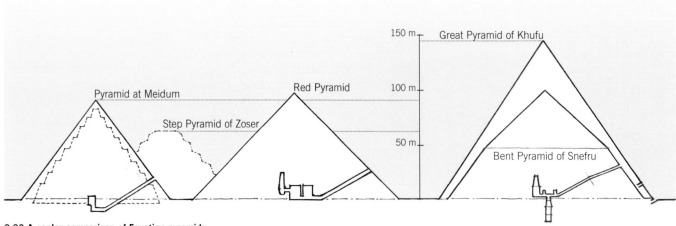

2.33 A scalar comparison of Egyptian pyramids

After Zoser, the pharaonic institution began to assert its cosmological narrative with ever-greater force and precision. One of the places where this manifests is a cult center for the falcon-god Menthu not far from Medamud, a provincial town 5 kilometers northeast of Karnak at Thebes. The original sanctuary, which dates from about 2500 BCE, consisted of a roughly lozenge-shaped enclosure 83 meters at its widest, surrounded by a high wall with a gate to the east. The interior contains a grove of trees and two burial mounds that could be interpreted as the primeval mounds appearing above the waters of chaos. This cult site contains features that would continue to be part of later temple architecture. The mounds become pyramids, the enclosing wall becomes a square, and the entrance courtyard becomes the pyramid temple.

With Snefru (2613–2589 BCE), who ruled during the Fourth Dynasty, one sees the rapid maturity of the Medamud prototype. But it took Snefru several tries. His first project was the step-faced pyramid at Meidum. The location of the two tomb chambers was innovative. Separated horizontally in the Zoser temple complex, here they are placed one on top of the other, the lower one representing the chthonic aspect of the Egyptian religion. Snefru abandoned the building after fifteen years of work and started another, larger pyramid complex 50 kilometers north, near

Dahshur. Originally planned to be a towering 150 meters high, it was too bold, and the ground gave way under part of it. In an effort to save the building, the designers added a kink or bend to reduce the weight and angle of the slope, which is why it is today called the Bent Pyramid.

The failure forced Snefru to ask his builders to return to the Step Pyramid at Meidum. They added a layer that transformed it into a true pyramid, but this time only after careful preparation of the ground. (In Roman times, the stone facing was removed to be made into stucco. Hence it is possible to see the original form.) Still, it was not enough for Snefru. He constructed a third pyramid two miles north of the Bent Pyramid. Not as steep as the earlier ones, it is called the Red Pyramid because of the reddish cast of the stone. This is where Snefru is actually buried. It is the first true pyramid. The harmonious proportions of the form and the perfection of the system of tomb chambers made it the model for subsequent tombs. Construction was so well thought out that despite the weight of the 2 million tons of stones on the roofs of the chambers, cracks have yet to appear.

Pyramids at Giza

Though the pyramids today are seen as freestanding, they were actually surrounded by a wall that defined the sacred precinct. On the eastern side stood an altar on the base of the pyramid, and on the western side, a mortuary temple. At the ceremonial center of the temple complex was the Ka statue that embodied the still-living spirit of the king. The statue had to be tended to and provided with food and drink. Though a Ka statue might have been placed near the altar, others were placed in the mortuary temple. If anything were to happen to the Ka statue, the spirit of the deceased would never gain entrance to the heavenly realm.

The mortuary temple was connected to a so-called valley temple placed along the Nile River. The pharaoh's body would be brought there on a funerary ship. Once the body had been properly prepared, the coffin was sledded up to the mortuary temple, where other rituals would take place, including daily prayers, incantations, and offerings. The coffin, attended by a lavish funerary cortege, was then brought into the pyramid and placed in the stone sarcophagus that was built into the burial chamber of the pyramid. The pharaoh and the canopic jars that contained his entrails, along with various assorted possessions, were placed in the tomb chamber, and offerings were made. Then the funerary party exited the pyramid

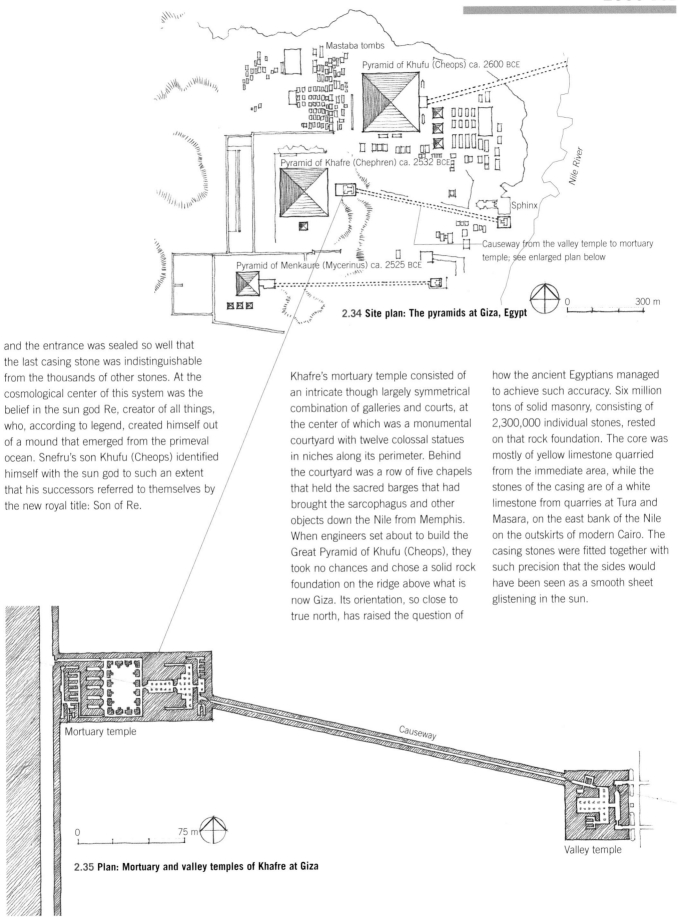

Mastaba tombs

Pyramid of Khufu (Cheops) ca. 2600 BCE

Pyramid of Khafre (Chephren) ca. 2532 BCE

Nile River

Sphinx

Causeway from the valley temple to mortuary temple; see enlarged plan below

Pyramid of Menkaure (Mycerinus) ca. 2525 BCE

2.34 Site plan: The pyramids at Giza, Egypt

0   300 m

and the entrance was sealed so well that the last casing stone was indistinguishable from the thousands of other stones. At the cosmological center of this system was the belief in the sun god Re, creator of all things, who, according to legend, created himself out of a mound that emerged from the primeval ocean. Snefru's son Khufu (Cheops) identified himself with the sun god to such an extent that his successors referred to themselves by the new royal title: Son of Re.

Khafre's mortuary temple consisted of an intricate though largely symmetrical combination of galleries and courts, at the center of which was a monumental courtyard with twelve colossal statues in niches along its perimeter. Behind the courtyard was a row of five chapels that held the sacred barges that had brought the sarcophagus and other objects down the Nile from Memphis. When engineers set about to build the Great Pyramid of Khufu (Cheops), they took no chances and chose a solid rock foundation on the ridge above what is now Giza. Its orientation, so close to true north, has raised the question of

how the ancient Egyptians managed to achieve such accuracy. Six million tons of solid masonry, consisting of 2,300,000 individual stones, rested on that rock foundation. The core was mostly of yellow limestone quarried from the immediate area, while the stones of the casing are of a white limestone from quarries at Tura and Masara, on the east bank of the Nile on the outskirts of modern Cairo. The casing stones were fitted together with such precision that the sides would have been seen as a smooth sheet glistening in the sun.

Mortuary temple

Causeway

Valley temple

0   75 m

2.35 Plan: Mortuary and valley temples of Khafre at Giza

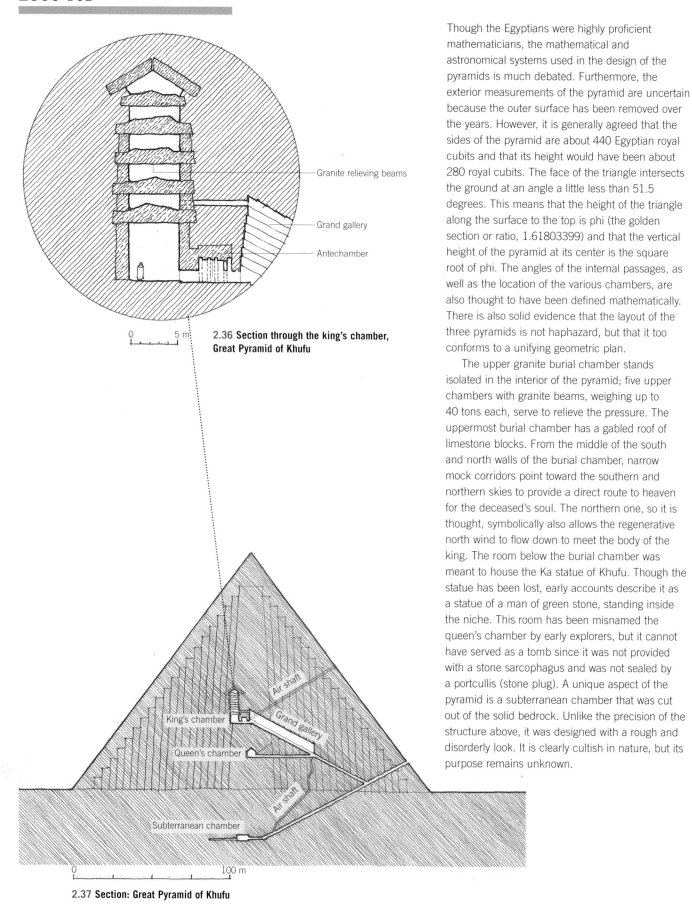

2.36 Section through the king's chamber, Great Pyramid of Khufu

— Granite relieving beams

— Grand gallery

— Antechamber

0   5 m

King's chamber

Queen's chamber

Grand gallery

Air shaft

Air shaft

Subterranean chamber

0   100 m

2.37 Section: Great Pyramid of Khufu

Though the Egyptians were highly proficient mathematicians, the mathematical and astronomical systems used in the design of the pyramids is much debated. Furthermore, the exterior measurements of the pyramid are uncertain because the outer surface has been removed over the years. However, it is generally agreed that the sides of the pyramid are about 440 Egyptian royal cubits and that its height would have been about 280 royal cubits. The face of the triangle intersects the ground at an angle a little less than 51.5 degrees. This means that the height of the triangle along the surface to the top is phi (the golden section or ratio, 1.61803399) and that the vertical height of the pyramid at its center is the square root of phi. The angles of the internal passages, as well as the location of the various chambers, are also thought to have been defined mathematically. There is also solid evidence that the layout of the three pyramids is not haphazard, but that it too conforms to a unifying geometric plan.

The upper granite burial chamber stands isolated in the interior of the pyramid; five upper chambers with granite beams, weighing up to 40 tons each, serve to relieve the pressure. The uppermost burial chamber has a gabled roof of limestone blocks. From the middle of the south and north walls of the burial chamber, narrow mock corridors point toward the southern and northern skies to provide a direct route to heaven for the deceased's soul. The northern one, so it is thought, symbolically also allows the regenerative north wind to flow down to meet the body of the king. The room below the burial chamber was meant to house the Ka statue of Khufu. Though the statue has been lost, early accounts describe it as a statue of a man of green stone, standing inside the niche. This room has been misnamed the queen's chamber by early explorers, but it cannot have served as a tomb since it was not provided with a stone sarcophagus and was not sealed by a portcullis (stone plug). A unique aspect of the pyramid is a subterranean chamber that was cut out of the solid bedrock. Unlike the precision of the structure above, it was designed with a rough and disorderly look. It is clearly cultish in nature, but its purpose remains unknown.

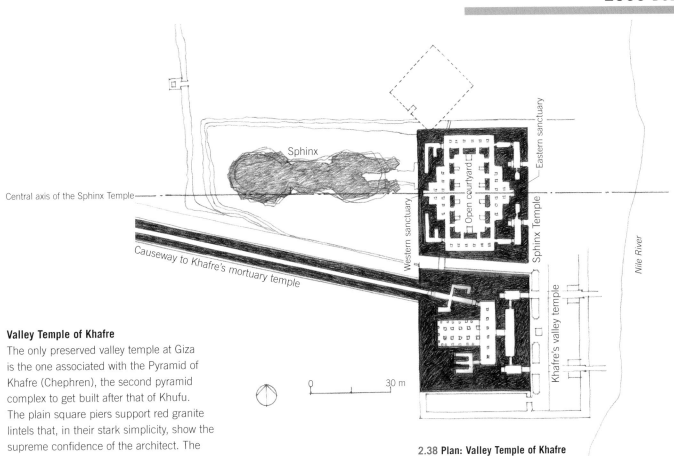

Central axis of the Sphinx Temple ——

Causeway to Khafre's mortuary temple

Sphinx

Western sanctuary

Open courtyard

Eastern sanctuary

Sphinx Temple

Khafre's valley temple

Nile River

0   30 m

2.38 Plan: Valley Temple of Khafre

Valley Temple of Khafre

The only preserved valley temple at Giza is the one associated with the Pyramid of Khafre (Chephren), the second pyramid complex to get built after that of Khufu. The plain square piers support red granite lintels that, in their stark simplicity, show the supreme confidence of the architect. The piers would have been highly polished. The rectilinear perfection of the piers contrasts with the more organic coursing of the gigantic stones of the wall. On the outside, the box-shaped form gives no indication of the complex internal layout. In fact, the space between the interior and the exterior is filled solid with enormous stones; the interiors would thus have seemed to be carved from the earth itself.

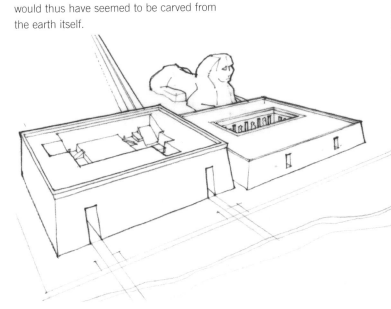

2.39 Overview of the Valley Temple of Khafre

2.40 Interior: Valley Temple of Khafre

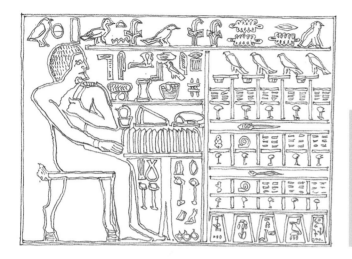

2.41 Egyptian slab stela
A slab stela shows a royal personage at a funerary repast sitting next to an offering table covered with the loaves of bread that have been brought to him. Next to him on the floor, on small platforms, are containers holding incense, ointments, figs, and wine.

Architecture and Food

For both Mesopotamian and Egyptian societies, food was not only the sustenance of humans but also of the gods. Offerings of food were laid out in front of the Ka statue in its niche to provide for the difficult journey ahead. They consisted of meat, roasted fowl, bread, fruit, vegetables, beer, and wine, all delivered out of the temple district's own gardens. The slaughter of the animals, out of sight of the gods, was supervised by the priests. From an anthropological perspective, one can say that this equation was necessary for social and political cohesion. There is also evidence of this in Mesopotamia, where the ziggurat was a type of elevated feasting platform. A text states, "In the first night watch, on the roof of the high temple of the ziggurat … when [the star of] the great Anu of heaven comes out," the feast was to be laid out upon a golden table for Anu and his wife Antum, as well as for the seven planets. The most exact instructions were reserved for the nourishment and entertainment of the gods. The flesh of the cattle, sheep, and birds, and beer of first quality, along with wine "poured from a golden ewer," was to be offered.

2.42 Statuette of a woman bearing offerings

Though both Mesopotamian and Egyptian food sacrifices emphasized breads, drinks, and the bounty of the land, the Mesopotamians rarely sacrificed animals, which were not plentiful in the alluvial plain. For the Egyptians, animal sacrifices were not uncommon, with offerings—especially of gazelles, antelopes, geese, ducks, and pigeons—coming mainly from hunting. The meat was offered in either boiled or roasted form. The shank and the heart were thought to have a particularly reviving effect for the Ka. Unlike the Greeks, the Egyptians did not perform the actual killing and bloodletting in "sight" of the gods; the meat arrived fully cooked. The difference is telling. The Ka is visualized as alive and sensitive, or at least as coaxed back to life by tasty morsels. The Greeks, as will be discussed later, saw the sacrifice very differently.

It was only at the time of the New Kingdom, the Mycenaeans, and later the Dorians, that one finds the multiple slaughter of large animals such as bulls. Furthermore, for the Greeks, the sacrificial animals could only be taken from domesticated herds, such as cattle and sheep. Sacrifice would remain important, but mainly in a symbolic sense, in Judaism and Christianity. Hinduism is one of the few modern religions that still preserves ritual food offerings to the gods, though meat sacrifices are forbidden.

2.43 **Stonehenge as it stands today, near Salisbury, England**

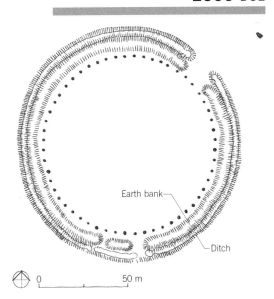

2.44 **Plan: Stonehenge, ca. 3000 BCE**

Stonehenge

Among Bronze Age sites in Europe, Stonehenge is preeminent. It has been wrecked by the Romans, who were trying to suppress local religions; chipped at by tourists; threatened with demolition in 1914; sold at auction in 1915 for £6,600; and, finally, its value as an irreplaceable relic of England's past understood, given to that nation in 1918. Today, this structure is one of England's most important tourist attractions. It is natural to compare Stonehenge with the megalithic temples in Malta, and in its early formation, there might have been some general connective thread. But the Maltese temples only underwent a process of refinement and enlargement, as one might expect from a rather static society, whereas Stonehenge underwent several revisions that significantly and purposefully altered its use and meaning. The structure as we see it today is in fact a combination of the last two phases and dates from between 2500 and 1800 BCE, making it more or less contemporary with Ur in Mesopotamia and the end of the age of pyramids in Egypt. This is important because there is a tendency to overstate the primitivism of Stonehenge, when in actuality it was a relatively advanced Bronze Age structure. Today, because Stonehenge is isolated in the landscape, it is difficult to visualize that the area was once densely settled. In the immediate landscape of Stonehenge one would have seen hundreds of burial mounds, some dating back to the fourth millennium BCE.

The first version of Stonehenge, dating to about 3000 BCE, was consistent with the circular henges of that age, except that this one was an impressive 100 meters across, with two or perhaps three spaces left open for access to the inside of the circle. At the center, archaeologists speculate, was a circular timber building about 30 meters across. A long avenue marked by stones ran up to the trench and alongside a single 4.9-meter-high stone just outside the circle. It has a pointed top and is known as the heel stone. Two alignments were built into it: one astronomical, at the northeast entrance toward the northernmost rising of the moon, and the other to the cardinal point to the south at the other causeway.

Around 2500 BCE, the structure was transformed by the Beaker People, so named because of the fine beaker vessels that they produced and that have been found in their villages and tombs. Having beliefs different from those who originally built Stonehenge, they changed the earthwork structure, and indeed the symbolic landscape associated with it, from a lunar to a solar monument. The origin of the Beaker People is much debated; the argument that they come from eastern Europe is strengthened by the fact that they were experts in the mining and trading of gold and copper. Metal ores had been discovered, perhaps by the Beaker People themselves, at several places in Ireland, as well as at Great Orme's Head on the north coast of Wales facing the Irish Sea.

The Beaker People integrated the geographically disparate technologies of mining, smelting, metal production, and trade into a single economic system and transformed Stonehenge from a local temple to a focal point for a larger civilizational entity. They filled the area for miles around with their circular burial mounds and founded a new city to the northeast of Stonehenge, now called Durrington Walls, which was defended by circular defensive walls 480 meters across. Their wealth shows up in their graves. In one grave, archaeologists found gold ornaments as well as bronze pins from Bohemia, blue faience beads from Egypt, and amber beads from northern Europe.

At the center of their cosmology was a connection between the smelting of ore and the sun. For this reason they had to redesign Stonehenge, transforming its orientation from the moon to the sun. To do this they rotated the axis an almost imperceptible 3 degrees eastward to coincide with the rising midsummer sun, according to the research of Gerald S. Hawkins in collaboration with John B. White. The Beaker People also imposed a rectangular shape measuring 33 by 80 meters onto the circle by adding four large stones that point to summer and winter risings and settings. Though the precise nature of how the stones worked is in dispute, Stonehenge's latitude, as it turns out, is the only one in Europe where this combination is even possible.

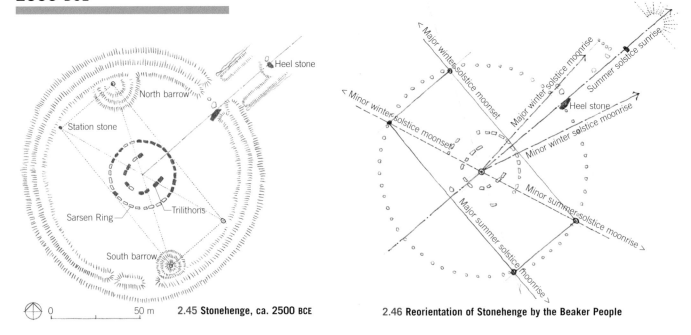

2.45 Stonehenge, ca. 2500 BCE

2.46 Reorientation of Stonehenge by the Beaker People

The most significant change attributed to the Beaker People was the addition of a ring of sixty large bluestones to the interior. They also constructed, about 1 kilometer north of Stonehenge, what archaeologists call a cursus—a 3-kilometer-long, 100-meter-wide rectangular form, slightly beveled toward the ends. Created by incising a ditch into the landscape, it lies in an east-west orientation. Though simply built, it is laid out with great precision. Its purpose is unknown, even though there are other cursi scattered across the region, some predating the arrival of the Beaker People. It certainly was not a running track, as the name implies. One can surmise that since the eastern sector was associated with the sunrise and the western side with the sunset, the cursus played an important part in the ritual expressions of life and death. Was it a pathway for the soul?

No sooner had the Beaker People completed their work, in or around 2300 BCE, then Stonehenge underwent yet another and even more impressive transformation. The new designers no longer belonged to the Beaker Culture. They were now working at the behest of a culture represented by chieftains whose numerous cemeteries were added to the landscape around Stonehenge.

Their origin is even more mysterious than that of the Beaker People. The new overlords removed the bluestones that had been put there by the Beaker People and added the now famous Sarsen Ring of trilithons, *sarsen* being the name of the local sandstone boulders. The ring, 33 meters across, was composed of thirty enormous stones with an average weight of 26 tons. The transportation of the blocks from a site 30 kilometers away would have been a feat in itself. Particularly noteworthy was the effort made in the preparation of the stones. Moving in unison and using stone mauls swung on ropes, workers pummeled the surface of the boulders to pulverize protrusions, first with large mauls the size of pumpkins and then moving down in size to mauls the size of tennis balls. When the surfaces were finally flat, other teams were set to work rubbing the surfaces with large flat stones, back and forth like a woodworker with sandpaper. When they were done, the posts measured 4.1 meters high, 2.1 meters wide, and 1.1 meters thick. They were surmounted by thirty, 6- to 7-ton lintels that formed a continuous circle around the top.

The precision was remarkable. The tops of the lintels, once they were in place, never varied more than 10 centimeters from the horizontal. Such carefully worked stone is not typical of other English henges, whose stones not only came from closer sources but were left natural, perhaps because they were seen as possessing a magical, chthonic presence. The Sarsen Ring was architecture of a particular type, for it was in reality something akin to carpentry in stone: the sanding of the surfaces and the way in which the stones were fitted together seem to imply a direct application of the techniques of carpentry to stone. Possibly the designers were replicating in stone a wooden prototype, or perhaps they were seeking to enhance the power of the stone structure by embodying in it the more familiar techniques of woodworking.

Stonehenge went through yet another transformation. In this final phase, some of the bluestones that had been removed were

2.47 Distribution of the Beaker People, ca. 2000 BCE

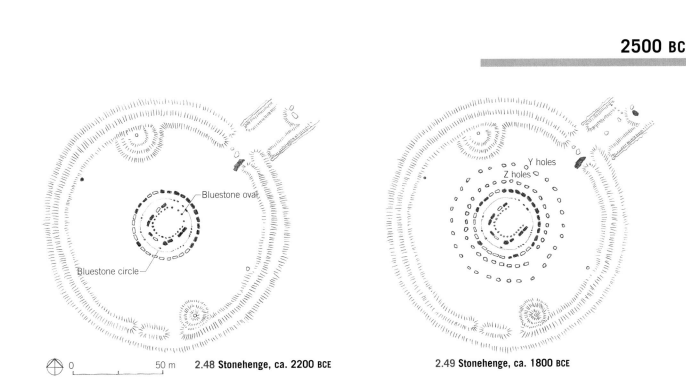

Bluestone oval

Bluestone circle

0   50 m   **2.48 Stonehenge, ca. 2200 BCE**

Y holes
Z holes

2.49 Stonehenge, ca. 1800 BCE

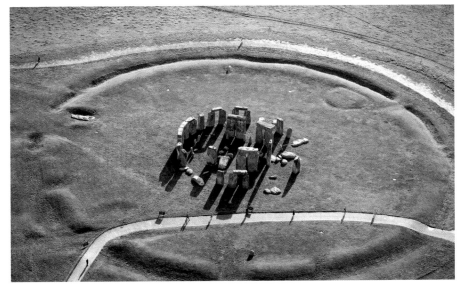

2.50 Aerial view of Stonehenge

brought back to the site, with some being erected within the Sarsen Ring and others placed in a horseshoe configuration. Such a horseshoe was uncommon in England but occurred more frequently across the channel in Brittany. The implications of this have yielded much speculation, but it is almost certain that southern England and French Brittany were at this time part of a single cultural province.

As a result, so it is thought, of climatic cooling, the culture that built Stonehenge devolved into a hamlet society, with little capacity to continue the great architectural accomplishments of its predecessors. In the shadowy remnants, a druid culture emerged that contributed practically nothing to the architectural legacy of England.

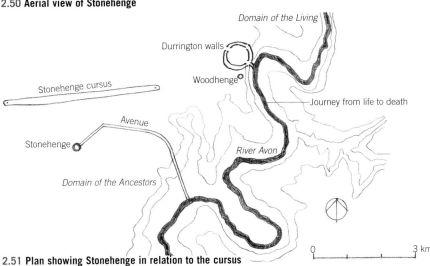

Domain of the Living

Durrington walls

Woodhenge

Journey from life to death

Stonehenge cursus

Avenue

Stonehenge

River Avon

Domain of the Ancestors

0   3 km

2.51 Plan showing Stonehenge in relation to the cursus

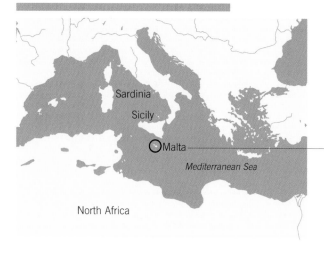
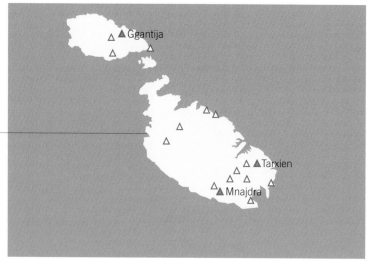

2.52 Temple sites on the island of Malta

Megalithic Temples of Malta

Around 4000 BCE, settlers arrived at the Maltese archipelago, a string of rocky islands between Sicily and the North African coast. There they set up farms and traded with Sicily and Sardinia for flint, obsidian, and other nonnative tools and materials. It is difficult to know the climatic and geographic conditions of the islands at the time. Today, without modern technology, the island would be relatively inhospitable, given that there are few trees and no natural water sources. But in ancient times there must have been natural springs and an environment suitable for agriculture, for the Maltese flourished for a thousand years, between 3500 and 2500 BCE, more or less contemporaneously with the Old Kingdom in Egypt.

In Egypt, there had been a rapid shift to a complex cosmology controlled by the elite. But in Malta, religion revolved only around the ancient mother-goddess cult. Malta should not, however, be seen as more primitive, but rather as a place where the goddess cult survived—something it did not in more industrialized areas such as Egypt and Mesopotamia. It is also unlikely that Malta was completely isolated. In fact, its drive for monumental expression conforms to parallel drives in Egypt.

The temples that have been unearthed both inland and along the coast share common characteristics. The outer walls were made of raw, undressed megalithic stones set vertically in the ground and forming an oval. How the massive, multi-ton stones were brought to the sites remains a mystery. Archaeologists have found parallel ruts along which the stones might have been pulled, possibly on round stones used as rollers, but these ruts do not lead to the temple in efficient lines (they zigzag through the landscape), nor are they always parallel.

In the interior space of the temples, the stones were meticulously dressed and set up to create lobed chambers, the surfaces of which were sometimes finished with plaster. The space between the outer and inner walls was filled with dirt and rubble, and on the outside the whole was mounded over to form an artificial hill. How the spaces were roofed is still debated. Corbelled Neolithic tombs can be found in Spain and Portugal, but given the absence of such stonework, it seems likely that the roofs were supported by timber beams not unlike those in the early tomb structures in Egypt. A model of a tomb, made by the ancient builders themselves, shows that these buildings were not arbitrarily formed but conformed to a prototype of planned symbolic spaces. The nature of the rituals for which these structures were built has been lost to history. But statuettes of heavyset earth goddesses found on the sites are evidence of a cult dedicated to fertility, death, and renewal. The deities, some sitting upright, others lying asleep, look not unlike the plans of the temples themselves—a squat rounded figure harboring a mysterious, bodily

2.53 Interior of Hal Saflieni Hypogeum, Malta

2.54 Figure of the earth goddess

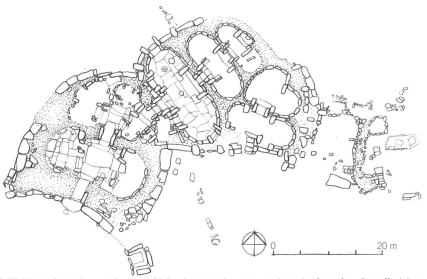

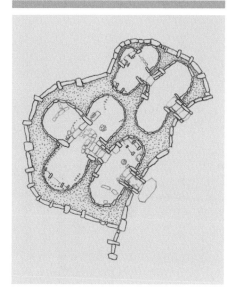

2.55 Plans of temple complexes on Malta drawn at the same scale and orientation: Ggantija (above left) and Tarxien (above right)

inner world. Animal bones and statuettes testify to the ritual offerings and sacrifices that were likely associated with the cult. Many temples contained carved or freestanding stone altars, and most had libation stones with wells for liquid offerings to the earth. The later temples have a type of plaza in front and were equipped with stone benches, indicating that the temples were used for communal gatherings.

The earliest and best preserved temple on Malta is Ggantija, part of a cluster of temples situated on the nearby island of Gozo. This temple was used continuously for hundreds of years, with the earliest material possibly dating to around 3500 BCE. Ggantija was a double temple, nearly 30 meters long. It had a floor of crushed limestone slurry that formed a hard, concrete-like surface. The

portals from chamber to chamber were huge post-and-lintel configurations of megalithic stones. The exterior was monumental and simple. The core cloverleaf configuration to the west was built first. Two more lobed chambers were then added along its entry passage. Later, a second temple was built adjacent to the first and enclosed within the original mound. The reasons are unclear. Perhaps the local population expanded and exceeded the original temple's capacity. Perhaps a plentiful harvest year prompted the farmers to renew their thanks to the earth goddess. Whatever the reason, generations of Maltese continued to regularize and expand the design, testing, refining, and reproducing the archetypal shape at different scales, with different orientations, and with varying numbers of chambers.

The temple at Tarxien, built around 2500 BCE, is the most complex of the surviving temples. The imposing concave facade of the main temple was composed of finely coursed stone, with larger blocks at the base and smaller blocks at the roof, which corbelled outward to form a small cornice. Within, pairs of symmetrical chambers were built successively deeper over the centuries, one connected to the next by dual trilithon portals and connecting passageways. At nearby Mnajdra is a complex of three temples of the same period, overlooking an oval court. The southern temple is aligned such that the equinox sunrise illuminates its main axis.

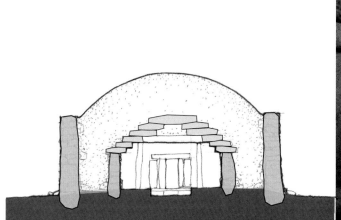

2.56 Section through a typical Malta temple

2.57 Temple complex at Mnajdra, Malta

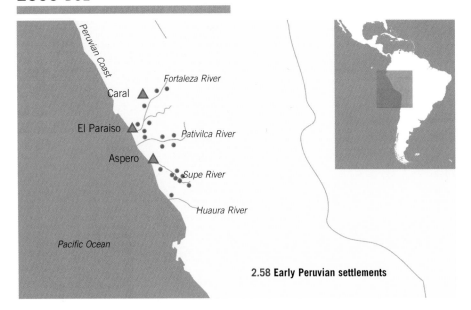

2.58 Early Peruvian settlements

First Civilizations of the Americas

During the Ice Age, between 30,000 and 10,000 BCE, nomadic populations from China and Mongolia crossed the then existing Bering Strait land bridge, moving first into the Great Plains of North America and then south along the shore of the Pacific Ocean. By 10,000 BCE they had reached the southern tip of South America. (Recently, it has also been proposed that another stream of people may have come westward from Europe, following the edge of the Atlantic ice shelf. This is based on the similarities of arrowheads in both locations.) Throughout the Americas, the social structure of the native Americans remained that of hunter-gatherers until sometime between 5000 and 3400 BCE when, in Central America, the first attempts were made to create permanent settlements and cultivate crops such as corn, avocados, chili peppers, amaranth, squash, and beans. By 2500 BCE, villages appeared with shelters made of wattle and daub, and by 1500 BCE we see the first examples of pottery.

The indigenous people of the Americas are generally called pre-Columbians, a term that refers to the arrival of Christopher Columbus in 1492. This text will generally refer to them as native Americans, to recognize the ancient continuities between the civilizations of North, Central, and South America.

The thin sliver of the South American coastline sandwiched between the Pacific and the rising peaks of the Andes Mountains turned out to be particularly suitable for the development of the earliest advanced native American settlements. It was home to a wide array of ecological life zones, ranging from the tundra of the upper valleys to the grasslands of the middle altitudes to the deserts of the northern coast. There, once the domestication of plants and llamas had taken place, one sees the rapid growth of settlements into medium-size villages with populations of up to three thousand. One of the earliest sites to be developed was a stretch of coast about 200 kilometers north of Lima, Peru, with sites that date back to 10,000 BCE. Four fast-flowing rivers converged on the site, from north to south: the Huaura, the Supe, the Pativilca, and the Fortaleza.

There were, however, drawbacks to this landscape. Because of the direction of the prevailing air currents, moisture-laden winds skip over the coast until they hit the high peaks of the Andes. The area close to the ocean is thus, for all practical purposes, a desert. These conditions would have the makings of an inhospitable environment were it not for the warm Pacific Ocean coastal currents that supported a rich marine life. Thus the earliest Andean settlers lived principally off the ocean, the only civilization of this age to do so.

But the ocean alone was not likely to have been enough to support the large, concentrated populations that would have been required for building and maintaining the hundreds of huge ceremonial complexes that dot the high river valleys of Peru. These date to later times, when the native Americans learned to canalize water and cultivate the lower reaches of the narrow valleys. But what was grown was not primarily food, as one might expect, but cotton, and in this the early civilizations of the Andes differed remarkably from the great river civilizations in Eurasia, which concentrated on food production. Cotton served not only for clothing but also for nets used in fishing—and as a trade item. (Though cotton today is a common commodity, one has to remember that when the Spaniards invaded Peru they would have known it as a luxury item. Their clothing was made of flax and coarse wool.) Irrigation was in the form of weirs—diversions from the river that follow the contours of the land and thus, like a spider web, distribute water into the fields. These small channels did not require much labor to build and maintain. Apart from cotton, the locals grew beans, potatoes, peanuts, and avocados. At the same time, aided by the versatile llamas, travel along the coast became easier and more frequent. This irrigated agricultural phase is usually dated to about 1500 BCE, but in 2001 archaeologists found that the carbon dating of organic fragments from the Supe River valley of Peru dated to 2620 BCE. Since this discovery, the chronology of civilizational development in South America has been keenly debated and is presently undergoing significant revisions.

The societies in the Americas did not have pigs, sheep, or cattle, and therefore did not need fenced enclosures, which were at the root of almost all non-American societies from their early stages onward. Whereas in Africa and Eurasia, land was divided between farming and grazing, and fences were needed to identify ownership and protect property, in the Americas there were no domesticated animals, and therefore, no such need. Native American societies thus developed along very different lines than in the rest of the world. They survived by cleverly exploiting their natural environment, especially their water resources. And they centered their agriculture on a region's diverse assortment of trees and plants, in conjunction with organized planting, hunting, and fishing.

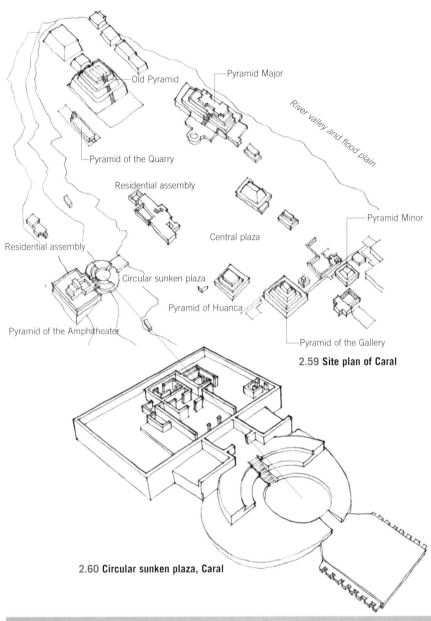

Old Pyramid
Pyramid Major
Pyramid of the Quarry
River valley and flood plain
Residential assembly
Pyramid Minor
Central plaza
Residential assembly
Circular sunken plaza
Pyramid of the Amphitheater
Pyramid of Huanca
Pyramid of the Gallery

2.59 Site plan of Caral

2.60 Circular sunken plaza, Caral

2.61 Central zone of Caral

Caral

Caral's location on a natural terrace 25 meters above the Supe River floodplain, and its size—65 hectares—point to a powerful aristocracy with extensive resources for construction. A huge central plaza, roughly 500 meters by 175 meters, is surrounded by an extensive array of buildings that include six large platform mounds, a range of smaller mounds, two major sunken circular plazas, various residential structures, and buildings whose purposes are not yet known. Each of the mounds is associated with formally arranged residential complexes. Although the ceremonial structures of the early Andean civilizations have the outline of a pyramid and are usually called pyramids, it is more accurate to refer to them as platform mounds. This is because they were conceptually conceived as a series of platforms, of which the earth was first, rather than as pyramids, with an implied internal volume. (The word *pyramid* is from a Greek word that describes Egyptian structures.) What the native Americans called their structures is unknown. The word *pyramid* will, however, be used here in cases where convention has already established it as part of a name.

Pyramid Major, Caral's dominant platform mound (160 by 150 meters and 18 meters high) is perched on the northern end of the site, at the very edge of the terrace from which it overlooks the valley. It was constructed in two major phases. First, the mound walls were built by filling in open-mesh reed bags with cut stones. The outer surface of the mound was then covered with multiple layers of colored plaster. Five other platform mounds join with it to form a C-shaped plaza facing south. Just beyond its open mouth, at the center of a low mound, is a sunken circular plaza 50 meters in diameter.

If the main plaza, surrounded by mounds high above the valley floor, creates the impression of a vast bounded space reminiscent of a high valley plateau, then the circular sunken plaza, reminiscent of the later kivas of North America, repeats that space on a smaller scale, perhaps corresponding to the lower elements of life. What is not

2.62 View of El Paraiso, Peru

present is what might be called art: there are no sculptures or wall paintings. Nor is it clear what the inhabitants' religious views were. Caral is still being excavated, but one can anticipate that the site was laid out facing toward celestial events, such as the rising sun and the movement of planets and stars. Caral's importance lies in its overarching influence. In Eurasia at this time, there were already many different competing world views. But all later Peruvian cultures were developments and elaborations of Caral.

El Paraiso

El Paraiso, spread out over about 50 hectares, is on the southern bank of the Chillon River, about 3 kilometers inland from the coast in an agricultural valley not far from Lima. It is sited at the southern end of the urbanization zone that developed during this time; its construction dates to about 1800 BCE. The two largest mounds run parallel to each other, with a scattering of smaller mounds to the southwest forming a U with a central plaza that is roughly 50 meters wide and 150 meters long. The plaza opens northeast, toward the river and a distant mountain peak. The mounds associated with the plaza are made of interconnected rectangular courts, rooms, and passages. The walls are 1.5 to 2.5 meters high and 1 meter thick and are made of stone blocks set in mortar and then covered by mud plaster that

shows traces of red and white pigment. The plaza, would, therefore, have been brightly colored in its time.

A residential structure at El Paraiso, probably for the aristocracy, consists of a complex maze of interconnected rooms that were added to over time by building new structures to the side or by filling in older rooms to enable rooms to be built at a higher level.

Like Caral, El Paraiso's economy was primarily cotton-based. The city, lying at the bottom of a coastal valley with wide floodplains, has an ideal location for growing this crop. Creating a city around such a specialized—and inedible—product indicates the presence of a broad, interdependent networked culture. Nonetheless, though huge stone structures dot the site, there seems to have been no central or hereditary ruler: there is an absence of elaborate burials. The city was, perhaps, governed on the model of an agricultural cooperative, controlled by an elite.

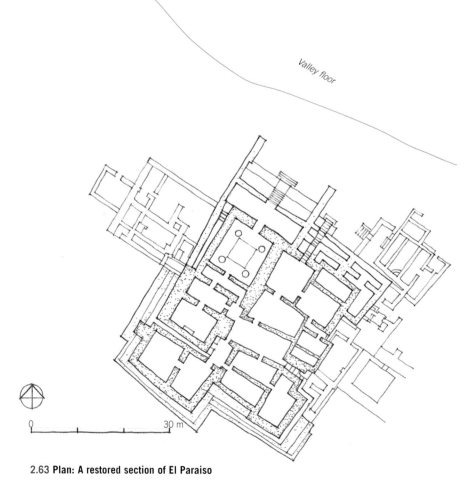

Valley floor

2.63 Plan: A restored section of El Paraiso

0   30 m

1500 BCE

In the middle of the second millennium BCE, Central Asia—from the Bactrian-Margiana Archaeological Complex society in Turkmenistan to the Indus Ghaggar-Hakra region in the south—went into a period of turmoil and decline. An ecological disaster—the drying up of the Ghaggar-Hakra River—certainly played a part in creating a political vacuum. During this period, large groups of people who called themselves Aryas, or Aryans as they are now known, moved into northern India and introduced novel cultural elements. Since their structures were built of wood rather than brick, very little tangible evidence of this period of conflict and turbulence has survived. The newcomers brought with them iron and sacred oral texts that are among the oldest in the world. Around 1500 BCE these were assembled and written down. This was the so-called Vedic period, named after a Sanskrit Indo-European word that means "knowledge"; this period lasted to approximately 500 BCE.

West Asia also experienced a state of flux and instability. Assyria, Babylon, and other Mesopotamian cities were overrun by invaders of unknown provenance, the Mitanni and Kassite people, who had moved in from the north and east. A similar situation existed with the so-called Sea People, who progressed eastward along the coast of the Mediterranean, conquering the Nile Delta. Among the newcomers there were also the Hittites, who settled in Anatolia. There, in the north-central region, they founded Hattusas, a capital with numerous temples. They brought in scribes from Syria to maintain their records in cuneiform script, creating voluminous state archives. They also recognized the importance of the camel as a beast of burden: by the middle of the second millennium BCE, caravans with as many as six hundred animals were plying trade routes across the desert plains. The Hittites and the Egyptians became the preeminent land powers in western Asia, with Egypt embarking on a remarkable period of temple architecture epitomized by the constructions in Luxor.

In 1600 BCE, the Bronze Age Shang dynasty in China controlled a large area in northeast and north-central China, with cities such as Zhengzhou and Anyang arising—the former encompassing a region of roughly 1.5 by 2 kilometers; it was one of the largest planned cities in the world at that time. The period is noted for extraordinary bronze vessels used to hold wine and food in rituals linking rulers with their ancestors. Chinese iron technology differed from that of the West insofar as the Chinese did not forge the metal but cast it using multiple ceramic molds.

The region of coastal Louisiana today called Poverty Point, on the Gulf Coast of North America, emerged as the center of an important chiefdom. Its people built enormous earthworks as part of an artificially constructed, sacred landscape. Unlike other native American tribes in the region, who relied only on local raw materials, the Poverty Point people developed an extensive trade network. Meanwhile, in the Andes, improvements in irrigation technology enabled farmers to move upstream, away from the ocean, expand their economies, and build large sites such as Cardal in present-day Peru. Among the numerous aspects of their agriculture, it was the development of cotton that was most revolutionary. The ritual centers that were built involved enormous U-shaped complexes, the architectural elements of which would remain part of the Peruvian architectural language for millennia. The Andeans had neither the wheel nor beasts of burden.

China: Yangshao Culture
ca: 5000–1500 BCE

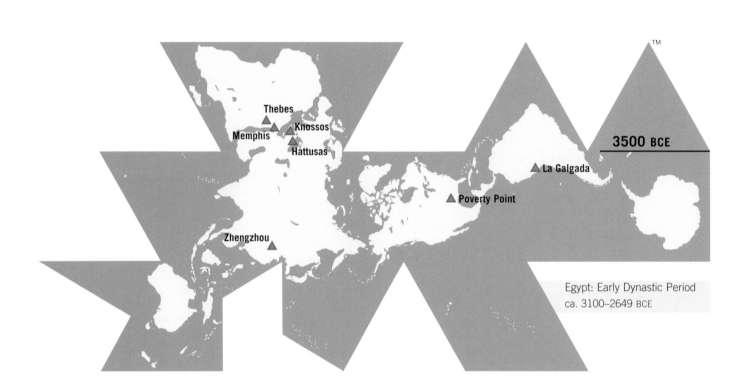

3500 BCE

Egypt: Early Dynastic Period
ca. 3100–2649 BCE

North and Central Andes: Valdivia cultures
ca. 3300–1500 BCE

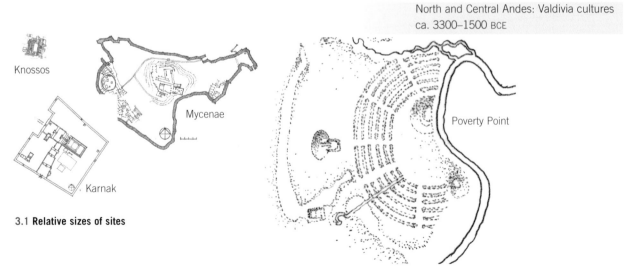

Knossos

Mycenae

Karnak

Poverty Point

3.1 Relative sizes of sites

Xia Dynasty
ca. 2070–1600 BCE

Shang Dynasty
ca. 1600–1050 BCE

Western Zhou Dynasty
ca. 1046–771 BCE

▲ Zhengzhou
ca. 1700–1400 BCE

▲ Shang tombs at Anyang
ca. 1400–1100 BCE

Minoan Culture
ca. 3000–1200 BCE

▲ Knossos
ca. 2000–1400 BCE

Mycenaean Culture
ca. 1600–1100 BCE

▲ Treasure of Atreus
ca. 1250 BCE

Nuraghic Civilization
ca. 1600–750 BCE

2500 BCE	1500 BCE	500 BCE

Middle Bronze Age
ca. 2000–1600 BCE

Late Bronze Age
ca. 1600–1200 BCE

Iron Age
ca. 1200 BCE

Egypt: First Intermediate Period
ca. 2150–2030 BCE

Second Intermediate Period
ca. 1640–1550 BCE

Old Kingdom
ca. 2649–2150 BCE

Middle Kingdom
ca. 2030–1640 BCE

New Kingdom
ca. 1550–1070 BCE

Third Intermediate Period
ca. 1070–712 BCE

Late Period
ca. 712–332 BCE

▲ Temple complex at Karnak
Begun ca. 1550 BCE

▲ Mortuary Temple of Queen Hatshepsut
ca. 1520 BCE

▲ Temple of Luxor
ca. 1350 BCE

▲ Abu Simbel
ca. 1300 BCE

▲ Hattusas
ca. 1800 BCE

Machalilla Culture
1500–1100 BCE

▲ La Galgada
ca. 2600–1400 BCE

▲ Huaricoto
ca. 2200–2000 BCE

▲ Salinas de Chao
ca. 1610–1300 BCE

▲ Cardal
ca. 1465–975 BCE

▲ Poverty Point
ca. 1800–700 BCE

3.2 Shang dynasty China

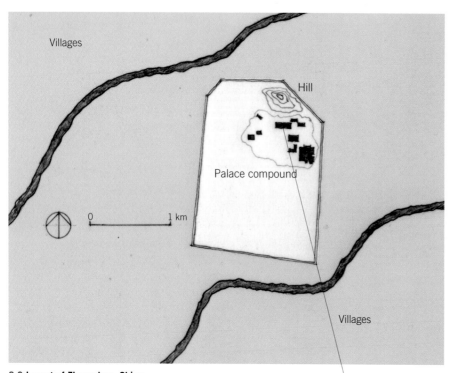

3.3 Layout of Zhengzhou, China

Shang Dynasty China

Ancient Chinese historians talk of the ten thousand kingdoms that existed before the Xia dynasty (ca. 2070–1600 BCE), and indeed, the rise of defensive fortifications around cities was a testament to intra-urban warfare. Among these numerous city-states, Xia came to control the territory on the Yellow River, paving the way for the rise of the Shang dynasty (ca. 1600–1050 BCE), whose first capital was Zhengzhou. Despite its importance, centralization of state power had not yet been developed. Nonetheless, it was during the Shang dynasty that the royal person became viewed as a symbol of cosmic powers. The theocratic order thereby established was to remain foundational to the Chinese definition of rulership.

Zhengzhou, on the Yellow River, was immense, with its east wall measuring 1.7 kilometers long. It was surrounded by small villages, workshop areas, and bronze foundries. In the northeast section of the city, just south of a small hill, was a palace and temple district where *han tu* platforms of different sizes have been found; they once were the bases of large buildings. The largest is 60 by 13 meters and is oriented to the cardinal points. That it is located just south of the hill is no accident, as that was and remained the preeminent position of Chinese palaces.

3.4 Reconstruction of Shang dynasty palace

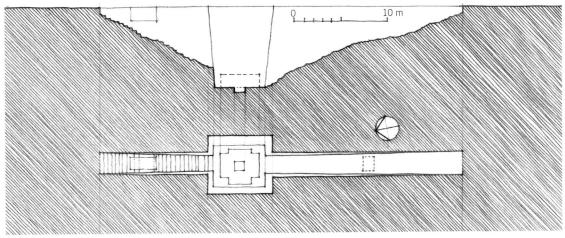

3.5 Plan and section: Tomb of Fu Hao, near Yin, Anyang County, China

The Shang moved their center several times, finally settling in Yin (present-day Xiaotun in Anyang County, Henan Province). The central complex (ca. 1275 BCE) at Yin consisted of a building with a 50-meter-wide courtyard, presumably a palace. Behind it was an open-air platform at the center of which rested a square, probably two-storied structure that served as the cosmological center of the kingdom and in which, or in front of which, sacrifices were made. A platform to the west side of the approach ramp was where blood sacrifices were made, as evidenced by special drainage tubes designed to catch the blood from slaughtered animals. In other parts of the world, function is often relatively easily determined, but in early Chinese architecture, this is not the case. All buildings are ritual structures, regardless of what practical uses may be ascribed to

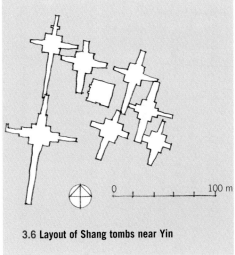

3.6 Layout of Shang tombs near Yin

them. From temple and palace to farmhouse, the most important part of the building is the spiritual center where ancestors, gods, or revered persons are venerated. The emphasis on cosmic symbolism also manifested itself in tombs that were mini cosmic diagrams. At the center of a royal grave, for example, is the wood-chambered tomb, decorated and painted and placed some 12 meters below ground. Two and sometimes four ramps lead down from the surface to the sides of the chamber, in the center of which the king was buried. In some tombs, guards were buried in the corners, each with a dog and holding a weapon. During this time, porcelain wares were invented and jade carving techniques perfected; silk weaving was of the highest quality.

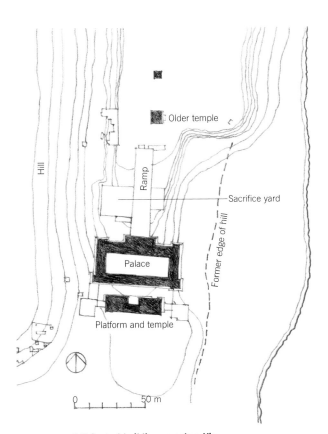

3.7 Central building complex, Yin

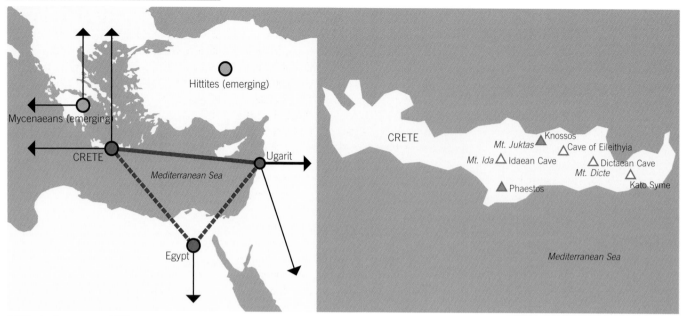

3.8 Trade diagram, ca. 1600 BCE

3.9 Minoan sites on Crete

The Minoans and Knossos

The turmoil in the Mesopotamian heartland benefited the economies of the eastern Mediterranean, and they gained in importance. Among the main beneficiaries were the Minoans on Crete, who developed the world's first thalassocracy, a maritime trading economy initially defined by Aristotle. With their trading acumen, they stitched together the Mediterranean economies of West Asia and Egypt with the emerging markets of Europe. Their palace architecture (Knossos, Phaestos, Mallia, and Zakros) was conceived according to very different principles than those of Mesopotamia. The Minoans appeared not to have been overly concerned with defensive installations, from which one concludes that their trading practices were peaceful in nature. The Minoans also never came under the same type of economical and political stresses that necessitated complex cosmologies. They thus emerge still clothed in chthonic religious practices, which were more intimate and less formal than the rigid system prevalent in Egypt and Mesopotamia; their holy places were connected to landscape features.

Nonetheless, during the Bronze Age, Cretan religion began to become more complex, and we see the emergence of strong male gods and, in particular, the Cretan Zeus, a fertility god who died annually

and was reborn in a sacred festival. He took the form of a bull, which was central to a festival known as the Thiodaisia, during which the cities renewed their oaths of alliance to each other. These rites included large-scale drinking and feasting and were staged in the open landscape or in front of the major palaces in special theaterlike settings. There was a joyful, life-enhancing quality to their festivals as well as to their artwork, as can be seen in the murals in their palaces. Three caves were particularly important in their cult: the Dictaean Cave on Mt. Dicte near the village Psychro, the Idaean Cave on Mt. Ida near Anogheia, and the Cave of Eileithyia, dedicated to the birth goddess. The Dictaean Cave, cold and moist even in the heat of summer, with a pool of water surrounded by stalactites, was the site of rituals dating back to the earliest time of Cretan habitation. The Cave of Eileithyia is now a Christian site and is still visited by Cretan women. A procession led up to the peak of the mountain to a special sanctuary where offerings were "fed" into a cleft in the rocks. Today an annual procession still makes its way up to the top of the mountain for the feast of Afendis Christos—an example of how Christianity often tried to nullify "heathen" cults by appropriating ancient rituals and customs. The cave most intimately connected

with the Cretan creation myth is the cave on Mt. Ida, where the earth mother Rhea gave birth to Zeus. Myth describes him as tended by nymphs and protected by youths against his father, the legendary Chronos. Zeus then fathered Minos, who became King of Knossos and of Crete.

3.10 Ruins of ritual structure: Cave of Eileithyia

The events involved a dance in which performers somersaulted over a charging bull, as represented vividly on the walls of the palace. Men and women are both portrayed performing the jump, a man in one case in midair, waiting to be caught in the open arms of a woman. Given that the entire landscape was sacred, the Minoans did not build temples but rather palaces, the largest of which was at Knossos, built around 2000 BCE on top of a prior Neolithic settlement. It was rebuilt and enlarged in 1700 BCE after a large earthquake, and rebuilt again in 1500 BCE after a fire destroyed it. The palace contained residences, kitchens, storage rooms, bathrooms, ceremonial rooms, workshops, and sanctuaries. There were sophisticated infrastructural installations, ventilation systems, and groundwater conduits. In storage basements, archaeologists have found elephant tusks from Syria and copper ingots from Cyprus.

Though we do not know what role the priest-king who ruled there assumed, it is clear that the palace, with its many different kinds and sizes of interior spaces, terraces, courtyards, and platforms, represented a mosaic of interwoven activities. It was part palace, part warehouse, part factory, part religious center. At the center of the palace, and of its communal life, was a large rectangular courtyard laid out on an almost perfect north-south axis, with several entrances converging onto it. The courtyard was surrounded by verandas at the upper levels, allowing views into its space. Because of the verandas, windows, porches, steps, and doors that folded open into the sides of the walls, the visual interrelationship between inner and outer space is particularly intricate—more so than in any other palace architecture of this period.

Flanking the courtyard was the throne room, which had gypsum benches on the north and south walls with a place for the insertion of a wooden throne, which was replaced with a gypsum one later. The red stucco walls are covered with images of griffins, legendary animals with the head and wings of an eagle and the body of a lion that are thought to have symbolized strength and vigilance. The floor seems also to have been stained red. The benches, though at seat height, were probably used to hold votive offerings. Opposite the throne was a lustral basin to which steps descended and which may have served for initiation rites. The low room, which was kept dark, was meant to simulate a sacred cave, according to some scholars. Around the room were the various storage rooms mentioned above, some of which were repositories for precious objects used in the ceremonies. The whole complex of chambers—sixteen in all—was designed as a self-contained unit that had both a public entrance from the courtyard and also a private staircase connecting to the floor above.

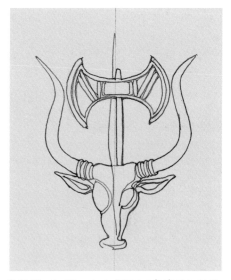

3.11 The double axe, or *labrys*, principal symbol of the Minoan-Mycenaean religion, standing erect on a bull's head

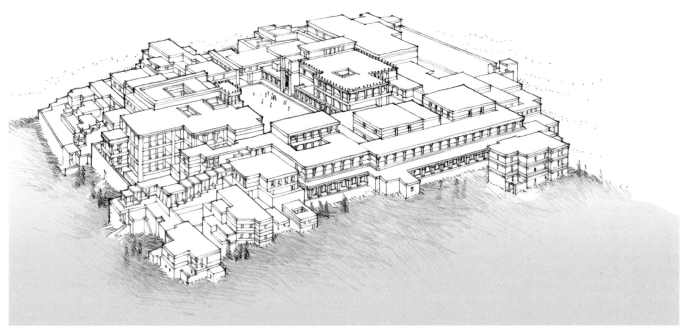

3.12 Overview of Knossos

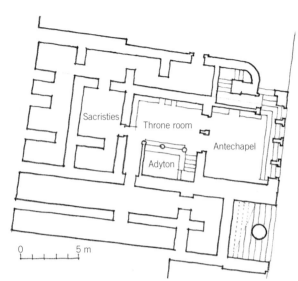

3.13 Plan of throne sanctuary at Knossos

3.14 Throne room, Palace at Knossos

Well-squared limestone was used for column bases, doors, and other supportive elements. The wooden columns, tapered toward the bottom, were painted blue; the capitals, painted red, had the profile of cushions. In the principal rooms, the stone rubble walls were finished with a fine layer of plaster painted in a fresco-like technique; they depicted scenes of animals and plant forms, and nautical life of remarkable vibrancy and beauty. Minoan art was among the first

to represent human movement. The main colors used were black (carbonaceous shale), white (hydrate of lime), red (hematite), yellow (ochre), blue (silicate of copper), and green (blue and yellow mixed together).

Though palaces by definition require controlled access, entry into the Palace at Knossos was more than a sequence of gates and antechambers; it was a linearly extended theatrical space. The starting point was the west porch, which consisted of a

single column standing between walls—an iconic representation of the mother goddess. From that point one walked south to a terrace that offered a broad vista to Mt. Juktas. No visitor would have missed the reference to the Cretan Zeus here. Through an opening midway down the terrace, one entered a series of state rooms that led to a great columnar hall illuminated by clerestory windows designed as a box within a box. It, in turn, opened up to a flight of steps flanked

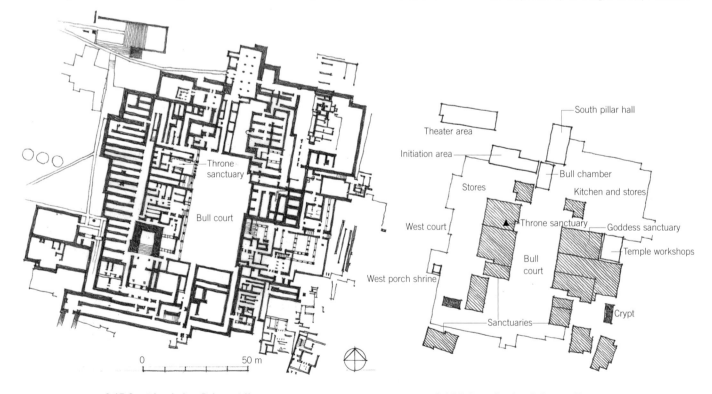

3.15 Court-level plan: Palace at Knossos

3.16 Schematic plan: Palace at Knossos

by a colonnaded veranda for spectators. At the top of the stairs was a lobby with two ceremonial doors right and left of the axis leading to another hall. At the back of this hall a door led to a staircase that descended at right angles in the direction of the processional way down to the central courtyard.

Descending the stairs, the visitor faced across the court to a goddess sanctuary, an imposing structure with a wide ceremonial staircase leading up through a colonnade to a landing in front of a pier-and-door partition. Inside was a spacious room 18.5 by 15 meters, with eight tapering pillars around a central square that was probably open from above. A statue was placed against the back wall, with the walls themselves richly decorated with scenes of boxing and bull-grappling, and more griffins. It is possible to imagine the central court as a plateau, positioned at the intersection of the sunken throne room on one side and the elevated cult space, with its skylight, on the other.

In the middle of the courtyard was a small altar for burnt offerings and, off to one corner, a large circular stone with concavities in it, probably also for offerings. It was perhaps in this space that the bull ceremony was performed with the spectators viewing it from the numerous balconies and verandas.

The palace was partially rebuilt under the supervision of Knossos's chief archaeologist, Robert Evans, in the 1920s. The rebuilt parts were made of concrete to protect them from earthquakes. Other palaces have been uncovered on the island, as have several peak sanctuaries, such as the one on Mt. Juktas, which was clearly linked to the cult practices at Knossos. It was the focus of pilgrimage ceremonies and was also probably associated with ceremonies legitimating the rule of the kings of Knossos.

The demise of the Minoans was largely due to the volcanic eruptions on the nearby island of Thera (modern Santorini) around 1600 BCE. It was partially rebuilt and then destroyed again by fires of unknown provenance. The destruction of the Minoan civilization created opportunities for the Mycenaeans on the Peloponnese, whose takeover of the sea trade in the Mediterranean was often intermingled with piracy. They set up posts on Crete and integrated Minoan cultural elements into their own aesthetic protocols.

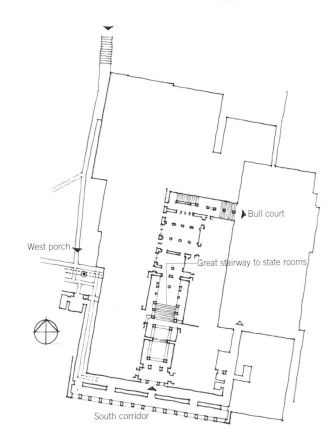

3.17 Diagram of entry sequence: Palace at Knossos

3.18 One of the grand stairways at the Palace at Knossos

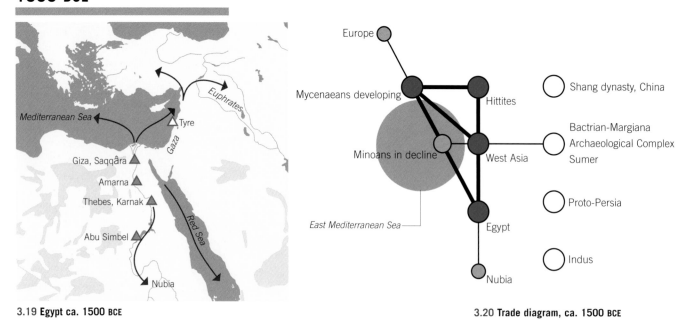

3.19 **Egypt ca. 1500 BCE**

3.20 **Trade diagram, ca. 1500 BCE**

Egypt: The New Kingdom

The middle of the second millennium BCE was a time of significant upheaval throughout West and Central Asia. The impressive urban developments in India, Margiana, and Mesopotamia either had come to a halt, as in India, or underwent important changes. The same was also true of Egypt, where around 1720 BCE, the Nile Delta was invaded and occupied by the Hyksos, who ruled Lower Egypt from their capital, Avaris, until driven out by Ahmose I of Thebes in 1567 BCE. The origin of the Hyksos, and even their name, remains the subject of scholarly debate. In 1550 BCE, Ahmose I, founder of the Eighteenth Dynasty (called the New Kingdom, a rule of dynasties lasting until 1070 BCE), was able to throw off the Hyksos and regain control over the country. The return of stability in Egypt meant the vigorous trade in goods on which so many Near Eastern societies depended could recommence. Furthermore, with the troubles in Mesopotamia and the decline of the Minoans, Egypt began to dominate the region. Seeking to guarantee the borders against the all-too-volatile political environment of western Asia, the Egyptians marched into Syria and besieged Nineveh and Babylon. No longer isolationists, as they had been in the Old Kingdom, they now became colonizers. The turquoise mines in the Sinai were reopened, and Ekron and other cities controlled by the Philistines traded with Egypt in pottery and metals.

An important change that came with the reestablishment of unity involved religion: no longer only the purview of the elite, it now comprised larger sections of society. Festivals, processions, and celebrations that could draw thousands of participants were introduced. The New Kingdom saw the rise of large temple institutions that played an important part in the life and politics of the times.

The Egyptian name for Thebes was Waset, the "city of the scepter." It was located on a small rise of the middle of the Nile floodplain that became, during the inundation of the Nile, a quasi-island. Thebes was the Greek name for the city that eventually stuck.

Waset (Thebes)

During the period of the New Kingdom, the capital of Egypt was Thebes, where the family that had thrown out the Hyksos came from. The consequence was that the Theban ram-god Amun-Re, the god of the sun and the heaven and the omnipresent father of the kings who guaranteed world order, was elevated to the status of a national deity. At least a dozen temples were built over a five-hundred-year period, from about 1500 BCE to 1000 BCE. The site spans both sides of the Nile and includes the Valley of the Kings, where many of the pharaohs were buried. Thebes had been used as a burial site since around 2000 BCE, but with its new prestige as imperial capital, it became also the royal site. The main components of this political/religious landscape was the temple complex of Karnak, the Temple of Luxor, and, on the western side of the Nile, the Mortuary Temple of Queen Hatshepsut and the Temple at Medinet Habu.

The earliest of these large construction projects was begun by Queen Hatshepsut on the west bank, where she erected her mortuary temple and Medinet Habu. Her successors continued her efforts. Thutmosis I began enlarging the temple complex at Karnak around 1530 BCE, while Amenhotep III started work on Temple of Luxor around 1350 BCE; the temple-building activity culminated in the efforts of Seti I and Ramesses II, who added significant parts to Karnak and Luxor around 1280 BCE.

Some sixty festivals were celebrated in Thebes annually. Some took place within the temple confines; others involved moving cult images form temple to temple. The three most important of these traveling festivals involved Amun; his wife Mut, the Egyptian mother goddess; and Mut's son Khonsu, the lunar deity.

1. Preeminent was the Opet ("secret chamber") festival during which the statues

West and the deified dead kings. The festival came to be associated with renewal and regeneration. It occurred during the second month of *Shemu*, the harvest season (roughly our April), and lasted for over twenty days.

3. Amun's cult image traveled every ten days from the Temple of Luxor on the east bank to the shrine of Medinet Habu (ca. 1460–1420 BCE) on the west bank. The original name was Djanet, and according to popular belief, it was the place where Amun first appeared. The cult images were transported to the various temples by means of a symbolic barque, which was carried on poles on the shoulders of devotees.

Queen Hatshepsut's mortuary temple played a key role in the processional events as the temporary resting place for the barque during the Beautiful Feast of the Valley. Hatshepsut, daughter of Thutmosis I, the fifth pharaoh of the Eighteenth Dynasty, was a charismatic and controversial figure in her role as a female monarch. She ruled for twenty years, during a particularly strong moment in the Egyptian economy. After her death, it is presumed that Thutmosis III, her stepson, ordered the systematic erasure of her name from any monument she had built, including her temple at Deir el-Bahri. Some of her monuments were destroyed outright. Such destructions were not uncommon in Egyptian history.

The temple, built by Senmut, her architect, went against the tradition of enclosed precincts. It combined mortuary temple, processional way, rock-cut tomb, and ancillary chapels into one synthetic unity with no parallel in Egyptian architecture. The original Egyptian name of the temple was *djeser-djeseru*, or "the sublime of the sublimes," because it is located in an area that was called Djeseret, or "sublime place," which was dedicated to Hathor, a mother goddess as well as the goddess of love and beauty. A preexistent Hathor chapel on the site was positioned directly under an impressive cliff and built partially into Hatshepsut's temple. The temple was approached by a causeway and a canal that allowed the sacred barque to be brought from the Nile. The temple did not contain her tomb, which was located in the Valley of the Kings and is concealed behind the cliff that looms over her mortuary temple.

3.21 Hieroglyphic relief of the Barque festival

of Amun, Khonsu, and Mut were escorted from Karnak to the Temple of Luxor. At a particular moment during the events, the deity "spoke" to confirm the legitimacy of the king. The god's legitimization of the king was reciprocated by gifts to the temple from the royal family. The festival took place during *Akhet* (roughly our September), the season when the Nile flooded, and lasted for eleven days, but as time progressed, the number of festival days grew. The journey from Karnak to Luxor was made over land along a processional street; the return journey was made along the Nile by means of boat.

2. The Beautiful Feast of the Valley coincided with a celebration of the dead in which Amun, Mut, and Khonsu would travel to the western shore to visit the gods of the

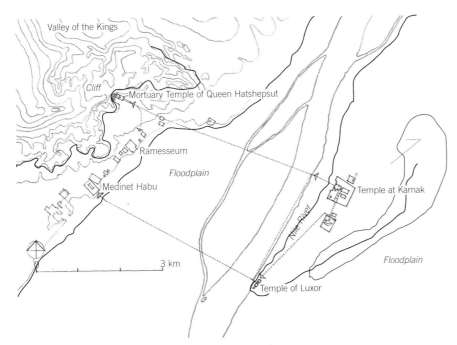

3.22 The principal temples and processional routes, Karnak

The axis of Queen Hatshepsut's mortuary temple was precisely aligned to the east with the temple complex at Karnak across the river and to the west with Hatshepsut's tomb on the other side of the cliff in the Valley of the Kings, which was to become the main burial place for the Egyptian royalty for many centuries. There was also a valley temple next to the Nile, but that structure has disappeared.

Particularly innovative was the use of terraces that reach out into the valley floor, prompting speculation about outside influences. The design consists of three of these terraces leading upward to the foot of the imposing cliff face. The first terrace contained trees and gardens. An axis runs through the entire scheme with ramps connecting the various courts. It was the second level that connects to a chapel of Hathor. On the opposite side is a chapel to Anubis, the jackal-headed god of the dead. The axis leads through a hypostyle hall to the last courtyard, with the cliff wall rising

3.23 Mortuary Temple of Queen Hatshepsut, near Karnak, Egypt

impressively above it.

To the left of the upper terrace there is a faux palace for Hatshepsut's ancestors, and to the right an open-air sanctuary dedicated to Re-Horakhty. (Re, the sun god, went through a daily cycle of death and rebirth, dying at the end of each day and being reborn in the morning as Re-Horakhty.) The rooms for the barque sanctuary, which terminate the axis, together with the room for the cult image, were carved out of the rock itself.

The Chapel of Amun on this upper terrace was the final destination of the holy process of the Beautiful Feast of the Valley.

The plan displays a brilliant use of symmetry and asymmetry based on the integration of different elements. Particularly noteworthy are the columns along the front of the temple which are part of a wall and pier system that foreshadows later development. Also, instead of using the usual lotus motives for the capitals, here the columns are fluted cylinders built out of drums.

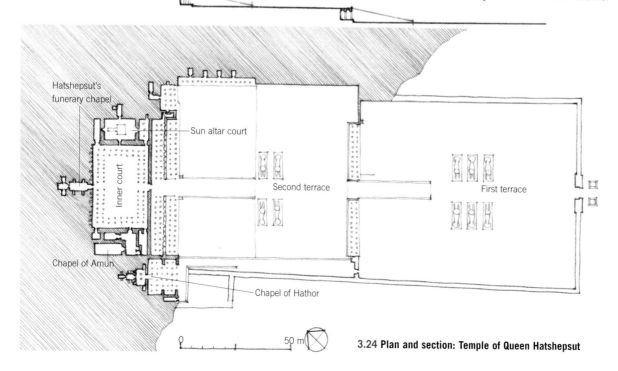

3.24 Plan and section: Temple of Queen Hatshepsut

Karnak

Karnak, the name taken from a nearby village, was known to the ancient Egyptians as Ipet-isut ("the most selected of places"). It consists of three districts. In the center stood the establishments of Amun-Re (begun around 1530 BCE); in the south, those of Mut, the mother goddess; and in the north, those of Montu, the god of warfare, strength, and virility. The temple has two entrances, one for those arriving from the direction of the Nile, to accommodate the barque procession, and the other from Luxor. The Nile entrance had its own harbor. Both entrances are defined by a series of majestic pylons. To the north of the enclosure is a small sanctuary to Ptah, who was sometimes seen as an abstract form of the Self-Created One. He was intimately connected with the plastic arts and especially with the mysteries of architecture and stone masonry.

The pylons are numbered in the order in which they are encountered when walking through the site. Here, the parts of the building are listed in order of their construction:

- Pylon 8, Hatshepsut, ca. 1479 BCE (Hatshepsut builds mortuary temple and Medinet Habu.)
- Pylons 5 and 6, Thutmosis III, ca. 1450 BCE
- Festival Hall, Thutmosis III, ca. 1450 BCE
- Pylon 7, Thutmosis III, ca. 1450 BCE
- Pylon 3, Amenhotep III, ca. 1350 BCE (Amenhotep III begins Temple of Luxor)
- Pylon 9, Horemheb, ca. 1300 BCE
- Pylon 10, Horemheb, ca. 1300 BCE
- Pylon 2, Horemheb and Ramesses I, ca. 1300 BCE
- Hypostyle hall, Seti I and Ramesses II, ca. 1280–70 BCE (Ramesses II added pylon and courtyard at Luxor.)
- Temple of Ramesses III, ca. 1150 BCE
- Temple of Khonsu, Ramesses III, ca. 1150 BCE
- Pylon 1, Thirtieth Dynasty, 350 BCE

3.25 Hypostyle hall of the Temple at Karnak

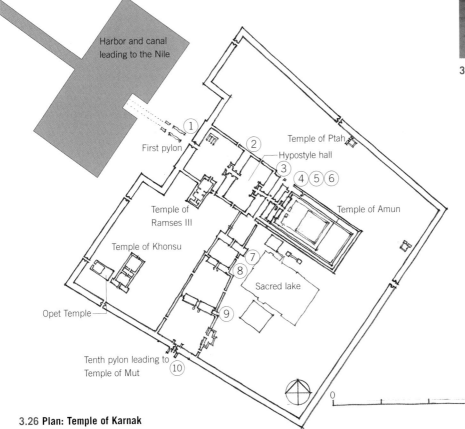

3.26 Plan: Temple of Karnak

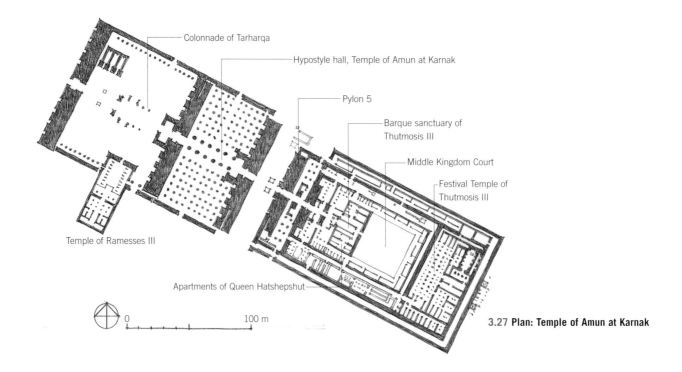

Colonnade of Tarharqa

Hypostyle hall, Temple of Amun at Karnak

Pylon 5

Barque sanctuary of
Thutmosis III

Middle Kingdom Court

Festival Temple of
Thutmosis III

Temple of Ramesses III

Apartments of Queen Hatshepshut

0   100 m

3.27 Plan: Temple of Amun at Karnak

The most important element in the design of this vast temple was the small shrine behind the fifth pylon, open at both ends, where the specially designed portable barque by which the image of Amun was carried outside the temple was stored. The structure that Queen Hatshepsut built on or close to this site, but which was dismantled by her successors, has been uncovered and reconstructed at Karnak, but not on the original site. It was made out of special red quartzite stone (thus its name, the Red Chapel) on a base of black diorite. The current structure, built by Philip III of Macedonia around 340 BCE, follows the original one, but it contains only two rooms: one where the offerings were presented, and one with a stone base on which the barque rested.

A pylon (from the Greek word for "gate") is a high, inclined, and slightly trapezoid-shaped wall with a large central entrance guarding a sacred precinct. It was often accented by tall flagpoles and obelisks whose tops were sheathed in gold plating. The two flanks of the pylon, formal and imposing,

symbolized the mountain ranges that hem in the Nile. Their form was a purely symbolical expression of Egyptian power. Though all architectural forms of the period—such as the ziggurat in Mesopotamia, the *megaron* in Greece, and the processional paths in Egypt—had symbolical value, the pylon gates were among the earliest architectural forms that condensed wall, gate, and cosmology into a single declaration of power. The Egyptian word for "pylon" was *bekhnet*, which implies vigilance. Thus it relates to the watchtower-like nature, if not the actual function, of these structures. Flagpoles were placed along the front of the pylons, the poles and flags representing, for the Egyptians, the presence of a sacred precinct at the most basic level.

Like huge billboards, the pylon also proclaimed, in image and text, important events in the role of the donor-king. On one, the seventh pylon of Karnak, a huge Thutmosis III is shown holding a club and taking a swing at a cluster of enemy soldiers—depicted smaller—whom he

seemed to seize by the hair. Beneath his feet, in three rows, are the names of the conquered cities and peoples, also listed in three rows. The conquest of the Lybians, Hittites, and Bedouins are particularly vigorously portrayed. The pylons were most often covered with a fine layer of stucco and painted white, while the figures and other pictorial elements were rendered in vivid colors.

The first interior space of the Temple of Amun, located behind the second pylon, was the so-called hypostyle hall, or hall with many columns. The intervals between the enormous columns are proportionately small, dwarfing visitors, who feel as if they are walking among colossal giants. The columns, 24 meters high, are more than just the structural supports for the roof; they serve as superdimensional history books: the scenes painted on them refer to the religious practices and great achievements of the king. At the bottom they are decorated with images of papyrus and at the top with offering scenes. These details were not actually

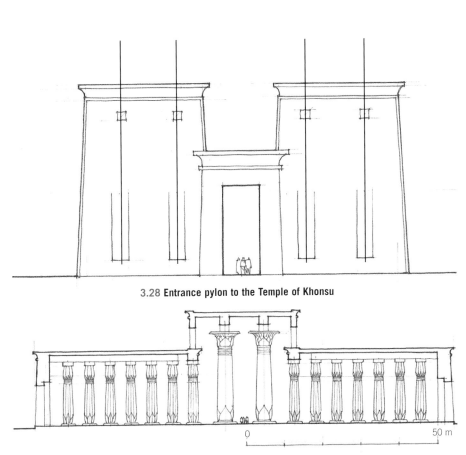

3.28 Entrance pylon to the Temple of Khonsu

3.29 Barque Sanctuary of Temple of Khonsu

0   50 m

meant to be read by visitors: the screened light coming from the clerestory windows high up under the roof would have created a shadowy environment, with the bulk of the columns rising majestically into darkness.

At the eastern end of the building is a festival hall, the exact purpose of which is open to interpretation. Most likely it served as a place for jubilee festivals for the procession, as well as for a type of hall of fame glorifying the deeds of the royal conqueror. On its walls are scenes of gardens and animals. Close to the south entrance there is a space into which the sacred boat was brought and turned to appear poised to go down the central aisle.

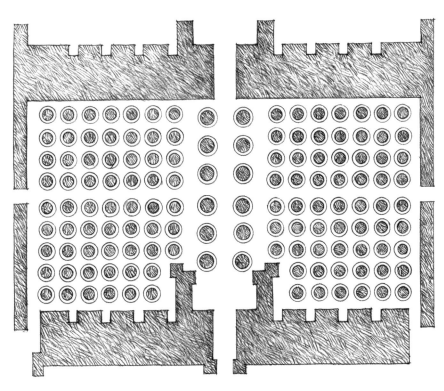

3.30 Plan and section: Hypostyle hall, Temple of Amun at Karnak

3.31 Temple of Luxor

One enters the Temple of Luxor through a rhomboid-shaped courtyard, built later by Ramesses II, that leads to a passageway of two rows of seven impressively scaled columns 21 meters high. That space opens to a court and a hypostyle hall, and finally to the sanctuary itself. A series of successively smaller telescoping rooms then leads to the sanctuary, where the barque was stored. From a door to the left, one gained access to the hall placed at right angles to the axis, which was defined as the mythical place of the path of the sun. Three doors opened to rooms, one for each of the cult images of the divine triad: Amun; his spouse, Mut, the mother of gods; and their son, the moon god Khonsu. They all "gathered" here during the Beautiful Feast of the Valley.

The temple is not axially aligned but follows the gentle easterly bend of the processional route, as it was extended in later building campaigns farther and farther toward the north. Egyptian temples, unlike Mesopotamian temples—or even later, Greek and Roman temples—were not conceived as finalities. Instead, they could grow, be changed, get rebuilt, and even be allowed to decay over time. In the case of Luxor, rulers added courts and hypostyle halls as indications of their support and patronage. The Amun-Re Temple, for example, grew steadily toward the Nile, with new gateways being added and others redesigned.

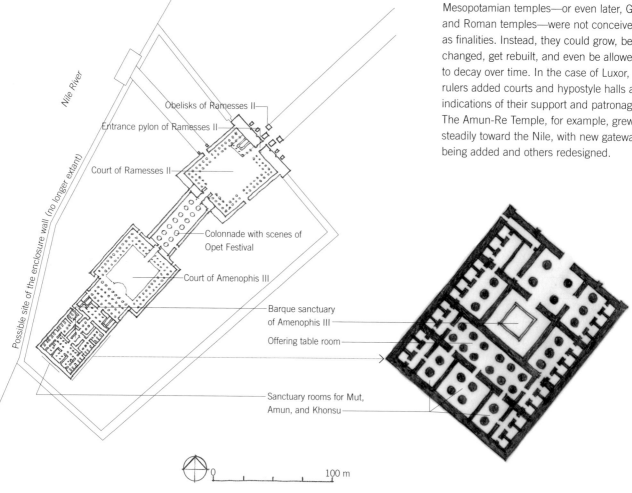

Nile River

Possible site of the enclosure wall (no longer extant)

Obelisks of Ramesses II

Entrance pylon of Ramesses II

Court of Ramesses II

Colonnade with scenes of Opet Festival

Court of Amenophis III

Barque sanctuary of Amenophis III

Offering table room

Sanctuary rooms for Mut, Amun, and Khonsu

0   100 m

3.32 Plan: Temple of Luxor

3.33 Temple at Abu Simbel, near Philae, Egypt

3.34 View looking toward the sanctuary: Temple at Abu Simbel

Abu Simbel

Ramesses II (1290–1224 BCE) was a pragmatic ruler who extended the sphere of Egyptian influence from the upper valleys of the Euphrates to the fourth cataract of the Nile. Nubian gold from the mines of Wabi el-Allaqui swelled his coffers. To protect the trade routes, he built a series of temple outposts that also served to spread Egyptian cosmological beliefs. His wealth enabled him to carry out numerous large-scale building campaigns, the most ambitious of which was the founding of the city of Ramesses (Pi-Ramesse). Close to the old Hyksos capital, Pi-Ramesse stood at the departure point of the increasingly important and well-fortified road to Palestine. The city was sprawling, crowded with temples to state gods, palaces, and military installations (including stables and weapons factories). Copper, the all-important raw material, was delivered here from the newly opened mines at Timma in Israel. Ramesses II's temple at Abu Simbel (1260 BCE) represents the pinnacle of Egyptian rock temples. The facade, carved directly into the sandstone cliff, takes the form of a pylon and is dominated by four colossal seated figures, 22 meters tall, all portrayals of Ramesses. On either side of the statues and between the legs of each are figures of Queen Nefertari and some of the royal children. Above the temples, Ramesses is shown sacrificing to the lord of the temple, Re. The cornice is decorated with a row of baboons, their arms raised in worship of the rising sun.

On the interior, the temple contains two pillared halls, storage rooms, and a sanctuary deep in the rock. The 10-meter-high walls are mainly covered with scenes and inscriptions relating to the king's military exploits against the Hittites and against the Kushites in Nubia. The axis ends in the sanctuary on the west wall with a row of four seated statues of Ptah, Amun, Ramesses, and Re-Harmachis. The small altar in front of them is where sacrifices were made when the light of the rising sun illuminated the sanctuary at dawn.

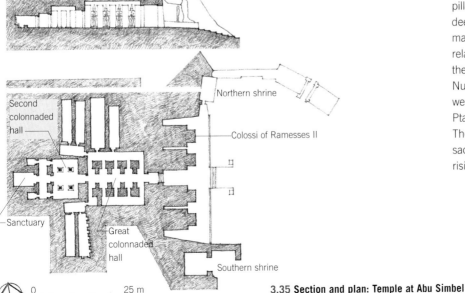

Second colonnaded hall

Northern shrine

Colossi of Ramesses II

Sanctuary

Great colonnaded hall

Southern shrine

0   25 m

3.35 Section and plan: Temple at Abu Simbel

3.36 **Relief of a Djed column**

3.37 **Papyrus, cluster-bud columns**

Egyptian Columns

The Egyptians were the first to develop the column as more than just a load-bearing device—it had symbolic importance. Reeds and flower stalks bundled around poles were used to demarcate sacred spaces. Mostly, the columns were covered with stucco and painted in vibrant colors. Because we tend to see columns as purely structural devices, we can forget that for the Egyptians, the column was a denotative form.

The most common plant themes for columns were the palm, the lotus, and the papyrus. For lotus capitals, there was the so-called bud form, which was usually used in outer courts, and the open form, found in a temple's central area. At the Hatshepsut mortuary temple, one finds fluted cylindrical columns, representing bundled reeds, with plain square capitals that were to have a profound impact on the columns developed by the Greeks.

The preferred structural support for columns was bedrock, but where that was not possible, they were rested on a broad base that in turn rested on a cone shaped stone below the surface of the floor to further distribute the weight. Foundations were often made of compacted sand several meters deep, the sand creating an even distribution of the forces.

The Djed pillar was the archetype of the Egyptian column. It emerged in the early history of ancient Egypt and, though

its meaning is much debated, it most likely derived from a harvest ritual and came to represent the creation myth. Its importance grew over time to represent the world holding up the sky, and as such it came to represent the idea of stability and permanence, important themes in Egyptian dynastic definition. The pillar as it was used in ceremonies was associated with the god Sokar in association with Osiris, the god of the dead.

3.38 **Papyrus, open-bud column**

3.39 **Hatshepstut mortuary temple columns**

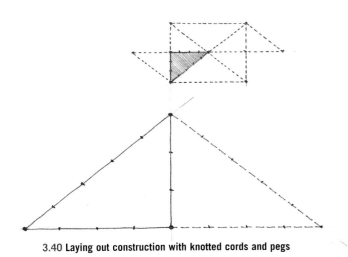

3.40 Laying out construction with knotted cords and pegs

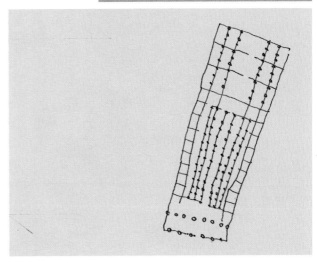

3.41 Low relief of a pylon: An early example of an architectural design

Egyptian Design Methods

Architecture, given its permanence, cost, and prestige, was an important subject in the discourse of the time. Texts relating to architecture, surveying, and town planning make it obvious that architecture had risen to the level of a distinct craft. Architectural plans, drawn on stones, some of which have survived—and most certainly on papyrus, though none of these have survived—indicate a high level of coordination between planning a building and its construction. Beside the titles of royal architect, builder, and overseer of works, there were also priest-architects who had access to secret books that had plans and specifications for buildings and statues. There was even a goddess of architecture and reckoning, Seshat, who begins to appear in Egyptian records in about 2500 BCE. She is depicted as bearing a seven-pointed star or rosette on her head, sometimes above a wand. She was also the goddess of the art of writing.

The king himself played an important part in the planning and the symbolic execution of a structure. In one mural, Thutmosis II is shown performing the ceremony of staking out the ground plan of a temple using a special "plan net," a netlike webbing of rope with knots that marked off locations. The procedure consisted of stretching a net along the axis and then spreading it

out to determine the basic points of the construction. To form a right angle, for example, the Egyptians used a cord with twelve intervals that was wound around three stakes at units of 3, 4, and 5. For construction, plans were certainly produced. Sketches have even been found on the walls of a quarry. On the pylon of the Temple of Khonsu at Karnak is a low relief of a pylon that could very well be one of the first surviving architectural design projects. Drawings from the roof of the hypostyle hall

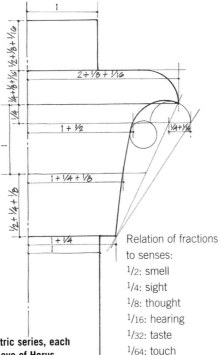

Relation of fractions to senses:
$1/2$: smell
$1/4$: sight
$1/8$: thought
$1/16$: hearing
$1/32$: taste
$1/64$: touch

3.42 Design of a column capital based on a geometric series, each fraction of which symbolizes a different part of the eye of Horus

of Edfu and elsewhere give us some indication of how columns were designed using a complex ordering of ratios in which a cubit was used in conjunction with a geometrical series of fractions. For example, to a column 9 cubits high, the architect would add $1/4 + 1/8 + 1/16$, each fraction symbolizing a different part of the Eye of Horus. Unlike later Greek and Hellenistic assumptions that positioned mathematics in relationship to cosmological spheres, Egyptian mathematics was connected to the physiology of the body. The eye was seen as one unit, with each of the parts measuring a fraction. This unit was named after Hequat, who was a goddess represented by a frog; she was also the sign of fertility. The name is fitting, since Egyptian mathematics involves a system of leapfrogging over various fractions to achieve the desired answer. The carving of a column and capital was thus a shortcut for these operations.

Though we do not know for certain the geometry of the pyramids, it has been ascertained with a fair amount of probability that height-to-width was determined through the ratio of 4:1 pi or sometimes 3:1 pi. Egyptian mathematics, as discussed by Corinna Rossi in her book on the subject, was the most advanced in the world at the time. By 1700 BCE, the date of various papyrus scrolls dealing with mathematical topics, various complex mathematical systems were being devised.

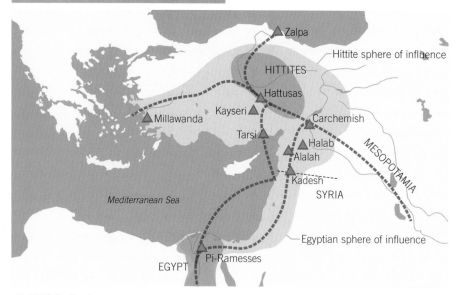

3.43 Hittite Empire

The Hittites, similar to the Mesopotamians, had a vast pantheon of intermarried gods and goddesses, in the center of which was the male weather god, symbolized by a bull. His consort controlled the rivers and the sea but was also sometimes known as a sun goddess. Even though temples were important for the Hittites, they also had outdoor sanctuaries. In this they were much more like the Minoans than either the Egyptians or the Mesopotamians. One such sanctuary is Yazilikaya, a little over a kilometer to the northeast of Hattusas, to which it was connected by a processional way. It had a pantheon of gods chiseled into the face of the cliff, perhaps showing them arriving at the house of the weather god for the spring festival.

Hittite Empire

The Hittites settled in Anatolia around 1600 BCE. To the amazement of scholars, they were revealed to be Indo-Aryan, once their language was deciphered. They must have chosen the site of their capital, Hattusas, with an eye toward dominating the intersection of two important trading routes. One ran from the Aegean coast, from a harbor later to become Ephesus, to the Black Sea. The other ran southward, from the Black Sea port of Amisus (Samsum) to the headwaters of the Euphrates. To further stimulate trade, the Hittites permitted Assyrians to set up posts for their donkey and camel caravans in eastern Anatolia, such as the one at Kanesh, 20 kilometers northeast of Kayseri and only 100 kilometers southwest of Hattusas. At its height, the Hittite Empire stretched into the Levant, leading to conflict with the Egyptians and to the famous battle for Kadesh (1275 BCE) in northern Syria. After the battle, which was a draw, the two parties wrote up a treaty that guaranteed peace and security throughout the area, allowing the cities along the Syrian coast to grow in importance and also creating a power shift away from Mesopotamia toward the eastern Mediterranean. A cuneiform version of this treaty, found at Hattusas, hangs today in an enlarged copy at the United Nations Building to demonstrate the age-old importance of international treaties.

Though the Hittite economy was basically agricultural, the Hittites conducted a lively export in copper, bronze, and later, most prized of all, iron. Many of the mines were in the vicinity of Bokar-Maden in the Taurus Mountains. The main military strength of the Hittites lay in the intensive development of new weapons, such as the light horse-drawn chariot with its six-spoked wheels. It contributed greatly to speed and mobility in battle. The Sumerians had already had chariots pulled by wild asses, but their wheels were made of solid wood. Egyptian chariots held only two men, while the Hittite's held three, the driver and two soldiers, one each for attack and defense.

Hattusas

Hattusas (modern Bogazköy), situated at the juncture of two ancient trade routes in north-central Turkey, lies on the northern slope of a ridge where a high plateau begins to descend toward the valley. Of the many temples in the city, the most notable was the so-called Temple I, squarish in plan with an annex in the back. It took up an irregularly shaped city block and was composed principally of storage cells for sanctuary treasure and food. Archaeologists have found jars of Cretan and Mycenaean provenance there. The storage room walls were very thick, suggesting that the building was two or three stories high. The entire complex, including the storerooms, measures 160 by 135 meters. The temple

3.44 Relief depicting twelve gods of the Hittite underworld, Yazilikaya, Turkey

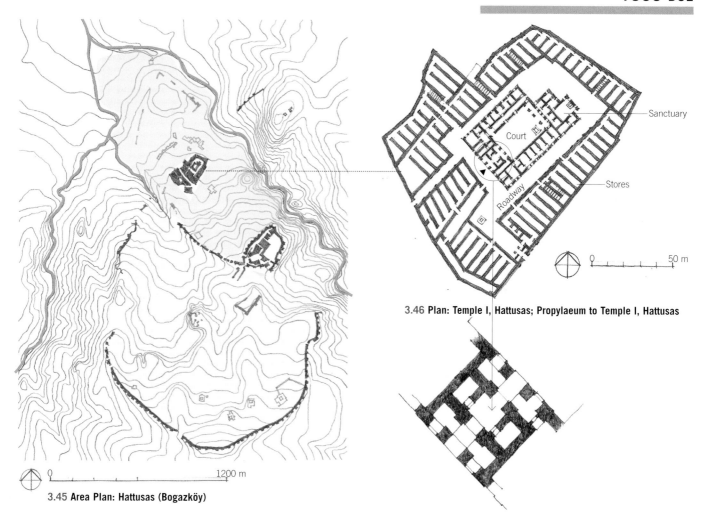

3.46 Plan: Temple I, Hattusas; Propylaeum to Temple I, Hattusas

3.45 Area Plan: Hattusas (Bogazköy)

was built of limestone, whereas the annex that contained the sacred statues was built of granite, indicating its special status. The courtyard in front of it was entered through a symmetrically laid out gate, square in plan and divided into nine spaces. In the rest of the plan there was an attempt to balance the right and left sides of the courtyard. In the northeast corner was a washhouse, while a portico at the far end gave access to the sacred spaces in the annex, consisting of two large rooms and several smaller ones. The cult statues were in the larger of the two rooms to the northwest and were dedicated to the sun goddess, while the other room was dedicated to the weather god. All in all, the building appears as an aggregation of different elements: the gate, the court, and the annex.

How the temple service was conducted has been partially clarified from various texts that have been found. The most important event was a springtime festival at which the combat of the weather god and a dragon

was acted out or recited. During the festival, the king and queen, accompanied by jesters and musicians, would enter through the ceremonial gate on the eastern wall and proceed to a stone basin, where the king would perform a ritual hand washing using water poured from a jar made of gold. From there he would enter the temple courtyard through the monumental gate. A master of ceremonies then prepared the king and the assembled dignitaries for a feast, perhaps in the colonnade of the courtyard or in the throne room itself. The Hittites, like the Mesopotamians, employed no columns or capitals in their architecture. Instead, they grouped rooms around paved courts. In contrast to Sumerian temples, however, in which rooms received daylight from windows high up in the walls, resulting in dark and mysterious interiors, the Hittite architects employed tall windows starting close to floor level. Such windows were placed on both sides of the cult statue and would have bathed it in brilliant light. The Hittites also

employed colonnades in a type of wall-and-pier system that enriched their spatial vocabulary considerably. And finally, Hittite architects strove for a deliberate tension between symmetry and asymmetry that has parallels, as we shall see, with Minoan architecture.

There are other differences with Mesopotamian temples. The *cella* of a Mesopotamian temple communicated with the courtyard through an intervening antechamber or antechapel, so that the congregation in the court would have a clear view of the god's statue in its niche. In Hittite temples, the entrance to the cella was not in the wall opposite the cult statue but in one of the adjacent sides. The cult room was approached indirectly, through side rooms, the statue would therefore not have been visible from the court. This has led archaeologists to conclude that the cella was reserved for priests or a corresponding elite who alone were admitted to the sanctum.

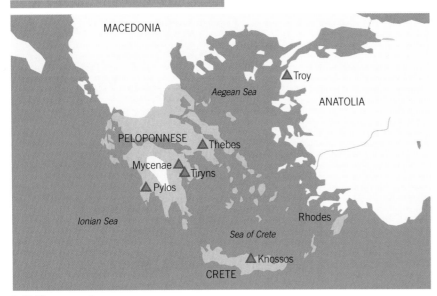

3.47 Mycenaean Greece

Mycenaean Civilization

The Mycenaeans, from parts unknown, settled in Greece around 2000 BCE. There, like the Hittites, they quickly coalesced into a unified Bronze Age social order. The numerous harbors and islands of the Peloponnese lent themselves to a system of regional chieftains or kings operating under the umbrella of the lord of Mycenae, to whom they were connected by ties of blood, old tribal loyalties, language, and old memories of origins as reflected in their myths. Commanding a powerful fleet, he could ensure that city-state's foremost position. After the decline of Minoan dominance over the Mediterranean, the reach of Mycenae extended to all the Aegean islands, including

Rhodes and Cyprus. The Mycenaeans traded with Sicily, southern Italy, Egypt, Sardinia, and the countries bordering the Black Sea, leaving trading outposts along the way. Their form of power was a novelty in world history. They were not centralized and had no land-based army. But it was precisely this that propelled them into world events. Tribal affiliations created small but fiercely loyal fighters. They developed their own export commodities. Their carpenters, for example, used ivory from Syria with great skill to adorn furniture. Their metallurgical skill was legendary; Mycenaean bronze swords have been found in Romania. There were obviously interactions with the Minoans,

from whose long culture the Mycenaeans borrowed elements of wall decorations and building techniques. Mycenaean architectural sensibilities were, however, their own and centered around the *megaron*, or great hall.

Nestor's palace complex at Pylos, of which we hear much in Homer's *Odyssey*, was built between 1300 and 1200 BCE. Predominant is the *megaron*, a square room with four fluted columns in the center of which is an elevated hearth 4 meters in diameter; the room was vented by a clerestory ceiling. The floor was plastered and decorated with a grid the fields that were painted with nonfigural patterns.

The walls were covered with an elaborate series of frescoes showing animals, musicians, and individuals carrying offerings and a bull sacrifice. On the wall near the throne (*to-no* in Mycenaean Greek, whence comes the word "throne"), was a drawing of an octopus with special symbolical meaning. Did the slippery, multi-armed organism resemble the adept, multi-zoned Mycenaean social structure? The throne was made of wood, plated in gold and ebony.

Behind the great hall were two storage rooms containing large pots for storing oil. The residential quarters were in a discrete block at the eastern corner. There was even a room with a bath made of terra-cotta. Access to the *megaron* was more direct than the labyrinthine approach at Knossos. From the outside, one entered through an H-shaped *propylon* (the word literally means "before the gate") with a single column dividing the path into two, much as one would have found in Crete. It did not lead to a hall or corridor but into a courtyard, where a porch of columns and a set of doorways formed the entrance into the *megaron*.

To the right of the entrance was the guard room, and to the left, the palace archives and records of trade transactions. Before entering the *megaron*, a visitor would first have been led to a room on the left side of the courtyard, which was a place for ritual preparation. The palace was located on a ridge with a protected port about 5 kilometers from the sea, right on the trade route that worked its way through the Peloponnese.

Mycenaean palaces were much more than residences; like at Knossos, they were administrative centers and the locus of the region's industrial production. The Palace of Pylos, for example, employed around 550 textile workers and 400 workers in the

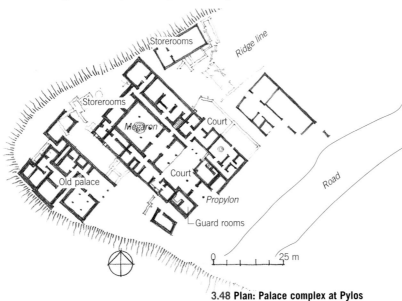

3.48 Plan: Palace complex at Pylos

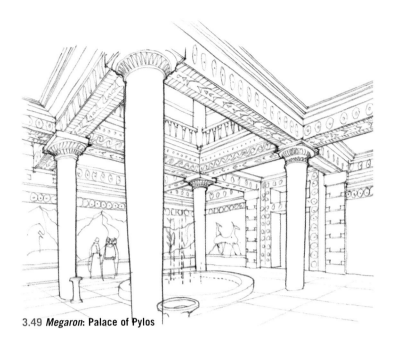

3.49 *Megaron*: **Palace of Pylos**

3.50 Mycenae, Greece, and environs

metallurgical industry. There were also other types of artisans, such as goldsmiths, ivory carvers, stone carvers, and potters.

The most dominant city of the time was Mycenae itself. Though today the city seems remote, this was not the case in 400 BCE. It straddled a shortcut through the Peloponnese between the broad and protected Argos harbor and a port on the Bay of Corinth, and thus connected Crete and the eastern Mediterranean with the markets in Italy and beyond. Situated on the side of mountain, it was easily protected.

Mycenae was defended by thick ring walls that were built around 1450 BCE. Part of this formidable defense work consisted of a cyclopean wall named for the seemingly superhuman strength it must have taken to move these immense boulders. In other parts one finds regular rows of blocks of stone fitted without mortar. One enters the citadel through the famed Lion Gate, which might imply a connection to, or at least familiarity with, Hattusas. Just to its right is a large circular burial *tholos*, the so-called Treasury of Atreus, which archaeologists found almost intact; it has six chambered tombs containing gold, silver, and bronze burial treasures. Entrance to this circle was restricted to the elite. Unlike the Egyptian pharaohs, who were placed in pyramids, and later in secret caves, the Mycenaean dead were displayed within the city at a place where memory and narrative were most likely to converge. Later Greeks would call the gathering of people in commemorating places a *choros*. Indeed, Homer would emerge, long after the Mycenaean Age had waned, recounting the tales of Mycenaean heroes, among them Agamemnon.

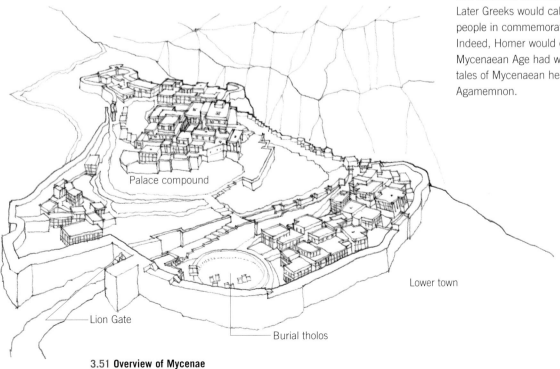

3.51 Overview of Mycenae

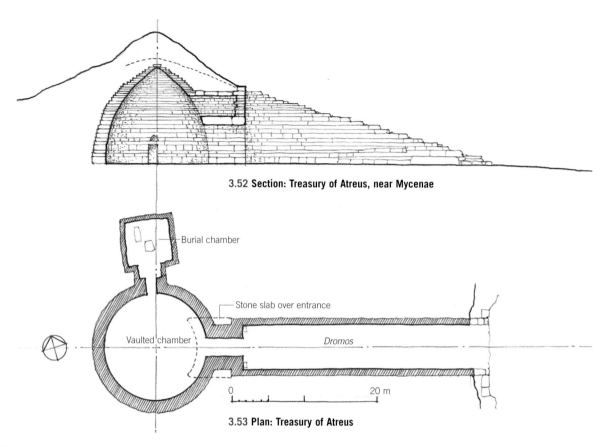

3.52 Section: Treasury of Atreus, near Mycenae

Burial chamber

Stone slab over entrance

Vaulted chamber

Dromos

0   20 m

3.53 Plan: Treasury of Atreus

Treasury of Atreus

Beginning in the late Bronze Age, the kings were buried outside the city in great beehive—or *tholos*—tombs, monumental symbols of wealth and power. The one at Mycenae, the Treasury of Atreus, is the most famous and the most finely built. It consists of a great circular chamber cut into the hillside, some 15 meters in both diameter and height, and entered by a corridor—a *dromos*—about 36 meters long and 6 meters wide. The tomb was roofed by a corbelled dome made of finely cut ashlar blocks. A rectangular room, the burial chamber proper, was tucked in next to the central one. The whole was covered with earth to form a conical hill. The high facade at the entrance was flanked by two half-columns of green porphyry—a stone native to Egypt—carved with chevrons and spirals. Though fitted with Minoan-style capitals, their bulbous proportions foreshadowed the transformation the capitals would undergo subsequent to the Dorian invasion. The stone lintel above the door was elaborately decorated with running spirals and other patterns.

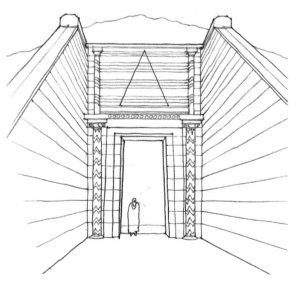

3.54 Entrance facade, Treasury of Atreus

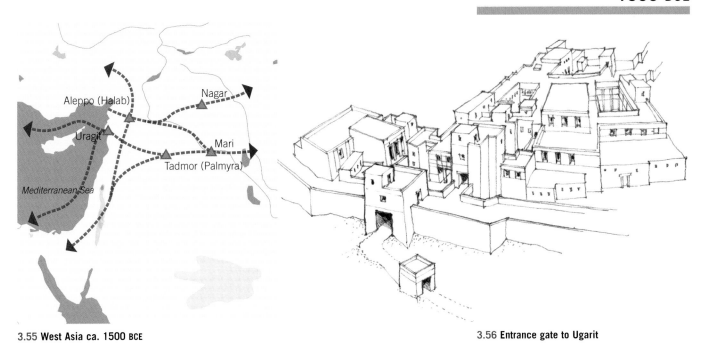

3.55 West Asia ca. 1500 BCE

3.56 Entrance gate to Ugarit

Ugarit and Mari

Ugarit, on the coast of Syria, profited from the atmosphere of peace that followed the Egyptian-Hittite accord. It became a major terminus for land travel to and from Anatolia, inner Syria, and Mesopotamia, as well as a trading port serving merchants and travelers from Greece and Egypt. Documents discovered at Ugarit mention a wide spectrum of trading goods—wheat, olives, barley, dates, honey, wine, and cumin, and also copper, tin, bronze, lead, and iron—coming from as far away as Afghanistan and central Africa. Though a trading city, Ugarit seems to have specialized in the Murex seashells that were used in the fabrication of much sought-after purple dye. Timber from the Levant's forests were another important Ugaritic export. Though the Ugarit kings were generally aligned with Egypt, the entrance to the palace, close to the western gate and with views of the Mediterranean Sea, had strong similarities to Minoan architecture—except, so it seems, that there were no open columnar loggias. In that sense, and in plan, with its courtyard, it was more Mesopotamian. One entered a *propylon* that led, after a turn, to the left, to a courtyard at the far side of which was the throne room. The private part of the palace, with a garden, lay to the rear.

Despite various problems with invaders, a few Mesopotamian cities were able to maintain themselves as centers of trade, the leading one at the time being Mari (in present-day Syria), a town that had been inhabited since the fifth millennium BCE but that grew in significance during the second millennium BCE, when it began to serve as a staging area for caravans heading across the desert to the Mediterranean. But around 2000 BCE, the population suddenly swelled as a result of the arrival of a confederation of tribes called the Amorites—perhaps from the Indus River valley—on their way west. Their numbers were such that they were able to subdue Mari and control the trade in copper and tin that passed through Persia and over the Euphrates. Zimri-Lim, who ruled from about 1779 to 1757 BCE, was able to wrest control back, and soon the city was as prosperous as ever, possibly because it was the center of a textile industry that made it less dependent on the vicissitudes of agriculture. It was protected by a 2 kilometer-wide moat that was fed by the Euphrates.

The Palace of Zimri-Lim contained over three hundred rooms and was possibly the largest single building in the world in its time. Supposedly, King Yahmad of Aleppo and the king of Ugarit both expressed their desire to visit the palace and see its splendor for themselves. The state archives, housed in the building, yielded some twenty-five thousand cuneiform tablets, which provide important information about the life and customs of Mesopotamia at that time. The entrance to the palace, from the north, led to a courtyard that was separated from the royal courtyard beyond by a laterally placed room with asymmetrically placed doors. Behind the official throne room were a series of storage rooms, as would have been typical, since the most precious commodities were stored close to the throne room. The palace bakery was located in the northeast corner. At the southeast corner was the palace temple. In typical Mesopotamian fashion, the inhabitants of Mari worshipped a vast array of gods and goddesses, such as Dagan, the deity of storms, and Ishtar, the goddess of fertility, both of whom had temples dedicated to them in the city. To get a sense of the growth of these palaces and the increasing centralization of power, one can look at the temple at Tell Chuera, in northern Syria, built about 2500 BCE. We also see the growing size differentiations of the various courtyards: the domestic and the official parts of the palace become more differentiated over time.

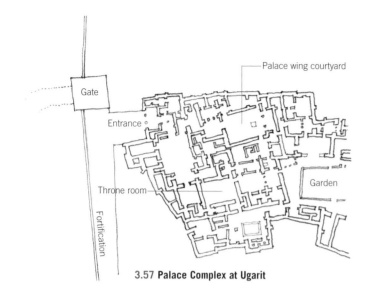

Palace wing courtyard

Gate

Entrance

Throne room

Garden

Fortification

3.57 Palace Complex at Ugarit

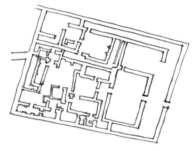

3.58 Palace in Tell Chuera

Private palace

0   50 m

Entrance

Bakery

Throne room

Palace temple

Slave quarters

Palace storehouse

Palace temple

3.59 Palace of Zimri-Lim at Mari

By the end of the 12th century BCE, the Mediterranean was in disarray, largely due to the incursions of the so-called Sea People. Though no one knows who they were or where they came from, it was clear they were not just warriors but entire communities on the move. Presumably, they were a coalition of different population groups. The Egyptians were able to repulse them only after several major battles, forcing them into the Levant. Simultaneously, the Dorians swept down from the north, destroying everything before them. The great citadels of Mycenae were set upon and suffered disastrous fires. The generally accepted date for the demise of the Mycenaean culture is around 1100 BCE. For several centuries, with Egypt weakened by its struggle against the Sea People and the invading Dorians bent on destruction rather than building, the eastern Mediterranean, on which so much had depended for so long, vanished as an economic entity, and a dark age prevailed.

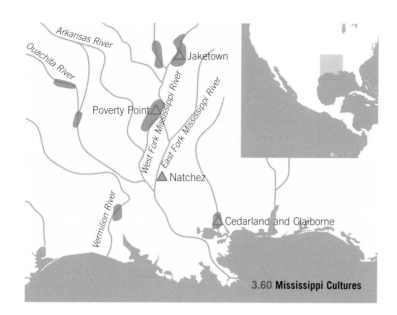

3.60 **Mississippi Cultures**

3.61 **Pictorial view: Mound A (Large Bird Mound), Poverty Point, USA**

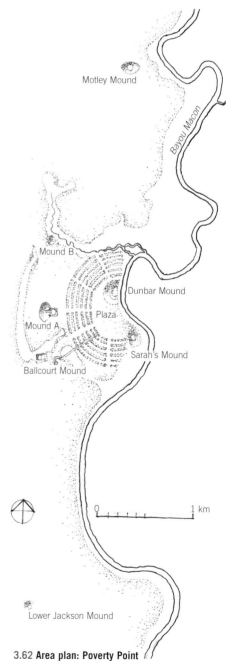

3.62 **Area plan: Poverty Point**

Poverty Point

First reported in 1873, the semi-elliptical ridges of Poverty Point were thought to be natural formations. It was only in the 1950s, when the site was viewed from the air, that archaeologists realized they were artificial constructions. Located in the lower Mississippi Valley of Parish County, Louisiana, near both the Gulf Coast and the confluence of six major rivers, Poverty Point is not a unique construction. Similar huge earth mounds have been found all over North America, particularly along the Mississippi and the coastal regions, some of them dating as far back as 2000 BCE, around which time the first settlements developed along the numerous rivers of the region. The Poverty Point people produced the largest and most elaborate earth mounds in North America. The mounds had both a sacred and secular significance, but whether the site was a city or a regional ceremonial center cannot be easily decided.

First settled around 1800 BCE, the Poverty Point area extended throughout the lower Mississippi Valley, from New Orleans to the southern tip of Illinois, a distance of about 800 kilometers. The people that lived near Poverty Point chose their locations carefully, linking the site to the waterways of the Mississippi River, which allowed for easy trade and communication. Trade was extensive and included chipped-stone projectile points and tools, ground-stone plummets, and shell and stone beads. This extensive trade network differentiates the Poverty Point people from earlier cultures in the area.

Six concentric semi-elliptical rings enclose a vast open plaza covering an area of about 34 acres. Aisle-like openings run between the rings, dividing them into six sections, which are thought to have stood over 2 meters high. In and around the complex are six to eight constructed earthen mounds. Besides providing protection from flooding, the rings may have functioned, at least partially, as living areas, since domestic objects have been found during the site's excavation. Nonsecular objects have also been found, indicating that the complex may have had a sacred, ritualistic function as well. The main plaza faces east. Someone looking along the aisles from the center outward would have looked toward the sun at the winter solstice in one direction, and toward the sun at the summer solstice in the other. The ceremonial center may have functioned as a cosmic instrument, but exactly how is still not known. It may also have served as a "protective" enclosure, keeping out evil spirits.

What is most astonishing is that Poverty Point was a society that had not yet begun to cultivate corn. Corn was raised in Mexico around this time, but it would take several centuries before it could be farmed in more northerly climes. A staple at Poverty Point was fish, augmented by venison and the meat of smaller animals. Plants undoubtedly provided the main part of Poverty Point food, but because their remains are rarely preserved, we have a limited view of their contribution. Nuts predominate, and include hickory nuts, pecans, acorns, and walnuts.

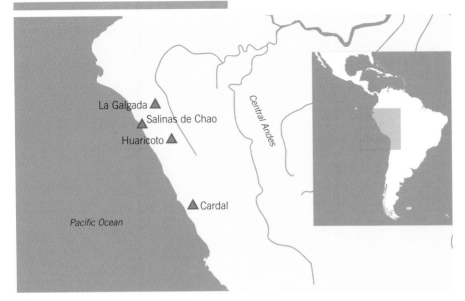

3.63 Peruvian civilizations, ca. 1500 BCE

Civilization of the High Andes

By 1500 BCE, the Andean cultures had moved into the higher valleys of the Peruvian mountains, from which trade routes, moving north and south, were much more easy to establish than they were along the coast. Aided by the versatile llama, the burgeoning trade enabled the development of a series of interconnected highland centers, such as Cajamarca and Ancash, and in the river valleys of the Moche, Casma, Chillon, Rimac, and Lurin. Each had large storage structures in which to accumulate agricultural produce. As large, centralized surpluses of wealth were generated, competition among the elites of the various centers pushed the development of ritual complexes into ever larger sizes and increasing complexity. In the period from 2000 to 1000 BCE, relatively simple and approachable ceremonial structures, such as the one at La Galgada, were replaced by a string of enormous U-shaped complexes, the largest of which was at Salinas de Chao.

At Huaricoto, from around 2200 to 2000 BCE, there are thirteen superimposed, deeply buried ritual structures. Relatively intimate in size, they were used by small groups for fire sacrifices, which were performed by their own members, rather than by a member of the priestly class. Each ritual structure, after being used for a while, became a burial site—presumably for the family or clan to which it belonged—and was then filled in to form the base of the next generation's ritual structure.

By this time, the sacrifice of living human beings and children had become a part of Andean social practices. Located along the Tablachaca River about 70 kilometers from the sea and in mountainous territory, La Galgada (ca. 2600–1400 BCE) consists of two mounds, a ring platform, and a low circular wall forming a plaza. As at Huaricoto, there are small circular masonry ritual chambers. But these are more formalized, complete with plastered interiors, niches, benches, and a central hearth with built-in ventilator shafts. The older chambers are scattered around the site. The mounds may also contain

superimposed layers of ritual structures, but those have not yet been excavated. The latest chambers are located on the north mound, organized in a loose U-shaped arrangement within a walled enclosure and accessed from a small plaza on the west by long, steeply pitched stairs.

Cardal (ca. 1465–975 BCE), located 14 kilometers from the Pacific Ocean on the Lurin River, consists of three large platform mounds made from irregular quarried stone set into clay mortar and arranged in a monumental U-shape open to the north. Dominating the site is the main platform mound, 145 by 60 meters and 17 meters high. A steep 6.5-meter-wide stairway leads up to the focal structure—an atrium—atop

3.64 Site plan of Cardal

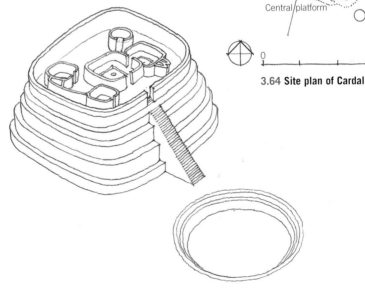

3.65 Pictorial view: North mound at La Galgada

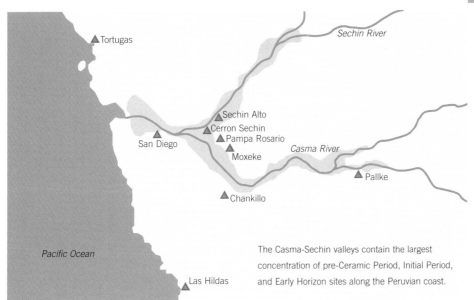

The Casma-Sechin valleys contain the largest concentration of pre-Ceramic Period, Initial Period, and Early Horizon sites along the Peruvian coast.

3.66 The Casma-Sechin valleys

this mound. There are three subsidiary plazas to the north. Eleven circular sunken platforms are scattered across the site, some on top of the mounds, others around the plaza. Outlines of residential structures for about three hundred inhabitants are still visible at the site. Cardal was a major regional hub that functioned somewhat like a modern convention center, with multiple places designed to accommodate public gatherings of different sizes and compositions. Rituals performed in the sacred atrium would have been clearly visible in the plaza and, given the steepness of the slope, the position of the spectators, and the size of the mound, would have appeared monumental and impressive.

Besides Cardal, massive U-shaped ceremonial complexes were constructed in the Andean highlands at places such as Las Aldas (1600–1100 BCE), Sechin Alto (1800–1700 BCE), and Moxeke (1500–1300 BCE). Sechin Alto was the largest of these, with its biggest 300-by-250-meter platform mound rising an imposing 44 meters above the surrounding plain. Not built upon a preexisting hill, this mound contained 2 million cubic feet of fill, masonry, and conical mud bricks, making it one of the largest prehistoric constructions in the Americas at that time. It consisted of an almost kilometer-long series of axially aligned platforms, terraces, and circular pits.

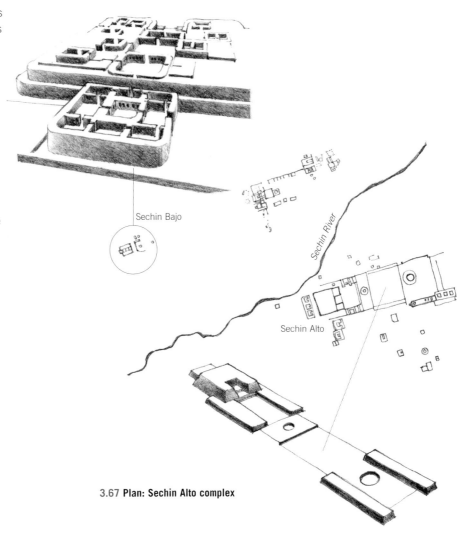

3.67 Plan: Sechin Alto complex

3.68 Pictorial view: Salinas de Chao, Isla Blanca, Peru

Salinas de Chao

Salinas de Chao (ca. 1610–1300 BCE), located 8 kilometers inland from the Pacific Ocean, shows the ritual complexes integrated within an urban fabric. Though the valley was narrow and not particularly productive agriculturally, the city controlled nearby salt mines. A haphazard residential order is punctuated by numerous ritual centers. Two of these dominate. Unlike at Cardal, the longitudinal axis is elongated and knitted together by sidewalls into a single unit terminating in the circular court. Entered from two opposing stairs on the diagonal axis, the circular court appears as a large open courtyard and terrace. The ritual structure is raised on three levels, exploiting the natural slope of the land. A series of symmetrical platforms and terraces and a central stair further magnify the central presence and the upward monumentalizing thrust of the focal structure, telescoping its presence into the plaza, in contrast with the enveloping negative space of the sunken court. Although the larger complex is built around the longitudinal axis and exploits the natural elevation of the hillside, its architectural expression points to a more monumental, processional order. The U-shaped spatial composition echoes the character of the river valleys in which it is located.

The creation of U-shaped complexes in the highland Andes inaugurated a new kind of ritual space that became the staple center of South American architecture until the arrival of the Spanish in the 15th century. While older Andean structures were intimate and focused on ritual theater to be witnessed by those below, the U-shaped complexes were much too large for bounded ceremonies. They would have required impossibly large populations to fill them; furthermore, the rituals on their mounds would not have been visible even from an average distance. However, many smaller ceremonies could have been carried out simultaneously in them; one possibility is that their lengths and sequences may have been designed to stage elaborate processions from one court to another. Yet their size also suggests that these complexes may have been conceived as embodiments of larger cosmic orders, of value simply in their creation.

Peru is an earthquake-prone zone. The effects of El Niño, flash floods, and landslides are periodic occurrences. Propitiating the gods of nature and carefully practicing a life in harmony with both agricultural and astronomical temporal rhythms was the keystone of not only early Andean beliefs but of most subsequent South American and Mesoamerican cultures. While archaeologists still debate the exact nature of their rituals, they seem to agree that they have been organized around the necessity of cyclical sacrifice and the ritual repetition of natural rhythms. Processional architecture would have facilitated such a ceremonial iterance of units of time. These complexes are not sacred structures per se. They are not houses of God. Nor are they landscaped gestures raised skyward. Rather, they are ritual theaters.

3.69 Reconstruction of a prototypical U-shaped monument complex

800 BCE

By 1000 BCE the agricultural and water canalization techniques that had been developed in the coastal communities of South America were also being applied in the highlands, from which it was easier to control trade. Several ritual centers were founded, such as Chavín de Huántar, which was located at the intersection of important trade routes. In Central America meanwhile, the Olmecs had drained the tropical, marshy lands of Veracruz and converted them into thriving agricultural fields, yielding surpluses. Around this time, and probably because of Olmec ingenuity, maize (corn), which was to change the culinary history of the Americas, was first cultivated. The resulting prosperous trading economy formed the basis for the first major ritual centers of Central America, such as San Lorenzo and La Venta in modern-day Mexico.

Whereas Mesoamerica had just entered the Bronze Age, the Eurasian world was entering the Iron Age. By 1000 BCE iron smelting had become fairly widespread, having been introduced by the Hittites. Its usage spread all the way to China. Iron weapons changed the power structure and was presumably the cause for much of the period's upheaval and displacement. New cultures arose and flourished, almost all of them iron-making cultures. In northern Italy, we find the Etruscans; in Greece, the Dorians; along the coast of Turkey, the Ionians; in Armenia, the Urartu; and in southern Egypt, the Nubians. In the eastern Mediterranean, cities like Byblos and Sidon flourished, as did the Israelite kingdom centered in Jerusalem.

It was within this context of improved weaponry that the Dorians established their hold on the Mediterranean ports and extended their power toward the west by founding colonies in Sicily and Italy to secure the newly developing, grain-producing regions. Magna Graecia, as it was called, was so strong that by 500 BCE it had become a single economic and cultural continuity. It was thus in Sicily and Italy that one finds some of the most developed early Greek experiments in stone architecture. The 9th and 8th centuries BCE saw the rise of the regional importance of Palestine in relationship to the Kush in Nubia and the Sabaean kingdom in Yemen. Kush was an important source of metal, and for a period its kings took control of Egypt. The Sabaean kingdom in Yemen had a monopoly on the production of frankincense, an oil derived from a plant that grew only there. Frankincense, which was very expensive, was a requirement in many religious ceremonies. In order to reach the markets, it was brought to Palestine, with its connections to ports and trade routes.

Between the 8th and 6th centuries BCE, the Assyrians and Babylonians established themselves as the controlling powers of western Asia, but though their empires were extensive and their new cities famous, their inability to establish coherent financial and trade policies made them vulnerable. The fall of the Babylonian Empire to Persia in 539 BCE marked the beginning of the end of a Mesopotamian-centered culture that had, for over two millennia, been one of the dominating regenerating forces—culturally, economically, and politically—in Eurasia. With this collapse, and the power shift to Persia, it can be argued that East and West developed along different tracks from this point onward.

Further to the east, in India, the Vedic Indo-Aryan invaders who had imposed themselves as a ruling class in previous centuries had by this time occupied large sections of the Indo-Gangetic Plain, where they established sixteen *mahajanapadas*, or kingdoms. Initially, the state of Kashi, with its capital at Varanasi, gained supremacy, but it was subsumed by Koshala. Varanasi, however, remained an important center of learning and became home to scholars from all the *mahajanapadas*.

In 1046 BCE the Zhou replaced the Shang, establishing the longest-lasting dynasty in Chinese history. They built two of China's four great cities, Xi'an and Luoyang, codifying urban planning principles that were cited, if not always adhered to, in all subsequent Chinese capital cities. Little, however, remains of these cities, since they were constructed largely of wooden buildings on earth platform foundations. The Zhou created the ideology of imperial rule as the "mandate of heaven," which was later to be extolled as the model of governance by Confucius and others. They also began a process of consolidation, which resulted in the exile of "barbarian" tribes, mainly to the south, who became the ancestors of the Thai, Burmese, and Vietnamese.

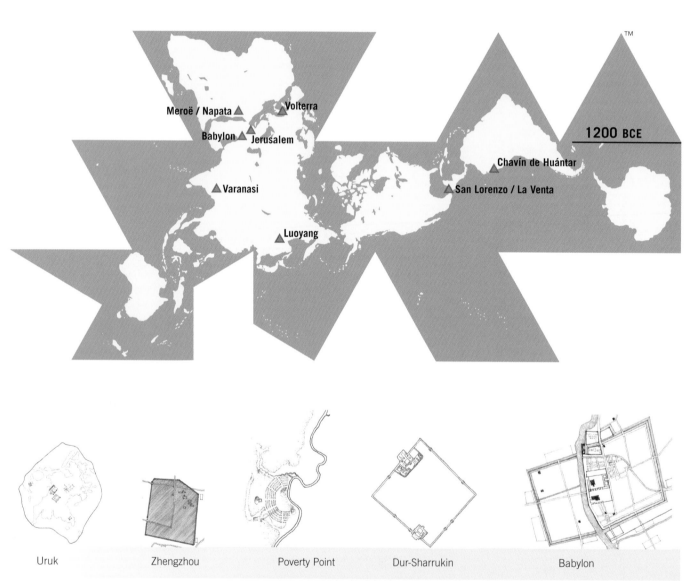

▲ San Lorenzo
1500–900 BCE

Meroë / Napata ▲

▲ Volterra

Babylon ▲ ▲ Jerusalem

1200 BCE

▲ Chavín de Huántar

▲ Varanasi

▲ San Lorenzo / La Venta

▲ Luoyang

Uruk

Zhengzhou

Poverty Point

Dur-Sharrukin

Babylon

4.1 Relative sizes of sites

Aryan Invasion
ca. 1200 BCE

Olmec Cultures
ca. 1500–400 BCE

▲ **La Venta**
1000–400 BCE

Chavín Culture   ▲ **Chavín de Huántar**
ca. 1000–400 BCE   ca. 900 BCE

Western Zhou Dynasty   Eastern Zhou Dynasty
ca. 1046–771 BCE   771–256 BCE

▲ **Ritual Complex at Fengchu**
ca. 1000 BCE

1000 BCE   **800 BCE**   **600 BCE**

Iron Age II
ca. 1000–586 BCE

Etruscan Culture
ca. 750–90 BCE

▲ **Banditaccia**   ▲**Volterra**
8th to 3rd centuries BCE   5th to 4th centuries BCE

Balkan Peninsula: Mycenaean Era
ca. 1600–1100 BCE

Greece: Geometric Period   ◉ ca. 776 BCE   Greece: Archaic Period
ca. 900–700 BCE   Olympic games founded   ca. 700–480 BCE

▲**Temple of Hera at Samos**
8th century BCE

Temple of Apollo at Thermos ▲
630 BCE

▲ **Temple of Solomon**   ▲**Temple of Poseidon at Isthmia**
953–586 BCE   7th century BCE

▲ **Mahram Bilqis**
9th century BCE

Kingdom of Kush
ca. 760 BCE–350 CE

▲ **Napata**
ca. 900–300 BCE

Neo-Assyrian Empire
ca. 911–612 BCE

▲ **Dur-Sharrukin**   ▲ **Babylon**
717–705 BCE   Rebuilt 605 BCE

▲ **Nineveh**
705–612 BCE

▲ **Varanasi**
ca. 1000 BCE–present

4.2 Urbanization of the Americas, ca. 800 BCE

North ◯ Poverty Point Culture (ending 700 BCE)

Central ◉ Olmecs

South ● Chavín de Huántar

4.3 Trade in the Americas, ca. 800 BCE

Olmecs

The Olmecs (ca. 1500–400 BCE) were the first culture in Central America to produce a formal architectural vocabulary out of permanent materials; their heartland extended in an arc of about 200 kilometers along the southern shore of the Gulf of Mexico, on the coastal plains of Veracruz and Tabasco. The Olmecs (a name given to them by modern archaeologists—their real name is unknown) converted a swampy land to their advantage. They first cultivated the ground on the natural damlike elevations that rose above the land. Eventually, by dredging and piling up earth to heighten and extend these land swells, they could not only create cultivatable land but also harvest fish, clams, and turtles from the waterways. It was around this time that we see the emergence of a permanent leading class, who, of course, lived on the highest land created by extensive modifications of the earth. By 1000 BCE, the principal city, San Lorenzo, had substantial reservoirs and drainage systems integrated into a palatial complex with causeways, plazas, and platform mounds. Other Olmec cities were La Venta, Tenochtitlán, and Laguna de los Cerros. These places were focal points for the developing trade throughout Central America. The jade used for figurines and in rituals originated in Guatemala, for example. Perhaps because of its greenish color, which could be associated with water or vegetation, jade was symbolically associated with life and death.

The scale of the agricultural revolution that the Olmecs created is only now becoming clear. Aside from the rubber tree, which they isolated and developed, there was also corn, which was, however, a product of genetic engineering; it had to be created artificially from its predecessors. In this it was very much unlike rice, millet, and other grains in Eurasia, which were variants of natural plants. So aware were the Olmecs of the significance of the maize revolution that corn was represented in the headdress of the king. Later in the Mayan creation story, humans were literally created from maize. The Olmecs had the advantage of a vast variety of natural plants that could be farmed, such as avocados, beans, tomatoes, chilies,

4.4 A characteristic motif of Olmec art was the were-jaguar, a human face with the mouth of a jaguar.

and squashes. But it was the development of maize, rich in vitamins and sugars, that propelled Mesoamerican agriculture. It was planted very differently from a European crop. In Eurasia, farmers rotated crops each year, growing a different plant until the soil was exhausted and then leaving it fallow for a period. But in Mesoamerica, farmers developed a system by which several crops could be planted alongside each other in an elaboration of the natural situation. In this way, fields could be used for thousands of years. This revolution in agricultural techniques gradually spread across the entire continent. By the time the Pilgrims arrived in Massachusetts in 1620, fields of maize, beans, and squash lined the New England coasts. Maize also made its way south into Peru, even though the potato was at the center of the Andeans' agricultural system. It has been suggested that the sudden emergence of an organized and cohesive culture was also due to a lively trade in salt and the discovery of methods to process salt for medicinal, religious, and culinary purposes. Salt was eventually used as money by the Maya.

The religious life of the Olmecs centered on caves, springs, and volcanoes. The volcano, a frequently used symbol in Olmec imagery, was associated with the world being born from below but was also viewed as the home of the storm clouds, lightning, and rain. It was depicted as a dragon with a gaping mouth representing

4.5 Colossal monolithic head uncovered at San Lorenzo, Mexico

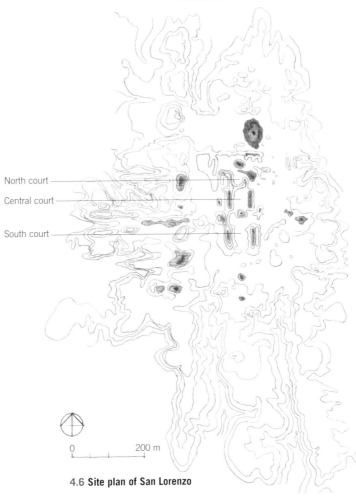

North court
Central court
South court

0   200 m

4.6 Site plan of San Lorenzo

the portal to the underworld. The sky was ruled by a bird monster or sun god whose energy powered the cosmos and made the plants grow. Underneath the dragon, the Olmecs visualized a watery void out of which the world was formed. The main deity in their mythology was the rain god, depicted as a jaguar, a shamanistic symbol of transformation. This jaguar could assume other forms—even human ones. The sexual union of a woman and a jaguar gave birth to a special class of gods that were represented in sculpture as having a snarling mouths, toothless gums, fangs, and a cleft head. The Olmecs learned to drag and float stones and columns of up to 40 tons over a distance of 160 kilometers. Most were chiseled into jaguars or human heads by Olmec sculptors. Unlike the angular and sharp features of later civilizations, the Olmec heads were round, soft, and very lifelike. They were also quite large—some of them over 3 meters high.

San Lorenzo

Olmec ceremonial structures were located on islands or on elevated lands that remained dry during the rainy season. This was true for one of their principal sites, San Lorenzo (1500–900 BCE), named after a nearby modern village and located in the lower reaches of the Coatzacoalcos River, some 60 kilometers to the southeast of the volcanic mountains of Santa Marta and San Martín. The Coatzacoalcos River is the only tropical river system in Central America. During the

dry season the water flows mainly in the river channels, but in the wet season the river overflows to form a vast fluvial network.

In 1000 BCE, San Lorenzo was basically an island hill, created by large-scale reengineering of the swampy lowlands through a process of cut-and-fill—all done without the aid of beasts of burden or wheels. The final shape, covering an area of about 7 square kilometers, resembled that of a bird. Though the wooden architecture has long since disappeared, the use of a scarce basaltic stone, brought from the distant Tuxtla Mountains, for steps, columns, and aqueducts provides a vivid picture of the scale and grandeur of Olmec engineering skills. The main ceremonial complex consisted of a series of modified earth platform mounds arranged north-south in a series of courts. Huge monolithic heads, most likely representations of the rulers, stood in the middle of the courts. These heads were

not idols to be worshipped but, so it seems, representations used to reenact mythological or historical events. Cut-stone cisterns collected water for the dry season. Drainage was through a network of canals built of large basalt blocks.

From the central court, six long artificial ridges projected outward on the north, south, and west sides of the mound. The only one that has been excavated so far reveals that the Olmecs had to have transported 67,000 cubic meters of soil to create a platform about 200 meters long, 50 meters wide, and 6.5 meters high. While the exact purpose of these ridges is still in dispute, the current thesis is that they may have been the sites of palace complexes, as evidenced by their sheer size, the basalt thrones that were found there, and the 200-meter-long drainage system.

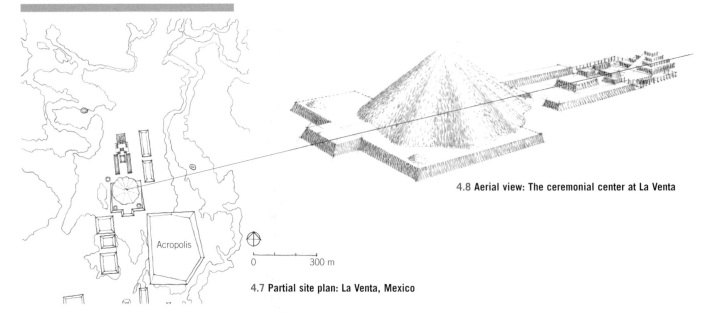

4.8 Aerial view: The ceremonial center at La Venta

4.7 Partial site plan: La Venta, Mexico

Acropolis

0   300 m

La Venta

For unknown reasons, San Lorenzo went into decline. La Venta, 80 kilometers northeast of San Lorenzo and closer to the shore of the Gulf of Mexico, took its place around 900 BCE as the leading Olmec center. With a population of about eighteen thousand at its height, it was located on a 5-kilometer island in a coastal swamp overlooking the then active Río Palma. Since there was little locally available stone, most of the city was built from earth and clay. Large basalt stones were brought in from the Tuxtla Mountains, but these were used nearly exclusively for monuments, including the colossal heads, the "altars" (actually thrones), and various stelae. Beneath the mounds and plazas, archaeologists have found sculptures and ritual objects, often of a particular type of blue-green jade, the source of which has recently been determined to be located in Guatemala. La Venta was abandoned around 400 BCE, its sculptured monuments apparently intentionally defaced by its own inhabitants for reasons not yet fully understood.

La Venta Pyramid, about 30 meters high and 150 meters in diameter, is the largest of the Olmec pyramids. It was constructed from 130,000 cubic feet of beaten earth and clay to form an unusual fluted conical shape rising from a rectangular base; a series of unique flutings, or depressions and protrusions, make up its surface. No other structure built by native Americans is known to have these flutings, the meaning and

purpose of which are unknown. The pyramid was part of a ceremonial complex arranged along a north-south axis. The court at the northern end was originally surrounded by an enclosure of prismatic basalt columns. Recent archaeological evidence suggests that the fluted pyramid may have been the terminus of the structures, not as it might at first appear, to its north, but to a larger group of platform mounds to the south, which are presently under excavation. As at San Lorenzo, excavations at the so-called Acropolis (which may have been the base of a palace complex) show a complex drainage

system, with stone troughs and collecting basins.

Excavation crews at El Manatí, a boggy site at the foot of Cerro Manatí, 32 kilometers from San Lorenzo, have recently uncovered at least forty life-size, carved, wooden human heads that date to about 1200 BCE. Unlike San Lorenzo and La Venta, this site was not a populated settlement but an isolated ritual center, where the heads were part of ritual sacrifices performed to please the water gods. Skeletons of sacrificed children, as well as seven rubber balls used in ritual games, have also been found there.

4.9 Olmec wooden figurines at El Manatí

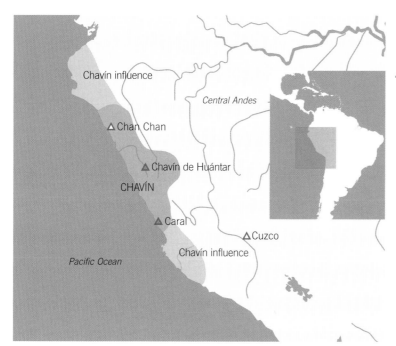

4.10 **Chavín culture along the Peruvian coast**

Chavín de Huántar

By 800 BCE, Andean civilization had spread further into the highlands of the Andes, with new towns and ritual centers located at higher elevations. One of these, Chavín de Huántar, appears to have been founded around 900 BCE. It is located at a place where the Mosna River narrows dramatically into the precipitous gorges of the Cordillera Blanca in northwest Peru. The city was a trading center, where highland people exchanged meat for seafood with the people from the coast. Though seemingly remote, it was only about a six-day walk to the Pacific Ocean to the west and to the tropical forests to the east. At its peak, the city supported about three thousand people, small by today's standards but large for the time.

The first ceremonial structure that was built there was a U-shaped pyramidal platform mound called the Old Temple. Facing east, it consisted of a large circular sunken plaza, with the customary dual stairs on axis and a centralized main staircase leading to the raised terrace. The platforms are imposed one above the other and may have been built up over time because they are of different heights; the highest is about 16 meters over the sunken plaza onto which they face. The walls of the platforms are adorned with gigantic grotesque heads, carved in the round and inserted in the massive masonry. Chavín art bears some resemblance to Olmec art, suggesting a link

between the two cultures.

The plaza, sunk 2.5 meters below the surface of the court and with a diameter of 21 meters, could have held about five hundred people at one time. Two thin horizontal slabs, alternating with single rows of large, precisely cut rectangular slabs, line the wall edge of the plaza. The lower of these slabs depict seven jaguars, with the corresponding upper slabs displaying matching pairs of mythical figures, all of which seem to be marching toward the main staircase leading to the platform mound. The walls of the court bring the steep slopes of the surrounding mountains directly into the visual space of the temple. It is presumed that priests communed with supernatural forces in the form of a jaguar. Hallucinogenic drugs played a role in these rituals.

The platform mound of the temple is honeycombed by a windowless labyrinth of corridors, staircases, and air ducts so complex that no adequate plan has yet been published. The passageways, no more than a meter wide and varying in height, are large enough for a single person to walk through and were undoubtedly used for ceremonial purposes. Some of these galleries span several floor levels and are connected by stairways. An initiate would probably have been led down the corridor, which would have reverberated with the echoes from the rushing water. At the end

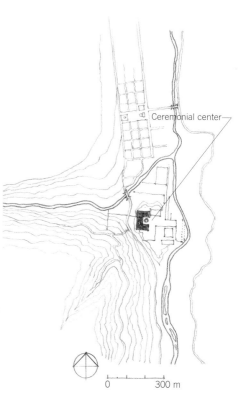

4.11 **Area plan: Chavín de Huántar, Peru**

of the corridor and illuminated by flickering torches, there was a 5-meter-high statue of a divinity with a catlike face and long hair. Immediately above it, hidden from view, was a priestly functionary who provided the god's oracular declamations. Known today as the Lanzón, its presence is still awe-inspiring. People regarded the deity as a potent source of prosperity and brought offerings to it to strengthen the relationship between communities and the supernatural world.

Chavín was a ceremonial center and not an urban temple. But as it attracted ever larger numbers of pilgrims, it changed in a proto-urban environment. Its prosperity is reflected in the remodeling of the temple precinct into a structure known as the New Temple, which consisted of a platform on the summit of which were two, two-roomed structures. No stairways led to the platform: priests would appear from concealed

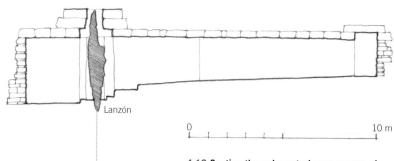

4.12 **Section through central passageway of the Old Temple leading to the Lanzón at Chavín de Huántar**

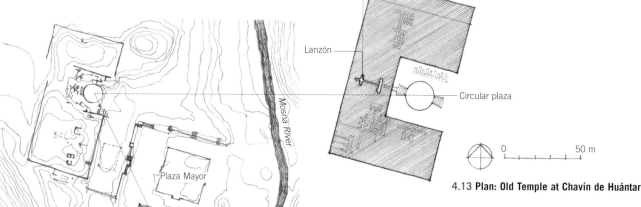

4.13 **Plan: Old Temple at Chavín de Huántar**

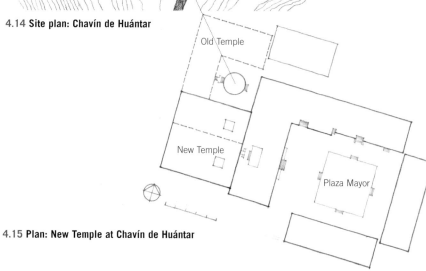

4.14 **Site plan: Chavín de Huántar**

4.15 **Plan: New Temple at Chavín de Huántar**

staircase instead. The two temple buildings of cut-and-dressed stone would have been visible far into the distance. The long maze of galleries from the Old Temple was extended into the platform. There does not seem to be a new central gallery room, however, indicating the continued reign of the old deity in the cruciform chamber.

To the east, on axis with the New Temple, is a square semisubterranean ritual court, Plaza Mayor, about 20 meters wide, with shallow stairs in the middle of all its sides. The court is flanked on the north and south by two additional platform mounds, completing the complex. Construction in and around these complexes came to an end between 700 and 500 BCE. The reasons are unclear, as is so much about early Peruvian civilization.

4.16 Zhou dynasty China

Zhou Dynasty China

The Zhou were most likely tribes from northwestern China who adopted modern Shang weaponry—in particular, the bow and arrow and the chariot—to conquer the Shang. The dynasty is divided into the Western Zhou (1046–771 BCE) and the Eastern Zhou (771–256 BCE). The Western and Eastern Zhou periods are distinguished by the relocation of the capital city from Hao (near the present city of Xi'an) in the west to Luoyang in Henan Province. The move was apparently prompted by the need to stabilize the eastern provinces. The Zhou soon entered into a period of internal strife, known as the Warring States Period (475–221 BCE). Despite this, the Zhou made the transition to iron, developing cast-iron production (as opposed to forged iron in the West) around 500 BCE. They also established the first imperial cities, two of which—Xi'an and Luoyang—are still major urban centers today.

Though it might seem that China has been "Chinese" from early on, there were, prior to the Zhou dynasty, several regional and linguistic groups (somewhat similar to what one might have found in South Asia). In their conquests, the Zhou enforced the use of the Chinese language, part of an effort that they perceived to be a civilizing agenda.

Those who did not want to succumb moved southward, displacing or integrating into local populations to become the ancestors of modern Thai, Laotians, and Burmese. During the Zhou dynasty, many of the cultural and political ideals that were to pervade Chinese imperial society were established. Rites of worship, an ideology of harmony, and the sacrifices to ancestral deities all served to link political and religious authority. The Zhou articulated this as the "mandate of heaven" (*tianming*).

It was in this context that the philosopher K'ung-fu-tzu, known to the West as Confucius (551–479 BCE), proposed an ethical philosophy based on the principles of proper conduct. Before Confucianism, Chinese rulers had governed by principles that assumed a direct relationship between power and punishment. Confucius argued that good governance was linked to adhering to traditional customs. The ideal Confucian man had to earn the right to authority by strict self-criticism and self-renovation; the cultivation of music and the arts were also important. The Zhou rulers began to incorporate some of Confucius's ideas into state religious practices, using ritual (*li*) as a sign of aristocratic behavior. Several Zhou

4.17 Ritual wine container, late Western Zhou dynasty

period texts, including *Zhou li* (Rituals of Zhou), *Yi li* (Ceremony and Ritual), and *Li jie* (Record of Ritual) detail the organization at the early Zhou court and the duties that governed every rank and office.

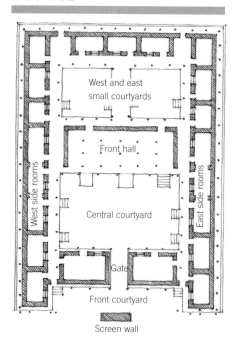

4.18 Plan: Ritual complex at Fengchu, Shaanxi Province, China

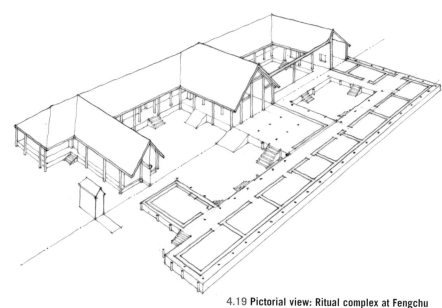

4.19 Pictorial view: Ritual complex at Fengchu

The Ritual Complex

Under the Zhou, ritual halls became part of the standard architectural vocabulary. These halls were places where the elite assembled according to their status in the social hierarchy. Assemblies could take place for political purposes or to commemorate the kingdom's royal ancestors. The rituals were accompanied by chimes that marked noble rank. A chime of sixty-five bells, which would have required six musicians standing and kneeling on both sides of the bell-chimes, was recovered from a Zhou dynasty tomb. The components of the temple were a gatehouse, a large central court, the ritual hall, and its flanking halls. The overall plan was governed by a strict adherence to geometry and was designed so that the position and role of each participant was spelled out precisely. A reconstruction of the ritual complex at Fengchu (1100–1000 BCE) shows an axially and symmetrically arranged series of buildings and courtyards framed on three sides by a walled enclosure. The entrance was defined by a gate in front of which was a freestanding wall, which, as in later Chinese structures, served to prevent unwanted spirits from entering the complex. Behind the gate was a large courtyard framing the main hall, elevated on a platform,

and accessible by three flights of stairs. Excavations beneath some of the rooms to the rear have uncovered inscribed tortoise shells and oracle bones, whence comes the presumption that this was a ceremonial complex. The main construction was of wood, with bronze used to bind and reinforce structural elements at the joints.

To protect themselves from invaders from the north, the Zhou began to erect large walls, which were later added to and combined to form the famous, 4,800-kilometer-long Great Wall. The base of some parts of this wall was nearly 7 meters wide. On the large stones that were its foundations, earth was rammed layer upon layer. Traces of wood—possibly the remains of posts used to hold the wall in place—have also been discovered. Walls were not only defensive elements but also a symbol of a ruler's power and nobility. The city was, in fact, defined as a wall. The three words *cheng*, *du*, and *jing* are each commonly translated into English as "city," but *cheng*, as a verb, meant "walling a city." Later, in imperial China, *cheng* referred to a walled administrative city. Even in common parlance today, *cheng* is translated as "city wall" or simply "wall."

Wangcheng Plan

Although the only physical evidence of Zhou cities are earth foundations, there is an important description of an ideal city, accompanied by an illustration, in the *Rituals of Zhou*. The description is presumed to be of Luoyang, capital of the Eastern Zhou dynasty, but is better known as Wangcheng, or "Ruler's City":

The *jiangren*, or master craftsman, builds the state, leveling the ground with the water by using a plumb line. He lays out posts, taking the plumb line (to ensure the posts' verticality) and using their shadows as the determiners of a midpoint. He examines the shadows of the rising and setting sun and makes a circle that includes the midpoints of the two shadows.

The master craftsman constructs the state capital. He makes a square nine *li* of each side; each side has three gates. Within the capital are nine north-south and nine east-west streets. The north-south streets are nine carriage tracks in width. On the left (as one faces south, or to the east) is the Ancestral Temple, and to the right (west) are the Altars of Soil and Grain. In the front is the Hall of Audience and behind, the markets.*

*Nancy Shatzman Steinhardt, *Chinese Imperial City Planning* (Honolulu: University of Hawaii Press, 1990), 33.

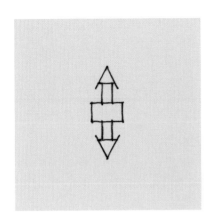

4.20 Chinese pictograph for "walled city"

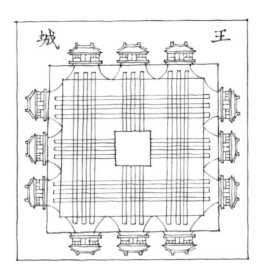

4.21 Idealized plan of Wangcheng

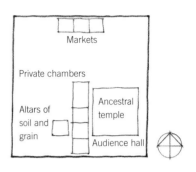

4.22 Inner city of Wangcheng

Drawings of Luoyang from the 15th and 17th centuries illustrate its salient features, with the addition of the inner city walls. Not far from the temple one finds soil and grain altars, the private or sleeping chambers (*qin*), and the markets. Although no single Chinese city of later date seems to actually have been built according to the Wangcheng plan, it can be argued that most subsequent major Chinese cities developed along its basic principles. Wangcheng in particular symbolizes the notion that the Chinese emperor is at the center of the world; in addition, the number nine, which sounds like the word *long-lasting* in Chinese, was habitually associated with the emperor.

In 1038 BCE, the Duke of Zhou founded a new city, Chengzhou ("The Accomplished Zhou"), to the north of the Luo River. It was intended to be the capital—something that did not take place until 770 BCE. The city, which closely resembles the ideas of the Wangcheng plan, had a palace at the center, three markets to the north and to the south, an ancestral temple, and, next to it, altars of soil and grain. It was destroyed in a civil war in 510 BCE and rebuilt with a modified design and with a new name, Luoyang, which is its current name.

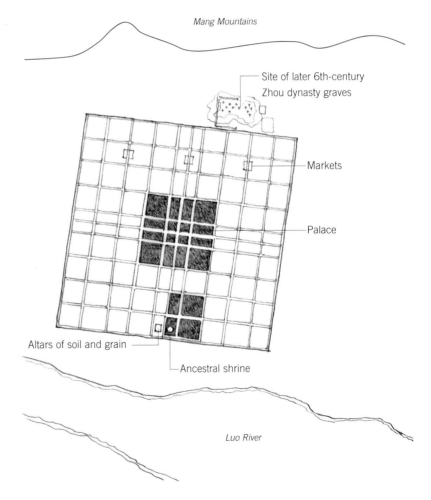

4.23 City plan of Chengzhou (Luoyang)

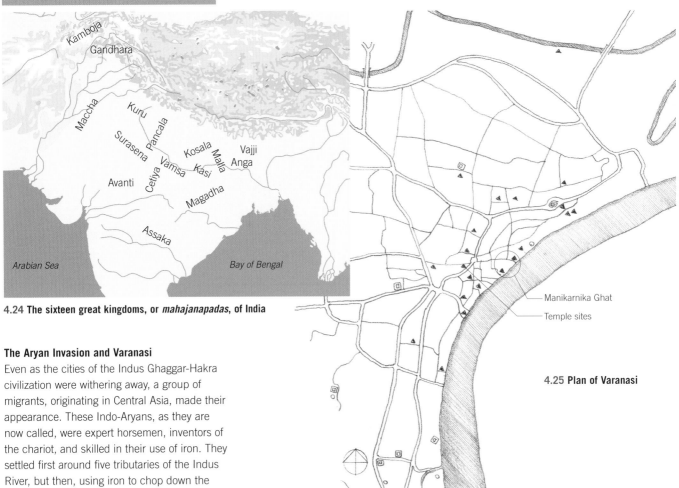

4.24 **The sixteen great kingdoms, or** *mahajanapadas*, **of India**

Kamboja

Gandhara

Maccha

Kuru

Pancala

Surasena

Cetiya

Vamsa

Kosala

Malla

Kasi

Vajji

Anga

Avanti

Magadha

Assaka

Arabian Sea

Bay of Bengal

— Manikarnika Ghat

— Temple sites

4.25 **Plan of Varanasi**

The Aryan Invasion and Varanasi

Even as the cities of the Indus Ghaggar-Hakra civilization were withering away, a group of migrants, originating in Central Asia, made their appearance. These Indo-Aryans, as they are now called, were expert horsemen, inventors of the chariot, and skilled in their use of iron. They settled first around five tributaries of the Indus River, but then, using iron to chop down the forests, moved into the fertile Gangetic Plains around 1200 BCE. Of the numerous cities that came to be built, little remains, since everything was built of wood. By the year 1000 BCE, sixteen kingdoms and semirepublics, known as *mahajanapadas*, had developed. Warfare among them was constant, with victors absorbing the vanquished and destroying their cities. By 500 BCE, four mahajanapadas dominated: Magadha, Kosala, Kasi, and the republican Vrajji Confederacy. Around 450 BCE, Magadha became the dominant power by defeating the Vrajji Confederacy as well as Kosala and Kasi. Kasi's capital, Varanasi was spared the normal fate a conquered city and granted special status as a pilgrimage site. It was here that codification of Aryan rituals, as elaborated in their oral treatises, took place. What emerged was not a single doctrine, but competitive philosophical schools ranging from the materialist to the atheist.

Varanasi was so important as a center of religious learning that in the 6th century BCE, the famed Shakyamuni Buddha made Varanasi his first stop after his self-enlightenment. Numerous other influential thinkers came to the city as

4.26 **A contemporary Vedic fire ceremony**

well, including Adi Shankara (9th century CE), whose teachings and writings laid the foundations of Hinduism, which relied heavily on Vedic ideas.

Vedic rituals did not require temples or even the creation of statues. They were based on fire sacrifices of various kinds that needed only brick platforms. Fire was the agent that enabled the transformation of the sacrificial food (matter) into smoke and air (energy). Though no early Vedic altars have survived, the legacy of their rituals is still alive in Hinduism, which views this city as one of its most sacred. At dawn every morning, thousands of devotees gather on ghats—steps leading down to the shore—to face the sun that rises across the broad expanse of the Ganges River and is reflected in its waters. Half immersed in the river, they greet the sun by cupping the water of the Ganges into their palms and pouring it back into the river with arms extended. This is followed by a slow turn of 360 degrees while standing in place, a miniature act of circumambulation. A quick dip in the river completes the ritual. This ritual can be repeated many times or performed with greater elaboration that includes long chants and sequences of yogic postures.

Varanasi is built on the western side of the river on a high, natural berm at a curve in the river. Behind the berm, in a semicircular arch, lies the dense fabric of the medieval city, with twisting narrow streets and a multitude of temples, water tanks, and street shrines. The eighty-four ghats that line the river's edge are accessed at more than fifty locations along the berm. In the midst of all this, one can see rituals pertaining to every aspect of human life: the shaving of a newborn's head, the first blessing after a marriage, the penances of old age. The Manikarnika and Harishchandra ghats are particularly important, as they are dedicated to the ritual of cremations; it is from these ghats that the ashes of the dead are immersed into the Ganges River. To be born and, more importantly, to be cremated at Varanasi is to attain the highest aspiration of Hindu practice: *moksha* or nirvana—freedom from the cycle of birth and death.

Most of the temples and ghats that one sees today date from the 18th and 19th centuries. In the 9th century BCE, there was a much simpler—but no less symbolically powerful—relationship between land and water.

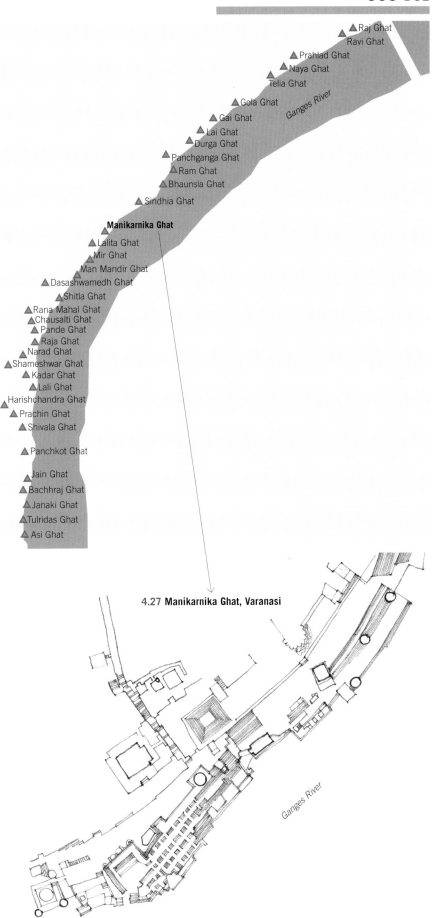

4.27 Manikarnika Ghat, Varanasi

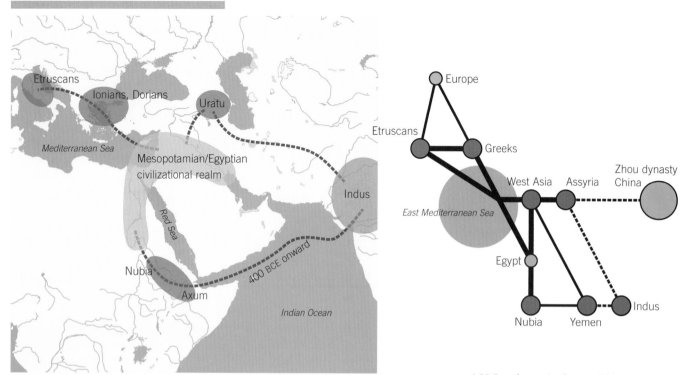

4.28 West Asian and African metal centers, ca. 800 BCE

4.29 Eurasian trade diagram, 800 BCE

The Iron Age

Scholars generally think that the forging of steel was developed by the Hittites, who kept the technique secret. Its development had taken thousands of years of familiarity with kilns, metals, and extraction methods, until high-temperature smelting could be mastered. But after the downfall of the Hittites in 1200 BCE, the art of forging spread, reaching China around 600 BCE.

Apart from China, there were five newly emerging metal-oriented societies: the Urartu in Armenia, the Nubians in the Sudan, the Etruscans in Italy, the Dorians and Ionians in Greece, and, somewhat later, the Mauryans in India. As these cultures were all marginal to the Mesopotamian/Egyptian civilizations, the consequences were enormous. Iron, in other words, completely changed the political and civilizational landscape; areas once peripheral to the urbanized Mesopotamian/Egyptian heartlands had now become important, if not dominant, players in the world economy.

Iron was used to make weapons, of course, but was also superior for crafting agricultural implements like plows and wheels. With these new iron plows, the plains of Sicily, the north coast of Africa, and even the high plains of eastern Anatolia became major grain-producing regions,

significantly lessening the need for grain from Mesopotamia and Egypt. Iron farm implements also had a profound impact on the development of agriculture in sub-Saharan Africa, where for the first time, large-scale agriculture and land clearing could be undertaken. The African connection—which was centered around Nubia and later, Aksum—exhausted itself around 800 CE largely because deforestation led to serious environmental degradation, making both mining and agriculture difficult with permanent negative consequences for the economy.

The Urartu were conquered by the Assyrians in order to secure a steady supply of metal for their army. There is little left of Urartu architecture, apart from remnants, most of it having been destroyed by centuries of warfare. The Nubians, who produced extensive architectural works, continued Egyptian traditions. The Etruscans and the Dorians were, however, newcomers, having moved into the Mediterranean from the north. Their views on the world were different from that of the Egyptians and Mesopotamians, leading them to create a highly refined civic-legal description of the divine that was to impact European architecture for centuries. (Many Etruscan and Greek concepts were

taken over by the Romans.)

In eastern India, the discovery of iron in the Barabar Hills was to have a global impact. The Indo-Aryans had brought iron to India, but it was only in the 5th century BCE, with the rise of the Mauryan Empire, that the extensive use of iron spread, first along the Ganges River, and subsequently into Central Asia by means of trade corridors connecting Africa and China. As a consequence, Central Asia, which was not an iron-producing area, became ever more dependent on trade to stay up to date.

By the 6th and 5th centuries BCE, the most powerful forces in the global economy emanated from India, Europe, and eventually China, with Central Asia becoming important mainly as a transit region. Disadvantageously, this region could also be attacked from many sides; indeed, for the next thousand years, until the modern era constructed fixed boundaries protected by international law, the borders in Central Asia were in continual flux, as state after state attempted to secure a dominant role in cross-Asian trade. This was not yet a problem in Europe, where Italy and Greece were the rising powers and where trade with the hinterlands in the north would not develop until the Roman invasion of Gaul in the 1st century CE.

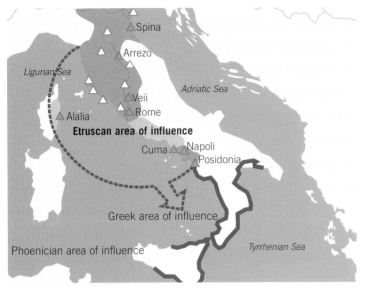

4.30 Etruscan Italy

4.31 Detail of an Etruscan capital

The Etruscans

The origin of the Etruscans is hotly debated. Their language, which has only been partially deciphered, does not belong to the Indo-European language family. They settled predominantly in the north part of the Italian peninsula, between Arno and Tiber rivers and on the west side of the Apennine Mountains. This territory provided plenty of metal ore, such as copper, iron, lead, and silver, but they appear to have acquired the skill to exploit these metals prior to settling in Italy; indeed, the presence of these ores might have attracted these settlers in the first place. For example, Volterra, one of their main cities, twelve of which formed the Etruscan League (Dodecapoli) was close to Colline Metallifere (Metalliferous Hills). The Etruscan city of Vulci, also part of the league, was especially noted for its bronze work production.

It was not just the Etruscans' economic acumen that differentiated them from the surrounding tribes but also their fantastic belief structure, which relied heavily on omens. The Etruscan aesthetic, as displayed in the decoration of their graves, was spontaneous and vivacious and open to the appreciation of other cultures—especially that of the Greeks, whose goods and vases they freely imported and copied. As a group, the Dorians, Ionians, and Etruscans all played an important part in restoring the Mediterranean to economic and cultural viability after the disruptions of the preceding centuries.

Despite the settlements of the Greeks in the south and center of Italy, the Etruscans were able to maintain their hold over the northern half of the Italian peninsula. There they had a vibrant interaction with Rome, the ascendant power, until they were finally absorbed into the Roman Empire, to which they contributed substantively. Many Etruscan cities, like Veii, north of Rome, were, in their heyday, as big as Athens, with a population estimated as high as one hundred thousand. Though the physical fabric of Etruscan cities has largely been lost, much can be discerned from the multitude of tombs that dot the hillsides, veritable cities of the dead, all executed in skillful masonry and richly decorated interiors. Many Etruscan walls and gateways in Rome, Perugia, Cortona, and other places still exist today.

At Velhatri (today's Volterra), sections of the formerly 7.3-kilometer-long enclosure,

built during the 5th and 4th centuries BCE, as well as the Porta all'Arco and the Porta di Diana, still bear witness to Etruscan skills. The city gate of Perugia in particular exhibited a bold use of the arch, a building element that, along with the vault, was introduced by the Etruscans and became one of their main contributions to Roman architecture. In Rome itself, several famous structures, including the Circus Maximus and the Cloaca Maxima, the Roman sewage system still in use today, were built by Etruscan masons. The deft and unfailingly secure use of arches that emerged in Etruria was to have a tremendous impact on Roman architecture, as is evidenced by the Roman aqueducts. Even the Greeks had not equaled this skill, remaining content with what was basically a simple post-and-lintel system in the construction of their temples.

4.32 Etruscan tomb, Tarquinia, Italy

Etruscan Religion

The outward aspect of Etruscan religion
was its scrupulous adherence to ritualistic
formulas. And yet, through Etruscan art and
painting, one senses a lively appreciation of
individuality. This vibrancy did come at the
expense of stylistic unity—something that
lent their art an unmistakable, and in some
sense unusual, receptivity toward outside
influences. Elements of the Corinthian,
Ionian, and Attic are all in evidence in
Etruscan art and painting. This is also true
of their religion—so much so that their own
deities came to be fused with, and coalesced
around, Greek ones, paving the way for the
later Roman assimilation of Greek culture.
Unlike the Greek pantheon, however, the
Etruscan's included supernatural and
chthonic beings whose number and nature
are still unknown to us. The Etruscans also
had a complex system of augury (such
as the study of the entrails—especially
the liver) and of sacrificial animals. They
studied and interpreted natural phenomena,
such as comets or the flight paths of
birds (a practice known as *auspicium*, or
divination). A 3rd-century BCE bronze model
of a liver (found near Piacenza, Italy) has
been recovered was perhaps used to train
Etruscan priests (haruspices) in the art of
interpretation. The upper surface is divided
into forty sections, corresponding to the
celestial zones of the Etruscan pantheon;
these have the names of gods, including
many with whom we are unfamiliar, engraved
on it. The particularities of the animal's liver
told the priest which deity to invoke. It was
probably meant to be aligned north-south.

One of the words used to describe this
liver was *templum*, which could refer to the
sky, to a consecrated area on earth, or to a
much smaller surface, such as the liver of
an animal used in divination, as long as the
orientation and partition of the area followed
the celestial model. A *templum* could thus be
a physical space (in which case it would be
marked or enclosed), but it could also be an
area of the sky, in which the birds would be
observed.

A *templum*, in other words, was a space
where humans, represented by priests
(augurs), could interact with the gods. In all
ancient Mediterranean and Mesopotamian
cultures, nature was associated with divine

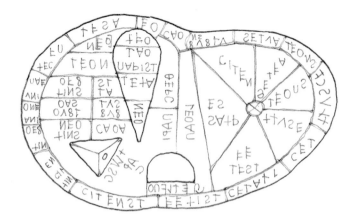

4.33 Bronze Etruscan model of a liver, 3rd century BCE

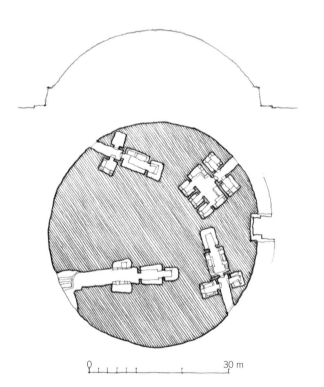

4.34 Tumulus mound, Etruscan necropolis of Banditaccia at Cerveteri, 7th to 5th centuries BCE

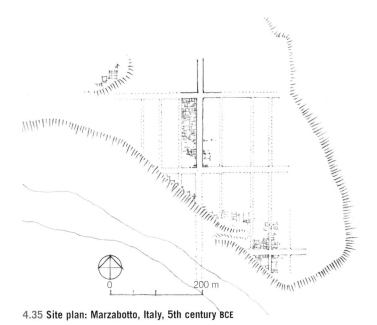

4.35 Site plan: Marzabotto, Italy, 5th century BCE

4.36 Example of an Etruscan arch

presences, but for the Etruscans, the gods spoke through signs. This was not the case in Mesopotamian religions, where gods spoke more directly, through priests. For the Minoans, religion centered on nature's life cycles, with the gods representing the stories associated with those cycles. But for the Etruscans, religion was a practice of translation. Unlike the more fearsome and arbitrary gods of the Mesopotamians, Etruscan gods readily communicated their intentions. Disaster could come about just as much from the actions of the gods as from a misunderstanding of their messages.

The orientation of Etruscan temples was of critical importance and was determined by the intersection of two axes, one north-south, called *cardo*, and the other, east-west, called *decumanus*. The idea was employed later by the Romans in setting up military camps according to strictly standardized rules and subsequently became fundamental to Roman town planning. Apparently these orthogonal lines were closely connected to Etrusco-Italic religious iconography. The observer's place was at the point where the two lines crossed; he stood with his back to the north. The eastern sector to the left (*pars sinistra*) was of good omen and superior gods; the western sector to the right (*pars dextra*) was of ill omen and for the infernal deities. The vault

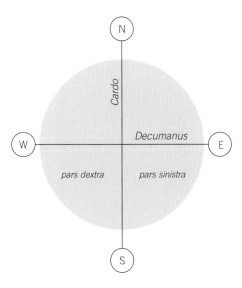

4.37 Diagram of *cardo* and *decumanus*

of heaven, thus quartered and oriented, was further subdivided into sixteen minor sections in which were placed the habitations of many divinities. This plan corresponds to the outer ring of sixteen compartments of the Piacenza liver.

The position of signs manifested in the sky, thunderbolts, flights of birds, and other portents, as studied by the augur, would indicate which god was responsible for a particular message and whether it was a good or a bad omen. This process was called *auspicium*, a word that was a combination of *avis* ("bird") and *specio* ("to see"). The priest and soothsayer watched the flight and feeding of birds, listened to their cries, and even examined their entrails. From this came words like *contemplatio*, meaning literally "with a template." There was also the distinction between whether the message was an order or a friendly reminder. All in all, the *templum* (as a type of three-dimensional template) stood between the ephemeral and the real, linking the invisible absolute realities of the divine with the real needs of the supplicants. The consecrated ground on which this took place was expressed in Etruscan language by the word *sacni* (becoming the Latin *sancti*). When the temple was finished, the opening was presided over by the augur in a ceremony called the *inauguratio*.

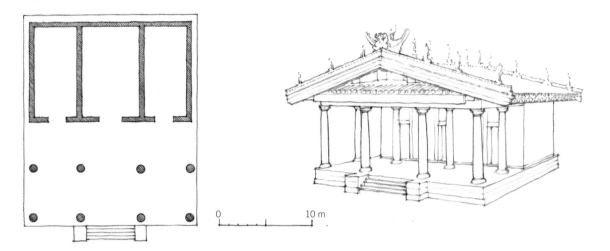

4.38 **Plan and pictorial view: An Etruscan temple, based on descriptions by Vitruvius**

Etruscan Temples

The form of Etruscan temples paralleled certain aspects of Greek temples, but there are several important differences. The Etruscans never made the leap to stone. Except at a very late period, the Etruscan temple was not thought of as requiring permanence. The podium that raised the temple above the surrounding ground level, however, was often of stone, with stairs or ramps leading to the top. The temple proper was built of mud, brick, and timber. Though similar to Greek temples in that respect, Etruscan temples were meant to be viewed only from the front and sides, rather than stand as an object in the landscape; they therefore have no rear facade. The pitch of the roof was relatively low, and they had overhanging eaves. The pediment was originally open so that the roof timbers could be seen. Also distinctive was the roomy colonnaded porch, known as the *pronaos* (meaning "in front of the naos") that stood in front of the *cella*. Etruscans often organized gods into a trivium, erecting temples with three *cellae*; their overall shape was rectangular, tending toward square. Etruscan temples introduced the principal of an axial connection between temple and altar, which the Greeks eschewed until very late, and probably then under Italian influence. Also characteristic was the striking use of color for the various temple elements, and the way the mass was broken up by antefixae, *acroteria*, and sculptural groups.

The Etruscans experimented with a range of columns, including the Ionic, until, by the 5th century BCE, they developed the Tuscan column, as it was later called by Vitruvius. This was a smooth, wooden column with diminution toward the top and a capital, akin to the Doric, consisting of a round cushion (echinus) and a square abacus. The bases, however, were inspired by the Ionic order (Doric columns had no bases). Because these structures were of wood, Etruscan temples had wide intercolumniations.

The habit of ornamenting the temple with decorative terra-cotta elements may have been taken over from the Greeks but was implemented by the Etruscans with particular showmanship.

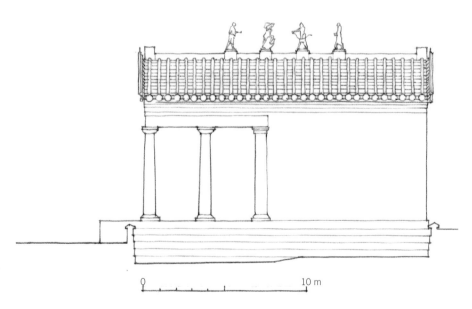

4.39 **Side elevation: Portonaccio Temple at Veii, Italy, 515–490 BCE**

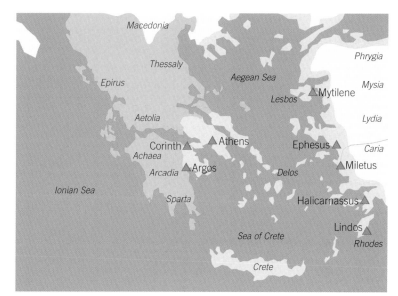

4.40 **Greece in the Archaic period**

4.41 **Geometric period Greek vase, typically serving as a monumental grave marker**

Greece: The Geometric Period

Post-Mycenaean Greece was a period of migrations, confusion, and poverty. But over time, the Dorians in Greece and the Ionians along the Turkish coast came to develop common cultural practices that fused elements unique to them with residues of the Minoan and Mycenaean cultures. This explains some of the differences in their development from that of the Etruscans. The Minoans and Mycenaeans, having had no temples in the technical sense, held caves and mountains sacred, with worship augmented by shrines. Homer represents the gods as highly mobile creatures constantly visiting each other in their palaces. The early Dorian religious practices took place in natural settings, which made it easy to incorporate some of the features and even locations of Minoan religion into their own. These rites, as described by George Hersey, also often involved trees, or groves of trees, that were fenced off and decorated with materials used in sacrifices—bones, horns, urns, lamps, weapons, fruits, and vegetables. Trees held a special place in Greek culture, and almost every god was associated with one. Athena was, for example, associated with the olive tree. The altar dedicated to a god was set out in front of his or her particular tree or grove.

The participants would bathe and dress in special clothes and, accompanied by flutists, sing while processing to the place of sacrifice. They were led by a girl carrying a basket of grain on her head. Under the grain, and concealed from view, was the slaughtering knife. The sacrificial animal, decorated with wreaths on his horns, was then led up to the altar with a fire already burning on it. Gathering in a circle, the participants would then wash their hands by pouring water from a jug, which they would also sprinkle on the animal. The barley grains from the girl's basket would be flung over the animal, altar, and earth. Once the knife was revealed, the priest would step forward, take it, and prepare for the sacrifice.

The beast, which had to be a prime specimen from the domestic herd, rather than a wild animal, had to be willing to

4.42 **Statue of a calf-bearer**

submit to the sacrifice, so the priest placed a bowl of milk at the base of the altar. As the animal stepped forward, it would bow its head to drink, which was interpreted as a sign of submission. Another indication of its assent was its shivering in the sight of the god, a process helped along by the liberal use of cold water. As the blood was held to be precious, it was drained into conduits and pits beneath the altar. The animal was then carved up; special meaning was given to various parts, with the liver being, of course, particularly important for the augur. Some parts were chopped up and wrapped in fat to form a type of reconstituted body. Sometimes the skull was placed on a stake near the altar and draped in an animal skin. Representations of this type of sacrifice extended to trophies and spoils taken from the conquered in battle, to assuage the spirit of the dead.

After carving the animal, the flesh was roasted and eaten. The communality of the meal bound together social units, from the family to the city. The gods received the act as devotional; as the smoke, immaterial, rose up from the altar, it was, so the Greeks thought, a sign of reverence. In exchange for this act of devotion, the humans could then read the message of the gods embedded in the physical shape of the liver. As mentioned earlier, the animals sacrificed to the gods had to be prime specimens from the domestic herd rather than wild animals.

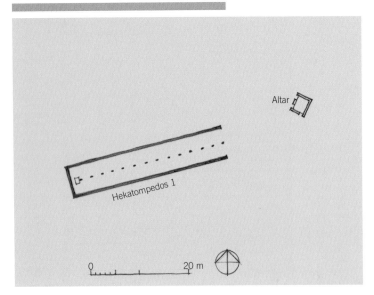

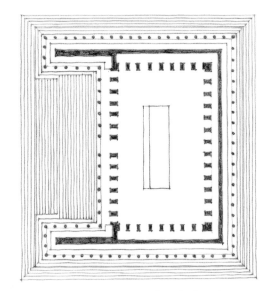

4.43 Plans: The Temple at Samos, Greece (above), and the Altar of Zeus at Pergamon (upper right), drawn at the same scale and orientation

The meaning of this sacrificial process is explained in the myth of Prometheus, who stole fire from the gods and brought it to mankind. In so doing, he made it possible for humankind to civilize itself. The gods did not take the fire back but punished Prometheus by chaining him to a cliff and having an eagle eat his liver. His liver would grow back every day, only to be eaten again. The sacrifice was thus part of a ritual remembrance of humankind's emergence into civilization and of their dependence on the gods for the regulation of their lives. But the sacrifice also marked the difference between humankind and gods, for unlike the gods, who existed in an ethereal form, humankind had to work and show sincerity to keep the communication alive. Only by making a sacrifice—in some ways a labor of love—could men demonstrate that they were thankful to the deities. That is why a skinny bull or decrepit goat would not do: the animal had to be the best of the lot.

4.44 Scene depicting early Greek sacrificial rites

Nevertheless, Dorians, Minoans, and even Etruscans had somewhat differing notions about sacrifice. Etruscan sacrifice was more formulaic and Minoan sacrifice more intimate than that of the Greeks. Unlike the Egyptians, Greek sacrifice was connected to the principles of farming and herding, rather than to the palace garden. Bread and meat were at the center of Greek sacrifice. Even in the Christian Eucharist, which developed later, we encounter, in veiled form, the importance of bread and meat, and indeed, even of wine, a comparison that raises important questions about the influence of Greek practices on early Christianity. The importance of the Greeks' attitudes toward sacrifice might easily be overlooked because so many of their altars were removed when Christianity tried to destroy any evidence of heathen practices. In fact, in the early days of Greek religion, there were no temples, only altars built out in the open.

One of the earliest and most sacred of the Greek altars, on the top of Mt. Lykaion in the Greek Peloponnese, dates back to 3000 BCE—Mycenaean times. It eventually became associated with Zeus, the king of the Greek gods, but whether that was true in the earlier period is unknown. Below the summit there was a stadium, indicating the site's association with an athletic festival, a combination that was to become another important element of many Greek sanctuaries.

The Mt. Lykaion altar, like the Temple of Hera at Samos (ca. 950 BCE) consisted of

no more than a low enclosure of flat stones forming a rectangle of about 2 by 3.5 meters. Altars became larger as time progressed; the one on the Acropolis at Athens, for example, from the 5th or 4th century BCE could hold a dozen bulls at one time. The Altar of Zeus at Pergamon, now in the Pergamon Museum in Berlin, was the most spectacular of all. Built from 197 to 159 BCE, it featured a flight of steps on its west side and flanking Ionic colonnades. It stands on a five-stepped, almost square plinth. The altar proper was inside the court.

The altars were not necessarily aligned symmetrically on axis with the temple, especially during the Archaic period. At Samos, the altar with its sacred tree, stood at first at an oblique angle, referring perhaps to a different celestial moment than that of the temple.

The emergence of the altar-plus-temple form coincided with the personification of gods in statues and, once again, seems to have been part of the assimilation process the Dorians underwent when they came into contact with older Mediterranean practices. Early Greek representations of their gods show influences from both the Mesopotamian and Egyptian cultures. But Greek representations were rarely as diminutive as the Mesopotamian and Minoan statues could be, nor as large as the Egyptians' often were. And perhaps therein lies the origin of the Greek advancement of the depiction of the human figure. The earliest three-dimensional representations of divinities known as kore

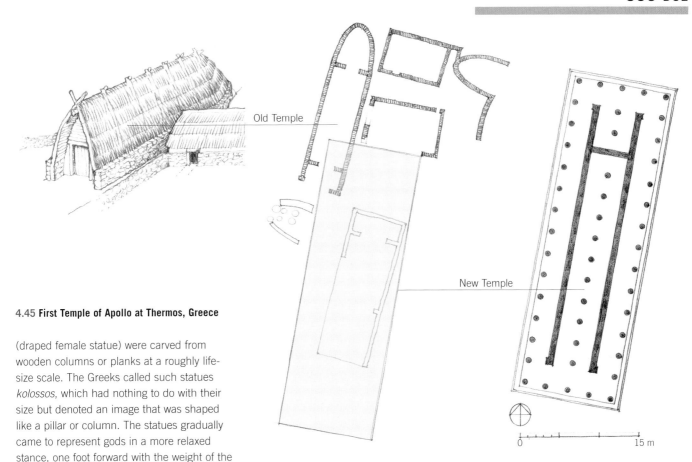

Old Temple

New Temple

0 — — — — — 15 m

4.45 First Temple of Apollo at Thermos, Greece

4.46 Plan: Later Temple of Apollo at Thermos

(draped female statue) were carved from wooden columns or planks at a roughly life-size scale. The Greeks called such statues *kolossos*, which had nothing to do with their size but denoted an image that was shaped like a pillar or column. The statues gradually came to represent gods in a more relaxed stance, one foot forward with the weight of the body balanced naturalistically on the rear leg.

Emergence of the Greek Temple Form

The earliest temples, built of mud bricks and thatched roofs, were modeled, presumably, on chieftains' houses and consisted of a single elongated, windowless room—a *naos* or *cella* (from which the word *cellar* comes)—that was eventually divided into a *pronaos* and *naos*. An example is the Temple of Apollo at Thermos (ca. 950 BCE) in the area of Aetolia in western Greece, where a low stone wall supported a high, steeply pitched thatched roof. There were no side chambers, ancillary spaces, or storage rooms. Soon a continuous porch was added around the body of the building to form an oblong shape, which over time became regularized and systemized. Later (ca. 630 BCE) we see, in the successive rebuilding of the temple, the development of the temple form over time, ending in the regularized form of later temples. The last temple had an elongated form, with proportions of almost 5 to 1 and a row of columns down the center.

Though Greek temples can be found facing the various directions of the compass, more than 80 percent were laid out to face

the sunrise, and most, more specifically, toward the sunrise on the actual day of their founding, which in turn coincided with the festival day of the divinity to which the temple was dedicated. From this custom arises the term *orientation*, primarily applied to the direction of the axis of a temple. Temples, however, were also sometimes oriented to elements in the landscape, to a solitary peak that suggested the presence of Zeus, or to double peaks, which, reminiscent of a bull's horns, were equated with Zeus. The Greek sanctuary was far from being a detached and spiritual sphere. Symbolically, it was representative of political, economic, and military life as well as the well-being of the city and the region. Many temples served as war museums, holding the spoils of conquest as well as serving as armories.

The word *temple* is widely used to describe Greek—and even often non-Greek—religious structures, though that word, which is derived from the Etruscan, came to be used only later by the Romans. For the Greeks, the structures were considered a

type of house (*oikos*) for the deity, who was represented inside the temple by his cult statue, originally made out of wood. But unlike Mesopotamian and Egyptian temples, the Greek temple had no storage rooms, preparation rooms, courtyards, or ancillary spaces. The temple was an integrated architectural unit, the main purpose of which was to house the divine statue. The *cella* was used primarily to store gifts to the temple and even war booty. Unlike in Egypt, the statue was not mobile: it was not paraded from site to site. Furthermore, the main religious events took place outside the temple, in front of the altar, and not within. Of particular sacred importance was the idea of the *temenos*, the boundary around the temple precinct. It could only be crossed at one point, marked by a gate, or *propylon*. The *temenos* did not necessarily have to be a wall, and could be nothing more than a row of stones on the ground. Its sanctity was inviolate, as it was a piece of land cut off from secular reality and reassigned to the divine.

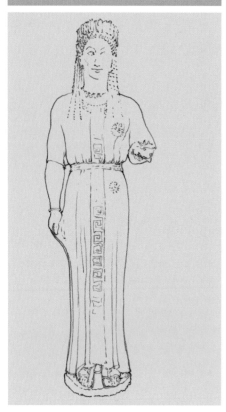

4.47 Slightly bigger than life-size female figure, mid-6th century BCE

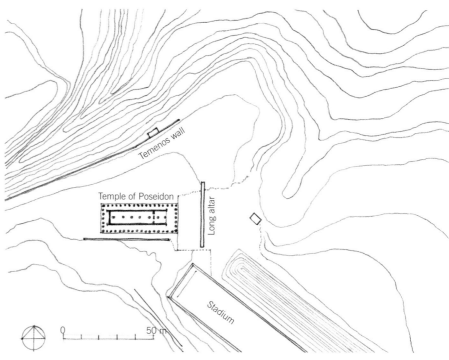

4.48 Site plan: Temple of Poseidon at Isthmia, Greece

Temple of Poseidon

The Temple of Poseidon at Isthmia (ca. 700 BCE), not far from Corinth, is among the earliest known Greek temples. Its podium measures 14 by 40 meters, with a central row of five columns within the *cella* and two in the *pronaos*. The *cella* was of stone, but the columns and entablature were of oak; the roof was low pitched and covered in fired terra-cotta tiles—a Greek invention. This temple represents an important break in the development of temple design. Whereas the stones for Egyptian temples were of irregular size, the ashlar blocks of this temple were laid in regular courses all the way to the roofline—a standardization of masonry elements. Furthermore, in Egypt, a wall was typically composed of two separate walls, the gap between them filled with rubble. Here the wall is a single vertical element. As with Egyptian temples, however, the wall was covered with a thin coat of plaster that would present to the viewer a smooth, continuous surface broken only, in this case, by a series of pilasters on the walls that responded to the rhythm of the colonnade along the outside of the *cella*.

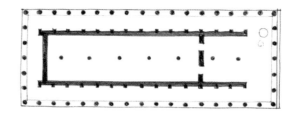

4.49 Plan and pictorial view: Temple of Poseidon at Isthmia

The site was fortified in about 1200 BCE, and ritual festivities were performed from the middle of the 11th century BCE onward. The Temple of Poseidon eventually attracted the Panhellenic Games, called the Isthmia, which took place every two years in honor of Melicertes-Palaemon, or Poseidon. The altar was a 30-meter-long structure in front of the temple, with the sports field and stadium just to the south.

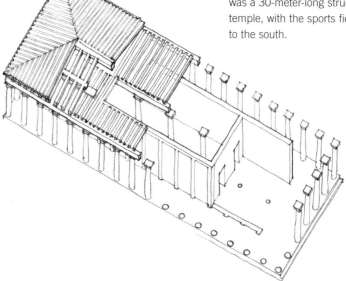

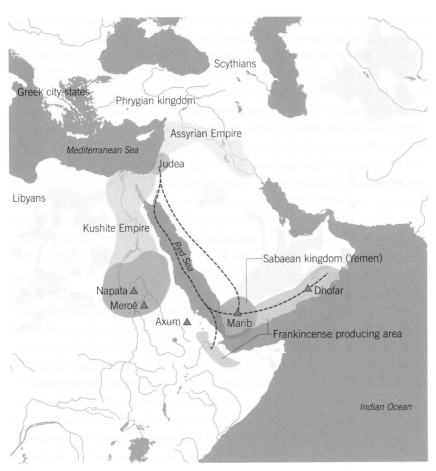

4.50 Economic zone comprising Judea, the Kushite Empire, and the Sabaean kingdom

In the 9th century BCE, the leading supplier of frankincense was the Sabaean kingdom (southwestern Yemen), whose capital was at Marib. The oil was brought up to the Levant, its prime outlet to world markets. Though the Sabaean area is now barren, it was then a lush oasis irrigated by means of a massive dam, the largest engineering work in the world at that time. Marib's main temple, Mahram Bilqis, or "Temple of the Moon God," was situated about 3 miles from Marib. It was so famous that it remained sacred even after the rerouting of the spice trail caused the collapse of the Sabean kingdom in the 6th century BCE. The dam, left in a poor state of repair, collapsed, causing the emigration of fifty thousand people and the abandonment of the city.

The temple was a rectangular structure with an inner peristyle. It was located at the perimeter of a large walled enclosure. There is still much archaeology that needs to be done on this site. While the temple may have been dedicated to a moon goddess, this has not yet been ascertained for certain; it could also have been a sun temple.

Saba/Sa'abia

A much desired commodity during this time was frankincense, derived from the sap of the *Boswellia sacra* tree, which grew mainly in Yemen. Since its aroma was thought to be life-enhancing, it was used to anoint newborns. It was also used in burials to embalm corpses. The Egyptians used it to make the distinctive black eyeliner seen in many Egyptian paintings. The Egyptian queen Hatshepsut sent an expedition to Punt (believed to be either Somalia or southern Arabia) in 1500 BCE; it returned with thirty-one frankincense trees, as depicted on the walls of her mortuary temple at Deir el-Bahri near Thebes. In fact, the demand for frankincense was staggering. Cities like Sumhuram and Ubar in Dhofar (southern Oman) were reported to export the equivalent of 3,000 tons of it every year. The desertification of the caravan routes and changing religious practices led to the decline of the trade by the 4th century CE.

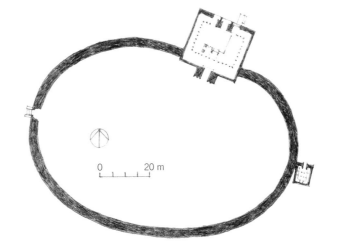

4.51 Plan of Mahram Bilqis

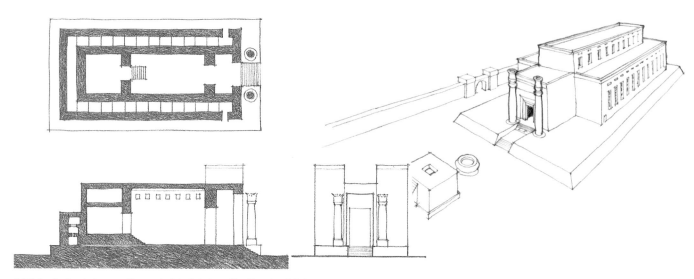

4.52 Conjectural plan, section and pictorial view: The Temple of Solomon

Temple of Solomon

With the Egyptian kingdom centered in its far south, the Levant experienced a moment of semiautonomy, with the Israelite kingdom, which had been established in the late 13th century BCE, rising to the level of an important regional power. One of Judaism's great contributions to the world was its concept of ethical monotheism, which became the basis of both Christianity and Islam. But though these religions played major roles in the history of architecture, the development of Judaism's own architecture was cut short by the destruction of the Second Temple and the forced diaspora of the Jews by Emperor Titus in 70 CE. Without a land of their own, and facing restrictions on their life and customs throughout Europe that lasted into the 20th century, Jewish architecture was restrained from developing its own distinct character.

The Jewish conception of religious space is a complex one. The Jahweh of the Israelites is an invisible, unrepresentable entity, a purely ethical force that is not permitted to be called by name. The mental image of the Israelites' self-identification was that of desert tribes living in tents in which permanent buildings played no role. Indeed, it has been held by some scholars that Moses refused to bring his charges across the Jordan into Canaan for fear that they would become concretized—that is, tied to property and agriculture.

After Moses's death, the Israelites entered Palestine and founded Jerusalem as their capital. A threshing floor was brought from the Jebusite "Zion" on Mt. Moriah as a place for carrying out the traditional sacrifices and as a place to display the ark. As described in the Bible, the ark was a gold-plated, portable chest containing the two stone tablets of Moses on which were inscribed the Ten Commandments. On top of it sat the images of two winged cherubim facing each other, the only kind of bodily representation permitted. Their outspread wings formed the throne of God, while the ark itself was his footstool. Wherever the Israelites went, the ark was carried in front by priests, especially in wars where its leading presence was viewed as a blessing for the enterprise. It was veiled in badgers' skin and blue cloth so that even the Levites, who were the only ones allowed to handle it, could not see it. As a more symbolic statement of permanence, Solomon, King David's son, built the First Temple for the ark (dedicated in 953 BCE). It was built with substantial help from Hiram of Tyre, who not only delivered the famous cedars of Lebanon used in its construction, but also, so it is suggested by specialists, his favorite architect, Chiram Abiff.

Because Solomon married the daughter of Amenhotep III, one could expect a certain amount of Egyptian influence at the Solomonic court. Even though the temple had an altar in front for animal sacrifices, the temple was not viewed as the residence of a god but as an elaborate container for the ark in the windowless Holy of Holies (Kodesh Kodashim). This room, in which, it was thought, one could speak to God directly, contained no furniture, but had, guarding the ark, two tall statues representing cherubim, whose outspread wings met in the center of the room. Over the centuries, many attempts at a reconstruction have been made from the sketchy descriptions given in the Bible. Details as to the temple's features are given in 1 Kings 6:19 and 8:6: "And the house, when it was in building, was built of stone made ready before it was brought thither: so that there was neither hammer nor axe nor any tool of iron heard in the house, while it was in building." The temple was destroyed in 586 BCE by the Babylonians, and the Jewish population was taken into the Babylonian Exile (597–537 BCE). Today's Wailing Wall is a remnant of the foundations of the Second Temple (515 BCE), built by the Israelites after they had returned from their enforced exile to Babylon. It was that temple that was destroyed, in 70 CE, by the Romans. Hadrian built a temple to Jupiter on the site. That building was, in turn, demolished and replaced by the Dome of the Rock.

Kingdom of Kush

As a consequence of the imperial expansion of the New Kingdom dynasties of Egypt into Nubia, Libya, and Syria, the subjugated peoples often adopted Egyptian religion, culture, and weapons of war. The Nubians, for example, who served as valued mercenaries in the Egyptian army, worshipped Egyptian gods and built pyramids in which to entomb their rulers. Nubia was rich in natural resources, notably gold, with mines numbering in the hundreds scattered over the desert. The New Kingdom pharaohs asserted strong control over Nubia to guarantee the flow of gold to support their imperial ambitions in Asia. To extract the metal from the veins of the quartz rock, the rock was first cracked by means of fire, then crushed into a powder by mills, and finally washed to separate the ore, which was melted into small ingots. The system was hugely labor intensive but yielded, by one estimation, 40,000 kilograms of gold a year, an amount that would not be exceeded again until the 19th century CE. With the demise of the New Kingdom, Nubia, also known as Kush, was free to assert itself and, during the reign of Piye (747–716 BCE), conquered Egypt and ruled there as the Twenty-fifth Dynasty.

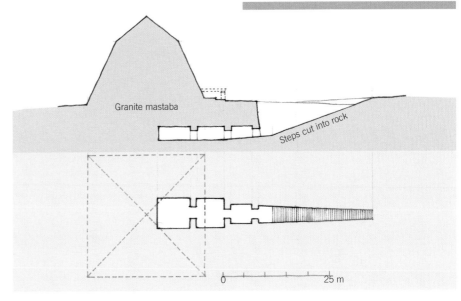

Granite mastaba

Steps cut into rock

0   25 m

4.53 Section and plan: Typical Napatan royal tomb

Iron played an important role, for the Kushites had learned the techniques of iron-working from their Assyrian enemies. Though the Kushites had iron, they did not have the fuel with which to smelt it. For that they had to turn southward, to the area around the city of Meroë, where the ancient, largely unexcavated slag heaps are still visible today. There the Kushite pharaohs promoted the Egyptian religion and embarked on programs of temple restoration.

At first, the center of the Kushite state was at Napata, lying just above the fourth cataract in the Nile River. Its focal point was the sacred flat-topped mountain of Jebel Barkal, which stands like a natural altar in the landscape a few kilometers from the northern bank of the Nile. In its shadow Ramesses II had already built several temples, one of which was the rather substantial Temple of Amun. The tombs at Napata are sited on both sides of the Nile; they are all that is left of the Nubian capital. The early tombs were round mastabas. These gave way to pyramids mounted on high bases with distinctive porches. During the last phase, at the height of Kushite control over Egypt, the rulers simplified the form to a pyramid and porch. A group of these are located not too far from Napata, near the modern town of Nuri. They form a tight cluster, with the bigger ones loosely lined up in row.

4.54 Overview of Napata tombs

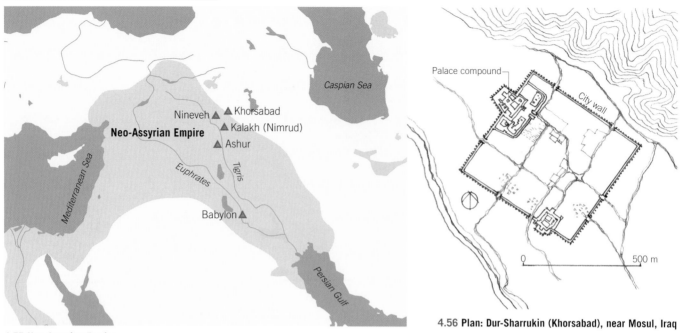

4.55 Neo-Assyrian Empire

4.56 Plan: Dur-Sharrukin (Khorsabad), near Mosul, Iraq

Neo-Assyrian Empire

The open terrain of the Mesopotamian heartland exposed the Assyrians, who controlled the northern river regions, to the seminomadic intrusions of the Kassites, the Hurrians, and subsequently, the Mitannians, whose kingdom was to extend over all of northern Mesopotamia. Assyria remained under Mitannian rule until early in the 14th century BCE, with only the core of its kingdom more or less intact, forming a narrow strip of land 150 kilometers long and only 40 kilometers wide along the western bank of the Tigris River. After the Mitanni defeat at the hands of the Hittites, the Assyrians reasserted themselves, invading Syria and compelling Mediterranean coastal cities like Tyre, Sidon, Byblos, and Arvad to pay tribute. In 663 BCE, the Assyrians were even able to sack the Egyptian city of Thebes. They were the first to command a truly Iron Age army. Though linked to Mesopotamian religious practices, the neo-Assyrians, with the god Assur at the top of their pantheon, imposed a particularly strict rule of divinely sanctioned warfare. Their engineers built bridges, tunnels, moats, and weapons of various sorts. By the year 668 BCE, Assyria had control over Egypt and the Nile River valley.

Because Assyria's first capital, Ashur, on the west bank of the Tigris, was open to the western steppe, it was relocated by Assur-Nasir-Pal II to Old Kalakh, now Nimrud, 64 kilometers to the north. But shortly thereafter, Sargon II (r. 722–705 BCE) designed the remarkable Dur-Sharrukin (Fort Sargon) near the present-day village of Khorsabad. Located 24 kilometers northeast of Nineveh, it was not yet finished when Sargon died. The city controlled the main pass route coming down from the mountains to the north, and its founding was probably intended to fend off any threat of invasion by the northern tribes. In plan, the city was a squarish parallelogram, with the palace, temples, and government buildings all compressed into an autonomous unit straddling the walls. In all, it covered 740 acres of ground. On the northwest side, half within and half without the circuit of the walls, protruding into the plain like a great bastion, stood the royal enclave. It rested on a 16-meter-high, 25-acre platform overlooking the city wall and comprised more than two hundred rooms and thirty courtyards. The palace in the center opened around a large inner court. It contained the public reception rooms, which were elaborately decorated with sculptures and historical inscriptions representing scenes of hunting, worship,

feasts, and battles. The harem, with separate provisions for four wives, occupied the south corner. The stables, kitchen, bakery, and wine cellar were located at the east corner. In the west corner stood the temple with a multistage ziggurat, its seven floor levels painted in different colors and connected by ramps. Below this enclave, on the inner side, was a zone surrounded by its own walls that held the administrative heart of the city and the sumptuous houses of high-ranking officials. For some reason, it was not acceptable to Sargon's son and successor, Sennacherib, who moved the capital once more to the old established city of Nineveh, when Dur-Sharrukin appears to have been largely abandoned.

The Assyrians, though possessing a formidable military machine, were unable to translate military success into economic stability. This was largely because they relocated vast numbers of people—estimates are as high as around six million—in their effort to thwart rebellion. Not only were the resettled peoples unfamiliar with their new lands, but many of their skills were no longer appropriate. In essence, the Assyrians obliterated their own tax base and quickly ran out of money.

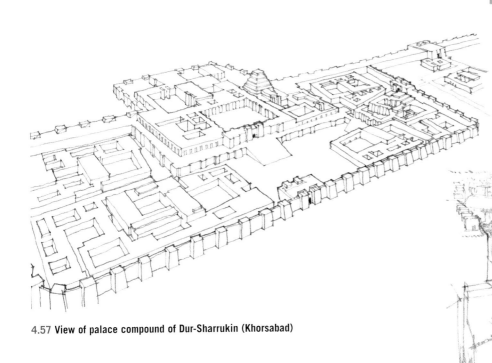

4.57 View of palace compound of Dur-Sharrukin (Khorsabad)

Babylon

Even at the height of Assyrian power, Babylonia remained the ceremonial center of southern Mesopotamia. By the mid-7th century BCE, however, as Assyria went into decline, the city began to assert itself, sacking Nineveh in 612 BCE and initiating a new era of prosperity. Nebuchadnezzar, who ruled between 604 and 562 BCE, started massive building projects. By 560 BCE, Babylon was certainly the most spectacular city in all of Western Asia if not the world, its forces marching even into Egypt and the city amassing huge wealth. Though Babylon was the last great Mesopotamian city-empire of the ancient age, the forced resettlement of conquered populations, the Israelites among them, left large territories untended or improperly governed.

Much as in Assyria, slaves were often used as farmers. Furthermore, as the Greeks no longer needed Mesopotamian grain, having developed Sicily for that purpose, and being distant from the metal-producing regions, all led to an untenable economic situation. Eventually, Persia to the east, having a more coherent sociopolitical system, was better able to control the emerging trade routes between east and west and became the dominant regional player. Babylonia was folded into the Persian Empire in 539 BCE.

Spanning the Euphrates, Babylon had two principal residential districts, with the palace and ziggurat compounds located along the shore. The palace reputedly had a garden on a high terrace some 18 meters above the river. It came to be known already in ancient time as the "Hanging Gardens." A pump brought water up from the river.

The Ishtar gate, brilliantly decorated with animal figures in yellow and white glazed brick against a vivid blue background, conveys a sense of the splendor of the city. It was the terminus of a processional way that led from the palace to the temple of Ishtar of Agade (Bit Akitu) that was used during the New Year festival.

4.58 Ishtar gate leading into Babylon from the north

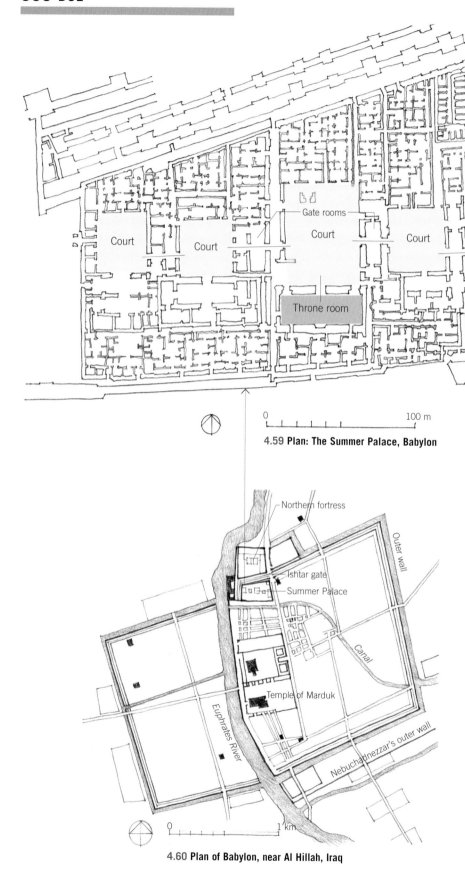

4.59 Plan: The Summer Palace, Babylon

0   100 m

4.60 Plan of Babylon, near Al Hillah, Iraq

Northern fortress

Ishtar gate

Summer Palace

Outer wall

Canal

Temple of Marduk

Euphrates River

Nebuchadnezzar's outer wall

0   1 km

The Summer Palace was located on the northern side of the city between the Ishtar Gate and the Euphrates. Similar to Assyrian tradition, the palace was not in the city but at its perimeter, but unlike Assyrian practices, the religious precinct remained in the center. The palace was constructed on high terraces and overlooked the plain and river below, but whether it was the location of the famous hanging gardens is not known. There were five courtyards at the core of the palace, each serving a different register of rooms in the north-south direction. The throne room was located lengthwise to the largest. It might have been barrel-vaulted, given the size of the walls. Typically for the age, the courtyards are not symmetrically aligned with each other. Access was from one to the other through a type of gate room.

400 BCE

From China to Greece, religious, ethical, and social thinking was undergoing various evaluations that contrasted with centuries-old traditions that had accepted the notion that power was imposed from the top, rather than that it should be examined from a theorized point of view. In the 6th century BCE, ethical and civic notions of government and personal conduct began to take root in many parts of Eurasia. In China, for example, Confucius (551–479 BCE) envisioned a world governed by reason and proper conduct, while Daoism, which existing alongside Confucianism, stressed a sort of quietistic noninterference and the paradox of complementary opposites. In India, Buddha and Mahavira challenged the highly stratified world of the Vedic orthodoxy, emphasizing the discipline of self-abnegation. Buddhism might have remained tangential to history had it not been made a state religion by Asoka (304–232 BCE), the creator of the first empire of South Asia. Since Buddhism at the time was largely an ascetic practice, Asoka did not order the construction of large temples, but set up pillars with the teachings of the Buddha etched onto them. In western and Central Asia we find Zoroastrianism, an ethically based religion that perceived the world as a struggle between good and evil. Man is viewed as a potential helper of God, capable of eradicating evil. And in Greece, Socrates, Plato, Aristotle, and others engaged in vigorous debates about democracy, law, and social philosophy. Athens, adopting democracy, became seminal in prefiguring the modern state.

Politically, the major player in western and Central Asia was Persia. Filling the vacuum created by the collapse of the Egyptian, Assyrian, and Babylonian empires, it extended its reach from northern India to Greece, giving rise to new architectural forms in the expansive capitals of Pasargadae and Persepolis. The Mediterranean, however, remained firmly under Greek control, with the Greeks, in the 5th century BCE, developing an architectural vocabulary that was to become foundational for European and West Asian architecture. Persia's unsuccessful attempt to conquer Greece, however, was to have unintended consequences. It stimulated the fantasy and ambitions of Alexander (356–323 BCE), who conquered Persia and its territories with the help of the highly trained infantry of hoplites and their fearful phalanx fighting techniques. For a while it seemed that the Greek Empire would stretch all the way to the Indus River, but Alexander's ambitions were cut short by his premature death in Babylon in 323 BCE. The conquered lands, divided among his generals, turned into quasi-independent states and regional power centers. The strongest of these was Egypt, ruled by the Ptolemies, who governed from Alexandria. An equally important city was Pergamon in Anatolia. The tiny island trading city of Delos overtook Athens as the cosmopolitan trading hub in the Mediterranean. The aesthetic of the time, in retrospect called Hellenism, tended toward realism, delicacy, and emotional expression; it left its imprint, especially on architecture and sculpture, on countries as far away as India and China.

In China, during the unstable later Zhou period, warring regional entities competed against one another in the construction of large palaces, introducing the imperial tomb as a sign of prestige and power. By the 3rd century BCE, the various factions were unified by the Qin (Ch'in) dynasty, which gave China its name.

In North America, the first complex cultures developed in the eastern woodlands along the Ohio River and its tributaries. The ground was fertile, fish and game abounded, and the waterways facilitated trade. In this environment, the people known as Mound Builders emerged. In South America, the most important cultural developments were well-organized societies that inhabited the Peruvian lowlands: the Moche civilization to the north, and the Nazca tribes to the south. The Olmecs, who had been the most influential culture in Mesoamerica for some time, were in decline by 400 BCE, having been replaced by the Maya and Zapotec peoples, who were making the transition from chiefdoms to small states.

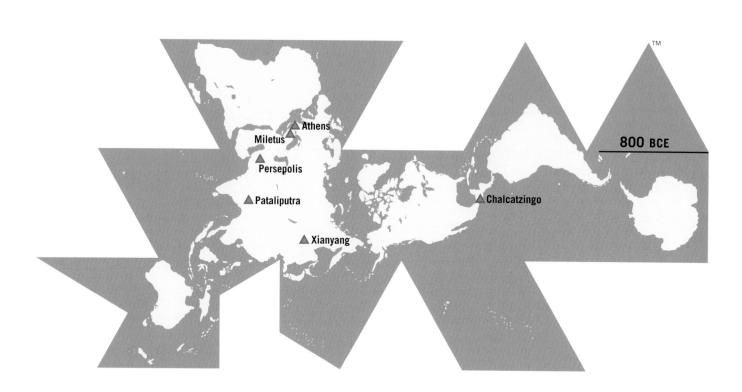

Athens

Miletus

Persepolis

Pataliputra

Xianyang

Chalcatzingo

800 BCE

Olmec Cultures
ca. 1500–400 BCE

Achaemenid Dynasty
ca. 559–330 BCE

Alexandrian Empire
334–ca. 301 BCE

Seleucid Period
ca. 305–247 BCE

▲ Pasargadae   ▲ Persepolis
ca. 546 BCE   ca. 518 BCE

Greece: Archaic Period
ca. 700–480 BCE

Classical Period
ca. 480–323 BCE

Hellenistic Period
ca. 323–31 BCE

▲ Temple of Poseidon at Isthmia
ca. 600 BCE

▲ Parthenon
ca. 447–438 BCE

▲ Athena Polias at Priene
334 BCE

▲ Temple of Artemis at Corfu
ca. 580 BCE

▲ Erechtheum
ca. 421–405 BCE

▲ Temple of Apollo at Didyma
ca. 313 BCE–41 CE

▲ Temple of Athena Nike
ca. 427 BCE

Sanctuary of Athena at Lindos ▲
ca. 190 BCE

▲ Miletus
Founded ca. 500 BCE

▲ Priene
Founded 334 BCE

▲ Dura-Europos
Founded ca. 300 BCE

600 BCE   **400 BCE**   **200 BCE**

Egypt: Ptolemaic Dynasty
323–40 BCE

▲ Temple of Horus
Begun 237 BCE

◉ Gautama Buddha
Born 566 BCE

Rise of great states in South Asia
8th to 6th centuries BCE

Mauryan Empire
ca. 323–185 BCE

▲ Lomas Rsi Cave
ca. 300 BCE

Pre-Classic Mayan Culture
ca. 1000 BCE–250 CE

▲ Chalcatzingo
ca. 400 BCE

▲ Teopantecuanitlán
ca. 400 BCE

▲ Kaminaljuyu
ca. 400 BCE

China: Eastern Zhou Dynasty
771–256 BCE

▲ Tomb of Zeng Hou Yi
ca. 433 BCE

▲ Xianyang Palace
4th century BCE

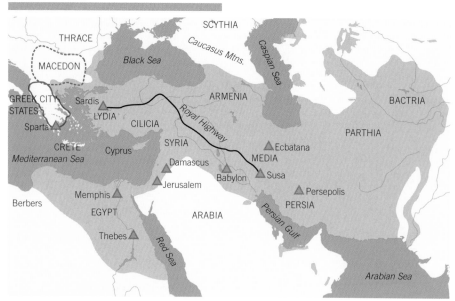

5.1 The Achaemenid Empire

Achaemenid Dynasty

Settlers arrived on the Iranian plateau sometime before or during the fifth millennium BCE, with one of the their ancient cities, Tepe Sialk (in central Iran, near the present-day city of Kashan) experiencing various occupations until about 800 BCE. By that time, the area had become known as Mede, and powerful kings extended control southward over the Elamite civilization located in the plains around Susa. With the weakening of the Assyrians to the west, one of the Median kings, Cyaxares (625–585 BCE), invaded and destroyed their capital, Nineveh, marching all the way to the gates of Sardis, where he turned back when a solar eclipse, interpreted as a bad omen, occurred. The capital of the Median kingdom at the time was Hagmatana ("the place of assembly"), a city dating back millennia; it is located under the modern city of Hamadan. The Median kingdom, however, underwent an inner transformation when the Persians, a branch of the Medians, took control under Cyrus the Great (559–530 BCE), who picked up where Cyaxares had left off and, in effect, united the Elamite, Median, and Babylonian realms into a region that extended from Anatolia to the Persian Gulf.

Though the famous military campaigns of both Darius and his son Xerxes I (in 490 and 480 BCE, respectively) against the Greeks were unsuccessful, the Persians, in alliance with the Phoenicians, who contributed substantially to their fleet, brought prosperity

to the Levant and its cities along the eastern Mediterranean coast. Temples were restored and monumental buildings erected. Phoenician cities like Byblos and Sidon experienced a renaissance. The Persians, seeing for the first time the great buildings of Egypt and western Asia, were eager to match these accomplishments. From the Ionians, Persia not only collected taxes but took their famously skilled craftsmen. An inscription of Darius's relates that the stonecutters who worked on his palaces were from Ionia, and the wood craftsmen were brought in from Lebanon, along with large loads of lumber.

By the year 500 BCE, the Persian Empire had grown to become the largest and most important realm in Asia, especially under Darius (522–486 BCE), who extended the boundaries of the empire into the heart of Egypt; the Zhou dynasty in China, by comparison, was still relatively isolated. The numerous city-states in India were occupied fighting each other. Unlike the Assyrians, Persian rulers attempted to gain the good will of their subject nations. Darius, for example, allowed Jews to rebuild the Temple of Jerusalem, which was finished in 516 BCE, the sixth year of his reign. Weights and measures were standardized, and an extensive road network was built—the first organized system of roads in history. The Royal Highway ran from Sardis, on the coast of Anatolia, to Susa, where it linked up, by means of western extensions, to the silk routes and to Pasargadae and Persepolis, the newly constructed Persian capitals. In fact, apart from the Greece, India, and Egypt, Persia was to a large extent surrounded by nomads and pastoralists, none of whom had extensive use of iron. It therefore stands to reason that Persia was eager to bring all of the Mediterranean into its realm of influence. Its failure to do so resulted in a double world: the linear geography of the Persians brought together by the Royal Highway and the network geography of the Mediterranean controlled by the Greeks and Phoenecians.

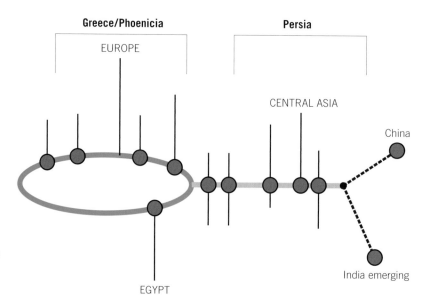

5.2 Trade diagram, ca. 400 BCE

5.3 Column capital from Persepolis, Iran

Pasargadae

In 546 BCE Cyrus established Pasargadae as
his capital, locating it at one of the starting
points for the caravan route northward
across the Great Salt Desert. The city's
administrative core is remarkable for its
spaciousness; palace, audience hall, altars,
and pavilions, are ll distant from each other
yet integrated into a parklike setting with
shady trees, watercourses, and gardens.
The Egyptians and Babylonians had palace
gardens, but such an expansive landscape of
palaces, gardens, and orchards was certainly
quite novel. It was also a sacred landscape,
for to the north there was a sacred enclosure
consisting of a walled precinct with a series of
flat terraces supporting an open altar.

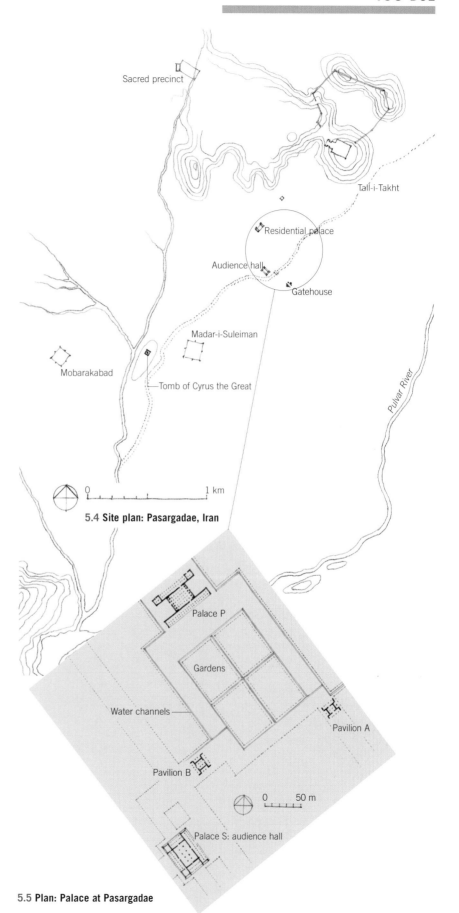

5.4 Site plan: Pasargadae, Iran

5.5 Plan: Palace at Pasargadae

5.6 Tomb of Cyrus the Great at Pasargadae

Not far from Pasargadae is the Tomb of Cyrus the Great. Its *cella* is 6 meters high and rests on a six-level stepped plinth that measures 13.5 by 12.2 meters at the base. The entire 13-meter-high edifice is of white limestone. Five huge stones, slanted to shed heavy rains, make up the roof. The monument, sitting boldly in the landscape, is an elegant combination of sepulcher and sanctuary. The building, with its cyma around the top, recalls similar, though more modestly scaled, Greek Ionian tombs. It was probably enclosed by a courtyard.

Pasargadae as a capital was relatively short-lived, for Darius designed his own capital city, Persepolis—"the city of the Persians," as the Greeks called it—located 10 kilometers to the southwest and closer to the fertile lands along the coast. It is a dramatic site at the edge of a large plain, the Marv Dasht basin, surrounded by cliffs. The palace is located directly under the west-facing slope of one of those cliffs. Construction went through several phases between 515 and 330 BCE. The first one involved cutting into the irregular and rocky mountainside to level a large platform 10 to 20 meters above the ground and measuring about 300 meters in length and 450 meters in width. The foundations contained complex drainage systems and water channels. Of the buildings themselves, however, little remains, since most of the walls were of mud brick. What we see today are the sections that were built in stone: the columns, foundations, and carvings.

Access to the terrace was provided by a double staircase with steps flat and deep enough to allow important guests to ride up on their horses. At the head of the staircase was a gate, its sockets still visible, guarded by a pair of large bulls to the west and bulls with the heads of bearded men to the east. Black marble benches line the wall. The largest building, the Apadana ("castle" in Persian), served as the main reception hall; it had seventy-two fluted and tapered limestone columns 7 meters high surmounted by bull- or lion-shaped capitals. The ceiling beams of cedar, ebony, and teak were gold plated and inlaid with ivory and precious metals. The general concept of a columnar hall dates to early Median architecture: a palace-citadel in Gobin Tepe from the 8th century BCE had a hall with thirty columns, as did Cyrus's palace in Pasargadae.

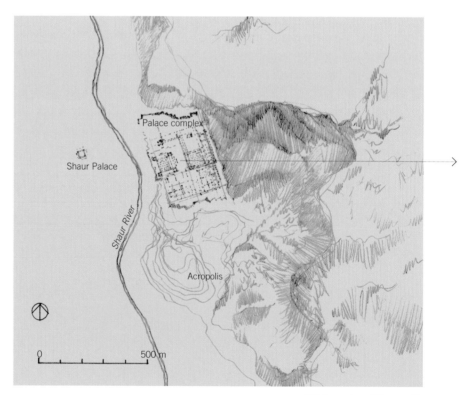

5.7 Area plan of Persepolis

5.8 Staircase at Persepolis

5.9 Staircase at Persepolis

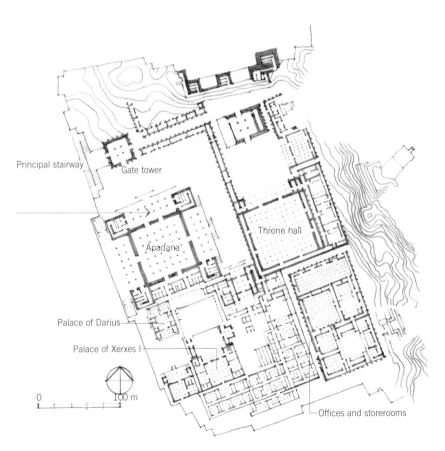

5.10 Plan: Palace complex at Persepolis

The reliefs on the staircases leading to the Apadana, the great audience hall of Persepolis, which is part of the oldest section of the palace, depict rows upon rows of emissaries, soldiers, and chariot drivers. It is a virtual film strip from which we can see how the various peoples of the vast empire dressed and what kind of ornaments, weapons, and hairstyles they sported. These and other sculptural elements and reliefs emphasize the formal and the imposing, in contrast to the lively movement and zest of the Assyrian and neo-Babylonian art. The northern part of the terrace, which included the throne room (known also as the Hall of a Hundred Columns), measured 70 by 70 meters and represented the main section of the complex, which was accessible only to a restricted few. The southern section contained the palaces of Darius and Xerxes I, the harem, a council hall, and storerooms. The storerooms also held the war booty, as well as the annual tributes sent by subject nations. Records found show that in the year 467 BCE, no less than 1,348 people were employed in the treasury.

5.11 Part of the palace complex at Persepolis

The whole scheme reflects, however, only the secular power of the empire, for as yet no shrine or temple has been identified. The question as to where the court lived is also still being debated. Some argue that there was a royal palace somewhere in the plan. Others claim that Persepolis was only a temporary residence for kings who had their major seat of power elsewhere and that, when in use, the court and the army camped in tents.

Persepolis was not only a grand palace complex but also a dynastic burial place. On the hillside above the palaces are tombs ascribed to the last Persian kings, Artaxerxes II and III, and Darius III. Persepolis's influence extended as far as Pataliputra in eastern India. It was looted and burned by Alexander the Great from 331 to 330 BCE.

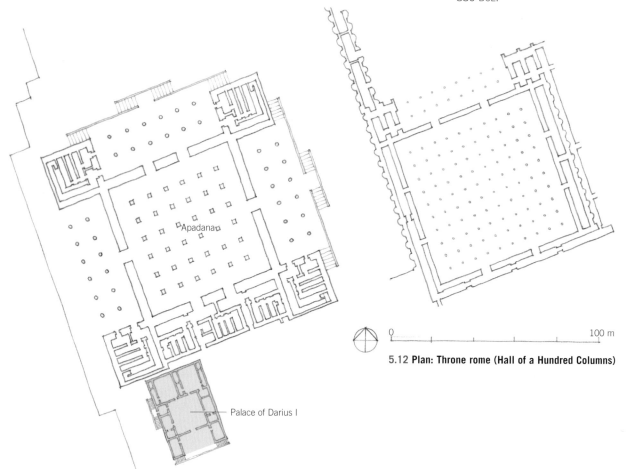

Apadana

Palace of Darius I

5.12 Plan: Throne rome (Hall of a Hundred Columns)

0   100 m

5.13 Plan: Apadana, the principal audience hall of Darius I

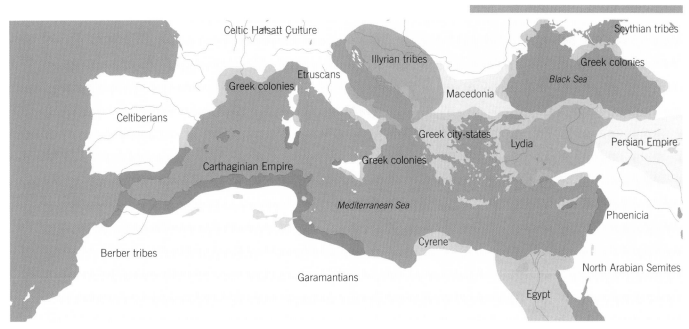

5.14 Greek and Phoenician colonies around the Mediterranean, 550 BCE

Greece and the Mediterranean

If Persia's empire was based on a comprehensive network of roads, the Greek enterprise was based on sea trade. Greeks plied the Mediterranean all the way to Gibraltar in the west and the Black Sea in the east, founding dozens of cities and trading posts. This trade network was a consequence of competition among Greek cities and of the gradual opening of the European hinterland to commerce. Massalia (now Marseilles, France), for example, was founded in 600 BCE as a trading outpost to facilitate commerce with the Gauls. Many of the city-states had their own colonies, with Miletus alone having no less than some ninety colonies spread around the Mediterranean. When viewed together, the two contrasting systems—the landlocked one of Persia and the maritime one of Greece—constituted a large east-west geopolitical continuum that remained viable until the breakup of the Roman Empire in the 5th century CE.

The Greek Temple

Greek temple design changed considerably in the middle of the 6th century BCE, as wood was increasingly abandoned for stone. This may have been partially due to a desire for permanence, but it may also have been spurred by the influence of Egyptian architecture, with which the increasingly came in contact.

At the time, the northern part of Egypt had been divided among vassals of the Assyrian Empire. Around 664 BCE, an Egyptian prince named Psamtik was banished to the marshes. Plotting his return, he allowed the Dorians to settle in Naucratis, on the western edge of the Nile Delta, around 620 BCE, on the promise that they help with his military ambitions, which were indeed successful. He was able to defeat his rivals, break with Assyria, and reunify Egypt. This opened a series of mercantile exchanges between Egypt and Greece that was profitable to both. Naucratis became a type of duty-free zone, with the Greeks setting up factories to produce pottery and ornaments in an Egyptian style for the Egyptian market. They also imported silver, which was still rare in Egypt; in return they appear to have received Egyptian grain.

When the Greeks, accustomed to small wooden temples and simple outdoor altars, first encountered the enormous Egyptian stone temples and pyramids, they were certainly amazed, and lost no time in studying Egyptian construction techniques. They also had ample opportunity, since Psamtik had embarked on an extensive building campaign. The impact of these lessons must have been immediate, for there is very little evidence that the Doric order existed before the Greek experience in Egypt. The Greeks were, however, not unfamiliar with stone and had already begun using it for the walls of the *cella*, as we have seen at the Temple of Poseidon at Isthmia. But to make columns and even the roof of the colonnade out of stone was a different matter.

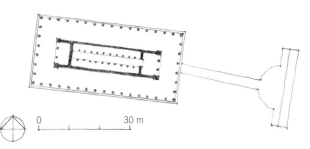

5.15 Plan: Temple of Artemis at Corfu (Kerkira), Greece, ca. 580 BCE
The earliest known Doric temple completely of stone

5.16 **Temple of Segesta, Sicily, Italy**

5.17 **Plan: comparison of Temple C at Selinus, Sicily, Italy, with the Temple of Poseidon, at Paestum**

One can follow the development of the Doric order at the Temple of Poseidon at Isthmia, where, by the time of its completion around 600 BCE, the oak columns were replaced by stone columns. (A Roman visitor in 176 CE reported a peculiarity: one oak column was still standing.) Some of the first stone columns were huge monoliths; others consisted of superimposed drums of varying heights and diameters.

There was an important difference between Greek and Egyptian stone preparation. In Greece, stones were brought to the construction site in an almost finished state, whereas in Egypt, stones for columns arrived at the site still quite rough (apart from horizontal cuts), with much of the finishing taking place when the stones were in situ. This difference would have significant impact on Greek architectural developments, as it would allow for an ever increasing elaboration of detail, proportion, and form.

The first Greek colonies were established around 770 BCE by the Euboeans on the island of Ischia (Pithekoussai) near Naples; Cumae in central Italy; the island of Naxos in the Cyclades; and Leotini in eastern Sicily. Around 710 BCE, the Achaeans founded Sybaris and Croton in southern Italy. The Spartans founded Tarentum around 650 BCE, while Syracuse was founded by the Corinthians in 743 BCE. All in all, in a span of one hundred years, some thirty colonies sprang up. The settlers maintained close relationships with their mother cities

and often appealed to them in times of war. But the colonies also began to flex their own military muscles. In 480 BCE, Syracuse defeated Carthage in the Battle of Himera and in 413 BCE inflicted catastrophic damage on Athenian forces during which the Athenians lost two hundred ships and thousands of soldiers. The wealth of these colonies helps explain why many of the early Greek temples were not in Greece, but in Sicily and Italy. At Selinus, on the southern coast of Sicily, seven temples were lined up on the acropolis and a nearby ridge. They date from 570 BCE to 409 BCE. At Paestum

in central Italy, there arose a temple of Hera (550 BCE), a temple of Demeter (520 BCE), and a temple of Poseidon (460 BCE). In contrast to the early temples at Selinus, the later temple of Poseidon in Paestum opened up the *cella* by means of an inner colonnade and achieved closer interaction between the body of the temple and the *pteron*, or columnar surround.

5.18 **Greek temple sites**

The *cella* ends with either columns in antis or a prostyle portico.

Anta refers to the thickening of the projecting end of one of the lateral walls. If columns are set between them, then the columns are said to be in antis.

A prostyle portico has columns running across the entire front.

An amphiprostyle temple has prostyle porticoes at both ends.

5.19 A comparison of Greek temple types

Greek Architecture and Language

Greek and Roman temples are described according to the number of columns on the entrance front, the type of colonnade, and the type of portico. The Parthenon, for example, is an octastyle peripteral temple with hexastyle porticoes at both ends. The Temple of Zeus at Olympia is a hexastyle peripteral temple with distyle in-antis porches at both ends. The basilica in Paestum is a rare enneastyle pseudodipteral temple with a tristyle in-antis portico.

Almost all surfaces of the temple—the steps, columns, capitals, walls, even the figures on the pediment—were painted in bright reds, blues, blacks, and yellows. What we know about the colors used for the temples comes from both archaeological and literary sources. The pigments were made from minerals, soot, ground stones, vegetables, and animal matter. The purple dye, for example, came from shellfish; the yellowish color that was applied to columns and beams came from saffron. The colors were applied sometimes with wax but usually on stucco.

Though today we may perceive Greek temples as isolated objects, they were actually framed in the landscape by a *temenos*, or sacred precinct, which could consist of something as simple as a row of stones but could also be a built-up wall. The *temenos* was the territory of the deity and had to be approached in a prescribed manner and entered only at a special place defined by a *propylon* (i.e., *pro-pylon*, or "before the gate").

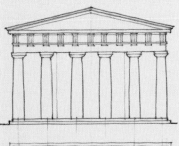
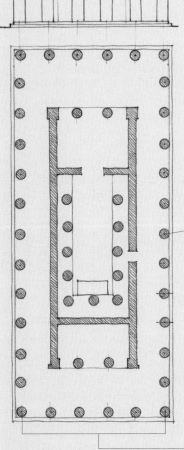

5.20 Greek temple terminology

The most basic element of the temple was the colonnade. Though so common today that it might seem to be a natural architectural form, it was actually a unique innovation of the Greeks. Called a *pteron*, it was a sacred form always reserved for temples. *Pteron* means "wing" or "fin," but also "oar" and "sail." It perhaps refers to early awnings placed against buildings. But it also indicates that the Greeks saw the building as a dynamic location—as something that literally catches the wind and hears the voices of the gods. The *pteron* also evoked the idea of a grove of trees, especially because columns were originally made of wooden trunks. The *pteron* has also been associated with stout soldiers forming a phalanx—a rectangular military formation—symbolically protecting the statue within the *cella*.

The following terms describe the type of colonnade surrounding the *naos* of a Greek temple:

- Peripteral: one row of columns
- Dipteral: two rows of columns
- Tripteral: three rows of columns
- Pseudodipteral: suggesting a dipteral colonnade, but without the inner colonnade

The following terms refer to the number of columns on the entrance front of a Greek temple:

- Henostyle: one column
- Distyle: two columns
- Tristyle: three columns
- Tetrastyle: four columns
- Pentastyle: five columns
- Hexastyle: six columns
- Heptastyle: seven columns
- Octastyle: eight columns
- Enneastyle: nine columns
- Decastyle: ten columns

A corona is the projection at the top of a cornice; the word was associated with the forehead and with controlling things from above. It was also associated with the eagle, the bird of omen and Zeus's favorite bird. For these reasons it became the appropriate element with which to top off a temple.

On the abacus of a capital rests the architrave, the main stone or marble beam running from column to column. Above the architrave is the frieze, which consists of alternating triglyphs and metopes. Beneath each triglyph, on the face of the architrave, is a smooth band—the regula—on the underside of which hang six stone pegs, or guttae. There is normally one triglyph to each column and one to each intercolumniation. The metopes were often decorated with paintings or relief sculpture depicting stories of the local hero or episodes from the myths associated with the god to whom the temple was dedicated.

Cornice
Triglyphs
Frieze
Metope
Guttae
Architrave
Regula
Guttae
Abacus
Capital
Echinus
Necking
Shaft
Base

5.21 Elements of the Doric order

- Pycnostyle: 1.5 diameters
- Systyle: 2 diameters
- Eustyle: 2.25 diameters
- Diastyle: 3 diameters
- Araeostyle: 3.5 diameters

Intercolumniation refers to the space between columns, expressed in column diameters. This systematization applies mainly to Hellenistic and Roman temples.

The temple rested on a *crepis*, the base of a building but also a shoe or sandal—a footing, in other words, proper to the divine presence. This foundation was constructed from roughly dressed masonry that was not concealed below the ground but was designed to appear as steps leading up to the platform on which the temple's columns rested.

The capital, which derives its name from the Latin word *caput* ("head"), was in Greek terminology the *kranion*, which refers to the top of the head or skull. The Doric capital, carved out of a single stone block, consists of a spreading convex molding, the echinus—a word that was applied to almost anything curved and spiny found in nature—and a low square block, the abacus.

The column shaft tapers from the bottom upward in the form of a delicate curve called an entasis, or swelling. The shaft of a Doric column almost always stands directly on the floor, without a base. Early columns from the 6th century BCE are often monolithic, but later the shaft came to be composed of superimposed drums, which were rounded by turning them on a lathe. The drums were doweled together with wooden or bronze spikes enclosed in concavities at the center. The shafts were fluted after the columns were in place. There are usually twenty broad and shallow flutes that meet to form sharp edges, or arrises. The joints between the columns would have been concealed by marble stucco.

The steps were often too tall to ascend comfortably, so a flight of stairs or a ramp was provided at the entrance. This demonstrates that the steps had nothing to do with the necessities of construction, for they could easily have been designed with more risers. Instead, the steps were intentionally built to make the temple appear as if it were rising on a natural outcropping, cleaned and smoothed in preparation for the building.

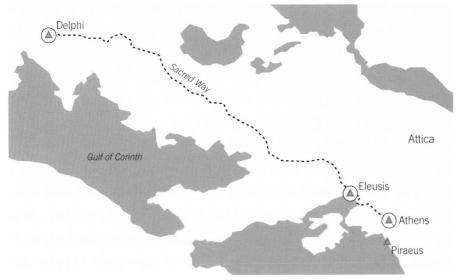

5.22 Sacred Way from Athens to Delphi

5.23 Plan: Telesterion at Eleusis, Greece

Telesterion at Eleusis

Festivals were an important part of Greek political and religious life similar to the Middle Kingdom practices of Egypt, except that Greek festivals were considerably more folksy in nature. The temple at Isthmia, for example, was the center of a festival that involved a major athletic contest. In Athens, festivals accentuated the flow of the year, and in fact filled 120 days, or one-third of the calendar year.

One of the oldest of these festivals, and one possibly once linked to the Eleusinian Mysteries, was the Thesmophoria, a harvest festival (*thesmoi* meaning "law," and *phoria* deriving from the word for "carrying"). It was celebrated by the married women of Athens whose husbands were Athenian citizens. The festival centered on the earth goddess, Demeter, whose daughter, Persephone, had to spend one-third of the year in the underworld with her husband, Hades. During these dry summer months, Demeter abandoned her function as harvest goddess and mourned for her absent daughter. The women set up makeshift shelters outside the sanctuary, purified themselves, sat on the ground, and fasted in commiseration with Demeter. On the third day, a meat celebration was conducted named after Kalligenaia, the goddess of beautiful birth and an ancient term that alludes to the very antiquity of this rite, which quite possibly antedates even the Greeks: this festival, if it can be called that,

had at its roots the ancient Mediterranean-wide mother cult.

Another important Greek festival, one that indeed exemplifies the very essence of Greek religiosity, was the celebration of the Great Mysteries at Eleusis, which took place in that city. Dating back some two thousand years, probably to Mycenaean times, this city was located some 25 kilometers distant from Athens and became part of the Athenian state festivals in the 6th century BCE. It was a seven-day celebration in September, officially the fifteenth day of the Greek month of Boedromion. People streamed to it from all of Greece, and even slaves were admitted. This festival was so deeply entrenched in the folk practices and the communal memory that it continued on into early Christian times—until the early Christian fathers put a stop to it. The procession followed the sacred road from Athens to Delphi that had, according to myth, been traveled by Apollo. The route started at the sacred gate in the city walls of Athens and proceeded through Eleusis to the sanctuary of Demeter on the Thriasian Plain.

Every September a great torch-lit procession wound its way along this route. Two days before it was to begin, the *hiera* (sacred objects) were brought in baskets to Athens by young Athenians in military training. The initiates met their *mystagogus* (a person initiated previously who helped them through the process) and took piglets

down to the sea, bathed with them, sacrificed them, and purified themselves with their blood. On the fifth day, they made the long 25-kilometer march to Eleusis. The statue of Dionysus was carried at the head of the procession. Then came the priests with the sacred cult objects hidden in baskets and finally a huge crowd of *mystai* ("initiates"). The high point of the festival took place in the Telesterion at Eleusis, a square, windowless building arranged in its final configuration with tiers of seats to accommodate some three thousand people.

The Anaktoron at the center of the great hall housed the hiera, the inner sanctum that, though small and windowless, was precious and of venerable age. The renovations and additions that were made to the Telesterion changed only the space around it, not the Anaktoron itself. The building in its final form (ca. 435 BCE) was designed by Koroibos. In the 4th century BCE, a colonnaded porch known as the Stoa of Philon was added to the southeastern side of the building. Though the songs and offerings were public, the experiences of the *mystai* during the rites were secret, and access to the inner sanctum of the Telesterion was restricted to initiates. Despite how long they lasted and the huge number of people who took part, the secrecy surrounding these rites has been preserved; one can only guess what the mysteries involved.

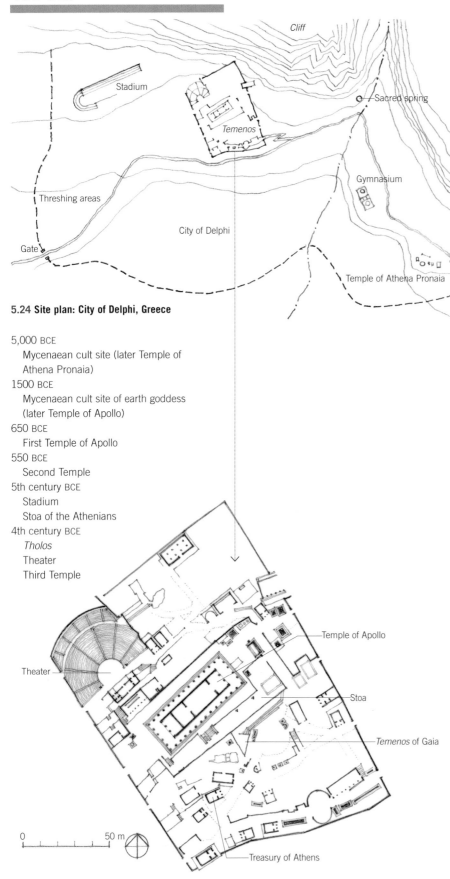

5.24 Site plan: City of Delphi, Greece

5,000 BCE
    Mycenaean cult site (later Temple of
    Athena Pronaia)
1500 BCE
    Mycenaean cult site of earth goddess
    (later Temple of Apollo)
650 BCE
    First Temple of Apollo
550 BCE
    Second Temple
5th century BCE
    Stadium
    Stoa of the Athenians
4th century BCE
    Tholos
    Theater
    Third Temple

5.25 Plan: *Temenos* at Delphi, Greece

Delphi

Delphi was without doubt the most sacred of the religious sites in Greece, with its own festivals and celebrations. One approached it from Eleusis on the sacred route that crosses the Boeotian Plains, passes the city of Thebes, and courses its way through increasingly rugged and remote territory filled with history and myth. Finally, the dramatic scenery of the limestone cliffs, from which gushes the Castalian Spring with its great cleft, comes into view, the buildings of the sanctuary rising up against the base of the cliff. The early history of Delphi is the story of a struggle between different types of religious practices. Initially, the site was dedicated to the great mother goddess in the Minoan tradition. With the arrival of the Dorians we see their paternalistic practices superimposed on the existing maternalistic social structures. Nonetheless, despite the seizure of the shrine by the followers of Apollo, the new concepts did not totally obliterate the old; rather, the maternalistic elements were subsumed. The mother goddess was transformed into the serpent, Python, slain by Apollo and is said to be buried there, but she retained her ancient *temenos* close to the Temple of Apollo, near the Rock of the Sybil. The temple foundations come close to her spot but do not obliterate it. Apparently, the Apollo cult was forced to compromise with the older deities as two population groups made their accommodations.

5.26 Delphic Pythia sitting on a tripod, attended by a supplicant

5.27 Treasury of Athens, Delphi

5.28 Pediment: Temple of Apollo at Delphi

Temple of Apollo at Delphi

During the three winter months, Dionysus shared the temple sanctuary on the Parnassos slope with Apollo, a reference to some of the ancient chthonic elements connected with the cult of Persephone, who, according to the Orphic myth, was the mother of Dionysus. Out of the ecstatic dances and choruses of Dionysus, the Greek drama was born, and at Delphi, above the great Temple of Apollo, there lies on cross-axis to the temple and facing straight down the slope a brilliant example of such a theater. Filling and defining a natural concavity at the base of the cliff, the natural and man-made merge into one majestic swath—one great hymn to the creation cycle of life.

From just inside the wall of the *temenos*, the viewer would see the silhouette of the Temple of Apollo floating against the backdrop of the cliff. The path to the temple was not a direct one but rather snaked its way upward past the various treasuries—many of distant colonies—to emerge just below the broad terrace built up against the slope. A supplicant, guided by an assistant of the Delphian cult, would have been led to the temple terrace to await his turn with the oracle. He would have had the opportunity to look straight down into the ancient precinct of Gaia. He might have spent some time regarding the temple itself.

What we see today is the last temple, the site having been occupied earlier by two previous Doric temples. The first one, a

structure from the 7th century BCE, burned in 548 BCE and was replaced by a larger one in 525 BCE, which itself was replaced in the mid-4th century BCE. On the east pediment facing the altar in front of the temple, sculptures portrayed the arrival of Apollo at Delphi, shown with his mother, Leto; his sister Artemis; and his companions, the Muses. At the opposite pediment, Dionysus, Apollo's brother—both having been fathered by Zeus—occupied the center, establishing a principle of balance, Apollo representing music and poetry, Dionysus, wine and ecstasy. The Dionysian and the Apollonian were not perceived as opposites by the Greeks but rather as complementary; together they embodied the wholeness of life. Below the east pediment hung the golden shields from the spoils of the Persian War, a gift to the temple by the Athenians.

The most important festival associated with Delphi was the change of rule that took place between Apollo and Dionysus at the appointed time. It was enacted in the great open-air theater above the temple with its thronelike overview of the sanctuary and surrounding landscape. The sports events that accompanied these festivals took place in the heights above the *temenos*.

Once inside the temple, the supplicant would smell the meat burning on the hearth and see the smoke rising toward the opening in the roof from which shafts of sunlight penetrated down into the gloom. Visitors

also mentioned a perfumed smell. The supplicants would have seen tripods, statues, pieces of armor, even entire racing chariots, brought as donations from the entire world of Magna Graecia, and often from foreign countries as well. After depositing his own offering, the supplicant would be led toward the far end of the chamber, where steps descend to a sunken area a meter below the level of the floor. From there he made his way into the adytum, at the back wall of which was a bench close to the branches of a laurel tree as well as a golden statue of Apollo. There, the prophetess, on a tripod and hidden from him by a curtain, was positioned over a crack in the rocks from which, according to some visitors, emanated that sweetish smell. An attendant, drawing back the curtain, would relay the question of the petitioner and from the depth, the prophetess received a reply to the question, often equivocal, which she conveyed back to the petitioner. Whatever the response—which often required a large amount of interpretation—it probably necessitated further donations. What caused the sweet smell has not been determined with scientific accuracy. Recent archaeological studies point to the possibility that it might have been ethylene, a common vapor in natural tar pits that produces euphoria, which is used today as an anesthetic.

5.29 Ionic capital from the temple at Neandris **5.30 Bronze female figure with headdress** **5.31 Treasury of Siphnos at Delphi**

Ionic Order

Though usually discussed after the Doric, the Ionic should not therefore be regarded as later. The development of the Ionic and the Doric orders paralleled each other, but stylistically there are notable differences. First, Ionic columns rest on molded bases that stand on square plinths. These moldings consist of combinations of tori, scotias, and rondels, often in pairs. The capital has different front and side views and is meant to be seen chiefly from the front and back. At the base of the capital there is a flat-topped molding with a profile like that of the Doric echinus, but it is usually carved with egg-and-dart moldings. Above this lies the volute, its loose ends winding down in dropping spirals on each side of the shaft and ending in buttonlike *oculi* (eyes). The entablature usually consists of three bands of fasciae of unequal height, each projecting a little beyond the one below it. Above it runs a band of egg-and-dart molding and over that a row of dentils, superceded by a projecting cornice often decorated with lions' faces and plant motifs.

The Ionic capital came into its own during the 7th century BCE. Unlike the Doric, the Ionic did not derive from a structural system, but perhaps from symbolic headdresses or from poles surrounded by bundled vegetation marking sacred areas. The capital consists of two large spirals that spring upward and outward from the shaft, as if a pliant stick were split at the ends and each curved outward halfway to form a spiral. The space between the spirals was decorated with a fanlike pattern. Capitals of similar form were found on the island of Lesbos.

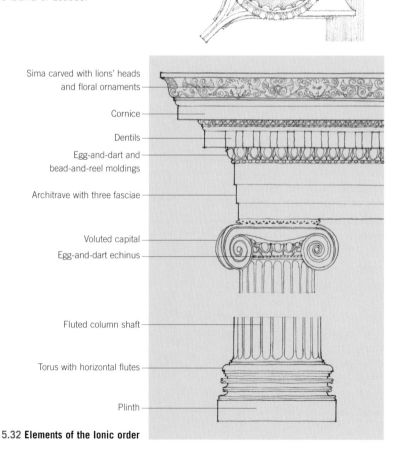

Sima carved with lions' heads and floral ornaments

Cornice

Dentils

Egg-and-dart and bead-and-reel moldings

Architrave with three fasciae

Voluted capital

Egg-and-dart echinus

Fluted column shaft

Torus with horizontal flutes

Plinth

5.32 Elements of the Ionic order

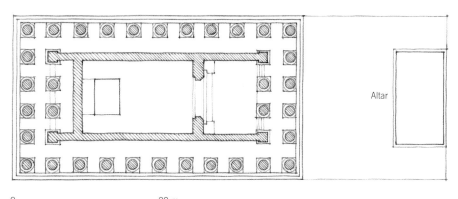

0   20 m

5.33 Plan: Temple of Athena Polias at Priene, Turkey

To construct the volutes, craftsmen devised a system of gridded holes into which pegs were inserted and around which a cord was wound and then, with a stylus attached, unwound. In essence, the spiral was a series of interconnected quarter circles and semicircles. One of the most elegant Ionic temples is undoubtedly the small Temple of Athena Nike (ca. 425 BCE) at the Acropolis in Athens.

Though proportional systems were most certainly in play in the design of the Doric order, the formalization of the system began with the Ionic. A temple of the Ionic at its most classic is the Temple of Athena Polias at Priene (ca. 334 BCE) by the architect Pythius, who wrote a book explaining the proportions of this temple. The larger proportions were worked out in similar ratios of 1:2. The overall dimensions of the stylobate measured 19.5 by 37.2 meters, for a ratio of 11:21. The axial spacing between the columns was twice the width of the square plinths. The antae of the porch and the *opisthodomos* in the rear stood opposite the penultimate columns of

the ends and sides and enclosed a rectangle measuring 12 by 30 meters, for a ratio of 1:2.5. No longer did architects manipulate the form to adjust for optical illusions; geometrical precision was now in order. The Ionic was codified further around 150 BCE by the architect Hermogenes, also of Priene. He worked out a series of ideal proportions that were to influence Vitruvius a century later. According to this system, the height of the column varied inversely according to the axial spacing, so that the sum of axial spacings and height was always 12.5 column diameters.

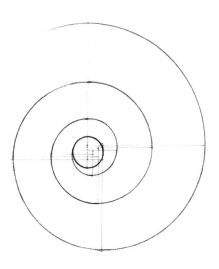

5.34 Development of the Ionic spiral

5.35 Temple of Athena Nike, Acropolis, Athens, Greece

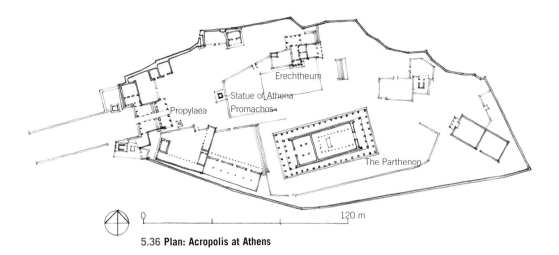

5.36 Plan: Acropolis at Athens

The Parthenon

Over the course of two generations, beginning in 550 BCE, the people of Athens would establish democracy (510 BCE), win the battle of Marathon (490 BCE) over the Persians, and build an economic and political empire within mainland Greece. The outstanding political figure of the time was Pericles, who was responsible for rebuilding the Parthenon as a Panhellenic sanctuary clad in the white marble from nearby Mt. Pentelikon. The building, replacing the one that had been destroyed by the Persians, was designed by Ictinus (with advice from Callicrates and Phidias) and built in less than ten years, between 447 and 438 BCE. It was perched at the prow of the ancient hilltop of the gods, facing Mt. Hymettos to the east and the Bay of Salamis to the west. It stood as a grand monument and votive to Athena, the city's patron deity. The Parthenon was bigger than any temple ever before built on the Greek mainland, its stylobate measuring 30.9 by 69.5 meters. Early accounts of the temple call it Hekatompedos, or "hundred-footer," referring either to its overall width or the length of the large eastern room of its *cella*, also know as the *hekatompedos*.

Because of the constant warfare in ancient Greece, almost every city was divided into a lower town and an acropolis, which literally means a "city on the height." The acropolis of Athens was no exception. It sits on a great isolated slab of limestone, tilted toward the west side from which it had to be approached. Already fortified with a wall by

the Mycenaeans, it was held to be invested with divine presences from ancient times. The waters from a spring on its southern flank are today still considered to have healing powers. But size was not its only unusual feature: the east and west facades were lined with eight towering Doric columns, making the Parthenon the only octastyle, peripteral temple built in ancient Greece.

The interior of the *naos* has been variously reconstructed, in some places with a standard roof and in others with an opening in the center. The columns in the *naos* supported a second tier of columns above, and there was a shallow rectangle in front of the statue of Athena, possibly used as a reflecting pool. Underlying the construction is a system of precise refinements that control the delicate curvature of horizontal lines, the elegant convergence of vertical lines, and the nuanced size and spacing of the fluted marble columns. In no other temple was this visual tension as subtle and refined as in the Parthenon.

The stylobate was not a flat plane but rather like a section of a very large sphere; it curved upward toward the middle, rising 41 millimeters on its short sides and 102 millimeters on its long flanks. This curve was carried upward through the entire structure, imparting a subtle upward curvature on the architrave, the cornice, and nearly every "horizontal" line of stone. Every column demonstrated entasis, or a slight bulging of the middle of the column's shaft.

Entasis is a countermeasure that corrects for an optical distortion: numerous parallel vertical lines appear slightly concave. The entasis here measured only 20 millimeters of deviation from a straight line—much more subtle and restrained than the entasis of earlier temples. Moreover, each of the

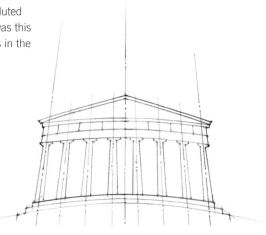

5.37 Diagram of the curved stylobate and inclined vertical axes of the perimeter columns of the Parthenon

5.38 **Approach to the Parthenon from the Propylaea**

5.39 **Detail of the pediment of the Parthenon**

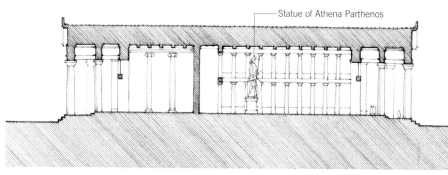

Statue of Athena Parthenos

Section

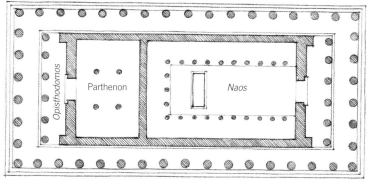

Opisthodomos

Parthenon

Naos

Plan

0   30 m

5.40 **Section and plan: The Parthenon, Athens**

forty-six perimeter columns was tilted slightly inward, with the corner column tilting on a diagonal. If the columns of the short sides were extended upward, they would meet around 4.8 kilometers above the roof.

While each of these refinements have functional advantages—the curvature to shed water, the angling to increase lateral structural support during earthquakes, and the corner adjustments to maintain proper column alignments with the metopes above— scholars, beginning with the Roman architect and historian Vitruvius, have argued that the nuances were mostly for aesthetic effect. The plastic quality of the architecture befits a building so rich in sculptural detailing. The artisans behind the Parthenon's sculptural program are not known. It is generally assumed that Phidias led a large team of sculptors who carved the pediments, metopes, and frieze. Much of the sculpture has been lost due to looting, defacement by Christians, and the explosion that nearly destroyed the Parthenon in 1687. But the drawings of French architecture student Jacques Carrey made in 1669 have been invaluable in reconstructing the form and meaning of the original sculpture. Thomas Bruce, the Seventh Earl of Elgin, dismantled about two-thirds of Phidias's frieze and had it shipped to England between 1801 and 1806, and today the so-called Elgin Marbles are in the British Museum, to the outrage of many.

5.41 Caryatid porch, Erectheum, Acropolis

Erechtheum

Unlike Egyptians, Greeks never added new elements to a temple. New structures, of course, could be added to the precinct, but the temple itself was not changed, unless it was somehow destroyed and rebuilt. It would be wrong, however, to assume that Greek architects were unable to think beyond the inflexibility of the temple form. The Propylaea and the Erechtheum on the Athenian Acropolis are examples of rather complex buildings whose architects had to accommodate a range of programmatic and ritualistic purposes. The Erechtheum wraps up different mythical narratives into a single composition. It was built on two levels with three porticoes of different designs; there were four entrances beside the subterranean one under the north porch. This irregularity was due to the necessity of designing a building around the spots that were essential to the narrative of the founding of Athens. Erechtheus, after whom the Erechtheum is named, was the mythical founder of Attica and the "earth-born king of Athens." At that time, it was believed that gods challenged one another to be honored by cities. Unfortunately, both Poseidon and Athena aspired to control Athens, so Erechtheus set up a contest in which each had to make a gift to the city. Poseidon drew saltwater by

striking the ground on the Acropolis with his trident, while Athena grew the first olive tree on its slopes. Erechtheus judged Athena's gift to be the most useful to the people of Athens and the city was named in her honor.

The central elements of the drama can be read by entering first through the north porch dedicated to Poseidon. Its expansive design takes in the grand vista and can be seen from the agora below. On the floor, to the left of the door, a type of window looks down at the bedrock, where one can see the indentations of Poseidon's trident. An opening in the roof above indicates the space through which the trident was thought to have flown. The great door leads to a narrow room that contained a shrine to Erechtheus. Under the floor was a cistern containing the saltwater of Poseidon. A door to the right leads to the sacred court containing Athena's olive tree. Continuing on the axis made by the porch of Poseidon, one goes up the flight of stairs to the caryatid porch, which today sits isolated in the field of ruins.

Although the plan of the building may seem chaotic, the temple not only graces the Parthenon with charm and wit but also makes sense as a three-dimensional celebration of the founding myth of Athens. The north porch is the largest and projects forward two intercolumniations, the height of its roof being almost level with the eaves of the central block. The south porch is less than half as high, but it is raised upon a terrace. Instead of columns, there are caryatids—columns in the shape of young

5.42 Erectheum from the south, as it stands today

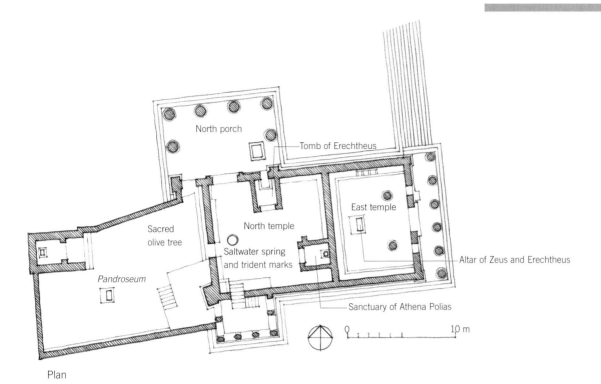

North porch

Tomb of Erechtheus

East temple

Sacred olive tree

North temple

Saltwater spring and trident marks

Pandroseum

Altar of Zeus and Erechtheus

Sanctuary of Athena Polias

0   10 m

Plan

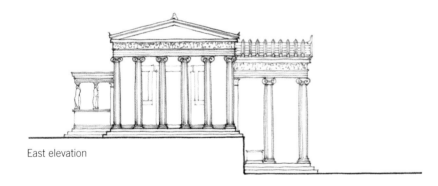

East elevation

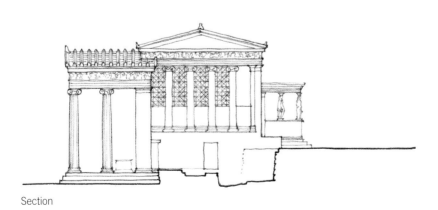

Section

5.43 Erectheum, Acropolis

women—carrying the load of the entablature on their heads. The east porch consists of six Ionic columns. The central block that holds all this together has two levels corresponding to the north and east porches. Three doors lead into it: the great door of the north porch, a plain opening at the bottom of the west wall, and a small door on the south side, to which a staircase leads down from the interior of the caryatid porch.

Rising up over the entire story and at a 90 degree cross-axis is the edifice of the victor, Athena, facing east. At the diagonal, upon descending the external stairs on the northern side and before entering the north porch, was an area dedicated to Zeus, the ultimate arbiter of the contest. His position seems to address the dynamic northeasterly pull of conical Mt. Lykabettos, for it, too, plays into the story. According to legend, Athena was absent from her city to retrieve a mountain to use on the Acropolis. Her sisters were curious about the chest in which Athena was protecting the young Erechtheus and opened it, contrary to Athena's orders. She became so angry that she dropped the mountain. How this plays out in the design is unknown, but from the agora below the Acropolis, the mountain and the Erechtheum are clearly in dialogue.

The propylon that defined the entrance to a *temenos* was more important for its symbolism than for protection. Its design is unmistakably reminiscent of Minoan and Mycenaean architecture, and there can be no doubt that it was incorporated into the Greek architectural language for its legitimizing allusions to an age that the Dorians themselves perceived as heroic.

5.44 Longitudinal section: The Propylaea at the Acropolis

Athenian Propylaea

The Propylaea (437–432 BCE) is approached by a massive ramp 20 meters wide and 80 meters long. It enters into a U-shaped structure with a Doric facade. The road continues through the building and is flanked by slender Ionic columns. The central parts are ceremonial and symmetrical; the outlying spaces serve various functions. To the left was a banquet hall, or *pinacotheca*, that reached to the very edge of the Acropolis wall. In it were spaces for seventeen couches. It is known to have contained paintings on the walls, thence the name. The area to the south led to the Temple of Athena Nike (ca. 427 BCE), which was the first construction on the Acropolis following the devastation by the Persians. It was also the first temple on the Acropolis to be built in the Ionic style and the first temple built entirely of Pentelic marble. In this area there was also a statue to Hermes, a god traditionally associated with boundaries.

Remarkable is the intricate play of solid and void spaces. The building itself is like a bracket yielding to the thrust of the ramp. The interior Ionic columns are much more slender than their Doric counterparts and impart a lightness to the shadowy interior that contrasts with the sturdy exterior and the brightness in front and back. Cross views were also important. From the door of the *pinacotheca*, for example, the view falls directly across the front of the main colonnade, positioning a viewer both inside and outside at the same time.

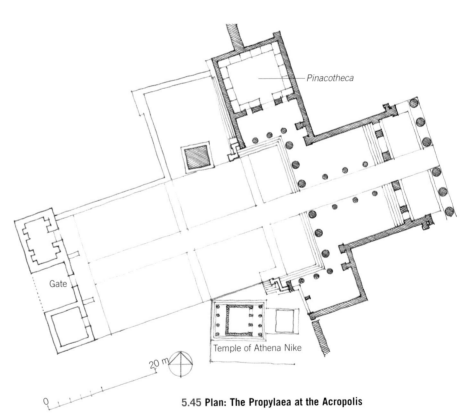

Pinacotheca

Gate

Temple of Athena Nike

20 m

0

5.45 Plan: The Propylaea at the Acropolis

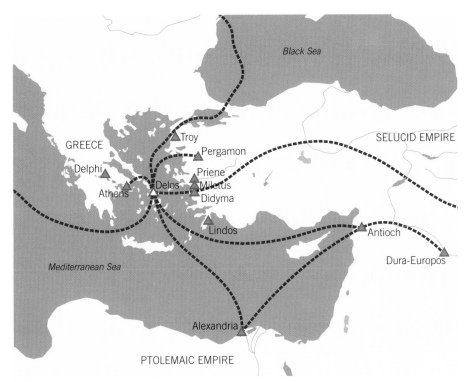

5.46 Greece and West Asia, 4th century BCE

The Hellinistic Age

Alexander the Great (356–323 BCE), son of Philip II of Macedon, assumed the kingship over the newly consolidated mainland Greece after his father's death, continuing his expansionary policies. He crossed the Hellespont in 334 BCE with his troop of Greek hoplites, defeated the powerful Achaemenid Empire, and went to the border of India founding many fledgling cities stocked with some of Alexander's Macedonian Greeks, awaiting—in vain as it turned out—his return with new troops and settlers to sustain his eastern empire. His empire fell apart after his sudden and unexplained death in 323 BCE in Nebuchadnezzar's palace in Babylon. Strife broke out among his potential successors, but eventually three realms emerged: the Antigonid Empire (Greece), the Seleucid Empire (Mesopotamia and Persia), and the Ptolemaic Empire (Egypt, Palestine, and Cyrenaica). All are part of what is called the Hellenistic Age, the enormous impact of which can be felt as far as India and China. As an art form, Hellenism had lost some of the discipline of its origins and in temple construction tended to gigantism and spatial experimentation; in sculpture, it is noted for the portrayal of emotions and empathy as, for example, in the Dying Gaul. Old cities like Athens, which for a while became part

of the Kingdom of Antigonus, were given new buildings. Some were paid for locally; some funds came from foreign donations. The enormous Temple of Zeus at Olympia in Athens, begun in 170 BCE, was paid for by Antiochus IV (d. 164 BCE) of the Seleucids of northern Syria. A new harbor, council hall, and residential quarter were added to the city of Miletus. Assos redesigned its central agora with a long two-story-high stoa. New cities were laid out, some as far away as Ai Khanum on the Afghan bank of the Oxus River.

Though planned cities go back millennia, the architecture of cities and the architecture of palaces or temples were, until then, generally speaking quite distinct. In Hellenistic cities, urbanism and architecture begin to overlap for the first time. Theaters, temples, villas, palaces, libraries, stadia, and streets are all equally important in such Hellenistic cities as Priene, Pergamon, Alexandria, Dura-Europos, Delos, and Rhodes. Rhodes was so wealthy that, when an earthquake destroyed the city in 225 BCE, citizens were able to rebuild speedily.

The economic engine that drove this tremendous expansion was not Athens but Egypt, the economic marvel of the Mediterranean. By the time of Ptolemy III (245–221 BCE), Egyptian fleets controlled most of the shipping lanes of the eastern Mediterranean. Building on the old pharaonic tradition of state control, the Ptolemaic kings updated technologies and production systems, transforming the country with its population of seven million into a grain-producing machine of unprecedented proportions. The Ptolemaic rulers introduced the water screw of Archimedes and built machines with drums or wheels driven by humans for raising water and pushing back the desert. Salt production was escalated. Mines and quarries, as well as the development of a state-run bank, were integrated into the system. It was in some respects one of the first examples of state-supported modernization.

5.47 Dionysus Theater, Athens

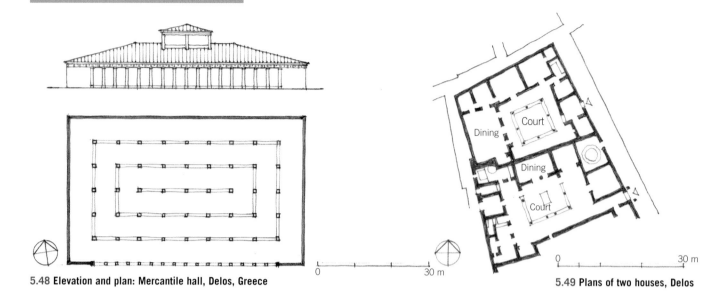

5.48 **Elevation and plan: Mercantile hall, Delos, Greece**

5.49 **Plans of two houses, Delos**

Delos

One of the places that most quickly adapted to the new world order was Delos. Though the island was small—one of the smallest in the Aegean—and though it had no local economy to speak of, it was almost equidistant from the various ports in the Aegean Sea. It entered into economic relations with Egypt and Macedonia to become the leading Mediterranean trading station. The tradition that had begun with the Minoans was perfected by the rulers of Delos. Money was made in the transfer of goods rather than in their manufacture and sale. Delos was also a holy place, considered the birthplace of Apollo and Artemis.

On one side of its harbor was a special landing place for pilgrims visiting the sacred sites; on the other side, the large and new mercantile harbor fringed with storage houses, wharves, and commercial buildings. The Egyptians, bringing their grain for redistribution, built shrines to their gods. Phoenicians came to sell ivory. Jews built a synagogue. And the Italians were on the scene as well, building an agora of their own. Everything could be exchanged, including slaves and spices. A mercantile hall measuring about 60 by 35 meters was built in 210 BCE, with houses for the merchants laid out with unprecedented richness.

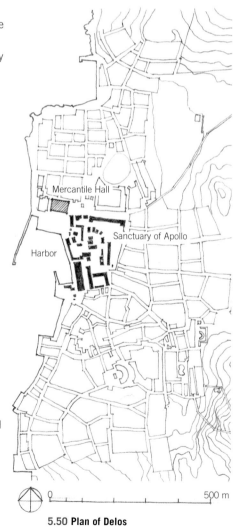

5.50 **Plan of Delos**

Priene

On the eastern coast of Anatolia, Miletus, Priene, and Heracleia were all part of an inlet that has long since silted over. Together with Didyma and with the ancient sanctuary of Samos as a type of gateway, this area was a major religious and economic center. Priene, founded in 334 BCE, occupies a sloping ground beneath a fortifiable acropolis. The streets run east-west along level ground and are about 4.5 meters across. From south to north, with the ground rising steeply, the streets are mostly narrower. The principal civic elements of the city are embedded in the structure of this grid and yet in dynamic resistance to it. The agora, for example, juts out from the grid to the south and does not align with the side streets. Across from it is a three-block-long stoa. Up the hill a few blocks to the west is the platform with the temple of Athena, and a block higher yet but to the east was a theater with spectacular views into the valley below and the mountains across. Farther northward yet, where the city ends and the steep slope of the acropolis begins, is a sanctuary dedicated to Demeter. A stadium and gymnasium define the lower edge. The city, because of its composite character, might appear to have been built up over time, but it is in actuality a skillful play of solids and voids and of private and public zones, spread out over a difficult terrain.

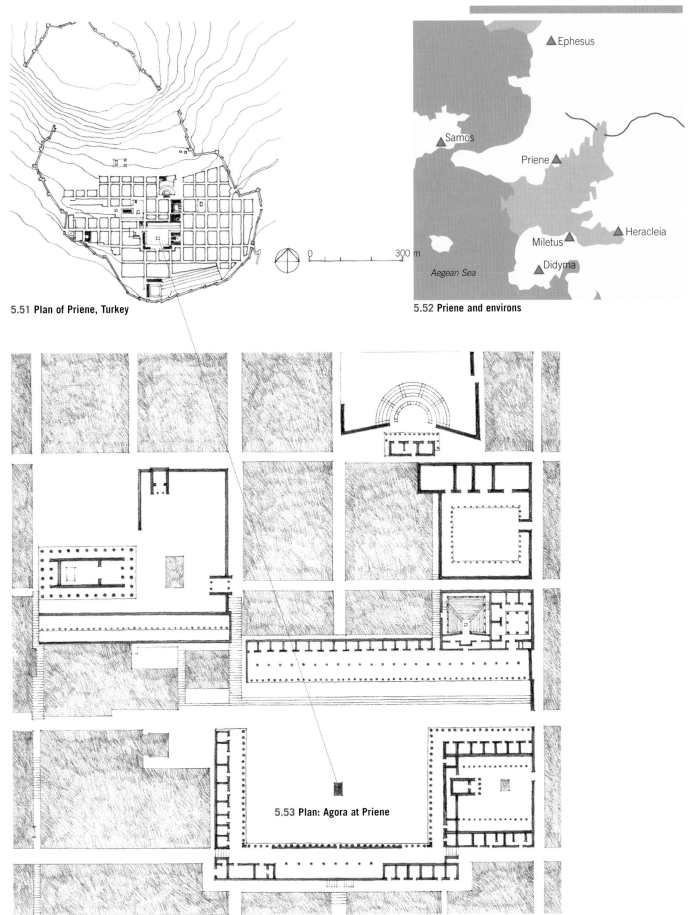

5.51 Plan of Priene, Turkey

5.52 Priene and environs

Ephesus

Samos

Priene

Miletus

Heracleia

Didyma

Aegean Sea

0   300 m

5.53 Plan: Agora at Priene

Pergamon

By the year 281 BCE, the city of Pergamon had become the center of a small but powerful city-state rivaling Athens and even Alexandria as a center of Greek culture. It is estimated that at its peak, it had a population of three hundred thousand people spreading from the mountaintop site to the southwest, across the Caicus Plain. Overlooking the city was an acropolis decked out with an assortment of structures that show the Hellenistic spatial aesthetic at its best. The object of the overall composition was not simply to work with the contours, almost instinctively, as was traditional in Greek planning, but to exploit them for their inherent sculptural qualities. At the heart of the acropolis stood a temple to Athena, the protectress of the city, dating from the beginning of the 3rd century BCE and most likely the oldest structure on the acropolis. It is one of the very rare Doric temples in Asia Minor and was no doubt built as an homage to the Parthenon. It was enclosed in a *temenos*, with stoas on three sides that clamp it into the hill. Just behind the stoa was the palace of Eumenes II. Behind another wing of the stoa but at a higher level was the famous library built around 190 BCE, which held up to two hundred thousand volumes. Yet farther up is the military zone of the acropolis with its storehouses, officers' housing, barracks, and arsenal.

The theater, resting against the slope of the mountain, is one of the most spectacular in the Hellenic world. It was originally constructed in the 3rd century BCE, rebuilt around 190 BCE, and refurbished in Roman times. The cavea, or auditorium, forms part of the natural contour of the west-facing slope and has room for ten thousand spectators, with the king's marble box just at the center of the front row. A comparison of Pergamon with Priene is instructive, for it shows that, as important as the Hippodamian city grid plan was, Hellenistic town planners also saw its limitations and, as at Pergamon, adopted a method that followed the lay of the land and indeed exploited it with great skill.

Toward the south, at the edge of the acropolis and on a terrace 25 meters below the Athena temple is the Altar of Zeus, built for Eumenes II soon after his victory over

5.54 Plan: Pergamon, near Bergama, Turkey

0   200 m

5.55 Remains of the theater at Pergamon

5.56 Propylaea on the acropolis at Lindos, Greece

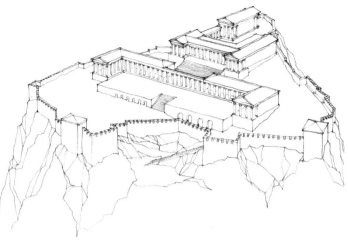

5.57 Pictorial view: Sanctuary of Athena on the acropolis at Lindos

the Gauls in 190 BCE. The Gauls had been sweeping southward from western Europe, and even though they would continue to harass the northern borders of Mediterranean countries for centuries, Eumenes II had managed to hold them at bay, at least for a while. The altar was a U-shaped, Ionic, stoalike structure perched on top of a high socle, with a vast flight of stairs leading up its west side to the level of the colonnade. On its enormous socle level was a frieze representing the mythical battle between the Olympian gods and the ancient giants, symbolizing the triumphs of the Pergamon kingdom over the Gauls.

The altar stands in a courtyard atop an almost square plinth. It was surrounded by a colonnade that sheltered a wall on which there was another frieze celebrating the legitimacy of the Pergamon kings. This altar was not only the traditional end point of the sacrificial procession but also a political monument and even a war memorial. These are roles that had been in earlier days connected with the temple—the Parthenon being an excellent example. But here the altar reverted to an autonomous cultural object.

Sanctuary of Athena at Lindos

Though Pergamon is a masterpiece of adaptation to the landscape, resulting in a multifaceted architectural environment. Another example is the acropolis of Lindos (ca. 190 BCE) on the island of Rhodes, built around an older temple to Athena (ca. 300 BCE). The first terrace is framed out over the landscape by an outward-facing winged stoa, opened at the center by a broad flight of stairs. The stoa's front row of columns holds its edge to form a screenlike passage across the front of the steps. The steps lead to the top level and to a broad porch that, in turn, opens into a courtyard with an altar in the middle. The old temple is sited to the left of the courtyard, in dynamic tension with the altar.

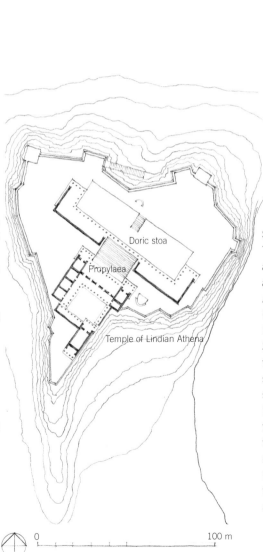

Mediterranean Sea

Doric stoa

Propylaea

Temple of Lindian Athena

0   100 m

5.58 Plan: Sanctuary of Athena on the acropolis at Lindos

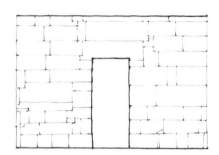

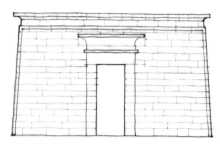

5.59 Comparison between Middle and New Kingdom walls and Ptolemaic walls

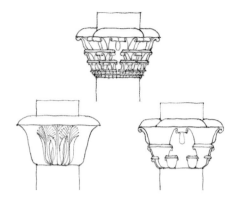

5.60 Examples of Ptolemaic capitals

Ptolemies

Alexandria was one of the principal Hellenistic cities. Situated on the western extremity of the Nile River delta, the city was founded in 332 BCE by Alexander to serve as a regional capital. It soon became the largest city in the Mediterranean basin, and it was unlike any other, with libraries, museums, and a rich cosmopolitan culture. Though little is left of the ancient city, the Ptolemaic period left a vibrant record of its art and architecture in many parts of Egypt, including the construction of about fifty medium-size and large temple complexes, not to mention smaller architectural works. The Ptolemies and their queens had no misgivings about following Egyptian tradition, and set up statues of themselves as cult images. In architectural terms, not only did spatial arrangements change but so, too, did construction elements. In older times, a wall was fitted together from stones of different shapes, with the surface treatment unifying the appearance. The stones were

laid in regular courses, creating a clarity and precision, or, depending on one's taste, monotony and rigidity. But true to the Hellenistic desire for complexity, the new temples introduced a feature rarely explored in older Egyptian architecture: the section.

The outside of Middle and New Kingdom buildings offered relatively flat volumes; very little could be learned about the interior arrangement of the temples from the point of view of an outside observer. But Ptolomeic buildings were set up with disparate volumes. There were contrasts between the towering pylon, the surrounding walls, and the hypostyle hall peaking over the top of the wall. To add to this contrast, Ptolemaic architects did not place windows on the top

of walls, as the earlier Egyptians had done: their hypostyle halls are pitch black if one closes the doors. Ptolemaic architects also added ambulatories around the temple, making it an autonomous object within the confines of the outer walls. Much innovation focused on the elaborations of columns and their capitals. The capital could be round or single-stemmed, quatrefoil or even eight-stemmed. The plant motifs are palm, papyrus, lotus, and lily, even though the lily was not a native Egyptian species. The plants' leaves could then appear stacked variously, from two to five. The richness of form was augmented by lively coloring.

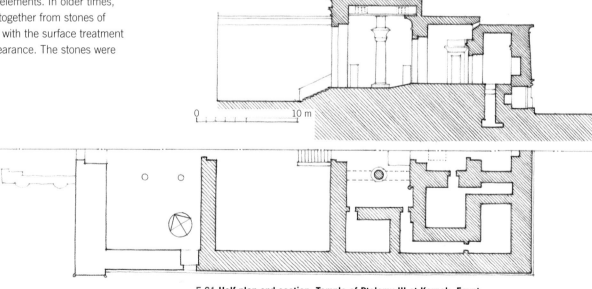

0   10 m

5.61 Half plan and section: Temple of Ptolemy III at Karnak, Egypt

5.62 *Pronaos* at the Temple of Horus, Edfu, Egypt

5.63 Hypostyle hall, Temple of Horus

Temple of Horus

The Temple of Horus (begun 237 BCE) is an excellent example of these tendencies. The building had not only to reflect the needs of the cult of Horus but also had to serve as a pantheon for the cumulative aspects of Egyptian religion. The entrance is marked by a grand pylon 62.6 meters across and 30.5 meters high, leading to a court colonnaded on three sides, a very un-Egyptian motif. The colonnade not only frames the entrance of the temple but also constitutes a type of extended porch that, along with the perimeter walls, forms a passageway. That passageway connects to the ambulatory between the temple and its enclosing wall. In true Hellenistic fashion, nearly every surface of the temple is covered by carvings and hieroglyphics (some of which were later defaced by early Christians, who were intolerant of pagan imagery). There were two hypostyle halls. The second one had two rooms on the sides; the room to the west was used for the preparation of sacred ointments, and the one to the east as a treasury for cult implements and clothes. Past the two hypostyle halls is an inner court, in the center of which is the freestanding sanctuary of Horus. The court also gives access to thirteen small chapels for the pantheon, all windowless and completely dark except for tiny slit entries. Great care was given to align the pylon with the noontime sun at the midsummer solstice. At that particular moment, the pylon does not cast a shadow.

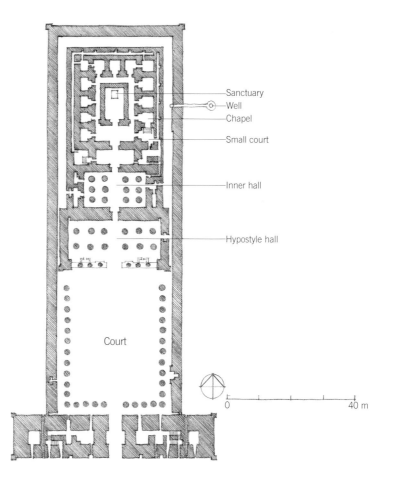

Sanctuary
Well
Chapel

Small court

Inner hall

Hypostyle hall

Court

0   40 m

5.64 Plan: Temple of Horus

5.65 Temple of Apollo, Didyma, Turkey

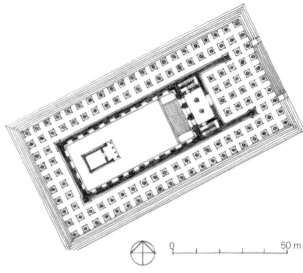

5.66 **Plan: Temple of Apollo**

Temple of Apollo at Didyma

It is difficult to speak of the Hellenistic temple as a single aesthetic form. In the cosmopolitan environment of western Asia, one sees different tastes in different places as well as variable influences. In Egypt, buildings of the Hellenistic era were designed in an Egyptian revival style. Such neoarchaisms were not outside the aesthetic interests of the Greeks. The Hellenistic aesthetic did, however, draw on centuries of experience in creating complex, composite relationships between space, landscape, and mythical narration—organizing it, as at Priene, into unified aesthetic expressions. One of the most spectacular of Hellenistic temples in this respect is the unfinished Temple of Apollo at Didyma, 14 kilometers south of Miletus. Sitting on a gentle hill and exposed on all sides, it contained the unusual feature of an open court, planted with bay trees, among which stood a shrinelike Ionic temple. Though several Greek temples—possibly even the Parthenon—had open interiors, this was something altogether different. The architects are said to have been Paeonius and Demetrios of Ephesus. Though much of the plan may have been laid out by them around 313 BCE, the work took well over three hundred years to complete and was abandoned in 41 CE.

The temple's Ionic double *pteron* stands on a stylobate accessed by seven huge steps. After ascending the steps, one enters the deep porch of the *pronaos*, behind which is an antechamber. The antechamber is actually higher than the *pronaos*, with its door serving as a window from which the oracles were delivered. Standing among the *pronaos*'s treelike columns—the tallest of any Greek temple's—the windows would have appeared to be the mouth of a cave. Access to the inner courtyard was by way of small doorways on either side of the window, through sloping, dark tunnels roofed with barrel vaults.

Penetrating through this dark "grotto," one enters the sacred grove. But this "inside" was in fact an outside. The artificial grove of trees, which is how the columns would have appeared from the outside, gave way to real trees on the inside. Furthermore, within that grove was another temple, with its axis oriented toward the entry; this small Ionic temple at the far end of the open *cella* faced a grand staircase leading back up to the antechamber from which the priests could officiate. Folding one temple compound into another was a consummate example of Hellenistic brilliance.

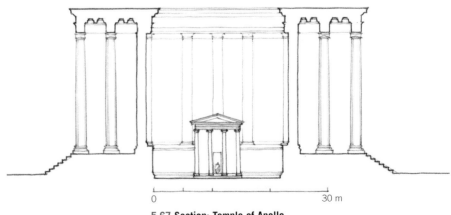

5.67 **Section: Temple of Apollo**

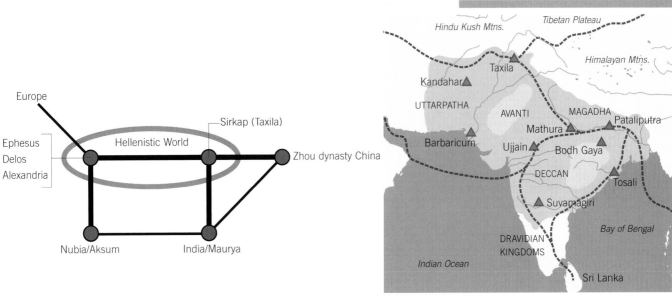

5.68 Eurasian trade diagram, ca. 300 BCE

5.69 Mauryan Empire, India

Mauryan Dynasty

In the period prior to about 300 BCE, connections between India and the rest of Asia had been somewhat tentative, as India, despite its vibrant urban culture, had remained relatively isolated from the Hellenistic economies that linked Delos and Pergamon in the west to China in the east. This situation changed rapidly when the Mauryan kings unified the Indian subcontinent, forming a new and potent economic force in the Asian world. Maurya, centered on the fertile plains of the Ganges River, had under its control not only a rich agricultural basin, but also the Barabar Hills to the south of the Mauryan capital Pataliputra, where copper and iron could

be mined. Consequently, India could begin to compete in the global politics of iron, and thus emerge from its relative isolation.

The Mauryan kings expanded their territory westward and southward until, at its height, the empire stretched northward along the natural boundaries of the Himalayas and westward to Kandahar, which had been founded by Alexander in the 4th century BCE. This brought India into full contact with Greek and Persian culture, and soon Indian spices, copper, gold, silk, and rice began to appear in distant places. The impact of this contact manifest in Indian buildings in a shift from wood to stone architecture, initially in the form of monumental columns and rock-cut Buddhist caves. Chandragupta

(340–298 BCE), the founder of the Mauryan Empire, located his capital at Pataliputra, at the confluence of the Ganges and one of its tributaries, the Gandak. Not much has been recovered of this city, but an account by Megasthenes, the Greek ambassador at Chandragupta's court, describes it as about 15 kilometers long and 2.5 kilometers wide, girded by a moat and a wooden wall with 64 gates and some 570 towers. Excavations at the site have so far uncovered what appears to be a hypostyle audience hall on a grand scale, as indicated by 80 highly polished stone pillars, severed from their bases, set about 5 meters apart.

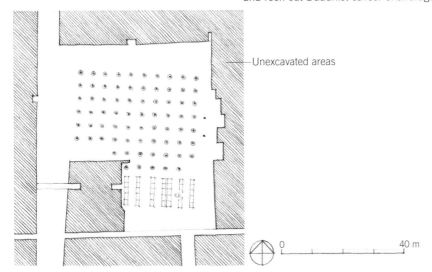

Unexcavated areas

0   40 m

5.70 Plan: Audience hall at Pataliputra, India

5.71 Capital from Pataliputra, 3rd century BCE

5.72 Asokan pillar at Vaishai

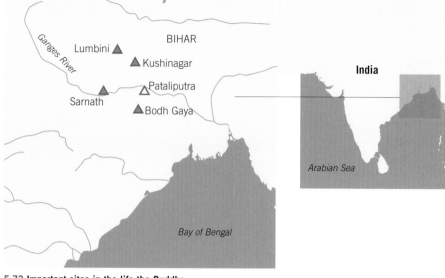

5.73 Important sites in the life the Buddha

Asokan Pillars

The rise of Buddhism can be traced to smoldering divisions within the Aryan polity. Large Aryan kingdoms like Magadha rose to power supported by a Brahamanical elite. Brahmins were the lawmakers, scholars, preachers, and advisers to the rulers, who occupied the highest position in the Vedic caste system. Since the caste system controlled the lives and destinies of everyone, there was little individuality. In the 6th century BCE, two men, Siddhartha Gautama (the Buddha, or "enlightened one") and Mahavira Jain, both from marginal clans, asserted the idea of an independent and individual journey to spiritual bliss, or nirvana, that contradicted not only the principles of warfare, but also the highly regimented Vedic rituals that required the leadership of the Brahmins. Nirvana was accessible to all, but it was not an easy to reach, as it required a commitment to rigorous asceticism. The main difference between the two men was that while meditation-based practices were at the core of the Buddha's teachings, Mahavira Jain insisted on a radical vegetarianism that including a prohibition on farming, since that inadvertently killed soil worms.

Buddhism might have remained just another intellectual stream of the Aryan world had it not been adopted as state law and moral order under Asoka (r. 272–231 BCE), the most famous of the Mauryan kings. After a particularly brutal battle, Asoka lost faith in the traditional Aryan order, and after more than a year of consultation with

various philosophers, decided to convert to Buddhism. Asoka was not the first Mauryan leader to be interested in Buddhism. At the end of his life, Chandragupta Maurya, founder of the Mauryan Dynasty, abdicated his throne and became a Jain ascetic. His son, Bindusara (r. 298–272 BCE) became a follower of an even more extreme ascetic movement known as the *ajivikas*. The ascetic interest of these rulers derived from the fact that they were not born into the Aryan Kshatriya (warrior) caste, but were low-caste upstarts who became Kshatriya after seizing the Magadha throne. The difference between Asoka and his predecessors was that he adapted Buddhist teachings into a new moral and social order for his empire that he called the *dhamma*. In essence Buddhism became a state religion.

5.74 *Vajrasana* ("Diamond Throne") at Bodh Gaya

Though most of Asoka's *dhamma* derives from Buddhism—including vegetarianism and belief in nonviolence—it was not identical to Buddhism. In fact, Asoka rarely mentioned the Buddha while describing his *dhamma*, which, significantly, included respect for all religions as a core part of its tenets. To promote his *dhamma*, which consisted of about thirty-three edicts, Asoka had them etched in stone tablets, on the side of prominent rocks, and inside cave sanctuaries, all in the vernacular language of his kingdom. He also carved them on the sides of pillars, about twenty of which have survived. One such pillar, in Lauriya Nandangarh (in Bihar), made from a single piece of polished sandstone, rises 12 meters above the ground and extends 3 meters into the earth. Though it is surmounted by an ornate capital, it is the shaft with the inscribed edicts that is of primary significance. The Asokan pillars consist of a stylized lotus base that supports an ornamental drum on which there are sculptures of animals ranging from the bull to the lion signifying royal authority. Most famous is the pillar found at Sarnath, the site of the Buddha's first sermon, the lotus base and drum of which is topped by a capital of four lions. Surmounting all this, at least originally, was the Buddhist wheel of law, which has, in turn, been adopted as the symbol of the modern Indian nation.

To further promote the Buddhist order, Asoka convened a council of all significant Buddhist practitioners, whose mission it was to codify the Buddha's teachings. Asoka also memorialized the major sites associated with the Buddha—in particular his birthplace (Lumbini), the site of his enlightenment (Bodh Gaya), the location of his first sermon (Sarnath), and the place of his death (Kushinagar). He sent emissaries throughout the empire and abroad, including to Sri Lanka, Afghanistan, Persia, and Greece. Most importantly, he collected all the known relics of the Buddha and distributed them to about eight sites, at which the first centers of Buddhist learning were established. The Buddha was never represented as a human figure in Asoka's time. Representations of the Buddha began to be made in the 1st century CE and have become important in the Buddhist tradition ever since. Asoka did build the diamond throne at Bodh Gaya to stand in for the Buddha and to mark the place of his enlightenment.

5.75 Barabar Hills Caves, two of the austere *ajivika* caves

Barabar Hills Caves

Buddhist ascetics were responsible for the oldest rock-cut caves in India, which date to the mid-3rd century BCE. They are located in the Barabar Hills of Bihar, 20 miles north of Bodh Gaya, at a prominent cluster of rock outcroppings in an otherwise flat landscape. There are four caves, consisting of two chambers each: a rectangular hall followed by a round room with a hemispherical ceiling. Inscriptions in three of them note that they were dedicated by Asoka for use by the *ajivikas*. Unadorned, with crisp rectangular openings punched into the rock, they are carved out of the granite with exacting precision and with a highly polished internal surface. One of them, the Lomas Rsi Cave, is incomplete. It was probably abandoned after the interior rock sheared and the roof partially collapsed. This cave has deeply carved openings and a wooden roof outline with a finely etched elephant frieze centered on a stupa. Since this cave has no inscription, it probably dates to Asoka, though its exterior may well have been carved later.

Rock-cut architecture had a long tradition in Egypt, Anatolia, and Patra, so the technique was most likely brought to India through Persia, particularly after Asoka. The word *cave*, which is used to describe these and subsequent such structures, is misleading, since these are constructed structures, and as such a form of architecture. In the centuries to come, this simple beginning was to flower into a tradition of rock-cut buildings that spread throughout South Asia and China.

5.76 Plan, section, and interior: Lomas Rsi Cave

5.77 Entrance, Lomas Rsi Cave

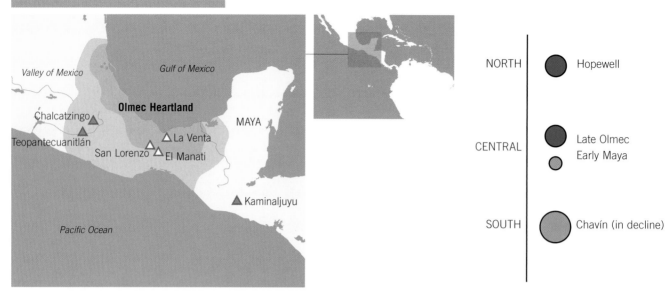

5.78 Mesoamerica, ca. 400 BCE

5.79 Urbanization of the Americas, 400 BCE

Late Olmec Centers

In the central Mexican highlands' Amatzinac Valley, about 65 kilometers southeast of Cuernevaca, lies Chalcatzingo, situated dramatically at the foot of one of three 300-meter-high volcanic cones that were considered sacred by the Aztecs, and probably also by the Olmecs. The area holds remnants of various cultures from 3000 BCE to the present, with the settlement reaching its peak of cultural development between 700 and 500 BCE, during the Middle Formative Period of central Mexico. Olmec traders of ceramics, agricultural goods, and raw materials are thought to have used the settlement as an outpost and trading center. The site consists of platform mounds and terraces, but most notable are a series of

5.80 Bas-relief from Chalcatzingo, Morelos, Mexico

bas-reliefs on several large boulders and on the cliff face, depicting mythical and religious themes associated with agriculture, rain, and fertility. One of the carvings portrays a woman ruler enthroned in a stylized cave with clouds floating out of it.

Like the special reverence reserved for caves as places of origin in Hindu culture and the architecture of South Asia, caves associated with female deities were especially revered in early Olmec culture and remained a force until much later in Mesoamerican civilization. One example of their abiding importance is the extraordinary clover-leaf-shaped volcanic tube cave that lies on axis beneath the base of the Pyramid of the Moon at Teotihuacán. Teopantecuanitlán ("the place of the temple of the jaguar-god"), lies in a remote area of western Mexico, about 160 kilometers south of Cuernevaca, at the confluence of the Amacuzac and Balsas rivers. It had two ball courts, a stone-lined aqueduct, and a large stone pyramid. Though Olmec, it lies far to the west and is indicative of the expanding range of Olmec influence. The site occupies about 90 square kilometers and shows three phases of occupation. In the earliest period (1400–1200 BCE), construction was with clay walls. Between 1200 and 800 BCE, an irrigation system was put in place with fitted stonewalls, aqueducts, and a stone-lined sunken court with drains. Four inverted T-shaped monumental

sculptures bearing Olmec-style zoomorphic representations have also been found from this period. Finally, from the period between 800 and 600 BCE, there are six structures built in a semicircle.

The Early Mayas

With the Olmecs in decline, a new power emerged, but along the Pacific coast in today's Guatemala. Known as the Mayas, they developed in an area where seasonal marshes enabled intensive agriculture. The Mayas had inhabited the area since 1500 BCE, and by 1200 BCE, extensive trade networks were in place. Each village was linked to the next by causeways, which were paved with white stones—thus their Mayan name, *sacbe*, or "white way." The Mayan heartland today is covered with forest. One might assume that, once cleared, it could have sustained a large civilization's enterprises; in actuality, the Mayas succeeded because they were able to manage what is, in fact, a relatively harsh ecological environment. The main problem is that the ground is of limestone, which absorbs rainwater: without artificial water management, crops would therefore be hard to grow at a large scale. Furthermore, where there were swamps, the water was too salty for use, and it rarely rains from January through April. The solution was to elevate the fields, carve out rain-retaining terraces,

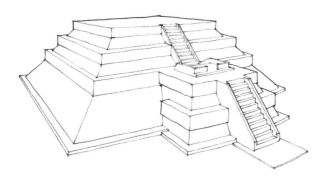

5.81 Reconstruction of an early Kaminaljuyu temple

5.82 Kaminaljuyu Stela 10

and create reservoirs connected by canals. Revamping the landscape allowed the cities to expand, but it also made them more vulnerable in times of war and draught.

The roads formed a network that extended hundreds of kilometers. Cities exchanged salt for maize and obsidian for foodstuff. Oyster shells were prized, and stingray spines, shark teeth, conch shells, and turtle shells were all in demand for rituals. By 1000 BCE, members of the Mayan elite were beginning to live in separate compounds, where they developed a highly esoteric religious philosophy.

Kaminaljuyu, an early Mayan site, is situated just outside Guatemala City. The city, at a strategic location between the Pacific coast and the Mayan lowlands, had a flourishing trade in salt, fish, and shells coming from coast, and in cacao, jaguar skins, feathers, and other commodities, which came from the jungles to the east. The obsidian beds 20 kilometers northwest of the city were a major source of its economic success. The site, which dates back to the pre-Classic period (800 BCE–300 CE), originally consisted of more than one hundred platforms and mounds distributed over an area of 5 square kilometers and organized around plazas that opened off wide avenues. Kaminaljuyu had its largest population and dominated the highlands of Guatemala between 300 BCE and 150 CE. Its people were early practitioners of irrigation

agriculture, using aqueducts to distribute water. Around 400 CE, Kaminaljuyu came under Teotihuacán influence.

The rise and fall of the various cities, kingdoms, and empires in the Americas is a matter of much debate. Regional strife and changing economic realities played a part. So, too, it is likely, did the degradation of the environment as result of deforestation and farming that for a period created surpluses but that over time depleted the soil, producing a weak and vulnerable economy.

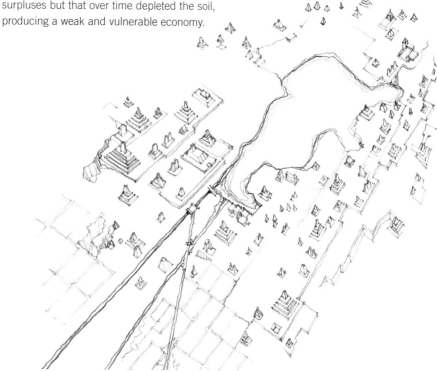

5.83 Site plan: Kaminaljuyu, Guatemala City, Guatemala

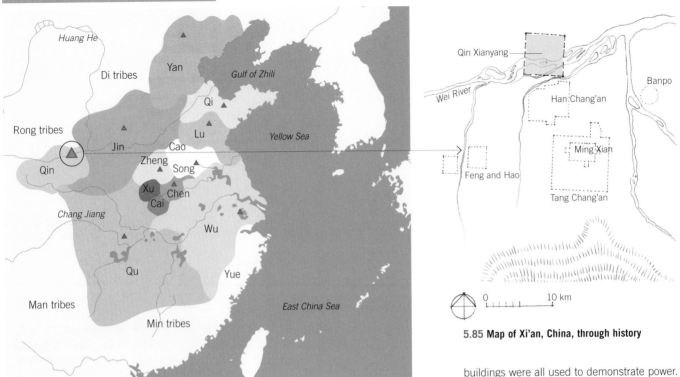

5.84 China during the Warring States period

5.85 Map of Xi'an, China, through history

China: The Warring States Period

In the Warring States period (481–221 BCE), the old league of cities ruled by the Zhou nobility was replaced by a system of territorial states (seven major and about seven minor ones) under the command of monarchs who seemed to have engaged in feverish construction activity. They fortified existing city walls, multiplied enclosures and barricades, and established satellite towns, all primarily for the purpose of defense. Prior to the Warring States period, cities were cultic and political entities inhabited by the nobility and their followers. Populations at most were in the tens of thousands. During the Warring States period, as cities became capitals of states, their nature changed, becoming divided between a political center and an economic center, the two holding each other in mutual suspicion. This suspicion was articulated in laws that attempted to control the actions and influence of merchants. The result was that new and sharp boundaries were drawn within the city between the political district, which was protected with its own wall, and the merchants' district. New architectural elements appeared that, through height and verticality, emphasized the ruler's authority. Towers, pillar gates, and raised buildings were all used to demonstrate power. When Shang Yang began constructing the new Qin capital Xianyang, the first items built were the gate towers.

Stepped terraces—called *tai* platforms—surrounded on all four sides by the wooden columns and beams of the palace, could give the impression of multiple-storied buildings. In an age that lacked the ability to construct true multistoried buildings, this design allowed for structures that seemed to rise above the city. The ruler was both all-seeing and yet invisible. Furthermore, it was believed that the ruler should move in secret to avoid evil spirits and that he should live as much as possible in towers. For this reason, Shi Huangdi, the First Emperor, built elevated walks to connect all 270 of his palaces and towers. Anyone who revealed where the emperor was visiting was put to death. This withdrawal from the gaze of the populace, and even from the court, became an essential attribute of Qin and Han imperial personages. In Rome and India, a ruler's person had to be visible. But in China, his status was derived from being hidden and remote.

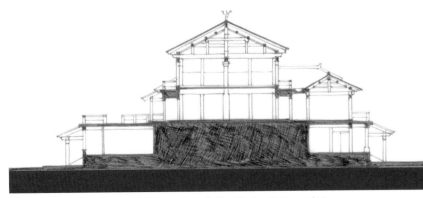

5.86 The monumentality of palace complexes in the Warring States period

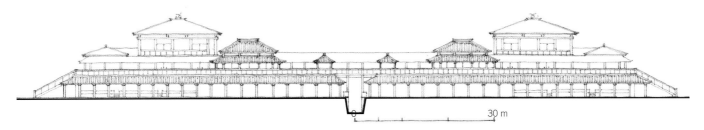

5.87 Elevation: Xianyang Palace No. 1, Xi'an, China

Xianyang Palace

Unlike the enclosed and understated ritual complexes of old, these new palaces projected themselves into space as imposing three-dimensional structures. In general, the higher the *tai*, the more assertive the claim to power by the ruler who had commissioned it. In a time when rulers and states were constantly at war, claiming authority through buildings was critical for a ruler's image. For instance, a Zhou king constructed an imposing platform at the site of his meeting with other lords. History reveals that his guests, struck with awe at the sight of this platform, agreed to join the Zhou alliance.

A dramatic terrace pavilion, the Xianyang Palace No. 1 consisted of a series of rooms and corridors built one on top of another around an earthen core, giving the impression of a multilevel structure of great volume and height. While this structure has been identified with the Xianyang Palace of Qin Shi Huangdi, first emperor of Qin, recent evidence suggests that it was first built during the Warring States period and subsequently integrated into Shi Huangdi's palatial complex. Located north of the Wei River, the palace's foundations are 60 meters long east to west, 45 meters wide, and about 6 meters high. The reconstruction suggests that

the palace superstructure was symmetrical, having had two wings. The earthen core was surrounded by bays on all sides, creating the image of a three-story building of immense size. A drainage system guided water into underground pipes. The chambers were connected by intricate passages, and balconies were decorated with elaborate bronze accessories and colorful murals.

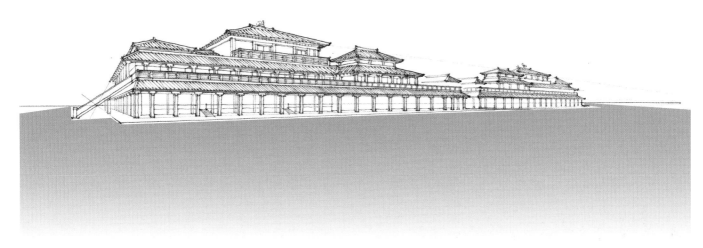

5.88 Pictorial view: Xianyang Palace No. 1

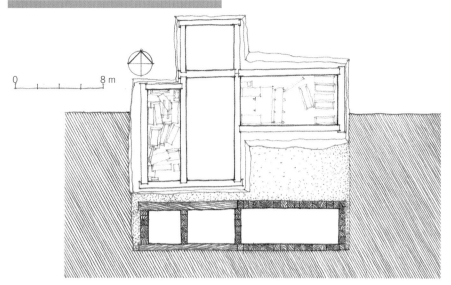

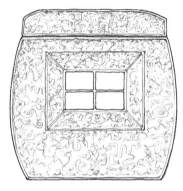

5.89 Plan and section: Tomb of Zeng Hou Yi, Sui Zhou, China

5.90 Coffins with windowlike and doorlike openings found in the Tomb of Zeng Hou Yi

Tomb of Zeng Hou Yi

The architecture of tombs and graveyards became increasingly important at this time. Texts compiled during this period distinguish between rituals performed within the city in ancestral temples and others performed outside the city at graveyards. The most visible remnants of Zhou architecture are, in fact, tombs, of which more than six thousand have been discovered. The tomb of Zeng Hou Yi (Marquis Yi of Zeng) attracted international attention when a large collection of bronze objects was found there, including a set of sixty-five bells weighing a total of 2,500 kilograms. The tomb consisted of an irregularly shaped vertical pit, 13 meters deep and more than 200 square meters in area. It was divided into four chambers by wooden planks, with the principal chamber, on the east, containing the marquis' body. The body was placed in a coffin that, in turn, was encased in another. The space between the outer coffin and the chamber walls was filled with charcoal, clay, and earth to seal it as completely as possible. The eastern chamber also had coffins for eight women—possibly musicians who were sacrificed at the time of the burial (although human sacrificial internment was almost over by this time in Chinese history). The western chamber held skeletons of thirteen young women, who may have been the ruler's concubines. The remaining two chambers were filled with ritual objects and weapons made of bronze, gold, copper, lacquer, wood, jade, and other materials.

A curious aspect of this tomb is that small windowlike openings connect all four chambers. Even the marquis' outer coffin bears a rectangular hole, and his inner coffin is painted with doors and windows with lattice patterns. Similar openings have been found in other Zhou tombs. According to Chinese Daoism, when a person dies, his *hun* (the spiritual soul) would leave, but his *p'o* (the earthly soul) would remain attached to his body. The series of doorways in this tomb might be there to facilitate the movement of the *p'o* in its underground "palace."

5.91 Bianzhong bells found in the Tomb of Zeng Hou Yi, along with a 125-piece orchestra and 25 musicians

0 = 4239: Egyptian calendar
3763: Jewish calendar
756: Roman calendar
752: Babylonian calendar
547: Buddhist calendar
1 of the Yuanshi era of the Han dynasty
The Chinese calendar begins afresh with
each dynasty.
1 Anno Domini of the Christian calendar

The following equivalents may vary a bit since New Year's Day falls on different days in these calendars.

Though today the Gregorian calendar, established in 1582, is widely used around the globe, notions of time were once just as diverse as culture itself. The Egyptians, who were the first to shift from a lunar to a solar calendar, were also the first to understand that a year was 365.2 days long. But this awareness was lost by the end of the Roman era. The Romans were not particularly nuanced timekeepers, and not only created months like July and August (to commemorate Julius Caesar and his successor, Augustus) for political reasons, but gave them both thirty-one days to demonstrate the rulers' importance as well. The Chinese counted their years not consecutively, but with each new dynasty. Though the Anno Domini ("the year of our Lord") dating system (often abbreviated AD) was adapted from the Julian calendar established by Julius Caesar in 44 BCE, it was not until the 8th century that western Europe began to adopt it. The concept of BC—"before Christ"—was a 9th-century development. Today that idea is usually expressed (as it is in this book) as BCE— "before the Common Era."

There is, of course, no year zero in the Gregorian calendar. The oldest known use of a decimal place-value system that included a zero dates from 458 CE in India. From there it spread via Arab mathematics to arrive in the West in the 13th century.

At this time, Eurasia was dominated by China and Rome, interconnected by a vast system of land and sea trade routes known in their entirety as the Silk Route. As a consequence of these far-flung trade systems, two cultures came to the fore: the Gandharans in Afghanistan and the Nabataeans in Jordan. The latter served as the connecting link to India, allowing the Roman traders to avoid Parthia.

The Nabataeans were remarkable for their spirit of innovation regarding architecture. Initially, the economic ascendancy of Rome cast a pall over West Asia, and very little of consequence was built during the 1st century BCE. But soon Rome was able to impose a cohesive appearance over its expanding domains. Roman emperors from Augustus to Trajan changed the architectural face of the European and West Asian world, building impressive temples, forums, villas, and cities, all with the typical Roman imprint. In China, the Qin dynasty, systematically annexing all competing states, created a centralized government with a corresponding bureaucracy. For this achievement the Qin emperor, Shi Huangdi is known as the First Emperor. It is, in fact, from the word *qin* (or *ch'in*) that the name *China* derives.

After Shi Huangdi's death, the dynasty quickly collapsed and was replaced by the Han dynasty (202 BCE–220 CE), which was marked by a long period of peace; it is traditionally referred to as China's imperial age. Although more transparent and accountable, the Han maintained the Qin's ambition for a unified and centralized empire. Han architecture established precedents

that were followed by subsequent dynasties. Little remains of the actual palaces, cities, and monumental stone sculptures, but clay models and literary references contain vivid descriptions, as, for example, those of the "spirit roads" of the 1st century CE, with their stone monuments that line the approach to imperial tombs. In Central Asia, because of the disintegration of the Mauryan Empire in India around 200 BCE, the nomadic Yueh-chi from Mongolia established the Kushan Empire (1st century BCE–3rd century CE) that stretched from parts of Afghanistan and Iran to Pataliputra in the central Gangetic Plains in the east and down to Sanchi in the south. Due to its unique location, this empire became a melting pot for people and ideas from India, Persia, China, and even the Roman Empire.

In the Americas, the Hopewell Culture became the first large-scale culture in North America, spreading a web of cities and villages along the Ohio River. In Mexico, Teotihuacán in the Valley of Mexico and Monte Albán in the Valley of Oaxaca had rapidly risen to power. A network of villages in the Yucatán Peninsula had also begun to develop into the distinctive Mayan culture that would dominate Central America in the coming millennium. On the Mexican Pacific coast, in the area around central Jalisco, shaft tombs reveal a new culture of death. Built into the heart of settlements, these tombs integrated the dead into the daily life and activities of the community. In Peru, the Chavín were in decline, with the pieces redefining themselves under the Moche and Nazca.

0

Roman Republic
509–27 BCE

◀ **Pompeii**
From 6th century BCE

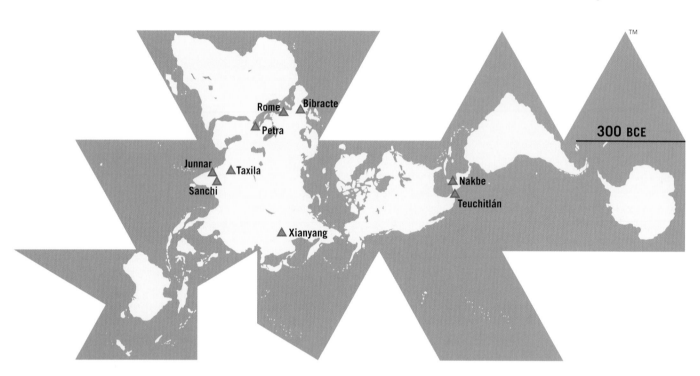

300 BCE

Eastern Zhou Dynasty
771–256 BCE

Qin Dynasty
221–206 BCE

◀ **Xianyang Palace**
4th to 3rd centuries BCE

▲ **Nakbe**
350 BCE–250 CE

Roman Empire
27 BCE–393 CE

▲ **Temple of Zeus Olympia**
Begun 170 BCE

▲ **Colosseum**
72–80 CE

▲ **Pantheon**
126 CE

▲ **Imperial Forums**
48 BCE–112 CE

▲ **Domus Aurea**
ca. 65 CE

▲ **Pergamon**
From 3rd century BCE

▲ **Temple of Fortuna at Praeneste**
40 BCE

▲ **Palace of Domitian**
92 CE

▲ **Bibracte**
ca. 1000–30 BCE

▲ **Petra Rock-Cut Tombs**
312 BCE–106 CE

200 BCE	**0**	**200 CE**

4239: Egyptian calendar
3763: Jewish calendar
756: Roman calendar
752: Babylonian calendar
547: Buddhist calendar
1 of the Yuanshi era of the Han Dynasty: Chinese calendar

▲ **Taxila**
150 BCE–100 CE

Mauryan Empire
ca. 323–185 BCE

Kushan Empire
2nd century BCE to 3rd century CE

▲ **Stupa Complex at Sanchi**
ca. 100 BCE

▲ **Rock-Cut Caves at Junnar**
100–25 BCE

Wang Mang Interregnum
9–25 CE

Western Han Dynasty
206 BCE–9 CE

Eastern Han Dynasty
25–220 CE

▲ **First Emperor's Tomb**
246–210 BCE

▲ **Mingtang-Biyong Ritual Complex**
ca. 1st century BCE–1st century CE

Teuchitlán Tradition
ca. 300 BCE–900 CE

▲ **El Openo**
300 BCE–200 CE

Pre-Classic Mayan Culture
ca. 1000 BCE–250 CE

▲ **El Mirador**
150 BCE–150 CE

0

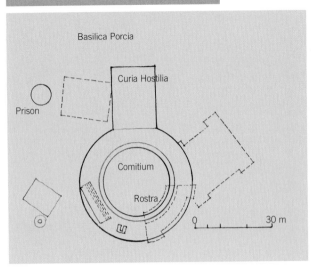

6.1 Plan: Forum Romanum, Rome

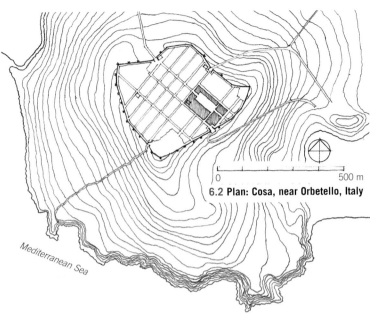

6.2 Plan: Cosa, near Orbetello, Italy

The Founding of Rome

The founding of Rome remains shrouded in myth. From Plutarch, Virgil, Titus Livius (Livy), and other Roman authors, there emerge colorful tales that ascribe the founding to Aeneas's descendant Romulus. Aeneas, after fleeing the burning Troy and various adventurous voyages, arrived on the Latin shores, where he founded a dynasty with Livia, daughter of Latinus. From them sprang, generations later, the twins Romulus and Remus, with Romulus eventually founding Rome, an event that is said to have occurred around 750 BCE. The judgment of modern scholars is that the tales constitute

a summary of folk memories enhanced by wishful thinking. Nonetheless, archaeological evidence has not yet been able to undermine this general narrative. Around the 4th century BCE, Rome became conquest-oriented, and one by one, the neighboring cities and tribes were brought under its control. When the Greek city of Tarentum in southern Italy (Apulia) fell in 272 BCE, Rome enslaved all its citizens. The fall of Syracuse in Sicily followed in 212 BCE. The sack of the Greek city of Corinth in 146 BCE brought Greece itself under Roman control, and with the conquest of Carthage on the north coast of

Africa, Rome assumed uncontested control over the Mediterranean basin. The religious life of the Romans centered around the Temple of Saturn (498 BCE) and the Temple of Concord (367 BCE) on the Capitoline Hill. Little is known about these temples, but they were most probably Etruscan in style.

The civic heart was the Comitium (whence comes the word *committee*), a meeting place located on the forum just below the Capitoline Hill. It had a speaker's platform, the rostra, named after the ships' prows that were hung there following the Battle of Antium in 338 BCE. It was a shallow circular amphitheater in front of the council chamber, or curia. Though not a building, it was nonetheless a *templum*, or sacred space laid out on a north-south axis. To maintain control over its far-flung territories, Rome built garrisons, fortifications, and even cities, like Cosa, which was laid out in 273 BCE. It occupies a high, rocky site on the coast of Etruria, 100 kilometers north of Rome. It was connected to its harbor below by a road leading down a sharp incline. Roughly trapezoidal in plan, at its highest point the city contained a long rectangular forum in its northeastern corner. The forum was an enclosed outdoor space, accessed by gates and containing the religious, mercantile, and governmental institutions. The Comitium, with its circular steps and a curia behind it, on the model or Rome, was on the longer northeastern side of the forum. Near it was a basilica, built in 150 BCE, and used as a law court.

6.3 Map of Rome, ca. 4th century BCE

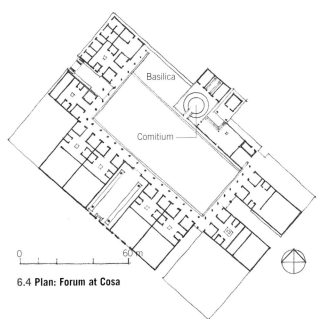

6.4 Plan: Forum at Cosa

6.5 Basilica of Pompeii, Italy

Pompeii

New Roman cities initially fell into two categories: a Roman colony and a Latin colony. Roman colonies, like Ostia (350 BCE), Rimini (268 BCE), and Cosa, were often built near the sea in order to guarantee access to ports. The citizens of these colonies had the full rights of Roman citizen as well as a senate of their own. Latin colonies were military strongholds near enemy territory. Their inhabitants did not have Roman citizenship. Later, colonies were founded for veterans—an example is Pompeii, which was resettled with veterans in 80 BCE. As a result, it was rebuilt to make it conform to Roman expectations. The history of Pompeii before the Roman takeover in 80 BCE is obscure. It was probably founded in the 7th or 6th century BCE by central Italian tribes and subsequently came under Greek control. Thus, long before the Roman period, it was an old and flourishing town. The Romans transformed it into a bustling port and resort until its life was snuffed out by an eruption of Mt. Vesuvius in 79 CE. Beginning in 80 BCE, the Romans began to rebuild its forum. At the narrow southern end were the municipal offices, including the senate house, and to the east, around the corner, a squarish, unroofed building with its own *temenos*, used as a law court. Built around 100 BCE, it was unroofed, so as not to violate the ancient Greek rule that trials be held in the open air. In the center of the forum, the Romans added the Temple of Jupiter (80 BCE), rising high on a podium, with two equestrian

statues flanking the steps and the altar in front. Seen from the southern end of the forum, it closes the sweep of the open space, drawing in Mt. Vesuvius, which rises behind it. The Romans also reworked the eastern flank of the forum, adding a vegetable market and shops (*macellum*), and a sanctuary to the city's *lares* (guardian deities). Next to it one finds the small Temple of

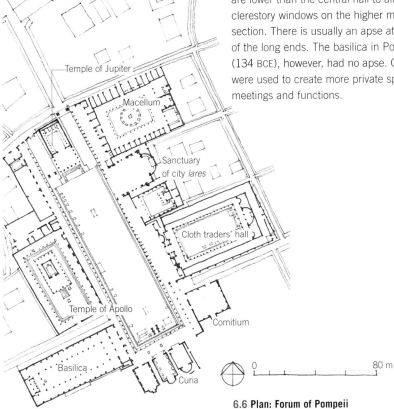

6.6 Plan: Forum of Pompeii

Genius Augusti, flanking the Porticus Eumachiae. Tying everything together was a two-story colonnaded portico. One of the essential aspects of Roman civic architecture is the basilica. This building type appeared in Rome— apparently full-fledged—with the basilica on the forum (184 BCE). A basilica generally consists of a wide elongated hall with two or four side aisles separated from the main hall by columns. These side aisles are lower than the central hall to allow for clerestory windows on the higher middle section. There is usually an apse at one of the long ends. The basilica in Pompeii (134 BCE), however, had no apse. Curtains were used to create more private spaces for meetings and functions.

0

6.7 Sites of Roman cities and colonies

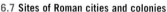

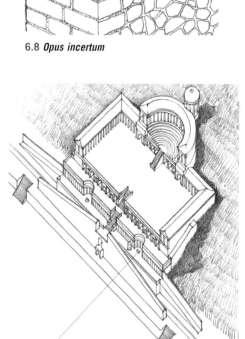

6.8 *Opus incertum*

Temple of Fortuna at Praeneste

The town of Praeneste (Palestrina), which has existed since the 8th or 7th century BCE, owes its reputation to its strategic, defensible position on a spur of the Apennines some 35 kilometers east of Rome. The temple built there was dedicated to the goddess Fortuna Primigenia. Her oracular answers were read by a gifted boy who randomly chose from among oak sticks inscribed with oracular pronouncements. One of the reasons for the longevity of the building—and of subsequent examples of Roman architecture—was the use of concrete. Though concrete had been known to Romans since 190 BCE, it was not able to support great weight. During the period of Praeneste's construction a new form of cement came into use. Pozzolana was made from a volcanic ash from the Vesuvius area—especially from the city of Pozzuoli, from which it took its name. Roman architects might not have understood the chemistry causing the bonding of concrete, but they were well aware of its exceptional properties—especially of its ability to set underwater, which facilitated the design of ports and harbors. Though the famous Roman architectural theorist Vitruvius was still highly suspicious of the material when he wrote his treatise in 40 BCE, the architects of the Temple of Fortuna Primigenia showed no lack of confidence. The temple's symmetrical arrangement, inspired by Hellenistic design notions, rose up the side of a hill 60 meters from the bottom. The uppermost terrace was crowned by a double L–shaped Corinthian colonnade that framed a semicircular theater, which was itself surmounted by a colonnade. Behind this, on the central

6.9 Pictorial view: Temple of Fortuna at Praeneste

6.10 Section of hemicycle: Temple of Fortuna at Praeneste

0   20 m

axis, stood a small round temple, or *tholos*, cut partially out of the rock, indicative of a particularly sacred site. The upper terrace and the theater were used for festivals, dances, and rituals. Except for the columns and other architectural elements, the structure, including the support vaults, was built entirely of concrete. Exploiting the potential of the new material, several kinds of vaults were used, including ramping and annular forms. That the facade of the upper level rested on a vault, rather than on the wall beneath it, would have been unthinkable in the days before concrete.

156 ■ Europe

The Roman Urban Villa

Until the 2nd century BCE, Roman houses followed the old Mediterranean plan, with rooms grouped around a tall, dark atrium. Eventually, however, with increased prosperity, private houses became ever more luxurious. Colonnaded gardens, inspired by Egyptian architecture, were added behind the house. Exedrae and libraries were installed, as well as fountains, summer dining rooms (some upstairs to allow views), and even private baths. Windows became bigger, and walls were ornamented with illusionistic pictures. In Pompeii, some families bought out their neighbors to increase their living space and create a grand house. Compare this with Sirkap, in present-day Pakistan, founded by the Greeks in around 190 BCE; while there is a similarly dense fabric of houses, there is little differentiation in their scale. But in Pompeii, after the abovementioned consolidation had taken place, a single villa could be as large as an entire city block in Sirkap. The owners of these houses, based on Etruscan traditions, placed great value on the social importance of feasting. Meals were elaborate affairs prepared by professional cooks and served on silver plates, with occasional bouts of drinking. In 182 BCE, the senate passed a law regulating the size of parties, but this did little to stem the tide. Villas grew to enormous size and can be found in the Campagna, or by the coast.

6.11 Residential fabric of Pompeii

Villas were embellished with dining pavilions, towers, colonnades, fish ponds, and formal parks. During this time, wealthy Romans began sending their sons to Greece to learn rhetoric, leading to careers in law or politics. Also admired was Greek art and architecture, although there was less interest in Greek literature, music, and science. Sundials were brought from Greek cities in Sicily, but it took Romans a hundred years to learn that, having moved the sundials northward, they had to adjust their markings for the change in latitude.

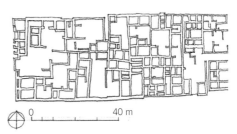

6.12 Plan: Portion of the Taxilan city Sirkap, Pakistan, at the same scale as Pompeii, for comparison

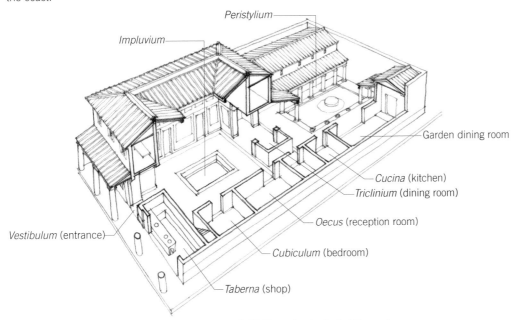

6.13 Elements of a typical Roman house

6.14 Tomb of Marcus Vergilius Eurysaces, Rome

6.15 Monument of the Julii, St.-Rémy, France

Republican Tombs

The rise of an affluent merchant class combined with Hellenistic emotionalism led to the emergence of a funerary architecture that became an autonomous form of architectural expression. Although tomb design can easily be dismissed as a minor architectural typology, it played a key role in offering a field of experimentation in which architects could work out, in miniature certain architectural problems or themes. The tomb of Marcus Vergilius Eurysaces (30 BCE) is a case in point. A wealthy Roman baker, he asked the architect to design something on the theme of a *panarium* (a tube for storing bread). The exterior is decorated with rows of these tubes—carved in stone—that are framed by pilasters at the corners. The top has been lost, but it was most likely a pyramid. Grave monuments of the leading class were, of course, more monumental and dignified, conforming to the deceased person's status in life. The Monument of the Julii in St.-Rémy, France, for example, is sedate and consists of three superimposed zones: a socle, or foundation zone; a four-sided arch; and a delicate round tempietto on top.

6.16 Tomb of Absolom, Jerusalem

The so-called Tomb of Absolom in Jerusalem, 20 meters high, is a mixed construction. The lower part is carved out of the bedrock, while the remainder is constructed of ashlar. In the lower part, a socle supports a cubic-shaped box, the faces of which are decorated with half-columns. Though the bases are Ionic, the entablature is Doric. On the box there rests a plain and unornamented attic element that in turn is the base for the drum; the roof is in the shape of a tent. Though traditionally considered to be the tomb of King David's son Absolom, who lived in the 10th century BCE, this cannot be accurate. Most scholars date it to the 1st century CE.

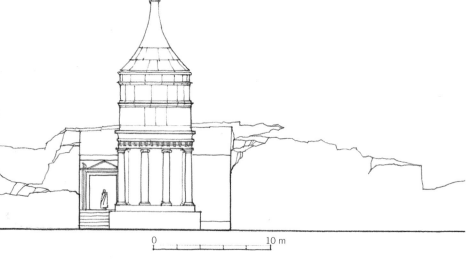

0   10 m

6.17 Tomb of Absolom, Jerusalem

6.18 Kbour-er-Roumia ("tomb of the Christian woman"), Algiers

Tholoi Tombs

In Algiers, in northern Africa, one finds several tumulus tombs that obviously harken to ancient traditions. Particularly impressive is the Kbour-er-Roumia ("tomb of a Christian woman," 19 BCE), located in Algiers, west of Tipsa. It has a diameter of 60 meters and rests on a low square base. A three-stepped *crepis*, or foundation, supports a ring of sixty slender Ionic half-columns that decorate a drum, from which rises a stepped conical hill terminating in a circular platform 32 meters above the ground. The top was ornamented by a sculptural element that has since disappeared. A spiral corridor gave access to the tomb's interior. Though such a tomb might strike one as alien and not in tune with classical sensibilities, the type actually served as model for the mausoleum of Augustus in Rome, which Augustus had built in 28 BCE shortly after his victory at Actium. This imposing structure, though badly ravished by time, has a tall circular base 87 meters in diameter that was covered with travertine. Flanking the entrance were two obelisks taken from Egypt, as well as bronze tablets summarizing the emperor's achievements. On top of the base there was a tumulus planted with cypress trees, at the top of which stood a cylindrical structure. The building was thus a blend of architecture and landscape, of building and mountain. In 410 CE, during the sack of Rome by Alaric's Goths, the golden urns, containing the ashes of Augustus and his family members and deposited in niches in the inner sanctum, were emptied of their contents and plundered.

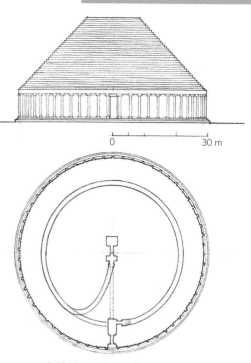

6.19 Plan and elevation: Kbour-er-Roumia

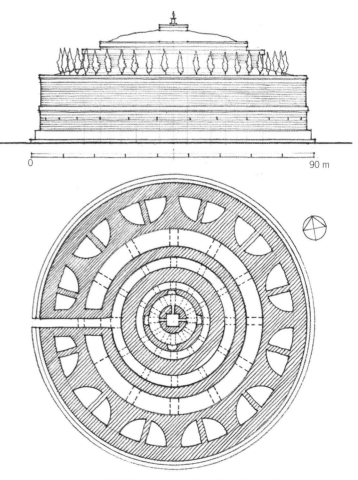

6.20 Plan and elevation: Mausoleum of Augustus, Rome

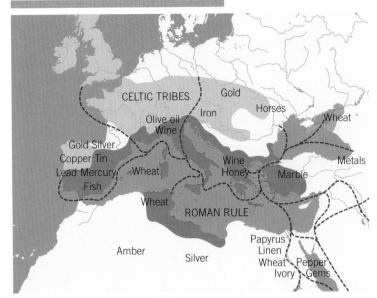

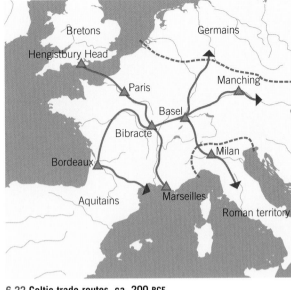

6.21 Leading trade products, ca. 200 BCE

6.22 Celtic trade routes, ca. 200 BCE

Bibracte

Originating from areas to the north and west of the Black Sea, the Celts began to spread westward across Europe around 1000 BCE and soon dominated the area from Switzerland and northern Italy to France and southern England. As a clan-oriented society interconnected by trade, the Celts were suited to the complex and disparate landscapes of the region. They were also excellent agriculturalists, organized around networks of small settlements and farms. Large cities developed during the 1st century BCE. These included, from east to west, some cities that are still inhabited, such as Kelheim in Germany, Bern in Switzerland, and Reims and Paris in France. Most others have long since disappeared back into the landscape, such as Hengistbury Head on the cliffs of the southern coast of England and Manching Oppidum in Bavaria. These cities, the first efforts at urbanization in Europe, were located on flat-topped hills or along ridges that could be easily defended by the addition of earthen berms.

In the cities of Gaul, there was a shift from a largely agricultural and self-sustaining local economy to one based on regional and transregional trade and industrial specialization, such as metal and cloth making. The principal trading partner was, of course, Rome to the south. Most maps of Europe show only the Roman Empire, but viewing the Roman and the Celtic areas together provides a sense of the scale of Celtic territories. Celtic metalworking was facilitated by the presence of extensive forests, even though archaeologists believe that good parts of southern England, as well as locations elsewhere, became deforested as a result of these activities. The Celts also exported salt, tin, and amber. The principal import from the Greek and Roman territories was wine, transported northward with great difficulty in large amphorae. The Celts had a polytheistic and animistic religion, with shrines situated on hilltops, in groves, and on lakes. They worshipped both gods and goddesses, many associated with natural features like springs and mountains. Gods also possessed particular skills, like blacksmithing, healing, and warfare. Some gods were local to a particular area; others were shared. Priests were not only religious officials but also judges and calendar keepers, as well as guardians of the communal memory.

Though life in these Celtic areas was hardly static, with raids, expansions, and contractions occurring in many places over the course of time, by the 1st century BCE, the situation had become increasingly unstable. A set of tribes from Germany and Denmark began to move southward into areas held by the Helvetii. The Helvetii themselves also were on the move westward, for unknown reasons; to the south, the Romans had begun to chip away at Celtic territory, taking Milan and Marseilles. In 51 BCE, the Romans took Bibracte, one of the largest of the Gaulic cities, and by 79 CE, most of Gaulic territory had been incorporated into the Roman Empire. Bibracte stood halfway on the trade route between Marseilles and Paris to the north and, across the English Channel, to Hengistbury Head. Bibracte was also the jumping-off point eastward to Germany. The original name of the city was probably Éduens, the name of the regional tribe.

At over a square kilometer in size and straddling the ridge of one of the tallest mountains in the area, it was the same size as Rome, though considerably less dense—it contained space for farm animals and the houses were rarely more than one or two stories high. The city had a population of several thousand, but there were numerous smaller satellite villages. Despite being at the top of a mountain, several artesian springs fed the city with water year-round. The city also served as a refuge for the local villagers in times of warfare, which might explain the construction of the second fortification ring in the 1st century BCE, about a hundred years after the construction of the first ring. These rings, which are log-reinforced earthen berms some 5 kilometer in length, were not insignificant engineering feats. They required twenty thousand logs as well as tons of earth

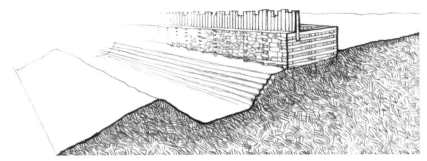

6.23 Section through fortification wall of Bibracte

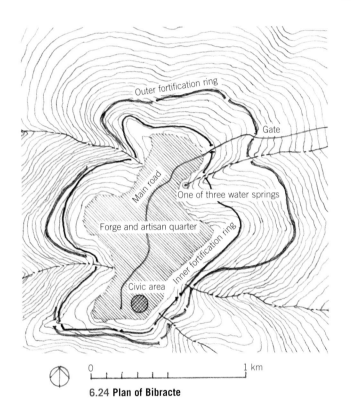

6.24 Plan of Bibracte

and rocks to be packed together to form artificial ridges. A wide road led through a gate to the center of the city, where the civic buildings were placed including, at the city's peak, an open platform that served communal purposes. The houses were all of wood, though later houses, built by the Romans, were sometimes built of stone and stucco. The city has been only partially excavated, but a forge and its associated artisan quarter have been revealed along its main road.

In his *Roman History*, Cassius Dio wrote, "Caractacus, a barbarian chieftain who was captured and brought to Rome and later pardoned by Claudius, wandered about the city after his liberation and after beholding its splendor and magnitude he exclaimed: and can you then who have got such possessions and so many of them, still covet our poor huts?" But it was not the huts that the Romans coveted—rather, it was Gaul's extensive agricultural and mining network. At first the Romans were occupiers, but by the 1st century CE, the two cultures were highly interwoven. The Romans, however, preferred to build their cities in plains, as they were more conducive to the movement of their armies. For that reason, many of the Celtic cities died out and disappeared. Bibracte was typical in that respect. It was eventually abandoned, with the nearby Roman town Augustodunum, today's Autun, taking its place as the regional center.

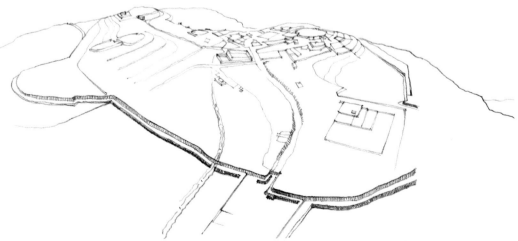

6.25 Pictorial view of Bibracte

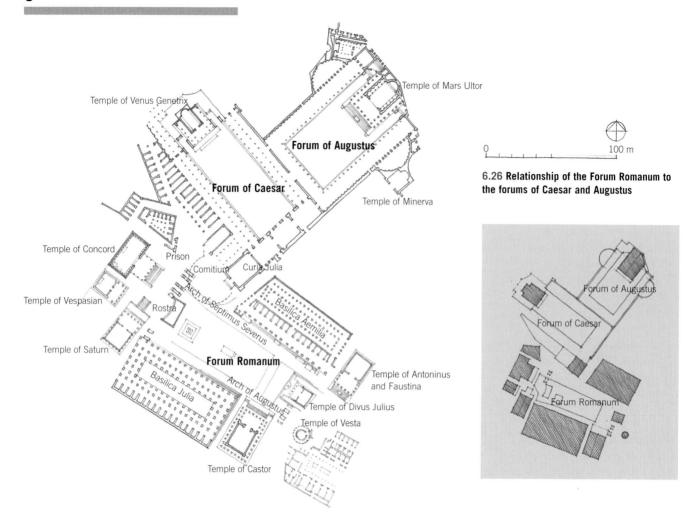

6.26 Relationship of the Forum Romanum to the forums of Caesar and Augustus

Augustan Rome

The shift from republic to empire coincided with the trend of deifying rulers. Caesar was the first to experience such an apotheosis; after that, it became common practice for emperors to be equated with divinity. Emperor Augustus, who followed Caesar, changed Rome. It is said that he found Rome a city of brick, but that when he died, he left it a city of marble. This is not far from the truth, for in the forty years of his reign, Augustus practically rebuilt the entire city, and more than anything, he remodeled the Roman forum.

To understand the magnitude of these efforts, we have to remember that before Augustus's long tenure (27 BCE–14 CE), Rome was an unattractive and even unsafe city. It had a population of one million; crime, corruption, speculation, and mismanagement caused the temples to be neglected and the public structures to crumble. Many parts of the city were slums. Fires broke out continuously—in 16, 14, 12, and 7 BCE—while floods ravaged low-lying areas. Among Augustus's efforts was an attempt to bring order to the core of the city. After a major storm, he asked for a study of roof tiles. He also created a new water system, restored eighty-two temples, increased spending on public building and street repairs, and even established a fire brigade of six hundred slaves.

One of his first efforts was to complete the Forum of Caesar, which was left unfinished at the latter's assassination in 44 BCE. Rectangular in shape, it was similar in scale to the old forum but enlarged to the north and connected to it by a portal. The Temple of Caesar, built in white marble, sat on a high podium at the narrow end of the forum. The building had columns on three sides, making it appear that the *pteron* and the *cella* had been snapped into each other. The fundamental idea of the composition was once again Hellenistic, but its simplicity and orderliness established it up as a prototype. The new forum, encroaching on the old Comitium, had to be moved further to the south. The senate house, where Caesar was murdered, was rebuilt so that it fit neatly along the new forum's perimeter, at the southern corner.

Another of Augustus's building projects was the Basilica Julia, which served as a courthouse for the 180 members who sat in four panels and dealt with wills and inheritance matters. The building is 101 meters long and 49 meters wide, with its long side defining the edge of the forum. August also rebuilt the Basilica Aemilia, which had been restored by Caesar. It had a sixteen-bay, two-story facade, richly articulated with columns and marbles, and was considered one of the most beautiful buildings in Rome.

Forum of Augustus

Apart from the efforts in the old forum, Augustus decided to lay out a brand new forum (10–2 BCE), which was located to the east of the Forum of Caesar and along the city wall to the west. Since it was in a thickly settled area, houses had to be purchased and cleared away. One entered the forum from the south side, on axis with the temple, which was placed at the far end of the forum. It seems Augustus was not able to purchase all the land he needed, even though the area behind the forum was one of the poorer sections of town. A large wall was erected behind the building, to serve both as a firewall and to shield against the squalor on the other side. To resolve the irregularity of the site, the architect added porticoes to conceal back entrances to the right and left of the temple.

The northern portico ends in a square room that contained a colossal statue of Augustus. The temple was dedicated to Mars the Avenger (Mars Ultor) in accordance with a vow made by Augustus before the Battle of Philippi (42 BCE) in which Brutus and Cassius, the assassins of Julius Caesar, were killed. There are eight Corinthian columns in front and along the flanks. The plan is nearly square, measuring 38 by 40 meters. Omitting two rows of columns created space for a generous entrance. Inside the

6.27 **Temple of Mars Ultor, Forum of Augustus, Rome**

temple, in the apse, elevated five steps above the floor, were statues of Mars, Venus, and the deified Julius Caesar. Forming a cross-axis are two large exedrae. Their purpose was to hold statues that tell the narrative of Romulus and Aeneas, the great men of Rome's founding. The Augustan Empire was depicted as the culmination of this history, with Augustus himself presiding over this portrait gallery in the form of a bronze statue on a pedestal in the middle of the forum. Apart from the religious ceremonies that took place here, the forum became the starting point for magistrates departing for the provinces and the repository of the triumphal banners. It was also the place for senate meetings when reports of military successes were expected.

6.28 **View eastward into the Forum Romanum**

Vitruvius

The Augustan Age was a boon for architects, leading Marcus Vitruvius Pollio (ca. 70–25 BCE) to compose a treatise entitled *De architectura* ("On architecture"), known today as the *Ten Books on Architecture*. Though the book contains a vast amount of useful information on construction materials, choice of site, and even the education of an architect, Vitruvius was generally critical of the architectural developments of his age. He was hesitant to accept concrete and felt that many of the new buildings commissioned by Augustus were built without guiding principles. In attempting to reestablish these principles, he argued that the three orders—Doric, Ionic, and Corinthian—should be governed by proportions unique to each. Vitruvius also differentiated between *firmitas*, *utilitas*, and *venustas* ("durability," "usefulness," and "beauty"). Each building, he argued, needed to be designed with these criteria in mind. A warehouse, for example, should be built with usefulness in mind, but not be unpleasant to look at, whereas a palace should be built with beauty in mind, but nonetheless designed for the ages.

The impact of Vitruvius on Roman architecture was minimal, but when a copy of his treatise was rediscovered in 1414 in the monastic library of St. Gall in Switzerland, it became the foundation of architectural theory in Europe for the next three centuries.

What follows are some quotes from chapter 2, book 1 of Vitruvius's *Ten Books on Architecture*:

"Architecture depends on fitness (*ordinatio*) and arrangement (*dispositio*); it also depends on proportion, uniformity, consistency, and economy."

"Arrangement is the disposition in their just and proper places of all the parts of the building, and the pleasing effect of the same; keeping in view its appropriate character."

"Proportion is that agreeable harmony between the several parts of a building, which is the result of a just and regular agreement of them with each other; the height to the width, this to the length, and each of these to the whole."

6.29 Corinthian capital: Temple of Athena, Tegea

6.30 Corinthian capital: Temple of Castor

Corinthian Capitals

Among the major orders, the Corinthian capital was a latecomer. Its first appearance in architecture, so it is now thought, was at the Temple of Apollo at Bassae (420–400 BCE), where Corinthian columns stand framed at the end of the *cella*. They appear for the first time on the exterior at the Temple of Zeus at Olympia (begun 170 BCE), a huge Hellenistic-era temple in Athens. The use of Corinthian columns remained intermittent until the age of Augustus, at which time they became synonymous with the young empire. The conceptual origins of the Corinthian capital are obscure. Vitruvius tells the story of a Corinthian girl who died. Her nurse put various pots and cups into a basket and placed it on her tomb. The following spring, an acanthus root that had been under the tomb began to send sprouts through the

basket. The architect Callimachus happened to pass by and decided to model a capital on the arrangement. There is no way of knowing if this is accurate, but the themes of purity and death were certainly important attributes of the column, and the acanthus had long been associated with immortality. Unlike the Doric and Ionic, which could be transformed only in subtle ways, the Corinthian capital tolerated numerous variations that are usually described by the number of rings of acanthus leaves (typically two). From behind these rise the stalks, usually springing in pairs at the corners and curving into volutes (literally "turns") under the abacus.

At the center of the abacus, one often finds a blossom. The Corinthian capital of the Temple of Athena in Tegea (350 BCE) is shorter and has stalks with greater definition than Augustan-era Corinthians (as at the Temple of Castor, from 6 CE), which emphasize the leaves. Sometimes an Ionic capital is added to the Corinthian to make what is known as a composite capital. At the Temple of Apollo at Didyma, the architect added a palmette between the stalks.

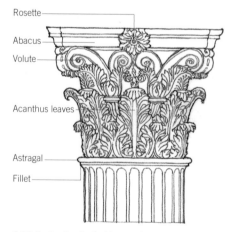

Rosette
Abacus
Volute
Acanthus leaves
Astragal
Fillet

6.31 Parts of a Corinthian capital

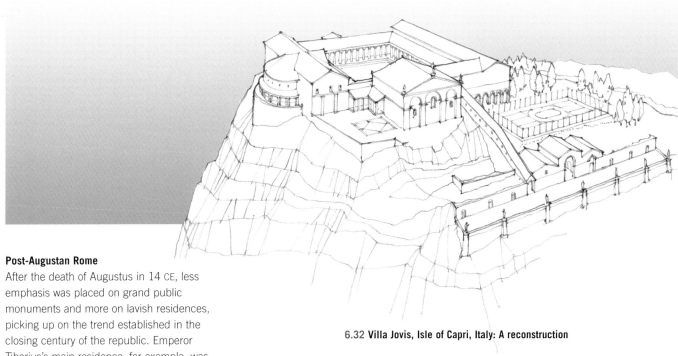

6.32 Villa Jovis, Isle of Capri, Italy: A reconstruction

Post-Augustan Rome

After the death of Augustus in 14 CE, less emphasis was placed on grand public monuments and more on lavish residences, picking up on the trend established in the closing century of the republic. Emperor Tiberius's main residence, for example, was the Villa Jovis ("Villa of Jupiter") on Capri, perched on top of a sheer cliff at one end of the island. It was built around 30 CE on an enormous vaulted concrete undercroft that served as a cistern, the only source of water for the villa. A semicircular hall and dining pavilion looked eastward, directly over the cliff's edge. A loggia was to the north of the courtyard, the baths to the south, and the service rooms and a kitchen were in the wing to the west. It was from this grand perch that Tiberius ruled the far-flung empire.

The great fire of 64 CE completely destroyed more than four of Rome's fourteen regions, clearing large areas of land in the city center. Nero, who was always rumored to have set the fire, immediately cleared a place for his new residence, a type of villa grafted into the urban landscape and the stage for complex rituals and ceremonies involving the imperial person. The grounds filled the valley between the Esquiline, Caelian, and Palatine hills. There was an artificial lake in the middle where the Colosseum now stands. Suetonius's description of Nero's palace complex gives some impression of the splendor. Its vestibule contained a colossal statue (40 meters high) of himself. The area covered by the vestibule was so great that it had a triple portico a mile long; it also had a pool which looked like a sea, surrounded by buildings that gave the impression of cities. There were rural areas with plowed fields, vineyards, pastures, and woodlands filled with all types of domestic animals and wild beasts. Walls were inlaid with gold and highlighted with gems and mother-of-pearl; the dining room ceiling had rotating ivory panels that sprinkled flowers and perfumes on those below.

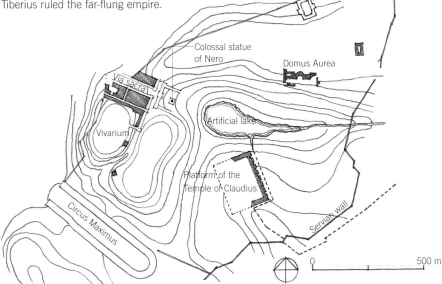

6.33 Area plan: Nero's palace complex, Rome

6.34 Interior: Octagonal room of the Domus Aurea

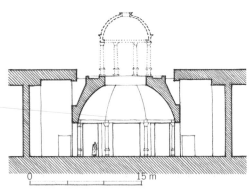

6.35 Plan and section: The octagonal room, Domus Aurea

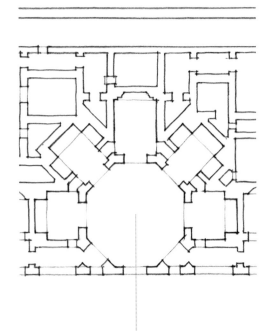

Only one wing of the palace complex remains, the Domus Aurea ("Golden House"), which rests against the side of the Esquiline Hill and is in itself a remarkable piece of architectural ingenuity. It is a combination of small scale and tactically applied axial units. To the east, an octagonal room is woven into a register of rooms to the rear. The vault of the octagonal room was designed so that light could filter in from behind the shell of the vault, which in turn is supported by eight brick-faced concrete piers originally dressed with marble and stucco. Though it begins as an octagon, the vault blends into a sphere at the top, where a wide oculus 6 meters across brings light into the room. Based on iconographic and literary evidence, some scholars have suggested that the oculus was covered by a lantern dome. Equally ingenious is the waterfall room on the vault's northern axis. Further to the east, a large, open pentagonal court intrudes into the building from the south and pushes the rooms once again toward the service rooms to the back. On axis is a vaulted room flanked by a suite of supporting rooms. The western wing contains a particularly elegant sequence of spaces that, like pistons, connect the front with a courtyard to the rear, ending in a chamber with fountains. The long axis of the courtyard ends in a large vaulted dining room that also seems to back its way into the side of the hill. The brick walls that we see today would have been covered with marble and painted stucco.

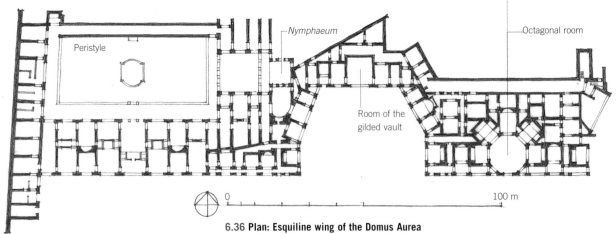

Peristyle

Nymphaeum

Octagonal room

Room of the gilded vault

0   100 m

6.36 Plan: Esquiline wing of the Domus Aurea

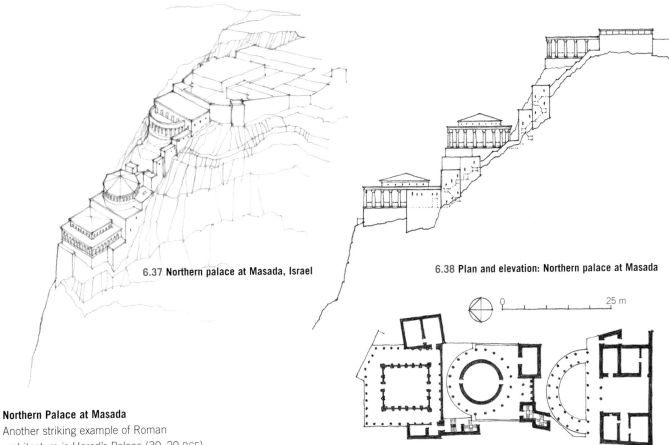

6.37 **Northern palace at Masada, Israel**

6.38 **Plan and elevation: Northern palace at Masada**

Northern Palace at Masada

Another striking example of Roman architecture is Herod's Palace (30–20 BCE) at Masada, a mountaintop fortress city rising above the shores of the Dead Sea in the Judaean Desert, 20 kilometers southeast of Jerusalem. This palace is a synthesis of Roman and Hellenistic design principles. The main residential part of the palace is at the top of the acropolis, while the rest of it descends down the steep northern slope of the cliff in a tour de force encounter between architecture and nature. On the upper terrace, rooms were grouped around a large hall that opened onto a semicircular pavilion or balcony, offering a fine view over the almost vertical drop of the cliff. Steps led down to the middle terrace, dominated by a rotunda and used, perhaps, as a dining room. Behind it, carved out of the cliff face, was a library and an enclosed room, possibly a treasury. Below that was another terrace with a hypostyle hall and a bath complex. Herod built several other spectacular structures. The so-called Herodion, south of Jerusalem, built around 24 BCE as both a palace and a fortress, lies atop an 80-meter-high semiartificial hill. Two concentric walls contained the palace.

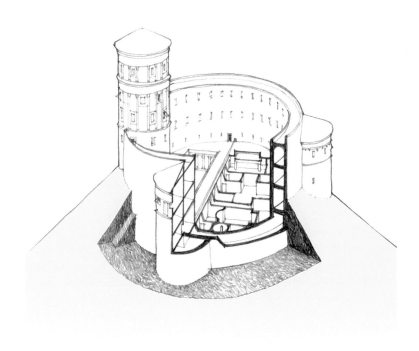

6.39 **Herodion palace/fortress**

6.40 Water garden, Palace of Domitian, Palatine Hill, Rome

6.41 View into court, Palace of Domitian

Palace of Domitian

Following a period of violence and anarchy after the death of Nero, stability returned with the rule of Vespasian (r. 69–79 CE) and a century-long sequence of rulers whose policies, broadly considered, brought peace and unity to the ancient Mediterranean world. Peace for Romans, of course, came at a price for others. In 70 CE, Vespasian destroyed the second temple of the Jews in Jerusalem and forced the Jews into slavery. About ten thousand Jews were transported to Rome to be used as workers to help build the Colosseum. In the wake of these and other victories, Vespasian's son Domitian (r. 81–96 CE) began a new imperial palace (also known as the Flavian Palace or Domus Augustana), which, on the eastern ridge of the Palatine Hill, was to become the permanent residence of the emperors. It was still in use when Narses, the conqueror of the Goths, died there in 571. Domitian imposed his absolutist tendencies upon society to a degree previously unknown. Under his rule, the lingering pragmatism of Roman culture became increasingly infused with an ideology of Near Eastern flavor with implications of the quasi-divine nature of the ruler. The new palace had to reflect the new notions of power and majesty. The tight, almost chaotic

jumble of conflicting axial realities that made Nero's palace so startling gave way to a more controlled expressions when Domitian's architect, Rabirius, cut a great step into the hillside to create a split-level palace.

The palace was in the upper part, the residence in the lower. Though there is a great deal of spatial innovation, everything is thought through. There are no awkward or surprising collisions of space, as one finds in Nero's palace. The entrance is on an axis that lead through two peristyle courts and into a structure that is at first symmetrical but, at its right and left perimeters, connects fluidly into other spatial configurations. Helping to negotiate the spatial transitions is the ingenious use of curved and rectilinear geometries. The entrance, for example, is marked by a curved vestibule that leads through a series of spaces that expand and contract based on the theme of the vaults above and on openings of different sizes and qualities that lead to side rooms.

The more the plan is studied, the more combinations can be made of these spaces, depending on whether they are read as recessive or dominant. At the far end of the axis were two summer houses, located at the top of the large curve of a gallery overlooking

the Circus Maximus. On the east side of the palace one finds another register of spaces dominated by a hippodrome, the floor of which is some 10 meters lower. A viewing box forms the terminus of a cross-axis connecting the garden fountain and the peristyle court. The *aula regia*, or audience hall, overlooked the forum.

A staircase leads to the lower level, where the residence of the emperor was located, just at the seam between the two buildings. Roman stairs were never very elaborate, and this was no exception. The principal rooms are arranged around the court with its fountain, while the emperor's private chambers are on the northwest. The central room projected out into the space of the courtyard's ambulatory. To the right and left were fountain rooms. The entire suite was separated from the retaining wall by a service corridor. To the northern side three remarkable rooms with niches, *aediculae*, and complex vaulting formed another unit—a palace within a palace.

To the west is another axis, but one that is enclosed. This is the part dedicated to the imperial state and is conventionally called Domus Flavia. A gate leads to a peristyle court. To the north are three state chambers:

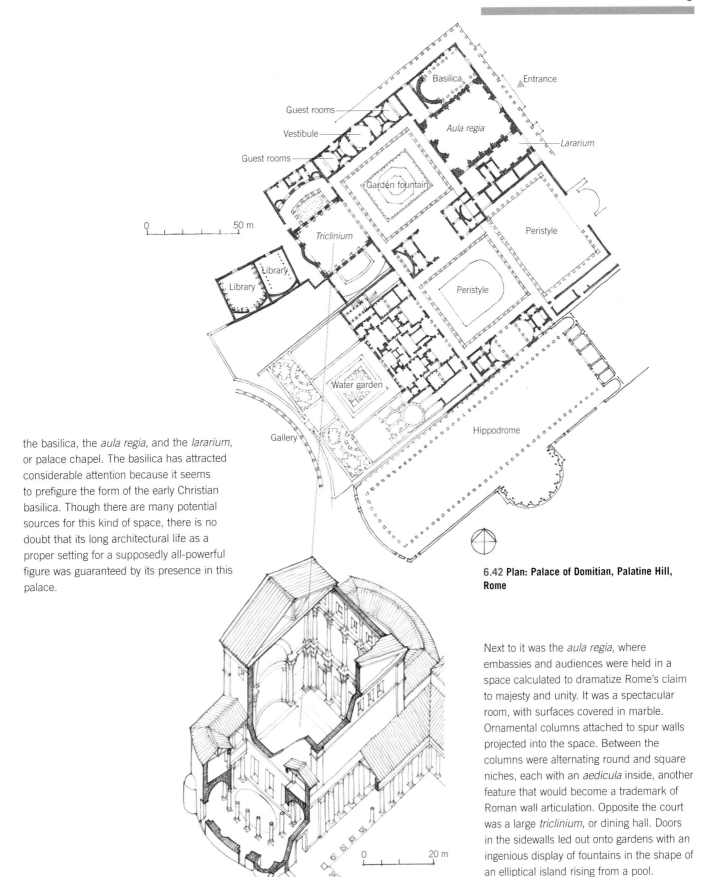

6.42 Plan: Palace of Domitian, Palatine Hill, Rome

the basilica, the *aula regia*, and the *lararium*, or palace chapel. The basilica has attracted considerable attention because it seems to prefigure the form of the early Christian basilica. Though there are many potential sources for this kind of space, there is no doubt that its long architectural life as a proper setting for a supposedly all-powerful figure was guaranteed by its presence in this palace.

6.43 Pictorial cutaway: The *triclinium*, Palace of Domitian

Next to it was the *aula regia*, where embassies and audiences were held in a space calculated to dramatize Rome's claim to majesty and unity. It was a spectacular room, with surfaces covered in marble. Ornamental columns attached to spur walls projected into the space. Between the columns were alternating round and square niches, each with an *aedicula* inside, another feature that would become a trademark of Roman wall articulation. Opposite the court was a large *triclinium*, or dining hall. Doors in the sidewalls led out onto gardens with an ingenious display of fountains in the shape of an elliptical island rising from a pool.

6.44 The Colosseum, Rome

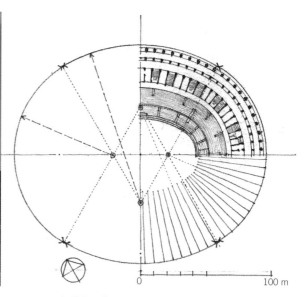

6.45 Possible method for laying out the Colosseum

The Colosseum

The Colosseum (72–80 CE), much like the Temple of Fortuna, derives its structural strength from its concrete vaults. If the building, after earthquakes, fires, and lootings, today still conveys its onetime grandeur and even retains, up to a point, its usability for open-air functions, we have the ancients to thank for their bold use of that material.

Though theaters were a common element in Greek and Roman cities, this was the first one that was designed as a freestanding object. An earlier design dating from 80 BCE in Pompeii and another from 56 BCE in Lepcis Magna in North Africa were similar in plan, but both were partially carved into the rock. The Colosseum sits in a shallow valley between three hills, making it visible from all directions, which gave it the status of a landmark from the very beginning.

It is elliptical in plan and could hold fifty thousand spectators, with boxes for the emperor and dignitaries at the centers of the longer sides. Gladiatorial combats and the exhibition of wild beasts did not stop with the Christianization of Rome. Romans remained Romans. While gladiatorial combats were abolished in 404 CE, games came to an end only in the middle of the 6th century. And it remained a place of public punishment well into the 8th century. The masses of stone that came down in earthquakes in 1231 and 1349 provided Rome with building material for more than four centuries.

If the undercroft shows once again the skill of the engineers in designing and organizing a building on this scale, its facade shows the architects' confidence in their use of the orders in relationship to the building's solids and voids. Though ornamentation is minimal, the system of attached columns and arched openings allows for a balanced interpretation of structure and mass. The 53-meter-high wall was divided into Doric, Ionic, and Corinthian layers. The fourth story had no openings, but brackets in the cornice allowed large masts to be clamped against the building to support awnings.

The capitals were stripped to their elemental form. While this may have been for economy, it also kept the columns from becoming merely ornaments. Instead, they seem to be infused with the same purposefulness as the vaults, even though they belong to a different structural system. Furthermore, the arches have an architectural profile created by the way a molding separates each arch from its supporting pier at the impost blocks and lightens the appearance of each arch from the heavy voussoirs of which it is composed. The columns look more structural than they are, and the arches less so. A less skilled hand could easily have tipped the balance the wrong way.

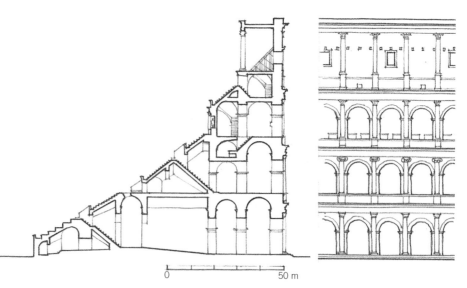

6.46 Partial section and elevation: The Colosseum

Imperial Rome

At the beginning of the 2nd century CE, under Trajan (r. 98–117 CE) and then Hadrian (r. 117–38 CE), Rome was at the height of its power. Trajan defeated the Dacians in Romania (101–6 CE) to dispossess them of their plentiful gold mines. Other campaigns led into Armenia and Mesopotamia. The wealth that flowed back into the capital restored the public treasury and insured vigorous implementation of architectural programs. And the rulers set a determined pace. Trajan rebuilt Ostia, Rome's harbor; established a new public bath; and repaired or extended existing streets. Above all, he ordered a new forum to be built. Attributed to the architect Apollodoro of Damascus, it was a complex larger than any of the other forums. Three hundred meters long, it covered more than three times the area of the Forum of Augustus. To prepare the site, the engineers had to chop away a section of a hill that connected the Quirinale to the Campidoglio. The Forum of Trajan was entered through a gateway located in a gently bulging wall. At the far end was the sideways-oriented Basilica Ulpia (107–13 CE), whose apses on both ends echoed the ones built into the colonnade of the forum that, in turn, emulated the ones in the Forum of Augustus.

Apart from the size of the basilica, it was designed in a traditional manner. Two rows of gray granite columns lined the aisles, with light filtering down, as usual, from a roof that covered the central space. The roofs of the side aisles were covered by concrete vaults rising directly from the architraves, while the roof over the central aisle was probably

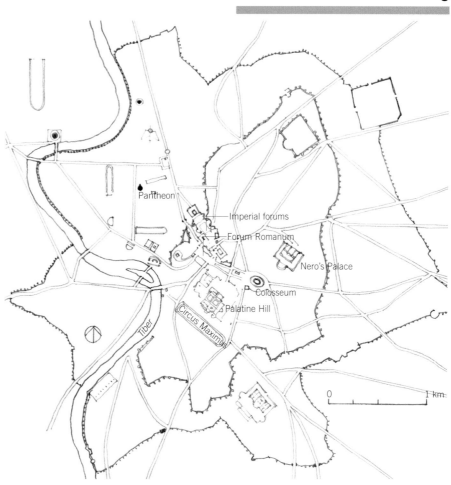

6.47 Plan of imperial Rome

spanned with wooden timbers. Sculptures and relief panels show the campaigns and triumphs of the emperor. On the main axis just behind the basilica stands Trajan's Column, with a spiral sculptural relief reading from the bottom to the top that depicts the various important events of Trajan's campaign in Dacia. At the top was a bronze statue of Trajan himself. The column contained an interior staircase. The freestanding column, an unconventional feature in its own right, was also unusual for Roman architecture, insofar as it interrupted the axial flow to the temple. But it also highlights the central role of the forum as a war memorial. The column is flanked by libraries: one for Greek scrolls, the other for Latin. The whole complex ended with Trajan's temple, which was enormous, with columns measuring 2 meters across. The forum's unusual design may possibly derive from its emulation of the central administrative area of a military camp: Trajan's Column and flanking libraries seem similar to the location of the general's standard and military archives, which were set up behind the basilica. Trajan was born in Spain and was raised as a soldier; the military iconography has thus been suitably translated into a civic monument.

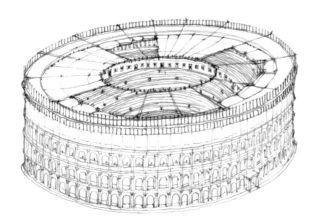

6.48 Aerial view of the Colosseum

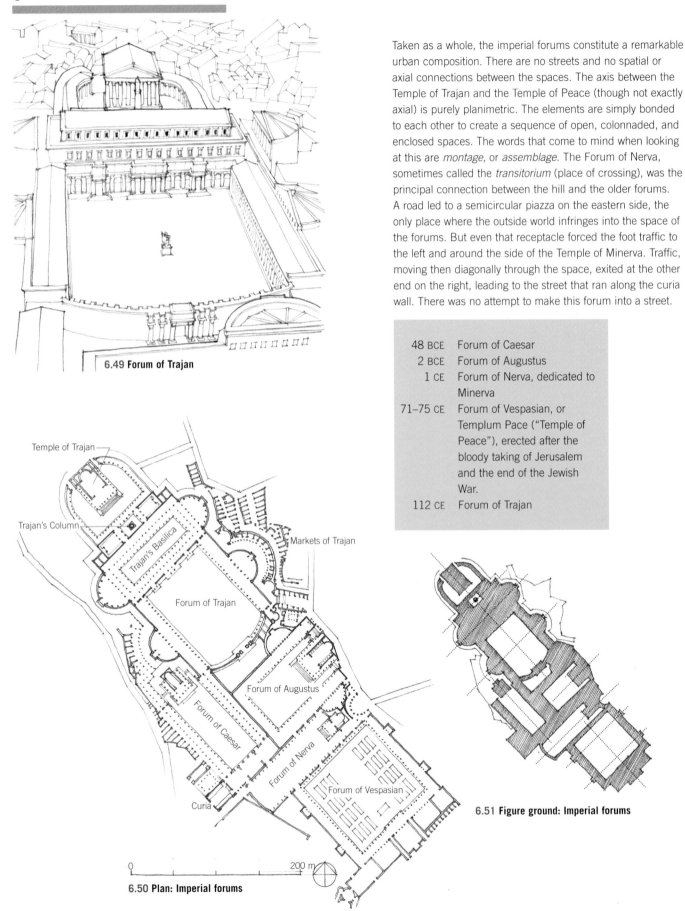

6.49 Forum of Trajan

Taken as a whole, the imperial forums constitute a remarkable urban composition. There are no streets and no spatial or axial connections between the spaces. The axis between the Temple of Trajan and the Temple of Peace (though not exactly axial) is purely planimetric. The elements are simply bonded to each other to create a sequence of open, colonnaded, and enclosed spaces. The words that come to mind when looking at this are *montage*, or *assemblage*. The Forum of Nerva, sometimes called the *transitorium* (place of crossing), was the principal connection between the hill and the older forums. A road led to a semicircular piazza on the eastern side, the only place where the outside world infringes into the space of the forums. But even that receptacle forced the foot traffic to the left and around the side of the Temple of Minerva. Traffic, moving then diagonally through the space, exited at the other end on the right, leading to the street that ran along the curia wall. There was no attempt to make this forum into a street.

48 BCE	Forum of Caesar
2 BCE	Forum of Augustus
1 CE	Forum of Nerva, dedicated to Minerva
71–75 CE	Forum of Vespasian, or Templum Pace ("Temple of Peace"), erected after the bloody taking of Jerusalem and the end of the Jewish War.
112 CE	Forum of Trajan

Temple of Trajan

Trajan's Column

Trajan's Basilica

Markets of Trajan

Forum of Trajan

Forum of Augustus

Forum of Caesar

Forum of Nerva

Forum of Vespasian

Curia

0   200 m

6.50 Plan: Imperial forums

6.51 Figure ground: Imperial forums

Rock-Cut Tombs

The idea of making rock-cut tombs is an ancient one. Hittite rock-cut sanctuaries, for example, date back to 1250 BCE. Rock-cut tombs can be even found in Italy dating from the Etruscans. The custom was brought eastward by Darius I, whose own tomb (486 BCE) was carved out of the cliffs near Persepolis. The rock-cut tombs in Lycia on the southern coast of Turkey date from the 4th century BCE; on the front of many of them are temple facades in miniature. Though rock-cut architecture is made in imitation of traditional buildings, construction techniques are very different. Masons must start from the top so that the discarded stones do not fall on the heads of their compatriots or damage the new building elements. Working from the top down requires a different type of planning and thinking. The technique was used not only for tombs, but also for Buddhist and Hindu temples, and later even for churches. A large necropolis of rock-cut tombs exists in Cyprus near the town of Paphos. Several are designed in the form of an *impluvium*.

6.52 **Plan and elevation: Lycian chamber tomb**

6.53 **Lycian tombs, Dalyan, Turkey**

6.54 *Impluvium* **of a rock-cut tomb, Paphos, Cyprus**

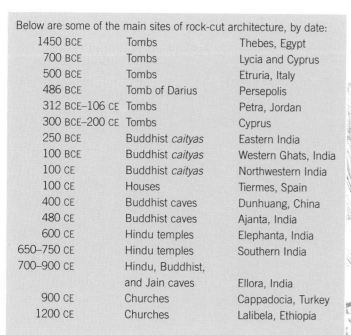

Below are some of the main sites of rock-cut architecture, by date:

1450 BCE	Tombs	Thebes, Egypt
700 BCE	Tombs	Lycia and Cyprus
500 BCE	Tombs	Etruria, Italy
486 BCE	Tomb of Darius	Persepolis
312 BCE–106 CE	Tombs	Petra, Jordan
300 BCE–200 CE	Tombs	Cyprus
250 BCE	Buddhist *caityas*	Eastern India
100 BCE	Buddhist *caityas*	Western Ghats, India
100 CE	Buddhist *caityas*	Northwestern India
100 CE	Houses	Tiermes, Spain
400 CE	Buddhist caves	Dunhuang, China
480 CE	Buddhist caves	Ajanta, India
600 CE	Hindu temples	Elephanta, India
650–750 CE	Hindu temples	Southern India
700–900 CE	Hindu, Buddhist, and Jain caves	Ellora, India
900 CE	Churches	Cappadocia, Turkey
1200 CE	Churches	Lalibela, Ethiopia

6.55 **Rock of Naqsh-i-Rustam, near Persepolis, Iran**

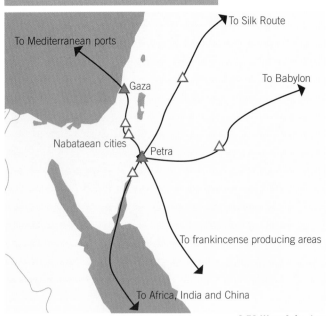

6.56 **West Asia, 1** CE

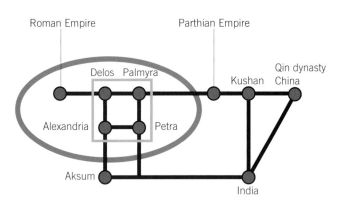

6.57 **Eurasian trade diagram, 1** CE

Petra

Temples in Rome, because of their location, tended to be relatively conservative architecturally, whereas in the former Hellenistic areas, there was always a sense of experimentation; there, Roman architecture became less "Roman." This was certainly true in Petra, the trade headquarters of the Nabataeans, whose fame spread as far as the Han dynasty in China. They were middlemen in the trade of luxury items, including frankincense, myrrh, gold, and camels, which they bred extensively. They moved in caravans and maintained a nomadic ethos that did not require the building of permanent houses. Eventually, however, the Nabataeans established several cities that linked Petra with the Mediterranean port of Gaza, including Avdat and Shivta. They rose in importance because they provided the Romans an alternative to the Silk Route, which had to go through the unstable Parthian kingdom. To secure this connection, the Romans, instead of invading the Nabataean area, offered them Roman citizenship, with its much coveted privileges.

Nabataean architectural legacy is best preserved in the city of Petra, meaning "rock" in Greek. On this site, temples, theaters, and hundreds of tombs—all cut into the living rock of the steep mountains that surround the Petra Valley—still stand in testament to this largely forgotten culture. It is located in the area of Jordan called Edom, meaning "red," from the color of

the Shara Mountains that ring the Petra Valley, which is only accessible through the 1.6-kilometer-long canyon. The site was fitted with well-developed systems of water control and storage, including rock-cut cisterns and ceramic pipes. There were no houses, as the Nabataeans lived in tents, but the dead were given monumental tombs, the smallest and most abundant of which date from the early decades of the 1st century CE. Their facades

reveal a range of cultural influences. Some are framed by pilasters and topped with stepping "crow's-feet" ornamentation, a motif of Assyrian and Babylonian origin. Still others are massive, largely unadorned facades with small, clearly delineated entrances recalling an Egyptian pylon.

The beautifully preserved, deep-pinkish facade of the Khasneh al Faroun was probably built for King Aretas III (87–65

6.58 **El-Deir, Petra, Jordan**

6.59 Khasneh al Faroun, Petra

BCE), but most scholars date it to the 1st century CE. Standing an astonishing 30 meters high, it recalls the massing and intercolumniation of Hellenistic temples. Twelve columns, six on the lower level and six above, are capped with Corinthian capitals and highly ornamented moldings and friezes. The upper columns are shorter than the lower, but from the perspective of a viewer on the ground, they seem well proportioned.

6.60 Plan and facade: Khasneh al Faroun, Petra

The spaces between the attached columns contain high reliefs depicting Nabataean deities and animals. The griffins that decorate the frieze are derived from Mesopotamian lore. The facade's culminating feature is a round *tholos*, standing largely free and framed by broken pediments.

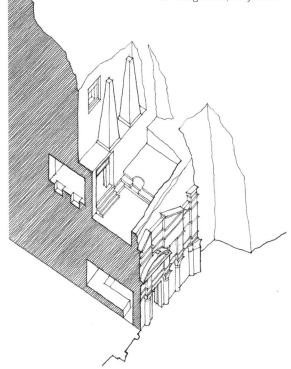

6.61 Cutaway: Obelisk Tomb, Petra

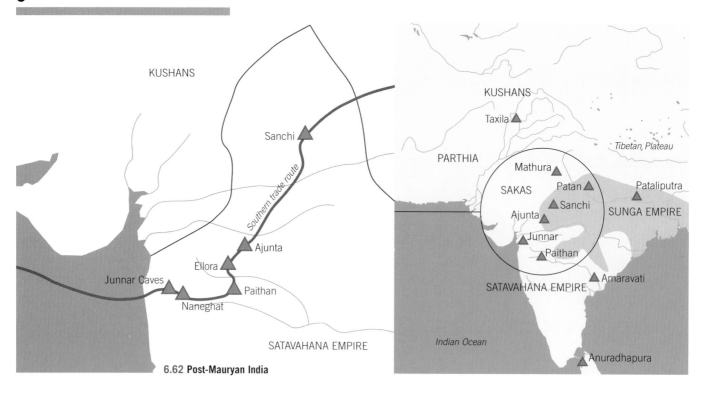

6.62 **Post-Mauryan India**

Development of Mahayana Buddhism

Late in the 2nd century BCE, Asoka's Mauryan Empire began to disintegrate, resulting in the formation of a series of smaller kingdoms: the Sunga in the west, the Satavahanas to the south, and in the north, the Shakas. This transformation paralleled an equally important transformation within Buddhism that had important implications in the field of architecture. As originally conceived, the Buddhist monkhood was strictly mendicant. Its members lived itinerantly in poverty and survived by begging; they were not allowed to erect shrines, acquire property, or deify the Buddha. This form of Buddhism was subsequently referred to as Hinayana (or the "Lesser Vehicle"). In time, as Buddhism began to receive royal patronage and its practitioners became more diverse, a more monastic and populist form of Buddhism, known as Mahayana (or the "Greater Vehicle") emerged that required the establishment of institutions where monks could live and study.

The transformation from the initial mendicancy to monasticism can be tracked through the four great Buddhist councils called to reconcile differences in interpretation. King Ajatsatru convened the first Buddhist council in the 5th century BCE soon after the Buddha's death,

in order to record the extant sayings of the Buddha (sutras) and to codify the rules of mendicancy. Continuing conflicts between the Hinayana and Mahayana schools of Buddhism prompted the convening of the second Buddhist council in 383 BCE. That council ended with the victory of the mendicants. But by the time Asoka convened the third Buddhist council in 250 BCE, the tide was beginning to turn. In anticipation of extensive royal patronage, the council prepared the definitive treatises of Buddhism, in particular the Tripitaka (the "Three Baskets"), the three texts considered to be directly transmitted by the Buddha himself. A fourth council was eventually convened around 100 CE, at which three hundred thousand verses and over nine million statements were compiled and written in Sanskrit. These became the basis of Mahayana Buddhism, which soon began to flourish and spread into Central Asia, China, Korea, and Japan.

Significant parts of the Mahayana credo were articulated by Nagarjuna, the 2nd-century Indian philosopher and the most influential Buddhist thinker after the Buddha himself. Nagarjuna promoted what is known as the Middle Path, a compromise between the ascetic and the worldly sects

of Buddhism. He argued that Asoka, as a virtuous Buddhist king, was a *cakravartin*, and should thus be considered to have direct access to nirvana, or Buddhahood. Nagarjuna's definition of kingship served as a model for generations of rulers throughout Asia, including the 18th-century Qin dynasty emperor Qianlong and today's Dalai Lama.

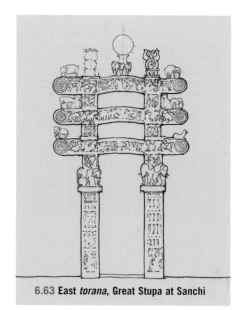

6.63 **East *torana*, Great Stupa at Sanchi**

6.64 **Stupa II at Sanchi, near Bhopal, India**

Sanchi Complex

The most important of the remaining Sunga period Buddhist complexes is Sanchi, which was founded by Asoka and flourished for thirteen centuries. The complex is located near the ancient town of Vidisa, along the fertile river valleys of the southern trade route (or *dakshinapatha*). It is located on a hill that rises sharply above the valley, making its three stupas distinctly visible from afar. The surrounding hills are also surmounted by stupas, all of which establish the area as a sacred landscape. Originally, the stupas were plastered and painted, and on festival days were gaily decorated with flowers and other ritual offerings. Large groups of visiting monks and laity alike came to Sanchi in processions.

Stupas started out as reliquary mounds, or *caityas*, which can denote any sacred place—such as where a funeral pyre or consecration had occurred; they were usually marked off by a wooden railing. Asoka had the Buddha's bodily remains divided into eight parts and distributed throughout his empire as relics, with their location marked by ceremonial mounds. (*Stupa* means "piled up.") Built by the thousands and becoming the dominant symbol of Buddhism, stupas came to embody many meanings, some standing in for the body of the Buddha, others for his enlightenment, and yet others serving as a cosmic diagram.

Conceptually, a stupa is a cosmological diagram linking the body of the Buddha to the universe. The fundamental elements of a stupa are present in the oldest of

Sanchi's stupas, the so-called Stupa II (ca. 100 BCE). The central mass consists of an earthen hemispherical mound faced with fired bricks, with a shallow berm (or *medhi*) ringing its base. This round structure is then surrounded by a stone balustrade (or *vedika*) that replicates a construction out of wood. Both the interior and exterior surface of the *vedika* are carved with shallow reliefs and medallions depicting scenes and events of Buddhist significance. The *vedika* has openings on four sides, aligned to the cardinal directions. These are accessed not on axis, however, but at right angles, through bent entrances, all of which open in a counterclockwise direction. The cross-axis of the cardinal directions, coupled with the directional openings, form a space-time cosmological diagram, or mandala, in the form of a *svastika* (or "swastika"). The directions represent space, and the bent entrances, replicating the movement of the stars, represent time. The purpose of the *vedika* is to give spatial definition to the ritual counterclockwise circumambulation of *parikrama*. A Buddhist monk, or a pilgrim, in performing the *parikrama*, engages in a haptic reenactment of the fundamental order of space and time, and in the process, brings his or her body into harmony with that larger order. In Buddhism, as in Hinduism, *parikrama*, along with the mandala and the *svastika* (totally unrelated to its Nazi appropriation), are still fundamental to architectural expression.

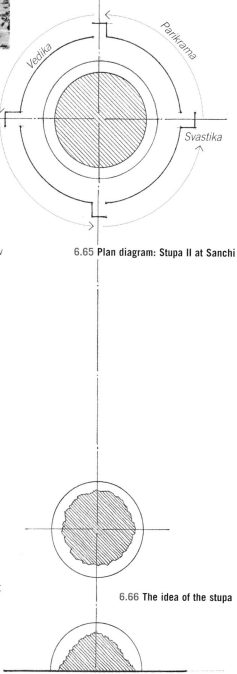

6.65 **Plan diagram: Stupa II at Sanchi**

6.66 **The idea of the stupa**

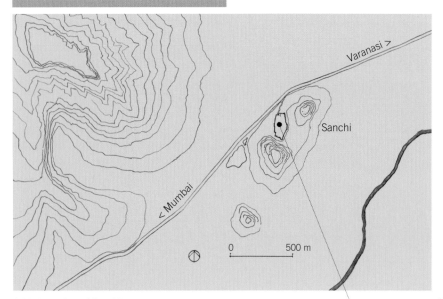

6.67 Area plan of Sanchi

Stupa I is the largest stupa at Sanchi; it is
also known as the Mahastupa, or the "Great
Stupa." Begun by Asoka, it was enlarged to
its present diameter of 36 meters late in the
Sunga period. It is a solid mass built up in
the form of hundreds of stone rings that were
surfaced with plaster and painted. (This outer
surface has eroded away and has not been
replaced.) The significance of the Mahastupa
is highlighted by the rare presence of one of
Asoka's pillars at its southern entrance. The
Mahastupa is essentially a magnification of
Stupa II in plan, with the addition of another
vedika around the inner *medhi*, which is also
accessible by stairs on the south. This makes
it possible to conduct a double *parikrama*
around the stupa.

At the top of the stupa is another *vedika*—
the *harmika*—that is inaccessible and serves
only symbolic purposes. In the middle of the
harmika is a finial, with three stone discs of
diminishing size, called *chattris*, balanced on
a columnar support. The *harmika* and the
chattris collectively denote the stupa's vertical
axis, echoing Asoka's pillar and completing
the cosmic connections of the stupa. The
other innovation at the Mahastupa are the
monumental stone gateways called *toranas*.
The *toranas*, imitating wooden construction,
consist of two vertical pillars supporting
three horizontal bars that are slightly bent at
their center and that project well beyond the
posts. The beams end in volutes that connote
the sacred scrolls, the treasured objects of
the Buddhist *sanghas*. Like the *vedikas*,

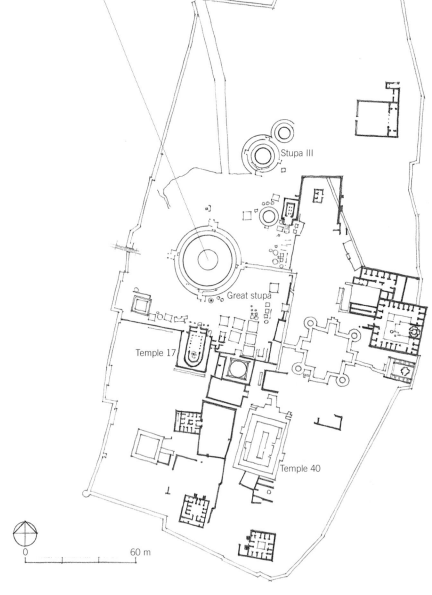

6.68 Plan: Stupa complex at Sanchi

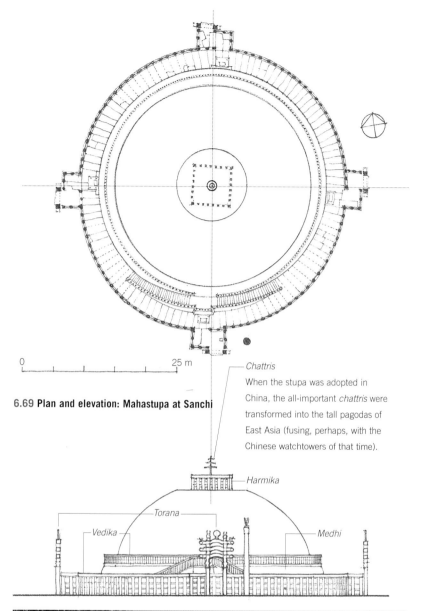

6.69 Plan and elevation: Mahastupa at Sanchi

Chattris

When the stupa was adopted in China, the all-important *chattris* were transformed into the tall pagodas of East Asia (fusing, perhaps, with the Chinese watchtowers of that time).

Harmika

Torana

Vedika

Medhi

6.70 Mahastupa at Sanchi

the surface of the *toranas* are elaborately decorated, depicting Buddhist themes and events, completing the classic stupa as we know it.

Sanchi enjoyed extensive patronage and grew into a large monastic complex of Buddhist learning and worship that included subsidiary structures where the monks lived. Over time, a number of small stupas were added to the complex. The more important the person whose relics were contained in these stupas, the closer that stupa was to the Mahastupa. (During excavation in the mid-19th century, most of these relics were, unfortunately, removed.) The Hindus also recognized this site as important, and one of the oldest Hindu stone temples—from the 4th century CE—is to be found there, close to the southern entrance of the Mahastupa. A relief on the northern *torana* of the Mahastupa depicts a large ceremonial procession, complete with musical instruments and offerings and led by elephants, on its way to the Mahastupa. One has to imagine Sanchi thus—not as a remote monastery populated by mendicant Buddhist monks totally disassociated from ordinary life, but as a bustling center of religious activity where the monks and their patrons enjoyed extensive contact and communication.

Abhayagiri Vihara

A monastic complex, designed around similar principles to Sanchi, was founded in the 2nd century BCE on the island of Sri Lanka. Known as the Abhayagiri Vihara, it was located north of the Sri Lankan capital, Anuradhapura, and became, by the 1st century CE, a major Buddhist institution. At its center was a huge *dagoba* 107 meters in diameter and a colossal 120 meters high. Around it were clustered an image house, a series of assembly halls, general purpose halls, a refectory with the communal rice trough, bathrooms, and multistoried residential dormitories, or *viharas*. In the 4th century CE, Abhayagiri became the center of Mahayana Buddhism, which opposed the more officially sanctioned Theravada sects of Sri Lanka.

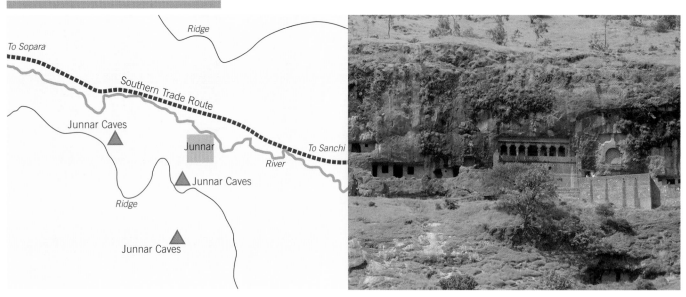

6.71 **Junnar Caves area**

6.72 **View of Junnar Caves, near Naneghat, India**

Junnar Caves

Seven sets of early Buddhist caves in the outer reaches of the Satavahana kingdom are all that remain of the early mendicant, Hinayana phase of Buddhism. Dating from the 1st century BCE to the 1st century CE, they are close to Naneghat, a remote place at the head of a mountain pass linking the Satavahana capital, Paithan, to the port of Kalyan. Junnar was important because it connected the Satavahanas to the important maritime trade with Egypt and the Mediterranean, which flourished after about 150 BCE. One of the Junnar Caves contains an inscription from about 100 BCE listing all the major rulers of the Satavahanas; it is considered to be the definitive record of their lineage.

The Tulija Lena (100–25 BCE) is significant because its *caitya* hall is completely round in plan, as if the *parikrama* plan of the stupa chamber at Kondivte had become the complete *caitya* itself. By way of comparison, a similar circular *caitya*, but without the *parikrama* pillars, was also excavated at Guntupalli, in the Krishna River basin of Central India. These two caves define the moment when Buddhists considered adopting an alternate expression of their main worship space, exploring the possibilities of the circular areas excavated in the earliest *caityas*.

6.73 **Entrance to Bhuta Lena cave (No. 26), Junnar**

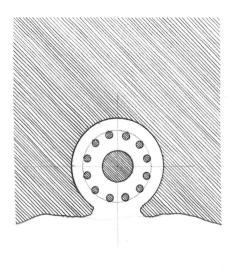

6.74 **Plans of *caitya* halls: Lenyadri, India**

Tulija Lena, India

Guntupalli, India

6.75 **Plan:** *Caitya* **hall at Kondivte, India**

6.76 **Entrance to the** *caitya* **hall at Kondivte**

Caitya Hall at Kondivte

In the 2nd and 1st centuries BCE, rock-cut Buddhist architecture became elaborate in concept and execution. Caves were excavated all over South Asia, but in particular in the passes of the Western Ghats, a mountain chain in western India running some 45 to 90 kilometers inland from the Arabian Sea. The largest concentrations of rock-cut architecture are in Bhaja and Pitalkhora. These were of two types: a *caitya*, or meditation hall, consisting of an apsidal hall focused on a stupa, and a *vihara*, or living quarter, consisting of a number of cells organized around a rectilinear, columnar court. The *caitya* hall at Kondivte, Maharashtra, (100 BCE), just north of Mumbai, marks an important moment of transition. Like the Lomas Rsi Caves, the stupa is contained in a circular enclosure, leaving barely enough room for one person to perform *parikrama* around it. Unlike Lomas Rsi, this *caitya* hall is entered on axis, rather than from the side. All subsequent rock-cut *caitya* halls are entered on axis as well.

6.77 **Cross-section:** *Caitya* **hall at Bhaja**

6.78 **Interior:** *Caitya* **hall at Bhaja, near Lonavla, India**

The *caitya* hall at Bhaja, Maharashtra (100–70 BCE), besides being much larger than the rest, dissolves the distinction between the stupa chamber, with its *parikrama* path and antechamber. It fuses them into one large space while maintaining the distinctive presence of the *parikrama* path by creating a long, U-shaped colonnade that extends the entire length of the hall. The consequence is a simple and elegant building that has the effect of separating an independent three-dimensional form from within the larger excavation.

The hall's presence is projected at the entrance in the form of a large opening with a horseshoe-shaped top, reflecting the vaulted ceiling of the hall. As is the case with all Buddhist rock-cut architecture, the *caitya* hall at Bhaja is carved out to faithfully imitate wood construction, complete with ribs, inward leaning columns, and traces of joinery. The exterior facade carved around the central opening consists of a number of miniaturized faux building facades, complete with carved human figures leaning over railings.

O

Taxila: The Gandharan Cosmopolis

In the period from 150 BCE to 100 CE, the Gandharan region of the upper Indus Valley—now in Pakistan—was ruled by the Shakas from Sogdiana and the Parthians, who took over this region from Alexander's governors. The Shakas and the Parthians adopted Buddhism, cultivated Hellenistic workers, and brought their own Persian and Central Asian backgrounds to the mix, creating an architecture that was an international synthesis of varying tendencies. Located on a major tributary of the Indus River, the Gandharan capital city, Taxila (also called Sirkap), was positioned at the meeting point of three trade routes, one extending east to the Indian heartland, a second west to Bactria and Persia, and a third to Central Asia and the northern path of the Silk Route. Taxila was rebuilt several times, until an earthquake in the 1st century CE prompted a complete rebuilding.

The urban layout of Taxila is rigidly rectilinear in plan, with a 700-meter-long street running through its center. The whole was bound by a high wall. Dense courtyard housing of various sizes is organized in blocks around a main street. A number of religions seem to have commingled in Taxila. The city was celebrated in the ancient world as a prestigious center of learning, and for the next eight hundred years or more Buddhist shrines continued to be built here. One of the city blocks was given over to what is known as the Apsidal Temple, which is like a *caitya* hall of the type that was pervasive throughout South Asia at the time. But this temple was constructed as a freestanding object. Sitting in the middle of an open courtyard, measuring about 40 by 75 meters, the temple was raised on a high plinth and accessed by a large axial stair. The stair was flanked by two stupas on square bases. (Only the bases survive.) To the southeast of the city, on another plateau, is the large Dharmarajika Stupa. The mound on which it sits is surrounded by a multitude of monks' cells.

North of the city, on a high rocky outcrop, is a Jandial temple, a Greek peristyle temple complete with a *pronaos*, *naos*, and *opisthodomos*. The base of this temple, however, is thicker than structurally necessary, promoting speculation that there may have been another superstructure above the main walls and that the temple may have been a fire temple of the Zoroastrians.

0   10 m

6.79 Plan of a Jandial temple

6.80 Plan: Dharmarajika Monastery, Taxila, Pakistan

0   50 m

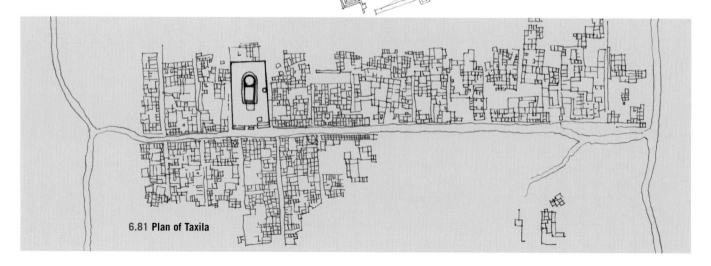

6.81 Plan of Taxila

Xiongu Khanate

Long (Great) Wall

Route to West Asia

Gobi Desert

Taklamakan Desert

CHINA

Yellow River

Yellow Sea

Extent of the
Han Empire

Xianyang

Luoyang

Qin dynasty

Tibetan tribes

Chengdu

East China Sea

Yangtze River

Route to India

6.82 Qin dynasty China

Qin Dynasty China

After almost two hundred years of civil war, China was unified by the short-lived but supremely despotic Qin dynasty (221–206 BCE). The first ruler of the dynasty, Ying Zheng, renamed himself Shi Huangdi ("First Emperor") and justified his ruthless suppression of opposition on the grounds that he had a divine mandate to reunify China. After victory over the last of his enemies, Shi Huangdi put in place a centralized bureaucracy and administration that could account for the diverse sections of the empire. The system of writing was standardized, as was the language. A single currency was introduced—a copper coin with a hole in the middle so it could be strung on a string. Shi Huangdi also connected the existing defensive fortifications in the north of China to form the first Great Wall to fend off invading "barbarians" from the north. Despite these accomplishments, Shi Huangdi was unpopular in his time; he raised taxes, deprived the nobility of power, was ruthlessly intolerant of those who opposed him, and suppressed the writings of alternative philosophers. Although Shi Huangdi's short-lived dynasty was controversial, Qin (pronounced "chin") is the origin of the Western name China ("land of the Qin"). The Chinese themselves referred to their domain as the Middle Kingdom.

The ideal of a unified China, which was to persist throughout Chinese history, can be contrasted with the histories of South Asia and Europe, where, even though emperors were periodically able to conquer large territories, the idea of a single, unified empire

was always keenly contested. It was only as a consequence of European colonialism in the 18th and 19th centuries that India, for example, became a single nation.

The Qin capital, Xianyang, about 28 kilometers west of present-day Xi'an, was built in a very unusual manner as a microcosm of the Chinese empire. Each time Qin conquered a warring state, the palace of the enemy was destroyed, and a replica was built on the northern bank of the Wei River, facing the new palace to the south. These replica palaces were then connected by covered walkways and filled with musical instruments and singing girls from the vanquished states. The emperor also resettled over one hundred thousand people from these conquered states to Xianyang. This policy was meant to reduce the possibility of rebellion by placing dangerous elements within the purview of the emperor.

Though the Qin palaces were destroyed in dynastic wars, they are described extensively in the literature, and excavations in the late 1970s discovered that these palaces are quite similar to those descriptions. One of the most impressive was the palace of Qin Shi Huangdi himself. Three large groups of palatial foundations have been discovered in Xianyang. The oldest (Palace No. 1) is a two-level structure, with the upper level imposingly raised 6 meters above the lower. The upper level is L-shaped and extends 60 meters east to west and 45 meters north to south. At its center is the principal hall, with a large pillar right at its midpoint. A smaller hall

to the southeast is thought to have been the emperor's residence. The L shape suggests that another similar complex was to be symmetrically placed to the east.

In 212 BCE, Shi Huangdi commissioned the construction of an enormous palatial complex, Zhao Gong ("Shining Lord"), on the south side of the Wei River. The rammed-earth foundations of the complex measure about 1,400 meters by 450 meters and 7 to 8 meters high. According to the Shiji:

Then he had palaces constructed in the Shanglin Gardens, south of the Wei River. The front palace, Epang, was built first…. The terraces above could seat 10,000, and below there was room for banners [20 meters] in height. One causeway round the palace led to the South Hill, at the top of which a gateway was erected. A second led across the Wei River to [the capital]….*

*Sima Qian, *Selections from Records of the Historian*, trans. Yang Hsien-yi and Gladys Yang (Beijing: Foreign Languages Press, 1979), 179.

When Shi Huangdi died, construction of his tomb was delayed. The Qin's ambitious building program in Xianyang had, however, not been completed in 206 BCE, when most of the capital was destroyed by the Han dynasty. Since the Wei River has since changed course many times, always shifting toward the north, the old Qin capital is drastically eroded today.

6.83 Terra-cotta warriors in the Tomb of the First Emperor

Tomb of the First Emperor

The Tomb of the First Emperor, one of the most celebrated archaeological finds in China, is located in Lishan, just south of Xi'an. Sited on a plain with a wall of mountains framing its southern view, it is probably the largest and most costly tomb in history, even compared with the Egyptian pyramids. Its outer perimeter wall, 6 meters thick and constructed of rammed earth, encloses an area of approximately 2 square kilometers. The main entrance is on the east. Within the perimeter there was a second walled enclosure with four more gates, one on each of the four sides.

Outside the eastern entrance, archaeologists have uncovered more than 8,000 life-size terra-cotta figures, grouped in battle order, rank by rank, some mounted on horse-drawn chariots, others in infantry groups armed with spears, swords, and crossbows (although the spear shafts, bows, and other wooden objects have decayed away). Vault no. 1 is the largest, measuring 60 by 210 meters. In eleven parallel trenches there are over 3,000 terra-cotta foot soldiers arranged as an infantry regiment, facing away from the emperor's tomb. In the eastern gallery are bowmen and crossbowmen in a formation of three rows, making a total of almost 200 sharpshooters. Most were armed with actual crossbows with a range of 200 meters. Archaeologists once believed that each warrior had individual traits—that they were portraits of the emperor's guard of honor—but it now seems that there are about one hundred different types of faces.

Vault no. 2 contains a formation of chariots and cavalry with supporting troops, all turned toward the east. There are 1,430 warriors and horses divided into four groups. Vault no. 3 seems to be the headquarters of the terra-cotta army, with a commander along with 68 officers. This vast buried army was meant to accompany the emperor in death and protect him. Other vaults contain acrobats, musicians, and craftsmen.

The 76-meter high mound remains unexcavated but recent tests have shown that it is a building of extraordinary dimension and design, covered completely over by tons of earth. The building consists of two bracket-shaped structures, probably of rammed earth, that define and tower over a large central room that serves as the tomb chamber. The Shiji contains a description of this burial monument. For a long time it was thought to be an exaggeration, but now seems to be quite plausible:

…Qin excavations and building had been started at Mount Li, while after he won the empire, more than 700,000 conscripts from all parts of the country worked there. They dug through three subterranean streams and poured molten copper for the outer coffin, and the tomb was filled with models of palaces, pavilions, and offices, as well as fine vessels, precious stones, and rarities. Artisans were ordered to fix up crossbows so that any thief breaking in would be shot. All the country's streams, the Yellow River, and the Yangtze, were reproduced in quicksilver and by some mechanical means made to flow into a miniature ocean. The heavenly constellations were above, and the regions of the earth below. The candles were made of whale oil to insure the burning for the longest possible time.

Sima Qian, Selections from Records of the Historian, trans. Yang Hsien-yi and Gladys Yang (Beijing: Foreign Languages Press, 1979), 186.

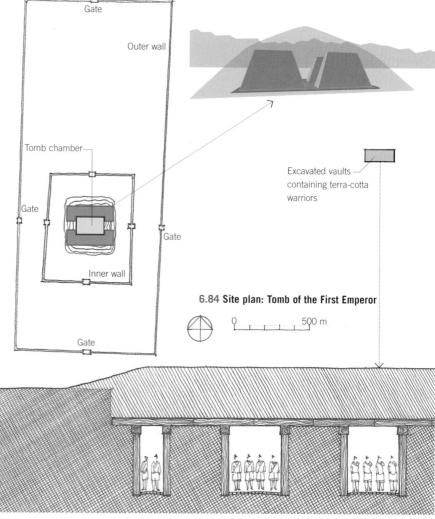

6.84 Site plan: Tomb of the First Emperor

6.85 Section through vaults: Tomb of the First Emperor

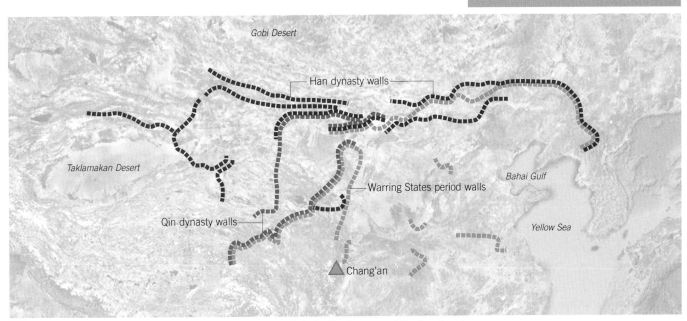

Gobi Desert

Han dynasty walls

Taklamakan Desert

Bahai Gulf

Warring States period walls

Yellow Sea

Qin dynasty walls

Chang'an

6.86 **Construction of the Great Wall during the Warring States period, the Qin dynasty, and the Han dynasty**

Great Wall of China

The empire created by Shi Huangdi had few serious enemies to its south, and to the west, the enormous Taklamakan Desert served as an impediment to all but the heartiest of traders. But to the north, the nomadic Mongol tribes were such a threat that they embodied for the Qin and Han dynasties the quintessential "barbarians." The Mongols' skill with horses gave them a military advantage that would, under Chengiz (Ghengis) Khan, not only yield China to them but indeed take them to the very doors of Europe. The Chinese response to the Mongol threat was to reach for a radical option that could only be mounted by a highly organized empire—the creation of a vast defensive wall, the *wanli qangqeng* (10,000-li-long wall), popularly called the Great Wall since colonial times. Small segments of earthen ramparts had been constructed along the northern frontier in the Warring States period under the Zhou. Shi Huangdi conceived of connecting and extending these segments, and the idea was realized by the Han emperors. The resulting fortification is not a single continuous structure but rather a network of walls and towers. Whenever possible, it was backed into mountains or otherwise located to take advantage of naturally occurring defensive formations.

To maintain its integrity, the Great Wall was constantly patrolled, and signal systems were set up to transmit messages from one watchtower to another. As the counterpart to the unified empire, designating the barbarians beyond, the Great Wall is the symbol of the Middle Kingdom. In spite of being expanded and reinforced repeatedly, the Great Wall was repeatedly breached by northern nomadic civilizations, many of which went on to establish successful ruling dynasties in China, such as the Jin, the Liao, the Yuan, and the Qing. These supposedly "barbarian" dynasties, of course, had less interest in reinforcing the wall.

Extending from contemporary North Korea all the way to the Jade Gate in Gansu Province, the Great Wall had several architectural components:

- Border towns: Of varying shapes and sizes, these towns were small and defensible, complete with moats, walls, streets, dwellings, and watchtowers.
- Fortifications: Small forts, 50 to 150 square kilometers in area and protected by moats and high walls, served as military stations.
- Check points: Two- to three-story watchtowers were built everywhere the wall encountered intersections or was open to movement.
- Beacon towers: Watchtowers on platforms from which lookouts could spot approaching enemies and alert adjacent towers by smoke signals were located about 130 meters apart.

Most of the Qin and Han sections of the Great Wall were made of pounded earth and paved with stones. Some parts, however, were made of Chinese tamarisk and reeds that were arranged in a checkerboard pattern and then filled in with sand and stone. While much of the ancient wall of Shi Huangdi has disappeared, most of what was built in the Ming dynasty (1368–1644), following a route different from that of Shi Huangdi's fortifications, survives today.

6.87 View of the Great Wall of China

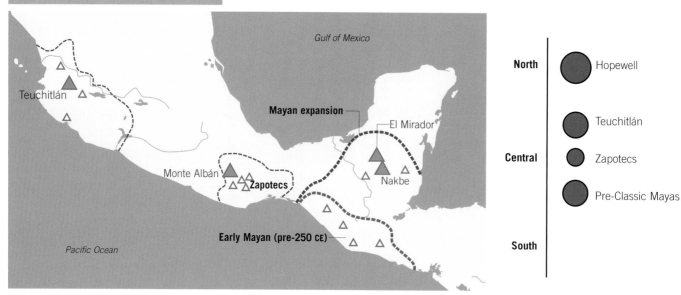

6.88 Urbanization of the Americas, 1 CE

North — Hopewell
Teuchitlán
Central — Zapotecs
Pre-Classic Mayas
South

6.89 Trade in the Americas, 1 CE

Shaft Tombs of Teuchitlán

At the turn of the millennium, Central America was dominated by the Zapotecs, who had replaced the Olmecs, now in serious decline. In the Yucatán Peninsula, in the meantime, the Mayan culture had begun to take root, developing monumental platform-and-pyramid complexes in the El Mirador basin and Tikal. At the edges of these great civilizations, in the high lake valleys of western Mexico, we find a relatively minor but fascinating civilization at Teuchitlán, around the slopes of the extinct volcano Tequila. The remains today consist of funerary shaft tombs accompanied by corresponding surface-level ritual architecture created as integral parts of small chieftain settlements, the largest of which probably had about twenty to thirty thousand inhabitants. Though burial chambers were a constant in western Mexico, significant here is that no pyramids or images of the usual deities have been found. The origin of this particular culture and the reasons for their autonomous architectural development are not well understood. *Ancient West Mexico* (edited by Richard Townsend) contains some of the more recent studies.

For the residents of Teuchitlán, funerary tombs were a critical part in establishing the connection between the living and their ancestors. They were used by hereditary chieftains and their families and became the symbolic center of the society's communal life. The earliest type of tombs (1500– 800 BCE) consisted of a round opening surrounded by a low platform, from which a short, stepped passage led into the mortuary chamber. Such small tombs from all periods are found everywhere in western Mexico. Little is known of the tombs from the period between 800 and 300 BCE, since none have been scientifically excavated, although tombs are found throughout the lake-basin district.

0
10 m

6.90 Plan and pictorial view: Shaft tomb at El Arenal

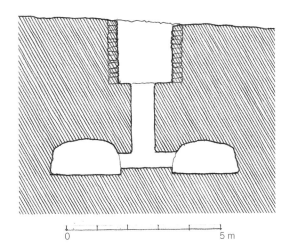

6.91 Section through shaft tomb at El Arenal

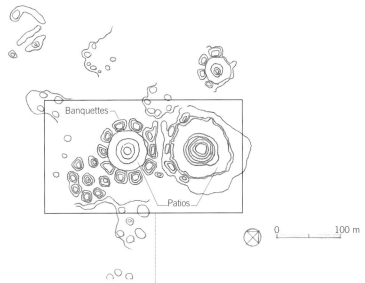

6.92 Site Plan: Guachimonton precinct at Teuchitlán, near Ameca, Mexico

In the period 300 BCE to 200 CE, the shaft tombs used by hereditary chieftains and their families became the symbolic center of the society. Carved into volcanic tuff, the tombs are generally boot- or bottle-shaped. Vertical shafts are cut anywhere from 1 to 21 meters below the surface before opening into one or more side chambers in which the dead were interred, along with a large offering of hollow ceramic figures, shell jewelry, obsidian jewelry, ground stone, and other items. There is evidence that the tombs held burials from different times and were therefore reopened as necessary.

Of the shaft tombs of the period between 300 BCE and 200 CE, the largest, at El Arenal, has an 18-meter shaft and three burial chambers. Two other shaft tombs are located within the same ceremonial area. On the surface, the shaft emerged at the center of a circular stepped mound that was surrounded by an elevated circular patio, at the edge of which were eight to twelve evenly spaced rectangular platforms. Made of rubble and packed earth, the larger complexes of the later phase (300–800 CE) range from 28 meters at Potrero de las Chivas to well over 100 meters at Guachimonton, the largest of the Teuchitlán ritual sites. The circles were often found in groups of two or three, with some of the circles overlapping. Ball courts were also found in association with these circles. Later, in the period from 300 to 800 CE, shaft tombs became less important, and huge surface circles, along with ball courts, came to dominate the construction, to the point that their burial chambers are as yet undiscovered.

6.93 Plan and section: Central circular structures of the Guachimonton complex at Teuchitlán

The graves of El Arenal, like most shaft tombs, have been looted or destroyed. One that has been excavated intact at Huitzilapa is a shaft tomb 8 meters deep, with two burial chambers, several burials, and about sixty thousand artifacts. The tomb sits at the western end of the 50-by-200-meter settlement. At the eastern end is a large, elongated ball court. The center of the settlement is dominated by a religious complex consisting of eight platform mounds surrounding a circular pyramid. This complex abuts another, smaller circular complex to its west consisting of four platform mounds fronting onto a square court with a small circular pyramid in the middle. The shaft tomb is located in one of the mounds. Low abutments indicate that the four platforms were linked together in a ring at their base. The shaft tapers about one-third of its way down and then opens into two domical chambers, oriented north-south, which are entered through narrow openings and stairs. Within, six skeletons, one of which is clearly that of the chieftain, are laid out with their heads toward the entrance, surrounded by offerings.

Clay models found with the offerings testify to the self-consciousness of the designs, linking community festivals to the order of the cosmos, the rhythms of the seasons, and the cycle of life and death. The circle replicates the encompassing ring of the horizon; cardinal and intercardinal orientations are established by pyramid stairways along axes related to the path of the sun. The models show a tall mast rising from the central pyramid, which in mystical parlance would be the axis mundi, connecting the apex of the sky to the central point of the earth's surface and to the underworld nadir. These sites were also the location of observations and rites on the day of the summer solstice, the annual time of the sun's zenith passage, the beginning of the rainy season, and the renewal of the earth's fertility.

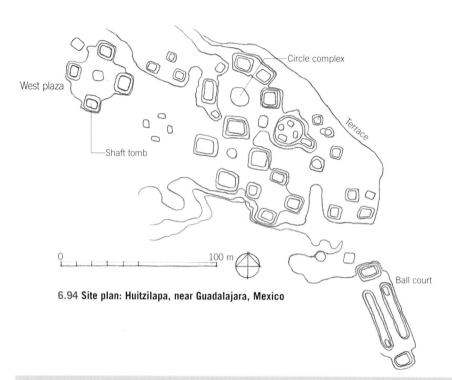

6.94 **Site plan: Huitzilapa, near Guadalajara, Mexico**

6.95 **Pictorial view of Huitzilapa**

Nakbe

The Mayan civilization, centered initially on the coastlines of Guatemala and El Salvador, spread northward between 250 and 900 CE into the Yucatán Peninsula. At its peak, it was one of the most densely populated and culturally dynamic societies in the world. Many of the pre-Classical sites declined by the 3rd century CE, leaving the cities in northern Guatemala dominant. The Mayas developed a religious philosophy controlled by a professional priesthood built around the importance of astronomical manifestations that were part of the eternal struggle between the powers of good and evil. The benevolent gods brought thunder, lightning, and rain, and insured abundance, whereas the malevolent ones brought death, destruction, hurricanes, and war. The religion developed into a worship of time in its various manifestations; it was highly esoteric in nature, requiring priests, mathematicians, and prophets. Dancing was an important aspect of religious ceremonies, as was the giving of sacrifices. These ranged from food offerings and ornaments (like feathers and shells) to the practice of human sacrifice.

This specialized production and dependency on foreign trade might have been the reason for both the success and the eventual demise of the Mayas. Trees were felled to fuel the kilns in which limestone was burned. Deforestation, it has been suggested, led to a gradual erosion of both land and wealth. By 350 BCE, a centralized elite was able to control large labor populations whose rapid rate of production was aided by the development of standardized construction modules and faster stonecutting techniques. It is during this period that monumental Mayan architecture—at a scale never seen previously—emerged in the Yucatán Peninsula. An abundance of massive architectural assemblages, ranging from 40 to 72 meters high, are found in the Mirador basin. Since they are located in marshes, all the major building groups were raised on large platforms that were then connected by elevated causeways.

Located in the Petén region of Guatemala, habitation at Nakbe started about 1400 BCE, reaching its height between 600 and 350 BCE. Its central area was constructed on a massive man-made platform surmounted by three mounds. The mounds contained clusters of temples, with the tallest structure, at 150 feet, on the west platform; the one on the east platform was 100 feet high. Nakbe was linked by causeways made of white crushed rock to adjoining settlements, including the one at El Mirador, its rival to the north.

In general, the organization of early Mayan ceremonial complexes was devoted to creating distinct visual hierarchies by means of a system of interconnected raised platform terraces surmounted by temples. The central ceremonial complex at Nakbe consists of two major, connected, built-up platforms (the eastern one 32 meters high, and the western one 45 meters high), on top of which the principal structures are clustered.

6.96 Stela 1, the Hero Twins, Nakbe, Guatemala

6.97 Site plan of Nakbe

O

6.98 El Tigre, El Mirador, Guatemala, as it stands today

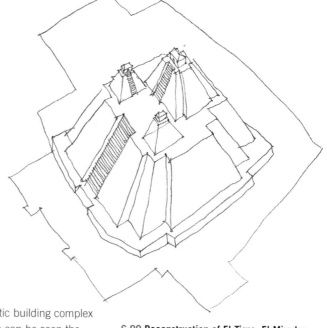

6.99 Reconstruction of El Tigre, El Mirador

The eastern platform has two parts. One is a cluster of low-platform structures on a terrace, creating a court that is anchored on its west side by a large freestanding pyramid. The other part has a larger pyramid, which is visible from the court, but whose access was restricted to priestly use. Thus a complex ceremonial whole was formed—with multiple hierarchically organized spatial and visual centers—that was used for multiple ceremonial functions.

Across the causeway is the western platform, which consists of three terraced courtyards, the highest of which supports the large pyramid; as with the others, access is restricted through the small courtyard in front of it. Since the function of Mayan pyramids was to support the temple, they were always flat-topped. The pyramid itself consisted of tightly compressed layers of stones and clay sealed by a brick casing.

El Mirador
Just north of Nakbe, El Mirador (Spanish for "lookout") was an early Mayan city that reached its cultural high point between 150 BCE and 150 CE. Though the city was spread out over an area of 16 square kilometers, the center was a crowded constellation of sacred and secular buildings. Here the platforms have been built up successively over time, comprising the largest set of platforms found anywhere in the Mayan world. The entire site was dominated by the

so-called El Tigre, a gigantic building complex covering 5.6 hectares. We can be seen the emerging Mayan typology of the triple summit structures. These generally consisted of a steep platform mountain having at its summit two smaller buildings facing each other in front of an axially placed stepped pyramid temple. Archaeologists believed that this arrangement represented the three stars in the constellation of Orion—known as Alnitak, Saiph, and Ligel—within which was supposed to burn the fire of creation.

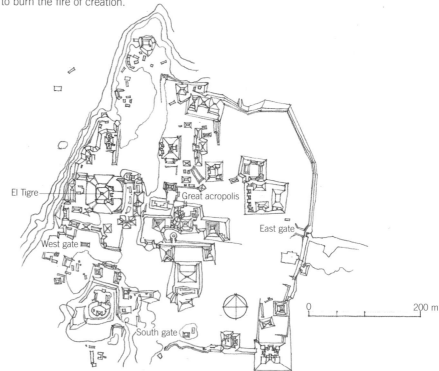

6.100 Site plan: The west group at El Mirador, Guatemala

200 CE

In the year 200 CE, Rome, Chang'an, and Teotihuacán were the world's megacities; all three were the capitals of vast empires. Imperial Rome, with more than a million inhabitants, had the largest population, whereas Teotihuacán, at 20 square kilometers, covered the largest area. By the 8th century, however, both Rome and Teotihuacán had been overtaken by Chang'an, which had become the largest city on the planet, drawing almost the entire Asian world into its economic orbit.

Between 100 and 300 CE, the Roman Empire grew into one of the greatest and most extensive empires in the world, and yet it was on the brink of disaster. During this time, wealth was lavished on temples, palaces, baths, viaducts, libraries, courts, streets, theaters, and amphitheaters. The development of Roman architecture, the most extensive urban architecture of any civilization to that date, reached from England to North Africa and from Spain to the Levant, and would have a profound impact on subsequent developments throughout Europe and beyond for centuries to come. The Han dynasty was also building cities, palaces, and tombs on a colossal scale, helped by remarkable advances in technology and mining. Its western capital, Chang'an, was built as starting point for caravans heading westward over the Taklamakan Desert. Situated between China and Rome were the Parthians, a horse-based tribal culture of former nomads who established themselves as a ruling elite in Mesopotamia and Central Asia. They were not an architecture-oriented culture and allowed local cults to continue temple building in the Hellenistic tradition.

But they were keen traders and played an important part in creating the Silk Route; their capital, Hecatompylos, became one of its prime stopping places.

At this time, an important religious transformation was taking place in western Asia, one with long-term ramifications beyond its immediate geographical range. The old Mesopotamian religions were superceded by Hellenistic and Iranian mystery cults, by sun cults, by Zoroastrianism's fire worship—and by Christianity. Novel religious concepts spread throughout northern India, the birthplace of the Buddha, as well. Generally, these new religious practices were more personal and mystical than their forerunners. Another emerging religion, Mithraism, was increasingly practiced by the soldiery in the far-spread provinces of the Roman Empire. Buddhism, which has to be understood as part of this search for ethical self-transformation, was developing rapidly, moving deeper and deeper into China and Southeast Asia in the form of monastic schools located along trade routes.

In any discussion of the global encounter between East and West, one has to mention the Kushans, a Mongolian people that had been pushed out of China into present-day Afghanistan, supplanting the Gandharan Empire. Living at the crossroads of the region, between Persia, India, and China, and adopting Buddhism, they produced stupa complexes that were Hellenic in articulation and Indian in form, with certain elements of Zoroastrian influences. During this time, the southern maritime trade routes from Egypt by way of the eastern coast of Africa to India, Indonesia, and China were beginning

to develop into a trade network as important as the land-based Silk Route. Like Petra in Jordan, Aksum in modern Ethiopia became a significant regional force, trading with India and, northward, with the Roman Empire.

In Peru, one sees several regional states emerging: the Moche in the north and, in the south, the Nazca, who produced large pilgrimage centers such as Cahuachi, where mysterious patterns on the ground later appeared, celebrated today as the Nazca Lines. The purpose of these elaborate designs, whose full impact can only be appreciated from the air, remain unresolved, as do questions about the nature of the Nazca's religious practices, to which they seem related. In Mexico, the superpower of the region was unquestionably Teotihuacán, the capital of an empire that encompassed most of Central America and that was the center of a trading network extending from the Mississippi Delta to the Peruvian coast. Teotihuacán was the largest and most influential city of pre-colonial America. All subsequent architecture in Central America was impacted by its legacy. In North America, originating along the Ohio River valley, we find the so-called Hopewell Culture, a loose confederation of tribes that shared a belief structure and burial practices not dissimilar to those in Poverty Point farther south. They created earthworks such as mounds, fenced-in hilltops, and geometrical configurations on the ground that served as gathering places and ceremonial locations. Unlike the people at Poverty Point, they were agriculturalists, with a far-flung trading network that ranged from the Atlantic Ocean to the Rocky Mountains and the Gulf of Mexico.

Roman Republic
509–27 BCE

▲ **Miletus**
479 BCE–250 CE

▲ **Ephesus**
270 BCE–420 CE

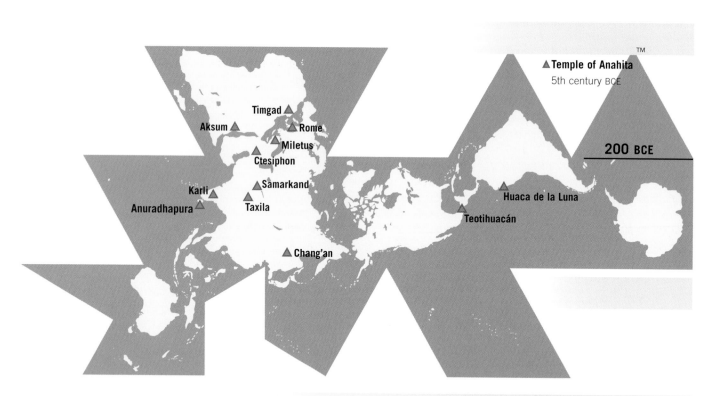

▲ **Temple of Anahita**
5th century BCE

200 BCE

Timgad ▲

Aksum ▲   ▲ Rome

▲ Miletus

Ctesiphon

▲ Samarkand

Karli ▲

Anuradhapura ▲   ▲ Taxila

▲ Chang'an

▲ Huaca de la Luna

▲ Teotihuacán

China: Western Han Dynasty
206 BCE–9 CE

▲ **Han Tombs**
3rd century BCE to 3rd century CE

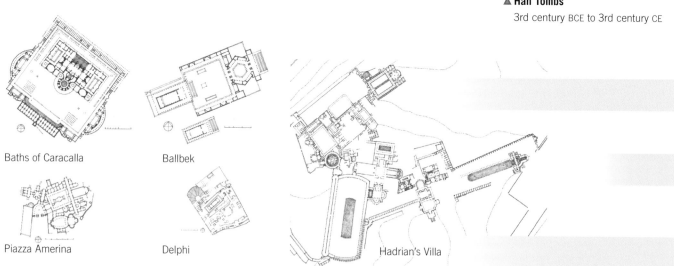

Baths of Caracalla

Ballbek

Piazza Amerina

Delphi

Hadrian's Villa

7.1 Relative sizes of sites

Roman Empire
27 BCE–393 CE

▲ Hadrian's Villa
118–34 CE

▲ Bath of Caracalla
212–16 CE

▲ Temple of Jupiter at Baalbek
Begun ca. 10 CE

▲ Pantheon
126 CE

▲ Baths of Diocletian
298–306 CE

▲ Library of Celsus at Ephesus
110 CE

▲ Diocletian's Palace
300 CE

Parthian Empire
247 BCE–224 CE

Sassanian Empire
224–651 CE

▲Takht-i-Suleiman
ca. 300 BCE–110 CE

▲ Palace of Ardashir
ca. 224 CE

Aksum Prominence
1st centuriy CE

0   **200 CE**   **400 CE**

Satavahana and Ikshvaku Dynasties
2nd century BCE to 4th century CE

◀ Amaravati Stupa
ca. 3rd century BCE

▲ *Caitya* Hall at Karli
ca. 2nd century CE

Kushan Empire
2nd century BCE to 3rd century CE

▲ Kushan Temple at Mat
1st century CE

▲Takht-i-Bahi
2nd century CE

▲ Jetavanarama Stupa
3rd century CE

Wang Mang Interregnum
9–25 CE

Eastern Han Dynasty
25–220 CE

Sixteen Kingdoms Period: North China
25–220 CE

▲ Mingtang-Biyong Ritual Complex
ca. 1st century BCE–1st century CE

Nazca Culture
300 BCE–200 CE

Moche Culture
ca. 200 BCE–700 CE

▲ Huaca del Sol and Huaca de la Luna
ca. 100 CE

Teotihuacán Culture
ca. 150 BCE–650 CE

▲ Pyramid of the Sun
ca. 200 CE

▲ Pyramid of the Moon
ca. 250 CE

Hopewell Culture
200 BCE–500 CE

7.2 **Roman Empire, ca. 200 CE**

Roman Empire

By the 2nd century CE, the Roman Empire extended as far north as Gaul and across the channel to England. Under Hadrian, North Africa was absorbed. Inroads were made into western Asia in order to secure trade links to the East. The eastern reaches of the empire were defined by older cities like Petra, Antioch, and Alexandria as well as by newly expanded cities like Palmyra and Duros Europus. The development of cities was now at its peak, and the consequences can be seen throughout Europe and the Mediterranean. The list of Roman foundations includes Aosta, Bordeaux, Florence, London, Mainz, Mantua, Paris, Milan, Silchester (Hampshire, England), Trier, Cologne, Turin, Verona, and Vienna, to name only a few. Many cities, like Florence, Milan, Paris, and Trier, still carry the imprint of the Roman grid to this day. Though the paradigm for the city was the *castrum*, or military camp, which was divided by two intersecting main streets, the *cardo* and *decumanus*, this model was used mainly in the initial phases of the colonization in Europe and North Africa. In Europe, though some of the Gaulic cities remained in use, many, because they were on hilltops, were evacuated by the Romans, who preferred valleys and river towns, which were easier to defend and more amenable to Roman practices of camp organization. The *castrum* model, however, was rarely used

in the East, where cities were already well established.

North Africa is an excellent place to study Roman urban concepts; it supplied the capital with staple crops and luxury goods. Hadrian was eager to develop this area and offered free tenancy and a period of tax exemption to anyone who would agree to reside permanently on marginal land and put it under cultivation. It was a successful policy that encouraged the establishment of rural trading centers, many of which developed into urban environments. In some places

a new town was founded, like Timgad, a gridded city roughly the size of Florence; in others, such as at Lepcis Magna, an existing Phoenician city (east of Tripoli), the planners adopted a flexible and additive approach.

Roman cities were more differentiated than Greek cities, which were defined by a central agora and temple precincts. A Roman city had streets, squares, fountains, gates, memorial columns, and public buildings that formed a type of armature around which the rest of the city grew. At Palmyra and Ostia we can see the attempt to graft this armature

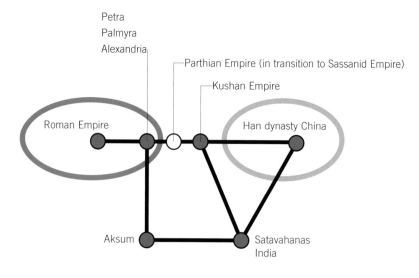

7.3 **Trade diagram, ca. 200 CE**

7.4 Principal temple of Djemila, Algeria

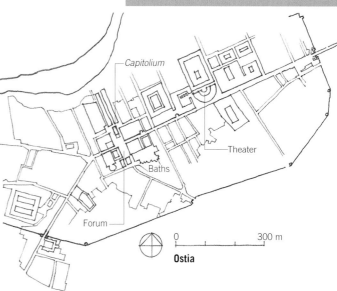

7.5 Plans of three Roman towns drawn at the same scale and orientation

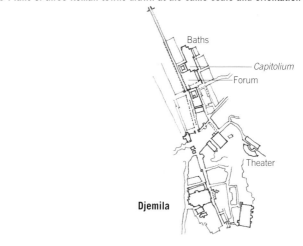

onto places that had been founded at an earlier date, when they were more towns than cities. Djemila, in Algeria (96 CE), is typical; its elongated shape is a result of the terrain. The first part of the city to the north shows a relatively systematized layout, with the forum at the center of the town along the main road. But when that proved inadequate, a new forum, temple, and theater were built in a southward extension that followed the curves of an existing road. Though Timgad (100 BCE) is often given as a typical example of the rigorous application of the grid, the original town soon outgrew its borders. In fact, the elements of the armature that were originally left out of the design—the baths, the gates, even a *capitolium*—were grafted onto the fabric of the city. A new arch, the Lambaesis Gate, demarcated the limits of the development. These urban extensions show a willingness to negotiate with the landscape and existing features such as roads. In some places, the Romans were even willing to work within the Hellenistic design mold; the most spectacular examples of this are at Ephesus and Miletus.

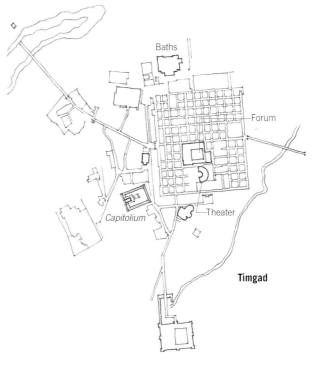

7.6 Main road of Timgad, Algeria

7.7 Plan: Ephesus, Turkey

Harbor

0   1200 m

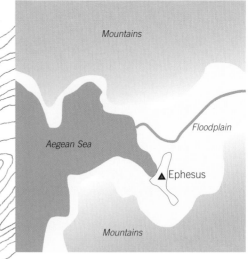

7.8 Area plan of Ephesus

Mountains

Aegean Sea

Floodplain

▲ Ephesus

Mountains

Ephesus, a small town and religious center on the shores of the Cayster River near its mouth on the Turkish coast, was settled in the 9th century BCE and began to develop into an important port. Because the river was silting over, the city was abandoned and rebuilt at its current location 2 kilometers to the east around 270 BCE. It was designed not from the top down, as was Pergamon, but horizontally, in a protected, curving valley that opens in dramatic fashion onto the new harbor. By the end of the 5th century CE, the port of this city, just like that of the first one, silted up and the city fell into disuse. Today the harbor is 5 kilometers inland.

	Ephesus rebuilt	ca. 270 BCE
1	Theater	100 BCE
2	Agora	4 CE
3	Stadium	54 CE
4	Fountain	86 CE
5	Gymnasium	90 CE
6	State agora and odeum	100 CE
7	Temple of Domitian	96 CE
8	Nymphaeum	102 CE
9	Library of Celsus	110 CE
10	Temple of Hadrian	120 CE
11	Gates of Heracles	150 CE
12	Gymnasium of Vedius	150 CE
13	Pollio Fountain	150 CE
14	Temple of Serapis	170 CE
15	Palace of the Proconsul	300 CE
16	Baths of Scholastica	370 CE
17	Arcadiane	395 CE
18	Marble Way	420 CE

7.9 Theater at Ephesus

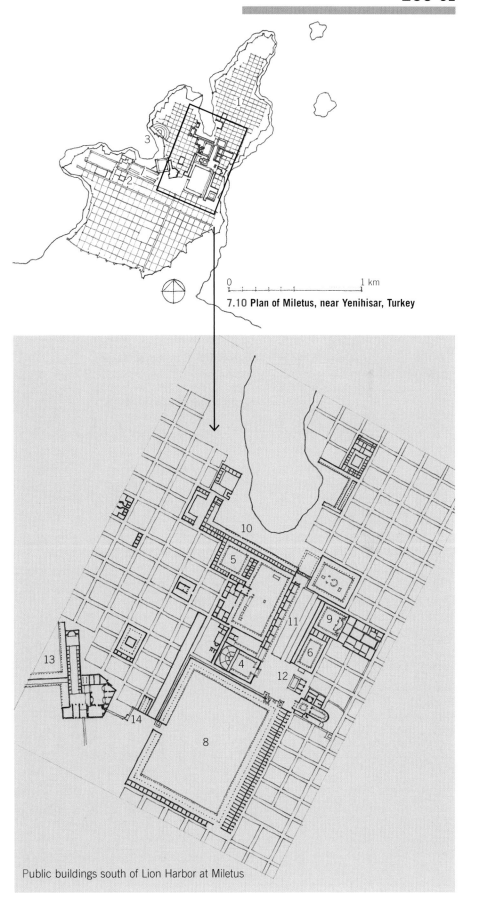

7.10 Plan of Miletus, near Yenihisar, Turkey

0   1 km

Miletus, on the western coast of Anatolia, went through three distinct phases. First it was a Greek colony; then it was a quasi-independent city-state, prospering during Hellenistic times; and finally, it became part of the Roman Empire. In the latter phase, the designers worked sometimes with, and sometimes against, the established pattern; some of the older buildings, like the Bouleuterion (175–164 BCE), were preserved, while others were destroyed. They also inserted an intricate web of public buildings, streets, gates, and spaces that linked the old harbor with the new extension to the south. The dates show the pace of construction.

	Miletus founded	479 BCE
1	Northern street grid	470 BCE
2	Temple of Athena	450 BCE
3	Theater	450 BCE
	Rise to prominence	
4	Bouleuterion	175 BCE
5	North agora	170 BCE
6	Gymnasium	150 BCE
7	Stadium	150 BCE
8	South agora	150 BCE
	Imperial era	
9	Baths of capitol	50 CE
10	Harbor stoa, redesigned	50 CE
11	Processional way	150 CE
12	Nymphaeum	150 CE
13	Baths of Faustina	170 CE
14	Temple of Serapis	250 CE

Public buildings south of Lion Harbor at Miletus

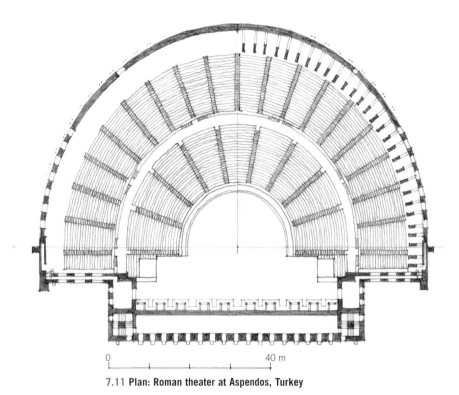

7.11 Plan: Roman theater at Aspendos, Turkey

0   40 m

The Roman Theater

Almost all Roman cities had a theater used for both popular and religious purposes. In the days of the republic, the Romans were somewhat skeptical of theaters—which were common in Greek cities—concerned about their potentially corrupting influences. One decree forbade sitting at theaters, since it was deemed more manly to stand. As a result, theaters built during the Republican period were temporary structures built of wood. The first permanent theater was ordered by Pompey in 55 BCE. Its design was what could be called transitional; it included a temple of Venus at the top of the seating area so that the rows of seats appeared to be steps leading up to the temple. Gradually this subterfuge fell away once theaters were built in the colonies, where the emphasis was on the theater as a public amenity.

Whereas Greek theaters were carefully and strategically inserted into the natural landscape and often had dramatic views, the Roman theater was conceived as an urban architectural element, its magnificence and splendor a token of Rome's imperial status. The slope of the seating was steeper than in Greek theaters, possibly for acoustic reasons. Initially, Roman theaters were hollowed out of a hill or slope, as at the theater at Aspendos, a Roman colony in Turkey. Over time, however, Romans viewed their theaters as regular urban structures. All of the theaters built within the city of Rome were made without the use of earthworks. Also unlike Greek theaters, the auditorium, though not roofed, was covered with awnings, *velaria*, which could be stretched out from tall poles to provide shelter from rain or sunlight. The stage building (*scaenae frons*) was usually three stories high, with the theater divided into the stage (orchestra) and the seating section (auditorium).

7.12 Roman theater at Aspendos

7.13 The Pantheon, Rome

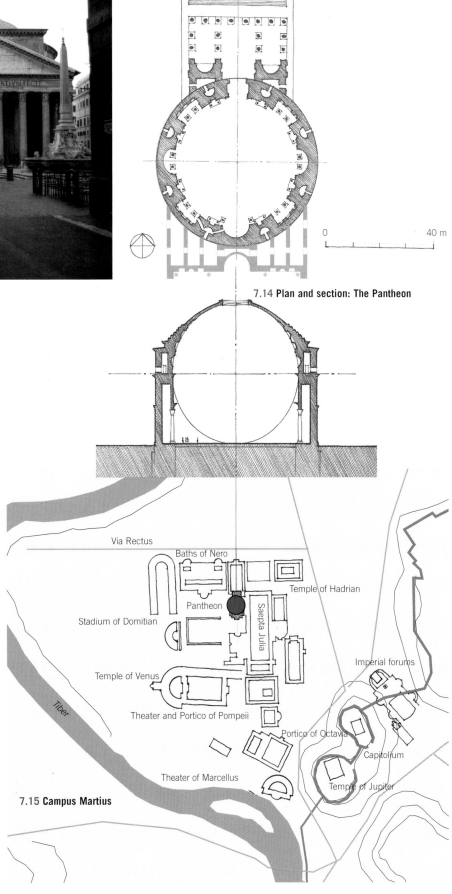

7.14 Plan and section: The Pantheon

7.15 Campus Martius

The Pantheon

Hadrian (76–138 CE) had, of all the emperors, the deepest personal interest in architecture; he was also a poet and a painter—as well as a competent commander. His reign was generally a peaceful one, except for the role he played in the Bar-Kokhbar Revolt in Judaea. Reneging on his promise to let the Jews rebuild their destroyed temple, he planned to replace it with a temple to Jupiter and turn Jerusalem into a Roman city, the Aelia Capitolina, named after his own name, Aelia, and that of the Roman god Jupiter Capitolinus. The resulting revolution was brutally repressed. Hadrian's effect on architecture was felt in all corners of the empire, including Rome, where he built numerous buildings, but none more significant than the Pantheon (126 CE). Though it has been repaired many times, the Pantheon has served as a church for centuries. Although it has lost its original marble cladding and lacks the impressively dimensioned court that once framed the entrance of its facade, it is still an impressive building. However, what one sees today from the outside is nothing like the original, which was not a freestanding building but embedded in the urban fabric. Its principal view would have been from within a long, colonnaded forecourt.

The building was sited in an area north of the old city center known as Campus Martius (the "Field of Mars"), that was, before the founding of Rome, used for pasturing horses

7.16 Oculus of the Pantheon

and for military exercises. During imperial times, it became the site of Rome's urban expansion, with baths, theaters, and temples, including a large open courtyard building known as the Saepta Julia, where Romans voted.

Though much of the Pantheon's bulk is overdimensioned, one cannot fault its architects for wanting a building that would last through the ages. Its bold interior space was, even for the Romans, an innovation. Though domed spaces were not uncommon, none compared to this one. It derives conceptually from Greek and Egyptian mathematical interest in spatial geometry, which was introduced by Hadrian, who was familiar with Egyptian practices, having lived in Alexandria. It was Archimedes, a Greek, who had solved the problem of measuring the volume of the sphere and cylinder in relation to each other. Romans contributed practically nothing to analytical geometry. In that sense, the building is relatively un-Roman. While the classical *cella* had always been a dark and mysterious place oriented east to the rising sun, this building rejects that tradition.

Jupiter is here represented not by a statue but by the abstraction of light itself. It was a remarkable anomaly in Roman thinking, for while smaller domed oculus structures had been built earlier, they were for bathhouses, like the one that still stands at Baia, on the

north shore of the Bay of Naples. These places might have been a good place to work out technical issues, but they were certainly not models in the symbolic sense. The octagonal room in Nero's palace brings us closer, in that it ended in an oculus and descriptions emphasize its symbolic purpose. Perhaps seventy-five years later, with Hadrian, Roman architects had an emperor who, like Nero, had a verve for architectural experimentation and an interest in the Hellenistic East, where sun worship first came into its own in Egypt and Syria.

Against the vertical alignment of the half-spherical dome, one has to add the startling dynamic of the sun's rays as they move slowly through the space like a searchlight, illuminating one by one elements of the architectural interior—sometimes the floor, with its pattern of orange, red, and white marbles brought in from all over the empire; sometimes the orange marble columns; sometimes the coffering of the dome itself. The building probably had an astronomical dimension, but nothing about that is known for certain.

Unfortunately, no Roman text has yet been found that explains the interior in respect to the arrangement of the divine statues, the ritual practices undertaken in the building, or even the symbolism of the oculus. But it is likely that the building alludes to the unity of the divine and the imperial realms. Apart from sun temples that were beginning to be built in Syria (where Hadrian was the governor in 117 CE), there are mystery cults that emphasized light and darkness, like the Eleusinian Mysteries practiced in Greece, into which Hadrian had been initiated. In that sense the building can be perceived as an import of Eastern religious ideas into the very heart of Rome. Originally, a flight of five steps as wide as the entrance portico led to the floor level of the interior. The monolithic shafts of the facade are of gray Egyptian granite; the four inner columns are reddish Egyptian granite; and the capitals Pentelic marble. The porch leads

7.17 Interior of the Pantheon

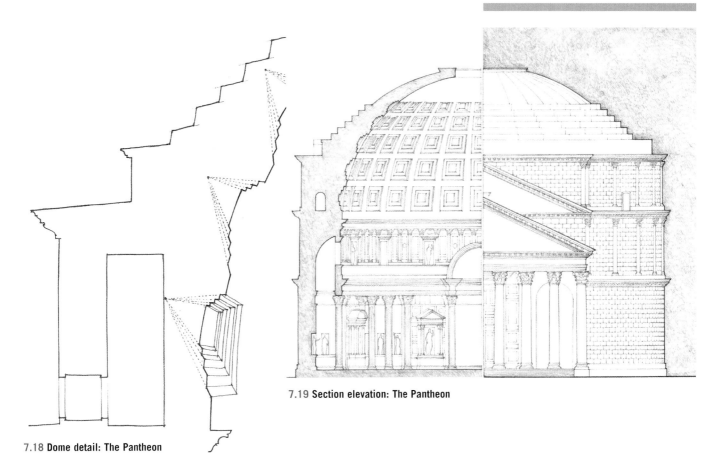

7.18 Dome detail: The Pantheon

7.19 Section elevation: The Pantheon

to a barrel-vaulted entranceway, flanked by niches. Between the porch and the rotunda are areas for stairways to reach the spaces that honeycomb the cylindrical structure. The threshold is defined by a huge block of Portasanta marble. The walls, carved out by alternating square and round niches, form four axial connections through the center space.

The niches of the interior are screened by columns and flanked by pilasters of yellow-orange marble under a continuous entablature. The apse alone is marked by freestanding columns, which interrupt the entablature running along the back of the niche. The dome presents itself on the interior as successive rings of coffering that diminish in size and depth as they near the oculus. They end, however, not at the mouth of the oculus but well short of it, leaving a smooth, platelike area around the opening. The concrete surface of the dome visible today is, however, not what contemporaries saw. The edges of the oculus, and the coffering as well, were probably gilded, with

rosettes filling the centers of the coffers and creating a much more ephemeral, and less structural, impression, than what can be observed today.

Though the Romans are often praised for structural innovation, they could easily make structure subservient to architectural vision. The lower half of the coffering, in fact, bears no relationship whatsoever to the structure behind it. In that sense, the architects were willing to work with the illusion of structure, or at least wanted to separate the visual vocabulary of a dome's structure, from the hard reality of the structural support. The coffering should therefore not be seen as a three-dimensional concrete space frame in the modern sense, for even the coffering was designed from an optical point of view. The steps are shallower on their lower edge and steeper on the higher so as to appear the same height when viewed from the center of the floor.

The lower part of the structure is brick-faced concrete, with voids serving to reduce the overall weight. Massive curving vaults

direct the forces to the ground. For the dome, only concrete was used. The pour, made against a temporary wooden formwork, had to be seamless, placed bottom to top without pause in order to guarantee the cohesion of the whole. Organizing the production of the concrete, its immediate transport to the level of the dome, and its distribution to the right places by men carrying small batches was quite a feat. The width of the dome at the bottom is 6.15 meters. It thins to only 1.5 meters at the level of the oculus, which is 8.3 meters across and open to air and weather.

Despite the powerful evocations of the building, Hadrian's experiment would not be repeated, at least not in a way that can be confirmed. Though Roman architects continued to work with domed spaces, as in the Baths of Caracalla, the dome-and-oculus combination remained rare.

The original intermediary frieze was replaced in 1747 with one far less delicate in proportion. In the early 20th century, a small section of the original frieze was rebuilt based on Renaissance-era drawings.

Hadrian's Villa

Hadrian's other major contribution to architecture was an extravagant villa complex, a miniature world that he built for himself (118–34 CE) at the top of a hill about 25 kilometers east of Rome. It is not a single building, but a series of interconnected structures and gardens. Unlike the Palace of Domitian, with its compressed orderliness, the villa returns to the more freewheeling texture of Nero's palace. There are dozens of distinct elements separated from each other in the landscape and yet linked in surprising ways, so that the whole design unfolds only gradually. Some of the parts were meant to evoke memories of distant lands from Hadrian's far-flung travels. The residential parts were to the north. To the south was the stadium followed by a series of baths ending in the spectacular structure known as the *canopus*, which was lined with copies of the caryatids of the Erechtheum in Athens.

The whole was meant to evoke the international—and particularly Greek and Egyptian—flavor of Hadrian's trips. In that sense the villa was a collection of memories and allusions. The *canopus*, for example, refers to a particularly bright star that was often used in navigation by Mediterranean sailors. It appears in numerous Greek legends and was also the name of an Egyptian port near the mouth of the Nile. The *canopus* at Hadrian's Villa is designed as a long lake decorated along its edges with columns supporting alternating arches and lintels. The Shrine of Serapis (Serapeum) on the southern end of the complex was built against a steeply sloping hillside, creating the impression of a grotto or miniature gorge with a waterfall at the back. It was dedicated to Serapis, the syncretic Hellenistic-Egyptian god who was the protector of the city of Alexandria. With water from an aqueduct above flowing through the gorge and around a crescent-shaped masonry reclining seat toward the long, riverlike pool, diners on the curved bench seats would have had a cool and enjoyable meal, even in the heat of summer. A small semicircular pool where food could be floated back and forth further added to its charm. The vault's surfaces were covered with blue and green mosaics. And the walls of the exedra were decorated with semicircular niches that held statues.

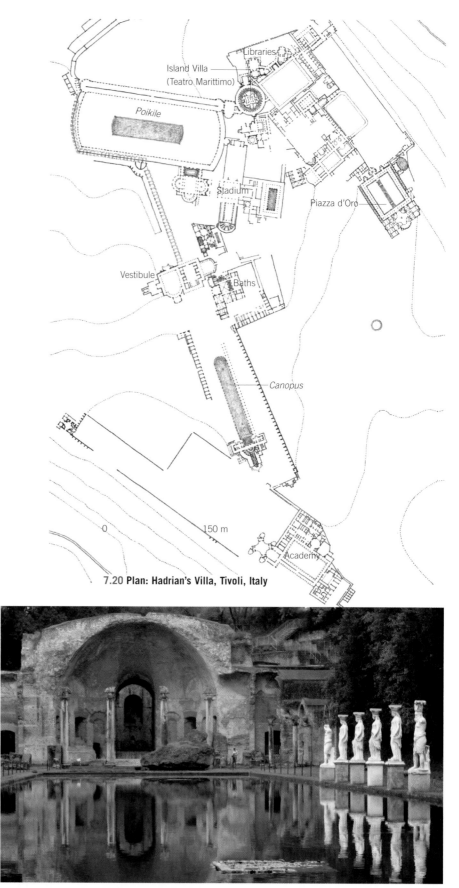

7.20 **Plan: Hadrian's Villa, Tivoli, Italy**

7.21 *Canopus*, Hadrian's Villa

7.23 Island Villa, Hadrian's Villa

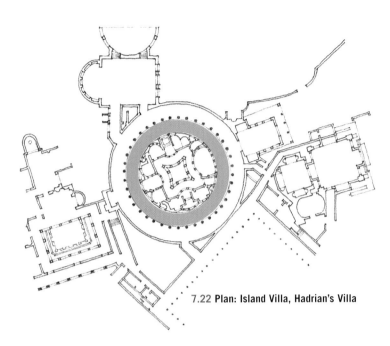

7.22 Plan: Island Villa, Hadrian's Villa

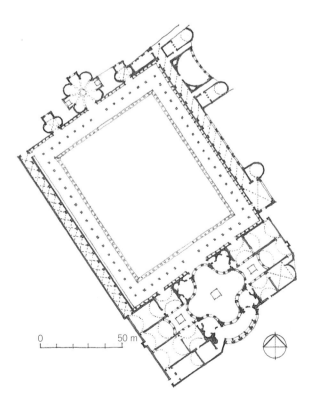

7.24 Plan: Piazza d'Oro, Hadrian's Villa

The so-called Island Villa, surrounded by a moat and a colonnade, is among the many astonishing elements of the villa. Access across bridges leads into an intricate architectural composition of concave and convex curves. The apparent symmetry at the center, typical of the spatial imagination of Roman architects, feathers out toward the perimeter, as if the architect had less and less control over the more marginal volumes—in a sense a metaphor for the Roman Empire itself. The two bedroom suites were on the east side; the dining room on the south. The western side was taken up by a small bathing suite. At the center of the compressed peristyle court was a fountain, its sound filtering its way through the rooms.

The Piazza d'Oro, another element in the villa, consists of a large, nearly square peristyle court, with a pool at its center. At the far end is a pavilion, or *nymphaeum.* The main room is composed of rounded "walls" turned concave and then convex to form a flowing, four-armed space. (These were not walls in the strict sense, but curved colonnades.) The room was open to the sky. The four ancillary spaces at the corners are all identical. The concave side leads to rooms with fountains in the floors, whereas the one on the principal axis leads to a curving space, the back wall of which is lined with fountains. Hadrians's Villa shows the Roman spatial imagination at its best. Order is balanced against complexity, as is architecture against landscape.

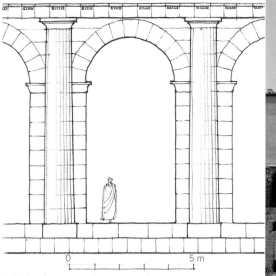

7.25 **Fornix system of the** *tabularium*

7.26 **Arch of Septimus Severus, Rome**

Roman Vertical Surface

Since the Egyptians covered their temple walls with images or historical reliefs, there was no opportunity for architects to think of the wall as anything other than a definer of space. In Greek architecture, walls were often hidden behind columns, and even though the Greeks invented the pilaster in the form of columns in antis, and sometimes even articulated walls with shallow panels, they never saw the wall as anything other than a wall. But by the time of the Colosseum, Roman architects were beginning to experiment with complex articulations of the vertical surface. For the first time, the wall became an architectural element per se. The technique of framing arches within engaged half-columns supporting an entablature, called the fornix system of ornamentation (*fornix* meaning "vault" or "arched room"), dates back to about 150 BCE. The amphitheater of Nîmes (in France) recapitulates the theme, as do numerous triumphal arches, such as the Arch of Titus (81 CE). Eventually, *aediculae* and niches were added to the vocabulary, as can be seen at the Arch of Trajan at Timgad (100 CE), a path-breaking design. The central arch is flanked by smaller arches surmounted by *aediculae* flanked by their own columns. The two sides are then organized by enormous columns that reach to the top of the *aediculae* and that, with the help of imposts, rise to a level where the arches can spring over them. The two side elements are then

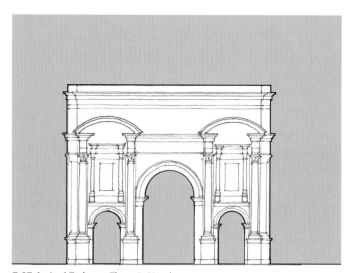

7.27 **Arch of Trajan at Timgad, Algeria**

united by an entablature that is reduced to a thin projection. It is perhaps a bit awkward, but certainly kinetic.

To get a sense of the level of experimentation that this opened up, one can turn once again to the rock-cut tombs of Petra in southern Jordan. The so-called Palace Tomb, which has been variously dated to the second half of the 1st century CE or early 2nd century, for example, shows a stratified design, with the lower register of four doors framed by round-headed and pedimented *aediculae* with unusual, abstracted capitals. The whole is tied together by an unbroken entablature on which rests

a row of half-columns, the last ones being pilasters; above that is an accordion-style entablature with the pilaster order shadowing its way through to the top.

The Tomb of Sextius Florentinus is particularly refined. Above the lower register is a pilaster order and a second set of capitals. This interpenetration of horizontals and verticals shows a capacity to see in the x- and y-axes simultaneously. Such a degree of visual complexity would not recur until the Italian Renaissance.

During the 2nd century CE, richly elaborated architectural fronts that had once been associated with the prosceniums in theaters sprouted forth in public spaces. This is true of the facade of the Library of Celsus at Ephesus (110 CE), which stands on the western end of a marble courtyard and is approached by a flight of nine steps. The three entrances, with large windows above them, are flanked by four niches that contain statues personifying the virtues of Celsus, Roman senator and proconsul of Asia. In front of the facade are four double-story pairs of columns; the capitals of the lower story are Corinthian, and those of the upper story, Ionic. In a further display of design skill, the architect changed the pairing between top and bottom. At the top, the columns are brought together with pedimental and rounded arches spanning the gaps. The end columns stand almost free against the facade. Such displays were more than just architectural excess. They conformed to the Hellenistic desire for immediacy and were meant to express the qualities and generosity of the patron.

7.28 Library of Celsus, Ephesus, Turkey

7.29 South market gate, Miletus, Turkey

At the *nymphaeum* of Nîmes, France, the columnar elements form an exoskeleton against which presses the mass of the walls. The search for complex and imaginative formations reaches a climax at the stage for the South Theater in Gerasa. Though the first floor has been reconstructed, it shows a row of paired columns on dadoes forming a screen in front of pedimented doorways with *aediculae* between them; the base of the *aediculae* rests atop of the dado. A similarly well-thought-out scheme prevails at the court of the Temple of Zeus at Baalbek. Two Corinthian columns in antis work with two pilasters to create the semblance of a screen unit. The *aediculae*, roundheaded at the bottom level and pedimented at the top level, are squeezed in between the pilasters, practically hiding the wall surface behind. The theme continues in the large niche behind the columns. The whole is tied together by a single unbroken entablature.

Entablature

Pedimented niches
Columns in-antis

Round-headed *aediculae*

Pilasters

7.30 Facade detail: Court of the Temple of Zeus, Baalbek, Lebanon

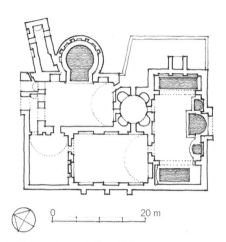

7.31 Plan: Agora Baths at Ephesus

0   20 m

Roman Baths

Although wealthy Romans had baths in their townhouses and country villas, the heating of a series of rooms, or even an entire separate building especially for this purpose, was usually reserved for public bathhouses, which were available in cities and towns throughout the empire. These baths, called *thermae*, were owned by the state and often covered several city blocks. Entrance fees were quite reasonable and within the budget of most free Romans. The area in these baths that was actually covered with water was relatively small, for the bulk of the structure was filled by exercise spaces, lounges, and places to stroll. Since the Roman workday began at sunrise, work was usually over at a little after noon. At about 2 or 3 PM, men would go to the baths, staying for several hours of sport, bathing, and conversation, after which they would be ready for a relaxing dinner. Republican bathhouses often had separate bathing facilities for women and men, but by the time of the empire, the custom was to open the baths to women during the early part of the day and reserve them for men from 2 PM until closing at sundown.

The baths were secular spaces not associated with altars or divine patronage. Some of the thermal or mineral baths, however, might be associated with local river nymphs or the gods of medicine. Baths offered an environment that was both sensual and social. Some baths had lecture halls and libraries. The origin of these institutions goes back to the beginning of classical culture and the emphasis placed on physical fitness by the Greeks; bathing was viewed as a part of the hygienic rituals associated with sports. Gymnasiums, in which sports and education were combined, were reserved primarily for the sons of citizens and as a place for military training. Under Alexander the Great, however, the baths of Greek gymnasiums became a more social environment— and the Roman bath even more so. In fact, few citizens were so poor that they could not afford the entrance fee. Aware of the beneficial role these institutions played in the health, education, and entertainment of the people, the Roman State allocated considerable resources to their maintenance. The larger buildings were also the perfect vehicle for state propaganda. Their lavish interiors were decorated with trophies, inscriptions, and sculptures reflecting the reach and power of the emperor.

The Baths of Caracalla (212–16 CE) are recognized as the best developed example of the Roman public bath. The main building (200 by 114 meters) was set in an enclosure (328 by 400 meters) that contained cisterns, running tracks, gardens, libraries, and shops. The facade was relatively austere and had only a few doors; by contrast, the internal spaces were open and sunny. The main

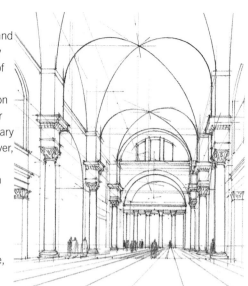

7.32 Interior scale: Baths of Caracalla, Rome

pool was the *natatio*, or swimming pool. Though it had no roof, the towering walls on all sides provided cooling shade in the afternoon. The *frigidarium* was at the center of the composition. It was covered by three cross-vaults that soared above the level of the surrounding rooms. Clerestory light would have filtered down into the space. The right and left rooms led to the *palaestrae*, the exercise courts. Then came the *tepidarium*, with small plunge baths of warm water

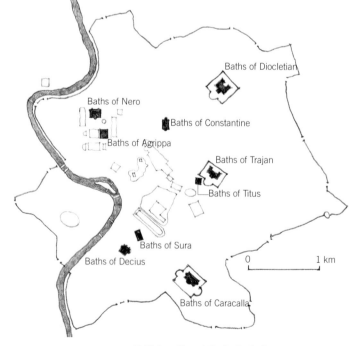

7.33 Location of the baths in Rome

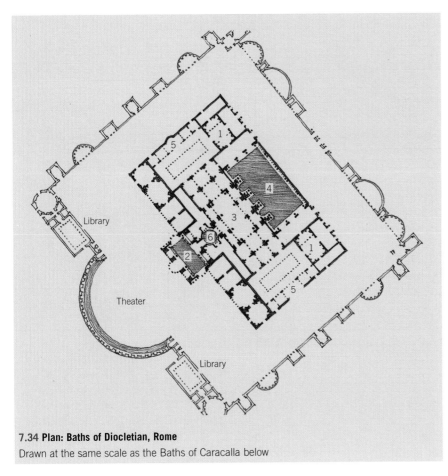

7.34 Plan: Baths of Diocletian, Rome
Drawn at the same scale as the Baths of Caracalla below

on both sides. The climax was a circular *caldarium* 35 meters across, with large windows in the walls. Heat was supplied by hypocaust ducts from below.

There are eight major public baths in Rome; they covered a significant proportion of the city by the time of the end of the empire.

25 CE	Baths of Agrippa
64 CE	Baths of Nero
80 CE	Baths of Titus
104 CE	Baths of Trajan
ca. 100 CE	Baths of Sura
212–16 CE	Baths of Caracalla
ca. 250 CE	Baths of Decius
298–306 CE	Baths of Diocletian
320 CE	Baths of Constantine

Parts of the Roman Bath

1 *Apodyterium*: Dressing room/locker room
2 *Caldarium*: Main hot room
3 *Frigidarium*: Main cold-water hall, often containing several unheated pools
4 *Natatio*: Large unheated swimming pool
5 *Palaestra*: Exercise yard
6 *Sudatorium*: Sweat chamber
7 *Tepidarium*: Warm room and bath, often a type of "heat lock" between the *caldarium* and *frigidarium*

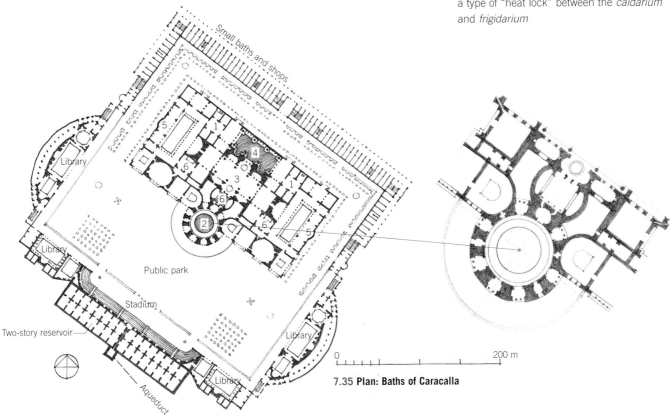

7.35 Plan: Baths of Caracalla

Diocletian's Palace

In 166 CE, Germanic tribes breached Rome's frontier along the upper Danube, and in 172 CE the Moors from northern Africa invaded Spain. In 253 CE, the Franks from the middle and lower Rhine regions began to launch intermittent attacks on northern Spain. In 257 CE, the Goths raided Greece and Asia Minor. Although the empire was under siege, there were also problems within Rome itself. In the decades before Diocletian (r. 284–316 CE) became emperor, there had been no less than twenty successive emperors proclaimed by the senate, and at least as many usurpers and pretenders. To restore order in Gaul and to prevent usurpation of the throne, Diocletian drastically changed the governance of the empire, a move that had profound historical implications for the rest of Europe. He split the empire into two, and then into two again, with his friend Maximian serving as co-regent in the western part of the empire. The four rulers had their respective capitals at Nicomedia, Greece; Mediolanum (modern Milan); Treveri (today's Trier, Germany); and Sirmium (in modern-day Serbia). Diocletian governed the Asiatic part of the empire and Egypt from Nicomedia, using the Persian model of rulership, implementing other territorial partitionings of the empire, and separating military from civilian administration. Initially these efforts were successful. In 296 CE, Britain was restored to the empire; in 298 CE, the Persians were subjugated and the Germans were expelled. Although tolerant of Christianity, which was growing in momentum, Diocletian issued an edict in Nicomedia in 303 CE in which he prohibited it. This brought about numerous executions, the confiscation of property, and the destruction of churches. On May 1, 305 CE, he abdicated and retired to the palace he had prepared for his retirement in Split (Spalato) on the Bay of Aspalathos, on the coast of what is today Croatia.

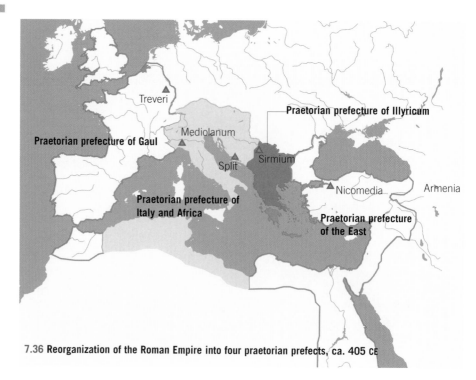

7.36 Reorganization of the Roman Empire into four praetorian prefects, ca. 405 CE

Diocletian and Maximian both built sumptuous palaces. The Piazza Armerina by Maximian, located in eastern Sicily near Catania, follows some of the conventions of Hadrian's Villa, though with less overall compositional quality. The various elements seem to be stuck together relatively arbitrarily around a large open courtyard. Nonetheless, the composition is not without order. From a curved entrance courtyard, the visitor turns right into a series of slightly disjointed spaces leading up to the audience hall at the east. The composition is tied together by a type of "street" running north and south linking the principal elements of the program.

In contrast to Piazza Armerina, Diocletian's Palace in Split, Croatia, is part fortified camp, part city, and part villa. It is in the form of a slightly irregular rectangle (175 by 216 meters) protected by walls and gates, with towers projecting from the western, northern, and eastern facades.

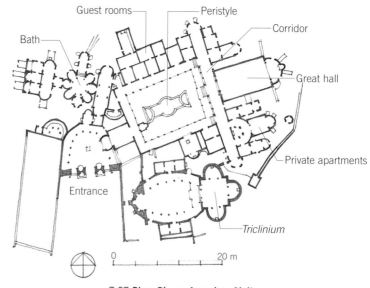

7.37 Plan: Piazza Armerina, Sicily

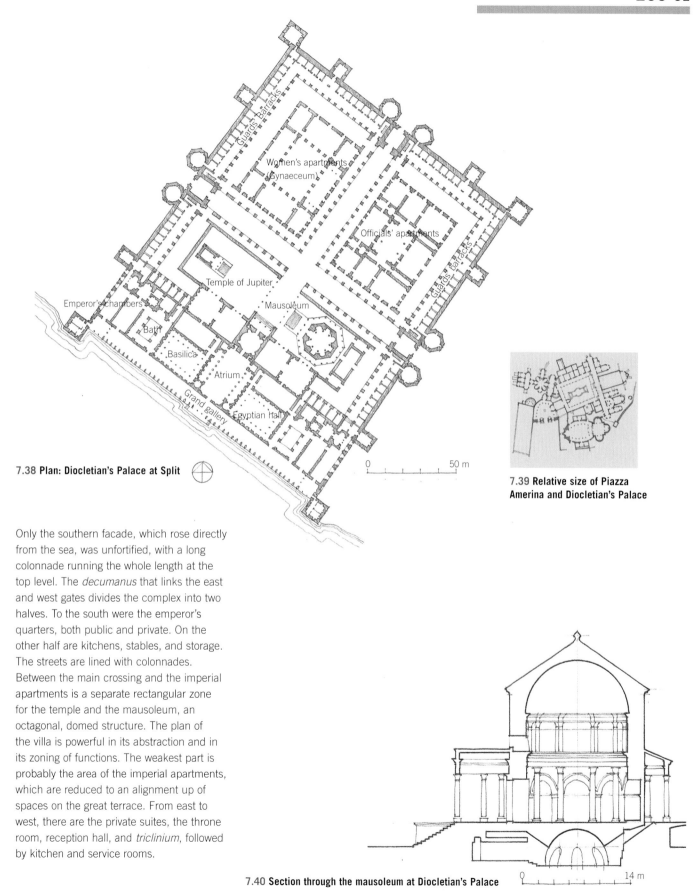

7.38 Plan: Diocletian's Palace at Split

0   50 m

7.39 Relative size of Piazza Amerina and Diocletian's Palace

Only the southern facade, which rose directly from the sea, was unfortified, with a long colonnade running the whole length at the top level. The *decumanus* that links the east and west gates divides the complex into two halves. To the south were the emperor's quarters, both public and private. On the other half are kitchens, stables, and storage. The streets are lined with colonnades. Between the main crossing and the imperial apartments is a separate rectangular zone for the temple and the mausoleum, an octagonal, domed structure. The plan of the villa is powerful in its abstraction and in its zoning of functions. The weakest part is probably the area of the imperial apartments, which are reduced to an alignment up of spaces on the great terrace. From east to west, there are the private suites, the throne room, reception hall, and *triclinium*, followed by kitchen and service rooms.

0   14 m

7.40 Section through the mausoleum at Diocletian's Palace

7.41 Location of Baalbek, West Asia

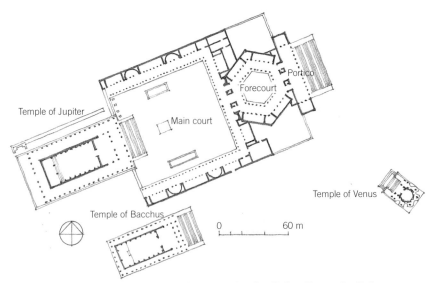

7.42 Plan: Sanctuary of Jupiter Heliopolitanus, Baalbek

Baalbek

The supreme deity of the Canaanites was El, the sun god who also carried the bull as an attribute. The fertility goddess Ashera was his companion. Worshippers were not allowed to pray directly to the couple but could use the mediating influence of their son, Baal, the master of rain, tempest, and thunder. This was typical of Hellenistic religions, which saw the emergence of several sons of deities. The principal site of the worship of Baal was near a natural rock fissure some 15 meters deep, at the bottom of which was a small rock-cut altar. Since the altar was difficult to access, another one was constructed above it on the hill. This was then augmented with protective gates and towers. Eventually a temple was added, built on a high undercroft. The Temple of Jupiter, the final temple on that site, was begun during the reign of Augustus (27 BCE–14 CE); it was constructed on a scale unknown in Rome until then. Some of the foundation stones weighed 800 tons. Nonetheless, it was not as big as some of the enormous Hellenistic temples, such as the one at Dydima, which sat on a podium 17 meters high, with columns reaching another 22 meters. (Size was an element typical of the colonies but looked down upon by the homeland as a sort of barbaric excess.)

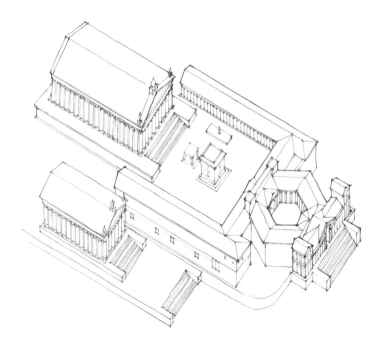

7.43 Pictorial view: Sanctuary of Jupiter Heliopolitanus

The temple's entrance was demarcated by two buildings: the propylaeum (3rd century CE) and a hexagonal court (2nd century CE). The latter opens onto a court surrounded by porticoes and rooms serving various functions. The creative combinations of columns, attached columns, arches, and *aediculae* with round or pedimental tops would all be rediscovered only in the age of the Baroque. Trajan visited the shrine around 115 CE to consult the oracle before his Parthian campaign, and it may even have influenced him in the design of his forum. In 195 CE, Septimus Severus (r. 193–211 CE) bestowed upon Baalbek the title *jus italicum*, moving it up into the most prominent class of Roman cities. Construction at the site continued during the rule of Caracalla (211–17 CE), a member of the Syrian dynasty of emperors.

Nearby is the Temple of Venus (3rd century CE), an extraordinary building composed of a round *cella* with a porch. The *cella* on the exterior is ornamented by columns attached by scalloped entablature, creating a dynamic play between the round and rectilinear geometries. Building activity in Baalbek was still taking place when Emperor Constantine declared Christianity the official religion of the Roman state in 330 CE, putting an end to one of the largest and longest building projects in the Levant.

7.44 Temple of Venus, Baalbek

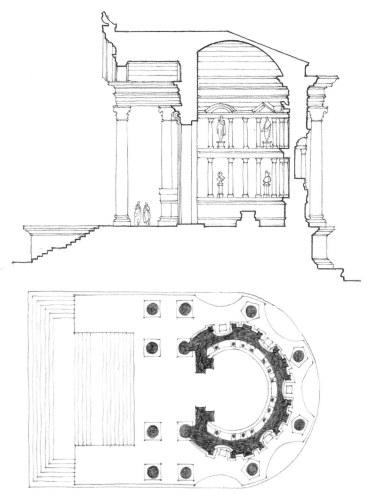

7.45 *Cella* of the Temple of Bacchus, Baalbek

7.46 Plan and section: Temple of Venus

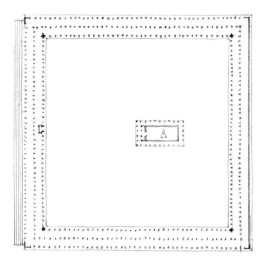

7.47 Possible plan: Temple to Anahita, Kangavar, Iran

7.48 Horse statuette of Parthian warrior

The Parthian Empire

The Parthians, about whom actually very little is known, took over the Hellenistic Seleucid Empire; originally they were nomads from northern Iran and Central Asia, but because of their trading skills, the Parthian Empire (247 BCE–224 CE) became the glue that held together the vast Central Asian trade networks. They brought with them, however, little in the way of architectural culture, and so for the most part adopted the Hellenism of the Sassanians before them, blending it with their own particular aesthetic. As a result, there is remarkably little architecture to show for some five hundred years of Parthian rule. Remaining consummate and feared horsemen, they governed as a military elite, leaving, by and large, the local administrations intact. There were, as a consequence, several regional capitals. Though warfare with the Romans and with nomadic invaders from the north was more or less constant, the 2nd century was a time when the caravan cities of Palmyra, Hatra, and Mesene (formerly Characene), situated at the confluence of the Tigris and Euphrates rivers, grew in wealth and influence. It was also a time in which, given the lack of centralized authority, different religious practices began to flourish simultaneously. Iranian sun, fire, and mystery cults took the place of ancient Mesopotamian practices.

Christianity, Judaism, and various baptismal sects expanded into Mesopotamia. Strong relations between the Parthians and the Chinese resulted in envoy exchanges.

When the Chinese envoy arrived at the Parthian border, he was greeted by an escort of twenty thousand horsemen. Parthian elites, on the whole, adopted Zoroastrianism (see 400 CE), an emerging religious practice based on fire worship. This they fused with certain Hellenistic practices, creating fire sanctuaries dedicated to specific divinities, saints, or angels. Parthian fire altars served as regional and national pilgrimage sites. One such site, Takht-i-Suleiman, in western Iran, around the rim of an extinct volcano with a lake at its core, was frequently visited by the royal Parthian elites. The architectural expressions, however, tended to be modest. Only later, during the Sassanian period, when Zoroastrianism became a state religion, did the large and grand architectural works such as those at Takht-i-Suleiman begin to emerge.

The most important urban Parthian founding was Ctesiphon (see "400 CE"), on the east bank of the Tigris at its confluence with the Diyala River, 32 kilometers south of Baghdad. Originally a garrison city, it developed into a regional capital, as it was situated on the so-called Royal Road, which connected Susa with Anatolia.

The road, begun by the Assyrians, was set up with guard posts and stables to facilitate fast communication. It is not clear when Ctesiphon became important, but it seems that the spoils of a large campaign against the Roman Empire in 41 BCE were invested in the new capital, which had become the winter residence of the kings after 129 BCE. The Romans sought to take the city and did so in 116, 165, and 198 CE, but in 224 CE, Ardashir overthrew the Parthian monarchy and established the Sassanian Empire, with Ctesiphon remaining one of its capitals.

Though its date is much in dispute, there exists a temple thought to be dedicated to the ancient deity Anahita, the divinity of water—and hence associated with fertility, healing, and wisdom. The building, located at Kangavar in western Iran, next to a sacred spring, became prominent in the Sassanian period in the 4th century CE, when it served as a summer resort for Sassanid kings. The temple, however, predated the Parthians, who possibly did little more than rebuild the interior. The outer precincts certainly appear Hellenistic or Sassanian in tone. It is a vast, almost square structure, just over 200 meters on a side, with a continuous double-aisled colonnade set on a plinth and with access on one side by a continuous flight of steps.

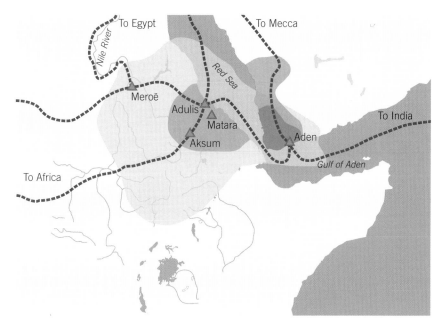

7.49 Area of Aksumite influence, 200 to 500 CE

The Aksumite religion was related to Mesopotamian and Arabic religions insofar as it was polytheistic: deities were perceived as controlling the natural forces of the universe. In the 4th century, King Ezana converted to Christianity and declared Aksum a Christian state—the first Christian state in the history of the world. The city contained several large palaces that, unlike the more rambling palaces of western Asia, tended to be highly symmetrical. They were approached by broad staircases that led to a forecourt with more stairs leading to a central throne or reception room. Construction material was stone and brick, probably covered with plaster. The roofs were wooden.

Aksum

By the 4th century BCE, the area of what is today northern Ethiopia had come to enjoy a strategic position in the developing sea trade routes between Africa and points east in Arabia, India, and even China. With the decline of Kush, perhaps because deforestation led to the loss of wood for smelting, this area, controlled by the Aksumites and with its own vast forest reserves (now, of course, completely nonexistent) was primed to become a regional powerhouse. Though Aksum was an inland capital, its port cities, Adulis and Matara, were cosmopolitan centers. The rulers imported silver, gold, olive oil, and wine while exporting luxury goods of glass crystal, brass, and copper. Other important exports to the Greek and Roman world were frankincense, used in burials, and myrrh, which had important medicinal properties. Both these highly valued products were obtained from the resin of particular trees that grew mainly in the mountainous regions of Aksum and southwest Arabia. The quality of Aksumite metalwork in gold, silver, bronze, and iron attests to the skill of their craftsmen.

The significance of Aksum in global trade should not be underestimated. With the Romans eager to seek alternative trade routes to the East to get around the Parthians, they had developed relationships with Petra. Aksum, much like Petra, was a part of this

southern trade network, and should be understood in the context of developments in India. There is little of the original Aksum left today, apart from some impressive stelae, the largest being King Ezana's Stele, erected in the 4th century CE and named after the first monarch of Aksum to embrace Christianity. It is decorated at its base with a false door and apertures resembling windows on all sides. The city was originally impressively located in a gap between two prominent rock outcroppings. The remains of a vast palace and a smelting factory have recently been uncovered.

Across the Strait of Hormuz lay the Himyarite kingdom, or Himyar. Formerly a trader in frankincense, the decline in demand for that product led to trade in ivory exported from Africa to be sold in the Roman Empire. Ships from Himyar regularly traveled the East African coast, where Himyar exerted a considerable amount of political control over the trading cities of East Africa. Himyar was independent until taken over by the Aksumites in 525 CE. Aksum remained a strong empire and trading power until the 6th century, when deforestation led to its decline (much as it had in Kush)—a decline accelerated by the rise of Islam and the resulting shift in trade routes. The area's arid geography today gives little indication of this once lush and forested territory.

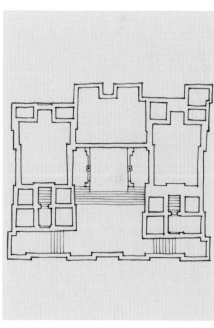

7.50 Plan of an Aksumite palace

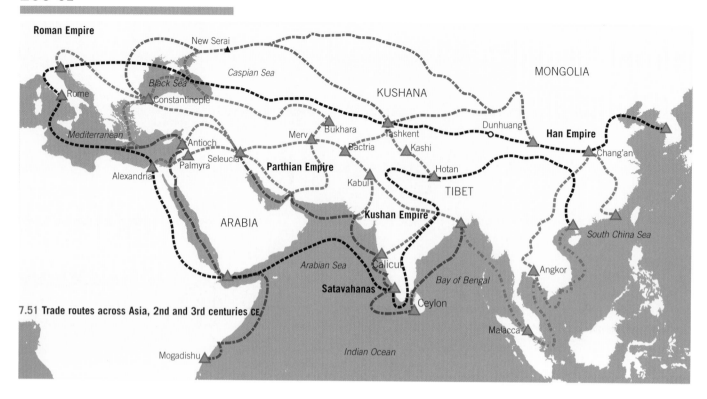

7.51 Trade routes across Asia, 2nd and 3rd centuries CE

Amaravati Stupa

In the 2nd and 3rd centuries CE, South Asia was dominated by two major dynasties: the Satavahanas, who controlled central and southern India, and the Kushans, who, although having recently migrated to the region, ended up ruling a vast area stretching from Central Asia to northern India. The Satavahanas were former Bactrians, feudatories of the Mauryas in the Gandharan region who moved down to central India around the 2nd century BCE. The Kushans were Mongolians who emigrated to Gandhara in response to the building of the Great Wall by the Qin. Both had their roots in trading communities and extensive trading networks both within and beyond South Asia. Both were predominantly Buddhist, although the Satavahanas were already witnessing a reemergent Hinduism and the Kushans continued to practice aspects of their older beliefs. Outstanding traders, the Satavahanas called themselves the *dakshinapath-pati*—"the rulers of the southern trade route"—which linked Egypt, controlled by the Romans, with the Han rulers of China. The route went from ports along the Indian Ocean to the west, across India in a northeasterly direction, to ports on the Bay of Bengal. Buddhist monasteries beame catalysts for

this mercantile development, serving as resting places and transition points for the traders.

The most famous of the Satavahana merchant constructions, the Amaravati Stupa (3rd century BCE), was dismantled in the 19th century, its artwork distributed to the museums of Europe. Like the earlier ones at Sanchi and Bharut, the Amaravati Stupa, when first built under the Mauryas, was a simple mound, but it was significantly enlarged under the patronage of the merchants. The elaborately carved railings and gateways that have been preserved depict scenes of a bustling city. Turban-wearing people fill every panel; musicians play for well-endowed dancers; richly adorned women lean from barrel-vaulted balconies; horses, bullocks, and elephants crowd the streets, along with oxcarts. In the distance, large ships with open sails are ready to take to the sea.

7.52 Carved slabs from the Amaravati Stupa, near Guntur, India

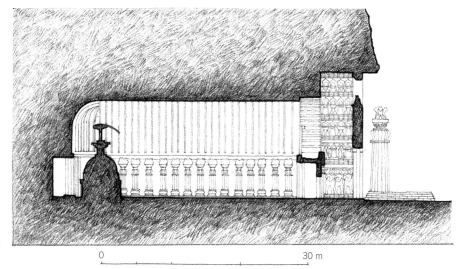

7.53 Longitudinal section: *Caitya* hall at Karli

0   30 m

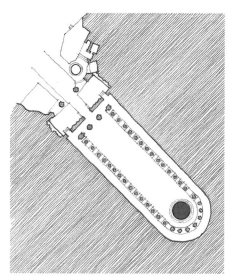

7.54 Plan: *Caitya* **hall at Karli, Maharashtra, India**

7.55 Interior: *Caitya* **hall at Karli**

Caitya Hall at Karli

One of the largest and most impressive of the Buddhist *caityas* was built in 120 CE at Karli, on the western Deccan Plateau. About 40 meters deep and 12 meters wide, the Karli cave is fronted by a recessed entrance of stone screens that has holes in it, indicating that originally, a larger wooden construction was added to complete the building. Just beyond the screen, on the left, is a large pillar carved from the same matrix as the rest of the cave. The end wall of the entrance portico displays a stamped-out, repeated set of horseshoe-arched building motifs that sit atop a plinth composed of life-size elephants, as if they were supporting the weight of the superstructure (as at Pithalkhora). The central panel of the cave entrance is dominated by several panels of male-female couples, known as Mithuna couples, holding each other affectionately with a distinctive touch of sensuality. According to one source, Mithuna couples represent "the notion of the individual's reintegration with the Universal principle, expressed through their affectionate gestures and implicit sexuality." (The entrance panels also contain bodhisattvas, but these were carved in the late 5th century CE, when the iconography was "modernized.")

Karli is famous for its interior, in part due to its sheer size, but more so because of the balanced and measured nature of the overall composition of its elements through which Karli brings the *caitya* vocabulary to one of its finest resolutions. Compared to earlier *caitya* caves, the width of Karli's central space is much more generous in relation to its height and depth. The Karli stupa is no longer the incidental center of a crowded array of elements, but the focus of a hierarchical composition. The stupa itself is relatively simple in form. An unadorned, simple hemisphere sits atop a slightly tapered base, ornamented with carved *vedikas*. At the same time, it is much bolder than most earlier stupas, as its *chattri* rises simply from a rectangular base, or *harmika*, which expands into mushrooming tiers of horizontal bands. But then it suddenly projects into space on a high vertical *stambha*, upon which sits the final *chattri*, which becomes the focus of the entire composition. The *chattri* catches the light in the dark surroundings and thereby appears as a horizontal flash in the vertical composition. (The *chattri* denotes the umbrella of the Buddhist ideal under which the monk finds shelter and faith.)

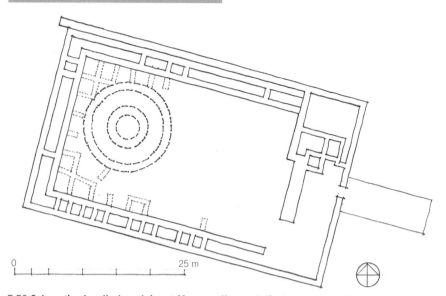

7.56 Schematic plan: Kushan shrine at Mat, near Kanpur, India, based on remains

0   25 m

Kushan

With the weakening of the Parthians, the Kushans in Central Asia came to dominate Asian trade. They were not native to the land, but, like the Parthians, nomadic invaders; they were originally a Mongolian tribe known as the Yueh-chi, who were driven west into northwest Afghanistan and Tajikistan around 135 BCE by the Chinese. They ruled from two capitals: Purushapura (now Peshawar) near the Khyber Pass, and Mathura in northern India. The Yueh-chi, like the Satavahanas, became traders, particularly engaged in the sea trade with the West as well as in the silk trade with China. They enjoyed a flourishing urban life. They adopted Buddhist thought and culture as their core belief system, although they added their own distinctive elements to it. The Kushans can be imagined as a three-pronged hinge connecting Persia to the west, Aksum and India to the southwest, and China to the east. Perhaps for this reason, the Gandhara region under the Kushans continued to be home to a multiethnic society tolerant of religious differences. A distinctive aspect of Kushan art and architecture was its emphasis on the emperor as a divinity.

At Mat, just north of their southern capital in Mathura, are the ruins of one of the few Kushan temples (1st century CE) to have survived. It is a large rectangular structure, oriented eastward and built on a high plinth. One entered on axis but had to maneuver around a baffle before coming into the main courtyard. The shrine, defined by two concentric round walls, was at the far end. A large statue of the Kushan king, Kanishka, more than 2 meters high, was found at this site; it probably stood at the center of the walls.

In the Afghan region to the north, the Kushans constructed large numbers of stupas and Buddhist monasteries, only a few of which survive. Kanishka built a huge stupa at Shaj-ji-ki Dheri, in Peshawar, Pakistan, of which only the base survives. A stupa at Guldara (2nd century CE), near present-day Kabul in Afghanistan, has survived largely intact. Oriented to the east and accessed by a large stairway, the round stupa is raised on a very high rectangular base, unlike the stupas farther south, so that the emphasis on the base becomes equivalent to the stupa itself. The cardinal directions are marked by deep niches with rounded arches, which are further embellished by ogee-shaped arches and pilasters. Otherwise, the structure is completely solid. The entire base and stupa is divided into panels by pilasters of distant Hellenistic derivation. On this rests a cylindrical structure, also ornamented with pilasters. It was most likely surmounted by a semispherical top.

The masonry technique of construction is of Parthian origin. It consists of flat slabs of sedimentary rock, piled in even, horizontal rows, with the decorative elements, such as the pilasters and their capitals, formed by protruding, carefully orchestrated rocks beyond the main surface.

7.57 Stupa at Guldara, near Kabul, Afghanistan

7.58 Aerial view: Takht-i-Bahi, near Peshawar, Pakistan

Takht-i-Bahi

Just northeast of Peshawar, on the spur of a hill overlooking the critical trade route over the Khyber Pass, lie the ruins of the Kushan monastic complex Takht-i-Bahi (2nd century CE). Commanding a dramatic view of the valley below, it consists of a stupa court that faces, on axis, a *vihara* cloister, also clustered around a courtyard. The stupa is at the highest level and is enclosed on three sides by alternating large and small niches. The fourth side, where the main entrance is located, is plain. The stupa and *vihara* courts are connected by flights of stairs to a central intermediate court that splays out in an east-west direction; it is mostly covered by a series of platforms of various sizes that originally would have held small stupas and shrines. The edges of this intermediate court are defined by niches that may have originally held statues or functioned as small shops or storage compartments.

All that remains of the stupa at Takht-i-Bahi is its rectangular platform and the stairs leading up to it. One can imagine what the stupa might have looked like by studying the small votive stupas found in the region. One example, preserved in the Indian Museum in Calcutta, consists of a square base, upon which the hemispherical stupa rises in several stepped levels, each one adorned with a different iconographic program. The *harmika* has five stages, each slightly larger than the previous; from the middle of the *harmika* rises the central pillar that carries

a seven-stage *chattri*, diminishing in diameter. The Kushan stupas of the Gandhara region fall somewhere between the stupas of central India—which are dominated by the girth and body of the main stupa and surmounted by a small symbolic *harmika* and *chattri*—and the Chinese pagodas—which are almost entirely composed out of the *chattri* conceived on a grand scale. They faithfully reflect their location as the halfway house—the intermediate space through which diverse ideas passed and were in the process transformed and renewed.

7.59 Kushan votive stupa

7.60 Plan: Monastic complex of Takht-i-Bahi

Anuradhapura

From the 4th century BCE to the late 10th century CE, Anuradhapura was the capital of the island of Sri Lanka, its economic heart, and the font of Sri Lankan Buddhism. It was located in the central lowlands of Sri Lanka, in the midst of agricultural land. Irrigation systems were key to the prosperity of Anuradhapura and its surroundings and were already being developed at an early time. The Malwaty Oya River connected Anuradhapura to the city of Mahathia (modern-day Manner), a major port trading with India, Rome, and Southeast Asia. Buddhism was brought to Anuradhapura in the 3rd century BCE by Mahinda, Mauryan emperor Asoka's son, who also brought with him from India a sapling of the original Bodhi Tree from Bodh Gaya. This sapling planted in Anuradhapura is the oldest continuously documented tree in the world. Anuradhapura soon became a major center of Theravada Buddhism, a relatively conservative form of the religion.

The city has at least five major stupas, each with its own monastic complex. They were each built by kings keen to support a particular Buddhist sect. Overall, the historic core of the city is a historical palimpsest; the principal stupas are Thuparama (245 BCE); Ruvanvelisaya (140 BCE), which stands 90 meters high; Lankaram (85 BCE); Abhayagiri (final form 4th century CE); and Jetavanarama (ca. 280 CE), the largest stupa of them all, at 115 meters in diameter and originally 120 meters high. Just to the west of the city, a renegade set of ascetics built a "wilderness monastery," centered on a sacred quadrangle within a moated compound. All the Anuradhapura stupas are placed in square, walled compounds. Unlike in India, they have cores made of brick, not earth or stone. Only the outer bricks, however, were fired. The Sri Lankan architects developed an unusual stupa type, which was protected by a wooden domed roof supported on stone columns. It is known as the Thuparama. The core was built in 245 BCE, but the superstructure was added in the 7th century.

From the 7th to the 10th centuries, Anuradhapura was successively invaded and sacked by the Pallavas, Pandyas, and Cholas from southern India. In 1017 CE, the capital was moved to Polonnaruwa, under a vassalage of the Cholas.

7.61 Jetavanarama Stupa, Anuradhapura, Sri Lanka

7.62 Thuparama Stupa, Anuradhapura

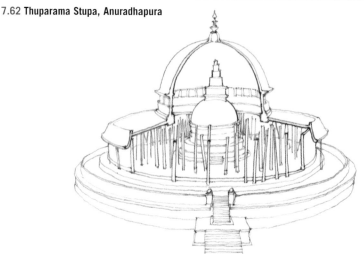

7.63 Pictorial section: Thuparama Stupa, Anuradhapura

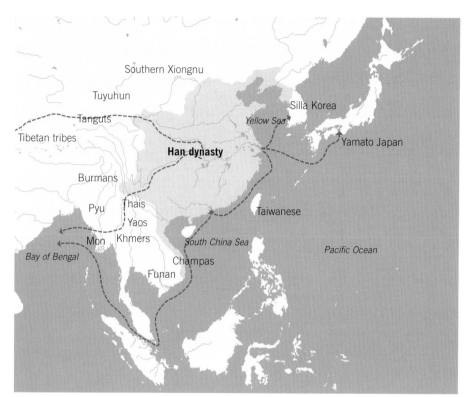

7.64 Han dynasty China

By the 3rd century CE, paper was widely used in China, replacing bamboo, wood, and silk slips. Paper was exported to Korea and Japan in the 7th century, and then to Europe, most likely through Central Asia and Arab intermediaries, in the 12th century. The existence of water clocks, sundials, astronomical instruments, and even a seismograph in 132 CE attest to the Han's technological and scientific sophistication.

Even though they came from the south of China, the Han built their capital, Chang'an, not far from Xianyang, on the other side of the Wei River, within the Qin heartland. They used one of the Qin palaces, the Xingle Palace, as its core, renaming it Changle ("Long Joy") Palace. This astonishing break of geographical ties was also the first step in the creation of an artificial—one might even say universal and divine—imperial culture.

Han Dynasty China

By the turn of the millennium, the Han dynasty (206 BCE–220 CE) ruled an area larger than the Roman Empire. They abandoned Shi Huangdi's absolutism for a more balanced philosophy of governance, even though they held on to the Qin idea of a unified and centralized China. Emperor Wudi (141–86 BCE) established new commanderies in Korea, and his conquest of Ferghana and neighboring regions in 101 BCE gave China control of the trade routes running north and south of the Taklamakan Desert, its gateway to the west. In return for its silk and gold, China received wine, spices, woolen fabrics, grapes, pomegranates, sesame, broad beans, and alfalfa. Under the Han, poetry, literature, and philosophy prospered, and the voluminous *Shiji* ("Historical Records"), written by Sima Qian (145–80 BCE), set the standard for later government-sponsored histories. By 100 CE, trade along the Silk Route began to flourish, with caravans reaching Luoyang almost every month. International diplomatic exchanges became common, including those with Emperor Andun (the Chinese name for the Roman emperor Marcus Aurelius Antoninus) in 166 CE.

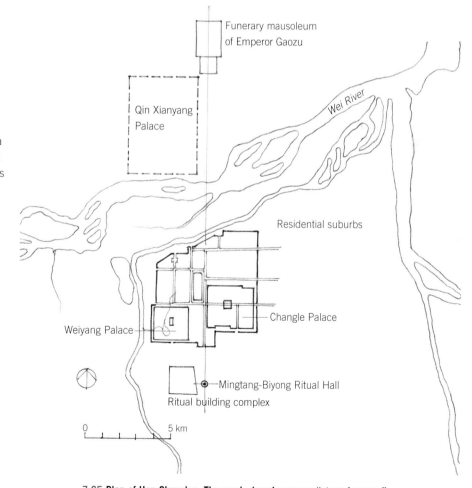

7.65 Plan of Han Chang'an. The word *chang'an* means "eternal peace."

The shape of the new city, with its twelve gates, was irregular, with almost half of the area filled in with huge palaces connected by two-story passageways with bridges crossing the streets. These passageways allowed the emperor to move among the palaces unseen. As the city grew, a suburb developed to the east.

To the west of Changle Palace, the new Weiyang Palace was constructed, with an immense audience hall. (The word *weiyang* means "maintaining the dignity of the law.") Because the emperors lived there, this building had a particular prominence. Like the Qin palaces, these gigantic Han palaces were built of wood around a solid earthen core. The Han also constructed a major palace complex west of the city at Shanglin Park, along with an artificial lake, the Kunming Chi. The lake, which symbolized the world's oceans, had at its center the statue of a whale. Very little survives of the vast wooden constructions of the Han. However, funerary objects placed in royal tombs often contained models of structures for use in the afterlife. These models show multistory timber-frame watchtowers with corner piers and upper levels generally smaller than the lower ones, resulting in tapered profiles. At each level, widely overhanging roofs and balconies were supported by elaborate bracket sets and braces.

Mingtang-Biyong Ritual Complex

If the Qin capital was designed as a microcosm of the Chinese empire, nearby Chang'an was designed to represent nothing less than the heavens themselves. For the Qin, rituals tended to include disparate rites from China's far-flung geography. According to the *Shiji*, the sacrificial rituals, known as *zhi*, were meant to be performed on high grounds in forested areas, where offerings were made to the four deities of the directions, represented by the colors white, azure, yellow, and red. The Han multiplied the Qin rituals and offered sacrifices to the gods of heaven and earth, mountains and rivers, the sun and the moon, and the stars and the planets, but they built artificial replicas of natural altars in the capital itself.

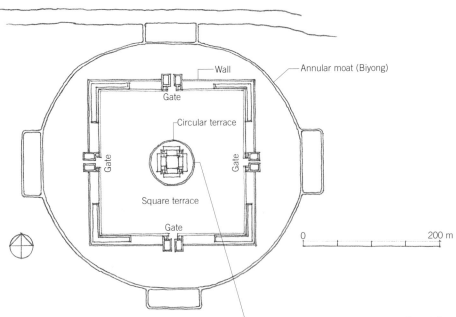

7.66 Plan: Mingtang-Biyong Ritual Complex, near Xian, China

These ritual structures to the south of Chang'an, known as the Biyong ("Jade Ring Moat") and Mingtang ("Bright Hall," 141–86 BCE), were designated as the intersection of heaven (circle) and earth (square), oriented around the four cardinal directions. The circular moat of Biyong that defines its outer perimeter is bridged by paths coming in from the cardinal directions and heading into a square enclosure in the center of which,

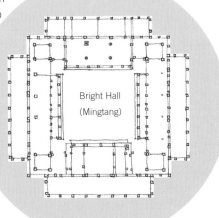

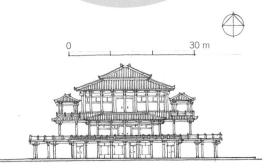

7.67 Plan and elevation: Central structure of Mingtang-Biyong Ritual Complex

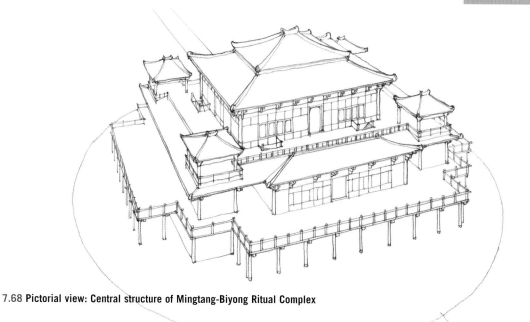

7.68 Pictorial view: Central structure of Mingtang-Biyong Ritual Complex

on a round terrace, was the main bilevel sacred hall (*mingtang*). The walls of the four outer chambers were painted with colors associated with each direction: east, green; south, red; west, white; and north, black. The structure was aligned with the mausoleum of Emperor Gaozu, the founder of the Han dynasty, which was located on the north side of the Wei River. (See plan on page 219.)

The building is a diagram of Chinese imperial philosophy. The human realm was seen as a land mass surrounded by water, with the empire in the center, and with peripheral territories occupied by barbaric people at the edges. At the conceptual center of it all was the emperor, who ruled by divine mandate and was the Son of Heaven. From this spot, the calendar was regulated and its knowledge disseminated.

Adjacent to the metropolitan area to the north lay one of the most fertile areas in the Wei Valley, with canals expanding its capabilities. Huge storehouses of grain were constructed. Two centuries of resettlement had increased the population of Chang'an and its surrounding territory. Unlike many regions of China that were relatively self-sufficient, this one soon became increasingly dependent on imported grain. The strengthening of the city drained the will of peripheral regions to challenge imperial

authority while creating a distinctive capital culture. The rulers were careful, however, to make it appear as if the city were isolated from the rest of China. They therefore maintained important ritual sites across China, such as at Yong, Fenyin, and Mt. Tai in Shandong. The emperor was expected to travel to these places and perform rituals there.

Like the Qin before them, the Han emperors, both at Chang'an and Luoyang, allocated significant wealth—perhaps up to one-third of their revenues—to tombs for themselves. Unlike the Qin, they also

constructed tombs for their empresses— usually as a smaller nearby building. The tombs of nine of the eleven emperors of the Western Han are spread along the north bank of the Wei River. (The other two were built southeast of the capital.) These Han funerary complexes were associated with their own cities: the funerary city of Emperor Wudi is said to have had about three hundred thousand residents. The result is that the entire local geography around Chang'an was, in a sense, a sacred landscape. The tomb of the Shi Huangdi, the First Emperor, was the farthest away to the east.

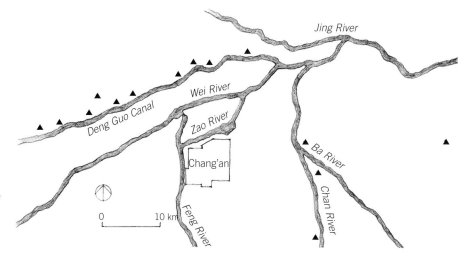

7.69 Imperial funerary mounds of the Qin and Western Han dynasties

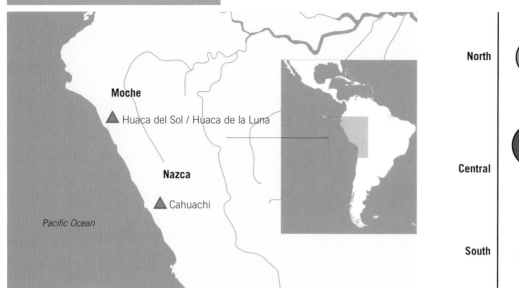

7.70 **South American civilizations, ca. 200 CE**

7.71 **Urbanization of the Americas, ca. 200 CE**

Moche and Nazca Civilizations

Two South American civilizations rose simultaneously in Peru during this time: the Moche on the north coast, and the Nazca in the south. (They are known by the current names of the rivers in whose valleys their ruins are located.) Very little is known about their political and social organization. The Moche were, however, outstanding metalworkers, and both the Moche and the Nazca were potters and weavers.

The Moche Valley on the northern Peruvian coast had been occupied for a long time. The largest of the pre-Moche settlements were made by the Salinar (450–200 BCE). The period was one of turmoil, and for that reason large protected cities developed, one of which, known as Cerro Arena, sprawls for 2 kilometers along a ridge on the south side of the Moche Valley, overlooking a trade route. Its two hundred structures made of quarried granite range from small one-room residences to elaborate twenty-room buildings. Strangely, the Salinar seem not to have built any ceremonial structures.

About 100 CE, construction began on the ceremonial complexes of Huaca del Sol and, 500 meters away, Huaca de la Luna, in the center of the Moche Valley. About ten thousand people are believed to have lived in the neighborhood of these two huge platform mounds. As was the tradition in Mayan structures, Huaca del Sol, sited along

the river, was successively expanded; it was rebuilt in eight stages, the last in 450 CE. Little remains of their gigantic (345-by-160-by-40-meter) pyramid, apart from one edge. But an analysis of the adobe shows that each brick had a mark on it, generally believed to be that of the bricks' builders and suppliers. This indicates the presence of a complex, highly organized building guild or similar social organization. In building this giant structure, the builders decided

not to construct a single piece, but instead placed segments next to each other, thus improving its resistance to seismic activity. In an earthquake, the independent sections might collapse, but the overall structure would remain intact. The sides of the stepped pyramid were decorated with colorful patterns and images. The whole was topped by small buildings that formed a sacred precinct. The original name of the structure is not known.

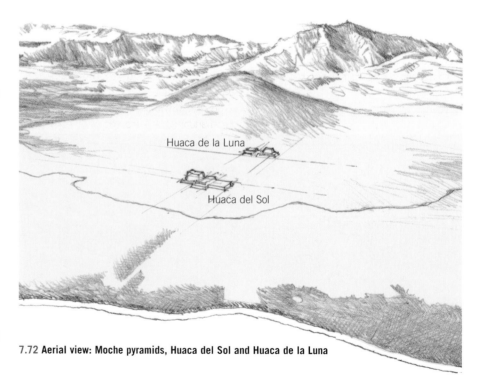

7.72 **Aerial view: Moche pyramids, Huaca del Sol and Huaca de la Luna**

7.73 Examples of figures from the polychrome friezes on the courtyard walls at Huaca de la Luna

Nearby is Huaca de la Luna, sited at the northern base of a tall mountain. Built in six stages, its extension (290 by 210 by 22 meters) consisted of three platforms and four plazas. It is generally believed that Huaca de la Luna served as the region's paramount shrine and the setting for ceremonies of human sacrifice. In an enclosure behind the temple, archaeologists found the remains of over forty men, their bones buried in a thick layer of sediment, indicating that they were sacrificed during periods of heavy rain. Sacrifices in periods of drought were also evident. The principal deity behind this practice was a half-human, fanged god often shown holding a ceremonial knife in one hand and a severed human head in the

other. The city's main buildings were located in the plain between the two temples.

Andean metalworking reached its height at this time. It had developed from a long-standing metallurgical tradition of the Lambayeque region, with its gold, silver, and copper mines. Gold had a special status, not as money, but as a symbol of power. Smiths developed elaborate techniques for making and working the alloys, including the equivalent of electrochemical replacement plating: they dissolved gold in acidic solutions so that it would attach to copper surfaces, thus creating stronger and longer-lasting alloys with shiny golden surfaces. The metal was used by priests in headdresses and as ornaments, and possibly on the surfaces of buildings as well.

By the 7th century, the site had begun to be abandoned. It is thought that a thirty-year drought, in combination with devastating mountain floods, weakened the legitimacy of the Moche rulers.

Nazca Lines

Unlike the large centralized societies of the north, the Nazca civilization consisted of a loose federation of allied communities; they lived on the Paracas Peninsula from around 300 BCE to 200 CE. Religious life centered on pilgrimage centers such as Cahuachi, which owes its significance to its geographical location: because of its geological path, the Nazca River goes underground midvalley and emerges at a point just below Cahuachi. In a water-scarce region, the reappearance of the river would have been viewed as miraculous. Cahuachi's adobe platform mounds are much smaller than those of their Moche neighbors, and they cap some forty low-lying hills overlooking the Nazca River. Like Chavín de Huántar, Cahuachi was a pilgrimage site that became ever more urbanized. Even after the Nazca declined in the 5th century, the city remained an important site for rituals and burials. The Nazca built over fifty underground water channels; many of them are still in use by the local communities.

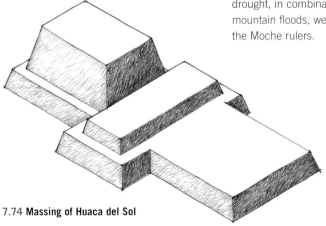

7.74 Massing of Huaca del Sol

The Nazca people also etched gigantic patterns in the ground. In this extremely dry region, manganese and iron oxide deposits covered the stony desert surface over the millennia with a thin patina. The Nazca created their markings by removing this darker surface to expose the lighter soil beneath and then enhancing the outline by laying the cleared stones along the edges. These large-scale drawings, which are in fact visible only from the air, are of animals such as birds, a spider, and a monkey, as well as of straight lines and geometric shapes. Their purpose is unknown, but celestial orientation and ritual walks along the paths have both been suggested. These lines and figures cover an area of about 50 square kilometers and are unique in the world.

North Amazon Societies

Along the border between Brazil and Bolivia, researchers have recently discovered evidence of mounds and earthworks, and even a ring of megaliths used for celestial calculations, dating to about two thousand years ago. The ring comprises 127 granite blocks, each about 3 meters high. This indicates that settled societies had by this time penetrated the Amazon rain forest along the various rivers where fertile floodplain soil for agriculture was available in abundance. The people who lived here seem to have specialized in planting fruit trees, capitalizing on the rich soil quality to survive during the dry season and in periods of drought. An extensive network of low, water-controlling dams indicates the practice of fishing on a large scale. In fact, experts now estimate that a significant portion of lowland forests in this area was organized to benefit humans. It has been suggested that the diseases that came with the arrival of Europeans wiped out this civilization, and that the forest consumed the physical traces.

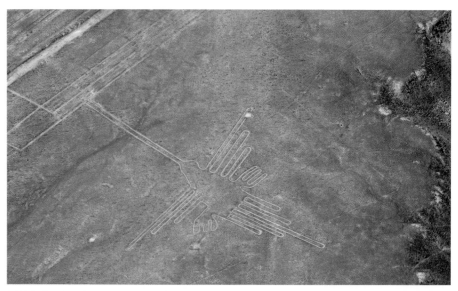

7.75 Aerial view: Nazca ground drawing, Peru

7.76 A Nazca figure of a monkey

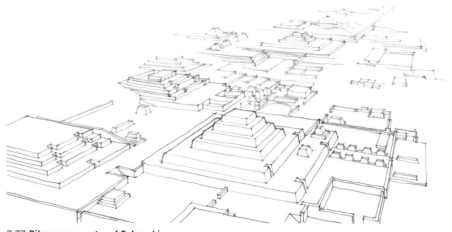

7.77 Pilgramage center of Cahuachi

7.78 Influence of Teotihuacán's empire

Teotihuacán

Teotihuacán was the largest and most impressive of America's cities until modern times. Located in the highlands of central Mexico, Teotihuacán existed for a period of eight hundred years, growing from a large village of about 6,000 people into a metropolis of 150,000 to 200,000 inhabitants around 600 CE, with an urban core extending across 20 square kilometers. It was the center of an empire that dominated the culture and politics of even the furthest Mayan city-states and kingdoms. Third-century inscriptions on stelae at Tikal and Copán record that Teotihuacán controlled their dynasties. They may have also influenced the mound cultures of the Mississippi. In spite of its size and magnificence, little is known of Teotihuacán's multiethnic inhabitants. Evidence of a writing system is only just coming to light, most of it seemingly destroyed when the city fell. The city was a type of "forward capital," in so far as it was an exposed outpost on the northern edge of the Mesoamerican cultural realm. Beyond it to the north stretched the arid wastes of the Mexican plateau. The Aztecs were to eventually master that plateau with their water systems.

The Mayas called the city Puh ("place of the reeds"), but the name *Teotihuacán*, "the place where men become gods," was given to it later by the Aztecs, who built their own capital, Tenochtitlán, farther to the south a millennium later. (The original name is not known.) By the time of the Aztecs, Teotihuacán, by then abandoned, was already a place of legend and mystery. Today, there are many ongoing debates about the nature of the city and the purpose of its structures. Though at its height Teotihuacán was roughly contemporary with the early stages of the Mayan cities located to the south, there were distinct differences between the cultures and, so it seems, only minor evidence of interaction.

Archaeologists believe that a four-chambered cave, discovered by local residents in the early years of the 1st century BCE, marks the beginning of Teotihuacán's rapid growth. Caves played an integral role in the Mesoamerican religions; they were considered places connected with the origin of gods and ancestors, as well as portals to the underworld, the world of demons and other potent beings. The Teotihuacán lava cave may have held particular significance, as its four lobes could represent the four parts of the Mesoamerican cosmos. It was a focal point of fire and water rituals. In the 2nd century CE, Teotihuacán's largest pyramid, the Pyramid of the Sun, was built directly over the cave.

7.79 The Citadel of Teotihuacán, Mexico

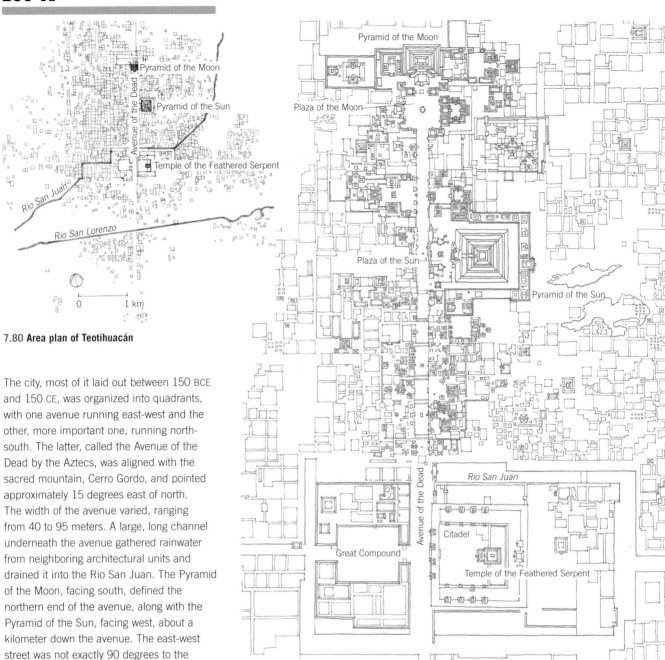

7.80 Area plan of Teotihuacán

The city, most of it laid out between 150 BCE and 150 CE, was organized into quadrants, with one avenue running east-west and the other, more important one, running north-south. The latter, called the Avenue of the Dead by the Aztecs, was aligned with the sacred mountain, Cerro Gordo, and pointed approximately 15 degrees east of north. The width of the avenue varied, ranging from 40 to 95 meters. A large, long channel underneath the avenue gathered rainwater from neighboring architectural units and drained it into the Rio San Juan. The Pyramid of the Moon, facing south, defined the northern end of the avenue, along with the Pyramid of the Sun, facing west, about a kilometer down the avenue. The east-west street was not exactly 90 degrees to the north-south avenue, but lay 16 degrees, 30 minutes north of west, once again for reasons having to do with astronomy. Farther south there was a great sunken plaza, known as Ciudadela.

The Pyramids of the Sun and the Moon, echoing the shapes of the mountains surrounding the valley, were constructed by hauling millions of cubic yards of sun-dried bricks, all without the help of wheels and beasts of burden. Beneath the pyramids are earlier structures, perhaps the tombs of Teotihuacán rulers. The first to be built was the Pyramid of the Sun, completed around 200 CE. One of the largest structures in the

7.81 Plan: Central zone of Teotihuacán

ancient Americas, it was 215 meters square and some 63 meters tall. The profile as it exists today is misleading and a product of the imagination of its reconstructors in the early part of the 20th century. The pyramid originally consisted of four stepped platforms surmounted by a temple and an Adosada platform, which was built over what was the pyramid's principal facade. Its exterior was originally covered with a thick layer of smooth plaster and was probably painted red.

The Pyramid of the Moon at the northern end of the Avenue of the Dead was completed around 250 CE. Recent excavations near the base of the pyramid staircase have uncovered the tomb of a male with numerous grave goods of obsidian and greenstone, as well as sacrificial animals. One of the most significant tombs yet discovered at Teotihuacán, it might indicate that even more important tombs lie buried at the heart of the pyramid. At the foot of the Pyramid of the Moon, there is a plaza (204 by 123 meters) surrounded by platforms that in ancient times were stuccoed, painted, and topped with temples. A low platform at the center of the plaza and visible from all the surrounding platforms served as an important ritual site.

Temple of the Feathered Serpent

After the Pyramid of the Sun and the Pyramid of the Moon were completed, construction shifted to the south, where a large ritual complex and palace compound called the Ciudadela—a sunken plaza large enough to hold most of the city's inhabitants—was centered on the Temple of the Feathered Serpent (Quetzalcoatl). Completed in the early 3rd century CE, the temple is flanked by two apartment compounds where the city's rulers may have lived, as well as fifteen smaller stepped pyramids—three at its back on the west, and four each on the other three sides.

7.82 The feathered serpent god (Quetzalcoatl), Teotihuacán

The initial construction phase of the Temple of the Feathered Serpent appears to have been marked by several mass burials of people who were apparently sacrificed, their hands tied behind their backs, during the construction of the pyramid. They seem to have been killed as part of a warfare cult that, according to archaeoastronomers, was regulated by the position of the planet Venus in the heavens during its 584-day celestial cycle. The Temple of the Feathered Serpent may have marked the first use of

the distinctive Teotihuacán architectural profile known as *talud-tablero*, in which a rectangular panel (the *tablero*) sits atop a sloping panel (the *talud*).

The surfaces were decorated with murals. All the platforms at Teotihuacán have this profile, and its presence at other sites is generally an indicator of Teotihuacán influence throughout Mesoamerica. The balustrade and *tableros* of the Temple of the Feathered Serpent featured large, tenoned serpent heads with low-relief bodies upon which elaborate mosaic headdresses appear at intervals. The headdresses, with their prominent eyes and fangs, were integral to the military iconography at Teotihuacán and were used throughout Mesoamerica.

By 200 CE, all major construction at the site had been completed, and the Puh Empire attended to building and improving the city's residential areas. Teotihuacán's complex urban grid was filled with single- and multifloor apartment compounds. This grid, the only one known in Mesoamerica before Tenochtitlán, the 14th-century Aztec capital, implies a high degree of social control.

From 200 to 600 CE, Teotihuacán continued to flourish, with long-distance trade becoming an important factor in its prosperity. But its success did not last. Around 750 CE the city burned to the ground, possibly torched by invaders from the city of Cacaxtla, 210 kilometers to the east.

7.83 Detail: Temple of the Feathered Serpent

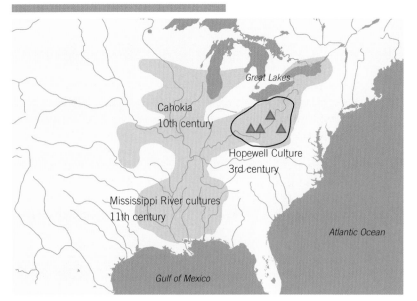

7.84 Hopewell Culture

7.85 Copper falcon and mica hand, Hopewell Mound Group

Ohio's Hopewell Mounds

The term *Hopewell* refers to a culture that flourished along the rivers of the northeastern and midwestern parts of North America from 200 BCE to 500 CE. The term is based on the name of a farmer who owned the land where one of the mound complexes is located.

At its greatest extent, the Hopewell Culture stretched from western New York (including the shores of Lake Ontario) to Missouri and from Wisconsin to Mississippi. Though spread across a vast region, the communities of the Hopewell Culture were interconnected and actively communicated and traded with one another. The largest cities, however, were found in the Ohio region, with urban development spreading westward and southward into the Mississippi Valley. The Hopewell communities built large mounds to mark the sites of their elaborate funerary rituals. Some of their most famous mounds are in Ross County, Ohio, where there is a huge rectangular earthwork within which is another enclosure with rounded edges. Other enclosures are in the shapes of octagons, ellipses, and trapezoids. At Mound City, as one of the Ohio sites is called, there are about twenty-three mounds, each built over the remains of a charnel house, a structure specifically created for mortuary services.

The charnel houses were used for both cremation and for defleshing the body, before the whole structure was burnt down. The Hopewellians placed artifacts, such as copper figures, mica, arrowheads, shells, and pipes, in the mounds. As some of the material in the mounds, such as black volcanic glass, or obsidian, are not local, it is clear that the Hopewell communities had extensive trade networks. The mounds might also have served to fix the movement of the sun or the moon through the seasons, but their poor condition today makes it difficult to ascertain their original purpose.

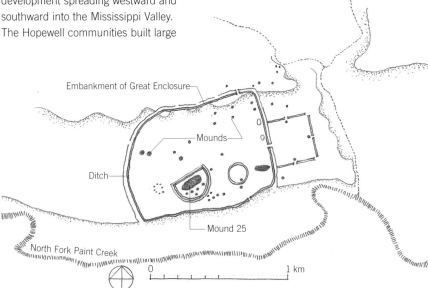

7.86 Plan: Hopewell Mound Group, near Hopewell, Ohio

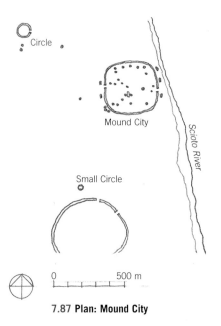

7.87 Plan: Mound City

400 CE

The decline of Europe culturally and economically paralleled the shift of the Roman power base to Byzantium and western Asia. The other main centers of power were the Sassanian Empire in Central Asia, the Gupta Empire in India, and the Han dynasty in China. The Sassanians, who replaced the Parthians and reduced the reach of the Kushites, established their capital in Firuzabad, in present-day Iran; they ruled from the Mediterranean to the borders of China. Eurasia finds itself in a moment of adjustment in 400 CE, as the South Asian, Chinese, and Roman worlds were all being transformed by new religious ideas. South Asia experienced the rebirth of Hinduism, China came under the sway of Buddhism, and the Roman world was in the process of coming to terms with Christianity. Aksum, in northern Ethiopia, was also still a force to be reckoned with, although it was by then in decline.

In Central Asia, the most impressive buildings were made by the Sassanians in Iraq and Iran, where Zoroastrianism still prevailed. Little remains of the Zoroastrian fire temples, however, creating a gap in how the history of architectural development of that time is understood. Farther east, in South Asia, the Gupta rulers had built an empire that by 400 CE controlled all of north India. They saw it as their mission to revive old Aryan theologies, but they did so in a manner that incorporated Buddhist practices. In the process, they created a new religion that we now call Hinduism. The emergence of Hinduism under the Gupta was, in fact, simultaneous with an efflorescence of Buddhist practice in places such as Ajanta and Nalanda. Alongside the Gupta's first brick Hindu temples, some of the earliest Buddhist brick temples were also being constructed, such as at Bodh Gaya, the place of the Buddha's enlightenment. Mahayana Buddhism continued to flourish in the remnants of the Kushan Empire, which was located at the intersection of the Eurasian trade routes. There, colossal rock-cut Buddha figures were built that were to have a profound influence on the development of Chinese, Korean, and Japanese Buddhism.

In China, the Han dynasty collapsed in 220 CE; it was superseded by the Sixteen Kingdoms, with the Chinese religious world impacted by the arrival of Buddhism brought in by traders and monks from India. At Dunhuang, located at the western end of the Great Wall—where the Silk Route splits into its northern and southern arms, winding around the Taklamakan Desert—Buddhist monks built one of the largest cave complexes in the world. Hundreds of caves, carved out of the sheer cliff face, functioned as a publishing house, where thousands of copies of the sutras from India were copied for distribution throughout China. Japan, during this time, had its first encounter with centralized government, following the ascent of the Yamato clan. In a related development, Southeast Asia was on the verge of rapid expansion, with Indian and Chinese traders plowing the waters in search of markets. The Puy in Burma (modern-day Myanmar), who adopted Buddhism, were the first in the region to develop large fortified cities built in conjunction with the extensive irrigation of local streams.

In Rome, Emperor Constantine issued the Edict of Milan in 313 CE, which decreed religious tolerance towards Christians. The foundation of Constantinople, Constantine's city, was, however, a hybrid of Christian and pagan motifs. The Christianization of the empire continued after his death, as "heathen" altars and temples were destroyed and new forms of architecture, suitable for the religious needs of Christianity, were established. Architecture centered to a great extent on great martyr cities such as Rome and Jerusalem. At the same time, invasions from the Russian steppes were taking their toll on the unity of the empire, which was now split into different jurisdictions. However, cities in the eastern provinces, like Antioch and Constantinople, with their strong Hellenistic traditions, remained relatively wealthy and would become, for a while, the key to the survival of European learning.

Climate seems to have played an important role in the developments of this period. The volcanic eruption of Krakatoa in 416 CE created years of famine and disruption around the globe.

Kushan Empire
2nd century BCE to 3rd century CE

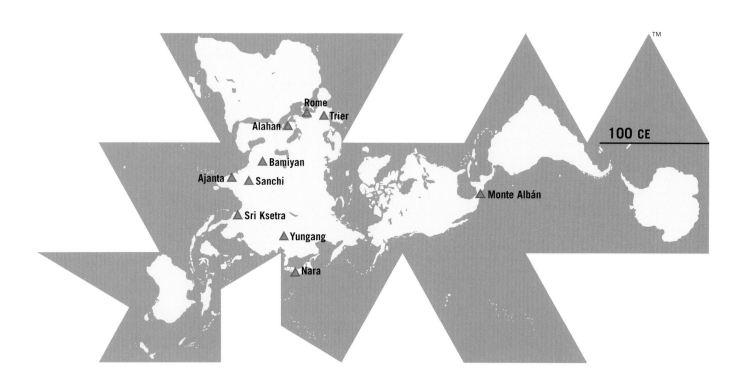

100 CE

Parthian Empire
247 BCE–224 CE

Sassanian Empire
224–651 CE

▲ **Palace of Ardashir**   ▲ **Palace at Shapur I**
ca. 224 CE   ca. 260 CE

Gupta Empire
ca. 321–500 CE

▲ **Temple at Bhitargaon**   ▲ **Mahabodhi Temple**
400–50 CE   Late Gupta period

▲ **Gupta Caves at Udayagiri**   ▲ **Ajanta Caves**
Early 5th century   Mid-5th to late 6th centuries CE

China: Eastern Han Dynasty
25–220 CE

Sixteen Kingdoms Period
304–439 CE

Period of Northern and Southern Dynasties
386–589 CE

▲ **Mogao Caves**   ▲ **Yungang Caves**
4th to 14th centuries CE   Mid-5th to late 6th centuries CE

200 CE	**400 CE**	**600 CE**

Funan City-States
est. 1st century CE

Pyu City-States
ca. 100 BCE–840 CE

◀ **Sri Ksetra**   ▲ **Oc Eo**   ▲ **Sigiriya**   ▲ **Bamiyan Buddhas**
1st century BCE   1st to 7th centuries CE   5th century CE   6th century CE

Roman Empire
27 BCE–393 CE

Western Roman Empire
393–476 CE

Merovingian Dynasty in Central Europe
482–751 CE

▲ **Basilica at Trier**   ▲ **St. Sabina**
ca. 310 CE   425–32 CE

▲ **Basilica of St. Peter**   ▲ **Santa Maria Maggiore**
ca. 320 CE   ca. 432 CE

▲ **St. John Lateran**   ▲ **St. Stefano Rotondo**
ca. 314 CE   468–83 CE

Byzantine Empire
330–1453 CE

▲ **Church of the Prophets**
465 CE
                    ▲ **Qalb Lozeh**
▲ **Qalat Siman**   500 CE
470 CE

▲ **Church of Acheiropoietos**
470 CE
                              ▲ **Tomb of Theodoric the Great**
                              ca. 520 CE

▲ **Alahan Monastery**
5th century CE

Monte Albán Culture
ca. 500 BCE–900 CE

Japan: Kofun Culture
ca. 3rd century to 538 CE

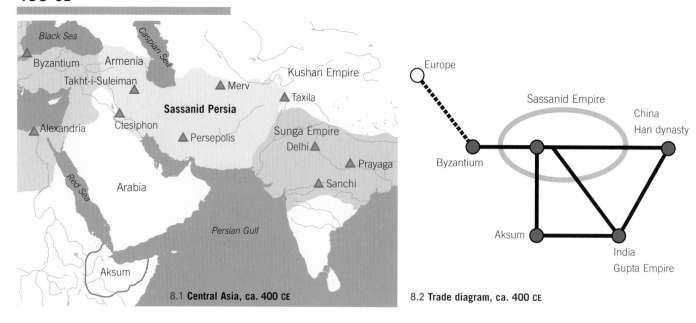

8.1 Central Asia, ca. 400 CE

8.2 Trade diagram, ca. 400 CE

The Sassanian Empire

With the weakening of the Parthian rulers, the Sassanians asserted themselves. They were led by Ardashir I (226–41 CE), a descendant of a line of priests serving the goddess Anahita in Istakhr, Persis (Pars), who, at the beginning of the 3rd century, had acquired the governorship of Persis. Unlike his predecessors, Ardashir had a strong interest in architecture and urbanism, and founded numerous palaces and cities. The Hellenistic tradition of monumental architecture was revised and given its own Persian perspective. Ardashir rebuilt Ctesiphon, but little remains, as it was constructed using the traditional mud brick.

Elements of a palace made by Ardashir's successor, Shapur I (241–272 CE), imply that it was a massive palace complex, but only the central vault remains. Spanning 28 meters, it is possibly the largest vault in ancient history. It is thought that the arch was built without wooden supports during its construction. The thin, unfired mud brick is laid on a slant, its weight transferred to the sidewalls. Architecturally, the arch is a pointed ovoid peculiar to Mesopotamia.

Visitors to the throne hall during the reign of Khusrau I (r. 531–79 CE) tell that the vast floor was covered with a splendid "winter carpet" of heavy woven silk adorned with

gold and jewels. Its pattern was supposed to represent a beautiful pleasure garden with running brooks and interlaced paths. Though never equaled, it became the model for garden carpets. The winter carpet was confiscated by Arab conquerors when they took Ctesiphon in 638 CE. Scornful of the display of royal luxury, they cut it up and divided it among their warriors. But the idea of a carpeted floor was soon to become a permanent fixture of Islamic mosques.

Ardashir's capital was Firuzabad, located in an easily defensible valley. At the front of Ardashir's palace was an open, arched throne room, or *iwan*, flanked by side chambers. To

8.3 The only visible remains of Ctesiphon today is the great arch, Taq-i Kisra, of Khusrau's palace.

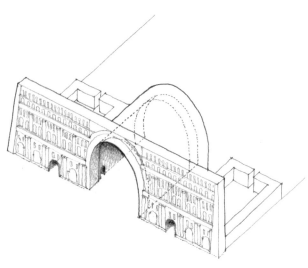

8.4 Pictorial view: The Taq-i Kisra, the *iwan* of Khusrau I, Ctesiphon, Iraq

8.5 Firuzibad and its area

The desolate area of present-day Ctesiphon gives little indication of its once lush orchards and rose gardens. The Parthians established other cities as trading centers, such as Hecatompylos (Šahr-e Qumis) in eastern Iran, but little remains of their past splendor.

In celebration of his victory over his Roman adversaries, Shapur I (r. 241–72 CE) built the city of Bishapur 135 kilometers north of Firuzabad, on the route to Susa. Like Firuzabad, it was located in a narrow fertile plain surrounded by mountains. Founded around 266 CE and constructed partly with the forced labor of Roman captives, the city covers an area of about 1 by 2 kilometers and is surrounded by a city wall with closely spaced round towers. Since only part of the site has been excavated and studied, we have only a piece of a larger whole—one that was developed and expanded over time. One of the largest buildings on the site was a cruciform hall with massive walls indicating vaulting, but its purpose, whether a palace or temple, is still unclear. Nearby is a square building that was presumably a temple, but that, too, is not yet certain. Another important Sassanian city, used as a summer capital, was Shushtar, in Iran, about 56 kilometers east of Susa. There, extensive irrigation works that included a dam and bridge were built. One of the principal crops of the area was sugarcane, which had been brought over from Egypt.

the rear were three domed rooms and behind them, a courtyard and garden. Most of the structure was mud brick dressed with stucco and stone elements. The *iwan* was a building innovation of the later Parthian era that is found in Sassanian palaces and buildings of importance; it was to remain an important typological element in Persian architecture. The palace lay to the south of Ardashir's planned circular city, over 2 kilometers in diameter, at the center of which was a large tower that, so it is thought, served as a Zoroastrian fire temple.

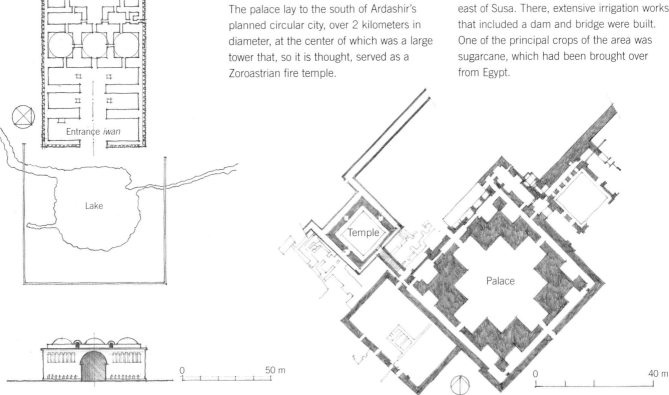

8.6 Plan and front elevation: Palace of Ardashir

8.7 Plan: Palace/temple complex at Bishapur

8.8 Fire temple in modern-day Iran

Zoroastrian Fire Temples

It is presumed that Zoroaster (Zarathustra) lived around 600 BCE, but no one knows exactly when or where he lived or died; there remain only traditions. And there is just as much ambiguity about the fire temples that were built for the faith he developed. Fire was ranked according to its uses, from the lesser fires of potters and goldsmiths, through cooking fires and hearth fires, up to the three great symbolically perceived eternal fires of the farmers, warriors, and priests. Zoroastrianism was opposed to the use of images, and during the Sassanian period, cult statues were removed, although anthropomorphized divinities remained.

Zoroastrian fire rites were performed in the open on hilltops and platforms, and also in enclosed temples. As the rituals and practices became canonized, the corresponding religious architecture was standardized, and a complex network of temples resulted. The role of the fire in the religious services was mainly symbolic and served the purpose of consecration, much as the cross does in a Christian context. Though each king had his own royal fire, there were also fires corresponding to the three classes of society: rulers, warriors, and farmers. There was a prescribed ritual for reigniting the home fire from the city fire and the city fire from the royal fire. Rituals together with the rites of purification were in essence all part of state bureaucracy. Some have drawn parallels to the Hindu caste society and to Mandarin China.

It is difficult to construct a clear architectural history of the fire temples since only about sixty ruinous examples remain for the entire 1,200-year period from 550 BCE to 650 CE. At their peak, fire temples ranged from Azerbaijan to Osh, Kyrgyzstan, on the Chinese border, where pockets of Zoroastrian beliefs still linger at Stakhra, 20 kilometers south of Persepolis—and even farther at Taxila in Pakistan. Some of the fire temple ruins belong to the Sassanian era (224–642 CE), during which Zoroastrianism flourished as the official religion, but others date to the earlier Achaemenian, Seleucid, and Parthian periods. Many fire temples were built in the vicinity of geothermal springs. This is certainly the case in Azerbaijan, where burning eruptions of gas from the numerous mud volcanoes still light up the sky today and are linked to the fire temples at Nush-Dzhan-Tepe, Adurgushnaep, Surakhany, Pirallahi, Hovsany, Shakhdag, and elsewhere. An important fire temple site is Takht-i-Suleiman ("Throne of Solomon"), near Mt. Zindan in southern Azerbaijan. Tradition has it that it was thought to be the birthplace of Zoroaster. It is a spectacular site, consisting of the much worn crater of a former volcano that still spews out blasts of sulfuric air. Though little remains today, we know from descriptions that the temple was in use for several hundred years, beginning from around the 5th century BCE. It rose to particular prominence under the Sassanians. The demise of Zoroastrianism was sudden. To

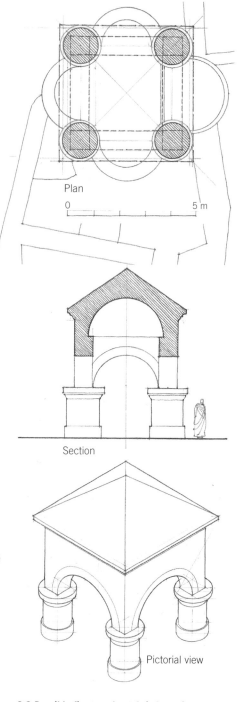

Plan

0   5 m

Section

Pictorial view

8.9 Possible fire temple at Ani, Armenia

the west, Christianity vigorously suppressed it. Islam effectively chased it from the realm, destroying its temples and dispersing their congregations. Today, most remaining believers live in Hindu areas in India, with a large community, for example, living in Mumbai. There are also residual communities in Iran where there are important fire temples in Yazd, Kerman, and Tehran.

Ajanta Caves

In 390 CE the Gupta king Vikramaditya arranged the marriage of his daughter Prabhavatigupta to Rudrasena II, the prince of the vassal state of Vakataka, through which went the *dakshinapatha*, the southern trade route. The Vakatakas' gratitude for their status as guardians of the *dakshinapatha* is recorded in their lavish patronage of Ajanta, the largest assemblage of Buddhist rock-cut *caityas* (meditation chambers) and *viharas* (dormitories) found anywhere in South Asia. These *caityas* and *viharas* are collectively called caves even though they are not caves but rock-cut architecture.

Like the Sunga period Sanchi complex, Ajanta was a kind of college monastery, affording accommodations for up to several hundred teachers and pupils. Chinese pilgrim Hsuan Tsang (Xuanzang) notes that Dinnaga, a celebrated Buddhist author of books on logic, resided there. Though his books are lost, the Ajanta Caves have survived; even their paintings are relatively intact. Though somewhat difficult to access, the location alongside the *dakshinapatha* meant that the caves could effectively serve the needs of both the Mahayana Buddhist monks and their students; the names of many of the latter are inscribed within the caves. As Mahayana practitioners, Ajanta's monks were allowed and encouraged to create Buddha figures and thus to propagate the concept that many had attained nirvana even before the historical Buddha. Since virtuous worldly acts were a way of attaining nirvana, or Buddhahood, the laity's patronage of the Ajanta monks helped them in their own quest for nirvana.

The Ajanta Caves are located along the sheer rock wall of a dramatic C-shaped chasm carved by the Waghora River. The Waghora, a mountain stream, forces its way into the valley and forms in its descent a series of waterfalls 60 meters high, which must certainly have been audible to the monks in the caves. The thirty-odd caves vary from 10 to 33 meters in elevation above the river. Their *caitya* window, originally an imitation horseshoe-shaped wooden window, has now been transformed into an abstract representation of the Buddha, with a prominent topknot and elongated "ears" reminiscent of the ears of earlier statues of the Buddha.

8.10 The cliff edge containing the Ajanta Caves

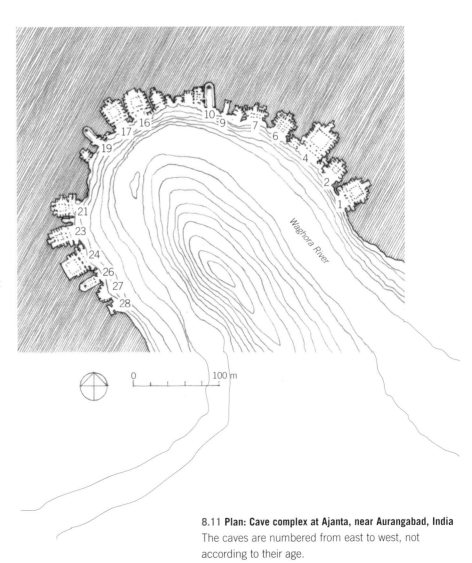

8.11 Plan: Cave complex at Ajanta, near Aurangabad, India
The caves are numbered from east to west, not according to their age.

8.12 Paintings from Cave 2 at Ajanta

The Gupta Empire, with its capital at Pataliputra, is considered to be the classical age of Hindu and Buddhist art and literature. The arts, architecture, science, and literature were given strong support. The decimal system, which is still in use, was an invention of this period. Aryabhatta's expositions on astronomy in 499 CE, moreover, gave calculations of the solar year and the shape and movement of astral bodies with remarkable accuracy. Though the empire was relatively decentralized, one should consider the Gupta, the Sassanian, and the Byzantine empires as a continuous regional unit.

The columns are richly sculptured with floral and figural representations symbolic of the gardens where the Buddha preached and gained enlightenment. The column capitals and bases bulge like the folds of the corpulent Buddha. The stupas are also richly ornamented, with Buddha statues attached directly to their surfaces, presaging the eclipse of the stupa as the primary representational element, particularly in China and Southeast Asia. The oldest pre-Vakataka *caityas* (Caves No. 9 and 10, located almost in the middle) were relatively simple, with an apsidal colonnade marking the circumambulatory route around a largely unadorned stupa at the end. However, Caves Nos. 19 (450 CE) and 26 (490 CE), from the reign of Harisena, take on Mahayana overtones. Both have an elaborate forecourt open to the sky, with side chambers hewn directly out of the rock. Unlike the great *caitya* at Karli, whose entrance replicates a wooden assemblage of *caityas*, these are covered by large and small Buddha figurines and stupas. No longer imitation-wood stage sets, they are symbolic entities in themselves.

As Mahayana Buddhism became ever more popular, it developed a more elaborate liturgical practice that supported a richer artistic program. Evidence of this can be seen in Ajanta's *viharas*, which served as the monks' residences. Over time, the *viharas* at Ajanta changed from simple dwellings for the monks to full-fledged ceremonial spaces, but the basic form, a rectangular colonnaded hall preceded by a portico and surrounded by cells, persisted. The Ajanta

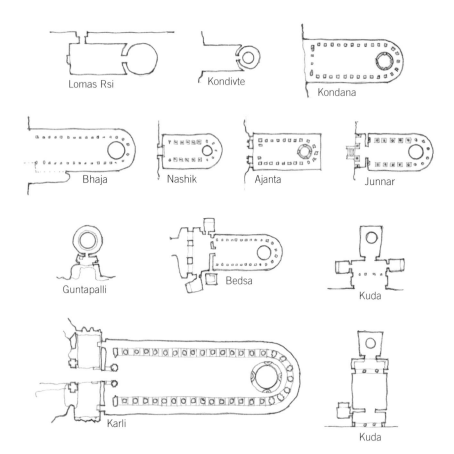

Lomas Rsi

Kondivte

Kondana

Bhaja

Nashik

Ajanta

Junnar

Guntapalli

Bedsa

Kuda

Karli

Kuda

8.13 Comparative plans of *caitya* halls, based on drawings by Christopher Tadgell

viharas have a broad veranda, the roof of which is supported by pillars that open into a central pillared hall averaging about 6 by 10 meters. The cells open to this hall. The number of the cells vary according to the size and importance of the *vihara*. Some of the cells associated with particularly significant monks were transformed into shrines with their own votive Buddha statues (like at Caves Nos. 2, 6, and 17). Some *viharas* even acquired multiple stories (Cave No. 6) and circumambulatory routes (usually defined by a colonnaded passage). As they began to house more ceremonies, they also became more ornamental and decorative, with images depicting scenes from the life of the Buddha and from Buddhist treatises painted onto the walls. A certain nonmonastic sensuousness pervades the images, which are not confined to designated panels. Despite the dim light, every surface of the *viharas* was painted over. Art, sculpture, and architecture, in other words, comingle to create a seamless, sensory experience. Structural expression is denied. Like the imitation-wood construction present in the older *caityas*, the essential symbolic message of the Ajanta *viharas* was

to display the profound beauty of the life and world of the Buddha and, at the same time, underline its character as an illusion, or *maya*—a fundamental doctrine of Mahayana Buddhist practice on the path to nirvana.

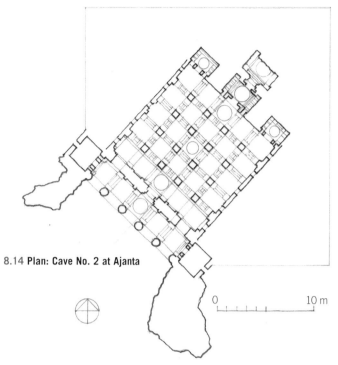

8.14 Plan: Cave No. 2 at Ajanta

0   10 m

8.15 Interior of Cave No. 26 at Ajanta

8.16 Interior of Cave No. 19 at Ajanta

8.17 Entrance to Cave No. 2 at Ajanta

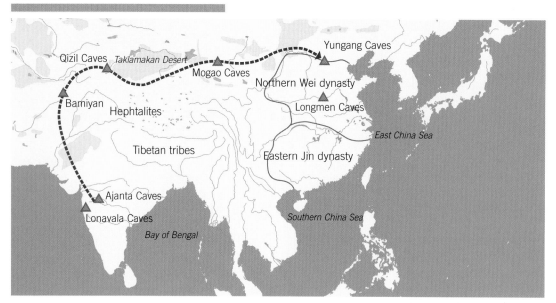

8.18 Buddhism in Central Asia

Establishment of Chinese and Central Asian Buddhism

By the 6th century CE, Mahayana Buddhism had made its way into China and Korea, and from there crossed into Japan. Never accompanied by the sword, Buddhism was spread along the trade routes, benefiting from the symbiotic relationship between monastic monks and itinerant traders. Traffic between China and South Asia in the 7th century was heavy. (In Chinese literature, it is India—not Europe—that is referred to as the "Western Kingdom.") Besides silk, which was the prime luxury commodity, South Asian kingdoms imported camphor, fennel, vermilion, fine leather, pears, and peaches from China. The Chinese, who were much more self-sufficient, seemed to be interested mostly in Buddhism. The Han emperor Ming-di was the first to officially invite Indian Buddhist monks to China to translate Buddhist sutras into Chinese. In 64 CE, after the long and arduous journey, Dharmaratna and Kasyapa Matanga arrived in Luoyang, the new Han capital, with a white horse laden with sutras.

The Han emperor built a monastery for them called the Baima-si (or the White Horse Monastery). Although the current structure dates mostly from the 14th century, Baima-si is by reference the oldest surviving temple of China. In the millennium after the arrival of Dharmaratna and Matanga, hundreds of Indian monks came to live in China. Not as many Chinese traveled to India, although those who did were very well-known, even in their own time, because they kept extensive records of their travels and actively interpreted Buddhism for the Chinese. These include Faxian in the 5th century and Hsuan Tsang (Xuanzang) and Yi Jing in the 7th century, both of whom made the long and arduous journey to South Asia and back. Although Buddhism spread rapidly across East Asia, its translation into relevant Chinese concepts took time.

Buddhism, however, was only one among many competitive intellectual traditions prevalent in China at the time. Not everyone was convinced that Buddhism was an improvement over local Confucian and Daoist principles. Confucianists, for instance, challenged Buddhism's inability to set out principles of an organized social and political order—which was, of course, Confucianism's strength. (Buddhism, in contrast, is introspective and personal.) Competition between these two divergent philosophical traditions remained a hallmark of Chinese history for the next two thousand years. There were several attempts at mediation between them—most famously the Qing emperor Qianlong's creation of a Tibetan Buddhist model of governance, with the emperor in a central role, in the 18th century. In general, however, Buddhism governed the temples and monasteries, while the court still operated on Confucian principles. Buddhism, in other words, had to prove its way into China. In that process it was translated into Chinese both literally and conceptually. The stupa, for instance, became contracted to the *ta*. Thus East Asian Buddhism has a distinct flavor, different from the Buddhism of South Asia and even Southeast Asia. As a result, esoteric Chinese schools of Buddhism, such as Pure Land Buddhism, founded in the 3rd century CE, began to develop. It was Chinese Buddhism that was exported to Korea and Japan, where it also took on a local flavor but remained based largely on the Chinese mold as distinct from that of the South Asian.

In 400 CE, Buddhism was supported by the Northern Dynasties (386–581 CE). In the Southern Dynasties (420–589 CE), Confucianism was still dominant, even though some learned monks attempted to make Buddhist ideas compatible with Daoist philosophy. The end of the Northern and Southern Dynasties saw the beginning of a large influx of foreign immigrants, most of whom were traders or Buddhist missionaries from Central Asia. Some settled in China and held official posts; they adopted the Chinese way of life but maintained their own social customs and practiced Buddhism. By the time China was united again under the Sui (581–618 CE), the country had already experienced decades of relative political stability and social mobility. This prepared the way for one of the most prosperous epochs in its history—that of the T'ang dynasty (618–907 CE).

emperors of the Southern Dynasties. While most of the caves at Yungang are focused on the image of the Buddha, one of the caves (No. 29) has a vertical column rising from the floor to the roof, articulated as a multistory tower with a series of projecting eaves. Small images of the Buddha are located between the floors. This is an early manifestation of the Chinese pagoda (or *ta*) conceived, in Mahayana Buddhist thinking, as a magnification of the *chattris* of the South Asian stupa. Under Mahayana Buddhism, the esoteric abstractions of the stupa were slowly replaced by a more graphic and literal iconography. First, the figure of the Buddha was considered to be equivalent to the stupa, an idea that was often expressed by superimposing a Buddha figure directly onto the stupa, as at Ajanta. In China, as the *ta* emerged as the dominant form, the figure of the Buddha was inserted into the pagoda, either as a single colossal standing figure or with several at each level. (See the discussion of the Mu-ta in "600 CE" and the Guanyin-ge in "1000 CE.")

8.19 Mogao Caves: West wall of Cave 285

Yungang Caves

Some 1,000 kilometers east of Mogao, in present-day Shanxi Province, the Yungang caves were constructed in the late 5th to early 6th centuries CE under the imperial sponsorship of the Northern Wei dynasty (386–534 CE). Unlike the Mogao Caves, which were inhabited by monks on a trade route, those at Yungang were a new type of cave, being built adjacent to the Wei capital Datong. They had only a small resident monk population and were meant for worship, primarily by the urban population of Datong. A Northern Wei minister ordered the construction of the first five of the caves. These contained colossal statues of the seated Buddha, in the manner of the Bamiyan. In an environment in which imperial patronage of the Buddha was fiercely contested, these caves may have been intended as representations of the five Northern Wei emperors as a way to compete with Confucian ideologies or even deified

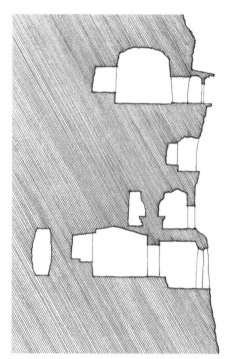

8.20 Section through cliff at Mogao Caves

8.21 Interior, Cave No. 10, Yungang Caves

8.22 Partial plan: Yungang cave complex

8.23 **View of some of the more than five hundred Mogao caves at Dunhuang, China**

Mogao Caves

Carved out of the cliffs on the western bank of the Dunhuang River, the five hundred or so Mogao caves document the first millennium of Buddhism in China, from roughly 300 to 1350 CE. As one would expect, the caves are located at an important junction in the Silk Route, right at the western end of the Great Wall. Surrounded by desert, at Dunhuang the Silk Route breaks into its northern and southern paths. West of Dunhuang begins, or ends, one of the most arduous parts of the journey, through the harsh Lopnar and Taklamakan deserts. Abandoned in the 14th century, the Mogao Caves were rediscovered in the early 1900s, yielding a spectacular find of fifty thousand manuscripts in just one of the caves. Intentionally sealed in the 11th century, this cache held thousands of copies of sutras, letters, contracts, poems, prayer sheets, and various official documents. In some cases, there were multiple copies of the best-known sutras, handwritten with brushes dipped in lustrous black ink on paper, establishing that Mogao was a critical center for the dissemination of Buddhist knowledge. Large quantities of these manuscripts were distributed to Japanese and European museums before the Chinese government intervened and took the rest to the national museum in Beijing. The work of properly translating and understanding the significance of these manuscripts is still ongoing.

The architectural significance of the Mogao Caves lies as much in their individual characteristics as in their collective presence as a marvelous city of caves. Visible from the distance in the arid landscape, one sees three to five tiers of caves carved into a long cliff face, all fairly close to one another. Some are small niches with room enough for a single monk to sit in meditation, whereas others have lofty ceilings and are large enough for a procession of a hundred or so worshippers. Changes in dynasties marked new beginnings in different parts of the Dunhuang cliff. The earliest caves were simple chambers with niches and sculptures of the Buddha.

8.24 **Cave No. 10, Yungang, near Datong, China**

By the Northern Dynasties period, the caves became more complex and took the form of short corridors leading from the entrance hall to a transverse chamber with a simulated gabled roof. Opposite the entrance, the principal Buddha image was placed against a central pillar, allowing the worshippers, as at Ajanta, to perform *parikrama*, or circumambulation, around the central image. Cave No. 285 (539 CE) has its sidewalls lined with niches in which monks could sit and meditate. Cave No. 428, the bequest of the governor of Dunhuang, Prince Jian Ping, (565–76 CE), is one of the most elaborate of this period, with each of the four niches of the central pillar featuring statues of the Buddha and three bodhisattvas. The "gabled" roof is divided into panels by bands painted brown that mimic the structure of a wooden hut.

Like contemporary caves in South Asia, most of the Mogao cave walls are covered by paintings describing the life of the Buddha and various manifestations of Buddhist doctrine. The predominant colors are blue, green, red, black, white, and gold. Stylistically, the art is an amalgam of Indic, Central Asian, and Chinese influences, although the overall style is far more South Asian than is later Chinese Buddhist art and architecture.

Kushans of Bamiyan

Bamiyan was at the center of the 5th-century Eurasian world. Trade routes from China, India, and West Asia came together in this valley, located in the middle of contemporary Afghanistan. The site was protected by a large Buddhist monastery, with more than a hundred caves of various sizes carved out of the sheer cliff face of the nearby mountains. In their midst, separated by about 1 kilometer, the Kushan emperor Kanishka initiated the construction of two gigantic Buddha statues, known as the Bamiyan Buddhas. They were completed in the 4th and 5th centuries, under the Sassanians. Colossal Buddhas, never built in India, were a Kushan invention that was widely imitated throughout China, Korea, and Japan for centuries to come. Although the Bamiyan Buddhas were among the first of their kind, in March 2001 they were destroyed by the Taliban, who perceived of them as idols.

8.25 **View of Bamiyan, Afghanistan**

The Bamiyan cliff rises sharply at the northwestern edge of its wide and expansive valley. To the north toward China and to the east toward India, the valleys approaching Bamiyan are narrow and sharp. The traders coming upon Bamiyan would have encountered a dramatic change in landscape. The traders' attention, however, would have been focused on the imposing sandstone cliff that rises sharply at the northwestern edge of a wide valley. As seen from across the valley, the 1.6-kilometer-long cliff, pockmarked by the caves, rises to a peak in the middle. Behind it, one after another, rise successive layers of the Himalayas, with the most distant ranges perpetually clad in snow.

Even from this distance, the Bamiyan statues would have been clearly visible and would in that sense have conversed with the distant Himalayan peaks.

The bodies of two Bamiyans were first cut directly from the stone and then molded with a mixture of mud and straw to create the folds of the robes, the hands, and the details of the face. The drapery was made by suspending ropes from the stone surface of the upper body. At the base the ropes were held in place by wooden pegs and then covered over with mud plaster. The entire surface was originally painted in gold and other bright colors. The outward expression of the statues, in particular the folds of the

garments, has a Hellenic character. Most of the smaller caves at Bamiyan were covered with paintings, very similar in style to those one found in the caves at Ajanta. The origin of the idea of building colossal statues is as yet unknown. The only known precedents of this type are from pharaonic Egypt.

8.26 **Bamiyan and environs**

8.27 **Bamiyan Buddha**

Mahabodhi Temple

Bodh Gaya, the garden in Gaya near Patna where the Buddha is said to have attained enlightenment while sitting under a pipal tree, is one of the most venerated pilgrimage destinations of the entire Buddhist world. The Mahabodhi (literally "Great Buddha") Temple at this site was begun by Asoka, who ordered the construction of a simple stone platform, known as the Vajrasana ("Diamond Throne"), to mark the spot where the Buddha supposedly sat. In accordance with the nonrepresentational requirements of Hinayana Buddhism, Asoka had no other representation or temple built at the site. The pipal tree itself is said to have been cut down by zealots, first in the 4th century BCE and then again in the 7th century CE. But a sapling from the original tree, taken to Sri Lanka by Asoka's daughter in the 4th century BCE, still thrives. In the late Gupta period, the Mahabodhi Temple (late 5th or 6th century) was constructed next to the tree. The temple has been renovated repeatedly over time, and it is difficult to be absolutely certain what part of it is original to the Gupta period. Nonetheless, its contours today are not that different from its description by Hsuan Tsang (Xuanzang) in 637 CE.

Hsuan Tsang recorded that the Bodhi Tree was enclosed by a strong, high brick wall (originally built by Asoka) 500 paces in circumference. Rare trees offered shade, while fine grasses, flowers, and strange plants covered the ground. The main gate opened east toward the Niranjana River, while the south gate connected to a large lotus tank, the sacred tank where it is believed that the Buddha spent a week. The north gate opened into the grounds of a large monastery. Inside there were innumerable stupas and

8.28 Mahabodhi Temple, Gaya, India

shrines, built as memorials by sovereigns and high officials. In the center of the Bodhi Tree enclosure—defined by a stone *vedika* or fence (like the one around the Sanchi stupa)—was the Vajrasana, sandwiched between the Bodhi Tree to its west and, to its east, the Mahabodhi Temple, 48 meters high with a width of 20 paces.

The temple was made of bricks coated with lime. It had tiers of niches with gold images, its four walls were adorned with exquisite carvings of pearls, and at its top was a gilt-copper stupa. Hsuan Tsang separately also recorded that south of the Bodhi Tree was an Asokan pillar more than 30 meters high. The Mahabodhi Temple is today clearly

similar to this description. It is surrounded by four subsidiary shrines at its corners that were added in the 19th century. The central chamber houses the image of the enthroned Buddha of the temple. The brick *shikhara* contains another *cella* at the upper level with a secondary image of the Buddha.

Along with the Bhitargaon Temple, the Mahabodhi Temple is among the oldest multistory brick temples in South Asia. Although they went out of fashion in India once stone temples began to be constructed, it is also possible that the development of the Buddhist pagodas in China may have in part been inspired by Hsuan Tsang's description of this temple, which was widely circulated.

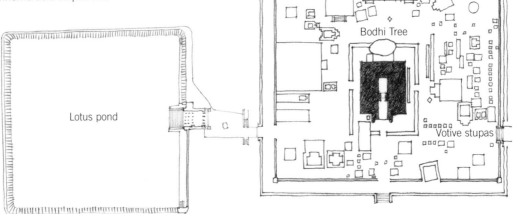

Lotus pond

Bodhi Tree

Votive stupas

8.29 Plan: Mahabodhi Temple

Sigiriya

On the island of Sri Lanka, in 477 CE, Kasyapa Matanga assassinated his father, Dhatusena, and usurped the throne. But because his brother, Mogollana, challenged his accession and escaped to India to amass an army, Kasyapa Matanga left the capital city, Anuradhapura, and built for himself a defensible palace-fortress atop Sigiriya—a striking tabletop rock rising 370 meters over the plain. Inhabited since the 5th century BCE by a Buddhist community, Sigiriya under Kasyapa Matanga was redesigned into a full-fledged city. When Mogollana returned to Sri Lanka and defeated Kasyapa Matanga in 495 CE, he reinstalled himself at Anuradhapura, leaving Sigiriya to became a Buddhist monastery; it remained active until the 14th century.

The palace and gardens were constructed on three surfaces: atop the rock, at midlevel on a shoulder of the rock, and on the plain surrounding the rock. An ingenious stair, hacked out of the rock, connected the various levels. The top level, which slopes gradually north to south, is divided into a terraced palace complex to the west and a series of interconnected water cisterns and gardens to the east. Artesian wells supply water year-round, thus making the whole palace possible. The midlevel structures were built around a series of rock-cut caves that were used by the Buddhist monks. At the base of the hill, a huge rectangular garden, irrigated by a system of hydraulics, is enclosed within ramparts and moats. A man-made lake just to the south of the rock feeds the moats and its related canals. The lower garden is a Zen-like blend of a strict geometrical plan overlaid by the boulders and other natural forms that are sprinkled across the site. Five gates regulated entry. Entering from the west, there was first a square garden with a central island that was linked by causeways, and surrounded by L-shaped pools. This was followed by a long garden, divided into two levels that included two long pools with fountains fed by shallow serpentine streams. The sequence concludes

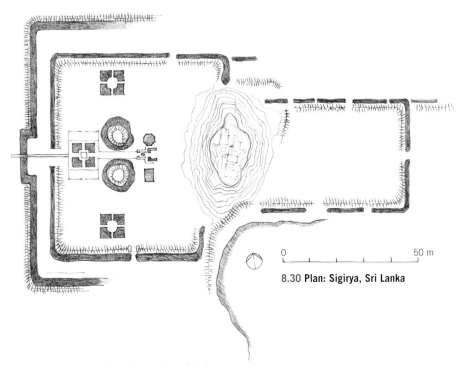

8.30 Plan: Sigirya, Sri Lanka

0   50 m

at the stairs that lead up the rock and that is guarded by a pylons ornamented by the gigantic claws of a lion, sculpted from the rock—thus its name, Lion's Gate. It seems that the western face of the rock was covered by paintings, most of which were destroyed once the palace became a monastery, so that they would not disturb meditation.

8.31 View of Sigirya from the garden

8.32 Lion's Gate, Sigirya

Hindu Renaissance

At the very time Buddhism was gaining new converts across East Asia, India saw it gradually waning. This transition took place during the Gupta Empire, when Buddhist practices began to fuse with the surviving Vedic practices of pre-Buddhist times, creating a new and well-organized religion that we now call Hinduism. The Gupta revival of a transformed Vedic Hinduism was a skillful exercise in adaptation and invention. It was not a simple revival of pre-Buddhist Vedic practices. Rather, Vedic institutions were reinvented to serve the purposes of their new champions. Old fire sacrifices were transformed into courtly ritual; oral Vedic literatures were rewritten to integrate contemporary social and cultural norms; and Vedic gods were supplanted by new, more agential and personal gods—particularly Shiva and Vishnu. Sanskrit became the language of the court and the medium of an official high culture that revolved around the reinvented institution of the temple.

Though the new Hinduism challenged Buddhism theologically, the latter's institutions and practices were assimilated into the Hindu temple. Unlike the Mauryas and the Han Chinese, the Gupta maintained subject kings as vassals and did not consolidate every kingdom into a single administrative unit. This enabled them not only to maintain and profit from the trade routes that were still controlled by the Buddhists but also to exploit Buddhist institutions for Hindu purposes. Buddhist practices were not prohibited—in fact, their institutions continued to thrive. The interblending of Buddhist and Vedic cultures was described by Fa Hein, the famous Chinese pilgrim to the Gupta state from 399 to 414 CE. He talks of a magnificent procession of about twenty wheeled stupas with figures of seated Buddhas attended by standing bodhisattvas coming to the Gupta capital of Pataliputra, where it was received by the Hindu Brahmins and ushered into the city with great ceremony. By this time, the Buddhists were themselves routinely making stone images of the Buddha. In some instances, a Buddhist *caitya* hall would be reused for Hindu gods. And in a stroke of genius, the Buddha himself was deified as another manifestation of Vishnu from the Hindu pantheon.

The basic configuration of the Hindu temple can be seen at the so-called Temple 17 at Sanchi and the Kankali Devi at Tigawa, both from the early 5th century CE. Both consist of a flat-roofed *garbha-griha* and *mandapa*, linked by a simple stepped stylobate and architrave. The *garbha-griha* (literally "womb chamber") is usually square and unadorned. The *mandapa* is essentially a place for the worshipper.

In Hindu worship, the *antarala* (doorway or threshold) between the *garbha-griha* and a *mandapa* marks the all-important moment of transition at which the worshipper and the deity come into direct visual contact and enact the critical transaction called *darsana* ("beholding of an auspicious deity"). Indeed, the whole temple can be considered a two-way portal between the worlds of the worshipper and the deity. In essence, the deity descends into the lingam or statue while the worshipper ascends to the sacred threshold. The deity is considered to be a guest in the world of the worshipper. In a ritual called *puja*, the worshipper offers the deity food (and, at times, such gifts as clothing and ornaments) on a tray. The pandit, or priest, who stands at the threshold and mediates the ritual takes the food from the tray and touches it to the mouth of the deity. He keeps a portion for the temple, returning the rest, with some additional special food from the temple, called *prasada*, for the worshipper.

Another example of an early Gupta period Hindu temple is the brick-and-mud mortar temple at Bhitargaon (400–50 CE). Here the *garbha-griha* is surmounted by a large tapering superstructure, called the *shikhara*. The *shikhara* marks the vertical axis in the form of the cosmic mountain. Its purpose is to enable the worshipper to visualize the

8.33 Temple 17, Sanchi, near Bhopal, India

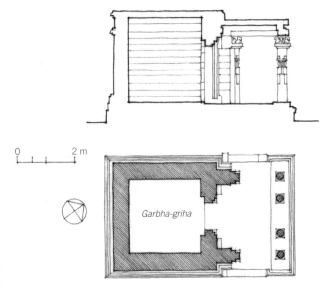

Garbha-griha

8.34 Section and plan: Temple 17, Sanchi

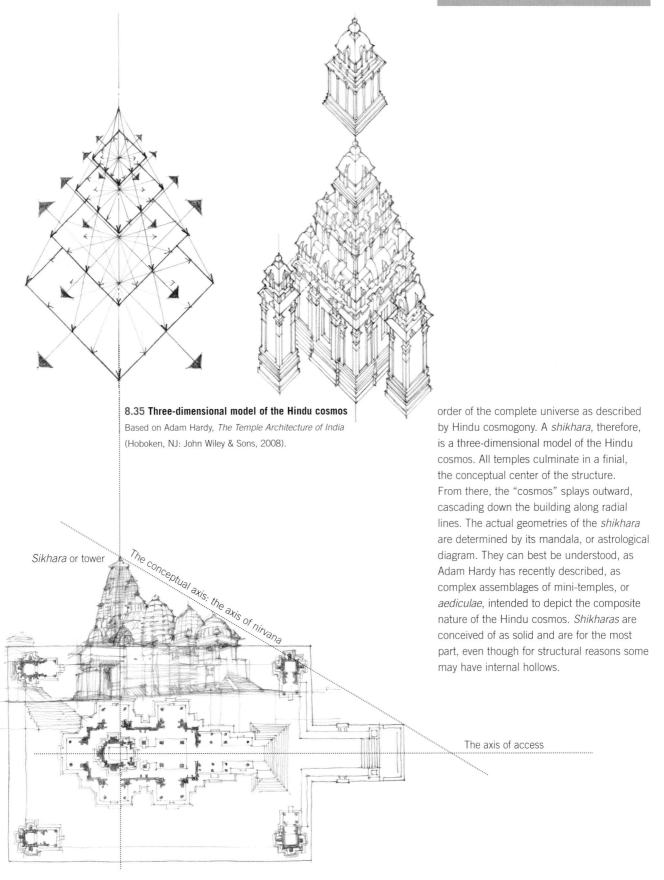

8.35 Three-dimensional model of the Hindu cosmos

Based on Adam Hardy, *The Temple Architecture of India* (Hoboken, NJ: John Wiley & Sons, 2008).

Sikhara or tower

The conceptual axis: the axis of nirvana

The axis of access

8.36 The vertical axis: the mountain as a link between the upper and lower worlds

order of the complete universe as described by Hindu cosmogony. A *shikhara*, therefore, is a three-dimensional model of the Hindu cosmos. All temples culminate in a finial, the conceptual center of the structure. From there, the "cosmos" splays outward, cascading down the building along radial lines. The actual geometries of the *shikhara* are determined by its mandala, or astrological diagram. They can best be understood, as Adam Hardy has recently described, as complex assemblages of mini-temples, or *aediculae*, intended to depict the composite nature of the Hindu cosmos. *Shikharas* are conceived of as solid and are for the most part, even though for structural reasons some may have internal hollows.

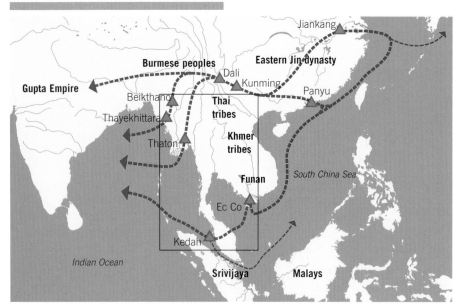

8.37 The Pyu, Mon, and Funan cultures in Southeast Asia

The Pyu, Mon, and Funan

Southeast Asia was influenced by two related factors: the Indianization of its culture and the trade routes that ran from the Bay of Bengal across to southern China and that moved around the Malaysian Peninsula. China, under the Han dynasty (205 BCE–220 CE), sought to control the southern Silk Route, which ran through the cities of Kunming and Dali to Burma (modern-day Myanmar) and India. Around 200 CE, the Chinese established Pany (now Guangzhou) on the Pearl River delta for the purpose of expanding this system of trade routes, a policy furthered by the Jin dynasty—especially because in the 4th century, northern China was largely overrun by nomadic tribes. The Jin capital at the time was Jiankang (present day Nanjing). The Indianization of Southeast Asia, which began in the 1st century CE in Burma and reached the southern coast of Vietnam by around 500 CE, was a complex process that involved both Buddhism and Hinduism. With these new religions came a temple architecture that intermixed Indian concepts with local traditions of woodworking.

Among the earliest Buddhist civilizations to develop in that way was the Pyu, in the central and northern regions of Burma and usually dated from about the 1st century BCE to the 9th century CE, and the Mons, who were located farther to the south in modern Myanmar and Thailand. The Pyu controlled

the trade along the Irrawaddy River, which was one of the prime routes between India and China. This area is quite dry, and agricultural production would have been poor had it not been for highly effective irrigation systems that distributed water from the numerous streams. The Pyu constructed low weirs just below natural bends in the streambed; these directed part of the water into diversionary canals that then followed the contours of the landscape to deliver water to the fields. The Pyu established several major

towns and cities, the principal ones being Thayekhittaya (Sri Ksetra, 9 kilometers east of Pyay), which controlled the trade routes to the south, and Beikthano and Halin (Halingyi, near Shwebo) in the north.

Thayekhittaya is an oval-shaped city some 120 kilometers to the south, controlling access to the Irrawaddy River delta. The city is quite large—about 3.5 kilometers across—and was at its height during the 5th through the early 9th centuries. It has some of the earliest Buddhist shrines in Burma. Bawbawgyi, located just outside of the town, is 60 meters tall and has a bell-shaped body that is hollow up to about two-thirds of its height. In this respect it differs from most stupas in Burma, which are typically solid and cannot be entered. There is an opening at the base on one side and another aperture high up in the opposite wall. The interior contained a ceramic vase in which there were twenty sheets of gold and silver embossed with excerpts from Buddhist manuscripts. The exterior we see today may not reflect the original, which was probably plastered and painted.

Beikthano, 30 kilometers to the west of the Irrawaddy and sited along one of its tributaries, was defended by two walls forming a squarish shape with rounded corners. Huge, specially shaped bricks were produced for the fortification. The buildings

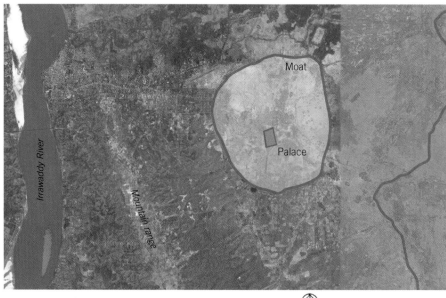

8.38 Area plan: Thayekhittaya (Sri Ksetra), Myanmar

0   4 m

in the city were, as was common, built of wood and bamboo (whereas the monasteries were of brick). There was also a sizable palace more or less at the center of the city. An account of Beikthano was recorded in the T'ang dynasty (618–907 CE) chronicle Man Shu that notes that the walls of the city were built of greenish glazed titles and that there were twelve gates and three pagodas at each of the four corners. There were a hundred monasteries built with bricks and "embellished with gold and silver, vermilion, gray colors, and red kino." Since no Buddhist artifacts have been discovered in the city, it has been surmised that the inhabitants were Andran Buddhists, a form of Buddhism that predated the adoption of iconic representations of the Buddha.

Further south, the Mon had become similarly Indianized and had begun to develop their own urban planning. Thaton—located in modern Myanmar—is thought to have been founded by King Siharaja during the lifetime of the Buddha, which would place it in the 5th century BCE. A trading port, it has a quadrangular city plan that enclosed the walled palace compound located at its center.

Another important kingdom in the trade network link across Southeast Asia was Kedah, on the western coast of Malaysia. It was used as a shortcut over the peninsula to the port of Langkasuka. At Kedah one finds some of the earliest Hindu temples in Southeast Asia. One of the differences in the Buddhism of the Puy was the Hindu Kedah; built around a sacred landscape centered around Mt. Jerai, it would also have served as a landmark for ships from India. The temples, built at the base of the mountain, as was Hindu custom, faced east and were square in plan. The sacred landscape would become an increasingly significant element in Southeast Asian architecture and urbanism, especially in Vietnam and Cambodia. When ships were able to successfully navigate the trip through the Straits of Malacca—which became the norm around 700 CE—the importance of Kedah diminished. It eventually became part of the Srivijaya Empire.

Oc Eo

The Mekong River flows south between flanking mountain ranges to turn eastward near the modern city of Phnom Penh into open flat land that, because of its yearly inundations, numbers among the great fertile river deltas of Asia. Though it is difficult to know with certainty what this part of Asia looked like around the turn of the first millennium CE, archaeologists are relatively confident that it had developed into a strong network of village communities organized loosely around kingdoms, the principal one being Funan, with its homeland in the flatlands to the south of the Mekong Delta. One of its principal cities by the 2nd century CE was Oc Eo. A gold coin depicting the Roman emperor Antonius Pius from 125 CE makes it clear that Oc Eo was already connected to the Asian trade circuits. Gold jewelry and gems were imported from India, while pewter, iron, and bronze work, as well as ceramics, were exported. By the 4th century, numerous canals were dug, and prototypes of religious buildings—both Buddhist and Hindu—began to appear by the end of the 5th century CE. The Indianization of South Asia had begun. By the 6th century another city, known as Vyadhapura, or the "City of Hunters" (now known as Angkor Borei), had also risen to prominence. It was a port linked by canals to Oc Eo and the river Bassac, a branch of the Mekong. It was for the region quite large, enclosed by a squarish wall 2 kilometers in area. This cultural district extended to the port city of Kampot in Cambodia where, in the hills nearby, one finds several early Hindu cave shrines.

The name *Funan* is Chinese and derives from the Khmer word *phnon*, or mountain. The Funan had a strong trading relationship with the Chinese. In fact, much of what we know about Funan, apart from archaeology, comes from Chinese descriptions. The Hinduism that established itself there was not built around a caste system that was difficult to export. Hinduism did, however, allow for a strong centralization of power that appealed to the elites of these emerging kingdoms. One of the earliest temples, dating to the early 6th century, is on a hill near Angkor Borei. Called Ashram Maha Rossei, it is a compact stone temple with its roof built up as a series of horizontal layers. The portal is flanked by columns and a tall arch—not a real one, but one carved from horizontal slabs of stone. The development of architecture from wood to brick and from brick to stone was by this time more or less complete.

8.39 Angkor Borei, Takeo Province, Cambodia

Mithraism

Beginning with Hellenism in the 2nd century BCE and on through to the 5th century CE, western Asia was a hotbed for religious experimentation. Among the dozens of cults that developed, there was the cult of Cybele, which was structured around the annual death and rebirth of her husband, Attis; the cult of Isis, originating in Egypt, which promised immortality and was associated with the death and resurrection of her consort, Osiris; and the cult of Mithra, which involved a sacred seven-day celebration of the winter solstice and a ritual meal that included bread and wine. The Roman policy was usually to accept these cults as long as their believers also recognized the official Roman gods, along with the patriotic gesture of the worship of the divine Augustus. To refuse to recognize the Roman gods, as both Jews and Christians often did, was interpreted as an affront to the authority of the state, which was one of the reasons Jews, and later Christians, were persecuted. From among the myriad of cults and religions, Mithraism was the most widespread throughout the Roman occupied lands thanks to soldiers who carried its teachings back home with them. It reached its widest popularity during the 3rd century CE.

Mithra was the god of light, but whether there was a connection to the Vedic semi-god Mithras of 1000 BCE has not been established. Mithraism appealed to soldiers because Mithras was associated with fidelity, manliness, bravery, and good fellowship. The cult excluded women. The emperor Commodus was publicly initiated into its mysteries. Emperors Diocletian, Galerius, and Licinius all built Mithra sanctuaries called Mithraea, usually in cavelike settings or underground. There were seven degrees of initiation into the Mithraic mysteries, leading to father (pater). The chief of the fathers, who always lived in Rome, was called Pater Patrum or Pater Patratus, terms later applied to Catholic priests. The ceremonies of initiation were elaborate and included lustrations and bathings, branding with red-hot metal, and being anointed with honey. A sacred meal was celebrated consisting of bread and haoma juice for which, in the West, wine was substituted. This meal

8.40 Interior of a Mithra cave temple

was supposed to give the participants supernatural virtue, perhaps similar to the concept of grace. Prayer was offered three times a day toward the east, south, or west, according to the hour, following the sun's path. The sacrifice of a bull played a central role. According to Mithraic narrative, Mithras and the bull were alone in a barren world.

Mithras killed the bull to release the life force within it. As the bull's blood spilled upon the earth, all forms of life sprang into existence. Thus Mithraism was already syncretic, containing traces of bull worship and sun worship. The widely spread but secret Mithraic practices facilitated the almost contemporaneous spread of Christianity.

8.41 Mithra slaying the bull, bas-relief, 2nd century CE; in the Städtisches Museum, Wiesbaden, Germany.

Emergence of Christianity

When Constantine officially recognized Christianity in 326 CE, it did not instantly spell the end of paganism, and many traditions were carried over. Nonetheless, Christianity's monotheism, with its stress on ethical values, imparted an authenticity to religious practice that previously had been equaled only by Judaism, of which it was an offspring. Initially, Christianity might have appeared to be just another of the numerous Hellenistic religion and cults, such as the cult of Isis and Dionysus, Mithraism, the Gymnosophists of Upper Egypt, and the Theraputae of Alexandria. Few could have predicted the way Christian beliefs would sweep across the Western world as it spread in the footsteps of Roman occupation and took hold in Rome itself. Constantine, prodded by a dream, converted on his deathbed. From then on, the Roman title Pontifex Maximus signified that the Roman emperor was simultaneously head of the Church and the vicar of Christ. As for the Church's competitors, they were folded bit by bit into the Christian world—or condemned as heresies. The religious pluralism that flourished in the 5th century, and out of which Christianity itself had emerged, ended by the end of the 6th century. Judaism alone was given some leeway, but it, too, was under pressure. Christians were forbidden to marry Jews, and synagogue building stopped for the most part. Debates raged about the nature of Christ and his cosubstantiality with God, about the Trinity, about Mary, about the wording and the nature of the Eucharist, and about many other issues.

The choice of architectural style must also have caused considerable discussion. One thing was clear: it was impossible for the new religious architecture to follow in the footsteps of temple architecture. The wide variety of building types from the early days of Christianity are a result of the search for a proper fit between architecture and liturgy. In an earlier age, a tomb could not possibly have been mistaken for a basilica or a bathing establishment. Roman architecture created clearly defined architectural environments for the various urban functions. But by the 3rd century CE, distinctions were rapidly disappearing and being reformulated, as with Maxentius's "basilica," which was

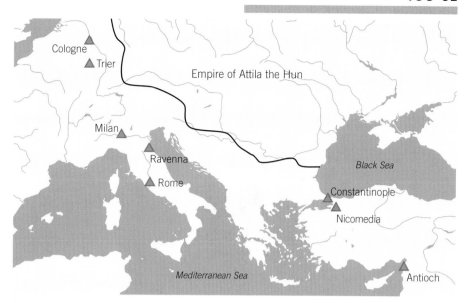

8.42 Roman capitals, 4th century CE

modeled on an imperial bath building. In early Christian architecture, when house-churches were no longer needed, this trend accelerated as various forms were studied and reevaluated for their compatibility with developing liturgical needs.

The impact of Christianity on Roman buildings was, of course, a negative one. The imperial forums were abandoned, temples were chopped down for building materials, and walls were added between columns to transform temples into churches. More often than not, stones from Roman buildings were fired in large kilns to make lime for mortar. As late as 1606, Paul V demolished the Temple of Minerva in the Forum of Nerva to obtain building material for the construction of the Aqua Paola fountain. Christian fanatics went to Baalbek to destroy idols, but they were initially beaten back; pagan rituals continued there until about 380 CE. But bit by bit, the Christian emperors tightened their grip. The sanctuary was eventually destroyed and its remnants redesigned as a relatively humble church. The liquidation of sculptures was so complete that not a single example has survived. So devastating was the destruction of the pagan world that it took a thousand years, until the 15th century, before interest in its existence was anything more than fleeting.

To add to the complexity of the times, when Constantine left Rome in 326 CE and formally dedicated Constantinople as the

"new Rome" in 330 CE, the city of Rome became a backwater almost overnight. Constantine founded his new city not so much as a Christian one, but rather as a place where Christianity and paganism could coexist. This was not possible in Rome, where Christians demanded complete allegiance from their sovereign. Seen from the perspective of Rome, the construction of Constantinople was a disaster. But seen from the perspective of the eastern provinces, it was a natural re-ascendancy. Unlike the European parts of the empire, which were spread out and had many different tribes laying claim to various regions, the east was naturally cohesive. The division of the empire had other consequences as well, for suddenly there was not one capital, or even four, but actually six: along with Constantinople, there was Antioch, Nicomedia, Milan, Trier, and Cologne, all of which were now refurbished as imperial residences. Milan was an imperial residence from 353 CE onward and suddenly became a major architectural center. Five new churches were built; three of them stand to this day, at nearly their full height.

In 380 CE, however, Emperor Gratian made Trier his residence, bringing the flow of money to the north. Emperor Honorius favored Ravenna and transferred the Imperial See there in the early 5th century; it became the residence of the Christianized Ostrogoths under Theodoric (490–526 CE) and his successors. Sumptuous new buildings

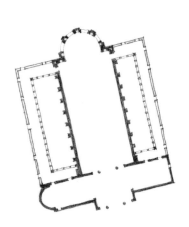

8.43 **Plan: Basilica at Trier, Germany**

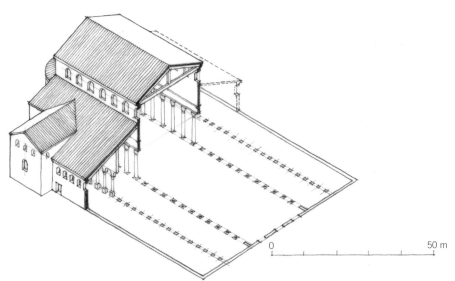

8.44 **Cutaway view: St. John Lateran, Rome, Italy**

0   50 m

8.45 **Interior: Basilica at Trier**

were soon on the drawing boards. Of Constantine's considerable building activities in Constantinople, however, little remains. Most of what is known of the architecture from this early period of Christianity derives from the remnants that have survived in Syria and Egypt, and in Jerusalem itself.

Without an imperial presence, Rome had to fend for itself. In 410 CE, the city was sacked for three days by a band of Visigoths. The emperor of the West, Honorius, sat helplessly in Ravenna, and the emperor of the East was even farther away, in Constantinople. For protection, the Romans hired Odoacer, a German chieftain, but in 476 CE, he proclaimed himself king, defeated the Roman general Orestes at Piacenza, took Ravenna, and deposed Romulus Augustulus, barely more than a child, who was the last official emperor of the West until the coronation in 800 CE of Charlemagne.

The Roman administration of Italy continued to function under Odoacer, who retained the chief officers of state. In 488 CE, Zeno sent Theodoric the Great, king of the Ostrogoths, into Italy to expel Odoacer. In 493 CE, Odoacer consented to a treaty and was invited to a banquet where he and his officers were assassinated, leaving Theodoric master of Italy. Theodoric eagerly imported the most skilled masons and mosaic artists from the east, while adopting the conservative Roman basilica-styled plan for his churches. But this did little to calm anxieties in Constantinople, and in 534 CE, Justinian

sent an army to bring Italy and North Africa into his sphere of control. In 536 CE, even Rome was taken, but in 568 CE, the Visigoths were back and laying waste to northern Italy. As water poured into Rome from the aqueducts that had gone into disrepair, the unused land reverted to swamps, spreading malaria that made large parts of the area surrounding Rome into the disease-ridden plane that it remained until the 20th century. In 680 CE, the bubonic plague broke out. Rome's population dropped from about a million at the time of the Roman Empire to as low as thirty thousand by the 6th century. The large parts of Rome that were now abandoned or used as farms came to be called the *disabitato* ("uninhabited areas").

It has long been held that early Christian architecture evolved out of the atrium, or *tablinium*, of the Roman houses where early Christians met. Admittedly, until the 4th century CE, Christian architecture as such did not exist, as services were held in houses and in catacombs. But the argument that the basilica emerged out of the Roman house, persistent in ecclesiastical circles, creates the illusion of a linear evolution of form that the physical evidence does not support. The basilica that imposed a pattern on church buildings by Constantine was the Church of St. John Lateran, transformed from an imperial palace in Rome in 314 CE. For this church, the basilica was a logical choice. Though little of the original building is left, its form is well established. It consisted of five aisles, the central one higher than the others to let in light from a clerestory. Two rows of fifteen huge columns created the 75-meter-long colonnade. The whole was covered with a wooden roof. At the end was a large apse where the clergy would sit. They were separated from the populace by a columnar screen. The transept that one sees today is a medieval addition. There were no columnar embellishments, and the facade—and indeed the entire outer surface—were of little architectural significance. In fact, it would be several centuries before the idea of a representative facade, which had previously been nurtured by the Romans, would return as an important design element in Western churches.

Though the exterior of the building might seem primitive, the interior was opulent. The roof beams shimmered in gold foil, and the walls were ornamented with mosaics high above the red, green, and yellow marble columns of the nave. Seven golden altars and offering tables stood in the sanctuary, which was lit by chandeliers of gold and silver. A hundred years later, Rome saw the construction of St. Sabina (425–32 CE), a mature and stately replica of St. John Lateran. Its larger windows show a greater familiarity with masonry construction.

Martyria

Though the city of Rome was no longer a political or economic power, it became an important religious and pilgrimage center much like Jerusalem, for it had the burial places of St. Peter, St. Paul, and other martyrs. In making their tombs an important part of veneration, the notion of a dark and uneventful Hades, and the idea of death as a privileged realm of pharaonic afterlife, were obliterated. Tombs were perceived as a site of reawakening on the day of the Last Judgment, when all of humanity was to be judged. Visiting a tomb was in a sense an anticipation of this event. The cult was to become such a strong part of Christian religious folk practice that a church's possession of even a piece of a saint's or martyr's body, such as a finger, displayed in a reliquary, bestowed an aura of sanctity to the edifice. This went so far that entire body parts and even bodies were snatched away, such as that of St. Mark of Venice, which was taken from Alexandria.

The precedent for this type of veneration can be found in Buddhism, which, around the 1st century BCE, had already begun reliquary practices—certainly an innovation in the history of religion. This folk practice, which apparently arose spontaneously, was soon recognized as a boon by the Church establishment, as it attracted the pious, and as such was a public demonstration of Christianity's validity. Indeed, the new notion of history made by simple people doing heroic things—far different from history as mythology or history as royal lineage—would have a profound impact on later developments.

St. Peter's in Rome

Since many of the graves in Rome were at the outskirts of the city or in cemeteries outside the walls, the Christianization of Rome created an entirely new geographical profile previously unheard-of in the history of Western urbanization. It was no longer a forum, agora, or palace that dominated the city and its image, but rather the dozens of monasteries, baptisteries, and churches scattered in clusters in the farthest reaches of the city and its environs. Whereas the Church of St. John Lateran in Rome is a basilica that had been established by imperial fiat as the official ecclesiastical seat of the Pope, Bishop of Rome, it continues to serve as the political, religious, and administrative center of the Church.

Constantine founded the original church over the tomb of St. Peter around 320 CE. Though a basilica, St. Peter's had a slightly different shape than St. John Lateran, reflecting its status as a martyrium. A broad flight of stairs led to the atrium, built on a vast platform over the sloping ground. The platform itself was constructed over a Roman necropolis, with the tops of the various tomb structures cut off and the intermediate spaces filled in. The church itself, because of its use, was 112 meters in length—considerably longer than St. John Lateran. The nave can be described as a covered street with colonnades on both sides. The columns were not built for the church but were taken from pre-Christian Roman buildings. The nave became a place where those who could afford the cost could be

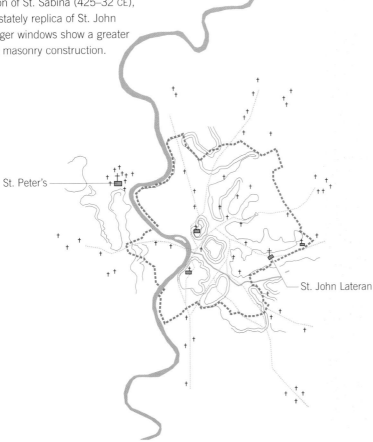

8.46 Christian sanctuaries outside the city walls of Rome

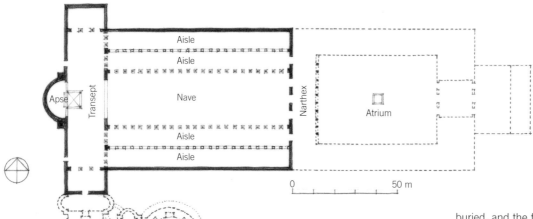

8.47 Plan and cross-section: St. Peter's in Rome, Italy

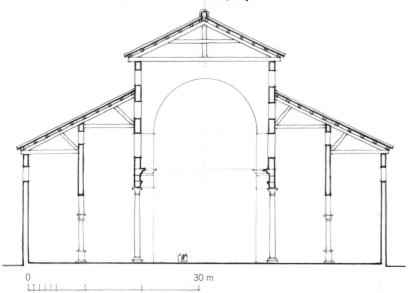

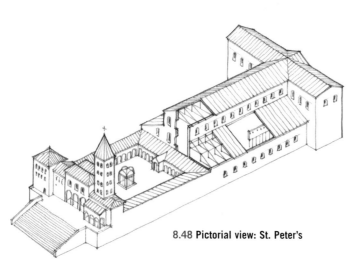

8.48 Pictorial view: St. Peter's

buried, and the floors were soon carpeted with graves. Part street, part graveyard, and part sanctuary, on feast days, it became the site of boisterous family celebrations (a practice that was eventually banned).

The rather dark nave, illuminated only by high clerestory windows, led not to an apse, as at St. John Lateran, but to a large transept, which was a unique space. At its focus, over the tomb of St. Peter in the crypt below and just in front of the apse, was a *baldachino*, or canopy, resting on four columns. Though today the nave-and-transept combination might seem common, that was not the case in the 4th century. The transept only became ubiquitous after the Carolingians made it a central part of their churches in the 9th century. At St. Peter's, the transept differentiated the more popular martyrium church from an imperial basilica like St. John Lateran. The building's significance lies in part in the difficulties involved in its construction. The use of concrete had by that time been forgotten, and vaulting was thus impossible. The art of stone masonry itself was diminished; even for a building commissioned by the emperor, the columns had to be taken from Roman buildings. Despite these limitations, and perhaps even because of them, the building achieved directness and majesty—it was one of the first buildings in the evolving Mediterranean world that was meant from its inception to highlight the mass appeal of the new religion. This was no dark and intimate "house of the gods" in the Hellenistic tradition, nor was it a place of personal reflection in the Buddhistic sense. Rather, it was a space in which large-scale communal ritual overlapped with the message of imperial glory.

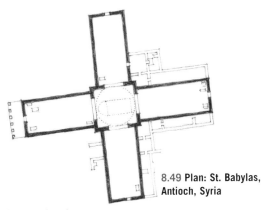

8.49 Plan: St. Babylas, Antioch, Syria

First Baptisteries

In Antioch, St. Babylas (378 CE) was composed of four aisle-less arms with timber roofs converging on the center square. A baptistery was built against one of the side arms and a sacristy against the other. These were, of course, new types of spaces, and they challenged the architectural form of the basilica, which was in its Roman days a structure without side rooms. Fitting these spaces into the basilica scheme was to become a main design problem in the coming millennium; at St. Babylas, they are simply stapled to the side of the building. At St. John in Ephesus (450 CE), they are bent around the northeast corner, whereas at St. Mary in Ephesus (400 CE), they were appended to one side of the atrium.

Baptism is one of the seven sacraments every member of the Christian community is subject to—as well as the first and most important one. Without being baptized, even an innocent baby may, after death, remain in limbo, as it has not been cleansed of original sin (according to St. Augustine). Because baptism symbolizes entry into the community of the Church, baptisteries were given special architectural importance. Some baptisteries were square, others rectangular; some had apses, others none; some were vaulted, others not. Soon, however, baptisteries became recognizable architectural elements. The baptistery at Ravenna is an early example (400–450 CE). Its octagonal shape came to be emulated throughout Italy and elsewhere. The baptistery at Nocera (5th century), east of Naples, has a cupola that rose directly from a circular drum buttressed by the walls and arches of an ambulatory defined by column pairs. It is similar to St. Costanza in Rome (330 CE), which was, however, not a baptistery but rather a tomb that was converted to a church in the 13th century.

8.50 Interior: Baptistery at Ravenna, Italy

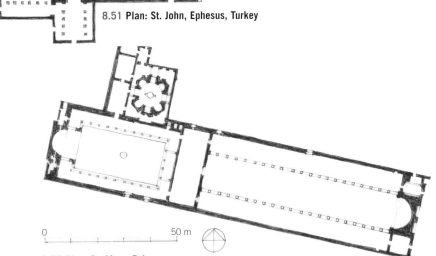

8.51 Plan: St. John, Ephesus, Turkey

0   50 m

8.52 Plan: St. Mary, Ephesus

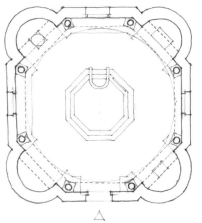

8.53 Plan: Baptistery at Ravenna

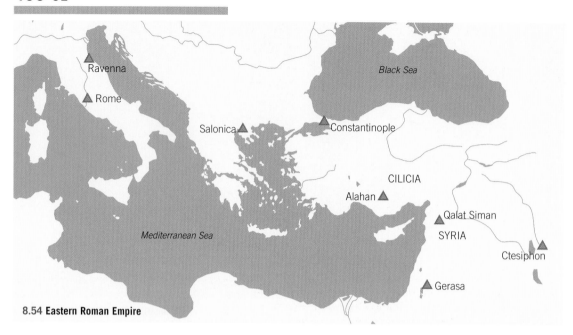

8.54 Eastern Roman Empire

Post-Constantinian Age

Splitting the Roman Empire into four parts under Diocletian in 293 CE was envisioned as the creation of a partnership that would increase responsiveness in case of a local crisis within the empire. When the Christian emperor Theodosius reformalized that division into east and west one hundred years later, in 395 CE, it ultimately led the empire into a schism. The rapidly shrinking importance of the western empire forced it into dependency on the East—and not without a good deal of resentment. It was sacked in 410 CE by the Visigoths and again in 455 CE by the Vandals, who had set up their kingdom in North Africa. And when central and northern France was lost to the Franks after 460 CE, northern Italy was opened to invasion by various groups, including the Ostrogoths; they converted under Theodoric (495–526 CE), who set up his rule in Ravenna. In the East, the Christian empire remained relatively unscathed. Nonetheless, the 5th century was very different from the Constantinian age that preceded it. The unity in theology and in architecture that Constantine had sought to impose on his dominions broke down, leading to an era in which each region began to develop its own particularities.

In the East, *martyria* became large freestanding structures. In the West, martyrs' graves were enclosed within churches. The architects in some places preferred columns,

in others piers. Some architects used transepts; others did not. The location of rooms like the sacristy, the archives, and the library added further variations.

The Church of the Acheiropoietos in Salonica (470 CE) is almost classical in its clean lines and broad command of space. The White Monastery (Deir-el-Abiad, ca. 440 CE), not far from the city of Suhag in Egypt (about 500 kilometers south of Cairo), takes on an Egyptian flavor in its compact, boxlike shape; its various rooms include an unusual triconch at the head. The narthex is

placed not to the west, but along the south, with the baptistery at one end. The Church of the Prophets, Apostles, and Martyrs in Gerasa, Jordan (465 CE), is a brilliant essay on the theme of a square within a square. In Rome, St. Stefano Rotondo (468–83 CE) embodies a complex intersection of cross and rotunda. St. Stefano notwithstanding, the Roman churches tended to be the most conservative. St. Sabina (425-32 CE) and Santa Maria Maggiore (ca. 432 CE) preserved the Constantinian tradition of a colonnaded basilica.

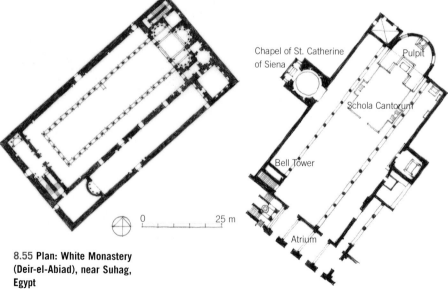

8.55 Plan: White Monastery (Deir-el-Abiad), near Suhag, Egypt

8.56 Plan: St. Sabina, Rome, Italy

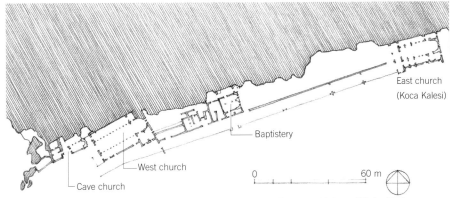

East church
(Koca Kalesi)

Baptistery

West church

Cave church

0   60 m

8.57 Site plan: Alahan, Cilicia, Turkey

8.58 Structure of Koca Kalesi, Alahan

Alahan Monastery

For a brief and fragile moment in history, the art of stone masonry that had been perfected by the Egyptians and Greeks hung in a precarious balance. In Constantinople, stone was replaced by brick. Even the Hagia Sophia made only sparing use of structural stone. Further to the west, because of the use of concrete, Roman architects had not built with stone for centuries; it was only used as a veneer. When the art of mixing concrete was forgotten, European architects resorted to rather primitive-looking rough stone walls. In 633 CE, Islamic armies conquered Syria, and,

not yet having established the architectural traditions for which they would become famous, drove the masons into exile. The use of dressed stones remained restricted to a small geographical location that stretched from Cilicia, along the southeastern coast of Turkey, to northern Syria, and across to Armenia.

The region is now split into Syria, Turkey, Georgia, and Iraq, and a comprehensive history of its architecture is still lacking. But around 400 CE, it was in this small region that the most skilled

masons in Eurasia were working, and their efforts would have important influences on Islamic and Christian practices alike. The skills of Cilician and Syrian masons were known long before the region became Christian, and so it is no wonder that Cilicia soon developed a thriving Christian architecture, especially after the ascendancy of Emperor Zeo (r. 474–91 CE), who came from the Cilician city of Tarasis. Cilician builders had the advantage of a local volcanic mortar similar to the pozzolana that was used by the Romans in the making of concrete.

One of the most important Cilician sites created during the reign of Zeo was at Alahan, where several churches were built along a terrace against a rocky hillside. It includes a cave church at the western end of the terrace, near a basilica, with the eastern basilica 140 meters away. The eastern basilica, with a facade that is still relatively intact, is built next to the cliff wall, with part of the narthex carved out of the rock. The western part of the church contains two transeptlike bays that probably supported a central tower with triple-arched windows punctuating the north and south faces. The inner corners are filled with squinch arches, supported by slender colonnettes. The whole is too light to support a dome of stone; it is therefore thought that it either supported a light, brick dome, or perhaps a wooden one.

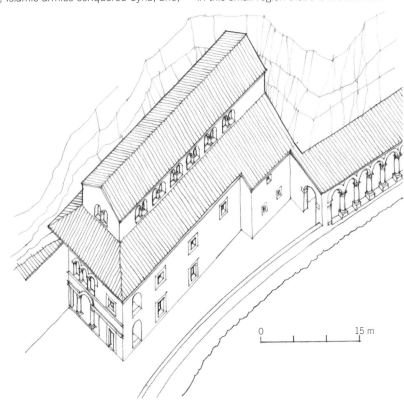

0   15 m

8.59 Pictorial view: Koca Kalesi, Alahan

8.60 Ostrogoth and Visigoth territories

Tomb of Theodoric the Great

The Ostrogoths, a tribe from the Russian steppes, had moved into Europe and settled in northern Italy. They establishing a relatively short-lived state under their king Theodoric the Great (454–526 CE) that included, at its zenith, Italy and the Balkans; its capital was at Ravenna. In 402 CE, Ravenna had become the capital of the Western Roman Empire. The transfer had been made primarily for defensive purposes: the city was surrounded by swamps and marshes. But the move

failed to hold back the Germanen, who took the city. This led the Byzantine emperor Zeno to commission Theodoric to conquer Italy. But once installed, Theodoric created his own kingdom and purposefully sought to revive Roman culture and government as best as he could. Theodoric converted to a form of Christian belief called Arianism, which held that Jesus was not equal to God, as mainstream Christians believed, but somewhat lesser. This caused a major controversy and increased the rift with the Byzantines. Theodoric commissioned architects to build a palace that, though it has not survived, is known through frescoes to have had a colonnaded front with a four-columned, pedimented center.

The calm manner in which the large ashlar stones and arches are articulated in the tomb that Theodoric built for himself (ca. 520 CE) suggests the presence of Syrian stone masons. It is located 1 kilometer from the center of Ravenna, beyond the ancient town walls, in an area used as a graveyard by the Goths. Though the foundation was of concrete, the construction itself is of dry masonry, indicating that no mortar or cement was used. The lower story forms a decagon containing, in each of its sides, a recessed rectangular niche with an arched head. Internally, it has the shape of a cross with equal arms. The upper floor is similar, except that it has a circular interior. It is thought that the upper floor had a continuous balcony

8.61 Tomb of Theodoric the Great, Ravenna, Italy

all the way around, the columns resting on the top of the wall of the lower part. Since there are no stairs leading to the upper floor and traces of an access stairway have never been found, it is presumed that the upper room was the funeral chamber, to which the remains of the king were perhaps brought by a temporary stairway. The dome, 10 meters in diameter, consists of a huge single piece of Istrian limestone with twelve handles on the top, used, no doubt, to lift the stone into place.

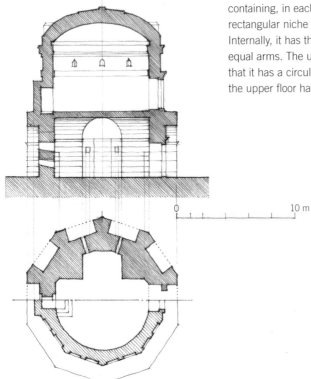

0   10 m

8.62 Plan and section: Tomb of Theodoric the Great, Ravenna

8.63 Mosaic depicting the palace of Theodoric the Great in his palace chapel of San Apollinare Nuovo

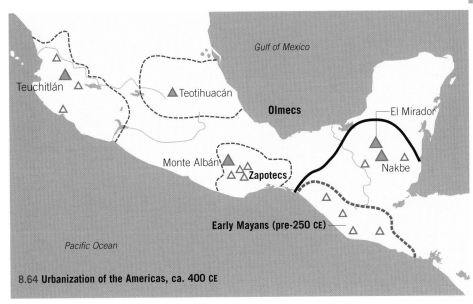

8.64 **Urbanization of the Americas, ca. 400 CE**

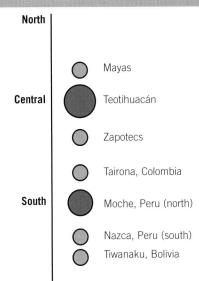

North

Central

South

○ Mayas

● Teotihuacán

○ Zapotecs

○ Tairona, Colombia

● Moche, Peru (north)

○ Nazca, Peru (south)

○ Tiwanaku, Bolivia

8.65 **Trade in the Americas, ca. 400 CE**

Zapotecs of Oaxaca

In a valley formed by the convergence of three mountains 480 kilometers south of Mexico City lies the dramatic and spectacular Zapotec capital, Monte Albán. The entire semiarid valley of Oaxaca was inhabited by the Zapotec people from 1500 BCE up until the Spanish invasion. By 1000 BCE, a Zapotec elite had emerged, with connections to the Olmecs in the north. By 500 BCE, the valley had an estimated twenty-five thousand residents, making it one of the largest population centers in America. It was supported by several types of irrigation projects, including artificially terraced hillsides watered by canals fed from permanent springs. The ubiquitous forest of today is far different from the tended former landscape of the Zapotecs.

The Zapotecs believed that the universe was divided into four great quarters, each associated with a color—red, black, yellow, or white. The center was blue-green, which they considered a single color. The east-west axis of the sun was the principal axis of their world. Their religion was animistic. They believed that everything was alive and deserving of respect. As in Hindu cosmology, the Zapotecs distinguished living things from inanimate matter by the possession of a vital force called *pee*, or wind, breath, or spirit. *Pee* made things move to show that they were alive—like a bolt of lightning, clouds moving in the sky, a tremor of the earth, the

wind in one's hair, and even the foam on a cup of chocolate. Inanimate things could be engaged with technology, but those with *pee* had to be approached with ritual and sacrifice, especially involving something living, like a beating heart. Zapotecs recognized a supreme being—without beginning or end—with whom no human came in contact. It was never represented. Humans did, however, interact with natural forces, the most powerful and sacred of which were Cociyo (lightning), the angry face of the sky, and Xoó (earthquake), the angry face of the earth—two of the four quadrants. Even time was alive and considered cyclical. The Zapotecs had two calendars—a solar calendar with 18 months of 20 days, plus 5 days to bring it to 365, and a ritual calendar, or *piye*, composed of 20 hieroglyphs or "day signs," which combined with 13 numbers to produce a cycle of 260 days.

Social structure was stratified into two layers: the commoners and the nobility. They had different origins. Commoners were born of commoners; they lived, worked, and died. Members of the nobility were descended from venerated ancestors; they conducted wars, brought home captives, and were buried in tombs from which they ascended to the sky to become "cloud people." Men had multiple wives, and under ideal circumstances, primogeniture was the law.

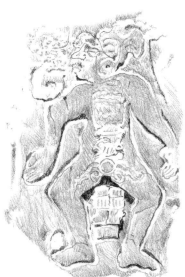

8.66 **A "dancing" figure actually showing the mutilated remains of an enemy king**

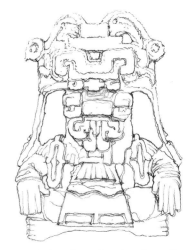

8.67 **Xoó: Lightning and earthquake motifs in Zapotec culture**

8.68 Monte Albán, near Oaxaca, Mexico

Monte Albán

Around 500 BCE, at the height of their prosperity, the Zapotec elite constructed a new administrative center, picking a previously unoccupied escarpment located dramatically in the heart of the valley of Oaxaca. The valley is composed of three sub-valleys that join together in the shape of a Y, with the 400-meter-high, 4-kilometer-long escarpment more or less in the center and visible from miles around. The city, known as Monte Albán, was built along the terraced slopes. It has long since disappeared; however, the temple precinct at the top of hill remains. Its oldest structure is the Temple of the Dancers (Monumento de los Danzantes, ca. 400 BCE), which consists of a triple set of platforms in the southeastern corner of the site. It is decorated by a series of "dancing" figures, so-called because they depict men in strange, rubbery postures as if they were acrobats of extraordinary ability. Despite the name, they are probably not dancing as we might interpret that word today. Given their closed eyes and exposed, mutilated genitals (a sign of ritual humiliation), these figures are believed to represent the earliest set of rulers subjugated by the Zapotec elite. Between 100 BCE and 200 CE, Monte Albán rulers expanded their control throughout the Oaxaca Valley and constructed a grand plaza by leveling an area of 300 by 200 meters. It was oriented to the cardinal directions and paved over with white stucco.

The huge terraced platforms that are part of palace enclosures are on the northern and southern ends of the plaza. The northern platform, which was repeatedly enlarged and modified, has two sunken patios, each with steps and platform mounds on axis. The southern platform, which was smaller, was built by incorporating older platforms into its design. The period 200 to 700 CE finds the Zapotecs at the height of their prosperity, and this is the phase to which most of the surviving structures can be dated. In the center of the plaza is a group of three conjoined buildings facing east-west; they were indisputably the focal temples. While the platform of the central temple has steps on both sides, it actually opens only to the east and consists of a double chamber separated by a partial wall and columns. Later Zapotec temples had two chambers: an outer, less sacred chamber to which worshippers could come, and an inner, more sacred chamber where the priests performed their rites. Those rites included burning incense and both animal and human sacrifice. Priests also performed autosacrifice, offering their own blood by piercing parts of their body. Some rituals involved the use of hallucinogenic mushrooms and drugs.

There are three large complexes on the western side of the plaza, known as L, M, and IV, consisting of more platforms, temples, and enclosed forecourts. One platform contains an internal stairway leading to the top of the building; the stairway is reached by an underground tunnel that passes beneath the plaza to the central range of buildings, allowing the priests to reach them unseen. One structure detached from the main group, Building J, is a rarity in Zapotec architecture: it is set at a 45-degree angle to the site's main axis. Its ground plan resembles an arrowhead, with the steps forming the blunt end. It opens to the northeast and may have been oriented to the bright star Capella and used for astronomical purposes. A vaulted tunnel crosses the front part of the structure and leads upward.

Monte Albán re-creates the Zapotec conceptual order on several different scales. It is primarily the place of privilege at the center of the cosmological landscape. The complex also replicates, on a diminished scale, the very relationship of the escarpment on which Monte Albán was built to the larger valley of Oaxaca, with the main ceremonial temple in the middle surrounded by a "mountainous" ring of platform mounds. The sunken patios in the north platform repeat the order of a valley surrounded by pyramids, again with a central platform. Unlike the artificial mountain volcanoes of the Olmecs, the Zapotecs created here a miniaturized landscape that is both a sacred geography and its representation.

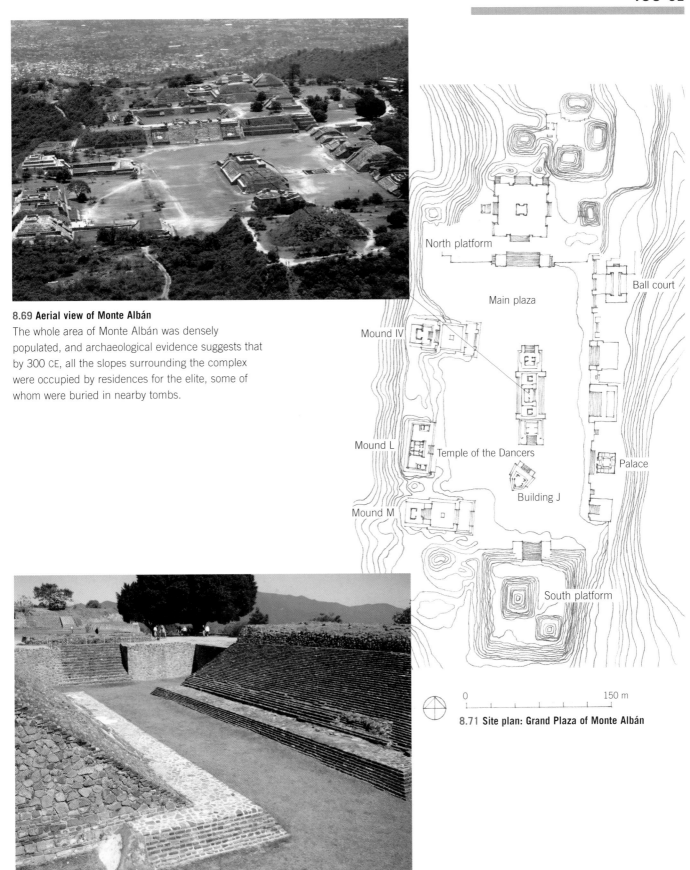

8.69 Aerial view of Monte Albán

The whole area of Monte Albán was densely populated, and archaeological evidence suggests that by 300 CE, all the slopes surrounding the complex were occupied by residences for the elite, some of whom were buried in nearby tombs.

North platform

Main plaza

Ball court

Mound IV

Mound L

Temple of the Dancers

Building J

Palace

Mound M

South platform

0   150 m

8.71 Site plan: Grand Plaza of Monte Albán

8.70 Ball court, Monte Albán

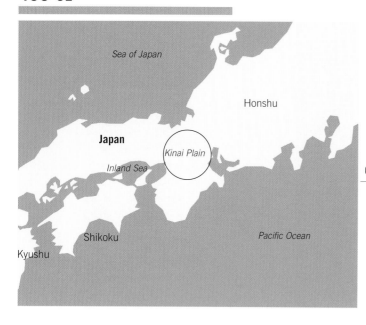

8.72 5th-century Japan

Kofun Period: Japan

In the late 5th century CE, Japan's Yamato clan managed to wrest control over much of Honshu and Kyushu islands, thereby establishing Japan's first royal family, a bloodline that has continued unbroken to this day. The Yamato centralized the government and, most importantly, organized the collection of grain. Each new king built a new palace and was buried in his own huge earthen tomb. By the 8th century, Buddhism had come to Japan and the tomb building came to an end. This pre-Buddhist era from 300 to 700 CE is known as the Kofun period.

In plan, made in the shape of a keyhole, Kofun tombs were constructed by modifying a small hill and were generally surrounded by a moat. The round part held the tomb, and the rectangular portion was used for rituals and ceremonies. They were generally 100 meters long, with the largest, the Hashihaka Tomb in Nara, measuring almost 280 meters. The hill was designed as a truncated cone that intersected with an elongated stepped pyramidal form. The reason behind the complex geometry is not known; dozens of variations on it exist. The wooden coffin was

8.73 A *haniwa*, or funerary statue

usually buried directly at the summit, often in a pit lined with stone slabs and rocks. Later, stone coffins were used, and, finally, in the late Kofun period, stone chambers with horizontal entrance passages were constructed. These allowed reentry into the chamber, leading to their development as family repositories with multiple burials.

Today, the mounds are overgrown with trees, but originally the tops were filled with clay figures, called *haniwa*, that served as substitutes for burial sacrifices and also served to mark the borders of the gravesite. Some, simple cylinders 40 to 50 centimeters in diameter and about a meter tall, were stands for weapons and armor; others were of soldiers and even horses. Because the horse- and animal-shaped *haniwa* were neatly arranged in rows, it is believed that they were part of a sending-off ceremony, or perhaps served as guardians.

8.74 Aerial view: The burial mound of Emperor Nintoku, Osaka, Japan

600 CE

In 600 CE, on the eve of Teotihuacán's collapse, the civilizations of Central and South America were at their zenith. With Monte Albán still a powerful state farther north, a host of Mayan city-states—Tikal, Calakmul, Copán, Tonina, Palenque, and Yaxchilan—arose in the Yucatán. Although bound by trade, family ties, and a common culture, these states competed ferociously for dominance. The main achievement of the Mayas was the development of the most advanced calendar in the world. In the Andes, around Lake Titicaca, Tiwanaku emerged at the center of an extensive empire.

In Eurasia, this period was a time of consolidation during which the newly arising world religions were changing and being tested. The Byzantines, for example, were in the process of adapting Christianity to establish the basis from which imperial power could draw its authority. New architectural forms, such as the brick dome, were developed, concrete by this time having been forgotten. The Hagia Sophia was the most ambitious and splendid architectural accomplishment of the age.

Ruling from Constantinople, the Byzantines were the dominant force in the Mediterranean, but even they had to negotiate with hordes of invaders from the north and deal as best they could with the Ostrogoth rulers of Italy. The plains and deserts of Syria and Persia, though still nominally under the control of the Sassanians, were in a state of unrest. Muhammed founded the last of the great modern religions, Islam, taking Mecca in 630 CE. With the Syrian heartland in turmoil, Armenia experienced a moment of growth, mediating between East and West. Especially in architecture, it played an important role of cultural transmission by preserving the ancient Greek and Hellenistic traditions of fine masonry craftsmanship (in contrast to the Byzantine workmen, who had reverted to brick). Otherwise, architecture in the European West was usually made of roughly hewn stones. In the area that is now northern Syria, eastern Turkey, Georgia, and Armenia itself, precision-built stone churches arose, with important implications for Islamic and Christian architecture in the following centuries.

The South Asian dynasties were accelerating their transformation of Buddhism into Hinduism and engaging in experimental temple design in response to the liturgical demands of Hinduism. The Kalcuris, and then the Chalukyas in the Deccan Plateau and the Pallavas in the south, developed a range of rock-cut and structural stone temples. But while Buddhism was slowly disappearing from India, it was emerging as a powerful force in China, Korea, and Japan. The T'ang emperors invested heavily in large public works projects such as roads and canals aimed at enabling trade. As a consequence, engineering skills matured. New monasteries were built, and a new building form, the *ta*, or pagoda, emerged out of the Indian stupa. Meanwhile, in Japan, Buddhism, which had entered from Korea, fused with preexisting Shinto concepts to produce a unique brand of Buddhism that, from the start, was allied with high architectural accomplishment, such as the Horyu-ji Temple in Nara. The first building of Ise Jingu, Japan's holiest Shinto shrine, also dates from this time.

◀ **Tiwanaku**
First settled 400 BCE

Southern Andes: Peak of Wari and Tiwanaku cultures
6th to 10th centuries

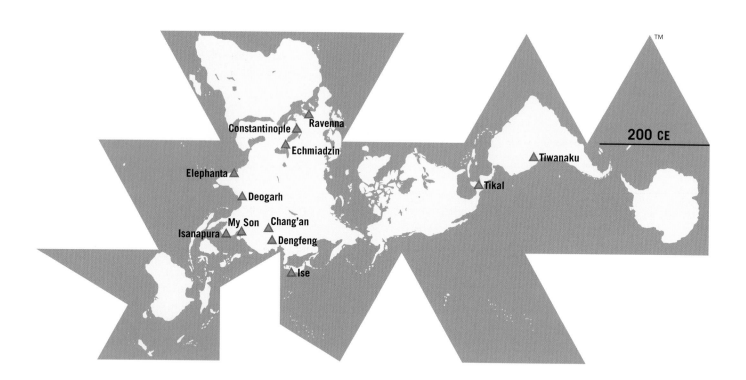

200 CE

China: Eastern Han Dynasty
25–220 CE

Sixteen Kingdoms Period
304–439 CE

◀ **Ise Shrine**
Rebuilt every twenty years since ca. 500 BCE

Mayas: Dynastic City-States
ca. 250–900 CE

▲ **Tikal Temple Complex**
700–900 CE

Byzantine Empire
330–1453 CE

▲ **SS. Sergius and Bacchus**
525–30 CE

▲ **Hagia Sophia**
532–37 CE

▲ **St. Vitale, Ravenna**
538–45 CE

▲ **St. Hripsime Church**
7th Century CE

400 CE   **600 CE**   **800 CE**

India: Rise of regional states
500–1300 CE

▲ **Vishnu Temple at Deogarh**
Early 6th century CE

▲ **Five Rathas**
7th century CE

▲ **Shore Temple at Mamallapuram**
700–728 CE

▲ **Shiva Temple at Elephanta**
540–755 CE

▲ **Durga Temple**
675–710 CE

▲ **My Son**
4th to 14th centuries CE

Period of Northern and Southern Dynasties
386–589 CE

T'ang Dynasty
618–907 CE

▲ **Songyue Temple Ta**
523 CE

▲ **Daming Palace**
Begun 634 CE

Korea: Koguryô Kingdom
37 BCE–668 CE

▲ **Hwangnyongsa Temple**
Begun ca. 553 CE

Kofun Culture
ca. 3rd century to 538 CE

Asuka period in Japan
ca. 538–710 CE

Nara period in Japan
710–794 CE

▲ **Horyu-ji Temple**
7th century CE

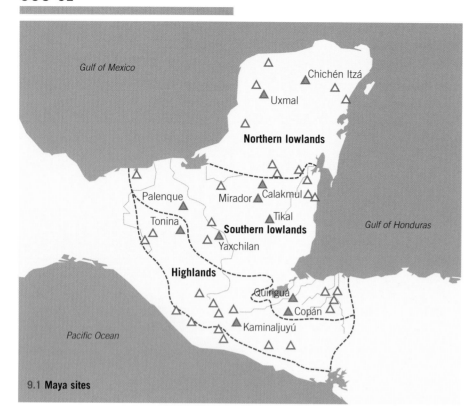

9.1 Maya sites

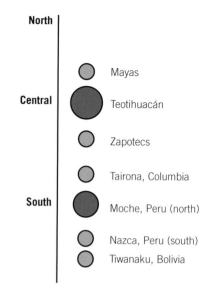

9.2 Urbanization of the Americas, ca. 600 CE

Tikal

Tikal's recorded history begins in 292 CE, when Balam Ajaw ("Decorated Jaguar") came to power. At its peak around 700 CE, Tikal was home to about eighty thousand people. Surrounded by corn fields cultivated with intense labor, the houses of its residents were spread evenly over a 16-square-kilometer area. They were clustered into groups of about four to seven, all raised on high platforms and organized around a courtyard. A high level of civic organization and hydraulic engineering was critical to Tikal's survival. The swampy land had to be sectored by raised causeways that provided access to the cultivatable land and also allowed for travel and transport. For dwellings, more permanent stone platforms had to be built, and for fresh water, stone-lined cisterns were constructed. Like Uaxactún before it, Tikal was built on a set of hills, located on the watershed between the Gulf of Mexico and the Caribbean Sea. Perched at the high point of the region, therefore, Tikal's temples enjoyed a commanding view of their surroundings.

Though the central buildings of the Mayas were used for ceremonial and religious functions and also sometimes as markets, the city itself was spread out in the form of an urban settlement. Whereas the priestly class and ruling elite probably lived in the palaces associated with the shrines, the rest of the Mayas visited the centers sporadically for distinct purposes. Though temples were constructed with specific orientations and functions in mind, ceremonial centers as a whole were not expanded according to preplanned rules or geometries, giving them a somewhat ad hoc appearance. There may, of course, have been reasons for the slightly disjointed and angular arrangement of buildings and open plazas, but these have been lost to time.

The North Acropolis, Tikal's oldest complex, was "reskinned" many times. When a ruler of some significance died, he was buried in the acropolis, and a new stone layer was added to it. The new mass was carefully set to ensure that the addition did not damage the older structure. Small vaults were built for the burials, each with its own shrine. Stairs provided access to these chambers for ancestral rites, which had to be performed by later rulers. A section through the acropolis, therefore, is a veritable textbook of Tikal's thousand-year history. The plaza is a flat stone platform approached by climbing six wide steps. A set of stelae describing Tikal's rulers and dating their achievements are lined up along its northern edge. Temples I and II were constructed simultaneously from 734 to 736 CE by Yik'in Chan K'awiil. (K'awiil also built Temples IV and VI.) The Tikal ruler Jasaw Chan K'awiil I died in 734 CE and was buried beneath Temple I in a spectacular ceremony.

Unlike most Central American platform mounds, whose colossal size completely dwarf the shrine that sits atop them, the shrines of Tikal dominate their substructures. The width atop the shrine of Temple I is just a little less than that of the structure's base. This makes for an extremely steep profile. As a consequence, the visual focus of the entire composition is the shrine's entrance, which is wider than the steps leading to it. Nowhere else in Central American architecture does one find this particular set of architectural proportions at work. Unlike the clay and stone interiors of earlier Mayan pyramids, the interior of this one was built with large blocks of stones, carefully and accurately fitted in the supporting walls. To keep water from leeching into the interior, the surface

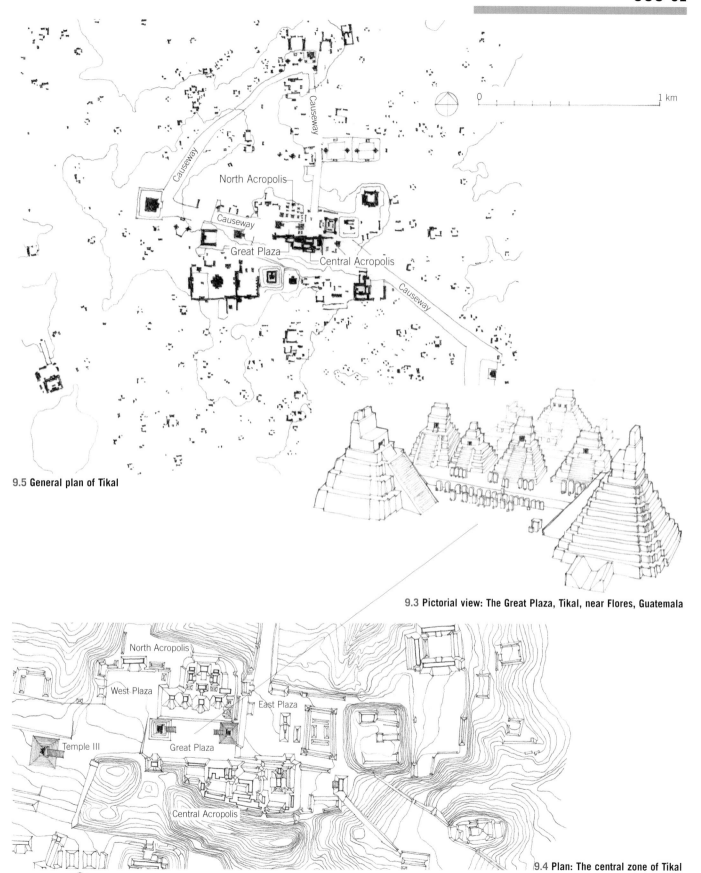

9.5 General plan of Tikal

North Acropolis

Causeway

Causeway

Causeway

Causeway

Great Plaza

Central Acropolis

9.3 Pictorial view: The Great Plaza, Tikal, near Flores, Guatemala

North Acropolis

West Plaza

East Plaza

Temple III

Great Plaza

Central Acropolis

9.4 Plan: The central zone of Tikal

0   300 m

0   1 km

was sealed with mortar. The brickwork that covered the entire pyramid served more for decoration than for protection.

Southeast of the Great Plaza is the so-called Central Acropolis, which held the royal courts and residences. It consisted of a series of courts connected at the corners, with simple adjoining buildings sitting on platforms. The palace courts, although they adjoined the central ceremonial complex, were visually screened off from their surroundings. They were entered at the corners. Tikal's urban core is a spectacular assembly of more than a hundred stone temples. Their engineers constructed Tikal's base by building up the higher zones into platforms with mud and stone. Three zones in the middle were linked over time by causeways to form a triangle. Additional causeways connected to adjoining platforms and the rest of the urban area.

The largest of these zones is focused on a giant stone platform, the Great Plaza. To its north is the North Acropolis, which faces the Great Plaza. Its eastern and western ends are anchored by the so-called Temples I and II, respectively. Farther west and slightly to the south is Temple III, and even farther west, connected by a causeway, is Tikal's largest temple, the 70-meter-tall Temple IV.

Astronomy determined the location of the main temples. They are linked by sightlines. Standing on top of Temple I looking west, the peak of Temple III marks the setting of the sun at the equinoxes. From the same position, a sightline to Temple IV marks sunset on August 13, the day the world began, according to the Mayan calendar. Farther north, two adjacent platform mounds, called the Twin Pyramid complex, are oriented exactly along the cardinal directions. Their collective steps add up to 365, corresponding exactly to one calendar year. They were constructed at the end of a twenty-year period of the Mayan calendar, signifying the successful completion of that period.

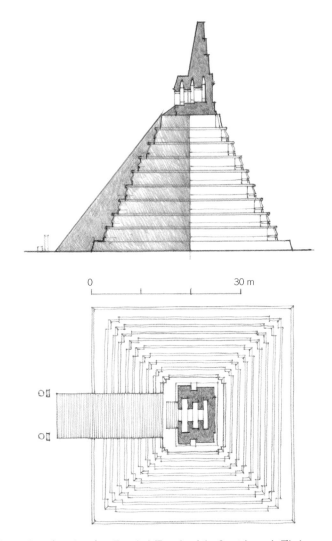

0   30 m

9.6 Plan and section-elevation: Temple I (Temple of the Great Jaguar), Tikal

9.7 Temple I (Temple of the Great Jaguar), Tikal

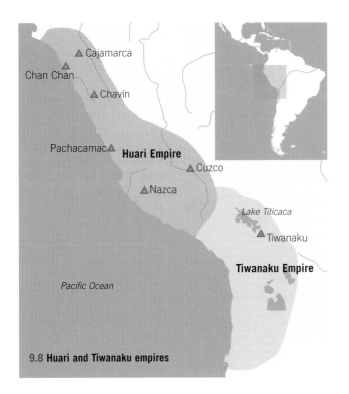

9.8 Huari and Tiwanaku empires

Tiwanaku

Tiwanaku lies in a highland valley in the southern Andes 3,660 meters above sea level, near the south shore of Lake Titicaca. Inhabited from roughly 1000 BCE to 500 CE, it was not only the capital of a network of cities but also the regional ceremonial center, maintaining its preeminent position as such until about 1000 CE. It was not so much the city that was important but the lake, which was seen as the place of origin whence the primeval couple were sent out to call mankind forth from the springs, rivers, rocks, and trees. Lake Titicaca was known as a *taypi*, or the zone of convergence between the principles of *urco* (the west, high, dry, pastoral, celestial, male) and *uma* (the east, low, agricultural, underworld, female). If Tiwanaku was the central representation of the *taypi*, the elite who lived there were viewed as the guardians and representatives of this sacred order.

The ceremonial center was surrounded by an immense artificial moat filled with water diverted from the Tiwanaku River, which evoked the image of the city's core as an island. Upon crossing the moat and entering Akapana, the main temple, a visitor moved from the space and time of ordinary life to that of the sacred. Akapana was a low-terraced platform mound with a base 200 meters square and a height of 17 meters.

9.9 Megalithic entrance to the Kalasasaya Mound, near La Paz, Bolivia

Vertically placed stones, approximately 3.5 meters on center and joined with characteristic Andean precision, mark the edges of the terraces and form the retaining walls. The topmost terrace was covered by thin layers of a bluish-green gravel, brought in from the Quimsachata Mountain Range just south of Tiwanaku. A complexly engineered drainage system connects the top of Akapana to the Tiwanaku River and ultimately to Lake Titicaca. On the summit of Akapana was a sunken court. Associated with the Akapana are four temples—the semi-subterranean, the Kalasasaya, the Putuni, and the Kheri Kala. The semi-subterranean temple is open to the sky, a negative space lined with standing sandstones and masonry infill and axially linked to the Kalasasaya—a large, terraced platform with a megalithic staircase on the south centered on the Portal of the Sun, and a monumental stone sculpture, the so-called Ponce Monolith. The Kalasasaya was also furnished with its own central sunken court, like the Akapana. On the morning of the spring equinox, the sun beam bisects the semi-subterranean temple and appears in the center of the Kalasasaya's staircase.

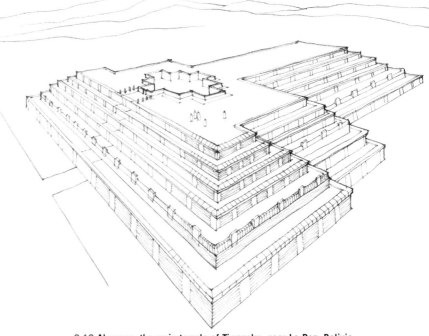

9.10 Akapana, the main temple of Tiwanaku, near La Paz, Bolivia

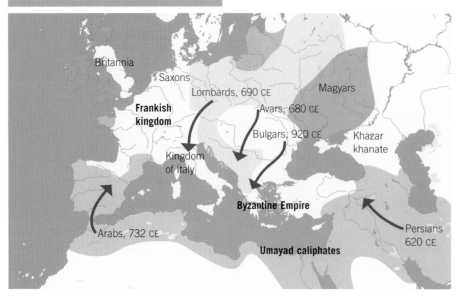

9.11 Justinian Europe, showing movements ca. 600 CE

Age of Justinian

The time period between Constantine the Great (272–337 CE) and Justinian (483–565 CE) was one of consolidation. For Justinian, the Romanum Imperium was to be identified with the Christian *oikoumene* (the known inhabited areas of the world), and the triumph of Christianity was as sacred a mission as the restoration of Roman supremacy. To this end, he reintroduced Roman law, but with the dogmatic primacy peculiar to the Christian religion. All other religions were denied legal protection. Pagan temples were torn down and strict laws passed to consolidate and unify the Christian domination of the empire. In 529 CE, Justinian closed the Academy in Athens, largely to stem the multiplication of ideas and theories in theological debates and to enforce a unified doctrine. Many of its scholars had to seek refuge in Persia, taking with them the fruits of Greek learning.

Justinian was able to recover Italy and Africa. Bridges, fortifications, aqueducts, churches, markets, and whole cities sprang up in the wake of his conquests. But the situation was tenuous. East Europe was still in turmoil, with the Avars and Bulgars moving into Greece and the Lombards into northern Italy. The newly Christianized Frankish kingdom, along with Italy, formed only a thin civilizational wedge into a still barbaric Europe. Newly developing, however, were trade links up the Volga River into the Russian steppe, facilitating trade that had become disrupted by the advances of the Islamic armies.

An excellent example of Justinian's architecture can be seen in Constantinople in the church dedicated to Sergius and Bacchus, two soldiers in the Roman army who were martyred in the early 4th century CE and became the official patrons of the Byzantine armies. Certain changes to its environs should, however, be kept in mind. The building, now a freestanding structure, was originally part of a larger complex that included Justinian's private residence and palace. Furthermore, the slightly thicker walls to the south belonged to another church dedicated to St. Peter and St. Paul, begun in 518 CE and built by Justinian's uncle, Justin I. When Justinian became Caesar in 525 CE, he appended the new construction onto that one.

The two churches were connected at ground level by means of three large arched openings that later changed into windows when the Church of SS. Peter and Paul was removed. (Such church composites were not uncommon in the East, though they were rare in the West.) The narthex on the west extended across both churches, which shared a common atrium in front. To the north was a monumental entrance, presumably from the former palace, creating a cross-axis from north to south linking the two buildings. For reasons unknown, the Church of SS. Peter and Paul fell into disrepair and was demolished; by the 16th century, it was gone, as were most of the remnants of Justinian's palace.

SS. Sergius and Bacchus's original context is important, as it explains some of the curious—and also sometimes overlooked—aspects of its design. To provide an entrance for the priests from the southwest into the apse at the back of the church, the eastern facade was tilted a bit, with the space left for a porch perhaps still visible in the setback of the facade at that corner. The resultant tilt impacted the orientation of the apse and thus of the central nave. To the west, the tilt was not implemented, because the narthex had to align with the Church of SS. Peter and Paul. The plan is distinguished by its extraordinary openness. Unlike Western churches, which channel the churchgoer into the nave from the west, here is a system that permits more fluid pathways into and through the church. Another remarkable feature of the plan that applies to both SS. Sergius and Bacchus and the Hagia Sophia is that there are no separate rooms to the right or left of the altar—rooms for the preparation of the sacred meal and where the bishop dons his garb. Such spaces, the *prothesis* and the *diaconicon*, respectively, are typical in later Byzantine churches, but they are not present in early Justinian ones. The result in both buildings is that the central structure holding the dome is freed from the surrounding architecture in a way that is uncharacteristic of Byzantine design. The presence of multiple doorways, and the absence of a *prothesis* and *diaconicon*, requires some explanation, as does the liturgical use of these buildings.

One could compare SS. Sergius and Bacchus and Hagia Sophia with the plan for the Roman basilica, which is distinguished by its simplicity. Byzantine churches had galleries; Roman churches did not. Furthermore, the apse was not a podium with an altar, as is the case in the West, but a semicircular tier of benches called a *synthronon*. One is still visible in the Church of St. Irene, which stands just to the northeast of the Hagia Sophia and was used before the Hagia Sophia as the city's principal church. A final component of Justinian liturgical space was an elevated *ambo*—a

9.12 Interior: SS. Sergius and Bacchus, Istanbul, Turkey

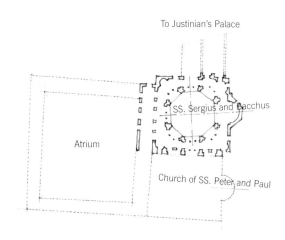

9.13 Original context for SS. Sergius and Bacchus

reading desk or pulpit—approached by stairs from east and west, from which the Bible would be read. (The word *ambo* is derived from the Greek verb *amabainein*, which means, "to go up.") It was usually set near the center of the nave but often slightly to the east of the axis. The ambo was surrounded by a low screen and a slightly elevated path to the altar, often marked out by a low screen as well.

It would be a mistake to project current medieval liturgical uses in Greek Orthodox churches onto these spaces, even though there are clearly numerous similarities. In Justinian's day, the populace gathered closely around the ambo in the nave. In addition, the preparatory rites of the *prothesis* for the First Entrance that are common today were not practiced. The entrance ritual was more straightforward but also grander. The people gathered in the courtyard, and there they made their offerings of bread and wine to the church. Once the bishop had blessed the entrance and had himself entered, he was followed by the deacon, who carried a bejeweled and bound volume of the Gospel—which stood for Christ

himself—accompanied by candle-bearers, incense-bearers, and a subdeacon carrying a cross. The rest followed. This entrance, the First Entrance, had numerous symbolic meanings, including the rejection of disbelief, and signified the first appearance of God and the conversion to faith. In Rome, the order is reversed. The priests enter first and await the arrival of the bishop. In Constantinople, the bishop would go past the *ambo* and into the sanctuary—defined by the short barrier of the iconostasis—to the altar where the Gospel would be placed, and then to the *synthronon*, where he would give the initial blessing signifying the glorification of Christ.

If the emperor, who was the head of the Orthodox Church, was present, he would arrive earlier than the bishop and join him at the narthex, at the head of the procession. His honor guard, consisting of soldiers and cross-bearers, would have preceded him into the church to define the path. After leaving a gift of gold at the altar, he would proceed to the south aisle, where his throne was located. The interaction between emperor and priesthood was an essential and defining moment in the integrity of the empire and the Church, with their meeting and common participation in the ceremony a sign of the unity of the earthly and divine realms. At SS. Sergius and Bacchus, the emperor's spot was in the northeast of the gallery, from where he could overlook the proceedings.

9.14 Plan: SS. Sergius and Bacchus

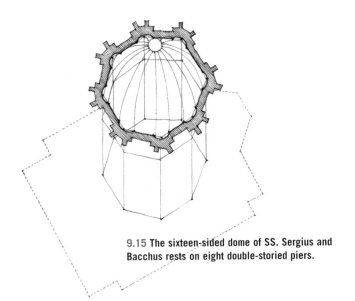

9.15 The sixteen-sided dome of SS. Sergius and Bacchus rests on eight double-storied piers.

Today, a table or niche on the north side serves as the *prothesis*, but there is no evidence that this custom existed in Byzantine times. It seems that the act of bringing offerings of bread and wine by the congregation started outside the church, in a special room of a building called the *skeuophylakion* that was used to hold the sacred vessels in which the food was transported. In other words, during the service, the wine and bread brought by the congregation was prepared out of sight and, in the process, "became" the flesh and blood of Christ, and was then carried into the church. The bishop made his entrance already vested—thus the absence of the *diaconicon*, which came only later. The atrium served as a place for people to gather. The narthex was a more formal space used to organize the procession once it had arrived. Once the procession had commenced, the congregation could also enter, which it did by streaming into the space from the various entrances, in a manner of popular commotion.

Following the blessing, the readings took place from the altar and from the *ambo*, the Gospel having been carried to the *ambo* with great solemnity and excitement. After the reading and the sermon came the Great Entrance, or as it was called at that time, the Entrance of the Mysteries, during which the Eucharistic bread and wine were transferred from their place of preparation to the place of offering on the altar.

At the Hagia Sophia, the *skeuophylakion* was located north of the building and was most likely the round building at the northeast corner. The bread and wine were brought in through a side door. At SS. Sergius and Bacchus, the atrium and the *skeuophylakion* are no longer extant, and additional archaeological work will be necessary to determine the location of the latter. The space inside the church was used to segregate men from women, but how, exactly, remains unclear. It seems that the empress and her court viewed the liturgy from a special place in the gallery, but whether all women were in the gallery or only in some part of it, or whether women had a place on the ground floor, has not been fully determined.

Over the center of the space itself rises a sixteen-sided pumpkin dome brought down on eight double-storied piers, screened in the interstitial spaces by pairs of columns on both levels. These screens alternate in a rhythmic manner: straight in the direction of the principal axis, and curving outward on the four spaces at the corners. The novel plan type had been developed in Cilicia at the so-called Domed Ambulatory Church in Dag Pazari, which some scholars date to the 480s CE and which has an ambulatory. Another church even farther south, dedicated to the Virgin Mary, is also of the same box-in-a-box type; it dates perhaps to the 420s CE. Also similar is the cathedral in the city of Bosra (511–12 CE), located 140 kilometers south of Damascus and dedicated to the same saints. Those buildings, however, were of stone, whereas SS. Sergius and Bacchus was built of brick embedded in a thick mortar. Much lighter, these bricks were probably easier and quicker to build with (although they were also susceptible to lateral forces and earthquakes). This also meant that the supporting walls could be opened up with windows and that the buttressing could, in effect, be concealed in a supporting cast of semi-domes and quarter-domes. There is considerable debate as to whether this technique came from Mesopotamia or whether it was homegrown. Whatever its source, once established here the technique would soon be developed still further, as in the Hagia Sophia. Another earlier source might come from late Roman times: an

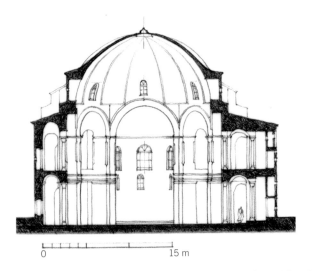

9.16 Transverse section looking toward the sanctuary: SS. Sergius and Bacchus

9.17 Interior: St. Vitale, Ravenna, Italy

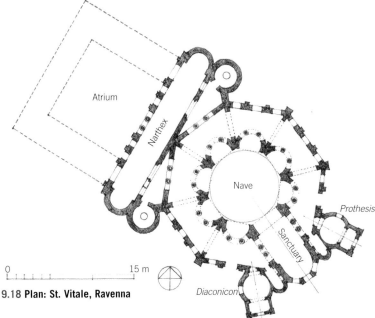

9.18 Plan: St. Vitale, Ravenna

octagonal "church" was found in Gadara, but excavations have shown that this building, like a similar one in Gerasa, was originally a market that had been converted into a church.

St. Vitale, Ravenna

A building that is often quoted as a parallel to SS. Sergius and Bacchus is the Basilica of St. Vitale (538–45 CE) in Ravenna. It was built during the brief time in the 6th century when Ravenna was the seat of Theodoric's rule as titular head of the Western Empire.

It was financed by a wealthy local banker whose monogram appears on the capitals of the ground floor. St. Vitale, known as a prime example of Byzantine architecture in the West, is clearly linked iconographically to Constantinople.

The central area is an octagon supported by piers, between which double-height bays swell out and away from the center. The surfaces were richly decorated with marble panels and mosaics of extraordinary splendor and grandeur, in the Byzantine style. Though the double-shell plan with its wedge-shape

piers is similar to SS. Sergius and Bacchus, at St. Vitale a *prothesis* and *diaconicon* were added to the north and south of the apse. The sanctuary is also given greater prominence and is more remote from the central space. The ambulatory and gallery were originally not vaulted (the present vaults are medieval), placing greater emphasis on the piers, which are buttressed to their backs. To compensate for the mass of the piers, the architects replaced the rhythmic alternation of semicircular and straight screens with a continuous row of semicircular niches, which are deeper than the ones at SS. Sergius and Bacchus and thus give the space an airier feeling. The dome of St. Vitale has more or less the same width as that of SS. Sergius and Bacchus. It is, however, considerably higher and more vertical in proportion: the bottom of the dome and the top of the arches underneath are separated by several meters and do not touch, as they do at SS. Sergius and Bacchus. The exterior is of plain brick, as was typical of Byzantine architecture, but unlike Armenian architecture, the dome is not visible from the outside. Today the basilica is most famous for its Byzantine-type mosaics showing a solemn and stately procession in which Emperor Justinian and his consort, representing regal authority, bring offerings.

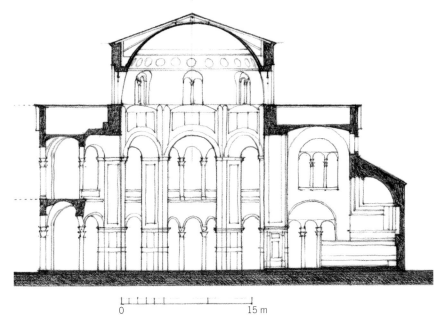

9.19 Section: St. Vitale, Ravenna

9.20 **Narthex: Hagia Sophia**

Hagia Sophia

The Hagia Sophia ("sacred wisdom," 532–37 CE) in Constantinople was, from the date of its opening, considered one of the greatest buildings in the Western world. Little is known for certain about its predecessor, which was dedicated by Constantine in 360 CE but damaged in civil strife. For the new church, Justinian called in Anthemius of Tralles and Isidore of Miletus, who produced a daring and lofty domed structure still largely intact today. Sheathed in marble and gold, its splendor made it one of the most talked about buildings in the Christian world. One visitor, Procopius, writing in the 6th century, when the building was newly finished, stated, "The dome must surely seem not to rest upon solid masonry but to cover the space beneath with its golden dome suspended from heaven." Some skeptics thought they had been right when an earthquake destroyed the dome in 557 CE, barely twenty years after its dedication. But undaunted, Justinian had a new one built, though the second one was more steeply pitched.

The structural system is simple but ingenious. A 30-meter square forms the center. At the corners, piers rise up to support four arches, between which are pendentives that hold a dome scalloped with forty ribs. Windows line the base of the dome, making it seem to float. The east and west arches are closed off with a screen of columns and windows. The undersides of

9.21 **Interior: Hagia Sophia, Istanbul, Turkey**

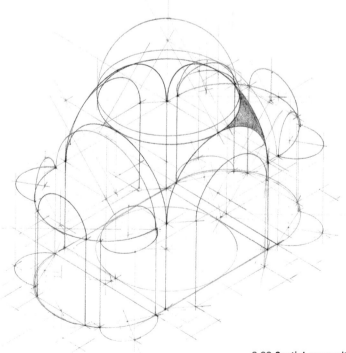

9.22 **Spatial composition: Hagia Sophia**

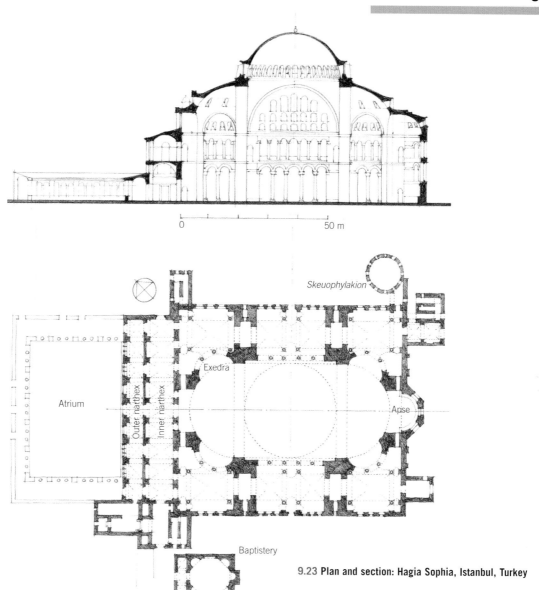

9.23 Plan and section: Hagia Sophia, Istanbul, Turkey

the east and west arches, however, seem to have blown away, allowing one to look into vast, three-apsed buildings on both sides. The only difference between east and west is that on the eastern side, the final 8 meters of the apse boldly project from the perimeter wall that otherwise, like a box, contains its precious spatial cargo. The deep galleries on the north and south, which form spacious corridors parallel to the nave, help create the sense of drama that pervades the building. From a structural point of view, they serve to divide the buttressing into segments.

The vaults, made of brick, are thin and lightweight. There is still considerable uncertainty about the statics that govern the building's integrity, because the semi-domes

are too thin to be of much assistance. But the combination of supporting half-domes, quarter-domes, and massive piers were enough, and in the days before computers and earthquake impact studies, the audacity of the system is remarkable. Later, from the 8th century on, various types of buttresses were added to the exterior to prevent problems.

The use of windows is similarly complex. The window at the east end of the apse, the lights along the base of the dome, and those on the north and south all allow light to stream directly into the nave. But the large windowless openings under the supporting arch at the west end are filled only with grille work. Under the north and south

tympana, the colonnaded columns stand in the shadows, backlit from the windows in the outer wall. Impressive as the complex structural system of the Hagia Sophia is, the architects made every effort to make it appear effortless. The marble cladding and the mosaics would have obliterated any sense of oppression or weight. From the dark-gray marble of the pavement to green marble with white veins, dark-blue marble with yellow veins, and reddish columns, to the silver and gold of the mosaics, the eye moves from surface to surface as if structure simply did not exist.

9.24 View of the semi-dome, Hagia Sophia

The first dome was covered with a gold mosaic. The second one had a large figure of a cross embedded in its decoration. The windows were filled with glass tinted blue, red, green, brown, yellow, and purple. The light was thus a subdued one. Even the patterned marble floor, unlike the floor of the Pantheon, denies a sense of stability and has been described by ancient commentators as a wavy sea. Though a good deal of the marble panels have survived, few of the mosaics have, since most were taken down or plastered over during its conversion to a mosque. (The Hagia Sophia was secularized in 1935.)

From the outside, with its staggered heaping of volumes, a visitor would not expect an interior space of this dimension and scale. In fact, past the narthex the space rises forcefully, creating the feeling of being at the bottom of a vast canyon, with the church floor a type of stage on which the Entrance of the Mysterires was performed. Nighttime illumination must also have been impressive. From the base of the dome, brass chains swept down to support a metal ring equipped with flat silver disks pierced to hold glass vessels for oil lamps. Within this vast candelabrum hung another, smaller crown of lights, while higher up, a great silver disk acted as a reflector.

The church was sited just north of the palace complex at the terminus of the main avenue that ran through the city. Apart from the Hagia Sophia, very little of the palace survives today.

9.25 Palace area of Constantinople

9.26 **Detail of capital, Hagia Sophia**

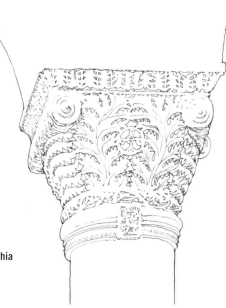

9.27 **Examples of Byzantine capitals**

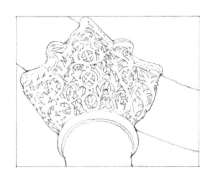

Byzantine Capitals

There are two types of capitals used at Hagia Sophia: composite and Ionic. The composite capital that emerged during the late Byzantine Empire, mainly in Rome, combines the Corinthian with the Ionic. Composite capitals line the principal space of the nave. Ionic capitals are used behind them in the side spaces, in a minor position relative to the Corinthian or composite orders (as was their fate well into the 19th century, when buildings were designed for the first time with a monumental Ionic order). At Hagia Sophia, though, these are not the standard imperial statements. The capitals are filled with foliage in all sorts of variations. In some, the small, lush leaves appear to be caught up in the spinning of the scrolls—clearly, a different, nonclassical sensibility had taken over the design. At SS. Sergius and Bacchus and other churches of the time, we see the full emergence of this experimentation.

Post-Renaissance classicism in Europe dismissed these efforts as radically outside the norm of the "classical" tradition. But the classical tradition was more open to experimentation than one might at first think. Furthermore, after the fall of the Roman Empire, in which standardized models were often used, local craftsmen were invited to test their skills. That many of these craftsmen were using northern motives or were themselves Christianized Visigoths is more than obvious. The Visigoths invaded Byzantine territories in the 5th century, with many of them staying on to be conscripted into the Byzantine army. They tended to use vine and plant motifs for their ornamentation, as can be seen in their belt buckles. Most of the Visigoths eventually went on to settle in southern Spain.

The capitals at St. Vitale in Ravenna show wavy and delicate floral patterns similar to decorations found on belt buckles and dagger blades. Their inverted pyramidal form has the look of a basket. At the Basilica Eufrasiana in Parenzo, Croatia, along the Adriatic Sea, we find a double-tier design, with birds at the corners and delicately carved grapevines below. At Salonica, Greece, we encounter capitals that also consist of abstract curved patterns, in conjunction with some that have leaves that look as if they are being tossed around by the wind. The capitals at SS. Sergius and Bacchus have a delicate stenciling that allows the swirling tendrils of acanthus to stand out against the blackness of a deeply cut background.

9.28 **A Visigoth ornament**

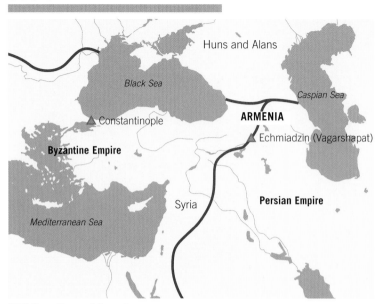

9.29 Byzantium and Armenia

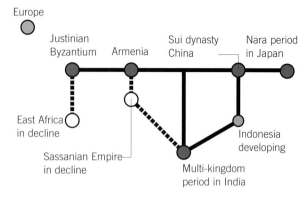

9.30 Eurasian trade diagram, ca. 600 CE

Armenian Architecture

The area defined by the Caspian Sea to the east and the Black Sea to the west was an important geographical hub. Merchants could unload goods from China on the shores of the Caspian, where they would be taken through Armenia to the Black Sea, from which almost any destination in Europe was reachable. The trip from China to Rome would have gone through fewer contested territories in the year 600 CE than it does today; the location was, however, both the cause for the rise and the fall of the Armenian kingdom. Descended from the Urartu, the Armenians were in turn controlled by the Persians, by Alexander the Great, by the Romans, and then by the Persians again. Despite all this, the Armenian desire for autonomy was strong, and the period between the 4th and 9th centuries saw Armenia at its creative best. In the 6th and 7th centuries, with Arab regions to the south and Vikings to the north still in disarray, Armenia was a safe link between East and West. But by the 10th century, with the expansion of Islam and Christianity into large, far-flung yet interconnected domains, trade increased—to the detriment of Armenia, which was able to survive only until 1375.

The significance of Armenia in the history of architecture lies, once again, in the high quality of its stonework. In Constantinople, stone had given way to brick. (The Hagia Sophia is basically a brick building.) The use of concrete, furthermore, had been forgotten by this time. Only the Armenians had

maintained the classical Hellenistic tradition of clean surfaces, volumetric complexity, and a strong focus on a compact, objectlike effect of the building in space. This would have an important impact on the later development of church architecture in Europe, when Armenian masons were in demand in the west, particularly in France.

The history of Armenia's Christian architecture begins in 301 CE, when Dertad III (the king of Armenia under Roman suzerainty) was converted to Christianity by St. Gregory the Illuminator, a native Armenian who made Christianity the state religion. In general, the Armenian liturgy resembles that of the Eastern Church, except

that its language is classical Armenian rather than Greek. The distinctive look of Armenian architecture developed quite rapidly. Buildings tended to have forms that were simple and solid-looking. From the earliest date, they were volumetric and planimetric masterpieces. Furthermore, the carving and placement of the stones was excellent; indeed, at the time, these buildings would have been far superior to other stone buildings in Europe and Asia. Though Byzantine architecture introduced the dome as an important potential element in Christian architecture, the Byzantine dome was externally not visible. Armenian architecture, by way of contrast, pushed the dome up over the mass of the building. Though the dome itself was covered with a light wooden conical roof, the silhouette achieved would have a profound impact on future church design.

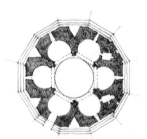

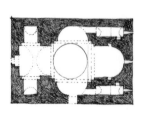
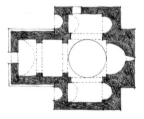

9.31 Typology of Armenian churches

9.32 St. Hripsime, Echmiadzin, Armenia

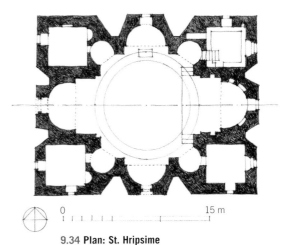

9.34 Plan: St. Hripsime

The Armenian word *gmbet*, usually translated as "dome," means more precisely "the vault of heaven." The vision of Gregory the Illuminator (b. 239 CE), the patron saint of Armenia, also played a part in the acceptance of the dome. He wrote that he saw a figure of light descending from heaven associated with a magnificent building that had the form of a dome on four columns.

St. Hripsime

One of the most refined examples of Armenian architecture can be found in Echmiadzin. St. Hripsime was the second church built by St. Gregory the Illuminator during the first quarter of the 4th century. It was replaced in 395 CE by a small chapel. The present edifice was built in 618 CE. The building is constructed of dark, ash-colored tufa bonded on the interior with concrete-like mortar. The whole rests, like a Greek temple, on a stepped stylobate. The interior is organized on a quatrefoil plan, with niches in the cardinal directions. In addition to these, there are niches on the diagonal corners, creating a fluid and dynamic interior space. The diagonal niches, having the form of three-quarter cylinders, may also have been intended to strengthen the abutment of the dome. They give access to four subsidiary chambers that flank the eastern and western niches. Barrel vaults intervene between the axial niches and the central square.

These vaults, which are wider along the main axis, accentuate the east-west direction. The whole composition is bound together to form a well-proportioned rectangle with large triangular recesses on the exterior that impart a rhythmic impression of the composition. The dome rests on a sixteen-sided windowed drum that has twelve windows at its base. Four windows are obscured by small cylindrical towers that were added later as buttresses. The entrance porch on the west is also a later addition. The beauty of the St. Hripsime edifice derives from the simplicity and harmony of its different parts.

9.33 Interior: St. Hripsime

9.35 A Hindu mandala

9.36 Vishnu Temple, Deogarh, India

Vishnu Deogarh and Elephanta

During the 6th and 7th centuries, with Buddhism marginalized, Hindu architecture in South Asia entered an experimental phase, and rock-cut temples competed for prominence with the new structural-stone and brick temples. The plethora of styles and approaches was a product of the numerous kingdoms, that of Harshavardhana (606–47 CE) in the north, and, moving southward, the Chalukyas, the Pallavas, the Cholas, and the Pandyas. Although an invasion of north India by the Huns dispersed the Buddhist monks from Kashmir, they continued to prosper in major universities like Nalanda, Ujjain, and Sirpur. Typical for the syncretism of the time, Sirpur had shrines dedicated to Hindu deities such as Shiva and Vishnu adjacent to compounds dedicated to the Buddha. One of the oldest statues of a female deity, Haritiki, has also been found at Sirpur.

An interesting comparison can be made between two 6th-century Gupta period temples: the Shiva shrine on Elephanta Island, a rock-cut structure built by Shaivite monks for their own use, and the Dasavatara Vishnu Temple at Deogarh, a brick-and-stone structure built for a large devotee population. Elephanta is a Hindu shrine adapted from the older Buddhist rock-cut structures, while Deogarh is a new invention—a shrine constructed with rock to appear as if it is monolithic (i.e., rock-cut). The latter has a representational mountain as its *shikhara*, while the former has a real mountain in which it is embedded. Both begin with a square *garbha-griha*, but while Deogarh would have had originally held an image of Vishnu, Elephanta still has the Shiva Lingam at its center. From the middle, four axes radiate out, defining access paths. Deogarh, however, is accessible only from the west (the direction of Vishnu) and has three implied doors (*ghana-dwaras*, literally "blind doors") along its remaining cardinal directions.

9.37 **Vedic altar, the origin of the Mandala diagram**

9.38 **Plan: Vishnu Temple, Deogarh**

Ghana-dwaras

9.39 *Garbha-griha*, Cave of Shiva, Elephanta, near Mumbai, India

9.40 Lingam, Cave of Shiva at Elephanta

Elephanta is open on all four sides, though east is its primary direction of access. Deogarh's main shrine is at the center of a nine-square mandala, with four subsidiary shrines interlocked at its corners. Elephanta has a much more complex geometry, with four sets of nine-square mandalas interlocking to define two major axes of access, one from the west and the other from the north. The north-south axis, aligned with the main entrance, terminates in three gigantic Shiva sculptures in deeply recessed niches. This triptych, much celebrated in the annals of art history, occupies the entire width and height of the end wall, and, compared to the rough-hewn character of the rest of structure, was carved with greater care.

The cerebral exploration of interlocking geometries based on mandala diagrams was to become the defining characteristic of Hindu temple form in the centuries to come. Mandalas are derived from original Vedic altars and are used in both the Hindu and Buddhist religions as diagrams to map the cosmos for astrological observations. These diagrams are abstract, without scale, and can take any number of forms derived from a combination of superimposed squares and circles.

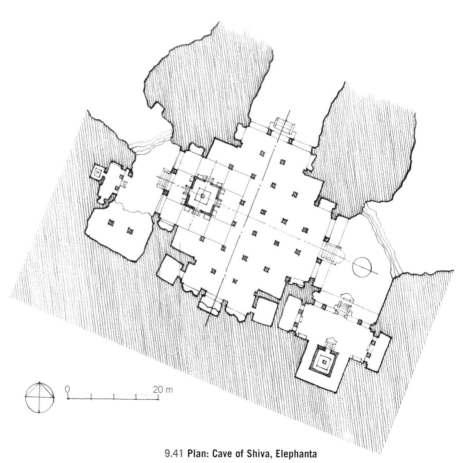

0   20 m

9.41 Plan: Cave of Shiva, Elephanta

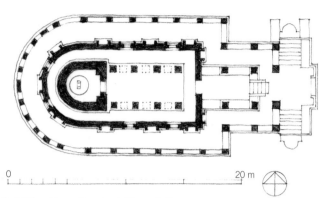

9.42 Plan: Durga Temple at Aihole, India

9.43 Five Rathas, Mamallapuram, India

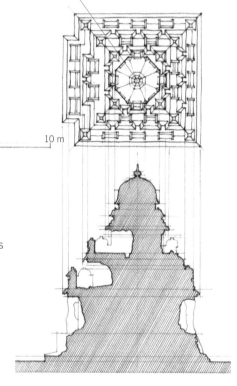

9.44 Plan and section: Dharmaraja Ratha, Mamallapuram

Durga Temple and the Five Rathas

One of the most experimental of the Chalukyan temples in western India is the so-called Durga Temple (675–710 CE) at Aihole. It is unusual in two respects: it has an apsidal end clearly derived from the Buddhist *caitya* halls, and it ably accommodates the *parikrama*, or circumambulatory function, by providing an enclosed corridor around the general arc of movement. There are a few examples of similar apsidal temples in India, but they are rare. Furthermore, the Durga Temple has a secondary envelope wrapping around the main shrine, which is unique in Hindu temple architecture. Usually the plinth, at most, will echo the outline of the main shrine, but at the Durga Temple, a second aisle was created and left largely unadorned, with large openings formed by simple piers. The veranda created by the intermediate space makes for an interesting study, with a simple but light-filled "functionalist" outer perimeter that contrasts with—and protects—the heavily ornamented and sculpted interior wall, which belongs to the main body of the temple.

Contemporary with the Chalukyas, with whom they had frequent commerce, the Pallavas are one of the most distinguished dynasties of the South. The second Pallava ruler, Narasimhavarman II, built at Mamallapuram not only one of India's largest port cities of the time but also a series of monuments that form something of a petrified stone city on the coast.

The oldest and most famous of his constructions are the so-called Five Rathas (mid- to late 7th century) and the Shore Temple at Mamallapuram. The Five Rathas are a group of five miniaturized stone temples accompanied by life-size sculptures of a bull, an elephant, and a lion. Four of the temples are carved out of a single, large piece of rock. It is unclear why they were made. They may have been an experimental study of typological possibilities or displays of sculptural prowess in stone intended to rival woodwork. Miniaturization is, in fact, a persistent theme in Hindu temple design. Every temple is a thought of as a miniature, or model, of the Hindu cosmic order. And the "decorative" module of a temple on a *shikhara* is also a miniature of the temple of which it is a part. In other words, on every scale—from the mini-temple on a *shikhara*, to the temple itself, to the full-scale reality of the Hindu cosmos—the same form repeats itself, as in fractal geometry. Beyond being a symbol of cosmic order, temples also project to the worshipper a sense of personal wholeness.

9.45 Shore Temple at Mamallapuram

Shore Temple at Mamallapuram

The Shore Temple at Mamallapuram (700–728 CE), so called because it overlooks the Bay of Bengal, is one of the oldest structural stone temples in southern India. It is attributed to the Pallava king Narasimhavarman II. Originally, it was part of a series of temples that belonged to a former port city that has long since disappeared into the waves, leaving the building isolated on the beach. The temple is actually an amalgam of three different shrines. The main shrine is dedicated to Shiva and faces east. The second shrine, with a smaller *shikhara*, is also dedicated to Shiva, but faces west. Between the two, attached to the back wall of the smaller Shiva shrine and entered from the east, is a small third shrine with no superstructural presence, dedicated to the reclining Vishnu. The Vishnu shrine, probably the oldest on the site, is on axis with the larger Shiva shrine, although there is no direct communication between the two. The entrance is through a gateway, or *gopuram*, covered by a transverse barrel vault.

Although most of the exterior arrangements of the temple have eroded, there is ample suggestion that water may have been channeled into pools in the temple and may indeed have also entered into the Vishnu shrine—which would have been appropriate, since the reclining Vishnu figure is described in mythology as lying in the primordial ocean. The *shikharas* are similar to those of the nearby Five Rathas, with a strict pyramidal outline and a pilastered wall. The individual tiers of the Shore Temple's *shikharas* have been kept distinct and separate, with the deep overhanging eaves casting dark shadows without blurring the levels. Both *shikharas* resolve themselves into octagonal capstones with long finials.

Most later Hindu temples, dedicated to more than one deity, are lined up hierarchically or organized radially around a dominant center. The Shore Temple's biaxial configuration of the two Shiva shrines, which are separated and yet linked by the small Vishnu shrine, represents an effort to balance the multiple competing liturgical requirements.

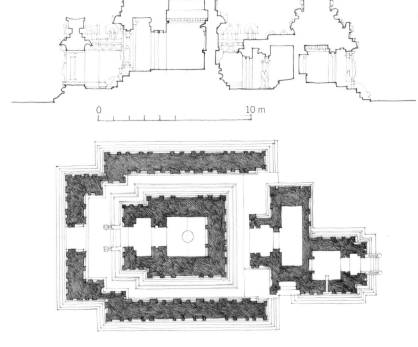

0   10 m

9.46 Plan and section: Shore Temple at Mamallapuram

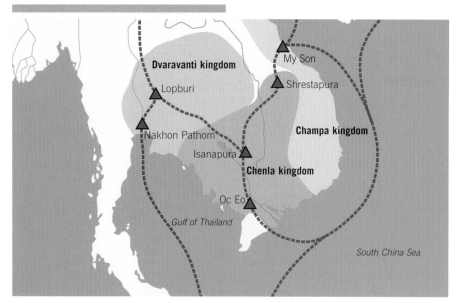

9.47 Zone of development in Southeast Asia, 600 CE

Southeast Asia

Between 300 and 600 CE, there was a marked transformation of the Irrawaddy and Mekong river hinterland in areas that are today Thailand and Cambodia. River water and floodwaters were brought under control, and increased centralization allowed for the exercise of authority. In the Mekong River area, *barays* were created. These water pools, formed by large enclosed dikes, were flooded naturally by the Mekong River, and after the floodwaters receded, retained water in the basins for irrigation during the dry season. By means of this hydroengineering, rice production increased and new cities sprang up.

Among the larger of these new cities were Nakhon Pathon and Lop Buri in Thailand, and Isanapura and Shrestapura in Cambodia and Laos. All were carved out of the jungle and surrounded by newly created agricultural zones. It is clear that the Southeast Asian hinterland was becoming interconnected with trade routes that worked their way both east-west and north-south, with China consequently gaining in importance. Politically, the area was divided between the Dvaravanti in Thailand, the Chenla in Cambodia, the Champa along the Vietnamese coast, and the emergent Srivijaya kingdom in Malaysia and Indonesia. These kingdoms were heavily influenced by Indian religious ideas. The Dvaravanti were Buddhists, whereas the Chenla, developing form the Furnan, were Hindus; the Champa, who were

closest to China, blended their Hinduism with Chinese notions about landscape and state representation.

In 618 CE, the Chenla king Isanavaram I (r. 616–35 CE) established Isanapura—the suffix *pura* means "city"—as the capital of his kingdom, 20 kilometers northeast of Kompong. (The city is now called Sambor Prei Kuk.) It was about 2 kilometers square and contained approximately 150 temples all dedicated to Shiva or one of his numerous forms. Though the city has not been thoroughly studied archaeologically, the brick temples show considerable sophistication. The Chenla had originally built their temples of wood but made the conversion to brick around this time. The brick was covered with stucco and decorated with lacquer and gilding. Among the three main temples, one—called the North Group—consists of a 100-meter-square platform about 1 meter high on which rest five shrines, a standard prototype for Hindu temples that represent the five peaks of the mythical Mt. Meru, the abode of the gods. The central shrine contained the Shiva Lingam, but unlike most shrines it is open on all four sides. It rests on a terrace about 50 meters square. Small shrines define the corners. The whole is contained by an enclosure wall.

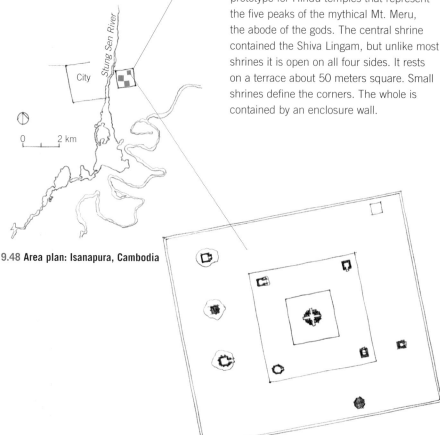

9.48 Area plan: Isanapura, Cambodia

9.49 Plan: Prasat Sambor (North Group), Hindu temple complex of Sambor Prei Kuk, Isanapura

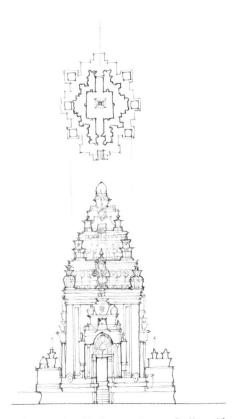

9.50 Elevation and plan: My Son temple, near Da Nang, Vietnam

9.51 My Son temple

My Son

The idea of a sacred landscape also took root in the Champa kingdom. The coast of Vietnam that it controlled had for centuries been developing as an important regional economic zone, its numerous bays and inlets accommodating trade with Chinese and Indian vessels. Initially, the Champa, as a set of federated cities, were closely tied to Chinese cultural and religious traditions, but in the 4th century, there was a strong infusion of Indian culture. Sanskrit was adopted as a scholarly language, and Hinduism—especially Shaivism—became the state religion. Toward the end of the 4th century, in a somewhat unusual move perhaps reflective of Chinese notions of kingship, a valley known as My Son (69 kilometers southwest of Da Nang) was set aside for religious purposes and as a memorial site dedicated to the noble achievement of the royal dynasty. My Son ("Beautiful Mountain") was located near the Thu Bon River and to the west of Indrapura, now known as Hôi An, a city that at that time possessed a large harbor and was an important trading center. The valley, hidden from the plain and with only one entrance, is surrounded by hills and mountains. The site was envisioned as a sacred one. The highest mountain of My Son, the Rang Meo, or "Cat's Teeth Mountain" (800 meters), symbolized Mt. Meru, the residence of the god Shiva, the main deity worshipped by the Champa.

The earliest temples, built from wood, have not survived. Brick masonry was introduced toward the end of the 7th century. The temples all followed a similar Indian model: a square ground plan with a platform and shrine proper, and a high, stepped roof. The external surface was often plastered and painted. Eventually, stone was also used for decorative purposes around lintels and door jambs, as well as for columns and pilasters. There is a blind portico facing east, also lavishly ornamented. The interiors are plain, with small niches for lamps. The Shiva Lingam, symbolizing the divine force, was situated on a plinth in the center.

A decorated frieze connected the tower with its roof (*suarloka*). Each tower had three stories, forming a stepped pyramid that represented Kailasa, the abode of Shiva. Many of the roofs were originally covered with gold or silver leaf. In front of the *kalan* stood a smaller gate tower (*gopura*), built from brick, with stone pillars. Most of the temple complexes also had long buildings (*mandapas*) with tiled roofs adjacent to the gate towers, used for religious ceremonies. In many cases there were smaller, two-roomed temples (*kasagraha*) around the *kalan* for the worship of lesser deities. Each complex was surrounded by a thick wall of brick, but these have almost entirely disappeared over the centuries.

As was the case in all Hindu temples, only the Brahmin were allowed to enter the *cella*, or inner sanctuary, and minister to the god with food, music, and other offerings. Pilgrims could pray outside, leaving their gifts with the religious authorities.

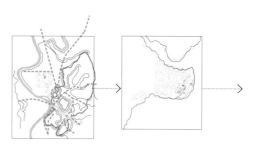

9.53 The sizes of Rome and Constantinople relative to that of Chang'an, shown on facing page.

9.52 T'ang dynasty China

Sui and T'ang Dynasties

After a long period of competitive warfare, the Sui (581–618 CE) and the T'ang (618–907 CE) succeeded in establishing centralized dynasties that controlled much of the Chinese territories. In an effort to integrate the economies of their territories, they made determined investments in public works—in particular the building of canals and roads. Their engineering achievements can be seen in the segmental stone-arch bridge they built over the Jiao River near Zhaozhou on the main north-south trade route. The Jiao River was more than 40 meters wide at this point. The steep approaches of their older, semicircular bridges were impractical for wheeled vehicles, while their post-and-lintel technology was not sufficiently advanced. The problem of sinking multiple stone piers into the swiftly flowing river made a multiple-

arched structure impractical. Li Chun, the engineer of the bridge, constructed the Zhaozhou Bridge using a series of twenty-eight adjacent arcs, each containing forty-three wedge-shaped stone voussoirs tied together with nine reinforcing iron rods to pull the stones together. Over the next four centuries, T'ang engineers constructed bridges using not only the segmental arch and open spandrel construction but also arched, suspension, and cantilever technology.

Daming Palace

Though the Sui and T'ang emperors were generous patrons of Buddhism, their own authority continued to derive from the Confucian ordering of the world that had been established during the Han dynasty.

Spatially, the authority of the emperor was, of course, represented by the palace, constructed axially at the head of the city. In the long reign of Gao Zong (650–83 CE), the power of the emperor was further magnified by the creation of another palace beyond the boundaries of Chang'an. The Daminggong (*gong* means "palace"), or "Palace of Great Light," is in its own special compound covering 3 square kilometers. It was organized axially in a series of interconnected courts forming a four-part complex:

1. Entry square, about 500 meters square
2. Hanyuan Hall (Hanyuandian) in front (south side) of the entry square
3. Xuanzheng Hall at the back (north side) of the square
4. Northern third, containing the emperor's court, reception areas, residences, gardens, and temples

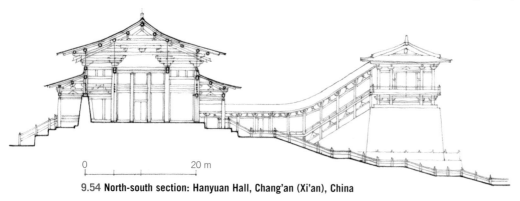

0   20 m

9.54 North-south section: Hanyuan Hall, Chang'an (Xi'an), China

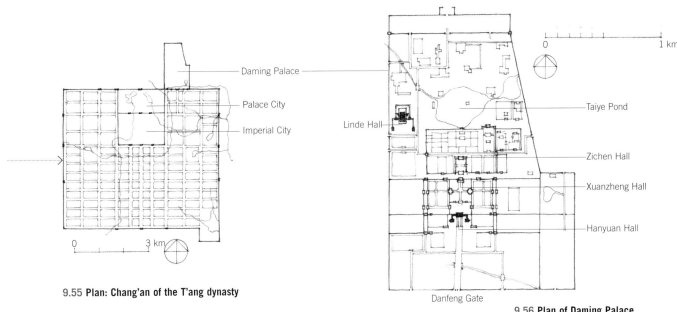

Daming Palace
Palace City
Imperial City

9.55 Plan: Chang'an of the T'ang dynasty

0   3 km

Linde Hall

Taiye Pond
Zichen Hall
Xuanzheng Hall
Hanyuan Hall

0   1 km

Danfeng Gate

9.56 Plan of Daming Palace

First in Daminggong's axial sequence was the Hanyuandian, or the "Enfolding Vitality Hall," the main gate where imperial rites were performed. This huge, imposing gate faced a gigantic square where ceremonies with a large number of participants and spectators were held. Fifty-eight meters wide, the Hanyuandian, quite large in itself, had a vast stair at its center, the Dragon-Tail Way, that was a classic example of the Chinese horizontal elongation of space. The gate's 11-by-4-bay structure supported a double-hipped roof and was flanked by high pavilions on either side that were raised, on their own bases, higher than the main hall. Three-hundred meters beyond was the Xuanzheng ("Political") Hall, from whose sides extended walls that defined the palace complex. Here the emperor held court on the first and fifteenth day of each lunar month. Beyond its arcades lay all the main offices of

the imperial bureaucracy. Two gates led to the internal compound of the palace, which consisted of a series of pavilions strung together by rectilinear arcades. Beyond the palace lay the Taiye Pond and a large open area with pavilions and garden compounds. West of the main palace area was the Linde ("Unicorn Virtue") Hall, which was used for banquets and less formal receptions. It consisted of three interconnected structures that abut one another on their long sides to form a larger complex 58.2 meters wide and 86 meters deep, accompanied by a panoply of surrounding arcades and pavilions. Literary sources record that theatrical performances were held in the arcades and polo matches took place in front of the first hall.

9.57 Pictorial view: Hanyuan Hall, Chang'an (Xi'an), China

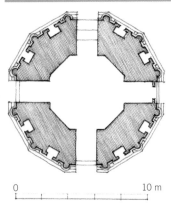

9.58 Plan: Songyue Temple Pagoda, Dengfeng, China

Songyue Temple Ta

Architecturally, the Chinese translated the South Asian stupa into the *ta* (or pagoda, a Portuguese-derived word). While the stupa is a round earthen mound, the *ta* is a tower. Both the *ta* and the stupa serve the same purpose: to house a buried relic at their core. But the *ta* is a tall, multistoried structure, whereas the stupa is squat and solid. The stupa emphasizes the fullness of the mound's body and focuses on the mystery within its earthen core; the *ta* magnifies the vertical axis and makes a display of the many levels of heavens inhabited by many Buddhas.

Though the form may have been inspired by Han Chinese watchtowers, the *ta* never functioned as such. Rather, it served as a beacon visible from a distance. The *ta* was no mistranslation, however; it was how the Chinese chose to represent the stupa. This may be because stupas began during a phase of Buddhism that deemphasized representation, while the *ta* emerged after the establishment of Mahayana Buddhism, which permitted representation. The *ta*, in fact, symbolizes outright the multi-heavened cosmology of Mahayana Buddhism. In the stupa, this cosmology is referred to through the small *chattris* ("umbrellas") at the summits. The *ta*, essentially, is a *chattri* magnified to huge proportions. Even Hsuan Tsang, who had seen and carefully recorded innumerable stupas in India, specifically chose the form of a *ta* when building his own monastery in Chang'an, the Wild Goose Pagoda (652–704 CE), a seven-story, 20-meter-high structure originally made of mud and brick.

9.59 Songyue Temple Pagoda

The Songyue Temple Ta (523 CE), in Dengfeng, Henan Province, is China's oldest and largest surviving *ta*. Located in the middle of a river valley, it is a twelve-sided, 40-meter-high polygon consisting of fifteen bodhisattva levels, surmounted by an obtuse finial. The whole is made of brick, including the corbelled overhanging eaves of the main body. The overall form is parabolic, with a slight suggestion of entasis. The unornamented lower story of the base has an entry facing south. The second story is slightly cantilevered, with engaged columns at the corners and lotus-bud capitals that seem to be of Indian origin. The four sides face the cardinal directions and have openings leading to a central space; the other sides have arched niches, like the Mahabodhi Temple complex in India. The arches are decorated with lion motifs.

The Songyue Temple Ta was originally plastered, possibly white, and would have stood out against the hills. As it is, the pagoda, along with others with which it forms a family, sits in dramatic relation to its surroundings. Unlike most later pagodas, the Songyue Temple Ta is inaccessible. The individual stories—much too small to ever have been intended for human occupation—are entirely representational, complete with a door and two windows carved into each of the twelve sides at each story.

9.60 Location of Nara and Ise Jingu

9.61 A Shinto shrine

Nara Period: Japan

By the 8th century, the various clans of Japan had cohered into a single political unit under an emperor; the northern islands were the last to be brought into this unity. Rice was the principal commodity. Japan's native religion at the time was Shintoism, a form of animism in which every aspect of nature was revered. There were no creeds or images of gods, but rather a host of kami, or sacred spirits. Kami were both deities and the numinous quality perceived in objects of nature, such as trees, rocks, waters, and mountains. The kami are still venerated at more than one hundred thousand Shinto shrines throughout Japan and are considered to be creative and harmonizing forces in nature. Humans were seen not as owners of nature, or above and separate from it, but as integral participants in it—and indeed derived from it. The Buddha was received as a "great kami," but a kami could also be attributed to the spirits of deceased emperors, heroes, and famous persons. In the 6th century, the emperor came to be deified as a living kami, and his divinity surpassed that of other kami. One honored kami in the form of food offerings, music, dance, and the performance of traditional skills such as archery and sumo wrestling. Ceremonial purity was strongly encouraged, and bodily cleanliness was an absolute necessity.

Only priests could approach the kami during special rites, since they alone were the mediators between the human and the kami. The earliest Shinto sanctuaries were simple piles of boulders or stones that marked the sacred dwelling place of the deity and the place where the kami were thought to reside. Kami could also live in a constructed shrine, usually a simple, unadorned structure before which there stood a detached portal, known as a torii.

Ise Jingu

The unification of Shinto's animism with the spirit of the emperor set the stage for a remarkable building, the Ise Jingu ("Shrine"), dedicated to the tutelary kami of the Japanese imperial family. It has no parallel in the entire history of global architecture. Every 20 years for the last 1,500 years, the shrine has been rebuilt, identical to the one before, but with virgin old-growth timber.

9.62 South gateway to the Ise Inner Shrine, Ise, Japan

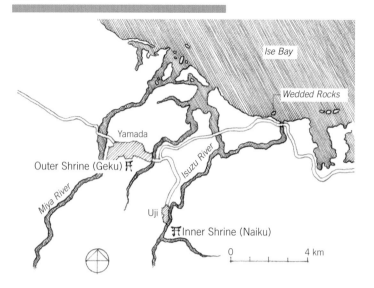

9.63 Location Map: Ise Jingu, Ise, Japan

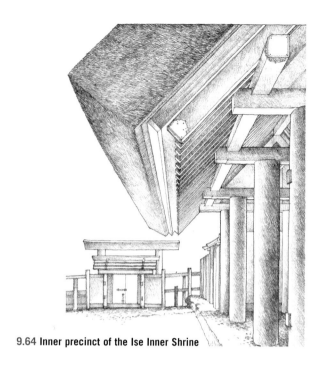

9.64 Inner precinct of the Ise Inner Shrine

The Ise Jingu that stands in Japan today was built in 1993. In a sense, it is therefore practically new. Yet, at the same time, it can be dated to the year 500 CE. The sacred necklace of *magatama* (jewels representing the soul spirit, which enter the body of the possessor) is the symbol of succession from the sun goddess and is the emblem of the emperors of Japan even today. This necklace is kept at Ise. As such, Ise Jingu is Japan's most revered shrine.

Set deep in a forest at the mouth a river valley south of the town of Ise, the shrine consists of two primary structures—the Inner Shrine (Naiku) and the Outer Shrine (Geku)—as well as a wide array of lesser sanctuaries distributed around a narrow, verdant coastal plain on the east coast of the Kii Peninsula in southern Honshu. The area, relatively warm even in winter, is crossed by the fast-flowing Isuzu River. Naiku is dedicated to Amaterasu Omikami ("Heaven-Illuminating Great Kami"), the traditional ancestral deity of the imperial house, and Geku is dedicated to Touke Okami ("Abundant Food Great Kami").

Originally unconnected, the two were joined into an institutional unit in the 9th century. Of the two, the Inner Shrine became the more important, its complex now containing about 120 separate shrines, including a number of tiny sanctuaries dedicated to the spirit of a single rock or the deity of a bubbling spring, as is Shinto practice.

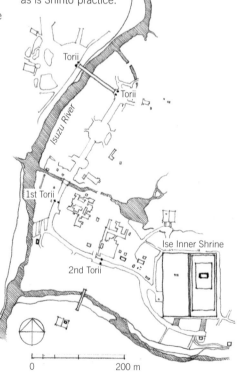

9.65 Area Plan: Ise Inner Shrine

The path to the Naiku is carefully scripted, marked today by a series of torii (derived from the Sanskrit *torana*, for "gate"). One accesses the Naiku precinct by crossing the Uji Bridge, which is constructed from fragrant cypress wood, over the Isuzu River. At each end of the bridge is a freestanding torii, a symbol marking the presence of a sacred shrine. From the bridge, the pilgrim proceeds to the right along a broad street covered with gravel and flanked by carefully tended gardens. At its end is another torii, and after that there is a large stone basin with water for purification rituals. Then the path turns east and rises up the gentle slope through another torii, this time surrounded by tall cedars and zelkova elms that create the sense of entering a dense forest. Moss covers the ancient rocks along the path. Finally, the path curves to approach the Naiku from the south. The final approach is made by way of twenty-one stone steps that lead to the torii of the outermost fence. A fine silk curtain hanging across the entrance is all that marks the beginning of the prohibited zone. The innermost shrines are open only to the temple priests or the imperial family, and even then only in a highly regulated and hierarchical fashion. Only the reigning emperor has access to the innermost shrine, the Shoden, and the rest of the family's distance from the Shoden is a measure of their distance from the throne. Everyone else worships from the outside.

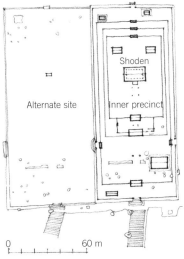

9.66 Plan: Ise Inner Shrine

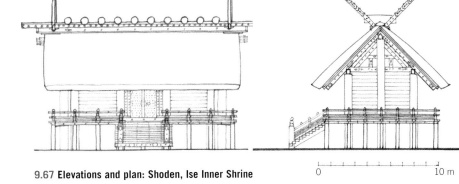

9.67 Elevations and plan: Shoden, Ise Inner Shrine

The Naiku contains three structures organized axially—the central shrine, the Shoden, and, behind it on either side, the two treasuries. The 15-by-10-meter Shoden sets the tone for the entire shrine. Raised off the ground by columns set directly into the ground (without a foundation), the Shoden is a meticulously crafted and ornamented wooden structure three bays wide and two bays deep, built entirely without nails. It has a deeply thatched reed roof and an entrance on its long side accessible via an external flight of stairs.

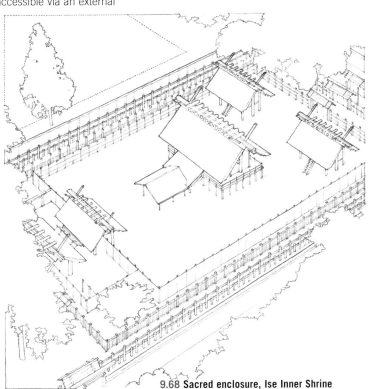

9.68 Sacred enclosure, Ise Inner Shrine

Straight, squared timbers are used for the rafters, which descend sharply from the ridgepole. The side gable ends have no openings. At the middle of each gable end is a freestanding solitary pillar that supports the ridgepole.

The ritual process of rebuilding the Ise every twenty years is known as *shikinen sengu* ("the transfer of the god-body to a new shrine in a special festival year"). The reconstruction alternates between two adjacent sites. While one site is in use, the other is thus always empty, covered by white gravel. When the floor of the previous Shoden is relocated, a small wooden pillar, known as the *shin-no-mihashira*, or "heart pillar," is left buried in the old shrine compound, and a small shed, the *oi-ya*, is built over it to protect it from the elements.

There could be several possible explanations for the *shikinen sengu* ritual. The most prosaic is the need for periodic maintenance of buildings made with highly perishable materials. The idea of renewal might also be tied to Shinto beliefs and could be described as the desire to show reverence to the Great Kami by revitalizing its earthly residence. In a metaphysical sense, a belief in the transience of material objects as opposed to the permanence of form, a metonym for the nature of the kami, is ritually enacted. But most fundamentally, perhaps, the rebuilding renews the social contract with the imperial family, the core of whose legitimacy lies in the long line of its unbroken ancestry.

Buddhism's Arrival in Korea and Japan

The arrival of Buddhism in Korea was not uncontroversial, as it upset long-established conventions, but by the 6th century, with the gradual unification of the clans of Silla under King Beopheung (514–40 CE) in particular, Silla became a full-fledged kingdom, with Buddhism as its state religion. One of the first Buddhist temples was the Hwangnyongsa Temple (553–644 CE). Hwangnyongsa, which means "Golden (or Imperial) Dragon Temple," was located near the royal palace, on a plain surrounded on all sides by mountains. The whole was enclosed and framed by a rectangular perimeter wall. An immense 80-meter-high, nine-story, wooden pagoda stood right in front of the entrance. Behind it were three halls.

From Korea, Buddhism crossed into Japan during the reign of the Emperor Kimmei (509–71 CE). Along with their teachings, the Koreans brought with them their architecture, which defined the early period of Japanese Buddhist architecture. Buddhism's introduction, as in Korea, was resisted by those who preferred traditional Shinto rituals. But here, too, as in Korea, Buddhism was only part of the larger transformation toward centralized authority. The emperor also introduced Chinese-modeled fiscal policies and established the first national treasury.

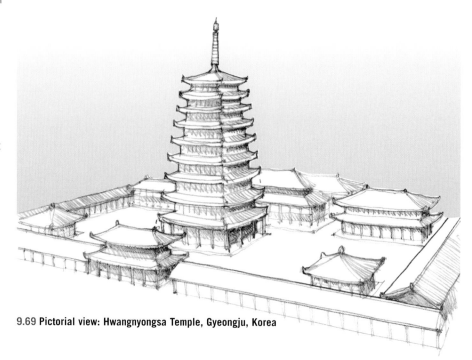

9.69 Pictorial view: Hwangnyongsa Temple, Gyeongju, Korea

The earliest Buddhist temples of Japan, such as the Monastery at Shitennoji (the "Temple of the Four Heavenly Kings," 593 CE) were derived from traditional Korean temple plans, with the pagoda and the main hall aligned on axis with the entrance or middle gate. The temple layout, though smaller than the Korean prototypes, is rigorously symmetrical along a central axis leading to the main hall.

There are seven basic elements known collectively as the *shichido garan* ("seven-hall monastery"). These are the pagoda (*to*), the main or golden hall (*kondo*), the lecture hall (*kodo*), the bell tower (*shoro* or *shuro*), the sutra repository (*kyozo*), the dormitory (*sobo*), and the dining hall (*jikido*).

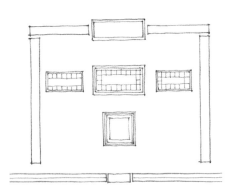

9.70 Plan: Hwangnyongsa Temple, Gyeongju, Korea; only the foundations exist today.

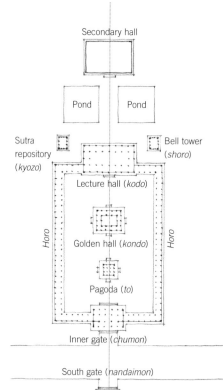

Secondary hall

Pond   Pond

Sutra repository (*kyozo*)   Bell tower (*shoro*)

Lecture hall (*kodo*)

Horo   *Horo*

Golden hall (*kondo*)

Pagoda (*to*)

Inner gate (*chumon*)

South gate (*nandaimon*)

9.71 Plan: Early Buddhist monastery at Shitennoji, Osaka, Japan

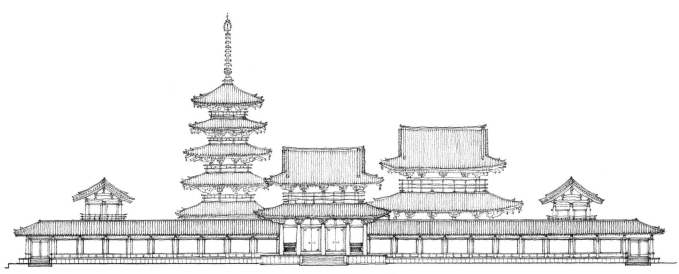

9.72 Elevation: West precinct of Horyu-ji Temple, Nara, Japan

Horyu-ji

Following the so-called Taika reform (645–49 CE), the Japanese royalty came to prefer the Chinese rather than the Korean precedents and adopted a degree of flexibility. This is reflected in Horyu-ji (*ji* means "temple") at Nara, built late in the 7th century, where the axiality of the components was abandoned. The golden hall and the pagoda were placed next to each other, the height of one balancing the width of the other. The cloister was wide enough to give both sufficient breathing room. The eastern wing of the precinct has one extra bay to accommodate the width of the golden hall. This created a dynamic balance between the verticality of the structures and the general horizontality of the forms. Inside the golden hall is the triad of the Buddha Sakyamuni with two attending bodhisattvas made by the celebrated sculptor Kuratsukuri no Tori in 623 CE to commemorate the death of Prince Shotoku. The Four Heavenly Kings were made around 650 CE by the sculptor Yamaguchi no Atai Oguchi.

The five-by-four-bay proportions of the hall make it appear almost square. It is a two-story structure with two deep, overhanging eaves, upturned at the ends, complemented by a shallow porch eave on the lower level that was built later. It sits on a low base, with small stairs on all four axes and a hipped gable roof marking the crest. Like in Greek architecture—and in most contemporary wooden temples—the columns at Horyu-ji display entasis, with their greatest dimension in the middle and their smallest at the top. The middle gate roughly repeats the organizational scheme of the golden hall, but on a simpler scale. It is four bays wide and three bays deep, and because it has a row of columns down the center, one enters the complex slightly off axis.

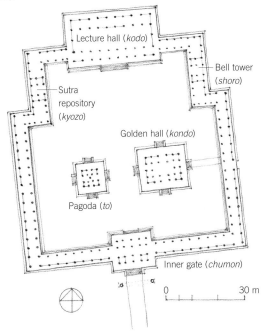

9.73 Plan: West precinct of Horyu-ji Temple

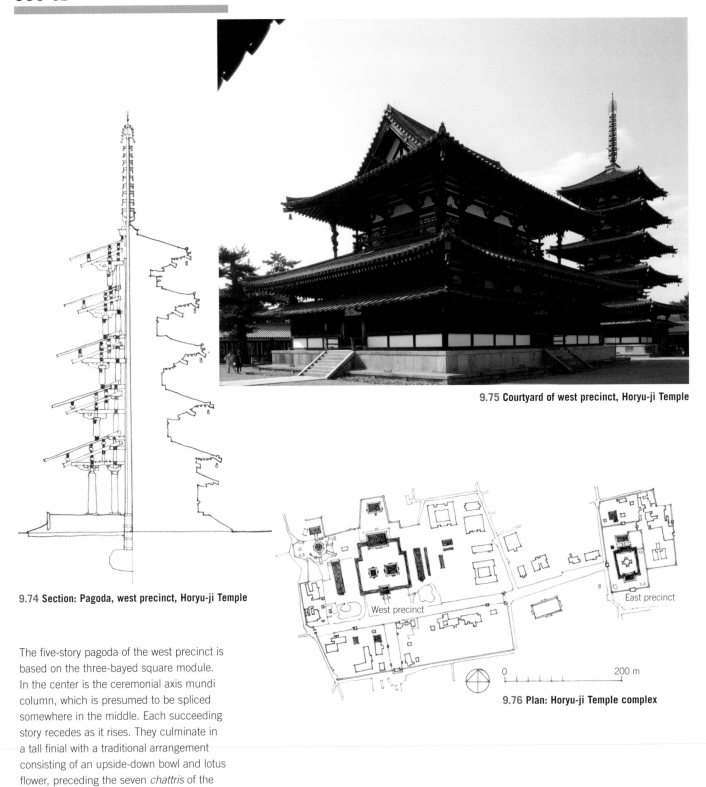

9.75 Courtyard of west precinct, Horyu-ji Temple

9.74 Section: Pagoda, west precinct, Horyu-ji Temple

West precinct

East precinct

0   200 m

9.76 Plan: Horyu-ji Temple complex

The five-story pagoda of the west precinct is based on the three-bayed square module. In the center is the ceremonial axis mundi column, which is presumed to be spliced somewhere in the middle. Each succeeding story recedes as it rises. They culminate in a tall finial with a traditional arrangement consisting of an upside-down bowl and lotus flower, preceding the seven *chattris* of the upper worlds, and finishing with water-fire and illumination finials. The original precinct was expanded by extending the northern end of the enclosure to include a lecture hall (*kodo*) in the early 8th century.

800 CE

In 800 CE, China's T'ang dynasty (618–906 CE) was one of the largest powers in the world, and the city Chang'an, at the eastern end of the Silk Route, was not only Eurasia's economic engine but also home to a large and varied populace of different intellectual persuasions and religions. T'ang buildings, however, having mainly been of wood, have all but disappeared but for a few surviving monastic halls that provide a glimpse of their architecture. Parallel in global importance was the new Islamic kingdom that stretched from Persia to the western Mediterranean as far as Córdoba in Spain. The architectural expression of Islam was the mosque, which in the early days of the new religion was a simple hypostyle hall oriented toward Mecca. But soon elaborate palaces and gardens arose, competing with the glamour and display of the Byzantine Empire. On the Temple Mount in Jerusalem, which had seen two Jewish temples and a Roman temple, a new structure was built, the unequaled Dome of the Rock, venerating the spot where Muhammed is said to have ascended to heaven. The Umayyad caliphs occupying the old Roman and Visigoth city of Córdoba in Al-Andalus on the Spanish peninsula developed a splendid and tolerant court, with a large mosque built on the ruins of a Roman temple. In 750 CE, the Umayyad dynasty was replaced by the Abbasids, whose new capital, Baghdad, made that city one of the great urban settlements of the age.

Meanwhile, South Asia, divided among several kingdoms, was a hotbed of intellectual and religious activity, leaving a substantial architectural legacy. The Hindu kingdoms' architects built in stone and brick, and by means of rock cutting, as is evidenced by their numerous temples. Simultaneously, Buddhist monasteries continued on and matured into universities of international repute. Monks from China, Sri Lanka, Japan, Southeast Asia, and Indonesia came to study at Nalanda, Paharpur, and Amaravati. Southeast Asia was also coming into its own, fed by the expanding trade links to China and India, and in particular by the Pallavas from India's east. In Indonesia, the Shailendra kings built Buddhist, and subsequently Hindu, stone temples of great accomplishment, including Borobudur, one of the finest Buddhist stupa shrines ever. To Indonesia's north, in Cambodia, the Khmer king Jayavarman III founded a new Hindu kingdom with a capital called Hariharalaya, on the floodplain of the Tonle Sap Lake, the largest freshwater lake in Southeast Asia. The city, a perfect square about 3 kilometers on a side, with a temple at its geometric center, rivaled the circular city of Baghdad as an urban enterprise. With an economy organized around rice production, the Khmer were to rule over Cambodia for six hundred years, their achievement largely due to their sophisticated irrigation technology.

Compared to the massive amounts of wealth that flowed from East to West and that filtered its way through Southeast Asia, the situation in Europe, after the collapse of Rome, was still rather tenuous. Europe was only coming into its own when Charlemagne was crowned Holy Roman Emperor by Pope Leo III on Christmas night of 800 CE. His capacity to organize the kingdom brought Europe back onto the global horizon. His architectural accomplishments, however, were relatively slight, as technology and the philosophical arts were still in serious decline. Nonetheless, Charlemagne, though himself barely literate, admired and sponsored learning and supported monasteries, which were the repositories of ancient texts and the only source of literacy north of the Alps. Eager to assume the legacy of the Roman Empire, he adopted the language of Roman architecture that would become the referent for architectural expression for centuries to come.

All in all, in the 9th and 10th centuries, the Eurasian map started to foreshadow the modern world, with distinct kingdoms arranged continuously from the Pacific to the Atlantic, linked to one another by trade and determined just as much by religion as by geography. This was also a period of urban innovation: Hariharalaya, the new capital of the Khmer; Baghdad, of the Islamic Abbasids; Córdoba, Spain; and Aachen, the capital of the Holy Roman Empire. Chang'an, however, still remained, along with Constantinople, among the largest cities in the world.

In America, a new generation of Mayan city-states had arisen in Guatemala, Honduras, and El Salvador starting around 250 CE. The impact of Central America's civilizations continued to be felt at its outermost reaches through the establishment of cities like Pueblo Bonito by the so-called Anasazi of North America.

Period of Northern and Southern Dynasties
386–589 CE

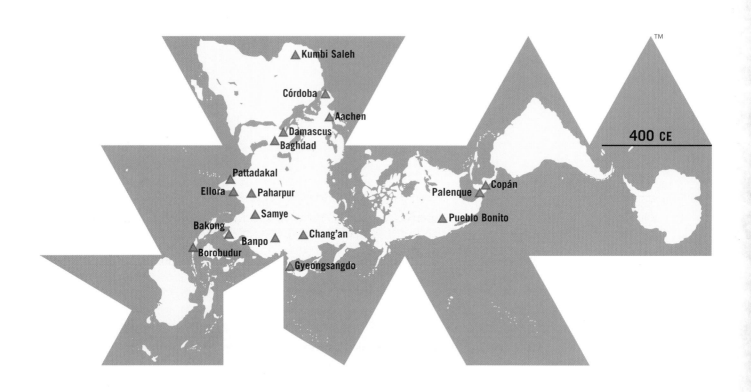

Kumbi Saleh

Córdoba

Aachen

Damascus

Baghdad

Pattadakal

Ellora Paharpur

Samye

Bakong

Banpo Chang'an

Borobudur

Gyeongsangdo

Palenque Copán

Pueblo Bonito

400 CE

Pre-Pueblo Cultures
ca. 1000 BCE–700 CE
▲ **Quirigua**
2nd to 10th centuries CE

T'ang Dynasty
618–907 CE

▲ **Chang'an: The T'ang Capital**   ▲ **Nanchan Temple**   ▲ **Foguang Temple**
581–906 CE   782 CE   857 CE

Silla Dynasty   ▲ **Buseoksa Temple**
668–935 CE   676–1000 CE

Umayyad Rule   Abbasid Caliphate
651–750 CE   750–1258 CE

▲ **Dome of the Rock**   ▲ **City of Baghdad**   ▲ **Great Mosque of Samarra**
632–91 CE   ca. 762 CE, capital of Abbasid Caliphate 852 CE

▲ **Umayyad Mosque**   ▲ **Great Mosque of Córdoba**
706–15 CE   784-87 CE

600 CE	**800 CE**	**1000 CE**

South Asia: Pallava Dynasty   Chola Dynasty
to 740 CE   ca. 860–1279

▲ **Kailasnath at Ellora**   ▲ **Virupaksha Temple**   **Sumstek Gompa**   ▶
600–1000 CE   733–44 CE   11th to 13th centuries CE

▲ **Mahavihara of Nalanda**   ▲ **Rajasimhesvara Temple**
6th to 7th centuries CE   Early 8th century CE

▲ **Somapura Vihara**
7th century CE

Pre-Angkor Period in Cambodia   Angkor Period in Cambodia
ca. 550–802 CE   802–1431 CE

▲ **Candi Prambanam**   ▲ **Phnom Bakheng**
835–56 CE   ca. 900–921 CE

▲ **Samye**   ▲ **Borobudur**
787–91 CE   ca. 760–830 CE

Byzantine Empire
330–1453 CE

▲ **Germigny-des-Prés**   ▲ **Theotokos Tou Libos**
806–11 CE   10th century CE

▲ **Koimesis in Nicaea**
9th century

Merovingian Dynasty in Central Europe   Carolingian Dynasty   Holy Roman Empire
482–751 CE   751–911 CE   962–1806 CE

▲ **Abbey of Fulda**   ▲ **St. Gall**
790 CE   816–36 CE

Abbey Church of St. Riquier ▲ ▲ **Palatine Chapel**
Completed 799 CE   792–805 CE

Mayas: Dynastic City-States
ca. 250–900 CE

▲ **Palenque**   ▲ **Copán**
ca. 600–800 CE   ca. 600–900 CE

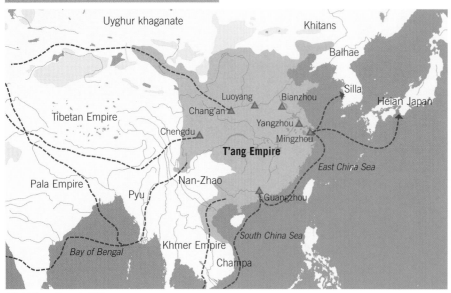

10.1 T'ang dynasty China

Chang'an

In the 9th century, the largest economic zones of Eurasia consisted of China, India, and the Islamic realm. Together they exerted a demand for trade that stretched from Córdoba to Chang'an. Trade was also developing with the west coast of Africa. But the relationship between southern India and Southeast Asia was becoming an increasingly important element in the global economy. In Europe, the Byzantines were impacted negatively by the advance of Islam. The Franks, who had settled in France and converted to Christianity, were in an expansionary phase, though they were still in many respects at the perimeter of the Eurasian world.

Located at the terminus of the Silk Route, Chang'an ("Forever Peace") was first established by the Han dynasty in 200 BCE, when it moved its capital west from Luoyang. But in 24 CE, in the middle of the Han reign, Chang'an was looted, burned, and reduced to a provincial city; Luoyang was reestablished as the Han capital. In the 4th century CE, Chang'an experienced a revival as a center of Buddhist learning. And then late in the 6th century, the first emperor the Sui dynasty reestablished Chang'an as an imperial capital. The Sui rebuilt the city a few miles south of the old Han city and called it Daxing ("Great Prosper"). This was the city that, under the T'ang, was to become famous as China's *urb primus* of the 1st millennium CE. Developing both external and internal trade

was a high priority under the Sui, and then the T'ang linked Chang'an with Luoyang, Yangzhou, Chengdu, Guangzhou, Youzhou, Bianzhou (now Kaifeng), and Mingzhou (now Ningbo). Guangzhou and Mingzhou were ports that serviced Korea and Southeast Asia, respectively. An ancient form of bill of exchange, known as *feiqian* ("flying money") was introduced by the T'ang. Merchants who sold their goods in Chang'an could get *feiqian* drafts with which they could draw money in other places.

In 750 CE, Chang'an, with a million residents, was the largest city in the world.

A stela inscribed in 781 CE documents the introduction of Nestorian Christianity by Syrian priests in 635 CE. The last of the Sassanian princes, Firuz, found refuge there around 670 CE. Manichaeism arrived with the Persians fleeing Islam in around 694 CE. However, Chang'an remained predominantly a place of Buddhist scholarship. Thousands of Buddhist scholars and pilgrims, such as Faxian, came to live in Chang'an, with its hundreds of Buddhist monasteries. In 840 CE, the Japanese pilgrim Enin found monks from southern and northern India, Sri Lanka, Kucha (from the Tarim Basin), Korea, and Japan—as well as China—building pagodas, temples, and monasteries. Hsuan Tsang's Wild Goose Pagoda was constructed in the 7th century to hold all his manuscripts. Enin also noted that among the city's prized relics were four teeth of the Buddha, from India, Khotan, and Tibet—and the fourth, reputedly, from heaven. During festivals honoring these dental relics, each monastery was bedecked with offerings such as medicines and foods, rare fruits and flowers, and various kinds of incense. Individual donations were commonplace. One donor gave a hundred bushels of rice and twenty bushels of millet; others provided biscuits or cash.

Chang'an became the historical model for city planning, not only for later Chinese capitals like Beijing during the Ming and Qing dynasties but also for the capital cities of Korea and Japan, such as Nara, Kyoto, and

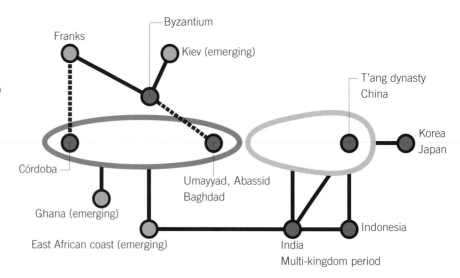

10.2 Eurasian trade diagram, ca. 800 CE

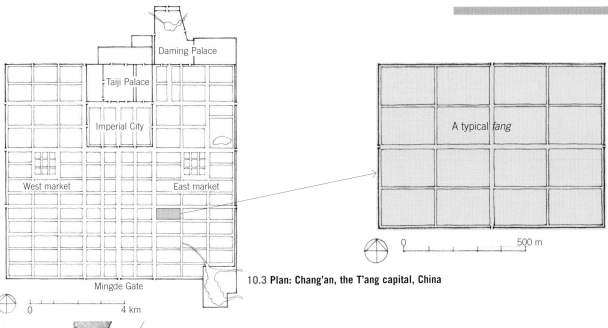

A typical *fang*

0   500 m

10.3 Plan: Chang'an, the T'ang capital, China

10.4 Outline of Manhattan, drawn at the same scale as Chang'an above

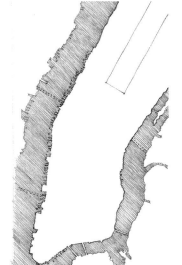

Palace

Ukyo (Right capitol)

Sakyo (Left capitol)

Kamo River

Eastern market   Western market

0   3 km

10.5 Plan grid: Heian-Kyo (Kyoto), Japan

Kyôngju. The construction of Chang'an was overseen by the Sui imperial engineer and planner Yuwen Kai (555–612 CE). Kai had already engineered the Grand Canal (605–6 CE) to facilitate the transport of grain from the alluvial southern plains to the relatively impoverished (but militarily strong) northern areas. Although overscaled, Chang'an's master plan was based on Zhou period descriptions of the Wangcheng ideal city (see "800 BCE"). Some 8.65 kilometers by 9.72 kilometers in size, the city's outer walls were punctured by three gates on the western, southern, and eastern walls. The southern gate, Mingde—the main entrance—opened onto a monumental street 220 meters wide, while the streets leading from the rest of the gates measured about 140 meters each. Four canals distributed water to the city.

The city's module was based on the dimensions of the imperial palace. The Taiji Palace (the palaces and halls for imperial meetings) was located at the north end of the central north-south axis, occupying no less than 5 percent of the entire city. Just south of it was the Imperial City (offices of the government and national ceremonial halls). The rest of the city was divided by east-west and north-south avenues into 108 neighborhood blocks called *fangs*. In spite of its population, the colossal spread of the city ensured that the density of the *fangs* was not very high, especially compared to that of Teotihuacán and Rome at their height.

The *fangs* contained temples, commercial buildings, public parks, and housing. Each *fang* was a mini-city with its own inner transportation network, walls, gates, and corner towers. There were two major commercial areas in the outer city referred to as the west and east markets, each occupying two *fangs*. These markets were the subject of many literary descriptions, often devoted to the global range of goods available there. The areas around Quijan Lake and the Xingqing *fang* were famous scenic districts.

In China, a capital city was dependent on the fortunes of the dynasty, as each dynasty established its own capital. So after the T'ang were defeated in 907 CE, the city lost its capital status. A series of rebellions resulted in an officially sanctioned persecution of its population, particularly of Buddhists. Another factor in the decline of the city was a global warming trend that made travel through the Taklamakan Desert increasingly difficult. The age of the Silk Route was at an end. Trade now increasingly went south, through Southeast Asia, or north, through the Russian steppes, even though it was the former that first reaped the benefits of this change.

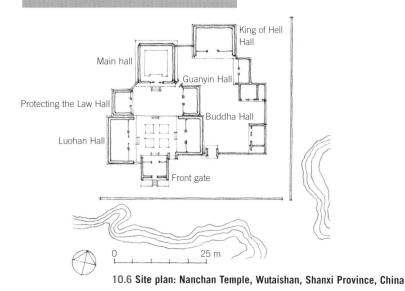

10.6 **Site plan: Nanchan Temple, Wutaishan, Shanxi Province, China**

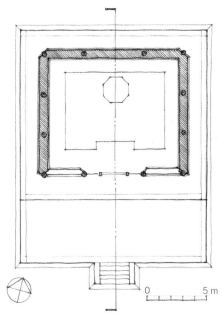

10.7 **Plan and section: Main hall, Nanchan Temple**

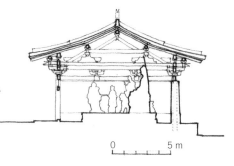

Nanchan and Foguang Monasteries

Of the thousands of wooden monasteries built during the Sui and T'ang periods, the Nanchan and Foguang monasteries, located far north of the capital on Wutai Mountain in Shanxi Province, are two of the few to have survived into our time. The older Nanchan Temple is a relatively modest structure from the T'ang period that was rebuilt in its present form in 782 CE. Its main hall was dedicated to the bodhisattva Manjusri, who was, according to tradition, a disciple of the Buddha and was seen as the personification of transcendent wisdom. Bodhisattvas were seen as beings who, like the Buddha, had attained enlightenment, but had stayed on in the world to show others the way before attaining nirvana. The temple rests on a low, 1-meter-high platform, its precinct defined by a wall.

The Foguang Temple (857 CE) was a more ambitious construction. Unlike the three-bayed hall of Nanchan, with its simple hip-and-gable (*xieshan*) roof, the Foguang hall is seven-by-four bayed and has a roof format known as first-class hip style. The columns divide the hall into an inner and outer *cao* ("space"). Just as they transformed the stupa to a *ta*, or pagoda, the Chinese also transformed the monastery format; in this case, it clearly derived from the palatial architecture of the time. Monasteries generally consisted of a Buddha hall framed by a courtyard within a colonnaded enclosure, with a north and a south gate. The larger ones had east and west gates as well. The courtyards were named after their principal buildings; for example, the pagoda courtyard, the *chan* ("meditation") courtyard, the *vanaya* ("discipline") courtyard, the *purea* ("land") courtyard, and so on. The overall styles of Nanchan and Foguang temples, however, are very similar, with low-pitched roof slopes, deep eaves, and dominating brackets. (The current building is a reconstruction from the 1970s.)

10.8 **Main hall, Nanchan Temple**

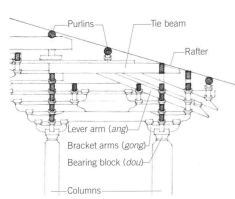

Purlins
Tie beam
Rafter
Lever arm (*ang*)
Bracket arms (*gong*)
Bearing block (*dou*)
Columns

10.9 Detail of bracket system: Main hall, Foguang Temple

Chinese wood roofs are described by the number and types of bracket sets and beams deployed. While bracket sets are a complex addition to the number of horizontal, vertical, and diagonal composite elements, called *dou-gong*, the beams are designated by their position and the number of rafters they span. *Dou-gong* bracket sets differ in size and number depending on their position and location, the size of the roof, and the stature of the building. Bracket sets of this complexity never developed in India, Mesopotamia, or areas to the west, where walls played a more important role in the structural stability and expression of a building. In the West, wood beams needed to be attached with skill, but architects did not have to worry about a building twisting, which is a common problem with structures set up on columns or posts. The brackets keep the top part of the building stiff against rotational forces while supplying enough flexibility in case of earthquakes. The technology was developed early on by the Chinese, but it was by no means static. It went through several developmental stages. By the 15th century, engineers had learned how to simplify the bracketing systems and began using them more for the purposes of tradition than out of structural necessity.

10.10 Main hall, Foguang Temple, Wutaishan, Shanxi Province, China

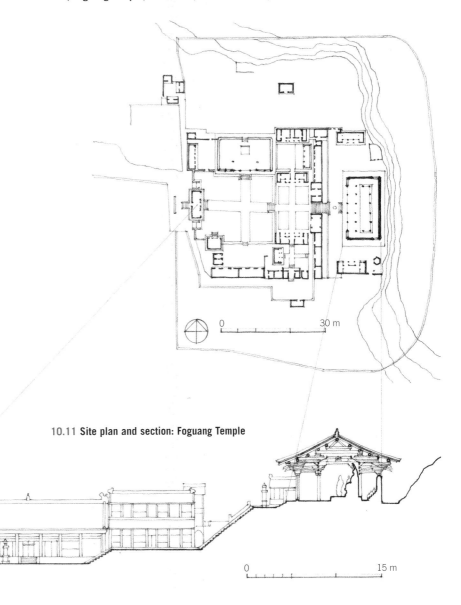

0   30 m

10.11 Site plan and section: Foguang Temple

0   15 m

10.12 Buseoksa Temple, Gyeongsangdo, Korea

Korean Buddhism

By the end of the 7th century, the Silla dynasty (668–935 CE), which had initiated the introduction of Buddhism into Korea, controlled most of the Korean Peninsula. It defeated the Kaya Federation in 562 CE, and thanks to an alliance with the Chinese T'ang court, it also succeeded in conquering the kingdoms of Paekche in 660 CE and Koguryô in 668 CE, thereby unifying Korea for the first time under a single kingdom, with its capital at Kyôngju. Even after the Chinese troops had withdrawn into Manchuria, the Silla maintained close ties with T'ang China through trade and diplomatic exchanges. The Silla made Buddhism the state religion, causing it to spread rapidly as far as Japan. Nonetheless, the introduction of Buddhism into Korea was met with some resistance, which was only resolved when native gods were in essence seen as apparitions into which Buddhist gods had temporarily projected themselves. Certain shamanistic gods, for example, were made into bodhisattvas incarnate. A similar tension persisted in Japan between Shinto traditions and the new modern Buddhist concepts. As Mahayana Buddhism evolved in India and China, several different sects accessible only to initiates evolved in Korea as well, particularly those influenced by Tibetan and Chinese esoteric or Tantric Buddhism.

Among the various temples that were built during this period was Buseoksa Temple (676–1000 CE), which was the center of Silla Buddhism. It was established by the monk Uisang, the founder of the Consciousness-Only School, an idealistic system of thought in which sense perceptions have no objective reality. Instead, it is the mind or the consciousness of the perceived that holds and contains the universe. Buseoksa, or "Temple of the Floating Stone," is so-named because of a large rock beside the western

hall that appears to float above the stones underneath, perhaps symbolizing its defiance of gravity.

The monastery rests on a forested slope defined by a series of terraces accessed by paths, stairs, and gate houses. There are 108 steps between the Cheonwangmun Gate and the Anyangmun Gate, the number of steps representing redemption from agony and evil passions through 108 cycles. The Anyangmun Gate is actually a pavilion floating out over the edge of a terrace; the terrace is entered from underneath. *Anyangmun* means "entrance to heaven," and the gate is the culmination of the spiritual path. With spectacular views into the valleys and landscape beyond, it sits opposite the Muryangsujeon Hall, with its Buddha; it dates from about the year 1000. (The temple was burnt by the Japanese in 1593 and restored from 1969 to 1973.)

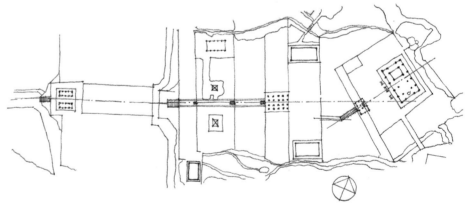

10.13 Site plan: Buseoksa Temple

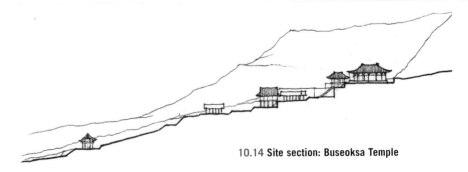

10.14 Site section: Buseoksa Temple

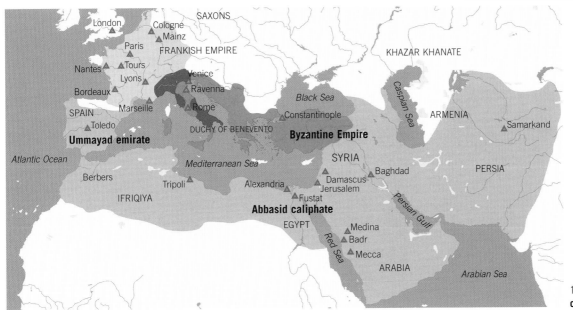

10.15 Islamic territories, ca. 800 CE

Rise of Islam

Arabia, on account of its extreme climactic and geographic conditions, was at the periphery of the great cultural centers of its age. It was mainly inhabited by nomadic Bedouin Arabs who served as traders or lived off the land's meager resources. The center of Arabian religion, which focused on nature and heavenly bodies, was in Mecca. Muhammed (ca. 570–632 CE) began a bitter and prolonged struggle with Arab tribes and their polytheism, advocating instead a brand of monotheism based on universalist and egalitarian sociopolitical ideas that conflicted with traditional tribal politics.

Born in Mecca in 570 CE, Muhammed was an orphan raised by his uncle. When he was forty years old, he retreated into a cave near Ramadan, where he received his first illumination. After further revelations, he began preaching monotheism. Successful in attracting followers, he eventually conquered Mecca and transformed it into Islam's holy of holies that all adult Muslims are required to visit at least once in their lives. He died in 632 CE after having converted most of Arabia to the new creed. Beyond being a prophet, Muhammed was also a farsighted statesman, a political arbitrator, and a gifted military commander, setting the stage for a fusion of religion and politics that was to define Islamic culture for centuries to come. By 711 CE, Muslim Arab armies were attacking north India to the east as well as North Africa to the west, and by the end of the 9th century,

Islam had grown into the largest political entity west of China.

Since Muhammed made no arrangements for a successor, dissension arose after his death as to how to govern this vast territory, and the conflict between the Abbasids and Umayyads created a divide in Islam that persists to this day. The Abbasids, descendants of Muhammed's uncle, al-Abbas, based their claim to the caliphate on the theological aspects of their rulership. The Shi'ites joined with the Abbasids in the 8th century, as they, too, believed that the caliphs ruled by divine designation and thus possessed spiritual authority. The Umayyads also saw themselves as heirs to the Islamic state but interpreted the caliphate as a constitutional necessity working for the temporal welfare and protection of the community. The conflict between the theological and political interpretation of rulership continues to be contested. It was initially the Umayyads who were dominant, governing from their capital in Damascus. Able administrators, they ruled for a brief but important period over the whole of the Islamic realm—the only time that it was so unified.

Muslims do not require a building, or even a consecrated space, to worship; rather, Islam is based on five "pillars," the most important being the five daily prayers performed while facing Mecca. The month of Ramadan is also important; during that time, Muslims commune with themselves,

give thanks to God through fasting, and make donations to the needy, fulfilling the commandments of the third pillar.

The typical mosque has a courtyard through which one enters and that contains a well or fountain for washing the hands and feet. In the first centuries of Islam, the hall of worship was, in most instances, a space consisting of rows of columns so that the congregation could face the *qibla* wall—a wall that stands at right angles to a line drawn to Mecca. The imam, or prayer leader, stands in front of a mihrab, or niche, in the middle of the *qibla* wall. In some mosques, the bay just in front of the mihrab is elevated and roofed with a dome. To the right of the mihrab is a stepped pulpit, the minbar, made of wood or stone, from which the imam can deliver a sermon (*khutba*), usually on Friday. Almost all mosques have a minaret from which the faithful are called to prayer. There is no prescription as to where they should be located or how many there must be.

Tarik Khana (ca. 760 CE) in Damghan, northern Iran, is one of the oldest extant mosques. Its rectangular shape encloses a courtyard and prayer hall. Massive round brick columns almost 2 meters in diameter support arcades of tunnel vaults. The Aksa Mosque in Jerusalem (702 CE) shows the development of an axis and transept emphasizing the *qibla* that becomes even more pronounced in the El-Hakim Mosque (991 CE) in Cairo.

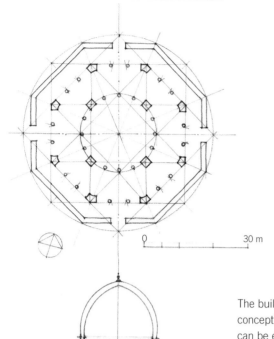

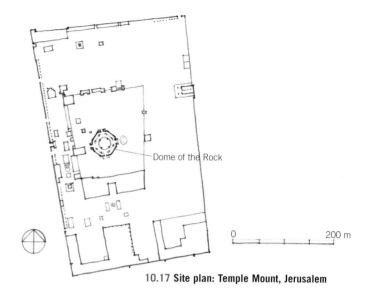

10.17 Site plan: Temple Mount, Jerusalem

10.16 Plan and section: Dome of the Rock, Jerusalem

Dome of the Rock

With the Islamic conquest of Palestine and Jerusalem in the third decade of the 7th century, Caliph Abd al-Malik brought in the best masons and craftsmen available to design the Dome of the Rock, or in Arabic, the Haram al-Sharif (the "Noble Sanctuary"), which is today the oldest Islamic building to have survived intact in its original form. Completed in 691 CE, it encloses a huge rock at its center, the highest point of Mt. Moriah, from which, according to tradition, the prophet Muhammed ascended to heaven at the end of his Isra' (or Night Journey) to Jerusalem. In the older, Jewish tradition, this is the Foundation Stone, the symbolic underpinning upon which the world was created, as well as the place of Abraham's binding of Isaac. This same location is also where numerous important events in the life of Christ are believed to have occurred. The site is therefore holy to the Jewish, Christian, and Islamic religions.

The building, which is Byzantine in conception and Sassanian in ornamentation, can be entered on all four points of the compass. The dome reaches 20 meters across the rock and is borne on a drum that rests on a double system of pillars and columns, the middle one circular, the outer one octagonal. The two rings, composed of piers and columns, are rotated so that the four piers of the inner ring face the arches of the outer octagonal ring, creating a dynamic interplay between square and circular geometries.

The dome and drum are not of brick or stone, but of wood. The dome is covered with golden copper-alloy plates, and the drum with shimmering mosaic patterns of blue, red, green, and gray. The interior, in the Byzantine manner, was decorated with mosaics, with a marble veneer in the lower section. Though technically a mosque, the building is much more. It is not only a geometrical and paradisiacal enclosure and a celebration of a spot of particular reverence but also a parallel to the Ka'aba in Mecca. Unlike that building, which can be circumambulated but not

10.18 Dome of the Rock

entered, this one can indeed be entered—yet because of the presence of the rock, the center of the building remains inaccessible. Furthermore, one gazes not at a rock, but at the peak of the mount; the architecture thus creates the feeling of suspending the viewer in space around that peak.

The history of the building site has been much debated. It was first consecrated by the Israelites when they built the First and Second Temples. After the Second Temple was razed by the Romans in 70 CE, Emperor Hadrian built a temple to Jupiter there that was perhaps connected to an octagonal structure that served as the foundation of the Dome of the Rock—but this has not yet been archaeologically proven. The crusaders consecrated the building as a Catholic church, but with their defeat, the site reverted back to Islam.

10.19 **Courtyard, Umayyad Mosque, Damascus, Syria**

Umayyad Mosque

Though the Arabs were initially illiterate, their conquests put them in contact with a multitude of civilizations, many features of which they began to assimilate, much as the Romans had done with Greek and Oriental cultures—except that the Arabs' transition occurred with astonishing rapidity and determination. From the Indians, who at that time were leaders in the field of mathematics, they adopted numbering systems; from the Persians, skills in construction; from the Byzantines, skills in vaulting; and from the Armenians, skills in stonemasonry. The center of this learning was Damascus, built up by al-Mansur, who lavished the wealth and power of the new empire on the city.

To house translated books from Greece, Byzantium, and India, as well the growing collection of works by Arabic scholars, Caliph al-Ma'mun ordered a library to be built. Known as the House of Wisdom (opened 1004 CE), it became the most outstanding single repository of knowledge since the Great Library of Alexander. Libraries were set up in other cities as well. Soon Arab scholars were making breakthroughs in everything from medicine and chemistry to optics and philosophy. In 807 CE, Sultan Harun al-Rashid (766–809 CE) sent Charlemagne a brass clock with a moving ball and brass horsemen who stepped out of windows on the hour. There was then nothing remotely similar in all of Europe.

The Umayyad Mosque in Damascus (709–15 CE), another monumental work of Islamic architecture, was built on a religious site dating back to an ancient Aramaic temple dedicated to the god Hadad. The Romans built a Temple of Jupiter on the site, a building that was, in the 4th century, transformed into a church (the Cathedral of St. John) situated on the western side of the temple. The church was then incorporated into the design of the mosque, which consists of three parallel ranges of space facing onto a large, enclosed courtyard.

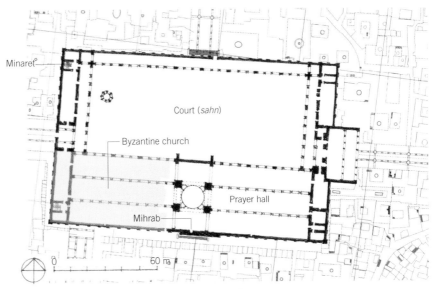

10.20 **Plan: Umayyad Mosque, Damascus**

After the Islamic conquest of Damascus in 661 CE during the reign of the first Umayyad caliph, Mu'awiya Ibn Abi Sufiyan, Muslims at first shared the church with Christians. The caliph eventually negotiated with Christian leaders to take over the space; in return, he promised that all the other churches in the city would be safe and that a new church, dedicated to the Virgin Mary, could be erected. Damascus itself was completely rebuilt in the shape of a rectangle bisected by a Hellenistic-inspired colonnaded road running north and south and crossing at the center, where the principal buildings were positioned.

The plan of the mosque is a 97-by-156-meter rectangle with three gates that connect the building to the city from the northern, eastern, and western sides. The mosque is defined by three halls, or *riwaqs*, that run parallel to the *qibla* wall. They are supported by two rows of stone Corinthian columns. Large and classically proportioned arches support a second, smaller colonnade, on which the massive wooden beams of the roof rest. The location of the mihrab is enhanced in the center by the octagonal, 36-meter-high Nisr Dome ("Dome of the Eagle"). In the eastern part of the mosque, a small marble structure between the columns of the *riwaq* holds the tomb of St. John the Baptist, who in Islamic tradition is known as the prophet Yahya. The building was richly outfitted with marble paneling and mosaics. In the

beginning of the 8th century, Caliph al-Walid ibn Abd al-Malik addressed the citizens of Damascus thus: "Inhabitants of Damascus, four things give you marked superiority over the rest of the world: your climate, your water, your fruits, and your baths. To these I wanted to add a fifth: this mosque." Originally, the mosque was abutted by a palace on its southern flank, with a special entrance next to the mihrab.

Baghdad

The Umayyad dynasty, which had its center in Damascus, fell in the mid-8th century. The new rulers, the Abbasids (r. 758–1258 CE), eventually became the champions of Sunni orthodoxy—a policy that helped them to unify an increasingly cosmopolitan Muslim empire. They constructed a new capital city, Baghdad, to the west of Damascus and on the banks of the Tigris River. Engineers from the entire Islamic world were called to the site to help in its planning and construction from 762 to 766 CE.

The layout, one of the most remarkable examples of town planning in history, was a simple circle about 3,000 meters across. The walls were built of bricks and ornamented with colorful tiles. Two rings of residential zones lined the inside walls, leaving a vast area open in the middle for the palace and mosque. The walls were punctured by four gates. Though there are other smaller, regional examples of circular cities, this was

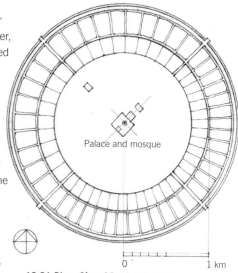

10.21 Plan: City of Baghdad, Iraq

by far the most elaborate. The city prospered, and with a population of about two million, it became a center of science, literature, and art, like Damascus. However, nothing of the city remains: it perished as a consequence of numerous sieges and inundations. The Abbasid dynasty ended when Baghdad fell to the Mongols in 1258.

Made possible by the wealth of the Abbasid rulers, Palaces of great size sprang up throughout the region, such as the fortified Palace of Ukhaidir in the desert about 200 kilometers south of Baghdad. It consists of a rectangular enclosure approximately 175 by 170 meters, with a gateway at the center of each of the round towers at the corners and semicircular towers spaced regularly between them. The main entrance led to an autonomous royal enclave (approximately 60 by 80 meters) positioned close to the north wall. It had a large courtyard and a barrel-vaulted *iwan* throne room, behind which was the royal apartment. Around that complex were four residential suites, each with its own courtyard. The palace possessed its own mosque; a bathhouse was located in the southeast of the complex. In the space between the palace and the outer walls, there would have been gardens. Though today only the mud brick of the interior construction remains, these surfaces would have been lavishly decorated with carved stucco and paintings, often of flowers and vines arranged in panels.

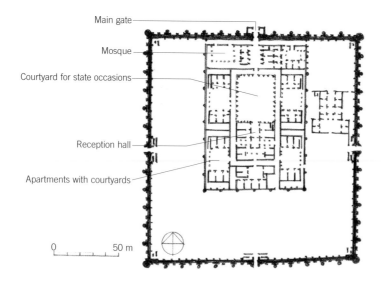

Main gate
Mosque
Courtyard for state occasions
Reception hall
Apartments with courtyards

0   50 m

10.22 Plan: Palace of Ukhaidir, Iraq

Great Mosque of Samarra

In 836 CE, the Abbasid capital was moved to Samarra, some 40 kilometers north of Baghdad. Samarra soon ranked among the greatest of the early Islamic cities. Though it remained the capital only until 892 CE, it prospered for centuries, reaching an area of 50 square kilometers. The caliph's residence itself took up 173 hectares on a cliff overlooking the Tigris River. Equally impressive were the two mosques, the Great Mosque of al-Mutawakkil (848–52 CE) and the Mosque of Abu Dulaf (860 CE), both designed to look like desert fortresses. The bastioned walls of the Great Mosque of al-Mutawakkil measured 240 by 156 meters, and for centuries it was the largest mosque in the world. There were sixteen doorways that fed into the vast interior. On the inside, four hypostyle structures (one prayer hall and three porticoes) were arranged around a large courtyard. Unlike in Damascus, where the three minarets were placed in the corners of the enclosing wall and one in the middle of the wall, here the minaret was a freestanding element placed on axis in front of the principal north entrance of the mosque. It had a helicoidal shape that reached 50 meters to the summit, with an external staircase.

Though contemporary texts are silent about the architectural articulation of these mosques, they may reflect the evolution from a more egalitarian society of early Islamic times to the more hierarchical society of the Abbasid period, when Persian ideas of kingship were increasingly adopted by Islamic rulers. Another reason for the silence may be that the mosque as an institution was less attached to the ruler than to the ulama, or religious leader, indicating a split between religious centers like these and the desert palaces, which were the centers of secular power.

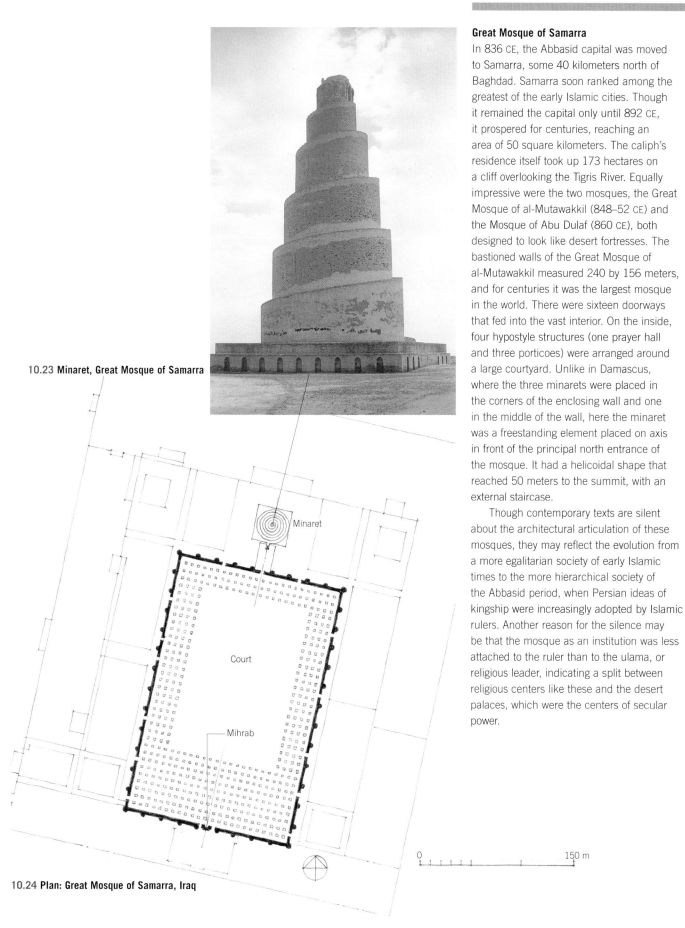

10.23 Minaret, Great Mosque of Samarra

10.24 Plan: Great Mosque of Samarra, Iraq

10.25 Spain (Al-Andalus)

10.26 Roofscape, Great Mosque of Córdoba, Spain

Great Mosque of Córdoba

Arab forces occupied Alexandria in 643 CE and crossed the Straits of Gibraltar in 711 CE. From there, they made forays over the entire Mediterranean into Italy and France, driving out the monks from Monte Cassino, south of Rome, in 883 CE. By the mid-7th century, however, the Muslim world had lost any real political unity: the Abbasid caliphate began to disintegrate, and in the mid-10th century, rival caliphates established themselves in Cairo and Córdoba. Originally, the Spanish territories were administered by a provincial government established in the name of the Umayyad caliphate based in Damascus. But when that dynasty was overthrown, its last surviving member, Emir Abd al-Rahman I, fled to Spain. Under him, Córdoba became the quasi-autonomous capital of a vibrant Islamic culture. By the end of the 10th century, it had become the largest city in Europe, with a population of about one hundred thousand. It was also an important center of Arabic learning, making crucial contributions to European civilization.

The first building of significance designed under Abd al-Rahman I was the Great Mosque of Córdoba (784–87 CE). Only the southwest part, the original prayer hall, still survives more or less unaltered. The mosque, modeled loosely on the Umayyad Mosque in Damascus (706–15 CE), consisted of a walled-in courtyard opening onto a hypostyle structure consisting of twelve bays with ten columns each.

At the time of its initial construction, the Great Mosque and the Dome of the Rock in Jerusalem were among the earliest examples of monumental Islamic architecture. There was nothing equal in scale and detailing in Europe. The wooden roof of the mosque was eventually replaced by a two-tiered arch system. The principal shape of the arch was that of a high horseshoe. In it, however, were nested free-spanning, buttressing arches. The voussoirs, alternately of red and white stone, created dramatic three-dimensional diagonal vistas.

Some of the capitals are spoils taken from destroyed churches and Roman civic buildings, and indeed, the unusual siting at the perimeter of the city may be due to its being built over the ruins of a Roman warehouse. The building thus signals that the rulers had come to terms with certain aspects of the existing architectural tradition, which they incorporated with great ingenuity into their design. The horseshoe-shaped arches are thought to have been adapted from the remains of local Visigoth architecture.

10.27 Dome structure, Great Mosque of Córdoba

10.28 Hall of the Great Mosque of Córdoba

10.29 Entrance facade, Great Mosque of Córdoba

Over time, the structure was lengthened and widened, but always with reverence for the initial design. The minaret, topped with a domed pavilion, was one of the first tower minarets in Islam. It was constructed to replace the Christian bell towers, which had been pulled down. A particularly important part of one of the later additions is the remarkable set of three domes added to the bay in front of the mihrab (962–66 CE), the central one quite spectacular. Unlike Roman domes, which were primarily spatial elements, or Byzantine domes, which were props for spatially ambiguous mosaics, this dome emphasized a combination of geometric logic and decorative detail. The octagonal base closes itself toward the peak of the dome with the help of lobed arches to form two intersecting squares. These squares, in turn, create an octagonal frame that holds a petaled, umbrella-shaped dome. The result is not a dome in the sense of a unified object, but a series of spatial layers that act horizontally and vertically. Light filtering in through the screens of the lower register of arches contrasts with the dark niches at the corners. The mosaics, executed by Byzantine craftsmen, are of plants and vines in geometric patterns.

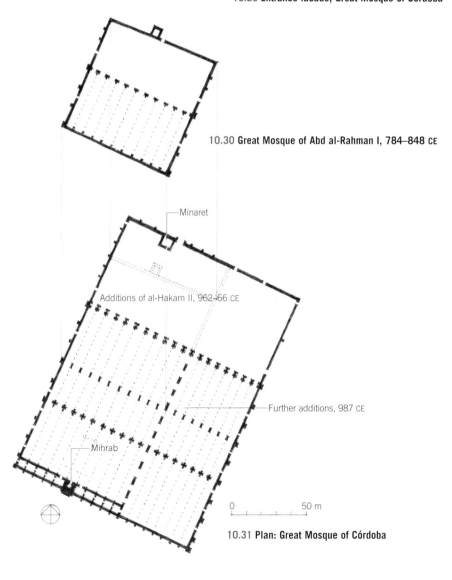

10.30 Great Mosque of Abd al-Rahman I, 784–848 CE

Minaret

Additions of al-Hakam II, 962–66 CE

Further additions, 987 CE

Mihrab

0   50 m

10.31 Plan: Great Mosque of Córdoba

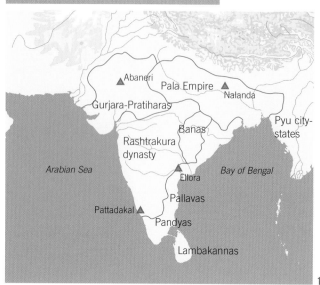

10.32 **India ca. 800 CE**

Basic Vocabulary of Hindu Architecture

Garbha-griha: Literally, "womb chamber"; innermost sanctum

Lingam: Literally, "phallus," but also "mark" or "sign"; the symbol for Shiva. (Shaivite temples face east; Vaishnavite temples face west.)

Shikhara: Literally, "mountain peak"; the rising tower of north Indian temples

Gopuram: A monumental tower at the entrance of south Indian temples

Pradakshina: Circumambulation

Prasada: Literally, "palace"; temple precinct

Mandapa: A pillared hall in front of the temple and sometimes connected to it; if a temple has more than one *mandapa*, each is allocated a different function and given a name to reflect its use.

Rajasimhesvara and Virupaksha Temples

While India was ruled by a series of diverse kingdoms, the competition in south India between the Chalukyas and the Pallavas intensified. Victorious kings routinely carried the other's masons and temple builders back home with them. The consequence was a cross-fertilization of temple design. As a temple inscription notes, the Rajasimhesvara Temple (700–730 CE)—built by the Pallava king in his capital, Kanchipuram—was the model for the Virupaksha Temple (733-44 CE), built by the Chalyukyan queen at Pattadakal. Workmen from Rajasimhesvara also worked on the Virupaksha; the two make for an interesting comparison.

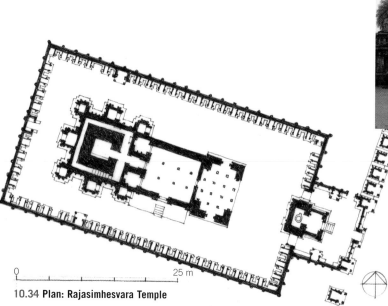

10.33 **Rajasimhesvara Temple, Kanchipuram, India**

10.34 **Plan: Rajasimhesvara Temple**

0   25 m

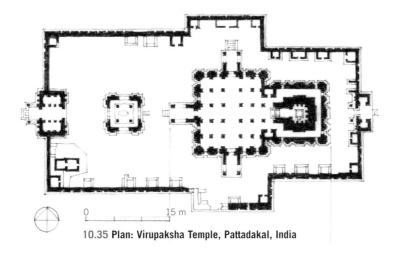

10.35 Plan: Virupaksha Temple, Pattadakal, India

The two temples' similarities involve their size and organizational type, rather than their appearance and formal order. Though most Hindu temples face east, Virupaksha, being a Shiva temple, faces west. The *garbha-grihas* of both temples are surrounded by a well-defined and fully enclosed *parikrama* path, but Rajasimhesvara has nine subsidiary shrines arrayed in constellation around it, while the Virupaksha establishes the presence of subsidiary shrines through articulations of the outer wall. Both have attached *mandapas*, but while Rajasimhesvara's two enclosed *mandapas* set up a single longitudinal axis, Virupaksha's single *mandapa* is fully pierced and sets up a cross-axis with spatial dynamism. Both temples are located with their own precincts of roughly equivalent size, and both have large entrance *gopurams*. But while Rajasimhesvara's precinct is packed with a phalanx of subsidiary shrines, and in fact has the beginnings of a second precinct enclosure also made of subsidiary shrines, Virupaksha's precinct has only an episodic collection of subsidiary shrines attached to it and breaks to respond to the cross-axis of the *mandapa*. The Virupaksha, being a Shiva shrine, also has the requirement of a Nandi pavilion for Shiva's bull; the pavilion sits as a separate element in its forecourt.

Unlike earlier Hindu temples in which the *garbha-griha* is framed by its plinth and precinct walls, here the outer frame and the inner *garbha-griha* are locked into each other by means of spatial intermediaries, including the *mandapa*, that allow for both axial and circumambulatory readings. Overall, the geometric order of the Virupaksha is more articulated than that of the Rajasimhesvara, as is evidenced in the ordering of the of twelve freestanding columns of the *mandapa* that are extended into the edges, either by pilasters or by columns, and arranged to clear the path of the cross-axis. The inner columns of the Rajasimhesvara, by contrast, are laid out by a simple arithmetic geometry.

10.36 Virupaksha Temple

10.37 **Two views: Temple of Kailasnath at Ellora, near Aurangabad, India**

Kailasnath at Ellora

Control of the Deccan Plateau was wrested from the Chalukyas around 750 CE by the Rashtrakutas, who ruled for about two centuries, until 973 CE. The Rashtrakutas quickly established their military superiority and captured the all-important trade routes that connected the western region to the rest of the subcontinent, in particular, the *dakshinapatha*, or southern route. On the *dakshinapatha* at Verul (contemporary Ellora), the Rashtrakuta ruler Krishna I ordered the construction of what was to become the largest rock-cut temple ever. Fifty meters wide, more than 90 meters deep, and 20 meters high, Kailasnath is in the middle of the 3-kilometer-long wall of basalt that has thirty-four caves carved out of it (twelve are Buddhist, seventeen Hindu, and five Jain, dating from 600 to 1000 CE). Kailasnath is conceived as a representation of the mythological mountain abode of Shiva, Mt. Kailash. Unlike the Buddhist rock-cut structures that essentially had always been elaborations of a cave, Kailasnath is an independent entity, a freestanding colossal sculpture revealed from the matrix. Since it is still surrounded by the rock from which it was hewn, there is a palpable sense of excavation to Kailasnath, as if it were still a work in progress.

Two "victory towers" have been left on either side of the mass of the Nandi chamber. They not only provide the vertical axis of the composition, but their length also visibly measures the mass of the rock that has been excavated. From outside, the temple is almost entirely obscured

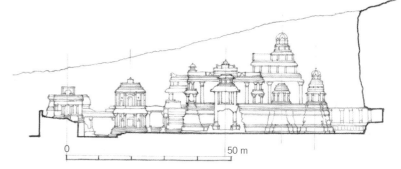

10.38 **Longitudinal section: Kailasnath, Ellora**

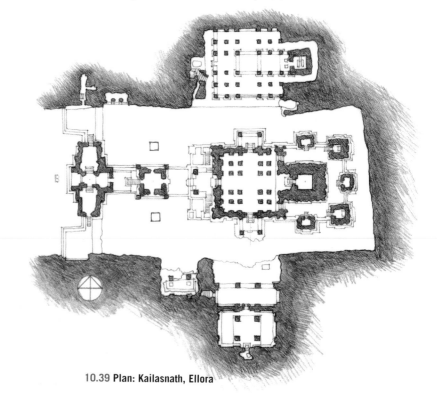

10.39 **Plan: Kailasnath, Ellora**

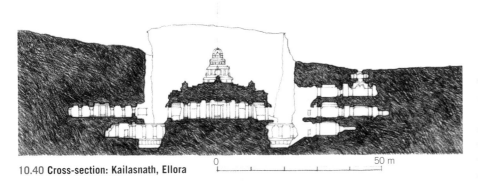

10.40 Cross-section: Kailasnath, Ellora

0   50 m

by its two-storied entrance *gopuram* (flanked on either side by Shaivite and Vaishnavite figures) on the west that leads, through a vestibule, into the main space. The ground floor is dominated by the immense presence of the excavated mass, since the body of the temple at this level is mostly solid and cannot be entered. Toward the back, the perimeter is ringed by a colonnade of square pillars whose only purpose seems to be to support the overhanging rock. In the midst of an elaborate sculptural program, the lower rock mass of the main shrine has life-size elephants carved into it, as if they were supporting the temple above.

Access to the main level of the temple is from a pair of symmetrical stairs on the west that emerge into the entrance vestibule of the shrine. The *mandapa* has sixteen columns clumped into groups of four, creating a cruciform central space that opens into smaller porches on the north and south. The *garbha-griha* has no inner *parikrama*; it is instead on the outside, defined by five subsidiary shrines. Bridges connect the main shrine with the Nandi chamber and the entrance *gopuram* as well. The *shikhara*—or tower—of the main shrine has a four-tiered pyramidal shape resolving into an octagonal finial. The subsidiary shrines use the same vocabulary. Toward the north, on the cross-axis with the *mandapa*, there is another rock-cut temple, Lankesvara, complete with a sixteen-pillared *mandapa* and *garbha-griha*, that almost rivals the main shrine. And to the south there are two additional shrines, also rock-cut, one of which extends almost 25 meters into the rock.

Most discussions of Kailasnath's construction process assume that gigantic trenches were dug into the rock to clear out the main mass of the temple; this would have been followed by a process of excavating and sculpting. A counterintuitive possibility is suggested by the subsidiary shrines—in particular the one to the north—which are excavated so deep into the rock; the same process might have been employed for the main shrine. Since Kailasnath is derived from rock-cut cave temple precedents, excavating the sacred cave and then, in an act of superseding the infinity of the mountain around the traditional caves, "uncovering" the exterior in the form of a complete temple,

makes sense conceptually as well. There would have been no room for error, since rock cannot be replaced. Making the temple had to have been an act of skilled and deliberate craftsmanship. The Rashtrakutas would, of course, also have been very familiar with the constructed temples of the Chalukyas, their predecessors, and the Pallavas and Pandyas, their contemporaries to the south. The reason for their decision to dedicate the full extent of their resources to the creation of a gigantic rock-cut structure is unknown, but it must have had to do with reasserting the value of the traditional way of making a monumental ritual structure in the face of the imminent modernity of the structural stone temple.

10.41 Detail: Temple of Kailasnath, Ellora

10.42 Detail: Temple of Kailasnath, Ellora

10.43 Mahavihara at Nalanda, Bihar, India

Mahaviharas at Nalanda and Somapura

Mahavihara (literally "great *vihara*") was the term used to designate the huge Buddhist universities that were established by the Guptas in the 5th century and that flourished until the 12th century. The most famous of these was Nalanda. Almost every Buddhist pilgrim to India made a stop at Nalanda. Mahaviharas like Nalanda were multidisciplinary universities devoted not only to the preparation of Buddhist practitioners but also to the study of secular disciplines. Officially established by the Gupta king Kumara Gupta I (415–55 CE), Nalanda boomed in the reign of Harshavardhana. Nalanda had more than two thousand senior monks and about ten thousand disciples. Theravada, the school of Buddhism followed mainly in Sri Lanka, Burma, Thailand, and Cambodia, developed here. Besides the various schools of Buddhism, including Hinayana, Mahayana, and Tantric, courses on the Indo-Aryan Vedas, *hetu vidya* ("logic"), *shabda vidya* ("grammar"), and *chikitsa vidya* (medicine) were also taught at Nalanda. The Chinese pilgrim Hsuan Tsang spent most of his time at Nalanda studying law.

Aryabhatta, the 5th-century astronomer and mathematician (born in 476 CE in Kerala, India) came to Nalanda as a boy to study astronomy. He was one of the earliest people to support the theory that the earth is a sphere, preceding Copernicus by a millennium. His main work, known as the Aryabhattiya, was translated into Latin in the 13th century. It included methods of calculating the area of a triangle, the volume of a sphere, and square and cube roots. Aryabhatta also wrote about eclipses and proposed the sun as the source of moonlight. Another 7th-century Indian astronomer, Brahmagupta, calculated the circumference of the earth as 5,000 *yojanas*, or about 36,000 kilometers, only 4,000 short of its true distance. The number zero, called *sunya*, (meaning "void" or "empty") was invented at this time. *Sunya* passed into the Arabic as *sifr*, meaning "vacant." In about 1200 CE, this word was transliterated into Latin but its original meaning was lost, resulting in the words *zephirum* or *zephyrum*.

Nalanda consisted of ten quadrangles covering 14 hectares, all lined up in a block and packed next to each other. Made of brick, each *vihara*, 50 to 60 meters long, had a central courtyard (some with a shrine) ringed by two or three stories of cells for the monks, who lived about thirty to a floor. The *viharas* faced a row of freestanding stupas (sometimes described as *caitya* temples) also made of brick, each with long central stairways leading to a platform on which stood the main shrine, with subsidiary shrines at the corners. In its time, the street between the *viharas* and the stupas would have been packed with monks and their disciples.

After Harshavardhana, the Pala kings of Bengal maintained Nalanda for four centuries, until the 11th century. In fact, the surviving ruins date from the Pala period. The Palas were the patrons of several other monastic universities, such as at Vikramsila and Somapura. So numerous were the *viharas* that the name of the modern state in this region, Bihar, is a contraction of the Sanskrit for "Land of the Viharas."

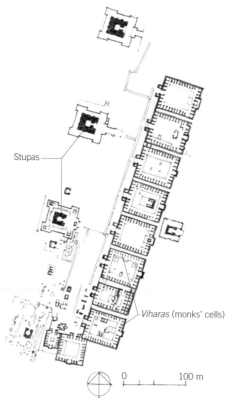

Stupas

Viharas (monks' cells)

0   100 m

10.44 **Plan: Mahavihara at Nalanda**

At Somapura (800 CE) the accretive character of Nalanda's plan was rationalized by the Palas into a single gigantic order. With a distinct cruciform shape, its *caitya* temple is more than 100 meters from north to south and sits in the middle of a vast quadrangular courtyard 300 meters on a side, the edges of which contain 177 cells that may have served as shrines or monk cells. Facing north, the stupa sits on three terraces with jagged edges constituting a stage for the central shrine (which is missing). The whole complex is made of burnt brick with decorative terra-cotta finishes that narrate Mahayana tales from the life of the Buddha and other bodhisattvas. The sculptures reveal the sex-based nature of Tantric Buddhism, which relies on the release of human energy through sexual intercourse. The order and configuration of the terraced stupa are based on Mahayana mandala diagrams of the kind that are still found in Nepal and Tibet.

The Sumstek Gompa in Alchi, Kashmir, built on a smaller scale, has survived largely intact. Located on the high-altitude road from Srinigar to Ladakh, the shrine is a three-tiered structure, the interior of which is profusely adorned with murals depicting Buddhist motifs and bodhisattvas. Its adjoining *dukhang* ("assembly hall") contains a statue of Avalokiteshvara made of pure gold. In a style reminiscent of Ajanta, its walls are painted with scenes of turbaned men and multiple-braided women drinking, riding, fighting, and wearing garments of Central Asian origin, although their features are decidedly South Asian. Most of what survives dates to the 11th century.

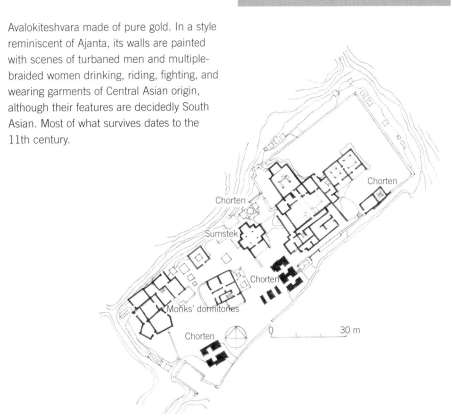

10.45 Site plan: Sumstek Gompa, Alchi, India

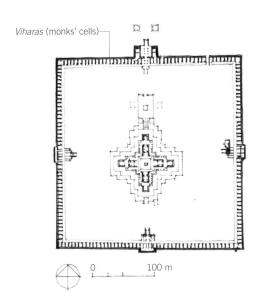

10.46 Plan: Somapura Vihara, Paharpur, Bangladesh

10.47 Sumstek Gompa

10.48 **View of Borobudur, near Yogyakarta, Indonesia**

Indonesia at a Crossroads

By the 9th century, the entire region of Southeast Asia had begun to cohere as a series of relatively stable states linked by trade and religion. Guangzhou was the primary entry point into China. Kunming, a quasi-independent state (to become the Kingdom of Dali) was the primary land-based entry point. Particularly important was the development of trade around the Straits of Malacca. Ships no longer unloaded at Kedah for the portage across the peninsula. With the sea route now becoming the norm, Sumatra and Indonesia quickly became a strategically important area. The Hindu-Buddhist Shailendra kings of 9th-century Indonesia used their new wealth to catapult their kingdom from one of the farthest outposts of seaborne trade between China and India into a conceptual center of the Hindu-Buddhist cosmological universe. Within the short space of a hundred years, and funded by trade revenues and their own rice production, they built not only one of the finest Buddhist stupa shrines ever, Borobudur, but also, a scant 20 miles away, one of the largest and most complex assemblages of Hindu temples of the time, the Prambanam complex.

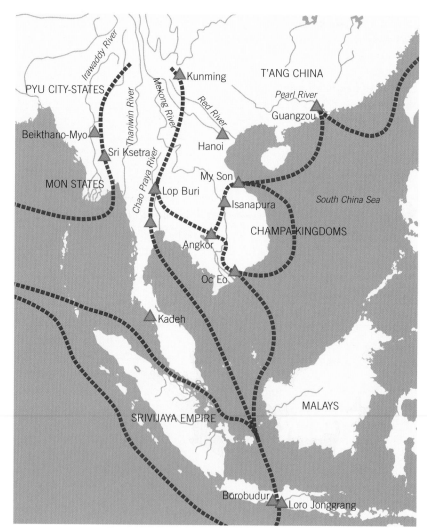

10.49 **Rivers and cities of Southeast Asia**

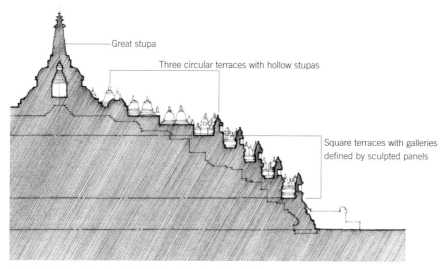

Great stupa

Three circular terraces with hollow stupas

Square terraces with galleries defined by sculpted panels

10.50 Partial section showing the three levels of Borobudur

Borobudur

The great "cosmic mountain" at Borobudur (ca. 760–830 CE) was started in the reign of the Shailendra king Indra and completed in that of Samaratunga. Though based on earlier experiments, Borobudur is unique in its formal organization and articulation. It is approximately square in plan (122 meters north to south and 116 meters east to west), and it is roughly aligned to the cardinal directions. The plan follows a typical Buddhist mandala diagram, with a biaxial symmetrical order composed of a series of jagged terraces giving way to round ones in the middle.

Borobudur is at one level a quintessential stupa, having been built onto a solid mound; at another level, it is a three-dimensional pedagogical process. The building is neither a temple nor a monastery. Rather, it is something of a university that one goes to, not to invoke divine beings but to participate in a didactic journey, to learn—by moving through its spaces—a progression of lessons through which the successful student can attain a state of *bodhi*, or perfected wisdom, just as the Sakyamuni Buddha did 2,500 years prior. The essential experience consists of an orchestrated sequence of four galleries followed by three terraces, preceded by one large plinth, or pre-terrace. The first four terraces are square, and the latter three are round. The whole experience culminates in the central stupa, which is completely solid and cannot be entered. As the Buddhist pilgrim approaches it, the complete profile of Borobudur is clearly visible, its levels of galleries and rounded stupa terraces

orchestrated hierarchically around the central stupa, forming the outline of a gently swelling mountain. The destination, the central stupa, seems evident. As the pilgrim gets closer, however, the central stupa disappears and seems to retract into the monument, and it is replaced by a forest of smaller stupas and sculptures on a more human scale. Since nirvana is not a place or a thing, it has no physical dimension that can be described. Rather, it is an inner state that must be achieved by the pilgrim by means of a personal journey. As governed by the mandala, this journey must be completed by a pilgrim in sixty conceptual steps.

The journey begins by circumambulating the four lower galleries, which have two rows of sculpted panels on each side, recounting sequentially stories from the life of the Buddha. These narrow galleries are staggered to block all lines of sight, in order to focus the pilgrim's attention on the panels. Only after having cleared these four levels can pilgrims ascend to the round upper levels, where there are no enclosing walls. Instead, they encounter the bell-shaped hollow stupas, each one of which contains a different sculpture of the seated Buddha displaying one of the mudras, the characteristic symbolic gestures of Buddhism. The openings on the lower stupas are diamond-shaped and large, while those on the ones above are square, smaller, and fewer in number. While each side of the *candi* ("temple") in the lower level is one step, each bell-shaped stupa takes a whole step toward the end. At the final stage, pilgrims arrive at the stupa whose solidity symbolizes the *shunyata*, or "nonpresence," aspired to by the Buddhist pilgrim who seeks nirvana. The lowest terrace of Borobudur, probably added to stabilize the structure, was constructed at a later date; it hides a row of friezes behind it. One of the unresolved controversies surrounding Borobudur is whether it was originally planned with a large stupa in the middle that would have dominated the whole edifice.

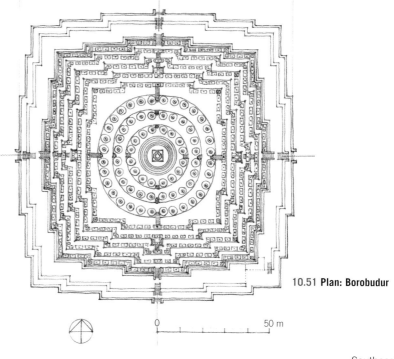

10.51 Plan: Borobudur

0   50 m

10.52 **Loro Jonggrang, Prambanan, Indonesia**

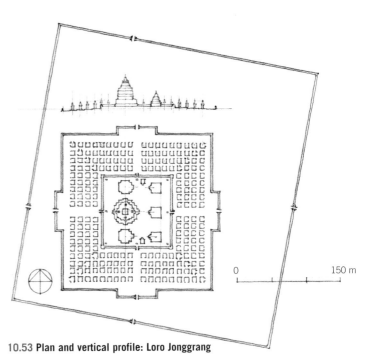

10.53 **Plan and vertical profile: Loro Jonggrang**

Candi Prambanam

In about 835 CE, after Samaratunga's death, his young son Balaputra's right to accession was usurped by his sister's father-in-law, Patapan of Sanjaya. Patapan replaced Buddhism with Hinduism in the Shailendra kingdom and began the construction of a series of Hindu temples that was continued by his son, Rakai Pikaton (or Jatiningrat). One of the most impressive of these is Candi Prambanam, known popularly as Loro Jonggrang ("Slender Virgin"). Built around 850 CE, Loro Jonggrang's three central shrines, facing east, are dedicated to the Hindu trinity, Brahma, Vishnu, and Shiva, with Shiva at the center. (Ideas of divine kingship were also attached to the temple, especially after the burial of the remains of the king of Mataram Balitung [d. 910 CE], who claimed to be a reincarnation of Shiva. Three subsidiary shrines, for the corresponding animal "vehicles," or *vahanas*, of the temple deities, face westward, toward the main group.)

The shrines sit on a platform, accessible from all four sides. Around the platform, 224 small shrines are arrayed in concentric rings, with extra widths for passages leading to the center. These small shrines are oriented in ranks of 18 to face outward, with the ones at the corners designed with two orientations. A wall encloses the complex with access gates on each side. Originally, this whole complex was surrounded by another perimeter wall,

oriented not to the cardinal directions but northeast and southwest and measuring about 390 meters on a side. Except for its southern gate, not much of this enclosure has survived. It is not certain if this area was a sacred park or whether it also contained school buildings.

Prambanam's shrines are articulated as two-story structures divided by a band of molding. Their profiles are most like those of the Pallavas of southern India, which emphasize slender verticality with distinct and clear horizontal layers, as in the Shore Temple. Prambanam's two-storied base, however, is significantly taller than its South Asian precedents. The bulbous profile of the individual *salas*, or superstructures, of

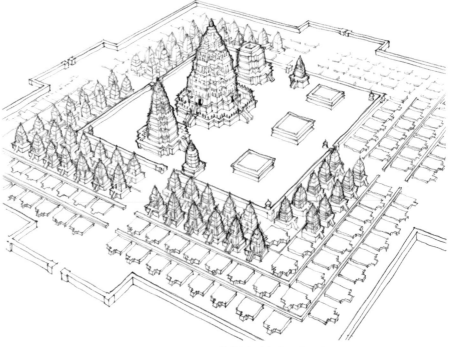

10.54 **Aerial view: Loro Jonggrang**

Prambanam is also a nod in the direction of Borobudur, not far away. The plans and tripartite elevational orders of Hindu and Buddhist structures of Southeast Asia were—probably quite purposefully—very similar. The two cosmologies were often articulated in parallel as well. As a consequence, it is not unusual to mistake a Hindu temple for a Buddhist one, and vice versa, especially in contemporary Cambodia.

Samye, Tibet

A century after the introduction of Buddhism into Tibet, King Trisong Detsen formally established Buddhism as the state religion by building the Samye Monastery. Its full name is Bsam yas mi 'gyur lhun grub gtsug lag khang, or the "Temple of Unchanging Spontaneous Presence" (founded 775 CE, constructed 787–91 CE). The first Tibetan monks were ordained here, and it was the seat of Tibetan Buddhism until the establishment of the Potala Palace by the fifth Dalai Lama in the 17th century. Located in the Chimpu Valley just south of Lhasa, the monastery was laid out in the form of a mandala, with a circular perimeter wall about 300 meters in diameter; the main temple, the Utse, representing Mt. Meru, is in the center. The wall is topped by 1,008 tiny chortens with gates at the four cardinal points. The four continents in the ocean around Mt. Meru are represented by temples at the cardinal points, each flanked by two smaller temples to symbolize islands. The Utse has three main stories, each of which was designed in a different traditional architectural style—Indian, Chinese, and Tibetan. The first floor is dominated by the main assembly hall; the second is basically an open roof area where monks and locals carry out the craftwork for the temple; and the third is the palace of the Dalai Lama, with a small anteroom, throne room, and bedroom. Four chortens at the corners of the Utse are brightly colored black, white, red, and green. Each has stairs and small chapels. There is a *nyima* ("sun") temple in the north and a *dawa* ("moon") temple to the south. Though all Buddhist temples are modeled on an imaginary mandala, this one has the mandala as it basic plan, writ large in the landscape.

10.55 Samye Monastery, Dranang, Tibet

10.56 Samye Monastery, Dranang, Tibet

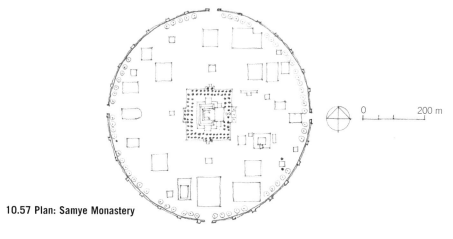

10.57 Plan: Samye Monastery

Hindu Kingdoms of Cambodia

In 802 CE, Jayavarman II, who had united the various Chola kingdoms in Cambodia and southern Vietnam, became king and supreme ruler over his vast new territory. The coronation ceremony took place on Mt. Mahendraparvata overlooking the Angkor Plain. It was, for the region, a new type of kingdom. The traditional trade route from Kunming had gone through Burma and through cities on the Irrawaddy River, like Biethano-Myo. And the shipping lanes that developed around 400 CE hugged the coast to the benefit of cities like Oc Eo. The Khmer controlled a large inland area that they made fertile with their irrigation technology. In a century, it was to make them the wealthiest kingdom in Southeast Asia. The rise of the Khmer was also spurred on by the trade between China and India. The rule of the Song dynasty (960–1279 CE) conforms quite closely with that of the Khmer, and with the Chola in India (860–1279 CE). Both China and India exerted powerful economic influences in the Southeast Asian areas, although, from a cultural point of view, it was India that won out, with its variants of Buddhism and Hinduism spreading throughout the region. To the east in Vietnam, there were the Champa, whom the Khmer tried several times to conquer in order to gain access to their ports. To the south was the Srivijaya Empire, founded in the 8th century on the island of Sumatra, which controlled the Straits of Malacca. Also to be factored in is the Dali kingdom in Yunnan Province in southern China. From 900 until 1253 CE, when it was conquered by the Mongolians and brought back into the fold of the Chinese Empire, it was an autonomous state; with the disruptions of the trade routes that came with the Mongolian expansion into Asia, the southern route, which went right through the Dali heartland, proved to be a viable alternative. The Khmer sold specialty items to the Chinese, such as spices and wood, in exchange for metal items such a bronze pots as well as silver and gold.

10.58 **View of Bakong Temple Mountain, near Siem Reap, Cambodia**

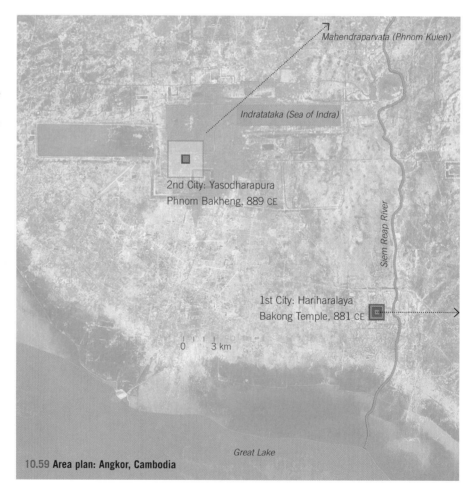

Mahendraparvata (Phnom Kulen)

Indratataka (Sea of Indra)

2nd City: Yasodharapura
Phnom Bakheng, 889 CE

Siem Reap River

1st City: Hariharalaya
Bakong Temple, 881 CE

0   3 km

Great Lake

10.59 **Area plan: Angkor, Cambodia**

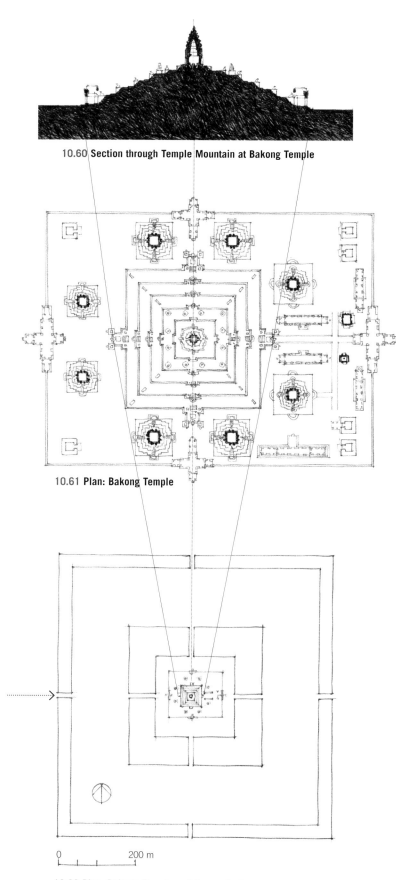

10.60 Section through Temple Mountain at Bakong Temple

10.61 Plan: Bakong Temple

0   200 m

10.62 Plan: Bakong Temple and its precinct

Hariharalaya

The city called Hariharalaya was laid out as a perfect square about 3 kilometers on a side. The name *Hariharalaya* is derived from the name of the Hindu deity Harihara, who was prominent in pre-Angkorian Cambodia. The name *Harihara*, in turn, is a composite of *hari* (meaning "the Hindu god Vishnu") and *hara* (meaning "the Hindu god Shiva"). The name thus means something like "the City of Vishnu and Shiva." The city was not as dense as medieval European cities, since it were interspersed with gardens and small fields.

That Jayavarman II chose this site to the north of the Great Lake for his capital was no coincidence. Apart from a steady supply of water for rice growing, the place was seen as a local holy land that, with relatively modest enhancements, could be transformed into *the* holy land of the Khmer. Angkor spiritual geography, as would have been typical in Indic mythology, was defined around three primary elements: the mountain, the river, and the ocean—or Mt. Meru, the Ganges River, and the Indian Ocean. Each had its own translation in the local Angkor geography.

Mahendraparvata (Mt. Meru)

Mt. Meru, the abode of the gods, lies at the center of the physical and spiritual universes. For the Khmer, its incarnation was Mahendraparvata, "the Mountain of Indra, the King of Gods." Known today as Phnom Kulen, it is located about 25 kilometers to the northeast of Angkor. Jayavarman II built several temples on the mountain to house the lingam. It was also from this mountain that the stones for the Angor temples were quarried. In that sense, the stones possessed a spiritual charge.

Siem Reap (Ganges River)

The mountain is the source of the Siem Reap River, which in its numerous offshoots drains most of the plateau before reaching the Great Lake. It is the water from this river that feeds the complex system of canals and *barays*. The river was identified with the goddess Ganga.

Indratataka (Sea of Indra)

The "ocean" was built in Jayavarman II's city immediately after he become king. This vast *baray*, the largest of its kind at the time, was called Indratataka, or "Sea of Indra," and was 3.8 kilometers long and 0.8 kilometers wide.

Bakong

Jayavarman II may have founded the city, but his state temple was some 20 kilometers away, back in Phnom Kulen. For this reason, his court remained at Phnom Kulen until 802 CE, when he finally moved to Hariharalaya. The next king, Indravarman I ("Protected by Indra"), built a new state temple, but in the very center of the city. The temple (881 CE), which had long avenues extending from it in the cardinal directions, sat in a moated enclosure that would have contained palaces and royal storehouses. Dedicated to Shiva, it measures 900 by 700 meters and consists of three concentric enclosures separated by two moats. The innermost enclosure, which measures 160 by 120 meters, contains eight towers and the central temple, which has a single tower on its top platform. The plan of the temple is square and consists of five levels. Though not complicated compared to subsequent temples, the design is quite refined. The levels become successively shallower, and the staircase narrows as it ascends. The culminating tower is thought to have replaced the original one, since its architectural style corresponds to that of the 12th-century temple city Ankgor Wat.

Stone was used for the platforms, whereas brick was used for the architectural parts. The brick was covered with bas-relief carvings in stucco depicting scenes from Hindu mythology. Large stone statues of elephants are positioned as guardians at the corners of the three lower levels of the pyramid. Statues of lions guard the stairways.

What often makes Khmer temples seem alien to Western perceptions is that they are not set *against* the landscape. They are both a form of architecture based on a complex application of geometry and site planning and a constructed landscape; all these temples are not only in a sacred landscape but are themselves copies of the symbolic landscape of mountain and ocean. The moats that surround the temples do not serve a protective purpose but represent the primeval oceans in which the treasure of immortality was hidden. The water also visually echoed the temple's image, making the temple-mountain appear linked with its inverted reflection. On a practical level, these waters are integrated into the *baray* system, literally nourishing the land. This mutually reinforcing relationship between a symbolic landscape and its real-life model is continuously at play in these temples.

The temple represents a combination of these five principles:

1. The sacred mandala/mountain/ocean of Shiva and the Hindu pantheon
2. An intensified model of the scared landscape in which they are sited
3. The home of the god(s)
4. The omnipotence of the king
5. The economy of the Khmer people

Around the year 900 CE, King Yasovarman I ("Protected by Glory"; r. 899–917 CE) created yet another new city, along with a new state temple and a new and significantly larger *baray*. The city, Yasodharapura ("Glory-Bearing City"), was, like its predecessor, perfectly square, but it was much larger: about 4 kilometers on a side. The new state temple, Bakheng, located at the center, was known originally as Yasodharesvara—the "Lord of the One Who Bears Glory." It is also referred to in inscriptions as Phnom Kandal ("Central Mountain"). Yasodharesvara is built on top of a sizable 60-meter-high rock outcropping, the top (and perhaps even the slopes) of which had been shaved down to suit the design. Whereas Bakong was more of an artificial mountain than a real one, Bakheng was a mountain augmented by a temple to become a type of supertemple/mountain. The whole was surrounded by a moat measuring 650 by 436 meters. Avenues radiated out in the four cardinal directions from the mount, with a causeway running in a northwest-southeast orientation from the old capital area to the east section of the new capital's outer moat and then, turning to an east-west orientation, connected directly to the east entrance of the temple. The temple faces east, measures 76 meters square at its base, and is built in a pyramid form of six tiers. At the top level, five sandstone sanctuaries stand in a quincunx: one in the center and one at each corner of the level's square. The quincunx represents the five peaks of Mt. Meru.

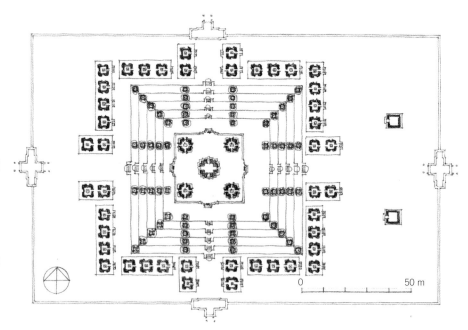

10.63 Plan of Phnom Bakheng

East Africa

By the 6th century, iron technology had begun to proliferate throughout much of Africa. The Bantu, who had spread through East Africa in the first few centuries of the common era, were particularly noted for their ironwork, and they created a system of exchanges that saw the development of Swahili culture along the coast. Maritime trade was stimulated by the arrival of Arab Islamic traders on the coast beginning in the 8th century. They became quite prominent in the economy of Africa by the 11th century. Slaves, bananas, and cattle were the prime commodities. A result was that Islam was slowly adopted by coastal Africans, although it did not become dominant until the 12th century.

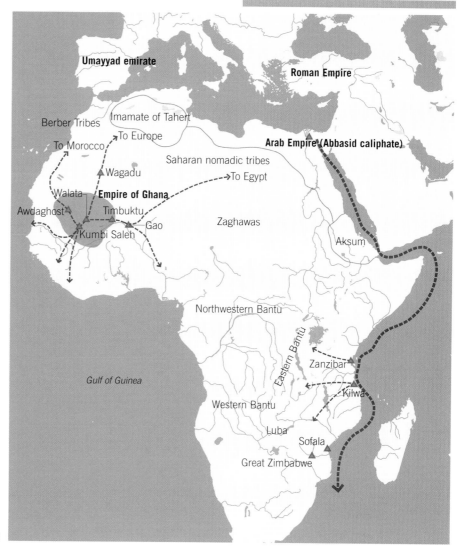

10.64 **Africa, ca. 800 CE**

Ghana

By the 9th century, the Kingdom of Ghana had become one of the most powerful states in East Africa. Its actual name was Wagadu, the word *ghana* being the title of the king. The kingdom was located on the north bank of the Senegal and Niger rivers (in present-day southeast Mauritania and southwest Mali), approximately 500 miles northwest of the modern nation of Ghana. The land was known for its gold, but Ghana itself did not produce the gold that came from Bambuk, which lies to its south. To get to the markets it had be brought through Wagadu. Around 970 CE, Ghana conquered Awdaghost, giving it control over the trade route from the north. Several oasis towns were then created, such as Alata, 170 kilometers to the northeast of the capital.

The transformation of Ghana from a city-state into a centralized kingdom with a sizable army seems to have taken place in the 5th or 6th century. Salt was one of the main commodities exchanged for gold. According to travelers, the king held audience in a domed pavilion surrounded by ten horses covered with gold-embroidered cloth. Behind the king, ten pages held shields and gold-mounted swords; on his right were the sons of the vassal kings of his country, wearing splendid garments, their hair plaited with gold.

The capital, Kumbi Saleh, founded in southeast Mauritania in the 7th century, was a double city. It consisted of the original town surrounded by a palisade and a merchant town, which had a population that was for a long time mostly Muslim, judging from the twelve mosques it contained. At its peak, it had as many as twenty thousand residents. The royal city was located in its own precinct.

In 1076, the Sanhaja Berbers—the Almoravids—invaded and razed the city. Excavations have revealed a vast set of stone ruins, including a square tomb chamber measuring just over 5 meters on each side with a column recessed into each of the external corners. There were originally four openings into the chamber, but three of these were subsequently blocked up, leaving a single entrance on the east side. Just inside, the entrance steps made of brick led down into a subterranean chamber containing spaces for three sarcophagi. Elsewhere excavation has revealed a row of shops connected to houses.

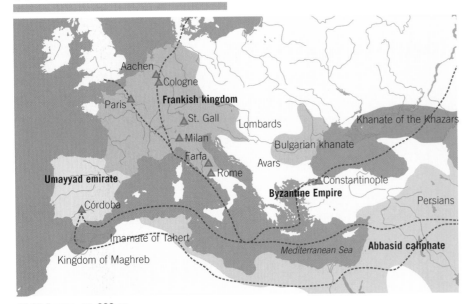

10.65 Europe, ca. 800 CE

10.66 Theotokos, icon of the Virgin Mary

Byzantine Empire

With the creation of the alliance between the Roman papacy and the Frankish kingdom, the Byzantine Church became increasingly isolated from Europe. As a result, despite some successes against the Arabs to the south and the Bulgars to the north, Byzantium experienced a period of decline that began at the end of the 6th century. During this time, paintings known as icons became an important part of religious ritual. Painted on panels or in the domes of churches, the icons usually depicted Christ or Mary and were considered to be holy objects. Their use was not uncontroversial, with theological arguments being developed both for and against them. In 843 CE, however, the use of icons was officially permitted. Nicephorus I (r. 802–11 CE) was able to introduce a period of relative stability, especially once the Slavs had converted in the 10th century, choosing Byzantine orthodoxy over the Latin church in Rome. By the time of Basil I (r. 867–86 CE), there was an upward trend in politics, literature, and art. A great deal of effort was made to expand the imperial palace in Constantinople. In 830 CE, a Byzantine envoy sent to Baghdad was so impressed by the splendor of Arab architecture that he urged the emperor to build a similar palace. The palace soon became one of the great architectural complexes of the world. Though still somewhat isolated from the massive flow of trade from China through the Islamic regions,

the opening up of trade along the Volga River and the stabilization of Italy and France positioned Byzantium as a hinge between West and East.

The revival brought with it important changes in the political-architectural relationship. Unlike in the Justinian era, during which most of the major architectural monuments had been conceived as public buildings, the architecture of this period served the imperial elite, who sponsored their local monasteries. As a result, major architectural projects were rare. The churches of this period were considerably different from their Western counterparts insofar as they were not firmly linked to each other. Instead, they were relatively autonomous, privately endowed units performing important local services, such as running orphanages and hospitals. In exchange for the endowment, the donor obtained the right to perpetual memoriam Masses and services and the right to participate in the monastery's internal affairs. Though schools were sometimes associated with these monasteries, they were located outside of the walls, together with the administrative offices.

Today, most of the monastic enclaves have disappeared, leaving only the churches as freestanding objects. Originally, however, the church would not have been visible over the monastic walls. Unlike the Roman model, there were no atrium structures attached

to the building. This change reflects the individual patronage system, which brought with it a shift toward an internally oriented, pietistic practice. For this reason, religion in Byzantium was still so attached to devotional practices that the powerful relationship between religion and learning developing in other parts of the world—including the great learning centers in India, Spain, and the Benedictine monasteries of the Carolingians—failed to take root.

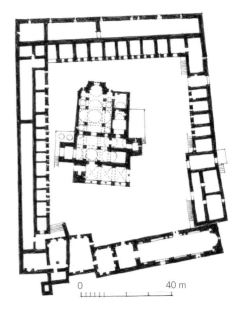

10.67 Plan: Monastery of St. Meletios on Mt. Kithairon, Greece

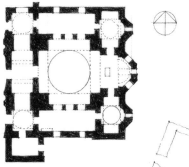

10.69 Plan and section: Koimesis at Nicaea, Greece

0   10 m

10.68 Pictorial view: The Monastery of St. Meletios on Mt. Kithairon
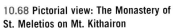

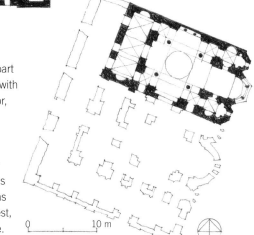

0   10 m

10.70 Plan: Theotokos Tou Libos, Istanbul, Turkey

Theotokos Tou Libos

By 800 CE, the Byzantine church style had begun to take on its characteristic form of a dome resting on four columns placed in a square. The interiors were outfitted with sumptuous mosaics. Having been despoiled over time by the Venetians, Mongols, or Turks, there are a few remaining for study today. Many surviving examples are not in Istanbul: the Capella Palantina in Palermo, Italy (1132–89); the Monreale Cathedral, also in Palermo (1172–89); and San Marco in Venice (12th to 13th centuries) represent Byzantine art at its pinnacle. A prototype of the domical or Greek-cross church plan is Koimesis in Nicaea (Iznik), Greece, from the 9th century. Four strong piers mark the corners. They shelter small groin-vaulted bays of equal depth. A dome on pendentives rises from the peaks of the barrel vaults and is enclosed in a low drum that is pierced at the cardinal points by small windows. The eastern arm opens to the chancel, which is flanked by side chambers with apsidioles that, on the outside, register as polygons. This cross-shaped domed nucleus is enveloped north and south by barrel-vaulted aisles and galleries. To the west, there is an esonarthex surmounted by a gallery. The exterior, typical of post-Justinian architecture, reads as a graduated mass culminating in the dome, but the parts are tightly fused into each other. A more developed version of the cross-domed plan was used by Emperor John II Komenos in his Church of Christ Pantokrator (Zeyrek Camii, built 1118–43).

The dome was not only the dominating part of the composition but was also painted with a large frontal image of Christ Pantokrator, or Lord of All. For the Byzantines, art was inseparable from theology, and they used icons either on the surface of walls or as separate devotional objects in their churches. The scale of the churches thus emphasized spatial intimacy. Subtlety was valued over size. More so than in the West, the church was an image of the universe. The bishop's entrance into the church symbolizes Christ's coming into the flesh. Candles, incense, music, reliquaries, gold and silver utensils, and shining mosaic walls helped create a world infused with mystery and awe.

Another example of Byzantine church style is the Church of the Theotokos Tou Libos (now called North Church and part of St. Mary Panachrantos), built in 907 CE by Constantine Lips, a high official. It was associated with a convent and a hospice for travelers. The sacristy and vestry to the right and left of the apse are still pronounced, but compared with the Church of Christ Pantokrator, they are now more organically fused into the side aisles. The church had an upper level with two small chapels above the two corner bays at the west end of the *naos*. A south church was added some eighty years later.

10.71 Interior: Theotokos Tou Libos

Europe and the Carolingians

Around the year 800 CE, the architectural hot spots were in Indonesia, China, and the Islamic world. In Europe, the situation was still bleak. Stability had improved somewhat with the Christianization of the Franks when Clovis I adopted Catholicism in Reims, France, in or around 496 CE; as was then the practice, all the Franks then adopted Catholicism as well. The king of the Visigoths, Theodoric I, along with other Germanic tribes, finally stopped the invasion of the Huns in Chalons, France, south of Reims, in 451 CE. But the onslaught of steppe tribes was not over yet. With their families and herds, the Lombards had moved into northern Italy. The Ungars and Bulgars were on the move as well, dispersing into Greece, and some even into Italy. This meant that a huge swath of territory, from the tip of Greece northward all the way to the Baltic Sea was still in a state of flux. The settlement of the Franks, who had moved into France from the lower Rhine only a few centuries earlier and who were now starting to farm the land previously known by the Romans as Gaul, was the only bright spot.

Though they had been Christianized by the 7th century, the Franks rarely had periods in which there had just one ruler. Furthermore, southern Spain had been lost to the Islamic armies, as had the Christianized areas of the eastern Roman Empire in Syria. The Armenians, with their vibrant architectural culture, were also dispersed, many fleeing westward to Constantinople and Italy. Byzantium itself was under continual threat of invasion by Islamic armies, and even the Mediterranean was largely controlled by Islamic ships. Nonetheless, the Franks eventually consolidated their hold to become the dominant force in Europe. Together with the Byzantines, the Christian civilizational area formed a tenuous U, from Denmark down through France and Italy, around Greece, and into Anatolia. The invasion of northern Italy by the Lombards threatened to cut Italy off from France, but in 774 CE, Charlemagne, by then king of the Franks, conquered the Lombards and brought them into the Christian fold. The Frankish, Italian, and reduced Byzantine areas now formed the core of the Christian world.

Charlemagne (747–814 CE), was by all accounts an unusual man. The eldest child of Pepin the Short (r. 768–51 CE), he introduced new financial regulations, took a serious interest in scholarship, and promoted the liberal arts at his court. With all this in mind, Pope Leo III realized that in order for Europe to survive, he would have to share power with Charlemagne. Thus was born the idea of the Holy Roman Empire. To their mutual benefit, it in essence had two rulers: a religious one and a secular one, the military power of the latter protecting the existence of the former. On Christmas day of the year 800 CE, in Rome, Leo crowned Charlemagne Emperor of the Empire. It was a unique arrangement for its age, and one that would have long-term consequences. The title would be handed down and fought over for centuries and officially dissolved only in 1806.

Long before Charlemagne's coronation, the Carolingian Church had established a close relationship with Rome, but it was only with the coronation that the Roman liturgy became the norm. For this, Charlemagne turned to the monastic rules of St. Benedict (489–543 CE), who had live three centuries earlier. He had formulated his rules during an age in which temporal rule had broken down. As a counterbalance to the chaos, Benedict envisioned the monastery as a devout Christian family of men. The monks' waking hours were devoted primarily to worship and manual labor. But over the centuries, the system was inconsistently applied. Charlemagne reaffirmed the rules as a way to regularize monastic life from the patchwork of devotional practices it had become while simultaneously bringing the Church closer to imperial policy by making it the basic financial, territorial, and educational institution of the land. Christianity, which had formerly lived within the limited confines of what was left of the Roman Empire, was now becoming a broad European phenomenon. A new unified era was thus created.

The seat of religious power was still, however, in Rome, and therein lay a peculiar ambiguity about the location of power that was to beset European politics for centuries and would not be resolved until the Enlightenment in the 18th century.

At the time of Charlemagne, however, the careful balance between the secular and the religious was still perceived as a mutually beneficial cooperation. The type of government Charlemagne set up developed into a feudal system, with a strict hierarchy linking serf, landlord, and count to the king. (It did, however, lack a firm centralized administrative structure.) Charlemagne moved from place to place to assert and expand his authority. The result was an important expansion of architectural works that imprinted his rule on the landscape. In Italy, just north of Rome, he rebuilt the monastery at Farfa as a southern outpost of the empire while to the east, he relied on the monasteries at Lorsch and Fulda.

Plan of St. Gall

A 9th-century plan for a medieval monastery at St. Gall in Switzerland provides direct insight into the organization of the medieval monastery. Drawn with red lead on smooth calfskin, the plan provides a remarkably comprehensive snapshot of an institution of about forty buildings inhabited by about 110 monks, with an equal number of laypeople who served as support staff. The site is organized into three zones: to the west, at the bottom of the plan, are the areas open to the lay population; the monastery proper is in the middle zone; and to the east, at the top, are the garden, infirmary, and cemetery. To the left of the road that accesses the church entrance, a reception hall and a dormitory for pilgrims was foreseen. To the north of the church there were special buildings for the abbot and novices. St. Gall was a nave church, with no transept. Its rounded entrance was flanked by freestanding towers. These were not bell towers—those were a later development. At the top of one tower was an altar to St. Michael, and on the other was an altar to St. Gabriel, the celestial guardians representing the forces of light against those of darkness and evil.

Though the draughtsman did not show the thickness of the walls, he did show doors, chimneys, and ovens and labeled each room. He even labeled the vegetables that were planted in the garden, such as onions, leeks, radishes, and fennel. The monk's cloister,

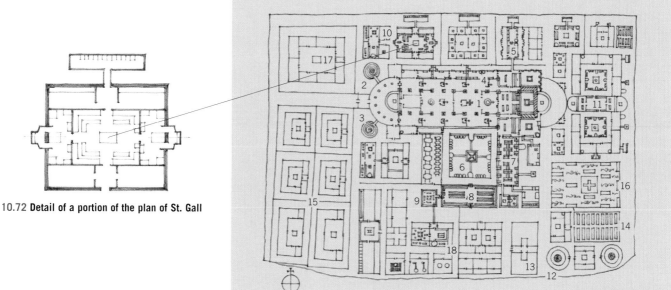

10.72 Detail of a portion of the plan of St. Gall

10.73 Plan of St. Gall, St. Gallen, Switzerland

the spatial core of the plan, was an open yard about 30 meters square, with arcaded walks giving access to surrounding buildings such as the dormitory, refectory, and the storehouse for the wine and beer kegs. The north walk, broader than the rest and fitted with benches, was used as a chapter house for daily meetings. It was connected to the east wall of the church by a special entrance that allowed the monks access to the altar, which was screened off from the public. The plan was drawn using a module of 40 Carolingian feet, the *numeri sacri*, as that is the dimension of the crossing of the church's altar. The church length was 5 times that amount, or 200 feet, and the depth of the side aisles half that amount, or 20 feet. By means of further halving, the draughtsman arrived at 2.5 feet, the smallest base measure applied in the plan.

1. Church
2. Tower of St. Michael
3. Tower of St. Gabriel
4. Guest lodgings
5. Abbot's house
6. Cloister
7. Monks' dormitory
8. Monks' refectory
9. Kitchen
10. Brew house
11. Novitiate and infirmary
12. Henhouse
13. Granary
14. Monks' garden
15. Monks' orchard and cemetery
16. Sheep, goats, and cows
17. Unknown function
18. Workshops

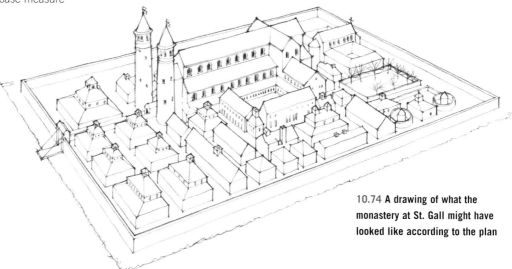

10.74 A drawing of what the monastery at St. Gall might have looked like according to the plan

The Palatine Chapel

The Palatine Chapel consists of a tall octagonal shaft of space, surrounded by annular galleries. At the ground floor, the octagon is defined by plain, undivided arches holding a cornice that separate the lower from the upper arches. On that cornice, the openings consist of elegant arcade screens between tall arches leading up to a groin vault. To fight the lateral thrusts of the dome, the architects added lateral vaults at the gallery level that seem to have been inspired by observing Roman theater construction. The design, in its simple organization of piers and columns, has the appearance of a Carolingian attempt to revive Roman aesthetics. The use of variegated marbles for the paneling and the voussoirs also reflect an awareness of St. Vitale in Ravenna, with which this building most certainly sought to compete, even though at St. Vitale, the shimmering and curved surfaces create a more ephemeral effect. Nonetheless, at the Palatine Chapel we see the beginnings of an internal facade and of the search to bring unity to various architectural elements—the openings, cornice lines, revetments, and columns—while still providing for liturgical needs.

As the burial place of Charlemagne and the setting for imperial coronations, the Palatine Chapel became, in time, a dynastic shrine and an icon of imperial power. It was likely also viewed as an incarnation of the heavenly Jerusalem: it cannot be a coincidence that the circumference of its inner octagon comes to 144 Carolingian feet, just as the walls of the heavenly Jerusalem described in the book of Revelation come to 144 cubits.

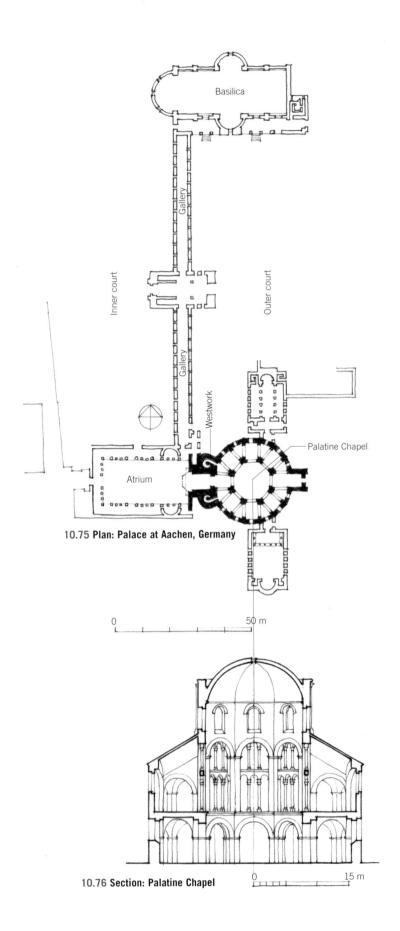

10.75 Plan: Palace at Aachen, Germany

0   50 m

10.76 Section: Palatine Chapel

0   15 m

10.78 Pictorial view: Abbey Church of St. Riquier, near Amiens, France

10.77 Interior of the dome, Palatine Chapel

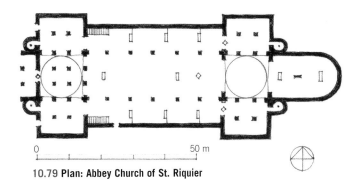

10.79 Plan: Abbey Church of St. Riquier

0   50 m

Architects could, of course, no longer rely on concrete, the production techniques for which had been forgotten, and so churches of this era tend to be stark and simple volumetrically. Windows are small, round-headed, sparsely ornamented, and positioned high in the wall. It was an architecture that did not tax the spatial imagination yet one that yielded stable, solid forms and dark, mysterious interiors. It spoke a language of clarity. Walls were not only thick but solid-looking. The transept, a minor element in the 5th-century basilica churches of Rome, became integral to the design. This would set in play the need for innovations in vaulting and then for an increasingly intricate relationship between inside and outside that would become the fundamental issue of subsequent medieval European architecture. But vaulting at the time was to a large extent a thing of the future: most Carolingian buildings had wooden roofs.

The Abbey Church of St. Riquier in northern France, not far from Amiens, though it is no longer extant, can be reconstructed from descriptions and old views. Completed in 799 CE, it followed the basic plan, with towers soaring from cylindrical bases. The external appearance was of clear geometry, solid walls, and small windows. The building was accessed in the Roman manner via an atrium as well as transept entrances. The atrium stood in front of a massive structure surmounted by a cylindrical tower. The monastery had a population of about three hundred monks and one hundred novices, in addition to the servants and serfs. The abbey was dedicated to the Holy Trinity and was connected to two smaller sanctuaries dedicated to St. Benedict and the Virgin Mary, all connected by walls and porticoes.

Conforming to the new liturgy, there was a processional path through the church, which was designed to allow the various altars to be visited in sequence. (The church contained a collection of twenty-five relics.) This processional movement through the church was to become a mainstay of medieval religious practice. Also new was the addition of an autonomous spatial zone behind the altar that accommodated the monks. This church-behind-a-church, or choir, was to become an important element in the church design of the Middle Ages. Also significant was the design of the tower over the transept crossing.

10.81 Temple of the Inscriptions, Palenque, near Chiapas, Mexico

10.80 Mayan territory

Mayan City-States

In the 8th and 9th centuries, the Mayan city-states of the Yucatán dominated the peninsula. In the period from 600 to 750 CE, the city of Palenque, located in the foothills of the Chiapas *altiplano*, began to expand under the leadership of the king Pacan and his two sons. Palenque is set into the hillside and laid out to take advantage of the contours and natural cleavage formed by the Otulum River, which passes through the city; water from it was diverted to the Palenque's central palace, the city's most remarkable building, via a long corbel-vaulted tunnel. The Palenque architects set corbeled vaults parallel to one another, which not only created greater interior spaces unlike the solid masses of most Mayan buildings but also stabilized the whole structure. This is one reason Palenque's buildings have aged so well. Their rooftop ornamental superstructure was also made as a roofcomb, which further reduced the structure's overall weight.

Palenque's palace sits on a broad platform that is centrally located to visually command the site. On one side, the palace dominates the edge of the Otulum River; on the other, its platform and profile define the edges of Palenque's central plaza. The palace complex opens toward the hills, although the monumental stairs are on the north and west sides. This indicates that access to the palace, as one might expect, was carefully regulated. The interior is dominated by two courts that take up half the complex and are separated by a long double-vaulted building that was the palace's original core. The south half of the palace is labyrinthine, with a dense network of interconnected chambers.

Visually, the palace's most recognizable structure is the four-story tower that rises just outside the west courtyard. It is unique in Mayan architecture, and its purpose is still undetermined. To the southwest of the palace complex is the so-called Temple of the Inscriptions (683 CE), which is famous because its foundation contains the tomb of K'inich Janaab Pakal. Unlike most tombs in the base of pyramids (as at Tikal, where they are completely interred within their superstructure), Pakal's tomb remained accessible from a stairway at the top of the temple. In the access stairway, can therefore be found the explicit spatialization of one of the cardinal ideologies of Mayan religious practice: that rulers and generations to come ruled because of their connection to their ancestors, and that honoring and maintaining an ongoing relationship with those ancestors was critical to their being and welfare. The stelae on Pakal's sarcophagus show him passing through the underworld in the process of becoming an ancestor. During the 8th century, the city came under increasing stress, in concert with most other classic Mayan city-states, and there was no new elite construction in the ceremonial center. Palenque was eventually abandoned.

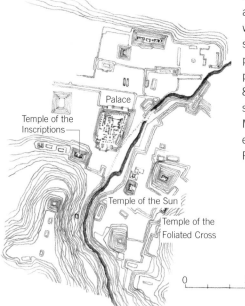

10.82 Plan of Palenque

10.83 Ball court, Copán, Honduras

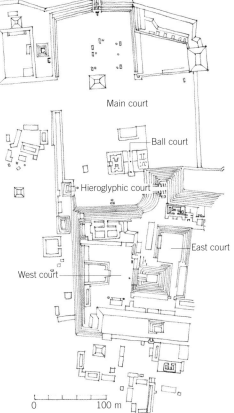

10.84 Plan of Copán

Copán

Located in a mountain valley of the Copán River on the western edge of Honduras, Copán is the southernmost of the major Mayan cities. One of the largest Mayan centers, Copán was the capital of a state covering several hundred square kilometers between 400 and 820 CE. The site is about 600 meters above sea level, above the jungles and rain forests of the lowland Mayas. Although occupied for about two thousand years, the main visible buildings were built in the period between 600 and 900 CE. The excavated ruins cover about 40 acres and consist of the main acropolis and five plazas. Like the ancestral complex of Tikal, the main structure at Copán is an agglomerative megacomplex, built over a period of six hundred years, which has formed into a gigantic platform with an assorted collection of masonry temples, palaces, ball courts, plazas, tombs, carved stelae, and altars, all dating mostly from between 695 and 800 CE.

Like the acropolis at Monte Albán, the surrounding mountains of the Copán River valley offered rich possibilities for dramatic landscape alignments. In particular, the Copán ball court, which sits between the main plaza and the acropolis, is aligned so that a view through it, which is also the main view from atop the acropolis, seems to exactly echo the angles of the steep hills beyond. The Copán main group, as is typical of Mesoamerican ceremonial centers, is oriented to the cardinal directions along the longer north-south axis, with the heavier concentration of built-up terraces and palaces to the south and a main plaza to the north. The main plaza is entered from the east. A subsidiary plaza leads into the vast rectangular space of the main bounded plaza, with a low, three-level platform mound in the middle. A ball court and subsidiary platform abut the south end of the main plaza, just before a monumental set of stairways leads up to the higher levels of the royal complex. A platform pyramid sits in the middle of the high terrace, which is edged by a series of palaces and tombs. The northern edge of the main plaza extends out into a T, forming another pyramid. The steep western stairway is a famous hieroglyphic stairway whose 2,200 glyphs relate the story of the last Copán dynasty.

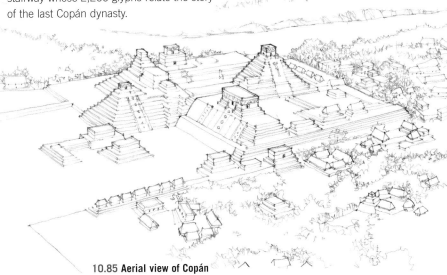

10.85 Aerial view of Copán

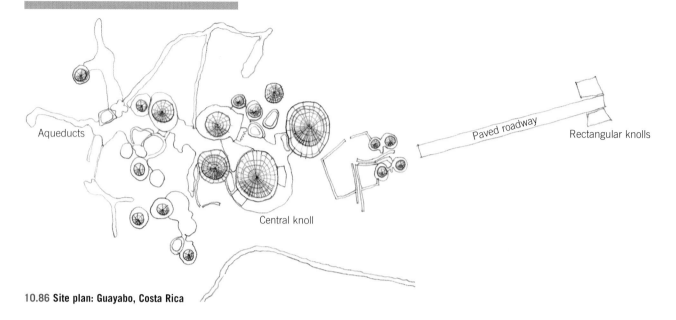

10.86 Site plan: Guayabo, Costa Rica

Aqueducts

Central knoll

Paved roadway

Rectangular knolls

Quirigua

Cauac Sky became king of Quirigua in 725 CE, while it was still a part of the state of Copán, but after he defeated and captured Eighteen Rabbit, king of Copán, in 738 CE, Quirigua became independent. The city, which rests in the floodplains of the Motagua River, has at its core a gigantic rectangular plaza, oriented north-south and studded with some of the largest Mayan stelae and monoliths ever discovered. Its main platform mounds and palace group are clustered at its south end. A freestanding, solitary pyramid sits off-center at one end of the great plaza; its other side lines up with a much smaller, better defined plaza, with a ball court in its center. A monumental flight of stairs at the southern edge of this ball court plaza leads to the main set of terraces and platform mounds that support the principal palaces. The Jade Sky Palace at the southernmost and highest point of the complex lines up on axis with the great plaza, forming its visual terminus, although access to it is carefully regulated. Both the palaces front their own private raised plaza, which they share with another, the so-called Palace 1B5. The embankments and shape of the western edge of the acropolis indicate that the Motagua may have flowed along its edge at one time, so that the palaces would have directly overlooked the river.

Guayabo

South of Mexico, in Costa Rica, archaeologists have uncovered traces of a significant urban settlement near the town of Guayabo. Human occupation of the site dates back to 1000 BCE, but the most recent studies reveal that Guayabo reached its peak from 300 to 700 CE. The culture was influenced by the Mayan's and belongs to the southernmost edge of what is known as Mesoamerica. The city consisted of large, conical wood-and-thatch houses with several internal stories built on stone foundations. Paved roads connected the city to the fields and the aqueducts that brought water into the city center.

10.87 Pictorial view of Guayabo

1000 CE

The turn of the millennium saw extensive temple-building programs throughout South and Southeast Asia. Thousands of temples arose. They were not built by one single kingdom; rather several kingdoms used temple architecture to vie for wealth and influence. Among them were older kingdoms, like the Pratiharas, and new kingdoms, like the Gangas, the Chandellas, and the Solankis. Eventually, the Cholas in south India would control a territory that reached from the Ganges in the north to the island of Sri Lanka in the south. The Khmer in Cambodia were also building grand temples in their capital city on the Angkor Plain; the Srivijaya in Indonesia were great temple builders as well. All of this was to some degree a consequence of the weakening of the Silk Route, a result of political disruptions in north China that forced the Song to look to the south for economic leverage and trade. While the Song territories, crisscrossed with a network of newly established towns, developed a strong mercantile economy, the Liao in the north, who had adopted Lamaist Buddhism, created new hybrid monasteries, thereby establishing the first firm Chinese connection to Tibet. In Japan, meanwhile, a shift in power from the emperor to the aristocracy was accompanied by the growth of a new form of Buddhism, popular in contemporary Song China, known as Pure Land Buddhism.

In the Islamic world, the political and religious patterns that were to determine the power gambits of these regions for centuries to come began to emerge. Islam had divided itself into different political entities, with the differences between Sunni and Shi'ite becoming irreversible. From west to east we find the Berber Almoravids, who took control of Spain and linked it with their home base around Marrakech; the Shi'ite Fatimids, who controlled Algeria and Egypt; the Sunni Seljuk Turkomans, who had subdued Persia and whose leader became the new caliph in 1055; and the largely Sunni Ghaznavid Empire, stretching from Afghanistan to northern India. All were great mosque and palace builders. The Seljuks remain the most impressive, however, as they imposed a particularly coherent political, religious, and economic architecture on their territory. The Silk Route, though diminished, continued to flourish, with the Armenian capital, Ani, becoming a significant stop. Another important city was Cairo, which had, under the Fatimids, been provided with several new mosques and palaces.

In Europe, the struggle for dominance was led by the Ottonian kings in Germany and the Normans in England. Both used a combination of religious and military institutions to stamp their authority on the land. The Ottonians combined monasteries with local market towns, whereas the Normans reorganized the entire legal and religious landscape of England. The visible result, in architectural terms, was the appearance of cathedrals, castles, and monasteries that tended to blend continental and Islamic features, partially creating the base of what would later be known as Gothic architecture. Also developing was a complex monastic network, with the Cluniacs, in particular, controlling monasteries across France, Italy, Germany, and Spain and creating a rapid development in architectural language. At the same time, another type of religious geography emerged as a result of the developing pilgrimage routes that linked distant destinations and spread architectural knowledge from place to place. Italy was slowly developing its own architectural expressions, including the baptistery, which was located at the center of the town next to the duomo, or cathedral, and was paid for with city funds rather than—as was common in France and England—through royal patronage and taxes.

In the Yucatán Peninsula, the Mayas were at their height. In the valley of Oaxaca, the Zapotecs continued to construct new cities, and in the north, the Toltecs were in the process of building a powerful new dynasty destined to define the form and shape of the cultures that the Spanish conquistadores encountered five hundred years later.

Dynastic City-States
ca. 250–900 CE

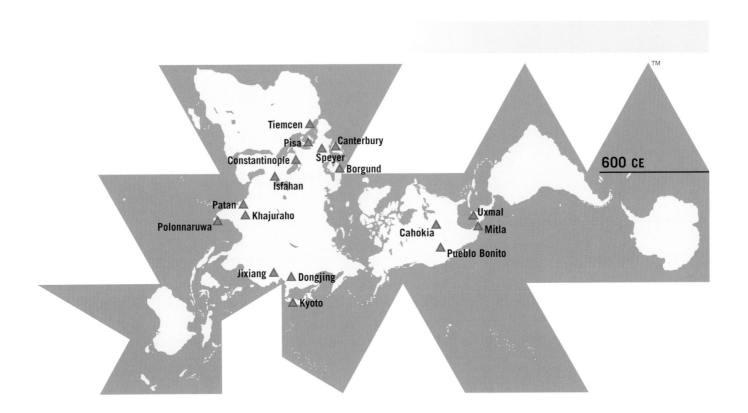

TM

Tiemcen ▲

Pisa ▲ Canterbury

Constantinople ▲ Speyer ▲

▲ Borgund

Isfahan ▲

600 CE

Patan ▲

Polonnaruwa ▲ Khajuraho ▲

Uxmal ▲

Cahokia ▲ Mitla ▲

Pueblo Bonito ▲

Jixiang ▲ Dongjing ▲

Kyoto ▲

Mosque at Qayrawan ▲
670–863

Toltec-Chichén City-State
ca. 1000–1200

▲ **Mitla**   ▲ **Uxmal**
750–1521   800–1000

Pueblo Cultures   Mississippian Cultures
ca. 700–1600   ca. 800–1600

▲ **Cahokia**   ▲ **Pueblo Bonito**   ▲ **Serpent Mound**
ca. 700–1400   Begun 920   ca. 1060

South Asia: Rise of regional states
ca. 500–1300

▲ **Rajarajeshwara Temple**   ▲ **Sun Temple at Modhera**   ▲ **Lingaraja Temple**
Late 10th century   1022–27   ca. 1100

Lakshamana Temple ▲   ▲ **Khandariya Mahadeva Temple**   ▲ **Jain Temples on Mt. Abu**
ca. 950   1000–1025   10th to 16th centuries

▲ **Parakramabahu Palace**
12th century

800 CE   **1000 CE**   **1200 CE**

T'ang Dynasty   Northern Song Dynasty   Southern Song Dynasty
618–906   960–1127   1127–79

▲ **Dulesi Monastery**   ▲ **Yingxian Timber Pagoda**
ca. 984   1056

Japan: Late Heian Period   ▲ **Byodo-in**
ca. 900–1185   1053

Byzantine Empire
330–1453

Cathedral of Ani ▲ ▲ **Sanahin**   ▲ **Church of Christ Pantokrator**
989–1001   10th to 13th centuries   1118–43

Kievan Russia   ▲ **Church of the Tithe**   ▲ **Borgund Stave Church**
ca. 860–1240   989–96 CE   12th century

Ottonian Dynasty
936–1024

St. Michael in Hildesheim ▲   ▲ **Speyer Cathedral**   ▲ **Abbey Church of St. Foy**
1001–33   1040–1137   Begun 1050

▲ **Canterbury Cathedral**   ▲ **Krac des Chevaliers**
1042–1185   ca. 1100

Norman rule in England   ▲ **Durham Cathedral**
1066–1154   1093–1133

Italian City-States
Late 11th to early 16th centuries

◄ **Church of the Holy Sepulcher**   ▲ **Cathedral of Pisa**   **Baptistery of Parma** ▲
ca. 335 to 12th century   1063–1118   1196–1270

▲ **Santiago de Compostela**
1075–1128

Abbasid Caliphate   Fatimid Caliphate   Umayyad Caliphate
750–1258   969–1171   929–1031

▲ **Great Mosque of Isfahan**   ▲ **Al-Azhar Mosque**   ▲ **Mosque of Tinmal**   **Sultan Han** ▶
8th to 16th centuries   970–72   1153–54   1229

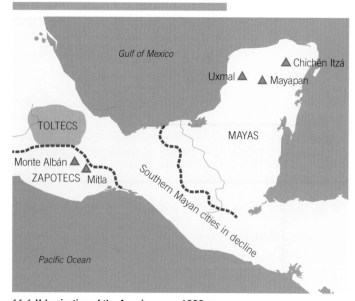

11.1 Urbanization of the Americas, ca. 1000 CE

North
● Pueblo Culture
● Cahokia
● Mississippi cultures

Central
○ Zapotecs
○ Toltecs
● Post-Classical Mayas

○ Tairona, Columbia

South
○ Chimor, Peruvian shore
○ Chachapoyas, Peruvian mountains
○ Aymara kingdoms, Bolivia
○ Mapuche, Chile

11.2 Trade in the Americas, ca. 1000 CE

Mayan Uxmal

Uxmal was one of several Mayan city-states competing for territory, but by 900 CE it had become the regional capital and most likely the largest of the Mayan cities. A network of stone roadways, called *sakbehoob*, connected Uxmal to Nohpat and Kabah. Chichén Itzá was a major ally. Uxmal's elite lived in a sprawling palace complex located on the area's highest ground. A stone wall with regularly spaced openings enclosed the area. At the southern end of the complex, built into a small mound, was the main platform mound, wedged between a gigantic platform with the so-called Governor's Palace to its east and a series of rectangular courts to its west. The platform mound faced north, its broad stairs visible from a great distance. The northern edge of the palace complex was dominated by a huge quadrangular palace, called the Nunnery (890–915 CE). To its immediate east, the largest structure, a steep platform mound with a rare oval-shaped base, was the so-called Temple of the Magician. Scores of other buildings, arranged in quadrangles of various size and shape, were distributed through the complex; most were residential units, and a few were platform mounds. Similar structures outside the wall were dispersed across a much larger urban residential area. The currently used names for many of the structures were coined by the conquering Spanish and do not indicate the actual functions of the buildings.

Chan-Chaak-K'ak'nal-Ajaw (9th century), who ruled the city, commissioned the Governor's Palace, the Nunnery quadrangle, and very likely a rebuilding of the Temple of the Magician. The latter, originally built in the 6th century, was reconstructed at least four times. While the exact reasons for its unusual shape are still uncertain, its dramatic profile dominates the setting, contrasting with the orthogonal geometries of the Governor's Palace and the Nunnery quadrangle. Its limestone core was originally covered with smooth plaster and painted red with accents in blue, yellow, and black.

11.3 Uxmal palace complex, Mexico

11.4 Temple of the Magician, Uxmal

11.5 Ball court at Uxmal

The Governor's Palace, standing as a clearly defined entity in its own right, was both the royal residence and a sort of council house. Its huge terrace was linked to the main platform mound at the corner, signifying their continuity. Although the platform was accessible only from the west, from the middle of the complex, the main structure of the Governor's Palace, an astonishing 100-meter-long building, faced east, away from the center, and overlooked a distant vista from across a vast platform. The rising sun would have brightly illuminated its twenty-four rooms, which were clustered into three compartments. Narrow passages with steep triangular roofs separated them. Each room was a set of two, one opening onto the front, and the other behind it, against a blank back wall. The broad frieze on the Governor's Palace is its chief glory. Made from over twenty thousand individual stones depicting serpents, thatched huts, masks of the rain god Chak, human busts, and geometrical motifs, the frieze is a kaleidoscope of Mayan mythology. A gigantic stone sculpture above the main entrance shows Lord Chak on a throne surrounded by serpents. The friezes on the four buildings of the Nunnery quadrangle together depict the Mayan cosmography, or the order of the universe as conceived by the Uxmal. The southern building—also known as the *itzam nah*, or "conjuring house"—bears the icons of the Lords of Xibalba, the underworld.

The south building of the Nunnery quadrangle aligns axially with the ball court, the symbolic gate to Xibalba. The eastern frieze depicts the cyclic themes of world creation, while the western frieze depicts scenes of war, sacrifice, death, and rebirth. Together, the eastern and western friezes symbolize the diurnal and annual journeys, or "lives," of the sun, and its compact with the earth, inhabited by humans. The northern building, erected on the highest platform of the quadrangle, has a frieze that depicts celestial figures symbolic of the world of "heaven." In the middle of the quadrangle stood a stone column, representing the *wakaj-chan*, or "world tree," and an altar representing the first stone of the cosmic hearth.

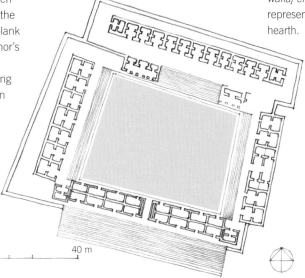

0   40 m

11.6 Plan: The Nunnery quadrangle at Uxmal

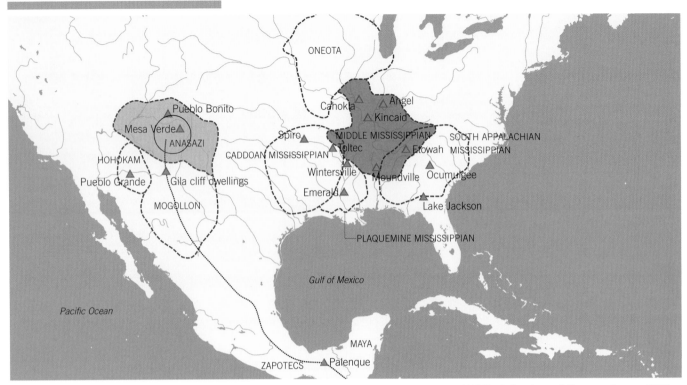

11.7 North America and Mesoamerica, ca. 1000 CE

Cahokia

By the 11th century, Hopewell Culture cities had fallen on hard times. The new power centers were now farther west along the Mississippi River. This change coincided with the emergence of a chiefdom society that adopted a comparatively large-scale, intensive, maize-based agriculture. It had taken about a thousand years for corn cultivation to make it this far north, and its impact was quite dramatic. For the first time there is a clear settlement hierarchy and the construction of truncated pyramid mounds, with temples or burial buildings atop such mounds. Soon a network of larger and smaller city cultures developed in a large triangular area down the Mississippi River at its western edge and eastward into Georgia, along other rivers. Farther to the west, in more arid conditions, were the equally strong pueblo cultures.

One of the most important of the new cities was Cahokia (700–1400, near St. Louis). Its residents benefited from the Mississippi's alluvial deposits as well as from the trade that brought copper from the upper Great Lakes, mica from the southern Appalachians, and seashells from the Gulf of Mexico. Twenty thousand people lived in Cahokia at its peak in the 12th century,

making it the largest city north of Mexico. Its center of its religious precinct was the so-called Monks Mound. Begun around 1000 CE, it was surrounded by terraces and smaller mounds roughly on axis. The Cahokians, who seemed to have known of Central American advances in astronomy, built several calendrical circles with posts of

red cedar. A circle of 24 posts was enlarged to one of 36, then to one of 48, and finally to one of 60 posts. Their last and largest circle was built only to an arc of 12 posts, but if completed, it would have had 72 posts. At the equinoxes, the post marking sunrise, due east, aligns perfectly with the front of Monks Mound. The city was abandoned in

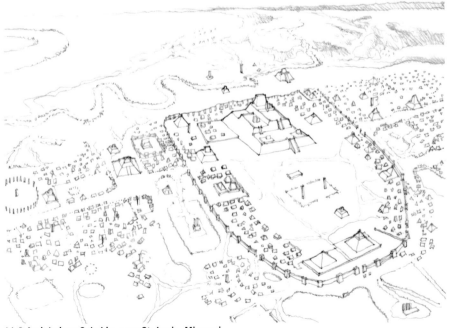

11.8 Aerial view: Cahokia, near St. Louis, Missouri

the 15th century. Overhunting, environmental degradation, and social conflict may have all played a part. Whereas Mississippi cultures in Ohio faltered, they continued to thrive farther south in Georgia and Alabama until the arrival of the Europeans.

Serpent Mound

In Ohio, where there had once been the Hopewell Culture, a new and more modest culture emerged, known by archaeologists as the Fort Ancient Culture (1000–1650). Settlements composed of circular and rectangular homes constructed of twigs and thatch and situated around an open plaza were enclosed by stockades, suggesting an increase in the level of conflict that perhaps accounted for the breakdown of the Hopewell Culture. Settlements were rarely permanent, usually shifting to a new location after one or two generations when the resources surrounding the village were exhausted. The diet was composed mainly of maize, squash, and beans, supplemented by hunting and fishing in nearby forests and rivers.

Though this culture was a step down from Hopewell Culture, it nonetheless managed to construct some remarkable earthworks, including Serpent Mound (ca. 1060), in Adams County, Ohio. The mound consists of a low berm made of stones and compacted clay placed on a promontory that rises 30 meters over a small river. Measured along its coils and curves, it stretches 400 meters. The head of the serpent was placed at the crest of the bluff. Several theories have been proposed as to the meaning of the mound. For some American tribes, the serpent was considered evil, but for others, it was thought of as beneficial. In all cases, however, the snake was considered a potent force. (The Hopi snake dance was used principally as a prayer for rain.) Astrological alignments have been proposed, and indeed, the snake's head is aligned to the summer solstice and the various curves to other celestial events. The village was located across the river from the mound. The fate of the Fort Ancient people is not know for sure, but there was a period of depopulation shortly before the appearance of early European explorers and missionaries, during which the Wyandot, Delaware, Shawnee, and Miami tribes, among others, moved into the area.

11.9 Serpent Mound, Adams County, Ohio

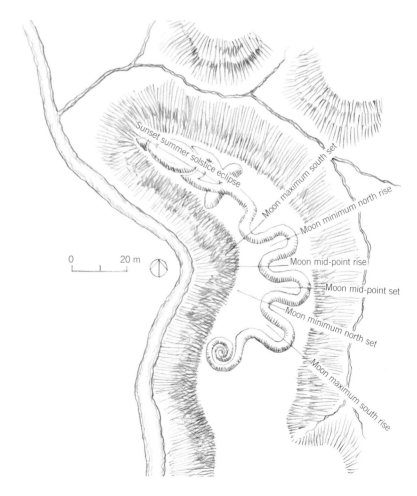

11.10 Plan: Serpent Mound

Pueblo Bonito

Modern borders cause the ruins of the southwestern United States to be viewed as discrete from those of Mesoamerica. In reality, the settlements in places such as Chaca Canyon and Mesa Verde made up the northern frontier of the Mesoamerican world and were not separated from its influence. However, because of their unique climatic circumstances, they developed a very self-defined culture. By 600 CE, the area came to be occupied by three distinct groups: the Hisatsinom (also called Anasazi) to the north and the Mogollon and Hohokam to the south, the latter seemingly having originally been Mayas. They had begun to change from a migratory farming culture to a sedentary one, building permanent houses with an increasing level of sophistication. One of the reasons for this change was the rapid increase in population beginning around 700 CE due to improved weather conditions and more copious rainfall—the dry and arid conditions of today were not those of the 9th century. By 1100, there were twelve major Pueblo cities and hundreds of small clutches of houses—one of the most impressive urban structures north of Mexico bespeaking a high level of social organization.

One of these groups has traditionally been known as Anasazi, but since that is a Navajo word meaning "ancient enemy," the Pueblo people prefer to use the Hopi word *Hisatsinom*, meaning "the old ones." What they called themselves is not exactly known. The largest Hisatsinom settlement was Pueblo Bonito (Spanish for "beautiful town"). Located beneath a massive cliff, part of which has since caved in, the city had a D-shaped plan, with masses of rooms and circular ceremonial structures called kivas surrounding two large plazas. The rows of rooms each rose one story before stepping back from the one below, giving the whole an impression of a terraced amphitheater. Indeed, it has been suggested that one of the city's functions was to provide a place for viewing ritual dancing.

Kivas, a local building type with a very long history and broad distribution, were an essential part of the Hisatsinom culture and architecture. They originated as circular storehouses, often nothing more than deep-

11.11 Pueblo Bonito, Chaco Canyon, New Mexico

pit houses, plastered on the inside with smooth adobe. But they soon became semi-subterranean temples, serving as communal spaces for the performance and viewing of ritual dances. Each kiva was the province of a social unit, and there were several kivas in each village. They were only for men; women were allowed in only on special occasions. In Pueblo Bonito, among the regular-size kivas, were two that were over 18 meters across and that probably served the entire city. Though these kivas were built above ground, the subterranean effect was maintained by

constructing rooms all around and filling in any empty space with earth. Kivas were equipped with a central fireplace, a low masonry bench around the wall, and four wooden posts. Some kivas had an underfloor ventilating system and a subfloor vault to the west of the fireplace. Their flat roofs had a smoke hole in the center and served as an entrance by means of a ladder. The sandstone masonry walls at Pueblo Bonito consisted of a loose rubble center-faced on both sides with artfully placed sandstone bricks.

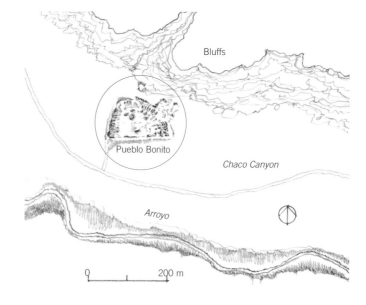

11.12 Site of Pueblo Bonito

Construction of Pueblo Bonito began in about 920 CE, and the city was modified over the course of three centuries. Early research attempted to relate its construction directly to more contemporary Pueblo architecture, whose structure reflects the social order of its inhabitants. The evidence, however, indicates that this was not the case at Pueblo Bonito. Nonetheless, its construction would have required a complex coordination of labor and materials. Tens of thousands of pine beams, used for wall supports and roof structures, came from a forest 90 kilometers away. Pueblo Bonito's overall orientation is north-south, which became typical of all structures erected by the Hisatsinom, but the architecture integrates the midpoint and extremes of the cycles of the sun and the moon into its layout. Though the highly disciplined architecture could suggest a strong hierarchical social order, the Hisatsinom are believed to have had a fairly egalitarian society.

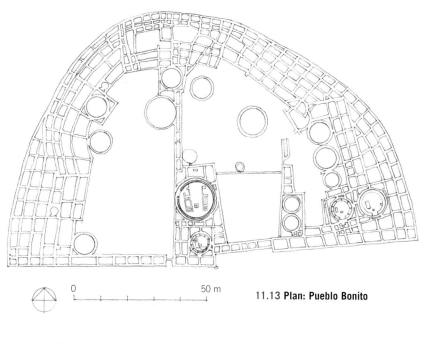

0   50 m

11.13 Plan: Pueblo Bonito

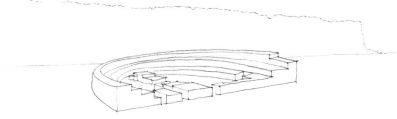

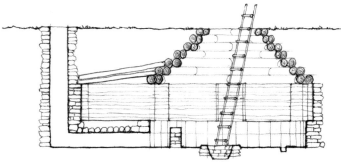

11.14 Plan and section: Traditional kiva

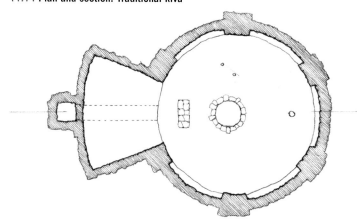

The Hohokam also soon began to design cities, such as Casa Grande (in Arizona, ca. 1100), having developed canals to bring water to their fields. Archaeologists have discovered hundreds of miles of these canals in the Gila River valley, as well as the Salt River valley of Phoenix and elsewhere. By the 13th century, long periods of drought brought that culture to an end and changed the social landscape of the region. They were replaced by the Pima and Tohono O'odham tribes. It was the Pimas who called their predecessors the Hohokam, meaning the "vanished ones."

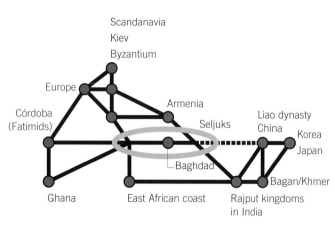

11.15 Eurasian trade diagram, ca. 1000 CE

11.16 South Asia temple sites

Rise of the Rajput Kingdoms

Between 800 and 1000 CE, the Gurjara-Pratiharas from the west, the Rashtrakutas from the Deccan Plateau, and the Buddhist Palla kings from the east were locked in a battle for control of the central Gangetic Plains. Kanauj, through which all of the major trade routes south, east, and north passed, was the prized possession. The three contenders, by turn, had all managed to capture Kanauj, but two centuries of warfare weakened all three to such a degree that they all eventually collapsed. The resultant power vacuum in northern India led to a series of new kingdoms. Some of these, like the Chalukyas, were former vassal states that now declared independence. More significantly, a large number of semitribal and tribal communities that had previously been subjugated emerged as kingdoms in their own right. These are known collectively as the Rajput kingdoms because of their shared caste identity (*rajput* means "royal son"). Among these, the Solankis (western and central India), the Chandellas (north-central India), and the Orissans (east and central India) were eminent temple builders. The capital of the Solankis, Patan, was the largest city in India and the tenth-largest city in the world.

Most of the tribal communities were of the lowest caste, so their new kings had to acquire the Kshatriya, or warrior caste. To accomplish this, the kings laid claim to a mythical lineage and, more importantly, began to build and support temples as a way to legitimate their rule. The result was one of the largest temple-building campaigns in India, with new forms coming into being. Regional deities and gods were accepted into the expanding Hindu pantheon, and worship was conducted in regional languages. Other than the introduction of Islam, which was yet to come, the patchwork of regional identities that is modern India was established at this time. Contemporary India still has twenty-two official languages (and over five hundred dialects) with clear geographical divisions. It is therefore useful to think of India as one does of Europe: as an interrelated network of distinct regional areas. While the various regions share certain cultural aspects, their identities are as diverse as those of European countries. The same applies to their architecture. To think of a unified Indian architecture is as useful and as useless as thinking of "European architecture."

Rani-ni-Vav at Patan

Access to and distribution of fresh water played a critical role in all of Indian society, where water had both an economic and a symbolic value. But Solanki wells were no simple affairs. The step well called the Rani-ni-Vav, or "Queen's Step Well," was built at Anhilwara (Patan) in the 11th century, in memory of Bhimdev I (1022–63) by his widowed queen, Udaymati. It consists of a long stairway leading down to the water table. The entire excavation is lined with a multitiered colonnaded "facade" supported by elaborately carved stone columns and beams. It was partially roofed, with light filtering even into the deepest parts 28 meters below the surface. The reason for such splendor was that the Rani-ni-Vav (*rani* means "queen"; *vav*, "well") served as a supplementary palace for the queen and her attendants. The natural temperature of the earth, combined with the evaporative effects of the wind passing over the water, turned the step well into a subterranean world of cool repose during the blistering summer months. Since the well went so far down, its walls had to be buttressed against implosion. This was achieved by building heavy stone buttresses at the well's mouth and bracing its interior.

In a more symbolic sense, the step well was also another version of the ghats of Varanasi or the water tank of the Sun Temple at Modhera, except that the step well was fully inhabitable. Much of Solanki architecture was eventually destroyed by invading Islamic armies. The Rani-ni-Vav survived intact because it was intentionally filled in with earth by the retreating Solankis.

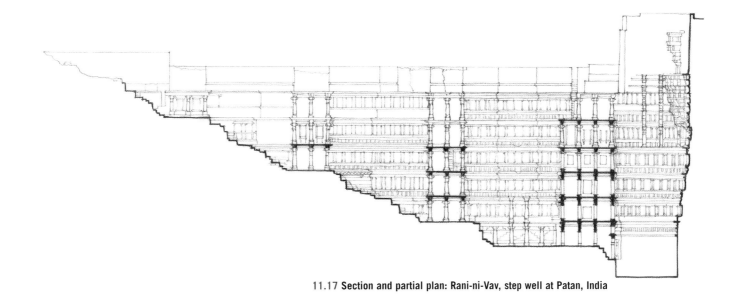

11.17 Section and partial plan: Rani-ni-Vav, step well at Patan, India

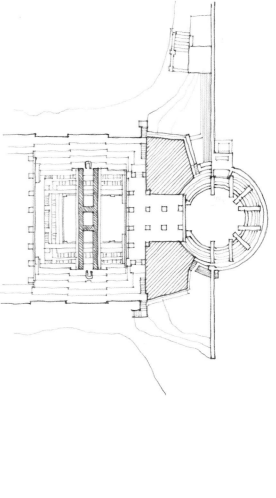

11.18 Rani-ni-Vav, step well at Patan

Sun Temple at Modhera

Of the various Rajput kingdoms, the Solankis, who ruled in Rajasthan and Gujarat, were among the most zealous temple builders. They traded not only with the other kingdoms of South Asia but also with Central Asia. Though principally worshipers of Shiva, they claimed lineage from Pandu, a mythological king during ancient Vedic times. Through that connection, they legitimized their tradition of solar cults. The Solanki royal temple, dedicated to Surya, or the sun, was made from golden sandstone in a tripartite axial arrangement. The main shrine is in the west, a rectangular water tank in the east, and a *mandapa* in between, all integrated into a single composition. The *mandapa* is connected to the steps surrounding the water tank by a freestanding gateway, or *torana*, that marks the top of a flight of steps. While the aesthetic expression of all the temple's elements is in itself quite remarkable, it is the delicate richness with which all the columns, brackets, cusped and wavy arches, and roofs are carved that stands out. Their distinction lies in how they function optically to connect the building's elements. Standing on the western edge of the tank and looking eastward toward the main temple, the view seems to be of one building composed of the steps leading upward to the *mandapa*. But the conical top belongs to the shrine in the distance, and the entrance of the *mandapa* is actually the *torana* in the foreground.

11.19 **Sun Temple at Modhera, India**

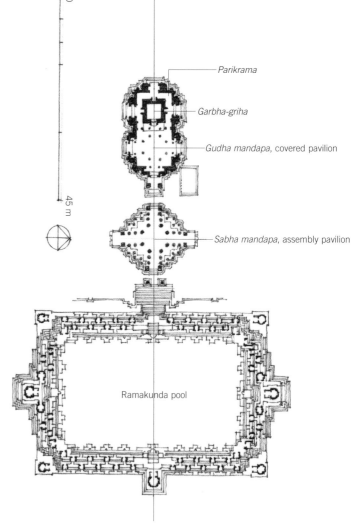

Parikrama

Garbha-griha

Gudha mandapa, covered pavilion

Sabha mandapa, assembly pavilion

Ramakunda pool

11.20 **Plan: Sun Temple at Modhera**

That this effect is deliberate is evidenced by the access steps, which are a separate element excavated from the ground between the edge of the tank and the *torana*, thereby establishing an optical connection between the two. There is also an echo effect between the implied triangular profile of the temple and the inverted V of the steps, and also between the conical dome above and the steps at the base of the inverted V, which widen out into the tank. The entirety creates an uncanny reflective effect, even when there is no water present.

11.21 Detail: Sun Temple at Modhera

11.22 Ramakunda pool, Sun Temple at Modhera

11.23 Lakshmana Temple *sikhara*

11.24 Lakshmana Temple at Khajuraho, India

Chandellas

In a brief period of about 175 years, the Chandellas, who called their kingdom Jejakabhukti, built more than eighty temples in and around their capital of Khajuraho (ancient Khajjuravahaka). The crispness of their architectural forms and the close continuity in their order and language indicates that there must have been a core group of architects, or perhaps even a single architect-in-charge. Two of the main royal temples of the Chandellas were the Lakshmana (ca. 950 CE) and the Khandariya Mahadeva (1000–1025) temples.

Dedicated to Shiva, the Lakshmana rises on a high platform ensuring that, like all other Khajuraho temples, it is visible in the surrounding flat countryside from afar. Independent subsidiary shrines are located at the four corners of the platform, suggesting a sense of enclosure and defining a sacred precinct without the actual existence of a wall. Access is highly dramatic, via an axially placed stair to the platform and another set of stairs to the temple. The profile of the temple was itself something of a "stairway to heaven." The temple consists of three *mandapas* preceding the main *shikhara*. The *mandapas* are articulated in horizontal layers, while the main *shikhara* emphasizes the vertical. One of the key architectural issues is that the *mandapa* is no longer just a flat roofed box in front of the temple: it now has its own pyramidical roof that competes with the *shikhara* of the main shrine. From this time on, one of the main characteristics of Hindu temples is their silhouette.

One distinguishing feature of the Khajuraho temples is the manner in which their architects orchestrated the front elevations—not mathematically or geometrically, but perspectively. The front elevations of the *mandapas* are designed so that at eye level they all appear to nestle into each other perfectly. (This is similar to the design of the Sun Temple at Modhera.) The objective was not just aesthetic. The superstructure of every Hindu temple is conceived as a model of the universe; its purpose is to disclose to the believer the inherent order and beauty of that universe.

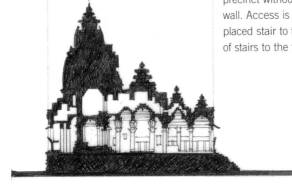

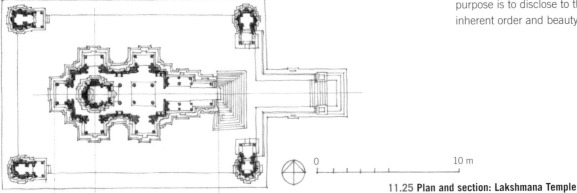

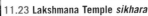

0   10 m

11.25 **Plan and section: Lakshmana Temple**

11.26 **Khandariya Mahadeva Temple, Khajuraho, India**

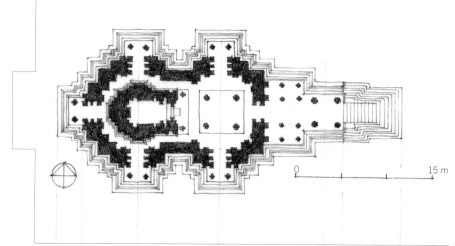

11.27 **Plan: Khandariya Mahadeva Temple**

Khandariya Mahadeva Temple

The Khandariya Mahadeva Temple (1000–1025), like the Lakshmana, sits on a high platform that it shares with another smaller temple, the Jagdambi, dedicated to the goddess Parvati. There are no corner shrines, so the profile of the Khandariya and its partner is silhouetted against the sky without distraction. Balancing the composition between the two temples is a small shrine resting on its own plinth. At 30 meters, including the 4-meter-high platform on which it rests, the Khandariya rises higher than all the other temples, but its strength lies not in its size, but in the quality of its architecture. Its profile is designed to represent the rhythms of a jagged mountain range, both in its outlines and in the composition of its parts. Unlike the Lakshmana, the Khandariya's four *mandapas* are articulated with distinctive mini-*shikharas* that cluster around the main *shikhara*. These mini-*shikharas* produce the sense of a rising wave while still being fully geometrical. The slight widening at the base, the strong horizontal protrusions of the porches, and the tightly bound faceting at the intersection of the *shikhara* and the *mandapa* make for an extraordinarily powerful composition. Because of their height, the porches give the visitor a sense of elevation above the quotidian. The interior of the sanctuary, however, is appropriately deep and dark, like a cave.

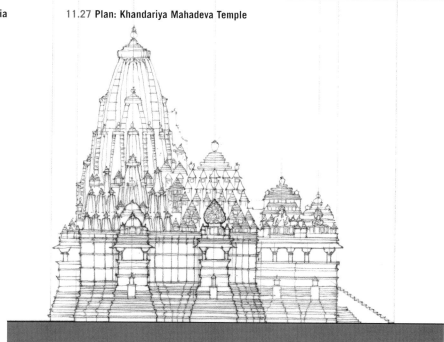

11.28 **Elevation: Khandariya Mahadeva Temple**

Unlike many Hindu temples, the Khandariya is lit by large openings located well above eye level. The effect is particularly spectacular in the circumambulation route, where the light coming from a high source casts dark shadows between the folds of the sculptures, bringing them into sharp relief. The openings are furnished with platforms and steps for attendants and musicians.

The Khajuraho temples are famous for their so-called erotic sculpture. Sexual acts of almost every kind are carved with the same attention to detail and fullness as all the other sculptures, underscoring the Chandellas' interest in Tantrism. This sexual sculpture, while present in abundance, is neither highlighted nor hidden; it is both an important part of the assemblage and a part of the wider variety of life depicted in the sculptural program.

11.29 **Tantric sculpture from Khandariya Mahadeva Temple**

Tantrism

The Chandella Rajputs, who were Gond tribesmen brought from obscurity into the caste through the bhakti cults, remained invested in aspects of their old animism—particularly in the rites associated with female fertility. Their practices therefore found sympathy among Tantra (anglicized as "Tantrism") practitioners, who held that veneration of the female deity was critical to attaining nirvana. Tantrics believed that through ascetic practices and esoteric rituals they could use the inherent divine power (*prana*) that flows through the universe (including one's own body) to attain spiritual goals. For this reason, Tantric worship makes elaborate use of mantras, or symbolic speech made up of words or phrases that are repeated over and over. Tantric practices required secret initiations by a guru or leader. A woman had to be present at every ritual because the female was the initiator of the action; the male could only be activated through union with a female. Routinely condemned by more orthodox Hindus, the Tantrics gained widespread acceptance among the nobility of the time, particularly the Rajputs. Tantrism was also an important force in contemporary Buddhism.

An example of an early Chandella Tantric structure is the Chausat Yogini Temple (mid-9th century), located 1 kilometer from Khajuraho. Its name literally means the "temple of sixty-four women saints." One of many such temples found in northern

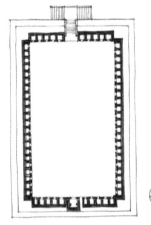

11.30 **Plan: Chausat Yogini Temple at Khajuraho, India**

India, it consists of an empty quadrangular enclosure surrounded by sixty-four small shrines, each with their own individual pyramidical *shikharas*; the main opening is on one of the smaller sides to the north. The center of the Chausat Yogini is visibly empty or open, in contrast to a typical Hindu temple dedicated to a male deity, in which the dominant temple would be in the middle. Unlike the Vaishnite and Shiavite temples, the Chausat Yogini Temple is oriented north-south.

11.31 **Chausat Yogini Temple**

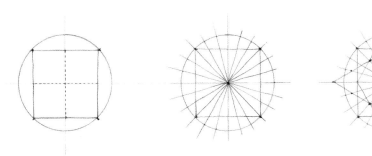
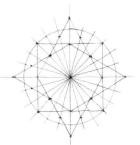
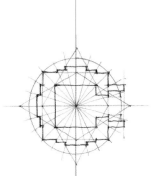

11.32 Geometric evolution of an Orissan temple plan (after Andreas Volwahsen)

Vastu-Shastras

In the 10th and 11th centuries, a series of technical manuals was published under such titles as *Vastu Shastra* ("Construction Treatise") and *Shilpa Shastra* ("Sculpture Treatise"); they provide insight into the highly codified language of temple design and construction. From these texts we know that a temple's overall design was handled by a chief Brahmin, known as a *sutradhar*. He based his work on an astrological diagram called a mandala, a graph that mapped the positions of stars, planets, deities, and the sun with respect to a particular site. Its design is based on the overlay of a square and a circle. The *sutradhar* chose from hundreds of mandalas, depending on the deity of the temple and the religious persuasion of the community. The temple's actual form was derived through a series of geometrical maneuvers designed to express the potency of the various planets and deities occupying the grid of the mandala. Radiating lines, the weight given to the primary directions, and special triangles all determined the location of the building's various parts. A complex system of faceting, known as *rathas*, determined the detailed articulation of the temple's surface. The purpose of the *rathas* was to enable multiple deities to share a single surface——in the vertical and horizontal plane—by suggesting superimposed layers. The final form was inevitably a heavily faceted pyramid. Once

the design had been determined, it was relayed to the master builder, whose craft was handed down through oral tradition. Sculpture and paintings were then finished by independent *shrenis* ("artisans").

The cosmic order expressed by a temple offers a vision of a pyramidal universe cascading downward in conceptual waves from a single point of origin that in itself is without form or substance. The objective of the worshipper, in apprehending this vision, was to devote himself or herself to ascending to that formless center, a task assisted by devotion to the temple's resident deity.

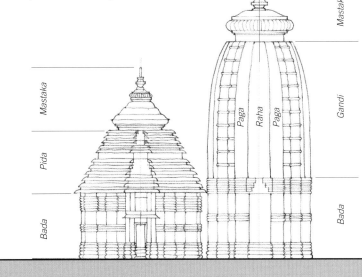

11.33 Orissan temple elements

Orissa and Lingaraja Temple

Another important kingdom was Orissa, located in eastern India south of Bengal, whose fertile rivers and ports were key to its wealth. Over the centuries, various dynasties ruled from its capital, Bhubaneshwar, which came to be home to about seven thousand Hindu temples, many of which were distributed around a sacred pool. A few hundred still stand. As Hinduism matured, the ruling dynasties grew in power, and their ritual practices became more and more elaborate, the temples of Bhubaneshwar grew in size and complexity. The temples were unique, as the *mandapa* was given its own pyramidical roof that had to be harmonized with the rising *shikhara* of the *garbha-griha* (which the Orissans call *rekha deul*). The emergence of this attempt at integration is seen at the Rajarani Temple (ca. 1000 CE).

11.34 Rajarani Temple, Bhubaneshwar, Orissa, India

Jagamohan   *Rekha deul*

11.35 Plan: Rajarani Temple

Rathas are the projections and recesses that form the *pagas*.

11.36 Lingaraja Temple, Bhubaneshwar, Orissa, India

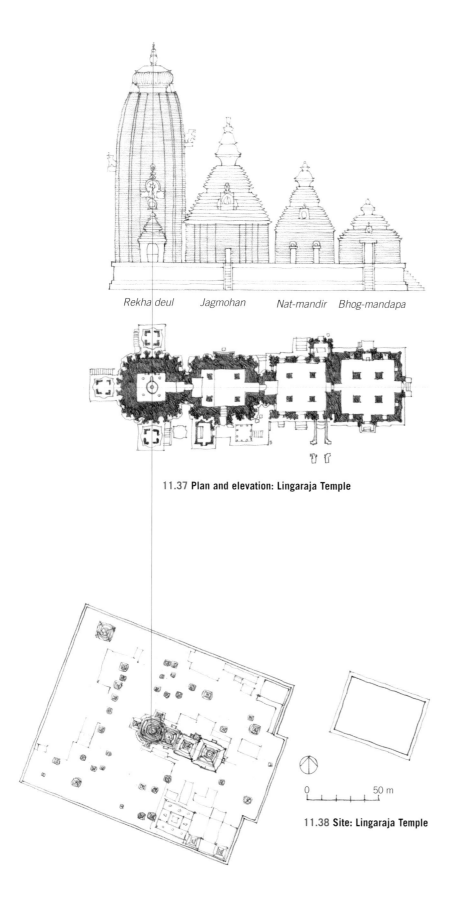

Rekha deul   *Jagmohan*   *Nat-mandir*   *Bhog-mandapa*

11.37 Plan and elevation: Lingaraja Temple

0 ⊢——————⊣ 50 m

11.38 Site: Lingaraja Temple

As the "king" of the Bhubaneshwar temples, the Lingaraja (literally, "the Phallus King," ca. 1100) was distinguished not only by its size but also by the presence of a row of three *jagmohans*. The rituals that would normally have been conducted in a single hall were here separated, enabling several rituals to occur simultaneously and creating the sense of a mini-pilgrimage in their performance. These *jagmohans*—a primary *jagmohan*, a *nat-mandir* ("dance hall"), and a *bhog-mandapa* ("collective ritual performance hall")—were about the same size, though each has a distinctive plan suited to its function. The *jagmohan* has a fully articulated exterior, making it a shrine in itself. The *nat-mandir* is airy and open so that its activities could be seen and heard in the surroundings. The *bhog-mandapa* duplicates the *jagmohan* and was probably added later to facilitate rituals by larger groups that could not access the innermost shrine. The Lingaraja's 37.5-meter-high *rekha deul*, which dominates the silhouette, has a distinctive profile, first rising almost vertically and then, only toward the top, curving inward, before yielding to a recessed neck that supports a wide *amalaka* resting on the backs of lions (an indication of royal patronage).

The Lingaraja sits in the middle of a quadrangular compound dotted with numerous small subsidiary shrines that were added over time to the main sequence in order to increase its potency. This proliferation is common in active Hindu temples and is described as the *parivar* (literally, the "family") of the main shrine, which is expected to change and grow in time as does a prosperous family around a reigning patriarch. Though the Lingaraja is now decommissioned, the nearby Jagannath Temple in Puri, also built by the Gangas in the 12th century, is still in use, and as a result, its *parivar* has grown. The compound is now completely saturated with subsidiary shrines, many built recently.

11.39 *A Teaching Session* (detail from a Shravanabelagola painting)

Jains

Many of the ministers employed in the Rajput courts were neither Hindus nor Buddhists but Jains, who were often the best financial experts and bankers available—an unintended consequence of their religion. Jainism originates in the teaching of the Mahavira, a contemporary of the Buddha from the 6th century BCE. (*Jain* is a corruption of the Sanskrit word *jina*, meaning "conqueror," the title given to Mahavira in Jain texts.) Like the Buddha, Mahavira preached a doctrine of asceticism and meditation, but Mahavira insisted that all forms of life were equivalent and that respect for life was essential for the purification of the human soul. Strictly ascetic Jains, known as Digambaras ("sky-clad," or naked), were thus expected not only to be vegetarians but also to eat only a fruit or vegetable that had broken off its plant of its own accord. Root vegetables like potatoes and beets that entailed killing the whole plant were also prohibited. Nor could Jains be farmers, since working the land inevitably harmed insects and worms. As a consequence, they turned to professions such as jewelry making, trading, and banking and were thus highly sought after by the courts. They also often became great librarians and patrons of the arts.

Like the Mahayana Buddhists of Central and East Asia, the Jains built colossal monolithic statues of their Tirthankars (literally, "ford finders," or "those who cross the river of human misery") and spiritual leaders. In 966 CE, Chamundaray, a Jain minister of the Ganga dynasty, built at Shravanabelagola, Karnataka, a 17.38-meter-high statue of a naked Gomteshwara Bahubali, the first man said to have attained enlightenment through Jain practice. It sits on top of a hill visible from a distance. Every twelve years the statue is covered with milk, yogurt, ghee (clarified butter), and saffron, as well as with gold coins.

Like the Buddhists, the Jains challenged Hindu caste hierarchy and refuted Vedic orthodoxy, particularly the Brahmin's claim to privileged access to higher knowledge. So Jain ideas and institutions, like those of the Buddhists, were severely attacked by the Hindus in the 9th and 10th centuries. Followers of the Shaivite and Vaishnite bhakti cults blamed them for negating life and being too abstract and impractical for the common man. But unlike the Buddhists, who wilted under the critiques and eventually disappeared from India, the Jains managed to survive the rising tide of Hinduism (and later iconoclastic Islam), in part because of their economic and political clout.

11.40 Statue of Gomteshwara Bahubali

Today there are almost three million Jains in India, mostly in the western provinces and in Karnataka. That Hindu India today is largely vegetarian is mainly due to their influence. The Jain believe in the leadership of twenty-four Tirthankars who, after having totally conquered vices such as anger, pride, and desire, are said to have appeared on earth to show Jains the way to the true religion. The original twenty-four Tirthankars were expanded to fifty-two and then seventy-four after the 12th century.

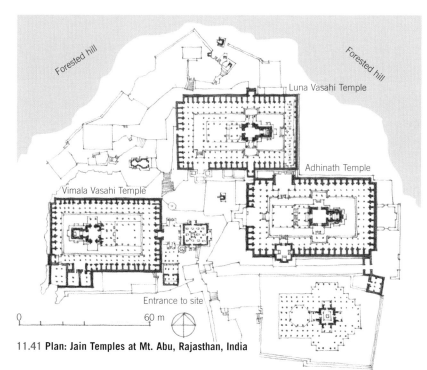

11.41 **Plan: Jain Temples at Mt. Abu, Rajasthan, India**

11.42 **Interior, Vimala Vasahi Temple at Mt. Abu**

Jain Temples at Mt. Abu

From the 10th through the 16th centuries, Jain ministers employed in Rajput courts used their wealth to build a set of five temples at Mt. Abu, Rajasthan, 170 kilometers north of Ahmedabad. Known collectively as the Dilwara Temples after a near-by town, they are clustered on a hill located on the high plateau summit of the mountain. Each temple sits high off the ground on its own terrace and is accessed on its flank by steps spilling out from a multitiered porch. The plans are modeled on Hindu precedents, with a main *garbha-griha* preceded by a *mandapa*. The central deity of the site is Adinath, one of the Tirthankars; shrines to all the Tirthankars were added to each temple later on. As a result, the individual temples came to be surrounded by a quadrangle composed of rows of mini-shrines. The *mandapas* of the mini-shrines were joined to form a cloister. Into the residual space between the quadrangle and the temple, the architects inserted a pavilion held up by highly ornate columns of lavish sculptural detail. The temples, of local white arasa marble, are carved as if made of wood. The columns and ceilings of the open pavilion are the climax of the sculptural program.

At the Vimala Vasahi, twelve multifaceted piers, linked by flying arches, hold up a domed ceiling. Sixteen female figures, personifying various aspects of learning, are attached in a ring around the perimeter. The exterior wall, by contrast, is restrained in its ornamentation, masking the rich articulations of the interior.

11.43 **Dilwara Temple at Mt. Abu**

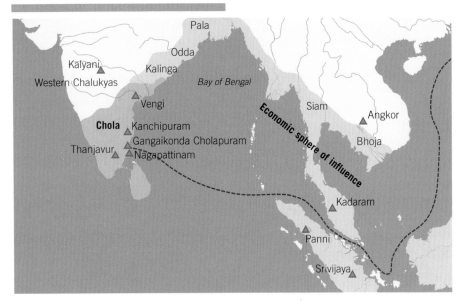

11.44 Chola and its economic sphere of influence

Cholamandalam

India's south came to be dominated by a single power, the Cholas, who combined military strength with an effective strategy of wealth generation and governance to bring about a social and economic revolution of their own. Building for themselves a new capital at Thanjavur, they eventually came to control all of peninsular India, becoming the largest power on the subcontinent. They lost no time in embarking on an aggressive campaign of temple building, not only to spread Shaivism, but also to consolidate their economic base. The Chola king Rajaraja I (985–1004) turned his attention to the trade routes and soon brought the Arabian shipping lanes under his control. Sri Lanka became a vassal state. His son, Rajendra I (1014–44), with his eye on the lucrative sea trade with China, sent his fleet to conquer Malaya and Shrivijaya, leaving the Cholas the controlling superpower of Southeast Asia. The Cholas, who called their sphere of influence the Cholamandalam, the "Chola Vision-World" possessed the largest naval force India was to have until modern times.

The Cholas chose the image of Shiva Nataraj, who orders the movement of the world with his dance, as their representative royal deity. The temple itself was an extension of the royal ordering of the world. The word "temple" in Tamil is *kovil* (*kov* meaning "god-king," *il* meaning "home");

it connotes both temple and palace and thereby serves a range of functions, from the religious to the judicial. For every economic unit (like a village or a district), the Cholas built a temple. While the temple's basic endowments of agricultural land or villages were made by the king, the actual land for the building was donated by the local elite. Donations for building materials were made by the merchants. Provisions, such as images, lamps, and oil were obtained through individual donations. Temples were also run like a corporation. They had the authority to make land grants and to invest their assets as they considered fit. They even became banks, with major contributions and

investments inscribed on the walls of the temple for all to view. In this way, the Chola temples became the financial centers of the community. Village assemblies were held in them, and they were often responsible for the education of upper-caste boys. The temple's administration, however, was controlled by the king, and Brahmins were the only ones allowed to conduct rituals. Temples maintained a huge permanent staff that included musicians, artists, artisans, and dancers (including *devadasis*, women dancers dedicated to the temple for life.) The community's cultural institutions, in other words, were also the preserve of the temple.

Dakshinameru (Rajarajeshwara Temple)

While regional temples served the more quotidian purposes of governance, Rajaraja I's royal temple at Thanjavur, the Chola capital, embodied a vision of kingship at the scale of an empire. Rajaraja I projected himself as a *cakravartin*, a king destined to bring order to the world, a demigod in the grace of Shiva Nataraj. He called his temple the Dakshinameru, the "Mt. Meru of the South," distinguishing his world from that of the north. (Dakshinameru is now generally know as the Rajarajeshwara or the Brihadeshwara Temple). Major ceremonies of royal initiation and legitimation were held there, linking deity and king. The daily rituals of the deities mirrored those of the king, including his morning round of the sacred enclosure and his sunset retreat to his bedroom. Dakshinameru maintained a

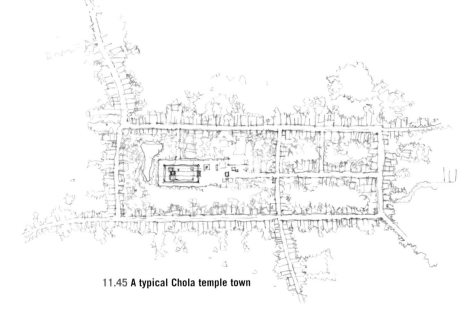

11.45 A typical Chola temple town

staff of six hundred *devadasis*, treasurers, accountants, record-keepers, watchmen, musicians, readers of texts, and craftsmen of every sort—in addition to scores of Brahmin priests. To this day it remains the largest temple in India.

Situated next to a river that was channeled to form a moat symbolic of the cosmic ocean, its outer enclosure was built like a fortress. It was entered on axis through a five-story *gopuram*. A second, three-story freestanding *gopuram*, set on a long, low platform, gave access to the main quadrangle. The towering, sixteen-story mass of the main *shikhara* dominates the view, with pilasters, piers, and attached columns articulating the entire surface. In the interior, the circumambulation route that goes around the massive lingam in the *garbha-griha* is repeated on the upper story, which is inhabitable. This is a rarity in Hindu temples, an allusion to the idea that Rajarajeshwara offered access to the realm of the gods. The ground story (which symbolically corresponds to the earthly realm) is therefore articulated as two stories, indicating more than one celestial dimension of the royal temple. The main temple is preceded by two cojoined, dimly lit hypostyle halls: the *antarala*, or vestibule, where the priest would be, and the *mandapa*. In the *mandapa*, the columns are exquisitely and intricately carved—showing the potential for refinement—whereas in the *antarala*, the columns are left as massive and plain monoliths: the first manifestation of form emerging out of the formless.

11.46 **Dakshinameru (Rajarajeshwara Temple), Thanjavur, India**

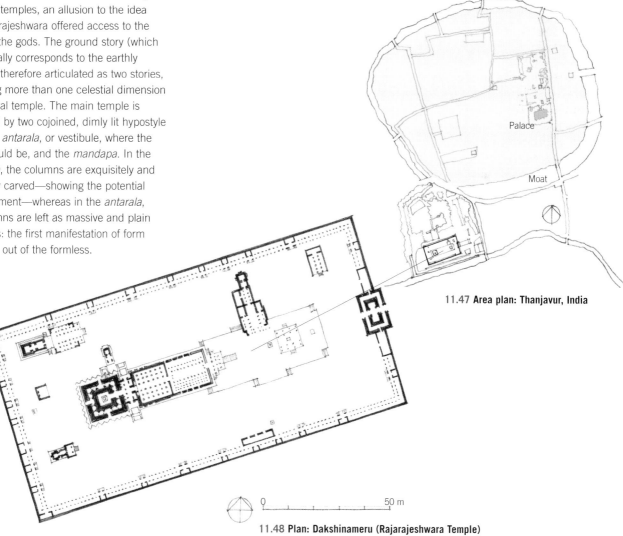

11.47 **Area plan: Thanjavur, India**

Palace

Moat

0   50 m

11.48 **Plan: Dakshinameru (Rajarajeshwara Temple)**

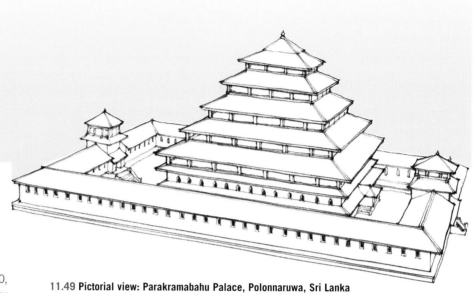

11.49 Pictorial view: Parakramabahu Palace, Polonnaruwa, Sri Lanka

Polonnaruwa

In 993 CE, Rajaraja I invaded and sacked Anuradhapura, the Sri Lankan capital, and annexed the island to the Chola Empire. He created Polonnaruwa, just southwest of Sigiriya, as the new capital of Sri Lanka. Even after the Cholas were defeated in 1070, Polonnaruwa remained Sri Lanka's capital for the next two centuries. Most of Polonnaruwa's most important buildings were erected during the thirty-three-year reign of Parakramabahu I (1123–86), who consolidated Sri Lanka into a centralized kingdom and reformed the Buddhist sects along more traditional lines. Like Anuradhapura, Polonnaruwa was located on the west bank of a lake that had been dammed for irrigation and water management; the lake was a tributary of the Mahaweli River, Sri Lanka's largest. Though Hindu temple construction ceased under Parakramabahu I, he continued to build monumental stone structures in emulation of the Cholas. The architecture at Polonnaruwa thus is a mix of Cholan and more local Sri Lankan sensibilities.

Parakramabahu I's largest structure was a seven-story palace located where the river flowed out from the lake. Part of larger complex that included subsidiary palaces and water tanks, the main part of the palace was an exact square surrounded by a quadrangular enclosure. With its main entrance to the west, the palace's seven diminishing stories rested on a massive solid masonry core at its center. The rest was supported by columnar structures with wooden roofs. There was a massive audience hall on the ground floor.

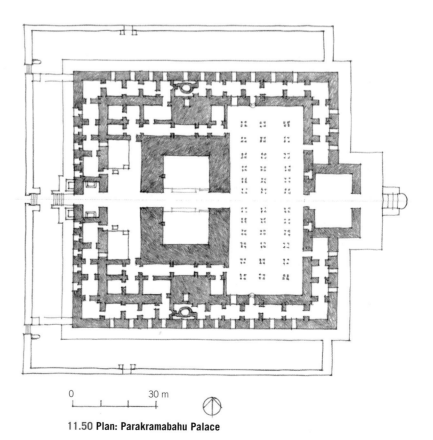

```
0          30 m
```

11.50 Plan: Parakramabahu Palace

Just north of the palace complex was the walled sacred enclosure, the centerpiece of Parakramabahu's attempt to reform Buddhist practices in Sri Lanka. Gates define the main east-west path through the enclosure. The two main structures are the Vatadage, which housed a tooth of the Buddha brought from Anuradhapura, and the Hatadage, a massive Chola-style temple with its own enclosure and gate. The Vatadage followed the design of the Thuparama at Anuradhapura, with a circular platform leading to a trabeated circumambulation hall around the solid mass of the stupa. Four seated Buddhas on the cardinal axes face out toward the access stairs. A seven-story mini-palace and a series of smaller temples and halls are spread through the rest of the enclosure.

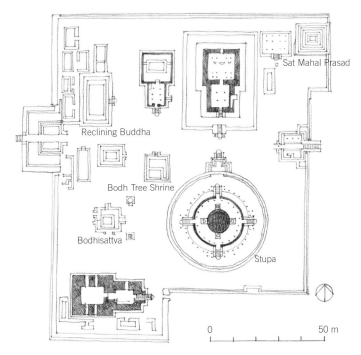

Sat Mahal Prasad

Reclining Buddha

Bodh Tree Shrine

Bodhisattva

Stupa

0   50 m

11.51 Plan: Polonnaruwa stupa complex

11.52 Polonnaruwa stupa

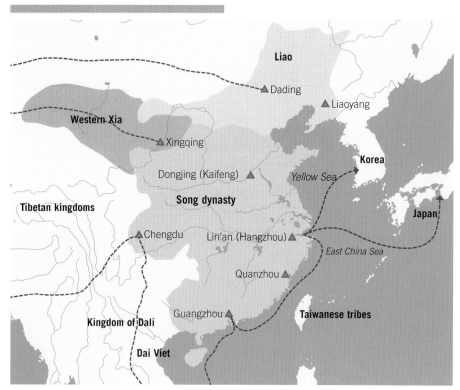

11.53 Song dynasty China

Song Dynasty China

The Song dynasty (960–1279) reunited most of China proper. The Song period divides into two phases: Northern Song (960–1127), and Southern Song (1127–1279). The division was caused by the forced abandonment of north China in 1127 by the Song court, which could not push back the Jin invaders. The northern Song capital was in the city of Dongjing (now Kaifeng); the southern capital was established at Lin'an (now Hangzhou). Though much weakened, the economy was still powerful, and the use of a new type of early ripening rice from Southeast and South Asia created abundant food surpluses. Confucianism was reinforced, and foreign relations were established with India, Indonesia, and Fatimid Egypt.

The 11th-century Song dynasty cities were the largest and most complex cities in the world. Among these, Dongjing (present-day Kaifeng City), with close to a million residents of diverse faiths, was perhaps the largest. Unlike the cities of the T'ang, Song dynasty cities were more than just administrative centers; they also served as a locus of trade, industry, and maritime commerce. Dongjing lay at the intersection of four major canals connecting to other cities and feeding into the Yellow River. Because the city was not divided into activity-specific wards, merchants could set up shop anywhere they pleased. Paintings from the time reveal that all the major streets and intersections were alive with activity. (A Song scroll, *Upper River during Qing-Ming Festival*, contains a detailed description of bustling Dongjing.)

Though Chinese authorities often preferred highly regulated cities, Dongjing shows the development of more flexible, wardless cities such as Lin'an, another center of culture on the southern coast of China during the 10th and 11th centuries and—following the defeat of the Song by the Jin in 1123—the capital of the so-called Southern Song Dynasty. Song cities were very cosmopolitan, with large populations of non-Chinese merchants. The new concept of a cultural entertainment area, a *wazi*, became popular, especially with the creation of night markets. The Song created extensive road networks between their large and small cities. The use of paper money facilitated the mercantile economy. The cultivation of tea and cotton became widespread; gunpowder was used for the first time.

One of the leading scientists and statesman, Shen Kuo (1031–95), a mathematician, astronomer, cartographer, and encyclopedist, also served as finance minister. Through experimentation with suspended magnetic needles, Shen discovered magnetic declination toward the North Pole—and the concept of true north, a revelation that made the compass useful for navigation. He also wrote extensively about movable type printing, which had been invented by Bi Sheng (990–1051). Under the Song Dynasty, Daoist and Buddhist traditions became closely aligned. But it was Confucianism, influenced by Buddhist practices, that reemerged as a major ideological force. Though having different emphases, the two were not seen as discordant.

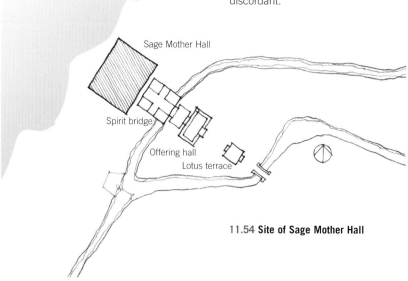

11.54 Site of Sage Mother Hall

Sage Mother Hall

Song cities, as had been traditional since the Han, had elaborate open-air sacrificial altars used for imperial sacrifices to the heaven, earth, sun, and moon. There were also magnificent roofed *ci*, temples with columnar interiors that were constructed for commemoration and veneration, often in connection with Confucian learning. During the Song dynasty, such structures also served as sites of imperial sacrifices. One of these was the Jinci, built at the site of three springs that had been worshipped since ancient times and famous in Chinese literature for its pastoral beauty. It is located at the base of a mountain 25 kilometers southeast of Taiyuan, an important regional city. Whereas most Chinese temple compounds followed a conventional pattern of south-facing halls preceded by courtyards, the entirety framed by a wall with a gate, this sanctuary, dedicated to the springs' spirit, was built with the landscape in mind. Though over time numerous buildings have been added to the site, it originally consisted of a southeast-oriented series of buildings and bridges that crossed two canals, all set between two springs with the Sage Mother Temple set directly behind the middle and third one. The sanctuary was seen as a celestial court reigned over by a supreme goddess. For that reason, the Sage Mother hall (1038–87) at the apex of the composition was built in the imperial style: it has a timber-framed, double-eave hip-and-gable roof with dramatic, five-*puzo* eaves.

Since the Sage Mother was seen as important in providing rain as well as spring water, the lotus terrace, the first structure in the sequence, was, so it is thought, the site of ritual offerings and ceremonies dedicated to rain. This open-air platform is followed by a roofed offering hall that leads to the remarkable Spirit Bridge, which traverses one of the springs. It actually consists of two bridges that cross each other at 90 degrees, meeting at the center. They are set in front of the hall itself, which is a single-story building; but because it was built with an encircling veranda with its own set of brackets, it appears as if it were two stories. The eight dragons of gilded wood that wrap themselves around the front columns are a marker of the Sage Mother's identity as water goddess and as a provider of rain. Columns were eliminated to allow for more room in the veranda, where it is two bays deep. The wall of the open U-shaped enclosure of the shrine has embedded within it, as is typical, the columns that support the roof. The inner walls, which were completely painted with themes associated with the goddess, had life-size statues of attendant women standing along them. The Sage Mother is clothed in elaborated robes but is in a seated Buddha position—no accident, as hers was meant to compete with Buddhist shrines.

11.55 Detail, Sage Mother Hall, Jinci Temple, Taiyuan, China

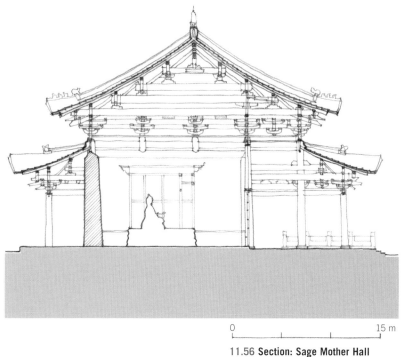

0   15 m

11.56 Section: Sage Mother Hall

The Iron Pagoda

The architecture of the *ta*, or pagoda, developed rapidly under the Song. Pagodas had first emerged during the Han dynasty (202 BCE–220 CE) as wooden structures, and then during the T'ang dynasty (618–907 CE) as stone and brick buildings that could more easily survive lightning strikes. Though Buddhism in China had waned after the late T'ang period, during the Song dynasty Buddhist pagoda towers continued to be built—often in the countryside instead of within city walls, perhaps so as to not compete with the cosmic-imperial authority that was represented by the cities' drum and gate towers. An exception to this is the Iron Pagoda of Youguo Temple in Dongjing (present-day Kaifeng), which gets its name not because it was made of iron but because the color of the building resembles that of iron. It is an octagonal brick structure about 57 meters high built around a solid core, with a spiral staircase circulating between the core and outer shell. The use of brick allowed the architects to achieve an elegant, thin shape that would not have been possible in wood, even though the building was designed to imitate a wooden structure with densely positioned eaves (*miyan*) and wooden brackets (*dou-gong*). The glazed bricks on the exterior are richly decorated with images of the Buddha, monks, singers and dancers, flowers, lions, and dragons and other legendary beasts. Under the eaves, 104 bells ring in the wind.

11.57 Silhouette, Iron Pagoda, Kaifeng, China

Liao Dynasty

A tribal clan known as the Khitan created the Liao dynasty (947–1125), which stretched from Korea and Mongolia in the north to Beijing in the south. The Liao was the first of China's several so-called foreign dynasties. In response to the dual nature of the area—with nomads to the north and settled Chinese populations in the south—the Liao created a double government, building a series of cities through which this duality was expressed. Its capital, Shangjing ("Supreme Capital"), near modern city of Lingdong, was located at the headwaters of the Shira Muren River, a site hallowed by the Khitan people. It served as the administrative center of the empire and included a commercial district, called the Chinese city, made of permanent materials; the ruling Liao, however, continued to live in their traditional urts in their own part of the town. Eventually, more than thirty walled cities were built, including four subsidiary capitals for the four regions of the empire, serving as centers of commerce; the southern capital was a predecessor of Beijing. The cities were square (or almost square), with a separated walled palace city within the city adjacent to the north wall. The Liao embraced Buddhism with such vigor that it is estimated that 10 percent of the population were monks and nuns. Nonetheless, most Khitan still adhered in one way or another to the traditional animistic religion in which the sun was worshiped. Thus, the Khitan emperor faced the east, where the sun rises, rather than the south, as Chinese emperors did.

Though the Khitan accommodated themselves to the Song dynasty architectural and urban traditions—as they had no such traditions themselves—they transformed Chinese building conventions to develop their own style. The buildings they commissioned were made by Chinese and Korean craftsmen. Nonetheless, their buildings were in many respects different, if not superior, to those of the Song. Whereas the Song aspired to a clarity of structure, the Liao reveled in the complexity of brackets and joinery that were not only more durable but lent a more majestic tone to their buildings. One of their innovations was to remove central columns in the halls to allow more space for the statue of the Buddha. This partially explains the need for a more complex roof structure, which had to span greater distances. It was primarily during the reign of the sixth Liao emperor, Longxu (Shengzong, 971–1031), that the most Liao wooden architecture was constructed.

Mu-Ta

More than one hundred early pagodas from the Song, Liao, and Jin dynasties have survived into modern times because most were made of brick. Of the timber buildings, few have survived, apart from the Liao structure known as the Yingxian Timber Pagoda, built in 1056. It is often referred to simply as Mu-ta, or the "Wooden Pagoda." The Mu-ta was built to commemorate Xinzong (1031–55), the seventh Liao ruler. Access to the 67-meter-high *ta* was through

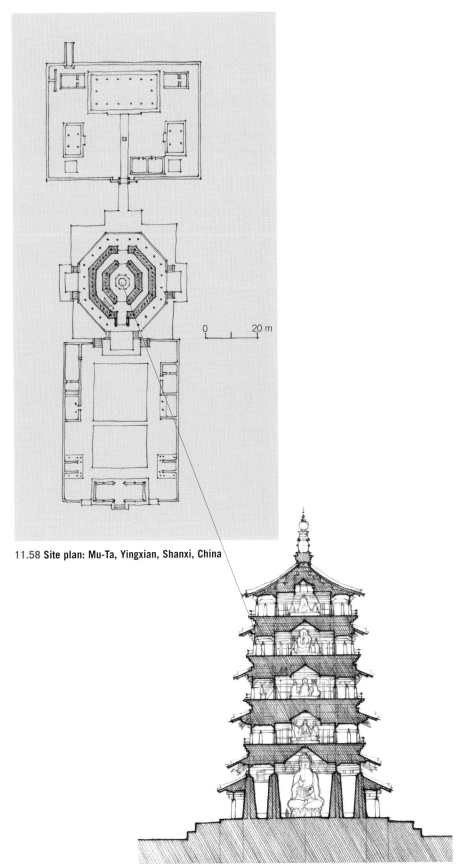

11.58 Site plan: Mu-Ta, Yingxian, Shanxi, China

0   20 m

11.59 Section: Mu-Ta

a monastic enclosure with a monumental mountain gate (*shanmen*) and a large, 55-meter-long forecourt that is no longer extant. The building was elevated on four "moon terraces" (*yuetai*), each with a pair of side stairs. The *yuetai* were a standard feature of Liao buildings but at the time were not used in Song architecture.

The lowermost story of the building consists of three independent rings of wooden pillars. The smallest pillars in the outermost ring support the lowest eaves. The two interior rings form the inner and outer cao, with a giant seated Buddha figure in the center. With the exception of the lowermost level, where the columns are encased in a wall to create an enclosure, all the upper stories are open. There are three primary levels, each being a temple unto itself and each with a Buddha statue.

A skyscraper of sorts in its day, the Mu-ta was one of the most advanced structural achievements of its time. Like the Guanyin-ge of Dulesi Temple, each story of the Mu-ta is a separate structural entity (none of the pillars rise more than a story) tied together by fifty-four different types of bracket sets. On the exterior, each story of the Mu-ta is represented by eaves, held up by a neat arrangement of structural *dou-gong*. In the interior, however, the structure is held together by a complex mesh of posts and beams, radial *dou-gong*, and cross-bracing that ultimately forms a thick nest in the form of a torus between the external skin and the central space. It is this mesh of cross-reinforcements that has enabled the Mu-ta to endure for a millennium unharmed by numerous earthquakes.

Dulesi Monastery

In about 984 CE, Hebei, a Liao nobleman from Jixian, built a Buddhist monastery, Dulesi ("Solitary Joy"), dedicated to Guanyin, the bodhisattva of compassion and mercy. Dulesi Monastery was rebuilt several times, but its central structures, the main gate (*shanmen*) and the prayer hall (Guanyin-ge) are original to the Liao. (The suffix –*ge* refers to multistory buildings that are accessible only from the front and that, like this one, house colossal statues.) Thirty meters separate the *shanmen* from the Guanyin-ge. The line of sight is such that the top of the roof of

11.60 **Dulesi Monastery, Jixian, Hebei Province, China**

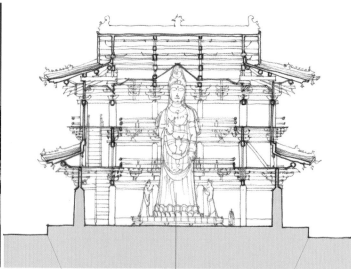

11.61 **Section through Guanyin-ge, Dulesi Monastery**

the 22-meter-high Guanyin-ge is distinctly visible from the entry portal of the *shanmen*, allowing the entire structure to assert its full impact upon entry. As in the Mu-ta, each story of the Guanyin-ge is a distinct structure wedged into the one below. It is a three-story building, though on the outside it appears to have only two stories so that Guanyin's eyes can be seen through the upper-level windows when one enters the compound.

Wood roofs are described by the number and types of bracket sets and beams deployed. Bracket sets are classified by the number and complexity of their horizontal, vertical, and diagonal elements. Beams are designated by their position and the number of rafters they span. In the *shanmen*, four four-rafter beams and four two-rafter beams hold up the roof. The structure uses an astonishing twenty-four different types of bracket sets, the most complex ones at the corners. The building is raised on a polished stone base about 1 meter in height. The plan is divided by columns into an inner, triple-high space and a circumambulatory vestibule, known as the outer and inner *wai* and *nei cao*, respectively. The second-floor ambulatory is accessible by stairs. In addition, the Guanyin's eyes align with a masonry pagoda—the White Pagoda (reconstructed 1058) located 350 meters away on axis. This visual connection was a reinterpretation of the Mahayana Buddhist practice of superimposing statues of Buddhas on stupas to emphasize the commonality between the two.

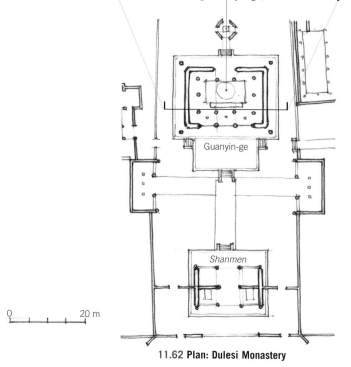

11.62 **Plan: Dulesi Monastery**

Located just outside their cities, Liao tombs consisted of multichambered underground burial vaults and several platforms above ground on which descendants could perform sacrifices to appease the spirits of the dead. Accessed by a long "spirit path," a paved road leading to the tombs, they were flanked by larger-than-life-size statues of mythical and real animals and other ceremonial objects meant to guard and guide the spirits. Interiors were painted to imitate the interiors of tents and wooden structures. Curiously, the Liao tombs all contain one panel with the painting of a woman in the act of stepping through

a door; their meaning remains unclear. Bodies were drained of fluids and filled with vegetable products, embalmed, and often covered with a suit made of fine metal.

The Liao dynasty began to decline in the 12th century. In 1120, the Song made an alliance with the newly founded Jin dynasty and attacked the Liao regime. In 1125, the last emperor of Liao, Tianzuo, was captured by the Jin army, ending the Liao dynasty. The Jin, who were related to the Mongolians, turned out to be more formidable than the Song anticipated, and soon controlled much of the former Liao area in northern China.

11.63 **Japan: Location of Kyoto and Nara, Japan**

11.64 **Phoenix hall at Byodo-in, near Kyoto, Japan**

Pure Land Buddhism

Around the year 1000 CE, as power shifted from the upper classes to the aristocracy, a new form of Buddhism known as Pure Land Buddhism came to dominate Japan. Since Pure Land Buddhism was open to all, it offered a means by which the Japanese aristocracy could gain access to Buddhist teachings without having to live in monasteries. Originally developed in India in the 2nd century CE, Pure Land Buddhism was based on the concept that a devotee could attain rebirth in a *sukhavati* ("equanimous or pure land") of his or her choice by following a designated set of personal meditations. These meditations were to focus on a particular set of visualizations—a set of prescribed scenes that took the worshipper to that place through a series of steps. Its core teachings were contained in the "Visualization Sutra," a sermon believed to have been given by the Buddha to the virtuous Lady Vaidehi, who sought to be released from her world full of material attachments and demons. Because of its association with Lady Vaidehi, Pure Land Buddhism was promoted, in particular, by women. Pure Land visualizations were usually depicted in paintings, sculptures, and mandala diagrams. The act of transcribing sutras and redrawing visualizations was enough to earn a devotee merit. These transcriptions were ultimately done as architecture by remaking plans implied in mandalas into real buildings. This made the temple itself into an object of worship.

In 1053 a nobleman, Fujiwara no Yorimichi (990–1074), converted a preexisting villa in Uji, near Kyoto, into a transcription of the Taima mandala. This visualization is known as the Byodo-in, the "Temple of Equanimity." In Buddhism, *byodo* ("equal") refers to the condition of possibility that is open to all. The Phoenix hall (Hoo-do) is all that remains of the original temple. Hoo are mythical phoenix-like birds, sculptures of which top the roof of the hall.

The Taima mandala depicts the Buddha seated on a C-shaped platform on a lake surrounded by bodhisattvas. Built on an artificial island in a lake, the Phoenix hall replicates the Taima mandala in plan, with winglike extensions on the right and left. The Phoenix hall was meant to be viewed primarily from across the lake, as a visualization for a devotee to focus on during meditation.

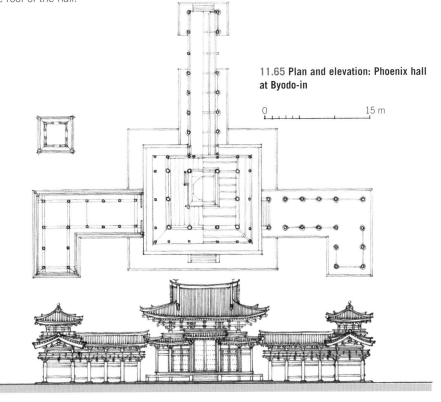

11.65 **Plan and elevation: Phoenix hall at Byodo-in**

0   15 m

11.67 Byzantium and eastern Europe

11.66 Interior, Church of Christ Pantokrator, Constantinople

Byzantine Revival

By the year 1000 CE, the Byzantine Empire had rebounded under Basil II, due to successful military campaigns and a restructuring of its administration. Among the reasons for its new success was the rise of trade with Novgorod and Kiev, which created a circular trade flow that included Armenia while avoiding still-volatile central Europe. Church building also began to rebound. Formally, little changed: the central element was still a dome resting on four columns placed in a square. New, however, was the desire to create compound churches by adding new ones to older ones through opening a passageway between them and uniting them by means of a new narthex. This can be seen at the Church of Christ Pantokrator (known in Turkish as Zeyrek Camii), a complex of three churches (1118–43) that was completed by Emperor John II Komenos. The south and north churches were built first by Empress Eirene. After her death, John decided to join the two churches, with a third dedicated to the archangel Michael but also serving as a mortuary chapel for his family clan, the Commenus. Over the centuries, many Byzantine emperors were buried there. The building thereby became much renowned in Constantinople. It was, as was customary, associated with a monastery and a hospice—in this case one for old men. The south church is a four-column type. The columns, now gone, were of red marble. The north church is similar, with a dome carried on a high drum. The middle church also had a dome, creating a complex labyrinthine interior. The building was made of brick with a plastered wall that was painted.

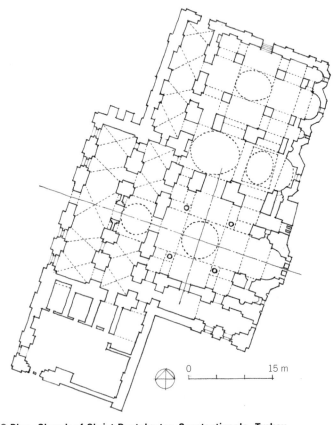

11.68 Plan: Church of Christ Pantokrator, Constantinople, Turkey

Kievan Russia

Centralization of power under the Rurikovichi dynasty, of presumably Norse origin, accelerated the decline of the patriarchal clan organization and gave rise to the development of a trading class ruled by noblemen. Kiev soon became the center of a great waterway system of rivers, principally the Dnieper, linking Scandinavia and Byzantium. This allowed for a consolidation of trade routes—the Dnieper and the Volkhov rivers connecting the White Sea to the Black Sea, and the Volga River connecting the Caspian Sea to the north, serving as the highways of the age. Trade in furs, hides, wax, honey, wheat, spices, metals, and fabrics contributed to the increase in the wealth of the cities along these routes. Though the Hungarians made an alliance with the Latin Church, the Slavs and Rus converted in the 10th century to the Eastern Church centered in Constantinople. The decision, according to legend, was inspired by the beauty of the Hagia Sophia and the elaborateness of the religious rituals as reported back to Russia by emissaries sent to compare the two religions. The connection to Byzantium is borne out architecturally: the first masonry structure in Russia, the Church of the Tithe in Kiev (989–96 CE), was erected by Byzantine masons. Though little of it is preserved, 20th-century excavations revealed fragments of mosaics and fresco decorations and allowed for a reconstruction of the plan—an inscribed cross—that served as a prototype for Russian medieval masonry churches. Another important church of the time was the Hagia Sophia in Novgorod, a stone building consecrated in 1052 by the Novgorod prince Vladimir Yaroslavovich. The church became a main center of Christian spirituality in northern Russia. Though influenced by Byzantine architecture, Russian churches began take on a unique style. Unlike Byzantine churches, which do not have particularly pronounced silhouettes, Russian churches often had domes set high on tall drums. Furthermore, four domes were set in a tight cluster around a central one. The churches were bulky with small windows, making the interior all the more mysterious. A narthex helped negotiate the transition between outside and inside.

Vladimir-Suzdal was a principality that succeeded Kievan Rus as the most powerful Rus state in the late 12th century; it lasted until the late 14th century. Its fortification possessed a so-called golden gate (1158–64), one of the best-preserved instances of the ancient Russian city gates. It was modeled on similar golden gates in Jerusalem, Constantinople, and Kiev. It is probable that the masons were invited from Byzantium, as they used Greek measures rather than Russian ones. The structure was topped with a church dedicated to the Deposition of the Virgin's Robe.

11.69 Golden Gate, Vladimir, Russia

11.70 Elevation: Church of the Tithe (Desyatinaya). Kiev

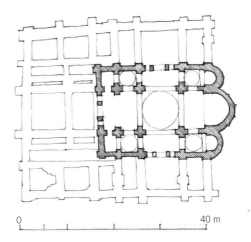

0   40 m

11.71 Plan: Church of the Tithe (Desyatinaya)

Armenia

An important influence on Byzantine architecture came from the direction of Armenia. During the period of the Arab caliphate (654–861 CE), all church building in Armenia had stopped, but when its independence was regained, Armenia saw a reawakening of its architectural culture until 1045, when it was invaded from the north by the Turks. But in 1080, Prince Ruben founded a new kingdom in Cilicia and Armenia (sometimes known as the fourth Armenian kingdom). The close relations this kingdom established with European countries played an important role during the Crusades. Intermarriage with European crusading families was common among its aristocracy. Many French terms entered the Armenian language. To the north of this Christian realm was the empire of the Khazars, and to the south, the Islamic caliphate of Baghdad.

Sanahin Complex

A well-preserved monastic compound, Sanahin (also known as St. Amenaprkitch), 2 kilometers southeast of the town of Alaverdi, is an example of an Armenian monastic institution. Unlike Byzantine aggregates, in which buildings tend to fuse into each other, the complexes in Armenia maintained volumetric and functional clarity. The composition in this case is designed along two rectangular lines, with facades facing westward. The churches (begun 934 CE) have between them a barrel-vaulted corridor, or *academia*, where pupils could sit on stone benches while the teacher walked up and down the space, as was the custom in peripatetic schools. Appended to the front of both churches are *gavits*, dating from about 1210, which came to be used around that time. In these vaulted spaces on the west side of the church, novices could assist during Mass. Their principal utilization, however, was as meeting halls, and laws and ordinances were carved on the internal walls. They also served as special places to bury nobility. The southern church has four columns, whereas the northern one has three naves. They were illuminated by an oculus in the vault.

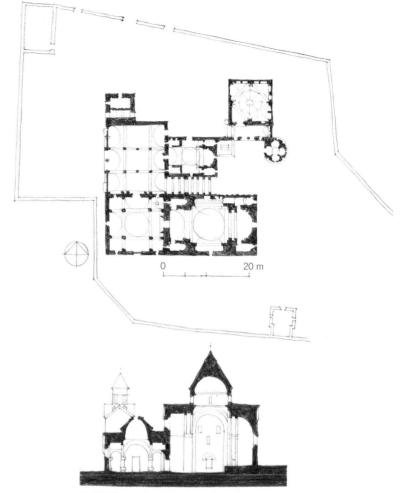

11.72 Plan and section: Sanahin complex, Lori, Armenia

11.73 Interior of Sanahin church

Armenian stonework was the best in the world thanks to the long Hellenistic tradition on which it was based. During this period emerged decorative detailing based on floral and geometric designs to form blind arcades and articulate openings and cornices—another design feature that would to spread to the West, and to Italy in particular.

The Church of the Holy Cross on the island of Aght'amar (consecrated 921 CE), originally unencumbered by ancillary buildings, makes its impression through symmetry and equilibrium. Unlike Byzantine churches, which were composite in nature, Armenian churches aimed to maintain a tight bond between interior and exterior. The sacristy and the vestry, instead of being separate spaces to the right and left of the altar, are therefore embedded in the mass of the wall. The interior, however, was never just a reflection of outer form.

11.74 Church of the Holy Cross on the island of Aght'amar in Lake Van, Turkey, near Gevash (Wostan)

0   10 m

11.75 Plan: Church of the Holy Cross on the island of Aght'amar

The church, as is also typical of Armenian architecture, presents the buildings in simple elemental forms: cubes, cylinders, cones, and pyramids. The dome is conical on the outside but hemispherical within. Walls are made of an aggregate of pebbles and mortar much like concrete and dressed with blocks of closely fitting pink sandstone. The plan, with its four apses, is known as a tetraconch, even though the east and west exedrae are deeper than those on the north and south. The exterior is decorated with bands of bas-relief sculpture depicting biblical scenes. The lighting on the interior is indirect, and the windows are small. The main light source is around the drum, above which the dome seems to float, as if it were on a ring of light. The wide side apses swell the space outward at ground level, with small concavities at the corners, between the piers, adding further illumination. The entire interior was originally painted with religious scenes.

11.76 Church of the Holy Cross on the island of Aght'amar

By the 10th century, Ani had risen to become one of the leading cities of West Asia. Located on what is now the border between Turkey and Armenia, it was sited on a long promontory defined by the Akhurian River. Its defensive walls were built in 963 CE, but the city quickly outgrew them to reach a population of about one hundred thousand. Though the city was taken by the Byzantines in 1045 and then the Seljuks in 1064; it was restored to local rule under Zak'are Mxargrjeli in 1199 and flourished until being sacked by the Mongolians in 1236. The chapels and churches numbered in the hundreds.

The Cathedral of Ani (989–1001) deserves to be listed among the principal monuments of the time because of its pointed arches and clustered columns and piers. It was spectacularly sited at the center of town on a bluff overlooking the Arpa and Akhurian rivers. The architect responsible for the building was Trdat, whose fame was such that he was summoned to Constantinople to repair the dome of the Hagia Sophia, which had been damaged by an earthquake in 989 CE. Continuing the tradition of Armenian architectural innovation, Trdat rested the dome on a drum with four pendentives descending between the arches, which rest on four piers. Smaller arches span the side aisles. It is not a copy of earlier prototypes. Because the dome is independently supported, the rest of the structure is larger than the size of the dome would permit. This creates a more airy relationship between dome and perimeter than was the case in earlier Armenian churches, which were more compact in nature.

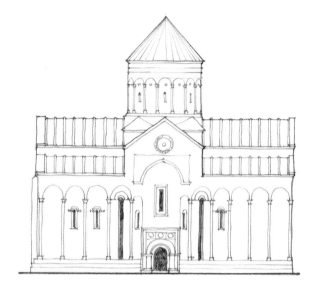

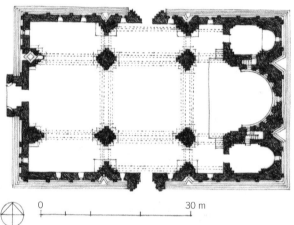

11.77 Plan and elevation: Cathedral of Ani, Armenia

0   30 m

11.78 Cathedral of Ani

11.79 Holy Roman Empire

11.80 St. Cyriakus, Gernrode, Germany

Ottonian Germany

For several decades under Charlemagne (742–814 CE), virtually the entire Western world—such as it was defined at that time—had been brought together into a single political entity governed by a homogenous group of bishops and judges, scions of the dominant families. But with the division of Charlemagne's empire after his death, the Viking raiders in the north, and the Muslim incursions in the south, the quality of life in Europe deteriorated. Communities were scattered, libraries destroyed, and monasteries ruined. By the year 1000 CE, however, the situation had begun to improve, partially because by then the feudal system had been established throughout most of Europe. Society fell roughly into three groups; the serfs, attached to the land; the members of the religious establishments; and the aristocracy, whose power was hereditary: they collected the taxes and took responsibility for the military protection of the land.

By the year 1000 CE, the balance of power had shifted from France to the eastern part of the kingdom and the Christianized Germans under the Ottonian dynasty (919–1024). The princely realm of Germany, like that of France, had no capital city in the modern sense. Rulers moved from place to place, adjudicating legal cases as they went, trying to hold together the network of relationships on which the kingdom depended. The absence of a single capital city differentiated the European notion of governance at that time from almost every other state in the world. The German Empire aspired to be the heir of the Roman mantle even more than the Carolingian Empire had. Though Charlemagne was bestowed the title of Imperator Augustus by the Pope, the phrase Romanum Imperium only began to appear on documents after 1034.

Despite the overt connections to Rome, Ottonian rulers admired Constantinople. Mothers and wives of the aristocracy were often Greek princesses, and the emperor took over the Eastern notion of *basileus*, or sovereign, complete with the concomitant conception of authority and its emblems of power—the golden cape and the sphere held in the right hand. These Eastern connections brought with them artisans as well as Byzantine and Armenian architects and stonemasons, whose quality of workmanship had a positive impact on Ottonian architecture. Near Quedlinburg in Gernrode stands the only fully preserved church from the early Ottonian period, the Collegiate Church of St. Cyriakus. Different from Carolingian architecture, these churches, though still volumetrically powerful, demonstrate much more skilled stonework, along with a desire for verticality. Like Carolingian churches, Ottonian ones consisted of volumetric masses.

As a way to cement imperial control over their territory, the Ottonian kings combined the founding of monasteries with the founding of market centers. But the uncluttered external surfaces and the integrated relationship between the crossings and transepts of St. Cyriakus in Gernrode (960 CE) and St. Michael in Hildesheim (1001–33), for example, impart to these buildings a complex simplicity that earlier Carolingian churches, such as St. Riquier, lacked. St. Michael was sited not far from the newly developing market city of Hildesheim, defined by it broad street onto which the shops faced. The church was not in the city proper, as that was not yet very common; instead, it was in its own precinct outside of town. Unlike Roman churches, the entrance was broadside, from the south, leading up from the marketplace.

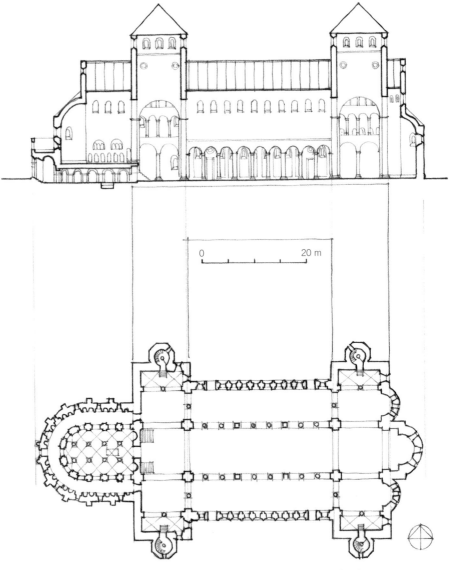

11.81 Plan and section: St. Michael in Hildesheim, Germany

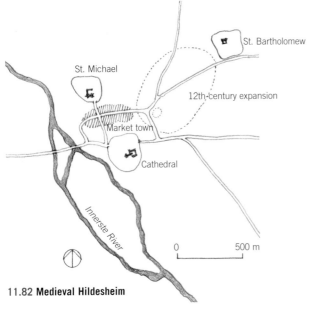

11.82 Medieval Hildesheim

Stretching between two almost identical transepts, the nave has a ratio of 3:1, the rhythm established by piers with two columns interspersed between them. The building, which has no westwork, reflects the gradual reduction of its importance. The crypt, with its ambulatory, is at ground level, with the high altar located above. The cloister to the north has been lost over time. The roof was supported by wooden trusses.

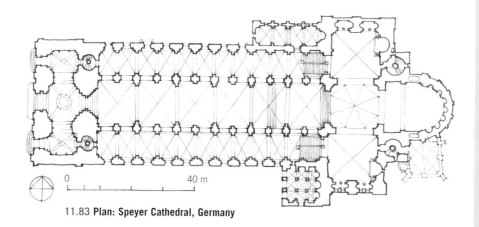

11.83 Plan: Speyer Cathedral, Germany

The word *cathedral* derives from a Greek word that designates a professor's chair from which a lecture was given. Early Christian bishops used a cathedra not only as a symbol of their power but also as a place from which to preach, even though that practice was eventually abandoned. The first use of the word in regard to architecture dates from around 800 CE. A cathedral, in that etymological sense, is thus an elaborate framing device for a bishop's chair. Some ancient chairs still exist, such as the so-called Chair of St. Peter, which is preserved in the Vatican Museums.

Speyer Cathedral

Despite the problems of the times, increased trade and competition among cities led to a rapid increase in architectural production and to an experimentation with new forms. Particularly important was the introduction of stone vaulting. The implications were profound—spatially, structurally, and symbolically. To support the vault, the builders could have decided to build thicker walls, but instead they interpreted the side aisles as structural buttresses for the vault, transforming the interior of the building into a tripartite space visually coordinated with the vaults over the aisles.

One of the earliest churches built in the new manner was the Speyer Cathedral, begun around 1040, with the vaulting completed around 1137. Abandoning the squat compositions of Carolingian and Ottonian architecture, the nave elevation of Speyer was defined by a series of high arches reminiscent of a Roman aqueduct. Windows at the top bring light into the nave. Even more significant was the presence of a single attached column that rose some 32 meters from the floor to the base of the vault—higher than any other vault at the time. The crossing is defined by an octagonal tower. The tall proportions allow the building to seem more compact and controlled, and to some eyes, more Roman, especially when compared to Hildesheim's static arrangement of volumes. There can be no doubt that the third Abbey Church of Cluny, begun about 1088, was erected in open rivalry to Speyer. The interior nave of Speyer has since been rebuilt, but St. Étienne in Nevers (1063–97) is more or less comparable.

Despite its innovations, Speyer can also be seen as the end stage of the Romanesque style, for at that very same time, a remarkable new development was taking place at the Abbey Church of St. Foy at Conques, begun around 1050. As at Speyer, the tall, soaring barrel-vaulted nave creates the impression of a single structure, as opposed to a box with a roof on it. As at Speyer, the high side aisles serve as buttresses for the vault. And, as at Speyer, the nave, at least in the lower part, combines its structure with arcaded openings. But the architects here added buttresses on the outside to further strengthen the walls. Though small, they are enough to effect the clear differentiation between wall and column that defines Carolingian and Romanesque architecture. The wall begins to look more and more like a series of piers.

11.84 Abbey Church of St. Foy, Conques, France

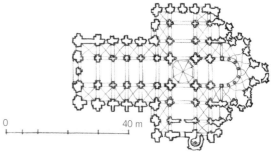

11.85 Plan: Abbey Church of St. Foy

11.86 Norman England

The Normans

In 911 CE, Charles the Simple validated the Norman possessions around Rouen, France, which the Normans had begun to occupy in the 9th century. The Normans, with amazing adaptive energy, renounced paganism and absorbed local customs and language. They also furthered the development of the Romanesque style, of which the Cathedral of Caen is the prime example. In 1001, Richard II, duke of Normandy, invited the Italian abbot William of Volpiano—accompanied by a colony of Benedictines, with their well-established traditions of design and masonry construction—to restore the Abbey of Fécamp. Soon a uniquely Norman style developed that incorporated Norse decorative motifs while drawing on the Islamic influences brought to England and France from the Norman holdings in Sicily.

A warrior people from the northern French coast, the Normans overran England and southern Italy and settled in Scotland, Wales, the Byzantine Empire, and (after the First Crusade) the Levant. Norman power was extended by strategic marriage alliances. In a series of waves, the Normans conquered parts of southern Italy and Sicily (1061), and then England, following the Battle of Hastings (1066). The new rulers transformed the entire religious, mercantile, and political geography of England. But their holdings were far-flung, from England and northern France to southern Italy and Sicily; the Normans consequently became a clearinghouse of

different stylistic and cultural trends that bridged many classic divides.

Most importantly they transformed the village- and agrarian-based geography of the Saxons into one based on towns in the middle of large farming districts or boroughs, with castles at their centers to serve as the basic instrument of government. Unlike in Germany, where castles were generally on defensible ridges or mountains, in England, where mountains are not a prominent geographical feature, they were built at the core of the urban layout. Town markets were created and an aristocracy took shape, promoting an international luxury trade in commodities such as fine cloth and wine. It has been estimated that about four to five hundred new towns were laid out in this manner, creating a pattern of urban centers that was to survive virtually unchanged until the Industrial Revolution and, in parts of the country, survives even today.

The Normans introduced not only a strong mercantile society but also a change in the notion of kingship. Roger the Great, in the chronicles of the time, is represented as the royal deputy of Christ. The small Saxon churches that dotted the English landscape could no longer measure up to such grand claims. Most were torn down and in their stead, the Normans designed a religious landscape around powerful state-supported bishoprics, each of which needed a sumptuous cathedral. Architects and masons

were brought in from the continent, as were successive waves of continental monks—Benedictines, Augustinians, Cistercians, Cluniacs, and Carthusians—who were just as important from a religious point of view as from an economic one, as their well-organized farms produced surpluses for the markets. The Cistercians, for example, were associated with irrigation and large-scale sheep farming. By the end of the 12th century, six hundred new monastic institutions of varying practices had been set up.

Durham Cathedral

Durham Cathedral (1093–1133) is important for its architectural features, specifically, its rib vaulting (the first of its kind in England), its pointed arches, and its high standard of masonry. Durham shows the specific Anglo-Norman style as a blend of the English decorative tradition with Norman architectural skills, and it marks the transition from a more monumental and simple scheme, as is seen in Gloucester Cathedral (begun 1089). The choir and the nave of the three-aisled church were built between 1093 and 1133, but the west towers were not completed until 1220. In comparison with the nave of Gloucester, which also has heavy round columns carrying the arcades, Durham, in the manner of Speyer, introduces the idea of attached half-columns that guide the eye to the ceiling. The loftiness of both churches had always been a feature of Romanesque architecture; what is novel here is the structural openness of the walls. A basic principle of Norman building was the reduction of solid walls to a thick but open skeleton of arches. The arches were not just interruptions in the wall but were defined in a regularized way, with surrounds framed by attached half-columns and horizontal string courses. The openings do not deny the weight and mass of the wall, as would become the tendency later, but rather, illuminated from behind, they seem to release their load gradually as the wall ascends.

The decoration of the columns, with its zigzag and chevron motifs, also made extensive use of color, specifically black and red, which was an influence from Islamic

11.87 Durham Cathedral, England

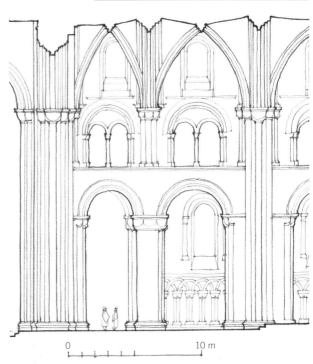

11.88 Partial section through the nave of Durham Cathedral

architecture that came to the country through the Crusades and the Norman-Arab connections in Sicily and northern Africa. Geometric patterns, such as those seen in Peterborough Cathedral, and other features of the inner decoration can later be found in several other cathedrals in northern England, suggesting that the same masons moved on to work in Scotland.

Durham Cathedral is considered a forerunner of what is now called the Gothic style, largely because of the fusion of the ribbed vault and the pointed arch, which are considered essentially Gothic features.

The building does not have buttresses and so appears from the outside quite boxy, unlike later Norman cathedrals, such as Canterbury Cathedral, where buttresses contribute to a vertical articulation. The so-called Galilee Chapel (1153–95) in front of the west facade is unique, with its five parallel halls and longitudinal arcaded walls without any subdivision into bays. This layout resembles one encountered in Islamic mosques and once again shows the cross-fertilization of ideas introduced from the Mediterranean.

11.90 Nave of Durham Cathedral

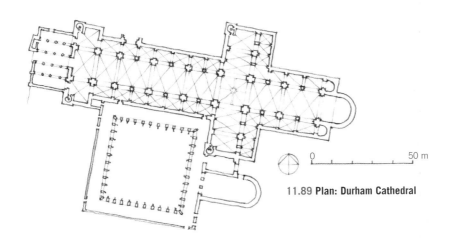

11.89 Plan: Durham Cathedral

Canterbury Cathedral

Among the new bishoprics Canterbury was the most important, as its bishop served as vice-regent of the king. When Canterbury Cathedral was destroyed by an accidental fire in 1067, one year after William the Conqueror landed on the south coast of England, Lanfranc, the first Norman archbishop of Canterbury, initiated a rebuilding that was based on the new cathedral of St. Étienne in France. When a fire destroyed the choir in 1174, the architects, William of Sens and William the Englishman, erected a new choir and a presbytery that doubled the length of the church. The newer part existed on a higher elevation, with the stairs serving to separate the more sacred areas to the east. The project shows how England adopted French construction techniques—specifically the flying buttress and the six-partite vault— while the nave itself remained from the time of Lanfranc. (The nave was, however, rebuilt in the late 14th century.) The church houses, among other sacred objects, the relics of St. Thomas, originally placed at the center of the round chapel at the eastern end of the building. The cloister and monastic buildings are placed on the north, instead, as is more frequently the case, on the south of the church. There were not buttresses on the Durham Cathedral, which gives it a resolute boxy form compared with the more vertical articulation of the wall surface at Canterbury.

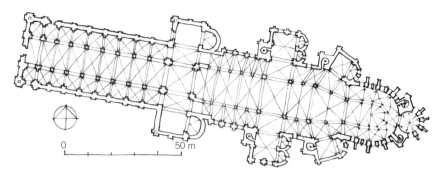

11.91 Plan: Canterbury Cathedral, England

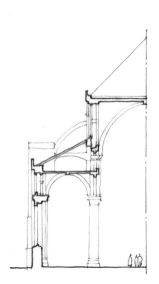

11.92 Partial section: Canterbury Cathedral

11.93 Interior vaulting: Canterbury Cathedral

Cefalù Cathedral

When Roger d'Hauteville conquered Sicily in 1060, he found a culture that had been under Arab influence since the late 9th century. The Normans not only availed themselves of the practical and technological innovations of the Muslims but also integrated them into their administration and even into the army. Soon Apulia, Capua, Sicily, and finally parts of northern Africa came under Norman domination. As a consequence, the Normans controlled the trade route to the Bosporus.

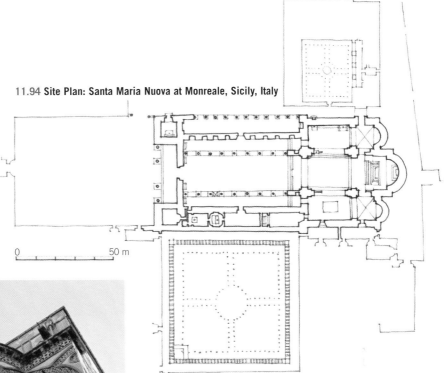

11.94 Site Plan: Santa Maria Nuova at Monreale, Sicily, Italy

0   50 m

11.95 Exterior detail: Santa Maria Nuova at Monreale

The first major Norman church in Sicily was built at Cefalù (begun 1131); it followed a typical early Norman footprint, with a nave with side aisles, a wooden ceiling, and a massive transept in the east. It is a heavy and somber building that contrasts sharply with Santa Maria Nuova at Monreale (from the Latin *mons regalis*, "royal mountain"), south of Palermo on the slopes of Monte Caputo, that was started only a hundred years after Cefalù. Islamic influences are apparent in the outside decoration of the apse, with its intertwined arches and terra-cotta ornamentation. The Great Mosque of Córdoba (10th century) and the Bab Mardum Mosque in Toledo (around 1000 CE) show similar interlocking arches. The cathedral also shows Byzantine influences, such as the exquisite mosaics that cover the interior walls of the cathedral and are second in quality only to those in the Hagia Sofia in Istanbul.

This stylistic synthesis is also evident in the areas of western Italy that the Normans controlled. Amalfi became a seafaring republic, rivaling Genoa, Venice, and Pisa, from the 9th to the 11th centuries. At its height it had trade representatives in Mahdiya, Tunisia; Kairuan (Cairo); Alexandria; Beirut; Jerusalem; Antioch, Syria; and Constantinople. At the Cathedral of Amalfi, the original Norman building underwent various expansions, including the Cloister of Paradise, which is clearly influenced by Islamic motifs.

11.96 Aerial view: Cefalù Cathedral, Sicily, Italy

Pilgrimage Churches

The 11th and 12th centuries saw a growth in the popularity of religious pilgrimages, usually to sites where miracles were believed to have occurred. Pilgrims sought out these churches mainly for the relics they housed, which were thought to emit a benevolent or curative aura. Possessing relics—a finger, a foot, or even a head of a saint—became central to a particular church's identity, and churches vied with each to collect as many such relics as possible. Major ones were the tomb of St. Peter in Rome, the tomb of St. James at Santiago de Compostela, and the Church of the Holy Sepulcher in Jerusalem. Most pilgrims traveled of their own volition, but some pilgrimages were acts of penance imposed for exceptional misdeeds. The trips, exhausting and often dangerous, became the source of stories and ballads, such as Geoffrey Chaucer's *Canterbury Tales*. Other accounts give us some of the earliest descriptions of church architecture in the West.

The most venerated pilgrimage site was the Holy Sepulcher in Jerusalem. The original church, constructed by Constantine, was consecrated in 335 CE to protect a tomb thought to have been that of Christ. Constantine's church was torn down by the Persians. The Crusaders then began a church that, with changes and additions, is the basis for the church as it stands today. Originally, the entrance from the main street led to a courtyard and then to a basilica with two side aisles. This opened onto an inner atrium (the holy garden) and the rotunda (the anastasis), which had a conical roof. The shrine itself, a rectangular structure, was destroyed by fire in 1808; the current one dates from shortly thereafter.

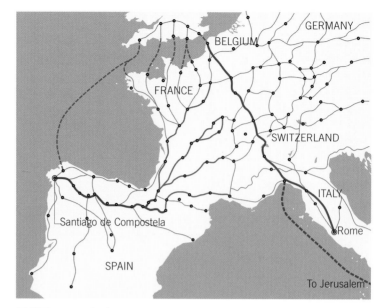

11.97 European pilgrimage routes

Descriptions of the Holy Sepulcher from visitors led to the construction of models in the West, such as St. Bénigne at Dijon (1001), Neuvry-St.-Sépulchre (1045), and the Church of La Vera Cruz in Segovia. As none of these replicas are alike, it is clear that a precise imitation was not as important as other features. Among these copies is the frequently restored Church of San Stefano at Bologna. Erected in the 5th century, it was rebuilt in 1180 in the shape of a dodecagon. The tomb chamber has an altar on top and is approached by two staircases.

The churches begun in the 11th century were significantly different from their Romanesque counterparts. Whereas in the earlier churches the nave was for the public and the apse for the monks or priests, the newer churches, which had sacred relics, were built for movement through the church and around the back of the high altar, where many of the relics were displayed.

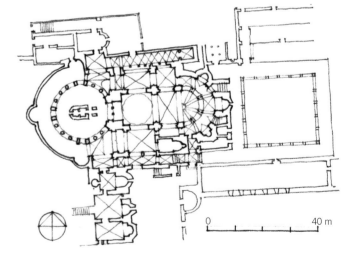

11.99 Plan: Church of the Holy Sepulchre, Jerusalem

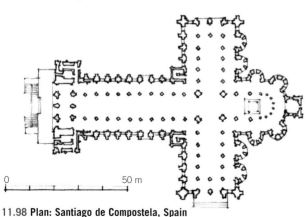

11.98 Plan: Santiago de Compostela, Spain

11.100 Krac des Chevaliers, west of Homs, Syria

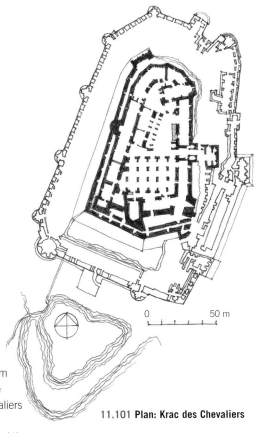

11.101 Plan: Krac des Chevaliers

Dover Castle

In the British Isles, castles had become a necessity in the late 9th century as a response to Viking incursions, but under the Normans, castles, built on licenses extended to loyal vassals by the king, played an important part not only in warfare and in deterring local rebellion but also in protecting and strengthening the economic fabric of the kingdom. Each major landowner had a castle as his principal seat. Many fortifications were near a river, which provided water for the moat. Protecting roadways, river crossings, or ports, castles were designed with different degrees of complexity, depending on cost, need, and the constantly evolving state of the art, which in turn was a response to evolving weapons technology.

Dover Castle, overlooking a busy port, was begun around 1180; it is almost cubical in form, measuring roughly 32 meters in all directions. There was a well in the basement to guarantee a water supply and chambers in the interior for storage of supplies. The idea was to minimize the size of the openings, or loops, as they were called. The loops were in this case not planned for positioning armaments; that would be a later development. The principal defensive position was the roof. Eventually, by the early 13th century, the square plan had to be abandoned because advances in siege technology made corners vulnerable to attack.

The Normans were not slow to profit from the military experiences gained from the Crusaders in the Levant. Krac des Chevaliers (Qalaat al-Husn, ca. 1100), located 65 kilometers west of Homs, Syria, embodied the best of the military thinking of the day. The castle, controlling a strategic corridor known as the Homs Gap—50 kilometers northeast of Tripoli and 30 kilometers west of Tortosa, where the principal Templar stronghold was located—was built to isolate the Syrian hinterland from its maritime outlets and was thus of crucial importance to the Crusaders in their control of the coast. Sited on top of a ridge, it consisted of a walled enclosure with rounded projections protecting the well-crafted fortress, whose steep stone glacis made it appear to be built into the top of an artificial hill. It contained a well, kitchens, armories, a chapel, and an inscription warning against pride. In such a massive fortress, the Crusaders might indeed have felt pride—at least until 1271, when it was taken by Sultan Baybars.

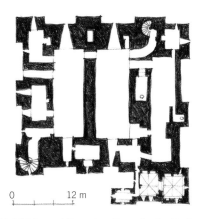

11.102 Second-floor plan: Dover Castle, England

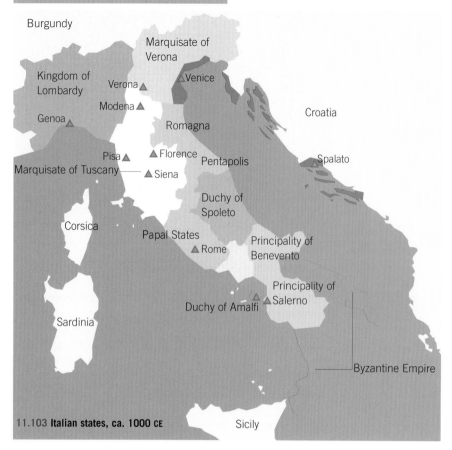

Burgundy

Marquisate of Verona

Kingdom of Lombardy

Verona ▲

Modena ▲

Genoa ▲

Pisa ▲

Marquisate of Tuscany

▲ Florence

▲ Siena

Romagna

Pentapolis

▲ Venice

Croatia

Spalato

Corsica

Duchy of Spoleto

Papal States

▲ Rome

Principality of Benevento

Principality of Salerno

Duchy of Amalfi ▲

Sardinia

Byzantine Empire

Sicily

11.103 Italian states, ca. 1000 CE

11.104 Modena Cathedral, Italy

Tuscany

Charlemagne traveled to Italy only four times, each trip lasting less than a year, setting a precedent of absentee monarchism that persisted for centuries. This allowed north Italian states, seen by the kings as the southern fringe of their empire, to survive as neither quite independent nor fully integrated into the empire. Nevertheless, their cities were bustling places. Lucca was growing so fast that houses were being built along the approach roads; soon a good portion of the population lived outside the walls in so-called bourgs. And between the cities, villages—called variously *vici, loci, casalia,* or *villae*—came to be established. As a result, monasteries—with some exceptions—were unable to develop the hold on the local population that they had in northern Europe. To be sure, the cities did not look very impressive. Roman civic buildings and temples had been left to rot, or they were used as quarries. Churches built after 600 CE were small. Only a limited amount of farming occurred within city walls. The forums had lost their civic value and became marketplaces. In 1006, a series of disastrous famines and plagues killed thousands of

people. The weak centralized power of the emperors combined with the rising status of the cities; consequently, more and more power was ceded by the emperors to the city bishops in order to maintain control.

The bishops of Modena, Reggio, Bergamo, Cremona, and other places were given unprecedented powers. In 904 CE, the bishop of Bergamo, for example, was granted the right to build city walls and to rebuild them with the help of the citizens. The result of this transfer of authority was dangerous to the imperial state, as bishops were not able to maintain their hegemony over urban society. Cities now began to vie with each other, however, in the construction of cathedrals and baptisteries that showed off the wealth of the city and the status of the church. The principal churches during this time were in Venice (begun 832 CE), Pisa (begun 1063), Modena (begun 1099), Cremona (begun 1118), Siena (begun 1196), and Verona (begun 1139).

The architect of the Modena Cathedral was Lanfranco, called *mirabilis artifex, mirificus aedificator* ("marvelous creator, wonderful builder"), about whom, however,

little is known except that he came from Como, where a school of builders had been established. Compared to other Romanesque buildings of the time, the structure is lighter and the lines stripped to their essentials. The building was clad in white Istrian stone and articulated by blind arcades. The central division is emphasized by a rose window and a baldachino-style central portal. The rose window on the facade was added in the 13th century. The work is ornamented with sculptures by the stonemason Wiligelmo; it depicts, among other things, Adam and Eve working the land to gain redemption. The portals also portray biblical and mythological events, including monsters and centaurs that warn not only of the diabolic threats awaiting man outside the city of God but also the threats that come from outside the Christian world, a reminder that Sicily had already fallen, first to Islamic troops, then to Arab colonizers. The archbishop's palace and administrative center was connected to the cathedral by means of a private passage. The building was commissioned by Queen Matilda di Canossa (1046–1115). One of the most powerful women of the

11.105 **Detail: Cathedral of Pisa, Italy**

11.106 **Cathedral of Pisa**

Middle Ages, she had a fortress in the heart of the Emilian Apennines and was a strong supporter of papal policy against the emperors. Matilda ruled over Tuscany, which extended from Siena and Pisa to Modena in the north. She commissioned, or had a hand in the commissioning of, several other buildings in the Po River valley, including the Rotunda of San Lorenzo in Mantua (1083), the Benedictine abbey of San Benedetto in Polirone (1077), as well as Cremona Cathedral (1107–17) and Piacenza Cathedral (1122).

Cathedral of Pisa

Construction on the Cathedral of Pisa began in 1063 after the victory of the Pisan fleet over the Saracens near Palermo. Pisa could now attempt to fulfill its ambition to become the Venice of the western Mediterranean and to develop a greater visual presence. The cathedral was consecrated in 1118, but it was completed only after considerable alterations in the 14th century. Stylistically it is a variation of the Mediterranean basilica plan, with influences from Armenia, Syria, and Islamic architecture. The building also had imperial Lombard overtones, especially in its facade, with its four registers of freestanding gallery work. The granite columns in the nave were taken from Roman temples on the isle of Elba; the capitals range from imperial Roman to Byzantine temples. The walls have marble paneling inspired by Byzantine practice, and the shape and manner of construction of the dome, rising on the inside from very high and narrow pointed arches, looks Islamic.

The building does not follow the trend of the great pilgrimage churches, in which structure and surface were becoming increasingly unified. In fact, it defied that trend in its celebration of surface. The elegant and costly marble sheathing that wraps around the exterior has little if any correlation to inner structure. The massive volume of the building becomes light and airy even though the openings are few and small, in the typical Romanesque manner. The plan is also far different from French cathedral architecture, which aspired to a unity of form and structure. Here the double-aisled nave is intersected by a transept formed by two single-aisled minor basilicas, set front to front, with a domed crossing between. Each of the minor cross basilicas is provided with an apse of its own. The plan is thus a type of composite of basilicas that, on the exterior, gives the illusion of a nave with transept.

The baptistery in front of the cathedral was begun in 1153. In 1173, the foundations were laid for the campanile, known now as the Leaning Tower of Pisa. In 1278, the tombs that cluttered the area around the church were gathered together and placed into a separate structure, the Camposanto, to the north of the church.

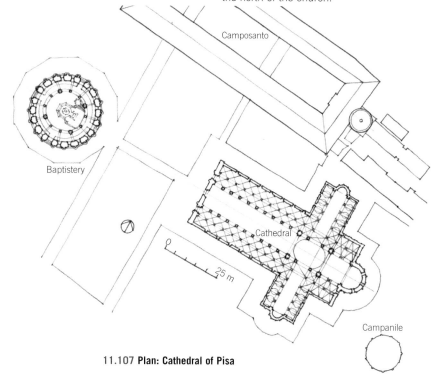

11.107 **Plan: Cathedral of Pisa**

11.108 Baptistery of Florence, Italy

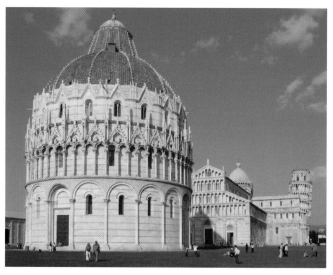

11.109 Baptistry of Pisa, Italy

Baptistery of Parma

Parallel to the emergence of the Italian urban cathedral was the urban baptistery, conceived as a bold, freestanding structure in the piazza in front of or next to a church. Their typically octagonal shape had its roots in early Christian mysticism and imperial Roman symbolism. By the 10th century, with the revival of learning, came a rise in numerology—a science of its own at the time built on the numbers embedded in the concept of the Trinity, the twelve apostles, the Holy Spirit (3 + 4), the number of perfection (3 x 4 x 5), and so forth. The number 8 and the octagonal form were especially important. In an inscription on the cathedral baptistery in Milan, the connection between number, geometry, and architecture is aptly expressed:

> "He erected an eight-choired temple for use by the saints, and an octagonal font is worthy of its number. This number proved fitting for the elevation of a housing of the holy baptism, which gave back to the people true deliverance, raising them again in the light of Christ, who loosened the bonds of death, and [who] from their graves raised the lifeless...."

Architecturally, the most significant baptisteries are at Florence (1060–1150), Pisa (1153–1265), and Parma (1196–1270). The Baptistery of Parma, modeled on the Rotunda of the Anastasi in Jerusalem, has corners that look like giant-order piers, with loggias and a blind arcade on top spanning

the interstices. The lower level consists of generous arched openings and blind arches. The eight great piers and the sixteen columns on each register are standard referents to the Holy Sepulcher in Jerusalem. Although the imposing mass of the building is Romanesque, its sculptural decoration reflects French Gothic elements. This is most clearly seen in the prominence accorded the Virgin Mary—the main portal is dedicated to her—and in the changed representation of Christ from a severe judge to a more humane figure, which was the sign of the new religious mentality.

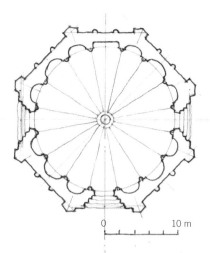

11.110 Plan and section: Baptistery of Parma

11.111 Baptistery of Pavia, Italy

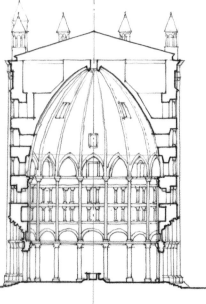

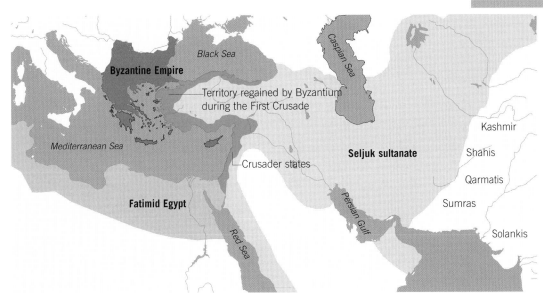

11.112 West Asia, ca. 1000 CE

Seljuk Turks

Turks in the 10th century were a pastoral people living in Central Asia east of the Caspian Sea. Abandoning their homeland, they moved into Afghanistan and Iran. Accepting the faith of Islam along the way, they created a number of Turkish-Islamic states, one being the Ghaznavids, who settled in what is now western Afghanistan. Another tribe, the Seljuks (named after a tribal leader), drove further westward, into Iran, Syria, and eventually the ethnically diverse Anatolia, held nominally by the Byzantines. The Seljuks consolidated their power over eastern Anatolia in 1071; their presence was a major factor in bringing about the Crusades. Despite the problems with the Crusaders, the Seljuk period was one of relative calm, with Persia seeing one of its most prosperous periods.

The stability and success of the Seljuk regime was the achievement of the politically skilled Vizir Nizam al-Mulk, a cultured Persian, a brilliant administrator, and a significant political philosopher, whose *Book of Government, or, Rules for Kings* is a classic of Islamic literature. At its peak, the Seljuk Empire spanned a region from northern India to the Aegean Sea, allowing the ancient trade routes of Anatolia to be connected with those to China. The strengthening of the Silk Route not only brought in enormous wealth but also promoted the development of industries, like

the manufacture of paper. Paper originally had to be imported from China, but in the 8th century, it was being produced in Baghdad and Damascus and exported to Europe.

The Seljuks distinguished themselves from earlier Islamic societies by their strict military hierarchy and attendant financial and landholding prerogatives, which were closed to all but a few exceptional local recruits. The principal elements of their political program were the mosque; the madrasa (Arabic for "school"); the *ribats* and *khanqahs*—the Sufis' lodgings; and the mausoleum, which commemorated their deeds.

The Seljuk architecture of Iran is characterized by elaborate brickwork and the development of the four-*iwan* plan. The Seljuks rulers in Anatolia used a vocabulary characterized primarily by stonework. Tiles were important decorative elements of Seljuk architecture. The technology for tile-making emerged out of a century-old tradition in Iran and Iraq, which was brought to Anatolia by the Seljuks. The tiles consisted of an underlying paste with a high silicate content over which a thick mixture containing kaolin and feldspar was spread. Monochromatic tiles were used for fill and borders; others were designed as large custom-made plaques for a particular place in the composition.

During Seljuk times, textile and leather exports were also important, as they were shipped to both Europe and the East. Once a year there was a vast commercial fair called Yabanlu Pazan ("Bazaar of the Foreigners") held for forty days not far from Kayseri, in the center of Anatolia, at a place where several caravan routes converged.

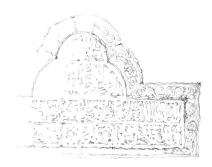

11.113 Seljuk calligraphy
Representations of the human form are banned in Islam, but images of birds and animals as well as sphinxes and centaurs—often linked to ancient totemic worship still prevalent in Anatolian lands—were frequently embedded in the composition of Seljuk art. Calligraphic inscriptions of Koranic verses were often used along the cornices or to frame portals.

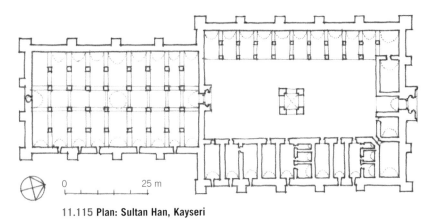

11.115 Plan: Sultan Han, Kayseri

11.114 Entry portal, Sultan Han, Kayseri, Turkey

Sultan Han

Among the finest and most characteristic of Seljuk buildings are the caravansaries (derived from two Persian words meaning "a palace for caravans"), or *hans*, constructed during the 13th century to encourage trade throughout the empire; several dozen of them survive in good condition. These buildings, some 119 of which are known to have been erected, were made to shelter and protect not only the caravan drivers but also their camels, horses, and donkeys, along with their cargoes, and to provide needed services. Though caravan resting places had existed for centuries, this was the first large-scale systematization of mercantile transport across a desert. The services offered were free of charge for the first three days. One of the basic rules was that travelers who came to the establishment were to be treated equally, without regard to race, creed, or social status.

Though plans of caravansaries may vary, they were typically square or rectangular buildings with thick stone walls and a large courtyard in the center surrounded by one- or two-story arcades; they accommodated bathing services, storage, a treasury, and stables, and had rooms for physicians, cooks, blacksmiths, and musicians as well. Though the exterior walls were plain and devoid of decoration, the portals were elaborately embellished with bands of geometrical designs and Koranic inscriptions. At the center of the caravansary was often a small mosque or prayer room, usually raised above ground level on a stone platform. At the far end of the courtyard, opposite the main portal, was a large vaulted hall, usually with a nave and three side aisles. Lit by narrow windows in the stone walls, it had a stone cupola centered above the nave and served as a shelter for goods and men during bad winter weather.

The Sultan Han, the grandest caravansary of all, covering 4,500 square meters, is west of Aksaray, a center in the Cappadocia region on the Konya Highway. Designed by a certain Muhammet of Syria, the doorway is particularly spectacular. The outer frame is covered with a delicate floral pattern. The tympanum over the door, which has an abstract geometrical pattern, looks as if it were eaten away by the encrustations of an open conically shaped stalactite vault. There are two parts to the design: a courtyard building and a hall. The courtyard building contained a bath and kitchen, and a room for special dignitaries. The large hall, entirely covered in vaults, consisted of one principal aisle and two symmetrical side aisles. There are windows at 4 meters high in each of the bays. The animals remained in the raised areas closest to the sidewalls; the middle was reserved for the travelers and communal functions.

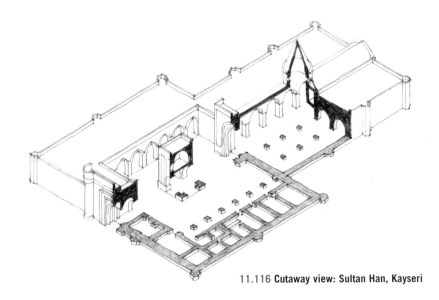

11.116 Cutaway view: Sultan Han, Kayseri

11.117 Gök Madrasa, Sivas, Turkey

11.118 Courtyard, Madrasa al-Firdus, Aleppo, Syria

First Madrasas

If the caravansaries were the central element of the Seljuk economic policy, the madrasa was an important element of Seljuk political ideology, initially serving to promote the Islamization of the Anatolian population, which until the 13th century had been predominantly Christian. The madrasa served subsequently to enforce and unify the Seljuk's Sunni beliefs. The madrasas were thus an important element in the campaign against the Shi'ite Fatimids of Egypt. Though many mosques had spaces and annexes that were used for classes as well as for residences for students and teachers, separate institutions for higher studies were still relatively rare prior to the Seljuks.

Madrasas were built in almost all parts of Asia Minor, but their origin is unclear. Some link it with the Buddhist *vihara*—and given that the eastern areas of Islam had been saturated with Buddhism for centuries, there is some plausibility to that argument. Another possibility is its association with the courtyard house, a tradition that goes back to ancient times. A madrasa was usually founded by a sultan or nobleman, who would generously endow it to meet its expenses. As with the caravansaries, the Seljuk madrasa followed a standard form. They were rectangular, compact, and relatively windowless, appearing as solid objects in the landscape. Portals, however, were often grandly and

richly carved. Most, like the Ince Minare Madrasa (1260–65) in Konya, Turkey, had a central courtyard lined with classrooms around a central *iwan* opposite the entrance. Others, like the Madrasa al-Fridus (1235–41) in Aleppo, Syria, had no *iwan*.

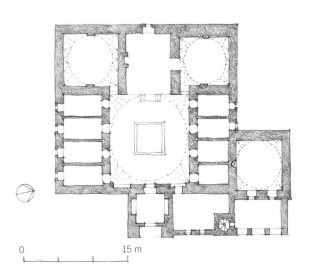

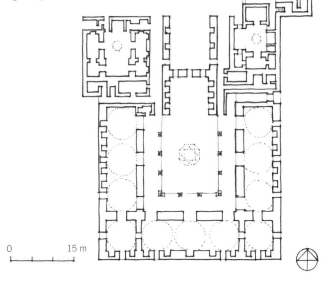

0   15 m

11.119 Plan: Ince Minare Madrasa, Konya, Turkey

0   15 m

11.120 Plan: Madrasa al-Firdus, Aleppo

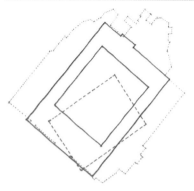
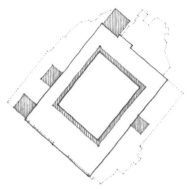
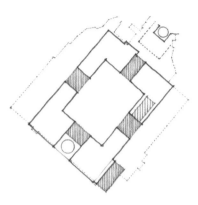

11.121 Development of the Great Mosque of Isfahan, Iran

Great Mosque of Isfahan

The Great Mosque of Isfahan (Masjid-i Jome, or Friday Mosque), in the northern part of the city, was one of the most influential of all early Seljuk religious structures. Though the building is known as a four-*iwan* type because the *iwans* face each other across an open courtyard, the building is, in actuality, the result of numerous architectural transformations. The primary building substance dates to a mosque built in the 840s CE that stood over an even earlier mosque, built in 772 CE, which in turn was built over the foundations of a Christian church. The mosque was a conventional hypostyle-courtyard mosque, typical of early mosques. But beginning around 870 CE, it was thoroughly revised. The central space was reduced somewhat by the addition of a new facade running around all four sides. An elegant *qibla* dome was built and, to the north, an annex with a domed sacred area, the original purpose of which is not precisely known.

In the time of Sultan Sanjar (1096–1157) four *iwans* were added to the courtyard, in essence imposing them on top of the older system. The old columns were thickened or removed, as was required; the original columnar rhythms are still best visible in the areas to the right and left of the northern *iwan*. In the 1350s, buildings were joined to the outer flanks of the structure, a madrasa was added to the western flank, and a *musalla* (a temporary place in which worshippers congregate to perform their prayers) to the eastern one, to name only the most prominent changes made to the building over time.

In its original pre-Islamic form, the *iwan* was a type of stage for the enthroned king, but the Seljuks used it for several purposes; in a madrasa, for example, it was a lecture room. At the Isfahan mosque, the *iwans* are grand portals, becoming the very symbol of the mosque on the other side. The Isfahan *iwans* are not identical. The main one, at the southwest, leads to the dome in front of the *qibla*. The side *iwans* have no particular relationship to the spaces behind them and lead nowhere except through doorways at the sides.

To the north, the *iwan* with its barrel vault points in the direction of a *haram*—a special sanctuary where contending parties could meet to settle disputes—which had originally been freestanding on three sides but was eventually roofed over and connected to the neighboring buildings. The particular reason why the mosque orientation was interrupted by the use of the four *iwans* is not known, but the building is an ideal space composed of principal elements, with the *iwans* a symbolic armature arranged in precise relationships to each other.

11.122 Courtyard, Great Mosque of Isfahan

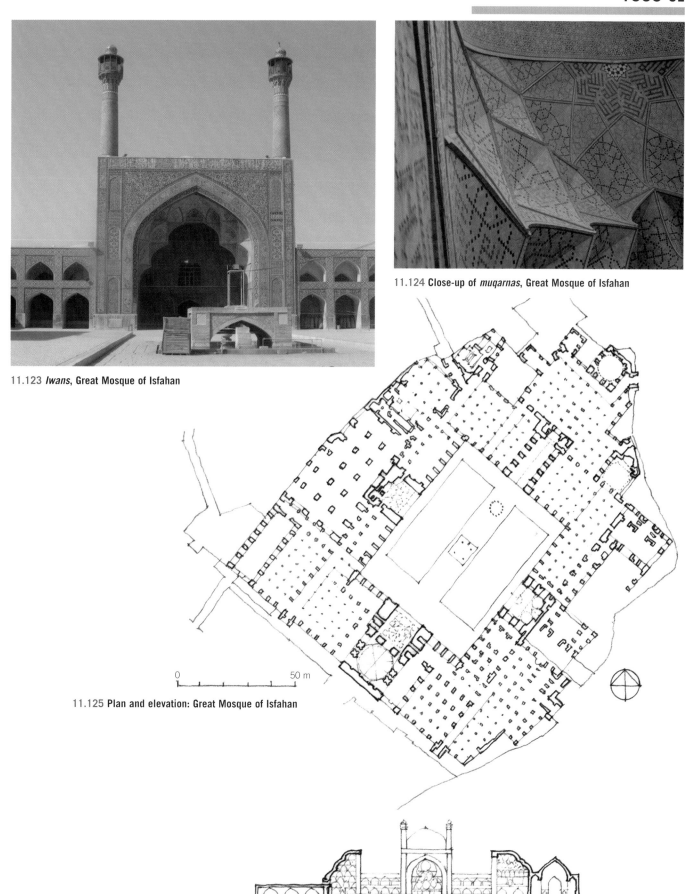

11.123 *Iwans*, Great Mosque of Isfahan

11.124 **Close-up of** *muqarnas*, **Great Mosque of Isfahan**

0   50 m

11.125 **Plan and elevation: Great Mosque of Isfahan**

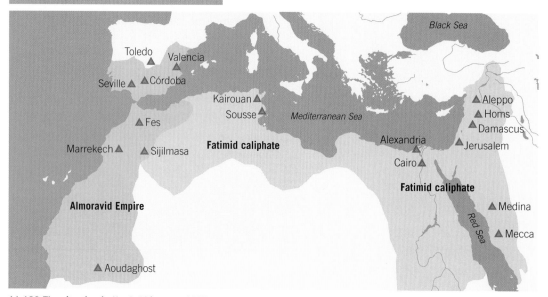

11.126 The situation in North Africa, ca. 1000 CE

The Fatimids

The Fatimids, who had established themselves in Tunisia, eventually lost Algeria and points to the west. But they were successful in their expansion to the east, sweeping through the Nile Valley, across Palestine, and into southern Syria to control a considerable part of the Middle East for more than two hundred years. Most Egyptians at that time were Sunni Muslims, whom the Fatimids—Shi'ites of the Isma'ili sect—opposed. The Fatimid caliphs, who considered themselves to be divine rulers sent by God to ensure the prevalence of Islamic justice, refused to recognize the legitimacy of the Sunni Abbasid caliphates ruling from Baghdad. It was the Fatimid vision and mission to convert the whole Muslim world to its faith and overthrow the Sunni caliphate. One of its principal architectural expressions was the construction of the city of al-Qahira, which became the heart of the modern city of Cairo, a few kilometers to the north of the old early Islamic town. At the core of the city, which was bisected by a main road, was a palace district with an east and west palace separated by a large square; nearby were the office of the state bureaucracy and the military. Al-Azhar Mosque (970–72 CE) was built to the southeast. Though it has been much renovated and enlarged, the mosque still maintains its North African hypostyle hall with wooden roofs. A striking feature is its central axis, which breaks

the rhythm and emphasizes the *qibla*. The minaret is placed on axis on the south side of the courtyard. The mosque in its final form, with various functions appended to its rectangular hall, almost became a city unto itself. It still remains an important center for Islamic theological scholarship in the Muslim world. The building is named "the radiant" in honor of the prophet Muhammed's daughter, Fatima al-Zahra, from whom the Fatimid dynasty claims descent.

Though descriptions testify to the sumptuousness of the Fatimid palaces, little of that palace architecture survives, but a sense of Fatimid era architectural skills can be gained by studying the facade of the Aqmar Mosque in Cairo (1125). Based loosely on the triumphal arch motif from classical times, it has a central portal flanked by tall niches that are surmounted by *muqarna* panels and by blind niches. An inscription runs across the top. Moldings and decorative friezes are used to tie the parts together.

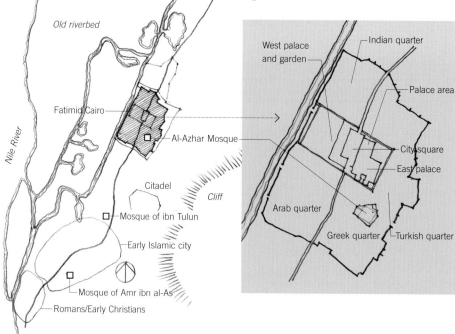

11.127 Cairo and environs

11.129 Al-Azhar Mosque, Cairo

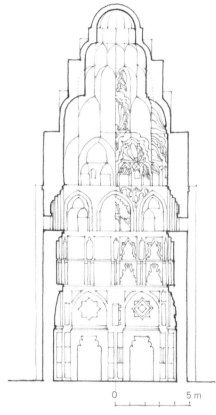

0   5 m

11.130 Section: Shrine of Imam Dur, Samarra, Iraq

Muqarnas

Muqarnas, also called stalactite or honeycombed vaulting, are one of the most ubiquitous features of Islamic architecture between the 11th and 15th centuries. They appear around the Islamic world, including South Asia, in a variety of materials, including brick, stone, stucco, and wood. The term's origin and meaning, as well as the historical development of the form, are not known for certain and are much debated. They originally developed out of squinches that eased the transition between the square and circle of a dome, but they became an articulation of the fascination among Islamic artists for complex geometrical patterns, which were being applied to the surfaces of doors and window moldings. Though they do not have an explicit symbolic value, they allude to the geometry of the heavens and the wonders of God's creations.

An early example is the Shrine of Imam Dur, in Samarra, Iraq (1085). The building consists of an elongated cube on which rests a series of octagonal tiers that telescope and rotate toward the final dome. Among the more developed example is the dome (*qubba*) of al-Barubiyyin in Marrakech, Morocco (1117), another early example of a complex dome structure. Its eight-pointed star seems to almost float free from its enclosing frame. The four corners have *muqarnas* of their own, producing a dynamic three-dimensional effect. One of the most spectacular of these domes is in the Alhambra palace in Granada, Spain, over the Hall of the Two Sisters (1356–59), which projects both chaos and order at the same time.

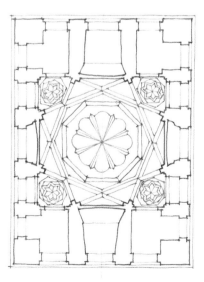

11.131 Plan of *qubba*, Al-Barubiyyin, Marrakech, Morocco

11.132 Mosque at Qayrawan, Tunisia

Mosque at Qayrawan

By the middle of the 9th century, Muslims were the uncontested rulers of North Africa and its Saharan and trans-Saharan trade routes. But given the heterogeneous population of Berbers, Romans, Christians, Africans, and Arab conquerors and their families, turbulence was ever-present. The Almoravids, Berbers from the western Sahara, eventually came to control Spain, so that by the year 1000 CE, a single Moorish empire spanned the Straits of Gibraltar, circumscribing the area of Morocco, Algeria, and Tunisia, an area known as the Maghreb (Arabic for "west"). They founded the city of Marrakech in 1062 as a portal to the southern trade routes. (The name *Marrakech* derives from *marra kouch*, which means "Land of the Kouch-men"; the Kouch were warriors with dark complexions from modern Mauritania.) It was, however, the subsequent rulers, the Almohads, who began construction of the Kutubiyya Mosque.

North African mosques have a plan that developed from the Spanish prototype, with the Mosque at Qayrawan (constructed in stages from 670 to 863 CE) serving as a particularly important model. The Kutubiyya Mosque in Marrakech, though built four hundred years later, differs little from the Qayrawan mosque. It has a low hypostyle hall organized around a T shape composed of the raised aisle facing the *qibla* wall

and a central axial aisle that connects the *mihrab* to the courtyard. Even the number of aisles—seventeen perpendicular to the *qibla* wall—matches that of Qayrawan. This is clearly an intentional link to a more ancient brand of Islam. But the rough quarry stone minaret, square in plan, towers 70 meters in the air, nearly twice the height of the minaret at Qayrawan. The result is that the square minaret, with its vertical emphasis, balances the horizontality of the prayer hall. The tower is five times taller than it is wide, with a slim

lantern at its top. Each of these five units, which correspond to five stacked interior rooms, is articulated on the facade with a framed register. Each register is different, though a motif of interlacing poly-lobed arches and blind openings is consistent throughout. The stone patterning, unlike that of the Almoravids, is not floral; the patterns result from the interlacing of simple repeated geometric shapes to create the appearance of a light web or net texture, known as *shabka*.

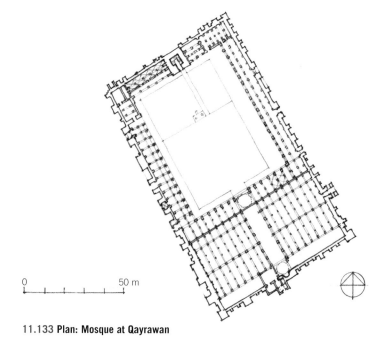

0   50 m

11.133 Plan: Mosque at Qayrawan

11.134 Mosque of Tinmal, Morocco

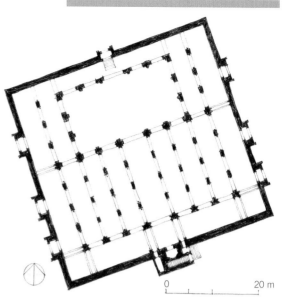

11.135 Plan: Mosque of Tinmal

Almoravid Dynasty

The Almoravids who ruled Spain and Morocco were replaced by another Berber tribe, the Almohads, whose base was even farther south in the Atlas Mountains. The economic center of both regimes was Fes, with its cosmopolitan populations of Berbers, Arabs, Andalusians, and Africans. The Almohads were active builders of religious, military, and civilian structures, as well as powerful promoters of crafts. Almohad textiles were shipped throughout the Islamic world and were sold in Christian Europe as well. The architectural styles of the Almoravids and Almohads are related, but there are important differences. The Almoravids adopted the more refined Spanish style, as in the great mosque in the city Tlemcen (1082) on the Moroccan-Algerian border, an important nexus in north-south/east-west trade routes. Inspired by the Mosque of Córdoba. The *qibla* dome is supported by slender ribs with delicately carved filigree patterns in between, making it seem to float in the open sky. The Almohads, who espoused a particularly puritanical form of Islam, developed a mosque type that adhered to a strictly circumscribed architectural plan, such as the Mosque of Tinmal, (1153–54), located 100 kilometers southeast of Marrakech in the Atlas Mountains. The wider central aisle and transept in front of the *qibla* wall, combined with the entrance courtyard, create a spatial figure within the plan. There were no minarets on the front, but rather a square tower directly over the *qibla*. The fortlike exterior belies the delicacy of the interior articulation.

11.136 Plan: Al-Azhar Mosque, Cairo

11.137 Locations of stave churces, Scandinavia

11.138 Kaupanger Stave Church, Norway

Medieval Scandinavia

Most stave churches in Scandinavia were built during the 12th century, after the Viking campaigns had come to an end. The conversion of Norway to Christianity was not due to missionary activity, as in Ireland and elsewhere, but came about through the efforts of the Viking kings. Olav Trygvason, who was king toward the end of the 10th century, was the first to build churches in Norway, probably with the help of a master builder brought over from the British Isles. Gradually, however, local craftsmen were drawn in, and wooden buildings appeared. Once totaling about eight hundred, today there are only about thirty of these unusual buildings extant.

Like the Viking ships, the stave churches derive from a building tradition developed to defy the harsh elements. A low wall of flat stones raised the buildings above ground level. Beyond that, columns, planks, and supports were dovetailed, pegged, and wedged—never nailed. Thus the structures were flexible and could expand or contract in damp or dry weather. To tighten the structure, a continuous belt of cross-braces was added to the periphery of the buildings. The interiors were modestly ornamented and very dark, with small strips of light occasionally forcing their way from the window in the west gable or from the small peepholes along the top of the longitudinal walls. Religious services were intimate and illuminated by candlelight. Psalm books were not yet in use.

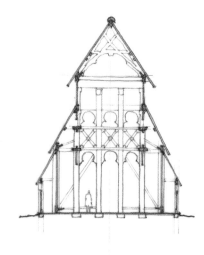

11.139 Borgund Stave Church, Norway

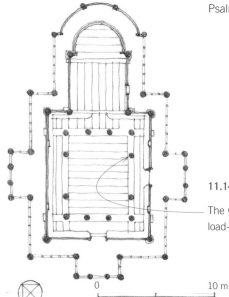

11.140 Plan and section: Borgund Stave Church

The word *stave*, from the Nors *stavr*, refers to the load-bearing posts that make up the structure.

1200 CE

The history of religions is never static, and this is especially true during the 13th and 14th centuries. In Japan, Buddhism developed into a variant known as Pure Land Buddhism, which is based on the concept of visualizations as the path to liberation. The Itsukushima Shrine in Japan brought out the delicate balance in Pure Land Buddhism's attempt to achieve a balance between outer landscape and inner meditation. In China, Mahayana Buddhism continued to take the form of large state-sponsored monasteries, with the pagoda (or *ta*) serving as a vertical representation of the many levels of enlightenment. In Pagan, in modern-day Myanmar, Buddhism came to be associated with didactic panels placed inside the temple superstructures. Buildings that were once meant to be solid now had dramatic internal illumination. In Cambodia, the Khmer rulers shifted from Shaivite Buddhists to Vishnavites, the latter better serving their developing ideology of royal divinity. Scale was no issue: Angkor Wat remains one of the largest religious buildings in the world. In South Asia, Hinduism continued its transformation into a religion with a multifaceted pantheon. The Orissan kings emphasized the sun god in a temple that had at its symbolic center an enormous stone chariot. The Hoysalas developed temples with a star-shaped plan to accommodate multiple deities.

In the Christian world, the situation was equally diverse and fluid. Large urban cathedrals that required the coordination of the powers of the Roman Church with those of the state (such as Gloucester Cathedral in Norman England); pilgrimage churches, with their emphasis on the Virgin Mary (such as Notre-Dame of Reims in France); and churches belonging to a new type of religious order—the mendicants who renounced the wealth and ostentation of the great cathedrals, preferring instead simple and modest buildings (such as the Dominican Church of Toulouse in France)—all developed nearly simultaneously. In Italy, the urban cathedrals and mendicant churches formed composite, though somewhat contradictory, liturgical spaces. The Ethiopians, who maintained the great tradition of rock cutting, created an entire liturgical landscape based on distant Jerusalem.

Following the dots on the map, it becomes clear that there is a major gap in the area from Central Asia to the Near East, in largely Islamic lands, where architecture was in a virtual standstill from 1220 to about 1330 because of the Mongolian disruptions. Mongolian armies invaded south into China and Burma and westward into Russia and Anatolia, altering the economic and political landscape everywhere they went. The Song in China, the Seljuks in Anatolia, the Delhi sultanate in north India, and the Novgorod Empire in Russia all came to a rather sudden end. The only Islamic region to prosper, well out of the range of the Mongolians, was Spain and North Africa, where in Granada and Fes new mosques and palaces were built. The most spectacular of the palaces was the Alhambra.

Once the destructive fury was over, the Mongolians were quick to adapt to local customs and ways, becoming Buddhist, Confucian, or Muslim—both Sunni and Shi'ite—depending on where they were. In China, they founded the Yuan dynasty. By eliminating regional rivalries, at least for a while, the Mongolians lowered the risks of trade across the great distances of the Eurasian continent. This enabled the quickening of the Eurasian economy that reached its zenith in the 15th and 16th centuries. One of the consequences of the 13th-century Mongolian domination of the Eurasian north was the rapid development of a sea-based southern economy that stretched from Africa, India, and Indonesia to China. Southeast Asia, in fact, now became an economic zone all its own, with the Burmese in Pagan, the Khmer in Cambodia and the Srivijayan Empire in Malaysia and Sumatra controlling trade between India and China, and becoming themselves major rice producers. The coastal ports extending from southern China to eastern Africa were now all part of a single trade network.

This was the time period of an amazing cast of architectural patrons, including Emperor Huizong (1100–25) in China; Prime Minister Taira no Kiyomori (1118–81) in Japan; Suryavarman II (1113–45) in Cambodia; King Kyanzittha (1084–1113) of Burma; Qutb-ud-Din Aibak (1150–1210) in northern India; King Narasimhadeva (1238–64) of Orissa; King Lalibela (1185–1225) in Ethiopia; Mohammed I (1238–73) of Islamic Spain; Frederick II (1194–1250) of the Holy Roman Empire.

In Central America, the Toltecs, claiming descent from Teotihuacán, established a militaristic culture that was to define the region's civilizations right up to the Spanish conquest. In the Yucatán, Chichén Itzá emerged as the primary city-state, the final moment of Mayan development before its final collapse around 1250.

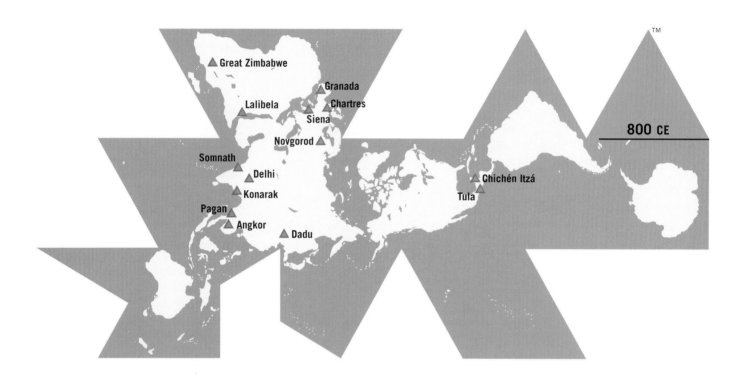

800 CE

Great Zimbabwe
Granada
Lalibela
Chartres
Siena
Novgorod
Somnath
Delhi
Konarak
Chichén Itzá
Tula
Pagan
Angkor
Dadu

Khmer Kingdom: Angkor Period
802–1431

▲ **Angkor Wat**
802–1220

▲ **Lokesvara Temple**
Completed 1191

Kingdom of Pagan
802–1431

▲ **Ananda Temple**
1090–1105

▲ **Shwezigon**
Late 11th century

Japan: Late Heian Period
ca. 900–1185

Kamakura Period
1185–1333

Nanbokucho Period
1336–1392

▲ **Itsukushima Shrine**
6th to 13th centuries

Northern Song Dynasty
960–1127

Southern Song Dynasty
1127–1279

Yuan Dynasty
1279–1368

◉ *Yingzhao Fashi* **published**
1103

▲ **Dadu**
Rebuilt 1264

1000 CE   **1200 CE**   **1400 CE**

India: Hindu States
10th to 12th centuries

Delhi Sultanate
1210–1526

▲ **Quwwat-ul-Islam**
ca. 1193–1315

▲ **Sun Temple at Konarak**
Late 13th century

▲ **Vadakkunnathan Temple**
11th to 19th centuries

▲ **Kesava (Somnatha) Temple**
ca. 1268

Zagwe Dynasty
ca. 1137–1270

Mamluk Sultanate
1250–1517

▲ **Great Zimbabwe**
ca. 1250–1450

▲ **Churches of Lalibela**
13th century

▲ **Mosque of Djenne**
13th century

Holy Roman Empire
962–1806

▲ **St. Denis**
1144

▲ **Chartres Cathedral**
1194–1220

▲ **St. Croce, Florence**
Begun 1294

Crusades
1096–1270

▲ **Notre-Dame, Paris**
1163–1250

▲ **Notre-Dame of Reims**
1211–90

Black Plague
1347–1352

▲ **Fontenay Abbey**
Founded 1119

▲ **Amiens Cathedral**
1220–35

▲ **Castel del Monte**
ca. 1240

▲ **Exeter Cathedral**
1280–1300

▲ **Palazzo Publico, Siena**
1297–1310

Republic of Novgorod
12th to 15th centuries

▲ **Intercession of the Virgin**
1165

▲ **St. Paraskeva Piatnitsa**
1207

Nasrid Sultanate
1298–1492

▲ **Alhambra**
13th to 14th centuries

Toltec-Chichén City-State
ca. 1000–1200

▲ **Tula**
ca. 950–1150

▲ **Chichén Itzá**
ca. 7th to 13th centuries

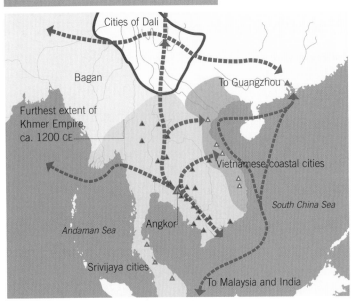

12.1 Southeast Asia, ca. 1200 CE

12.2 Vrah Vishnulok (Angkor Wat), near Siem Reap, Cambodia

Vrah Vishnulok (Angkor Wat)

The Song dynasty (960–1279) in China and the Chola in India (847–1249) exerted powerful economic influences in Southeast Asia, even though it was India that won out from a cultural point of view, with its variants of Buddhism and Hinduism spreading throughout the region. Another factor in the area's geopolitics was the Dali kingdom in southern China's Yunnan Province. From 900 CE until 1253, when it was conquered by the Mongolians and brought back into the fold of the Chinese empire, it was an autonomous Buddhist state and served as an overland passageway to southern China. Its primary city, Kunming, had long been the main stopping point along the route to India by way of Burma. The disruptions of the Silk Route that were the result of the Mongolian expansion into Asia made this alternative route especially important. In the 9th century, Dali, a nearby city, took control of Kunming and unified the area, building new temples and palaces.

A more distant development was the integration of the East African coast into the circuits of Arab and Indian traders, which created a continuous fabric of ocean ports from Africa to China. These regional and global events were highly advantageous to the Khmer, who were now at their height militarily and economically; they sat at the center of north-south and east-west trade in addition to having become one of the great

rice produces in all of Asia. By the 11th century, Yasodharapura, the Khmer capital located just north of the Tonle Sap Lake, had grown into a major city with about a million inhabitants; it was certainly the largest city in South or Southeast Asia, and maybe the second or third largest in the world.

The reason for its success was a *baray* system; its controlled release of water for irrigation increased rice production. King Rajendravarman (r. 944–68 CE) extended the city to the east with the construction of new temples. King Suryavarman I (r. 1001–50)

added new palaces to the north and a vast new *baray* some 7 by 2 kilometers to the west. He also created a large new temple, Baphuon (ca. 1060), just outside the gates of Yasodharapura. Baphuon became the center of a new square city, about as big as, and overlapping, Yasodharapura. But all these temples paled in comparison to the one now known as Angkor Wat, built by King Suryavarman II (1113–50). For its construction, a large part of Yasodharapura had to be cleared. The temple's probable original name, Vrah Vishnulok, was dedicated

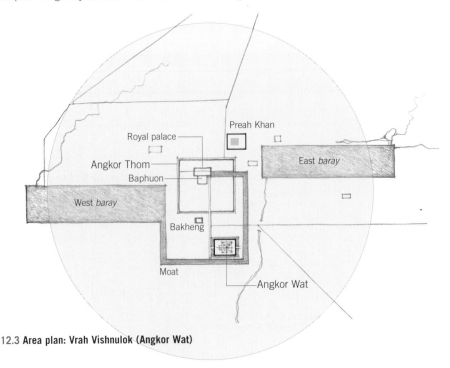

12.3 Area plan: Vrah Vishnulok (Angkor Wat)

to both Vishnu and Suryavarman himself; its *garbha-griha* once held a statue of Vishnu represented as a facsimile of Suryavarman. There is much that is still unknown about the temple—archaeological work on the Khmer civilization is still in its infancy. The building's astrological notations (such as the columns on its balustrade, which equal to the number of years in a Hindu age), as well as its esoteric astronomical measurements, are still being decoded. It is therefore generally assumed that the building is a map of cosmological space and time as understood by the Khmer.

The outer surface of the shrine did not look as it does today. Along with its four corner towers, it is presumed to have been gilded and would have shone brightly, especially when illuminated by the western sun. The stone would have been covered with a thin layer of stucco and painted. A causeway in the form of a raised path 9.4 meters wide and 350 meters long leads across the "ocean" and then across an open field to the front of the temple compound. The causeway terminates at the bottom of an elevated cruciform altar in front of the entrance to the temple. This was as far as the commoners could go. Both the causeway and the altar are edged by a balustrade designed as long serpents, a reference to Shesha Naga, the celestial serpent with seven heads. A critical role in the story of the cosmic ocean is played by Shesha, for it is on the coiled body of Shesha that the sleeping Vishnu dreams the universe. While he was dreaming, a lotus on a stalk emerged from Vishnu's navel, on which sat the god Brahma, who actually created the universe. The word *shesha* means "remainder," and Shesha is supposed to be made of what remains after each cosmic cycle comes to an end. The destruction of everything produces a remainder, which is the critical scaffold from which the "dream" of life comes into being. The Shesha Naga was one of the most prominent symbols of the Khmer.

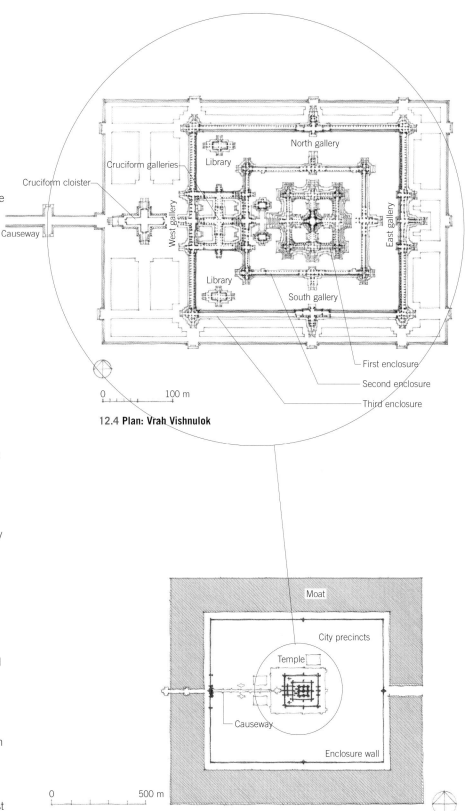

12.4 Plan: Vrah Vishnulok

12.5 City of Vrah Vishnulok

12.6 Cruciform courtyard, Vrah Vishnulok

12.7 Third enclosure gallery, Vrah Vishnulok

After the Naga altar is a three-portaled gate that gives access to the third enclosure. The spaces beyond this were reserved for royalty. Along the walls of this enclosure, facing outward and protected by a colonnade, bas-reliefs tell of the various manifestations of Vishnu; they are interspersed with illustrations of the life and family of Suryavarman II. This is where the primary symbolic message of the temple—Suryavarman II as a manifestation of Vishnu—is made clear. Unlike Buddhist structures, in which one moves clockwise, the narrative works counterclockwise, starting from the northwest corner. The bas-reliefs were painted in strong hues and would have been visible from the ground below through the colonnade.

From here one moves up through the different levels, each a smaller version of the cosmic order of ocean and island precinct, one "world" resting on another. Unlike Bakong (see "800 CE"), which consisted of a series of terraces, the vertical scale of Vrah Vishnulok escalates and intensifies as it nears the central precinct in the final level, which looms above and is accessible only by a long and very steep flight of steps. It contains the central shrine, the climax of the whole arrangement: a tower that rises 43 meters above the floor of its gallery (that is itself 23 meters higher than the level of

the moat). It is surrounded by four smaller corner towers. The main *garbha-griha*, with its statue of Vishu/Suryavarman II, was originally accessible from all directions. There was also a 23-meter-deep well at its center into which offerings could be thrown. Wells, found in most Khmer temples, are not only a connection to the water-based authority of the Khmer rulers but also an inverted mirror of the cosmic mountain symbolized by the tower.

The influences of the 9th-century Temple of Prambanam are obvious, except here the various peaks are tied into a single, extraordinarily complex composition. Furthermore, movement into the structure is not only axial but also from the corners, which gives Vrah Vishnulok a more multidimensional aspect than earlier temples. But the use of square piers and Greek and Persian decorative motifs in the galleries indicate that Vrah Vishnulok's details might also be viewed from within the sphere of Hellenism. The cruciform structures known as libraries that flank the causeway seem particularly Hellenistic, right down to their use of attached pilasters on the entrance porches. A good deal of scholarly work still needs to be done to properly understand this building's importance as it relates to the flow of architectural thought through South and Southeast Asia.

Angkor Thom and Preah Khan

In 1181, King Jayavarman VII converted to Buddhism and embarked on a rebuilding of Yasodharapura. He relocated its center from Bekong to a new temple called Indrapattha, known today as the Bayon, located just outside the old city walls. Instead of the whole body, only the face of the Buddha was graphed onto the many towers of the temple, a reinterpretation of Mahayana Buddhist practice. The gigantic face sculptures give Bayon a unique, enigmatic character. Jayavarman VII's new city, known today as Angkor Thom, was smaller than Yasodharapura—3 kilometers square instead of 4—and it probably served primarily as a palace compound, since it incorporated the palaces that had been built there by previous kings. Among the other astonishing buildings erected by Jayavarman VII is a Buddhist university to the north of the city, originally called Lokesvara but known today as Preah Khan. At its height, the Lokesvara temple complex had one thousand students and teachers. Surrounded by a moat, this huge complex comprises a vast axial network of corridors, chapels, libraries, and pavilions, unified by the two axes that lead through numerous thresholds to the central sanctuary. The principal inner surfaces were covered with stucco (some traces still remain) and

12.8 Quasi-Hellenic details in the interior of the so-called Library at Vrah Vishnulok

12.9 Lokesvara Temple (Preah Khan), near Siem Reap, Cambodia

were presumably painted with didactic images in vibrant colors. One of the more interesting structures is a two-story building with round columns, perhaps dating from the 13th century.

Environmental degradation as a result of deforestation led to a rapid collapse of the Angkor aqua-engineering systems in the middle of the 14th century. The kingdom was eventually sacked by the Thais and its vast wealth plundered. After that, the Khmer abandoned Angkor and moved south to Phnom Penh in 1431. The collapse of the Khmer was also a consequence of the rise of the Mongolians, who organized their trade routes through Samarkand, much to the detriment of Southeast Asia.

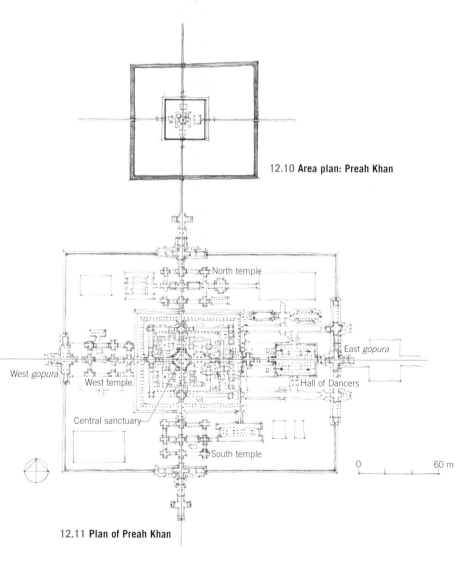

12.10 Area plan: Preah Khan

North temple

East *gopura*

West *gopura*

Hall of Dancers

West temple

Central sanctuary

South temple

0   60 m

12.11 Plan of Preah Khan

12.12 View of Pagan, near Nyangu, Burma (Ananda Temple in left foreground; Shwezigon in background)

Arimaddanapura was located on a bend of the Irrawaddy River to the west of an extinct volcano that had significant symbolic import. The earliest buildings were terraced stupas derived from Indonesian prototypes. The Shwezigon Paya (the word *paya* can be translated as "pagoda," "stupa," or "*zedi*"), for instance, is a solid-core stupa that rises steeply, like a stepped pyramid, through five square terraces, culminating in a stupa form so completely merged with the umbrellas

Kingdom of Pagan

The Khmer and the Kingdom of Pagan were the principal powerhouses of Southeast Asia. In the 12th century, the Pagan came to dominate the Puy cities and ruled over an area roughly equivalent in size to modern-day Myanmar (formerly Burma). Its capital was at Arimaddanapura (the "City of the Crusher of Enemies"), now known as the city of Pagan. For two centuries, Pagan waged war with the Cholas in peninsular India while maintaining a close but carefully guarded relationship with India's eastern kingdoms. Unlike the Khmer Empire, which was first Hindu, then Buddhist, or the Srivijayan Empire, which built both Buddhist and Hindu structures, the Pagan were Theravada Buddhists, a traditional form of Buddhism that was practiced in Sri Lanka. Between the 12th and 15th centuries, Pagan kings constructed more than two thousand structures, stupas, and temples. Despite their Buddhism, the Pagan kings, like the Khmers of Cambodia, adopted the Hindu idea, modern for its time, that the Buddha was a manifestation of Vishnu and that a virtuous king could also be a manifestation of Vishnu. Unlike the Khmer, however, the temples of the Pagan kings were not dedicated to themselves as manifestations of Vishnu, but to the Buddha.

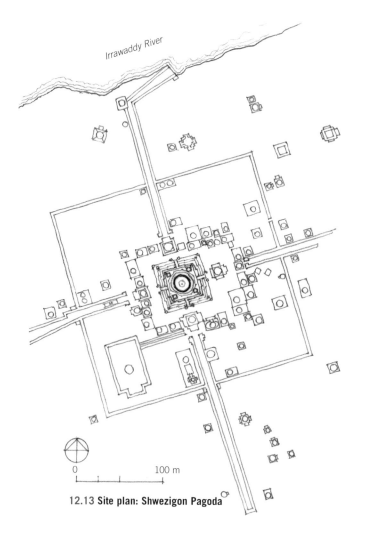

Irrawaddy River

0   100 m

12.13 Site plan: Shwezigon Pagoda

12.14 Shwezigon Pagoda, Pagan

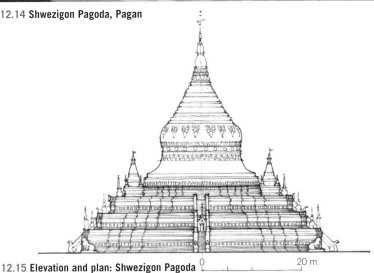

12.15 Elevation and plan: Shwezigon Pagoda

0   20 m

of its *chattri* above that the base forms an almost conical shape. Steep flights of steps at the center of the base's four sides gave pilgrims access to the terraces that, like those at Borobodur, contain didactic panels depicting tales from the life of the Buddha and other Buddhist texts. Though the stupa is intended to be conceptually solid, there is within it a complex network of narrow, interconnected corridors that were designed to enable postconstruction donors to gain merit by paying for dedicatory tablets embedded in its walls. The temple is presumed to have contained an important relic in its core, but it has not yet been found and is presumed stolen. Since the stupa was considered an extension of that relic, latter-day worshippers hoped to gain nirvana by embedding objects in its "force field."

Around 1100, soon after his ascension to the throne, Kyanzittha (1084–1113) began construction of several large stupas, among them the Ananda Temple (1090–1105). Though it has the customary square terraces, complete with glazed terra-cotta didactic tablets and corner stupas, it has no external staircases. From the square, ground-level substructure, the building rises in an escalating rhythm to the base of the superstructure and *shikhara*. In this building, the didactic galleries have been incorporated into the body of the temple in the form of two tall concentric ambulatories that are entered through broad, spacious porches at the center of each side. In no other Pagan temple is there so extensive a program of Buddhist education. Light comes through the thick walls into the outer ambulatory from high windows in a regular rhythm. Passageways cut directly in front of the windows allow light to filter further in. Nonetheless, at the core, the illumination is still rather sparse, and the atmosphere is meant to contrast with the light that comes dramatically into the space from hidden clerestory windows. This light illuminates the Buddha statues located in niches in the central core, facing out in all four directions. The clerestory light illuminating the innermost sanctum, never found in other Hindu temples, is a distinct Pagan invention. Almost all of the stupas were made of bricks produced locally from the alluvial soil.

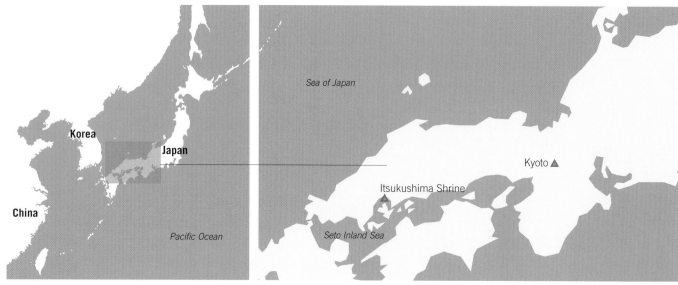

12.16 Location of Kyoto and the Itsukushima Shrine, Japan

Sanju-sangen-do

In Japan, frequent wars, natural disasters, and two attempted Mongolian invasions in 1274 and 1281 created a feeling of instability, which the Buddhists associated with the predicted end of the reign of Buddhism. This led to a period similar to that of the rise of the bhakti cults in South Asia. Charismatic Buddhist monks traveled the countryside popularizing Pure Land Buddhism, which promised enlightenment for anyone who devoutly repeated the name of the Amidaba Buddha. An arresting example of the architecture of Pure Land Buddhism was built in Kyoto in 1164 by Taira no Kiyomori (1118–81), an important general. Known as Sanju-sangen-do ("Hall of 33 Bays"), the structure was 120 meters long (33 by 4 bays), designed to display a thousand life-size statues of the thousand-armed Kannon (a bodhisattva goddess of mercy), five hundred on either side of a large central Kannon image. The statues are arranged in multiple rows and densely packed. Twenty-eight additional "attendants," many of them directly derived from the contemporary Hindu gods of India, are lined up in front. The forest of statues, arrayed as far as the eye can see, makes a strong impression, more fantastic than some earlier visualization structures, such as the Byodo-in.

12.17 Sanju-sangen-do, Kyoto, Japan

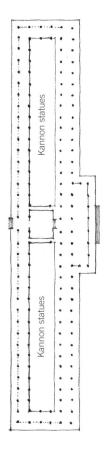

Kannon statues

Kannon statues

12.18 Plan of Sanju-sangen-do

12.19 Interior: Sanju-sangen-do

12.20 Itsukushima Shrine, Hiroshima Prefecture, Japan

west, or inland. Each shrine has a *haiden* (a worship or oratory hall), a *haraidono* (a hall for purification rites), and a *honden* (a main hall) in sequential arrangement. The timber columns are all coated with vermilion lacquer.

Torii gates have both Buddhist and Shinto associations. A torii is a reinterpretation of the Buddhist *torana*, or gateway. In Shintoism a torii also symbolizes the call to the god to come forth and grant the worshipper's prayers. Another meaning of *torii* is "bird perch," a term referring to a mythological story in which the gods attempt to lure the sun goddess, Amaterasu, from the cave in which she had hidden with the sounds of songbirds.

Itsukushima Shrine

Shintoism had by no means been weakened. In fact, Taira no Kiyomori also built a Shinto shrine on Itsukushima, one of the many islands in the Seto Inland Sea. A sacred site since the earliest times, it was home to Ichikishima-Hime-no-Mikoto, the kami "who ensures safety at sea," and her two sisters. The original shrine dating back to the 6th century was now rebuilt on a grand scale. In the main sanctuary Kiyomori also presented thirty-three illustrated scrolls of the Buddhist Lotus Sutra to the shrine, making Itsukushima a seamless blend of Shinto and Buddhist practices and architecture. Its solitary vermilion torii stand knee-deep in the sea at high tide, with the green mountain island as a backdrop; the shrine is regarded by many Japanese as an icon of their culture and identity. At high tide, it appears to float, and it is then that its Shinto character merges with Pure Land Buddhism's ideas, which would describe it as floating on the infinite ocean on a lotus plant. The beach shrine is connected by a *kairo* (a roofed, semi-enclosed corridor) to the two sides of the inlet. The *kairo* frame the relationship between water and land. There are two sanctuaries: the *honsha* (the main shrine housing female deities), which faces out toward the water, and on the east, roughly perpendicular to it, the *maro-do jinja* (the shrine for male guest deities) facing

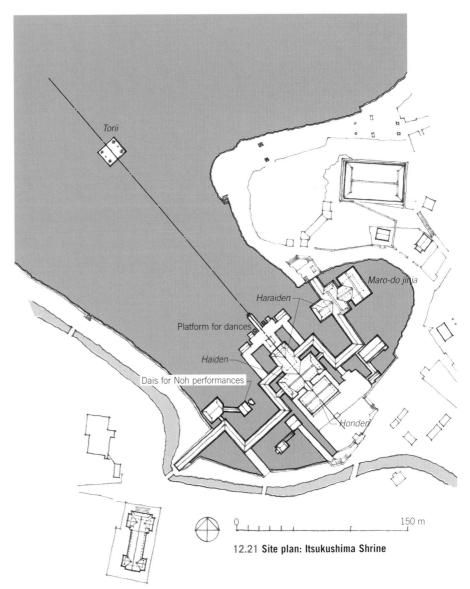

12.21 Site plan: Itsukushima Shrine

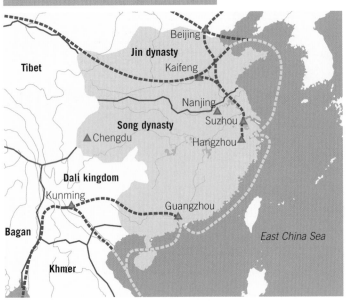

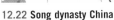

12.22 Song dynasty China

12.23 Garden of the Master of the Nets, Sozhou, China

Southern Song Dynasty

The Mongolian Jin and Jurchen dynasties to the north cut off trade along the Silk Route, forcing the Song to move their capital to Hangzho, south of modern-day Shanghai, their former capital, Nanjing, having been devastated by Jin dynasty raids. This move forced the Song to give up lucrative farming land for a terrain of mountains, lakes, and rivers all inhospitable to widespread agriculture, making them dependent on imported rice from Southeast Asia. The Song thereupon created a vibrant maritime trading network to India. Ships were built, harbors improved, and warehouses constructed. As the wealth poured in, powerful mercantile families began to establish large estates distinguished by elaborate private gardens. A garden at Dezhou, for instance, was renowned for its four distinct landscapes. Another garden had an artificial lake, with an island emerging from marshes and surrounded by artificial mountains and piles of rocks on which a palace was built. Little West Lake, a private garden in Lin'an, went so far as to "borrow" the views of an actual mountain outside its boundaries, splicing its view into its composition. The same is true for Genyue (1117–22), a Northern Song garden in Bianliang (modern Kaifeng) that is focused on a high peak, Longevity Mountain, in its northeastern corner. A multitude of lower peaks, called Ten Thousand Pines, are also visually "borrowed." Interspersed in the

garden are about forty structures, including verandas, lodges, towers, platforms, and rustic huts, all linked by pathways that move up and down and wind around, framing the architectural structures within and against each other and the landscape.

There are several estates in Suzhou, which became an important center for China's silk industry during the Song dynasty. The Garden of the Master of the Nets dates from this period. (Its name came from a subsequent owner of the garden.) It has three sections focused around an inner garden designed to enhance and intensify the essential qualities of the landscape and achieve a perfected, "natural" experience that was, nonetheless, imbued with didactic messages. In that sense the garden was both a visual and literary experience. The Song dynasty period, known for its literary achievements, was one in which storytelling became a popular form of entertainment. The stories told by professional entertainers were printed in storybooks, called *huaben*, which later inspired China's longer didactic novels dealing with the battle between the virtuous and the unscrupulous that teach the consequences of behavior. This was related to the ideals of Confucianism and, during the Song dynasty, neo-Confucianism, an aggregate of Buddhist metaphysics and Confucian ethics that taught that through reason and study, the whole world could be understood.

Yingzhao Fashi

The Song emperor Huizong (1100–1125) was an enthusiastic patron of the arts. A catalog of his paintings, the *Xuanhe Huapu*, published in 1123, lists over six thousand works in his collection. Art academies were established in his reign, which saw an increased interest in ancient history and culture; collecting antiques also became popular. Huizong also commissioned the *New Yingzhao Fashi* (1103), a detailed manual of architecture and construction. It was called the "new" *Yingzhao Fashi* because the previous one, dating to the T'ang, had become outdated. The manual was not, however, intended as an aesthetic or philosophical document, but rather to help the imperial administrators regulate, and reign in, the construction industry.

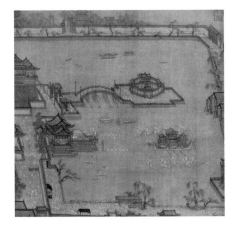

12.24 Mountain and river garden scenes from the Song dynasty

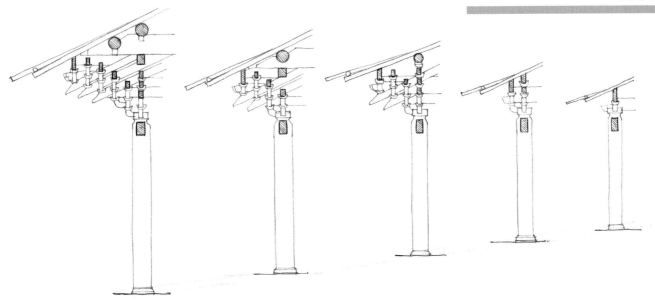

12.25 Hierarchy of the *dou-gong* (bracket system) according to the *Yingzhao Fashi*

Aesthetically, architecture under the Song and the Jin (and later under the Yuan) had become very ornamental and complicated. The size of the *dou-gong* decreased with respect to the overall column heights, but it increased in complexity and showmanship. The placement of columns was even occasionally disrupted to accommodate more ambitious spatial arrangements. While all these transformations made for a much richer and more expressive architecture, it also resulted in a great deal of waste and corruption. Because construction was controlled by powerful guilds that carefully guarded their knowledge, passing it on only in oral verse, buildings routinely ran over budget. The imperial court found that it could not reasonably predict the cost to complete buildings. Furthermore, the high demand for timber was causing rapid deforestation in the Song territories, and with the northern forests in the control of "barbarians," the court feared that it would soon run out of timber. The *New Yingzhao Fashi* aimed to solve both these problems. Li Jie was an intellectual, a painter, and an author of books on geography, history, and philology. In addition, as a superintendent for state buildings in the Ministry of Works (*Gong Bu*), he had carried out several building projects, which made him an ideal person for the job. For three years Li Jie systematically interviewed leaders of the construction guilds, documented their building principles and processes, and added his own rationalizations

and explanations. He finally presented his findings in 1105 in the form of regulations that the government administrators could use to monitor construction expenditures. Li Jie's *Yingzhao Fashi* consists of thirty-four chapters organized into five parts: basic data, regulations, labor work, materials, and drawings. Each part is subdivided into the following thirteen sections: moats and fortification; stonework; structural carpentry; nonstructural carpentry and joinery (doors, windows, partitions, screens, ceilings, staircases, shrines, etc.); stone carving and dressing; turnery; sawing; bamboo work; tiling; clay work and plastering; decorative painting and coating; brickwork; brick and tile making; and kilns.

The *Yingzhao Fashi* described eight types of buildings but was concerned primarily with imperial and governmental buildings, and not with buildings for commoners, since only the former would be paid for by the administrator. Most of the drawings are plans (determining the basic size of a building), sections (determining quantities), and wood sections (instrumental in determining costs). All these were regulated by a proportioning system, known as the *cai-fen*. A *cai* was 10 *fen*, and a *zu-cai* was 21 *fen*. The standard proportions were in the ratio 2:3. Thus a standard wood section would be 10 by 15 *fen*.

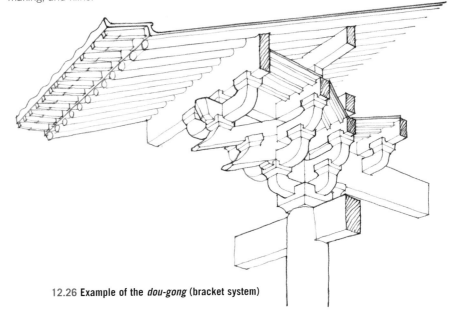

12.26 Example of the *dou-gong* (bracket system)

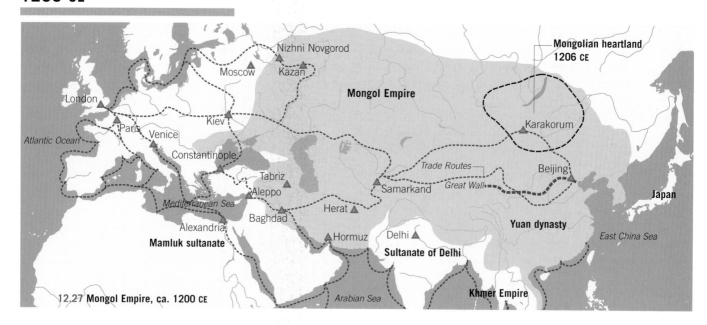

12.27 Mongol Empire, ca. 1200 CE

The Mongol Empire

By 1206, Temuchin, called Chengiz Khan ("Mighty Ruler") had united the dispersed and infighting Mongolian tribes, sending his armies south and west to create an expansive empire. Following his death in 1227, his son Ögedei advanced even farther west, taking Kiev in 1240. Kublai Khan, another grandson of Chengiz, completed the conquest of China in 1279, establishing the Yuan dynasty. The result was the largest empire in history, covering 20 percent of the earth's total land area and holding sway over a population of over one hundred million. Though it was not to last, it had important and numerous long-term effects.

Many accounts of the Mongolians focus on their ferocious fighting style and their barbarous looting of cities, palaces, and libraries. But most of the information that has been handed down about the Mongolians was written by the people who were conquered and who were not inclined toward more neutral assessments. One of the reasons for the Mongolians' success was their military style. Most armies fought with slow masses of soldiers. Many soldiers were farmhands with minimal skills and training. Mongolian soldiers, all excellent horsemen, had not only mastered a dynamic mode of attack but were also seasoned to cope with the brutal conditions of the steppe. A diet of meat and yogurt made them taller and stronger than many of their enemies. Furthermore, unlike in the West, where there were small groups of elite soldiers and large

masses of untrained combatants, the armies of the united Mongol tribes consisted of the entire adult male population under the age of sixty. Living in tents designed to allow the soldiers to follow the movement of their grazing horses, they had no urban culture and were interested primarily in the trappings of movable wealth, which they distributed with democratic even-handedness to all the tribes. When Chengiz Khan died, he was buried in a secret, unmarked location in the deserts of Mongolia, according to Mongolian tradition. (A team of archaeologists have recently located a site in Mongolia that is most likely Chengiz Khan's tomb.)

The word *yurt* is originally from the Turkic word meaning "dwelling place," in the sense of "homeland." The Mongolian yurt was easily transportable and yet solid enough to withstand ferocious winds. The basic element is an expanding wooden lattice that forms the circular walls. Poles from the sides rise up to connect to a compression ring, thus forming the roof structure. A band of rope is drawn around the top of the wall to bind it together. A fireplace was set out in the center. The wood structure is then covered with various amounts of felt, depending on climatic conditions. (Felt was made by pounding and rubbing wool—the Mongolians had no weaving skills. In fact, all their clothing was bartered for, bought, or came from war booty.) The yurt's entrance faced south so that the smoke from the fire could be better vented through the opening at the top. The

beds were on the north side and an altar with the gods was placed on the west, in front of which was a mat that was the seat of honor. A curtain could be drawn for privacy.

Yuan Dynasty China

When Kublai Khan (1215–94), Chengiz's grandson, ascended the throne of China, he chose the Chinese name *Yuan* ("original" or "prime") for his dynasty. By 1279, with the surrender of the last of the Song territories, all of China was under the Yuan. The Mongols divided society into four classes, with the highest reserved for themselves and the lowest for the southern Chinese from the former Song regions. Outsiders enjoyed the middle status in China, between the Mongols and the native Chinese, to the great irritation of the Song. Lamaist Buddhists—from Tibet and Nepal—and Daoists found particular favor with the Mongols, much as they had with the Mongolian-related Jin two hundred years earlier. Muslims were welcomed and happily tolerated at the western border. Under the Yuan, one of the oldest mosques of China, the tomb of Tughluq Temur was built in 1363 in Huocheng, Xinjiang.

The Mongolian capital was Karakorum, and it was from there that Chengiz Kahn would rally his troops. Chengiz's successor, Ögedei, erected walls around the city. Though nothing remains today, we know from descriptions that the city was square with gates in the cardinal directions and that it had Arab and Chinese quarters, several temples and mosques, and even a Nestorian church. When Kublai Kahn claimed the throne of the Mongol Empire in 1260, he relocated his capital first to Chengdu, and later to Dadu (present-day Beijing). While the Yuan introduced global civilization to China and modernized its military and its economy, they had no architectural culture. As a result, in building the new capital city, they adhered to the planning principles described in the *Rituals of Zhou*, which was a good political move, as it made them appear considerate of Chinese tradition. They also ordered the construction of numerous altars and temples throughout China dedicated to ancestors and local deities.

Dadu (from the word *ta-tu*, or "Great Capital") was known to the Mongolians as Khanbalig, the "City of the Great Khan." It was square with an orthogonal arrangement of streets typical of earlier Chinese capitals. The urban center, consisting of a palace and imperial quarters, was located south of the city center, with residential areas predominantly occupying the northern part. The name for the palace was *ta-nei*, or "great interior." It was surrounded by a 6-by-5 kilometer area reserved for the Mongolian overlords, who camped there in their yurts. To the south, in a separate rectangular precinct, was the "outer city" for the native Chinese, who lived in houses. A vast building served as the official site for ceremonies. Within it, Kublai Khan, like the Liao kings before him, lived in resplendent tents traditional to the Mongolians. Marco Polo, a visitor in his court, describes Kublai Khan's palace built in the Chinese manner:

You must know that it is the greatest palace that ever was. The roof is very lofty, and the walls of the palace are all covered with gold and silver. They are adorned with dragons, beasts and birds, knights and idols, and other such things. The hall of the palace is so large that six thousand people could easily dine there, and it is quite a marvel to see how many rooms there are besides. The building is altogether so vast, so rich, and so beautiful that no man on earth could design anything superior to it. The outside of the roof is all colored with vermilion and yellow and green and blue and other hues, which are fixed with a varnish so fine and exquisite that it shines like crystal and lends a resplendent luster to the palace as seen for a great way around.

Geomancy required that the palace face south against the slope of a hill, but since no hill was on the site, one was made—the Green Hill, about 100 meters high and 2 kilometers in circumference. It was planted with trees from every part of China and is thus a type of map of the Chinese world. Surrounding the hill was an enormous Divine Menagerie—a park for deer, stags, and other animals—with paved roads that led to a large lake with islands and pavilions. Little apart from the landscaping survives today, since it became the site of the vast Forbidden City, which was built after all the Mongolian buildings were torn down. Two particularly critical issues for the new city were water and grain: for such a big city, it was located far from the fertile grain regions in the south. These two problems were solved by the construction of a canal from the nearby Pei Ho River to the east, which allowed grain to be brought directly to the city gates.

The Grand Canal that wound its way northward from the fertile grain-producing areas of the south to the large cities of the north was one of the most important engineering works in the world. The goal was to make the movement of goods and grain independent of ocean transport. The first canal was begun in 613 BCE. In 206 BCE, the Lingqu Canal, which connected the Xingjiang and Lijiang rivers, was constructed. Another 200-kilometer section, completed in 589 CE, linked the newly constructed capital of Luoyang (Dongdu, or Eastern Capital) eastward to the confluence of the Wei and

12.28 Chinese canal system

Yellow rivers, thus overcoming the silting that plagued them. The Yuan dynasty continued these efforts, streamlining stretches of the canal by eliminating bends and consolidating the Jizhou and Huizong river systems, thus reducing the distance to be traversed from the southern end of the canal to the capital, Dadu, by almost 700 kilometers. The Ming dynasty (1368–1644) also committed large resources to canal maintenance and construction, keeping the canals clear of obstructions so that ocean transport was not required for grain distribution. The development of water locks and dredging techniques kept the canals in working order.

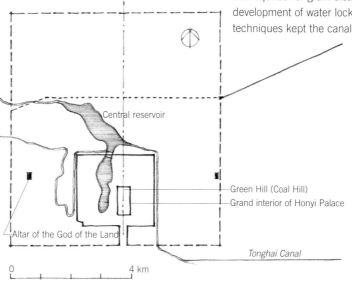

12.29 Plan of Yuan Dadu

Delhi

In the 12th century, South Asia was transformed by the arrival of the Islamic armies. They were led initially by Qutb-ud-Din Aibak, a Ghaznavid general from Afghanistan, who defeated the Rajput king and took over his territories in north India in 1192. His efforts were superseded in 1296 by Ala-ud-Din Khilji (1296–1316), who seized Ranthambhor, Chittorgarh, and Jaiselmer from the Rajputs and crushed the Solankis and the Pramars, going far south to conquer the fortress of Devagiri from the Yadavs.

Historians do not all evaluate the Islamic rulers' relationship to their Hindu subjects equally. Islamic rulers often massacred Hindus and systematically destroyed and desecrated Hindu temples. However, the Hindu population as a whole continued to thrive under Islamic rule, merging with it in many ways at the level of popular culture and thus underlining the more tolerant and even enlightened aspects of Islamic rule—particularly that of the Moghuls. (One of the eventual consequences of these underlying tensions was the partitioning of South Asia into India and Pakistan in 1947 by the British on the eve of their departure, an act whose ramifications are still in play.)

Qutb-ud-Din Aibak established his capital in Lahore but then moved to central India, taking over a Chauhan settlement called Tomar, to build Qila Rai Pithora, the first capital on the site of modern Delhi. Delhi was reestablished as a capital seven times on new sites in the same general region. These are:

1. Qila Rai Pithora, by Qutb-ud-Din Aibak (1192)
2. Siri, by Ala-ud-Din Khilji (1296–1316)
3. Tughlaqabad, by Ghias-ud-Din Tughlaq (1321–25)
4. Jahanpanah, by Muhammad bin Tughluq (1325–51)
5. Feroz Shah Kotla, by Firuz Shah Tughluq (1351–88)
6. Purana Qila, by Sher Shah Sur (1538–45)
7. Shahjahanabad (now referred to as "Old Delhi"), by Shah Jahan (1638–49)
   Early in the 20th century, Edwin Lutyens added New Delhi into the mix. All these are now integrated into modern Delhi.

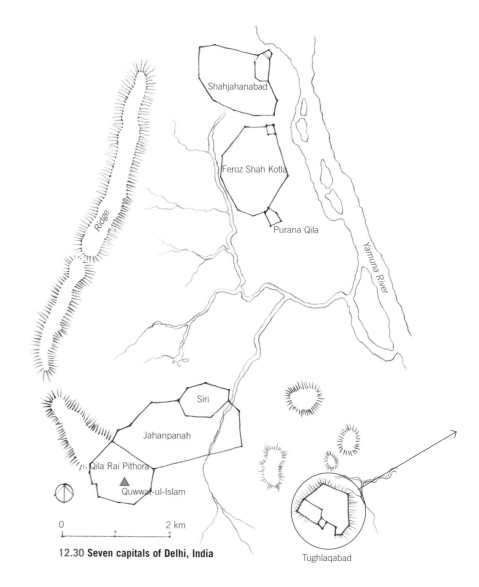

12.30 Seven capitals of Delhi, India

12.31 View of Tughlaqabad, Delhi

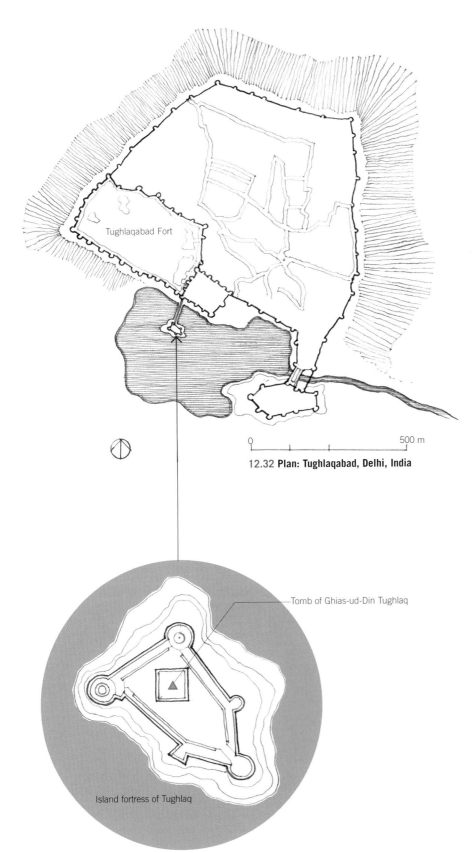

12.32 Plan: Tughlaqabad, Delhi, India

Tughlaqabad Fort

Tomb of Ghias-ud-Din Tughlaq

Island fortress of Tughlaq

0   500 m

Tughlaqabad

Ghias-ud-Din's Tughlaq's city, Tughlaqabad (1321–25), was a the largest of Delhi's fortress cities and a remarkable piece of engineering. To site his city, Tughlaq picked an irregular plateau that was difficult to work because it was very rocky but had the advantage of jutting prominently above the gentle westward slope of the floodplain of the Yamuna River. Tughlaq delineated his fort, which was made with local stone, in the shape of an irregular parallelogram with frequent circular turrets. The ground dropped quickly around the fort. Within, on the southwest side, he built his palace, enclosed within another fortified rectangle. At the junction of the palace and the rest of the fort was a sub-palace, a separate defensible entity in itself. One of the Yamuna River's drainage canals originally went right past the southern walls of Tughlaqabad; Tughlaq converted this canal into an artificial lake by building a dam linking a rocky outcrop just south of the city to the city itself. Tughlaqabad thus had valleys on three sides, and a lake toward the fourth. Within this lake Tughlaq built yet a another fortress, in the form of an island, linked to the main fort by a 220-meter-long elevated causeway. The lower level of this island fortress consisted of network of arched rooms with carefully controlled access. This was the treasury. On the roof of the treasury, Tughlaq built his tomb, a spectacular visual in the middle of the lake. There were additional hidden tunnels and causeways in the palace complex, adding to the secretive nature of the whole construction.

Quwwat-ul-Islam

The mosque of Quwwat-ul-Islam speaks unambiguously of its iconoclastic ambitions. It was begun in 1192 by Qutb-ud-Din Aibak, who placed it on the rise of land in the center of the city, the site of a former Hindu temple, and used as his raw material the stones from the city's twenty-seven Hindu and Jain temples. The pillars from the temples were used at times upside down or placed one on top of the other to raise them to the necessary height. The main *qibla* wall, on the west, consists of five corbelled ogee arches, presumably made by Hindu masons. Qutb's

12.33 Temple columns, Quwwat-ul-Islam, Delhi, India

successor, Iltutmish (1211–36) extended the qibla wall of the Quwwat-ul-Islam Mosque by three bays on either side and built a colonnade that enclosed the Qutb Minar on one side and his own tomb on the other. Iltutmish's was the first Islamic tomb in India. Built just west of the *qibla* wall, a small structure with a square base transforms into an octagonal dome on squinches.

A hundred years later, Ala-ud-Din Khilji (r. 1296–1316) decided to expand the complex by doubling the length of the *qibla* wall to the north. He also started construction of monumental *minar*, intended to be twice the height of the Qutb Minar, but which was never built beyond its first story. In 1311, Ala-ud-din Khilji constructed a gate, called Alai Darwaza (the "Gate of Allah") to the south of the mosque. This elegant cubic structure, with the proportions of a Roman triumphal arch, was constructed by Indian masons taking directions from their new Islamic rulers. A central arch dominates each facade. To the sides of the arches, windows in the lower register and blind windows above articulated in red sandstone are set against a white sandstone background. The dome sits atop squinches in a plain interior illuminated by small deep windows. The Alai Darwaza, exhibiting influences derived from Seljuk artisans, was among the first monuments in South Asia to signal the arrival of a distinctly South Asian Islamic architectural way of building, which was eventually perfected by the Moghuls.

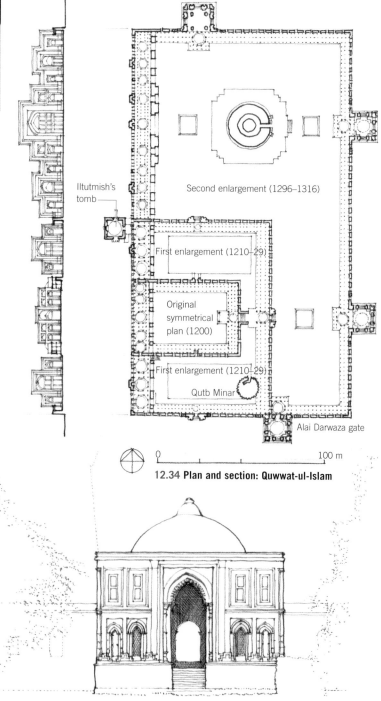

Iltutmish's tomb

Second enlargement (1296–1316)

First enlargement (1210–29)

Original symmetrical plan (1200)

First enlargement (1210–29)

Qutb Minar

Alai Darwaza gate

0   100 m

12.34 Plan and section: Quwwat-ul-Islam

12.35 Alai Darwaza gate, Quwwat-ul-Islam

Tomb of Ghias-ud-Din Tughlaq

Ghias-ud-Din Tughlaq began construction of a tomb of the saint Sheikh Rukn-I-Alam in Multan (ca. 1315), one of the finest pre-Mughal tombs in India. Clearly connected to the brick-and-tile building legacy of the Persians, this octagonal tomb had distinctly battered walls with corner turrets as its base and a high clerestory surmounted by a low dome finished with blue and white tiles. The Rukn-I Alam became the model for a series of tombs to come. Its form was developed from the language of the design of the Alai Darwaza, except that the walls are sloped and there is less overall ornamentation, apart from the white banding set against the building's red sandstone. The central arch has hints of Hindu detail, with its ogival-pointed arch form and crenelated outline. Similarly, its tall, marble-clad dome, imported straight from Persia, is topped with a form almost identical to the *amalaka* and *kalasha* found at the top of some Hindu temples. The interior of the tomb is a square box with a dome supported on pendentives—a construction system and symbolic language commonplace in the West but completely alien to the formal elaborations of Hindu architecture of that time.

12.36 **Mausoleum of Rukn-I-Alam, Multan, India**

Qutb Minar

Just outside his mosque, Qutb-ud-din Aibak built the tallest known brick victory tower (presently 72.5 meters), the Qutb Minar. Based on the Minaret of Jam in Afghanistan, which was also made of brick, both belong to a group of around sixty minarets and towers extending from West Asia to India built between the 11th and 13th centuries in the Islamic world. Most were erected as symbols of Islam's victory, though others were simply landmarks or watchtowers. The Qutb Minar was dressed in red and grey sandstone and white marble. Its inclined, conical volume gives it a dramatic presence. It is divided vertically into telescoping zones, each ending in a balcony supported by a multitude of small, highly ornamented brackets. Ala-ud-Din Khilji started a *minar* designed to be twice the height of the Qutb Minar. Little of this was realized, and only the short stub of the tower remains.

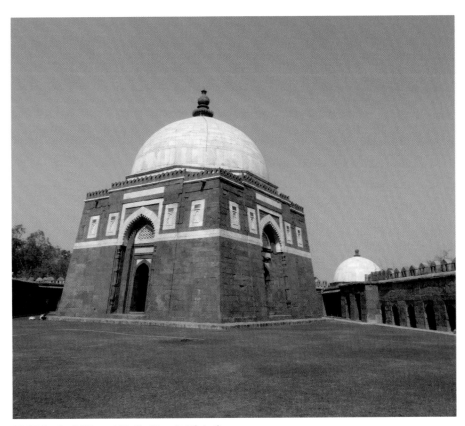

12.37 **Tomb of Ghias-ud-Din Tughlaq, Delhi, India**

12.38 **Qutb Minar, Delhi, India**

12.39 Chariot wheel, Sun Temple at Konarak, India

Sun Temple at Konarak

A new phase in Orissan history was ushered in by the Gangas, who, unlike their Shaivite predecessors, preferred the Vaishnavite religion. Under them, the Jagannath Temple in Puri (1174), the Sun Temple at Konarak (1258), and the Ananta Vasudeva in Bhubaneshwar (1278) were built. The Ananta and the Jagannath temples are similar to the earlier Lingaraja Temple, with a sequence of three *mandapas* leading up to the main shrine, or *deul*. The Sun Temple, however, assumes the single *mandapa* model of the Brihadeshwara Temple but magnifies it into a gigantic building. Whereas the *mandapa* survived intact into the modern era, the temple collapsed and only its base remains. It was begun by King Narasimhadeva (1238–64) who, after a series of successful battles, decided to dedicate the wealth he had appropriated from his conquests to build a temple to Surya, the sun god, instead of honoring the entire Shiva family, as had been the case with the earlier Gangas temples. Few Hindu temples are dedicated only to Surya; this is one of the only instances of a regional tribal god being paid homage on a royal scale. It was fused with Tantric themes visible in the sensual and erotic sculptural motifs.

Like the Cholas, the Gangas paraded their deities in procession, in huge wooden chariots shaped like temples. Narasimhadeva's Sun Temple, however, is designed around such an event. The giant

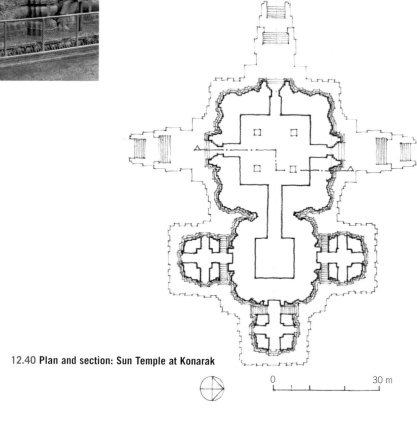

12.40 Plan and section: Sun Temple at Konarak

0   30 m

stone chariot carries the sun in its daily path across the sky. Twelve pairs of wheels, one for each month, were carved into the base and were accompanied by seven horses (three on the north, four on the south), one for each day of the week. The wheels, each more than 3 meters in diameter, had eight major and minor spokes, each with their own astrological significance. When seen from the side at some distance, the temple seems on the verge of movement. The *mandapa* has three sets of horizontal moldings in typical Orissan style, and the *deul* (which is now lost) was of the traditional vertical expression. It sits in the middle of a large compound

measuring 180 by 220 meters. Three subsidiary shrines, or *nisas*, facing north, south, and west, each with cruciform pre-chambers, are attached to the base of the *deul*. There are also a multitude of smaller independent shrines, constituting its "family," as is typical of Orissan temples. The stones at Konarak are not joined by any limestone or cement, a testament to the refinement of the builders' masonry skills. The site is associated with a sacred pond held to have curative powers. A major ceremony takes place there every February, with thousands of pilgrims converging on the pool to take a dip in its holy waters.

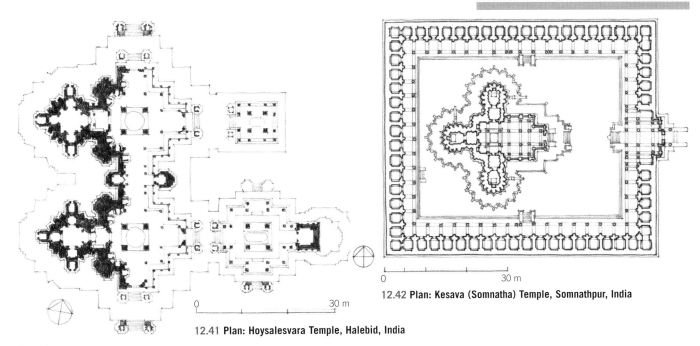

12.42 Plan: Kesava (Somnatha) Temple, Somnathpur, India

12.41 Plan: Hoysalesvara Temple, Halebid, India

Hoysalas

In southern India, after the Cholas' decline late in the 12th century, the Hoysalas declared their independence. They built about ninety temples from the late 12th to the mid-14th centuries. The important ones are at the two Hoysala capitals, Belur and Halebid. The Hoysalesvara Temple at Halebid (1121–60) is a composite of two identical star-shaped shrines of equivalent importance and complexity. Both face east and abut each other. Their cruciform *garbha-griha* is expressed on the exterior as a multifaceted star-shaped perimeter and three subsidiary shrines opening to the south, west, and north. On the east their entrance forecourts lead to a cruciform *mandapa*, one side of which is provided with an extra bay where two small shrines were inserted. The distance between the two shrines was calculated to ensure that each shrine could stand alone and be fully resolved (including in the full expression of its platform) and yet be linked at the first opportunity without any additional or superfluous bays. Even so, it could be argued that the Hoysalesvara Temple is really two distinct temples linked together by a corridor, rather than a single unit with multiple centers.

Most impressive with its multiple shrines is the Kesava (Somnatha) Temple at Somnathpur, India (ca. 1268). Part of a larger Vaishnavite complex, the temple is an ambitious structure, designed with three

shrines that retain their individuality and yet merge into a single expressive unit by sharing a *mandapa*. Enclosed by a low quadrangle with an entrance gate to the east, the temple sits on a low-stepped platform that follows its outline. Three star-shaped shrines, each with its own pre-chamber, open onto a square court elongated toward the east to form a colonnaded *mandapa*. Since each shrine is surmounted by a low superstructure and the *mandapa* is flat, the Kesava Temple does not have a dramatic skyline like those of the Chandella temples at Khajuraho. On closer examination, the plan and the detailing of the temple, however, are surpassed by none.

The Hoysala architects built with a hard, black schist that, though difficult to work with, could sustain deep cuts and take on a fine polish. With multiple tiers of deeply excoriated circular bands, columns seem to pulsate and swirl in space, as if they had just been removed from the wheel. Although most have been carved over, many of the columns have been left unadorned, which imparts to them an almost modern, mechanical quality, something rarely found in Hindu architecture.

12.43 Kesava (Somnatha) Temple

12.44 Vadakkunnathan Temple, Trichur, India

Vadakkunnathan Temple

Geographically the Western Ghats slice off the coastal region of Kerala from the rest of South Asia in the same manner that the Andes separate Chile from the rest of South America. Politically, however, Kerala's Chera kings reigned largely under the shadow of the greater powers of peninsular India, such as the Pallavas and the Cholas. Control of Kerala, however, was critical for trade and its climate ideal for growing spices, which were traded through ports in Cochin and Calicut, through Arab intermediaries, first with Byzantium, and later with China and Europe. In the 12th century, with the decline of the Cholas, Kerala broke into a series of small kingdoms and principalities dominated by high-caste Brahmins known as the Nambudiri. They maintained their cultural domination by marrying into local lower-caste families, establishing a culture that made significant accommodations to populist practices and local deities and cults that gave them a place of honor with Shiva and Vishnu in the temples they built.

The Vadakkunnathan Temple at Trichur, India, is one of the largest Nambudiri temples. It was begun in the 11th century but modified and added to until the 19th. Perched on top of a beautiful hillock at the center of the city, the temple comprises 9 acres surrounded by a reserved forest of hardwood teaks. The sacred area is defined by a rectangular enclosure. A secondary colonnade creates a circumambulatory around the inner edge of the temple precinct. The main entrances are from the west; three of them are directly aligned with the temple's three main shrines. The entrance farthest to the north is dedicated to Shiva and the southern one to Vishnu manifested as Rama. The one in the middle, though the smallest, is located at the most privileged place and given over to a shrine to Sankara-Narayana, the combined form of Shiva and Vishnu—a manifestation unique to Kerala. Although the *garbha-griha* of all three temples is square and built of stone, the outer forms are known especially for their graceful wooden roofs. Covered with copper sheets, the roofs have deep overhangs, their smooth, gentle forms contrasting with the richly crafted stone walls. The temple is famous for its annual Pooram festival, which was introduced in the 18th century, an event that combines elephant pageantry with the frenzied playing of drums and cymbals.

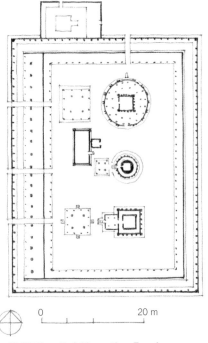

0   20 m

12.45 Plan: Vadakkunnathan Temple

provoked the interest of the Portuguese, whose subsequent arrival spelled the end of African control of the trade routes.) Its palace is situated on the rocky promontory of an island in Mso Bay. Husuni Kubwa, which means "large fortified house" in Swahili, had several courtyards for different functions, with a distinct progression from private to public. The king's private courtyard had a sunken pool with an audience court next to it. There was a protected harbor to the west.

North Africa was dominated by the Ayyubid sultanate in Egypt and the Almohads in Morocco and Spain. The once powerful Ghana Empire was in decline. The Almoravids, constituted of Saharan Berbers, had taken control of the trade routes through the Sahara and captured Koumbi Saleh, the capital of Ghana, in 1067. Furthermore, the expansion of the Sahara Desert led to further economic breakdowns and local power struggles. By the 13th century, however, a new power emerged: the Mali Empire. Centered to the north of Ghana, it was composed of several states that took control of the gold mines. Before the discovery of gold in the Americas, almost half of the gold in Europe came from Mali. The Mali Empire also controlled the salt trade in that region.

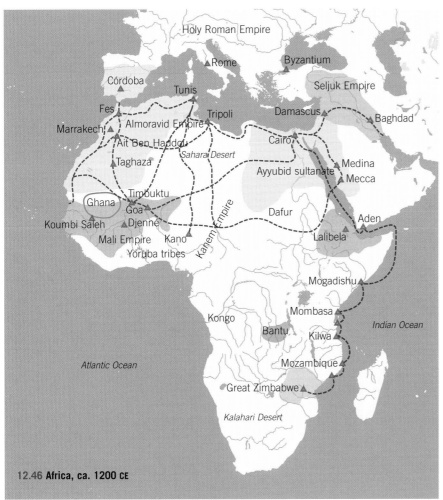

12.46 Africa, ca. 1200 CE

Africa

Prior to the 13th century, southern and eastern Africa were remote outposts in the global trade networks. But in the 1200s, the East African coast developed into an extensive trading zone linked to Arabian and Indian port cities and thus became the major distribution center for the African continent. Though the Arab traders were Muslims, Islam did not make much headway beyond the coast. East Africans sold gold, ivory, and slaves in exchange for metals, rice, and other commodities. One consequence of the cultural exchange was the emergence of the Swahili language, which combines African and Arabic linguistic elements.

Preeminent among the ports at this time was Kilwa, off the south coast of Tanzania. It was established in the 11th century by believers of Shirazi Islam, an East African variant of Middle Eastern Islam. The rulers controlled the sources of gold in nearby Mozambique. (In the 16th century, this

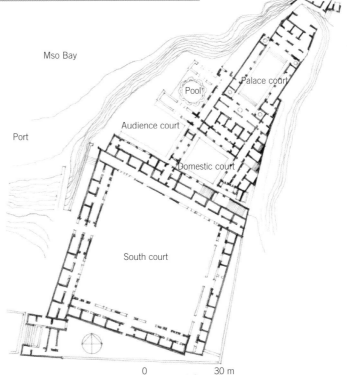

12.47 Plan: Palace of Husuni Kubwa at Kilwa, Tanzania

The Mamluk Sultanate

The Mamluks, who came to rule Egypt from 1260 to 1517, were not Arabs but originally Turkish, Kurdish, and Mongolian slaves who had been raised as fighters in the army of the Ayyubids, who were themselves Kurdish Turks from Syria. The word *Mamluk* comes, in fact, from an Arabic word meaning "the owned." But with the collapse of Shi'ite Ayyubid rule in Egypt, General Baybars al-Bunduqdari (1260–77) established Mamluk dominance over Egypt, pushing back the Mongolians as well as the Christian Crusaders in the Levant and Syria, and regaining control over the holy cities of Mecca and Medina. Under the previous Ayyubids, the center of power had been in Damascus, but under the Mamluks, Cairo's importance was restored; indeed, from a geopolitical perspective, Cairo was the prime link between India and Europe. Though a military elite, the Mamluks were savvy traders, establishing ties with Venice and Genoa as well as with Constantinople. Mamluk bureaucracy consisted mostly of Coptic Christians and Jews, who had filled such administrative roles for centuries.

During the 13th and 14th centuries at least five major madrasas were built in Cairo along a street close to the sultan's palace. Each of these was associated with a mausoleum. Normally, tombs, even for the rich, would be located outside of the city, but if the sultan gave an endowment to a madrasa he was granted an exception. Each madrasa is thus associated with a sultan's tomb. The buildings, sitting shoulder to shoulder, constitute one of the more important street environments of the age. As madrasas had to face Mecca, all the structures abut the street at about a 10-degree angle. The architects showed great adeptness at integrating the program into the complex and cramped urban site. Most impressive is the Madrasa of Sultan Qalawun (1284–85). Though the life of a sultan was continually beset by the possibility of internal rebellions testing his authority, he proved to be a capable ruler open to trade even with the Christians with whom he was fighting. He made trade alliances with the Byzantine Empire, Genoa, and the Kingdom of Sicily. The plan echoes the octagonal plan of

the Dome of the Rock. The wall of the mausoleum is divided into a series of pointed arched recesses, the hoods supported on marble columns. The portal, a remarkable piece of Gothic marble work, is a trophy seized from a church in Acre, the last Crusader stronghold in Palestine. The tomb chamber is an almost square plan, with four piers and four columns arranged in the form of an octagon supporting arches that in turn raise a high drum and above that, a dome. The rose granite pillars have Corinthian capitals. The walls are richly decorated with

marbles and mosaics. At its rear there was a hospital. The madrasa, which specialized in Sunni jurisprudence, has its own courtyard with student cells. Another important monument from this era is the Mosque of Sultan al-Nasir Muhammad (1318) built in the great citadel that protects the city. Though conventional in plan, the columns and capitals are mostly spoils taken from other buildings, including churches and even the ruins of ancient Egyptian buildings.

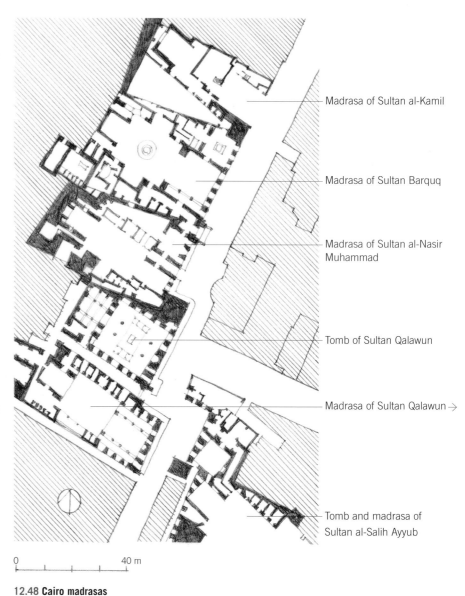

Madrasa of Sultan al-Kamil

Madrasa of Sultan Barquq

Madrasa of Sultan al-Nasir Muhammad

Tomb of Sultan Qalawun

Madrasa of Sultan Qalawun →

Tomb and madrasa of Sultan al-Salih Ayyub

0   40 m

12.48 Cairo madrasas

12.49 Tomb of Sultan Qalawun, Cairo, Egypt

12.50 View of dome, Tomb of Sultan Qalawun

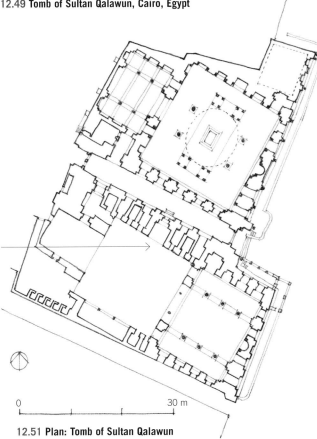

0   30 m

12.51 Plan: Tomb of Sultan Qalawun

12.52 Interior: Tomb of Sultan Qalawun

12.53 Giorgis, one of the rock-cut churches of Lalibela, Ethiopia

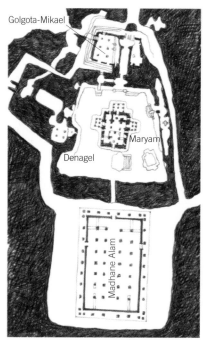

12.54 **Partial plan: Rock-cut churches of Lalibela**

Rock-Cut Churches of Lalibela

The collapse of the Aksumite Empire around 400 CE left the horn of Africa in the hands of various regional forces, but in the 13th century, the return of commerce to the shores and the transformation of Ethiopia into a Christian kingdom visited by pilgrims from far afield brought prosperity back to the region. The Zagwe dynasty (founded ca. 1137) capitalized on this, reaching its peak under King Lalibela (ca. 1185–1225), who is credited with building a set of eleven churches cut out of solid red volcanic rock in his new capital city, Roha, now called Lalibela (340 kilometers north of Addis Ababa). The city is located on a high ridge above the Takkaze River. Under threat from the forces of Islam from the north, the kingdom had

retreated into these ridges, from which they continued to control the Red Sea ports that linked central and southern African trade routes to the shipping lanes to India and beyond. The ridge had the added advantage of several springs that had both agricultural and symbolic value.

The churches are highly unusual in their overall conception. Not only do they constitute a holy land unto themselves, but they are a map of the holy city of Jerusalem, which King Lalibela had never seen, but imagined from descriptions in the Bible. The churches are divided into northern and eastern groups by a rock-cut channel called Yordannos ("Jordan River"). Bieta Madhane Alam is the largest and most impressive of

these churches. Bieta Giorgis (St. George), carved into the shape of a cross, is situated somewhat apart from the other churches to the west. Following a deep, narrow trench leads visitors in a wide circle through rock gates and chambers to its ground level. The building is approximately 12 meters in height, length, and width and rests on a triple-stepped platform. Though carved out of the living stone, it mimics a conventionally constructed building, replete with vaults and delicately chiseled acanthus leaves and gargoyles. The interior has a cruciform floor plan with a dome above the sanctuary in the eastern arm of the church. The building is associated with a sacred spring located just to the east of its entrance.

12.55 **Section: Rock-cut churches of Lalibela**

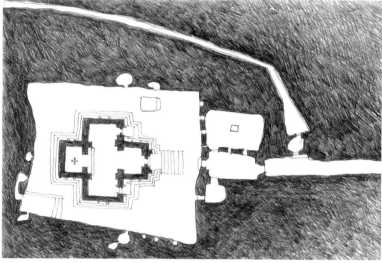

12.56 Plan and section: Giorgis, Lalibela

0　　　　　10 m

The Great Zimbabwe

The Great Zimbabwe ("Great Palace") is one of a group of fortress complexes dating from the 10th century; it is located on top of a granite bluff as well as in adjacent valleys in Zimbabwe, not far from Masvingo. The complex housed a large population as well as the royal court, markets, warehouses, and religious shrines. The number of ruins is substantial, and they have yet to be thoroughly studied. The kingdom drew its wealth from the abundant gold reserves in the region and from the good agricultural land. The blocks of the walls were skillfully laid without mortar and ranged from 1 to 5 meters thick. At the heart of the complex is the palace itself. The Karanga ethnic group, whose ancestors it is now thought built the structure, called it Mumbahuru, meaning "House of the Great Woman." The building was not constructed as an isolated object in space but as an extension of the natural landscape. Its oval-shaped walls enclosed a large area, within which were other stone wall enclosures that contained an outdoor living space (*kgotla*), a garden, and a place to keep livestock. The *kgotla* is also a place where descendants can establish communion with one another and with their ancestors. The visual focus of the building is a 6-meter-wide by 10-meter-high conical tower, the original purpose of which remains unknown.

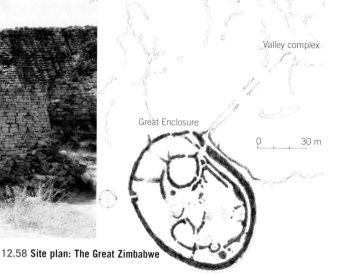

Hill complex (acropolis)

Valley complex

Great Enclosure

0　　　　30 m

12.57 The Great Zimbabwe, Masvingo, Zimbabwe

12.58 Site plan: The Great Zimbabwe

Mosques of Mali

Timbuktu was one of Africa's leading cities as well as one of the intellectual and spiritual centers for the propagation of Islam. It has three great mosques—Sankoré, Djinguereber, and Sidi Yahya—which form part of an Islamic university. By the 14th century, many books were written and copied there. The city lies at the intersection of the east-west and north-south trans-Saharan trade routes and was (and still is today) an important market for rock salt. The Djinguereber Mosque (first built in 1327) is the oldest of the mosques. Except for a small part of the northern facade, which is of limestone, the building is made entirely of sun-baked mud bricks called *ferey*, a mud-based mortar that is coated with a mud plaster that gives the building its smooth, sculpted look. The thickness of the walls depends on their height. There are three inner courts, two minarets, and a hypostyle hall with twenty-five rows of pillars that creates a space for two thousand people.

Thirty-five kilometers to the southwest of Timbuktu is Djenné, which was not part of the Mali Empire but an independent city-state. It is the home of a large mosque that was built in the 13th century, even though the current structure dates from around 1907. The *qibla* is dominated by three large, boxlike minarets jutting out from the main wall and eighteen buttresses. Each minaret contains a spiral staircase leading to the roof topped by a cone-shaped spire with two ostrich eggs. The logs that protrude from the building serve as scaffolding but have clearly been integrated into the design. Half of the mosque is covered by a roof, and the other half is an open-air prayer hall. The mosque's roof is supported by ninety wooden pillars. Roof vents allow hot air to rise out of the building. These buildings require continual maintenance in which the entire community participates, in preparation for the annual festival.

12.59 **Sankoré Mosque, Timbuktu, Mali**

12.60 **Mosque at Djenné, Mali**

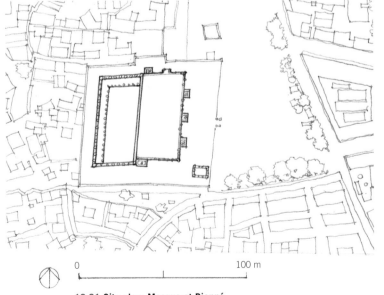

0   100 m

12.61 **Site plan: Mosque at Djenné**

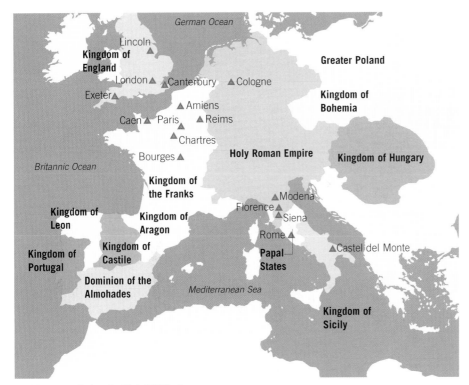

12.62 Europe during the High Middle Ages

Europe: The High Middle Ages

During the 13th century, the skyline of European cities underwent a profound change as the spires and towers of some six hundred major churches and cathedrals marked the location of cities in the landscape. This energetic building activity was driven by a combination of religious fervor and increasing wealth. Income from the selling of indulgences by the Roman Church was an important source of financing. It was a dubious practice that in the 16th century was to awaken the ire of Martin Luther and eventually lead to the Reformation. Another source of income was sending relics on tours. The bishops of Chartres, for example, sent the cathedral's relics as far away as England to solicit contributions.

The shift in focus dates to the Synod of Arras (1025), during which it was decided that sculptural programs could serve to help the illiterate visualize what they could not understand through the written word. Statues once used only sparingly, and usually in relation to aristocratic worship practices, now stood row upon row along church facades. Compared with the Norman facade of St. Étienne (1067–87) in Caen, France, with its small windows and imposing, solid-looking

wall of stone, St. Denis, with its broad and decorated portals seems to almost float above the ground. The church was begun by the Normans but was transformed by Abbot Suger (1081–1155). Actively engaged in France's political life, Suger played a leading role in running the kingdom while King Louis VI was away on crusade. He wanted cathedrals to accommodate large crowds that could then move easily past the relics. He thus created for St. Denis a space behind the high altar known as a chevet (French for "headpiece") where the church's more precious relics could be displayed. He also redesigned the cathedral's facade, introducing a triple portal that served as symbol of the Trinity. The Trinity had become important to theological speculation in the second quarter of the 12th century, and its restatement signified support for an orthodox interpretation of the Bible and for papal authority. The tympanum over the central door of St. Denis was the most important element of the facade, as it portrays Christ sitting in judgment. The sculptures were once again a concession to the unlettered, for few in the general population at the time could read and write. In this, St. Denis reflects a change in religious attitudes. Whereas Romanesque cathedrals were

designed primarily for the elite, St. Denis and later cathedrals were buildings meant to appeal to the popular imagination. On a more elevated plane, Abbot Suger held that the religious experience was one of transcendence, symbolized by disembodied light. The rose window in the center of the facade, for example, was one of the first of its kind—a grand wheel of light. The function of the facade, so Suger held, was to foretell the program of the interior. "By what shines here within, through palpable visual beauty, the soul is elevated to the truly beautiful and, rising from the earth where it was submerged, an inert thing, it is resuscitated into heaven by the radiance of its glory." For Suger, the use of precious materials in the furnishings of the church was also important, as it served as a presentiment of the splendors of heaven.

For all these reasons, St. Denis broke new ground and is thus heralded as initiating the Gothic style. For the first time, features such as cross-rib vaulting and flying buttresses (although present in prior churches) were here all combined into an integrated stylistic statement along with sharply pointed spires, a rose window, clustered columns, pointed arches, and a stress on luminosity.

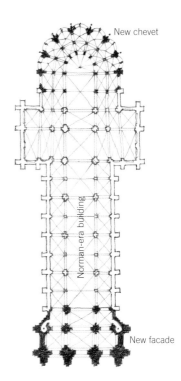

12.63 Reconstruction: St. Denis at the time of Abbot Suger

Citeaux and the four great daughter
abbeys of the Cistercian Order

Paris △ △ Clairvoux
Pontigny △ ▲▲ Morimond
La Ferté △▲ Citeaux

12.64 Area of Cistercian monasteries

12.65 Interior: Fontenay Abbey, near Montbard, France

Fontenay Abbey

Against the backdrop of 11th-century religious populism and the increasing laxity of the religious elite, especially in the monasteries, a countermovement sprang up headed by St. Bernard of Clairvaux. He urged a return to the austere rules of the early monastic days of St. Benedict, who had conceived of the church as a workshop for prayer. Among the most prominent of the new reform orders were the Carthusians, founded in 1084, and the Cistercians, founded in 1115. The Cistercians had four so-called daughter houses: Clairvaux, Morimond, Pontigny, and La Ferté. These in turn promoted the creation of other daughter houses—so many, in fact, that by the close of the 12th century there were 530 Cistercian abbeys in Europe, forming a powerful monastic network. Though Cistercians had a large number of recruits from the feudal nobility, one of the reasons for their success was that they conceived of manual labor as a form of prayer, and therefore opened their doors to artisans and peasants. The workmanship in their buildings—even in places that are normally not visible, like certain roof sections—was therefore executed with attention to the minutest detail. Such details were not meant for the eyes of men but for the all-seeing eye of God. The monasteries were organized as a farm, with all the monks participating in the chores. Cistercians soon became known for their innovations in farming and herding. Their

vineyards in Burgundy and the Rhineland became legendary.

Under St. Bernard's influence, all the details of monkish existence were rigidly prescribed, and there were frequent inspection visits. Cistercian monasteries were not sited along pilgrimage routes but in inhospitable, often swampy and inaccessible land. They had no crypts or towers and were built on rigorous geometrical principles, some by the monks themselves. They had simple vaulted naves; lighting was dim and limited by rule to only five candles. Wall surfaces were clean and simple. Sculptural embellishments, such as those found in St. Denis, were forbidden. The capitals of the

columns were kept as plain as possible. Bold proportions and architectural bravura were not tolerated; even ornamental pavements were frowned upon. The plans had square east ends in defiance of the ambulatory design of the great cathedrals.

Even though they were slow to explore its possibilities, the Cistercians' adoption of the ribbed vault around 1150 was an act of major architectural importance because they disseminated this feature across Europe. The building that best represents the Cistercian aesthetic is the Fontenay Abbey near Montbard, in the département of Côte-d'Or in France, founded in 1119—the oldest ensemble still in existence. Since there is

12.66 Monastery, Fontenay Abbey

no clerestory, the interior gets most of its light from facade windows and from the corresponding ones at the crossing and in the sanctuary. A tunnel vault with transverse arches defines the space of the nave. The building, though its design was controlled by a proportional system, was conceived in opposition to the technical virtuosity and the decorative program of the great cathedrals. On account of the tunnel vault, the nave possesses remarkable acoustical qualities. The refectory was placed in the customary Cistercian position opposite the fountain house on the south side of the cloister, with the axis perpendicular to the church.

There are several factors that determined the monastery's location. Because it was remote from nearby cities, distractions were few. But the Cistericans were not idle monks, and this particular monastery was based around metal production: it was just as much a monastic complex as an industrial one. Ore in the rocky hills just to the east of the monastery provided the raw materials, and

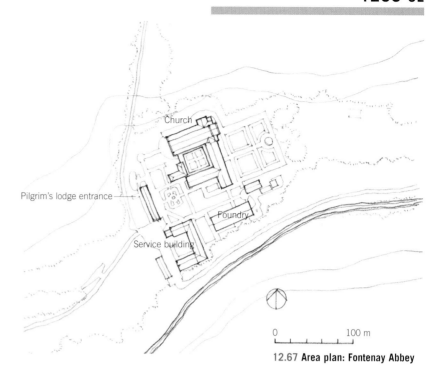

12.67 Area plan: Fontenay Abbey

a small but fast stream that ran through the valley could drive the forge's watermill, which in turn powered a gigantic hammer that pounded the metal. The tools that were made at the forge served not only the monks but were sold in the surrounding region. Apart from the forge, a large building which, at the time, was one of France's most productive, there was the monastic compound itself, a hostel for pilgrims, and an herb and medicinal garden.

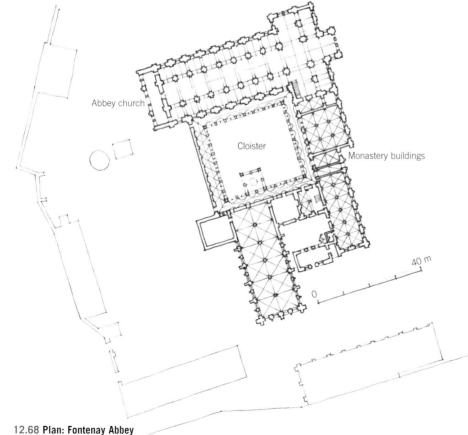

12.68 Plan: Fontenay Abbey

12.69 Interior: Fontenay Abbey

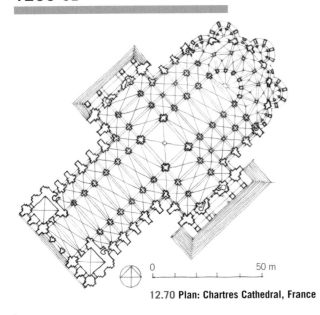

12.70 Plan: Chartres Cathedral, France

Cathedral Design

In the 13th century, cathedral building was by far the largest construction enterprise ever attempted in Europe. Chartres Cathedral, for example, was able to hold more than eight thousand people. Technologically complex and often dangerous, construction frequently took many decades and sometimes hundreds of years. Unlike Carolingian churches, with their imposing westworks, and unlike Ottonian monastic churches—which were associated with market towns and might not have had a facade at all—the facades on this new generation of cathedrals served as sacred thresholds to a mystic interior.

Among the various aspects of church design that changed during this period was the emergence of the interior elevation of the nave as an architectural unit in its own right, with architects seeking to balance the interplay of horizontal and vertical elements. At Notre-Dame in Paris (1163–1250), there are four discrete horizontal levels: the ground-level arcade, over which run two galleries—the tribune and the triforium—above which runs an upper, windowed story or clerestory. The windows of these cathedrals were not transparent but filled with stained glass, bringing into the interior a muted, shimmering light. To obtain the soaring height that the Gothic age aspired to, flying buttresses made their appearance. While they achieve the desired result on the inside, they tended to pose a problem on the exterior. At first the flying buttresses were a purely structural element, as at

St.-Germain-des-Prés, where they were added as reinforcements around 1180, but thereafter they were integrated into the plan from the start. Flying buttresses consist of a tower that supplies the necessary counterweight and an arch that transfers the lateral loads to the tower. Because of the flying buttresses, a church interior could become a spatial unit, although this occurred at the expense of the exterior's legibility.

The epitome of the new style was Chartres Cathedral (1194–1220), where the nave on the outside is almost completely obscured behind an intimate tangle of buttresses. The interior, on the other hand, is almost canyonlike. The nave elevation has only three levels, permitting a strong vertical extension of the bays. To compensate for the added height, two flying buttresses, one over the other, bring the load to the tower. The vaults, another important Gothic element, were composed of stone ribs with thin brick vaults in between, stretched like taut skin. The east end, with its rounded ambulatory, is modeled on St. Denis but goes further, adding five semicircular chapels. The piers were also innovative. Earlier piers often were composed of a cylindrical core at the level of the arcade and thin colonettes above. Here a continual line from the vault to the ground reduces the visibility of the column at the arcade level. Proportion and geometry were used throughout to organize all of the elements, from the small to the large. The length of the church, for example, is related to the transept in a ratio of 2:3; the length and width of the transept is 1:2.

The town of Chartres was, at the time, quite small, but among the wealthiest in Europe, with an important trade in textiles and metalsmithing. However, financing for the cathedral came not only from the local region but from almost all sectors of France, as St. Marie of Chartres had almost attained the status of a national deity.

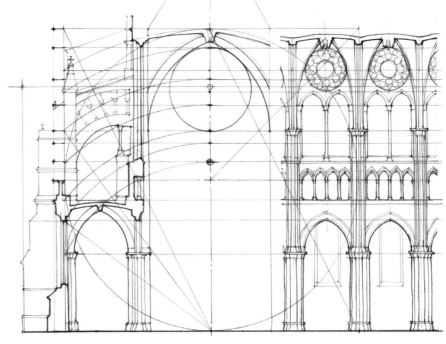

12.71 Partial interior elevation and section: Chartres Cathedral

12.72 Plan: Amiens Cathedral, France

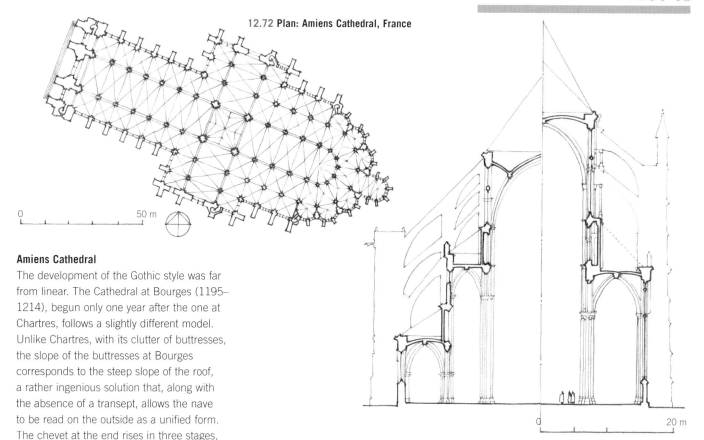

0   50 m

Amiens Cathedral

The development of the Gothic style was far from linear. The Cathedral at Bourges (1195–1214), begun only one year after the one at Chartres, follows a slightly different model. Unlike Chartres, with its clutter of buttresses, the slope of the buttresses at Bourges corresponds to the steep slope of the roof, a rather ingenious solution that, along with the absence of a transept, allows the nave to be read on the outside as a unified form. The chevet at the end rises in three stages, with small high-peaked chapels seemingly suspended between the buttresses' piers. The interior, with its tall arches, is not as canyonlike as Chartres because the tall arches create the illusion that the wall of the side aisle is the actual side of the nave.

12.73 Half-section: Naves of Amiens and Bourges cathedrals

0   20 m

At Amiens Cathedral (1220–35) the architects were more conservative than at Bourges, following the model of Chartres, with its calmer interior and soaring verticality. Amiens's impression of verticality is further enhanced by the integration of the crossing piers into the overall design of the nave's facade. The division of the upper window into four segments rather than the usual two increases the impression of verticality. Its tall nave arches and high clerestory windows combine elements of Chartres and Bourges while to some extent preserving the unity of the nave. The calm effect of the interior combines well with the luminosity of the chevet. A comparison of the sections of Amiens and Bourges shows that the interior of Amiens creates a greater vertical effect which is due to the lower arches along its nave and the absence of a second aisle, and is aided by better illumination. The consequence is that the buttresses of Amiens needed to be much higher to offset the weight, which annihilates the corporeal presence of the building that is still legible at Bourges.

12.74 Bourges Cathedral, France

12.75 Amiens Cathedral

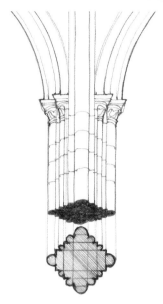

12.76 **Gothic compound pier**

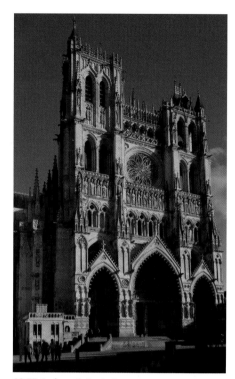

12.77 **Amiens Cathedral**

12.78 **Cathedral of Notre-Dame of Reims, France**

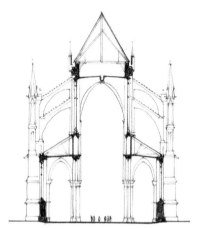

12.79 **Section and plan: Cathedral of Notre-Dame of Reims**

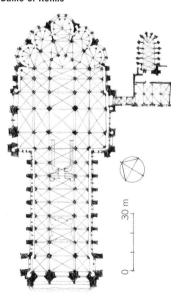

Whereas Romanesque churches had round columns in the nave, in Gothic churches from Speyer onward, columns that were composed of a columnar core with colonettes attached to it began to appear. The colonettes facing the nave continue upward to reach all the way to the vault, whereas the colonettes on the inside become part of the ribs of the vaults in the side aisles. As a result, Gothic supports were neither columns nor piers; rather, they were columnar bundles working not only in the vertical dimension but also in plan, as they would seem to be squares rotated 45 degrees, creating diagonals through the building.

Notre-Dame of Reims

By the second decade of the 13th century, the space of the church had changed from a place emphasizing the enactment of liturgical processes into a more public space where relics could be viewed and worshipped. On a philosophical level, the discussion changed from issues of liturgy to an emphasis on the transcendent and dematerialized quality of light (God) and geometry (the ordered universe). Robert Grosseteste, an English theologian and bishop of Lincoln, who read Greek and was familiar with Arabic scientific commentaries, argued that all of human

knowledge stemmed from the spiritual radiance of light. Rose windows appeared in almost every church, sometimes opening so wide that they touched the framework of the buttresses, as at France's Auxerre Cathedral (completed ca. 1234). Along with these new ideas was the emergence of the cult of the Virgin Mary. The mother of Christ, Mary had until then played a minor role in the Christian liturgy; she now captured the popular imagination, and we begin to see her image standing alongside those of the saints. At the Cathedral of Notre-Dame of Reims (1211–90), figures of Mary were visible in every part of the church, not only standing in for the saints but also for the Christian church itself. The building was, in comparison to Amiens, more airy in its detailing. The tall windows right and left of the rose window, which allow a view through the building, make the upper part almost seem weightless. The rosette barely fits in the narrow space allocated to it, and indeed the nave, though similar to that of Amiens, is considerably narrower in proportion. Chartres had its own prized relic, the tunic that had allegedly belonged to the Virgin Mary, a gift from Charles the Bald, who had obtained it from Constantinople.

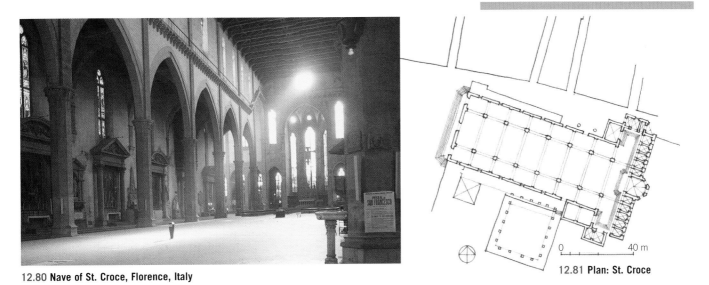

12.80 Nave of St. Croce, Florence, Italy

12.81 Plan: St. Croce

0   40 m

Mendicant Orders

At the beginning of the 13th century, the Roman Church saw its theological interpretation and hierarchical structure threatened by a series of so-called heresies, several of which revolved around an interpretation of the Gospels that held that access to the divine was through personal emulation of the deeds of Christ rather than through the complex liturgical demands of the church. Small wonder that this reading of the Gospels displeased the church fathers, who initially felt threatened by it. St. Francis of Assisi was on the verge of being branded just such a heretic in 1206 when he abandoned his privileged worldly life, became an ascetic, and preached the gospel of poverty. But Pope Innocent III, eager to bring the poverty sects under his control, allowed St. Francis to preach and informally approved his efforts in 1209 (and then officially in 1223), hoping to avoid a possible schism. Thus was born one of several mendicant orders that radically transformed church history and was to lead, some centuries later, to the Reformation triggered by the preachings of the German monk Martin Luther.

In the early Middle Ages, reclusive monastics preferred their monasteries in the quiet isolation of the countryside as a counterweight to what they saw as the decadence of Roman cities. As a result, inhabitants of cities and villages often had to walk long distances to go to a church and were thus remote from the cosmic principles that united them as members of

the Christian faith. The mendicant orders responded by setting up their monasteries in the hearts of cities or just outside their gates to make themselves humbly serviceable and approachable; in many places, religious services were within reach of the majority of Christians, both physically and conceptually, for the first time. Mendicant monasteries were not sites of calm reflection as Cistercian monasteries were, but served more as dormitories for the monks, who would leave in the morning to perform various duties. The Franciscans became specialists in architecture and construction, helping to build fortification walls and infrastructure. The Dominicans, another mendicant order, were known as doctors, lawyers, and teachers, and many became well-known philosophers. They were also closely associated with the development of Scholasticism during the 13th century and were prominent at the great universities of Europe. In a sense, the 13th century can be seen as the second Christianization of Europe. If the first was fought in the name of (often forcible) conversion and was largely dynastic in structure, the second was based on broad outreach and popular appeal.

Because mendicants had sworn an oath to poverty and consequently had no money, their churches were usually built for them by citizens. At first many were simple structures or converted barns. By 1250, there were Franciscan communities in almost every city in France, Germany, and Italy. Mendicant churches were by definition simple and

austere. The great ebullient forms of the cathedrals were spurned. The Dominican Church in Toulouse (1275–92), for example, had no flying buttresses and was built entirely of brick. At the Franciscan church of St. Croce (begun 1294), the architect Arnolfo di Cambio spurned vaulting and re-created the vast emptiness of Constantinian naves in a spare Gothic idiom. In many Italian towns, we encounter them as large plain brick buildings to this day.

12.82 Dominican Church, Toulouse, France

12.83 Castel del Monte, near Andria, Italy

12.84 Interior court, Castel del Monte

Castel del Monte

The Holy Roman Empire, which had been taken over by the Ottonians, existed more in name than in substance, with the German princes fighting among themselves for regional advantage. The church was eager to see the German Empire weakened in this way so that its own authority would remain preeminent. That changed with Frederick II (r. 1212–50), who was granted the Norman crown as king of Sicily, as his mother, the daughter of Roger II, had been a Norman princess. At the age of twenty-six, he also became emperor, being the son of King Henry VI of Hohenstaufen. At the time, just as new religious ideas were altering Christian religious practices, so too were new notions of kingship being developed, based to no small degree on the ideas of Aristotle, the bulk of whose writings were not known in the West until the end of the 12th century. These writings stimulated the development of a theory of state that required no appeal to theological premises. Though it would be centuries before that ideal could reach fruition, a generation of rulers now emerged who saw themselves as the head of their own institutional organization. In turn, for the first time, the Roman Church was asked to pay taxes on its vast land holdings.

Frederick II, who ironically had grown up an orphan in the streets of Palermo, Sicily, marched into southeast Italy accompanied by his army, which included many Arabs, and began an extensive building campaign, erecting some two hundred buildings—principally fortresses and palaces. The most impressive of his works is the Castel del Monte (1249) in rural Apulia, near the small Italian town of Andria. This fortresslike building, probably planned for his hawk-hunting expeditions, is located on top of a hill with commanding views of the surroundings. It is noted for its severity and compactness.

The Castel del Monte is a remarkably complex object with no singular precedent in Europe for the specificity of its shape. It has an equilateral octagonal exterior containing an octagonal courtyard and eight octagonal towers. Mathematically, the building is a monohedron, with eight reflecting planes and eight rotations forming a volume composed of eight symmetrical axes. The rooms surrounding the courtyard are necessarily trapezoidal, each containing a ribbed groin vault reminiscent of Cistercian architecture. Frederick II was a strong supporter of the Cistercians and their austere Christian aesthetic. The building was perhaps designed by the Cistercian architect Philippe Chinard. But Islamic influences are also present—no surprise, given Frederick II's familiarity with Islamic culture. Three of the eight towers contain staircases, while several others contain lavatory facilities; others serve no discernible purpose.

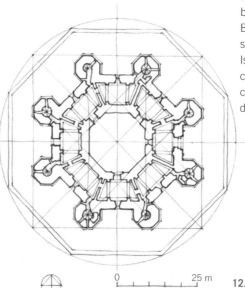

0   25 m

12.85 Plan: Castel del Monte

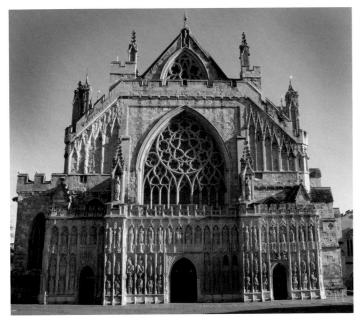

12.86 Entrance facade, Exeter Cathedral, England

12.87 Tierceron vaulting, Exeter Cathedral

Exeter Cathedral

The transition from the Romanesque to the early Gothic lies to some degree in the systematization of the nave elevation and in the integration of the nave with rib vaulting. By 1300, architects, increasingly confident, began to explore the decorative qualities inherent in structure, creating styles that historians variously call Decorated, Perpendicular, or Flamboyant Gothic. Scholars have long wondered if the emergence of this new stylistic direction coincided with increased contacts with the East. It is known, for example, that England's Edward I (1272–1307) sent an emissary to Persia. At any rate, Exeter Cathedral (1280–1300) shows a decorative unity and a fullness that earlier cathedrals did not have. The lower facade has become a veritable curtain displaying the figures of the saints. (The innumerable saints often have a special day allocated to them, and a child born on a specific saint's day would often receive that saint's name.) The gallery of saints at Exeter, with its abstract crenellations, stands as an almost independent screen in front of the building. On the inside, the crisply folded geometries of early 13th-century vaults have been replaced by the rippling shapes of fan vaulting, the origin of which is not known.

Buildings in this style do not represent a deterioration of the Gothic style, as is sometimes held; rather, they demonstrate a desire to integrate decoration and structure. One factor that contributed to the change was the fashion for more luminous interiors and more frequent use of white or clear glass, which enhanced the subtleties of a building's surface treatment. Furthermore, in England at least, cathedral builders did not aspire to the great heights that were typical of French churches, preferring instead wider windows, lower buildings, and taller steeples. Early 14th-century English cathedrals therefore tended to have more coherent and yet more dynamic silhouettes. This can be seen at the presbytery of Gloucester Cathedral (ca. 1350). Unlike those parts of the building that were already finished, the new extension, actually a structure unto itself, has huge windows that are clearly visible on the outside. The buttresses are kept tight to the body of the church. On the interior, facing the apse, the lightness and paperiness of the architecture has been so dematerialized that nothing is left except a thin filigree grid of supports. The new direction received its grandest manifestation at the Cathedral of Milan (begun 1387), a wide building with a vast orchestration of vertical elements in white marble, reaching a crescendo in an octagonal tower that rises almost magically from the center of the building.

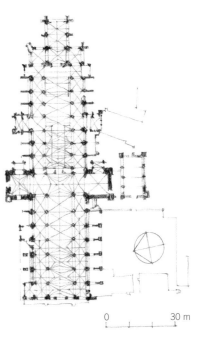

0   30 m

12.88 Plan: Exeter Cathedral

12.89 **View of Gubbio, Italy**

12.90 **Town Hall, Gubbio**

Italian Town Halls

In Italy, in the wake of faltering imperial control, a population explosion, and an expansion of markets, the artisans, guild members, and merchants known collectively as the *popolo* banded together with men of rank and property to dominate the political system. The rise of the *popolo* was rapid. In Milan, in 1190, the *popolo*, the main source of communal revenues, was entitled to only one-fifth of government positions. By 1198, they were the dominant political force in the city. Often the first acts of the *popolo* were to pass tax reform, systematize the law courts, and set up controls on public monies. Beginning with Pisa in the 1080s, Bologna in 1123, and Florence in 1138, these fledgling city governments laid the groundwork for an urban consciousness that was to become the hallmark of Italian politics for the next two centuries. The formal acceptance of this new arrangement came in the form of the Peace of Constance (1183), a much overlooked treaty that paved the way for the modern notion of civic governance. With the German emperors no longer in a position to assert their power, they gave the northern Italian cities the right to elect their own consuls, to govern their own lands, and most importantly, to make their own laws.

Central to the new notion of governance was a town hall in front of a public piazza (*campo*) where people could assemble. There was often also a special building for the head of the militia and police. For the first time in centuries—perhaps since the days of the

Romans—buildings were conceived and constructed as an ensemble with a public space. The earliest town halls date to the end of the 12th century and are at Brescia, Verona, Modena, Pavia, and Bergamo. These were followed in the 13th century by town halls at Volterra, Todi, Como, Ferrara, Siena, and Gubbio, among others. Most of these halls followed a simple prototype: a large meeting hall on the upper floor, with large windows facing the piazza and a balcony from which proclamations could be read. The ground floor was often open or had a loggia where silversmiths, gold traders, or other highly skilled craftsmen and merchants could work under the direct protection and supervision of the city. In the urban complex of Gubbio, the town hall and palace face each other across a piazza that is raised on a high undercroft looking out over the valley below. The new town halls were coordinated urbanistically with the cathedral buildings that were begun first at Pisa in 1063, followed by Modena in 1099, Verona in 1139, and Siena in 1196. The situation was, however, rarely peaceful. Milan, Brescia, and Piacenza were often at war with each other, as were Pisa, Genoa, and Lucca.

Siena

In the 13th century, Siena, one of the most important cities in Italy, controlled the southern Tuscan wool industry and dominated the trade routes between France and Rome. It was also home to Italy's richest

banks. Siena's power reached a zenith with the defeat of a much superior Florentine army at the battle of Montaperti in 1260. The city then embarked on unrivaled urban redevelopment, building a cathedral, a *campo*, and the town hall. The *campo* was constructed more or less at the center of the city, on unclaimed land that sloped steeply into a ravine. A large terrace was built over the ravine to form the *campo*. At the steep end, a town hall was constructed—the Palazzo Pubblico (1297–1310)—with four stories facing the *campo* and elegantly proportioned reception and councilor rooms, many decorated with frescoes recounting important events in the city's history. The curve of the piazza is lined with a continuous row of palace fronts, most dating from the 14th century. Opposite the town hall is the Loggia della Mercanzia (1417), for the merchants. The Duomo (1196–1215) a few blocks away dominates the town's silhouette. As was common in Italy, areas of towns were organized around mendicant churches. In this case the principal ones are San Domenico (1226), Sant'Agostino (1258), and San Francesco (1326–1475). The city's prosperity came to an abrupt halt with the arrival of the Black Plague, which reached Siena in 1348; by the end of that year, two-thirds of Siena's one hundred thousand citizens had succumbed. The city never recovered; what we see today is a snapshot of a late medieval Italian city.

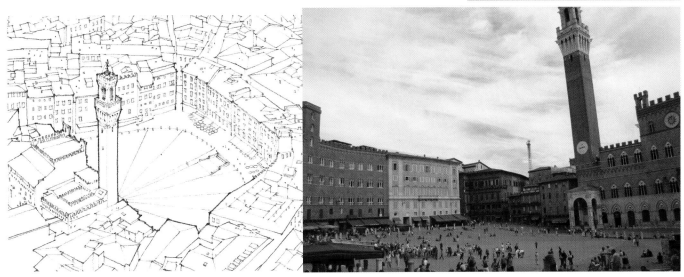

12.91 **Aerial view: Piazza del Campo, Siena, Italy**

12.92 **Palazzo Pubblico, Siena**

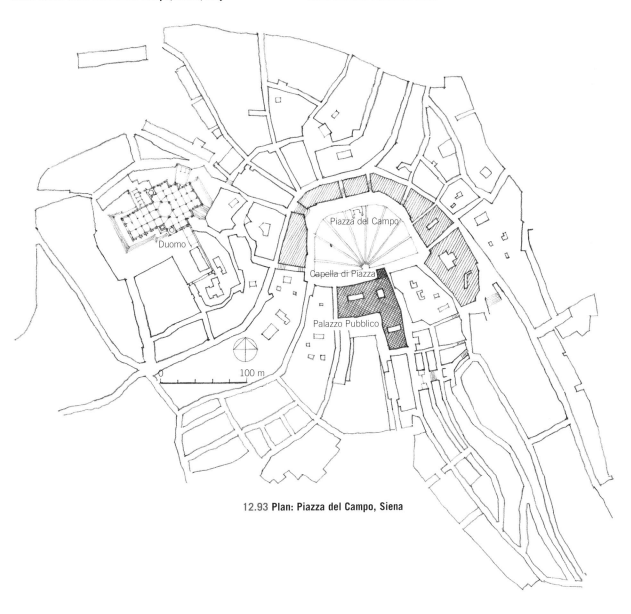

Duomo

Piazza del Campo

Capella di Piazza

Palazzo Pubblico

0   100 m

12.93 **Plan: Piazza del Campo, Siena**

12.94 Republic of Novgorod, Russia

12.95 Church of St. Paraskeva Piatnitsa, Novgorod, Russia

Republic of Novgorod

A gradual decentralization of power in the mid-11th century and the weakening of the Kingdom of Kiev gave rise to the development of autonomous cities and monastic complexes. The shift produced a church architecture suited to the tastes of each region. The greatest examples are found in the territory of Novgorod and in the area of Vladimir-Suzdal, where the monastic clergy, together with leading merchant families, took the leading role in church building. The Mongols had never quite reached Novgorod, stopping about 100 kilometers away, fearful of getting stuck in the marshes.

The Church of St. Paraskeva Piatnitsa, built in 1207 on the marketplace on the commercial side of the city, is dedicated to the marketplace's patron saint; it was built on the site of two earlier wooden churches, as noted by William Brumfield in his *History of Russian Architecture*. The building shows a departure from the cubic scheme of the earlier churches. The plan is still an inscribed cross, but its arms are emphasized in the north, south, and west by three large, covered porches, which are almost as tall as the church itself.

Another important regional center was Suzdalia, located in northeastern Russia in the upper reaches of the Volga River, an area that had been colonized by Slavic tribes in the 10th century. Among these early Suzdalian churches was the Church of the Intercession of the Virgin (1165). About 1.6 kilometers from the city of Bogolyubovo, it was commissioned by Andrey Bogolyubsky, who led a military campaign against both Kiev and Novgorod and subsequently established his power as the grand prince of all Russia. The church was built on an artificial hill overlooking the Nerl River. Paved with stones, the hill protects the church from the flooding on its marshland site and also accentuates the verticality of the design. The massing consists of a square base on which the church rests, with a tall drum and dome rising from the center. The elegance of the design is enhanced by the perfect sense of proportion established by the pilasters on the facade and the high apses that extend to the vaults of the *zakomary*, or arched gables.

In 1237, the Mongolians invaded the region and destroyed all its chief cities, with the exception of Novgorod and Pskow. They set up a state that lasted until 1480 in the south and east of Russia. Building activity during this period came to a halt, and most of Russia experienced cultural decay and isolation from Europe.

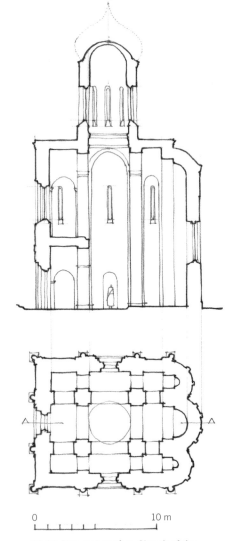

0   10 m

12.96 Plan and section: Church of the Intercession of the Virgin, Suzdalia, Russia

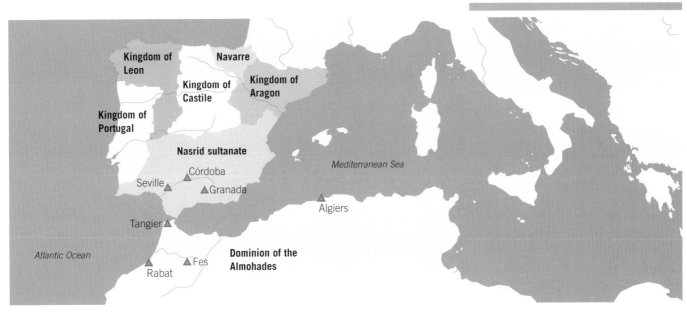

12.97 **Nasrid sultanate**

Nasrid Sultanate

In 1260, the Mongolians destroyed Aleppo and Damascus, massacring fifty thousand inhabitants. With the Arabian heartland in turmoil, there were only two places in the Islamic world where architecture could develop: northern India (which would eventually come under the sway of the Mongolian Timurid) and the Spanish-Moroccan area, which was far removed from Central Asia. The latter was extraordinarily prosperous, even though by the 11th century the unity of Spain and Morocco, as established by the Almohads, had dissolved. In 1228, the Almohad prince Idris departed from Spain to assume leadership over the Almohads in North Africa, and Ibn al-Ahmar moved in and established a vassal state under Ferdinand III; it became the Kingdom of Granada, the Nasrid sultanate, the longest lasting Moorish dynasty in Spain. (Northern Spain was controlled by various Christian kingdoms.) It was under the rule of the Almohads that the famed Alhambra was built. The Islamic areas of North Africa were still economically strong: Fes was a city of two hundred thousand and had some 785 mosques, including the Great Mosque of Fes (1275), modeled on Granada and the Attarin Madrasa (1323–25) with its finely carved capitals and delicate wall treatments. It was in Spain, however, where the spectacular Palace of Alhambra (Red Castle) was laid out in 1238 by Mohammed I (r. 1238–73).

It is first and foremost a fortification, defined by a defensive wall circuit mediated by towers and gates atop a natural acropolis surrounded by rocky terrain and the River Darro, which guards its northern side. Alcazaba, the citadel on the westernmost tip of the Alhambra complex, enclosed within an additional triangular wall circuit, exemplifies the military aspects of the complex. It served as an armory and was heavily fortified with a watchtower.

The palace was entered by a gate at the eastern end of the southern wall circuit. A second entrance, Bab al-Shari'a, the "Gate of Justice" (shari'a is Arabic for the body of Islamic religious law), stands at the western end of the same wall and is noteworthy for the carving of an outstretched hand in the keystone and that of a key above the portal. Various interpretations have been made of these symbols, which are probably intended to demonstrate the rulers' authority. The palaces were decorated throughout with colored tile and, up high on the walls, elaborately carved stucco. These designs combine geometric patterns, naturalist floral motifs, and a highly developed style of calligraphy through which Koranic verse and poetry became a visual art. The elaborate forms seen on the palace walls are often stylized script mirrored and transformed into an angular or curvaceous composition.

12.98 **Column capital, Court of the Lions, Alhambra, Granada, Spain**

12.99 Court of the Myrtles, Alhambra

12.100 Gate of Justice, Alhambra

Though the original purpose of most rooms in the palace has been lost, their purpose can often be extrapolated from the inscriptions on their walls. Floral motifs are found throughout the Alhambra, as are *muqarnas*, honeycomb projections from the ceilings that resemble stalactites.

The palaces are arranged to form a dense network of rooms, mediated by airy gardens with pools of water. Water was symbolically important and used throughout. The Court of the Lions has four channels of water representing the four "rivers of paradise" that extend near cardinally within the columnar portico surrounding the courtyard and into the palace itself on two sides. Some have suggested that the eponymous lions belie an intention to re-create the Temple of Solomon. The use of materials in the palace is varied. Some of the walls are made of a type of concrete; others are of brick. Ashlar stones were used at the gates and to reinforce the corners of the walls. The outside walls were stuccoed and sometimes painted to simulate stone or brick. Columns of marble are sometimes structural, sometimes decorative. The white marble imparts brilliance to the columns and gives them an elegant and ethereal quality. As in Greek times, the shaft was left plain, but the capital was painted in bright colors. Though similar to classical columns in their proportions, the Alhambra columns, like those in the Court of the Lions, have numerous annulets in the necking below the capital. Representation of the human form is forbidden in Islamic religious buildings, but geometrical designs are commonplace. In fact, those stemming principally from squares and the rectangular formations produced by the rotation of a radius from the base of the bisecting hypotenuse form the basis of most of the Alhambra's construction, in both plan and elevation. The two-dimensional ornament, particularly evident in the tile work, exemplifies this fascination with geometries stemming principally from squares forming eight-pointed stars. Geometric complexity is particularly evident in the ceiling of the throne room in the Comares Palace. As the *muqarnas* rise to the center of the vault, they obliterate the structural character of the space even though they are governed by an intricate and complex geometry of their own.

From 1492 to the 18th century, the Alhambra was the residence of the Spanish governors. In the 16th century, Charles V constructed a palace for himself that was grafted onto the fabric of the old structure. The mosque of the Alhambra, adjacent to this new palace, was refashioned as the Church of Santa Maria la Blanca in a Baroque style.

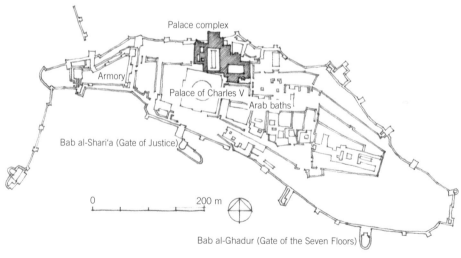

12.101 Plan of Alhambra

12.102 **Hall of the Ambassadors, Alhambra**

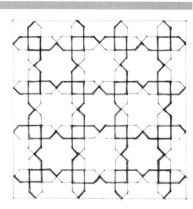

12.103 **Geometric motif, Alhambra**

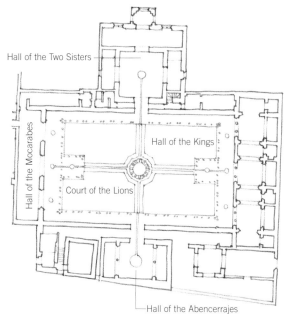

Hall of the Two Sisters

Hall of the Mocarabes

Hall of the Kings

Court of the Lions

Hall of the Abencerrajes

12.104 **Plan: Court of the Lions, Alhambra**

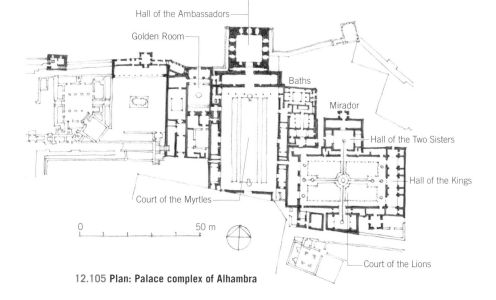

Hall of the Ambassadors

Golden Room

Baths

Mirador

Hall of the Two Sisters

Hall of the Kings

Court of the Myrtles

Court of the Lions

0   50 m

12.105 **Plan: Palace complex of Alhambra**

12.106 Mesoamerica, ca. 1200 CE

12.107 Giant Toltec figures at Tula, near Tula de Allende, Mexico

Toltec Empire

From the 9th to the late 12th centuries, the Toltecs, with their capital at Tula, located farther north than any previous pre-Columbian Central American capital, were the determining force of the region, taking over the role that had once been Teotihuacán's. They adopted an aggressive militaristic stance and practiced human sacrifice extensively. No subsequent dynasty failed to claim Toltec ancestry. Their myth of Quetzalcoatl (the "Plumed Serpent") was the likely cause of the Aztec's acceptance of the Spaniard Hernán Cortés in the 16th century, when the latter's arrival was mistaken as the prophesied return of Quetzalcoatl.

Tula had a population of about forty thousand by 1100 CE. The Toltec architects designed within established methods, such as placing buildings around large plazas, using many-tiered platforms as bases, building newer structures atop older ones, and painting colorful motifs on building surfaces. Their main sacred complex sat on a high artificial terrace, with the central plaza occupying an area 100 by 100 meters partly enclosed by pyramids, palaces, and ball courts. The substructure to Tula's pyramid was covered with thick white stucco, which may have symbolized the underworld. Although the temple at the top of the pyramid was destroyed, the stone columns that supported the roof still remain; they were carved with images of Toltec warriors. Unique to Tula was the Coatepantli, or Snake Wall—a

freestanding structure that encloses a passageway north of the base of the pyramid. Both sides of this passage are carved with identical friezes—bands of geometrically stylized snakes framing the central panels and depicting partly skeletonized men apparently being devoured by serpents. Only two other *coatepantli* representations are known to exist—at Tenochtitlán and Tenayuca—suggesting that they were a feature of Mesoamerica only from 900 to 1500 CE.

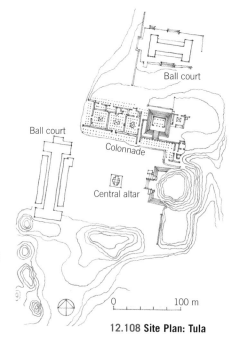

12.108 Site Plan: Tula

Chichén Itzá

The architectural ideas of Tula were reproduced and refined in Chichén Itzá, the main city-state of the Yucatán Peninsula in the 12th century. Because the city is very far from Tula, the mechanics of the influence between the two are still a subject of discussion. The sudden efflorescence of Toltec architecture in Chichén Itzá has led some to speculate that the exiled Toltec ruler, Topiltzin Quetzalcoatl, may have settled there. Although sacrifice and a militaristic stance were central to the Itzá elites, their ceremonial complex was much more about the cosmic calendar and its measurement and meaning.

The complex is organized around two *cenotés*, the Mayan word for the deep water-filled sinkholes that the Itzá associated with the underworld. These sinkholes are scattered across the Yucatán. The name *Chichén Itzá*, in fact, means "the opening of the wells of the Itzá." Since the soil and rock in the region is porous and does not hold water well, the eerie underground pools had both a practical and a religious meaning. Of the two in the city, the southern one was used for drinking water, and the northern one, connected to the surface by a ceremonial path, was used for sacrifices. The main structure, however, was the *caracol*, or observatory; it is circular, on a trapezoidal base, and raised on a rectangular platform. Its walls have tiny openings that allow the priest to track the movement of various stars

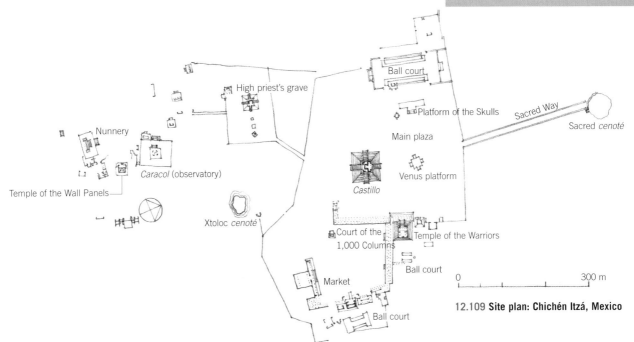

12.109 **Site plan: Chichén Itzá, Mexico**

and, in particular, the planet Venus. The northern complex is designed around an impressive biaxially symmetrical platform mound, known as the *castillo*. It hides within it an older platform mound, whose temple was accessed by a single stair. The temple, complete with its sacrificial sculpture, the *chacmool*, was carefully interred in the reconstruction, or the symbolic "reskinning," of the platform mound.

Besides being a sacrificial temple, the *castillo* also functioned as a solar calendar. It has 91 steps on three sides and 92 steps on the northern side, for a total of 365 steps, one for each day in the solar year. It is almost exactly aligned to the cardinal directions to enable the observation of solar events on solstices and equinoxes. The *castillo*'s best known calendar effect occurs on the equinoxes, when the balustrade of its northern stairway casts seven isosceles triangles as shadows that link together to form the body and tail of a serpent, with its head sculpted at the base of the stair. This is presumably a depiction of the ceremonial descent of Kukulkan, the Itzá's name for Quetzalcoatl, from the sky.

Kukulkan's descent is also presented in the Temple of the Warriors, marking the western edge of the plaza, a structure remarkably similar to the one in Tula. A forest of pillars, carved with warriors and originally roofed over with perishable materials, forms a long pre-chamber, presumably to restrict

access to the main pyramid, where the rulers would have held audience. A single flight of stairs leads to a temple whose threshold is marked yet again with a *chacmool* and two columns depicting Kukulkan's descent. In the back is a bench where the king may have sat as captives were sacrificed against the *chacmool*.

On the western edge of the plaza is the city's principal ball court, the largest known in pre-Columbian America. It is 146 by 36 meters, its hoops 8 meters high, making it almost the size of an American football field—so large that it is hard to imagine its being used for sport; it may, in fact, have been intended to depict a more ceremonial ball court of the gods. There are several other smaller ball courts in Chichén Itzá.

12.110 *Castillo*, Chichén Itzá

12.111 Ball court at Chichén Itzá

12.112 Temple of the Warriors, Chichén Itzá

The impaled heads of defeated warriors were displayed on a special construction in the middle of the plaza, just east of the ball court. At the middle of the northern edge of the plaza lies the entrance to the path that leads to the sacred *cenoté*. As was the rest of the Yucatán, Chichén Itzá was suddenly abandoned in the middle of the 13th century, for reasons that are still not fully understood. However, the *castillo* and its path to the sacred *cenoté* continued to be used by local inhabitants until the Spanish conquest of the region.

The *chacmool* was a Tula invention. These post-Classical Mayan stone statues depict a human figure reclining face up, its legs drawn in, its elbows on the ground, with its upper back raised and its head turned to a near right angle. It holds a vessel, disk, or plate on its stomach, where offerings may have been placed or sacrifices carried out. (It is presumed that the hearts of sacrificed victims were placed in the vessel.) Although the origins of the *chacmool* are undetermined, they proliferated during Tula times. Twelve have been found at Tula, fourteen at Chichén Itzá, and two more in the Aztec capital, Tenochtitlán. The ancient name for this type of sculpture is unknown.

12.113 *Caracol* (observatory), Chichén Itzá

12.114 A *chacmool*

1400 CE

In 1250, a century after the fall of the Toltecs, Chichén Itzá was abandoned. A migrant group from the north, known as the Mexica, settled into the central valleys of Mexico, establishing new cities. After two centuries of conflict, the city of Tenochca concluded a military alliance with the Acolhua of Texcoco and the Tepanecs of Tlacopan, forming a powerful bloc linking most of central Mexico. Their capital was Tenochtitlán, the site of contemporary Mexico City. To the south, the Chimu kingdom controlled the territories of coastal South America in the 13th and 14th centuries. There they exploited the arid climate to build one of the world's largest cities ever made from adobe, an ancient type of sun-dried brick made of clay, sand, and water, with some straw mixed in. In the middle of the 15th century the Chimu were displaced by the Incas, upstart rulers from the highlands of Peru whose capital was Cuzco. In their short rule before falling to the Spanish, the Incas dominated the trade routes of coastal South America, constructed long rope bridges, and built roads and cities with some of the most intricate and precise random rubble masonry in history.

The 15th century marks the end of the great conquests from the Russian steppes. The arrows on the maps showing invasions by the Gauls, the Huns, the Turks, the Mongolians, and other tribes from the steppes have disappeared. For the first time in over a thousand years, the Eurasian world was not beset by migratory invaders.

The impact of the invaders had not been entirely negative. Furthermore, many tribes began to make their own type of contributions and adopt local customs. For example, the Liao tribes in China adopted Chinese ways, and the Huns in eastern Europe converted to Christianity. But without these invaders and within a brief span of time, novel civilizational and aesthetical imperatives were underway, including the emergence of a new wave of global urbanism. In fact, many of the cities that today are at the very center of preservation efforts date from this period. In Korea, Seoul was transformed into a great and impressive capital. In China, Beijing's Forbidden City was built. Islam, of course, was also rebounding, expressing its wealth in mosques and schools and mausoleums from Egypt to northern India. Samarkand, the capital of Timurid, was expanded and became perhaps the leading economic city of the world. Close by was the bustling metropolis of Bukhara, the Shaybanid capital. Further to the east, the Mamluks were making considerable improvements to the city of Cairo. More or less absent from this urban expansionism is Southeast Asia. The decline of the Khmer sent the entire region into decline, with the exception of the Thai, who, at their new capital, Ayutthaya, were able to fill the vacuum. It is a great irony that the very increase in trade in the 14th century allowed the Black Plague to make its inroads, killing hundreds of thousands worldwide and placing a damper on European economic progress. Nonetheless, by the middle of the 15th century enough of a recovery had been made so that the true impact of the new global economy could be seen. Eastern Africa was bustling with trading ports filled with Islamic merchants who made the connection between Egypt to the north and India to the east.

The Italian Renaissance and the position of Italy also has to be understood within the context of this global economy. With the restoration of trade links to China, Italy, with its energetic mercantile city-states, was excellently positioned. Though far from unified, its rival city-states invested their newly acquired resources in art and learning and science, so that, as a totality, Italy became a dominant cultural force in Europe. The Venetian Republic, with its famed maritime fleet and trading posts throughout the eastern Mediterranean (some acquired during the Crusades), minted its own coins and secured its position as the world's leading gold market. Florence also began to assert itself, with the Medici becoming the leading bankers in Europe. While much building activity was occurring in Florence and Venice, cities such as London, Paris, and Aachen, Germany, were still at the relative periphery of the global economy.

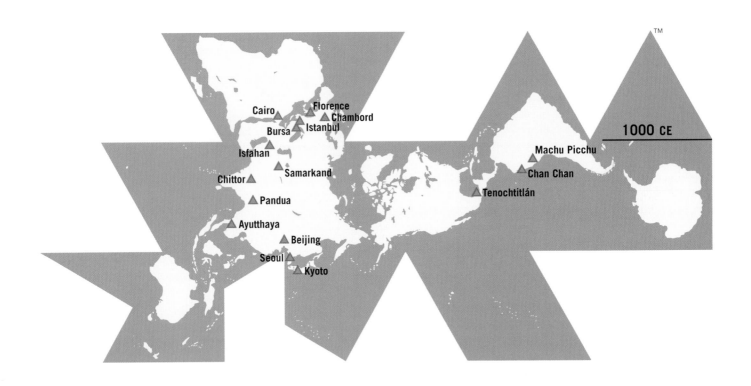

™

1000 CE

Cairo
Florence
Chambord
Bursa
Istanbul
Isfahan
Samarkand
Chittor
Pandua
Ayutthaya
Beijing
Seoul
Kyoto
Machu Picchu
Chan Chan
Tenochtitlán

Puebloan Cultures
ca. 700–1600

Iroquoian Language Cultures
ca. 1000–1550

China: Yuan Dynasty
1279–1368

Ming Dynasty
1368–1644

▲ **Forbidden City**
1420–1908

Joseon Dynasty
1392–1910

▲ **Gyeongbok Palace**
1394

▲ **Changdeok Palace**
1405–12

Japan: Kamakura Period
1185–1333

Nanbokucho Period
1336–1392

Muromachi Period
1392–1573

▲ **Kinkakuji**
1397

▲ **Ginkakuji**
1483–90

Black Plague in China
1330s

Black Plague in western Asia and Europe
1346–51

1200 CE   **1400 CE**   **1600 CE**

Ottoman Empire
1281–1923

▲ **Topkapi Palace**
Begun ca. 1459

▲ **Beyazit Medical Complex**
Completed 1488

▲ **Bibi Khanum Friday Mosque**
1339–1404

Timurid Dynasty
ca. 1370–1507

Delhi Sultanate
1210–1526

▲ **Friday Mosque of Gulbarga**
1367

▲ **Chittor Fort**
7th century to 1568

▲ **Jami Masjid of Ahmedabad**
1423

Egypt: Mamluk Sultanate
1260–1517

▲ **Complex of Sultan Hassan**
1356–63

▲ **Mausoleum Complex of Sultan Qaitbay**
1472–74

Italy: Papal and Autonomous City-States
12th century to 1870

▲ **Cathedral of Florence**
Begun 1294

▲ **Medici Palace**
1444–ca. 1460

▲ **St. Peter's Basilica**
Begun 1506

▲ **Sant'Andrea at Mantua**
1472–94

France: Valois Rule
1328–1589

▲ **Château of Chambord**
Begun 1519

Aztec State
ca. 1248–1521

▲ **Tenochtitlán**
ca. 1325–1521

◉ 1492
Columbus arrives in America

Conquest Period
1500–42

Inca Empire
ca. 1200–1532

◄ **Chan Chan**
ca. 1000–1400

▲ **Cuzco**
15th century

▲ **Machu Picchu**
15th to 16th centuries

1400 CE

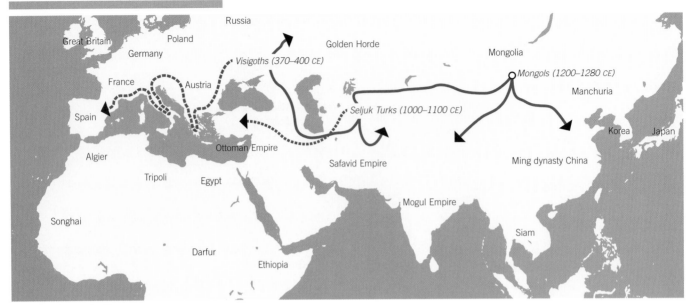

13.1 Eurasia, ca. 1400 CE

End of the Steppe Invasions

From the 2nd to the 14th centuries, Eurasian history was marked by a continual flow of humanity, first from the forests of Germany and then from the vast stretches of the Russian and Mongolian steppes. At first the great world powers, the Romans and the Chinese, attempting to keep the invaders at bay, erected fortified barriers. The Limes Germanicus, for example, ran roughly down the Rhine from the North Sea, following in Germany the course of the Danube River (Limes Rhaeticus). Its construction is contemporaneous with the beginnings of the more famous Great Wall of China. All these walls, of course, did not hold.

The reason for the expansionary turmoil among the largely nomadic tribes out of the Russian and Central Asian steppes are numerous. Climatic changes, overpopulation, internal stresses, and the desire for better farmland or plunder all figured into the equation. The Visigoths were particularly cruel in their zigzag route through Europe, finally settling in Spain, with their capital at Toledo; the Lombards, who conquered Italy around 568 CE, set up their capital at Pavia. The Normans, descendants of Viking raiders, negotiated with the Frankish kings to be allowed to settle in northern France, founding Normandy, with their capital at Rouen, and eventually conquering England in the Battle of Hastings in 1066. The Hungars, who had been a thorn in

the side of the Romans, made their peace with the Byzantine rulers and converted to Christianity. The Hephthalites, or the White Huns (as opposed to the Golden Horde, the color referring to how the Mongolians divided geographical regions) invaded Iran in the 5th century and proceeded into India, where they remained a distinct group. They were the first of several waves, culminating with the Seljuk Turks, who swept southward to dominate a belt of territory from Anatolia to western Iran. The greatest explosion out of the northeast was the Mongolians, who at their height around 1260 constituted an empire so vast that it defies the imagination, even today. They intermarried and ruled, adopting Christianity to the west, Islam to the south, and Buddhism in China. Their world was eventually transformed by the Timurid, descendants of the Mongols, who ruled from Samarkand and created an empire that ranged from northern Syria to western China.

As powerful as were the early civilizations in Mesopotamia, India, China, and the Mediterranean, the story of that world from about 400 to 1200 was associated with a different type of civilizational drive, one that at first glance seemed to be everything but positive. The Chinese, Romans, and Persians alike regarded the migratory peoples with horror and imbued them with the negative attributes of rootlessness and barbarism, even though more than a few of these tribes

possessed well-developed legal systems as well as agricultural, husbandry, and military skills, and occasionally brought novel inventions with them that were then widely adopted.

By the 15th century, migratory waves diminished, the great northern steppe having been emptied of its people. The impact of the Mongolian invasion was, however, still playing out. The rulers of the Shaybanid Empire in Central Asia, the Safavid Empire in Iran, and the Indian Mughal Empire were all descendants of Timurid rulers, producing a regional order that was amazingly stable for over two hundred years, leading to the flowering of Islamic civilization in all three empires. Eventually, in China itself, the Mongol example was repeated by the Manchus (from Manchuria) in the 17th century, who established China's longest-lasting dynasty. The Manchu Qing modeled themselves on the Mongolians, conceiving a multiethnic and pluralistic empire that withstood the great colonial invasions of Europe until the early 20th century.

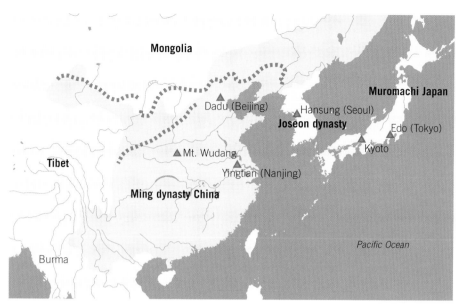

13.2 Ming dynasty China

Ming Dynasty China

In 1368, Zhu Yuanzhang defeated the last Mongolian Yuan emperor and established the Ming ("bright" in Chinese) dynasty. Initially, its capital was Nanjing, but the third Ming emperor, Zhu Di (r. 1403–24), moved the capital to Dadu, renaming it Beijing, meaning "northern peace." Zhu Di called himself the Yongle emperor, meaning the "emperor of perpetual happiness." The Ming (1368–1644) were Han Chinese; they considered the Mongolian Yuan foreign barbarians and were therefore eager to erase as many traces of Mongolian rule as possible. They tightened controls over the citizens and reintroduced Confucian practices. On the other hand, they continued the modernization programs of the Yuan, expanded urban centers, and maintained the traditional architectural construction styles. The bracketing system, however, had by this time become a largely ornamental device. Techniques in glazing evolved significantly; buildings such as pagodas, gateways, and arches, as well as screen wall facades, were decorated with color and elaborate carvings.

The Forbidden City

The Forbidden City, the enormous palace complex built by Emperor Zhengtong (r. 1436–49) in Beijing, is one of the most celebrated icons of imperial China. Its construction was a vast enterprise that involved rebuilding the Mongolian capital of Dadu. The palaces from that era were methodically destroyed, as would have been typical, apart from certain landscape features. At the core of the imperial compound was the Palace of Heavenly Purity—the residence of the son of heaven and the conceptual center of the empire. Since the emperor embodied both the authority of government and its justice system, access to him had to be carefully circumscribed and, at the same time, projected well beyond his actual physical presence. This, in essence, was the dual purpose of the Forbidden City.

The Palace of Heavenly Purity consists of three pavilions on axis, on an I-shaped, single-stepped marble platform, preceded by a terrace facing south. It is surrounded by a wall. Sixteen pavilions, housing for the royal concubines, extended to the east and west beyond this innermost sanctum. Imperial gardens and additional palaces for members of the royal family make up much of the remaining structures. South of the palace, a set of three halls perched on a three-step, I-shaped marble platform repeated the order of the innermost palace. This second set of buildings is the terminus and focus of the public sequence of the Forbidden City, and the conceptual center of the empire.

The emperor met daily with his officials in the Hall of Supreme Harmony. Only the highest officers had access to this hall, which was also the emperor's throne room. The halls behind it, the Hall of Central Harmony and the Hall of Preserving Harmony, only served supporting functions. Although the height, spans, and ornamentation of the Hall of Supreme Harmony are magnificent, the impact of the hall comes from the manner in which the roof's deep overhang projects its presence into the vast space of the courtyard that precedes it. In front of the emperor all supplicants had to prostrate themselves, or kowtow, facing north. Only the emperor faced south—an arrangement magnified by the orchestration of the roof and the courtyard. The Forbidden City housed the imperial bureaucracy and its millions of records. The daily communiqués that arrived from the most distant parts of the empire were catalogued, interpreted, and presented to the emperor and his counselors for action when necessary. The offices of the bureaucracy were located in the corridors on either side of the Hall of Supreme Harmony. Five marble bridges symmetrically straddle the Jinshahe, or "Golden Water River," that winds its way around the Forbidden City. Just beyond them, farther south, lies the imposing Meridian Gate, the designated entrance into the Forbidden City that aligns with the city's enclosing wall (with turrets in its corners) and moat. This was where high-ranking civil and military officials gathered to wait for the emperor and where large triumphant ceremonies were conducted.

13.3 Meridian Gate, Forbidden City, Beijing, China

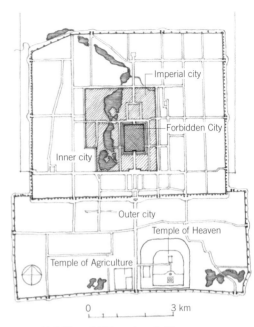

13.4 Plan of 15th-century Beijing

The U-shaped form (with five entrances and a tall platform with high pavilions) of the Meridian Gate connected the Forbidden City to the palaces beyond. The Gate of Uprightness, or Duanmen, was followed by Chengtian, from where the emperor issued imperial edicts, and then finally by the Great Ming Gate, or Da Mingmen, the main entry into the imperial city. As a visitor travels along the main axis of the Forbidden City toward its center, the elevation increases, each increase an indication of the power of the emperor. The first three gates rise high above the ground on imposing blank walls, giving the impression of being far below the zone of privilege. Beyond the Gate of Supreme Harmony, where the view opens up, the Hall of Supreme Harmony is raised

handsomely, an object in space on its three stately terraces and the highest point in the Forbidden City. The south view from the top of the third terrace was the emperor's privileged view, enabling him to see over the walls. From there all the gates and the length of the city could be apprehended in a single glance. Color played an important role. The podiums on which the buildings stood are a brilliant white; the wooden pillars are a dull red; finally, the roofs are tiled in imperial sun yellow.

That these palaces survive is itself of historical significance, as it was ancient practice in China for new dynasties to burn the capital of the former dynasty. This is one of the reasons there are so few historical structures, apart from temples, in China today. But in 1616, when the Manchu set up their dynasty on the ruins of the defeated Ming, they did not destroy the capital. Consequently, for five centuries, from about 1420 to 1908, the city was the hallowed seat of twenty-four emperors. The buildings seen today are not the original Ming-era buildings, but mostly relatively accurate reconstructions made by the Ch'ing Dynasty in the 17th and 18th centuries.

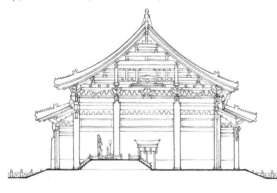

13.5 Section: Hall of Supreme Harmony, Forbidden City

13.7 Purple Heaven Hall, Mt. Wudang, China

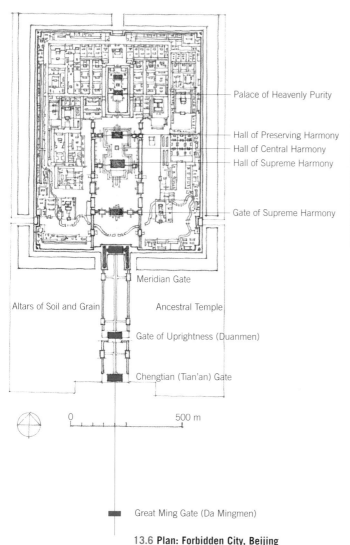

Palace of Heavenly Purity

Hall of Preserving Harmony
Hall of Central Harmony
Hall of Supreme Harmony

Gate of Supreme Harmony

Meridian Gate

Altars of Soil and Grain   Ancestral Temple

Gate of Uprightness (Duanmen)

Chengtian (Tian'an) Gate

0   500 m

Great Ming Gate (Da Mingmen)

13.6 Plan: Forbidden City, Beijing

13.8 Hall of Supreme Harmony, Forbidden City

Mt. Wudang

Zhu Di, the Yongle emperor, believing that his ascent to the throne had been aided by Zhenwu, a Daoist mythical warrior, dispatched in 1412 some three hundred thousand workers to Mt. Wudang in Hubei, where the Daoists believe Zhenwu had attained immortality. Mt. Wudang is in an area of precipitous cliffs and dramatic views, often covered in mist. Its thick forest is filled with caves, springs, and grottoes. Zhu Di's workers built a 60-kilometer-long pilgrimage path made of stone that winds its way up to the peak, aided by thirty-nine delicately constructed bridges. Along the way are nine temple complexes, two monasteries, and thirty-six hermitages, some perched over and along cliffs. The Purple Heaven Hall, Mt. Wudang's largest monastery, is farther up the slope. Two terraces (only one short of the Forbidden City's Hall of Supreme Harmony) elevate the elegant double-eaved, hip-and-gable five-bay hall. One of the main martial arts schools of China, Wudang kung fu, is associated with this area. Five hundred meters higher, the route culminates at Tianzhufeng ("Heavenly Pillar Peak") at the top of Mt. Wudang. Here sits a small Golden Hall (1416), its roof and the prominent parts of its three-bay structure executed in bronze. Within is the statue of the barefoot, long-haired Zhenwu surrounded by his Daoist retinue—the Dark Warrior, the tortoise entwined by a two-headed serpent, a golden youth, a jade maiden, and guardian spirits of water and fire, all cast in bronze. Above them, a bracket set more complicated than any found in the *Yingzhao Fashi* was built to signify their stature and royal favor.

13.9 Imperial Vault of Heaven, Temple of Heaven complex, Beijing

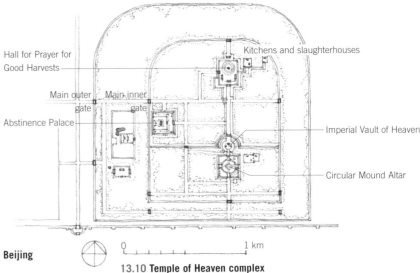

Hall for Prayer for Good Harvests

Main outer gate

Main inner gate

Abstinence Palace

Kitchens and slaughterhouses

Imperial Vault of Heaven

Circular Mound Altar

0   1 km

13.10 Temple of Heaven complex

Temple of Heaven

If the axis, courts, gates, great halls, and throne represented imperial authority, the emperor's connection with the altars and temples that he visited—which were all located outside the Forbidden City—was the concrete embodiment of his status as a son of heaven. The Imperial Ancestral Temple and the Altar of Soil and Grain, located just beyond the Meridian Gate, to the east and west of the major axis, were the oldest of the structures. The Altars of the Sun and Moon were located to the east and west of Beijing, and the Altar of Earth, to the north.

The south was reserved for the most important altars of them all in the Temple of Heaven complex: the Altar of Agriculture, intended to ensure the timely cycle of production, and the Circular Mound Altar, the enabler of the emperors' mandate. The Circular Mound Altar, also called the Altar of Heaven (Yuan Qiu Tan) is a three-tiered circular platform (the circle representing the shape of heaven) located in a square enclosure (the square symbolizing the earth). The altar, basically a type of ritual platform, was illuminated by hundreds of lanterns; incense burned everywhere. In the middle, facing south, was a tablet representing heaven, moved there especially from its resting place in the Imperial Vault of Heaven just beyond to the north. Before it, the emperor prostrated himself and kowtowed to the heavens more than fifty times in a carefully scripted ritual, witnessed by all present, that only he could perform. Heaven's displeasure with the emperor, manifested

by bad omens and natural or political catastrophes, was always considered a sign of the withdrawal of his mandate to rule.

Just north of the Circular Mound Altar is the Imperial Vault of Heaven, and farther north is the Hall of Prayer for Good Harvests (Qinian Dian). Elevated on three terraces of white marble, this temple has a triple set of conical roofs over a round space that is unique in Chinese architecture. The sacrifice there occurred on the winter equinox. The emperor prepared for the event by fasting for three days, living in the Abstinence

Palace located at the western edge of the complex. At three in the morning on the day of the equinox, the emperor traveled to the Circular Mound Altar, approaching it from the south—that is, facing north, in the position of a supplicant. The Abstinence Palace is one of the few Ming buildings made with stone vaults. Only the buildings for the dead (the Ming tombs) and this one were considered "unworthy" of a wooden roof, yet they were built with extraordinary care, showing that though stone architecture was not a tradition in China, it could be produced very skillfully.

13.11 Circular Mound Altar, Temple of Heaven complex

Joseon Dynasty, Korea

In 1392, Yi Songgye, with the aid of the Ming dynasty, seized the Korean throne and established the Joseon dynasty (also known as the Choson dynasty), which lasted until 1910. Korea was known under the Joseon as Daejoseonguk (the "Great Joseon Nation"). Though the Mongolians were defeated, aspects of Mongolian culture, here as elsewhere, remained embedded in Korean society. As in China, Confucianism was reestablished as the state religion. A new capital, Seoul, was built, situated not far from the peninsula's largest river and at the focal point of overland transportation routes. Several palaces were built in Seoul, the most important being Gyeongbokgung (or the "Palace Greatly Blessed by Heaven": *gung* meaning "palace," in 1394) and, a kilometer to the east, Changdeokgung (or the "Palace of Prospering Virtue," begun 1405, rebuilt 1592). The surrounding topography was carefully studied for the siting of the palace, from the standpoints of both Confucian ideology and feng shui, which also influenced the design of the principal roads connecting the main gates of the city by way of the four cardinal directions. Straight lines were not always the rule, as can be seen in the east-west and north-south thoroughfares, which are slightly curved.

According to feng shui, a building should face southward and should have mountains on the left and right that symbolize an azure dragon and a white tiger, respectively. The palace was thus situated in the north sector of the city, in the foothills of Paekak Mountain, facing south to the northern mountain peak called Nam Mountain. The deity on Paekak Mountain was female, whereas the deity on Nam Mountain was male. Paekak, which symbolized royal authority and was the most highly valued in terms of feng shui, was closed to the commoners and protected from any private use. Nam Mountain, however, was open to the common people. There was no natural mountain to the east of the palace, so an artificial hill was created to compensate for the topography's shortcomings.

In its original form, the palace had about five hundred buildings. They were burned during the Japanese invasions of 1592; about ten 19th-century reconstructions exist.

13.12 Gyeongbokgung, Seoul, Korea

Changdeokgung had a public portion (toward the south) and a more private part (toward the north) consisting of several stroll gardens strung together by a series of carefully composed follies for repose. One of these is particularly famous. Organized around a shallow quadrangular water tank, with a high ridge on one side and several small pavilions distributed along the tank's edges on the other three sides, the folly is skillfully understated, as if it were nothing more than a reinforcement of the natural elements already present in the landscape. The throne hall (*injongjon*), facing east and surrounded by its own wall, was a large two-story building,

built in 1405. It sits on the top of a series of low stone platforms that are particularly well proportioned in respect to the slope of the eaves. Stone tables in the courtyard indicate where each rank of official should stand for formal ceremonies. The bays are 5 meters square except for those on the central axis, which are 6.7 meters square. The throne sat on a high platform at the back of the middle bay. It was connected in the north to the government building, where the king worked, and in the south to a portrait hall, or *sonwonjon* shrine, where the former kings' portraits were displayed. On each king's birthday, a memorial rite was held there, emphasizing the principle of continuity.

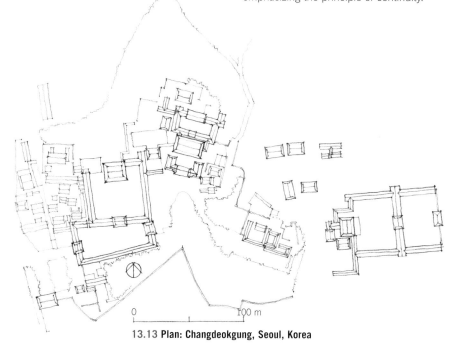

13.13 Plan: Changdeokgung, Seoul, Korea

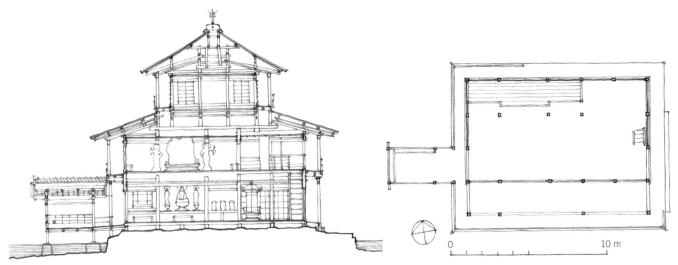

13.14 **Section: Kinkakuji, the Golden Pavilion, Kyoto, Japan**

13.15 **Plan: Kinkakuji, the Golden Pavilion**

Muromachi Japan

After two centuries of domination by aristocratic regents and military rulers, emperor Godaigo (r. 1318–39) enlisted the help of Ashikaga Takauji (1305–58) to reclaim the court in 1333. But when Godaigo refused to name Takauji as shogun after his victory, the latter forced the emperor into exile in 1335 and placed his own representative on the throne. As shogun, Takauji made two decisions that changed the course of Japanese history: he reinstated Kyoto as the capital and reestablished links with the Chinese Song dynasty—links that had been broken since Kublai Khan's failed attempt to invade Japan in the 13th century. Profits from the trade with China were important to the shogun's power. Song culture infused Japanese society, producing a blend of cultural elements that laid the foundation for a form of Buddhism known as Zen, the Japanese pronunciation of the Chinese kanji for *chan*. Chan, in turn, was a transformation of the Sanskrit *dhyan*, or meditation. Zen emphasizes sustained meditation rather than visualization as the way to nirvana. The Zen monasteries were built in the traditional Karayo style.

Kinkakuji

In 1394, the Muromachi shogun Ashikaga Yoshimitsu (1358–1408), Takauji's grandson, gave up his government position to become a monk and retired to his private estate, the central focus of which was a three-story viewing pavilion known as Kinkakuji, or the "Golden Pavilion." It sits at the edge of a carefully designed reflection pond. The first story contained a public reception room with a loggia along the water that served as access point for pleasure boats, its clearly defined wooden structural elements contrasting with the white plaster walls. The second floor served as a place for private discussions; it was protected by the gentle sweep of an upward-turning eave. The views into the landscape from the balcony were carefully designed—as was the rest of the estate—with small islands in the foreground framing and enlarging the background. (As in China, the surrounding distant landscape was also incorporated into the visual composition of the garden.) The third story, Yoshimitsu's private refuge, resolved the pavilion in an upwardly turning roof with a pronounced swell that culminated in a bronze phoenix finial. Yoshimitsu originally wanted to gild the pavilion (thus its name) but for most of its life it remained in wood. In 1950, the pavilion was destroyed by an arsonist. When it was reconstructed in 1955, its upper two stories were gilded to honor Yoshimitsu's original intentions.

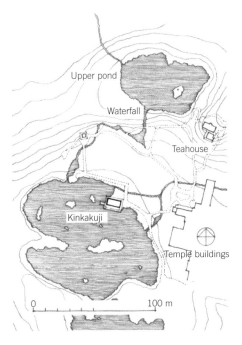

13.16 **Site Plan: Kinkakuji**

13.17 **Kinkakuji, the Golden Pavilion, Kyoto, Japan**

Ginkakuji

Ginkakuji ("Silver Pavilion") was built as a retirement villa by Yoshimitsu's grandson, the shogun Yoshimasa, in 1482. Yoshimasa wanted to cover two stories of his pavilion with silver, but his intention was never realized. In Yoshimasa's original design, the two-story pavilion stood at the edge of a pond set off against small bridges, tiny islands, and exactingly planted and pruned shrubs, all designed to generate carefully framed views that recalled descriptions from Japanese literature. Ginkakuji's fame lies in the additions made by Zen Buddhist monks during the Edo period in the 17th century, the palace having been turned over to Zen Buddhists after its patron's death. Since sand had to be stored on site to maintain the gardens, the Zen monks decided to use it to build two sculpted mounds next to the pond and in stark contrast to it. One is low and carefully raked to form a plateau, and it is called the Sea of Silver Sand, so named for its appearance in moonlight. The other mound rises as a perfectly shaped, truncated cone, arresting at first glance if only for its sheer size. The cone evokes the profile of Mt. Fuji but may also refer to the sacred mountain in the middle of a Buddhist mandala. As one walks around Ginkakuji and looks at it from different points of view, the cone, uniform in color and outline from all directions, functions as an object of constancy in the changing panorama. The two mounds set in play a drama of visual tension, the exact meaning remaining open to interpretation This type of meditational paradox is typical for Zen Buddhism.

In a sense it is Ginkakuji, more than Kinkakuji, that is more successful as a Zen garden. The assembly of its views is more restrained and subtle, and since they are bound by a much smaller space their experience is far more intimate and immediate. Together, they define the aspirations of the Muromachi warrior aristocracy as it changed under the influence of the Song and Zen.

13.18 **Ginkakuji, the Silver Pavilion, Kyoto, Japan**

Sea of Silver Sand

Ginkakuji

0   30 m

13.19 **Site Plan: Ginkakuji**

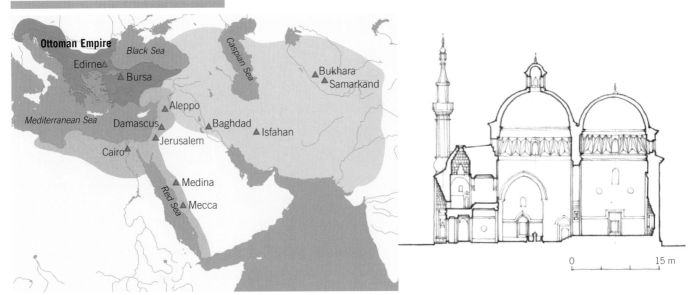

13.20 **West Asia and the eastern Mediterranean, ca. 1400**

13.21 **Section: Yesil Cami, Bursa, Turkey**

Ottoman Empire

Central and western Asia in the early post-Mongolian era were dominated by three new powers: the Fatimids in Egypt, the Timurids in Persia, and the Ottomans in Anatolia. The latter replaced the Seljuk Empire, which had been weakened by Mongolian attacks. The Osmanlis, or Ottomans, as they came to be known, were a Turkish tribe that captured Bursa from the Byzantines in 1326 and used it as their capital. In 1371 they reached Serbia, and in 1453 they conquered the main prize, Constantinople, bringing the Byzantine Empire to an end. The Ottomans were soon so strong that no single European country could challenge their position, despite repeated, coordinated attacks over the following centuries.

Ottoman mosques were not designed as introverted, walled rectangular enclosures, as the Seljuks had. Instead, they adopted the theme of the dome from the Byzantines, resting it on a square structure that was entered through a three-bay loggia with a minaret to one side. This prototype was expanded with side rooms, vestibules, and loggias. Sometimes the dome was given an enclosed forecourt. One of the best examples is Yesil Cami Mosque in Bursa (1412–19). From an ornate marble portal visitors pass a low, square vestibule that leads, by way of a short barrel-vaulted corridor, to the central hall. The main prayer hall, or *iwan*, behind the hall is raised from the central hall by four steps; the side *iwans*, by one step each.

Both domes sit on belts of "Turkish triangles" that negotiate the change from square to circles. At the center of the main hall, which has an oculus, is a pool. The royal family would have ascended the stairs near the entrance to gain access to the royal box. It is composed of two sections: a domed antechamber that opens onto a barrel-vaulted rear chamber that, in turn, looks onto the interior of the mosque. Whereas Seljuk buildings tended to be conceived as static rectangular objects that were brought

into relationship with each other by way of addition, from early on (and in step with the advanced architectural thinking of the 15th century in India and Italy), Ottoman structures were designed as institutional complexes that brought the building and public space into dialogue. At the Yesil Cami Mosque, the various parts of the institution—the madrasa, the imaret (or hostel for pilgrims), the hammam (bath), and the *türbe* (tomb)—are integrated in the city.

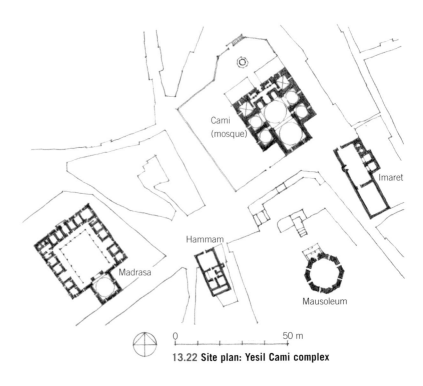

13.22 **Site plan: Yesil Cami complex**

13.23 Beyazit Medical Complex, Edirne, Turkey

13.24 Courtyard, Beyazit Medical Complex

Beyazit Medical Complex

In the spring of 1484, the thirty-seven-year-old Ottoman ruler, Beyazit II, on his way with his army to the Balkans, ordered the construction of the Beyazit Medical Complex (completed 1488) in Edirne (close to the modern border between Turkey and Bulgaria). The five principal elements of the composition are carefully walled off because of the number of horses, mules, and camels that would have been grazing nearby on the shore of the river. The buildings form an irregular U shape, with the mosque and its court at the center, facing in the direction of the street. The mosque is square in plan, half the width of the 50-meter-broad courtyard. The dome, lofty and rising dramatically over the entrance, was illuminated by a large central wheel carrying three tiers of oil lamps, all suspended by a single chain from the dome's center. Flanking the mosque are two square *tabhanes* with nine domes, each *tabhane* having four corner rooms opening onto *iwans* off a central court.

This plan is closely related to that of the Cinili Kiosk and is, therefore, distantly related to the architectural concepts of Central Asia. The minarets are set in the angle corners of the *tabhanes* and protrude from the walls of the courtyard. It is generally thought that these spaces served as temporary lodgings for members of the dervish orders, whose numbers were increasing in the 15th century. Dervishes are Sufi Muslims who commit themselves to poverty and austerity. They are similar to mendicant friars in Christianity or *sadhus* in Hinduism. Dervishes are prohibited to beg for their own good. They have to give the collected money to poor people. Given their obvious social usefulness, some Islamic rulers supported them. Beyazit not only supported their efforts, but was also not only a warrior but also someone who loved simplicity, peace, and retreat.

To the east of the mosque were two buildings that served as refectories and kitchens. The hospital on the western side of the complex is a hexagonal structure with its own small courtyard and forecourt. The hexagon was domed, and had a fountain in the center, the sound of which was intended to soothe the nerves of the ill. Musicians played in the principal *iwan*, which forms a stage at the far apse end of the hexagon. The whole complex employed 167 people and was staffed by three doctors, two eye specialists, and two surgeons, as well as a dentist.

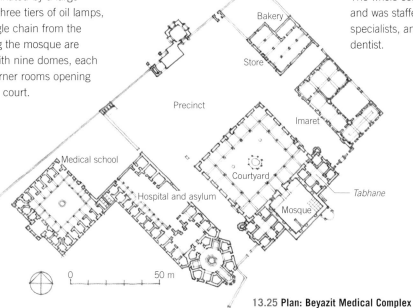

13.25 Plan: Beyazit Medical Complex

13.26 Topkapi Palace, Istanbul, Turkey

Topkapi Palace

On May 29, 1453, Sultan Mehmed II "the Conqueror" captured Constantinople after a fifty-three-day siege. For the Europeans it was a major defeat, as it brought to an end the Byzantine Empire and all that it represented. For the Arab armies, it was a long sought after prize that provided them with a major metropolis. Almost immediately, work was begun on the construction of mosques and other buildings, including the vast Topkapi Palace (begun ca. 1459) that served as the main royal residence and seat of the imperial Ottoman administration from the second half of the 15th to the mid-19th centuries. The palace, surrounded by water on two sides and by high walls on the third, was not based on a rational system, as a mosque would be, and is often seen as a haphazard aggregation of buildings. But this is not exactly accurate, since it was planned according to a logic related to the definition of a sultan. He was seen as beyond any relation of reciprocity, and ceremonies stressed the unbridgeable gap between master and subject—thus the insistence in this palace on the privacy of the sultan. The Mughals, elaborating on Timurid and Mongolian models, had more accessible private zones, much as in Europe, where the ruler could entertain guests. The Topkapi Palace, however, with its clearly delineated boundaries, was designed to instill a sense of sanctity and respect as much as fear and awe.

The main entrance of the palace was just behind the Hagia Sophia, now converted to a mosque. The Imperial Gate, the first of three main ceremonial double gates, led to the first court, which was comprised of workshops, storage areas, dormitories, kitchens, a bakery, and baths. It also contained a mint and various offices of the government. This court served as a waiting area for dignitaries as well as a staging area for processions and special ceremonies. Visiting ambassadors had to walk past the thousands of richly clad soldiers and courtiers standing in mandatory silence—an intimidating backdrop for diplomatic negotiations. The courtyard was also used for executions, which the sultan could observe from a window in the Tower of Justice.

At the second gate, the Gate of Salutation, the visitor would have had to dismount to gain access to the next court, called the Arena of Justice and the beginning of the palace proper. Unified by a continuous marble colonnade, it housed the Tower of Justice, the council hall, and the treasury, all clustered in the far left corner of the court. A loggia, raised on a platform in front of the council hall, overlooked the space. From the back of the inside of the hall, the sultan could watch the proceedings from behind a curtained window. The hall was low and unassuming because it was modeled on a tent known as the consultation tent, which was used by the imperial council during military campaigns.

The third gate, the Gate of Felicity, was especially sacred. On particularly important occasions, the sultan would greet visitors under its airy canopy. Behind the gate was the throne room or "Hünkar Sofasi," a square, one-story structure that served as an audience hall; the building is technically within the private precinct, yet it is conceptually part of the second courtyard. The third court was raised on high retaining walls, as the land slopes down below it toward the north. The throne room was located at the far left corner.

The buildings in this court were designed to take in the vistas of the surrounding landscape. The sultan, from his belvedere, could watch his flourishing capital and the port. The residential quarter was located to the east of the second and third courts in a compact mass huddled close to the walls of the court. There were special areas that housed pages and slaves—males, females, and eunuchs—who were all part of the sultan's retinue. It also housed the harem. In the northernmost corner were the royal apartments. The palace is not organized along an axis, nor are the buildings grand in the traditional sense. Rather, they are organized by diagonal vistas and angled approaches, the open areas of the courtyards meant to contrast with the ad hoc intimacy of the residential quarters.

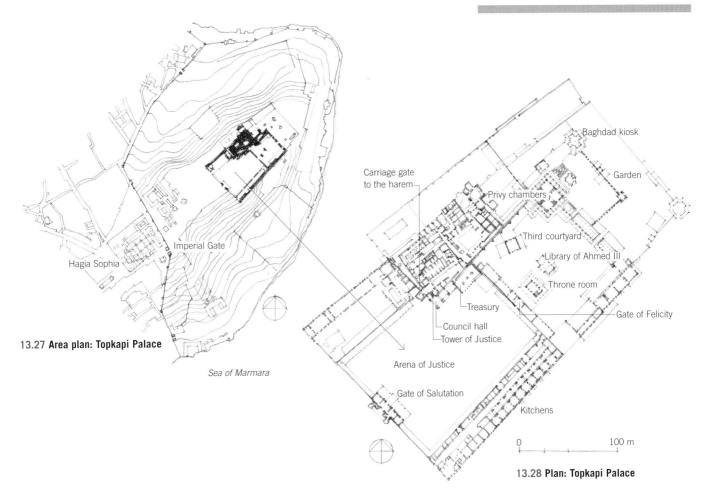

13.27 Area plan: Topkapi Palace

Hagia Sophia

Imperial Gate

Sea of Marmara

Carriage gate to the harem

Privy chambers

Baghdad kiosk

Garden

Third courtyard

Library of Ahmed III

Throne room

Treasury

Gate of Felicity

Council hall

Tower of Justice

Arena of Justice

Gate of Salutation

Kitchens

0   100 m

13.28 Plan: Topkapi Palace

13.29 Throne room, Topkapi Palace

13.30 Detail, Topkapi Palace

Timurid Dynasty

The occupation of Persia by the Mongolians and the fall of Baghdad in 1258 unleashed a period of disarray and confusion. One of the earliest post-Mongolian states to emerge was created by the Turkish-speaking Timur (1336–1405). A brave but notably cruel commander, he unified Persia, Iraq, and Transoxiana by expelling local potentates and clearing the countryside of robbers, increasing trade. While not themselves heterodox or Shi'ite, the Timurid rulers accorded respect to the Shi'ite figure Ali, the son-in-law of the prophet Muhammed, whom they considered the founder of their civilization's mystic brotherhoods. Furthermore, with a generosity unthinkable in later generations, Empress Gohar Shad built her Shi'ite subjects a splendid shrine in the city of Mashhad, still now a major pilgrimage center in modern Iran. Timur set up Samarkand, already a major metropolis along the Silk Route, as his capital. It soon possessed large suburbs with fountains and canals. In the factories, the citizens wove silk and cotton, worked leather, and decorated copper; Chinese craftsmen produced here the first paper outside of China itself. The 13th-century population exceeded half a million.

Consistent with Timur's passion for grand structures, imposing appearances became the main priority of his architectural program, with the facade developing into a virtual freestanding architectural form. High drums and external domes stabilized by brick ribs were often placed over the structural inner domes. The combination of portal and dome produced buildings of great spatial drama, such as Samarkand's biggest mosque, known as the Bibi Khanum Friday Mosque (1339–1404), which was entered through a high portal with round corner towers, its arches spanning nearly 19 meters. The principal elements of the plan—the entrance portal, the mosque, and the lecture halls—are all enlarged into monumental forms and then framed by the repetitive elements of the mosque. The colossal entrance portal protrudes from the exterior wall, with two minarets projecting out even further. The cylindrical shafts of the minarets, rising from the ground (rather than emerging from the top of the *iwan*) and sitting on decagonal socles, provide the earliest

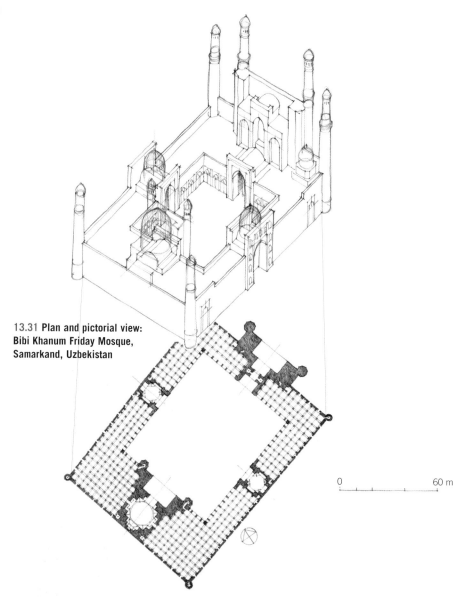

13.31 Plan and pictorial view: Bibi Khanum Friday Mosque, Samarkand, Uzbekistan

0   60 m

13.32 Portal, Bibi Khanum Friday Mosque

surviving example of minarets flanking a portal. Behind this lay a spacious courtyard, at the back of which stood the dome-covered main building of the mosque. The plan is the basic four-*iwan* type that had been developed in an ad hoc way in Isfahan some four hundred years earlier. But this building was a unit from the very start, and its hypostyle hall forms the connective tissue holding together the monumental elements. The *iwans* rise to an impressive 19 meters.

Of a similarly grand scale is the Ulugh Beg Madrasa in Samarkand (1417–20), which opens up to the main square on axis to the Bibi Khanum Friday Mosque. It is one of the largest madrasas in Central Asia, with an enormous entrance portal flanked left and right by dome-covered lecture halls with four axial niches. Slender round minarets mark the corners. The square courtyard has four *iwans* and a large mosque at the rear, with additional lecture halls to the right and left. The building became the prototype for many later madrasas. The domed corner rooms served as classrooms, while the court was enclosed by two stories of individual cells. The four colonnaded *iwan* porches, axially disposed and deeply recessed, served as meeting and discussion areas. The walls were decorated with marble panels and blue and purple bricks.

The Timurids developed a new type of dome support. Instead of the square hall and octagonal squinch, which had been developed by Islamic architects over the previous centuries, the dome was set on two pairs of overlapping arches. The dome was smaller than in the older system, but the whole had a dynamic plasticity, both outside and inside. This technique originated in Armenia, where it had been known since the 12th century. From there it spread to Russia, and it is quite possible that captured Russian or Armenian building masters might have been responsible for this aspect of Timurid architecture.

Though decorative tiles had been used in Islamic architecture from early on, their use was further developed under the Seljuks who completly sheathed buildings in colored tiles. Prior to the 13th century, most monumental decorations were made of stucco that was painted or gilded. But in the Timur period ceramic tiles were used to completely blanket the structure. Though the color blue predominates, the range of possible colors was quite wide, including turquoise, white, yellow, green, brown, purple, and black.

13.33 Ulugh Beg Madrasa, Samarkand

13.34 Timurid dome of the Bibi Khanum Friday Mosque

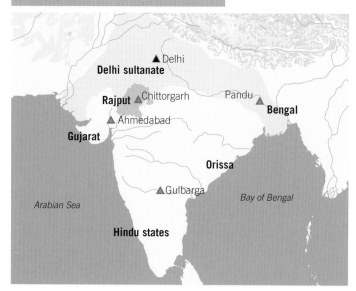

13.35 India, ca. 1400 CE

13.36 Interior arcade, Friday Mosque of Gulbarga, India

Deccan Sultanates

In 1400 central India was controlled by a familiar patchwork of diverse regional kingdoms, but for the first time most were ruled by Islamic kings, whose states were known as the Deccan Sultanates. With an opportunity to establish and build their new Islamic institutions, they conceived an array of innovative architectural projects.

Most of the Deccan sultans were affiliated with the sultans in Turkey for political reasons. Qutb-ud-Din Aibak's dynasty (1206–90) had controlled the entire Indo-Gangetic Plain of north India from its capital in Delhi. Its successor, the Khiljis (1290–1320), did spectacularly better, bringing central India—that is, the entire Deccan Plateau from Gujarat in the west to Pandua in the east and Gulbarga in the south—under their control. The Khilji's successors, the Tughlaqs (1320–1413), however, were unable to manage this vast empire and bungled a series of ill-conceived administrative projects. Timur, sultan of Samarkand, took the opportunity in 1398 to launch a raid from across the Himalayas and found Delhi bereft of its defenders. In the subsequent chaos, the governors and regents of the Deccan Plateau, many of them Khilji appointees, declared independence, establishing the Deccan Sultanates. The sultans took pains to distinguish themselves from the weak court in Delhi and instead turned to West Asia, not only for trade but also for occasional help in shaping their material culture and architecture.

Friday Mosque of Gulbarga

In Gulbarga, the capital of the Bahmanid sultanate (1347–1542), Sultan Muhammad I preferred his imported architecture as puritanical as possible. He used Rafi bin Shams bin Mansur, an architect from Iran, to build his Friday Mosque (1367). Without any courtyard or *iwan*, the mosque and its central hall (66 by 54 meters) is covered with sixty-three small cupolas; the *qibla* wall to the west features a high dome surrounded by twelve smaller, lower domes. An unusual aspect of the interior is the extremely wide span of the arcades, with very low imposts that were to become more common in south Indian Islamic architecture later on but were unheard of at this time. There is a Persian mood and even a basilica-like feel to this mosque.

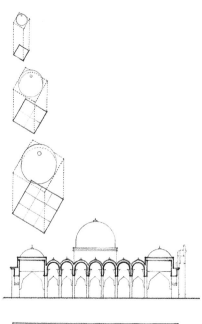

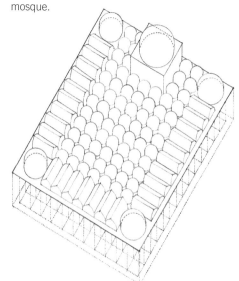

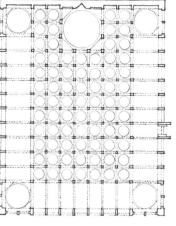

13.37 Plan, section, and pictorial view: Friday Mosque of Gulbarga

13.38 Mausoleum of Sultan Jalal al-Din Muhammad Shah

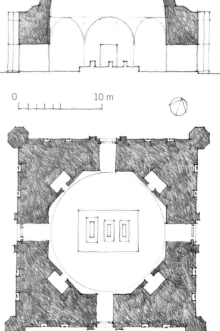

13.39 Plan and section: Mausoleum of Sultan Jalal al-Din Muhammad Shah

Pandua

One of the important kingdoms of the time ruled Bengal, in eastern India, from the 14th to the 15th centuries. Unlike some of the other Islamic sultanates, it readily adopted local practices, creating a style that is something of a fusion of the Islamic and Hindu. The Ilyas Shah dynasty, as it is known, constructed a new capital in Pandua in 1338. It is now a ruin a few kilometers north of Malda. The roads of the city were 4 meters wide and paved by bricks and stone materials taken from Hindu temples in Gaur. In 1420, the capital was moved to Gaur, but not before the construction in Pandua of a set of important monuments, mosques, and mausoleums.

The Pandua sultans started out building fairly conventional stone-clad buildings. But it rains incessantly in Bengal, and stone is scarce there. Brick had always been the material of choice, as we know from the Buddhist monasteries of the Pala kings. Even stone-clad mosques such as the Adina Mosque in Pandua (1364) have underlying brick structures. So in 1425, when Sultan Jalal al-Din Muhammad Shah (r. 1414–32) began construction on his mausoleum, he decided to make it out of brick. This square building with corner turrets and an octagonal room surmounted by a hemispherical dome has an unusual twist to it. Inspired by the curved roof of local vernacular bamboo-and-hay structures, Muhammad Shah's architects incorporated a curved cornice into the profile that not only helps shed water but gives the mausoleum a unique shape as well. From this time onward Bengal buildings began incorporating the curved cornice in every structure, creating a singular Bengali style that was imitated around South Asia in later centuries. The central chamber is octagonal, with a dome supported on squinches. Otherwise, the building is a solid and in that sense has characteristics of a Buddhist stupa. The exterior of the walls have niches and statues and are ornamented with delicate patterns on pillars at the four corners. It is assumed that the building was built by Hindu masons.

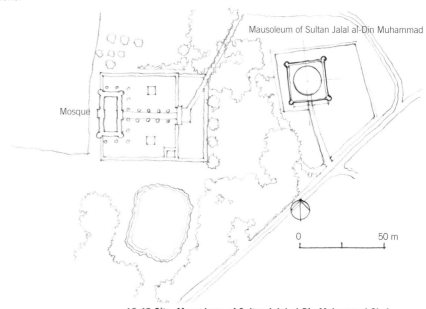

13.40 Site: Mausoleum of Sultan Jalal al-Din Muhammad Shah

13.41 **Inner court, Jami Masjid of Ahmedabad, India**

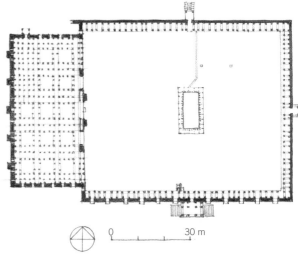

13.42 **Plan: Jami Masjid of Ahmedabad**

Jami Masjid of Ahmedabad

In 1398, Ahmed Shah (r. 1411–42), a former governor of the Tughlaqs in Gujarat, declared himself independent and in 1410 founded Ahmedabad on the Sabarmati River as his new capital. Ahmedabad went on to become very prosperous, particularly under Fath Kahn Mahmud (1459–1511), who expanded the kingdom in all directions. Under the Delhi sultanate and the Tughlaqs, it had been standard practice to demean demolished Hindu temples by reusing their columns, upside down or in pieces, to hold up a new mosque. The curious characteristic of Ahmed Shah's buildings is the manner in which this mark of repression became the expressive language of the new architecture. For his new Jami Masjid ("Friday Mosque"), built in 1423 in Ahmedabad, Ahmed Shah embraced the new aesthetic created by the demeaned Hindu columns and authorized the construction of new columns not unlike the ones that had been pillaged, thereby legitimizing this new architectural syntax.

The heavily ornamented columns not only peek through pointed arches of the court walls but are also magnified and attached to the sides of the central arch of the *qibla* wall in the form of minarets. The result is one of the finest mosques of western India, with the arched screen and pillar portico of the western *qibla* wall combined to create the effect of a finely composed and restrained but carefully detailed building, an effective combination of arch and trabeation. This hybridized way of building continued to characterize Ahmedabad's Islamic architecture, until it fell to the Mughals late in the 16th century.

13.43 **Court arcade, Jami Masjid of Ahmedabad**

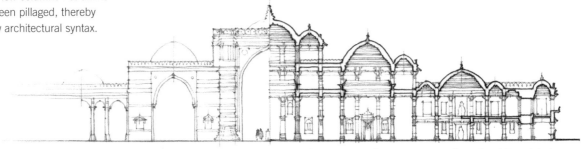

13.44 **Section through main prayer hall, Jami Masjid of Ahmedabad**

Chittor Fort

From Mauryan times onward, major Indian cities were defended by forts. In the plains these were made of mud and fired bricks, and protected by moats. In the hills, particularly in western India, engineers took advantage of slopes and cliffs. With the arrival of canons from the West, fort construction had to adapt, as can be seen at the Chittor Fort. It was built by the Guhilot Rajputs and located on a 200-meter-high escarpment. It consisted of seven successive gates. Pointed merlons, coupled with embrasures that splay out from narrow slits, were the means of deterring enemies from scaling the sheer vertical walls. Within the fort, a series of palaces was designed around water tanks. Temples built atop high retaining walls give the whole a rather dramatic silhouette. Two towers from the 16th century commemorating the victories over invading Muslim armies are rare examples of Hindu victory towers; they emulated the victory towers built by the Mamluks and the Lodis in Delhi.

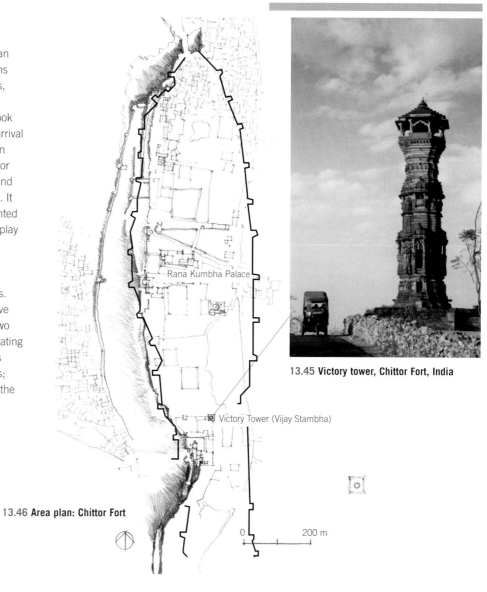

13.45 **Victory tower, Chittor Fort, India**

13.46 **Area plan: Chittor Fort**

13.47 **Chittor Fort**

13.48 **Water tank, Chittor Fort**

13.49 Southeast Asia, ca. 1400 CE

13.50 Ayutthaya temple complex, Thailand

Ayutthaya

The collapse of the Khmer Empire, combined with the related unraveling of the Srivijayan Empire in Malaysia, reduced the importance of Southeast Asia in the global economy. The Majapahit kingdom, which ruled from Java, and the Thai kingdom, with its capital in Ayutthaya, were the two dominant forces, both maintaining strong trade links with India and China.

The Thai kingdom was not a single, unified state, but rather composed of self-governing principalities and tributary provinces owing allegiance to the king. The name of the capital city derives from the Hindu holy city Ayodhya in northern India, which is said to be the birthplace of the Hindu god Rama. King Ramathibodi who established Ayutthaya, however, was Buddhist and made Theravada Buddhism the official religion of the state, indicating the close continuity between Hindu and Buddhist practices at the time.

The kingdom's wealth derived not only from its control of trade routes but also from its introduction of a new strain of rice. The Thais had traditionally planted glutinous rice that is still the staple in the north and northeast regions of the country. But in the floodplain of the Chao Phraya River, farmers turned to a variety of rice—the so-called floating rice—a nonglutinous grain introduced from Bengal. It grew faster and more easily, producing a surplus that was sold abroad,

even to China. An extensive set of canals was dug to bring the rice from the fields. Though inland, the city was essentially a port located on an island of the Chao Phraya at the intersection of the Lopbur and the Pasak rivers. The island was crisscrossed by a network of canals that ran alongside a rectilinear road system. Over time, five hundred temples, stupas, and palaces were built on this island by successive generations of kings.

Initially, Ayutthayas temples derived their form from architecture of the Khmers, but at a smaller scale and with a more deliberate staging of ancillary parts. The central stupa of Wat Rat Burana (1424) was not only surrounded by a geometrically configured cosmos of stupas but also had a colonnaded

arrival halls to its east and west. Immediately after his coronation in 1491, Ramathibodi II (r. 1491–1529) initiated the construction of Wat Si Sanpet, a spectacular triple-stupa funerary structure, to hold the remains of his father and brother; the third structure, built by his son after his death, contained his own remains. These three stupas, with their tall spirals on bell-shaped bodies, copied the Pagan prototype. An arrival hall to the east and a cruciform temple to the west framed the centerpiece of this unique compound, which was also surrounded by numerous small stupas, each with its own small funeral temple for the kings' extended families. As such, Wat Si Sanpet was singularly a royal precinct and, atypically, had no residential or meditation halls for the Buddhist monks.

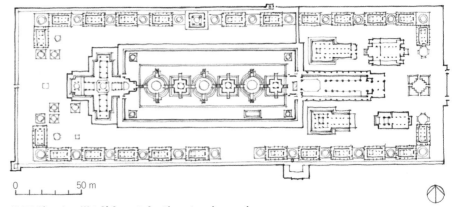

0   50 m

13.51 Site plan: Wat Si Sanpet, Ayutthaya temple complex

13.52 Italy, ca. 1400 CE

The Republic of Venice

The Black Plague (1350–1425) carried off 35 to 65 percent of the rural and urban population of Italy. Milan, for example, had a population of 150,000 before the plague in 1300. In 1463 its population was 90,000, and it was still under 100,000 in 1510. Only a handful of Italian cities rebounded, among which were Venice, Florence, Milan, Naples, and Genoa.

Following the Silk Routes westward across Asia, through the lands of the Timur, to the Ottomans, one comes to Islam's principal European trading partner, Venice, with its warehouses, and shipyards. Though a tiny city, Venetian influence, built up mostly through investments, stretched from Bruges and London to Aleppo and beyond. Almost all goods traveling to Germany, Sicily, and England had to pass through the port of Venice. By 1423, Venetian gold ducats were being minted at a million a year. The state budget of Venice at the time was equivalent to that of France and England combined. Given that Venice and its environs had a population of five hundred thousand, whereas France had fifteen million inhabitants, there is no doubt that Venice was Europe's economic hub beginning in the late 14th century and continuing for about a hundred years. After its last autocratic doge died, the city, a thalassocracy, became fiercely Republican, and an attendant—a spy, as it were—was present at all transactions and visits to the new doge. The latter was theoretically elected for life but was often removed for overstepping his authority. Over time, Venice acquired considerable Mediterranean trading posts, including Crete, Cyprus, most of the Aegean islands, and coastline stretches of Dalmatia, in addition to terra firma properties such as Bergamo and others up to Lake Garda and beyond. This allowed the Venetians to guard their land-based trading over the Brenner Pass and to grow their own wheat supply on Venetian-owned farms in the hinterland.

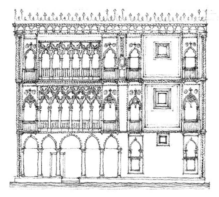

13.53 Facade: Ca' d'Oro, Venice

Among the new palaces that came to line Venice's canals is the most exquisite of all, the Ca' d'Oro, built between 1428 and 1430. It was named after the gold leaf that was applied to its exterior detailing. Stone for the facade was brought at great cost from Istria on the eastern Adriatic. The building, like almost all structures in Venice, had to be set on thousands of oak piles driven deep into the sand and mud of the city's lagoon. The facade consists of three superimposed galleries. Whereas the tracery of the loggias on the *piano nobile* and second floor has quatrefoil openings over the columns, the lower colonnade is noticeably more classical, with simple rounded and pointed arches. Though the exact origin of the quatrefoil shape is not known, the form was used on the Doge's Palace next to the Basilica di San Marco and was clearly meant to make known its owner's status as a member of the merchant elite. Decorative bands at the corners and edges and on various architectural elements of the facade make it seem like a curtain woven into place. The palace was built for Marin Contarini, a Venetian aristocrat and one of Venice's leading cloth and spice merchants.

13.54 Ca' d'Oro, Venice

Mamluk Sultanate

The Mamluks, with a ready supply of well-trained masons, extended and enhanced the tradition of Fatimid palace architecture, establishing a series of important new religious institutions along the main road leading to the citadel of Cairo. The greatest example is the Complex of Sultan Hassan, a colossal project begun in 1356. It contains a cruciform congregational mosque with four madrasas and a mausoleum, as well as an orphanage, a hospital, a bazaar, a water tower, baths, and kitchens. It was meant to house some four hundred students. The religious spaces are organized symmetrically to fit into the awkward site, which is defined by two major streets. The portal of the complex, rising 37 meters high, is crowned by a *muqarnas* cornice. The decorations include Chinese motifs such as chrysanthemums and lotus flowers. The open central court was paved and has a fountain at the center. The four madrasas are located in the corners between the arms of the *iwans*; each has its own small courtyard. The southeast *iwan*, the largest of the four, was spanned by an enormous vault, at the time considered to one of the wonders of the world. The mihrab and surrounding *qibla* wall are paneled in marble slabs of contrasting colors. Doors flanking the mihrab lead to the tomb beyond. In it, the walls are paneled with marble and the *muqarnas* of the dome are gilded and the whole illuminated by hundreds of specially designed glass lamps. The building not only makes maximum use of the site but redefines the Central Asian four-*iwan* type, making it more intimate yet also more monumental.

13.55 Complex of Sultan Hassan, Cairo, Egypt

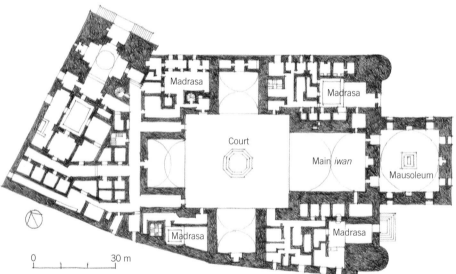

13.56 Plan: Complex of Sultan Hassan

13.57 Courtyard door (left) and entrance portal (right), Complex of Sultan Hassan

Mausoleum Complex of Sultan Qaitbay

Their designers' ability to impose order on complex urban sites was a unique aspect of Mamluk architecture in Cairo. No two buildings are alike, testifying to their architects' fluid imagination. But the asymmetry of these buildings was not always a matter of necessity, as can be seen at the Mausoleum Complex of Sultan Qaitbay (1472–74). Sultan al Ashraf Qaitbay (r. 1468–96) was known for the efficient manner in which he ran the country and the stability he created. He was particularly interested in architecture, promoting more than sixty projects, not only in Cairo but also in Mecca, Medina, Damascus, and Jerusalem. The mausoleum complex, with no other buildings surrounding it, houses the madrasa and the burial *qubba* of the sultan. Architecturally, it balances the minaret tower on the right with an open loggia on the left. The dome is made up of three separate elements: the square-planned building at the bottom; an intermediate volume with vigorously shaped scrolls at the corners that make the transition to an octagonal platform; and the dome, resting on a drum on that platform. Compared to the simple windows on the body of the building, some designed to look like they were carved out of the wall, the dome was given a particularly refined and elaborate decoration in which two patterns—an interlaced geometric star and a floral arabesque—are combined. On the interior is found *pietra serena* ("dark stone") paneling, a surface treatment similar to what would find in some northern Italian churches of this period.

13.58 Dome, Mausoleum Complex of Sultan Qaitbay, Cairo, Egypt

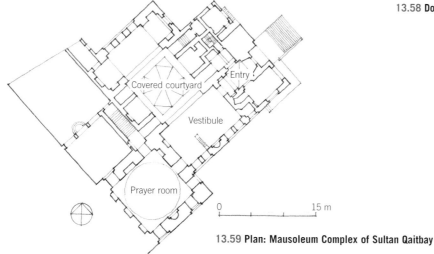

13.59 Plan: Mausoleum Complex of Sultan Qaitbay

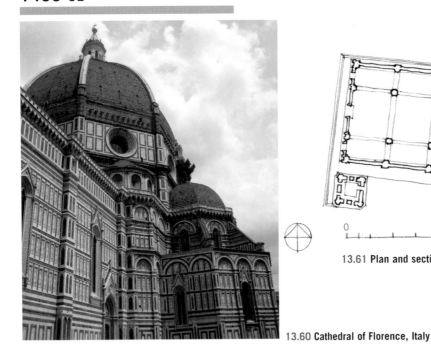

13.61 Plan and section: Cathedral of Florence

13.60 Cathedral of Florence, Italy

Cathedral of Florence

The Cathedral of Florence, begun in 1294, was among the last of the great Italian city cathedrals to be built. The plan, designed by Arnolfo di Cambio (1232–1300), was unusual, calling for a broad nave leading to an octagonal, domed apse. The fusion seems Eastern in concept and was perhaps meant as a homage to the city's patron saint, St. Reparata, who was martyred in 250 CE at Caesarea (in present-day Israel). Ultimately, however, the duomo was dedicated to the Virgin Mary, whose cult was then ascendant. The design specifications for the building explicitly banned exterior buttresses. (When Giovanni d'Ambrogio, the architect heading the construction in the latter part of the 14th century, attempted to introduce Gothic-styled buttressing, he promptly lost his job.) In the 1350s, the Florentines, wanting to outdo the churches of Pisa and Siena, decided to expand the length of the nave, which required that some already completed elements of the building be torn down. The basic design idea of a basilica-plus-octagon was retained, but on a larger scale. This, in turn, gave rise to problems with the dome; the new one was to be as wide as the Pantheon's in Rome and an astonishing 60 meters high, exceeding by far the Pantheon's 43 meters. The Romans had the huge advantage of having had concrete, which had by this time become completely forgotten. So without buttresses and without concrete,

how was the dome to be made? The Florentines were temporarily stymied. But construction continued with the three parts of the octagonal east end designed to appear closely packed to the body of the church, and the skin modeled on the 13th-century baptistery to the front of the building. By the time Filippo Brunelleschi was first consulted about the cathedral, the body of the church had more or less been finished, but there was a gaping hole where the dome was to be. To make matters even more difficult, a drum had been built with large round windows in its sides, meaning that lateral thrusts could not be brought to the ground through side vaults, as had been done at the Hagia Sophia.

Construction came to a standstill. It would have been impossible to build a wooden framework strong enough to support such a massive dome during construction,

which was why each successive architect concentrated his efforts on every part of the building except the dome. Finally, in 1418, a competition was announced—among the earliest public competitions in the history of architecture. Brunelleschi won by proposing an ingenious system by which the dome could be constructed with only limited use of wooden scaffolding. To deflect the lateral thrusts, Brunelleschi made a curving rib-lattice structure with an outer and inner dome of brick laid in herringbone fashion to ensure cohesion; a large metal chain laid at the base of the dome protected against outward expansion. This solution did not require a support structure during the initial construction phase since each vertical extension of the dome as it was being built, and as it spiraled closer to the center, would cohere to what was below. A centering platform was constructed only during the last phase, but it was suspended from the partially completed dome. The dome terminated with an oculus about 7 meters in diameter, superceded by a heavier than normal lantern (built in 1446) whose weight guaranteed that the ribs were in compression. The design was ingenious and one of the engineering marvels of the age. From here on out the dome would become an important element in monumental European architecture.

Florentine Loggias

The narrow streets of Italian cities consisted of hard materials, stone and brick, and because many of these cities were confined by city walls, open spaces were at a premium. Parks and gardens did not exist. Loggias—roofed-over open outdoor spaces—were highly valued and served both functional and symbolic purposes. Unlike an arcade, which covers pedestrian traffic, a loggia is a place to assemble rather than to traverse. The Loggia dei Priori (now called Loggia dei Lanzi, 1376–82) was built to service visiting dignitaries and ambassadors, and to facilitate the celebration of coronations and marriages of kings. It was constructed perpendicular to the entrance of the Palazzo della Signoria—the town hall—and consisted of three lofty arches rising from a stepped platform. The columns, sitting on a short, ornamented plinth, are composed of pilasters bound together into one massive shaft 10 meters high terminating in a rich and beautiful capital of the Corinthian order. This was probably the first attempt to re-create the Corinthian order since the time of the Romans.

Another type of loggia was for public services, like the one next to the Baptistery of Florence, which was used by the clergy to give out alms. But the most spectacular loggia was the one at the Foundling Hospital (Ospedale degli Innocenti, 1419–24, finished 1445), built by the Silk Guild, one of the most important guilds in Florence. Since 1294 the guild had committed itself to the care of infants (*innocenti*). Though it had set up wards and hospitals, this building was specifically for abandoned children. A special door with a rotating panel was built in the facade so that a child could be deposited anonymously. By the year 1640, more than 1,600 infants and children lived

there, along with forty priests, nurses, and administrators. The loggia that constitutes the building's facade was designed by Brunelleschi, and even though its prototype was medieval, its style was markedly new. The columns, modeled carefully on classical precedent, are the earliest examples of archaeologically correct Corinthian capitals in the 15th century. (Had Brunelleschi wanted to be more authentically Roman, however, he would not have set the columns on thin plinths only 5 centimeters high.) The facade consists of a long unbroken entablature. The arches are semicircular rather than pointed. Rondels depicting babies in swaddling clothes decorate the space between the arches. The vaults, also spherical, were originally covered with a sloping wooden roof. The attic level was added later.

13.62 **Foundling Hospital, Florence, Italy**

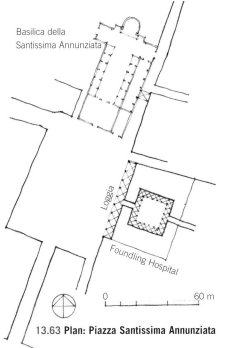

13.63 **Plan: Piazza Santissima Annunziata**

13.64 **Loggia dei Lanzi, Florence**

Italian Renaissance

The word *renaissance* (from the Italian *rinàscita*, "rebirth") was coined in the 19th century to describe the cultural and intellectual changes that took place in Italy during the 15th century. The term refers in particular to the growing infatuation of the Italian intelligentsia with Roman antiquity, whether it be with the writings of Cicero and his contemporaries or with the study of Roman ruins. It also refers, in the field of painting, to the discovery of perspective, the appearance of which had been approximated by painters like Giotto di Bondone (1267–1337), but which was first described mathematically by Leon Battista Alberti (1404–72) in 1435.

In painting, there is a clear progression that demarcates the Renaissance from the Middle Ages, but in architecture, the division between the two is more fluid. Medieval practices continued to intermingle with classically inspired ideas for a century. Nonetheless, the interior of the Pazzi Chapel, begun by Brunelleschi in 1429 but finished by other architects, set the tone for a type of architecture that emphasized the use of columns, pilasters, and entablatures all unified by a proportional system that governed the heights, widths, and intercolumniations of the pilasters. Though the detailing of the columns and bases was inspired by Roman buildings, Brunelleschi was still not using the orders in their distinctive categories of Doric, Ionic, and Corinthian. That emerged only somewhat later and was first insisted upon by Alberti in his treatise *De re aedificatoria* (1452), now known as *The Ten Books on Architecture*. Renaissance architecture is thus just as much about changes in practice as the emerging theories about the discipline. Key was the discovery (ca. 1415) of a copy of a manuscript of Vitruvius's *Ten Books on Architecture* in the Abbey Library of St. Gall in Switzerland; Alberti studied the manuscript and used it as an inspiration for his own work. Covering a wide range of subjects—from choice of materials to the history of architecture, and from different types of buildings to the philosophy of beauty— Alberti's treatise was written not only for architects but also for patrons eager to understand the logic of representation through buildings.

Other phenomena accompanied what is now defined by the words *Renaissance architecture*. The difference between the architect and the craftsman was now accepted, and architectural drawings became more common. Sebastiano Serlio (1475–1554) wrote a treatise, five books of which he finished, that was more visual than Alberti's treatise, which had no illustrations. Serlio's book has dozens of drawings, showing a variety of built and unbuilt projects. It was enormously popular among the many patrons and architects eager to emulate the splendors of antiquity.

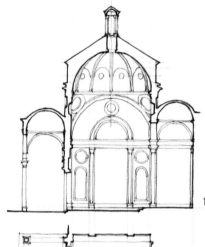

13.65 Plan and section: Pazzi Chapel, Florence, Italy

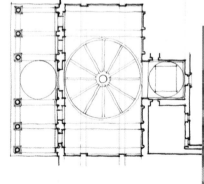

Questions about the nature of ancient Roman architecture and about the proportional systems that the Romans used were not easy to resolve and led to a wide range of interpretations. Some architects, like Brunelleschi, were less Roman than others, and, in fact, it was only with Neoclassicism in the 18th and 19th centuries that rigorous adherence to antique models was seen as a virtue. Nonetheless, the Renaissance did require a rigorous attention to proportion and as a result, facades become flatter and volumes more regularized. The vertical dimension began to be articulated by horizontal layers of columns, entablatures, and cornices. Niches and aediculae now entered the architect's vocabulary as secondary elements, to be placed between pilasters. Windows were framed and often pedimented.

13.66 Interior of the Pazzi Chapel

San Lorenzo

The drama of this building, which was begun in 1421, lies in the stark contrast of its interior between the *pietra serena* used for the pilasters, arches and entablatures, and the whitewashed walls. This creates the illusion of a structural system when in reality the pilasters are not at all load-bearing. Unlike French and English Gothic architecture, where the load-bearing function of architectural elements disappeared in column clusters, here the difference is clearly spelled out between what carries the load—or at least seems to carry it—and what does not. Even so, this is not a pure Roman-inspired building, for the prototype for the colonnaded nave is found in the early Christian basilica. The restraint and orderliness of the nave was also akin to Franciscan churches of the late 13th century, and the Latin cross plan, with its square chapels on the side, harkens back to the Cistercians. In that sense, this church can be seen as a complex fusion of early Christian, Cistercian, and Franciscan motifs, built according to classicizing rules.

Working within the constraints of the classical system forced Brunelleschi to confront the problem of "turning the corner," one of the persistent issues in classical architecture. On inside corners, only a few leaves of a pilaster are visible, implying the presence of a structural support hidden in the wall. Furthermore, the giant-order pilasters, in turning the corner between the transept and the nave, are partially obscured by the lower-order ones. Yet another problem is that the pilasters along the wall stand higher than the columns because the floor of the chapel is three steps up from the floor of the nave. This means that they should have been thinner—but that would have looked odd. To solve the problem without raising the nave columns on bases, Brunelleschi had the pilasters reach directly to the entablature, but on the columns in the nave he added dosserets above the capitals to equalize the distance. They are decorated with patterns that reduce their structural appearance.

The building has a complicated construction history. Though begun in the 1420s, little of it was actually built before Brunelleschi's death in 1446, when the job was handed over either to Antonio Manetti or to Michelozzo di Bartolomeo Michelozzi; scholars are not certain. Changes were made to the building design—the side chapels, for example, were not made as deep as they should have been—so the final result is only partially Brunelleschi's. Nonetheless, the idea of arches, spherical vaults, freestanding columns, and the use of classically inspired capitals, lintels, and cornices was, for the time, quite revolutionary.

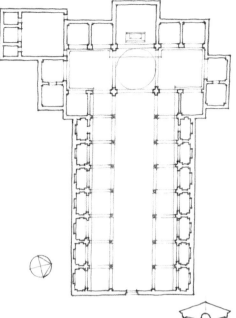

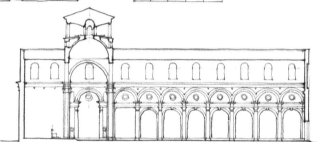

0   25 m

13.67 Plan and section: San Lorenzo, Florence, Italy

13.68 Nave of San Lorenzo, Florence

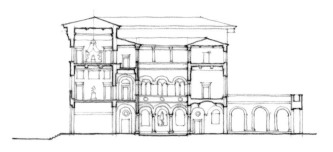

13.69 Medici Palace, Florence, Italy

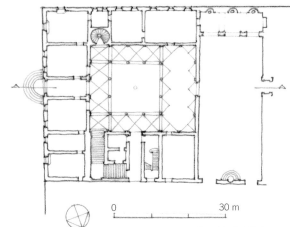

13.70 Plan and section: Medici Palace

The first Medici family member to come to prominence was Giovanni di Bicci (1360–1429), whose enormous fortune was passed on to his son, Cosimo I de' Medici (1389–1464), who ruled over a vast banking and mercantile organization. In 1422, a political crisis led to the expulsion of Cosimo and his family from Florence. But after a year away in Venice—and the consequent flight of capital from the city—he was invited back, and for the next thirty years he was the de facto ruler of the city, even though he never had an official title. Under the rule of his son, Lorenzo de' Medici (1469–92), the pretense of political liberty could no longer be maintained, but his tenure was one of great artistic sponsorship.

The Medici Palace (1444–ca.1460) was designed by Michelozzo di Bartolomeo Michelozzi (1396–1472), though heavily influenced by Brunelleschi's principles. The building is not what might be called classical or Roman, for it continued the prototype of three-story buildings established in the 14th century. This one, however, is topped by an enormous, classically inspired cornice that was meant to tie the volume together optically, though it makes the top floor appear to be almost crushed under its weight. The ground floor is heavily rusticated in purposeful imitation of the fortresses built by Emperor Frederick II in the middle of the 13th century. The windows have round-headed openings with strongly marked voussoirs; a string course separates the ground floor from the *piano nobile*. The story above that is entirely smooth, creating a strange effect in combination with the heavy cornice.

If the outside has a deliberately medieval aspect, the plan shows a new type of architectural thinking. The courtyard is arcaded on three sides, connecting on the fourth side to a reception loggia through which one can access to the garden behind the palace. Because of its scale, elegance, and built-in loggia, the courtyard has the appearance of a private piazza. A grand staircase leads up from the right side of the courtyard to allow direct access to the reception rooms on the *piano nobile* so that privileged visitors could avoid the lower floor's service areas. The location and character of this staircase, which introduces an asymmetrical element into the composition of the plan, became another issue that Renaissance architects struggled with: family bedrooms were usually on the third floor, while the attic rooms were allocated to the domestics.

13.71 Facade: Medici Palace

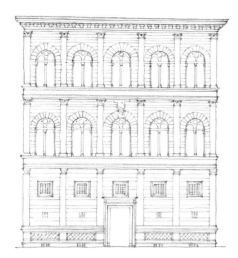

13.72 Elevation: Rucellai Palace, Florence, Italy

Rucellai Palace

Unlike most architects who rose up through the trades and guilds, Leon Battista Alberti had a law degree from the University of Bologna and was a noted humanist and scholar. He worked as an adviser and official in the papal office, a position that was, in essence, his day job. His real passion was studying the classics, producing treatises on topics that were of interest to him (such as painting and architecture), and writing dozens of small plays. His architectural treatise, *The Ten Books on Architecture*, remained a standard text used by architects and patrons for centuries. Drawing on Vitruvius's book of the same name, it was an up-to-date compilation of important information on almost all aspects of architecture and design. Adherence to classical ideas was important, but Alberti also wanted the architect to be responsive to the needs of the client. Above all, Alberti elevated architecture to a regular theoretical discipline, differentiating the architect, who gave the instructions, from the craftsmen who followed them. On a practical level, this differentiation already existed to some extent in the Middle Ages, but after Alberti architecture became for the first time a field of study differentiated from the crafts.

The Rucellai Palace (1446–50), designed by Alberti, gave to the Florentines their first taste of a truly "humanist" facade. It is, however, more show than reality, because it is little more than a stone veneer placed over a medieval palace. Nevertheless, it was a portent of things to come. All three of the facade's horizontal zones are articulated by

pilasters that, together with the unbroken entablatures that mark the different stories, form a grid over the entire surface. Window openings are placed within each intercolumniation. (There were, of course, no readily available models of a multistoried Roman building, so in some sense, this was conjecture.)

The initial design called for five bays; later, more bays were added to the right side of the facade. The pattern of the voussoirs, stones, and pilasters are grooved out of the variously shaped stones of the veneer. At San Lorenzo, the pilasters appear to be part of the structural system. But here, the pilasters, of the same material as the wall, read less forcefully and as less "real," evincing a desire to unify the facade in its two dimensionality. A coherence of this kind had so far been reserved for church facades and had until then not been applied to palace design. The palace was located on an extraordinarily tight site at a Y intersection of streets. For that reason, the facade can be seen only on the oblique. Set in front of the palace and at right angles to it is the three-bayed Rucellai Loggia, which was used for family celebrations, weddings, and occasional public meetings. Behind the palace is the Church of San Pancrazio, which was supported by the Rucellai family.

The palace exemplifies the difference between the humanistic and medieval mindsets. Whereas the humanistic mind demanded harmony of the elements, the medieval mind demanded a maximum

13.73 Rucellai Palace

of explicitness. The humanistic mind emphasized proportion; the medieval mind demanded visual coherency. In order to achieve proportional unity, Renaissance architects therefore had to sacrifice visual coherence by implying the presence of columns that became in reality thin pilasters. In a Gothic building, such a differentiation between the actually visible and the implied did not exist—nothing in that sense was "suggested." A smaller column could be just as structural as a larger one. Gothic architecture was a search for the clarification of form and in that sense was less suitable to respond to representational demands; it was at its best in churches. In Renaissance architecture, a few pilasters added to a facade might be all that was needed to differentiate a building belonging to an elite patron from a structure inhabited by lower-tier citizens. Renaissance architecture struggled to strike a balance between the real and the suggested. This played itself out in the facade—an unheard of "design problem" in the Middle Ages. Even though the relationship between the facade and what was behind it remained important, henceforth the facade was an architectural issue all its own. At its best, it was meant to symbolize and summarize the three-dimensional architectural program of the building it represented.

13.74 Site: Rucellai Palace

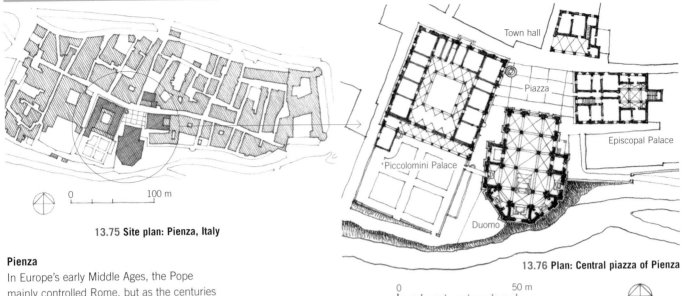

13.75 Site plan: Pienza, Italy

13.76 Plan: Central piazza of Pienza

Pienza

In Europe's early Middle Ages, the Pope mainly controlled Rome, but as the centuries progressed, the various popes cobbled together alliances with feudal lords that soon allowed them to control a territory reaching all the way to the Adriatic Sea. During the 14th century, when the Papacy, in a period known as the Schism, was split between two or more popes and pretenders, there was little the popes could do to profit from their territorial claims. But when the Schism was resolved in 1420, the popes began to feel the desire for grander architectural expression. The fabric of Rome had been seriously neglected over the centuries, and the papal palace was itself relatively shabby.

The first Pope to undertake serious architectural improvements was Nicholas V (1447–55), who rebuilt churches and planned improvements for the Vatican. It was, however, the next Pope, Andreas Silvius Piccolomini (Pius II), who integrated papal architectural ambitions with the emerging notions of humanist classicism. He built an elegant retreat for himself (1459–64) in his hometown Pienza, a rustic hilltop village south of Siena. The village's original name, Corsigniano, was changed to Pienza to reflect the new design. The task of grafting a papal retreat onto a medieval village was difficult: the center of the village, at the top of the hill where the views were best, was extremely narrow, necessitating the building of undercrofts to support parts of the new church and palace.

On the whole, the papal ensemble represents an idealized reconstruction of a late medieval town made with the intent to aggrandize the Pope's origins, but with buildings designed in the latest humanist style. The new duomo is at the top, with its piazza in front; the papal palace to the right of the piazza; and the bishop's palace to the left. A loggia and a "town hall" are at the front. The village, of course, had never had a town hall (since it was not a town but a mere village), and this one was built for the sake of imparting the impression of grandeur.

13.77 Cathedral of Pienza

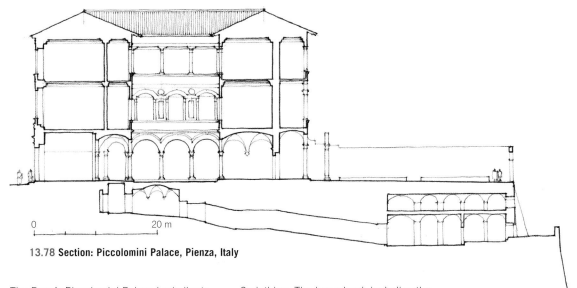

13.78 **Section: Piccolomini Palace, Pienza, Italy**

The Pope's Piccolomini Palace is similar to the Rucellai Palace; many therefore think that Alberti must have had a hand in the city's design, even though officially the architect was Bernardo di Matteo Gamberelli, better known as Bernardo Rossellino (1409–64), known more as a sculptor than as an architect.

Alberti served in the retinue of the Pope and frequently advised him on architectural matters. There is no attempt to unify the design of the various buildings by means of a single surface treatment. Instead, each building is clearly recognizable as belonging to a certain type or function. The trapezoidal shape of the piazza is partially explained by the topography. The road that cuts through the site is at the top of the curving spur of the hill, which falls off steeply to the south, so much so that the garden of the papal palace and the apse of the church had to be built up on massive foundations. It is also possible that the layout was meant to create a dynamic interplay among views along the street and the facades of the various buildings.

The palace rests at the very top of the hill so that the garden, supported by an undercroft that was used for stables and storage, seems to float high over the valley below. The facade is articulated by three stories of pilasters placed on continuous and unbroken entablatures similar to those at the Rucellai Palace. The lower order is Doric, while the upper two are a very simplified Corinthian. The lower level, including the pilasters, are covered with rustication, creating an ambiguity between structure and skin. The upper-level pilasters are more conventional. Unlike the Rucellai, each successive story is slightly diminished in height, grounding the whole in a way it might not be otherwise. The U-shaped palace has a square courtyard with a three-story garden loggia closing it off at the far end. This is emphasized at the corners where the facade meets the loggia so that the facade appears to be the thickness of a pier. The use of a loggia screen facing the distant hills reflects the emerging humanistic notion about the beauty of natural environments.

The facade of the church consists of four piers between which are nested arches supported by columns tied together by horizontal cornices at their top and midpoint. To accommodate the proportions of the attached columns, the architect set them up on high dadoes, which make the building seem unresolved. Integrating horizontal and vertical elements and unifying the diverse scales of a church facade would become one of the most important issues in Renaissance and Baroque church design. Despite this facade's problems, it is one of the earliest true Renaissance church facades. While it still builds on medieval prototypes, it reveals an attempt to integrate columns, piers, entablatures, niches, arches, and *aediculae* into a single compositional unit.

13.79 **Piccolomini Palace, Pienza**

13.80 Sant'Andrea, Mantua, Italy

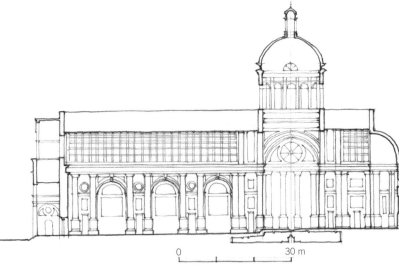

13.81 Section: Sant'Andrea, Mantua

Sant'Andrea at Mantua

At Sant'Andrea at Mantua (designed ca. 1470, built 1472–94), Alberti abandoned the tradition of side-aisled churches for a single barrel-vaulted nave with side chapels. Such a broad, open space, innovative for the time, could be easily justified for a church that was to hold large crowds of pilgrims that gathered for the annual showing of the blood of Christ. The blood, actually a dried substance held in a vial, is located in the crypt beneath the church and is retrieved during a ceremony through an opening in the floor at that spot. If the content of the vial turns to liquid, it is seen as a good omen. The facade—another early example of a true Renaissance church facade—faces onto a small piazza and is based on the theme of a Roman triumphal arch; the theme of triumph is carried into the interior elevations of the nave. Alberti's use of the giant order was novel for the Renaissance and one of its first attempted uses. The problem was how to coordinate the facade with the height of the barrel vault of the nave behind it. Alberti made no attempt to compromise the two disparate elements in the front, instead creating an arched opening that shields the upper-level window. The barrel vault on the interior was another Albertian novelty. Since there are no side aisles, the arches set between the giant order of the nave elevation simply open onto side chapels, which are also barrel-vaulted. The giant order, though not itself structural, at least marks the presence of buttress piers that support the vault. Integrating the buttressing into the building in this way demonstrates Alberti's talent in exploiting structural elements for spatial organization. The same is true for the pilasters in the side chapels that, together with the ribs, demarcate the geometry of the space. This is far different from Brunelleschi's "structural system," which is basically applied to the wall's surface. Strangely, the unity of the two scales at Sant'Andrea is avoided to some degree on the facade, where the lesser order is pulled away from the giant order by a few centimeters, perhaps to accommodate the necessary width of the opening—once again demonstrating some of the difficulties of working with the classical system. It is not known if Alberti's design called for a dome. (The current dome [1732–82] was designed by Filippo Juvarra.) The building, apart from the facade, does not set itself free from the maze of its medieval urban surroundings.

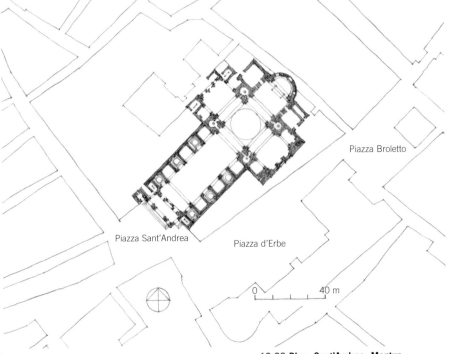

13.82 Plan: Sant'Andrea, Mantua

Piazza Broletto

Piazza Sant'Andrea

Piazza d'Erbe

Villa Medici

Though urban palaces were the norm for the elite, the Medici were among the first to create a villa that was not just a fortified stronghold. As ubiquitous as the villa building type became over time, in the 15th century it was quite a novelty. One of the villas' most important aspects are the gardens. During the Middle Ages, gardens as places of pleasure were rare: in the tight maze of medieval cities space was restricted by city walls, leaving little room for extensive gardens. In fact, because of their association with pleasure, gardens were often frowned upon. No doubt, visitors telling of the great gardens at the Alhambra in Spain played a part in establishing their legitimacy in Europe. By the middle of the 15th century, the idea of owning a place outside of town—perhaps in the hills where it was cooler in the summer and where the family could gather—became the norm for the elite. The use of the word *villa* to describe these places only came into use in the late 16th century, when the villas themselves became more elaborate. In the 15th century, they were still, at least to some extent, working farms that supplied the family, but outfitted with a manor house and garden.

Impacting this development was the revival of the old Roman notion of the bucolic country retreat as a place where one could enjoy music, poetry, and good company and play the gentleman farmer, away from the mercantile world of the cities. *Villa*, a treatise by Alberti, helped define the parameters of this humanistic lifestyle. For the new elite, the villa served practical goals as well: the artworks, sculptures, gardens, and buildings were all very much part of a system of wealth and prestige.

One of the villas used by the Medici family at Poggio a Caiano, was among the most important of that period. Standing on the top of a small hill a few kilometers to the west of Florence, it had a wide view over the plain between Florence and Pistoia. Originally a fortress, it was rebuilt, beginning around 1485, into a villa by Giuliano da Sangallo. It also seems to be the earliest attempt to re-create a classical *villa suburbana* as described in texts by Pliny and Vitruvius. The building rests on a large vaulted platform containing the service rooms and spaces

13.83 Villa Medici, Poggio a Caiano, Italy

needed for the farm. It is a two-story building with an H-shaped plan, set sideways to the axis. The whole, including its gardens, was framed by an enclosing wall. The curved double staircase replaced the initial design, which had a straight stairway leading to the top of the entrance platform. Functionally, the main rooms are aligned along the central axis with a large, barrel-vaulted room at the center straddling the two arms of the H. There were apartment suites with antechambers

and bedrooms located at each corner. The loggia, with its temple-front design at the entrance, was built for Giovanni de' Medici (son of Lorenzo, 1475–1521), who became Pope Leo X. The building was often used as a summer residence by the Medici family, for official receptions, and to welcome important personalities, such as Charles V, who stayed there in 1536. In the 1570s, frescoes alluding to the history of the Medici family were added to the walls of the great hall.

13.84 Lunette by Giusto Utens depicting the Villa Medici, Poggio a Caiano

13.85 Santa Maria dei Miracoli, Venice, Italy

13.86 Santa Maria del Calcinaio, Cortona, Italy

Miracle Churches

One of the consequences of the Black Plague was a surge of devotional practices, especially those associated with the Virgin Mary. Though this Mary cult had always been strong in France, in Italy a particular form of devotion developed in wihch paintings of the Virgin were accorded a magical power to heal. These paintings were not icons—that is, their artists did not intend for them to possess miraculous powers. In fact, most were quite humble—some old, some not—that instead became associated with miracles. In 1409, for example, a certain Francesco Madi commissioned a painting of the Virgin Mary holding the Christ child. He was proud of the painting even though it was quite modest and hung it on the street corner where he lived in Venice; it hung there for seventy years unnoticed. On the evening of May 23, 1481, a young lady was savagely attacked as she rounded the corner. After the attack, the crowd that had gathered to help her noticed that despite the knife wounds, she was unharmed. The next morning, the news had spread over the entire city, and soon large crowds convened under the painting hoping that its protective powers would also transfer to them. The number of people was such that the city had to move the painting and provide it with a church specially designed to allow it to be seen by all comers.

The plan of the building, Santa Maria dei Miracoli in Venice (1481), is very simple. But the rectangular, barrel-vaulted building

is clearly special. It is paneled outside and inside with rare multicolored marble and has the appearance of an enormous jewel box. The "box" is adjoined at its eastern end by a small quasi-centralized building that houses the painting, which is elevated on a high platform in order to be clearly visible from all parts of the interior. Unlike most Venetian churches that are at the center of their neighborhoods, this one was considered so important that it was placed alongside a canal so that more people could have access to it.

From the late 14th century into the 16th century, numerous churches in Italy were designed around similar miracle-working paintings. Why this practice reached so

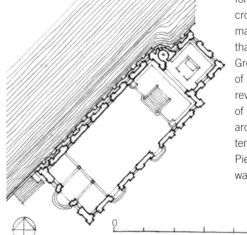

13.87 Plan: Santa Maria dei Miracoli, Venice

deeply into the popular imagination of the time is not known. Most of the buildings that house these images have plain, spacious interiors uncluttered by columns and aisles. In all of them, it is a painting of the Virgin Mary that presides at the altar. Many of these churches were centralized, but not all. Santa Maria del Calcinaio, at Cortona (1485), has a Latin cross plan. There are no external buttresses; only thin pilasters indicate its internal organization. The nave is generously proportioned and well illuminated from windows carved out of the thick walls.

Santa Maria della Consolazione

Renaissance architects were fascinated by the Greek cross format, largely because it was seen not so much as an icon—as it was for the Eastern Church, where the Greek cross plan was first established—but as a materialization of the mathematical ideas that bind the intangible to the tangible. In the Greek cross, architecture, with its equipoise of harmonic relationships and strict geometry, revealed the perfection and omnipotence of God's truth and goodness. Renaissance architects also rediscovered the circular temples of the Romans. The Tempietto of San Pietro in Montorio (1499–1502), a *martyrium*, was commissioned by Ferdinand and Isabella

13.88 San Pietro in Montorio, Rome

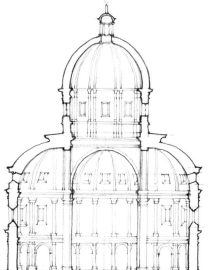

13.89 Santa Maria della Consolazione, Todi, Italy

of Spain. Designed by Donato Bramante (1444–1514), it is considered one of the first High Renaissance buildings in Rome. A ring of Doric columns topped by a balustrade surrounds a cylindrical volume that rises over the one-story high colonnade, which is topped by a dome. The site where St. Peter is said to have been crucified is accessed through the crypt. Bramante planned to rebuild the existing courtyard of the monastery in which the building is located in a circular form.

One of the important champions of the centralized church was Leonardo da Vinci (1452–1519), who experimented with a wide range of possibilities, most consisting of a square, almost cubical box with apses on all four sides. In some of his designs, the apse takes on a complex shape that allows for different formal arrangements between primary and ancillary spaces. All are surmounted by a dome—usually a replica of the Duomo of Florence.

The dome is such a ubiquitous element of the classical European tradition that it is easy to forget it was initially a revolutionary innovation. Its history as a symbolic form begins with churches in Armenia, where domes signified the heavens. Armenian churches had tall dome structures visible from outside the building, but the dome itself was rarely expressed as such and was instead usually hidden underneath a conical external form. Similarly, the dome

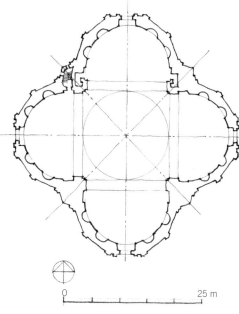

13.90 Plan and section: Santa Maria della Consolazione

of the Pantheon was impressive from the inside but had no exterior legibility. At San Pietro in Montorio, not only is the dome the culminating part of the composition, but it was meant to be seen and comprehended from both the outside and the inside. Later domes, like the one over St. Peter's Basilica in Rome designed by Michelangelo Buonarroti (1475–1564), were derivatives of this idea, even though for structural—and aesthetic—reasons, the outer and inner domes were rarely built as a single unit, but instead as two domes.

The form of the Greek cross received the greatest attention from architects who built churches for miracle-working paintings, as these churches did not need baptisteries, monastic appendages, or administrative buildings. One example is Santa Maria della Consolazione, a few miles outside of the town of Todi, Italy, built by the relatively unknown architect Cola di Caprarola but almost certainly influenced by drawings of Leonardo. The plan consists of a square under the dome with semicircular apses on all four sides. Its "miraculous" painting sits on a special altar in the eastern apse so that the building, though biaxially symmetrical, has a clear east-west emphasis. The airy interior seems to push out against the bones of the pilasters and ribs. The interior is quite luminous thanks to a proliferation of windows—even in the base of the hemispherical apse vaults. On the exterior, the internal "structure" is replicated, except that the corner piers, perhaps for structural reasons, were thickened. There are no windows at the ground level, which creates a sense of mass and density that contrasts with the light-filled interior.

13.91 Model for St. Peter's Basilica in Rome made by Antonio da Sangallo the Younger

13.92 Medal showing Bramante's intentions for St. Peter's Basilica, 1506

St. Peter's Basilica

The history of the building of St. Peter's Basilica in Rome (officially the Basilica di San Pietro in Vaticano) is certainly one of the most complex in the history of Western architecture. The decision by Julius II to tear down one of the most venerated sanctuaries in Christendom and erect a new building was a bold one, and the Pope appointed Bramante, who had just finished designing the Tempietto of San Pietro in Montorio, to design it. Like the Tempietto, the new St. Peter's was a *martyrium*, but unlike that building it had to be large enough to accommodate huge crowds. And given that the Hagia Sophia, its counterpart in the East, had fallen into the hands of the Islamic Turks, the building also had to serve as a symbol for all of Christendom.

Bramante (who worked on the project from 1505 to 1514) made a series of plans; some of his drawings still survive, permitting a close look at his design progress. The buildings he proposed were suitably ambitious. They even ignored the siting of the Vatican Palace, which sat directly next to the old basilica, implying that he planned for the removal of the palace and its replacement by a new one. Bramante's first plan (ca. 1505) shows a four-sided building sitting in a large courtyard open on all four sides. Each arm of the Greek cross ended with an apse projecting outward from the surface of the building. Four large towers were to rise from

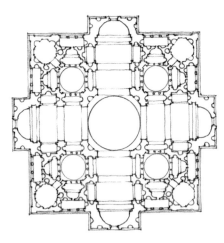

13.93 Plan of St. Peter's Basilica by Bramante

the corners. The building had remarkably little wall surface, the architectural structure being a type of residue between the spaces. The center was defined by a semispherical dome resting on columns.

A contemporaneous design was made by Antonio da Sangallo the Younger (1484–1546), who produced a large wooden model of the basilica. He thickened the piers to provide more support for the dome and added a T-shaped structure consisting of a facade and domed ceremonial space to the front, transforming St. Peter's into a longitudinal structure. Little was done, however, until the project fell into the hands of Michelangelo. By then the decision to transform the building into a combination centralized-longitudinal church had been made. A subsequent plan by Bramante (ca. 1512) thickened the walls to support the domes, a compromise in the direction of mass and stability that nonetheless underscores his skill at unifying space and mass. The four piers under the dome cohered into unified elements. The corner towers were balanced by luminous, domed ancillary spaces that have been cleared of columns so that they read as a fluid progression of niches and pilasters. The composition is dominated at the center by a Pantheonesque dome sitting on a forestlike ring of columns that served as a drum. The plan was approved in 1505, and in April 1506 the foundation stone was laid. For ideological and structural reasons, Bramante lengthened one arm of the building to form a nave with a centralized crossing.

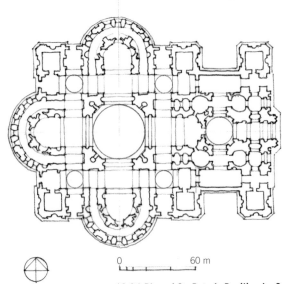

0   60 m

13.94 Plan of St. Peter's Basilica by Sangallo

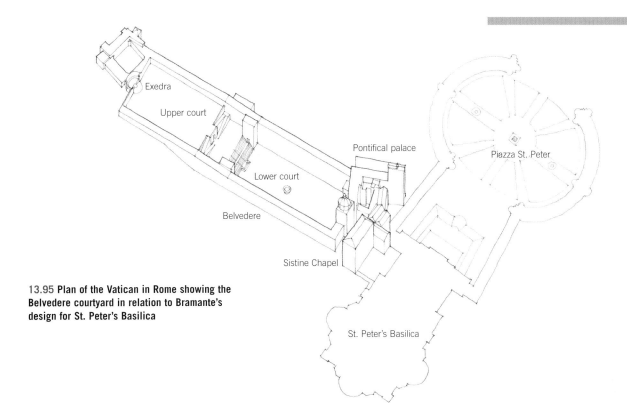

13.95 Plan of the Vatican in Rome showing the Belvedere courtyard in relation to Bramante's design for St. Peter's Basilica

At his death in 1514, he had, however, completed only the four main piers that were to support the dome. Even though the design would undergo subsequent revision by Michelangelo, these piers determined the basic spatial layout of the church.

Vatican Belvedere

Bramante's initial plan had called for a new papal palace as well as a new St. Peter's, but at some point the decision was made to keep the old palace, despite its awkward position in relation to the new church. In 1505, Bramante received the commission to design a vast rectangular courtyard that would connect the palace with a villa, the Belvedere, built some decades earlier and located some 300 meters to the north and up a hill. The part closest to the villa, which is at a higher elevation, was just one story high (a second floor was added later) and framed a formal garden. The two structures were connected at the center by a series of terraces. The lower space was a gigantic stage set, for the midlevel terraces and the lower level were connected by a large stretch of steps that served as outdoor seating facing the Vatican. The privileged viewing position, however, was from one of the upper-level papal apartments in the Vatican.

In the previous century, an architect would probably have designed the whole as a single colonnaded unit, but Bramante chose an approach based on a visual design methodology. The upper terrace has a triumphal arch motif that allows it to be seen from the distance of the papal window. The ground plane of the upper terrace is tilted slightly upward to the end wall so that the building does not seem to disappear into the perspective. Furthermore, the axis is designed as a series of interweaving forms and visual plays. The circular fountain in the lower court is answered by the apse in the nymphaeum in the retaining wall, which in turn is echoed by the large curved indentation in the facade of the back wall. Spectacular events were held in this space, from tournaments to mock naval battles, with thousands of spectators lining the galleries and sitting on the steps.

13.96 Belvedere courtyard, Vatican City

13.97 Château of Chambord, near Blois, France

The building consists of a square castle, or *donjon*, with round towers at the corners, the whole structure framed by a larger, rectangular building, still partially unfinished. The *donjon* is not in the center but on the inside of the square court, clamped against the northeastern side of the larger structure. The extraordinary, double helical staircase that rises through the center of the building, and which is attributed to Leonardo, leads to the roof of the building, a world unto its own. With its complex coves and turrets and views of the hunting grounds, it was used as a place for social events and outdoor entertainment. In a layout that was unique to the French, the central residential structure had four apartments, one in each quadrant.

The French Châteaux

In France, the 15th century and the first half of the 16th century was a period of relative economic weakness compared to the situation in Italy. The Black Plague had killed thousands, and due to the Hundred Years' War large tracts of farmland were left fallow. Furthermore, the struggle between the aristocratic classes had left the royal finances in disarray. High taxes fed a spirit of revolt. A turning point in France's fortunes came with the ascension of Francis I (r. 1515–47) who, though not a particularly astute military planner, did capture tracts of land in northern Italy—and in the process became a great admirer of Italian art and learning. In 1516 he invited the renowned Leonardo da Vinci to spend the rest of his life in his court, offering him his own little palazzo, Clos Luce, near the royal castle at Amboise, to which it was connected by an underground tunnel.

The kind of urban culture familiar to Italians did not exist in France. The kings did not even live in Paris, which did not become the capital until the 17th century. Instead, in a tradition dating back to Charlemagne, they moved from place to place, living in an assortment of châteaux, usually close to hunting grounds. While a villa is primarily a summer residence, the château is the residence of the lord of the manor—a country house for nobility and gentry. It is also often associated with a forest preserve used for hunting, an activity that only the nobility were permitted to engage in. Between 1527 and 1547, Francis I built no less than seven châteaux near Paris. Some were hunting lodges, others places of residence. Chambord (1519–47) was the largest and most elaborate of the chateaux of its age; it was so huge that it was uncomfortable to live in, and Francis himself inhabited it only for a few weeks. It is believed that Leonardo da Vinci had a hand in its design. (But since Leonardo died in 1519, the year it was begun, he could have been involved only in its planning stages.)

13.98 Staircase, Château of Chambord

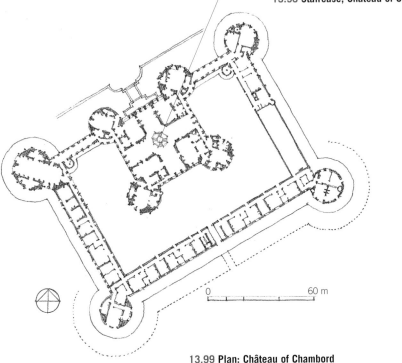

13.99 Plan: Château of Chambord

13.100 Urbanization of the Americas, ca. 1400 CE

North	New England cultures
	Mississippi cultures
	Hopis and Navajos (Southwestern U.S.)
Central	Triple Alliance (Central Mexico)
	Post-Classical Mayas (Southern Mexico)
	Tairona (Columbia)
	Chimor (Peruvian shore; conquered 1470)
South	Incas (Peru)
	Mapuche (Chile)
	Amazon cultures (Brazil)

13.101 Trade in the Americas, ca. 1400 CE

The Americas

The Americas in the 15th century were far different from the Americas in the 17th century, when disease killed off nearly 90 percent of the population. In the 15th century, from eastern Bolivia and Peru up through Central America and the western United States, eastward to the Mississippi and Georgia, and up to what is now New England, there was what the first Europeans sailing down the coast of New England described as a more or less continuous fabric of habitation. There were major cities that served as capitals of empires, like Qosqo in Peru and Tenochtitlán in Mexico; there were secondary cities that served as regional centers, like Chan Chan in Peru; Oraibi, a Hopi city in the United States; as well as other large cities in Georgia. In between, there were thousands of smaller villages. The spread of disease was so rapid that some cultures disappeared even before they themselves encountered the Europeans. There is a good deal of debate about the specifics of this terrible loss of life and culture, but the basic parameters of this tragedy are not in dispute.

The Hopis

In the 14th century, the Native Americans in North America were largely seminomadic except for the major city-dwelling areas in the Mississippi-Georgia region, which extended all the way to the Atlantic coast, and the southwestern and western areas controlled by the Hopis, who had been town dwellers for many centuries. The Hopi village of Old Oraibi in Arizona was founded about the year 1100. The Hopis' notion of urban culture had much in common with earlier urban cultures in the area dating back to the Anasazi and Hohokam. From 700 to 1130 CE, the area experienced a rapid increase in population due to consistent and regular rainfall. In the late 13th century, however, a severe drought, which seems to have put an end to the nearby Hohokam culture, forced the Hopis to abandon their smaller villages and

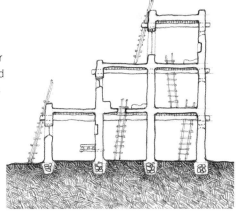

13.102 Section through a Hopi house

13.103 Taos Pueblo, New Mexico

consolidate their population in larger urban centers. When the the Spanish arrived, nine major towns existed: Sikyatki, Koechaptevela, Kisakovi, Sichomovi, Mishongnovi, Shipaulovi, Shungopavi, Oraibi, and Awatovi.

The word *Hopi* is a shortened form of *Hopituh Shi-nu-mu*, "the peaceful people" or "peaceful little ones." To be Hopi is to strive toward a state of reverence and respect for all things, to be at peace with these things, and to live in accordance with the instructions of Maasaw, the creator or caretaker of earth. The Hopis, like most Native Americans, assume the souls of the dead go to another part of the universe where they have a new existence, carrying on everyday activities as if they were still alive. Village life revolves around a series of ceremonies that are performed not only for the benefit of the village but also for the entire world. These ceremonies take place according to the lunar calendar and are observed in each of the Hopi villages. As with all pueblo cultures, most of the ceremonies take place in kivas. *Pueblo* is a Spanish word derived from the Latin word *populus* ("people"), and in this case means "village." The pueblos were, however, not villages in the European sense, but rather microcities with strong hierarchies and institutional coherencies.

Hopi cities were located at or near the edges of north-south running, flat-topped mountains known as mesas. The difficulty of transporting water up to the cities kept their populations small, but their location did allow for protection, with access paths to some pueblos purposely following narrow ravines. Houses were made of stone and mud and were often several stories high. The walls were constructed of undressed stones bound with mud plaster. Wooden beams rested on the tops of the walls to form flat roofs that were strengthened with grass thatching, a layer of plaster, and a covering of dry earth. The upper apartments were reached by outside ladders.

In the area to the south was another town, Acoma Pueblo, founded in the 12th century by the Acomas, who controlled a large area to the south and east of the Hopis. Though seminomadic, they eventually began to develop pueblo towns in the Arizona canyons. In the 17th century, the Navajos built even more pueblos, especially in their

13.104 An Iroquois village

native homeland in the northwestern corner of New Mexico, as part of their defenses against the Spanish invaders.

New England Societies

By the 14th century, the area of the United States now known as New England was home to dozens of Indian tribes. When seen from a larger temporal perspective of the Americas, the area had only been recently settled, perhaps as consequence of the decline of the Hopewell society in Ohio around 500 CE, which dispersed its populations in various directions. By the 16th century, about one hundred thousand people lived along the coasts, estuaries, rivers, and lakes from Maine to the Carolinas in settlements and villages organized around tribal affiliations. Contrary to what Europeans thought, the area was not a sparsely populated wilderness. Armed conflict was not unknown between the tribes, though such conflict was less about territory than about prestige. The absence of pigs and sheep—true across all of the Americas before the arrival of Europeans—meant that there were no fences, something colonialists misread as implying that the Native Americans had no concept of land ownership.

Villages were led by a sachem, the equivalent of chief or king, but each tribe had slightly different habits depending on its location and circumstances. Some were seminomadic, moving from winter to summer; others were not. Some planted in organized fields; others relied more

on hunting and fishing supplemented by agriculture. Trade was important, as it allowed for a certain degree of specialization as well as for exchange between areas. The forests were tended and underbrush cleared to improve hunting. Trees were pruned to create orchards of hickory, chestnut, and walnut, which produce edible and nutritious nuts. The area around a village would have been cleared to plant corn.

Villages were organized around clusters of hut-shaped houses (*wetus*) made of poles, with bark serving as walls. In winter, the *wetus* were covered with rush mats that were impervious to water; in summer, they were covered by thin sheets of flexible chestnut bark. A low fire burned in the middle and vented through an opening in the roof. The structures were well suited to the environment. One early colonist noted that they were warmer and less leaky than the houses of the English. The villages were protected by palisades of wooden poles, but moats and berms, such as were used in the larger villages and cities farther south in Alabama and Georgia, were not used. In 1616, Europeans brought an epidemic that wiped out 90 percent of the population in about three years. The result, from the European perspective, was a pristine land relatively untouched by humans. Plymouth Colony was established in 1620, for example, in an area that had been severely depopulated.

13.105 A *wetu*

Tenochtitlán

The fall of the Toltec capital of Tula (located about 100 kilometers north-northwest of Mexico City), led to the founding of a number of semiautonomous urban centers around Lake Texcoco. The city of Tenochtitlán (now Mexico City) was founded by one of these groups, the Mexica, on an islet in the western part of the lake in the year 1325. By the 14th century, war between the states had become systemic, leading in 1428 to an alliance between three of them that became the basis of the Aztec Empire. (Historians tend to shy away from the term Aztec because it only came into use in the 19th century.) At its height, the empire stretched across central Mexico from coast to coast. In 1521, the Triple Alliance was defeated by the Spanish conquistadores and their native allies under Hernán Cortés, who described the city before he destroyed it; his text and drawing were presented to the Spanish king and widely circulated in Europe, thanks to the printing press. Cortés told of a city of two hundred thousand inhabitants on an island in the middle of a lake, connected by causeways to the shore. Gigantic stone towers dominated the city's center, at the intersection of the causeways.

The Mexica were originally peripheral to the political world of that region, but under their general, Tlacaélel, who masterminded the Triple Alliance, the Mexica remodeled themselves after the Toltecs and claimed descent from Teotihuacán in order to legitimate their imperial claims. Their religion saw the sun as engaged in a violent and perpetual struggle for existence, a struggle that had to be nourished by human sacrifice. Several thousand were killed every year in such rituals. Though later European conquerors purported to be shocked at this, 17th-century Europe was, ironically, a significantly more brutal place; tens of thousands of people were hanged, quartered, burned, or impaled—often as part of great public spectacles—during the various religious wars.

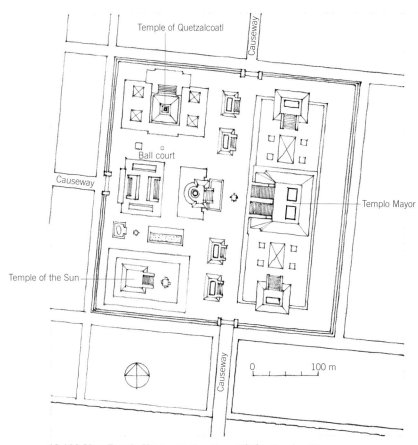

13.106 **Plan: Templo Mayor complex, Tenochtitlán, Mexcico City**

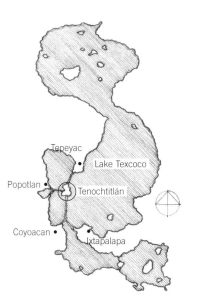

13.107 **Location of Tenochtitlán on Lake Texcoco, Mexico**

The Mexica settled next to a swamp but were able to drain the area to create a 10-square-kilometer lake with an island-city at the center linked to settlements on the mainland by three raised causeways. It grew to become an enormous city, much larger than any European city of the time. A gridded network of streets and canals teemed with boats transporting goods and people to its markets. Two aqueducts brought fresh water into the city. The ceremonial center consisted of two stepped pyramids rising side by side on a huge platform painted red and blue; nearby were palaces painted a dazzling white. Not far away were the schools for the sons of the nobility, the houses for the priests, a ball court, an intimidating *tzompantli* (or skull rack) displaying the severed heads of the sacrificed, and several other pyramids and temples, all surrounded by protective enclosures.

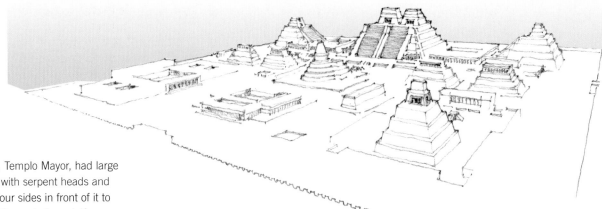

The main temple, Templo Mayor, had large incense braziers, with serpent heads and cauldrons on all four sides in front of it to receive offerings. It rose in four platforms, representative of the celestial levels of the cosmos, until it reached the top level where there were two temples dedicated to Tlaloc and Huitzilopochtli. Two parallel stairs led up to the summit. Huitzilopochtli, whose temple was to the south, was the Mayan warrior god who fought his brother Centzon Huitznahua and his sister Coyolxauhqui immediately after birth. He defeated them and threw their dismembered bodies down the mountain, a sacrifice marked by a round tablet at the foot of the stairs. Between 1325 and 1521, Templo Mayor was reconstructed seven times, with the older temple encased intact within each new larger building. Of all these, the second building has survived intact, including its two temples, complete with the stone to which prisoners were tied before being sacrificed.

13.108 Pictorial view: Templo Mayor, Tenochtitlán, Mexico City

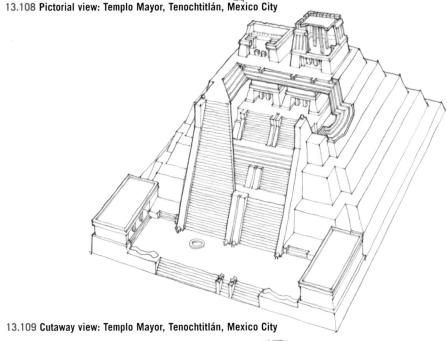

Like their predecessors, the Mexica were dedicated observers of the sun, the stars, the cycles of nature, the passing of the seasons, and the death of plant and animal life. And like their predecessors, their architecture and their rituals were intended to maintain the integrity of the cosmic order. Their science of observation was certainly very sophisticated, though today it is still incompletely understood. Templo Mayor pointed 7 degrees south of east, so that on the equinoxes the sun rises exactly between the temples of Tlaloc and Huitzilopochtli. A monolithic calendar stone 1.2 meters thick, 3.6 meters in diameter, and weighing over 24 tons, was found in 1790 under the main square. On its face is a representation of the sun god.

13.109 Cutaway view: Templo Mayor, Tenochtitlán, Mexico City

13.110 Calendar stone from Tenochtitlán

13.111 Chan Chan, near Trujillo, Peru

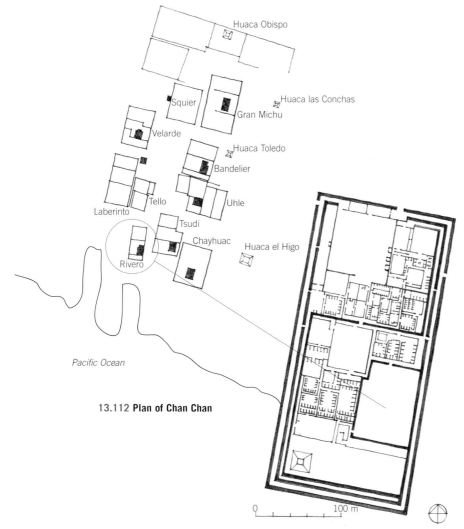

Huaca Obispo

Squier

Huaca las Conchas

Gran Michu

Velarde

Huaca Toledo

Bandelier

Tello

Uhle

Laberinto

Tsudi

Chayhuac

Huaca el Higo

Rivero

Pacific Ocean

13.112 Plan of Chan Chan

0   100 m

13.113 Plan: Rivero Citadel at Chan Chan

The Incas

In the coastal valleys of northern Peru, the collapse of the Wari kingdom around the year 1000 CE led to the emergence of the Chimu (850–1470), also called the Chimor, who in time came to control the entire northern coast of Peru from the modern border of Ecuador to Lima. Their capital, Chan Chan was spread out across a large plain of the coastal desert. Because the Chimu believed their kings continued to live even after death, a new king never moved into his predecessor's palace, but instead built a new one, which then became the home of his extended family after his own death. But the Chan Chan were soon subsumed into the world of the Incas. Not much is known about the prehistory of the Incas, except that like the Mexica, they were originally a small peripheral kingdom that became much more successful than those around it. The Incas borrowed form the Chimu their approach to royalty, with one exception: their king, or *inca*, was divine. One of their *incas*, Pachakuti, who ascended the Incan throne in 1438, quickly built an empire that brought the area of present-day Peru, Bolivia, Chile, Ecuador, and northern Argentina under Incan control. He did this by means novel to the South American political scene. In the previous era, regional expansionism had been limited due to the difficulties involved in marshalling large armies and moving them from place to place. (There were, after all, no horses.) The Incas expanded fairly peacefully by assimilating neighboring areas into their regime, offering stability and inclusion in exchange for services. Soon they were able to command enormous teams of people— many purposefully displaced from their homelands—to build roads and palaces, and work in craft industries and on farms. The consolidation of the empire was more or less complete by 1520. There was no money, no markets, and no land ownership: all land belonged to the king. It was a centralized system akin to modern socialism, except that the ruling Inca was a god. The result was that in just over a hundred years the Incas became the most powerful empire the Americas had ever seen, before they were conquered by the Spanish and depopulated by disease.

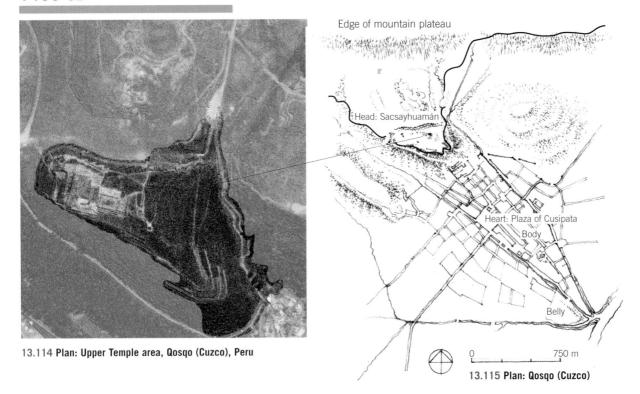

13.114 Plan: Upper Temple area, Qosqo (Cuzco), Peru

Edge of mountain plateau

Head: Sacsayhuamán

Heart: Plaza of Cusipata

Body

Belly

0   750 m

13.115 Plan: Qosqo (Cuzco)

The Incan capital, Qosqo (Cuzco), was located on the western fringe of the Peruvian highlands. Four major roads terminated in its center, the Plaza of Cusipata. Under Pachakuti, the first of the great Incan rulers, Qosqo was transformed from a village of clay and straw into a city of stone. Wedged between the Tullumayo and Huatanay rivers, the city's plan forms the body of a puma, or jaguar. The head was represented by the fortress, the heart by the central plaza, and the tail by the confluence of the two canalized rivers. The Plaza of Cusipata was surrounded by the main civic structure of Qosqo, the palaces, and three temples dedicated to the sun (Qorikancha), the creator (Kiswarkancha), and thunder (Pucamarka). The plaza was filled with pure white sand taken form the coast, and across the facades of the palaces were enormous plates of polished gold that reflected the setting sun. The plaza was the center of the Incan cosmos, with four highways leading to and from it demarcating the four sectors of the empire. Also radiating out from the city was a spider web of forty-one crooked spirit paths that connected holy features of the landscape such as springs, caves, shrines, and stones. The Incan calendar counted forty-one weeks, each eight days long.

Qosqo seems to have had no defensive wall, even though the impressively-scaled "head" of the puma, Sacsayhuamán, that overlooks the valley is presumed to have been a fortress. It could also have been a temple to the sun, a water reservoir—or all three. It has three platforms, one on top of the other, followed by a triple row of toothed walls made from gigantic blocks of granite. The walls were precise works of engineering.

Some of their granite blocks weighed up to 200 tons and had to be hauled large distances. Each block was shaped on-site to fit its neighbors exactly. Additionally, individual stones were shaped and aligned to create a ceremonial series of waterspouts and channels. There was also a large circular meeting plaza with ceremonial buildings perched at the lip of the cliff overlooking the city.

13.116 Aerial view: Qosqo (Cuzco)

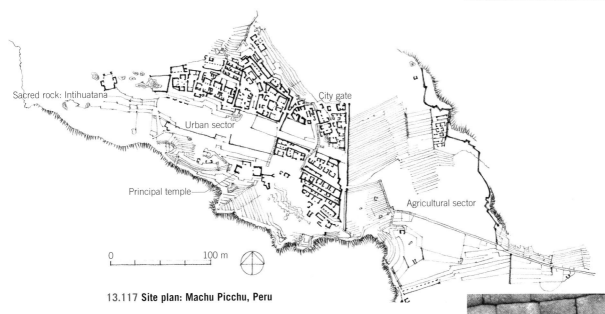

13.117 Site plan: Machu Picchu, Peru

13.118 Stonework at Machu Picchu

Machu Picchu

Machu Picchu, 70 kilometers northwest of Qosqo, is located between two steep peaks 2,750 meters above a gorge carved by the river Urubamba. It is the only Incan settlement to have survived intact, having been completely overlooked by the Spaniards. It was probably inhabited late into the 16th century, when it was gradually abandoned and forgotten. (There are other Incan sites in this remote area, but these have yet to be fully explored.) Some two hundred buildings arranged on a series of parallel terraces on both sides of a central plaza constitute the core of the small settlement that might have housed at most one thousand people. Access to the site was difficult; it was a long trek up the steep gorges, and entry was possible only from one carefully guarded checkpoint. Because it was a magnificent site for solar and stellar observation, some have argued that the city was a royal retreat, or perhaps even a special temple reserved for the elite. Key to the success of the site was the artesian spring at its top that supplied its inhabitants with water year-round. The genius of Machu Picchu lies in the terracing and partitioning of the site, which fills a saddle lying roughly east-west between the two peaks. The saddle rises sharply in the south and, after a crest and a short flat plain, slopes gently down toward the north and the east. It resembles a wave, with a stable spot at its precarious top. To shore up the land and to create spaces to build on, the Incan planners constructed terraces carefully, following the natural contours of the site. At the eastern end, there is a sector of terraces, presumably for cultivation, with a complex network of irrigation channels.

A long central plaza, gently terracing down toward the east, sets the stage. On either side of this plaza, accessed by a complex network of streets and stairs, are the main buildings. Most are single-room dwellings; some are clustered around courts, but most are arranged along narrow pathways limited by the terrace widths. They are all made of finely fitted stonemasonry, with wedge-shaped windows and monolithic lintels, and equipped with water drainage and harvesting systems. The granite used in the construction was quarried locally. Gable ends testify to perishable roofs long gone. There is, however, no evidence of any adobe construction, suggesting a highly elite and ceremonial function for the city. Nestled within this network are some surprising anomalies: a semicircular, turretlike structure unexpectedly abuts the residential fabric, and a series of baths line the central north-south pathway.

13.119 Passageway at Machu Picchu

The high southwestern edge of the saddle is reserved for a temple, accessed by a long stair from the east. At the foot of the stair lies what is assumed to be another temple, with three C-shaped rooms looking into a central court. At the top of the stair lies the main temple, the sacred center, dedicated to the sun. Three steps into an antechamber lead up to the final terrace, at the center of which lies a huge granite monolith known as the Intihuatana, or the "Hitching Post of the Sun." The Intihuatana stone is something of a miniature Machu Picchu, resembling the peak just beyond; it has a series of small "terraces" culminating in a dramatic outcrop. Intihuatana stones are believed to have once been dispersed throughout the Incan world, but they were destroyed by the Spanish, who considered them idolatrous. Their exact meaning is uncertain, but they were likely miniaturized replicas of a sacred peak to which the Incas imagined the sun could be tethered by a rope, enabling its circular journey through the upper and lower worlds. Perhaps Machu Picchu's peaks were as close as the Incans thought they could get to that sacred peak.

13.120 **Machu Picchu as it stands today**

13.121 **Close-up of the urban sector of Machu Picchu**

1600 CE

Thanks to the establishment of reliable cross-continental and coastal trade, the Eurasian world from Japan to western Europe had become a contiguous economic power bloc by the 17th century. Wealth and ideas traveled in the baggage or minds of traders, migrants, and armies. But this old-world order was now increasingly undermined by the newly arising, more efficient ocean trade. Imagine a traveler in 1652 starting a trip through Europe and Asia to study the latest developments in the field of architecture. Starting in Japan, he is led through the Ninomaru Palace in Nijo Castle, located in the heart of Kyoto, the capital of Japan. He then visits the austere Katsura Imperial Villa and is introduced by his hosts to the newly developed intricacies of the Zen tea ceremony. Crossing into Korea, he visits the Gyeongbok Palace in Seoul (begun 1394), led there by a Mongolian serving in the Manchu Empire, which had reduced Korea to a vassal state. Traveling with a Mongolian commander into the heart of Manchuria through Mukden, its capital, he visits the then still relatively recently constructed Forbidden City, which was then being refurbished by the new Manchu rulers who had just taken over Beijing, in the heart of which it is located. The times are just stable enough to travel to the nearby Ming Tombs. On the way, he discusses with his guides the pros and cons of the Chinese international seafaring voyages and whether or not they should be continued. He then works his way southward into the highland plateau of Tibet to visit the dramatic Potala Palace, built on a steep rocky crest for the fifth Dalai Lama, whose supporters had carved out an important political territory in the Lhasa Valley in the Himalayas. Descending to the fertile plains of the Ganges River, he now travels through areas controlled by one of the Islamized descendants of the Mongols, Akbar the Great. He makes his way past Man Mandir, one of the grand 16th-century palaces of the city of Gwalior in central India, and on to Delhi and its expansive palaces. He inspects the great planned city of Fatehpur Sikri, capital of the Mughal Empire from 1571 to 1585, laid out by Akbar himself, and then heads up the Yamuna River to see the just-completed Illumined Tomb, later known as the Taj Mahal. There he hears of new Portuguese settlers living in a small coastal town called Goa. He then heads for Kandahar and crosses into Persian territory, following the trade routes to Isfahan, where he sees that city's vast enormous city square, sumptuous mosques, and broad royal gardens. There he meets traders from as far away as England. From Isfahan, he crosses mountains and deserts into areas newly controlled by the Ottomans and, following the old Seljuk caravan routes, makes his way to Antioch on the Mediterranean Sea, where he boards a ship to Istanbul. This city, taken by the Ottomans in 1453, was in the process of being rebuilt by its new lords. He admires the great Hagia Sophia, but his guide points out to him the superiority of the mosques recently built by Mimar Sinan (1489–1588), the great architect and engineer. From Istanbul he departs on a merchant ship for the somewhat faded port of Venice and is told there of economic hardships and of Dutch competition while being shepherded to the church of St. Giorgio Maggiore by Andrea Palladio. He then follows a group of pilgrims to Rome, a city awash in Spanish money. The dome of St. Peter's Basilica, based on designs by Michelangelo and one of the most demanding and exciting building projects in all of Europe, was just being finished. In front of the church, he sees a vast area that has just been cleared to make way for Gian Lorenzo Bernini's colonnaded Piazza of St. Peter's. He takes the time to visit the recently finished building by Francesco Borromini, Sant'Ivo alla Sapienza, and to discuss with its priests their efforts to strengthen the Counter-Reformation. From the Roman port of Ostia he travels by boat to Marseilles and then northward, working his way through France. He admires the new wealth of the aristocracy and sees some of the great châteaux, such as the Château de Chambord of Francis I on the Loire River, whose double helical staircase may have been designed by Leonardo da Vinci (who, invited by Francis I, had spent his retirement years near the king). Our traveler also visits the Place Royale in Paris, stopping along the way to admire the great cathedrals. But to see the energy of the Europeans in action, he goes to Amsterdam, a world metropolis with neither grand palaces nor dominating churches but with a bustling port, testimony to Dutch mercantile prowess. He visits the new city hall and bank with the world maps inlaid in marble on the floor. He takes time to visit his first Protestant churches, plain and austere, and is told of terrible religious wars. In crossing the English Channel, he visits the newly built Banqueting House (1619–22). It is one of the first buildings in England to be designed in the modern Italianate manner, and the structure represents an ambitious but—from the point of view of the Chinese, Mughals, Ottomans, and Dutch—still relatively marginal power, for England's major export commodity was still wool, and its foreign policy was still driven more by piracy than by politics.

Muromachi Period
1392–1573
▲ **Himeji Castle**
1346–1610

Voyages of Zheng He
1405–33

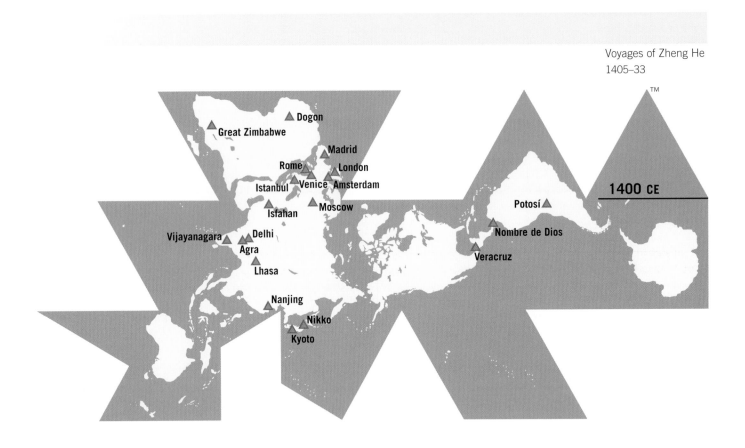

1400 CE

Momoyama Period
1573–1615

Edo Period
1615–1868

▲ Ryoanji Temple
ca. 1480

▲ Nijo Castle ▲ Katsura Rikyu
1601–3   Begun ca. 1615

◉ 1633
Closure of ports

China: Ming Dynasty
1368–1644

▲ Ming Tombs
1409–1644

▲ Potala Palace
1649–94

Mughal Dynasty
1526–1858

Humanyun's Tomb ▲ ▲ Fatehpur Sikri
1565   1569–74

▲ Taj Mahal
1632–53

1500 CE   **1600 CE**   **1700 CE**

Ottoman Empire
1281–1923

Safavid Rule
1501–1722

▲ Suleymaniye Mosque
1550–57

▲ Masjid-i-Shah Mosque
Begun 1611

▲ Cathedral of the Archangel Michael
1505–9

Russian Empire
1547–1917

Migration and establishment of the Dogon peoples
15th and 16th centuries

▲ Great Zimbabwe
16th century to ca. 1650

Kingdom of Spain
1516–1700

▲ El Escorial
Begun 1563

Italy: Papal and Autonomous City-States
12th century to 1870

▲ St. Peter's Basilica
1506–1615

▲ Villa Farnese
1547–9

▲ Il Gesù
1568–84

▲ San Carlo alle Quattro Fontane
1638–67

▲ Villa Rotonda
Begun 1566

▲ Sant'Ivo alla Sapienza
1642–50

▲ Uffizi
1560–81

▲ Sant'Andrea al Quirinale
1658–70

Netherlands: United Provinces
1581–1795

▲ Zuiderkerk
1603–11

▲ Amsterdam Town Hall
Begun 1648

France: Bourbon Rule
1589–1792

▲ Place Royale
Begun 1605

England: Elizabethan Age
1558–1603

▲ Hardwick Hall
1590–7

▲ Banqueting House
1619–22

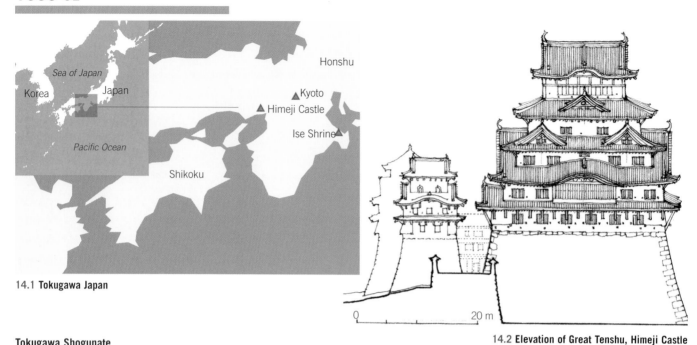

14.1 **Tokugawa Japan**

14.2 **Elevation of Great Tenshu, Himeji Castle**

Tokugawa Shogunate

By the early 17th century, the shogun commanders had unified and pacified Japan after a century of upheaval and civil war. They continued to patronize Zen Buddhism and reconstructed the major shrines and temples of Kyoto, such as Nishihonganji, Choin-in, and Kiyomizudera. In 1577, the shogun Oda Nobunaga (1534–82) sent his trusted lieutenant and the subsequent shogun, Hideyoshi, to construct a castle in Himeji, some 150 kilometers west of Kyoto, to control the routes connecting the newly acquired western territories. Two gently sloping hills overlooking the north end of Japan's Inland Sea serve as the locus of the castle compound, which consists of a *honmaru* ("inner citadel") and its defensive terrace. Resting on the top of a sloping stone base some 14 meters high, the main tower (known as the Great Tenshu) rises seven floors, a wooden skyscraper of its time. The entire structure is held together, from basement to the uppermost story, by two massive pillars that pass through and lock together each level of the building. The east pillar is made from a single trunk of silver fir 28.4 meters tall, while the second is a composite. This technology was taken from pagoda designs. Mastlike pillars at the center, known as the *shinbashira*, or "heart pillars," hold the structure together. The Himeji, in fact, is a type of bulked-up, inhabited pagoda—a symbolic allusion that certainly would not have escaped a visiting warlord.

Its exterior elevations consist of a carefully orchestrated rhythm of triangular and flaring gables, creating a visual signature for the Tenshu that eventually came to be imitated in all subsequent castles built in Japan. The walls are white, whereas the roofs are covered with gray tiles embellished with white plaster to secure them against the winds.

14.3 **Himeji Castle, Himeji, Japan**
The suffix *–jo* means "castle" in Japanese; Himeji Castle is thus known as Himeji-jo. (The suffix *–ji* means "temple.")

In Japanese, the relationship between power and architecture is often codified in language. *Mon*, or gateway, is part of the word *kenmon*, which describes a person of authority. It literally means "power gate." The word *mikado* ("honorable gate") is used in reference to the emperor. A *kinmon*, or "prohibited gateway," could only be used in the imperial palace where access was restricted. By the 9th century, the building of gates had already been forbidden to people of low rank.

14.4 **Yomeimon, Toshogu Shrine, Nikko, Japan**

Nikko Toshogu

It is testament to the power and ambitions of the Tokugawa shoguns that Tokugawa Ieyasu, soon after his death, was deified as a tutelary kami, or living spirit, of Japan in 1617. As such, Ieyasu was considered divine and on par with the emperor. As is appropriate to a kami, Ieyasu was buried high on the sacred mountain, Nikko. His mausoleum and shrine, known as the Nikko Toshogu, was built by his grandson, Iemitsu (1604–51), the third and most powerful of the Tokugawa shoguns. The Toshogu occupies the side of a hill and was built in the *gongen-zukuri* form, with extended verandas carried on bracket sets and paired triangular and cusped gables at the front. The access gate opens onto an irregularly shaped compound with a series of subsidiary buildings. From there the path moves left before turning north again to face the main shrine somewhat up the side of the hill. A torii marks the path that leads to the first terrace. Another stair through another gateway leads to the second terrace. From there, twelve steep steps lead up to the Yomeimon, the gate of the inner shrine. This was as far as the daimyo—the feudal overlords—were allowed to go to pay obeisance to Ieyasu. Only priests and members of the Tokugawa family were allowed to enter the shrine itself, just as the imperial family had sole access to Ise's inner shrine.

In the Yomeimon, the visitor encounters a spectacular display of color and structure. Two layers of highly ornamented bracket sets support a balcony and a tiled Heian-style, hip-and-gable roof. The pristine surfaces of the frame, painted with white lime, are accented with gilded metalwork. Phoenixes,

peonies, dragons in clouds, and birds of paradise compete for space with twenty-two figural compositions depicting Chinese themes. Shinto guardian angels sit on each side of the entrance, and a sculpture of Zhou Gong Dan, the Duke of Zhou, cited by Confucius as the paragon of the virtuous ruler, sits directly above the front entrance. The Nikko shrine is a three-part construction, with the worship hall (*haiden*) connected to the main hall (*honden*) by the *ishi no ma*, or stone-floored corridor. The shrine's decoration is more restrained and dominated by a single woodshop tradition. Forked finials (*chigi*) and billets (*katsuogi*) ride on the ridge of the *honden*, as was typical of all Shinto shrines.

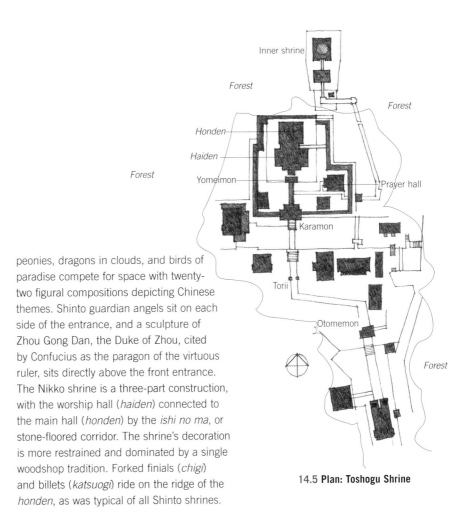

14.5 **Plan: Toshogu Shrine**

Nijo-jo

If Himeji expressed the authority of the shogun vertically, Ninomaru Palace in Nijo Castle (1601–3), located in the heart of Kyoto, was designed to stage authority through a carefully orchestrated syncopation of waiting rooms and meeting halls. Built by the shogun Tokugawa Ieyasu, it was the place where all of the region's generals would gather to pay obeisance. From 1624 to 1626, the palace was redesigned in preparation for a visit by the emperor Go Mizuno, the first visit by an emperor to a shogun's palace. The new design was coordinated by Nakai Masatomo, the master carpenter responsible for government projects in Kyoto.

A high stone wall with a moat surrounds the 500-by-400-meter site and contains two compounds, each within its own perimeter walls: one for a castle (now destroyed) and the other for the palace. The palace was capped by a series of massive clay-tiled roofs joined at various angles. Most of the woodwork was left unpainted. Entry is through a gate in the wall of the southern compound that leads into a courtyard with two additional gateways, one to the stroll garden on the left and the other to the palace, directly ahead but just off axis. The wall behind the gate steps back, suggesting the presence of hidden depths to the court, whereas the wall to the garden is angled, using perspective to create the illusion of a larger space.

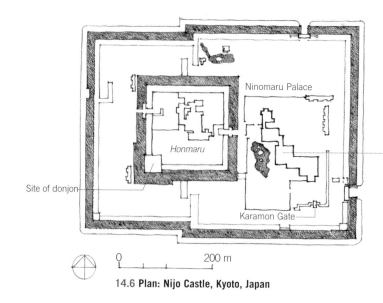

14.6 **Plan: Nijo Castle, Kyoto, Japan**

The Tozamurai (or waiting rooms and government offices), the Shikidai (or secondary audience hall), and the Ohiroma (or main audience hall) are the palace's three main buildings. Added to these are the Kuroshoin, meant for informal audiences with the shogun, and the Shiroshoin, the royal residence. There was also a service building in the back (at the north) with kitchen and baths, connected to the main structure by means of a network of corridors. In plan the palace functions as a series of layers organized by a diagonal spine—a corridor that defines the edge between the garden and the internal spaces. The main spaces

of the four buildings are connected to this corridor. Movable screens can be used to close or open any part of the palace or its corridors. Every plank of this garden corridor was fitted with tiny iron springs that creaked, even at the lightest of steps, so that when the screens were closed the occupants of the internal spaces would always know if anyone was outside, or if the shogun approached.

A visitor entering through the Kuramayose would be brought to one of the three waiting rooms of the Tozamurai. With the view of the garden screened off, the visitor would have been confronted with a large painting of life-size crouching tigers and panthers lurking in

14.7 **Entrance to Nijo Castle**

14.8 **Garden of Nijo Castle**

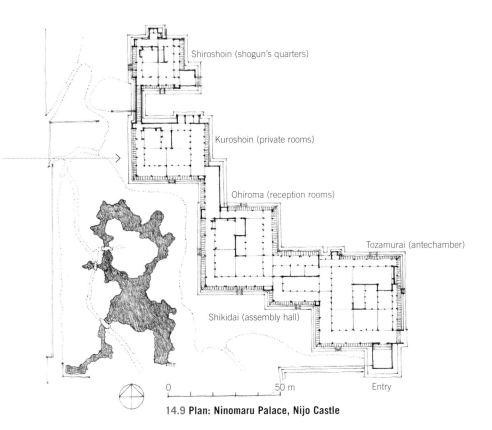

14.9 **Plan: Ninomaru Palace, Nijo Castle**

Shiroshoin (shogun's quarters)

Kuroshoin (private rooms)

Ohiroma (reception rooms)

Tozamurai (antechamber)

Shikidai (assembly hall)

0   50 m   Entry

14.10 **Ninomaru Palace**

bamboo groves. Here the hustle and bustle outside could be heard but not seen as the visitor waited to be called for his audience. This was the theater of intimidation. Most visitors would have their audience in the Shikidai with one of the shogun's councilors. The room, long and narrow and offering only a partial view of the garden, focused on the councilor, who would sit at one end. Behind him, the knotted branches of two large pine trees, evergreen and symbolic of the perennial authority of the shogun, were painted with bold strokes jumping freely across the structural elements in defiance of any containing frame. The three spaces of the Ohiroma were organized in an L shape to build in visual hierarchy. The visiting councilors sat in the *gendan no ma* (or lower chamber), separated from the *jodan no ma* (or upper chamber) by a single step. Lower-ranking visitors sat out of sight in the third chamber. The shogun entered from the north and sat in the middle of the northern half of the *jodan no ma*, facing south. There was thus considerable distance behind him and visitors.

Behind and to his east was the *chigidana* ("staggered shelves") gilded in gold, with a painting marking the place of authority. Directly behind him was a display space with a twisted bonsai pine, its highest branch rising vertically on center. When all the screens were shut, backlight from the sun would illuminate the shogun against the screen. Directly to the shogun's left, on axis, was an elaborately decorated door; above him, the coffered roof was raised; and to his right, if the screens were open, he would be able to see the island in the middle of the lake—the only spot in the entire palace from which this was possible. Thus, although the shogun sat on the floor on a mat at a spot that was not distinguished in any way, it was staged from every direction so that the moment he occupied it, his significance became clear immediately.

14.11 Suminoe pine, Katsura Imperial Villa, near Kyoto, Japan

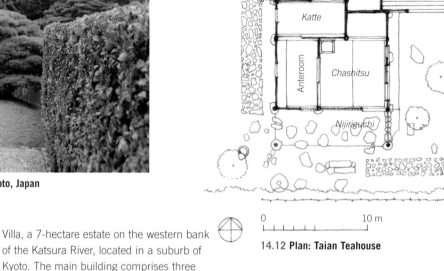

14.12 Plan: Taian Teahouse

0   10 m

Katsura Rikyu (Katsura Imperial Villa)

In contrast to the shogun military commanders who, in developing their political ambitions, created sumptuous displays of power, the older aristocratic families, now largely disempowered, began to adopt an introspective and pseudo-rustic aesthetic influenced by the ideals of Zen Buddhism. The most celebrated example of this new aesthetic—now considered by many modern architects to be the essence of Japanese architecture—is the Katsura Detatched Palace, better known as the Katsura Imperial Villa. It was built by the nobleman Hichijonomiya Toshihito (1579–1629) and his son Toshitada (1619–62). Underlying the design is the ceremonial teahouse. In the 17th century, serving and drinking tea had become the center of lavish rituals at courtly ceremonies, with the focus on the display of quality tea ware, the presentation ceremony often upstaged the tea itself. In the latter part of the 16th century, Sen no Rikyu (1522–91), a patron of the Zen monks in Ginkakuji, transformed the ceremony into a simple, precisely choreographed, and highly personalized exercise known as *wabi-cha*. His famous dictum was "one moment, one meeting." The goal of his ceremony, which contrasted with the extravagance of the shoguns, was to be free from all distractions—past and future—and to lead to a state of immediacy. Rikyu designed one of the first-known neo-rustic teahouses, Taian, in Yamazaki, south of Kyoto, but the form found its ultimate expression at the Katsura Imperial

Villa, a 7-hectare estate on the western bank of the Katsura River, located in a suburb of Kyoto. The main building comprises three interlinked *shoins* (or sections) referred to as the Old, Middle, and New Shoins, staggered at the western edge of an irregularly shaped pond with several islands. The Old Shoin, farthest to the north, was built by Prince Toshihito and the other two by his son, Prince Toshitada. The New Shoin, along with a

0   60 m

14.13 Site plan: Katsura Imperial Villa

14.14 Central Gate: Katsura Imperial Villa

14.15 Garden Gate, Katsura Imperial Villa

special gate and access path, was built on the occasion of the Emperor Go Mizuno's visit to Katsura in 1663. Seven teahouses are distributed in the garden in a semicircular arc and linked by a stroll path. In its outlines, therefore, Katsura is nothing more than a nobleman's country villa with a stroll garden. But it was also an ideological statement about the superiority of aristocratic society.

The palace has two main entry gates. The entrance into Katsura is through a gate at the far end of a purposefully simple bamboo fence. Nothing of the interior is visible from the outside. Even upon entering, the view is carefully screened by a hedge. Katsura's next gate was built for imperial visits. Yet it, too, was patently unassuming and opened onto a straight, unedged gravel path lined with trees leading to yet another gate. From there the gravel path turns right for 50 meters or so—the longest stretch of straight path at Katsura. Although the entire garden is to the left and the villa ahead, the view down this imperial approach is also carefully screened by bushes and trees. Small openings reveal views of the garden, a glimpse of the main teahouse, a look at the boathouse, and a bridge over a water view. When a visitor reaches the villa, there is a sharp turn to the left and a view along a promontory, edged by a thick hedge, with a miniaturized Suminoe pine tree. The framed view of the tree draws attention to, and blocks the view of, the garden beyond. The miniaturization of the tree also makes the promontory seem longer than it is and introduces the notion of self-consciously constructed symbolism in the landscape.

Tea pavilion (Gepparo)

Old Shoin

Middle Shoin

Music Room

New Shoin

14.16 Plan: Katsura Imperial Villa

14.17 Stepping-stones, Katsura Imperial Villa

To the right of the promontory, over an arched wood and earth bridge, is the Central Gate, a visitor's first encounter with architecture. A simple freestanding wall with a rectangular opening extends out to the west from a subsidiary building that contains the commoner's entrance. The gravel path terminates in a single large, uncut stone at the threshold, followed by four dressed stones arranged in a square. From there, a loose arrangement of uncut stepping-stones crisscrosses the straight path made by cut stones and signals one of the signature themes of Katsura's walkways: the studied orchestration of stepping-stones that generate a haptic and tactile experience. From the Central Gate, stepping-stones lead to the entrance of the Old Shoin, called the Imperial Carriage Stop. Here, another freestanding wall with an opening, projecting out from the Old Shoin to the north, offers an alternative route, a second carefully staged path leading east to the Gepparo, the teahouse closest to the *shoins*. The stepping-stones winding through the opening have the quality of mysterious footprints and invite the visitor to follow them. The final step up into the Old Shoin is another uncut stone dramatically set against the straight lines of the wooden steps of the entrance porch. Another of Katsura's signatures is the elaboration of the villa as a simple hut. Every entrance into the villa is from large, uncut stones, and every exterior post on the garden side sits directly on a stone foundation. All the wooden posts and beams were left unpolished, some with their bark intact.

The geometry that governs the plan of the three *shoins* is derived from the dimensions of the tatami and the sliding shoji covered with translucent rice paper. The spaces are orchestrated as a series of interconnected rooms, with all the important rooms facing east onto the garden. The supporting rooms are to the west and connected to secondary structures. The Middle and New Shoins are connected by an intermediate section called the Music Room. An external veranda runs along the eastern edge of the villa, edged by sliding screen doors that can be opened and shut to modulate the light and to connect the exterior and the interior.

The spatial and visual focus of the Old Shoin is an east-west cross-axis formed by the pantry, the Spear Room, and its main space (the "second room") with an external bamboo deck called the Moon-Viewing Platform. (The Katsura River was known as a scenic place for looking at the moon in August.) A miniature stone pagoda in a clearing on the southern edge of the Island of Immortals is the view's stable point amid a dense arboreal landscape. Its focus is the still water of the pond, which at night reflects the rising moon on the east and by day, the trees along its irregular edges. In autumn, the trees are ablaze with color and in winter, white with snow.

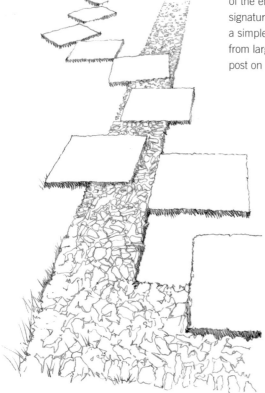

14.18 Garden path, Katsura Imperial Villa, Kyoto

14.19 Detail: Katsura Imperial Villa, Kyoto

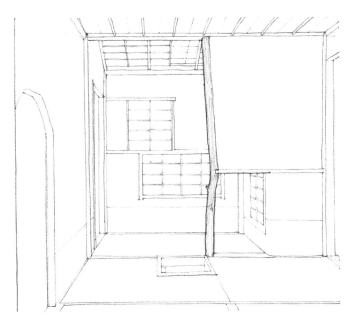

14.20 Interior of Tea Pavilion (Shokintei), Katsura Imperial Villa

14.21 Ceiling structure of the Gepparo, Katsura Imperial Villa

Katsura's main feature is the stroll garden. Its design is credited to Kobori Enshu (1579–1647), a tea master and garden designer, though that it is his design is not certain. Many walks are possible. The main walk circumambulates the pond in a clockwise direction, beginning to the north of the Old Shoin, winding around the shore to the main teahouse (the Shokintei), on to the large island with the Shoiken and Orindo teahouses, across the riding ground and moss garden, and back to the Middle Shoin. It is the journey, rather than the destination, that is important.

Much of the path is made of stepping-stones of uncut rock. Although each stone is completely horizontal and never more than a comfortable stride from the next, they do not form a continuous walkway and can suddenly make unexpected twists and turns. This forces visitors to become aware of not only where they are walking, but of the act of walking itself. When the dressed stones of the straight paths surrounding the *shoins* meet the stepping-stones, the latter dance around and through the former with a studied irreverence. But when they encounter the cascade of pebbles—the "sand" of the shore—they march through them like a determined walker on a beach. Sometimes they seem to have inherent purposes; the stepping-stones lead straight across the

wet moss garden, next to the Middle Shoin, whereas the straight path is forced to skirt around its edge. At other times, they seem more functional. Along the way, stone lanterns mark places of rest. One of the most famous uses of such a lantern is at the terminus of the spit of land that projects into the pond. The lantern, known as the Night-Rain Lantern, marks the terminus of the path not to be taken.

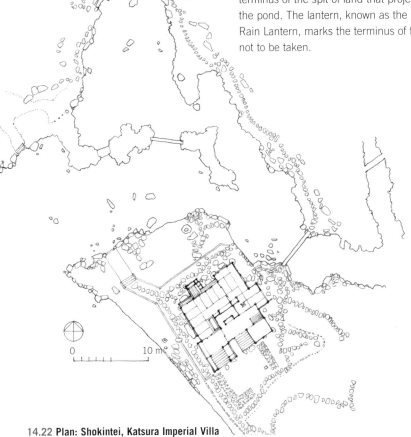

14.22 Plan: Shokintei, Katsura Imperial Villa

Ryoanji

Zen monks invented the dry meditation garden as a practical necessity. Earlier Japanese garden design had been based on Song Chinese examples, which were built on large estates with long stroll paths that had views created from the natural landscape and constructed ponds, islands, mountains, and even rivers complete with waterfalls. While the miniaturization of natural elements was a part of the design strategy, these gardens relied on size for their effect. In the 15th century, however, when the shoguns began to reduce plot sizes to accommodate their cities' larger populations, such full-fledged gardens became impossible. The newer generation of gardens, made by Zen masters, were designed around the principle of careful staged views. In the process, they created the dry garden, so called because they employed abstract means of representation, using, for example, white pebbles and moss to signify large bodies of water. The Zen monks particularly enjoyed creating visual koans, or quizzical conundrums, that could be meditated upon.

Ryoanji, the Temple of the Peaceful Dragon, contains the most famous of Japan's dry gardens, created around 1480 by an unknown designer in the estate of Hosokawa Masamoto, located in the northwestern foothills of Kyoto. The southern half of the estate contains a pond with an island and a circumambulatory stroll path, to which was added a rectangular dry garden with a bed of white gravel carefully raked to form east-west running bands. Within it were placed fifteen natural stones clustered in five groups. The gravel around them is raked in the manner of ripples in a pond. The precise meaning of this koan is left open. Perhaps the white field is an ocean and the rocks islands. The rocks could also stand for a tigress leading her cubs across a river—another common interpretation. Ultimately, the garden is not meant to convey a singular interpretation but to serve as an aid to meditation, with the empty space between the stones just as important as the stones themselves—or perhaps even more so.

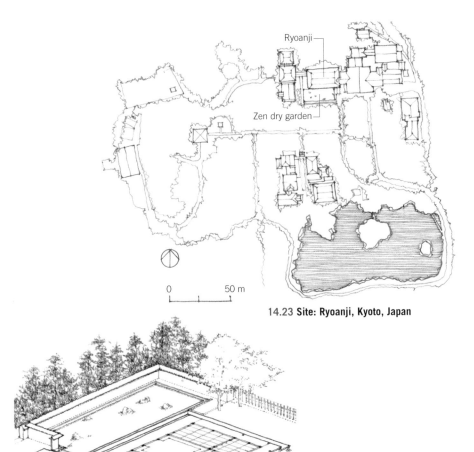

14.23 Site: Ryoanji, Kyoto, Japan

14.24 Pictorial view showing the relationship between Ryoanji and the Zen dry garden

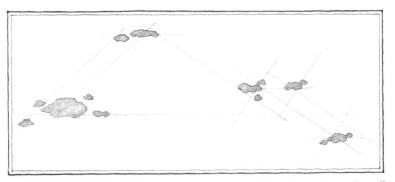

14.25 Dry garden at Ryoanji

14.26 Plan: Dry garden at Ryoanji

14.27 Ming dynasty China

The first Ming tomb built here was that of the third Ming emperor, Zhu Di, known as the Yongle Emperor, in 1409. Zhu Di moved the Ming capital to Beijing and built the Forbidden City. The Ming, continuing T'ang and Zhou funerary practices, designed their tombs in three parts—a long Spirit Path leading up to the tomb, a shrine for ceremonies and sacrifices to the dead, and the burial mound itself. However, unlike their predecessors, the Song, the Ming did not build a separate Spirit Path for each tomb; instead, they clustered all their tombs in a single valley off one Spirit Path with a single approach. The Ming also did away with the practice of sacrificing the emperor's "accompanying" concubines and servants and therefore did not need a separate chamber for them.

Ming Tombs

So efficient was the Ming bureaucracy that the reportedly indolent and pleasure-seeking ways of the seventh Ming emperor, Wanli (1573–1620), seems not to have affected the prosperity of his empire, and official ceremonies and presentations were often made to an empty throne. A large proportion of Wanli's time, along with an estimated eight million *taels* of silver, was spent in the design and construction of his tomb, which began in 1585, when he was only twenty-two years old. Much more than personalized egocentric attempts to guarantee an afterlife, tombs, and in particular royal tombs, were an integral part of the Chinese cosmology. Spirits of dead ancestors of even common people had to be fed and cared for, or else they were liable to visit misfortune upon future generations. The emperor's death, however, was particularly special, as he became part of heaven itself, and his tomb's architecture had to represent that transition. Many of China's royal tombs, going back to that of the First Emperor, Shi Huangdi, have still not been excavated. The thirteen Ming Tombs, of which only Wanli's has been explored, are among the most famous and best preserved. They are clustered in the valley of the Tianshou Mountains in Changping County, Hebei Province, about 80 kilometers northwest of Beijing.

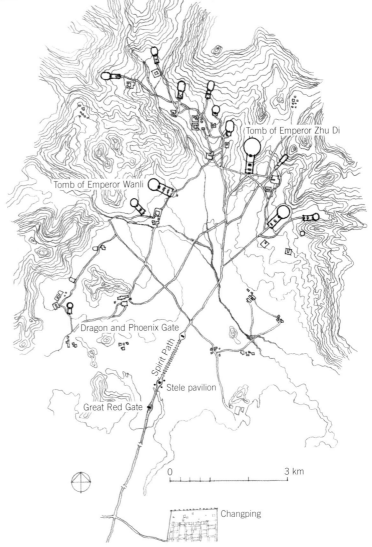

14.28 Area plan: Imperial Ming Tombs, near Beijing

The Yongle Emperor appropriated an area of about 330 square kilometers defined by a perimeter wall that encompassed a valley, the base hills of a mountain range, and rivulets feeding into a river running to the south. This area was protected by a prohibition against the cultivation or cutting of trees, and a village was established near the entrance to house people employed to maintain the land. About 1 kilometer beyond the *pai lou* was the Great Red Gate, the official entrance to the tomb grounds. (*Pai lou* is the generic term for gateways commemorating people who have led virtuous lives.) The building, square in plan, has a solid base, cut through with tall tunnel vaults in its axes that, at their center, frame a huge 10-meter-tall monolithic stele held up on the back of a tortoise. Poems, written by later emperors in praise of their ancestors, are carved on the stele. At this gate, the emperor dismounted and proceeded on foot. Just to the side of the gate, there was a pavilion, no longer extant, where the emperor and his retinue of about one thousand attendants rested and changed into the appropriate robes. From there, the emperor began his long walk down the Spirit Path.

As in earlier tombs, the main feature of the Spirit Path is its array of statues of mythical and real beasts and eminent nobles and generals, aligned on both sides. Twelve pairs of animals and six pairs of men symbolize an eternal guard, arrayed in the same manner in which the honor guard was prepared in the Forbidden City for ceremonial occasions. The animals are in pairs, one resting and one standing. At the end of this segment of the Spirit Path there is a small, three-portal gate, the center of which is blocked to prevent the entrance of evil spirits.

After passing through the sides of the gate, the Spirit Path continues in a gentle curve to the left and leads to a triple bridge across the river, straight to the Yongle Emperor's tomb. Subsidiary paths to the other tombs fan out from the main path like the branches of a tree. The tombs are a long distance from the main entrance—a walk of almost 6 kilometers from the *pai lou*. This walk, through a flat plain filled with carefully chosen fragrant trees, was often the subject of painting and poetry. As in the Forbidden City and Chinese imperial architecture in

14.29 Drum Tower of the Spirit Path, Ming Tombs

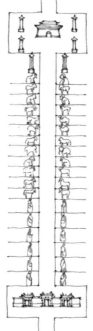

14.30 Spirit Path, Ming Tombs

14.31 Spirit Path, Ming Tombs

general, the path, as a monumental extension of space in the horizontal axis, was made at a scale appropriate only to the emperors. The horizontal extension of space was considered to be the measure of a building's significance. The Spirit Path thereby repeats the axis of the Forbidden City. But in another sense, it is the Forbidden City, with its fake mountain at the northern end, that copies the sacred axis embodied in the Spirit Path.

Conceptually, the Ming Tombs are a part of the same spatial-symbolic order as the Forbidden City and the Altar of Heaven. This order is in part feng shui but is mostly a spatialization of a social and spiritual order focused on the emperor: the symbolic order of Beijing was designed to enable the institution of the emperor, as a governmental and spiritual center, to be functional and visible. In the tombs, however, there were no quotidian needs, no citizenry to be governed. There, it was only the reigning emperor and his relationship with the ancestors, represented in the city by the empty space of the Altar of Heaven, which had to be spatialized, making for the purest representation of the intersection of the terrestrial world and the heavenly one. Each succeeding emperor was expected to visit the tombs of his predecessors on each of the anniversaries of their deaths. Site selection was critical. The Yongle Emperor picked a site for his tomb nestled at the base of the intersection of two low mountain ranges at the end of a hilly spur that points into a valley. This fit the dictates of feng shui, which required that two mountain ranges (the tiger and the dragon) provide a protective backdrop to the site to block evil northern spirits. (In the Forbidden City, the mountain is represented by the small artificial hill just beyond the north wall.)

14.32 Axial approach to the Ming Tombs

14.33 Underground chamber, Tomb of Emperor Wanli, Ming Tombs

The north-south axis was defined by the creation of the Spirit Path. As he did at the Altar of Heaven, a visiting emperor would have approached the site from the south, the direction of supplication. The entrance was marked by a stone ceremonial gate with five portals composed of six monolithic columns adorned with animals derived from native Chinese, Buddhist, and Indic sources. Unlike the Chinese convention that gave every important building a name that was then written on a tablet over its central entrance, the tablet on this particular gate was left empty, for it would have been inappropriate, so it was held, for mere mortals to announce the presence of the "sons of heaven."

14.34 Stele guarding the entrance to the tomb of Emperor Wanli

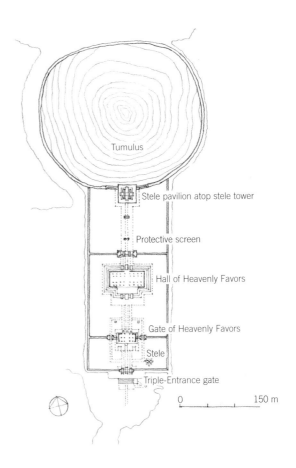

Tumulus

Stele pavilion atop stele tower

Protective screen

Hall of Heavenly Favors

Gate of Heavenly Favors

Stele

Triple-Entrance gate

0   150 m

14.35 Plan: Tomb of the Yongle Emperor (Changling)

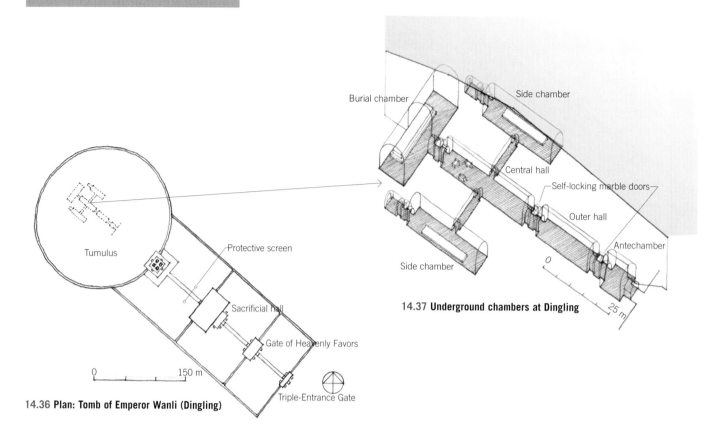

14.37 **Underground chambers at Dingling**

14.36 **Plan: Tomb of Emperor Wanli (Dingling)**

The thirteen tombs consist of a sequence of rectangular enclosures for rituals and sacrifices and a round or oval burial mound. The enclosures signify the terrestrial, and the circular mound the heavenly. Where the wall of the last enclosure and the wall of the circular enclosure meet is a stele tower with a pavilion on top of the base that permits access to the mound. Most of the tombs have only one or two enclosures, and only the largest three—Changling, Yongling, and Dingling—have three. Changling, the oldest and largest, begins with a triple-entrance gate leading into an enclosure that originally held a structure in which the emperor and his retinue could adjust their clothes. This led through a gate into the main court for sacrifices, which contained the Hall of Heavenly Favors—almost identical to the Hall of Supreme Harmony in the Forbidden City—replicating in death the architecture of life. Three marble terraces support the great hall (67 by 30 meters) with three stairs leading to it. Inside, sixty columns nearly 13 meters high each made from a single trunk

of old-growth timber called *machilus nanmu* support a double-eaved roof without any diagonal struts. The *dou-gong* on the exterior is ornamental, not structural. The coffered ceiling is painted blue, green, red, and gold. The Hall of Heavenly Favors and the Hall of Supreme Harmony are the two largest halls in China.

The tombs are defined by fortified earthen mounds with 3-meter-wide walls, buttressed on the outside to hold in the earth with no visible entry markers. They are planted with thujas and oak trees (since their roots are believed to be able to nourish the dead). At the apex of the hill is a small tumulus in the shape of a cone or long ridge. The tumulus is only representational; the actual tomb is far below the surface. Seen from the approach axis, the stele gate, the mound, and the mountain profiles are all part of one symbolic entity. The tumulus of Emperor Wanli's tomb, for example, lines up directly with the peak beyond. The approach to the offering table, which stands just in front of the base of the stele tower, is not flat, but actually a series of transitions marked by gates and thresholds.

The tomb of Emperor Wanli, located 27 meters below the surface, consists of three sacrificial enclosures and four interconnected barrel-vaulted chambers. Whereas the side chambers were empty and probably intended for concubines and family members, the central one contained three thrones for ritual objects. The burial casket of the emperor, the empress, and the highest concubine (elevated to empress when her son became the next emperor) were found intact in the main burial vault. The vaults were all made of white, polished marble. This tradition, which goes back to the tombs of the Han emperors, shows that although the Chinese had certainly mastered masonry skills, they chose to use them only for their tomb structures. One of the few places where a stone vault was used in a building above the terrain was in the Fasting Palace of the Altar of Heaven, where the emperor prepared himself for the all-important calendrical rituals. That room was, in essence, a type of tomb, for the emperor was expected to use it to purify himself through abstinence and fasting.

14.38 Potala Palace, Lhasa, Tibet (China)

Potala Palace

Buddhism was introduced into Tibet by
Mahayana monks traveling from India
and Nepal in the 8th century. By the
10th century, Nepal had begun to thrive
as a regional power, capturing significant
territories in Mongolia and China. The growth
of Tibet was, however, checked by the
Chinese well into the 15th century. Although
China's non-Han dynasties—the Liao and,
in particular, the Mongol Yuan—supported
Tibetan Buddhism, they made sure they
were politically subservient. The Ming paid
only lip service to Tibetan Buddhism since
their focus was on the revival of a Confucian
and Daoist state. As a consequence, the
Tibetans split into a number of competing
sects, variously identified by the color of
their habits as the red, white, and yellow
sects. But when the Ming dynasty began to
lose power, the Uigher Mongols under Altan
Khan, the descendants of the erstwhile Yuan
dynasty, converted to the Tibetan yellow sect;
after that, Tibetan Buddhism, or Lamaism,
spread quickly among the Mongols of Central
Asia. In 1641, Altan Khan's grandson, Gushri
Khan, defeated all the other Tibetan sects
and proclaimed Ngawang Losang Gyatso
(1617–82) the fifth Dalai Lama; he was not
only the spiritual head but also, for the first
time in Tibetan history, the political head of
Tibet. Just then the Mongolian Manchus had
taken over from the Ming, and one of their
first diplomatic acts was to invite the fifth
Dalai Lama to the Chinese court, where he
was received with full honors.

One of the fifth Dalai Lama's first acts was
to establish a new capital and build a new
palace that was identifiable as the seat of
both the spiritual and political power of the
Buddhist world. This was the Potala Palace, a
vast and majestic palace-mausoleum located
dramatically on a hill in the middle of the
valley of Lhasa, Tibet's "forbidden city."

The Lhasa River is a tributary of the
Tsangpo, which becomes the Brahmaputra
when it swings south around the Himalayas
and into India. At an elevation of 130 meters
above the valley, Marpo Ri hill stands above
a widened river bed at the bottom of a ravine
in the middle of which stand two steep, rocky
outcrops. On the higher and larger of these,
known as Red Hill, sits the Potala Palace,
360 meters long and 110 meters wide and
reaching to a maximum height of 170 meters.
It is oriented east-west, with the front facing
south toward the inner city. The setting is
dramatic. A jagged towering mountain range
forms a towering bowl. In the middle, the
rocky outcrop and the swiftly flowing Lhasa
are at the center of what literally seems like
the roof of the world.

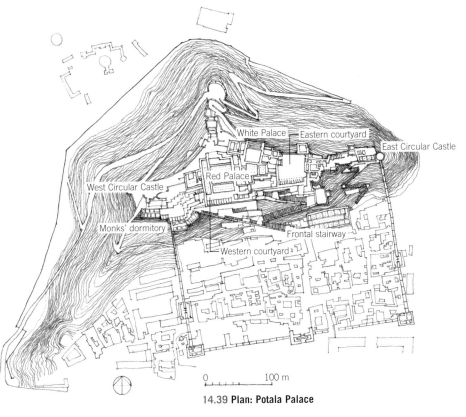

14.39 Plan: Potala Palace

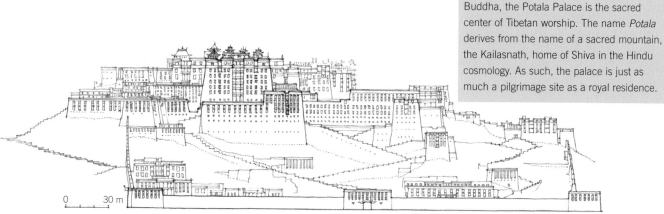

As the residence of the dalai lamas, considered to be living manifestations of the Buddha, the Potala Palace is the sacred center of Tibetan worship. The name *Potala* derives from the name of a sacred mountain, the Kailasnath, home of Shiva in the Hindu cosmology. As such, the palace is just as much a pilgrimage site as a royal residence.

0   30 m

14.40 South elevation: Potala Palace

Since it was meant to be defensible, the palace's primary massing is that of a fort. Thick, battered brick walls, painted white, rise steeply directly from the rock surface in a series of terraces that take over the entire summit of Red Hill. The walls step back and forth to accommodate the changing contours and to generate openings for the access paths. Solid and impenetrable at the bottom, the walls' higher reaches are punctuated by dark windows, which are few and simple at first but, at higher elevations, become larger and more richly embellished. The walls are topped by a prominent red coping. The visual terminus is a series of small, golden, Chinese-style roofs; not so large as to be the solitary focus, they are prominent enough to ensure that the eye comes to rest on them, providing a speck of metallic brilliance in a landscape dominated by gray rock. Long ramps, visible from the distance, wind their way up the side of the hill. Their slow ascents mark them as self-conscious processional paths leading to a place of pilgrimage.

The palace was built in two major phases. First the main ramparts and the western part, known as the White Palace, were built. Then this was partially rebuilt, and a Red Palace, which became the primary residence of the dalai lamas, was constructed. The White Palace houses large ceremonial halls for prayers, rooms for visiting dignitaries, and offices, while the Red Palace houses the audience hall as well as burial stupas for the dalai lamas. The roof of the palace opens onto a flat terrace where there are Chinese-style pavilions, gilded in copper, one for each dalai lama. At the foot of the Potala Palace, a square walled enclosure contains a network of governmental buildings.

Access to the Potala Palace begins at the end of the lower quadrangle, at a column erected to mark the completion of the Red Palace. The first ramp leads to subsidiary structures in the west, but then it switches back and heads up toward the White Palace. After another switchback, it comes to a point where the entrances into the Potala, which have been hidden until now, suddenly reveal themselves, nestled between the staggers of the walls. A stair to the east leads to the entrance of the White Palace and another, directly opposite, to the Red Palace. The high walls of the Potala itself are at hand, and for the pilgrim this is the first arrival threshold; several more follow. The usual entrance is through the White Palace. A tall rectilinear opening, with three open stories above, leads into a dark space with four columns.

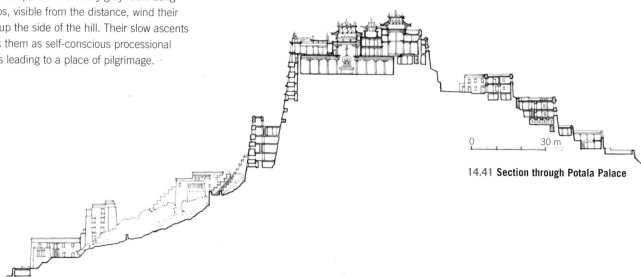

0   30 m

14.41 Section through Potala Palace

14.42 Potala Palace

From there the path turns left, proceeds down a narrow corridor, turns right, and arrives at a small curved court, where the second threshold to the palace is located. A flight of stairs and a two-column vestibule leads to another corridor that turns left into the eastern courtyard, the ceremonial arrival space of the Potala. This is the pilgrims' third and final threshold.

This courtyard is surrounded by a two-story enclosure and dominated by the canted mass of the White Palace at the northwestern corner. A central stairway leads into the six levels of the White Palace, highlighted by characteristic Tibetan windows made from brightly painted wooden frames and elaborately carved sunscreens. The elaboration and size of the windows increase with each story, the highest one terminating in the cornice. Internally, the main structural frame is made from wood, with rooms organized around a courtyard on the upper levels. This mode of construction and elevational representation is typical of Tibetan architecture, a consequence of its long intercourse with Nepalese architecture and culture.

The Red Palace contains pillared prayer halls and the salt-dried and embalmed remains of eight dalai lamas, marked by eight white stupas called *chortens*. The largest and most elaborate of these is the stupa for the fifth Dalai Lama.

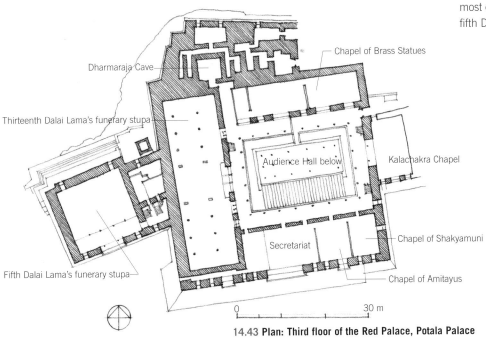

Dharmaraja Cave

Chapel of Brass Statues

Thirteenth Dalai Lama's funerary stupa

Audience Hall below

Kalachakra Chapel

Secretariat

Chapel of Shakyamuni

Fifth Dalai Lama's funerary stupa

Chapel of Amitayus

0 30 m

14.43 Plan: Third floor of the Red Palace, Potala Palace

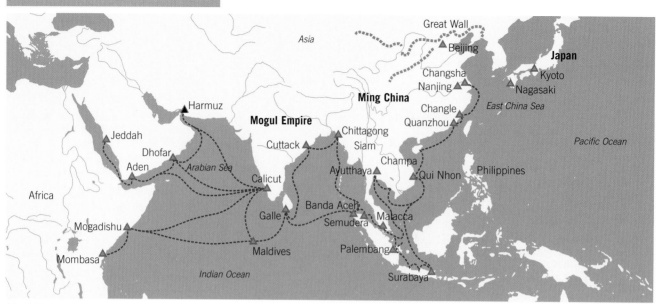

14.44 The voyages of Zheng He

Voyages of Zheng He

The first Ming emperor, Taizu, also called the Hongwu emperor, sponsored a series of famous naval voyages between 1405 and 1433 with at least seven of them traversing the "western ocean," which could be either the Indian or Pacific ocean. The voyages were commanded by Zheng He (1371–1435), a Muslim from China's Yunnan Province whose father and grandfather had made the hajj to Mecca and who, therefore, knew of Islamic cartographic advances. Zheng He's mission was not economic but diplomatic, seeking to establish ties with other nations. Some of the voyages had as many as three hundred ships and twenty-seven thousand sailors in all, and they reached as far as Mombasa in Africa.

The Chinese economy was integrally tied to trade, and these voyages were meant to expand China's trading horizons. The Chinese traded with the Dutch, who controlled Java, as well as with the Spanish and Portuguese. It is estimated that as much as one-third of all the silver extracted from South America was brought to China to pay for porcelain, silk, and other luxury goods. To feed this export economy, huge kilns were built at Jingdezhen in Jiangxi Province, which produced annually an estimated 100,000 small ceramic pieces and 50,000 larger pieces. Still preserved as ceiling decorations in the Santos Palace in Lisbon are 260 Chinese plates and bowls.

In 1449 the Mongolians ambushed an expedition led by Emperor Zhengtong, wiped out the Chinese army, and captured the emperor. Stability returned only in 1457 when Zhengtong recovered the throne. The Mongol threat, yet once again, shook the Ming court, which resolved to disband the expensive explorative sea voyages and concentrate instead on fortifying against the Mongolians. In 1474 the Ming general Wang Yueh insisted on and received approval to extensively rebuild the Great Wall. Almost forty thousand troops were set to work to build not only vast segments of the wall but also its accompanying fortifications, signal towers, and stockades. The Ming Great Wall occupies the rest of the last range of hills before the mountains level off in the northern deserts of Mongolia. And so the long-term possibilities of Zheng He's naval expeditions, were traded in for the immediate and urgent need to secure the Great Wall system. And as is so often the case, the wall system, ultimately did not work.

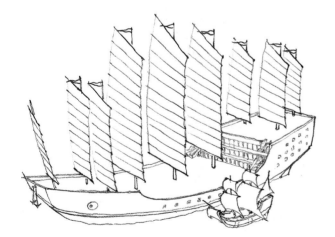

14.45 Ming dynasty treasure ship compared with Vasco da Gama's *São Gabriel*

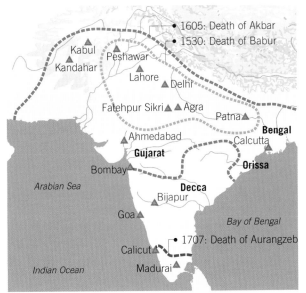

14.46 **Development of the Mughal Empire**

14.47 **Humanyun's Tomb, Delhi, India**

The Mughals

The Delhi sultanates, with their various competing interests, fell prey to an outside conqueror. Babur, a descendant of the Timur line, established the Mughal dynasty that, at the time of his death in 1530, comprised a huge empire that stretched from the Deccan to Turkestan. Babur's oldest son, Humanyun, lost the throne in 1540 to Sher Shah Sur, an Afghan and former ally, who, though he ruled for only fifteen years, established a centralized system of administration on the foundations of which later Mughals expanded. Humanyun regained the Delhi throne by 1555 but died a year later. He was succeeded by the eighteen-year-old Jalal-ud-Din Akbar (1556–1605), who laid the foundation of—and consolidated—the Mughal Empire. His grandson Khurram Shah Jahan (1628–57) was the beneficiary. One was an uneducated and idiosyncratic idealist, the other an indolent and cultured aesthete; both were responsible for using their vast wealth for two of the finest architectural creations of south Asia: the city of Fatehpur Sikri and the Taj Mahal.

Humayun's Tomb

Humayun's principal wife, Begai Begum, brought in a Persian architect living in Bukhara, Mirak Mirza Ghiyas, to design her husband's tomb (1570). It was located to the east of a tomb designed for one of Sher Shah's noblemen in 1547. Humayun's Tomb was to become the prototype that influenced the design of the Taj Mahal some fifty years later. Faced with red sandstone, it sits in the middle of a large square garden divided into quadrants by causeways; these are further divided into nine smaller sections in the manner of the *chahar baghor* four-garden plan of Persian provenance. Set into the axis of each causeway is a water channel with small, square lily ponds at the intersections. The eastern wall was built directly on the Yamuna River. (Over time, the river moved farther to the east.) Its main gate was on the south, although entrances were built in the center of all four walls. The building has two platforms: a low first platform with chamfered ends followed by the second main platform, which contains secondary arcaded and vaulted chambers.

Stairs from the central arch lead to the upper platform. The building itself is an octagon with eight surrounding chambers on two levels. A bulbous dome covered in marble sits on a high drum. Passageways connect all the chambers—an unusual feature that may be associated with the Sufi practice of circumambulating the burial chamber. A tombstone marker indicating the actual tomb below sits under the main dome that is raised on gigantic piers. The interior is plastered and painted in white and a delicate orange-red that closely matches the red sandstone used on the exterior.

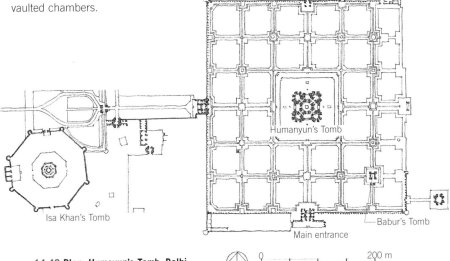

14.48 **Plan: Humayun's Tomb, Delhi**

Fatehpur Sikri

Begun in 1561 and abandoned a mere
fourteen years later due to lack of water,
Fatehpur Sikri's origins lie in Akbar's close
connections with Sufiism. Sheikh Salim
Chisti, a Sufi mystic, lived on a stony
escarpment 48 kilometers west of the capital,
Agra. Akbar traveled to Salim Chisti on foot
to beg for the gift of a son, who was born a
year later. To give thanks and to live in close
proximity to his mentor, Akbar decided to
build a new mosque and palace complex
on the long and narrow stony escarpment,
known then simply as *Sikri* (from *shukri*, or
"thanksgiving" in Persian).

The first structure built at Fatehpur Sikri
was the Jami Masjid, or Friday Mosque.
Because the mosque had to be oriented due
west, it is at an angle to the escarpment. The
multiple courts of the royal palace that were
built next were also are aligned with the Jami
Masjid rather than with the escarpment, so
that the whole complex staggers down the
axis of the ridge. The spatial implications
resulting from the shift in orientation are
immense. Because the center of the courts
are not aligned with each other axially, as is
the case in most courtyard-based complexes,
it makes for a dynamic diagonal sequencing
of spatial experience full of unexpected
expansions and contractions. Axial
expectations are manipulated to heighten
the surprises. For instance, the view from
Birbal's House, at the center of its court, into
the Pachisi Court, aligns with one of the arms
of Anup Talao. This sets up the expectation
that Anup Talao must also be at the center of
its court. Walking straight down the axis into
the Pachisi Court, however, reveals that Anup
Talao is at one end of its court, revealing the
diagonal character of the axis.

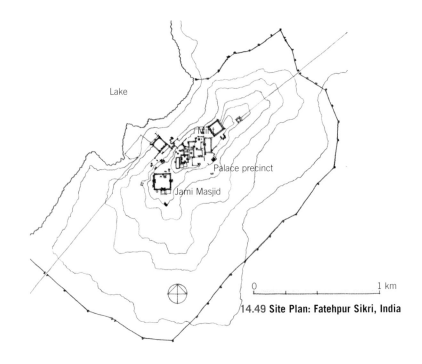

14.49 Site Plan: Fatehpur Sikri, India

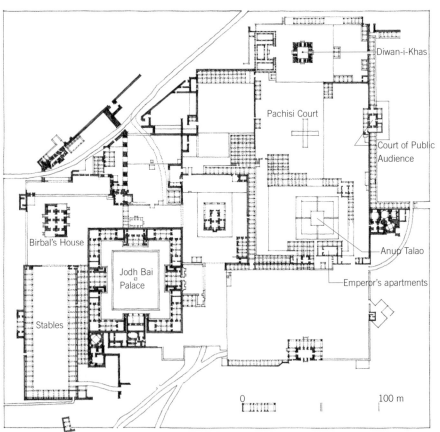

14.51 Plan: Palace precinct, Fatehpur Sikri

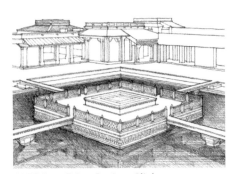

14.50 Anup Talao, Fatehpur Sikri

The 165-by-133 meter Jami Masjid has a huge courtyard, with gates on three sides and, to the west, the *qibla* wall, centered on an *iwan* with a central dome flanked by two smaller side domes. The *mihrab* and the western wall are elaborately decorated with inlay work of stone mosaic and glazed tiles with azure blue and gold inscriptions. Except for the *qibla* wall, the rest of the mosque is made of red sandstone with occasional marble inlay. The sandstone, faceted like wood, is used in the columns structurally and not as cladding, an innovation that gives to the colonnade a delicacy denied to clad stone piers. Indeed, structural red sandstone columns are used throughout Fatehpur Sikri, and where thicker walls were necessary, they were all clad with the same red sandstone (with the occasional marble and semiprecious stone inlay), giving the entire complex a unified impression.

Buland Darwaza

The Buland Darwaza (1573) is an ingenious work at the intersection of architecture and urban design. It was built in the Jami Masjid of Sikri, which was, until the late 19th century, the largest mosque in South Asia. In 1573, Akbar rebuilt the southern gate of the mosque after his much sought-after victory over Gujarat. Renamed Buland Darwaza, or Victory Gate, the 54-meter-high structure is so tall that it ran the risk of overwhelming the *qibla* wall of the mosque, for which it is just an entrance. The skill of Sikri's designers is evident in their handling of the building's section, which ensures a majestic reading on the outside but not on the inside. First, they exaggerated the external height of the Darwaza by building a lofty flight of stairs in front of it to take advantage of the mosque's location at the very edge of the escarpment. Its impact on the mosque is mitigated by the stepping down of the section; while the exterior elevation rises to the full height, the interior elevation finishes below the height of the *qibla iwan*.

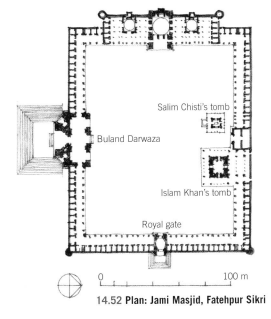

14.52 Plan: Jami Masjid, Fatehpur Sikri

Salim Chisti's tomb

Buland Darwaza

Islam Khan's tomb

Royal gate

0 — 100 m

14.53 Exterior profile: Buland Darwaza

14.54 Interior profile: Buland Darwaza

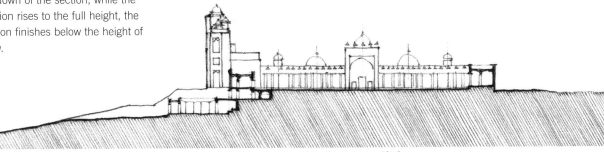

14.55 Section: Jami Masjid, Fatehpur Sikri

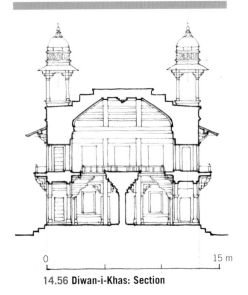

0   15 m

14.56 Diwan-i-Khas: Section

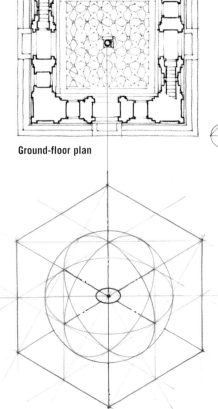

Ground-floor plan

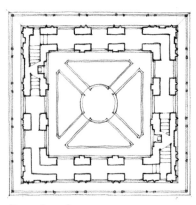

Upper-story plan

14.57 The emperor's seat, the conceptual center of Diwan-i-Khas

Diwan-i-Khas

Akbar's Diwan-i-Khas is a singular building in the history of architecture. It was conceived by Akbar, who was an exceptional and, in many senses, a very modern thinker. Although he was illiterate, he was very curious about the empire he had just created. He surrounded himself with philosophers and aestheticians, and searched for a philosophical and religious practice that could, to his mind, resolve the multiplicity of and contradictions among beliefs in his world. Akbar constructed a new syncretic and pluralistic cult, or religious practice, called the Din-i-Ilahi, or Divine Religion, with a fairly generic creed of abstinence, meditation, beneficence, politeness, and mystical monotheism. In 1582, at Fatehpur Sikri, Akbar officially proclaimed the birth of Din-i-Ilahi and called a general council meeting of members of all faiths to resolve all their religious differences. The core of Din-i-Ilahi was *sulh-i-kul*, or tolerance of all thoughts that benefit mankind. Akbar proposed himself, as a unique ambassador of God, as the central institution for resolving religious differences.

The concepts of Din-i-Ilahi are manifested in the Diwan-i-Khas, or "royal audience hall." It is the solitary object-in-space building in the main court, a two-story square box with four *chattris* at the corners made entirely out of red sandstone. A deep overhanging *chajja* casts a prominent shadow over the upper-story elevation. At 13.18 meters, the width of the building is the same as its height taken to the top of the *chattris*, making it symbolically a perfect cube. The drama of the Diwan-i-Khas is its interior. In its double-height space, located in the center of the overall volume and supported by a single pillar with a mushroom top of sandstone brackets, is a round platform that seems to hover in midair. It is connected at the corners with narrow bridges forming a cruciform pattern. A balcony runs around the interior at the second-story level. It functioned as an idiosyncratic audience hall, with the emperor listening to supplicants from above and consulting with ministers from the various philosophical and religious positions sitting at the ends of the bridges. The emperor's position, held up by a single column, was at the very center of the building, both in plan and section. Indeed, the emperor would sit at the very center of the cube and conceptual sphere implied by the building. This is a spatialization of the position occupied by the emperor, who was at the center—that is, equidistant from all philosophical positions—in Din-i-Ilahi. As a direct spatialization of a philosophical ideal, the Diwan-i-Khan can be described as a theoretical project. It had no known precedent and was never copied again.

14.58 Emperor's seat, Diwan-i-Khas

14.59 Taj Mahal, Agra, India

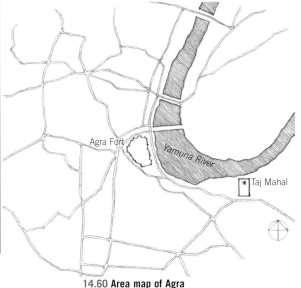

14.60 Area map of Agra

Rauza-I Munavvara (Taj Mahal)

Having inherited a vast and prosperous empire, Shah Jahan (1628–58) enjoyed the dividends of peace. He was dedicated to poetry, art, literature, and most of all to architecture, expending vast resources to build palaces, mosques, and tombs all across his empire, especially in Delhi, where he built a brand-new city called Shahjahanabad. In the latter half of his reign, however, the bulk of Shah Jahan's energies were devoted to the creation of the funerary tomb for Mumtaz Mahal, his favorite queen and granddaughter of the fabled Nur Jehan. The tomb was known to the Mughals as the Rauza-I Munavvara (the "Illumined Tomb") because of the luster and transparency of its marble. Later it was also referred to as Rauza-I-Mumtaj Mahal, which the English contracted to Taj Mahal in the 19th century.

Mumtaz Mahal died unexpectedly in 1631 while giving birth to her fourteenth child. Twenty-thousand workmen labored for fifteen years on her tomb. On every anniversary of Mumtaz's death, Shah Jahan staged the Urs celebration at the Taj Mahal. (Urs celebrations involve prayers and song in praise of the deceased, usually a saint.) The first Urs occurred on June 22, 1632, even before the tomb was completed. Shah Jahan was also buried on Mumtaz's right, feet facing south, and closer to the Ka'aba, as required by Islam. The Taj Mahal is thus truly the tomb of both Mumtaz Mahal and Shah Jahan.

Controversy surrounds the identity of the Taj Mahal's architect. Historical records list several people responsible for the tomb, or parts of it. Ismail Khan from Turkey may have designed the dome. Qazim Khan from Lahore cast its gold finial. Chiranjilal, a local lapidary from Delhi, was the chief sculptor and mosaicist. Amanat Khan from Shiraz was the chief calligrapher. Other specialists included sculptors from Bukhara, calligraphers from Syria and Persia, inlayers from south India, and stonecutters from Baluchistan. Thirty-seven men can be counted in its creative nucleus. In this sense, the Taj Mahal was a global project. Yet given that Shah Jahan personally supervised the design and approved every aspect of the project, he must be recognized as the chief architect of the Taj Mahal.

Although the bulk of the building material is from South Asia, the Taj Mahal's ornamental materials came from all around Eurasia. Its marble and red sandstone came from the hills of Makrana, near Jaipur, Rajasthan. From Central Asia came nephrite jade and crystal; from Tibet, turquoise; from upper Burma, yellow amber; from Badakhshan in northeastern Afghanistan, lapis lazuli; from Egypt, chrysolite; and from the Indian Ocean, rare shells, coral, and mother-of-pearl. Topazes, onyxes, garnets, sapphires, and bloodstones were among the forty-three types of precious and semiprecious stones from all around India that were used.

The main tomb is on the southern bank of the Yamuna River on a vast platform 103 meters square and 7 meters high, erected on arches. To its west stands a diminutive mosque, made of sandstone, with three modest marble domes. To its east is an identical structure, placed there to provide symmetry. Reflected in the wide waters of the Yamuna, which flows slowly in Agra, the Taj Mahal seems to be an apparition of domes and minarets rising above the plain. The side usually depicted today is actually the building's rear; the Mughal emperors accessed it from the water, arriving by means of a special barge that docked at the northeastern edge of the platform, from which a stair leads up to the tomb.

Land-based access to the Taj is from its southern garden. The simple and discrete red sandstone walls of its perimeter betray little of the drama that awaits inside. A small gate in the middle of the wall leads into a quadrangular enclosure with spaces for maintenance workers and shops. Stepping out beyond the wall is the main gate of red sandstone and marble, a rectangular *iwan* surmounted by a string of closely spaced *chattris*. In the center, a single large pointed arch opens onto the entrance bay, which telescopes down into the actual entrance arch itself. From there the main body of the Taj Mahal is perfectly framed.

The tomb sits at the end of a 300-meter square garden divided into quadrants (each further divided into further quadrants) known as the *char bagh* (meaning "four gardens"), which is a representation of the Islamic Garden of Paradise. Four channels, representing the four rivers of Paradise flow out from the center. The Islamic Garden of Paradise is a reinterpretation of the Garden of Eden from the Old Testament. Deciduous and evergreen trees fill the garden.

Once through the gate, the full frame of the Taj Mahal jumps into focus. Even at that distance the Taj Mahal fills the frame. The backdrop, given the hidden presence of the Yamuna River, is empty or, rather, always filled by the color of the sky. Water channels, with fountains down their middle, are wide and generous. They reflect the tomb and further magnify it. The slender three-story minarets create an implied cube that contains the Taj Mahal, making the tomb three-dimensional. The double dome of the tomb, however, rises above the minarets, so that it is only the dome (conceptually the dome of heaven) that rise above the imaginary plain supported by the minarets.

The translucent white marble that covers the entire surface of the tomb absorbs and reflects light. In the mornings and evenings, it has a reddish hue; during the day, it is a subdued white with a slight bluish tinge; and on moonlit nights, it is a brilliant white. On bright days, the light blurs the edges of the tomb, making it shimmer. Since every surface is covered in the same white marble, even the shadows are softened. At dusk and dawn, the Taj Mahal appears to float weightlessly, an ethereal, uncanny apparition.

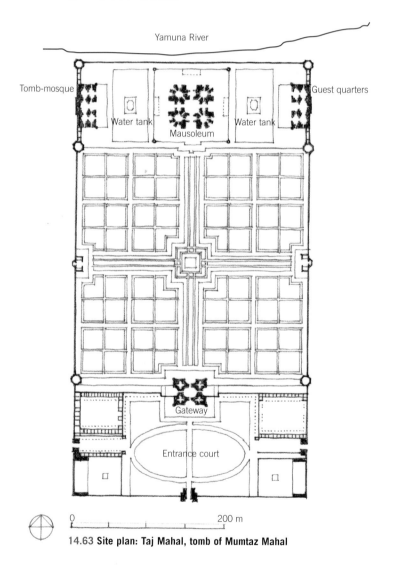

14.61 View of the main gateway to the Taj Mahal

14.63 Site plan: Taj Mahal, tomb of Mumtaz Mahal

14.62 Taj Mahal

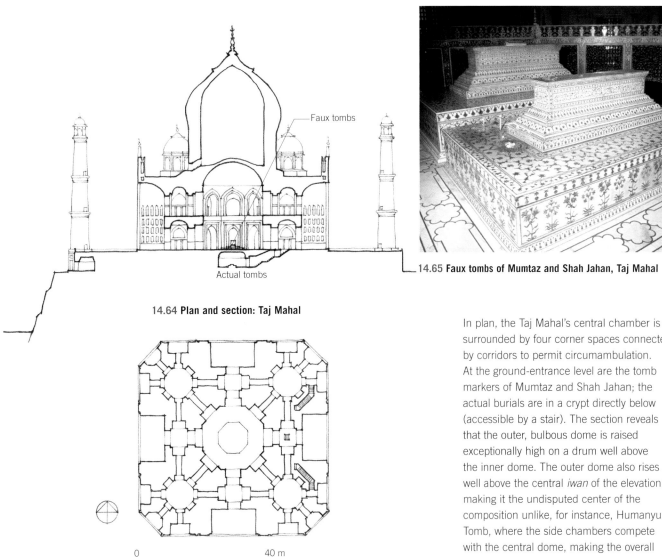

Faux tombs

Actual tombs

14.64 Plan and section: Taj Mahal

14.65 Faux tombs of Mumtaz and Shah Jahan, Taj Mahal

0   40 m

In plan, the Taj Mahal's central chamber is surrounded by four corner spaces connected by corridors to permit circumambulation. At the ground-entrance level are the tomb markers of Mumtaz and Shah Jahan; the actual burials are in a crypt directly below (accessible by a stair). The section reveals that the outer, bulbous dome is raised exceptionally high on a drum well above the inner dome. The outer dome also rises well above the central *iwan* of the elevation, making it the undisputed center of the composition unlike, for instance, Humanyun's Tomb, where the side chambers compete with the central dome, making the overall structure more squat than tall. The side *iwans* are faceted only on the outer side and not on the inner (as at Humanyun's Tomb), and the articulation of all the horizontal elements has been decidedly subdued in favor of the vertical ones. Indeed, a distinguishing characteristic of the Taj Mahal's massing is that in elevation, all the elements are clustered and hierarchically arranged to ensure that they do not compete with each other and instead build up the centrality of the main dome. Even the *chattris* have been clustered right next to the central dome, almost as if they were supporting domes themselves. Drawing an imaginary line along the edges of the central dome and the *chattris* yields a triangle or a pyramid framed by the four minarets.

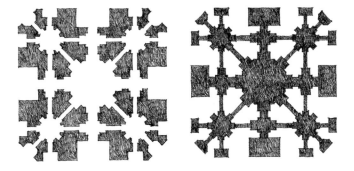

14.66 Mass and space rendered as figures, Taj Mahal

Vijayanagara

The brothers Harihara and Bukka escaped from captivity under Ala-ud-Din Khilji, to establish a new kingdom in the mid-14th century that resisted the rising tide of Islamic rule for 250 years. Consolidating Chalukyan, Hoysala, and late Chola territories, Vijayanagara built up its wealth by investing in Cholan decentralized temple-based administration and by irrigating new lands. A complex of canals, dams, and aqueducts irrigated the surrounding lands, bring water to the city, and fed the palace's tanks and baths. Commerce between the Portuguese, who captured Goa in 1510, and Vijayanagara was particularly important.

Its capital was located to maximize defense. Difficult to traverse rocky hills and the impassable Tungabhadra River provided defense from the north and west, the primary directions of a potential attack. The city itself was located on an uneven plateau, and the urban area was built into the gullies and valleys of the terrain.

Vijayanagara's temples and palaces were aligned to the cardinal directions, but three long market streets emanating from the temples are all mysteriously aligned about 2 degree south of east. The main temples are freestanding on the southern bank of the Tungabhadra, but the palaces and the city are enclosed in a fortified wall. The palace complexes are bound in their own enclosures. A "hundred-columned hall" and a huge platform, the Mahanavami Dibba, were designed to stage the frequent tribute ceremonies by vassals. An elaborate ceremonial tank and bathing pool, both fed by aqueducts, were part of the main palace. A long passageway sliced between two palaces gave public access to the Ramachandra Temple, the oldest and most sacred temple in Vijayanagara.

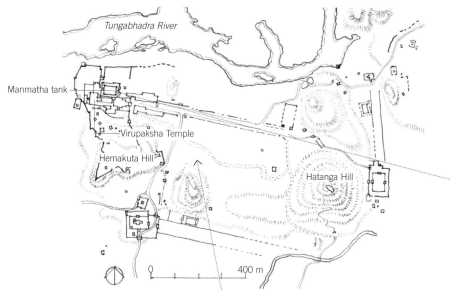

14.67 Site plan: Vijayanagara temples, India

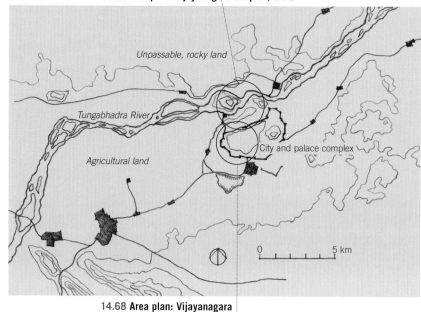

14.68 Area plan: Vijayanagara

14.69 Royal tank with aqueduct, Vijayanagara

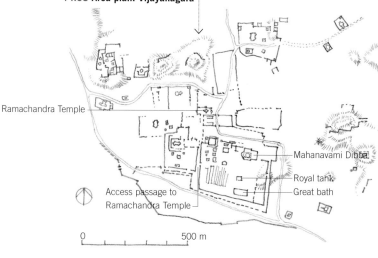

14.70 Site plan: Vijayanagara palaces

Tungabhadra River

Waterfront bathing ghats

Manmatha tank

Gopuram from ghats

Virupaksha lingam

Gopuram

Bronze *nandi*

To market street

0   80 m

14.71 Plan: Virupaksha Temple, Vijayanagara

The Virupaksha, Vijayanagara's most important temple, started as a small 10th-century Shiva shrine, with nearby ghats on the Tungabhadra. Over time it grew into a gigantic urban complex in itself, extending both to the water to the north and to the market street to the east. The *nandi* enclosure was added in the 15th century; the open *mandapa*, surrounding cloister, and the two *gopurams* were built early in the 16th century by Krishnadevaraya (r. 1509–29), Vijayanagara's main period of growth. Krishnadevaraya also formalized the tank and expanded the ghats. All the subsidiary shrines were integrated into the complex over time. The Virupaksha, like all other temples, opens into a long market street, effecting a direct connection between commerce and religion. All the temples also visually connected with each other and significant hilltops that themselves had small temples on them.

14.72 Market street in the landscape, Vijayanagara

14.73 **Bijapur, Vijayanagar, and the neighboring region**

14.74 **Tomb of Ibrahim II, Bijapur, India**

Bijapur

An alliance of the armies of Golconda, Bijapur, Bidar, and Gulbarga defeated and laid Vijayanagara to waste in 1565. The Bijapur dynasty, founded by Yusuf Adil Shah (1489–1510), benefited the most from the fall of Vijayanagara. Yusuf built Bijapur into a citadel with 10 kilometers of walls and six gates. Whereas his buildings were rather austere, those of Ibrahim Adil Shah II (1580–1627) are sumptuous and celebratory. Ibrahim II lavished attention on the tomb and mosque complex he built originally for his wife but that eventually held his own tomb and those of the rest of his family. The two square off on a single platform placed asymmetrically within a larger enclosure. The freestanding mosque has five arches three bays deep, with a bulbous dome over the central bays. A deep parapet supported by closely spaced brackets rounds out at the corners in a profusion of brackets; these spin tall, thin minarets culminating in small bulbous domes—almost complete rounds—supported like balls on a bed of flower petals. Similarly, the central dome appears to be a complete sphere, supported by tall lotus petals. The four corner minarets define a spatial field twice the height of the primary building at the center of which is the central dome with its own mini corner minarets. Ibrahim II's tomb, on the east side, abuts the edge of the compound. Although it has seven arches on each side in a varying rhythm of widths, the tomb's overall vocabulary harmonizes with the mosque.

14.75 **Section and plan: Tomb of Ibrahim II, Bijapur**

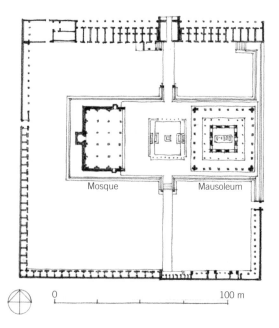

Mosque   Mausoleum

0   100 m

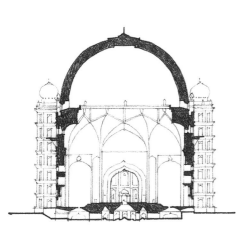

14.76 Section: Gol Gumbaz, Bijapur

14.77 Gol Gumbaz, Bijapur

The most unusual of Bijapur's buildings is the Gol Gumbaz, the largest single-chambered building ever constructed. It was a tomb built by Ibrahim II's successor, Muhammad Adil Shah (1627–57), for himself. Eight intersecting pointed arches, springing from two rotated squares, support both a round platform and the gigantic hemispherical dome. Built of brick, the dome is 3.5 meters thick at the base, has six small openings, and a flat section at the crown. Its supporting walls are largely plain and unornamented. The main entrance is to the west. In the middle, directly below the intersections of the arches, there is a simple platform with the tombs of Muhammad and his family at the center. Outside there are four corner turrets with simple domes articulated as towers.

Palace of Thanjavur

Thanjavur in southern India was taken by Vijayangara in 1535, but conquered by the rival Marathas in 1674. A palace begun in the 16th century was finished under the new Maratha kings. The entrance is through a large quadrangular courtyard leading to a remarkable—and unique—palace structure that simulates a Hindu temple. But whereas Hindu temples are solid, here the building has actual floors becoming progressively smaller and narrower as they rise. Nearby is a tower, the Durbar Hall, that was used as a watchtower and armory.

14.78 Palace of Thanjavur, Tamil Nadu, India

Isfahan

Throughout the 16th century in Persia, various dynasties vied for control, with the Safavids (who originated in Azerbaijan) led by Shah Ismail I (1501–24) finally winning out in 1501. The population of Persia until that time had been chiefly Sunni, but Ismail enforced adherence to the Shi'ite sect and began a campaign of conversion and unification. He also sought to retake what had been lost between 1501 and 1587 to the Ottomans. Under Shah Abbas (1587–1629), Isfahan—located almost in the center of Iran between Tehran and Fars—was made the capital (1598) and rebuilt into one of the largest cities in the world and the focus for all the artistic energy in the country. With a population of about half a million, Isfahan soon became a grand cosmopolitan center visited by English and Dutch merchants and European artists and diplomats—the latter hoping to secure alliances with the Safavid court against their common enemy, the Ottomans. A famous rhyme, *Isfahan nesf-eh jahan* ("Isfahan is half the world") was coined in the 16th century to express the city's grandeur. The new layout exemplified the most extensive urban planning in the world west of China.

Previously, the central part of the city lay next to the old Friday Mosque. Though many of the old buildings in that area were restored by Abbas, he instructed his planners to create a new urban center to the south and named it Naqsh-I Jahan ("Design of the World"). It consisted of a vast, rectangular open space that served as the city's new civic and commercial center. To its west was a monumental boulevard, Chahar Bagh Avenue, some 4 kilometers long, with canals, fountains, and trees, and flanked by palaces of the nobility. The boulevard stretched across the Zayanda River over a 300-meter-long multitiered bridge that connected the city to several garden estates (*chahar bagh* means "garden retreat") to the south. These estates were large, walled enclosures with pools, promenades, and pavilions. The central compositional element—and the link between the commercial district and the avenue—was the Imperial Palace in its own walled precinct, the Naqsh-I Jahan garden.

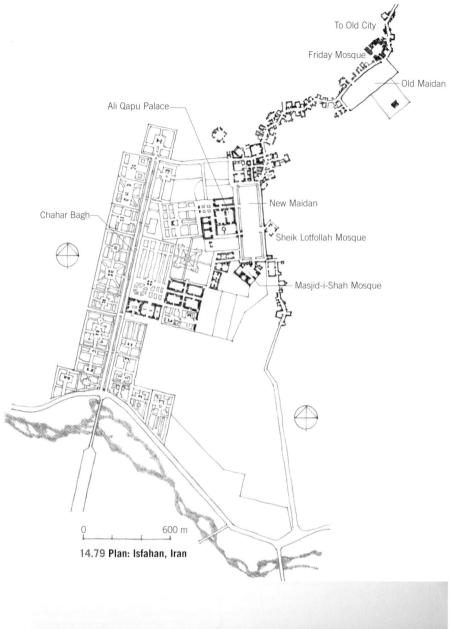

14.79 Plan: Isfahan, Iran

14.80 Main square of Isfahan

14.81 Masjid-i-Shah Mosque, Isfahan

The Masjid-i-Shah Mosque, begun in 1611, is set at a 45-degree angle to the square so it can face in the direction of Mecca. Its main portal mirrors the entrance to the bazaar to the north. The mosque, whose architect was Muhammad Riza, uses the four-*iwan* scheme, with a central courtyard 70 meters square surrounded by two-story arcades noted for a calm balance between volumetric organization, decorative detail, and unifying symmetry. (The plan is, in fact, distinguishable from many other such buildings by its unusual concern for such symmetry.) The domed sanctuary is flanked by rectangular chambers covered by eight domes that serve as winter prayer halls. These halls lead to rectangular courts surrounded by arcades that also serve as madrasas. The entrance portal is a tour de force of tile decoration, executed in a full palette of six colors (dark blue, light blue, white, black, yellow, and green). Glittering tiers of *muqarnas* fill the half-dome, some panels of which are decorated with stars and vines scrolling from vases.

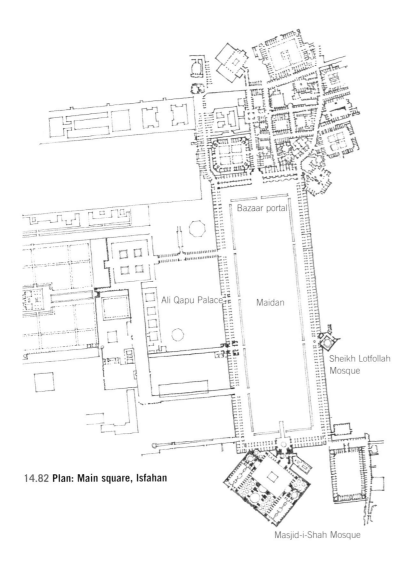

14.82 Plan: Main square, Isfahan

The new square—still today one of the largest in the world (512 by 159 meters)—was the symbolic center of the Safavid dynasty and its empire. It was used for festivals, markets, and games of polo. At night fifty thousand earthenware lamps hung from poles in front of the buildings to illuminate the square, which was designed with two stories of shops around its perimeter. The long, modular facades decorated with polychrome glazed tiles were broken only by the monumental entrances to four buildings: the Masjid-i-Shah Mosque in the south, the Sheikh Lotfollah Mosque in the east, the Ali Qapu Palace in the west, and the Great Bazaar to the north. A royal mint and a royal caravansary were also included in the ensemble, as well as baths and a hospital.

14.83 Interior: Masjid-i-Shah Mosque, Isfahan

Suleymaniye Complex

Suleyman I (1494–1566), the Ottoman sultan, not only expanded the reach of the Islamic armies but sought to turn Istanbul into the center of Islamic civilization through a series of building projects that included bridges, mosques, palaces, and various charitable and social establishments. He had the benefit of an extraordinarily gifted architect, Mimar Sinan (1491–1588), a contemporary of both Michelangelo and Andrea Palladio, with whom he is often compared. Sinan constructed nearly two hundred buildings in Constantinople alone, changing the face of the city and thereby creating Istanbul's unique silhouette of mighty domes and slender minarets. As an officer in the military and a trained engineer, Sinan assisted in the building of defense works and bridges and converted churches into mosques. With the capture of Cairo, he was promoted to chief architect and assigned the task of putting an Ottoman stamp on that city.

Though Sinan was consumed by the ambition to create a domed building modeled on the Hagia Sophia, his signature achievement was to fuse Seljuk features (with their emphasis on portals) with the stone mastery of Anatolia and the structural logic of Byzantine domes into a seamless and novel unity. This is nowhere better expressed than in Sinan's masterwork, the Suleymaniye Complex, begun in 1559, commissioned by Suleyman the Magnificent (1520–66) in the wake of his military successes in Iraq and the Balkans.

14.84 Ottoman Empire

The walled complex (216 by 144 meters) was terraced up a hill to take advantage of the view overlooking the Golden Horn to the north, and it contains, among other things, four madrasas, a medical madrasa and a hospice, a caravansary, a bath, and a bazaar. The spatial composition of the mosque is obviously modeled on the Hagia Sophia, following a trend already epitomized by the designer of the Beyazit Mosque (1501–6)—except that with Sinan as the architect, the composition is considerably tighter. The building is also, in many

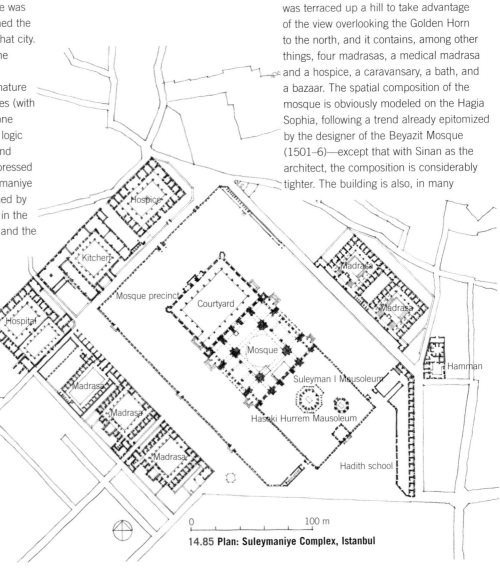

14.85 Plan: Suleymaniye Complex, Istanbul

14.86 Elevation and section: Suleymaniye Mosque

0   40 m

respects, very different from its Justinian model. It is dominated by a dome 48 meters high, with two flanking half-domes on the principal east-west axis and arches on the cross-axis. The weight descends to the ground by means of four massive columns of granite. On the exterior, the forecourt has a colossal portal with a tympanum framed by half-columns and minarets at the corners. Construction was organized by a court management office that, in consultation with the sultan, planned and oversaw the building project. Workers were Muslim as well as Christian and were organized according to

their skills. The decorative tiles were made in Iznik, the carpets in Anatolia and Egypt, and the colored and noncolored glass (the latter, a technological innovation of the time) in Venice. The limestone and granite came from the quarries on the Sea of Marmara, and the lead for the window grilles and doors from the Balkans.

While the Hagia Sophia was dark on the inside and designed to convey mystery, Sinan's building, lit from floor to dome in equal measure, is pervaded by a sense of clarity and discipline. The windows are numerous and wide, and since the galleries are pushed back, sunlight entering through

the windows of the sidewalls reaches directly into the central space. The architectural volumes are clearly legible and enhanced by a corbelled gallery at the level of the springing of the arches (somewhat similar in effect to the arch style at Santa Maria del Fiore in Florence) thereby unifying the spaces underneath the domes. By comparison, at the Hagia Sophia, the surface mosaics and gilding tend to blanket the form. Sinan's mosques served as models for Sultan Ahmed's mosque, built by Mehmet Agha, a student of Sinan; it is known as the Blue Mosque (1606–17).

14.87 Suleymaniye Complex

14.88 Vaulting in the Suleymaniye Mosque

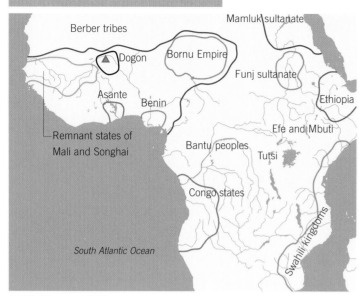

14.89 **Africa, ca. 1600**

14.90 **Dogon communal structure, Mali**

The Dogon of Mali

The African continent below the Islamic north consisted of a complex web of social and political organizations. Some societies, like the Asante, Yoruba, and Tutsi, maintained large states; others, like the Mbuti and Efe of Central Africa and the Kalahari Desert, continued a life of hunting and gathering. Despite the tendency to see African society as a collection of self-contained and self-supporting tribes, in reality, various groups had long and extensive contact with one another through trade. Neighboring societies may in fact have borrowed elements of each other's practices over the centuries, making it impossible to trace the precise origin of particular rituals. During the 1700s, aggressive Islamization from the north deeply impacted and changed West African nations but full Islamization, still a matter of political friction to this day, was never achieved; often a hybrid religious culture was created instead.

Western Africa was for a while dominated by the Mali Empire and then the Shonhai, both of which had strong trade connections to the north. But when the latter were defeated by Moroccan forces, the area was left to various regional powers, and the center of political and economic gravity moved to the coast (to the Asante kingdom in Ghana and, farther east, Benin, in the modern state of Nigeria) and eastward to the Bornu empire in Niger. The Mossi retained control of the Mali heartland in central Burkina Faso.

Between the 12th and 17th centuries, difficulties with the Mossi and with Islamic slave raiders forced several groups in Mali to move east, to more defensible positions along and below the Bandiagara Cliffs, a 150-kilometer-long sandstone escarpment in south-central Mali. The name *Dogon* was given to these people by the French in the early 20th century, even though they are not a homogeneous group, but a mosaic of different cultures, as is clear from their language, which consists of numerous dialects. In their new homes, the Dogon encountered a preexisting culture, the Tellem, whom they accepted into their society. The Tellem are the smithies for the Dogon, and they are responsible for making the important ancestor statues that are commissioned by Dogon elders for their ceremonies. The Tellem are held in awe because of their magical powers, but they are seen as lesser in the highly stratified society of the Dogon. Despite differences, the various groups have lived in remarkable peace over the centuries.

In Dogon society, an individual's status is determined by position within family groups and by hierarchies based on age and rules of descent. Religion involves the worship of ancestors as well as spirits. The Dogon believe, however, in one god, Amma, who is all-knowing and all-powerful and who upholds the balance between the living and the dead. Each clan has its own altar

14.91 **Dogon houses, Mali**

14.92 Dogon houses, Mali

14.93 Plan and section: A Dogon house in Mali (right) and a typical housing cluster (above)

Dogon society is spread out over a vast area of cities, villages, and clan compounds. Some of the larger cities have more than five thousand inhabitants and are composed of densely packed compounds. These compounds, called *ginna*, have different typologies, but they mostly consist of walled enclosures and squarish towers topped with conically shaped straw roofs. Another type is composed of two rectangular volumes separated to make a courtyard with an entrance at one end and a cylindrical kitchen at the other. In the cliffs, the compounds have a more compressed, arrangement, like a beehive. All compounds have granaries, divided up for different purposes. They are usually tall cylindrical structures with a door at the top and small portals below.

The word *ginna* also applies to the house of the eldest member of the clan, who descends from his clan's ancestral founder. This house will be larger and more complex than the others in the compound and will be based on the symbolism of the number one and the number seven, which is the sum of the female number, four, and the male number, three. At the social apex is the priest (*hogon*), whose house is appropriately large and visible, its facade painted with totem images. Civic buildings are known as *toguna*. They are basically artificial forests composed of high piles of sticks and straw held up on wooden, or sometimes stone, posts. They are low to the ground, so it is not possible to stand up under them: they are places for sitting and talking.

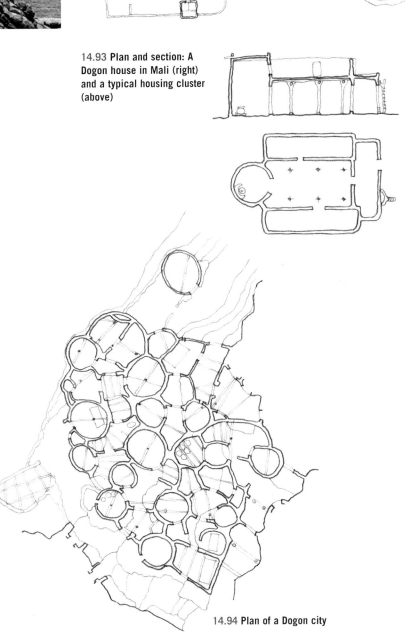

14.94 Plan of a Dogon city

14.95 Facade, Capitoline Museum, Rome

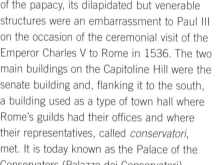

14.96 Plan: Piazza del Campidoglio, Rome

Italian High Renaissance

The seminal events of the 16th century, triggered by a recalcitrant German monk, were the Reformation and Counter-Reformation. When Martin Luther (1483–1546) nailed his ninety-five theses to a church door in Wittenberg in 1517, he only wanted to reform corruption in the Catholic Church. He had no idea that he was about to change the course of history. The rebellion against the Church spread and soon embroiled Europe in terrible wars for most of the next two centuries. Additional reform movements emerged, such as the Calvinists, who believed in a form of predestination. But all the various versions of countermovements can for the most part be summed up as *Protestant*, a word derived from *protest*. The response of the Catholic Church was called the Counter-Reformation, in which architecture played an important role, with great emphasis put on the attempt to reaffirm the splendor and dignity of the much-tarnished Roman Curia. Pope Paul III (Alessandro Farnese; r. 1534–49) initiated a series of bold building campaigns to this effect, chief among which was the construction of a piazza on the Capitoline Hill, the nominal site of the Roman senate. The papal route from St. John Lateran Church on the outskirts of Rome to the Vatican went through the Forum, up the hill, and over the Capitoline Hill. Though the area was of no particular importance to the political ideology of the papacy, its dilapidated but venerable structures were an embarrassment to Paul III on the occasion of the ceremonial visit of the Emperor Charles V to Rome in 1536. The two main buildings on the Capitoline Hill were the senate building and, flanking it to the south, a building used as a type of town hall where Rome's guilds had their offices and where their representatives, called *conservatori*, met. It is today known as the Palace of the Conservators (Palazzo dei Conservatori).

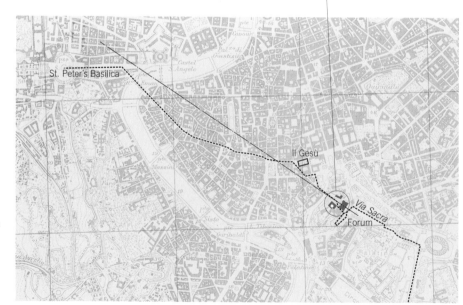

14.97 Location map: Piazza del Campidoglio

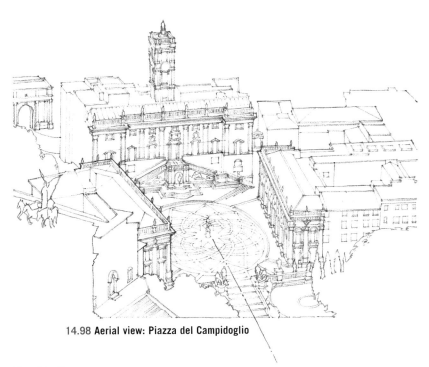

14.98 Aerial view: Piazza del Campidoglio

14.99 Arcade, Capitoline Museum

Campidoglio

Michelangelo Buonarroti (1475–1564) was put in charge of the transformation (begun 1538). He transfigured the disorderly complex into a symmetrical composition with a trapezoidal piazza and three palace fronts. The Via Sacra crossed the piazza, then descended a broad, gentle stairway also designed by Michelangelo. In the name of symmetry, Michelangelo added a building known as the Palazzo Nuovo (1646–50), with no programmatic requirements. This building, serving only as a framing device for the piazza, was erected by Carlo Rainaldi according to Michelangelo's designs. Although it looked like a habitable palazzo, it was in reality little more than a facade. The two palaces that define the cross-axis of the piazza have porticoes at their ground levels that extend the space of the piazza under the buildings. There are no arches, as would have been more common—and more structurally sound. But Michelangelo shunned the vault as an architectural form, preferring instead the pier and lintel. Also novel was the use of the giant order for the pilasters supporting an unbroken entablature, with a balustrade above the cornice to emphasize the principal rhythm of the facade. The white travertine pilasters are offset against the wall's orange-tinged bricks. The windows are mini-compositions in their own right, emphasizing the placement of the *piano nobile*'s great hall.

The trapezoidal shape of the piazza was unusual, and even though it was predicated to some degree by the existing context, it introduced a new and more dynamic notion of public space than was common in the Renaissance, which tended to favor more static, rectilinear schemes. At the center of the piazza is a shallow oval indentation out of which rises a slight swelling of the ground, its surface ornamented with a rotating twelve-pointed blossom pattern hinting at a zodiacal symbolism. The ideological content of the piazza was brought to the fore by the sculptural program. A sculpture of the emblem of Rome, a she-wolf nursing the twins Romulus and Remus, was placed over the entrance of the Palace of the Conservators. The most prominent sculpture—indeed the centerpiece of the piazza—is, however, an equestrian statue of Marcus Aurelius. It is one of the best preserved bronzes from Roman times and had been brought up from the Lateran Palace to emphasize the new civic nature of papal power. It escaped being melted down only because it was mistaken by the Church as representing Constantine the Great, held to have been the first Christian emperor. From an architectural point of view, the equestrian statue pulls together and animates the entire ensemble that now appears as a backdrop for the statue.

14.100 Partial facade: Piazza del Campidoglio

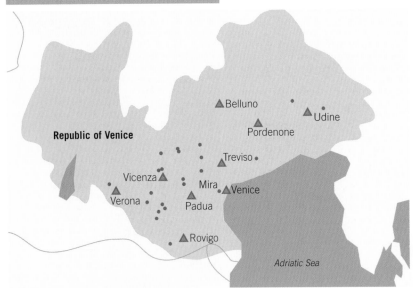

14.101 Sites of Palladian villas

Il Redentore (Church of the Savior)

Due to a combination of circumstances, the 16th century saw a dramatic decline in Venice's spice trade in the East. Genoese ships, preferred by the Spanish, replaced the Venetian galleys; Antwerp had become Europe's most important port; and Portugal, using its new shipping lanes around the Cape of Good Hope, had brought the cost of pepper down considerably. In 1505, for example, pepper imported from Venice over the old route cost 20 Flemish *groats* per pound, while Portuguese pepper cost only about 16 *groats*. Furthermore, Venice's immensely costly Turkish War (1570–73) was followed by a plague (1575–77) that overtook about one-third of the city's population. Nonetheless, Venice managed to hold on to its economic position, largely because of its mainland farms. (It has been estimated that by 1630 about 35 percent of patrician income came from Venice's mainland estates.) Gradually, the long-maturing crisis approached a climax. The Thirty Years' War (1618–48), another plague (1630–31), and the Turkish War of 1646 to 1669 left Venice a shell of its former self. The 1560s were thus the high before the low, and it was during this time that Andrea Palladio (1508–80) rose to prominence. He designed churches, villas, palaces, and the town hall of Vicenza. Even if he had not become a leading theorist, his work alone would have outnumbered that of any other Renaissance architect.

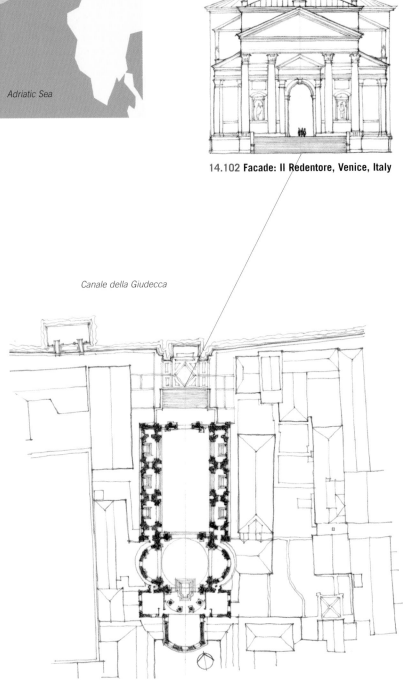

14.102 Facade: Il Redentore, Venice, Italy

Canale della Giudecca

14.103 Plan: Il Redentore

Palladio, originally named Andrea di Pietro della Gondola, was trained as a mason but under the influence of the humanist poet Giangiorgio Trissino, who became his first patron, the talented young mason was given a new name in honor of Pallas Athena. In 1541, he visited Rome with Trissino and made extensive studies of its ancient buildings, publishing his findings in 1554 in the treatise *Le antichità di Roma.* In 1545, he was given his first major commission, the rebuilding of the basilica in Vicenza. A flood of commissions soon followed for palaces, villas, and churches, leaving an indelible mark on Venice and the Veneto. In Venice, he designed the conspicuously located San Giorgio Maggiore (1565–80) on the lagoon opposite the Piazza San Marco. Its surprising facade superimposes a high, narrow temple front over the wider and lower one that extends laterally beneath it to cover the lower side aisles. Another church, Il Redentore, was built in fulfillment of a vow on the deliverance of the city from the devastating plague of 1575 through 1576, thus the name "the Savior." The facade's integration of the giant order with the minor order was, once again, a novel experiment. Palladio attempted—and succeeded—to integrate the different scales of pilasters, one of the principal problem of all Renaissance church facades. On the interior, the almost complete absence of nonarchitectural ornament and the uniform whiteness of the surfaces resulted in a sober luminosity.

Palladian Villas

The villas Palladio designed for the great Venetian families were far different from those of the popes in Rome or the Medici in Florence, which were designed for peace and tranquility. Palladio's were in part working farms that did more than just provide the villa with oil and grain; they were an important part of the new Venetian economy, and the nitty-gritty of farming life was encompassed in their aesthetics. To facilitate smooth traffic through the buildings, there are two staircases leading to the grain-storage rooms in the attic: one for those going up, and the other for those going down. From among Palladio's numerous villas, the most distinguished are Villa Barbaro (1549),

Villa Foscari (La Malcontenta, 1560), and Villa Emo (1599). All except Villa Barbaro have splendid, elevated temple-front facades giving access to a great hall. Their layouts are always symmetrical and simple, and the rooms, too, are governed by simple proportions (1 by 1, 2 by 3, 3 by 4, etc.). Windows and internal doorways are often aligned, adding even more cohesion to the interiors. Villa Foscari became a model for palaces, villas, and houses throughout Europe and the Americas. The inner planning was based on a large cruciform hall that reaches from front to back. Its dramatic temple front, accessed, however, from the sides, faces the river Brenda. Being so intimately connected with this gentle river imparts a special atmosphere of practicality to the villa. Not only could its owners easily commute to the Venetian lagoon, but its farm products could be transported to market. The villa was commissioned in 1550 and has in modern times again returned to members of the Foscari family, who have carefully restored it.

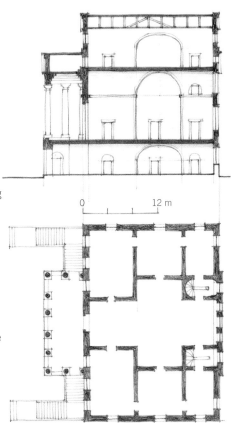

0 ⎯⎯⎯⎯ 12 m

14.104 **Plan and section: Villa Foscari, Mira, Italy**

14.105 **Villa Foscari**

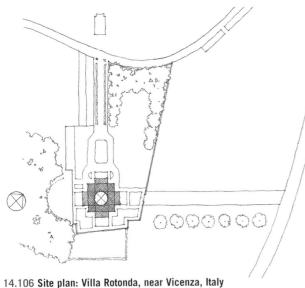

14.106 **Site plan: Villa Rotonda, near Vicenza, Italy**

14.107 **Villa Rotonda**

Villa Rotonda

Villa Rotonda (begun 1566), just outside Vicenza, though having many of the attributes of a working farm, was designed for the papal prelate Paolo Almerico as a retirement estate. The building's design is unusual for Palladio; it is symmetrical around both axes and stands on the top of a low hill artificially enhanced with retaining walls. The building's plan centered on a rotunda—originally planned with an open oculus—with identical suites of rooms at each of the four corners. Each of the four facades had a temple front. The villa is elevated on a basement that is disguised by its stairs. The principal material was brick covered with stucco painted white. Stone was used sparingly (given its cost in times of economic stress) for the capitals or for the ornamentation around windows. The entrance path facing the northwest loggia is recessed into the hill, so that from the villa looking back over the entrance one sees the chapel on the opposite side of the small road. To the north are orchards going down toward a river. Cut out of the woods to the south is a *giardino segreto*, an increasingly common feature of villa landscaping. Only on the east side is the view of the landscape unobstructed.

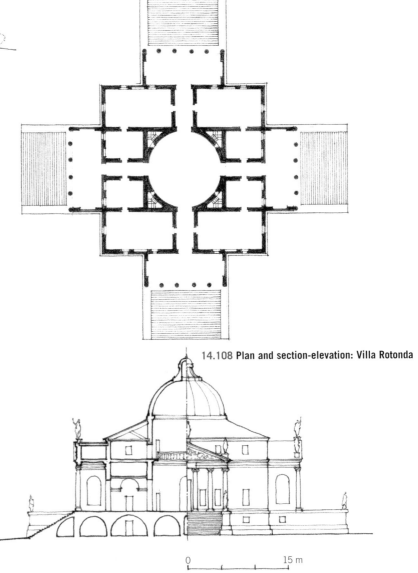

14.108 **Plan and section-elevation: Villa Rotonda**

0   15 m

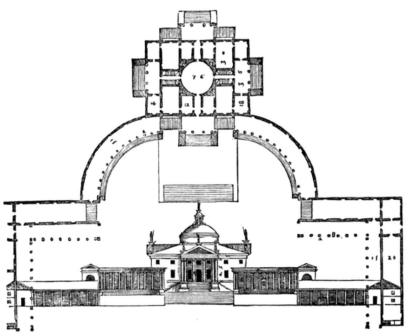

14.109 **Villa Trissino: From** *The Four Books on Architecture*, Andrea Palladio

Palladio was the most system-conscious of the great Renaissance architects, as evidenced by his *Four Books on Architecture* (1570). Leon Battista Alberti and Sebastiano Serlio had been forerunners with treatises of their own, but Palladio's approach was different. Alberti, in his *Ten Books on Architecture* (1452), attempted a comprehensive study of the field of architecture and dealt with everything from where best to get materials to the different types of buildings. There were no drawings. Serlio, in his *Five Books on Architecture* (the first volume appearing in 1537), had plenty of drawings, but his purpose was to show how the classical system could be put to use to generate an almost infinite variety of plans. This was in contrast to Palladio, who emphasized the systematization of the ground plan and its relationship to the section and elevation of a building. Whereas Serlio's treatise allowed the patron a good deal of options, Palladio's designs were much more circumscribed. Yet what made Palladio's architecture so influential was that it was despite its rigor it allowed for a good deal of variation. Method and system did not overshadow creativity. Important for Palladio was also the relationship between the building as an object and its broader framing. Courtyards and perimeter walls were integrated into the composition.

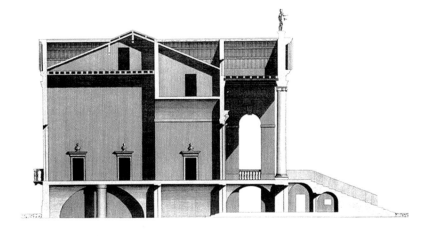

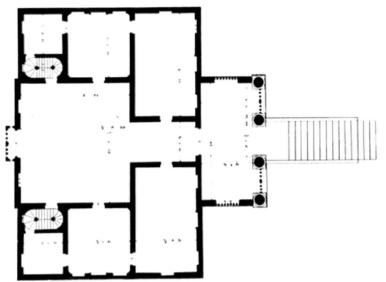

14.110 **Villa Chiericati: From** *The Four Books on Architecture*, Andrea Palladio

14.111 The Americas, ca.1600

Map labels: Santa Fe · Acoma · **New Mexico** · St. Augustine · Native American settlement area · Gulf of Mexico · **New Spain** · Mexico City · Mexica Empire at time of conquest · Caribbean Sea · Atlantic Ocean · Treaty of Tordesillas (1494) · Panama City · Caracas · **New Granada** · **Portuguese territory** · **Guiana** · **Spanish territory** · **Peru** · Lima · Cuzco · Pacific Ocean · Potosi · Inca Empire at time of conquest · **La Plata** · Santiago · Buenos Aires

Spanish Conquest of America

Spain's distress in the middle of the 14th century was largely due to the plagues of 1362, 1363, 1367, and 1374, which had taken a heavy toll on the country's economy; domestic production had ground to a halt, banks had collapsed, and the population was restive. The expensive campaigns of Ferdinand V and Isabella I of Castile (r. 1474–1516) against the Moors had further decimated the treasury, and a century and a half of great cathedral building had come to a halt. Unable to afford the highly taxed merchandise delivered overland by way of the eastern trade route that terminated in Venice, Spanish and Portuguese importers were, by the end of the 15th century, willing to sail westward to open a sea route to eastern markets. Christopher Columbus's discovery of the Americas in 1492 created excitement and hope, although initially it brought little to Spain's coffers. Matters improved only when Charles V (1500–58) was crowned Holy Roman Emperor in 1519. Due to a combination of unusual circumstances, this empire was huge—the largest in Europe since Charlemagne's. From his father Philip I of Castile, Charles had inherited

the Netherlands, Burgundy, Naples, and Sicily, and from his grandfather, the Holy Roman Emperor Maximilian I, the immense Habsburg possessions of Austria, Hungary, Tyrol, and Württemberg. Charles's prime interest, however, was northern Italy, which he came to dominate by 1530. Charles' dominion, which had no central capital, was a network of loosely interconnected self-contained political entities held together by a complex set of royal ties, inheritances, marriages, and economic interests. The vast holdings in the Americas were just one part of this rather unwieldy picture.

The huge empire of the Incas in South America, subdued by Francisco Pizarro, yielded more gold than the conquest of Mexico by Hernán Cortés. Not content with robbing the Incas of their gold, the conquistadores began panning for gold themselves, using tens of thousands of slaves. Rich deposits of silver were found in the city of Potosí in present-day Bolivia in 1545 and at Zacatecas (in what is now Mexico) in 1548. By 1650, Potosí was the largest city in the Americas, with a population of 160,000. Soon Spain became the world's

leading silver producer (the Spanish crown received one-fifth of the silver) and ultimately produced 50,000 tons of silver, a quantity that doubled the previously existing stock of silver in Europe. The result was that the entire economic structure of Europe, and indeed the world, had to bend to this new reality. And it was not only silver that contributed to Spain's newfound wealth: the salt flats in Portugal and in the Caribbean belonged to the Spanish crown as well, and they delivered most of the maritime salt consumed in the West. Furthermore, through Brazil, Spain also controlled most of the sugar imported to Europe.

The money from these enterprises filtered its way through the European markets, laying the foundation for the beginnings of Europe's commercialization and industrialization. The colonization of the Americas under the Spanish should, therefore, not be seen simply as one of conquest and subjugation in the traditional sense. Its military expenses for the colonization were relatively modest compared to its other expenses at the time, especially those required to fight the Ottomans. Instead, the Spanish empire—and later its rivals, the French and the Dutch—was brought into existence by a collaboration of powerful elites, international bankers, and enterprising traders who operated across national divisions. The traditional notion of production centers linked by trade routes had given way to an economic network that was energized by the flow of investment and debt. Credit in the form of promissory notes became the norm. The result of the initial success of the system was inflation the likes of which had never been experienced before.

When Hernán Cortés landed at Veracruz in 1504, he was mistaken by the Aztecs for the returning god Quetzalcoatl, whose return had been prophesied. When news of big ships with white men on horses reached the Aztec king Montezuma, it was inconceivable to him that these could be humans from another land. Cortés skillfully played up his reception as a returning god and rode into Tenochtitlán in 1519 to a heroic reception. He immediately imprisoned Montezuma, disarmed the population, and laid the city to waste. The rest of the Aztec kingdom was quickly brought under Spanish domination. Spain ruthlessly exploited its new American colony, an effort that went hand in hand with the forced introduction of Christianity. At the center of Spain's colonial system was a form of feudalism, in which Spanish settlers (*encomiendos*) were entrusted with large tracts of land (*encomiendas*) along with a population of not more than three hundred Indians. The natives retained possession of the land, which, however, officially belonged to the crown of Castile. The *encomiendos* were given the right of taxation and were allowed to demand labor services from the population. The Spanish *encomiendos* were supposed to keep order and convert the Indians under their care to Catholicism according to a papal bull of 1493. This, at least, was the theory; in practice, the system soon became corrupt and a tool for oppression and slavery. The *encomiendos* introduced European beasts of burden, farming techniques, and manufacturing processes, along with extensive mining facilitated by an unlimited supply of forced labor. New towns were created to support the *encomienda* economy and to connect it to the ports. The towns were laid out on a regular grid with a plaza in the center. Church and administrative buildings usually faced onto the plaza.

Hard on the heels of the conquistadores followed Catholic friars—Franciscans, Dominicans, and Augustinians—with the assignment to claim the natives for Christ. They were also the first to actually defend the rights of the native population. Central to that effort was Bartolomé de Las Casas, a former *encomienda* turned Dominican friar who vehemently protested the cruel and harsh treatment of the natives by the *encomiendos* to the Spanish crown. "Are they not human, children of God, deserving of our protection?" demanded de Las Casas. In response, the Spanish crown enacted a series of laws that prohibited the enslavement of the native peoples. In the effort to rapidly convert the Americans, the friars built many of the first churches, often intermixing the conventions of the Church's liturgy with local pre-Columbian practices.

Atrios

The Spanish-American churches built by the friars emphasized simplicity and directness. Straightforward boxes with thick walls, often buttressed on the exterior, provided a sturdy frame for the Franciscan house of God.

Windows were few and usually very high. The walls were unsegmented and left bare, or were at best painted with simple illustrations in a style not unlike that of the pre-Columbian temples. A simple stone table, raised up by a few steps, served as an altar, behind which might be a *reredos*—or ornamental screen—often painted pictures illustrating Christ's trials.

The real innovations were on the exterior. To accommodate large groups of worshippers, the friars developed the concept of the *atrio*, a large open court walled along the edges that used the facade of the church as a backdrop; there was an outdoor chapel to conduct Mass at the west end. In its entirety, the *atrio* was remindful of the plazas that fronted the pre-Columbian pyramids and therefore familiar to the native population. Within, the friars devised processions, complete with stopping places for the Stations of the Cross that began at the church and rotated counterclockwise around the *atrio*. The so-called stations were altars that represented the events that occurred as Jesus was brought to his crucifixion in

Jerusalem. Worshippers would stop at each, thereby reenacting the way stations of Jesus' suffering in a form of spatial prayer that had also become common in Europe during this time. Hundreds of such *atrio* churches were built by the Franciscans in the 1560s and 1570s, with some of the classic examples at Cuernavaca, Cholula, and Atlatlahucan. The Catholic Church, however, became increasingly uncomfortable with some of the lenient practices of the friars. The *atrio* churches contravened the basic principle of the house of God as a building with a roof. The friars also favored processional activities that often incorporated certain pre-Columbian songs and dances. Catholic icons often resembled older native images. All this made the Church in Rome nervous, opposed as it was to such hybridizations. In 1574, the monks' sacerdotal privileges were revoked, the building of monasteries was stopped, and the *atrio* churches were declared unfit for service. Their spirit, deeply ingrained in the native people's consciousness, nevertheless survived within the Latin American Church, imparting to it its unique character.

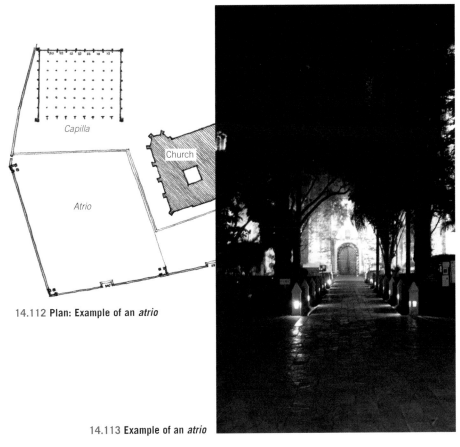

14.112 **Plan: Example of an *atrio***

14.113 **Example of an *atrio***

14.114 Santo Domingo, San Cristóbal, Mexico

Santo Domingo

One of the largest Spanish churches from this era is the Church of Santo Domingo in San Cristóbal. Built between 1547 and 1560 on the orders of Bishop Francisco de Marroquín of Guatemala, its present 17th-century facade is typical of the Mexican Baroque. The imperial double eagle, the coat of arms of the Emperor Charles V, can still be seen above the central portal and on the sides. The interior is lavishly decorated and contains a number of sculptures and wooden altars covered with gold leaf.

The city San Cristóbal de Las Casas was laid out on a grid according to the principles of the Law of the Indies, a series of codes that regulated social, political, and economic life in conquered areas. The grid facilitated land exploitation. A commons was always established in a city's center, in front of the church or cathedral. (The Church of Santo Domingo, however, was founded separately, to the north of the city center.)

Il Gesù

The major institution set up by the Church to fight the Reformation was the Society of Jesus, also known as the Jesuits. Despite its identification with Spain, the Society of Jesus was founded in France at the University of Paris. It was formed in 1534 by Ignatius Loyola (1491–1556), a Basque, and six of his followers, all students at the university. Loyola, a major force behind the Counter-Reformation, founded the Society of Jesus "to enter upon hospital and missionary work in Jerusalem and to go without questioning wherever the pope might direct." Though Pope Paul III recognized the Jesuit order in 1540, it was still relatively inconsequential until Loyola's death, after which it began to develop rapidly. The principal difference between the Jesuits and other orders that had traditionally emphasized communal religious devotion was Loyola's relaxation of a prescribed monastic life and an emphasis on a more active apostolic mission. The Jesuits were not lay brothers but priests organized around a centralized authority. Prayer and meditation had to be balanced with service and teaching. The Jesuits hoped to unify religious teaching with academic learning, and by 1575 they had already established

fourteen educational institutions in France with about one thousand members and with some of the colleges having a student population of more than eight hundred. At the time, by way of contrast, the universities of Europe, though controlled to some extent by churchmen, were relatively secular institutions.

The Jesuits also engaged in missionary activities and set up colleges in various parts of India, Africa, and the Americas. Their first missionaries arrived in Peru in 1568. In 1610, Philip III (r. 1598–1621), proclaiming that only the "sword of the word" should be used to subdue the Paraguayan Indians, made extensive use of the Jesuits in South America. In 1592, when Cardinal Odoardo Farnese visited the Jesuit college in the Piazza Altieri, twenty-seven languages were being spoken in the refectory.

From early on, the Jesuit order attracted important noble patronage, including Marguerite of Austria—wife of Octavio Farnese, the nephew of Alessandro Farnese (Pope Paul III), who supplied funds generously and gave to the Church the use of his architect, Giacomo Barozzi da Vignola (1507–73), to design Il Gesù, the Jesuit

14.115 Entrance facade, Il Gesù, Rome

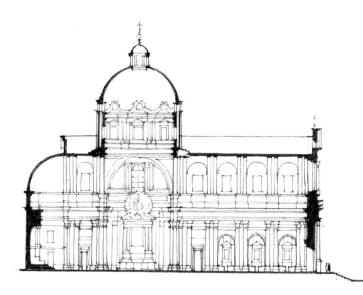

14.116 **Longitudinal section: Il Gesù**

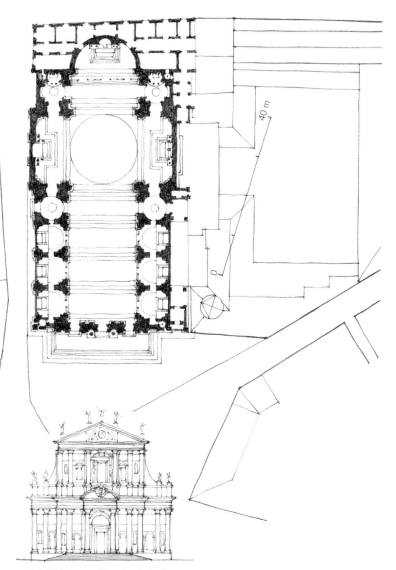

mother church, in Rome. The site for the church was a prominent one, just below the Campidoglio at an important intersection of the papal route through the city. Vignola's design was eventually modified, however, by Giacomo della Porta, whose facade was finished in 1577. In its plan and structure, Il Gesù was more influential than any other Roman church of the late 16th century. Its broad, barrel-vaulted nave facilitated preaching to large congregations. The choir was clearly cut off from the nave to emphasize the distinction between priests and laity. Side chapels, sold to individual families, ensured proper endowments.

The interior walls of the early Jesuit churches were simple, as mandated by the order's leadership. But the facades of Jesuit churches spelled out the transition away from the more restrained attitudes of the Renaissance. New formal problems were tackled and solutions proffered that were soon to be taken up by the great Baroque architects. For example, we see for the first time in Il Gesù the lower order, based on the theme of pilaster pairs elevated on high dadoes, with a similar dado zone separating the upper and lower orders. Energy seems to ripple horizontally and vertically across the facade. The central axis is emphasized by framed niches as well as by the attached columns to the right and left of the door.

14.117 **Plan and facade: Il Gesù**

14.118 El Escorial, near Madrid

El Escorial

The history of 16th-century Europe is in many ways the history of the predominance of the Spanish Empire, which stretched, by means of fortuitous marriages and inheritances, across Europe under the scepter of Spain's Charles V—who, to the shock of his Spanish subjects, could himself barely speak Spanish. (He was quoted as saying, "I speak Spanish to God, Italian to women, French to men, and German to my horse.") During his rule Charles V combined most of the predominant European dynasties. On his paternal side he fell heir to the Habsburg line of his grandfather Maximilian I, Holy Roman Emperor, and the house of Valois of Burgundy, while on his maternal side he was heir to Philip I of Castile and Juana of Castile, which encompassed the overseas colonies. Under his reign, the House of Habsburg reached its pinnacle, and Charles V himself attained the symbolic designation of Holy Roman Emperor.

The empire had, however, no unifying capital. Valladolid in the north of the Spain served for the most part as residence of the court. In 1526, Charles began to build a palace—never quite finished—inside the Alhambra fortification of Il Nasrid in Granada; it was designed by Pedro Machuca, who had been a painter practicing in Italy. Though elegant, it was too far to the south. So in 1562, Madrid was made the seat of Spain's royal court, with Philip II, the only son of Charles V, building for himself a vast palace, known as El Escorial (begun 1563);

it is located 50 kilometers northwest of the city on the slopes of the rugged Guadarrama Mountains that separate Madrid from the plains of Castilla y León. The word *escorial* ("slag heaps") refers to the heaps of scoria that were left by ancient iron miners on the site.

Philip II, a deeply religious king and a fierce advocate of Catholicism, designed his palace in the form of a monastery to symbolize the strength of his faith. Resting on a hill with broad easterly views, the palace covers a large area (205 by 160 meters), with the buildings laid out on a grid with inner

courts. Dominating the composition is the axially placed church and its forecourt. The church, built in somber gray granite, has a Doric order at ground level. All other pilasters are embedded in the articulation of the wall, giving the building a solid and massive appearance. Apart from the arcade below, the facade is reminiscent of St. Sebastiano in Mantua by Leon Battista Alberti. (Perhaps the reference to a saint who, despite being tortured, remained alive, was appropriate for a king who was known to have been brooding and obsessive.) The royal suite of apartments is located around a private courtyard, with Philip's bedroom, modeled on a monk's cell, looking out into the chapel. Through the centuries the palace has served as the mortuary for the Spanish kings, with stacks of sumptuous marble and bronze sarcophagi in the royal tomb chamber. The building is an anomaly when compared with contemporary palace construction elsewhere in Europe. Here, grandeur, splendor, ostentation, and ornamentation were eschewed. Instead the building was a self-conscious statement of an ideological return to a simpler life. It has been suggested that the building was meant as a model of the destroyed Temple of Solomon, its shape and form having been an important theoretical question at the time. Philip II's palace was a combination of royal retreat, heavenly city, and neo-medieval utopia.

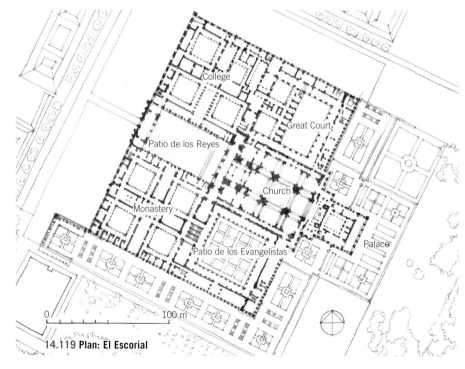

14.119 Plan: El Escorial

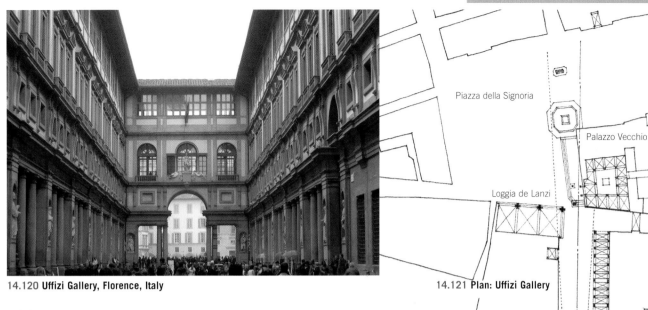

14.120 Uffizi Gallery, Florence, Italy

14.121 Plan: Uffizi Gallery

Uffizi Gallery

At the end of the 16th century, the vitality of life in Italian cities had been drained by the course of numerous wars as well as by the slow but inexorable drift of money and power to the northern European powers. Yet for the French economy, which was the principal European beneficiary of Spanish money, Florence was still an invaluable connection to the old Eurasian economy. Securing a link to Florence also allowed the French to monitor and control Italian politics. In 1533 Catherine de' Medici became the wife of Henri d'Orléans, the future king of France, and in 1600 Marie de' Medici married Henry IV of France. By the 17th century, it was French, not Italian, that was spoken in the drawing rooms of Florence. Cosimo I de' Medici (1519–74), seeking to balance the French influence by bringing in a Spanish wife, married Eleonora of Toledo, daughter of the Spanish ambassador to the kingdom of Naples. Cosimo set the style for his new absolutist rule by grafting onto the old city a new, quasi-royal profile.

Cosimo moved his residence across the river to the Palazzo Pitti, bought in 1549 and subsequently enlarged and remodeled several times by Cosimo and his descendants. He added the Boboli Gardens behind the palace between 1550 and 1558, but just as importantly, he built a private corridor from the Palazzo Pitti, over the Ponte Vecchio (which crossed the Arno River), to the Uffizi, and on to the Palazzo della Signoria, from which he ruled. Indicative of the new notion of statehood was the Uffizi ("offices"), which served as the administrative headquarters of the region. The Gallery (1560–65) was an unusual structure, built three stories high along both sides of a long, streetlike piazza that connects the Palazzo della Signoria with the river Arno. At its terminus is an airy loggia overlooking the Arno that was designed by Giorgio Vasari (1511–74), an artist who painted somewhat in the style of Michelangelo and is better known as the author of the *Le vite de' più eccelenti architetti, pittori, et scultori Italiani* ("The lives of the most excellent Italian architects, painters, and sculptors" [1550–68]). To this day the book is an indispensable source of information—even if it glossed over certain details or misrepresented others to increase the author's own importance. Vasari also undertook several architectural projects. But his sole major project was the Uffizi building in Florence. Rather than vaults on the ground floor, there are columns and entablatures remindful of the Campidoglio. The building is conspicuously grafted into the medieval fabric of the city that surrounds it.

14.122 Plan: Florence, Italy

Villa Farnese

The year 1559 saw the accession of Pope Pius IV (r. 1559–65) and the beginning of a new era of guarded optimism in Rome. When Queen Mary of England married Philip II in 1554, hope arose that England—which had split from Rome under Henry VIII—would be reunited with the Church and that nascent Protestant sympathies there could be crushed. At the time, Rome was a city awash in Spanish gold and silver. Rome thus also attracted the poor, and most probably had the largest collection of vagabonds of any major European city; some suggest that one in four of Rome's population was a beggar.

By the end of the century, the city had become a gigantic work yard. Architects, painters, and sculptors hastened to find employment. Technically, art was used not as an end in itself but as a battleground against the Reformation, a way of glorifying the splendors of the Church. In truth, by the end of the 16th century, power and money were held in the hands of a small Church oligarchy that was encouraged by the papal government to build fine houses and villas. These included the Villa and Palazzo Borghese (Cardinal Camillo Borghese, Pope Paul V, begun 1605); Palazzo Barberini (begun 1628); Villa Barberini (Cardinal Bonifacio Ferreri, enlarged 1641); and the Villa Pamphili (Giambattista Pamphili, Pope Innocent X, 1644).

Setting the tone for this building campaign was Alessandro Farnese (1520–89), grandson of Paul III, who commissioned a villa in Caprarola, to the north of Rome, while still a cardinal. Its designer was Baldassare Peruzzi. By no means a standard villa, it was designed as a *rocca*, a large fortified

14.123 Villa Farnese, Caprarola, Italy

14.124 Interior court, Villa Farnese

country residence, even though its castlelike attributes were more a result of style than necessity. The pentagonal shape with angular bastions may have come from designs made by Antonio da Sangallo the Younger, for whom Peruzzi had worked in the designing of St. Peter's in Rome. In 1556, Cardinal Farnese commissioned Vignola to complete the building and solve some of the as yet unanswered questions regarding circulation and planning, transforming Peruzzi's simpler building into one suited for papal life. (Vignola was also responsible for the street that was cut through the town.) Work was begun in 1559.

The building was positioned at the top of a hill, facing southeast over a wide terrace down a long, axially placed street that was carved through the center of the small town of Caprarola. In essence, the village became an extension of the palace's architectural layout. Farnese organized splendid hunts, and it is possible that the villa was built for this purpose. But the palace was also a place where dignitaries were to visit, and this may be the first building that was planned specifically for a carriage approach: from the piazza in front of the building, a large

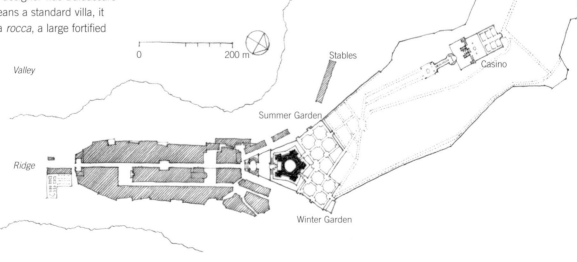

14.125 Plan: Caprarola and the Villa Farnese

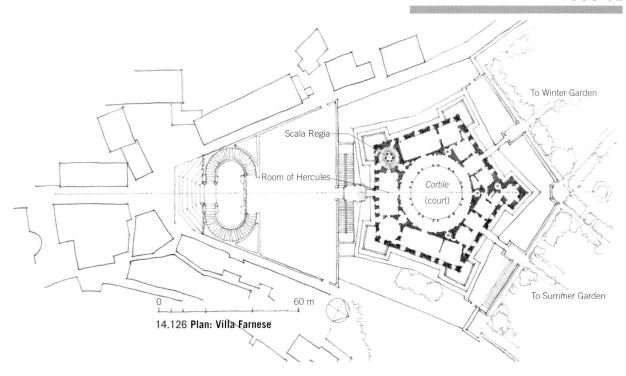

14.126 Plan: Villa Farnese

portal opened to a circular carriageway in the basement that allowed carriages to drop people off indoors at the foot of a grand spiral staircase and then drive around the corridor and out. Much of the basement was cut out of the tufa rock, including a great cistern underneath the courtyard. The basement also houses the major service rooms, and the kitchen, pantries, and ovens. On the exterior, a symmetrical pair of curving stairs, flanking and framing the carriage portal, mount to a polygonal terrace, at the back of which symmetrically designed switchback stairs lead to a small oval staircase that in turn gives access to the main door.

Overlooking the piazza from the level of the *piano nobile*—and the culmination of the arrival sequence—was a grand loggia with five open bays (now enclosed by windows) that offered a splendid vista of the city and the surrounding landscape. It was called the Room of Hercules, a classical theme associated, of course, with heroic deeds. Lavishly decorated with wall paintings

depicting Hercules—perhaps implying divine ancestry and thus the grandeur of the Farnese—it served as a summer dining room. At the opposite end from the spiral staircase is a round chapel.

There are two principal apartment suites on the *piano nobile* to the right and left of the great salon, entered from the circular courtyard. They form a linear chain of five rooms, with the more public rooms to the front. The three smaller rooms beyond served as the cardinal's bedroom, wardrobe, and study. From the dressing room, a wooden bridge over the moat provided access to two square gardens set into the hillside. The northern suite to the right of the entrance served as Farnese's summer apartment and the other as his winter apartment.

The idea that a villa should take into account the changing seasons had been a theory of Vitruvius's and was realized in the Renaissance in various instances. At Caprarola, this concept determines the layout of the entire complex.

Ingeniously inserted in the tower of the rear-angled bastion were the various private living conveniences required in a luxurious palace—the bathing rooms, a library, and, at the top, a dovecote. The circular court is two stories high, with a ground-floor arcade below and an arcade with coupled Ionic half-columns attached to the piers pierced by rectangular openings above.

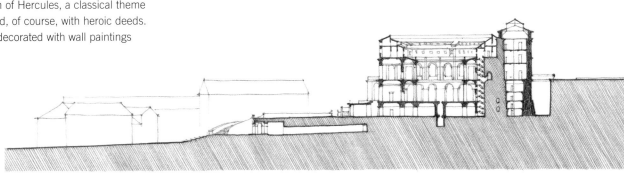

14.127 Section: Villa Farnese

14.128 **St. Peter's Basilica, Rome**

14.129 **Dome of St. Peter's Basilica**

St. Peter's Basilica

The Basilica di San Pietro in Vaticano, or St. Peter's Basilica in English, was erected during the successive reign of several popes each using their own architectural teams and is the combined effort of numerous architects. That in spite of this complex history, which entailed tearing down a previous basilica (started in 326 CE over the tomb of St. Peter under Constantine the Great) the building emerged as a success is nothing short of astonishing. The first architect, working under Pope Julius II, was Donato Bramante (1444–1514), whose plans won in a competition. The Pope himself laid the first stone in 1506 under the St. Veronica Pier. Bramante's plan was along the lines of a Greek cross of tremendous proportions. His design, however, was too grandiose even for the Vatican, and his successors spent half a century reducing its scale. Very little was done until 1535, when the work on a new model was begun, planned by a team of architects that included Baldassare Peruzzi and Antonio da Sangallo the Younger. But few of these plans were brought to fruition until 1546, when Michelangelo was made architect-in-charge by Pope Paul III—much against his will, as he was by then already 71 years old. By that time the piers of Bramante's building had been erected and Michelangelo had to work within that parameter. He did, however, tear down some of the walls that had already been constructed. By the time

of Michelangelo's death in 1564, the exterior and the interior of the south transept were complete. As it stands today, St. Peter's is the product of many architects working at different times who nonetheless largely followed Michelangelo's design.

Compared to Bramante's plan, Michelangelo's is strikingly simpler. No longer was there a proportional declination of space from large to small. Instead, there was a single square with four apsidal ends to the Greek cross. A longitudinal orientation was created by the addition of a colonnaded portico across the front. The correlation between inside and outside was obscured, however, by fattening the mass to the right and left of each of the external apses, creating the appearance of a continuous succession of pilasters. Compared with Bramante's design, which was intended to be read from the top down, its form dissolving into filigree patterns of niches, columns, and vaults, Michelangelo's building works from the bottom upward, with the strained relationship between the outside shape and the dome hinting at the mystery of the divine presence within. The walls were not the result of volumetric elements added together, as they were for Bramante, but a dynamic balance between form, structure, and space, with an alternating rhythm of dilation and contraction. Bramante's building would have appeared as a static mass, while Michelangelo's appears as an undulating cliff

surface that moves both toward and away from the center, especially when seen from the rear.

Michelangelo died without seeing his dome visualized. Giacomo della Porta, who inherited the project, changed Michaelangelo's intent and created an ogival form akin to the Duomo of Florence. He also raised the dome onto a higher drum so that it could be better seen from the piazza in front of the building. The windows between strongly buttressed fins are disguised by attached column pairs. When Michelangelo died, there did not yet exist a final plan for the facade. His relatively straightforward design was based on the Pantheon, but with six columns (instead of the Pantheon's eight) supporting a pediment. A series of architects were put in charge of the work, but until 1605 the front of the old basilica, astonishingly enough, was still in place and serving as the entrance. But that, too, was eventually demolished, and before long the last vestiges of the medieval basilica had disappeared. Maderno's facade elaborated on the themes of Michelangelo's building but it is not considered a success. The *aediculae* appear as if they barely fit in their respective spaces; the enormous attic story looms over the facade; and of the five entrances, three have lintels, as favored by Michelangelo, and two are round-headed, appearing awkward and small.

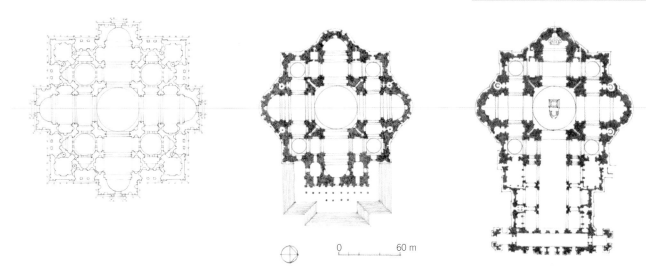

14.130 Bramante's plan for St. Peter's (above); Michelangelo's plan (center); Carlo Maderno's addition (right)

0   60 m

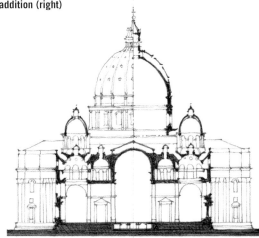

14.131 Section: St. Peter's Basilica

14.132 Interior, St. Peter's Basilica

14.133 Facade, St. Peter's Basilica

Baroque Italy

The Baroque style emerged in Rome essentially as a counterstatement to the Reformation; the architects who contributed most to its characteristics were Giovanni Lorenzo Bernini (1598–1680) and Francesco Castelli Borromini (1599–1667). Though it is now common to use the label *Baroque* to describe the architecture of the 16th and 17th centuries, this designation was formulated only in the late 19th century. Nonetheless, the word is valuable for pinpointing certain important changes in attitude about architecture—and indeed about life in general—during this period. Use of the term herein will be restricted to describe a style that developed as a medium for propaganda during the Counter-Reformation, spanning the decades between 1620 and 1670.

There is also an important difference between Roman Baroque and European Baroque. Baroque Rome waned after 1648 under Pope Alexander VII. From that time forward the papacy was no longer a major power in European architecture. With the ascendancy of France and Austria, the Baroque style began to change, assuming a more urban form and, in so far as it was now also applied to châteaux and princes' castles, it acquired elements such as public parks and waterworks. Approaches often extended far into the landscape with elongated perspectives. In France it is exemplified by the Place Vendôme in Paris and the Château de Vaux-le-Vicomte by André Le Nôtre (1656–61); in Austria, by the Schönbrunn Palace (1695). Eventually the Baroque became associated with the architecture of the late 17th-century European capitals—Rome, Paris, London, and Vienna—giving to these cities a profile that remains very much part of their identities today. On the negative side, many venerable old buildings of the Middle Ages were given new Baroque facades or makeovers, their interiors upgraded to conform to the "modernizing" trend of the Baroque.

The decade of the 1620s was a particularly promising moment in Church politics. Catholic forces destroyed an alliance of Protestant princes at the Battle of White Mountain (1620) near Prague, while missionaries were carrying the word of God to the Far East and the Americas. The relationship of the Church with Spain, the military enforcer of Church politics, was secure, or so it seemed at the time. There was a mood of celebration and a sense that the Protestant revolution could be contained, the heresies squashed, and the emerging generation of scientists silenced. (Galileo Galilei stood trial for heresy in 1633.) The heroes of the Counter-Reformation (many of them Spanish) were canonized—Charles Borromeo in 1610; Ignatius Loyola, Francis Xavier, Filippo Neri, and Teresa of Avila in 1622; and Gaetano da Thiene in 1629—and this in itself was a signal for new churches and chapels to be built, in honor of the new saints.

In church architecture, the Greek cross, which was sometimes favored in the Renaissance because of its symmetry, was rejected for the conventions of the Latin cross, which was liturgically more satisfying for Counter-Reformation purposes, as it allowed for a clear separation between clergy and laity, this being one of the distinctions between Catholic and Protestant churches of the time. The preference, as established at Il Gesù, was for a longitudinal nave unencumbered as much as possible by side aisles. Transepts were minimized or done away with, allowing the use of rectangles and ovals, which also helped to create a sense of community that these churches were to inculcate. Baroque architects preferred curves and ovals to straight lines, deploying niches, walls, pilasters, and attached columns in a seamless way that made architecture seem pliant and rubbery—not framing the liturgical but part of it. They also had an appreciation of rhythmic movement through space and intensified visual dynamics by using painting as well as sculptural putti (winged babies), which often inhabit the higher reaches of the space, sitting on

14.134 Sant'Andrea al Quirinale, Rome

ledges and entablatures. While in medieval cathedrals stained glass modulated the light, Baroque churches had plain glass devoid of tracery. Yet the windows were often unseen, designed to create a mysterious and diffuse light. One often finds a Baroque church quite luminous upon entering—without first noticing any windows at all.

Baroque architects did not hesitate to go from one medium to the other when asked to fulfill the Counter-Reformation's call to expound the mysteries of the faith and extol the virtues of the martyrs. Though treatment of walls and pilasters varied a good deal, careful thought was given to the effects of

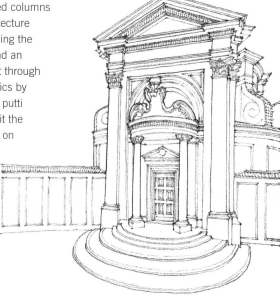

14.135 Sant'Andrea al Quirinale, Rome

14.136 Interior, Sant'Andrea al Quirinale

color and lighting. Italians preferred rose and pink marble highlighted by shades of white and black. They made use of gilded and coffered domes illuminated from a cupola. South Germans preferred a white- or cream-colored background accentuated with gilding, against which the furnishings were meant to stand out. Painters created elaborate ceiling frescoes portraying visions of the Church Triumphant. There was also a tendency to intensify color in the upward direction. The Baroque architect was an impresario of appearances, setting his stage with sculptures and paintings that were given just as much importance as the architecture itself. It was, however, not all show and no substance. Bernini and Borromini were both worldly and learned, and Camillo-Guarino Guarini was a theologian, philosopher, and mathematician. All were well-acquainted with classical architecture, using it in a deliberately new way to bring the articulation of space up-to-date with recent developments in mathematics and geometry.

Sant'Andrea al Quirinale

Up until the late Middle Ages in Europe, little if anything was known of architects in respect to their life and training. By the early 15th century, however, the leading artists and architects began to come into focus. Biographies of Filippo Brunelleschi were written, indicating his level of fame. Michelangelo and Leonardo da Vinci were famous by the ends of their lifetimes. But no artist of his time achieved the accolades and level of popular celebrity as Gian Lorenzo Bernini (1598–1680). When he was called to Paris by Louis XIV to submit a design for a contemplated new east wing for the Louvre, people lined the streets to see his carriage pass by.

The core architectural works of Bernini are San Tommaso da Villanova at Castel Gandolfo (1658–61), Sant'Andrea al Quirinale in Rome (1658–70) and Santa Maria dell'Assunzione at Ariccia (1662–64). All three have simple geometrical plans based on the architect's unqualified reverence for the Pantheon, and although Sant'Andrea is a transverse oval, its referent remains a classical one. The building had to be pushed back to allow for a small piazza in front of the church where carriages, which had become increasingly large over time, could pull up to the front. (The courtyard has since been removed.)

The church sits directly opposite the Palazzo del Quirinale, which was initially an official apostolic residence but is today the home of the president of Italy. Intended, as part of a monastic complex set up by the Jesuit order to train novices, the building was dedicated to recently appointed saints of the Jesuits—Andrea Avellino, Francis Xavier, Stanislaus Kostka, and Ignatius Loyola. It was thus, in Bernini's eyes, a type of Pantheon of the Jesuits. The massive Corinthian pilasters form the entrance, out of which projects a curved entrance canopy. The convex curve of the projecting porch is cradled in the middle of a concave-shaped piazza that mirrors the shape of the central oval in the interior. On the interior, a series of niches fill the body of the wall, with the central apse dedicated to St. Andrew and marked by flanking pairs of marble columns. The other four saints were positioned in the squarish niches on both sides of the principal cross-axis.

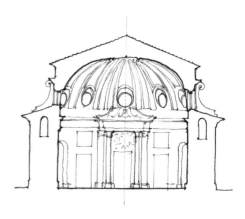

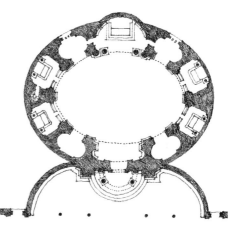

Roadway

14.137 Plan and section: Sant'Andrea al Quirinale

The color scheme and the use of light are striking. The Corinthian pilasters that mark out the principal spatial configuration are in white, whereas the spandrels, lesser pilasters, and freestanding columns on the side of the central apse are covered in delicate, white-speckled, rose-tinted marble. Light from a concealed window streams down into the apse, illuminating a spectacular picture frame supported by cherubs and solar rays, all in gold. The dome over the oval glistens with golden decorations ,evoking the heavenly space to which St. Andrew ascends. It is patterned between the ribs by finely worked hexagonal coffers. Perched over the windows at the base of the dome are figures of putti and the fishermen who were St. Andrew's companions.

San Carlo alle Quattro Fontane

San Carlo was dedicated to another newly created saint of the Counter-Reformation, St. Charles Borromeo, (1538–84), who had been archbishop of Milan and papal secretary of state under Pius IV. He was canonized in 1601. This church thus belongs to the new type of Counter-Reformation urban monastic order, in this case the Discalced Spanish Trinitarians, whose function was to collect money to buy the freedom of Christians captured by the Moors. Borromini was given the commission in 1634, but the building was not finished until 1667. The church is located at an intersection known for its four fountains—hence its name (*quattro fontane* means "four fountains").

14.138 **View of ceiling, San Carlo alle Quattro Fontane, Rome**

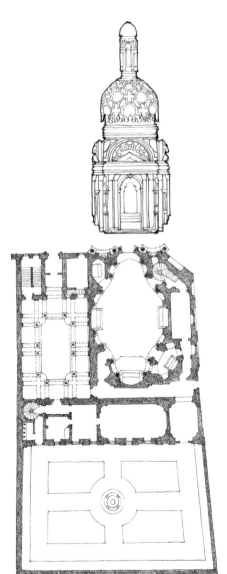

14.139 **Plan: San Carlo alle Quattro Fontane**

The body of the church is nestled in an L formed by the entrance to the compound on the left of the church and a back wing of rooms. Only the front facade of the church is visible, as the church engages the street at its narrowest. Though relatively flat, the numerous segmented curves of the bases and entablatures creates a dynamic tension between the columns and walls.

The design of the interior is an equally ingenious compromise between form and pragmatism. It is based on the prototype of a dome and four apses, but the apses have been flattened so that the spaces of the apses and that of the dome become almost one, brought into unity by means of a ring of Corinthian columns that appear embedded in the soft mass of the walls. The inner surface of the oval dome is coffered with interlacing octagons, crosses, and lozenges.

Though there is much that links these two great artists, Bernini and Borromini, the latter clearly worked unremittingly with the language of geometry. Bernini was also certainly most interested in geometry, but in many respects, he was more the classicist. It is Borromini who brings the classical orders and requirements into alignment with an almost medieval fascination with geometric complexity. If Bernini was attracted to the historical symbolism of Rome, Borromini was attracted to the symbolic potential of space itself.

Despite the spectacular nature of the facade of San Carlo alle Quattro Fontane, one has to recall that Borromini designed it to fit within a set of other facades that, though purposefully less remarkable, are all part of a single unit. One of the questions the design raises is, Where does one facade begin and the other end? The church facade hinges to the corner facade, with its fountain below and bell tower above, which in turn leads to the side facade of the monastic building, where the pilasters projecting only a few centimeters serve to create a background rhythm for the whole. To the right of the church facade, Borromini designed the monastery courtyard so that it ties in with the neighboring structure on its right. In fact, the church is remarkable precisely because it is not a freestanding element proclaiming itself as separate and distinct from the urban fabric; rather, it is consciously fitted into its environment. The two-story entrance courtyard to the monastery is also a play of geometrical inversions, but in keeping with the ideology of austerity, all its elements are plain white, giving the whole a strikingly modern aspect.

14.140 **San Carlo alle Quattro Fontane**

14.141 **View of ceiling, Sant'Ivo alla Sapienza, Rome**

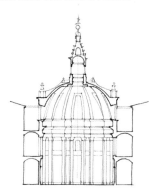

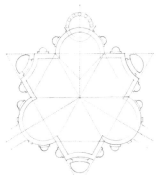

14.142 **Plan geometry: Sant'Ivo alla Sapienza**

Sant'Ivo alla Sapienza (1643–48) is somewhat different from San Carlo, from an urbanist's point of view, because the institution, a law school, filled the whole city block. La Sapienza was originally founded in 1303 by Pope Boniface VIII. The block was torn down and the new building constructed with a church dedicated to St. Yves (1253–1303), the patron saint of lawyers. Nonetheless, here, too, Borromini designed the building as if it were fitted into an older structure by using the institutional spaces as part of the "frame" for the church, which sits at the back of a long courtyard piazza, seemingly embedded within the fabric of the building. The church was designed in plan as two intersecting triangles, with circles added at the perimeter to add or subtract space. The result is a space that is centralized and yet axial. Its simplicity is ingenious. As at San Carlo, the facade and the space of the church just barely intersect. In fact, the church has no actual facade in the traditional Renaissance sense, since it is here nothing more than an elaboration of the courtyard's facade. The church has a high drum on which the dome is placed. The dome is surmounted by an ornate cupola with a spiraling top.

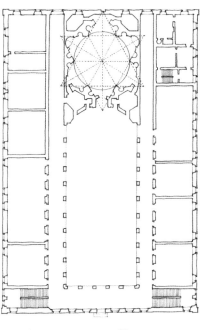

0   30 m

14.143 **Plan and section: Sant'Ivo alla Sapienza**

14.144 **Sant'Ivo alla Sapienza, Rome**

14.145 **View from the dome, St. Peter's Square, Rome**

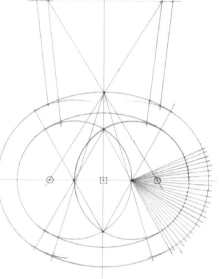

14.146 **Bernini's geometric solution for laying out St. Peter's Square**

St. Peter's Square

In 1626, Pope Urban VIII called upon Giovanni Lorenzo Bernini to begin work on the great baldachino over the papal altar of St. Peter's. So impressed was he that in 1629 he appointed Bernini the official architect of St. Peter's. Thereafter, for at least forty years, the greatest of the Baroque architects was engaged in the basilica's embellishment. The partnership between Urban VIII and Bernini matched that between Julius II and Michelangelo as one of the greatest patron-artist relationships in the history of architecture. But the scheme to redesign the grand piazza in front of St. Peter's came from Alexander VII. The first stone was laid in 1657, and the piazza was finished in 1666. A number of factors had to be taken into consideration. The old entrance to the Vatican was 120 meters northeast of the portico and had to be retained. Also, a covered processional way for state visits to the Pope had to be constructed, and the loggia for the time-honored papal blessing over the central entrance had to be kept within view of the greatest possible number of people, especially for the Easter celebration. Finally, there was a great Egyptian obelisk that had been brought to Rome in 37 CE that had to be moved to its present site (which occurred in 1586). Bernini's solution was to create and interlink two piazzas: a trapezoidal one in front of the church and

a great oval one opposite the facade. The trapezoidal space consists of corridor wings connected to the facade of St. Peter's. The basilica therefore seems to be brought forward and its height accentuated. The oval was constructed in a relatively conventional manner out of a series of circular arcs. The colonnade consists of two rows of column pairs that were designed to flair out from

14.147 **Aerial view of St. Peter's Square**

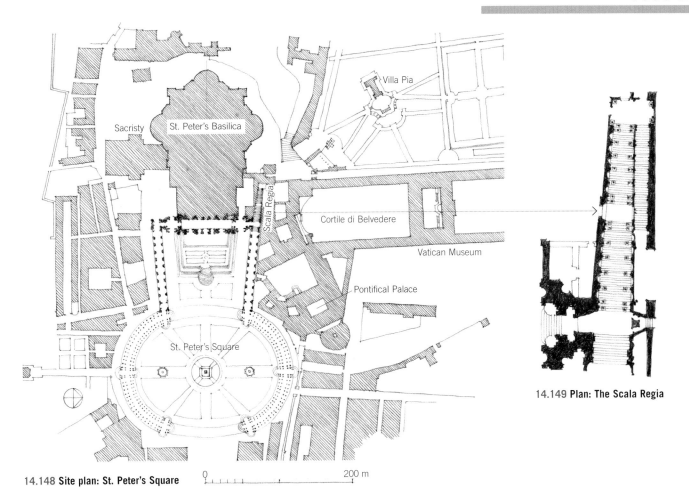

Sacristy

St. Peter's Basilica

Villa Pia

Scala Regia

Cortile di Belvedere

Vatican Museum

Pontifical Palace

St. Peter's Square

0   200 m

14.148 Site plan: St. Peter's Square

14.149 Plan: The Scala Regia

14.150 Colonnade, St. Peter's Square

the center, and because the side arms are farther out from the center, its circularity was emphasized. Bernini also experimented with a single large circle. Only over time did he come to the decision to make an oval; even so, the space is so vast that it is perceived as circular with the preexisting obelisk serving as its center; that may indeed have been Bernini's intent.

There had been nothing like Bernini's colonnade in any previous architecture, so his placement of an Ionic entablature on Doric columns seemed more than forgivable. The solid strength of the columns, in fact, contrasts with the verticality of the slender Corinthian columns of the facade. The program for the site required an important asymmetry in the plan to accommodate a suitable entrance into the Vatican Palace. Bernini solved this by incorporating the entrance into the northern colonnade. The entrance opens to the Scala Regia, (1663–66), which serves to bring dignitaries up to the papal palace. The aisled and vaulted

stairway is an architectural triumph over the awkward siting. Though the space provided was neither straight nor wide nor adequately lit, Bernini overcame each obstacle by using tricks of perspective that resulted in an impressive and dignified approach to the papal apartments.

When Bernini died in 1680 the connection of the great oval to the street leading up from the Tiber River had not yet been determined. Bernini had planned a building that would partially close off the piazza, creating a greater sense of enclosure, but it was never built. In 1935, under Benito Mussolini, the area was cleared out and given its current monumental design.

San Filippo Neri

Born in Modena, Guarino Guarini (1624–1683) taught mathematics after having joined the Theatine order, a Counter-Reformationist teaching movement founded in the southern Abruzzi. When the Theatines were invited to Paris, they introduced, to the astonished French, a new attitude toward religion involving elaborate representations and theatrical devices. The Theatines, unlike other orders, took their architects from members of their own order, and it was in this context that the young Guarini encountered the architectural profession. He also had the good fortune of studying in Rome in the 1640s, during the years in which Bernini and Borromini were the most active. His work, however, deviates from the trajectory set out by them in so far as it was influenced not only by medieval precedents, which he assiduously studied, but also by Islamic architecture. The telescopic disposition of vertical space characteristic of Mudejar architecture is exemplified in La Seo (the Cathedral of Saragossa), begun in the 12th century. Guarini also studied Gothic architecture, which, though much undervalued in Italy, had rebounded among intellectuals as part of a protest against the preponderance of Roman taste. Not Gothic, however, was Guarini's insistence that the upper ribs float in space, as at San Lorenzo in Turin (1668–87), where their support to the ground is visually incomprehensible. They are held up by four massive piers tied together at the level of the squinches by diagonal cross-arches, with the whole system disguised so well—and so purposefully—that the corner chapels' round openings seem to point to nothing behind them but thin air.

Guarini's centralizing urge in subsequent works was resisted by the Counter-Reformation clergy who argued that it did not fit their liturgically needs. The resolution created by Guarini and used subsequently by others was a type of elongated centralized system, either with an ellipse or by multiplying spaces along the axis. The Church of the Immaculate Conception in Turin is a case of the latter, whereas San Filippo Neri in Turin is an example of the former. There triangular projections break up the nave into three lozenge-shaped spaces.

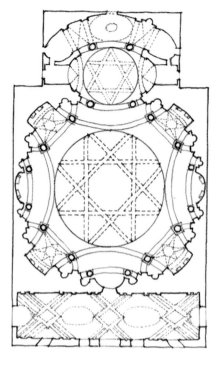

14.151 Plan: San Lorenzo in Turin, Italy

Though there are some similarities to a study plan that Borromini made for one of his churches, Guarini's plan is unmistakably different, not only in its separation and reintegration of the elements but also in the relationship between primary and secondary spatial elements. In Borromini, the secondary elements are still part of the inner spatial surface; in Guarini, the secondary spatial elements are almost autonomous, yet they appear continuous in the nave, suggesting a further continuation of space where there is none.

14.152 Interior: San Lorenzo in Turin

14.153 **Place Royale, Paris**

14.154 **Plan: 17th-century Paris**

Place Royale

When Henry IV came to power in France in 1589, Paris was not the city it is today. Despite the nominal authority of the crown, France essentially functioned as a highly decentralized confederacy of autonomous provinces. Paris had suffered several setbacks, such as the absence of the kings, who preferred to live in their countryside châteaux, and the general downturn of the economy in the 16th century. In Paris, there was not even a royal palace. With an estimated population of twenty million in the 1600s, France was, however, the most populous country in Europe and the third most populous country in the world—only China and India had greater populations. Despite this massive increase in urban populations, the rest of France remained a profoundly rural country. Economically, the glut of gold and silver from the Americas had led to inflation and created a huge underclass that would haunt French politics for another century.

In deciding to make Paris a capital city and the seat of a newly forming centralized nation-state, Henry IV initiated a series of urban projects that were also intended to boost the city's economic condition. One such project was the triangular-shaped Place Dauphine (1609–14), designed to provide accommodations for bankers and merchants. To make its importance a highly visible, it was located at the westernmost tip of the Île de la Cité; its narrow entrance formed a tranquil and enclosed precinct. Another experiment in urban design and mercantile enhancement was the Place Royale (today the Place des Vosges), begun around 1605 on open land at the edge of the city. It was originally planned with three sides for shops and apartments and the fourth for a range of workshops for the manufacture of silk. Though some silk was still imported from China, much of it now also came from Vigevano, Italy, where silk production was mastered in the late 15th century. Henry IV was eager to reduce France's dependence on foreign production, but French silk production never succeeded because of the climate, and eventually the whole square became a residential address that attracted the cream of Parisian society. Presiding over the square at both ends were special pavilions for the king and queen, as the place was intended as a setting for royal pageants. It was inaugurated in 1611 when a masque and a tournament were held there in celebration of the marriage of Louis XIII to Ann of Austria. As a setting it was well suited to the nobility and the rich bourgeois, who had taken to strolling and riding in carriages. Originally, therefore, the square was not paved but covered with a lawn and fenced in, an idea unknown to the Italian Renaissance.

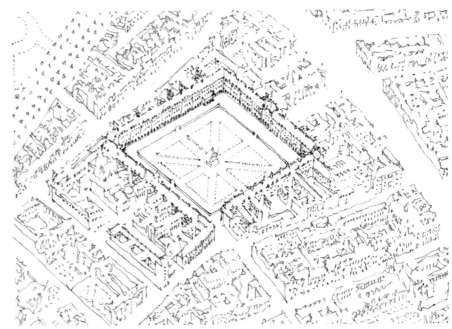

14.155 **Aerial view: Place Royale**

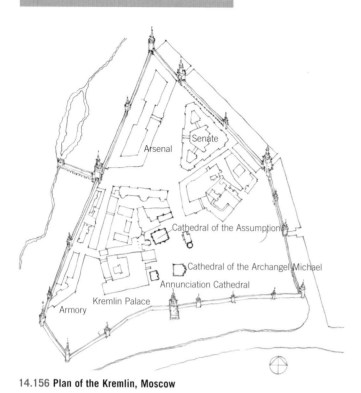

14.156 **Plan of the Kremlin, Moscow**

14.157 **Cathedral of the Assumption, Moscow**

Kremlin's New Churches

The Byzantine Church, in a desperate move to relieve Turkish pressure on Constantinople, agreed to reunite with the Roman Catholic Church (the Union of Florence, 1439). The Russian Church, a delegate from which was present at the signing in Florence, chose, however, to repudiate the treaty and to maintain the Russian Church as defenders of the Orthodox faith. This sense of renewal, along with the consolidation of central Russian lands in the face of the disintegration of the Mongol Empire, spurred an unprecedented building campaign, especially under Ivan III (1462–1505). Despite Russian insistence on a decoupled relationship with the West on matters of church doctrine, Ivan III sent an envoy to Italy in 1475 to seek out Italian architects who could assist in the planning and execution of his various construction projects. None was more important than the redesign of the Kremlin, the hilltop fortification compound at the center of Moscow that city rulers had used as their place of residence since the 12th century. Italian engineers began repairing and updating the Kremlin walls as well as parts of the palace within.

The most important Italian architect to arrive was Aristotile Fioravanti (1420–85), who had worked in the service of Francesco Sforza in Milan. He designed the Cathedral of the Assumption (Uspenskii Sobor), a church that became the location for the crowning of Russian rulers and the investiture of the patriarchs of the Russian Orthodox Church. The nave consists of a nine-square grid defined by four freestanding columns. The apse and associated liturgical spaces form a separate block, the whole packaged into a rectangle with only the apse projecting at the rear as in the Hagia Sophia in Constantinople. The principal dome is not at the center of the nine-square grid but over the intersection of the main east-west axis with the secondary north-south axis. On the outside, the building is segmented into tall round-headed bays marked by thin columns. A band of delicately articulated decorative arches defines the middle zone. The windows are slit-like and contribute to the building's feel of solidity. Five tall drums and their gilded domes project into the space above the building. This typically Russian pentacupolar silhouette brings the Italian and Russian elements together.

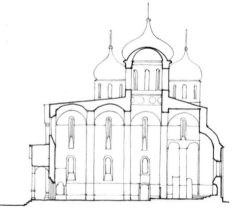

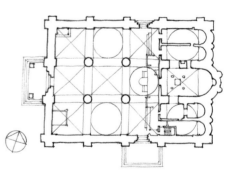

14.158 **Plan and section: Cathedral of the Assumption**

One of the final churches begun by Ivan III was the Cathedral of the Archangel Michael (begun 1505) on a site a 100 meters to the south of the Cathedral of the Assumption. It was to be used as the burial site for Russian rulers. The architect, Aleviz Novyi, arrived in Moscow in 1504 after completing a palace for the Crimean khan, Mengli-Girei, at Bakhchisarai. He was possibly Alvise Lamberti da Montagnana, a student of Mauro Codussi, the noted Venetian architect. The architecture clearly reflects a Venetian style, as opposed to the more medieval, Lombard style of Fioravanti. The facade is of a standard tripartite division, whereas the side facade has an ababa rhythm. Instead of unadorned piers, as at the Cathedral of the Assumption (in the city of Vladimir, 1158–60), there are two registers of pilasters, some of the earliest examples of the neoclassical style in Russian architecture. Much like the Cathedral of the Assumption, there is a fusion of Russian and classical motifs, especially in the series of shell arches that form the crown of the building. Indeed, it was the intent of Ivan's architects to remain firmly rooted in the Russian tradition, and classicism was therefore sublimated to regional idioms to maintain, for political purposes, a continuity with the past. Though the impact of Italian classicism was muted in subsequent decades by the return of the onion dome and the reintroduction of color, its impact is nonetheless undeniable.

Church of the Ascension

Following Ivan IV's conquest in 1556 of the Khanate of Astrakhan at the mouth of the Volga River on the Caspian Sea, one of the most important Eurasian trading arteries came into Muscovite possession. Just as importantly, the conquest gave a boost to the Russian Orthodox Church, which had been facing challenges to its wealth, institutions, and even to its doctrines from various religious groups. The churches being built at the time are known as tower churches and have become some of the more distinctive examples of Russian architecture.

14.159 **Cathedral of the Archangel Michael, Moscow**

One of the most noted examples is the Church of the Purification (latter half of the 17th century), which was built in Aleksandrova Sloboda, in the compound from which Ivan himself ruled. Built over an earlier structure, it consists of a two-story polygonal arcade supporting tiers of *kokoshniki*, an open octagon, and on top, a tent roof with cupola soaring to a height of 56 meters. The building thus moves away from the religious traditions embedded in the pentacupolar motif toward a dynastic message that reached its apotheosis at the Church of the Ascension at Kolomenskoe (1529–32) some 10 kilometers southeast of the Kremlin in Moscow. This church consisted of a two-tier arcaded church reached by external staircases, on top of which rose an astonishing structure comprised of the body of the church, three tiers of flattened *kokoshniki*, and an octagonal drum supported by a tent tower on top.

14.160 **Church of the Ascension, Kolomenskoe, Russia**

Amsterdam

Though Holland had the fastest-growing economy in Europe at the time, having become the mercantile hub of the Spanish Empire, this was not reflected in its architecture. Because the Dutch were for the most part Calvinists and their beliefs dictated simple structures, they did not build churches until they had gained their hard-fought independence from Spain in 1648. During this period Amsterdam was becoming one of the leading international ports of Europe, developing a cityscape that included the town hall in Dam Square (now the Royal Palace), the Westerkerk, the Zuiderkerk, as well as a large number of canal houses commissioned by leading mercantile families. Dutch naval power began rising rapidly in the late 16th century, and the Netherlands became the leader in global commerce during the second half of the 17th century. Its principal enemies in the contested ocean routes for sugar, slaves, and spices were initially the Spanish and Portuguese and then the English.

The first church in Amsterdam specifically built for the Protestant community was the Zuiderkerk (1603–11). It is a simple six-bay rectangle that is pseudobasilican in plan: although it has a nave and side aisles, it has no apse, thus reflecting the more community-oriented nature of its religious services. The priest gave his sermons from a pulpit attached to one of the columns more or less in the midst of the congregation. Music and especially communal singing were important parts of the liturgy. There is no crypt since relics and their worship are not part of the Protestant religion. The building has a wooden vault with a tower squeezed into one of the corners but positioned so that it dominates the view along a nearby canal. Although the building is relatively simple, the tower with windows, balustrades, and paneling is as extravagant as any of that era. On the interior, the columns are dark and contrast with the whitewashed walls in imitation of 15th-century northern Italian Renaissance churches. In this way the style harkened back to an ideal of a simpler late Medieval–early Renaissance life, presumed to have been untainted by the grandeur and corruption of the Church of Rome.

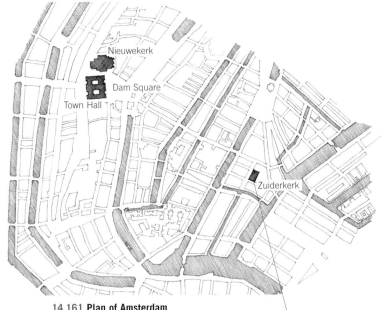

14.161 Plan of Amsterdam

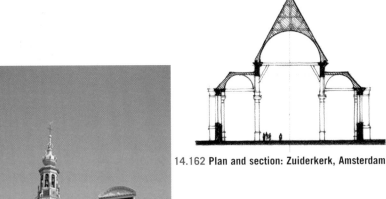

14.162 Plan and section: Zuiderkerk, Amsterdam

14.163 Zuiderkerk, Amsterdam

14.164 Amsterdam Town Hall (Burgerzaal)

14.165 Plan: Amsterdam Town Hall (Burgerzaal)

First floor

Ground floor

0   40 m

The Zuiderkerk was followed by the Westerkerk (1620–31), which created a more unified whole: there is a clear division between the main axis—where the tower serves as an entrance—and the cross-axis with the pulpit.

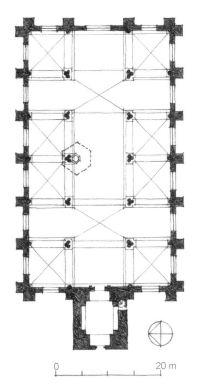

0   20 m

14.166 Plan: Westerkerk, Amsterdam

Amsterdam Town Hall

For the Dutch, it was not gold that was to be extracted from its colonies but cocoa, tobacco, and sugar, which turned out to bring more profit than all the bullion of the Americas combined. In Amsterdam, the new center of the Dutch world, and a city entirely dedicated to making money, palaces, monasteries, and castles were not part of the cultural fabric. Instead there were rows and rows of townhouses facing onto a relatively straight arrangement of parallel streets and canals. By the end of the 17th century, the city's population had grown from twenty thousand to two hundred thousand in the span of just over a hundred years. The city's exchange bank, Wiselbank, founded in 1609, was for a long time the greatest public bank in northern Europe. By the end of the 17th century, over 16 million Dutch florins were on deposit in its vaults—including the florins of other European governments. The bank was on the first floor of the new town hall, designed by Jacob van Campen (begun 1648). On the facade of the building, a statue of Atlas lifts the globe on his shoulders above a pediment in which the nations of the world offered up their goods to an allegorical

Amsterdam. Inside, the marble floor of the huge barrel-vaulted town hall, or Burgerzaal, lit from the sides by two courtyards, was inscribed with maps of both the heavenly and the terrestrial worlds. The building, though it is almost 100 meters long, its facade looks like two palaces stacked on top of one another.

It remains significant, however, as an expression of Amsterdam's ascension in world politics and as a statement of the burgeoning role civic architecture was to have in the future urban profiles of Europe. It was also one of the first applications of Italian Renaissance style to a monumental civic structure, and it was in many respects to remain the model for town halls well into the modern era. The building faced onto one of the city's few public squares, called the Dam, which had as its focus a tall square building known as the Wage (or the public weigh house). Here and in the nearby markets, as a description put it in 1664, the whole world seemed to be assembled to buy and sell— Poles, Hungarians, the French, the Spanish, Muscovites, Persians, and Turks.

14.167 Elizabethan England

14.168 Wollaton Hall, near Nottingham, England

Elizabethan England

Though England, too, benefited from the shift away from the Mediterranean to the Atlantic, its growth in the first half of the 16th century was hampered by complex internal conditions, poor management, and restrictive policies. Its maritime operation existed mainly in fishing, smuggling, and plundering. It was at best a regional force. This began to change during the reign of Queen Elizabeth I (1558–1603). She adopted modern notions of management, transforming feudal magnates into officeholders. Overseas foreign investments resulted in a growing propertied class, with wool and textiles becoming an increasingly large part of the economy, along with the production of lead, salt, and soap. The population increased from three to four million between 1530 and 1600, providing a large reservoir of potential indentured labor. The English destruction of the Spanish armada in 1588 established the country as a sea power to be reckoned with. The result was a thirst for a cultural equal with France and Italy, and 16th-century Englishmen were the first of their nation to become more aware of the vast world around them.

English architecture, however, had a long way to go. Houses were relatively plain and rugged and showed no fine paintings, apart from portraits. Nonetheless, the change in English culture was rapid and profound. Old houses were set out with chimneys, walls were paneled, windows glazed, and old timber-framed buildings were faced with

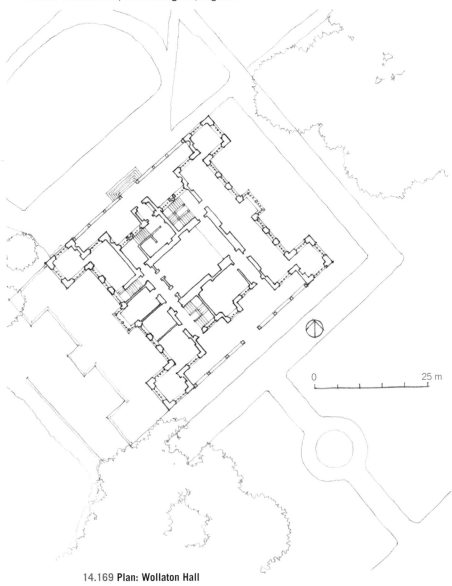

14.169 Plan: Wollaton Hall

14.170 Hardwick Hall, Bolsover, Derbyshire, England

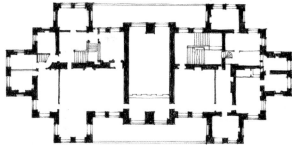

14.171 Second-floor plan: Hardwick Hall

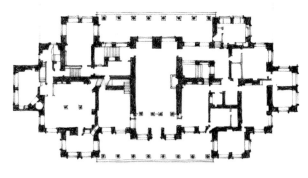

14.172 Ground-floor plan: Hardwick Hall

stone. A particularly important innovation at the time, and one that affected the development of Elizabethan-era architecture, was the use of coal in glass firing. And here, once again, immigrants played an important role. Jean Carré, who was from the highly contested area of Lorraine and whose patent for plate glass was granted in 1567 was attracted to England along with other glassmakers from Lorraine. Soon furnaces were being built in scattered parts of the country, and prices began to fall almost at once. The market responded with enthusiasm. Wollaton Hall (near Nottingham, 1580–88), the home of an important coal magnate, was already a splendid showcase for the new industry. It sported at the top a special "prospect room" that had no particular purpose other than to show off its towering fenestration. This type of fenestration can be contrasted with that of Titchfield Priory (Hampshire, 1537–40), which, even though it is only the gatehouse that survives, still has windows in the Gothic medieval manner.

Hardwick Hall

Hardwick Hall (1592–97) in the English heartland at Bolsover in Derbyshire is less ostentatious and more unified than Wollaton Hall. Its tall windows are simply and tightly framed against the unadorned wall. Volumetrically, the building is an ingenious fusion of a three-story building with six, four-story towers. As was characteristic for English manor houses, the symmetry on the outside was not enforced on the inside, where the designers preferred to operate with greater flexibility. Apart from the front and back porticoes and the connecting hall, the building, designed by Robert Smythson, was laid out to suit the needs of the client, Bess of Hardwick, Dowager Countess of Shrewsbury, a woman of considerable standing in Elizabeth's court. Upon the death of her husband, George Talbot, the 6th Earl of Shrewsbury, the biggest tycoon in England, Bess became one of the richest ladies in England, well able to dictate her preferences in architecture. The ground floor contained the kitchen and service rooms as well as a chapel. To the right of the great hall, a staircase led to Bess's principal quarters, with anterooms leading to her bedroom at the corner. On the other side there was a great chamber, which served as the dining room.

There was another suite for relatives and guests on the third floor. The second and third floors both have long galleries along the back facade. The long gallery on the third floor is fully integrated into the plan with the "withdrawing chamber" located on the central axis. The prototype for such a gallery was the queen's gallery in Hampton Court (1536–37), which was built as a place from which the ladies of the court could watch the hunting in the park. At Hampton Court, the great gallery was an independent wing attached to the queen's lodgings; at Hardwick, it is integrated into the design. The interior of Hardwick was mostly finished with whitewash. The color in the house was provided by the rich tapestries, the numerous table carpets, and the gilded and colored furniture. The floors were covered in reed mats, as was common at the time.

Banqueting House

Inigo Jones's second visit to Italy from 1613 to 1614, during which he studied the buildings of Andrea Palladio in particular, prepared the young architect (1573–1652) for his most ambitious project, the Banqueting House. The first Banqueting House, appended to the Royal Palace in London, was built in 1581 and served for dining and theatrical entertainment. A second one was built in 1606 but was destroyed by fire in 1619. The Banqueting House designed by Jones in 1619 was less a place for banquets than a royal audience hall, reflecting a greater emphasis on royal authority. This was the first public structure in England in the mature Palladian style. At the ground floor, the windows between the pilasters were an alternating sequence of triangulated and segmental pediments, while at the upper floor the windows are all unpedimented, yielding an intricate yet calm design. The central three bays are emphasized by the use of attached columns, and the corners by pilaster pairs. The whole is raised on a low rusticated basement that matches in height the balustraded frieze on top. The building's importance lies in the symbolic significance of its Italian motifs—an attempt to extend the architectural language born during Europe's mercantile revolution in the 15th century. But whereas Italian architecture originally developed in a culture of regional princes and rich merchants, it was now being associated with the centralization of the state.

14.173 Interior, Banqueting House, London

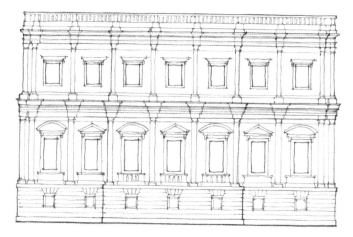

14.174 Plan and elevation: Banqueting House

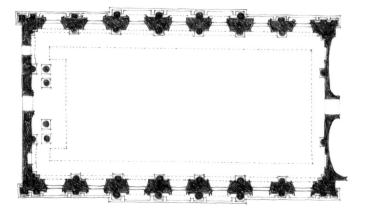

1700 CE

By the early 18th century, cities like Samarkand, Bukhara, and Aleppo, once at the heart of Eurasian trade, had become increasingly marginal to the new world economy centered on the maritime ports established by the European colonial powers. This phenomenon was global, spawning major new metropolises such as Macao, Hong Kong, Singapore, Bombay (now Mumbai), Calcutta (now Kolkata), Madras (now Chennai), Cape Town, St.-Louis (Senegal), Rio de Janeiro, Buenos Aires, Boston, New York, and Quebec City. At the foundation of the system was the fort and the plantation. Local populations were transformed into workforces and when these were in short supply, enslaved and indentured laborers from Africa and Asia were brought in on ships. In Europe, it was the French who first translated colonial power and wealth into large-scale architectural projects, none grander than Versailles (1661–1778). Aristocratic privilege and high-bourgeois mercantilism resulted in large residences reflecting the social pretensions of their owners and the new economic conditions. New building types, such as bourgeois apartments (or *hôtels*), coffeehouses, parks, and theaters sprang up.

It was also a time of unease. Religious persecutions in Europe were at their height, and tensions among the various powers over control of the global economy resulted in a series of costly wars. The Dutch War (1672–78) concluded in favor of the French,

but later the War of the Spanish Succession (1701–14) created an important power shift in the direction of Austria and England, paving the way for places like Schönbrunn Palace (begun 1695) and Blenheim Palace (1705–24). Russia, too, was a rising power, redefining itself in the European model both culturally and architecturally with its impressively scaled new capital of St. Petersburg, founded in 1703. Throughout Europe, the Baroque style, as it came to be known, was dominant, with thousands of churches built or refurbished in that manner. Huge palaces were also built, first in France and then in Austria, Italy, and Germany, with long allées and gardens stretching far into the landscape. The increased governmental centralization led to new state institutions such as hospitals and asylums.

China and Japan were, however, still economically and politically balanced against the colonizing West. The Qing annexed parts of Central Asia and Tibet to make the largest Chinese empire in history. To accommodate China's diverse populations, the Qianlong emperor developed a pan-Asian conception of empire, building dozens of new palaces and gardens and reestablishing the Yuan-era link with Tibetan Buddhism. Since Chinese currency was based on the silver standard, European traders, anxious for Chinese goods, poured silver into the empire. In Japan, the Tokugawa shogunates were in the midst of redefining the culture, creating a world that followed a strict code of behavior that was in

many respects astonishingly modern, as the rising middle class sought ways to articulate institutions suitable to its needs despite the restrictions placed on it by the shoguns.

In India, in the brief period of time as the Mughal Empire weakened and before full colonization by the British, local governors took the opportunity to proclaim independence. Shuja-ud-Daula in northern India, the Nawab of Oudh in Bengal, the Sikhs in Punjab, the Rajputs in Rajasthan, and the Marathas in the Deccan fought among themselves for power at the same time as European colonizers began to build on their coastal footholds and start to acquire hinterlands. As a result, though this was a turbulent period in India, it was also a time of tremendous cultural and architectural exploration. The Sikhs, a reformist movement, took root in northwestern India and established a formidable kingdom. Darbar Sahib ("Golden Temple") in Amritsar was their most important shrine. The Mallas of Nepal, meanwhile, enjoyed relative immunity from these global events next door, although their royal square in Patan embodied its own global history.

In contrast to the energy in Europe, India, and East Asia, building activity in West and Central Asia slowed down. This was so pronounced that most books dealing with Islamic architecture end around 1750. The result was that East and West, both strong and viable, split around an increasingly economically marginalized center.

▲ **Elmina Castle**
Begun 1482; taken over by the Dutch in 1637

Haciendas ▲
Begun ca. 1529

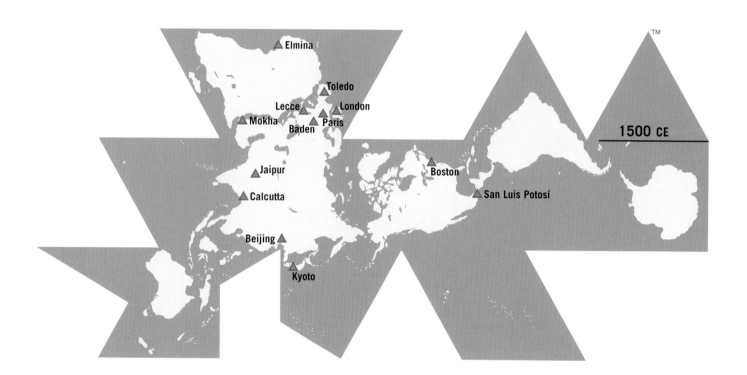

▲ **Elmina**

▲ **Toledo**

Lecce ▲ ▲ **London**

▲ **Mokha** **Baden** **Paris**

▲ **Jaipur**

▲ **Calcutta**

Boston ▲

▲ **San Luis Potosí**

Beijing ▲

Kyoto

TM

1500 CE

China: Ming Dynasty
1368–1644

▲ **Fort Manoel**
ca. 1682

Central America: Viceroyalty of New Spain
1535–1821

France: Bourbon Rule
1589–1792

▲ **Hôtel de Sully**   ▲ **Hôtel des Invalides**
1624–29   1670–76

     ▲ **Versailles**   ▲ **Place Vendôme**
     1661–1778   Laid out 1702

England: Stuart Rule   Hanoverian Rule
1603–1714   1714–1901

1600 CE	1700 CE	1800 CE

Sir Isaac Newton's *Principia* published ◉   ◉ Thomas Savery invents the steam engine
                              1687   1696

                                              ◉ Abraham Darby produces high-quality iron
                                                 1711
                                                                        ◉

▲ **St. Stephen Walbrook**   ▲ **Blenheim Palace**   Benjamin Huntsman develops the
1672–79   1705–24   crucible method for making steel
                                                           1740
     ▲ **St. Paul's Cathedral**   ▲ **Stowe Gardens**
     1675–1710   Begun ca. 1712

     ▲ **Schönbrunn Palace**
     Begun 1695

The Baroque Era   ▲ **Zwinger**   ▲ **Winter Palace**
Late 16th to early 18th century   1710–28   ca. 1730

                                            ▲ **Karlsruhe**   ▲ **Santiago de Compostela**
                                            Laid out 1715–19   Facade: 1738–50

                                                 ▲ **Vierzehnheiligen**
                                                 1743–72

Qing Dynasty
1644–1911
                                                         ▲ **Yuanming Gardens**
▲ **White Stupa, Beihai**   1720s
1651

Japan: Edo Period
1615–1868

     ▲ **Sumiya**
     1670s

South Asia: Mughal Dynasty
1526–1858

▲ **Meenakshi Sunderesvara Temple**
1623–59

     ▲ **Durbar Square**   **Darbar Sahib** ▶
     Rebuilt 17th century   Rebuilt 1764

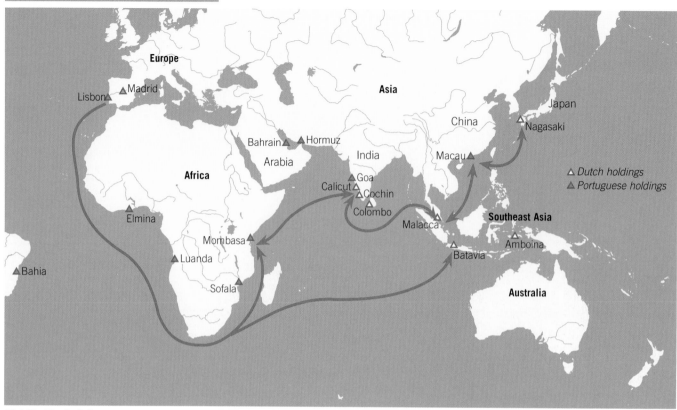

15.1 World colonialism

Colonialism

By the end of the 17th century, what had begun as risky sojourns to distant lands in search of less expensive spices developed into a struggle among the various European nations for control of foreign lands and their lucrative trading links. The principal competitors were Portugal, Spain, Holland, France, and Britain. The models of colonization differed according to circumstance. Africa's colonization was based almost exclusively on the extraction of gold and ivory—and on the export and enslavement of human beings. Local traders brought the "goods" to the ports where the exchange took place. The slave trade had been a part of African economy for centuries, even among Africans themselves, but the new colonial model, dependent on cheap labor, magnified it to such a degree that the history of Europe, Africa, and the Americas was irrevocably altered. It is estimated that more than twenty million people, and possibly as many as forty million, were forcibly removed from Africa; all the colonizing powers participated.

The first slaves were brought to the Caribbean in the 1520s. In 1619, the Dutch introduced slaves into North America to work on the plantations, replacing the decimated Native American population. The primary form of colonial intervention was the founding of plantations, which had to be managed with a firm grip. Their principal commodities were sugar, coffee, tobacco, cocoa, and tea. The plantation system was first installed by the Dutch in Indonesia, the Spanish in the Americas, and the French in the Caribbean—and then eventually in Africa itself. The legacy of this system was unambiguously negative and had consequences that are still playing out today. In Mexico, even by 1910, 70 percent of all arable land was held by just 1 percent of the population, and similar situations existed in South American countries. Almost every country or region that was colonized by the plantation system had to struggle later to create secular, scientific, and cultural institutions on par with those of the Europeans.

The situation in New England was different, even though there, too, the initial impetus for colonialization was economic. There were no large chiefdoms, as there were in Louisiana and Georgia, to stand up to the invaders, and this allowed settlers to nourish the illusion that they were occupying virgin territory. In addition, the influx was extraordinarily diverse. By 1700, from Maine to Virginia villages and towns had a mixture of Dutch and English Puritans, French Calvinists, Catholics, Swedes, Spanish Jews, and English Anglicans. By the early 1700s, a traveler would have found courthouses, schools, churches, roads, and two universities—Harvard, founded in 1636, and Yale, founded in 1701. New England was thus an international mercantile-agrarian project, unique in the colonial world.

India, because it was remote, densely populated, and largely urbanized, did not receive large influxes of European settlers and their slaves. Even though plantations owners could find inexpensive labor among the locals, officers of the British East India

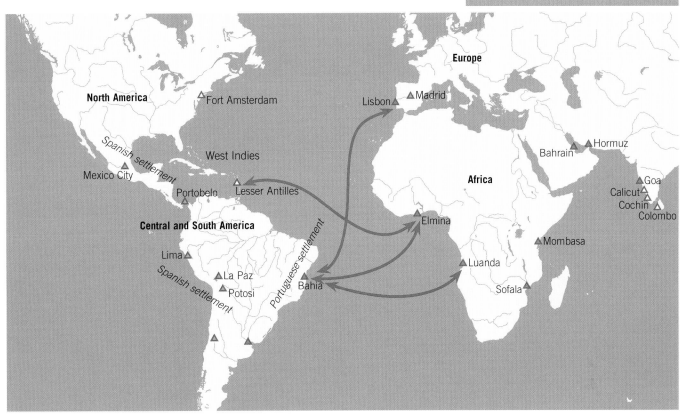

15.1 World colonialism

Company, at least initially, had to approach Indian rulers with the appropriate respect to negotiate trade—and protection treaties. In 1690, the then ruling Islamic Mughals allowed the English to found an outpost at Calcutta (Kolkata), at the swampy mouth of the Hooghly River. Security at Calcutta, however, was not a foregone conclusion. Just as the Dutch were having difficulties in Indonesia, Calcutta was sacked in 1756 by Siraj ud Daula, the regional ruler of Bengal. Taking their advantage, the English pitted one regional faction against another, and by successfully applying this practice soon became the masters of South Asia, ultimately partitioning the subcontinent some two hundred years later, along largely religious lines, into India and Pakistan. The consequences of that partitioning are still playing out today in seemingly unrelenting regional strife. (This is just one example of the problems caused by artificial boundaries created by colonial powers that ignored the ethnic composition and preferences of the indigenous population once colonial models had to be abandoned.)

China presents a different story. Under the Qing dynasty, the China's economy was thriving, and it neither wanted nor needed European goods. The English, however, wanted tea, which by the 19th century had become an important commodity in England. But instead of paying with currency, of which the English were in short supply, they wanted to trade tea for the opium that the English grew in India. The Chinese government naturally resisted and attempted to close its ports. Trade, nonetheless, was forced upon China. In the mid-19th century, following complaints of hardship by the English merchants and opium suppliers, the British invaded, launching the Opium War of 1839 to 1842, which forced China to open its ports and brought it to its knees—another sad chapter in the history of colonial arrogance. As in China, the Japanese economy was flourishing, and trade with Europe carried more obvious risks than benefits. Well aware of what was happening in India, Japan therefore also closed its ports beginning around 1639—with the exception of Nagasaki, where circumstances were kept tightly controlled.

The largely Arab and Islamic countries of West and Central Asia were of limited interest to the colonial powers. The Ottoman Empire was seen primarily as a convenient bulwark against czarist Russia. Persia was of even less consequence to the Europeans and slowly shrank under Russian pressure. The area did not to receive any strong interest from the Europeans until the the discovery of oil in the 20th century.

It is no accident that just as the colonial project was unfolding and flooding Europe with great wealth, the 18th century saw a philosophical movement emerge that challenged the arbitrariness of colonial power and its attitudes toward "primitive cultures." Based largely in France, England, and Germany and known as the Enlightenment, it tried to imagine alternative civil and institutional models in tune with new thinking about the rule of law, even though it did not reject colonialism as such. Its successes and failures in that respect are still being debated.

Colonial Forts

To protect ports and trade routes, the colonial powers embarked on a worldwide fort-building campaign. Many hundreds, if not thousands, were built—sixty alone along the West African coast. Africa had been a supply source of enslaved laborers for centuries. Islamic rulers, for example, owned slaves captured in holy wars. In fact, some of the first slaves brought to India were brought there by Arabs. For the most part, enslaved men were used in the government and by the military, and women as domestics in households or as field-workers. But in reaching around the west coast of Africa, Europeans opened a whole new chapter in the dark history of slavery.

Portugal's Elmina Castle in Ghana, on a promontory overlooking the mouth of a river, set the pattern for subsequent buildings. The rectangular castle was located within the protected core of a set of perimeter walls. A church and administrative center faced each other across the inner courtyard. Corner bastions projected past the surfaces of the building so gunners could protect the entrances and flanks. In 1637, it was taken by the Dutch, who rebuilt and expanded it as a slave collection point. By 1700, new technologies and military strategies required a different type of fort. Success now lay not in the height of the walls but in the ability to shoot sweeping fire from within the fort while deflecting mortars and cannon shots coming from the outside. Fort cannoneers did not want to lob the ball high, as it would merely plunge to the earth. Instead, the cannonball was shot low to the ground so that it would bounce and ricochet through enemy lines. Artificial sloped terraces, known as glacis, were built around the fort to expose attackers to cannon shot. When combined with ditches and bastions that provide raking angles, the

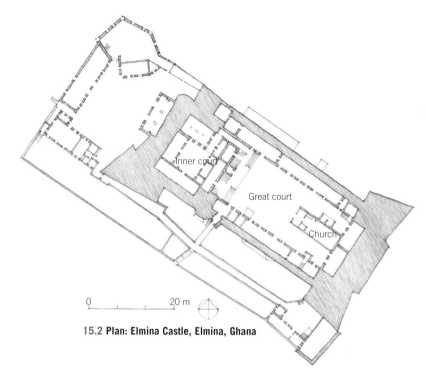

15.2 Plan: Elmina Castle, Elmina, Ghana

Inner court

Great court

Church

0   20 m

15.3 Elmina Castle

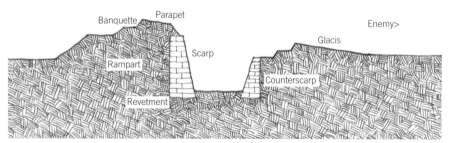

15.4 Section through fortification, Elmina Castle

Banquette Parapet

Rampart

Scarp

Revetment

Enemy>

Glacis

Counterscarp

geometry of an 18th-century fortification becomes quite complex, as can be seen in Fort Manoel, (ca. 1682). It was located in Marsamxett Harbor, to the northwest of the principal city of Valletta, which it protected in Malta. Fort Manoel was used as a model for forts built throughout the world, particularly by the English and French. For example, the English Fort Commenda in Ghana, begun in 1686, is a similarly advanced but somewhat simpler version. These forts would remain the norm for the next two hundred years, until the advent of aerial bombardment. One of the most complete 17th-to-19th century fortification systems that still exists can be found in Valletta, Malta.

Haciendas

The hacienda system is thought to date to 1529, when the Spanish crown granted to Hernán Cortés the title of marquis of the Valley of Oaxaca in the present-day state of Morelos, Mexico. The grant included all the Native Americans then living on the land and the power of life and death over them. The Native Americans, like the slaves who soon arrived from Africa, were bound to a particular hacienda for life, as were their descendants. By the 18th century, the system, stretching from Mexico to Argentina, was the primary means of export production and in some cases the core of urban developments. Included in this geography was Louisiana, which was settled by the French. Haciendas came in various sizes, and some were gigantic. Peotillos, 55 kilometers from San Luis Potosí in Mexico, for example, controlled an area of 193,000 hectares.

The word *hacienda* comes from an Old Spanish term (*facienda*) derived from the Latin *focere*, which means "to make something," and most haciendas specialized in one or two products—Peotillos, for example, specialized in grain. In the Andes, maize, wheat, barley, beans, and a variety of vegetables were produced; in areas where water was abundant, sugarcane was grown, which gave rise to rum and liquor production.

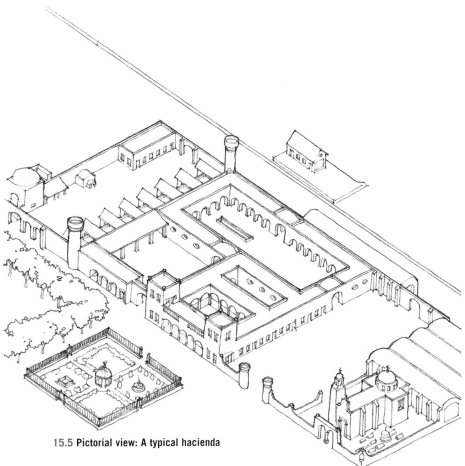

15.5 Pictorial view: A typical hacienda

Other haciendas focused on livestock, cacao, coffee, tobacco, cotton, rubber, and a variety of woods. Since the hacienda was often remote from metropolitan centers, it had to accommodate a wide range of functions. It had its own marketplace, cemetery, and jail. Layouts followed a common scheme involving courtyards for different purposes: for the workers and their families, for workshops, and for warehouses. The main residential building fronted onto a plaza, known as a *patio de campo*. The link between the *patio de campo* and the more restricted private areas of the master was through a corridor known as a *zaguán*.

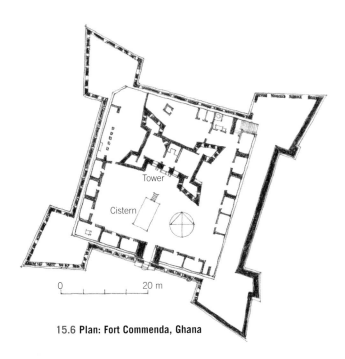

15.6 Plan: Fort Commenda, Ghana

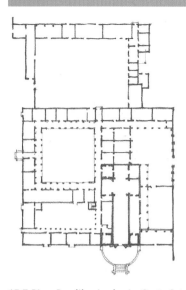

15.7 Plan: Brazilian hacienda, Santa Catalina

15.8 Example of a Brazilian hacienda

Brazilian Haciendas

In Brazil, the development of sugar and coffee plantations generated, as early as the 17th century, a proliferation of *fazendas* (the Portuguese equivalent of haciendas) in the northeast of the country. As in other places, the high death rate of the native population created a need for African slaves, and eventually over three million were brought to the country. Thus a new type of construction was added to the architecture of the *fazendas*—the *senzala*, or slave quarter, which was divided into small spaces to house the slaves and their families. The symbolic and economic center of the *fazenda* was the large patio where the coffee was dried. The master's house was located on one side of the square, usually positioned on higher ground overlooking the entire area.

Italian *Masserie*

Colonization was largely a European imposition on non-European lands. An exception was in southern Italy, which was under Spanish domination until the arrival of French troops under Napoleon. Lecce, an important center in Apulia, was an independent city-state until 1463, when it and the surrounding territory came under the control of the Kingdom of Naples, which in turn was an extension of the Spanish Empire. Anti-Spanish uprisings were brutally suppressed. The area, a leading producer of olives and wines, was organized into

a system of plantation estates known as *masserie* (or *masseria*, for a single farm). The buildings, like haciendas, had courtyards for agricultural purposes, but the main house was far different than the hacienda, with its roomy patio. Largely because of worries about raids by the Ottomans and resistance from the locals, the buildings were a cross between a palace and a fort. They were usually solidly built of stone, with few

windows and often a long external staircase leading to the *piano nobile*. The top of these stairs was sometimes constructed in wood so that in case of invasion, the staircase could be separated from the house in a last-ditch effort at defense. The farms, which dotted the landscape, brought wealth to their owners, who lived in cities such as Lecce and Bari, which were outfitted with Spanish-style Baroque churches and palaces.

15.9 Example of a *masseria* near Lecce, Italy

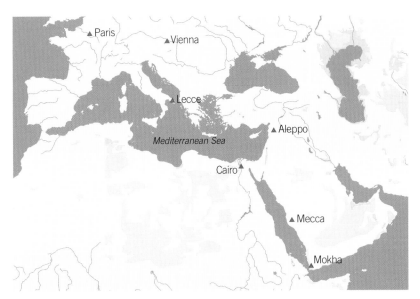

15.10 Africa, West Asia, and Europe, ca. 1700

15.11 Kaffeehaus Jüngling, Vienna, ca. 1838

Coffeehouses

The expanding middle class, with its ravenous taste for novelty food items and luxuries supplied by the colonies, rapidly reshaped European culture. Its diet changed considerably, with tomatoes, potatoes, and corn forming the new staples; chocolate became a luxury item, imported from the Spanish Americas, and sugar from the Caribbean became an indispensable consumer good in a very short time. Coffee, however, came to Europe from Africa by way of Arab traders. It is thought to have been first produced in Ethiopia and Yemen. The drink caused a great deal of controversy in the Islamic world, because some authorities thought coffee was intoxicating and therefore should be forbidden. As a result, its consumption was initially associated with subversive political activity, perhaps because it was drunk in the new all-male coffeehouses where intrigue might be brewing along with the beverage. From the beginning, then, the social significance of drinking coffee derived from its consumption in public by an exclusively male clientele in this new kind of establishment, the coffeehouse.

The coffeehouse of Ipshir Pasha in Aleppo, Syria (1653), is a rare early coffeehouse to have survived to present times. It consists of a courtyard and a covered hall, with windows overlooking the street to the south. Domes of varying shapes cover the hall. The end of the Turkish trade monopoly over coffee came in 1616, when the Dutch East India Company illegally exported and planted seedlings in Java and elsewhere. The French subsequently founded coffee plantations in the Caribbean, leading to a rapid expansion of the drink's popularity. The opening of the first Parisian café was in 1672. The Kaffeehaus Jüngling in Vienna, from about 1750, had a completely glazed two-story wooden facade overlooking a piazza provided with tables and illuminated by a large lamp (such outdoor lighting being at the time quite a novelty). By 1800, there were more than three thousand coffeehouses in England.

Tobacco smoking was brought to Europe by the Spanish army and was eventually taken up by men of the upper classes who were under the impression that it enhanced their reasoning capacities. Thus, along with coffeehouses emerged gentlemen's smoking rooms. Sugar, another colonial product, was also incorporated into newly emerging rituals of consumption. It was put into tea and coffee (first in France, so it is thought), thus combining—if one throws in a piece of chocolate—a culinary experience that flaunted Europe's global economic imperative. One also saw the emergence of professional sugar bakers, called *konditors* in southern Germany, who often created a whole sugar course, in which an entire meal was replicated in sugar for the guests to view—and to nibble on before it was taken away and the real meal served. No European city was complete without its *konditorei* serving sweets to ladies on cozy couches, forming the counterpoint to the bars for men, where coffee and liquor were consumed standing up. These socializing habits formed in the days of colonialism still continue today.

The times of meals began to change to accommodate these transformations in taste. Until then dinner, the principal meal, was served at midday, but the custom of drinking tea and eating chocolate in the afternoon caused it to be shifted to later in the evening. It soon became the custom to start the day with coffee and chocolate, a repast now called breakfast. Whereas coffeehouses were associated with boisterous male conversation and business deals, tea became domesticated into a ceremony presided over largely by women, who often served it on silver tea sets—silver being yet another colonial commodity. (In 1717, 700,000 pounds of tea were imported; 3 million pounds were imported by 1742.) Furniture was designed to accommodate the new rituals, including a "conversation chair" that allowed one to lean back in a more relaxed position; the high-backed padded chair also made its appearance. There were those who complained about the "modernization" of tastes, but there was no turning back, and many of these novel habits became permanent features of urban life.

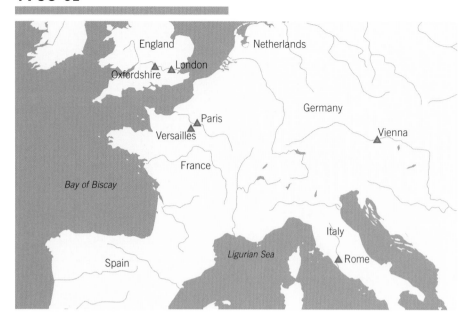

15.12 18th-century Europe

French Culture of Empire

With the decline of Spanish sea power after the loss of its armada at the hands of the English in 1588, France acquired the Isle of Bourbon (1642) for use as a commercial base in the Indian Ocean; took over the mouth of the Senegal River in Africa, where it became involved in the slave trade; and set up sugar plantations in the Caribbean. French fur dealers settled Canada, founding Quebec City (1608). Somewhat later, the French founded New Orleans (1718) at the mouth of the Mississippi River, forming a T-shaped area running through the heart of the vast North American continent. An important export from Canada was fur. (Large animals had been hunted to extinction in Europe centuries before.) Fur then became the new fashion requirement for the elites fetching huge sums of money. The money flowing into France, however, created an inflation the likes of which had never been experienced in the global economy before, making, in essence, the poor even poorer. For the elite, however, it brought unimaginable wealth, which was spent in lavish constructions beginning around 1660. This architectural bonanza was further by the optimistic mood of the 1680s, when France basked in a short-lived peace following the successful conclusion of the Dutch War in 1678, which made France and England the primary colonial powers of the world.

What the French brought to the colonial project, unlike the Spanish, was advanced planning. Their success, especially under Louis XIV, king as of 1661, lay in combining absolutism with an effective government bureaucracy, all supported by an elaborate tax collection system. The rationalization of the national economy was the undertaking of Jean-Baptiste Colbert (1619–83), Louis XIV's chief adviser on political, economic, naval, and religious matters. He was responsible for many of the innovations that, though cumbersome, created the base for France's economic prosperity. It also created the modern notion that the state should define and invest in its own economic interest. An edict was issued, for example, that all lace sold in France must be made in France. The freight tax was eliminated to lower the cost of transporting goods. Thanks to Colbert, there was a new understanding that there was a nexus between global trade and the national economy. Colbert also appreciated that economic power was dependent on knowledge. He therefore commissioned extensive studies of shipbuilding, navigation, and armaments to ensure that the French fleet remained the strongest in the world. He also founded the Royal Academy of Science (1666) and the Academy of Architecture (1671), among other institutions, to serve and advise government administrators and ministers.

As a consequence of these changes, a new social order emerged, known as the bourgeoisie. The nouveaux riches, as the French called them, adopted aristocratic airs but betrayed their origins through their lack of courtly manners and their ignorance of etiquette. Changes in fashion, hairstyles, cuisine, and lifestyles required constant attention. The emulation of the nobility also entailed conspicuous consumption, especially by financiers who bought ennobling titles and large country estates. When the French king Francis I (1494–1547) invaded northern Italy, he was struck by the level of decorum he encountered there, such as the use of elaborate introductions, the formalities of courtly interaction, and the public displays of power and wealth. Though the French quickly learned Italian manners, it was not until the explosion of wealth in the mid-17th century that there was an attempt to transfer these courtly protocols into the upper levels of society, where it was refashioned according to a different set of needs and expectations. Hunting, the principal pleasure of the aristocracy, was replaced by attending a theater, conversing in a parlor, strolling through a private garden, or waltzing in a glittering ballroom—endeavors that now defined the enrichments of bourgeois life.

As a result, there was a tremendous outpouring of artistic production. This was the age of the playwright Molière and the composers Henry Purcell, George Frederick Handel, and Johann Sebastian Bach. Antonio Canaletto amazed viewers with his highly realistic paintings of urban squares, and Giambattista Tiepolo excelled with his dramatic ceiling paintings of mythological events taking place among softly billowing clouds. Courts vied for the best painters, sculptors, and designers.

It might appear ironic that a century that saw the proliferation of flamboyant artistic excess and the emergence of harsh class distinctions, not to mention abject forms of colonial arrogance, was known as the Age of Reason. But the advent of European modernity derived from many sources and had many facets. Not all factors followed each other in logical sequence; they occurred in a sort of eruption of concurrent events and interlocked phenomena, such as the rise of philosophical rationalism and state-sponsored industrialization, theories about cause and effect, and philosophies of cognition. Francis Bacon (1561–1626) and René Descartes (1596–1650) with his famous declaration of self-discovery, "cogito, ergo sum," ("I think, therefore I am"), set the mood for a world of experimentation and deductive reasoning that tried to come to grips with an emerging awareness of the complexity of the world, whether in the realm of science or practical knowledge. Though Descartes' philosophy, known as Cartesianism, was condemned by the Catholic Church, its followers were legion, and Descartes' physics and "method" were broadly accepted, even by some churchmen, in the guise of Aristotelianism.

Nonetheless, the scientists of the age still kept their religious attachments in some form or other. Seventeenth-century rationalism should not, therefore, be confused with late 19th-century professionalism. While science and rationalism intruded into the social, intellectual, and aesthetic climate of the age, it often did so under the guise of traditionalism. Nonetheless, the 17th century was a time when almost every subject was analyzed. One saw the publication of René Descartes *Discours de la méthode* (1637), Thomas Hobbes's *Leviathan* (1651), as well as the *Théorie de la construction des vaisseaux* (Theory of the construction of the ships, 1667) by the Jesuit priest Pierre Hoste, a professor of mathematics who sought to improve the art of shipbuilding. The slide rule, the barometer, the thermometer, and the compound microscope all came into being in the first half of the 17th century. Generally speaking, 17th-century science stressed mechanics as a governing principle in the same way that governments began to stress and extend their bureaucratic reach, both ultimately promising efficiencies of production. The world was suddenly filled not only with agency but also with the means to control and define that agency and to give it spatial extension and measure.

Hôtels

The word *hôtel* refers to an apartment for the urban elite as it came to be developed around 1630. *Hôtels* were designed as showpieces of order and dignity in the otherwise chaotic and unregulated world of the Paris street. The reason for their sudden emergence was that Henry IV (1553–1610), unlike previous French kings who preferred to live in rural châteaux, moved his court to Paris and established a capital there. The result was that the wealthy wanted to now live in Paris as close as possible to the court.

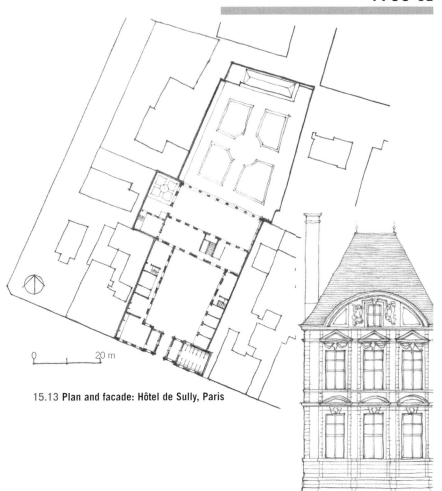

0   20 m

15.13 Plan and facade: Hôtel de Sully, Paris

15.14 Hôtel de Sully

The buildings were designed around a specific set of spaces. A *porte cochere* allowed carriages to enter the *cour d'honneur*, where the ritual of arriving, dismounting, and entering was played out. The stables were located to one side of the courtyard, along with special rooms for the carriages. The *corps de logis*—the principal living quarters—faced the court. To the rear of the *corps de logis* was a garden, perhaps with a gallery, a long windowed room for taking in the views and conversing. Visiting rooms, ballrooms, and dining rooms, part of the *appartements de parade*, were on the main floor. The family living quarters, which were usually above, consisted of an antechamber in which to meet visitors; the bedroom (*chambre*); and possibly a more private room for conversation or study known as the cabinet. Servants lived under the roof. In the arrangement of the elements, symmetry was preferred, at least for the entranceway and courtyard, with much creativity going into establishing the necessary imprint in the often irregular urban sites with which the architects had to work. One of the best examples is the Hôtel de Sully by Jean du Cerceau (1624–29). It was lived in by Maximilien de Béthune, Duc de Sully (1560–1641), superintendent of finances under King Henry III and later Henry IV's prime minister.

Place Vendôme

Most of the early 17th-century *hôtels*, though located near the Royal Palace, were built wherever land was available and were thus relatively isolated from each other. As the century progressed, architects sought to integrate hotels into real estate packages known as royal squares. Though these squares were called royal, they were usually built on the initiatives of private individuals or municipalities—even though the climate for their creation was fostered by the king—and they therefore had to be consonant with the principle of royal dignity. Between 1684 and 1688 there were many more proposals for such squares than were actually realized. The first in Paris was the circular Place des Victoires (1684–87) with an equestrian statue of the king in the middle. This was followed by the Place Vendôme (laid out in 1702) whose facades were all designed by Jules

Hardouin-Mansart (1646–1708) and his disciple Pierre Bullet. (It was only later that the actual houses behind the facades were executed by various architects.) The double *hôtel* for the wealthy financier Antoine Crozat (1702) and his son-in-law the Comte d'Evreux (1707) was located in one corner. Crozat was a leading figure in royal finances. Both *hôtels* have rooms in a remarkable variety of sizes and configurations, but typical of French design was the absence of corridors (except in the servants' quarters) to link the rooms, which were organized sequentially along the main facade. The building was designed by Pierre Bullet. Place Louis XV, now the Place de la Concorde in Paris (1763–72), linked the Tuileries Gardens and the Champs Élysées on one axis with the river, and the Church of the Madeleine, planned as a royal chapel (1806–42), on the other axis. Its central area was actually designed as an island of sorts, surrounded as it was by a moat (now filled in). Squares were also built in other French cities, such as the Place Royale (now the Place de la Bourse) in Bordeaux (1729) and the Place du Palais in Rennes (1721–30).

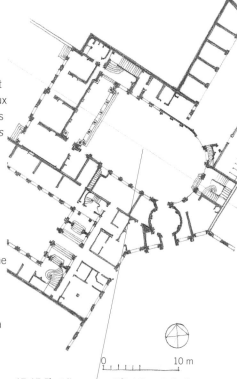

0   10 m

15.15 First-floor plan: Hôtel Crozat, Paris

15.16 Plan: Place Vendôme, Paris

15.17 Place Vendôme, Paris

15.18 Paris in the age of Louis XIV

East Facade of the Louvre

The Louvre was originally a small 12th-century fort built as a defense against the Normans. Charles V enlarged and improved it, but all of it was torn down in 1546 by Francis I, who commissioned a new hunting lodge to be erected by Pierre Lescot. Construction began and then stopped. Jean-Baptiste Colbert hoped that Louis XIV, after his marriage to the Infanta of Spain, Maria Teresa, in 1660 would make the Louvre the seat of the royal household and the court. As a result, in 1655, Louis Le Vau (1631–70), France's leading garden and château designer, took over the job of updating the Louvre into an urban palace, in collaboration with Claude Perrault. In 1664, a competition was held for the east facade of the Louvre, and submissions were made by Claude Perrault and even by Gian Lorenzo Bernini, who was invited to Paris to study the site. Bernini proposed a Roman-style facade that would hide all the previous construction. His design was rejected, however, for one that was a synthesis of the ideas of Perrault, Le Vau, and perhaps others.

Given the project's complex history and the number of architects involved in the final design, it is an astonishingly successful building. The high ground floor, with its narrow, minimally detailed windows, serves as a podium for the main floor, with ranges of coupled, freestanding columns that form a screen for the building behind, creating a linear loggia. A central pedimented projection was integrated, with the columnar screens

to its flanks. Unpedimented "pavilions" with pilasters instead of columns define the far ends. Such an arrangement was quite novel. It could be compared with the Palazzo Porto-Breganze designed by Andrea Palladio (built by Vincenzo Scamozzi, 1575), which is more unified in appearance, or the Villa Barbaro (1549–58), where the pieces are more differentiated. The Louvre struck a balance between unity and differentiation that was much admired in its own day—and much imitated. The building is also significant in the history of technology. The columns carry straight entablatures that are actually a series of disguised arches held together in part by tie rods. The structure was completed by 1670, but when Versailles was proclaimed the new royal capital in 1682, the funds for the remaining Louvre projects that had been foreseen began to dry up.

Château de Versailles

The site for the Château de Versailles was an old hunting lodge about 20 kilometers southwest of Paris. The redesign of the building into a grand palace by Louis Le Vau and Jules Hardouin-Mansart went through several phases, beginning in 1661, after André Le Nôtre had begun work on the gardens and fountains. The architects solved the problem of what to do with the old building by wrapping a new building around it. The original palace still stands, but it is embedded within the fabric of a new structure that consists of a series of forecourts, creating a telescoping U around a central court at the top of a gently sloping hill. In 1682, work had progressed far enough that the king could proclaim the palace the royal capital. Three avenues lead through the countryside to the front gate, but only the central and northern avenues lead to Paris; the southern avenue, 1 kilometer long, was added for the sake of symmetry. The avenues brought visitors to the first gate, through which the carriages passed. They were stopped at the second gate, and everyone except for the most distinguished had to proceed on horse or foot to the last gate, which led into the inner courtyard.

On the ground floor of the palace were apartments, mainly for the royal guards and administrators. One room to the right, however, was specially prepared for the reception of important visitors. It contained the grand double Stairway of the Ambassadors, resplendent with colored marble and wall paintings. The stairway led to the principal reception rooms where the king lived. There were no corridors.

15.19 East facade of the Louvre, Paris

15.20 Château de Versailles, France

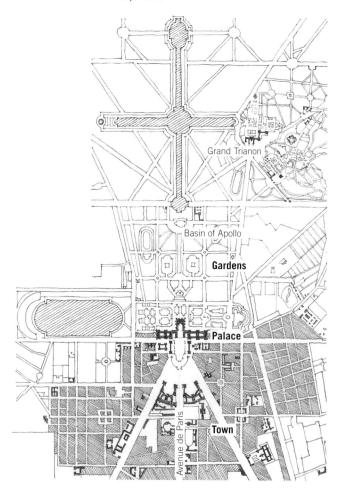

Grand Trianon

Basin of Apollo

Gardens

Palace

Avenue de Paris

Town

15.21 Plan of Versailles

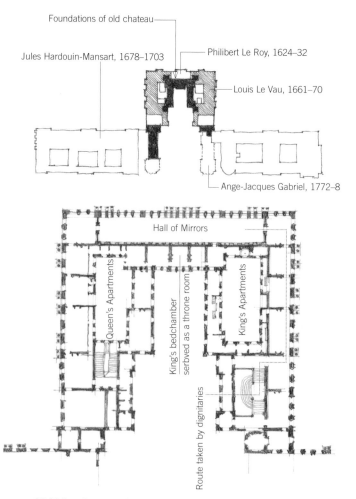

Foundations of old chateau

Jules Hardouin-Mansart, 1678–1703

Philibert Le Roy, 1624–32

Louis Le Vau, 1661–70

Ange-Jacques Gabriel, 1772–8

Hall of Mirrors

Queen's Apartments

King's bedchamber serbved as a throne room

King's Apartments

Route taken by dignitaries

15.22 Development of the palace at Versailles during Louis XIV's reign

15.23 **Hall of Mirrors, Palace at Versailles**

15.24 **Hardouin-Mansart's chapel at Versailles**

The apartments were arranged enfilade, meaning that the doors of the rooms lined up to provide a continual vista along the length of the suite. Facing the gardens to the west was the long Hall of Mirrors, which was where state receptions were held. Just off the hall, where it crosses the main axis of the palace, one finds the king's bedroom, loctated at the conceptual center of the palace's universe. The bedroom was not a private room, but a place where the king met friends and even important dignitaries.

The building was designed, planned and executed by the King's Buildings Office (Conseil des Bâtiments), which was set up by Jean-Baptiste Colbert and was so well organized that even after the untimely death of the palace's chief architect, Louis Le Vau, construction work was never halted. Le Vau's replacement was Jules Hardouin-Mansart, who was not only the architect but also the administrative coordinator of the system that had been devised by Colbert. (Ironically, though the King's Buildings Office set an astonishingly high standard of performance, the king's personal authority was often required to resolve even the most trivial of questions.) Le Vau based his designs to some extent on his landscaping of the Château

de Vaux-le-Vicomte (begun 1657) outside Paris, built for Nicholas Fouquet, Louis XIV's finance minister. There, using a hill, he created a series of terraces and slopes with views back to the building. The land around Versailles was much less auspicious. It lacked vistas, woods, and even water. Much of it was a bog. Water for the fountains and canals needed to be pumped uphill. The gardens were laid out on a grid and aligned with the palace at the far eastern end and aligned along a broad allée to a fountain at the far western end. Though no hill was available on the flat site, Le Vau was able to create subtle elevation changes by gently sloping the ground downward away from the palace toward the Grand Canal in the distance, creating a feeling of height and extension into space simultaneously.

At first the gardens were designed for traditional uses, like walks and pleasurable conversation, but Louis XIV introduced the idea of the garden celebration, or *fête*, which included horsemanship events, banquets, plays, music, and fireworks. These events were not just for the elite but were part of the king's publicity and propaganda apparatus to enhance the fame of Versailles. As tastes developed for ever grander displays, the

gardens went through several redesigns, particularly at the western end, where Jean-Baptist Tuby's Basin of Apollo, which shows Apollo rising from the sea was added. The theme of Apollo, elaborated on in a nearby grotto, was meant to emphasize the king's divine aspirations.

In the early 1680s, Louis XIV became increasingly religious due to the influence of his pious mistress, Madame de Maintenon, whom he secretly wed in 1684 after the death of his first wife, Maria Teresa. Though there were already several chapels in the Palace of Versailles, Hardouin-Mansart was commissioned to design an even grander one. His consisted of a rectangular nave with an apse, but without a dome. Gothic in its proportions, it was intended to demonstrate a connection with the Palatine Chapel. Much like Charlemagne's cathedral in Aachen, it has arched openings on the ground floor. The exterior is an elegant fusion of Gothic sensibilities with classical orders, a high pitched roof, large windows extending to the pilasters, and a buttresslike thickening of the apse walls. The main floor was articulated by freestanding columns holding a straight entablature, influenced by the Louvre's colonnade.

15.25 **Courtyard, Hôtel des Invalides, Paris**

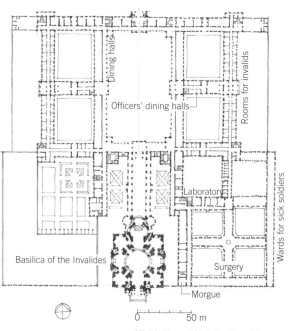

15.26 **Plan: Hôtel des Invalides**

Hôtel des Invalides

Hospitals had first appeared in Europe as a byproduct of pilgrimages and of the Crusades. There were several important hospitals in Italy. The Knights of St. John were well known for their hospitals on Rhodes and elsewhere. By the 18th century, however, hospitals were flooded not only with the thousands of soldiers who fought in the almost endless cycle of battles but also by the poor and the indigent, who formed an increasingly large lower class. Plagues and epidemics added to the problem. In Paris, a cholera epidemic in 1519 and the plagues of 1580, 1596, 1606, and 1630 struck down thousands. But because hospitals remained associated with religious orders and charitable institutions, there was practically no distinction between a hospital, a pesthouse, and a poorhouse. Conditions were so terrible that the sick were often unwilling to leave their houses for a hospital, concerned that while they were sequestered, their property would be pillaged or their income threatened. To combat these conditions, Henry IV decreed the construction of the Hôpital St.-Louis (begun 1607). It was

outside the city walls and easily accessible from major roads. The wards consisted of wide, open corridors, with patients' beds placed against the walls. Four of these corridor buildings were linked to form a large courtyard.

After the end of the Thirty Years' War in 1648, the thousands of former soldiers, many of whom had lived their entire lives in the military and were unaccustomed to civilian life, posed a threat to civil and moral authority. The Hôtel des Invalides (1670–76) aimed to address this problem in that it served as a military retirement dormitory. Behind its moat and expansive entrance lies a large court, while ranges of buildings to the right and left are grouped around smaller courts. The north facade is articulated in typical French fashion by central and end pavilions that project forward. Apart from the entrance porches, there are no columns or pilasters on the main facade. The court has two stories of arches on piers relieved only by the pedimented pavilions at the center along the axis. There were special areas for sick and wounded soldiers, for pauper soldiers, and a barracks for older veterans. There were

surgery areas and large mess halls where soldiers ate with their officers at the head table.

By way of comparison, hospitals in England, where there was a lot ambivalence about spending public money in a way that many thought would seem to reward poverty, tended to be simpler and less generous. Chelsea Hospital (begun 1682) shows, however, the first awareness in England of French innovation regarding the problems of former soldiers. Designed by Sir Christopher Wren, soldiers were sequestered in cells, showing a degree of unease about allowing them to socialize. The cells were placed in ranges, back to back. At the end of the range, a larger room was set out for the sergeants. Instead of an enclosed quadrangle, the wards faced each other across a courtyard open to the Thames River, with a great hall and chapel linking the wards at the far end. The hospital's governor and lieutenant governor lived in detached pavilions at the corners. The differences in the two hospitals speaks volumes about English and French attitudes about society and hierarchy at the time.

Basilica of the Invalides

The church at Les Invalides (1676–79), also known as the Soldier's Church, is actually a double church, a basilica attached to a centrally planned domed edifice. It was designed by Hardouin-Mansart. The facade's windows are not articulated with Italian-style balconied *aediculae*; instead, they are left to appear as mere openings carved out of the thickness of the wall. The dome sits on a high double drum and constitutes the culmination of the building's massing. The lowest dome is cut open to create a large oculus, revealing the underside of the dome above. It is painted with the sky and clouds, and allegorical religious figures from the Charles de Lafosse painting *St. Louis Giving Up his Sword to Jesus Christ*, which portrays a soldier's ultimate destiny. The uppermost dome is supported by a lightweight wooden structure.

Splitting the dome into several shells made it far different from Michelangelo's dome at St. Peter's, whose dome is doubled mainly for structural reasons. Here the dome is split not only to create an illusion on the inside—a type of vertical framing device into the glories of heaven—but also to enhance its visibility from the outside. Instead of being just a temple to martial glory, the church was a religious shrine dedicated to the sainted Louis IX, the 13th-century French king with whom Louis XIV was increasingly associated. The fortunes of the French government were decreasing toward the end of Louis XIV's reign and his reputation needed glorification, if not deification. Carrying over the theme on the dome's ceiling, the saint's statue appears in the left niche of the main facade; Charlemagne's is in the right niche.

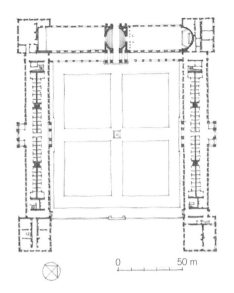

15.27 Plan: Chelsea Hospital, England

15.28 Dome, Basilica of the Invalides, Paris

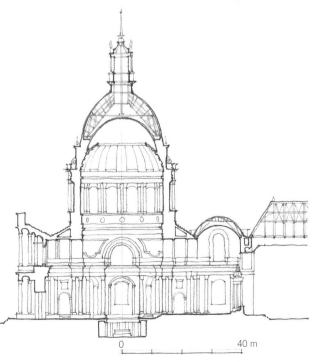

15.29 Section through dome, Basilica of the Invalides

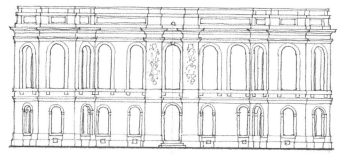

15.31 Elevation: L'Observatoire de Paris

15.30 L'Observatoire de Paris

L'Observatoire de Paris

The foundation for theoretical discourse in architecture had been laid in the Renaissance by Leon Battista Alberti, Sebastiano Serlio, and Andrea Palladio, among others. One of the beneficiaries of the work of these Italian theoreticians, and one of the most representative of the new generation of French theoreticians in the 17th century, was Claude Perrault (1613–88). Perrault was a fervent believer in the exalted position of the age in which he lived. For him, the age of Louis XIV had reached the equivalent of the age of Augustus. Perrault began as a member of the medical faculty at the University of Paris but shifted his interests to the realm of architecture. He was familiar with Greek and knew Latin, and his translation of Vitruvius's *Ten Books on Architecture* was brought out in 1673 in a spectacular folio edition dedicated to the king. Perrault also presented a copy to members of the French Academy of Sciences. It was the first authoritative and well-annotated French translation of Vitruvius, and it became the standard work on architecture in Europe. Though Perrault's own taste influenced the illustrations, he attempted to adhere as much as possible to the information in Vitruvius's text, setting an example for accuracy and attention to detail that was to become an essential aspect of the neoclassical mentality. His images emphasized the undecorated aspects of antiquity, resisting the temptation, prevalent in his time, to dwell on ornamentation and decoration. A particularly heated debate revolved around the question of whether the perception of beauty was a result of custom or a spontaneous response. Perrault argued that beauty was not a fixed property to be revealed by the artist but a variable depending on custom, pointing out, for example, that one can find neither two buildings—nor two authors—that agree on all subjects or always follow the same rules.

Though Perrault had a hand in the design of the east facade of the Louvre, his principal architectural accomplishment was the design of the Observatoire (1667–72) for the Royal Academy of Science (founded in 1671). Built in the southern outskirts of Paris, the building was by the standards of the day quite austere. There were no orders, no columns, and no pilasters. Simple string courses demarcating the stories, and openings are either slightly recessed from the smooth wall surface or surrounded by barely projecting moldings. Each side of the octagonal corner towers was aligned with the sun's position at solstices and equinoxes, and the eastern one was unroofed for the use of a telescope within. The building was put together with the greatest skill, and the staircase, with its complex three-dimensional curving surfaces—all in stone—still astonishes today. The roof was used as a platform from which astronomical measurements could be made. A hole in the center of the floors of the main chambers allowed the sun's zenith to be calculated.

England: House of Stuart

In 1536, the English king Henry VIII dissolved the Catholic monasteries and abbeys and created the Anglican Church. Although the Anglican Church has many liturgical similarities to the Catholic Church, it is the king of England, not the Pope, who is its head. It was thus in every aspect a state religion. Puritanism, however, gained many adherents, and they became a substantial force in Parliament. The English parliament became so strong that during the English Civil War (1642–51) it had Charles I executed in 1649 and set up Oliver Cromwell (1599–1658) as ruler of the Protestant Republic, as some term this interim period. In 1660, the monarchy was, however, able to reinstate itself under Charles II. Despite these troubles, the external policies during this period were marked by rapid growth of trade and colonization. The Navigation Acts of 1650 and 1696 aimed at protecting English shipping and ending Dutch dominance in world trade. In the second Dutch War (1665–76), New Amsterdam, founded in 1625 by the Dutch West India Company, fell to the English and was renamed New York, after the Earl of York. In 1670, the British East India Company was given the right to autonomous territorial acquisitions.

In the meantime, the antiquated housing stock in London gave rise to untold problems. London fell victim to no fewer than sixteen outbreaks of the plague, culminating in the Great Plague of 1665, which killed 17,000 people. The following year, London experienced the first great urban fire of modern times, which lasted for five days and destroyed almost all of central London.

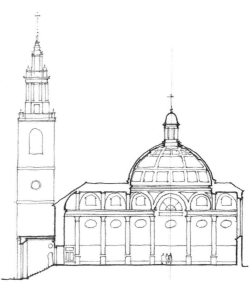

15.33 Plan and section: St. Stephen Walbrook

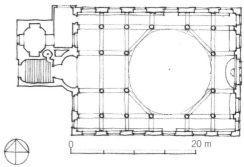

15.32 St. Stephen Walbrook, London

Some 13,200 houses were destroyed as were more than 80 churches, including St. Paul's Cathedral. (The fire also put an end to the plagues, apparently by killing off the rat population.)

Though the disaster presented an opportunity to rethink the layout of the city, it was decided to rebuild more or less along the lines of the old streets. Rebuilding the churches became an opportunity to place a strong Anglican imprint on the city. The Anglican Church was dominated by the landed gentry, and the church therefore became an extension of the interests of the ruling class. Sir Christopher Wren (1632–1723) was asked to design almost all of these churches—some fifty-one buildings—beginning in 1670. Having no recent English prototypes to fall back on, he relied on Italian notions but modified them to fit the more restrained tastes of the English.

The variety of Wren churches is immense, partially because many were built over the foundations of their predecessors, often on irregular lots and in cramped quarters. In a reaction against Puritanism, Anglicanism placed considerable emphasis on the dignity of the service as prescribed in the Book of Common Prayer. But unlike Italian Counter-Reformation churches, which emphasized the spectacle of devotion, Wren's churches possess some of the simplicity and openness of Protestant churches. The color pallet of their interiors was restrained; almost everything was white, with a few accents like gilded column capitals, string courses, and rosettes set against the dark wood of the altarpiece and furniture. Large windows brought in ample light. Wren experimented with a range of forms—centralized, longitudinal, and square. Some churches had galleries. The individually designed steeples,

however, became the most famous aspect of his designs. Steeples had been in disfavor since the introduction of the Italian Palladian style by Inigo Jones, who preferred towers and domes. Wren brought the steeple—a Scandinavian wooden architectural form—into the Palladian fold by creating a box for the bell chamber with openings and pilasters on which the steeple rested. St. Stephen Walbrook (1672–79) is a typical case. It is a cross-in-square church with a central dome, a forerunner of St. Paul's. The outside, mainly hidden behind the mansion house, appears plain, while inside is a bright classical interior. Eight Corinthian arches on high bases support the dome.

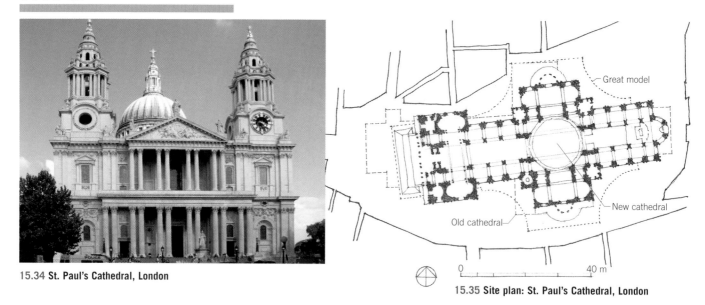

15.34 St. Paul's Cathedral, London

15.35 Site plan: St. Paul's Cathedral, London

St. Paul's Cathedral

After the destruction of St. Paul's Cathedral in the Great Fire of London, many wanted to rebuild it in the old Gothic style. Wren, however, envisioned a building up-to-date with European neoclassical sensibilities. Several plans and revisions were made, including one known as the great model, which had highly original large concave exteriors. It was rejected for a more conventional plan. The church fathers accepted the modern exterior but insisted on a medieval-style section, with low side aisles and a tall nave.

The building (1675–1710) is in the shape of a cross, with the dome, one of the largest in the world, over the crossing. It is surrounded by three galleries on different levels. To disguise the low side aisles, Wren created a blind second story that also conceals the buttresses holding up the vaults. Without the false second story, the dome would have looked astonishingly out of scale. Even so, it looms large, resting on a ring of columns with eight cleverly disguised buttresses. On the interior is a giant pilaster order for the nave and a lower order for the secondary spaces, modeled loosely on St. Peter's. But unlike Michelangelo's lower drum, which fits compactly onto the body of the building, St. Paul's drum is both lofty and airy, rising almost incomprehensibly out of the center of the building. While Michelangelo's lantern appears as a bundle of forces collected into a relatively tightly wound package, Wren's lantern sits serenely on top of the dome as a small centralized tempietto.

The outer dome, flattened on top, consists of a wooden frame with a lead surface supported by an invisible conical masonry structure. Below that there is a catenoid inner dome. To create the impression of height so that the inner and outer domes appear to match, the supporting columns lean toward the center. On the facades, which seem to resemble those of a palace more than a church, the paired pilasters and *aediculae* rely heavily on the themes set out by Donato Bramante, as does the ring of columns at the base of the dome, which—unlike the ones on the inside—are not structural (although they do add buttressing support to the base of the dome).

The pairing of the Corinthian columns on the facade is taken from the Louvre. Wren had made a trip to Paris and to Italy to see architectural developments in these places first hand. The building can thus be seen as a purposeful synthesis, if not a celebration, of different design ideas. Whether it transcends these can be debated. Unlike Hardouin-Mansart's dome for the Hôtel des Invalides, the interior of St. Paul's dome is painted to look like a colonnade supports a dome higher up. The upper part of the conical vault is painted to extend this illusion through the oculus.

A catenary arch is the mirrored upward projection of a suspended chain. It is the ideal basis for a vault or dome, as it supports itself without needing buttressing. This form of curve was derived from the mathematics of Jacobus Bernoulli.

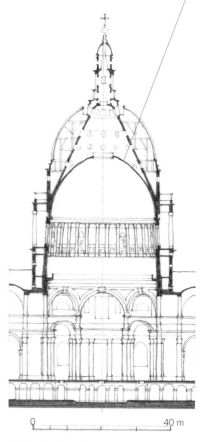

15.36 Section through dome of St. Paul's Cathedral

15.37 Dome, St. Paul's Cathedral

Blenheim Palace

The conclusion of the Wars of the Grand Alliance (1688–97), in which England, Austria, and others were successful against the French, resulted in a shift of power in the European world. The matter was not settled, however, until the War of Austrian Succession, which culminated in 1704 in a huge battle near the small German town of Blenheim. When it was over, the English, under the 1st Duke of Marlborough, had routed the French. Their success had clear implications for the global economy. Among other things, it enabled England to take over the lucrative French slave-trading network throughout the Caribbean.

As a token of her appreciation, Queen Anne, with Parliament's hearty approval, rewarded the duke with a 15,000-acre piece of land and the funds to build himself a castle. The building was designed from the start as a public monument to the English victory. In its great hall there is a painting of the duke in shining cuirass and blue mantle kneeling before Britannia, who, seated on a globe, offers him a victory wreath. At Britannia's feet sits the goddess Plenty, with fruits pouring out of her cornucopia. Mars and Hercules look on with wonderment. Off to one side Clio, the muse of history, holds a huge pen and is writing the words "Anno Memorabilia 1704" in a big volume. On the exterior, over the central portico, stands Minerva, the goddess of war, with a chained captive to either side. The corners of the towers are capped with 12-meter-high pinnacles that portray the duke's coronet crushing the French fleur-de-lis. Trophy piles carved out of stone, pikes, armor, cannonballs, and drums bristle atop the ends of the east and west pavilions, while ferocious lions sink their teeth into the ruffled feathers of French cocks. The building was designed by John Vanbrugh (1664–1726), a personal acquaintance of the Duke of Marlborough. Vanbrugh had no formal training as an architect, but he worked closely with Nicholas Hawksmoor, an architect who had apprenticed in the office of Wren.

During the Baroque period, the dome became a dominant theme for churches and even for secular buildings, like the U.S. Capitol. There are several variations, but unlike Palladio's dome, which has no drum, most post-Renaissance architects preferred the model set out by Donato Bramante: a dome resting on a short drum. Wren's dome for St. Paul's is clearly an adaptation of Bramante's.

15.38 **Blenheim Palace, near Oxford, England**

The plan for Blenheim Palace was designed as a showpiece of English might. The grand Roman imperial portico on the north entrance might seem obvious enough, but it only barely disguises the enormous hall behind it. The principal living suites in the rear were not connected enfilade, as they would have been in France, but were served by a circulation system that takes up quite a bit of space itself. On the west, there is a long gallery with views to a garden and a forest beyond. Though the building fulfilled the fantasy of domination, many even at that time thought it extravagant. But when Blenheim Palace came into being in 1705, absolute monarchy had reached its zenith in England and in France. Society believed in hierarchical order; reason, governance, and divinity had fused into one, and this was all reflected in its design.

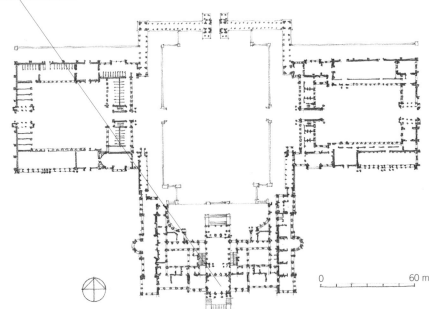

0   60 m

15.39 **Plan: Blenheim Palace**

15.40 **Blenheim Palace**

15.41 St. Mary Woolnoth, London

St. Mary Woolnoth

The most imaginative of the English architects of the early eighteenth century was undoubtedly Nicholas Hawksmoor (1661–1736). Wren shared with his apprentice an interest in the architecture of Asia Minor and in the then still barely known architecture of Greece and Egypt. But if Wren had an eye for compositional unity, Hawksmoor aimed to bring the elements of architectural composition into dynamic interrelationship. He pried features out of their expected contexts. Hawksmoor's buildings are often seen as examples of the Baroque or, in the case of St. Mary Woolnoth, the English Baroque, as it is sometimes called. Although Baroque religiosity was not a factor in his work, it nonetheless fit with the ambitions of Reverend Thomas Tenison (1636–1715), archbishop of Canterbury, who played a key role in rebuilding London after the Great Fire. He saw the fire as an opportunity to restore the luster of the Anglican Church, which had been weakened in an increasingly secular age, by emphasizing its basic theological tenets in combination with a grand architectural vision. The ascendancy of the Tory Party in 1710, with its strong attachment to the king and the Anglican Church, was a further factor in setting the stage for Hawksmoor's church commissions.

The strangeness of Hawksmoor's buildings is a result of a design process that emphasized esoteric historical and philosophical meanings. In that sense, Hawksmoor spoke to a generation of designers that attempted to distance itself from amateur architects. Unlike Wren, who wanted to place England on par with the great Baroque capitals of Europe, Hawksmoor was seeking a more personal idiom. His St. Mary Woolnoth (1716–24) is an astonishing building when compared with the stiff linearity of the English Palladian style that was starting to make its presence felt. The double-tower facade appears to be two buildings stacked on top of each other, the entirety surmounted by two symmetrically placed small bell housings. In the lower zone, the voussoirs around the openings are connected to horizontally banded rustication grooves that continue even around the corner columns. Over this structure, Hawksmoor placed a "base" on which rests an entablatured blind portico. It would be wrong to see this simply as playful when it is clear that he attempted to force the architectural elements—such as keystones, arches, pilasters, and columns—out of their traditional compositional contexts, emphasizing them and allowing them spatial and compositional independence.

French Baroque, as exemplified in the east facade of the Louvre, aspired to a unity of mass and surface decoration. Here the surface decoration and the massing battle for supremacy. Not adhering to the limited Palladian interpretation of the antique, Hawksmoor studied buildings such as the Roman Tomb of the Julii at St. Rémy, France. The two columns flanking the entrance are esoteric references to the Temple of Solomon, the reconstruction of which preoccupied many architects of the time, including Wren. Anglican theologians of the day were also interested in the Second Temple of Solomon as a way to reconnect to both biblical authenticity and the ethos of early Christianity. The upper portico was a reference to the Mausoleum of Halicarnassus, one of the ancient seven wonders of the world, which had been destroyed but for which Hawksmoor made a sketch based on descriptions by Pliny and Vitruvius.

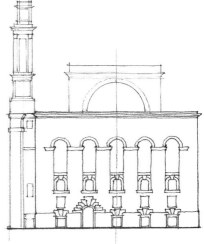

15.42 Plan and section: St. Mary Woolnoth

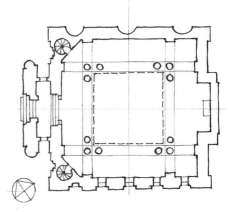

15.43 Baroque Europe

Spread of the Baroque

The eighteenth century may have been the beginning of the decline of French power, but under Louis XIV, Paris enjoyed enormous influence in the arts, which explains to some degree the spread of the Baroque palace from one European court to another, until it became a Europe-wide phenomenon: Sweden, Russia, Italy, Germany, and central Europe were all sites of numerous large-scale building projects. Leading the way were the Austrians, who, surviving their struggles with the Ottomans and emerging as victors along with the English in the Austrian War of Succession, entered into European politics with significant leverage. Among the several important architects operating in Austria, Johann Bernhard Fischer von Erlach (1656–1723) was the most outstanding. He studied art in Rome and later in Naples, in close contact with Gian Lorenzo Bernini. His design for the Schönbrunn Palace (begun 1695) set the tone for a wave of palace buildings in Austria and Germany, all taking their inspiration from Versailles. Most of the palaces featured a long approach axis that integrated the palace with the constructed landscape. The buildings had forecourts or a series of forecourts and were usually located near the perimeters of existing cities. The palace built in Karlsruhe (1715–19) in Baden, Germany, by Margrave Karl-Wilhelm von Baden-Durlach, with its *bleiturm* (*blei* means "lead") for the storage of ammunition, is another example of how palaces were meshed with their surroundings. The tower is at the center of a vast radiating road system that blends forests, gardens, palaces, and the urban surroundings into a single geometrical unit. The palace is in the shape of a V that opens itself toward the town.

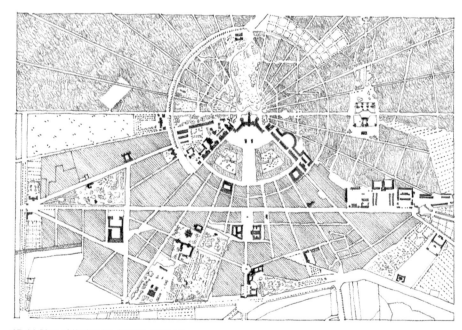

15.44 Plan of Karlsruhe, Baden, Germany

15.45 **Schönbrunn Palace, Vienna, Austria**

15.46 **Palazzo Farnese, Rome**

15.47 **Château de Maisons, Maisons-Laffitte, outside Paris**

15.48 **Lyme Park, Cheshire, England**

Baroque—and later, Neoclassical—architects experimented with different combinations of basic elements. The Palazzo Farnese (1484–1546) in Rome, a building without a pediment and a giant order, served as one potential model for palace fronts, but most Baroque and Neoclassical architects preferred pilastered fronts and in particular the model set forth by the Palazzo Thiene (1545) by Palladio which has a pilastered *piano nobile* resting on a rusticated arcaded base floor. The French added to this model side pavilions that are not freestanding but rather integrated into the scheme as end-pieces to the facade—as, for example, in Hardouin-Mansart's Château de Maisons (1630–51), whose roofs are articulated separately. Filippo Juvarra put the two together in his Palazzo Reale in Madrid (1735), but without the high roofs. There was, however, no pedimented front, as the Neoclassicists would have preferred. All these motifs come together at Lyme Park (1732) in England, the south front of which was designed by Giacomo Leoni. Here the Palazzo Thiene and the Palazzo Reale are combined, even though the side-pavilion motif is not strongly articulated—so as not to seem too French, no doubt.

15.49 Cathedral of Santiago de Compostela, Spain

Narciso Tomé's so-called Transparente (completed 1723) in a chapel in the Cathedral of Toledo is another example of Spanish Baroque. For its construction, a space in the medieval vault was removed and filled in with the new design. The Transparente caused an enormous sensation at the time it opened, an occasion celebrated with a bullfight and public rejoicing. Technically, it is neither an altar nor a chapel but a spatial-sculptural environment celebrating the theme of the Holy Sacrament. Its purpose is to frame the Eucharist, which "appears" in the opening at the back of the high altar of the cathedral. Two columns hold up an entablature but the ends of the cornice curve outward like a pair of horns, with angels flying and diving about above; the whole is framed by tall columns draped with vegetation. The entrance of the central cavity is crowded with figures, golden rays, and putti, all of unheard-of pomp. Higher up is a bas-relief of the Last Supper carved in alabaster and a representation of the Virgin's apotheosis. Higher still and beyond are more angels. Christ is seated on clouds, surrounded by prophets. The whole scene is lit by a large concealed dormer window from behind the onlooker.

Facade of Santiago de Compostela

Though the facade of a Baroque church was intended to announce the architectural themes of the interior, the facades of the Spanish Baroque were almost synonymous with the church itself, especially in instances where facades were added to existing structures to make them appear up-to-date. A prime example is the facade of the Cathedral of Santiago de Compostela (1738–50), which was added to a venerable Romanesque church. It is fronted by the small elevated Plaza del Obradoiro, to which it was connected by a grand staircase. At the lower level of the facade there are still some residual memories of Renaissance restraint. But these are quickly surpassed on the higher levels, which are formed by a crowd of volutes, balls, pinnacles, putti, and statues, giving way to the tower bases that stretch upward on attenuated pilasters and end, at their tops, in a veritable symphony of turrets and volutes.

15.50 Transparente, Toledo Cathedral, Spain

15.52 **Aerial view of St. Petersburg**

15.53 **Winter Palace, St. Petersburg**

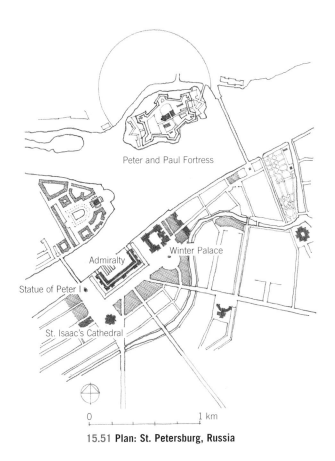

Peter and Paul Fortress

Winter Palace

Admiralty

Statue of Peter I

St. Isaac's Cathedral

0   1 km

15.51 **Plan: St. Petersburg, Russia**

St. Petersburg

Of the many Baroque projects of the period, none rivaled that of St. Petersburg in scale and complexity. At the start of the 17th century, Russia was a backward country, at the mercy of conflicting forces. There were urban riots in 1648, a revolt in 1662, a rebellion in 1669, and an uprising in 1668. Czar Peter Alexeyevich Romanov I (1672–1725), known as Peter the Great, reestablished order, modernized Russia, and pulled the country out of its isolation. Singlehandedly, he turned the Orthodox Muscovite state into a secular, Westernized empire—against considerable opposition from many levels of society. He accomplished this through massive forced-labor enterprises as well as a series of wars that consumed as much as 90 percent of the state budget. The result, however, was an empire that stretched from the Baltic to the Caspian seas. After his victory over Sweden in a war

that lasted twenty-one years, Russia could again sail down the Neva River to the Gulf of Finland. To safeguard his access to the Baltic Sea, Russia built the Peter and Paul Fortress, the cornerstone for which was laid in 1703. The project eventually grew into one of the biggest building sites in Europe. Forty thousand peasants were conscripted, along with Swedish prisoners of war. Work had progressed far enough by 1712 for relics from the Vladimir-Suzdal Monastery to be sent to the St. Alexander Nevsky Monastery, named after the 13th-century national hero who received his name after beating the Swedes on the Neva River. St. Petersburg now had its founding myth and was an instant religious as well as secular center. To speed things along, Peter, in 1714, even forbade masonry construction throughout the rest of Russia to ensure a supply of qualified workers and materials for St. Petersburg.

15.54 **Winter Palace, St. Petersburg**

15.55 Elevation and Plan: Vierzehnheiligen, near Bamberg, Germany

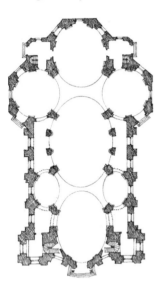

Below, the theme of the frescoes is usually the Church Militant, looking upward at the splendor of the Church Triumphant. Compositionally, the frescoes are exquisite, thanks to the way in which the figures of the apostles, saints, and church fathers are marshaled and in which more angels and putti—who fly, sit, or gaze adoringly among blue skies and puffy clouds, forming a playful expression all their own—are positioned at decisive points. The use of color is rich and various. Rarely is the treatment heavy, and for the most part it yields an astonishing thematic and symbolic unity.

Vaults were usually of brick, one layer thick, reinforced from the top with ribs. The bottom third of the vaults were often strengthened by an extra layer of brick mortar poured over the whole to produce a crudely reinforced concrete shell. Such vaults could be built quickly and were inexpensive to construct. Precise calculations were not required, nor were the elaborate lift machines that would have been necessary for heavy stones. They were also free from the problems of statics and often required support at only a few points.

Neresheim

The south German Baroque is mainly the story of a few eminent architects assisted by painters, stucco workers, and sculptors of no less distinction. Among the architects, Johann Michael Fischer (1692–1766) and Johann Balthasar Neumann (1687–1753) were the most prolific. Neumann's most extraordinary work is perhaps the Church of Vierzehnheiligen (1743–72) at a Franciscan monastery near the town of Bamberg that had become a pilgrimage church in the mid-15th century, following what was said to be a miraculous apparition.

Bavarian Baroque

Largely rural and possessing only three towns with a population over one hundred thousand, Catholic Bavaria in southern Germany had not only withstood the Reformation but was also resistant to the aristocratic urban Catholicism of nearby Austria. Bavarian architects transformed the Baroque style into an exuberant and colorful architectural idiom. The interiors of churches in villages and monasteries are usually painted white and are light-filled and airy, with gilded overlays contributing to a dematerialized, buoyant effect. The dome, such an important element in Italian architectural composition, plays no major role in Bavaria. Significant, instead, were the ceiling frescoes, painted so that the barrier between earth and heaven seems to dissolve into white, wispy cloudlets with teasing putti frolicking among them.

15.57 Painted vault of Vierzehnheiligen

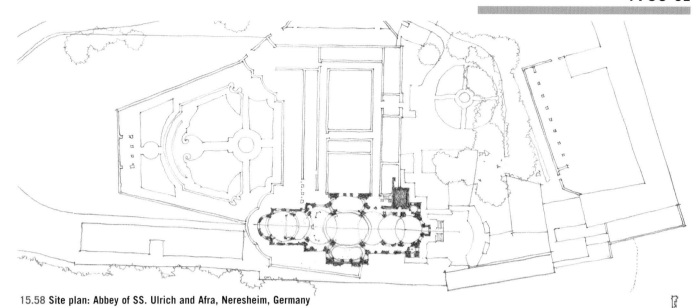

15.58 Site plan: Abbey of SS. Ulrich and Afra, Neresheim, Germany

Neumann's last and most comprehensively conceived major project, however, was the Church of Neresheim (1747–92). It is not freestanding, but integrated into the fabric of a Benedictine monastery, the Abbey of SS. Ulrich and Afra, and even includes at its choir end an old tower from an earlier Romanesque church. Oval and circular vaults are supported on an undulating frame of columns, pilasters, arches, and piers. Neumann was an officer in the engineering corps, and his buildings are just as much a testament to his engineering as to his designing skills.

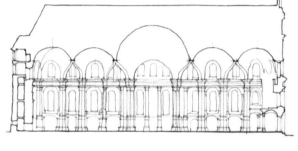

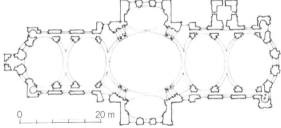

15.59 Plan and section: Church of Neresheim

15.60 Interior: Church of Neresheim

He used wall piers or short sections of wall turned at right angles to the nave as primary load-bearing elements, eliminating the necessity for a solid continuous outer surface. The oval at the crossing is placed lengthwise to the longitudinal interior, stretching between the part of the church that was used by the community and the choir at the rear reserved for the monks. The oval is counterbalanced by smaller ovals that evoke the tradition of the transept without interfering in the spatial liturgical rituals, which did not require such spaces. The ovals are connected by curving vaults that leave one in doubt as to how they work structurally, with light from the large windows visually dissolving the borders of the different spatial elements. Although its interior is cheerful, the exterior shell of the church is relatively plain.

15.61 Chinese Teahouse, Sans Souci, Potsdam, Germany

15.62 Sketch of Sans Souci by Frederick the Great

Sans Souci

The first detailed accounts of Chinese life arrived in the 1520s and were written by missionaries who had been sent to China, India, Indonesia, and Japan. In 1585, Pope Gregory XIII instructed the Spanish priest Juan Gonzalez de Mendoza to set down all that was known about China. *The History of the Great and Mighty Kingdom of China, and the Situation Thereof* was the first widely read treatise on the subject; de Mendoza mentions palaces and gardens and describes houses so grand that they reminded him of Rome. But these bits of information were (and remained) saturated with myths and legends. The first book with a more substantive content was *The History of That Great and Renowned Monarchy of China* (1655), written by Alvarez Semedo, who had spent twenty-two years in China. This was followed by a book by the Dutchman Jan Nieuhof, who took an interest in Chinese architecture. As a European accustomed to palaces in stone, he did not understand the Chinese custom of wooden architecture for its palaces, and therefore found it lacking. But he did produce several engravings of pagodas and palaces that fascinated his readers.

Soon European courts began to adopt certain Chinese themes for their gardens. In 1675, for example, Louis XIV built the Trianon de Porcelain, which, though in shape and form Western, had a roof with blue-and-white patterned tiles, creating what was thought to be a reasonable approximation of the porcelain pattern used at the famous pagoda at Nanjing. The building did not last long, partially because of leaks in the roof, but it set in motion a series of Chinese-styled pavilions, or what the Germans called *porzellankammern*, the most famous being the Chinese teahouse at Sans Souci Palace in Potsdam (1757) built by the Prussian emperor Frederick the Great (Frederick II). The palace, which served as the emperor's summer retreat, had a vast park that contained several pavilions, one of which was the Chinese Teahouse. The gilt columns, which support the roof, are in the form of palm trunks opening out in luxuriant sprays of shoots as they meet the entablature. Life-size gilt Chinese figures sit at the base of the columns, playing musical instruments and engaging in animated conversation. Chinese pavilions, as well as Turkish tents, soon became common in pleasure gardens of the time. Chinese porcelain was also making its way through the markets of Holland, adding more fuel to the fire, with members of the gentry creating collections of their favorite pieces.

15.63 Chinese Teahouse, Sans Souci, Potsdam

15.64 Stratford Hall Plantation, near Montross, Virginia

15.65 Interior: Stratford Hall Plantation

Georgian Architecture

With the ascent of King George I to the throne in 1711, significant changes began to take shape in England, leading to the rise of the political party known as the Whigs which, beginning in 1714, would dominate English politics for seventy years. George I ruled to a large extent through Robert Walpole, a Whig statesman and prime minister. He held his post through the reigns of George I and George II, maintaining a pro-mercantile policy with little interference from either king. Despite the free-flowing mercantile spirit of the age, architecture took on a notably uniform style known as Georgian. Though grand and stately, it was overtly simple and understated. Walls were usually of unadorned brick, and windows and doorways were framed in wood painted white. Facades were symmetrically arranged around the ground-level entrance or, on occasion, accessed by a short flight of steps. Grander houses might have a portico, pilasters, or corner quoins.

The Georgian style was England's first truly national style; it was unique to England and its colonies and arose out of the Protestant ethic of nondemonstrative simplicity. Functional and serviceable, it was adopted by the newly emerging mercantile class, which was heavily involved in coal and agricultural ventures not only in England but also abroad. (The expansion of the English aristocracy into mercantile endeavors contrasts with the approach of the French aristocracy.) Georgian-style buildings in England and Ireland range from Uppark (1690), built for the noted Whig politician

Forde Grey (later Earl of Tankerville) to Bellamont Forest in Ireland (ca. 1725) by the gentleman architect Sir Edward Lovett Pearce. Georgian-style architecture was also used throughout the English-controlled American colonies. The Stratford Hall Plantation (1738) in Virginia, at the head of a large estate that grew tobacco for export to England, was designed for Thomas Lee, a businessman in the Virginia colonies and for a time acting governor of the state.

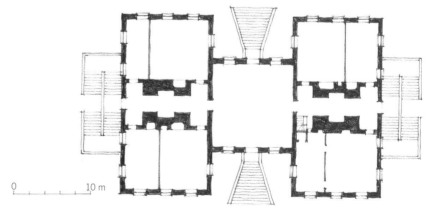

0   10 m

15.66 Plan: Stratford Hall Plantation

15.67 **Chiswick House, near London**

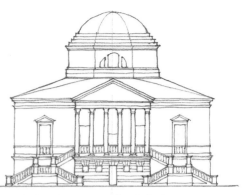

15.68 **Plan and elevation: Chiswick House**

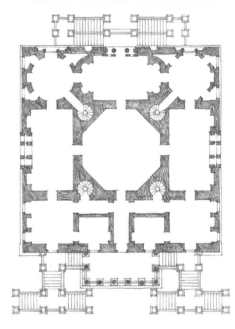

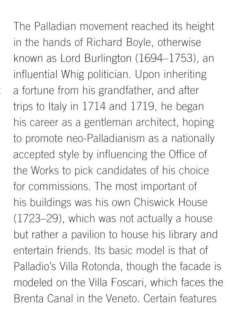

Chiswick House

Underlying Georgian architecture was the Palladian Revival, which blossomed after the 1715 publication of *Vitruvius Britannicus*, written by the Scottish lawyer and architect Colen Campbell, who proclaimed the superiority of antiquity over what he argued were the affected and licentious forms of the Baroque. In his eyes, the work of Inigo Jones should have been held in just as high esteem as that of Palladio. *Vitruvius Britannicus*, together with the publication of the three volumes of *The Architecture of A. Palladio* (1715, 1717, and 1725) by the Venetian Giacomo Leoni, sparked a movement that invested a great deal of energy in substantiating the idea of the primacy of the natural law of proportion—at that time still a rather novel idea in English design practice. Facade, plan, and volume had to be unified into a formal whole. Yet despite this penchant for abstraction, the external detailing had to adhere closely to Palladio's own works—thus the frequent use of rusticated bases, pilastered upper elevations, and pedimented entrances in the emerging Georgian style. Palladio's legacy bore an aura of authority and exclusion and thus played into the class consciousness of the gentry. Campbell's treatises offered relatively cheap but prestigious models to imitate, and, through the printed distribution of plans, plates, and treatises, helped to further Palladianism, a style that could be easily taught, mastered, and copied.

The Palladian movement reached its height in the hands of Richard Boyle, otherwise known as Lord Burlington (1694–1753), an influential Whig politician. Upon inheriting a fortune from his grandfather, and after trips to Italy in 1714 and 1719, he began his career as a gentleman architect, hoping to promote neo-Palladianism as a nationally accepted style by influencing the Office of the Works to pick candidates of his choice for commissions. The most important of his buildings was his own Chiswick House (1723–29), which was not actually a house but rather a pavilion to house his library and entertain friends. Its basic model is that of Palladio's Villa Rotonda, though the facade is modeled on the Villa Foscari, which faces the Brenta Canal in the Veneto. Certain features

were also taken from Vincenzo Scamozzi, such as the obelisk chimneys, the octagonal rather than circular main hall, and the string course at the balustrade level that wraps around the entire building. Palladian motifs also became common in the palaces on the Strand, a long street that ran along the north side of the Thames River and linked the old walled city of London, the country's economic capital, with Buckingham Palace (though it was still relatively modest at that time) and Westminster, the symbolic and political capital of the country. The presence of so many grand houses in this area gave London a very different character from Paris, where the *hôtels* had to be carved out of the urban fabric.

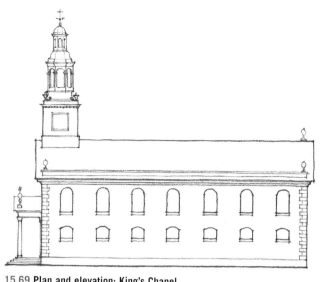

15.69 Plan and elevation: King's Chapel

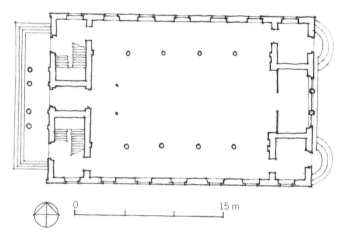

15.70 King's Chapel, Boston

0   15 m

King's Chapel, Boston

A list of items carried in British ships to the Americas can be quite revealing: drinking glasses, cups, teapots, pans, knives, candles, desks, paper, soap, medicines, and books. Such a massive export of cultural commodities not only for bare subsistence but also for the enhancement of daily life was a hallmark of the English method of colonial politics. Boston, one of colonial Britain's largest seaports, boasted an impressive set of houses, warehouses, shops, and meetinghouses. The number of Britons on the north Atlantic coast increased nearly twentyfold between 1660 and 1670. The city became so successful that in 1684 the Royal Crown, now considerably more powerful than it had been just a few decades earlier, took control of the colony, paving the way for the establishment of the first Anglican parishes modeled on those of Sir Christopher Wren's

in London. The most important of these was centered on King's Chapel (1749–54), designed by Peter Harrison, who had just recently arrived from England. He was not a gentleman architect like Lord Burlington and certainly not a brilliant designer like Nicholas Hawksmoor. He was, however, thoroughly committed to the Georgian spirit that had made Palladianism its central credo. Having learned Georgian Palladianism from books and publications, he eventually became its prime representative in North America.

In Newport, Rhode Island, Harrison built the Redwood Library (1748–50) and the Touro Synagogue (1759–63), the latter commissioned by descendants of Sephardic Jews who had been expelled from Spain, Portugal, and France in the 15th and 16th centuries. The members of the small congregation were attracted to Newport

because under Governor Roger Williams, the founder of Providence Plantations, they were assured freedom of religion. Harrison drew on the Bevis-Marks Synagogue of London (1701), which was a simple box with surrounding galleries on three sides; it, too, was designed for a Sephardic community. The twelve columns supporting the women's galleries on the interior represent the twelve tribes of Israel. They are each made of a single tree trunk. The lower ones are Ionic, and the upper ones Corinthian. There were no pews. Instead, the floor at the center was reserved for a table for the reading of the law. The men sat along the perimeter on the ground floor and the women above in the balconies. The building has a sense of intimacy and openness that Harrison had not been able to achieve in the King's Chapel.

15.71 **Stowe Gardens, Buckinghamshire, England**

The "picturesque garden," as it came to be known, was to no small degree a critique of the rationalism and modernity of Whig politics. In relation to painting, the term *picturesque* tended to commemorate instances of significant and unified human action, historical or mythical, that many of the conservative elite who favored a relationship between church and state thought had been lost in the corruptible world of the pro-mercantile Whigs. Key to the success of the new gardens was that they could be experienced not only by their owners and their friends but also by a wide range of personages drawn from the upper and middle class. At the time, garden tourism was on the increase and already an important part of upper-class social life. These gardens tapped into and furthered that phenomenon.

Stowe Gardens

There were two distinct architectural trends in England in the early decades of the 18th century: neo-Palladianism and the Baroque. (These are illustrated by two more or less contemporary constructions: Chiswick House, an example of the former, and St. Mary Woolnoth, an example of the latter.) By the 1730s, both styles came under attack by a movement known as the Picturesque. Though Protestantism, with its call for moral moderation, played a part in this movement, it was also enmeshed in the rise of English nationalism and, beyond that, in the political debates raging between Whigs and Tories. The Whigs favored free enterprise embodied in the philosophies of James Watt and Adam Smith, champions of policies that catered to the needs of aristocratic landowners who wished to be as free as possible from royal whim. The Tories saw the role of the king in more beneficial terms—as the symbol of all that was noble and lasting. Palladianism, generally speaking, had its supporters among the Whig elite, who saw in the style a parallel to their mercantile policies and social ambitions. It was a language of mathematics, proportion, and geometry unencumbered by the arbitrary and the whimsical. But by midcentury, even though the Whigs remained in power, they came to be criticized by those eager for a more principled accounting of England's colonial and mercantile policies. Corruption among the Whig elites made them an easy target.

Temple of Ancient Virtue

Temple of British Worthies

0   200 m

15.72 **Site plan: Stowe Gardens**

15.73 Temple of British Worthies, Stowe Gardens

15.74 Temple of Ancient Virtue, Stowe Gardens

15.75 Temple of Modern Virtue, Stowe Gardens

The theoretical origins of this garden movement lie in the writings and designs of Alexander Pope (1688–1744), eminent essayist, satirist, and critic of Whig policies. Among his achievements was the translation of the *Iliad* and the *Odyssey* into English, books that appealed to the English thirst for noble heroism. Pope, together with other literary friends of Lord Richard Temple Cobham (1675–1749), also helped articulate the governing iconography of the Elysian Fields, based on the myth of Elysium, the paradise for heroes. The imagery of the Elysian Fields was at the center of the development of Stowe Gardens from a modest parterre garden in the late-17th century to an English landscape park for Lord Cobham, field marshal and politician. Cobham, forced to resign his military commission in 1733, joined the ranks of Whig opponents. It was then that he decided to enhance and expand the Stowe Gardens.

One element in the gardens was the Temple of Ancient Virtue, a round Ionic tempietto honoring the great lawgivers and writers of the ancient world, among them Socrates and Homer; near it was as ironic commentary, the Temple of Modern Virtue, a ruined structure featuring a headless figure that was generally taken to represent Robert Walpole, the head of the Whig Party. The meaning of these two buildings is made clear to visitors by the presence of a Temple of British Worthies, a shrine to great Britons arranged in two groups of eight along a curving wall, honoring William Shakespeare, John Milton, Queen Elizabeth I, Inigo Jones,

and Alexander Pope, among others; not too far away is the Grenville Column, a memorial to Captain Thomas Grenville, who died aboard Lord Cobham's ship fighting the French in 1747. At the top of the column, the figure of Heroic Poetry fingers a scroll with the words *non nisi grandia canto* ("I sing only of grand things"), her face turned toward the Temple of British Worthies. Other elements were added to the garden later, including the Cook Monument (1778), commemorating Captain James Cook's discoveries in the South Pacific, and the Seasons Fountain (1805), honoring the visit by the Prince of Wales to Stowe Gardens.

To some extent the idea of a landscape—however artificial—conceptualized around a dignified, civilizational armature parallels the English colonial experience in the Americas. The French, who initially encountered strong resistance from the Native Americans and who, because they never had enough people in the colonies to suppress them, began to study and analyze their habits in order to gain their cooperation in trade and then lead them into conversion. But in their colonies, the English found little organized resistance (except in the Carolinas). While contact with the Indians led the French to ask questions about the origins of civilization, the English, at least those back home in their gardens, began to muse on the mythological underpinnings of European history. It may be in the English gardens, with their often pedagogical and ideological emphasis, that the first traces of what later was termed Eurocentrism began.

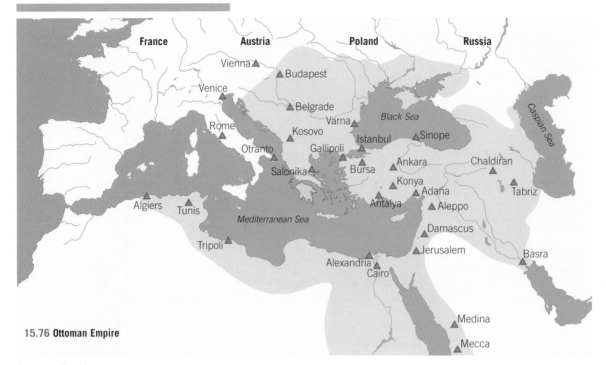

15.76 Ottoman Empire

Nurosmaniye Mosque

Faced with the transforming world economy, the Ottomans allied themselves with the French against England, Austria, and Russia. Although the Ottomans had lost their military advantage in Europe, they continued to be very strong financially. In fact, around 1700, they dominated the life and culture of the eastern half of the Mediterranean, controlling a vast territory that stretched from the Persian Gulf to Algeria. In 1703 Ahmed III moved the capital of the Ottoman Empire back to Istanbul (it had been in Bursa), which precipitated a major building boom. Instead of following the Suleymaniye canon established by Sinan, the architecture looked to external influences to generate new architectural expressions. For this reason, 18th-century Ottoman architecture is often described as being Westernized. But it is better thought of it as an early modern architecture in which Sinan's "classicism" was hybridized with European—and particularly French—Baroque architectural sensibilities and then mixed together with Persian and Indian precedents, the latter especially in palaces and gardens. (Two examples are the Sa'dabad Palace and the garden at Kagithane, Istanbul.) This amalgam contrasts with Russia's more aggressive and purist attempt to Westernize the state.

Mahmud I's Nurosmaniye Mosque (1749–55) combined a standard centralized domed plan with an unusually wide, highly fenestrated facade under a massive arch. A tightly clustered sequence of engaged pillars with capitals that unexpectedly merged with the cornice are complimented by European Baroque details, such as scrolls, shells, cable and round moldings, engaged pillars, and fluted capitals.

15.77 Nurosmaniye Mosque, Istanbul

15.78 **Qing dynasty China**

Qing Dynasty China

By the early 1600s, the Manchu, a seminomadic people closely related to the Mongolians, had built up a sizable kingdom at China's northwestern periphery. Seizing the moment, in 1644 they entered the Forbidden City to establish China's longest-lasting dynasty (1644–1911). Shun Chih (or Shunzhi, r. 1644–62), the first Manchu ruler of China, named their dynasty the Qing, or the "pure." It was China's third "foreign" dynasty. The Qing projected themselves not as outsiders but as the legitimate inheritors of the Yuan throne. Like the Ming, they built dynastic tombs with spirit ways and sacrificial halls nestled in the foothills. But the specific dedicatory decorations of some their tombs, in particular that of the Qianlong emperor (r. 1735–96) had Sanskrit incantations, diagrams, and decorations, a testament to his abiding faith in Tibetan Buddhism.

Under the Ming, Buddhism had waned, but in the 17th century, with the rise of the fifth Dalai Lama, Tibetan Buddhism experienced a resurgence, especially among the Mongolian Manchu. With their Chinese-style capital and manners and their Buddhist religious practices, the Manchu were something of a hybrid. Though Buddhism receive particular favor as the state religion, the Qing insisted that all religions and ethnic groups be recognized, and allowed Confucianism, Daoism, Buddhism, Lamaism, Islam, and even Christianity to be practiced. In 1651, Shunzhi invited the fifth Dalai Lama to visit Beijing. In connection with that visit,

Shunzhi ordered the construction of three Tibetan-style white stupas, two of them in the Imperial City. One of these is the bell-shaped White Stupa, the gigantic landmark of the Western Park or Beihai. Beihai, east of the Forbidden City but within the city walls, had first been developed by the Yuan and the Jin; under the Ming the waters were dammed to create three artificial lakes, with an island in the middle lake. Shunzhi placed the White Stupa on the highest point of the artificial hill on the island, so that it was clearly visible from a distance.

Unlike all previous Chinese dynasties, the Manchu did not automatically burn and pillage the Ming capital and establish a new one at another location. Instead, they reoccupied the Forbidden City at Beijing. One of the Shunzhi emperor's first decrees was to rebuild the parts of the Forbidden City that had been burnt by the retreating Ming. His only specification was that ducts be built into the Hall of Supreme Harmony so that heat could be pumped into it. To stamp their identity onto the city, however, they renamed all the major gates and pavilions and changed the ceremonies associated with the Temple of Heaven to reflect the new Manchu cosmic order. Non-Manchu, Han Chinese men were required to shave their foreheads and wear their hair in a long ponytail called the *que*. Differences between the Qing and the Han also played out in the urban fabric. In 1649, the Northern City, the traditional heart of Beijing, was reserved

only for Manchu. As a consequence, all the Han Chinese had to move into the Southern City, which had always been underdeveloped but that, as consequence of the new influx, developed into the commercial heart of the city. New temples and monasteries were built. Theaters, teahouses, shops of all kinds, guild halls, academies of classical learning, and public buildings were constructed. As wood became scarce, many of the residential and other secular structures were made from stone and brick.

By the middle of the 18th century, over forty new palaces had been built in the Forbidden City and in the privileged areas to its northwest. Unlike the Ming emperors, who confined most of their court activities to the Forbidden City and concentrated all major activities in Beijing, the Qing were avid travelers and built palaces and temples in distant parts of their empire. One of best-known Qing palace complexes is the Ningshougong (the "Palace of Tranquil Longevity," 1698–1772), built by the Qianlong emperor Ningshougong. Conceived as a mini Forbidden City within the Forbidden City, it consists of two sections: a set of three ceremonial pavilions (the Gate of Tranquil Longevity, the Hall of Imperial Supremacy, and the Palace of Tranquil Longevity Palace), followed by a denser living quarter consisting of a series of small and larger building arranged around a network of garden courts. The entire palace was completely screened from the rest of the Forbidden City.

15.79 **View from Qingyi's stroll path, Qingyi garden, Beijing**

15.80 **View from pavilion, Qingyi garden**

Yuanmingyuan

The area to the northwest of Beijing was a largely flat plain with a gentle gradient toward the southeast where the Yuan, Jin, and Ming had built summer retreats. The Qing converted these into huge garden-palace complexes, exploiting the numerous springs and rivulets that traverse the area. Waterways and reservoirs were built to ensure a perennial flow and distribution of water. The largest of these gardens was the Yuanmingyuan ("The Garden of Perfect Brightness," *yuan* means "garden"), built in the 1720s. Although its palaces and pavilions were similar to the axial courtyard structures of other palaces such as those in the Forbidden City, their distribution and layout is more relaxed. Entered from the south, the Yuanmingyuan was dominated by a palace with a small front lake and a larger back lake to frame it. The back lake had nine islands, each designed with its own pavilions, palaces, and scenic spots. North of this complex was a dense fabric of secondary buildings, laid out in a closely packed system of interconnected islands. The eastern half of Yuanmingyuan was composed around the large Fuhai Lake, in the middle of which were three small interconnected islands, representative of the three mythical Islands of the Immortals, supposedly located in the East China Sea. Fuhai Lake was also surrounded by a string of nine connected islands with pavilions and hills designed for scenic views and strolls. Yuanmingyuan had 350 buildings organized into 123 building complexes. Furthest east was the Chunjua Garden, with a palace in the middle of a large island. Emperor Qianlong added a long horizontal strip to the north for which he commissioned six European Baroque–style palaces designed by the Jesuit missionaries resident in his court. (Although the Qin court was not very interested in buying European products, it happily sold its goods, allowed trading posts, and entertained visitors, such as the Jesuits—contrary to the later colonial claim that the Chinese were completely closed to foreigners.)

Qingyi Garden

Later, Qianlong added a new garden, originally called Qingyi Garden (1750–64) and now known as the Summer Palace. It was designed as a series of palaces and pavilions around a large oval lake that was separated from two smaller lakes by long narrow islands. A stroll path went around the lake and across all the small islands. In the middle of the main lake was a small artificial island connected to the edge on the east by a long, arched, graceful bridge. The north edge of the lake was dominated by a huge palace and a Buddhist shrine complex raised high on a solid stone platform and on axis with the central island. In the west, the horizon was filled with a series of long mountains with distinct peaks. A pagoda and several pavilions were built on the crests of the peaks.

Chinese gardens were intended to evoke the order of nature distilled to its essence. The design skill lay in ensuring that every element functioned in a way that was harmonious with the whole from the perspective of viewing sites along the strolling paths. A garden's quality was described as a function of its scenic spots, which were thought of as embodied poems and three-dimensional paintings. Symmetry was abhorred. At the same time, all the expectations and conveniences of a royal palace and seat of government were to be fulfilled. There are three palpable visual foci at the Summer Palace: the island in the middle of the lake, the Buddhist shrine at the northern edge, and the tall pagoda on the hills in the west. Although the Buddhist shrine is the largest element, the island is in the middle and constantly attracts the eye. Yet while walking around, the pagoda in the distance always remains in view, becoming the best-remembered part of the garden.

The compositional ideas were derived from principles described in texts such as the Ji Cheng's *Yuan Zhi* ("Gardening"), written in the early 17th century. Ji Cheng invoked design concepts such as suitability, refinement, simplicity, and changeability or unexpectedness, which were to be used to create places that have qualities such as "the real and the false," "assembling and spreading," "unevenness and neatness," "connecting and separating," "open and closed," and "level and solid."

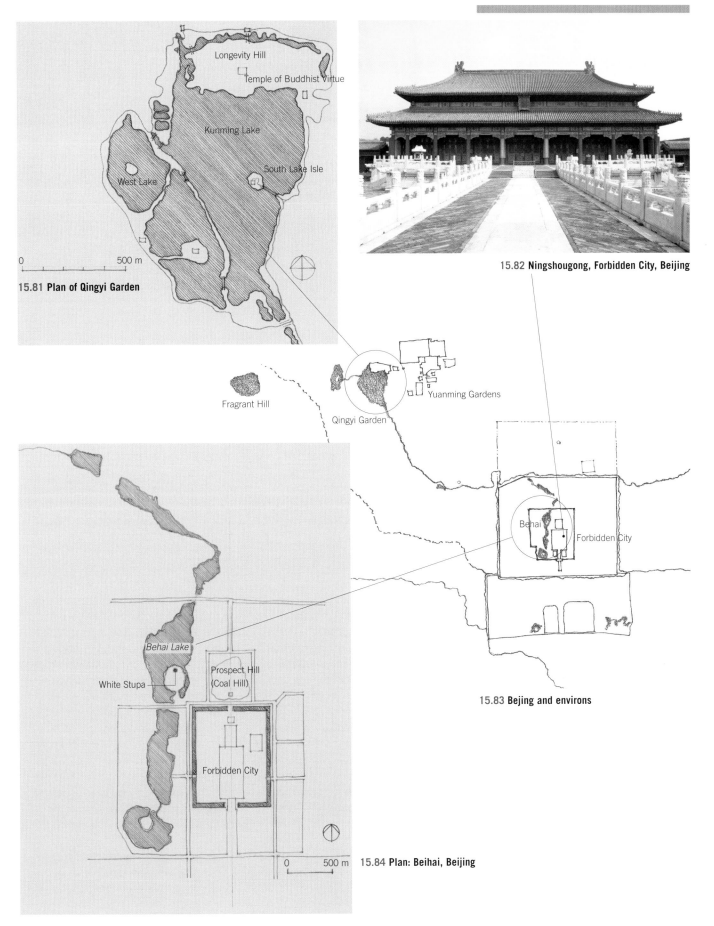

15.81 **Plan of Qingyi Garden**

15.82 **Ningshougong, Forbidden City, Beijing**

15.83 **Bejing and environs**

15.84 **Plan: Beihai, Beijing**

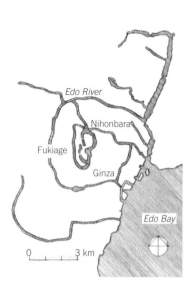

15.85 Original spiral plan of Edo (Tokyo), Japan

15.86 Architectural drawing of street in Edo (Tokyo) with shops, 1876

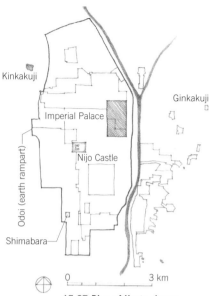

15.87 Plan of Kyoto, Japan

Edo, Kyoto's Odoi, and Shimabara

The Tokugawa shoguns' political strength created a period of relative peace that enabled trade and commerce to thrive, particularly with China, Holland, and Portugal—the latter having established a trading port, Nagasaki, in 1570. The shoguns' vision of Japanese society, however, was not drawn from a mercantile world but from a militaristic image of a lost, well-ordered past. They created the Bakufu code, a highly ceremonial, hierarchical set of guidelines that prescribed everyone's designated place in the social fabric. One of the shoguns' problems was how to define their difference from the imperial family, to whom they were subservient. Their solution was to distance themselves from the capital in Kyoto. And so in 1603, the first Tokugawa shogun decided to rule from a new city, Edo (now Tokyo). Conceived as a spiral, with accommodations made for geography, it was developed with both security and symbolism in mind, with its thirty-two major gateways guarding the various lines of approach to the center. Their locations were correlated with the twelve signs of the zodiac, integral to the astrological and calendrical system. The populace was not allowed to freely intermix, and each class was placed in different sections of the city. The vassals were located to the northeast of the castle. Lower-ranking samurai were located in a section all to

themselves; the merchants and artisans lived in the outermost, southwest parts of the city. Silver brokers lived in one neighborhood, gold brokers in another, and so forth.

Unlike Edo, where builders could start from scratch, the Tokugawa began to redesign Kyoto to meet the strictures of the Bakufu code. In the pre-shogunate period, its primary urban division lay between the imperial spaces and all the rest. Temples, noble houses, shops, and entertainment areas could all be found in the same neighborhoods. The shogun governor Maeda Gen'i (1539–1602) built a new north-south thoroughfare that cut through the old blocks. This opened up new street frontage, which was occupied by commercial establishments and houses. In 1591, the border of the city was defined by building an earthen rampart 9 meters at the base, between 3 and 6 meters high, and topped by a wood and bamboo fence. A miniature moat 6 to 18 meters wide was excavated outside. The world within was called the *rakuchu*, or the urbanized world, and the rest the *rakugai*, or the outside world. All forms of internal enclosures and fortifications were then demolished, erasing all signs of the localized authorities. Some of the major Buddhist temples were moved outside the walls, especially to the eastern hills. The members of the warrior class were made to settle right next to the Nijo Castle

and the Kyoto Governor's Palace, located just north of the castle. The members of the aristocracy were relocated to the peripheries of the imperial palace. Special quarters for the lowest classes—the *eta* ("the stained") and the *hinin* ("the nonhumans") were designated at the margins of the city.

Kyoto's prostitutes were a constant threat to the Bakufu code since they conducted their business in the mixed public space of the street. In 1640, they were confined to a single area that came to be called the Shimabara. Located in the southwest corner of the city far from its core, it was enclosed with its own wall, complete with a moat, whose purpose was not to prevent anybody from coming in, but to keep the prostitutes from leaving. A single gate on the east side controlled all movement in and out. With the merchants, warriors, and aristocrats sharing the same space and the same prostitutes, the Shimabara quickly became a place of sanctioned transgression. The more exclusive establishments of the Shimabara, the *ageya* ("pleasure houses"), catered to clients with high tastes. Accordingly, these places adopted architectural forms and decorations normally prohibited by their lower-class status that were here appropriate to the high status of the clientele. This double standard was managed by making the exterior simple, but creating individual spaces in the interior

15.88 Facsimile of Tobei Kamei's block print of the Shimabara geisha district

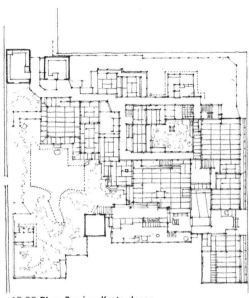

15.89 Plan: Sumiya, Kyoto, Japan

that were modeled on the residences of the upper classes, and even those of the shoguns. Indeed, to respond to the varied status and tastes of the clients, the interiors were often extremely eclectic, with individual entertainment rooms right next to each other built in completely different styles.

The only surviving example of a 17th-century *ageya* is the Sumiya ("Place of Peace and Long Life"), controlled by the Nakagawa family, which administered it for thirteen generations from its very beginning in 1641. From the street its facade is simple but cleverly designed. The outer walls of both its ground and upper story are recessed by half a bay and fronted by wooden screens that ensured no one could look in, but that the guests could see out. They were also removable, so that when street entertainers came calling or during festivals when the streets of the Shimabara became one big theater, the guests of the Sumiya could look straight out without hindrance.

In the interior are a range of styles taken from those of military mansions, town homes, and teahouses. They were, however, willfully decorative and colored with variety and exaggeration. The main reception rooms for guests were located behind the exterior facade on the eastern edge of the building. This position corresponded to the typology of the houses of rich merchants. As in

Shinden-style palaces such as Ninomaru at Nijo Castle and the Katsura Imperial Villa, the entertainment rooms located near the garden were stepped back to ensure that each room had a special relationship to the garden, with individually framed openings designed for each space. The second floor had smaller rooms for the more intimate relationships between the geisha and her clients.

15.90 Sumiya, Kyoto, Japan

15.91 **Pyoungsan Academy, near Hahoe Village, Korea**

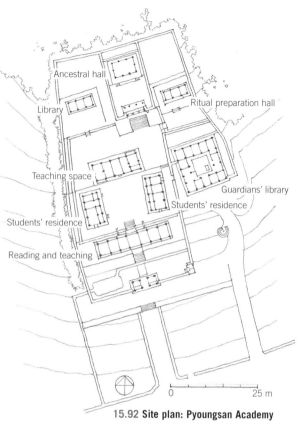

15.92 **Site plan: Pyoungsan Academy**

Joseon Dynasty, Korea

In Korea, the elite of the Joseon dynasty (1392–1910) attempted to suppress Buddhism in favor of Confucianism, but internal strife—as well as Japanese attacks in 1592 and 1597 and Manchu assaults in 1627 and 1636—ravaged the country's economy. Nonetheless, Korea rebounded in the 18th century due to the strict enforcement of a class system not unlike the Bakufu code and dominated by the *yangban*, who were government officials and administrators. Under them was a class of technicians, beneath them were the commoners (composed of farmers and merchants), and finally, at the bottom, "the despised people." In the strictest sense of the term, *yangban* referred to government officials or officeholders who had passed the civil service examinations that tested their knowledge of the Confucian classics and their neo-Confucian interpretations. They were the Korean counterparts of the scholar-officials, or mandarins, of imperial China. The term *yangban*, literally means "two groups," that is, civil and military officials. Though its members had to pass the civil service examination, family members could also become part of the *yangban* clan and thus share the aura of the elite, as long as they retained Confucian culture and rituals. Though neo-Confucianism became the official state religion, the lower classes clung to more traditional Buddhism.

15.93 **Section: Pyoungsan Academy**

Pyoungsan Academy, located picturesquely along a bend in the Nakdong River in south-central Korea, was a private Confucian high school for the sons of that region's *yangban* elite. It was erected in honor of Ryu Seong-ryong, who served as the prime minister during the destructive invasions led by the Japanese feudal lord Hideyoshi. The building, modeled on a *chôngjas*, a pavilion that the members of the *yangban* class had begun to erect (often along a stream or river at a particularly scenic spot) is an enclosed precinct rising up on a gentle slope.

One passes through a gate with a vista up the slope under the *chôngjas* and into the main court above, where the path leads. The view centers on the spot where the teacher would sit, with windows providing views into the landscape. Flanking the court are student quarters. Access to the *chôngjas*, which seems to almost float above the earth, elevated as it is on stout columnar logs, is along a simple narrow wooden plank. Behind the school is the shrine in a separate enclosure and, to one side, a library. The caretakers' house is in a separate enclosure attached to the walls of the school. The teacher did not live at the school but in the nearby village.

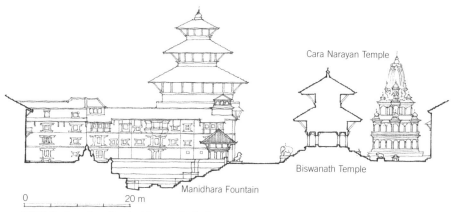

Cara Narayan Temple

Biswanath Temple

Manidhara Fountain

0   20 m

15.94 East-west section looking south: Durbar Square, Patan, Nepal

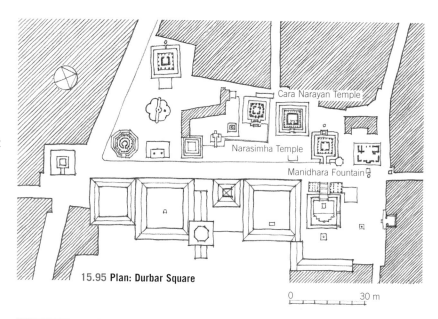

Cara Narayan Temple

Narasimha Temple

Manidhara Fountain

15.95 Plan: Durbar Square

0   30 m

Mallas of Nepal

Nepal was the midpoint along the north-south highway linking Tibet to India. Buddhist monks traveling through spread Indian- and Tibetan-style Buddhism in Nepal, creating a unique blend of the two. After Islamic invaders occupied northern India in the 10th century, fleeing Hindu priests, royalty, and merchants added a new Hindu layer to Nepalese culture and civic polity. In the 13th century, these Hindu kings established the long-lasting Malla dynasty, which ruled Nepal until 1482, after which it was divided into three independent kingdoms run by related Malla dynasties, with capitals in Patan, Kathmandu, and Bhaktapur. In the 17th century, the Mallas of Patan renovated and reconstructed their main royal court, known as the Durbar Square. Its oldest structure, the Manidhara Fountain, was built in the 6th century as a rest area for pilgrims. Under the Malla, the square grew in importance when royal palaces and temples were added to it. The eastern edge of the square was lined with a string of palaces abutting one another. On the western side an irregularly shaped open space is home to several freestanding temples. Dispersed throughout are many small shrines. At its northern end, just beyond the palaces, the Manidhara Fountain forms its own urban place. It is the delicate balance between structure and space that imparts to Durbar Square its unique urban character.

15.96 Durbar Square

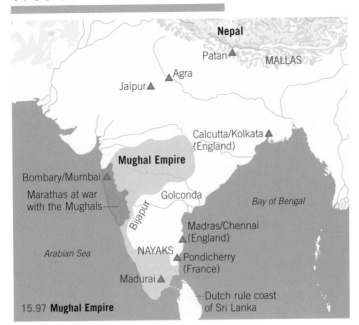

15.98 Meenakshi Sunderesvara Temple at Madurai, India

Nayaks of Madurai

In 1658 Aurangzeb deposed his father, Shah Jahan, and took over the Mughal throne. Under Aurangzeb's long reign (1658–1707), the Mughal Empire in northern India expanded to its greatest extent, incorporating the sultanates of Bijapur and Golconda in the 1680s. Unlike his father, Aurangzeb was a competent administrator, but he insisted on stricter adherence to Sunni morality, both personally and in official policy. Discrimination against Hindus increased, and all experimental hybridized religious practices were forbidden. Artisans and craftsmen fled.

Among the beneficiaries of this diaspora were the Nayaks, erstwhile governors of Vijayanagara territories who established a sort of confederation of autonomous kingdoms with capitals in Madurai, Tanjore, Gingee, and Ikkeri. The Nayaks, though nominally under the rule of Delhi, continued the Chola and Vijayanagara practice of treating temples as surrogate courts. In fact, the temples of Madurai and Tanjore became veritable cities unto themselves. Their gates were rarely closed, and urban life moved in and out at will. The Meenakshi Sunderesvara Temple (1623–59) has two main shrines, the larger one dedicated to Shiva in the manifestation of Sunderesvara ("the beautiful one") and the smaller to his wife Meenakshi ("the fish-eyed one"). Nonetheless, the temple's main deity is Meenakshi, a local regional goddess who is important to the Tamils. Though she was married to Shiva after the rise of the bhakti

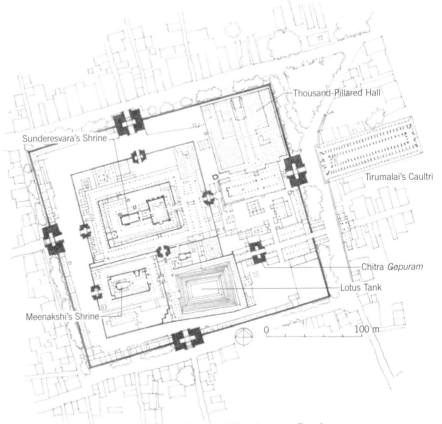

15.99 Site plan: Meenakshi Sunderesvara Temple

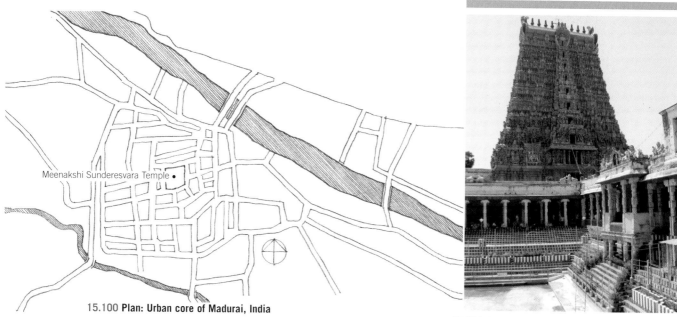

15.100 **Plan: Urban core of Madurai, India**

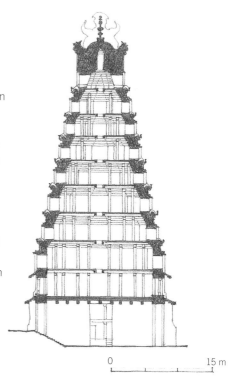

15.101 *Gopuram* of Meenakshi Sunderesvara Temple

cults, she maintained her dominance over the populace. Spatially this duality is represented in procession. Although Sunderesvara's shrine has a well-defined axis leading to it, it is Meenakshi's more informally defined access path that has the important historical locations along it, most importantly the Lotus Tank—the mythical origin of the temple—and a corridor with painted panels depicting stories from her life.

As it grew, the temple became a series of enclosures that nestle a diverse array of functional and ceremonial spaces such as pillared halls, open courts, inhabitable corridors, and shrines, all designed to accommodate the temples diverse civic and religious functions. In addition, it has markets, private shrines, places for resting, dwellings for priests, and ceremonial sites; a museum was added recently. Chief among the rituals is an elaborate annual procession meant to be visible to all, particularly the lowest castes, who were not allowed into the temple. This procession celebrated Meenakshi's divine wedding to Sunderesvara. Over a nineteen-day period in April and May, Meenakshi is taken out in a mobile structure in procession, into the crowded city streets, where she ceremonially defeats all the gods and earthly kings in one battle after another until she finally meets Sunderesvara, whom she almost defeats but suddenly realizes it is prophesied that she to marry him.

Seen from a distance, the Meenakshi Sunderesvara Temple's silhouette is defined by its *gopurams*, or gateways, the highest ones reaching 50 meters. Made of brick, they are largely solid and are ornamented with a myriad of vividly painted mythical deities and creatures. The *gopurams* increase in height the farther they are from the center. The gold-covered *shikharas* over the shrines are actually the temple's smallest superstructures. In part, the *gopurams*' function is to announce the temple's presence to the city, and when seen from a distance, they create a visual wave radiating out into the landscape. In other words, the mandalic universe that is usually condensed into the figurative representation of a Hindu temple's *shikhara*, was, under the Nayaks, expanded so far outward that it encompasses the geography of the entire city itself. And because Madurai sits in a river valley surrounded by a ring of low-lying hills, the hills can be imagined as the next layer of *gopurams*, implying mythical unseen mountains beyond.

0   15 m

15.102 **Section: The summit of a *gopuram***

Constantia

While the movement for Independence was gathering strength in America, the Tories found a hero in the figure of Robert Clive, a young officer of the British East India Company in India who, in spite of his small forces, was able to outmaneuver the French forces as well as those of Shiraj-ud-Doulah at the Battle of Plassey in 1757. Overnight, Clive became a celebrity in England, confirmation, it seemed, of the natural superiority of the noble aristocrat fighting in the name of the Crown. After his victory, the discourse justifying the colonization of India no longer remained economic, but incorporated issues of nationalism and Enlightenment rationality.

Before 1757, the English East India Company had essentially been a motley crew of enterprising mercantile traders. The first generations of English company officers had to be careful to maintain cordial relations with the Indians on whom they depended for trade. Many wore Indian clothes, and intermarriage was common. Thus the tomb of Job Charnock (d.1693) in Calcutta, the city he founded for the English, has no trace of English architecture. Based on Mughal prototypes instead, it is an octagonal structure with round openings on every side, with a higher story and crenellations. The finest example of this Anglo-Indian architecture, as it was subsequently (and sometimes derisively) called, was a sprawling palace called Constantia (1790), built by Claude Martin for the mixed-breed children who had been abandoned by their English fathers. Martin, a Frenchman, had amassed a fortune in trading and had aligned himself with the British as French fortunes declined. Constantia reimagined a Mughal tomb in the form of a multistory inhabitable space endowed with an eclectic range of contemporary European Baroque elements. Uncomfortably poised on a platform (with round arches and pilasters instead of pointed arches), Constantia was a symmetrical structure with the hint of a dome created by freestanding intersecting arches. The skyline is composed of *chattris* made in the European style and an array of statues, like in Italianate Baroque buildings.

15.103 **Constantia, Calcutta**

15.104 **Approach to Job Charnock's Tomb, Calcutta**

1800 CE

Although Europe was growing stronger and stronger, the largest world power in the year 1800 was China. It may not have manifested itself as such, since it had no colonies. Instead, it extended its borders the old-fashioned way, conquering Tibet, Turkestan, and Mongolia, and as a result, in size, population, production, and raw wealth, it had no equal. Its bold-thinking emperor, Qianlong, aimed to create a pan-Asian empire unified around the Indic notion of an ideal ruler, or *chakravartin*. Because the visual and formal vocabulary of Chinese architecture never underwent radical changes, there has been a tendency to see it as tradition-bound, but that would be far too reductive. Qianlong's purposeful use of imitation in constructing his new capital city, Chengde, was driven by the ideological innovation of constructing the city as a microcosm of the Chinese-Asian world. The Chinese empire, however, went into rapid decline once the British forced the Chinese to accept ever more opium—against Chinese imperial desires—in "exchange" for tea.

Europe was also undergoing a foundational revision as a consequence of the Enlightenment, the conflicting colonial ambitions of her various countries, and the rise of the Industrial Revolution, all of which fundamentally recast ideas about nature, law, government, and politics. With the French Revolution, aristocracy's stranglehold on everything from politics to architecture had been broken and its arbitrary aspects revealed. New building types relating to government and bureaucracy emerged, including the Somerset House in London (1776–1801), the U.S. Capitol in Washington, DC (1792), the Four Courts in Dublin (1786–1802), the Virginia State Capitol in Raleigh (1785), the Government

House in Calcutta (now Kolkata), and the new Houses of Parliament in London (1840–60). Landscapes were also being changed by the construction of factories and ports, with cities absorbing the growing population of the working class. Indeed, the Industrial Revolution would slowly and irrevocably change economic and political relationships the world over. The associated architecture of administration and control brought with it other new forms of architecture, such as the prison and workhouse. These negatives helped drive the neo-Gothic movement, which sought to restore moral compass to the times. The liberation of Greece from Ottoman occupation in 1829 spawned a vigorous neo-Greek movement not only in the United States but also in Germany, Scotland, and British India. In the United States, the Enlightenment was expressed with particularly utopian fervor, spurred on by the American Revolution and a sense that America was the land of untold opportunities. Science and research into the natural world expanded and touched on critical philosophical and political questions. New materials, particularly iron, forced architects to radically rethink architectural forms.

The utopianism of the European Enlightenment, however, was generally tempered, if not co-opted outright, by the lingering traditions of aristocratic privilege, producing an architecture generally known as Neoclassical, the history of which took many turns and in some cases retreated toward a more conservative Romanticism, especially in England. Nonetheless, traces of a vigorous and austere Neoclassicism, such as that pursued by the French architects Claude Nicholas Ledoux and Étienne-Louis Boullée, can be found throughout Europe

from 1800 onward. The reaction against Neoclassicism—first in the context of the Picturesque movement in England, then with the spread of Romanticism, which developed into national Romanticism after the Napoleonic Wars—became increasingly important as the century progressed. Instead of ancient Rome as the model of history and politics, national Romantics favored regional traditions that could serve to unify national sentiment. Architectural theory underwent important revision in the hands of Eugène-Emmanuel Viollet-le-Duc (1814–79) in France, Gottfried Semper (1803–79) in the German speaking world, and, in England, August Welby Pugin (1812–52) and John Ruskin (1819–1900).

Apart from China, Europe, and the European-controlled colonies, there were two areas that continued to develop architecturally, but in very different ways—Japan and Thailand. Japan, like China, tried to close itself off from European influence, maintaining in the process a strong architectural tradition and developing a "modern" architecture of the middle class, such as Kabuki theaters. Thailand, which was never colonized, was, by way of contrast, more than willing to open itself up to Western influence, unifying borrowed elements into regionally developed forms of practice. The story of 19th-century urbanism must therefore include not only such new cities such as Chengde, St. Petersburg, and Washington, DC, and the redesign of such older cities as Berlin, London, Paris, Dublin, and Athens, but also Bangkok, the newly founded capital of Thailand. This city provides a glimpse of what a modern Southeast Asian architecture would look like when it is beholden to neither an ideology of tradition nor a colonial imposition.

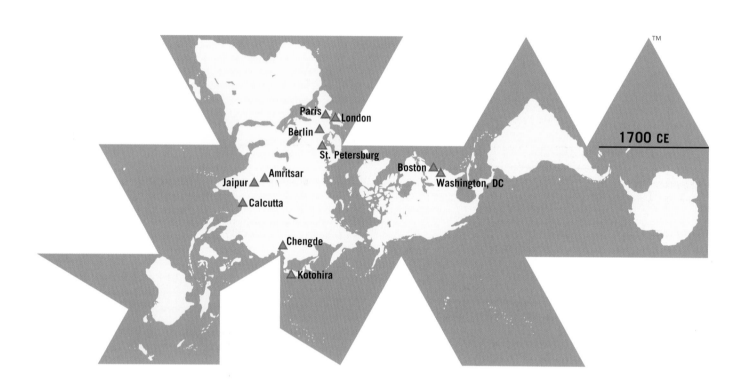

1700 CE

▲ **Bevis-Marks Synagogue**
1700

Japan: Edo Period
1615–1868

▲ Kanamaru-za
1835

China: Qing Dynasty
1644–1911

▲ Imperial Palace at Chengde
1703–80

▲ Putuo Zongcheng Temple
1771

Opium War
1839–1842

▲ Wat Pra Kaew
Begun 1785

▲ Hawa Mahal
1799

Neoclassicism
Mid-18th to mid-19th centuries

1750 CE	1800 CE	1850 CE

▲ Strawberry Hill
Rebuilt 1748–77

▲ Shelburne House
Begun 1763

▲ Government House
Begun 1803

Writers' Building ▷
1870

▲ Ste. Geneviève
1757

▲ Petit Trianon
1761–68

▲ Bibliothèque Nationale
1788

▲ Valhalla
1830–42

▲ Salt Works of Chaux
1775–79

▲ Père Lachaise
1804

Schauspielhaus ▲
1818–21

▲ Altes Museum
1823–30

▲ St. Madeleine Church
1845–51

Royal Scottish Academy ▲
1835

▲ Tennessee State Capitol
1845–59

▲ Beth Elohim Synagogue
1840

▲ Bibliothèque St. Geneviève
1845–51

Industrial Revolution
17th to 18th centuries

England: Hanoverian Rule
1714–1901

French Revolution
1789–1799

Napoleonic Wars
1795–1815

Victorian Era
1830–1901

American War of Independence
1775–1783

War of 1812

Joseph Bramah invents the water closet. ◉
1778

▲ Suffolk House of Correction
1803

▲ Pentonville Prison
1844

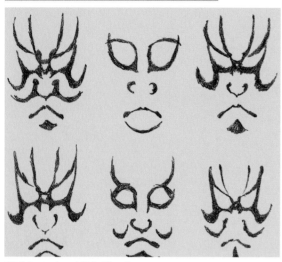

16.1 **Examples of Kabuki makeup**

16.2 **Facsimile of Nishimura Shigenaga's** *Interior of a Kabuki Theater*

Japan: Edo Period

In Japan the Tokugawa shoguns aimed not only to structure and ritualize society down to the last detail but also to close the country off against the outside world. Only some Chinese and occasional European vessels were allowed into the port of Nagasaki. While this insularity was motivated by the legitimate fear that Japan might become another India if it allowed Europeans free access, it was also partially aimed at controlling the population. This control even went into the creation of the Shimabara or courtesans' district in Kyoto (discussed in the previous chapter). A parallel consequence was the emergence of a type of theater called Kabuki. The word *Kabuki* connotes "out of the ordinary" and "shocking," and Kabuki theater involved a mix of the acrobatic, the comical, and the sensual—a fusion that had developed in the Shimabara district and had already been banned by the shoguns in 1652. However, the scandal associated with the Kabuki only assured its popularity. In the Shimabara, high officials interacted with theater people who, though beautiful, accomplished, and expensively dressed, were otherwise viewed as social outcasts.

The earliest theaters were temporary structures similar to those used for special public Noh performances, except that they were more plebeian than the high-class stages of the Noh. Noh performances, which can last all day, are an older form of theater which developed beginning in the 14th century. They were extremely codified in

themes and content and were supported by patronage from the government. Kabuki, by way of contrast, allowed for a greater degree of improvisation, even in its architecture where stages, in fenced-off outdoor areas took advantage of already existing situations or props, such as movable screens that enabled a street to quickly become part of the stage. Over time, the stages became more permanent when a wooden wall was added behind them. As Kabuki became popular with elite audiences, a separate space for them above that of the commoners in the form of raised boxes (*sajiki*) was added along the sides. These early theaters were equipped with dressing rooms, viewing boxes, teahouse additions, and corollary entertainment space which allowed a range of activities from genteel conversation to private performances of music, dance, storytelling, impersonations, and skits with risqué banter and sexual innuendo.

Kanamaru-za

The mature form of the Kabuki theater emerged in the late 17th century. With a solid wall running around the perimeter, it had only a single entrance, low and small, to regulate access. Only one person at a time could enter or exit, and then only by bending, just as one entered a teahouse. The facade had shoji screens and wooden slats to control sight lines. A small tower with a drum, vertical banners, and platforms extending into the streets furnished a framework for advertising.

There was no lobby. The audience entered directly into the main space, known as the *doma*, which was basically an open lawn. In front was the main stage, roughly 12 meters square. To the sides, lifted on stilts, were the cubicles, with access passages behind them, for the higher-class clients. The stage and the cubicles all had individual gabled roofs. The stage roof was held up by corner pillars with the gable end facing the audience, as in Noh stages. The stage, however, had an extensive backstage area, including side wings of different sizes, and an extensive preparation area almost twice as large as the stage itself. The backstage was independently roofed. The seating was divided into individual spaces, called *masu*, by means of low wooden separators arranged in a grid. By the 1740s, Kabuki stages were built throughout Japan. Over time, the facades became more elaborate, with up to three entrances—two large ones for the elite and a smaller one for commoners. An angled raised corridor led to the stage front. The stage became equipped with a revolving segment that could be used to execute quick scenery changes. There are only a few extant Kabuki theaters from the 17th and 18th centuries, among which the Kanamaru-za (1835) is the best preserved.

16.3 Interior of Kanamaru-za, Kotohira, Japan

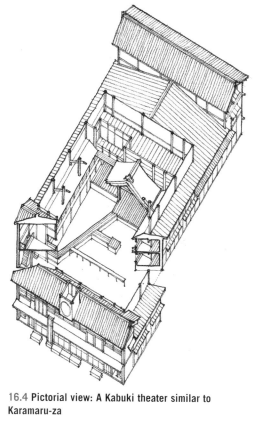

16.4 Pictorial view: A Kabuki theater similar to Karamaru-za

16.5 Kanamaru-za, Kotohira

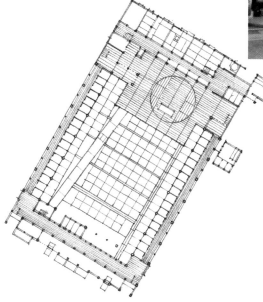

16.6 Plan: A Kabuki theater

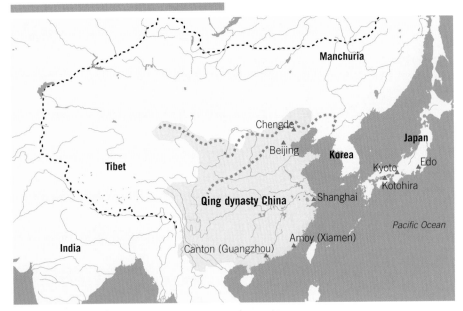

16.7 19th-century China

Emperor Qianlong

Though China increased its export of tea by more than 50 percent in the first third of the 19th century and quadrupled its silk exports, Chinese traders showed little interest in European merchandise. Indeed, they demanded hard currency payment in silver. The result of this asymmetrical trade relationship was that by 1800, almost half of the Spanish silver mined in America ended up in Chinese coffers. England, meanwhile, was having serious financial problems and began to force Chinese traders to accept opium in exchange for tea, a policy the English pursued so relentlessly that by the end of the 19th century, the Chinese economy went into a long-lasting tailspin. This is arguably one of the great civilizational tragedies created by European colonialism.

Back in the 18th century, the eventual reversal of China's fate would not have been conceivable. At that time, China under Qianlong (r. 1736–96) was the largest and richest empire in the world and from its perspective, contact with the outside world was unnecessary. Qianlong, not dissimilar to his contemporary, Napoleon Bonaparte, who pursued a pan-European ideal, saw himself as a pan-Asian emperor. And like Napoleon, he was a military commander of great skill. In ten campaigns between 1755 and 1790, he expanded the Chinese Empire, which reached its zenith when he brought Mongolia, Chinese Turkestan, and Tibet under his control.

Ruling over such a diverse population, and being a ruler of foreign origin himself, Emperor Qianlong aspired to establish a model of governance both pluralistic and moral. Qianlong's grandfather, the Kangxi emperor who was of Manchu origin, had chosen to practice Tibetan Buddhism in private, even though his governmental policy was based on Confucian ethics. Unsatisfied by this arrangement, Qianlong decided to govern along Tibetan Lamaist conceptions. His mentor in this endeavor was Rolpay Dorje, a Tibetan monk who became the grand lama of Beijing in 1736. Under Dorje's guidance, Qianlong adopted the model of the *chakravartin*, originally expounded by the Indian philosopher Nagarjuna, who founded the Madhyamika school of thought in the 1st

century CE. Central to being a *chakravartin* was that Qianlong act as a model Buddhist emperor would in his own time, rather than imitate past rulers. Qianlong tried to fit this role by casting himself as the mediator between the different peoples of his vast kingdom. He spoke several languages, and the court was officially polyglot: edicts were issued in at least three languages. Qianlong also set about creating a new architecture that took all he considered to be significant from the different traditions in his empire and modernizing them into a synthetic whole. As such, Qianlong offered a complex, multinucleated conception of empire and an ideal of modernity that contrasted with the colonial model of empire unfolding at the same time. While the English model eventually overwhelmed Qianlong's, the policies of contemporary China are still to some degree connected to his pan-Asian vision.

Chengde

As part of that pan-Asian vision, Qianlong embarked on an extensive building program that included the enlargement of Chengde, which had originally been planned by Qianlong's grandfather Kangxi only as a royal summer residence. The city is located north of Beijing, outside the Great Wall, thereby affirming China's claim of a Chinese-controlled, pan-Asian world. Under Qianlong, the city served three purposes. It was a summer residence, an administrative center for Mongolia and China's northern provinces, and an alternative religious capital for Tibetan Buddhism. The government, on the other hand, was still run from Beijing's Forbidden

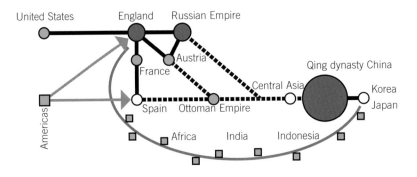

16.8 Eurasian trade diagram, ca. 1800

City. Besides building a road from Beijing to Chengde that continued into Mongolia and a dam to control the Wulie River, which ran through the city, Qianlong enlarged the palaces and gardens, and founded temples in the surrounding areas, including Puningsi (1755), the Puyousi (1760), the Anyuanmiao (1764), the Pulesi (1767), the Putuo Zongcheng (1771), the Shuxiangsi (1776), and the Xumifushoumiao (1780).

The Chengde temples, dedicated to a range of Confucian and Buddhist deities, are drawn from—and meant to represent—various parts of the empire. Together they form an arc that can be taken in at once from the main hill north of the palace. A self-conscious visual ensemble, Chengde was a veritable microcosm of the Qing Empire—a map of the land. But it was also an ordering of that map according to a Buddhist mandala. A critical feature of Chengde's landscape is a 60-meter-high rock formation called the Qingchui Peak. Wider at the top than at the bottom, Qingchui is at summit of one of the eastern hills. All the temples and palace complexes of the city can be interpreted as "facing" Qingchui—not

literally, but by the geomantic logic of Chinese and Tibetan landscape architecture. In this reading, Chengde as a whole was a mandala, with Quinchui standing in for Sumeru, the sacred mountain at the center.

The palace had three main groups of halls: the Main Palace (Zhenggong), the Pine and Crane Studio (Songhezhai), and the Eastern Palace (Donggong). The Main Palace, the principal living quarters, had nine courtyards representing the nine divisions of the celestial sphere. A wall enclosed a 4-square-kilometer area with several discrete landscape zones. The lake district had an island with buildings and courtyards that housed officials and was used for private activities. Further north was a site known as the Garden of Ten Thousand Trees, which was laid out beginning in 1703 and improved for decades. It contained a Prairie District that was a replica of the Mongolian steppe. Though used for horse races, military exercises, and fireworks, it had important political and ceremonial functions as well. On special occasions, the Qing created a simulated Mongolian camp site, complete with yurts.

16.9 Qingchui Peak at Chengde, Hebei Province, China

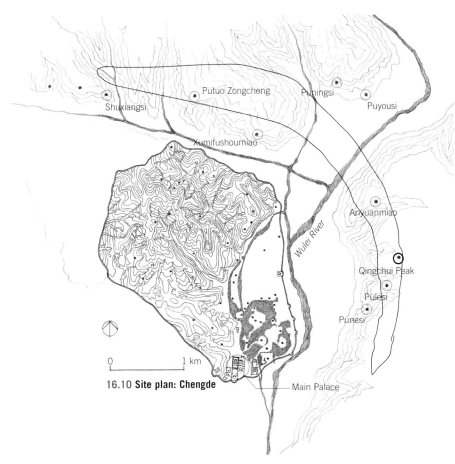

16.10 Site plan: Chengde

The twelve temples, of which only nine survive today, were designed as representations of other temples. The Pulesi ("Temple of Universal Happiness," 1767), for instance, is a hybrid building that merges the Tibetan conceptual order with Chinese formal expression. In appearance, the Pulesi is like the shrine at the Temple of Heaven in Beijing; it is a round temple with a double eave and conical roof. In plan, however, it replicates a Buddhist mandala with a series of stepped terraces. Chengde's most visible structure, the Putuo Zongcheng (1771) is a small-scale replica of Lhasa's famed Potala Palace. Like the Potala, the Putuo consists of a series of low white buildings rising up the side of a hill, culminating in the central red structure, the Dahongtai ("Great Red Terrace"), with the golden temple's roofs projecting over the summit. But the Putuo is not a pure copy. The original Potala's massive white walls enclosed a small courtyard. The walls of the Putuo, by contrast, enclose the Great Red Terrace, within which stood a huge Chinese-style temple pavilion suitable more for royal receptions than a hidden spiritual practice.

16.11 Pulesi, Chengde

16.12 Putuo Zongcheng, Chengde

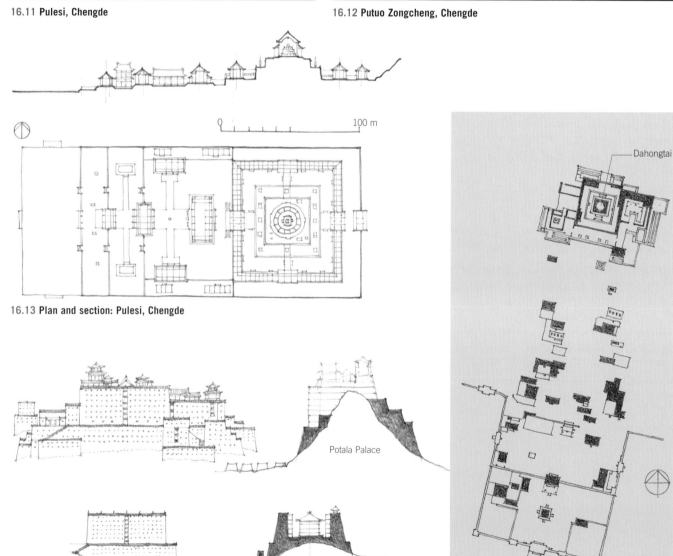

16.13 Plan and section: Pulesi, Chengde

Dahongtai

16.14 Diagrammatic comparisons of the Potala Palace at Lhasa and the Putuo Zongcheng at Chengde
Based on drawings by Anne Chayet

Potala Palace

Putuo Zongcheng

16.15 Site plan: Putuo Zongcheng

European Architecture: An Introduction

The terms *Neoclassicism*, *Romanticism*, and *Picturesque* are key to understanding the arts and philosophy of this period. (A more detailed discussion appears later in this chapter.) Neoclassicism, which began around 1700, refers to an Enlightenment-driven movement that emphasized the values of reason, order, and civility. In some instances, this came with an aristocratic slant; in others, with a progressive emphasis on science and egalitarianism for which it was viewed as a corrective aimed at the excesses of aristocratic culture. In architecture, it featured a turn away from the curves, inventiveness, and mysteriousness of the Baroque toward a more rectilinear and transparent organization of space. Unlike Baroque architecture, Neoclassical buildings were designed according to precedents from classical antiquity; such precedents served as proof of the continuity of history and the legitimacy of civil society.

The Picturesque, which began to take root around 1780 in England, challenged the Neoclassical ideal of permanence and order, preferring instead to emphasize mankind as subject to the unruly forces of nature and therewith to arbitrariness, disorder, and even decay. The Picturesque had its origins in painting, where it tended, as the name implies, to tell a story, as, for example, in Giambattista Piranesi's etchings of the great ruins of ancient Rome, which evoke the idea of loss—in this instance the lost monumentality of the heroic past. Gothic architecture, which was not particularly appreciated by the Neoclassicists, came into vogue in the Picturesque as something to be emulated partially because of its association with ruins. The Picturesque saw nature, and therefore landscape, as superseding the manmade: a consolation of sorts for the melancholic.

The Picturesque was a precursor of the broader movement known as Romanticism, which in the early decades of the 19th century grew into the main alternative to Neoclassicism. Beginning around 1820 and lasting until 1890, it sought to legitimize individuality and the power of imagination and thus stood in direct and indirect opposition to the rise of the industrial culture in Europe. One of its main representatives was the German painter

16.16 South front, Kenwood, Hampstead, London

Caspar David Friedrich (1774–1840). Unlike Neoclassicism, which saw nature in more passive terms, Romanticism challenged forth a personal and active response to the ideals propounded by the Enlightenment. (A famous example is the poet Lord Byron traveling to Greece to help that country in its fight for liberation from the Ottoman Empire.)

By the mid-19th century, Romanticism had begun to shape various populist nationalist discourses, finding its highest expression mainly in the fields of painting and literature. This first took place in Germany and England, and then in France and the United States, as well as in Poland, Russia, and Scandinavia. In the field of architecture, Romanticism favored not only the Neo-Gothic but also styles associated with natively rooted cultures: the Byzantine in Russia, the Norman in England, and the Gothic in France and Germany. The irony is that whereas Neoclassical architects had tended to resist modern materials, such as iron and glass, the Romantics—though usually critical of industrialism—were often more receptive, since they saw the new materials as part of the dynamic aspect of history.

Neoclassicism

The term *Neoclassicism*, in wide use today, was actually invented in the mid-19th century. Until then, critics, theorists, and artists called it simply the "true style" that challenged fluctuations in taste and, particularly, the extravagances of Baroque space. The heady mercantile era of the preceding century gave way to a desire for something perceived as authentic and stable. At its best, Neoclassicism shared the Enlightenment's spirit of reform, whether it was scientific advancement in the Age of Reason or the new political philosophy that stressed the principles of a socially regulated human action. In architecture, Neoclassicism initially played itself out in England, France, and Germany, although along different lines in each country. In England, Neoclassicism developed primarily in the domain of the private sector, with the great houses of the elite. In France, Neoclassicism was associated with the Enlightenment and the French Revolution and thus had a civic component. And in Germany it was linked with the rise of the nation-state and thus with its new representative institutions such as schools, museums, and theaters.

Robert Adam

Unlike in France, the royal court in England played only a marginal role in determining aesthetic norms; matters of taste were largely left to the members of the elite who, in turn, consulted with artists and architects. Best known among the architects of the time were the four Adam brothers, especially Robert (1728–92). The brothers were themselves members of the gentry, having learned about architecture as a matter of course from their lay-architect father and from a family friend, Sir William Bruce, a man of considerable political standing. The brothers were already successful architects when Robert made his first European trip. France left him disappointed, but in Rome he met and befriended Giambattista Piranesi, whose etchings of dilapidated Roman scenery were then wildly popular. When Piranesi published a portrait of himself and Adam on the dedicatory plate of what was to become his *Campo Marzo* etching, Robert Adam's fame was guaranteed.

Upon Adam's return from Rome, he realized that the Palladian manner he had used in his early career would no longer do. Ornament had to be based on antique precedent, not on Renaissance transmissions. Composition of the rooms would have to be tighter. The Adam brothers, now stimulated by Robert's insights gained in Italy, sought to create a totally integrated architectural and spatial environment. The standard practice at the time was for the architect to design the building but leave the interior finishing to specialists in the individual crafts, such as wainscoting, decorating, and plastering. Furniture was bought by the client and usually ordered from an existing stock. The Adam brothers now sought to control the entire production, down to the furniture and color schemes. They had a few copies of their collected drawings tinted so that other architects could imitate their method of coloring. Ceilings, rarely given much thought in Georgian domestic architecture—except perhaps for moldings at the perimeter and the articulation of corners—became an important element in the interiors designed by the Adam brothers. Robert Adam's ceilings were covered with panels consisting of framed small ceiling paintings.

16.17 Entrance facade: Shelburne House, London

The Adam brothers thus brought a sense of unity to the design. Shelburne House in London (begun 1763) was originally designed for John Stuart, 3rd Earl of Bute (1713–92), secretary of state under George III. When Lord Bute was toppled from power, the house was sold to the young and rich 2nd Earl of Shelburne (1737–1805), who served in the government in various capacities—even as prime minister. He thought of himself as a man of principle who supported Adam Smith's free-trade ideas, but he also had great respect for the monarchy and was thus held in suspicion by the Whigs.

The facade comprised a seven-bay, three-story central block with a four-columned pedimented temple front. It was a combination of Palladio's Villa Foscari and his Palazzo Thiene. The central temple front was set between two-story, three-bay pavilions. A rusticated, false-arcaded ground floor unified the composition. The frieze ornamentation was taken from the Temple of Concord in Rome. The use of precedents in this way was an important aspect of the Neoclassical architectural culture, which prided itself on being part of a European, historical continuum. The interior ornamentation was

16.18 An anonymous painting showing the Syon House before 1760

carefully planned and distinguished by delicate decorative pilasters and ceilings painted by Italian artists. The eating room had a series of niches in the walls for statues. The music room was oblong with a rotunda at each end, 11 meters in diameter. Some of the most important people in London society gathered at Shelburne House, among them Benjamin Franklin and David Hume. Much of the house was demolished in the 1930s. The eating room was rebuilt and is in the Metropolitan Museum of Art in New York.

Syon House

The Syon House (1762–63) in Brentford, London, was named after Mt. Zion, a onetime medieval abbey that had been closed down. In time it fell by dint of marriage to the 1st Duke of Northumberland, formerly Sir Hugh Smithson, who, even though his political role was marginal, wanted to be viewed as a man of taste and culture. Robert Adam was given the task of transforming the shell of the old nunnery into a grand house, which he accomplished by designing, in 1761, a series of rooms around a large domed structure that was to fill the courtyard. The entrance is on the long side of an apsed, double-square room kept in a grisaille color scheme, decorated in the Doric order. After turning right and going up the curved steps, one enters a green and gold square room decorated in the Ionic order. From there, one turns left to enter a long white and gold apsed room, Corinthian in style. Finally, by way of a red and gold, double-square room, one arrives at the great gallery, which has views into the garden. The residential areas were nested within the remaining part of the plan. The large, circular domed salon at the center was never built. The Adam brothers saw architecture as the backdrop for a hoped-for unification of life and space, of learning and politics, and of architecture and decoration. In that respect, their work can be seen in the context of the Picturesque, which emphasized the unique aspects of significant human action. Their architecture served to inscribe self-confidence and self-discipline into the psychology of the elite, thereby staking out a basis for the exercise of their authority.

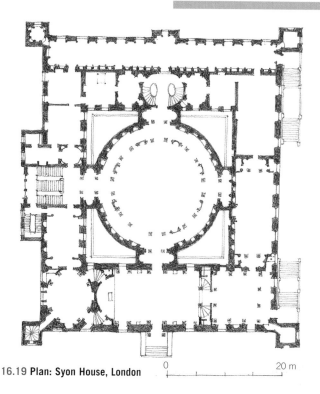

16.19 Plan: Syon House, London

16.20 Interior: Syon House

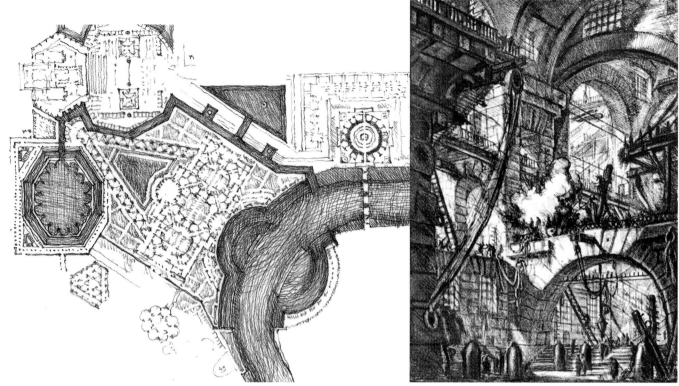

16.21 Drawing of a fragment of Piranesi's plan for Rome

16.22 Print from the *Carceri* series by Piranesi

Piranesi and Romanticism

In Europe, the 18th century was an expansionary age adjusting to the colonial project philosophically, economically, and politically. In particular, it was oriented toward accumulating wealth from far-flung global territories. Naive historicism, like that of the neo-Palladians, gave way to a search for more solid societal underpinnings that involved scholarly standards, academic affiliations, and incontrovertible historical facts based on proven archaeological discoveries. If the Adam brothers put this to work in their architectural practice, Giambattista Piranesi (1720–78) interrogated it in his engravings. Robert Adam worked for a secure elite and lived the life of an outward-looking member of an opportunistic colonial world. Piranesi lived surrounded by the faded glories of Rome in front of his eyes. But both, in different ways, confronted Europe's newfound role as the locus of the global colonial world with an as yet episodic sense of its own historical identity.

Copperplate engravings were all the rage at the time, but Piranesi elevated the art into an idiom all its own. Scouring the often malaria-infested Roman *campagna* for pictorial possibilities, Piranesi portrayed broken stones, crumbling bricks, collapsed vaults, and overgrown facades of haunting intensity, bringing unexpected and revealing angles into view. This was a Rome far different from the one imagined in England, where it was embedded in a rhetoric of order and manliness. Piranesi envisioned a cataclysmic end of time, with nothing left to show for Rome's erstwhile grandeur. The Colosseum is an empty crater; the foundation wall of Hadrian's Tomb a vast, battered cliff. Adam and Piranesi represented the two sides of the Romantic movement: Adam through his zest for the exotic, Piranesi through his moody melancholia. Both admired the heroic, but from different political perspectives. Adam saw the Roman past as the legitimization of English civilizational supremacy and as a living model for heroic action, while Piranesi rendered it as a meditative reflection on the short-sightedness of the powers currently in charge. These distinctions define the difference between neoclassicism and Romanticism, the former reflecting a historical optimism, the latter reflecting on the principle of historical loss.

16.23 Drawing made from a Piranesi print of Roman ruins

16.24 Strawberry Hill, Twickenham, England

16.25 Interior: Strawberry Hill

Strawberry Hill

Not all members of the English elite thought that Neoclassicsm was the answer. Protesting against its stiffness and artificiality, a group of intellectuals and aesthetes began to see the Middle Ages, not Rome, as more "authentic." Instead of the whites, soft blues, and golds used by the Adam brothers, they preferred reds, greens, and browns; purposefully dark and gloomy interiors; and asymmetrical ground plans. Horace Walpole (1717–97), builder of Strawberry Hill (1748–77), used the term *Gothic picturesque* to define this style. Walpole was in many respects a counterculturist. He was well educated; his wealth had been amassed by his father, the prime minister Sir Robert Walpole, who also secured his son's election to Parliament, a post that he held until 1768. The elder Walpole also arranged lucrative sinecures for his son in the Exchequer and Custom House that ensured a very comfortable income for life.

But public life did not appeal to Walpole, whose principal passion was writing Gothic novels, such as *The Castle of Otranto*. He also wrote a four-volume history of art entitled *Anecdotes of Painting* (1761–71). Upon the death of his father in 1745, Walpole settled at Strawberry Hill, an estate of some 40 acres at Twickenham, southwest of London, set among fashionable villas overlooking the Thames River and near the residence of his friend, the poet and garden enthusiast Alexander Pope. Expanding the existing house, he built a "star chamber" named after the golden stars that adorn the ceiling, and a "tribune," a square room with the ceiling copied from the Cathedral of York. He also built a library, an armory, a gallery, a china closet, bedrooms in several colors, and an oratory. There were towers, battlements, and stained glass windows rescued from demolished buildings. Walpole filled the house with art, paintings, sculpture, china, and heraldic symbols, both real and invented. Attention to structure was minimal: the fan vaulting in the gallery, a copy of that in Westminster Abbey, was made of papier-mâché.

If this was a gentleman's fantasy world, as has been claimed, the architecture of the Adam brothers was just as much a gentleman's fantasy, even down to the custom-designed chairs. Yet the contrast between Adam and Walpole could not have been greater. Robert Adam was the consummate tastemaker for the metropolitan gentry, insisting on a continuum between design and public life. Walpole created an aesthetic environment reflecting his personal choices. His house was much visited by the elite of the time: after 1763 Walpole even began selling entrance tickets. Adam and Walpole represent the paradoxes associated with emerging modernism. Professionalism, or at least the beginnings of what might be called a professional practice, in the former, and the deliberate and self-conscious search for personal expression and the desire for approbation in the latter.

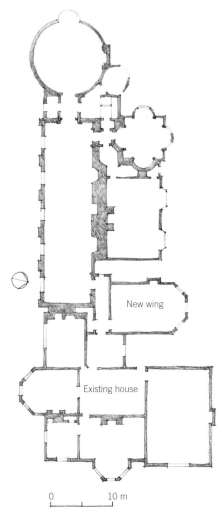

New wing

Existing house

0   10 m

16.26 Plan: Strawberry Hill

16.27 Reproduction of the frontispiece to Marc-Antoine Laugier's *Essai sur l'architecture*, from *Allegory of Architecture Returning to its Natural Model* by Charles Eisen

Marc-Antoine Laugier

Whereas in England, Neoclassicism was generally seen as the proper environment for the elite, the tone in France was more strident, assuming a subtext of antimonarchism driven in part by an emerging interest in rationalism and legalism and a desire to rethink the role of civic institutions. In architectural circles, this all came into the open with the publication in 1753 of Marc-Antoine Laugier's *Essai sur l'architecture*. Translated into English in 1775, it was a flashpoint of discussion about the nature of architectural production. Unlike Leon Battista Alberti's *Ten Books on Architecture*, Andrea Palladio's *Four Books on Architecture*, and Claude Perrault's French translation of Vitruvius, Laugier's work pointed not to a classical past but rather to an earlier, "rustic" past.

Laugier wrote neither as an architect nor as a gentleman connoisseur. He was a Jesuit priest and impassioned orator, having been invited in 1749 to preach in the presence of the king. He preached yet again to the king in 1754, one year after the publication of his book, in a climate of approaching revolt. Laugier, thinking perhaps of King Philip II of Spain and his humility, which was so forcefully expressed at the Escorial, thundered against the king's doubtful amusements and entreated him to give religion its due. His blunt address landed him in trouble with his Jesuit superiors, who were not keen on losing their political influence at the court. Unlike previous writers, Laugier interpreted the classical principle of the balanced interplay between the whole and its parts as formed by architectural elements that ensured the actual solidity of the building. As a result, he frowned on the use of pilasters, which had been a staple of architectural design ever since the Renaissance. Even though his image of the ideal building was not based on Roman models, Laugier admired the Maison Carrée at Nîmes, France, as the most perfect building of antiquity: "Thirty columns support an entablature and a roof which is closed at both ends by a pediment—that is all; the combination is of a simplicity and a nobility which strikes everybody." It was not the classical temple as such that needed to be imitated, but that which lay behind its design, the original "rustic hut," or *cabane rustique*, as he called it (and often mistranslated as "primitive hut"). This hut, according to Laugier, consisted only of columns, entablatures, and pediments. Vaults, arches, pedestals, and pilasters were not part of that system and, he argued, should not therefore be used. Even arcades, another important element in classical architecture, were listed by Laugier as "abuses."

Laugier's book was highly controversial. He argued that architecture should not be seen as representing a magical transition from the worldly to the heavenly, as had been implied by the Baroque style, but rather as a medium that told nothing less than the story of the "origins" of mankind. These origins had to remain embedded in architecture. They were similar to the notion of grace—a sign of divine approval that for Catholics is embedded in the human soul. In this sense, his argument echoed the 15th-century debate between Bartolomé de las Casas and Juan Ginés de Sepúlveda in Madrid, on the question of the status of Native Americans. Bartolomé de las Casas argued that Native Americans were free men, though not yet Christianized, and not slaves. The Jesuits, who held a similar view, were sent by the Church to the French colonies for the purpose of conversion. But they also studied and wrote about the life and work of the Native Americans. Laugier's hut was in many respects an indication of what the Jesuits had learned from people who in their eyes were not "primitive," as had originally been argued, but actually "noble;" it was this, they argued, that prepared them for Christ.

Influencing Laugier's writings was the just-published *Discourse sur les arts et les sciences* (1750) by Jean-Jacques Rousseau (1712–78). In this astonishing book, Rousseau critiqued what he saw as the naïveté of the Enlightenment's careless atheism. Not only had reason in the hands of the more powerful crushed individual liberty, but it had also replaced simple virtues with a labyrinth of false truths. Reason did not lead to knowledge but to hypocrisy, and civilization led to class division, slavery, serfdom, robbery, war, and injustice. The only real progress, he argued, was moral progress. It was a powerful and controversial critique of everything that the French intelligentsia had built up during the previous century. Rousseau, a native of the Calvinist city of Geneva, marveled at the civilizational and devotional virtues of Swiss farmers and Native Americans. It was Rousseau who coined the famous term *the noble savage* to describe the innate majesty of people like the Iroquois.

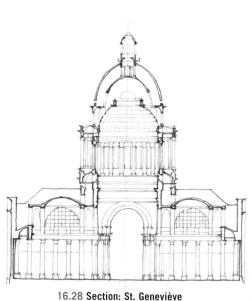

16.28 Section: St. Geneviève

16.29 St. Geneviève, Paris

St. Geneviève

Jacques-Germain Soufflot (1709–80) saw
in Laugier's argument the opportunity
for experimentation. The dome of his St.
Geneviève in Paris (1757)—now known as
the Panthéon—was derived from Bramante's
San Pietro in Montorio; its overscaled
relationship to the building on which it rests is
Baroque. The church, as a centralized Greek
cross, fulfilled a Renaissance aspiration.
Novel, however, and influenced by Laugier, is
the clean-cut, though gigantic, Neoclassical
temple front with Corinthian capitals modeled
on the Pantheon in Rome (though with six
rather than eight columns). On the interior,
Soufflot also adhered to Laugier's call for an
architecture in which every element had a
structural rationale. There are pilasters, but
they are clearly linked to the structural grid
established by the columns. The vaults have
a billowing lightness and are illuminated from
the side through large windows, concealed on
the exterior behind a parapet. The contrast
between the building's severe, clifflike exterior
and the luminous, airy interior was meant to
be a literal evocation of the Enlightenment's
transformative power. The building was
originally attached at its rear to a monastery
but made freestanding in the 19th century.

16.30 Interior: St. Geneviève

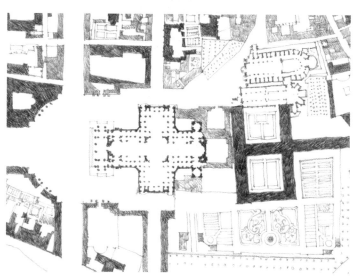

16.31 Site plan: St. Geneviève

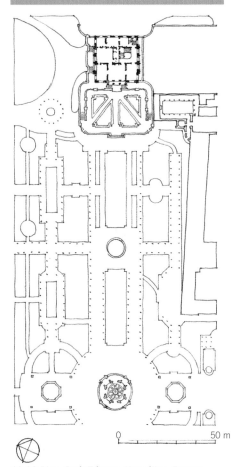

16.32 **Plan: Petit Trianon, Versailles, France**

16.33 **Petit Trianon**

Le Petit Trianon

French intellectuals were impressed by the English Picturesque and its mixture of elegance, informality, and exalted pedagogical mission. Voltaire, a Frenchman, was a fervent advocate of English culture and often insisted on speaking English at the dinner table. He was certainly no populist. For him, an enlightened monarchy was far superior to the chaos of democracy. This does not mean that Neoclassicism shied away from the fashion-conscious world of polite society. On the contrary, it profited from the strength of bourgeois networks. By 1763, ladies had their hair done *à la grècque*, and one writer complained that young French gentlemen were often affecting an English accent. Nonetheless, the work of the French Enlightenment philosophers was not completely antithetical to royal language, given the support it had from certain members of the French aristocracy. The critique of superficiality was expressed both outside and inside the court of Louis XV

(as we have already seen with Laugier), with many writers and artists calling for a return to the standards if not of the ancients, then at least of the time of Louis XIV. Ange-Jacques Gabriel's facade for the Petit Trianon in Versailles (1761–78) for Louis XIV shows just how quickly aspects of this new sensibility were realized. The volumetric simplicity, the absence of an axial imperative (as one might have expected from Hardouin-Mansart), and, equally, the absence of pilasters and quoins except for the central four pilasters, was accomplished without any loss of elegance. In plan, symmetry was preserved in the rooms behind the facade, but it purposefully breaks down toward the more private rooms to the rear.

In the European environment, where global realities had increasingly become part of upper-class life, Neoclassicism provided (as we have seen in the work of Adam) a language of stability and order that also reinforced the search for European self-understanding in the wake of the colonial experience. But Neoclassicism, as a language of self-mastery, was also a language of the master over the production of others. Neoclassicism thus provided an all too convenient legitimization of empire, harboring an underlying and suppressed contradiction between a civilizational ideal and the political expediencies that were necessary to realize that ideal.

Salt Works of Chaux

Eminent among the French Neoclassicists of the time was Claude Nicholas Ledoux (1736–1806), who designed for the French crown a series of gates and tollhouses—forty-five buildings in all—to mark the boundaries of Paris and to impress approaching visitors. The stations also served as places for the collection of a much-hated tax on the importation of salt (which had become very expensive) into the city. Like Christopher Wren's churches, each of the gatehouses was different and in its own way varied and forceful. A few are still extant, including the Barrière de la Villette (1785–89), which provides a good sense of Ledoux's austerely simplified architectural vocabulary. The central drum is supported by column pairs that serve as a screen holding the arcaded bottom of a cylinder, which is basically a circular building around a cylindrical light court. Windows are without moldings and ornamentation is held to a minimum. The wide and low pediment—compared with the more historically accurate pediment of St. Geneviève—and the astonishing, domeless drum are far outside the norms of classicism, but Ledoux, probably more than any other architect of his generation, was seeking to redefine architectural typology from top to bottom.

Ledoux also designed various buildings for the Salt Works of Chaux (1775–79), located in the east of France in the Franche-Comté region between two villages near the forest of

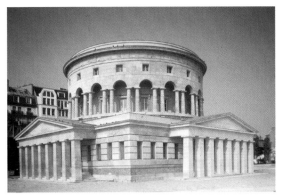

16.34 Barrière de la Villette, Paris

16.35 Salt Works of Chaux, Arc-et-Senans, France

16.36 Column of director's house, Salt Works of Chaux

The salt trade was among the grimmest aspects of life in 18th-century France; the forcible imposition of a tax gave rise to widespread smuggling and robbery, as salt was very much cheaper outside the country. The security of the salt works was therefore essential. The entrance contained guardrooms and a small prison and is marked by a dense peristyle of six baseless Tuscan columns, with a squat attic above. Along the walls are openings out of which flows, in a sculptural mass, the thick, saline water. The columns, with their alternating round and square stones, were quite novel. Interpretations vary, but it seems that Ledoux wanted to show the column as if it were in the process of being formed. This is perhaps the first architect-designed factory in history; what Ledoux hoped to demonstrate was the advantage of a rational and comprehensive solution to an industrial problem elevated to the level of the symbolic. Salt was produced there until 1895.

Chaux, not far from Besançon. The nearby forest supplied the wood needed to fire the kilns in which the salt was extracted from the brine. The factory replaced a previous installation some kilometers away that consisted of little more than a ramshackle assortment of sheds. The brine was brought to the site from its source miles away by means of wooden pipes. Ledoux's plan called for a semicircular arrangement of buildings, with the house of the director at the center and the salt-extracting buildings to both sides. The circumference is occupied by storage buildings, with the main entrance to the facility in the circle directly opposite the director's house.

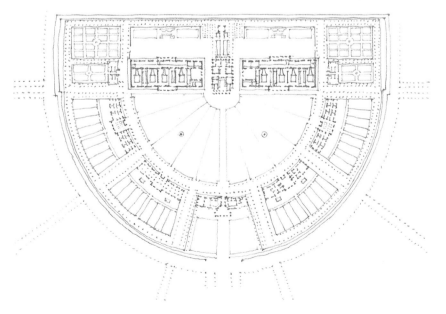

16.37 Plan: Salt Works of Chaux

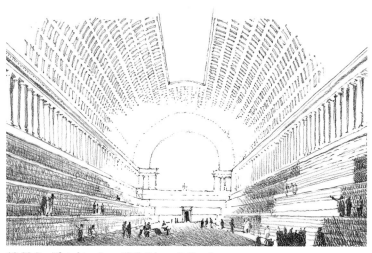

16.38 Boullée's idea for a Bibliothèque Nationale

The French Revolution

The events leading to the French Revolution (1789–99) were manifold. The successors to Louis XIV had become increasingly self-involved and rigid, leading a frivolous and wasteful life in Versailles: in 1751 the king spent 68 million *livres*, one-quarter of the government's total revenue, on the royal household alone. Wars further weakened the economy, and France's income from its colonies dropped from 30 million *livres* in 1755 to just 4 million in 1760. The descent was rapid. In 1760 the French commander in Canada surrendered to the English; in 1763 France lost the French and Indian War and had to abandon its forts. In 1770 the Compagnie des Indes Orientales (French East India Company) went bankrupt. The unmanageable national debt led to high taxes; thousands of acres of farmland reverted to wilderness. Unemployment in Paris was close to 50 percent, and prices soared. Under these stresses and the concomitant food shortages, rural disturbances were common, but the actual opening salvo of violence—the first confrontation with the regime—was the bloody storming of the prison fortress known as the Bastille on July 14, 1789.

Bibliothèque Nationale

More than any other architect, Étienne-Louis Boullée (1728–99), managed to straddle these complex political times successfully. He won widespread acclaim during his lifetime for his series of inspired drawings that seemed to envision a postrevolutionary world. Boullée's buildings have simple geometrical shapes, are monumental in scale, and often serve as backdrops for uncluttered, neo-pagan devotions. His project for the Bibliothèque Nationale (1788), though often classified as an example of the Neoclassical sensibility, actually has no standard classical features on its surfaces except for the entablature and the frieze of garlands. The main entrance, guarded by two large figures of Atlas, gives admittance to a vast barrel-vaulted space boldly slit open at the top. The books are arranged on shelves against the walls of continuous terraces on the two sides of the interior of the building. Even more spectacular is Boullée's cenotaph for Sir Isaac Newton (1784). A sphere that

represents the earth on the outside is on the inside a planetarium, with small holes forming the constellations. The entrance leads to a passageway that opens onto a shrine at the base of the inner void. Boullée's structures are always grand, both inside and out. For a theater, he designed a building within a building, a Pantheonesque interior placed inside a vast structure that itself encased in a dome.

Ledoux and Boullée are often called revolutionary architects, an appellation based on their architecture rather than their politics. Both architects straddled the fence in the French Revolution, even though they set in motion much of the aesthetic that for a short while governed the sensibilities of the age. Boullée probably made the transition better than Ledoux. He built little after the Revolution, but his place was more secure, and it was his vision that young architects in the Academy of Architecture, where Boullée taught, aspired to emulate. After the French Revolution, the history of Neoclassicism took many turns, fusing with the Greek Revival in Germany and Scotland and blending in with the eclectic stylistic preferences of the Victorians. Despite all of this, traces of a vigorous and austere Neoclassicism as pursued by Ledoux and Boullée could be found throughout Europe from 1800 onward.

As for Ledoux, his architectural practice dried up after the Revolution even though he struggled to redefine himself as an advocate of republican principles. He set to work to publish his architectural achievements in a book entitled *L'Architecture considérée sous le rapport de l'art, des mœurs et de la législation* ("Architecture considered in relation to art, morals, and legislation, 1804). It contained the plans not only of his built work but also of a remarkable set of

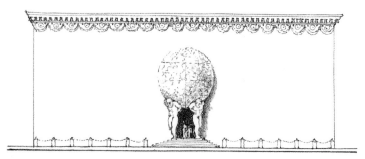

16.39 Facade: Bibliothèque Nationale

16.40 Boullée's cenotaph for Sir Isaac Newton

not only the rich and mighty should get the benefit of architectural speculation. Plans of even the most humble edifices were always symmetrical and concentrated on the efficient use of space.

Ledoux was responding to an incipient awareness that the complexity of society could be mapped architecturally, the underlying theme of the designs being human industriousness and the assumption that it deserves its own formal recognition. Though promising, it was not a line of reasoning that would have much traction in subsequent architectural speculation.

imaginary buildings. From the Renaissance onward, architects produced drawings that attempted to re-create Roman architecture based on ruins, some more accurate than others. Architects like Sebastiano Serlio and Andrea Palladio designed villas and palaces for imaginary clients, but no one had drawn a house for a humble woodsman, a house for a surveyor of dams, or a bordello, to list just a few of the buildings Claude Nicholas Ledoux designed. This made Ledoux's publication truly remarkable.

Though the structures may seem fanciful, even by today's standards, Ledoux aimed to make the ideals of classicism available to a broader spectrum of the social strata. The form of each building was directly themed to the occupation of its inhabitant. The head of a water canal system, for example, lived in a house that is shaped like a tube. This was what Ledoux called *une architecture parlante* ("speaking architecture"), through which buildings form a visual encyclopedia of the members of society and of their respective duties. There would be a temple of reconciliation, an asylum of happiness, and a temple of memory. His proposition was that

16.41 Ledoux's house of supervisors of the source of the Loue, a project for the ideal city of Chaux

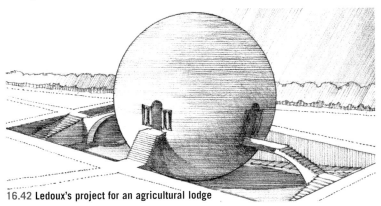

16.42 Ledoux's project for an agricultural lodge

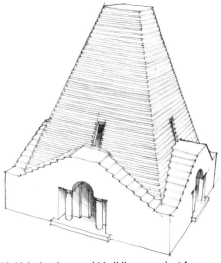

16.43 Ledoux's pyramid building, a project for a cannon forge

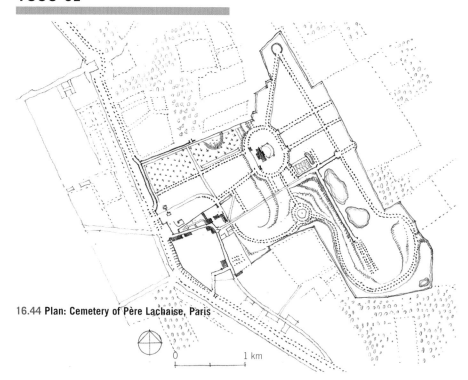

16.44 Plan: Cemetery of Père Lachaise, Paris

1 km

would gain in importance in the Romantic period to come. Consequently, military death achieved an honorable connotation that it had not had since antiquity. As are result of these changes, the cemetery known as Père Lachaise, which was laid out in 1804 outside of Paris, was opened to all citizens. Graves, however, were to last for only five years, unless the plot was bought by the deceased's relatives, who were also required to endow certain architectural features of the cemetery. This cemetery was also among the first examples of a "garden cemetery" laid out with trees, bushes, and winding paths; it had a central esplanade ending in a funerary monument. Père Lachaise became the model for cemeteries all over the world: the Glasgow Necropolis (1820), the South Metropolitan Cemetery at Norwood in London (1830s), and the Mt. Auburn Cemetery in Cambridge, Massachusetts (1831) are just a few examples.

Napoleonic Cemeteries

After the French Revolution, Napoleon sought to rebuild not only France but all of Europe along Enlightenment lines. He eventually succumbed to his overreaching ambition, making enemies of the Austrians, Russians, and English, who were all eager to keep Napoleonic ideas as far as possible from their domains. The impact of the Napoleonic era was, however, profound, bringing into parlance concepts like liberty and justice, abstractions that were presumed universal and strong enough to replace the defunct and self-serving regimes of the aristocracy. Napoleon proved that nations could function without the paternalism of kings and princes. Socially, he introduced many Enlightenment-influenced notions: the Napoleonic Code of 1804, for example, brought about the emancipation of the Jews in many of the lands under his control; it also modernized the school system.

One of his important contributions was in the architecture of cemeteries. Prior to Napoleon, the well-to-do were buried in or near a parish church. The poor were buried in paupers' graves. As for soldiers, they were easily dispensable figures, fighting often as conscripts or mercenaries; they were buried in unmarked graves on the battlefield. But in Napoleon's army, death in battle took on a new dignity, a notion that

16.45 View of the Cemetery of Père Lachaise

16.46 Mt. Auburn Cemetery, Cambridge, Massachusetts

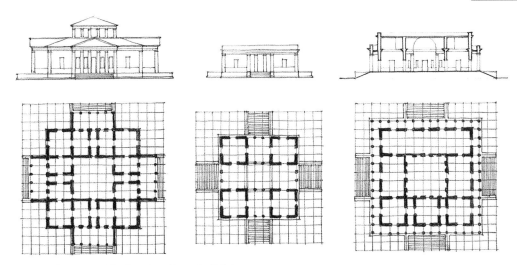

16.47 Horizontal combinations from Durand's *Précis*

Jean-Nicolas-Louis Durand

In France, the Romantic movement had many representatives among painters. Théodore Géricault (1791–1824), for example, used dramatic compositional techniques to bring out the themes of heroism, suffering, and endurance. In architecture, Romanticism was slower to develop. This was largely because in France, unlike in England and Germany, architecture remained under state sponsorship. For this reason, post-Napoleonic French architecture stayed on the course of Enlightenment rationalism. The most important proponent of this tendency was Jean-Nicolas-Louis Durand (1760–1834), a pupil of Étienne-Louis Boullée and a professor at the École Polytechnique (founded in 1794), whose work set the tone for more than a generation. The purpose of the École Polytechnique was to provide engineers capable of meeting the needs of the revolutionary armies as well as provide plans for civilian public works in the remote corners of the new republic. No such school existed in England, where the evolution of taste, remaining in the hands of the elite, was decentralized and thus often eclectic. Durand's book *Précis*, first published in 1802, became a reference used throughout Europe for half a century. In it, he rejected the standard Neoclassical emphasis on a historical relationship between contemporary architecture and antiquity and instead argued that even classical antiquity needed to be regularized according to the eternal principles of geometry.

Durand was opposed to historical classicism that only copied surface elements but that in plan was anything but rational— like the Capitol Building in Washington, DC, for example. He wanted the plan to be laid out on a grid and the function clearly expressed. "To please," he wrote, "has never been the purpose of architecture." Instead, the architect should provide "public and private utility," while aiming to serve "the well-being and the maintenance of individuals and of society." Durand's designs for walls, following Laugier, were freed from pilasters, moldings, quoins, and rustications. This was not stripped down classicism, but rather a linking of architecture with the presumed ideals of nature and reason. The square,

which has no dominant axis, constituted his ideological and figural building block, serving to link the columns in a grid and stabilizing the architectural formation. Like an ideal military unit, a building had to reflect order, clarity, and hierarchy. Rationalism and civic dispassion had to be evinced in order to demonstrate architecture's independence from aristocratic whim. In this respect, Durand represented a break from an insistence on tradition and literal historicism. Unlike Picturesque and Romantic notions of history as the ground on which the future projects itself, Durand's architecture was strikingly "modern," insisting on the primacy of program in the service of the state.

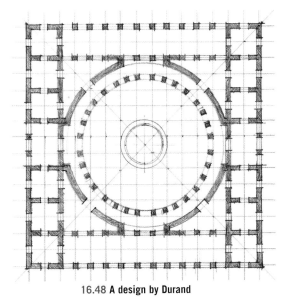

16.48 A design by Durand

16.49 Plan: Bank of England, London

0   40 m

16.50 Interior: Bank of England

Bank of England

By the early 19th century, the English economy was in a state of crisis, and the country had to borrow heavily from foreign banks. The French Revolution had spurred a major exodus of capital from London, and in the Napoleonic Wars (1799–1815), Napoleon had hoped to cripple English hegemony by closing off its European ports. Reconstituting the image of the Bank of England was therefore important, and a new building was planned. The commission went to John Soane (1753–1837), the son of a bricklayer who, as a young apprentice in an architectural firm, had earned enough to travel to Italy, where he was influenced by the work of Giambattista Piranesi. Soane eventually began to receive small commissions, until he was appointed to the Office of the Works in 1791. Even though the office favored the Neoclassical style, neoclassicism had not risen to the level of a state-sponsored aesthetic as it had in France during the time of Napoleon.

In designing the Bank Stock Office (1791–93), the first part of the bank to be built, Soane invented an architectural language based on flat vaults and pendentives to create a dynamic zoning of spaces. Other post-Enlightenment architects had a penchant for the appearance of mass and

weight, but Soane's interiors seem papery and light. The building is a labyrinth of cleverly interconnected public spaces that conform to the requirements of an oddly shaped lot. Soane's design, with its small passages that contrast with larger spaces, could be described as a picturesque form of classicism that surprises with unexpected juxtapositions.

The building was criticized by both the conservatives and the anticlassicists, though its inventiveness has been championed in recent years as proto-postmodern because of its quirky and arbitrary dealing with classical forms. Soane's work, however, should not be seen as more ornamental than that of John Nash (1752–1835), for example, for Soane was quite taken by the arguments of

16.51 Lothbury court, Bank of England, London, England

Laugier and, following him, omitted the use of columns and pilasters in the same facade. He also avoided the decorative use of Greek and Roman ornaments, believing them to be out of place in a modern society. His use of segmental and semicircular arches—shapes that do not go comfortably together but that draw attention to the dramatic effect of light and shade—was novel.

Soane was also an admirer of Sir John Vanbrugh (1664–1726), who in his estimation was the "Shakespeare of architects." In that sense he believed in the tragic nobility of architecture, but simultaneously (and this underscores the Romantic element in his work) in the break with the literal past. For that reason, Soane represented his bank as both a finished building and, remarkably, in a special drawing, as a ruin, anticipating the view backward from some future age.

Neoclassicism in the United States

When the sons, daughters, and grandchildren of the European settlers revolted against English rule, what had at first started as a search for economic freedom became one of the Enlightenment's greatest moments. In their search for antecedents, the American taste setters saw themselves as paralleling the early Roman republic rather than the Roman Empire. It was a subtle but important difference, based more on fantasy than historical accuracy. The style of French postrevolutionary Neoclassicism was taken up in particular by Thomas Jefferson (1743–1826), the drafter of the Declaration of Independence and the third president of the United States, who made a lasting imprint on American architecture of the period. Having lived in Paris for five years (1784–89) as ambassador to France, he came to admire philosophical developments in Europe and absorbed the idea that architecture was directly related to social reform. He was also the consummate gentleman architect, amassing a library of 130 books on the fine arts—certainly the largest in the United States at the time. As an amateur architect, Jefferson, together with Charles-Louis Clérisseau, fused the styles of Laugier and Adam in the design of the Virginia State Capitol (1785–92). It was modeled on the Maison Carrée of Nîmes, one of the few Roman buildings that was accepted by Laugier as true to the standards of the "rustic hut."

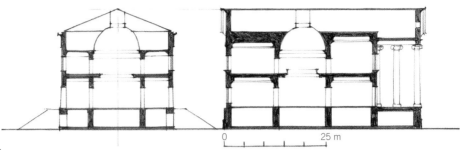

16.52 **Transverse and longitudinal sections: Virginia State Capitol, Richmond**

Clérisseau was a French architect prominent in the Neoclassical movement and author of a work that included the first measured drawings of the temple in Nîmes, which at the time was thought to have been a product of the earlier Roman republic, erected, so it was argued, by self-governing free men. The Virginia State Capitol is a literal interpretation of a classical temple as an embodiment of these republican ideals. It was also one of the first times a temple front was used as a model for a civic institution. The Virginia building was larger than its prototype, and the columns were in unfluted Ionic, as opposed to fluted Corinthian. Very different from the prototype is the circular space in the center with its vault (made of wood and stucco). It serves as a circulation space between the assembly rooms.

Both the Virginia State Capitol and the Government House in Calcutta are examples of an "applied" Enlightenment concept. In the United States, the Enlightenment project was mapped onto a largely open landscape, imparting to it a greater monumentality. This was not the case in India, where the cooperation of native populations was an integral part of the success of the colonial economy. Once it had become clear that buildings could not just be instruments of a superimposed regime, classical clothing was necessary to camouflage the colonial project behind a language of permanent principles. In the United States the situation was different, and neoclassicism could remain less ambiguous and associated with Romanticism, which, as it developed in the United States, emphasized the natural beauty of the landscape, empty of history. An example can be found in the paintings of Thomas Cole, such as *Landscape Scene from the Last of the Mohicans* (1827), which shows Native Americans more as decorative props than as individuals.

16.53 **Virginia State Capitol**

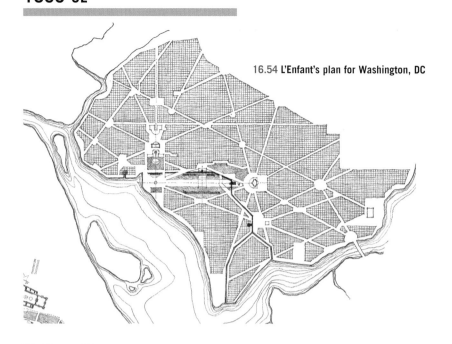

16.54 **L'Enfant's plan for Washington, DC**

pilgrimage sites of that city. In that sense the city blends aspects of Versailles and Rome, bringing the Counter-Reformation ideal of the freestanding monumental building in line with the notion of a city as a landscape traversed by grand ceremonial approaches. The siting of both the Capitol and the White House away from the river's edge and fronted by lawns derives from English country house prototypes. It might also point to the Hôtel des Invalides (begun 1670) in Paris, which, unlike the Louvre, was set at 90 degrees to the Seine River at the end of a park, connecting building and river. (In St. Petersburg, the Winter Palace, which is modeled on the Louvre, sits alongside the Neva River.)

Washington, DC

If St. Petersburg in Russia and Chengde in China were the great urban design projects of the mid-18th century, Washington, DC, played that role in the early 19th century. Designed by Charles Pierre L'Enfant (1754–1825) in 1792, it differed from St. Petersburg in that important buildings were placed as an ensemble around conjoining squares in the Italian manner, with radiating streets emanating from the center, resulting in a complex overlay of different geometries. Over the base pattern of the urban grid, L'Enfant imposed a Baroque-style web of avenues that is surprisingly idiosyncratic and that adjusts to the landscape and to the turns of the Potomac River. Over this, he imposed a third order, with the Capitol Building and the White House not facing each other across an open mall but placed at the ends of an L, with the Capitol at the end of the longer arm of the east-west facing L. The intersection of the two arms lies along the Potomac so that the two buildings, backing their way into the urban fabric from the river's edge, achieve a sense of parallel prominence.

L'Enfant's design calls to mind the gardens of Versailles because the grand avenues of the former are like the allées of the latter. However, the Capitol and the White House are also connected by one of several diagonals—Pennsylvania Avenue—a Baroque device first articulated for Rome under Sixtus V in his attempt to link the great

16.55 **United States Capitol Building, Washington, DC, 1846 (Library of Congress)**

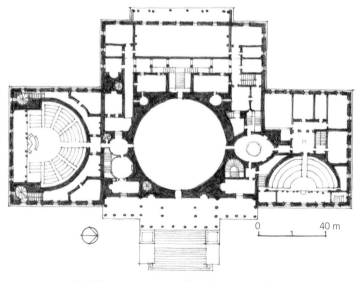

0   40 m

16.56 **Floor Plan: U.S. Capitol, Washington, DC**

16.57 **The U.S. Capitol today**

The U.S. Capitol Building, begun in 1793, went through several stages involving the architects William Thornton, Henry Latrobe, and Charles Bulfinch, in that order. It was difficult to design, since there was no clear prototype for a building with such a complex program. In the Thornton plan, the House and Senate chambers were placed right and left of a great rotunda that was envisioned as a museum, with niches sheltering statues of Revolutionary War heroes. The building seamlessly integrated allusions to a mythical Roman republic, to universal geometries, and to great historical events. The entrance was defined by a temple front with eight columns, modeled on the Pantheon, flanked somewhat unusually by columnar porches. Though the building was symmetrical on the exterior, it was not on the interior, where there was no attempt to balance the two chambers. This went against the neoclassical tendencies of the time. The building, set on a high ground-floor plinth, was topped by a Pantheonesque dome resting on an octagonal drum so that it would be easily visible from the surroundings. Beginning in 1855, the west front of the Capitol was rebuilt with a new dome (held up by a steel frame). Compared to the conventions set in play by Michelangelo's dome for St. Peter's in Vatican City, the dome is far out of proportion to the building below. Perhaps it is this strangeness that keeps the building from looking like a cathedral, imparting on it an unmistakable uniqueness.

Bullfinch, when left to his own devices, as at the Massachusetts State House (1795–98), was closer to the tradition of Palladio and Inigo Jones. Sited prominently on a hill, the state house is a brick structure with white woodwork and trim in the Georgian manner, but modeled loosely on Palladio's Palazzo Thiene and Robert Adam's Shelburne House. The upper floor is accessed by parallel stairs that flank the central space. A broad loggia with paired pilasters provide vistas down to the city and harbor. The wooden dome, originally painted gray to make it look like stone, was gilded in the 1890s. The style of the building is known as Federal, referring to buildings designed between 1780 and 1830 in the United States.

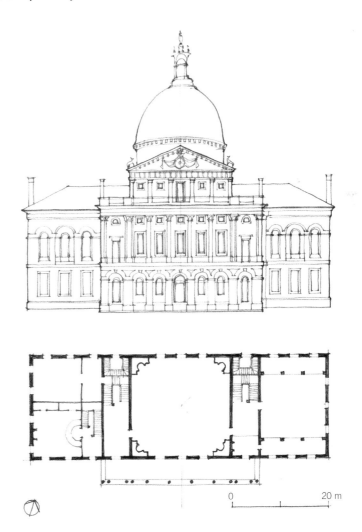

16.58 **Plan and elevation: Massachuesetts State House, Boston**

16.59 Royal Pavilion, Brighton, England

16.60 Site plan: Royal Pavilion

Royal Pavilion

Gardens of the period were often embellished with follies and other playful architectural curiosities, many of which evoked the themes of privilege, whether real or imagined. This was just as true for Sans Souci in Potsdam, Germany (near Berlin) as for the royal retreat at Brighton, England, then a small, fashionable resort used by the Prince of Wales, the future King George IV (1762–1830). The prince, who as regent sided with the liberal Whigs, built stables in the "Indian manner," modeled loosely on Shah Jahan's 17th-century Friday Mosque at Delhi. On the inside, the stables had a large timber-frame dome divided into sixteen lotus-leaf panels of glass. It was a remarkable structure and one of the first glass domes in the history of architecture. Designed by William Porden, the plan and general form were modeled to some degree on the Halle au Blé in Paris, a corn market that had a shallow wooden dome (built in 1782, destroyed by fire in 1803). But this was not a market hall, and the Halle au Blé lacked the grace and charm of the Brighton stables. What had begun as a curiosity—a playful extension of the colonial imagination—became something novel, neither Eastern nor Western, but that was nevertheless to presage a whole new level of spatial experimentation.

This was also true of the nearby Royal Pavilion (1818–22), which was built by John Nash. Though specializing in stiff, white Neoclassical palaces, Nash had also become something of an expert on the Chinese style.

As whimsical as the building may seem, it introduced a feature that was to announce the modern era. The dome was supported by a cast-iron structure, and indeed a good portion of the building was steel. Not having to design a Neoclassical building, which would have had to adhere to well-established norms about structure and *firmitas*, Nash, amazingly, created a building hung on a steel frame.

The Prince of Wales was a self-indulgent man who was allowed to have his eccentricities—including his mild support of the Whigs—as long as his father was alive. But once the prince became King George IV in 1820, he became a staunch defender of the Tory Party. He hired Nash again, but this time to redesign Buckingham House as Buckingham Palace (1825). The neo-Baroque eastern facade, designed by Thomas Cubitt, was added in 1847 in a manner thought necessary to reflect the power status of the king. In its design, the use of central and pavilion pediments draws on the East Wing of the Louvre, and the use of the giant order on Schönbrunn Palace in Austria. The windows reference Inigo Jones's Banqueting Hall. The English royalty finally had a residence on par with the great European palaces of the previous century.

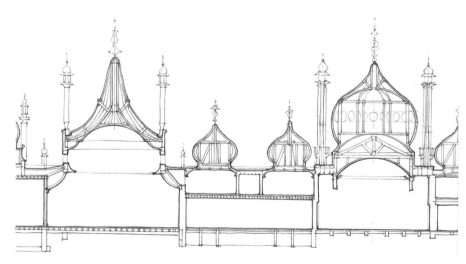

16.61 Partial section: Royal Pavilion

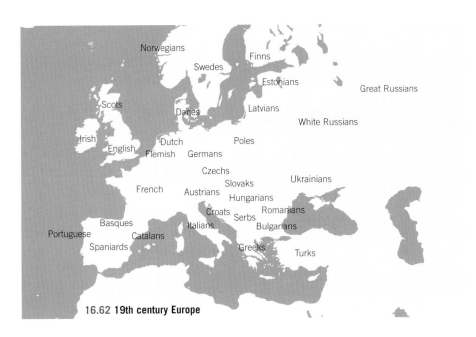

16.62 19th century Europe

Romantic Nationalism

Nationalism is such a ubiquitous idea these days that it is easy to forget that it is actually a modern concept, springing from the end of the Napoleonic Wars. As important as Napoleon Bonaparte was in spreading the ideas of liberty and justice throughout Europe, the consequences of decades of war left Europeans in desperate need of stability. In 1813 Europe's diplomats met in Vienna to discuss the political future of Europe in the hopes that its countries' borders could be stabilized. The Vienna Congress stipulated that countries were to create constitutions, if they had not already done so—a promise some rulers broke to create stronger bonds between the aristocracy and the bourgeoisie. It was hoped that countries with fixed national boundaries and a working legal infrastructure would avoid war—or have the means and recourse to avoid it. Though the ideals proved to be elusive, there is no doubt that the Vienna Congress helped to create the modern notion of a nation-state, and it was certainly successful in determining the future national boundaries in Europe—boundaries that drive European politics to this day. Though elsewhere in the world various regional wars broke out during the 19th century, the Vienna Congress created so little dispute that Europe did not go to war for a century.

The new spirit of nationalism found an easy alliance with Romanticism, especially in countries that had been victimized by the hegemony of other European powers. Romantic nationalism was particularly strong in Germany and Russia, which had been invaded by France under Napoleon. For the nationalists, history was more than just a gentleman's pastime. State boundaries had to make sense historically, linguistically, geographically, and now, ethnically, and this led to an interest in local history and the development of regional antiquarianism. Russia experienced a revival of the Russian language (until the defeat of Napoleon, the Russian aristocracy spoke mainly French). In Germany there was a fascination with the Middle Ages and with the imagery of the forest, but also with the ancient Greeks, with whom many Romantics felt an affinity. Romantic nationalism also emerged in Scandinavia as a protest against Russian occupation and took the form of a revival of Nordic mythology. Apart from the development of national languages, Romantic nationalists were interested in folklore and local customs, even if these had to be enhanced. A case in point is the "discovery" of *Beowulf* after the manuscript had lain as an ignored curiosity in scholars' collections for centuries. *Beowulf* quickly came to be seen as an English national epic. In architecture, Romantic Nationalism was slower to take hold due to the entrenched dominance of Neoclassicism, but as the century progressed, more and more examples could be found. One example, the Church of the Savior on Blood in St. Petersburg (1883–1907), was clearly meant to give impetus to a revival of Byzantine forms.

In recent decades, with the post–Cold War multiplication of new countries, Romantic nationalism has become a global phenomenon. Though it heralds the farmer and the workers, it often develops into an aesthetic that appeals to upper-class tastes. As a result, Romantic nationalism is generally a conservative response in the context of the lower classes and a seemingly liberal response in the context of the upper classes. The traits are clearly identifiable: passion for one's country combined with a feeling—factual or not—of past injustices at the hands of others. The past that Romantics point to is often bucolic and pre-modern—a cleaned-up fiction more than a reality.

16.63 Church of the Savior on Blood, St. Petersburg

16.64 **Schauspielhaus, Berlin**

Altes Museum

During the 17th century, the Kingdom of Prussia expanded its territory so that by century's end it had grown from a regional principality to a major state. And with the defeat of Napoleon at Leipzig in 1813, it became an important European power. Despite difficulties with France, infatuation with Napoleonic ideas led to a generation of German thinkers who hoped to retool the Enlightenment to fit the German context.

Energetic reformers, including the noted scientist Wilhelm von Humboldt, head of Prussia's department of education and arts, helped transform Prussia into a progressive state by abolishing serfdom and curtailing the privileges of the nobility, introducing agrarian and other social and economic reforms, and creating an exemplary system of universal education. After the victory over

Napoleon there was a gradual rise of the German Romantic movement—especially in poetry and philosophy, which envisioned nature as a manifestation of the divine. The greatest German Romantic painter, Caspar David Friedrich (1774–1840), created meditative landscapes that hover between mysticism and a sense of melancholy and solitude. Among the leading literary figures in Germany at the time were Johann Wolfgang von Goethe (1749–1832) and Friedrich von Schiller (1759–1805), who wanted to link German nationalism to the ideals of ancient Greece. This gave the German movement a different tenor than the nationalism in France, which emphasized the idealization of political institutions and social arrangements. In Germany, the Enlightenment emphasized culture and personal self-cultivation and was

thus drawn to the Greeks. To that effect, Goethe reformed the court theater of Karl August, Duke of Weimar, emphasizing the ennobling effect of the Greek playwrights.

The person who gave architectural shape to Romantic neo-Greek ideals was Karl Friedrich Schinkel (1781–1841). He completed his training as an architect in 1803 in Rome, where he met Wilhelm von Humboldt, with whom he became friends. It was Humbolt who helped secure Schinkel's position in the Prussian bureaucracy; one of his first public projects was the design of the Neue Wache, or New Guardhouse (1816–18), a monument to the new citizen's army of Prussia. Until then, the only significant Neoclassical building in Berlin was the Brandenburg Gate, inspired by the Athenian Propylaea. The Neue Wache is an austere building with a Doric porch with a relatively flat tympanum flanked by tower bases that make it appear to be a temple-gate combination. The tympanum shows the goddess of victory controlling and deciding a battle. The interior is a simple square room without a dome but with a round skylight at its center.

A few of Schinkel's other more prominent works include a theater, the Schauspielhaus (1818–21); the Altes Museum at Berlin (1823–30); Schloss Glienicke (completed 1827); and the Bauakademie (1831–36). No other architect in Europe, with perhaps the exception of John Nash, wielded so much influence. Schinkel's most visible commission

16.65 **Neue Wache, Berlin**

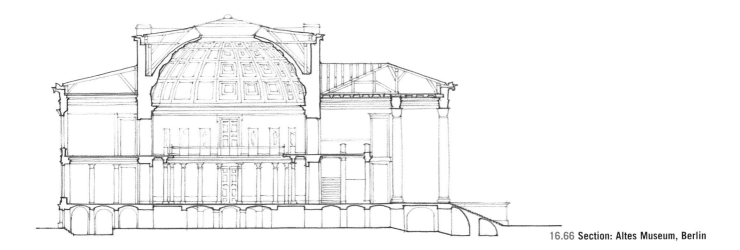

16.66 Section: Altes Museum, Berlin

was for a public art museum (1822–30) sited very prominently opposite the Schloss, or Royal Palace, in the very heart of Berlin. Now called the Altes Museum, it embodies Schinkel's commitment to monumental civic architecture as a vehicle of the Enlightenment's cultural imperative. Though museums were beginning to appear, most were refurbished palaces; the building type, as an institutional element in the urban landscape, did not yet exist, as up until this time art collecting had largely been a an aristocratic privilege. Schinkel designed the building as a great block with two interior courtyards and a central space, the interior of which is modeled on the Pantheon. The dome is not, however, visible from the outside. Instead, the front consists of a row of columns, like a great Greek stoa, elevated on a platform above the surroundings. At the top of the stairs, before entering the rotunda, there is a loggia with large open-air staircases to the right and left of the principal axis. Art works were exhibited in long rectilinear rooms with column pairs forming a passage down the middle. This was not a temple or sanctuary but rather a type of civic warehouse resembling an agora, with the central space fitted out with statues. The gallery spaces were designed for perambulating and conversing about art as much as one for looking at it. The plan was clearly influenced to some extent by Durand's call for the systematization between structure and program.

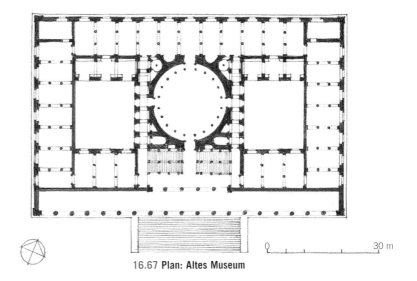

16.67 Plan: Altes Museum

16.68 Altes Museum

Jaipur and the End of the Mughal Empire

The Mughal Empire was at its largest under Aurangzeb (r. 1658–1707), who annexed all the Deccan sultanates. After his death in 1707, however, the empire quickly began to crumble. Taking advantage of the situation, a number of Mughal governors, particularly the Rajput ones, either moved toward independence or declared independence outright. The prosperity of South Asia actually increased at this time through growth in trade, including from the newly established European trading ports. If modernity can be understood as the forward thrust of transformation and as the production and exploration of the possibilities of the new in negotiation with the values of the status quo, then this was indeed a period of modernity.

Sawai Jai Singh II (1699–1743) utilized this opportunity to secure more autonomy for his own Kingdom of Amer (Bhopal). Since the 10th century, Amer had existed as a fortress town guarding in important pass on a trade route linking western India to Delhi. Amer Palace, located half way up a hill, consisted a series of interconnected courtyards protected by a fort. Three additional forts, strategically placed on adjoining hilltops, guarded the city. In 1727, Sawai Jai Singh felt sufficiently secure to establish a new capital on the unprotected plain, on the site of one of his garden palaces. Designed with the help of the architect Vidyadhar, Jaipur abuts the Amer hill on one side. The city was laid out on a grid to create a series of square neighborhoods divided by major arterials. Public amenities and markets hubs were located at the intersections, called *chokris*. The main east-west street was laid out to aligned visually with temples located on nearby hilltops. To entice settlers, Sawai Jai Singh ordered that shops be constructed along the entire length of the main streets so that the main arteries of the city were well defined. A consistent street section was maintained. The strategy worked, and Jaipur was fully inhabited in twenty-five years.

There is a theory that Jaipur was based on a nine-square mandala. Although not verifiable, the story is given credence because Sawai Jai Singh was an avid follower of Hindu astrology. In fact, to obtain the most precise observations of the planetary bodies,

16.69 **Amber Fort, Amer, India**

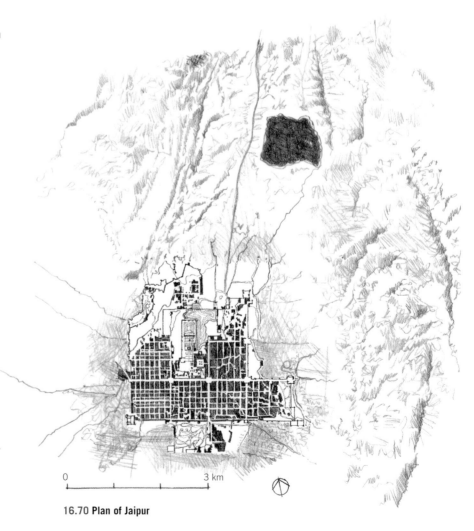

16.70 **Plan of Jaipur**

he constructed state-of-the-art observatories in Jaipur, Delhi (built for the Mughal emperor), Varanasi, Ujjain, and Mathura. Sawai Jai Singh's observatories were based on similar ones built by Ulugh Beg in the 15th century in Samarkand, only these were larger, and since they were spread apart, their observations could be cross-referenced for greater accuracy. Called Jantar Mantar, they make for a stunning, astonishingly modern sculpture park. (*Jantar Mantar* is a corruption of *yantra*, which means "instrument.")

In 1799, Sawai Jai Singh's grandson, Sawai Pratap Singh, built the Hawa Mahal, considered to be one of Jaipur's signature monuments. The Hawa Mahal (literally, "Wind Palace") gets its name because the building was considered insubstantial—or made of wind. It earned this title because

16.71 Hawa Mahal, Jaipur, India

the structure is essentially a five-story-high screen wall. Constructed at the edge of the palace complex, facing the street, it was built to enable the women of the royal household to watch the festival processions on the street while remaining unobserved themselves. Designed by Lal Chand Ustad, this structure derives from elements of Mughal palaces and mosques that often contained screened sections for women. At the Hawa Mahal, however, Ustad transformed the concept into a grand urban structure. Sawai Pratap Singh also constructed a palace on one of the artificial lakes of Jaipur.

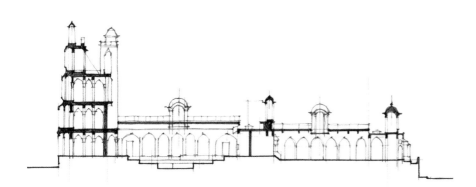

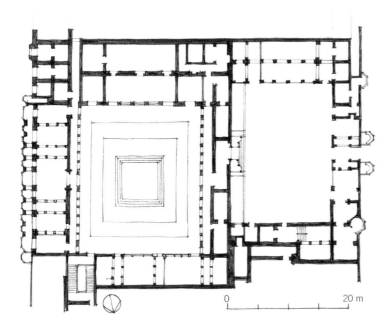

0   20 m

16.72 Plan and section: Hawa Mahal, Jaipur

16.73 Jantar Mantar, Jaipur

Darbar Sahib

In the 18th century, the Sikhs, under Maharaja Ranjit Singh (1780–1839), expanded into an empire encompassing the region of the five tributaries of the Indus, or the Punjab (literally "five rivers"). Founded by Guru Nanak in the 15th century, Sikhism is a mix of Islamic Sufi concepts and Hindu bakhti ideas. Critical of some Hindu practices, it eliminated idol worship and caste distinctions and emphasized the unity of God and the necessity of an intimate experience with the divine. The Sikhs offered themselves as an alternative to both Islam and Hinduism, and accepted converts from both. They were complexly involved in the political affairs of the Mughals, falling in and out of favor with the court at various times. In 1699, Guru Gobind Singh (1675–1708), the last of their gurus, formalized the Sikh religion, enjoining the faithful to defend it by arms if necessary.

Darbar Sahib, or Golden Temple, built in Amritsar in 1764 during the reign of Maharaja Ranjit Singh, had long been an important place of Sikh pilgrimage and learning. It was there that, in 1604, Guru Arjan Das installed the Granth Sahib, the Sikh holy book, after its compilation. The temple sits on an island in the geometric center of a sacred square pool, 150 meters on the side, that is surrounded by a marble walkway (for ritual circumambulation), which in turn is separated from the outside world by buildings that house the various functions of the institution, such as its administrative offices, including the Akal Takh, where

the highest priests have their offices. The Akal Takh a domed three-story structure is connected to the Golden Temple by a causeway. Every morning the Granth Sahib is ceremoniously carried from the Akal Takh to the Darbar Sahib to be installed; it is returned in the evening. Among the several affiliated structures that lie outside the compound is the Guru-ka-langar, a three-story building where 35,000 people are fed free daily.

The Darbar Sahib has doorless entrances on all four sides as an indication of the building's accessibility to all. No formal rituals are conducted there, but hymns are sung day and night. The lower story of the main structure is made of marble, whereas the upper story and domes are covered with plates of gilded copper. The low fluted dome is partially obscured by a high parapet with *chattris* at the four corners. The building's ornamentation and formal outlines are based on Mughal precedents, though the informality of the building's formal orchestration gives the Darbar Sahib a fluidity of expression associated more with Hindu and Jain temples than with the stately tombs and mosques of the Mughals. It is a unique structure, a product of one of the most determined attempts to bridge and synthesize the differences in Islamic and Hindu thought.

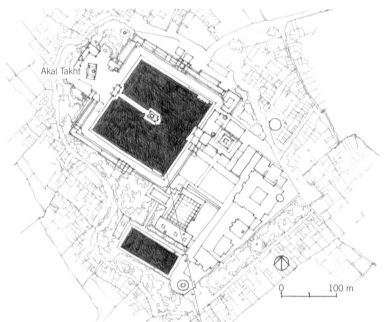

Akal Takht

0   100 m

16.74 Area plan: Darbar Sahib, Amritsar, Punjab, India

16.75 Darbar Sahib, Amritsar

Dakhmas

After Persia fell to Islam in the 7th century, the dedicated followers of Zoroastrianism fled to various parts of Eurasia, with the vast majority settling in India, particularly along its western seaboard. There they integrated into the diverse coastal trading communities. From the 18th century onward, the Parsi, as they are called in India, settled in large numbers in Mumbai and became very successful agents and trading partners of the British. They built large gated apartment compounds for their communities, and the wealthier Parsi built bungalows in or near the exclusive British enclaves. A prerogative of the wealthiest of the community was to commission a *dakhma*, or funerary tower. Unlike other religions that place the dead in the ground, Zoroastrians leave the body exposed to the elements and to vultures on funerary towers. In Zoroastrian scripture and tradition, a corpse is seen as a host for decay, and a series of rituals guarantee the purity of those who come in contact with it. The underlying principle is that the body, after its separation from the soul, should be disposed of in a way least harmful and least injurious to the living. Exposure is also considered to be an individual's final act of charity, providing the birds with what would otherwise be destroyed. In ancient times, towers were built atop hills or low mountains in desert locations distant from population centers. In Mumbai, many of the *dakhmas* were built on Malabar Hill, which is within the city but separated from the parts where people lived by a heavily forested park.

Only the corpse-bearers are permitted to enter the towers, which are built of stone, wood being considered impure. They are essentially elevated platforms in the shape of a ring, with a well at the center. The corpses are arranged on the platform in three concentric rings: men in the outer one, women in middle, and children in the inner ring. The platform slopes slightly toward the center to allow for the drainage of body fluids and rain into the central well. Large bones are disposed of in the central pit as well and are covered by a layer of lime to aid in their decomposition. The remaining material is run through multiple coal and sand filters before eventually being washed out to sea.

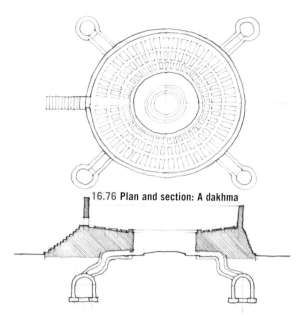

16.76 Plan and section: A dakhma

16.77 A dakhma

16.78 A dakhma

Colonial Calcutta: The Esplanade

That the European Enlightenment was born in the crucible of colonization had ramifications that are still being worked out by historians. Colonialism changed not only the lifestyles of the Europeans but also forced them to rethink their attitudes toward governance and the divine, as well as their role in history. One way to study this is to look at the English colonial project in India. The early days of the English colonists in India were far from idyllic. Calcutta was awarded to the British by the Mughals because it sat on one of the least desirable pieces of land: a marshy swamp. Cholera, typhoid, malaria, and tuberculosis were endemic. Particularly feared were the monsoons, when flooding increased health risks exponentially. But the deep waters of the river Hoogly allowed ocean-faring ships to travel 96 miles inland, enabling Calcutta to develop into a busy port. By 1780s the British East India Company army had become so large that several buildings had to be constructed outside the fort, which had been completed in 1773.

A huge open space was created, however, all around the fort to maintain defensive sightlines. This made the avenues lining the edge of the Maidan, as the open space was called, into prime sites for new mercantile and civic establishments. As Calcutta grew

in prestige and wealth, two-, three-, and even four-story mercantile establishments quickly filled in the avenue's edges, creating a continuous facade around the Maidan. Monumental loggia and pilasters, along with the occasional pedimented portico—all very visible (and designed to be seen)—rubbed shoulders, with crisp, white Italianate and Neoclassical buildings lined up to announce the English presence, forming what was called the Esplanade. Little of the Esplanade was made from stone, however. Most of it was brick-based construction with a generous coating of painted *chunar* plaster. The *chunar* looked good and shined in the sun but had to be constantly repaired, especially after the monsoons, when it often peeled away,

exposing the "sham" of the buildings—and by implication, of their nouveau riche occupants—much to the chagrin of derisive colonial commentators from the homeland. (This discourse of pride and shame as a function of appearance lingered around colonial architecture to its very end.)

Writers' Building

By the 1770s, faced with huge financial losses and the impending independence of America, the English parliament focused its attention on it colonies in the East, particularly in India, and found that in spite of its political successes and ample displays of wealth, the British East India Company, was nonetheless badly in debt, according to

16.79 View of *chunar* Calcutta from the Esplanade, ca. 1850

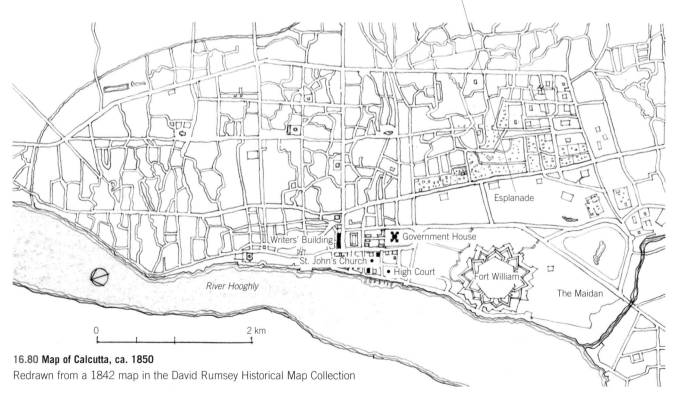

16.80 Map of Calcutta, ca. 1850
Redrawn from a 1842 map in the David Rumsey Historical Map Collection

the banking statements in London. Its officers were accused of corruption and profiteering, and in 1773 the company was reorganized in the hopes of establishing accountability. In addition, a governor general was appointed to ensure that besides becoming profitable, the company's administration over its territories was just and consonant with British ideals. A fair government in India was necessary not only to legitimize colonization but also to soften protest back in England. Thus was born the ideological project of colonization.

Warren Hastings, the first governor general of India (1772–85), was a capable and responsible administrator. He increased revenues exponentially (mostly from opium production set for export to China), expanded British territories, and, most importantly, ruthlessly enforced a strict administration with detailed accounting. His signature building was the gigantic secretariat and training school he had built for the clerks of the British East India Company. Known as the Writer's House (1780)—the "writers" were the clerks—this extremely long three-story structure lines one entire length of Calcutta's water tank. Given that it was the writers who enabled the rationalization of the company's

presence in India, it is only fitting that and their domain was a remarkable essay in rationalization and functionalism with a single cornice running the entire length of the perimeter, interrupted only slightly by the central facade. It was designed by a civil architect, Fortnam, and Thomas Lyon, an amateur architect and a carpenter. Hastings's approach to the problem of a just governance was supremely pragmatic. It was imperative that the English learn local languages, customs, and systems of government, he proposed, because it would enable them to know the people better and be able to govern with those systems. In 1784 he created the Asiatic Society of Bengal, with William Jones as its president, to study and translate the culture. For Hastings, Indian culture and civilization was a real and living thing—not something that he was interested in transforming or reforming, but only in governing, which he was wont to do with personal discretion and an iron hand.

St. John's Church

At the turn of the 19th century, English colonial policy changed again, this time under the influence of the Enlightenment's critique of the arbitrariness of power. Warren Hastings was impeached by Edmund Burke (1729–97), who argued that parliamentary oversight was not enough: there had to be a social contract attached to the principle of divine sanction; the purpose of the colonial administration had to be consonant with the "eternal laws" of good governance. For the Tories, good governance was ensured by the abiding prestige of the king and his aristocracy. The new governor general, Lord Charles Cornwallis (1786–93), in an attempt to replicate the European aristocracy in India, created a new class of landowners called zamindars.

Colonial architecture was called upon to signify the new "eternal laws." The Writer's Building was reskinned and acquired Doric porticoes. St John's Church (1787) was based on the late Georgian high steeple of St. Martin-in-the-Fields in London. A simple box (a three-bay nave and galleries) with a Tuscan portico and a stone steeple and spire, its symbolic importance equaled that of King's Chapel in Boston as a visible reminder of the authority of church and king. And this time it was made from real stone, not just *chunar*. Politically, the results of the new system were disastrous.

16.81 Writer's Building, as originally built and as re-skinned, Calcutta

16.82 St. John's Church, Calcutta

In the Mughal administration, land had been collectively owned at the village level, and zamindars were only tax collectors. Now that they owned the land, they could sell it in response to market opportunities. The peasantry was completely disempowered. Enterprising company officers exploited the opportunity, making quick fortunes.

Government House

By 1800, a new generation of company officers under the influence of the Romantics took issue with the Whig-backed zamindari system. They admired the Indian village (the country's ancient urban culture notwithstanding), thus enhancing the impression in Europe that the distinction between Europe and the colonies was a difference between cities and villages. They placed their faith in the paternalistic figure of the British officer, a man with great and concentrated authority who was highly paid but barred from obtaining any profit from company activities—and who was expected to be educated, enlightened, knowledgeable, and sympathetic. (The highest British officer was the governor general.) In 1798, when Lord Richard Wellesley replaced Lord Charles Cornwallis as governor general, he began construction of a new Government House (1803) to embody his authority. Its design, prepared by Charles Wyatt, was created with spectacle in mind. With a tall Pantheonesque central dome, each side of the facade is symmetrical and complete, and stands as an idealized object in space. The strict Neoclassical portico set up on a broad and imposing staircase sealed its identification with the eternal principles of Vitruvius, even though the entire structure was made in brick and *chunar*, and not Italian marble. However, the Government House's interior, unlike Kendleston Hall, which was segmented into rooms for privacy, was divided by perforated colonnades designed to ensure that the retinue of servants had constant, but screened, access to all spaces. Cornwallis's wife complained that the Government House had no place she could call her own.

Metcalfe Hall

From 1800 onward, great surveys were conducted in order to map every bit of land so that landholdings could be transferred to individual peasants. But this system could not be strictly enforced since land was held collectively in village trusts. As corruption again grew, critics of the Romantics arose: the new liberals who, from 1828 to 1856, the period of the governorships from Lord William Bentinck to the Earl of Dalhousie, drew inspiration from the Benthamite utilitarians. They believed that human nature was intrinsically the same everywhere and that it could be brought forth by education, law, and free trade. For them, passing on English civilization to the Indians, whose civilization was seen as defective, had a singular objective. They saw themselves as custodians of the Indian civilization until the Indians were sufficiently "civilized" and self-disciplined to maintain it themselves. This task was commonly characterized as the "white man's burden." In architecture the favored style was now the Greek Revival. Since the liberation of Greece from the Turks in 1830, English and continental archaeologists had been pouring over Greek ruins, measuring, copying, and studying them in great detail. Building from these accurate style sheets became the new clarion call of the 1840s. Sir Robert Smirke designed the British Museum in London (1823–47) in studied classicism. In Calcutta a fine Greek Revival building was designed for Metcalfe Hall (1840-44) by C. K. Robinson, with thirty huge Corinthian columns supporting a massive entablature.

16.83 Government House, Calcutta, India
Based on a map in the David Rumsey Historical Map Collection

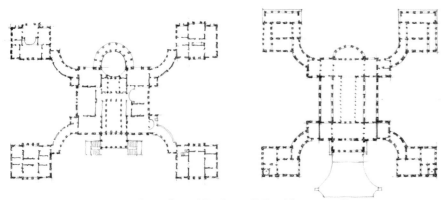

16.84 Plans: Comparison of Kendleston Hall and Government House

16.85 Metcalfe Hall, Calcutta

Khorezm

The discovery of gold on the banks of the Amu Darya during the reign of Peter the Great, together with the desire of the Russian Empire to open a trade route to India, led the Russians right to the Khanate of Khiva, just south of the Aral Sea. The khanate, known more accurately as Khorezm, was founded by the Uzbek leader Arab Muhammad Khan (1603–22), who built the city's imposing walls (1686–88). The nomadic Uzbeks were not interested in farming, which they left to slaves or local populations; their economy was based on trading and marauding, and Khiva became the site of a notorious slave market. The city (now in Uzbekistan) is split into two parts. The outer town, called Dichan Kala, was formerly protected by a wall with eleven gates. The inner town is encircled by brick walls whose foundations are believed to have been laid in the 10th century. In the 1830s, Alla-Kulli-Khan built a palace, Tash-Khovli ("stone country estate") in the eastern part of the inner city, just to the west of a large market. This complex has three yards arranged in a U with secondary spaces filling in the gaps. The southernmost is the receiving yard, where important visitors would be met. This is followed by a yard for entertainment. The last and most private yard was occupied by the harem. The outside walls of the palace were left plain, whereas the walls of the inner courtyards were decorated with blue and white majolica tile. The wooden pillars have distinctive bulbous bases carved with geometrical and plant decorations, and the ceilings are painted in a golden-red color. In 1873, the Russians, eager to control the trade routes to the south and east, took the city and created a quasi-independent state under their control.

16.86 Khiva, former capital of Khwarezmia

0   50 m

16.87 Area plan: Tash-Khovli, Khiva

16.88 Courtyard, Tash-Khovli

16.89 Wat Pra Kaew, Bangkok

16.90 Wat Pra Kaew

Wat Pra Kaew

By the late 18th century, the history of architecture becomes largely the history of European architecture, of European colonial architecture, and of Chinese architecture. Islamic architecture was on the wane, as was noncolonial architecture in India and elsewhere. There was one important and remarkable exception: Thailand. Thailand, or Siam, as it was then known, emerged as an important regional force in the 14th century under King Sukhothai, who controlled the area roughly encompassed by modern Thailand. His capital was the island city of Ayutthaya, about 100 kilometers north of Bangkok. Though the Thai culture was largely Indic in origin (*Ayutthaya* is Thai for Ayodhya, the sacred capital of Lord Rama), the Thai learned their Sanskrit and scripture from the Khmer of Cambodia, building several Angkor-inspired temples and stupas in Ayutthaya. The Chinese admiral Zheng He came to Ayutthaya and left behind a Chinese princess and her attendant, whose descendants still survive in Thailand as a distinct community and worship the princess and the admiral at a temple in the city. In the mid-15th century, the Thai sacked Angkor, and then in 1782, under King Rama I (1782–1809) of the Chakri dynasty, established the city of Bangkok, or Ratanakosin, on the Chao Phraya River as his capital.

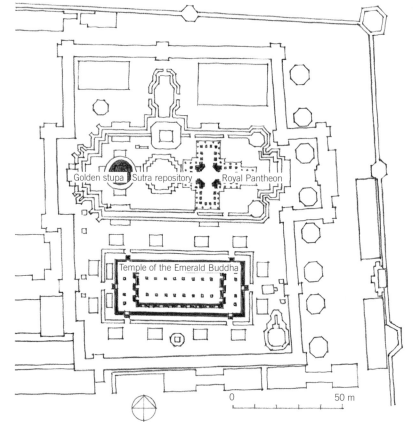

Golden stupa   Sutra repository   Royal Pantheon

Temple of the Emerald Buddha

0   50 m

16.91 Site plan: Wat Pra Kaew

16.92 Golden stupa, Wat Pra Kaew

The new royal palace was created as its new symbolic core in a compound a few hundred meters from the river's edge. Looking beyond the borders there was Cambodia, with Phnom Penh as its capital, and Vietnam, whose capital became Hué in 1802 under the Nguyen dynasty.

In the eastern section of the compound, a special structure was created to house the Emerald Buddha, a jade Buddha dated to 1434. Much venerated, it was brought to Bangkok in 1778 from northern Thailand. The compound is defined by a rectangular perimeter colonnade, with projections in the east and west, that contains a continuous wall fresco, painted on dry plaster, narrating the story of the Ramayana, the Hindu sacred text. At the center of the compound, on a raised platform running east-west, are three huge closely spaced buildings: a golden stupa, a square sutra repository, and a temple structure known as the Royal Pantheon. Also on the platform is a large stone model of Angkor Wat. Rama I had wanted the entire abandoned structure from Cambodia to be transferred to Bangkok, but when his emissaries returned with descriptions of its immensity, he decided to settle for a model. (Angkor Wat is itself, like any Hindu temple, a model of the cosmos, and as such the model is almost equivalent, in its philosophical significance, to the original.)

The close proximity of these buildings is not due to lack of space. Each building in Mahayana Buddhist symbolism is a representation of the other, and their proximity was intended to keep them from being seen as autonomous structures; instead, they were to be viewed as substitutes or even as metaphors for each other. Whereas the stupa is completely gilded, the other two buildings are decorated on the outside with lavish mosaics made of red, blue, and green tiles as well as fragments of glass and mirrors. The Wat Pra Kaew ("Temple of the Emerald Buddha") stands to the south of the platform. It has a single interior space undivided by partitions. The Buddha is at the far end in a resplendent setting, high above human height, enshrined in a small golden temple. The walls are covered with frescoes. The roof trusses are made of wood.

The building, and indeed the entire architectural ensemble, was one of the most important in its time in Southeast Asia, reflecting the cosmopolitan tastes of its patron. The tiles on the outside are laid out in a Persian style, the mosaics were made by Byzantine craftsmen, and the Buddha hall is a type of Sistine Chapel, its walls painted with religious murals. The placement of the Buddha on top of a golden structure appears almost Baroque. This should not be interpreted as a sign of "Oriental" eclecticism in the face of the rigorous historicism of the European Enlightenment, but rather as a modern fusion of different elements into something unique. Thailand was never colonized—a rarity in that part of the world—and thus its rulers had the freedom to explore and develop contemporary architectural ideas that were denied those countries placed under colonial imprint. Whereas native architectural traditions began to dry out or became fossilized with the introduction of European-style buildings in India, for example, such traditions continued to develop in Thailand, unfettered by any colonial overlords' offended eyes.

The Industrial Revolution

By the second decade of the 19th century, industrialization in England began to have global implications. A whole new society was being created, taking shape in a new type of city and new types of political and power relations. Unlike the great metropolises of old, factory towns like Manchester, Leeds, and Liverpool were not urban to begin with. There was no core of elegance, no great boulevards, no parks, churches, palaces, or cultural institutions. And yet these were cities competing in size and population with the likes of London and Paris. Manchester, nicknamed Cottonopolis because of all its cotton mills, became the second-largest city in England, after London. The industrial city was a novel urban landscape of people, traffic, and commerce—with a level of squalor never witnessed before. There was no urban planning: there was no sewage system, and water delivery was haphazard. Typhoid and tuberculosis outbreaks were common. Air pollution deriving from the foul smells of factories, sewage, and slaughterhouses was a given. (In London, the stench from the Thames River was so severe that work in the Parliament building, located right next to the river, was often impossible.) The cramped conditions of the workers were startling; life expectancy was twenty-eight years. During the Napoleonic Wars, the government paid little attention to these problems, and even after the war, despite growing unrest, the conservative Tory Party was resistant to change.

When the Whig Party gained a majority in the elections of 1830, things slowly began to change. The Great Reform Act of 1832 reapportioned city districts to reflect changes in the population; it also liberalized voting qualifications and defined the idea of democracy as we understand it today, even though voting rights were, for a long time, still reserved for men only. The Factory Acts of the 1830s reduced the hours of child labor; the Mines Act of 1842 prohibited underground work for all women and for boys under the age of ten; and the Ten Hours Act of 1847 limited the workday for women and young people to ten hours. Efforts were made to control sanitation. In the 1860s, Joseph Bazalgette, Chief Engineer of the Metropolitan Board of Works, designed an extensive series of underground sewerage pipes to divert waste downstream of the population center. The modern notion of infrastructure was therewith born; the system was soon expanded to include electricity and water. Despite these improvements, however, factory life remained afflictive and a major point of contention and political strife.

The Industrial Revolution's most important change to the architectural landscape was the emergence of the factory—in particular, cotton and clothing factories located near streams used to drive waterwheels. The buildings were uniform in appearance: most were rectangular blocks of unadorned brick or stone with wooden floors, usually four to six floors high. The power from the waterwheel was distributed through the building by means of a system of shafts, gears, and beltings. From the main shaft on each floor, power was distributed to smaller shafts. Belts from the shafts drove the individual machines. The longer the shaft, the more vulnerable it was to breakage; 30 meters was about the maximum length they could be, which limited the overall length of the mills. (The problem of mechanically distributing power over long distances was solved with the introduction of wire rope in around 1850.) The development of electrically powered machines at the end of the century brought more flexibility to factory design, and there was no longer a need to place them next to rivers.

At first these factories provided for local markets, but by the 1830s factories were oriented toward selling goods nationally and internationally. The early small factories employed families, often relying on the labor of children; larger factories often employed young women, usually between the ages of thirteen and twenty-five. Their lives were highly regularized, and most lived in boardinghouses that had strict rules of behavior. The scale of production can best be demonstrated by numbers. In 1860, England laid 17,000 miles of railroad track, compared with 10,000 miles of new track lain in France. By 1870, England controlled one-third of the world's overall production. English factories had 39.5 million cotton spindles, compared with just 5 million in France. Established in 1771, Arkwright's Mill at Cromford (just south of Matlock Bath) was the world's first successful large-scale cotton-spinning mill based on waterpower. Arkwright, who has become known as the father of the factory system, built the village of Cromford in order to house his mill's workforce. By 1790, the main buildings had been completed.

16.93 View of Manchester depicted in a painting by William Wylde in 1857

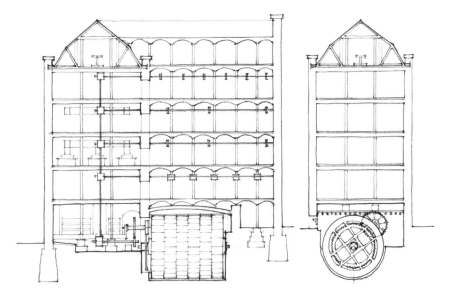

16.94 Jedediah Strutt's North Mill, Belper, Derbyshire, England

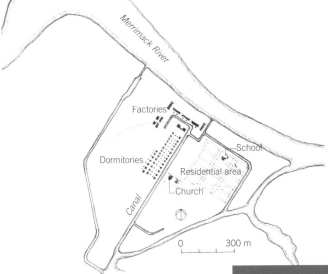

16.95 Plan: Lowell, Massachusetts

Lowell, Massachusetts

An example of an early planned industrial city was Lowell, Massachusetts, built by the Merrimack Manufacturing Co. It was the outcome of the efforts of Francis Cabot Lowell who, borrowing British technology, assembled the first successful, completely mechanized cotton mill in the United States. The city, established by a group of Lowell's partners after his death in 1822, was of unprecedented size and organization. The mills were arranged in a row along the canal with their backs to the Merrimack River; housing for the labor force was laid out in regular rows on a rectangular plan. In the town, to the east of the factory, was a church, a mansion for the director, a library, a school, and even a savings bank. The plan was very simple: a main street with shops and public buildings on both sides, and a cluster of identical houses for the workers, mostly girls between the years of fifteen and twenty-five years of age, leading off from the main street to the mills.

16.96 Suffolk Mills, Lowell, Massachusetts

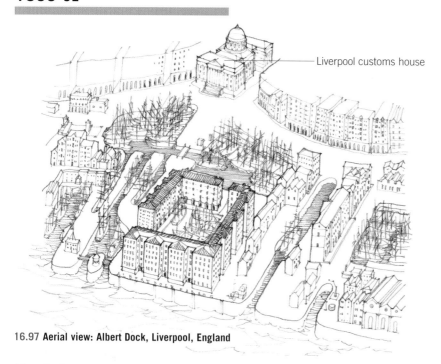

Liverpool customs house

16.97 Aerial view: Albert Dock, Liverpool, England

Albert Dock

The ports of London and Liverpool constituted cities unto themselves. At midcentury, the London docks, which were continually being improved and expanded, employed thirty thousand people. Liverpool witnessed a series of expansions, cementing its status as a global commercial power. By the 1890s, it had become the second-largest port in England, after London. Though trade through Liverpool dates back to the 17th century, the city now became England's main slave port, and the city's trade with Asia in the early 19th century widened its scope. Cotton, tea, rice, tobacco, sugar, and grain passed through

this port—as did immigrants. Specialized docks were built to house different types of merchandise, from palm oil, cocoa, and cotton to ivory and timber.

The Albert Dock (1846) in Liverpool, built of cast iron, brick, and stone and with no structural wood, was the first fireproof warehousing system in the world. Designed by Jesse Hartley, it also had the world's first hydraulic warehouse hoist system. Sited around a rectangular basin, the inner side had a ground-level colonnade of hollow cast-iron columns filled with masonry, with warehouses in the floors above. Tall windows allowed cranes to load and unload from

and to the floors. To make the building fully fireproof, the cast iron columns and beams supported shallow brick-arched floors. At a cost of £700,000 (approximately $100 million today), the Albert Dock, built to accommodate the trade with the Far East, was probably the most expensive structure in the world at that time. But within two decades, the entrance became too small for the ships, whose size had kept on growing, and it was converted to a warehouse. Next to the dock was a new customs house (no longer extant) designed by John Foster, with a grand and severe Ionic pedimented temple front (modeled on the Pantheon, but with Ionic capitals) and a Renaissance-style dome at its core.

16.98 Albert Dock

16.99 **Eastern State Penitentiary, Philadelphia**

16.100 **Suffolk House of Correction, Bury St. Edmunds, England**

Panoptic Prisons

The definition of criminality changed considerably between the 18th and 19th centuries. In the 18th century, criminals, the insane, the poor, and the indigent—that is, all "unwanteds"—were thrown together in large halls and corridors. The Lunatics Tower in Vienna (1784) was nothing more than a cylindrical fortress. Overcrowding, filth, and brutal conditions made them into terrifying places. Because their purpose was to protect the elite, there was little incentive to mete out any kind of nuanced justice. In England around 1819, there were 220 capital offenses, ranging from murder to stealing bread. With the Enlightenment came an attempt to refine the law. But it was not so much the squalor and mayhem of the prisons that so appalled the early 19th-century moralists as the fact that humanity could, in essence, be placed outside the reach of the moral life. A connection had to be made between the reform of the body and mind of the prisoner and the legitimacy of the state. This engendered the first modern jails, such as the Virginia Penitentiary (1798) by Benjamin Latrobe and the Suffolk House of Correction in Bury St. Edmunds, England (1803), where the governor's house was at the prison's center to demonstrate the new force of law that now ostensibly protected the prisoner from abuse while still enforcing its own code of behavior.

These new prisons were designed with isolated cells for inmates grouped along open corridors of buildings that were like the spokes of a wheel, allowing guards to observe all the prisoners easily and giving rise to the name panoptic prison. An exemplar of the panoptic system can be found at the Eastern State Penitentiary in Philadelphia (begun 1821), organized according to a philosophy set out by the Pennsylvania Quakers that presumed that isolation would promote monastic self-reflection. Prisoners lived in a cell and could go outside into a small private courtyard. They were allowed out only for infrequent baths or medical emergencies. Visits were permitted only from officials. Masks and the use of numbers rather than names ensured anonymity if inmates had to be removed from their cells. Even the sewer pipes were arranged to prevent communication from cell to cell. All the while, the prisoner's very movements were observed, either through the corridor or from the towers during exercises. Prisoners who were able were allowed to choose to perfect a few skills, such as shoe-making, basket-weaving, and broom-making; such humble activities, it was thought, would reconnect them with the principle that service to society was the primary reason for existence. This system was much admired despite the fact that it soon became obvious that quite few inmates went insane. Its English equivalent, the Pentonville Prison in London (1844), was designed according to a design by Jeremy Bentham: by which five radiating arms extend from a central hall from where the prisoners can be observed. Pentonville became the most copied prison in the world.

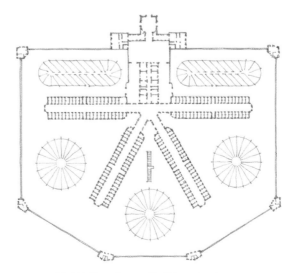

16.101 **Plan: Pentonville Prison, London**

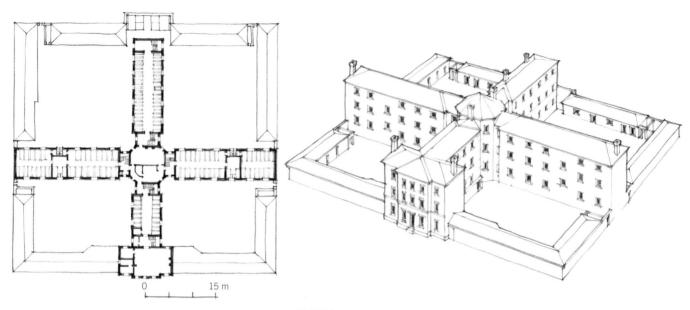

0   15 m

16.102 **Sampson Kempthorne's 1835 proposal for a "square" plan workhouse**

Workhouses

Many English cities had so-called workhouses that gave the poor work but that also served as religious boarding schools. The institutions were run by a parish as a type of charity work. From the perspective of their patrons they were designed as "large, spacious and we may say fairly elegant buildings," but the truth was far different. Frederick Engels wrote the following in his *Condition of the Working Class in England in 1844*:

> Below the bridge you look upon the piles of debris, the refuse, filth, and offal from the courts on the steep left bank; here each house is packed close behind its neighbor and a piece of each is visible, all black, smoky, crumbling, ancient, with broken panes and window-frames. The background is furnished by old barrack-like factory buildings. Here the background embraces the pauper burial-ground, the station of the Liverpool and Leeds railway, and, in the rear of this, the Workhouse, the "Poor-Law Bastille" of Manchester, which, like a citadel, looks threateningly down from behind its high walls and parapets on the hilltop, upon the working-people's quarter below.

By the 1830s there was a good deal of opposition to workhouses, given the hardship and brutality that they engendered. Though the government periodically attempted to reform their practices, their existence ended officially only in 1929. Workhouses came in different formats. Most were exercises in social geometry: square or rectangular, with courts that separated the men, women, and children and a chapel, infirmary, and administrative offices at the center.

0   20 m

16.103 **Plan: Bridge Street Workhouse, Manchester, Lancashire, England**

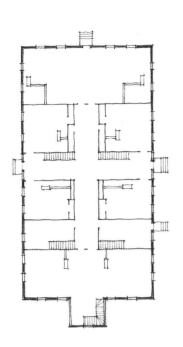

16.104 First-floor plan: A Shaker communal house

16.105 Interior of a Shaker house

The Shakers

The growing dissatisfaction with the grand Enlightenment aspirations about the unity of reason and nature spawned a generation of utopian thinkers, social philosophers, and cultural critics. Chief among these in France was Claude Henri de Rouvroy, Comte de Saint-Simon, an aristocrat, an officer in the American Revolutionary War, a real estate speculator, and a journalist. His writings, including *Memoire sur la science de l'homme* (1813), *De la réorganisation de la société européene* (with Augustin Thierry,1817), and *Le nouveau christianisme* (1825) were highly influential. He advocated a semimystical "Christian-scientific" socialism envisaged around an elite of philosophers, engineers, and scientists who would tame the forces of industrialization by means of a rational Christian humanism. Though Saint-Simon had adherents in Europe and even influenced the thinking of Karl Marx, his movement to create new communities was rarely brought to fruition there. In the United States, on the other hand, utopian ideals found a ready audience, with the founding of utopian communities reaching its height around 1840. Many utopian thinkers were U.S. citizens, but a substantial minority were emigrants from England, France, Germany, and Scandinavia. For most the ideal was a small tidy village with a range of craft industries.

The Shakers aimed at nothing less than transforming earth into heaven. They were celibate, and their daily work and religious rituals were designed to foster a belief in both the earthly sphere, envisioned as a rural settlement, and a heavenly sphere, envisioned as a New Jerusalem. Between 1780 and 1826 the Shakers founded twenty-five settlements from Maine to the Ohio frontier. Communities were organized into communal households called families, which consisted of thirty to one hundred persons. Shaker communities adopted names such as City of Peace, City of Love, Holy Land, and Pleasant Grove. Discipline was not imposed but a condition of divine respect. For example, anyone who slouched or nodded was required to make a public apology. Law required that one also sleep straight. Furniture reinforced the requirement for posture, and chairs were light and sturdy but had tall backs.

Shaker life was highly regulated. The women were responsible for sweeping the house, whereas the men cleaned the workshops. Drawers were often installed recessed into walls so as not to collect dust or create clutter. In the houses, an invisible boundary separated the men's rooms on the west from the women's rooms on the east. Double sets of stairs and doors articulated the division between men and women. The furniture, clothing, and even the buildings themselves were made by members of the community, who were therefore physically surrounded by the handiwork of other believers. Despite these constraints, Shaker rituals involved dance and pantomime. Shakers donned imaginary garments and sometimes saw "visitors" who appeared with particular messages to tell. Members who never raised their voices would suddenly begin singing, shouting, and whirling—hence the name of their sect.

The well-built and prosperous Shaker villages greatly enhanced the credibility of the communitarian strategy for social change. But the Shakers' unwillingness to engage in heavy industry eroded their prosperity after the Civil War, and their numbers declined sharply—due in large part because of their belief in celibacy and the subsequent lack of descendants.

August Welby Pugin

The two most important architectural theoretical works of the time came not from secularists but from secularism's—and industrialism's—critics: Marc-Antoine Laugier and August Welby Pugin (1812–52). Pugin's father, August Charles, Comte de Pugin, fled France during the Revolution and, as an authority on the Gothic style, took up work in the office of John Nash, who had to accommodate the growing demand for Gothic-style architecture even though he personally found it troublesome. The younger Pugin was already saturated in Gothic architecture and had even converted to Catholicism, believing it to be the only true religion. With little hope for a commission, he set about writing *Contrasts*, which he published in 1836 at his own expense because no publisher would agree to put out such an explosive work. The book made his reputation, and soon commissions for chapels, churches, and even private houses came his way. "The history of architecture is the history of the world," he wrote, and, turning to the work of his own day, he asked whether "the architecture of our times, even supposing it solid enough to last, hand[s] down to posterity any certain clue or guide to the system under which it was erected? Surely not…. It is a confused jumble of styles and symbols borrowed from all nations and periods." At stake was not just a style, he believed, but the history of civilization. Industrialism, greed, and secularism had isolated man from his fellow man.

Contrasts set the tone for a critique of industrialism that focused not on repairing the inequities that it precipitated by means of law and politics but by proposing a quasi-utopian alternative—one harkening back to the Middle Ages, for Pugin a time during which there existed a vibrant social conscience. The architect, he argued, should therefore not just adopt any style the client wanted; that would be equivalent to endorsing the arbitrariness of the modern world. *Contrasts* has a plate showing a town as Pugin imagined it in 1440 and another one showing it again in 1840. The former portrays a city with intact walls and a church in the foreground. The latter shows a cluttered river, a jumble of church spires and smokestacks, and, in the foreground,

16.106 **A plate redrawn from Pugin's** *Contrasts*, **showing a town in 1440**

16.107 **A plate redrawn from Pugin's** *Contrasts*, **showing the same town illustrated above in 1840**

a prison; the church is still there but is now overgrown and neglected. It was an accusation against rationalism that remains embedded in the image of modernity to this day, a touchstone for those who see modern life as a downward spiral into ethical and moral decline. Architecture had to be based on principles (and in this he was the child of the Enlightenment) that even included the use of local materials in accordance with local traditions. This was what made "true" Gothic different from what he saw as the shallow Gothic of Horace Walpole or worse, the cold rationalism of the neoclassicists. Only Gothic, he argued, could provide the moral compass that should be expected from a Christian society.

Despite Pugin's conservatism, he should not be seen as an antimodern. His convictions in respect to regional traditions and local climate, as well as his belief in "honest" construction, were all taken up by modernists once the Gothic imperative had played itself out. One of his arguments against Italianate architecture was that it did not suit England. A building, he maintained, had to show its various purposes, and this led to an appreciation for asymmetry and to an emphasis on articulating the differing parts of a building, an argument that modernists later would take up as well.

16.108 Houses of Parliament, Westminster, London

The debates that swirled around this building concerning the role and purpose of architecture were remarkable. The history of modern architecture is intertwined with the history of polemics, beginning with Claude Perrault's attack on beauty, carried forth by Marc-Antoine Laugier's attack on the classical orders, and extended into the 19th century by Pugin, who envisioned the building as a showcase of the Gothic style: a moral and aesthetic exemplar. Neoclassicism, with its cosmopolitan allusions that had met the expectations of the old elite, here gave way to a style that was associated not only with the new moralists but also with the monarchy of Queen Elizabeth I (1533–1603), whose rule was increasingly considered to be a golden age in which England saw the first flush of its global power. Neoclassicism, though once the favorite language of colonial authority, was increasingly seen as too generic and undifferentiated—as too Continental —to differentiate England, which was now the single most powerful colonial empire in the world, from its competitors.

It was because of this growing confidence in the legitimacy of the neo-Gothic as a genuinely English format that, after the old palace at Westminster burned in 1834, a parliamentary committee decided to rebuild in the Gothic style. Two hundred years earlier, a similar body had resolved to rebuild old St. Paul's in the neoclassical style.

A competition was announced for the commission for the new Parliament building; it was eventually given to Charles Barry, who worked closely with Pugin. Few can deny the brilliance of the plan, with its lucid hierarchies that differentiate between public and private areas and the grandeur of the approaches to the great octagonal hall that separates the House of Lords to the north from the House of Commons to the south. An internal spine, which allows for a special sovereign's entrance at the southeast corner of the building, is buffered by various open-air courts that allowed light into the various rooms. Offices, libraries, and meeting rooms are lined up along the principal facade toward the river. The exterior—done almost uniformly in a soft, yellowish limestone—was designed in a Perpendicular Gothic style that replicated the taste of the 15th century. Despite the monotone treatment of the building's external mass, Barry was able to introduce picturesque elements to the skyline through the asymmetrical positioning of the vertical elements—the Victoria Tower, the lantern over the octagonal room, and the spectacular Big Ben, Parliament's now-famous clock tower.

Thames River

1. Clocktower
2. Westminster Hall
3. Chamber of the House of Commons
4. Central hall
5. Chamber of the House of Lords
6. Royal gallery
7. Sovereign's entrance

0   80 m

16.109 Plan: Houses of Parliament

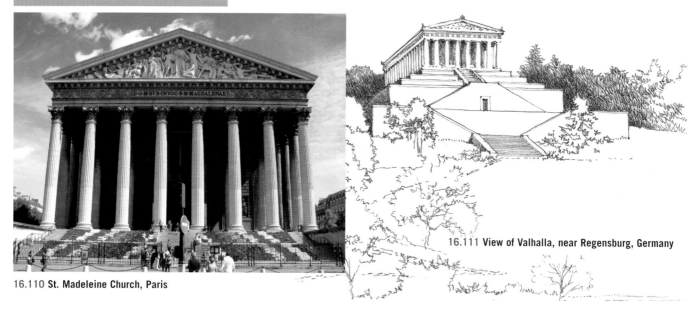

16.110 **St. Madeleine Church, Paris**

16.111 **View of Valhalla, near Regensburg, Germany**

Greek Revival

Although today the Parthenon is one of the most revered ancient buildings in Europe, its artistic prominence only slowly came into focus during the 19th century. In 1805, when Thomas Bruce, 7th Earl of Elgin, who had purchased the Parthenon frieze from the Ottomans, first approached the British Museum about buying the pieces, he encountered hesitation on the part of the authorities. A few years later, when Charles Robert Cockerell took the sculptures from the Temple of Aegina, the English showed no interest in their purchase, and he sold them to Ludwig I of Bavaria, where they now form the kernel of the Glyptothek Museum in Munich.

The fascination with Greece received a boost when hostilities ended between England and France in 1814, allowing Europeans to flock to Greece in unprecedented numbers. The country became all the more alluring in the 1830s, following the liberation of Greece from Turkish occupation. In 1830 England, Germany, and Russia signed the London Protocol, which recognized the independence of Greece. The Germans and Bavarians placed themselves in charge of the military operation that eventually freed Greece from the Ottoman Empire in 1833, putting Otto von Wittelsbach on the throne, his reign guaranteed by the European powers. The impact of the liberation of Greece on the European consciousness was profound. It breathed new life into the Neoclassical movement and into Enlightenment notions about freedom and progress. As a result, Neoclassicism, once associated with the heavy-handed world of imperial institutions, was now linked to the optimistic and progressive world of bourgeois industry.

Neo-Greek architecture took on a more strident form near Regensburg, Germany, at Valhalla (1830–42), designed by Leon von Klenze (1784–1864) as a hall of fame for German luminaries. Klenze, who had studied in Paris under Jean-Nicolas-Louis Durand, also designed the Glyptothek Museum in Munich (1816–30) with an archaeologically correct Greek front and a Roman-styled interior, following Durand's methodology. Valhalla, sited on a bluff over the Rhine River, was a relatively correct Greek-style temple placed on a series of terraces. Ludwig I also sent Klenze to help design Greece's new capital city, Athens, located to the largely uninhabited west and south sides of the ancient Acropolis. It became the first capital city built to reflect the fusion of Enlightenment and Romantic ideals.

The neo-Greek movement was relatively short-lived on the Continent, where it had to compete with other styles. But in Scotland, where the economy had rapidly developed in the middle of the 19th century due to its expanding hold on cotton trade and shipbuilding—Glasgow ships accounted for 85 percent of Britain's total tonnage—the country was eager to express itself as autonomous, even though it was part of England. The Greek style was thus an important expression of its national romantic fervor, as can be seen in the Royal Scottish Academy (William Henry Playfair, 1835) in Edinburgh, and St. Vincent Street United Presbyterian Church (Alexander Thomson, 1857–59) in Glasgow.

16.112 **Royal Scottish Academy, Edinburgh**

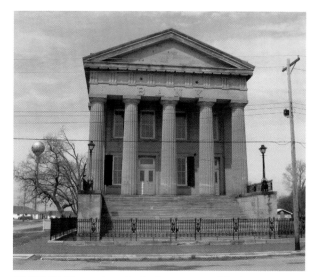

16.113 **Old Shawneetown Bank, Shawneetown, Illinois**

16.114 **Market Hall, Charleston, South Carolina**

Tennessee State Capitol

The most impressive examples of the Greek Revival were in the United States, where a particularly strong connection was made between Greece and America's own newfound nationhood. This was not a case of history simply being imported into the open landscape of the Americas; Americans saw their nation as the land of opportunity, where they could return to classical values without encumbrance of custom. The *Modern Builder's Guide*, which appeared in 1833 and ran through five editions until 1855, presented detailed engravings of the classical orders and their sources in ancient temples. The Greek Revival in the United States expanded on the Hellenistic leanings of the architecture of the so-called Federal era (1780–1830), but unlike the Federal style, which was best expressed in the great houses of the well-to-do, the Greek Revival was applied to institutional and governmental buildings: the Patent Office in Washington, DC (1836), which includes a copy of the front of the Pantheon as part of its facade; the Old Shawneetown Bank (1836) in Old Shawneetown, Illinois; the James Dakin Bank of Louisville (1834–36) in Louisville, Kentucky; the Market Hall (1840) in Charleston, South Carolina; and William Strickland's Tennessee State Capitol (1845–59) in Nashville. The latter combined a temple with a huge version of the Greek Choragic Monument of Lysicrates in Athens.

These were not isolated examples but part of a wave of neo-Hellenism that lasted for decades and stretched up into Canada; it can be felt in even humble buildings as far away as Oregon. When the Native Americans in the western half of New York State were conquered, place names were literally taken out of the Iliad. Today one can travel to Ithaca, Troy, Syracuse, Athens, Rome, Carthage, and even to Homer without ever leaving the state of New York. In Nashville, Tennessee, a full-scale replica of the Parthenon was built in 1897. It was not painted in the vibrant colors of the ancient Greeks but remained white, as the neo-Greeks preferred. The columnar Grecian mode was also easily adopted, especially in Mississippi and Louisiana, for plantation houses, where circumferential porches had been customary since the 18th century. Oak Alley (1836), near Vacherie, Louisiana, the home of planter Alexander Roman, is a well-known example of this style. The massive encircling columns support a continuous veranda on the second-floor level, and the twenty-eight columns are matched by an equal number of live oaks that line the formal approach to the house from the Mississippi River, literally playing out the relationship between nature and form—and reinforcing the ideology of elitism.

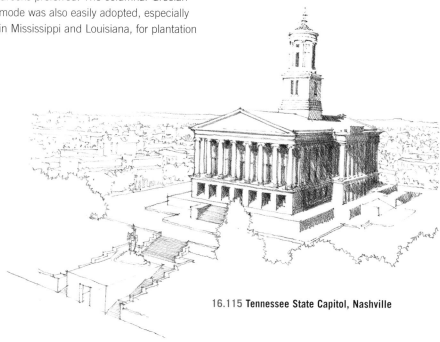

16.115 **Tennessee State Capitol, Nashville**

16.116 Oriel Chambers, Liverpool, England

Eugène-Emmanuel Viollet-le-Duc

The mid-19th century saw the rapid expansion of the middle class, the fitful demise of the influence of the landed gentry, and the rise of a professional class. The Geological Society upgraded its membership from the "interested" gentry to one based on merit and scholarly accomplishment. Arguments that fossils were planted in the ground by God—still a viable theory in the 1830s—were no longer accepted in 1850.

In architecture a similar revolution was taking place, led by a generation of theorists that included Eugène-Emmanuel Viollet-le-Duc (1814–79) in France, Gottfried Semper (1803–79) in the German speaking world, and John Ruskin (1819–1900) in England. Though different in many respects, all tried to rethink the principles of rationalism and technology, and all were writing at the same time. Ruskin's *Stones of Venice* appeared first in 1851, on the same date as Semper's *Die vier Elemente der Baukunst*. Viollet-le-Duc's *Dictionnaire raisonné de l'architecture française du XI au XVe siècle*, which was published in several editions, first appeared in 1854. Without a doubt, the period represented a turning point in architectural discourse. Of the three, Viollet-le-Duc was the strongest advocate of the modern material of iron. Unlike other architects of his time who were giving cast iron a Gothic flavor to appease the demands of the followers of August Welby Pugin, Viollet-le-Duc made no such demand. Nor was he advocating the technological rationalism of Sir Joseph Paxton in the Crystal Palace in London.

Cast iron, and then iron, had emerged relatively quickly on the architectural scene, but the application proper to its aesthetic was not yet obvious to midcentury architects. In the 17th and 18th centuries, Baroque architects, because of the large domes and complex lighting effects, operated in a realm between architecture and technology. Neoclassicism, with its emphasis on image, made much fewer technical demands on the architect. With the introduction of cast iron, that changed rapidly. The catalogues of architectural components published by the design office of British foundries began to grow thicker, and it was a short step from adding cast-iron balconies (excellent examples of which abound in the French Quarter of New Orleans, Louisiana) to designing entire houses and structures out of cast iron.

By 1850 some were arguing for a congruence between material and form, as can be seen in the remarkable Oriel Chambers (1864) in Liverpool, England, by the architect Peter Ellis. The thin cast-iron frame holds glazed bay windows with no concession to ornamentation. At the time, it was not well received; architects preferred to use cast iron mainly for floor supports. In that sense, the general approach of Quatremère de Quincy, who taught at the École des Beaux-Arts, still prevailed. He critiqued the use of exposed iron in anything other than industrial buildings, setting a tone with long-lasting consequences. Iron received strong support, however, from the Romantics, who saw it as an opportunity to escape the strictures of the classical orders and to introduce a more local or regional flavor to architecture. Viollet-le-Duc tried to hold a middle ground, arguing against both the academy, with its Neoclassical allegiances, and the autonomy of rational engineering. For him rationalism was not an instrument efficiency but the basis of a style that could emerge in concert with the visual and functional needs of the program.

Viollet-le-Duc's approach is best exemplified in his design for an iron armature for a concert hall (1886), which is striking and astonishing even today. Using the idea of a buttress but inverting it and placing it on the inside instead of the outside, he holds up a steel frame that in turn supports a thin masonry roof.

16.117 Viollet-le-Duc's design for a concert hall

Architectural Preservation

Today, architectural preservation is a major part of the architectural profession, although that was not always the case. Medievalists were especially concerned about the bad conditions many cathedrals were in, and the first preservation efforts were concerned with medieval buildings. Viollet-le-Duc played a large part in this movement, having been asked in 1835 to restore the Romanesque Abbey of Vézelay in France. This led to be restorations at Notre-Dame in Paris, Mont St.-Michel in Normandy, and the town of Carcassonne in Provence. Whereas John Ruskin advocated a restoration that preserved only the building's status quo, Viollet-le-Duc advocated a more aggressive form of preservation that included the possibility of rebuilding and even extending a building in the same stylistic manner. At Carcassonne, the high-pitched roofs and large parts of the Abbey of Vézelay are basically his designs.

In France, many of the cathedrals had been damaged during the French Revolution or had fallen into disrepair. On some buildings, Baroque and Neoclassical additions had been added. In dealing with such complex situations (and given that a medieval church might have taken centuries to complete and thus exhibit numerous styles), his approach was not to pick a particular time and restore it to that moment, but rather to synthesize the building and turn the restoration into a completion. This put a lot of power in the hands of the designer: the final result could be a building that never have existed prior to that moment. To advance his cause, Viollet-le-Duc made extensive studies of medieval building practices, not only so that his restorations could be accurate but also to ensure the conceptual and perceived authenticity of the new parts of the building.

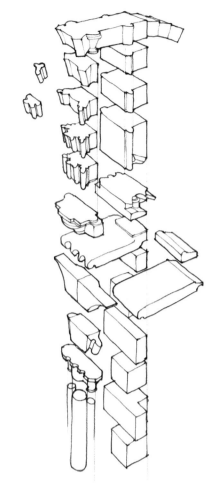

16.119 Viollet-le-Duc's analysis of a Gothic column

16.118 Abbey of Vézalay, France

16.120 Restoration in Carcassonne, France, by Viollet-le-Duc, begun in 1853

16.121 Bibliothèque St.-Geneviève, Paris

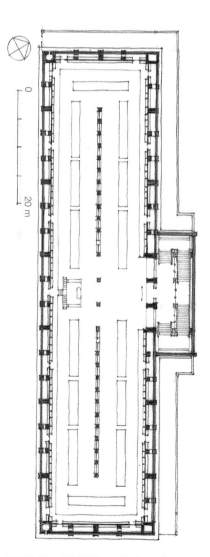

16.122 Transverse section: Bibliothèque St.-Geneviève

Bibliothèque St.-Geneviève

Among those who argued in favor of the use of iron in France was Henri Labrouste (1801–75). His Bibliothèque St.-Geneviève (designed 1843, built 1845–51), with its slender columns and billowing domes, coexists with stone walls, themselves without any trace of classical columns and pilasters. The distinction between the two floors is made on the outside by a thin entablature, with a continuous row of garlands suspended beneath it. Below, the wall is punctuated by relatively small, Romanesque-style round-headed windows. Above, from end to end, runs an arcade, with pilasters forming a regular rhythm across the facade; it is distinctly Roman in flavor. The lower two-thirds of the arcade are filled in to allow for a window in each bay. The whole is topped by a stripped-down cornice, lightly decorated in a neo-Greek manner. The building thus makes numerous historical references, but is no way historicist. Labrouste attempted to create an idiom that, through its reductivist aesthetic, could demonstrate a fluid connection between the old and the modern. To indicate the iron used on the interior (for those with a keen eye), Labrouste articulated the end bolts of the tie rods with round panels nestled between the archivolts. The building also has a Picturesque component, for inscribed onto the panels in the arcades are the names of the authors of the books held in the shelves within.

In Labrouste's hands, iron was a significant enrichment of the architect's toolbox. In the vestibule, for example, the tall, solid piers contrast with the spindly cast-iron arches. But these arches were meant to evoke the branches of a sacred grove, an image reinforced by wall frescoes that show treetops over the busts of famous literary figures. The vestibule thereby becomes a reference to the fabled Elysian Fields. Because Labrouste's position was not in line with the more conservative tastes of the academy, his career did not advance as fast as did those of his contemporaries. His use of iron as a form of vaulting became more common in the next decades and was used, for example, at Notre-Dame de la Croix (1870) in Paris. The building is sited with its back against the urban fabric and its long facade facing into the open square that flanks the Panthéon.

16.123 Plan: Bibliothèque St.-Geneviève

Semper made an equally bold argument: the origins of architecture lay not in the Greek post and lintel and not even in the need to add a roof to the post and lintel, as Laugier had argued. Architecture began, so he argued, through crafts. From weaving a basket, primitive humans learned how to weave branches into walls and then close off the gaps with mud. From pottery, they learned how to make tiles and bricks. The beginning of architecture therefore had less to do with archaeology than with anthropology. It was a radical rethinking of the origins of architecture and much discussed at the time. For Semper, nature was not an abstraction producing regular geometries that needed to be emulated, nor was it a biological force in the sense that Gothic architects understood it when, for instance, they modeled their vaults on tree branches. Instead, nature was wrapped up with our basic instinct for making things, which Semper understood as having both

an economical and a moral component. At the Great Exhibition of 1851, he lavished praise not on Sir Joseph Paxton's amazing technologically driven design of the Crystal Palace but on the display of houses from Trinidad, whose production yielded glimpses of an early stage of cultural development before industrialization derailed the processes by which craft develops form.

His theoretical opinions aside, when it came to architecture, Semper drew heavily on motifs from the Roman Baroque, using rusticated ground floors and pilastered upper floors. This is apparent in his design for the Swiss Polytechnical School (1858–64) in Zurich, where the domed rotunda, used as a reading room, is placed not at the center of the composition, as might have been expected, but along its facade as a dramatic accent to the entrance. It leads to a central hall defined by a restrained classical vocabulary.

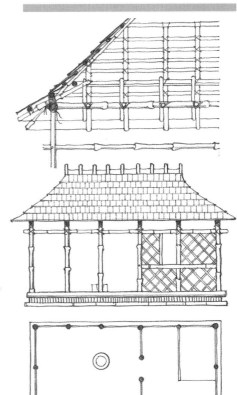

16.124 **Caribbean hut, by Gottfried Semper**

16.125 **Swiss Polytechnical School, Zurich**

16.126 **Touro Synagogue, Newport, Rhode Island**

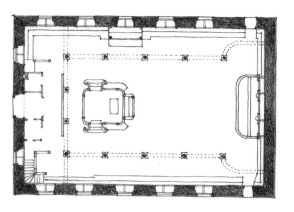

16.127 **Plan: Bevis-Marks Synagogue, London**

Synagogues

Until the end of the 15th century, most Jews lived within the footprint of the old Roman Empire, whether that be in Trastevere in Rome, in Spain, or in Thessalonica in Greece. This was the result of the great Diaspora imposed on the Jews by the Roman emperor Titus after his victory over them and the destruction of the Second Temple in 70 CE. Beginning with the Christian era, restrictions were imposed on Jews wherever they lived. They were not allowed to own land and were excluded from affairs of the military, thus denying them access to aristocratic privileges. But banking was one of the few trades they were permitted to engage in, and Jews were able to create a network that transcended local rivalries; in that capacity, they were often protected by kings and princes, who used them as private bankers. In Venice, Jews were allowed to come to the city principally because of their banking associations. They were assigned to live in an area known as the ghetto, a term from then on used to designate where Jews were required to live. An exception was in Lithuania where, from 1316 onward, Jews had a surprising amount of freedom.

With their expulsion by the Spanish in 1492 and by the Portuguese in 1496, the Sephardic Jews were forced to seek sanctuary in Poland, Amsterdam, Venice, Greece, Istanbul, and even Rome. In Amsterdam, a Sephardic synagogue was built in 1675. It has remained largely unchanged and is today one of the few tangible remnants of Amsterdam's once-thriving Jewish community. It is a large, rectangular brick building, with large round-headed windows on all sides that emphasize its vast interior space. It became the model for several later synagogues, including the Bevis-Marks Synagogue in London (1700) and the smaller Touro Synagogue in Newport, Rhode Island, the oldest synagogue in the United States. Jewish life in Germany improved slightly in the 18th century when courts invited Jews to come and serve as financial agents. In 1714, King Frederick William I of Prussia permitted the construction of a synagogue in Berlin.

The fate of Jews improved significantly under Napoleon, who passed a number of measures supporting the position of Jews in the French Empire and Austria—and just as importantly, in conquered countries. He began by abolishing laws restricting Jews to ghettos or to certain professions. (In 1797 when he invaded Italy, he threw open the gates to the ghettos.) In 1807, like his contemporary Qing emperors of China, he sanctioned several religions as "official"—a first for a European ruler—and these included Judaism, Roman Catholicism, Lutheranism, and Calvinism. As a result of Napoleon's initiatives, Jews in other lands sought and eventually received emancipation in Germany in 1848, Great Britain in 1890, Russia in 1917, and finally in Spain in 1930.

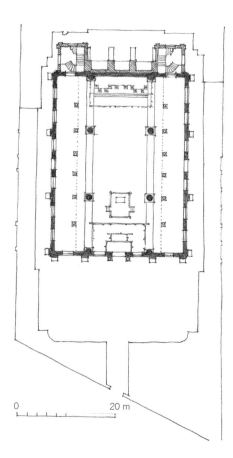

0   20 m

16.128 **Plan: Sephardic synagogue, Amsterdam**

16.129 Tempio Israelitico, Rome

16.130 Interior: Beth Elohim Synagogue, Charleston, South Carolina

The response by Jews to German emancipation was a synagogue building boom of unprecedented proportion. During the 19th century, more than two hundred large synagogues were built. Since there were few historical models to go on, synagogue architecture varied widely from place to place. This eclecticism was also a response to the new freedom from restrictions on what could be built. Furthermore, most of the architects were non-Jews who brought their own, often romanticized, expectations of what a Jewish space should look like to the project. Gottfried Semper designed a synagogue in Dresden (1840) that was Carolingian-Romanesque on its exterior, presumably to emphasize the aspirations of assimilation, but on the inside there was an order of columns with deep impost blocks copied from the Alhambra at Granada.

The emergence of Reform Judaism, intended to appeal to urban Jews, had a major influence on synagogue design. Reform Jews stressed the universal teachings of Judaism but also sought to modernize rituals that were difficult to maintain in a modern world. Reform Jews also held that Jewish people were not in a state of permanent exile but contributing members of their community and nation. They considered every house of worship a temple, as holy as the original temple in Jerusalem. Pews were permitted, and prayer was in German. The organ was introduced. The first Reform synagogue was opened in Seesen in central Germany in 1810, and it was called a temple in keeping with Enlightenment ideals. Some synagogues took up a classical theme and were designed almost literally as temples, as in

the Seitenstettengasse Synagogue in Vienna (1826) and the Beth Elohim Synagogue in Charleston, South Carolina (1840). Others were in keeping with the general 19th-century preoccupation with history and were developed along Egyptian and Byzantine lines, as, for example, the Princes Road Synagogue (1874) in Liverpool, which is a type of Norman Gothic with Oriental touches, and the Tempio Israelitico (1882) in Florence. Its prayer hall is almost square, with galleries on three sides supported by columns with Moorish cusped arches. Every square inch of surface is covered with patterns and colored designs of abstract configurations, creating a soft reddish-golden atmosphere.

16.131 Princes Road Synagogue, Liverpool, England

16.132 Beth Elohim Synagogue, Charleston, South Carolina

16.133 Memorial Hall, Harvard University, Cambridge, Massachusetts

John Ruskin

No Victorian era theorist was as widely read and discussed as John Ruskin, whose voluminous writings cover a host of topics. Ruskin preferred the simpler Italian medieval style to the more complicated northern Gothic because form, he argued, should be determined by the material of which it consists and by the way in which it is constructed. The early medieval period, he felt, embodied this ethos. Unlike Pugin, Ruskin was not opposed to the use of iron, even though he much preferred conventional materials. Disturbed by the rawness of industrialism, he wanted to bring a new awareness to the aesthetic intensity of the architectural surface. The fact that a wall is a series of layers, he argued, should be shown as distinctly as possible on its surface. Ruskin was not opposed to thin walls, for example, but wanted the thinness to be expressed in the paneling or in the use of a checkered pattern. Ruskin also asked his readers to

rethink their attitude about the past, looking not at the question of proportion and order in the neoclassical sense, nor at the question of Roman versus non-Roman motifs, but rather at the physical and material rationale that underlies architectural reasoning.

His concern for the visual led him to prefer monolithic columns. He rejected the use of piers and buttresses, as they interfered with the visual impact of a form. Mass was not to be constricted by cold geometry but was something to be molded freely with simple and grand outlines; he very rarely dealt with interiors and thus rarely asked questions about program and function. For Ruskin, the shape of a building—which would have been significant for Durand—was less important than the architect's attitude toward designing it, and a building's tactile surface and detail was just as important as the plan.

After Ruskin, a generation of architects began to design in a way that they thought conformed to his vision of the constructed world. This entailed a shift away from the enforced medievalism of Pugin to a more inventive style for which there is no particular name apart from the term Ruskinian Gothic. Among those who worked in this direction was the firm of Deane & Woodward, whose use of exposed Gothic-style iron in the design (right down to the rivets holding the elements together) on the interior of the Museum of Natural History at Oxford University (1853) demonstrated its expressive qualities. The industrial feel is offset by individually designed capitals with inventive floral motifs and the use of column clusters to create a light, transparent appearance. In the United States, one of the best examples of Ruskinian Gothic is Memorial Hall (1865–68) at Harvard University in Cambridge, Massachusetts, which houses a theater and a dining hall. It was designed by William Robert Ware and Henry Van Brunt. Most of the building is in red brick, accented in a lively manner with yellowish limestone. The roof is striped in grays, whites, and reds, with a massive tower rising over the ensemble.

16.134 Museum of Natural History, Oxford, England

1900 CE

Between 1840 and 1900, the European colonial powers, driven by a systematic policy of expansionism, increased their control of the world's land area from 60 to 91 percent. The new land acquisitions were used to raise cash crops and fuel industrialization at home. In the process, millions of people were disempowered, and indeed, the stain of this colonial era still haunts global political processes today. For England colonization ushered in an era of unbridled prosperity, making it the undisputed world power, especially after China was subjugated in the middle of the 19th century through a policy of military action and political intimidation—and by forcing the Chinese to purchase opium. Because of the long rule of Queen Victoria (r. 1837–1901), the second half of the 19th century has fittingly been called the Victorian era. By the late 19th century, Victorian England could act with impunity around the world. It invaded Egypt in 1882 to control the Suez Canal and South Africa in 1899 to take over the gold mines there. By the turn of the century, England's wealth set it up for a showdown with Germany, which did not have a major colonial empire but had industrialized heavily beginning late in the 19th century. By the end of the 19th century, in the race for colonial lands, France had begun to fall behind; its yield from its colonies had risen only slightly, while the cost of running its empire had escalated significantly.

Political philosophers, Karl Marx (1818–83) in particular, shed light on the emergence of the increasingly cozy relationship between government, power, and capital. Whereas Marx exposed the inner workings of capitalism, Charles Darwin (1809–82) introduced the theory of evolution and wrote about the inner workings of natural selection. Ebenezer Howard (1850–1928), witnessing the darker side the large English cities, challenged his contemporaries to leave the city, with its filth and grime, and design small cities closer in scale to human life. In the arts, the young generation of the 1880s, led by William Morris (1834–96), among others, began to rebel against the dehumanization fostered by industrial production and the

strictures of English society, and demanded a simpler and, for them, more authentic way of producing art and crafts. In the United States, Frederick Law Olmsted (1822–1903) led a movement to bring nature back into architectural and urban design.

Through all of this, the Victorian age in England saw the emergence of a new generation of urban building types, such as government buildings, court houses, post offices, law courts, museums, and railway stations. The architectural armature of the modern city was coming into focus. Debates raged about which style was appropriate and about whether, or how, iron was to be used. Generally speaking these buildings adopted a style that mixed various historical references that came to be known for its eclecticism. This was embraced by some, but critiqued by others. Though England played a dominant role economically and aesthetically and in matters of domestic and public architecture, the French, despite their economic problems, began to assert themselves in matters of urban culture. The center of Paris was completely rebuilt under Napoleon III. Never before had so much of a city been bulldozed away for new buildings. Thousands of new bourgeois apartments were built. It was an impressive undertaking and much admired world-wide. While Argentina's exports went largely to England, for example, when it came to building new streets and public buildings, that country's elite turned to Parisian models when it came to their capital, Buenos Aires. In the United States, the developments in Paris inspired the City Beautiful movement, which championed broad boulevards and monumentally placed buildings like museums, train stations, and courthouses. The firm of McKim, Mead & White (founded 1879) received dozens of such commissions and was for a period the largest architectural firm in the world. Concomitant with this in the late 19th century was the emergence of the first professional architectural associations in Europe and the United States. The turn of the 20th century also saw the flowering of a style known as Art

Nouveau, which with its rich materials and complex plant-like decorative forms, appealed to the elites of the industrial world, particularly in Europe. Its most active proponent architecturally was Victor Horta of Belgium. Developing his own style was the Spaniard Antoni Gaudí, whose colorful and fluid designs were undeniably unique.

Around the turn of the century, a perceptible split occurred between public and private architecture. Public buildings tended to be elaborate and yield to the monumental and the ornamental, whereas domestic architecture came to be dominated by the calmer ethos of the Arts and Crafts movement. Both, however, should be seen as part of the developing modernity of the times. Radical experiments were, however, continually being undertaken to invent new architectural styles and possibilities. In fact, between 1890 and 1910, architecture was significantly more experimental than it was in the 1930s. With the development of Art Nouveau and then Expressionism in combination with the spatial innovations of Frank Lloyd Wright in the United States, the foundations of what we now call modern architecture were set in place. New materials like concrete were used to build new types of enclosures. Simultaneously, the steel frame, developed in Chicago and New York, was challenging the norms of urban living and work. Steel became essential to factory design, but also to that most astonishing of new building types, the skyscraper. Particularly important to the transition to modernism was the Expressionist movement which, in the years before and after World War I, articulated the first coherent—though sometimes fanciful—alternative to traditional architectural practices. By the mid-1920s, however, the modern movement as it is generally understood began to take shape in the buildings and theorizing of Walter Gropius, Ludwig Mies van der Rohe, and Le Corbusier, among many others. The Bauhaus in Germany, the de Stijl architects in Holland, and the Constructivists in the newly formed Soviet Union became flashpoints for the developing aesthetic.

National Gallery, London ▲
1834–38

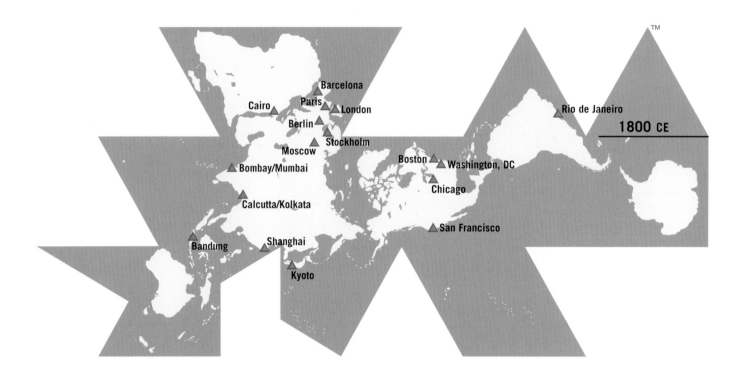

Barcelona

Cairo
Paris ▲ London
Berlin
Stockholm
Moscow
Bombay/Mumbai
Calcutta/Kolkata
Bandung Shanghai
Kyoto

Boston ▲ Washington, DC
Chicago
San Francisco

Rio de Janeiro

1800 CE

▲ Crystal Palace
1850–51

▲ St. Pancras Station
1863–76

▲ Amsterdam Stock Exchange
1898–1903

▲ Bandung Institute of Technology
1920

▲ Galleria Vittorio Emanuele II
1865–77

▲ Victoria Terminus
1878–87

▲ Shanghai Bank
1923–25

▲ Central Park
1853–83

▲ Reliance Building
1890–95

▲ Wrigley Building
1920–24

▲ Trinity Church
1872–77

▲ Boston Public Library
1888–95

▲ Pennsylvania Station
1904–1910

▲ Paris Opera House
1861–75

▲ Al-Rifaʻi Mosque
1869–80 and 1906–11

▲ Mubarak Mahal
1899

1850 CE　　　　　　　　　　**1900 CE**　　　　　　　　　　**1950 CE**

American Civil War
1861–65

World War I
1914–18

Great Depression
1929 to late 1930s

World War II
1939–45

▲ Cornell University
Founded 1865

▲ Winslow House
1893

▲ Robie House
1908–10

▲ Gamble House
1908–9

▲ Taliesin
Begun 1911

▲ Hollyhock House
1921

▲ Isaac Bell House
1882–83

▲ Maison Tassel
1892–93

▲ Glass House
1914

▲ Villa Müller
1930

▲ Casa Batlló
1904–6

▲ 25b, rue Franklin
1902–4

▲ Einstein Tower
1917–21

▲ Keith Arcade
1927

▲ Stockholm Public Library
1920–28

▲ Woodland Cemetery Chapel
1918–20

▲ Friedrichstrasse Office Building
1921

▲ Tatlin's Tower
1919

▲ Bauhaus
1924–26

▲ Villa Savoye
1928–31

17.1 Victorian England

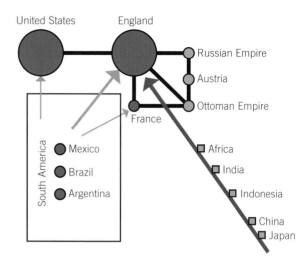

17.2 Eurasian trade diagram, ca. 1850

Victorian England

With Napoleon's final defeat at Waterloo in 1815, England became the undisputed master of the world, with only Russia posing a remote threat. Between 1815 and 1914, England added around 10 million square miles of territory, controlling about one-quarter of the earth's land area and roughly four hundred million people. China, by midcentury, had been brought to its knees by a series of wars the British waged against it that lasted from 1839 to 1860. Opium was at the heart of this conflict. Manufactured in India, opium was sold in China; to Chinese protests and edicts forbidding its use and importation, the English turned a deaf ear. As a consequence of the drug's debilitating effect on its population, half or more of whom became addicted, China, which had for centuries had a trade surplus, had by 1830 fallen into deficit. And by 1833, two-thirds of the English government expenditures were financed by tea revenue, which in turn relied on the vast profits made from the opium trade. In a single generation, the Chinese economy was devastated.

In 1857, the English government disbanded the British East India Trading Company and formally took control of India, with Queen Victoria becoming empress of India in 1876. Britain, due to its dominant position, now also effectively controlled the economies of many nominally independent countries. This was the case with Argentina, where British investors financed the

railroads and in return received favorable prices for the importation of beef. In 1875, England bought the indebted Egyptian ruler Ismail's shareholdings in the Suez Canal to secure control of this strategic waterway constructed in 1869. This led to outright British occupation of Egypt in 1882 and the conquest of neighboring Sudan in 1898. The brutal Boer Wars (1880–1881 and 1899–1902) were waged to control the gold mines of South Africa. For a while France hoped to keep pace with its own colonial empire, but by the end of the century it was no longer cost-effective. Even the British Empire was suffering by the end of the 19th century, given the inroads into the global economy made by countries such as Germany and the United States.

As a consequence of Britain's industrial expansion, the Victorian era was a period of unparalleled urban growth. In 1800, 90 percent of the population of Britain lived and worked in rural areas; by the end of the century the situation had dramatically changed, and 75 percent of the population was living in towns and cities. Improved steam engines and railroads and the construction of factories created the infrastructure for industrialization, in which England led the other European nations. But labor exploitation, poor housing, and the absence of social services created terrible situations, written about so poignantly by Charles Dickens in *Oliver Twist*. The situation

only began to change when the Whig Party gained a majority in the elections of 1830. The Reform Bill of 1832 reapportioned the parliamentary districts to reflect population changes and liberalized voting qualifications. In essence, this bill defined the idea of democracy as it is understood today (even though women were still excluded from voting and class inequities remained unresolved). The Factory Acts of the 1830s reduced the hours of child labor and began to correct some of the worst evils of the factory system. The Mines Act of 1842 prohibited underground work for all women and for boys under ten. And the Ten Hours Act of 1847 limited the workday for women and young people to ten hours.

Over time, city governments became stronger and were able to consolidate services and initiate major public works programs dealing with water, sewage, railroads, and ports. Nonetheless, the English cities remained largely unhealthy and uncontrolled, leading some to call for a new approach altogether: the Garden City, which could be built from scratch away from the pollution and turmoil of urban life. And even though the Anglican Church's authority was uncontestable, theological debates, the search for alternative religious experiences, and the rise of a professional class undermined established ways of thinking and created a period of continual debate and, for many, confusion. With the rise of

middle-class ambitions, new societal notions surfaced, including the separation of work and home, and the differentiation between the duties and tasks of men and women.

The Reform Club

The Reform Bill of 1832 was one of the most significant laws in the history of early modern government. It began the transformation from a medieval attitude toward industry to the more modern one that exists today. Its significance was not lost on its defenders, who created a Reform Club in London where members of Whig Party could meet and discuss. The building (1841), a political statement in and of itself, was designed by none other than Charles Barry, the architect of the Parliament Building. But unlike the Parliament, the Reform Club was in a Renaissance palazzo style with a Greek-style courtyard.

Why the double appeal of Greece and the Renaissance? Ancient Greece was seen as progressive, philosophically sophisticated, and militarily ambitious. Unlike the Middle Ages, which, for progressive Victorians, was often associate with old-fashioned thinking and a repressive religion, Hellenism was thus associated with an image—although one more fictitious than real—of the unity of reason, industry, and social harmony. And Hellenism was often fused with the Renaissance. Though today the concept of the Renaissance is widely accepted, it was not until the 1830s, just as the Reform Club was being built, that this time period was recognized as an independent moment in history. The Renaissance was interpreted as a moment of great artistic achievement. It was also seen as an age when the sciences were in ascendency and as a time confident in the values of urban living. The neo-Renaissance style thus carried a different set of connotations than the Neoclassicism of John Nash, with its elitist and aristocratic associations.

A massive set of drawings of Renaissance palaces made and published in the 1830s by Paul Letarouilly played an important part in establishing the Renaissance as a style—and political sensibility—all its own. The sober and unimpressionistic line drawings were meant to convey an ethos of clarity and precision.

17.3 Reform Club, London

17.4 Paul Letarouilly drawing of the Villa Giulia, Rome

The Athenaeum

By the turn of the century, the idea of associations—citizens coming together around a particular set of common interests—had become a social movement unto its own, reaching into the middle class. The theoretical underpinnings of this trend can be found in the writings of Alexis de Tocqueville (1805–59), the French philosopher and social scientist. He argued that associations were an important part of a healthy civil society. Given the modern world's contrary propensity for isolation, society needed to be bound together, he believed—not through the abstract authority of the state but through voluntary associations, educational institutions, newspapers, and even commercial and manufacturing associations. The idea never developed in France, where the tradition of state control was stronger. But in England, such associations proliferated. Most tended to be pro-urban, seeing the city, despite its faults and ugliness, as the symbol of civilization and the place where the virtues of polity, politeness, and urbanity could be exercised and maintained. Associations took many forms. Some were social, others political; some secular, others religious. A list would include the Natural History Society, the Mechanic's Institute, the Architectural Association, the Royal Victoria Gallery for the Encouragement of Practical Science, and a rich array of musical groups, library societies, and philosophical and charitable organizations. Preeminent among these was the Athenaeum, which, as its name suggests, was intended to promote learning and culture on the model of ancient Greece. (After the end of hostilities on the Continent in 1814, the English flocked in unprecedented numbers to Greece.) Its origins were in the late 18th century, and it carried with it the stamp of the Enlightenment. But by the middle of the 19th century, it had become less elitist and, in fact, a strong promoter of learning, education, and the arts in bourgeois society.

Athenaeum buildings tended to blend the Hellenic with the Italianate as with the London Athenaeum (1828–30), designed in a Neoclassical, Italian palazzo style by Decimus Burton (1800–81)—a protégé of Nash. It differs from the standard Italianate model in that the main entrance has a Doric

17.5 Finnish Athenaeum, Helsinki

17.6 Boston Athenaeum

portico with paired columns. On the inside, the main hall has a continuous frieze copied from the Parthenon. A statue of Pallas Athena stands above the porch. The original design was for two stories; the third was added later. The Boston Athenaeum building (1849) is a variation on this theme and is indicative of the ever-expanding importance of this institution. It was founded in 1807 by members of the Anthology Society, who wanted to create an establishment similar to that of the Athenaeum and Lyceum of Liverpool in Great Britain. The institution's library and art gallery were soon flourishing, and for nearly half a century the Athenaeum was the center of intellectual life in Boston; by 1851 it had become one of the five largest libraries in the United States. The building was designed in a Renaissance style by

Edward Clarke Cabot (1818–1901), modeled loosely on Andrea Palladio's Palazzo Thiene.

The Athenaeum was an international movement, with institutions not only in cities and towns in England and the United States but also on the Continent. The Finish Athenaeum (1887) in Helsinki, designed by Theodor Höjer, demonstrates the emerging scale and importance of these institutions. The facade is decorated with statues and reliefs along with busts of the architect Donato Bramante, the painter Raphael, and the sculptor Phidias. On the third floor, the caryatids that support the pediment symbolize the four classical art forms: architecture, painting, sculpture, and music. Between the second-floor windows there are reliefs that represent Finnish and international artists.

Public Sector Architecture

In London, prior to 1850, grand public buildings—apart from an occasional guildhall or market house from the 17th century—were rare. It was only in the 1820s that a modern civic architectural presence began to emerge, with the new Privy Council and Board of Trade Building (1822–27), the General Post Office (1823–28), and the British Museum (1823–46). Even so, metropolitan improvements were largely haphazard and impromptu affairs, and the amount of civic architecture remained meager at best: London was still basically run as a medieval corporation, with dozens of committees and organizations defending their turf and rarely working in unison. In 1855, in an attempt to rectify the situation, the government created the Metropolitan Board of Works to improve the process by which decisions regarding the commissioning and building of public buildings could be made. The result was immediate. In fact, most public buildings in Great Britain, whether municipal offices, post offices, fire stations, schools, or libraries, all date from after this time. Among the most important Victorian era governmental buildings that put a new bureaucratic face on the empire were the Admiralty (proposed 1852, built 1887), South Kensington Museum (1857), Colonial Office (1870–74), Home Office (1870–75), New Law Courts (1871–82), War Office (1898–1906), and New Public Office (completed 1908). The massing of these buildings tended to be heavy, usually in a Renaissance Italianate manner, with well-articulated quoins and voussoirs, such as at the India Office (1863–68) and the New Government Offices (1868–78).

Typical is the Inland Revenue Office (1852–57) by James Pennethorne. Educated by Nash, Pennethorne's style was nonetheless a bit looser: the building's giant order columnar porch rests on a tall, rusticated ground floor. The ideals of the neo-Renaissance social club are clearly at the root of the design, but are overlaid with Baroque elements to create a monumental form in agreement with Victorian preferences. The India Office (now the Foreign and Commonwealth Office) was designed around a large Renaissance style courtyard enclosed by a glass roof.

17.7 Foreign and Commonwealth Office, London

17.8 Interior courtyard, Foreign and Commonwealth Office, London

Cities began to compete for the top architects for their town halls, railroad stations, and commodity exchanges. Manchester, the great port city infamous for its gritty mills and open sewers, took the lead in the attempt to reform its urban image. Its grand town hall, designed by Alfred Waterhouse (1830–1905), is in a restrained Romanesque style, with a tall bell tower purposefully modeled on the Parliament Building in London. The city of Leeds followed suit in 1858 with a town hall designed by Cuthbert Brodrick. Four law courts were placed at the corners. Offices for the lawyers were located between the front and back facades. Its design featured a monumental Corinthian order with unpedimented entrances on all sides. The building opened with much fanfare— even Queen Victoria attended—and soon became the center of civic life in Leeds. It is reminiscent of the Grand Theater (1773–80) by Victor Louis in Bordeaux, France; indeed, its attempt to recall the virtues of the Enlightenment are quite evident. Different from the Grand Theater, however, was the addition of a huge tower modeled on the Hellenistic Mausoleum at Halicarnassus, which, oddly, was surmounted by an ornate domed top. This eclecticism, which was later to be critiqued, was, however, part of the exuberance of this new industrial era, which was seeking a freedom from a slavish commitment to history.

17.9 Manchester City Hall, England

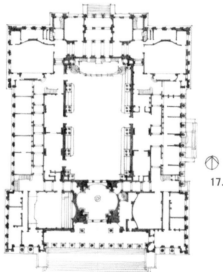

0   25 m

17.10 Plan: Leeds City Hall, England

17.11 Grand Theater, Bordeaux, France

17.12 Leeds City Hall

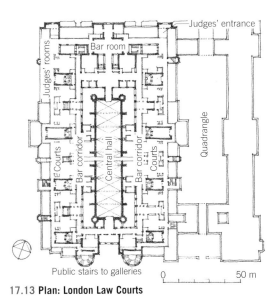

17.13 **Plan: London Law Courts**

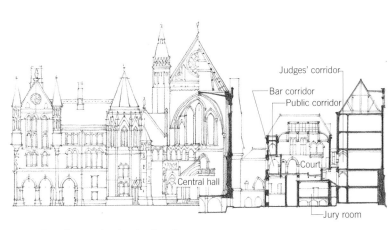

17.14 **Elevation-section: London Law Courts**

London Law Courts

On the whole, the Victorian era was still tied to the Picturesque ideal that architecture had to be linked creatively to the past in order to dignify the present. But the Victorians tended to be less attached to the purity of Roman or Greek prototypes than the generation of Robert Adam and John Nash. They experimented with historical styles that resonated with the increased archaeological erudition of the time and with the diverse philosophical persuasions of their clientele. George Edmund Street (1824–1881), who designed the London Law Courts (1870–81), for example, used an early medieval style, not August Welby Pugin's High Gothic. Street chose this style for its more stern and primitive associations. He and many of the young architects of the time were enthralled with the ideals of Gallic toughness. What today might be seen as medieval they saw as Saxon. The Saxons were not known for their architectural accomplishments, however, and here the added problem is that the precedents are more Franco-Norman than English.

The building's commissioning must be seen in the context of the Reform Bill of 1832, which eliminated many inequities not only in fact but also in representation. Police forces were made to function less haphazardly and were trained to differentiate between different types of criminal activity, as opposed to the more wholesale approach to crime of earlier generations. The 1846 County Courts Act, followed by the Judicature Act of 1873, tried to streamline the court system and make it more comprehensible while at the same time expanding its reach. Church courts were closed down and replaced by divorce and probate courts. The High Court also administered the voluminous new legislation dealing with property, bankruptcy, succession, copyrights, patents, and taxation.

With four different systems of circulation, the building was quite complex and mirrored the new and expanded horizon of law. It had eighteen courtrooms, two of them larger than the others for the more prominent trials. A private corridor for the bar circled the building between the courts and the central hall. Judges were provided with their own corridor circuit one-half level higher than that of the bar; it ran behind the courtrooms and gave direct access to the raised daises on which the judges sat in the courts. A circumferential corridor running just under that of the judges accommodated attorneys and had its own doorways into the courtrooms. The public, considered to be troublesome and boisterous, was segregated in its own corridor, which connected to the upper galleries of the courtroom. The large portal opening onto the Strand, one of London's most important streets, was used only infrequently for ceremonial purposes. One entered the building at specialized and monitored entrances that led to staircases and thus to the proper corridors. The great hall was not the central element of the circulation system but was used only by those already inside the building. Given the tight packing of rooms and corridors, ventilation was a major concern, and so spaces and gaps were left in the composition to allow for outdoor ventilation and ventilation shafts. Whether the building lived up to its ideology of transparency or obfuscated it in a labyrinthine system remains a topic of discussion.

17.15 **London Law Courts**

Railroad Stations

For most people in Europe, iron, a new material, was most prevalent in the spectacular railroad stations of the time. Representing a new culture of mobility and exchange, these buildings were not only marvels of engineering but also new and imposing additions to the urban environment. Civil engineers began to compete with architects as arbiters of taste. St. Pancras Station in London (1863–76), for example, contained a volume of space within its 80-meter span that defied anything architecture could previously have strived for. The large steel members were brought to the construction site by the railroad itself. In front of the shed, facing the city, was a building that contained baggage facilities, waiting rooms, and offices of various sorts. By the 1880s, terminals in England, Germany, France, the United States, and even in the colonies, such as Victoria Terminus in Mumbai (1888), had become the symbols of the age, leading one commentator to write that train stations were to the European 19th century what monasteries and cathedrals had been to the 13th century. Railroad stations also significantly changed the orientation and configuration of many cities, as railroad lines usually had to go near cities rather than through them because of the trains' smoky steam engines. Many of these peripheral railroad stations subsequently developed into urban hubs in their own right, with boulevards and rectangular urban blocks. In Paris, for example, there was the Gare de

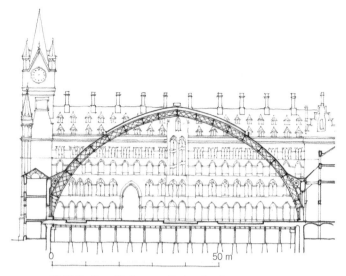

17.16 Section: St. Pancras Station, London

Lyon, the Gare du Nord, the Gare de l'Est, the Gare d'Austerlitz, the Gare Montparnasse, and the Gare St. Lazare, all of which changed the economic and social environment of the city. (*Gare* is the French word for "station.") The Anhalter Bahnhof (1872–80) in Berlin is another example.

The rise of the railroad station in England can be further explained by the fact that railroads were private companies in competition with each other, and therefore needed grand structures to distinguish them from their competitors. Although there were differences in the styles of the front building, with its portico and waiting rooms, the main prototype of shed-and-front building remained unchanged until well into the 20th

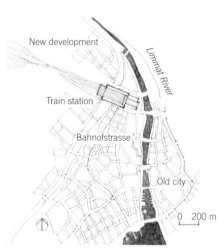

17.17 Plan of Zurich, Switzerland

century. In the colonies, where the English were monopoly owners of the railways, the stations were projected as symbols of civilizational advancement enabled by colonial rule. The Public Works Department of colonial India, staffed by officers of the trained English Corps of Engineers, took great pride in designing not only the large terminus stations but also the thousands of smaller stations that were needed throughout India for material extraction and the transportation of goods and people. While the larger stations were equipped with wide spans and rich decoration, the smaller ones were built using standardized and rationalized design schemes both to optimize functionality and to project a sense of militaristic order.

17.18 Anhalter Bahnhof, Berlin

17.19 **National Gallery, London**

17.20 **French-Egyptian Museum, Cairo**

National Museums

From the Renaissance on, history was more often than not explained as a sequence of great kings, queens, and military events. But beginning in the Enlightenment, history began to be perceived in terms of a civilizational dynamic and verifiable data. The original fixation on Rome and Greece expanded into a fascination with the history of Egypt, Mesopotamia, and India, with nations such as England, France, and Germany seeing themselves as the protectors and heirs of antique values. The national museums that now came into being exemplified the Victorians' desire—and capacity—to master the logic of the expanding concept of history. The Louvre was among the first of these new museums, having been transformed in 1793 from a private royal collection into a public art museum open to all citizens free of charge. Subsequently, Napoleon transformed the Louvre into an instrument of the state to strengthen the link between national identity and the history of civilization. The idea of the national museum was taken up by the Prussian king, Friedrich Wilhelm II, who built the Altes Museum in Berlin in 1829. By the end of the 19th century, the European conception of nation and empire were inextricably intertwined with displays of museums and exhibitions.

The discovery of dazzling, forgotten ruins, such as those at Angkor Wat by the French in the 1860s, became almost a competitive sport among nations. The principle of these discoveries was "finders keepers," with the finders often becoming more famous than their discoveries: the Elgin Marbles, from the frieze of the Parthenon, was named not after the temple, but after the man who had dismantled them and sold them to the British Museum, Thomas Bruce, the 7th Earl of Elgin.

The span of time encompassing the construction of the National Gallery in London (1838), the Kyoto National Museum (1898), the Estonian National Museum (1909), and the National Gallery of Art in Washington, DC (1931), demonstrates the expanding role of history and the collection of artifacts in the conception of national ideologies. At the same time, museums were built in the colonies to stress the legitimacy of the colonizer's presumed civilizing mission and to enable native peoples to recognize themselves as differentiated subjects under the overarching and unifying umbrella of empire. India's Government Museum of Chennai (1851) and Prince of Wales Museum in Mumbai (1914), as well as the French-Egyptian Museum in Cairo (1858), are but a few examples of the complex aspects of the history of colonialism.

In most cases, these museums were conceived as Neoclassical structures since the claim to classicism and its associated principles of order and system were so central to the concept of nationalism in the 19th century. The National Gallery of England had an octastyle temple front. The imprint of Neoclassicism was so strong that even in the 20th century, modernism—apart from a few exceptions—could do little to challenge it, at least in Europe and the Americas.

17.21 **Prince of Wales Museum, Mumbai**

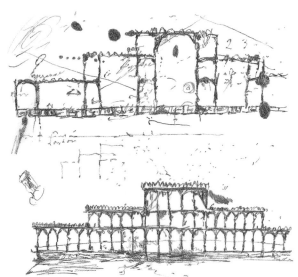

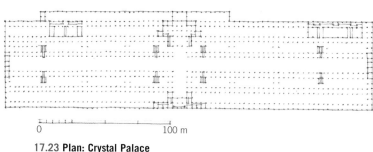

17.23 Plan: Crystal Palace

0   100 m

17.22 Sir Joseph Paxton's sketch for the Crystal Palace, London

World Fairs

The first industrial exhibition was held in France in 1801 to search for buyers of products during an economic depression that followed the French Revolution. The success of such fairs led Henry Cole (1808–82), a leading advocate of industrial design and well-known through his *Journal of Design and Manufactures* (1849–52), to argue that what was needed was not a national exhibition but a large international one that would showcase England's unique position in the global economy. The fair he organized was held in 1851 and took place in a building that came to be called the Crystal Palace.

The Crystal Palace was designed and engineered by Sir Joseph Paxton, an innovator of steel and glass greenhouses. Unlike Henri Labrouste's Bibliothèque St.-Geneviève, with its custom- detailed iron elements, or St. Pancras railroad station, with its massive beams, the Crystal Palace was composed of thin, lightweight elements that were mass-produced and assembled on site. Tension wires kept the structure from falling over. The effect was of a building that seemed almost to be woven; compression and tension forces were made visible as no other building had ever done before. Paxton also understood that the structure had to be inspiring and so designed its central element in the form of a long nave filled with exhibits, trees, and gardens. On display were machines and mass-produced products of all types. The colonies and distant lands were

also represented—but by their handcrafted products and raw materials. The contrast between the two reflected the intellectual mindset of the time. The industrial bosses marveled at the engineering and mass production; the Arts and Crafts enthusiasts, however, pointed to the colonial products as evidence of what was lost to England.

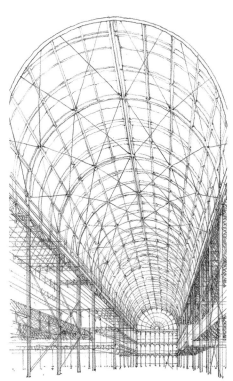

17.24 Interior: Crystal Palace

The Crystal Palace did have its critics, such as John Ruskin, who decried the building and its contents as representing the superficiality of modern culture. Nonetheless, no one had ever seen such a spectacle, and the fair was a phenomenal success: six million people visited in the six short months the exhibition was open. The fair's unprecedented triumph set the stage for a seemingly endless series of repeats: the Great Industrial Exhibition in Dublin (1853), the New York Crystal Palace (1853), the Palais de l'Industrie (1855), the International Exhibition of London (1862), the Dublin International Exhibition (1865), and London's Colonial and Indian Exhibition (1886). There were still others: the international exhibitions in Paris in 1855, 1867, 1878, 1889, and 1900; the Centennial Exhibition in Philadelphia (1876); the World's Columbian Exposition in Chicago (1893); and the World's Exposition at Melbourne, Australia (1880). There were also exhibitions held in the colonies and in non-European countries: in India (1883, 1883); in South Africa (1887, 1893); in Jamaica (1891); and in Guatemala (1897). A cultural history of these exhibitions would map out the core topics of 19th-century modernity, including the mass production of space and goods, the spectacle of display, the rituals of consumption, and the relationship between capital, nationalism, imperialism, and entertainment.

17.25 Galleria Vittorio Emanuele II, Milan

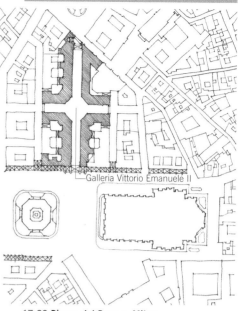

Galleria Vittorio Emanuele II

17.26 Piazza del Duomo, Milan

The *Passage*

Besides train stations and industrial fairs, the building type that best epitomizes the Industrial Revolution and its new culture of mass consumption was the shopping gallery. These were places where one could see firsthand not only the wealth of the global marketplace but also the use of new building materials: metal and glass. At the beginning of the 19th century, most shops differed very little from those of medieval times—a window or counter faced the street, with a small enclosure where business could be transacted. The fall in the price of glass made large shop windows possible, and they soon appeared at the end of the 1820s in London, Paris, and New York. In Paris, shopping streets—called *galeries* or *passages*—were soon designed with rows of shops under a single glazed roof. By the end of the 19th century, *passages* or their equivalents could be found in most European cities. At first they were on a single floor, but soon they were built on two or more levels. They provided security for shop owners as well as convenience for shoppers: most 19th-century cities were noisy and chaotic, and the streets unpaved. *Passages* offered protected enclaves for bourgeois patrons.

Marking the zenith of this building type was the extravagant Galleria Vittorio Emanuele II in Milan, a building that became a symbol of the young nation. Its entrance was located facing the piazza in front of the Duomo, the facade of which had only been finished in 1806. The planning of the piazza had been stalled for decades, but it was revived with the unification of Italy in 1859. Almost immediately the designing of the Galleria was put into motion, and when it opened in 1867, it was seen as an engineering and urban marvel.

The four wings of the building, meeting at a great, glassed dome, is completely regular on the interior, but it dovetails with the older existing structures around it. The building has seven floors, not including the cellar, with a network of concealed intersecting supports that allow for a flexible use of space. Staircases are located at the rear and are accessible through courtyards so as not to disturb the visual unity of the facades. The main staircases are located at the reentrant angles of the crossings. The third floor is reserved for club rooms, offices, and studios, while the uppermost floors are residential. More than just a shopping arcade, this building is an urban entity in itself and one of the boldest experiments in integrating the commercial and the private at that time.

17.27 Friedrichstrassenpassage, Berlin

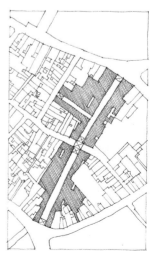

17.28 Galeries St. Hubert, Brussels

17.29 Interior of a Victorian-era house

Victorian Domestic Architecture

In France, state-supported architecture created an environment in which civic professionalism could flourish as practically nowhere else in Europe. In residential architecture, however, there was little innovation, except in the creation of urban apartments, until very late in the 19th century. In England, where civic architecture was not regulated by the state, architects turned to residential buildings as the primary way to enter the profession. The result was a rapid development of residential architectural thinking. The same was true in the United States, which is why much of the history of modern residential design focuses on these two places.

In the early decades of the Victorian era, the Renaissance was the preferred design model, especially since it had become, by the 1860s, associated with the ideals of humanism, grace, and aesthetic contemplation. A later generation would see the Renaissance's Italianate buildings as cluttered and spindly. For the Victorian architect, the value of these buildings lay not so much in their external appearance, as in their plans that offered flexible ways of organizing complex social and familial activities while providing coherence, ideologically and philosophically, to the ideals of the bourgeois family. The need for comfort also played a part. The Georgian architecture of the preceding generation was by way of comparison stiff and formal. In the 1880s, the English middle class, having

grown in wealth and sophistication, was at the height of its prosperity and financially able to provide a higher degree of personal comfort for themselves and their families. Due to the positive economic situation and the stable internal politics, the descendants of the Victorian era were noticeably less dogmatic than their parents. They preferred the intimate to the public scale. Chunky heavyweight furniture went out of fashion, and practical, lightweight furniture took

its place. Although this new generation may have broken with the past, in terms of technology it was noticeably critical and looked to the emerging rationalism of its age with a certain suspicion.

This generation was not one of ideological purists, even though it was the first English generation to be fully engaged in matters of social and political reform. A great emphasis was placed on education, and a tremendous number of schools were built in the latter part of the century. Though morality was strongly emphasized, religion itself was downplayed or replaced by a preference for spiritualism—or absented altogether. Life was not defined by abstract duties and obligations, but it was viewed as a domain of personal privacy, shielded against the ugliness and crudity of the external world. And it is for this reason that the movement produced comparatively little theoretical literature.

One of the Victorian-era styles that developed came to be known as Queen Anne. It featured pedimented gables, sash and bay windows, corner turrets, picturesque massing, and sometimes playfully conjoined elements. The brick flue of a chimney, for example, might appear to run through the bay window of an upper floor. Unlike the older Palladian prototype, it allowed for a lot of variation and site specificity.

17.30 S.R. Thompson House, a Queen Anne–style house

17.31 Plan of Central Park, New York City

Central Park

By the early 19th century, urban parks were recognized as an important indicator of a city's livability. The gardens of Versailles were opened to the public in the 1830s. But no park could measure up to New York's Central Park (1853–83). A treeless garbage dump and shantytown was converted by its designers into a park of some 2,170 square kilometers. A vast amount of earth was removed and the bedrock blasted away if it did not conform to the design. Four million cubic yards of soil and rock were then added, and four to five million trees were planted. The park, once matured, contained meadows, forests, hilltop lookouts, castles, sheep farms, skating rinks, and eateries, all accessed by curving paths with elegant bridges, underneath which was an elaborate drainage system. In 1872, its first year of operation, the park attracted ten million visitors.

It was designed by Frederick Law Olmsted (1822–1903) and Calvert Vaux (1824–95). Vaux, an English architect, came to the United States to work with Andrew Jackson Downing (1815–52), an advocate of landscape design and a famous critic of industrialization and urbanization. Olmsted, Vaux & Company, founded in 1861, also designed parks in Milwaukee, Wisconsin; Buffalo, New York; and elsewhere. In 1883, Olmsted established what is considered to be the first fulltime landscape architecture firm in the United States in Brookline, Massachusetts.

Downing, influenced by Picturesque ideas as well as the growing moralism of the early Victorian era, saw in landscapes as more than just a convenient stage used by the wealthy for setting up monuments to heroes, as it was at Stowe Gardens. Landscape, so

Downing held, strengthened character and supported the integrity of the family. Even the modest house garden, he argued, served as a civilizing purpose as it provided a protective veil around the house and helped it to blend into the landscape.

At the time, the area around most large cities in the United States had been radically deforested to make way for farms. In 1845, when Henry David Thoreau lived for two years in solitude next to Walden Pond in Massachusetts in an attempt to immerse himself in nature, the pond was one of the few areas for many miles around surrounded by trees. Downing believed that one could bring nature to the city in the form of parks, but only if they were big enough to simulate a landscape, albeit one that had been tamed and brought into balance with human needs.

17.32 Plan of Manhattan

École des Beaux-Arts

Throughout the 19th century, Europe's prime school for the study of architecture was the École des Beaux-Arts in Paris. Though intended for French citizens, it was, by the end of the 19th century, visited by students from around the world, creating a cadre of devotees who spread the school's pedagogical system and architectural style to places around the globe. Its influence could still be felt in American architectural schools well into the 1940s. The Beaux-Arts was originally founded as the Académie Royale d'Architecture in Paris in 1671 by Jean-Baptiste Colbert, finance minister of Louis XIV, who envisioned it as a place that would create the talent necessary for the king's complex building program. The French Revolution ended the royal academies, but in 1803, architectural education resumed, mainly to prepare students for state-sponsored architectural competitions. The founding of the Société Centrale des Architects in 1840 made architecture into an academic profession similar to law and medicine. The Société ended the aristocratic system of patronage; it was also the death knell of the gentleman architect (although that tradition had always been stronger in England than in France).

In the end, though the academic style of the French was much criticized by the moderns of the 20th century, the École elevated architecture into an autonomous and structured discipline. And with that autonomy came new and complex theoretical questions about the nature of architectural production. Should one use new materials like steel and glass? And if so, how? What is the relationship between the identity of a nation, its history, and its architecture? By midcentury these issues became quite divisive. On one side stood defenders of idealized classicism such as Quatremère de Quincy; on the other were the Romantics such as Henri Labrouste, with their flexible understanding of history. The conflict broke into the open with the École's appointment of Eugène-Emmanuel Viollet-le-Duc in 1863 as professor of the history of art and aesthetics. He supported the use of iron in buildings, which many French architects resisted.

His appointment was short-lived, however, and by the 1880s the school became known as a champion of an eclectic style that

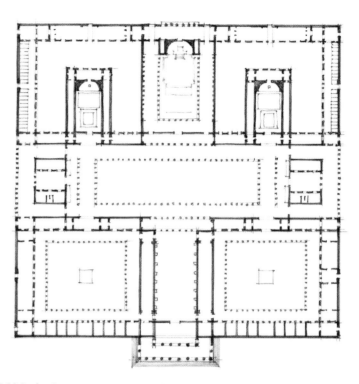

17.33 Design for a supreme court, Henri Labrouste, awarded the Prix de Rome in 1824

was Picturesque in its massing but that, nevertheless, remained committed to the tradition of clean and rectilinearly organized plans. Students who were enrolled in the school received much of their education outside of its walls. In fact, their principal learning took place in the atelier. The senior members of the field all employed students as cheap labor; in return, they educated them in the principles of design. Naturally, quality varied, as did style, and students therefore tended to choose those with whom they felt most compatible. Lectures were given at the École, yet attendance was voluntary, and no course examinations were given. Advancement depended on winning points in the monthly competitions in composition, construction, perspective, and mathematics.

For a student, the pinnacle of success was winning the annual Prix de Rome, permitting him to live and study at the Villa Medici for one year. The competition took place in three stages and lasted for

several months. Students had to develop a twelve-hour sketch (or *esquisse*) solving a design problem that had been set out by the professor of theory, leading to a more substantial presentation (or *charrette*), named for the carts in which the students carried their materials to school. The authors of the best eight were then given about three months, usually until the end of July, to develop a *projet rendu* (a "recorded project"). It was from these that a winner was chosen. Drawings made for the final stage of the competition could be very large; some measured 5 meters in length. Of particular importance to the Beaux-Arts conception of design was the ground plan. It had to be functionally clear and formally coherent, and it was usually composed of intersecting rectangles organized symmetrically along a central axis. There was a strong desire to balance buildings with courtyards and solids with voids. The arrangement of spaces—the differentiation between primary and secondary—was known as the *parti*.

Beaux-Arts plans have a set of unique characteristics:

1. Symmetry is stressed, and where there is asymmetry, it must be worked into the larger whole.
2. Axiality is important; the most important spaces must be on axis and clearly emphasized in space and proportion.
3. Cross-axes are used to distribute and organize the program.
4. There should be a clear hierarchy of the major and minor parts of the program. There should be no hidden spaces, but a gradation of importance.
5. At the center of the composition should be a great hall, the dimensions of which relate to the building's overall proportions.
6. Repeating elements should be unified to support the overall planning.
7. The relationships between open and closed spaces, and among building, courtyards, and surrounding gardens, should be resolved into an integrated whole.
8. The decorative elements should be in accordance with the program. Civic buildings would show restraint; opera houses, ebullience.

Henri Labrouste's proposed design for a supreme court from 1824 and Henri-Paul Nénot's design for an Athenaeum from 1877 exhibit similar characteristics. Nénot's project is designed around an assembly room that opens onto a grand longitudinally placed piazza that provides the outer dimension for the scheme. The assembly room is at the end of a series of halls to emphasize its importance. Secondary reading rooms are to the right and left of the main halls. The asymmetrical elements are balanced, and the gardens, which frame the entire building, are integrated into the scheme. Between the building and the boulevard is a grand plaza. The building, which is sited at a street intersection, is the culminating axial element of that street. Yet the presence of all these elements alone does not necessarily qualify the building as an example of Beaux-Arts. The design for the U.S. Capitol by Charles Bulfinch (1793), for example, is Neoclassical but has an asymmetrical interior with an oval space rather awkwardly lodged between the rotunda and the Senate chamber. From the perspective of a Beaux-Arts architect, this would be unacceptable.

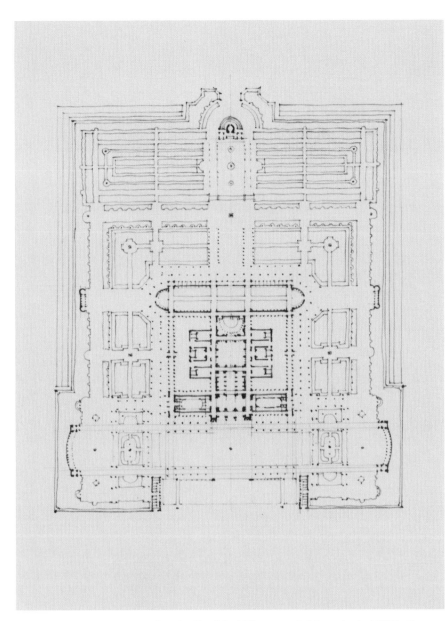

17.34 Athenaeum for a capital city, Henri-Paul Nénot, awarded first prize in 1877 by the École des Beaux-Arts in a competition for assembly rooms, a library, and a greenhouse.

Paris and Georges-Eugène Haussmann

In France, following a period of political
unrest, a plebiscite was held in 1852
that gave supreme power, with the title of
emperor, to Napoleon III (1808–73). He
promptly canceled the independence of
Parliament and rolled back advancements
that had been made in the name of universal
suffrage, free press, and education. Public
institutions were strictly supervised, the
teaching of philosophy in high schools
was suppressed, and the power of the
government was increased. The nation that
had been created in the name of the great
ideals of liberty, equality, and fraternity
had become, for all practical purposes, a
dictatorship.

Initially, the fortunes of France seemed
restored. The country emerged victorious
in the Crimean War (1854–56) and then
went on to build the Suez Canal (1854–69).
Napoleon III was eager to translate these
successes into architectural form and even
more than that, to transform Paris into the
leading capital of the world. For this he
turned to Georges-Eugène Haussmann
(1809–91), whose vision for Paris, like
Napoleon III's, was unmistakably big. Unlike
earlier urban design approaches in Rome
and elsewhere that used boulevards in
relationship to royal palaces or churches,
Haussmann's new streets were laid out
according to pragmatic and economic
considerations. They destroyed large parts
of medieval Paris, displacing thousands of
inhabitants, mainly from the lower classes.
Never before in the recent history had such a
large part of a city been leveled and rebuilt.

A typical plan would show a section of
the city overlaid by the new proposed streets
cutting through the dense old fabric. Though
there was some attempt to integrate the new
streets with the old, little was spared. The
new streets were lined with apartments and
provided with sewage pipes and gas lines. To
forestall conflagrations, the use of stone for
buildings, once the privilege of the rich, was
now used throughout the new parts of the
city. Haussmann's Paris would become the
model for cities around the world, such as
Buenos Aires, Cairo, Rome, and Saigon.

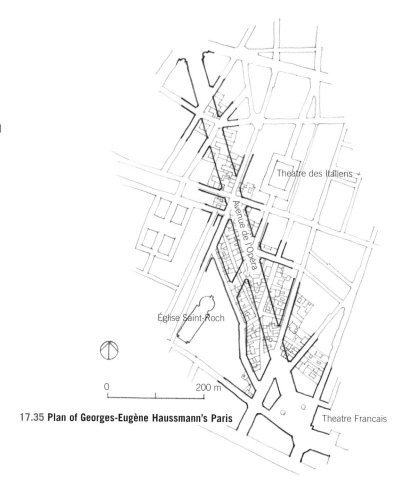

17.35 Plan of Georges-Eugène Haussmann's Paris

17.36 Street view: Georges-Eugène Haussmann's Paris

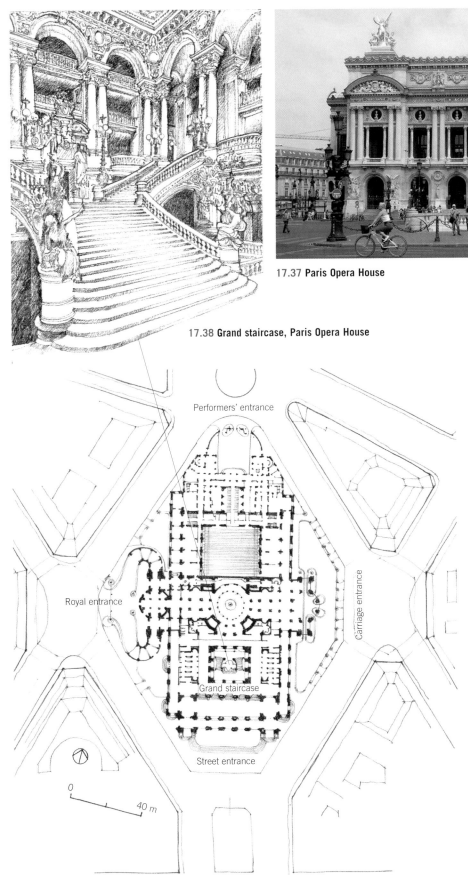

17.37 Paris Opera House

17.38 Grand staircase, Paris Opera House

Performers' entrance

Royal entrance

Carriage entrance

Grand staircase

Street entrance

0

40 m

17.39 Ground-floor plan: Paris Opera House

One of the centerpieces of the new Paris was the Opera House (1861–75), set at the intersection of several radiating streets. It was designed by Charles Garnier (1825–98), a young architect who was only thirty-six years old when he won the competition for its design. Earlier, he had won the Prix de Rome, demonstrating that, in France at least, even a workingman's son could gain access to the new professional class. Garnier's design blends the double columnar colonnade from the Louvre with elements from Michelangelo's facade on the Campidoglio, blending the royal symbolism that would have appealed to Napoleon III with the republican symbolism of Michelangelo's work. The front, when taken as a whole, could also be seen as a very wide triumphal arch. In this way, the building successfully negotiated the complex political situation in which it was situated without referring to Rome or Greece in any direct way. Like the London Law Courts, this building had multiple programs and circulation systems. The impressive front entrance was for the public arriving on foot. Those arriving by coach entered on the right side; performers and members of the opera administration entered at the rear. There was a special side entrance for the emperor, to which he could roll up in his coach and go directly indoors. Structurally the building is of steel, but the steel is rendered invisible by stone and brick. The staircase that lies between the entrance narthex and the theater is itself a three-dimensional theater intended to allow opera goers to see and be seen, the encounters themselves constituting an elaborate social ritual.

Colonial Bombay

In the first half of the 19th century, British India was administered by the British East India Company but regulated by the Crown and parliamentary policy. At this time English colonial ideology attempted to establish its right to rule by appealing to the "eternal laws" of institutions that it claimed could be derived from those of Greece and Rome. In May 1857, a widespread revolt broke out in almost all parts of British-ruled India. After a year, the revolutionaries were overcome; there was great loss of life on both sides. The revolt engendered many changes. Politically, India was transferred to the Crown: the British East India Company was dissolved, and a viceroy was established at the head of the Indian government. On the ground, the English used this opportunity to tighten their grip on India. Weak states were annexed, the Mughal emperor, nominally the ruler, was deposed, and old cities like Lucknow that had supported the revolutionaries were drastically rebuilt to ensure that British cantonments and forts could be defended with clear lines of sight.

The psychological trauma of 1857 was long lasting. For the Indians, the failed revolt initiated a long period of quiescence—an acceptance of English overlordship that would help transform large swaths of Indian urban populations into English-speaking urban elites, called babus, who worked hard to learn English and to internalize the culture and manners of their colonizers. Paradoxically, it was one of these babus who imagined a paradigm-shifting concept of resistance through nonviolence that triggered the process toward independence. For the English, who still had visions of establishing an empire that would last in perpetuity—and one that was both just and profitable—1857 brought home the central contradiction of imperialism in the age of the Enlightenment. Its "civilizing mission" had to be justified yet again, but this time, all lingering romantic ideals of a submissive and contented native population had dissipated.

Bombay (now Mumbai) emerged as British India's primary port, especially after the opening of the Suez Canal in 1869. The North's blockade of Southern cotton during the U.S. Civil War (1861–65) suddenly turned Mumbai into the world's prime exporter of

17.40 **Government Secretariat, Mumbai**

Indian cotton. New wealth made for new civic buildings. For the most, colonial architects continued to believe that the English national style of architecture was still the appropriate style for the buildings of British India, and in Victorian England, in the wake of Pugin's critiques, Gothic Revival was championed as the special preserve of Great Britain and its Christian culture. All of Mumbai's major civic structures were therefore Victorian Gothic in style: St. Clair Wilkins' Secretariat (1867–74) and his Public Works Offices (1869–72) were followed by John Begg's Post and Telegraph Offices (1871–74), and finally by the Law Courts (1871–78) by Colonel J. A. Fuller. Sir Gilbert Scott designed University Hall (1869–74) with a semicircular apse and a rose window in the French decorative style of the 15th century. His nearby library was completed with a 80 meter high clock tower (1878) modeled after Giotto's campanile

in Florence. With high-pitched roofs, crenellations, towers, dormers and Venetian arches, these buildings all assembled in a row defined Mumbai's image as the most distinguished colonial outpost.

The most spectacular of the Gothic Revival buildings was F. W. Stevens' Victoria Terminus (1878–87). The design derives from Gilbert Scott's St. Pancras Station in London, although with its fanciful Gothic detailing, polychromatic stone, decorative tile, marble, and stained glass, it exudes a certain non-English exuberance and excess—symptomatic, perhaps, of the growing English interest in Indian ornamental details. The largest British building in India at that time, it was a success with the English public and immediately became the iconic image of the city's ascendance as a center of import and export.

17.41 **Victoria Terminus, Mumbai**

The Chettinad Mansions

After the fall of the Cholas in the 14th century, the Chettiars, originally gem dealers, ship chandlers, and salt merchants in the Chola Empire, settled in about seventy-five villages around a temple near present-day Karaikudi in south-central India, in an area called Chettinad. They were among the first local communities to befriend the new English traders, and in the late 19th century they spread into Southeast Asia—particularly into Burma, Malaysia, Indonesia, and Ceylon—becoming wealthy moneylenders and diamond merchants and often working as official agents of the British East India Company. After World War II, when the British withdrew from India, the Chettiars were deported in large numbers from the newly independent countries of Southeast Asia, and they either returned to India or, in many cases, settled in the United Kingdom. Already in the late 19th and early 20th centuries, the Chettiars repatriated significant sums of money to their homestead villages, resulting in the construction of thousands of mansions. Designed to look European on the outside, they were on the interior distinctly more local, with a touch of the Indonesian in feel and design. The exteriors of the typically two-story structures were often Italianate in style, with columns and entablatures in painted stucco on brick. Inside there was usually a long *impluvium*-styled courtyard with columns made of Burmese teak, polished or lacquered in black or blue. Some columns were of Italian marble. The interior spaces was dominated by a high-pitched roof that dramatically sloped into the central courtyard.

17.42 **Courtyard, Chettinad house, Tamil, India**

17.43 **A Chettinad mansion**

17.44 Trinity Church, Boston

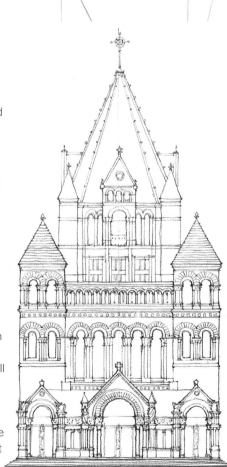

17.45 Plan: Trinity Church

0   20 m

Henry Hobson Richardson

By the late 1830s, the Greek Revival had become the adopted style of the United States, and it remained so up to the Civil War. The simplicity, ideological coherence, and ease with which its forms could be copied in brick and wood by local carpenters contributed greatly to its success. It had little competition from the Gothic style, which in the United States, unlike in Europe, had few major representatives. The result was a fluid movement from the Greek Revival to a French-derived style known as Second Empire, whose compositional emphasis was on vertical pavilions and classically derived ornamentation. It remained an important subcurrent well until the advent of modernism. In the 1880s and 1890s, a group of architects began to chart their own way, however, bringing out latent ideas of the Picturesque while trying to match this aesthetic with the needs of rising the mercantile class. These architects were Frank Furness in Philadelphia, Louis Sullivan in Chicago, and Ralph Adam Cram and Henry Hobson Richardson in Boston. All developed very distinctive approaches. Furness brought many of Viollet-le-Duc's ideas about integrating iron into design to the United States. Sullivan stressed bold simplicity combined with rich ornamentation in his buildings. Cram, who built several noted churches and schools, championed a neo-medieval style. Of them all, it was Richardson's work from the late 1870s to the mid-1890s that came to be seen by many as a style unto its own.

When Richardson (1838-1886) was young he intended to become a civil engineer, but he switched to architecture while studying at Harvard. In 1859, he began to study at the École des Beaux-Arts and remained in Paris for five years. Because of his Parisian training, Richardson was well suited to serve the needs of the rising class of new businessmen who wanted to see their success endorsed by the currently fashionable style of cosmopolitan Paris. But by the 1870s, Richardson was drawn increasingly to the English medieval style and to the Picturesque, attempting to synthesize their disparate and even contradictory aspects. Richardson's plans, for example, maintain the clarity typical of the Beaux-Arts, while his attention to the tactility and color of the building's stone surface evoke a tactility more in line with Queen Anne style and Ruskinian Gothic.

In 1872, Richardson achieved national prominence by being selected to build Trinity Church in Boston. It was designed on a triangular site in a soft pink limestone accented by dark brown stones for the columns, entablatures, and cornices. Though a small building, the generously scaled windows of the facade, compared to the small windows of the tower, make the composition seem both intimate and dynamic. Trinity Church's porch, facade, and crossing tower step back in a clear volumetric hierarchy. The porch, added after the building was built, but to Richardson's specifications, was modeled loosely on the Church of St. Trophime in

17.46 Porch, Trinity Church

17.47 Winn Memorial Public Library, Woburn, Massachusetts

17.48 Capitals, Winn Memorial Public Library

Arles, France, whereas the tower, very wide and across the entire width of the nave, was modeled on French and Spanish medieval buildings, including the 12th-century tower of the Cathedral of Salamanca in Spain. Though the building's style, in its massing and detailing, is neo-Romanesque, its plan is a Latin cross, with an apse at the eastern end. The focus of the church is the tall and airy crossing of the interior, which is one of the best-preserved examples of the Arts and Crafts style, consciously infused

here with a neo-Byzantine element. A huge candelabra originally hung from the center of the crossing. The interior, though relatively dark, is permeated by the muted light of stained glass windows in red, blue, and brown tones that washes against the walls' golden surfaces. Overall, building is an excellent example of a blend between the neo-Romanesque and the Arts and Crafts movement.

Richardson was fortunate that his mature career coincided with the rise of the American public library movement. The flowering of public education and the spread of interest in cultural developments in England and the United States led to the creation of many towns' lending libraries. It was a highly successful experiment in making the printed word accessible to a general audience—a unique idea in the world at the time. Richardson's libraries have a loose exterior picturesqueness meant to contrast with the clarity of the plan, as, for example, at the Winn Memorial Public Library in Woburn, Massachusetts (1876–79).

The plan is organized around a barrel-vaulted longitudinal library space with book-lined alcoves along the sides. It is adjoined by a transeptlike reading room at the head of which is a picture gallery and an octagonal museum. The building is entered from the side along a tall tower with Gothic-style tracery in its upper ranges. For the walls, Richardson, meticulous in his choice of materials, ordered red sandstone from a quarry in Massachusetts. The column bases and horizontal bands are of a cream-colored sandstone from Ohio, all set on a granite base. For the ornamental carvings of the capitals and corbels, Richardson brought in a Welsh sculptor.

17.49 Plan: Winn Memorial Public Library

17.50 Sultan Hassan, Al-Rafa'i, and Mahmoud Pasha Mosques, Cairo

17.51 Plan of Cairo, ca. 1874

0   1 km

Al-Rifa'i Mosque

Though the history of non-European modernism is generally thought to begin early in the 20th century with the spread of Art Deco (along Mumbai's Marine Drive, for instance), it actually commences in the second half of the 19th century, often still under the shadow of colonialism. This was true for Egypt, one of the first Arab countries to attempt to reinvent itself by means of modern ideas. Egypt, which had been under Ottoman rule, was able, under Muhammad 'Ali (1769–1849), to proclaim its nominal independence. Sa'id Pasha (r. 1854–63), Muhammad 'Ali's son and third successor, and especially Isma'il Pasha (r. 1863–79), his grandson, were the architects of Egypt's search for an image that was both modern and Egyptian. Isma'il was fascinated by French culture, so much so that he adopted French manners in his personal life and encouraged his entourage to follow suit. He was also an impatient modernizer who wanted to turn Egypt into an extension of Europe, despite adverse economic circumstances. The country's foreign debt, however, spun out of control. Bankruptcy was declared in 1879, leading to its occupation by the British in 1882.

Isma'il's passion for Europeanization was exemplified by his grand urban projects in Cairo, inspired by his visit to the Exposition Universelle in Paris in 1867. Back in Cairo, he tried to turn his own capital into another Paris, complete with wide, straight avenues planted with trees, palaces, planned gardens, pavilions, and all the amenities of modern city life, such as theaters, cafés, and even an opera house. He commissioned his minister of public works, 'Ali Pasha Mubarak, a member of the academic mission of 1844–49 to France and one of the most influential figures in modern Egyptian history, to draw up the city's new master plan.

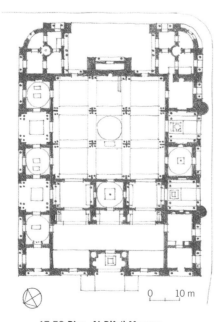

17.52 Plan: Al-Rifa'i Mosque

0   10 m

With the exception of two boulevards that cut across the old city's dense fabric and required the razing of many medieval structures, the new city extended westward toward the Nile along a north-south axis, with streets radiating from central squares to form star patterns à la Haussmann. This Parisian-style Cairo was built in haste to impress the European monarchs who had been invited to Egypt for the inauguration of the Suez Canal in 1869—among them Empress Eugénie, wife of Napoleon III.

The style that was developed during this period is known as neo-Mamluk style as it attempted to relate contemporary Egyptian architecture to a glorious phase of its history. One of the prime examples, as studied by Nasser Rabbat, the noted scholar of Islamic history, is al-Rifa'i Mosque, constructed in two stages, between 1869 and 1880, and 1906 and 1911. The first stage was designed and supervised by the Egyptian architect Hussein Fahmi, the second by the Austro-Hungarian Max Herz, with others hired as consultants and interior designers. The plan is clearly influenced by Beaux-Arts ideas: axiality, the rationalization of the spaces, and the interlocking of solids and voids. The decoration, however, is modeled on 13th-century Mamluk buildings. This building and Trinity Church in Boston are in many respects parallel—Beaux-Arts in plan, but in decorative detail and finish, purposefully historicist.

Arts and Crafts Movement

In England, the hopefulness of the 1870s began to evaporate by the end of the century. The emergence of Germany and the United States as political and economical rivals, the fiasco of the Boer wars, the stepped-up campaign for women's suffrage, and the continual drumbeat of workers' strikes and unrest had begun to sap the self-confidence and amiability of English society. The gulf between those clamoring for socialist reform and those arguing for a stronger imperial policy was creating bitter tensions. It was in this context that a movement sprang up that defined a middle ground between socialism and capitalism. Known as the Arts and Crafts movement, it appealed to individuality, novelty, and good taste, but it refined these ideals into a social and philosophical position that revolved around the critique of what many saw as the ethical vacuum at the center of England's mercantile culture. The concern of the Arts and Crafts was not on the end product, and certainly not on efficiency, but on the processes shaping the design itself: there had to be an intimate connection between design and production. This position was to have significant influence on later modernists, such as Henry van de Velde, Hermann Muthesius, Adolf Loos, and Walter Gropius.

The Arts and Crafts artists were, for the most part, resistant to making connections to industry, as they were frustrated by what they perceived to be the drift toward mechanization. Perfection of finish, symmetry, and precision were suspect, since they represented the denial of the human element. But just because the movement critiqued capitalism and industrialism did not mean it was a friend of the socialists, who for their part had little regard for the Arts and Crafts movement; their weapons were the trade unions, not guilds of bookbinders and furniture makers. In reality, the Arts and Crafts appealed more to the disenfranchised bourgeoisie, social utopians, and upper-class aesthetes than to members of the working class. In this it was, in essence, an extension of Victorian ideals that tried to educate the middle class on questions of taste. John Ruskin, for example, created a museum in Sheffield, England, that contained carefully assembled objects intended for the edification of local laborers and schoolchildren; it displayed paintings, sculptures, prints, and casts.

17.53 William Morris textile design

The Arts and Crafts movement became quite widespread, reaching Belgium, France, Germany, the United States, and even some of the English colonies, particularly India. Some of the Arts and Crafts enthusiasts, like John Lockwood Kipling (father of the author Rudyard Kipling), even moved to India to dedicate themselves to the cause of preserving and promoting Indian crafts. Kipling promoted a new journal on Indian crafts and even started a school to train young craftsmen.

William Morris and William R. Lethaby

When William Morris (1834–96) gave his first public lecture on "The Decorative Arts to the Trades Guild of Learning" in 1877, he was already known as a poet and decorator. That year he had already opened showrooms in London that displayed work from his business, known as the Firm. From it sprang the Arts and Crafts Exhibition Society (the source of the movement's name), launched in 1893 with a vigorous campaign of publication and exhibitions devoted to the applied arts. Louis Comfort Tiffany, famous for his lamps, was an admirer of Morris, as was Gustav Stickley, famous for his furniture. For these artists, the simple and the luxurious were not antithetical. Both sprang from the idea of the craftsman as

artist and from the belief in individualism and individual commitment, infused not the abstract deism of the Enlightenment, but an ethos of religiosity with strong leanings toward Christian simplicity and medieval quietude. Morris, who had initially planned to become a priest, was just as much a medievalist as a socialist.

Among the architects most closely associated with the Arts and Crafts were William R. Lethaby (1857–1931), Charles Francis Annesley Voysey (1857–1941), and, in the United States, the firm of Greene & Greene. Lethaby, who began his career working for Morris & Company, designed several houses, but it is his Brockhampton Church (1901–2) in Herefordshire, England, that is regarded as an important example of Arts and Crafts style. It is built of unassuming walls of red sandstone punctuated by a number of small, variously scaled windows. It is roofed with a steeply pitched concrete roof covered on the exterior with thatch—an unusual combination meant to protect the building against fire without compromising the overall effect. The tower was left without a steeple to augment the building's primitivism. (The steeple, after all, was a 16th-century invention.) And the entrance porch has a wooden bell tower that creates a perception of the building as a rebuilt "ruin."

17.54 Mubarak Mahal, Jaipur, India

17.55 **National Art Gallery, Government Museum of Chennai, India (formerly the Victoria Technical Institute Building)**

Indo-Saracenic Style

Late in the 19th century, Gothic Revival architecture, with its overt message of English nationalism, seemed increasingly out of place in India. It was now clear to the English that India had an architectural history that was as deep as it was complicated. With scholars now studying Indian art and architecture, a new generation of architects began to experiment with a style that came to be known as Indo-Saracenic, which adapted the architectural vocabulary of Islamic or "Saracenic" architecture to buildings such as town halls, libraries, and schools. The Indo-Saracenic paralleled the attempt in Egypt to create a neo-Mamluk style. Part of the Indo-Saracenic ideal was lodged in the colonial stereotype of the putative "decline" of Indian civilization. The English claimed that they had succeeded in conquering India because Indian civilization had begun to decay. One of the chief proponents of this idea was James Fergusson, the first historian of Indian architecture. Without any understanding of the functional or conceptual basis of Indian architecture, Fergusson classified and evaluated Indian buildings based on their formal properties and proposed that Indian architecture periodically went into decline and that it had thus to be revived by contact with foreigners.

For the Arts and Crafts high priest John Ruskin, the crucial index of decline could be mapped by differentiating between Indian craft and Indian art. While craftsmen, working in their native "innocence," were seen as a positive example for the English, the Indian arts had, in his opinion, begun a downswing accompanied by a downslide in morality. This decline, according to Ruskin, accounted for the "worse than bestial" acts that Indian revolutionaries had supposedly been responsible for in the violence of 1857. Yet at the same time, he feared that the decline in Indian crafts might be due to the corrupting influence of Europeans. His prescription was to reeducate native craftsmen in European aesthetics while preserving and reviving their craft traditions. European art with Indian craft in the service of modern colonial buildings was, therefore, the 19th-century recipe for a "modern" Indian architecture.

One of the most celebrated attempted translations of Arts and Crafts ideals into the practice of architecture in India was undertaken by Colonel Swinton Jacobs. An engineer by training, Jacobs worked in the "princely state" of Jaipur, in Rajasthan, for more than forty years, from 1867 to 1912. (Princely states were nominally independent but governed by local rulers who were subject to the oversight of the British Empire.) Jacobs believed that by training draftsmen to accurately copy full-size details from examples of Indian architectural history, they would come to appreciate the intrinsic quality of their own culture. His *Jeypore Portfolio of Architectural Details* (1890) was a collection of individual folio sheets that a craftsman could look at and study. All the examples were, however, drawn from Islamic architecture.

A building often attributed to Jacobs but probably designed by one of his personally trained disciples, Lala Chiman Lal, is the Mubarak Mahal (1899), located within the palace compound of Jaipur. A ceremonial reception hall, the Mubarak Mahal was also a museum comprising a two-story cubic volume with projecting porches. It is a case study in Indo-Saracenic ornamentation: on the upper story, a fanciful filigree of carefully executed embellishment outlines the cantilevered balcony that runs around the entire perimeter of the structure, and on the lower story individual bays, conceived as display cases, self-consciously stage distinct ornamental details. The entire program, layout, and proportions and divisions of the structure—in short, its aesthetic—derived from the European tradition. Only in its details was it Indian.

17.56 Robert F. Chisolm's winning entry for the Bombay Municipal Hall

17.57 Jaipur Town Hall, India

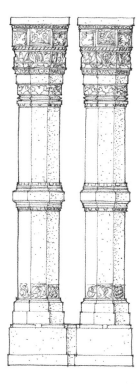

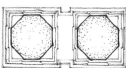

17.58 Sample drawing from the *Jeypore Portfolio of Architectural Details*

Robert F. Chisolm belonged to the generation of professional architects who believed more in exploring their professional freedom than in following designs from ideological strictures. It was this search that led him inevitably to eclecticism. His unbuilt design for the Bombay Municipal Hall competition, for example, called for a three-story volume with a large central dome that was based on the Taj Mahal. Chisolm widened the dome at its base with tall arched openings that necessitated an internal structural system made of steel. Smaller domes on octagonal bases terminated the corners of the main cubic volume. The corners were further emphasized by the suggestion of turrets created by faceting the edges, with a string of moldings close to the ground that flare out slightly at the base, as, for instance, in the Hindu Victory Tower at Chittorgarh. The overall conception of the massing is reminiscent of Henry Hobson Richardson's Trinity Church in Boston. The centerpiece of the elevation changes at every level: a porch supported by paired columns on the ground floor surmounted by a narrow balcony on the second floor and finished with a wide,

double-height arch surmounted by a Bengal-style drooping roof integrated into the cornice line. No part of the design was left untouched by careful attention to detail.

Arts and Crafts enthusiasts and the Indo-Saracenics did not make much of an impression on the local Indian maharajas in their personal commissions. Sawai Ram Singh (r. 1835–80) brazenly continued to have his workmen construct imitation, hybridized, European-style buildings, such as the town hall in Jaipur. Singh was a wily character. He had used the typical colonial misrecognition of his relationship with his feudatories to his advantage, making his feudatories, who usually served as checks on his authority, submissive to him on the basis of the representation that he had among his English backers. For maharajas who, like the babus, had no paternalistic project in mind, the identifiable style of power was European.

17.59 Isaac Bell House, Newport, Rhode Island

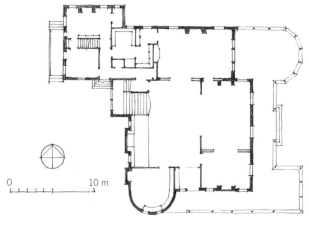

17.60 First floor plan: Isaac Bell House

Shingle Style

Unique to the United States was the development of what is now called the Shingle Style. It developed parallel to the Arts and Crafts movement but was more closely allied with Queen Anne style. Houses designed in this manner—often as summer homes for the New England elite—show an inventiveness in plan, with elements not merely touching each other but seeming to pass through each other or overlap. The firm that developed this style more than any other was McKim, Mead & White (founded 1879), which eventually became one of the leading design firms in the United States.

William Rutherford Mead (1846–1928), who had an affinity for the Renaissance, and Stanford White (1853–1906) had little formal training, but they worked their way up as apprentices. Charles Follen McKim (1867–70), by contrast, had studied at the École des Beaux-Arts. Between the three they produced a style of architecture that brought out the best in each of them. In their Shingle Style homes, they took the rooms of the servants' quarters out from under the attic and placed them in a compact block or wing against which the more openly designed living rooms of the first floor were contrasted. This can be seen in the Isaac Bell House in Newport, Rhode Island (1882–83), where the staircase was situated in a large room that served as a circulation center and as a spatial extension of the neighboring study and drawing rooms. This makes it different from the more

controlled and boxy spaces of Arts and Crafts houses. Even though it was common to raise the first floor above the level of the ground, the use of porches made the house appear as if it were resting on an elevated terrace, which was protected from the sun and rain by generously proportioned overhangs and roofs. The vertical surfaces of the houses were completely clad in wooden shingles; a variety of patterns were used to differentiate certain elements, like the gable front. The interior surfaces were usually covered with dark wooden paneling in combination with stucco, usually wallpapered but sometimes left plain.

By was of contrast, the Watts Sherman House (1874) in Newport, Rhode Island, designed by Henry Hobson Richardson, is closer to the Queen Anne and the Arts and

Crafts styles. The rooms are arranged in a more formal way and less open to the hall, and the servants lived in the attic. The overall massing is much more complex than the more volumetrically simple Isaac Bell House.

The Shingle Style began to fade in the late 1890s, by which time U.S. architects who had trained in Paris at the École des Beaux-Arts were returning home with a notion of architectural space that did not conform to the style's relaxed openness. The new preoccupation with monumentality in the United States met the expectations of the more class-conscious elite and ultimately put an end to Arts and Crafts and its related aesthetic phenomena. McKim, Mead & White played a dominant role in this shift, becoming the leading representative in the United States of the Beaux-Arts Neoclassical style.

17.61 First floor plan: Watts Sherman House, Newport, Rhode Island

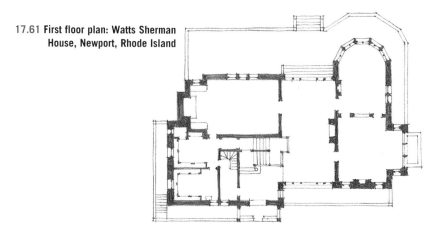

17.62 Gamble House, Pasadena, California

Arts and Crafts in California

In California, Arts and Crafts underwent its most vigorous transformation and its longest period of vibrancy. There it fused with Spanish-Mexican motifs, as well as elements from the Italian Mediterranean and the Far East. Linked to its development was a public school system strongly committed to manual-arts education and in particular to the belief that the union of head and heart through handicraft yielded therapeutic benefits. Local libraries organized sketch clubs and hosted exhibitions of local craft production.

Elements from the local landscape and flora were also quite strong in the California Arts and Crafts. Whether depicting the golden poppy, the Torrey pine, the redwood, or the sublime majesty of the Yosemite Valley, California's Arts and Crafts artists extolled the state's natural beauty and were much more intimately associated with the outdoors than their counterparts in England and the northeastern United States. Many of their houses exploited the fine views and outdoor living afforded by the landscape. These Arts and Crafts houses featured a deliberate blurring of interior and exterior space through the use of decks, pergolas, porches, and terraces. The English-style medievalism in these houses gave way to an aesthetic of primitivism embodied, for example, in the writings of Jack London, author of *The Call of the Wild* (1903). London's own house in Sonoma's Valley of the Moon was a prime example of Arts and Crafts domestic architecture: redwood, timber with bark left on, huge halls, and giant fireplaces.

The Gamble House (1908–9) by Charles Sumner Greene and Henry Mather Greene in Pasadena is an excellent example of the use of Japanese motifs. The stepping-stone path across the yard, the battered retaining wall, and an airy elevated porch are all inspired by Japanese precedents. Not a single detail is left unattended—not the lamps, the furniture, or the carpets. The house rests on a broad terrace that extends the space of the living rooms outward toward the gardens and lawns. The house also was designed in relationship to the existing majestic eucalyptus trees. As was common in Arts and Crafts (although rarely achieved on this scale), furniture, built-in cabinetry, paneling, wood carvings, rugs, lighting, and leaded stained glass were all custom designed by the architects.

The plan was unusual. A hall with a staircase bisected the entire building, with the living room and den on one side and the dining room, kitchen, and guest bedroom on the other side. The principal upstairs bedrooms had sleeping porches overlooking the garden. Unlike a Shingle Style house, with its steeply pitched roofs, the roofs here are very flat and seem to float over the building. This emphasizes the horizontal layering of space, as do the shadows from the overhangs. On the interior, the heavy wooden beams were left exposed, but they were smoothed and polished to bring out the material's yellowish warmth. The ceilings are plain white in the Japanese style and stand out against the wood framing. Art Nouveau touches—such as the lamps and stained glass and rugs—add a layer of urban sophistication. The house was designed as a retirement residence for David and Mary Gamble of Cincinnati. David, a second generation member of the Procter & Gamble Company, had retired in 1895. Procter & Gamble was a leading soap manufacturer.

17.63 First floor plan: Gamble House

The Bungalow

One of the most visible manifestations of the global colonial economy was the development and spread of the bungalow. The bungalow (the word derives from the Bengali word *bangla*) was first used by the English colonists in India as a type of garden and plantation house. Most had a single ridge roof that overhung the house, creating a porch called the veranda (originally a Hindi word). The veranda served as an intermediate space where colonizer and colonized could interact. In tropical climates it was also was the most comfortable space of the house. In time, bungalows added an entrance porch, which had to be large enough to receive a carriage. The interior space was designed around a central room, with bedrooms directly off to the sides and toilets and kitchens in the back so that they could be serviced by the native staff. Servant quarters were built at a distance in the back of the garden. The colonial bungalow spread as a type all throughout the tropical colonies in the late 18th and early 19th centuries.

A symbol of the good life, the bungalow was exported back to England. It could soon be found in the United States as well, in the form of the detached, single-family residential dwelling that could be easily built on small parcels. Climate and lifestyle dictates did not allow the core properties of the colonial bungalow to be exported, but its image was variously translated as it spread. The noncolonial bungalow was usually a single-story house (though it sometimes had two floors) of modest scale, with a low overhanging roof and a porch running along its front. Many subcategories evolved. The California bungalows, which were among the earliest in the United States (dating from about 1880s onward) commonly had wood shingles, horizontal siding, or stucco exteriors, as well as brick chimneys. The so-called Chicago bungalow, which was popular between 1910 and 1940, was often made out of brick. In many cases, the bungalow was inexpensive to build and did not need an architect. Furthermore, with its compact layout, it appealed to middle-class owners who could not afford live-in servants. The walls were usually wallpapered, whereas the trim for the doors and windows was dark-stained oak.

In the 1880s, the bungalow became associated with the Arts and Crafts movement, and indeed many bungalows were built in the so-called American Craftsman Style, which was a reaction against the overdecorated aesthetic of the Victorian era. Though the Arts and Crafts emphasized the handmade over the mass-produced, and some early bungalows followed this aesthetic, the bungalow was soon nothing less than an industrialized product. In fact, by the turn of the 20th century, an entire house could be ordered through catalogues; they were then shipped by rail or boat to be assembled on-site. Doors, windows, and built-in furnishings such as bookcases, desks, or folding beds could also be purchased from such mail-order catalogues. The bungalow spread as part of the suburbanization of the American city, with whole bungalow districts appearing in many U.S. cities.

17.64 Typical bungalow floor plan

17.65 Typical block of bungalows

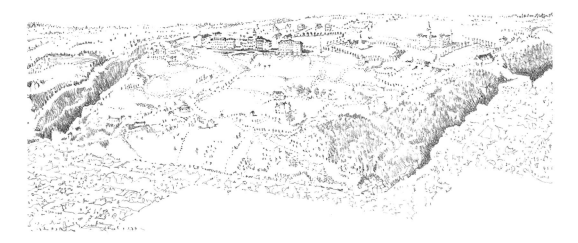

17.66 View of Ithaca, New York, in 1882, showing the early campus of Cornell University

Campus Architecture in the United States

The Land Grant Act of 1861, signed into law by President Abraham Lincoln, had a major impact on the history of U.S. education. It stipulated that each state have its own university, paid for by the sale of government land. No such educational policy had ever been attempted before, and no one could have foreseen its consequences in shaping advanced education in the United States. Despite differences from state to state, the early schools (known as land-grant schools) shared certain basic goals, including the promotion of practical education, the right of education for all social classes, and the freedom of students to choose their course of study. By the 1870s almost every state had one such university. Among the earliest were Cornell University in Ithaca, New York, and the University of California, Berkeley. By the turn of the century, dozens of private universities had also been built, and because of the rapid professionalization of the sciences in the 1880s, a new generation of technical institutions emerged. The Massachusetts Institute of Technology (MIT), founded in 1863, was among the first, but soon there were also the Illinois Institute of Technology (1890); the Carnegie Technical Institute (1900), which later became Carnegie Mellon University; and the California Polytechnic State University (1901). The net result of this combination of public, private, and technical universities was a university system unique in the world.

Architecturally, many universities at first looked to Germany, where state-sponsored institutions had large but often rather simple buildings. Students were expected to live in apartments, with relatives, or in clubs, and for this reason, German universities were located in major cities. In the United States, toward the end of the 19th century, the upper classes began to see higher education in a broader context as a maturing experience. This led to the design of campuses with sports facilities, dormitories, and a parklike atmosphere.

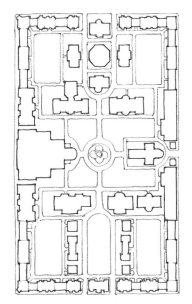

17.67 Early plan for the University of Chicago campus

Universities built in this period by the top firms in the country are still some of the most impressive accomplishments of that era. Designs came in three basic styles: Georgian, neo-Gothic, and Neoclassical. The Georgian style, leaning on the tradition of Harvard University, had individual buildings, usually raised in brick, arranged around a quad or "green," as at Cornell University. Differing from that was the Gothic style that offered an integration of study, life, and sports; examples can be found at Princeton University in New Jersey and at the University of Chicago, where there was no central quad but a loose arrangement of buildings in the landscape. The Neoclasssical was also used—as for example at Columbia University in New York City, with its centerpiece, Low Memorial Library (1903), designed by McKim, Mead & White; the University of Michigan (1904–36) by Albert Kahn; and MIT (1913–16), designed by William Welles Bosworth, with buildings arranged around a central axis and a domed library, modeled on the Pantheon, at the symbolic head of the composition. Though classical on the exterior, MIT was the largest building in the world at the time to have been built entirely of concrete.

17.68 Art Nouveau doorway in Paris

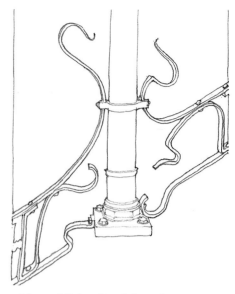

17.69 Ironwork on stairway of Maison Tassel, Brussels

Art Nouveau

By the 1890s in Europe, the supremacy of French Beaux-Arts and English Victorian styles were being challenged by architects in places that were somewhat remote from the English and French spheres of influence, such as Spain (Antoni Gaudí), Scotland (Charles Rennie Mackintosh), Holland (Hendrick Petrus Berlage), Austria (Otto Wagner and Josef Hoffman), and Germany (Peter Behrens). The state-directed architecture of France limited experimentation, but in these other countries are the sources of a movement that was to evolve into modernism. In the United States, where private commissions were more important than state-sponsored ones, the Beaux-Arts system that spread throughout by the first decade of the century had all but stopped independent developments, with the exception of the innovations introduced by Frank Lloyd Wright. It was in Belgium that a new style emerged. Known as Art Nouveau (or Jugendstil in Germany, named after the magazine *Jugend*, which initially promoted it), it built on a high-bourgeois aesthetic that had been developing since the mid-19th century. It had parallels with the Arts and Crafts movement in England, but there were important differences. Whereas the Arts and Crafts movement aimed to heal the alienation that had arisen as a consequence of industrialization, Art Nouveau stressed creativity. There were many overlaps, with not a few artists working in both camps. Art Nouveau artists, however, tended to avoid the heavy, neo-medieval look of the Arts and Crafts, preferring sinuous organic shapes and plantlike motifs. By the end of the century, Art Nouveau had drifted toward a virtuosic display of form, a complicated intermingling of materials, and an interlacing of structure and ornament. It was unabashedly expensive.

A great number of Art Nouveau artists were endowed with dual talents. Peter Behrens started out as a painter. William Blake, Dante Gabriel Rossetti, William Morris, and Aubrey Beardsley have left us poems of as great a value as their creations in the field of art. Algernon Charles Swinburne composed poems on paintings by James Whistler written on gold paper and displayed in specially designed frames. Oscar Wilde's *Salomé* became the libretto for an opera composed by Richard Strauss. Edvard Munch painted sound waves, and his paintings were once described in the leading Art Nouveau journal *Pan* as "emotional hallucinations of music and poetry."

Art Nouveau artists were also profoundly theoretical, seeking to answer questions about the nature of aesthetic production and its effect on the individual and society. Unlike previous theorists like Gottfried Semper, John Ruskin, and Eugène-Emmanuel Viollet-le-Duc, who emphasized the relationship between aesthetic and cultural production, Art Nouveau artists were intensely interested in the question of artistic creation. Walter Crane, August Endell, Hector Guimard, Henry van de Velde, and Adolf Loos all produced theoretical works in addition to their artistic creations. While the products promoted by the Arts and Crafts were by no means inexpensive, the movement carried with it spiritual and therapeutic connotations and a back-to-the-land naturalness that was ostensibly accessible to all; Art Nouveau appealed mainly to the wealthy.

That Brussels became a center for the Art Nouveau stands to reason: Belgium was the first Continental country to industrialize. It saw its proportion of world trade increase between 1840 and 1870—in particular in iron, steel, and coal—with Antwerp becoming one of the leading European ports to North and South America. By the 1870s, Belgium had its first generation of millionaires. Barcelona, Spain, where Gaudí received his main commissions, was also in an economic upswing, being one of the primary ports of the Mediterranean. This made the Art Nouveau a broader European phenomenon than the Arts and Crafts movement. It flourished in Glasgow, Vienna, Munich, Moscow, and Turin, and in the United States in New York and Chicago.

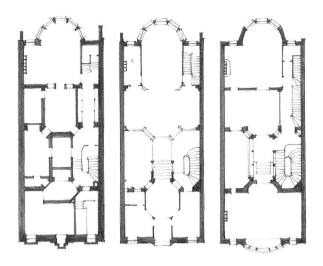

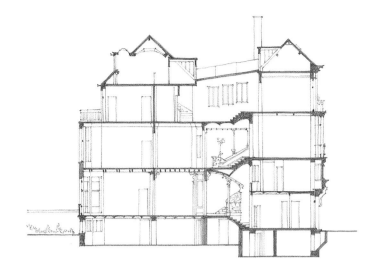

17.70 Floor plans: Maison Tassel, Brussels

17.71 Section: Maison Tassel

Maison Tassel

Though Westerners had purchased Chinese and Japanese tea sets, plates, and bowls for well over a hundred years and had tried to imitate certain Chinese building types like the garden pavilion, Art Nouveau artists were nonetheless stimulated by Japanese art, with its sinuous ornamental patterns. Indeed, the movement is named after d'Art Nouveau, the shop of Siegfried Bing, a Parisian importer of Japanese art and himself the owner of one of the important private collections of japonaiserie. In London, James Whistler was a brilliant promoter and adaptor of the Japanese style. He and others particularly admired the work of Kitagawa Utamaro, whose woodcuts were known for their curving lines and asymmetrical distribution of masses. Furthermore, the idea of coordinating a painting, its frame, its artistic effect on the room, and even the shape and proportion of the room itself, already put forward by William Morris, was reinforced by the perception of the coordinated unity of Japanese architecture. For Art Nouveau, purity of style was not important. Japanese themes could be fused with Greek, Celtic, and later, after Knossos was excavated in 1900, with Minoan motifs.

Though Art Nouveau expressed itself in the surface, it was far from superficial. In its rejection of depth and perspective and its insistence on flatness, it foreshadowed future dialogues on the validity of the representation of illusionary depth. Nature was no longer a remote system of regulating realities as it was for the Neoclassicists, but a sensuous evocation of living forms. Ornamentation was no longer a sin but the medium through which one could reach behind the static world of appearances. A door handle by Victor Horta (1861–1947) loops in and around itself like a piece of soft candy, one strand of which springs out into space to almost accidentally form a handle.

Victor Horta, active in Belgium, was probably the most influential of the Art Nouveau architects. In Maison Tassel (1892–93), Horta brought out the expressive quality of iron, which he used both inside and outside of the house in the form of ribbons that appear weightless, spiraling and twisting into space. Since the floors were supported for the most part by iron columns, rooms could open into one another and be distributed in a novel manner. Horta rejected the standard Brussels building type, with the staircase to one side of the building. Instead, the staircase, combined with a light well, is placed at the center. This allowed him to vary the elevations of the floors in the front and back, with four floors in the front along the street and three in the back, and the main rooms oriented to the center. Interpenetrating space, as well as the use of mirrors to enhance the feeling of space, make the interior seem like a world unto itself—a sanctuary from outside life.

17.72 Maison Tassel

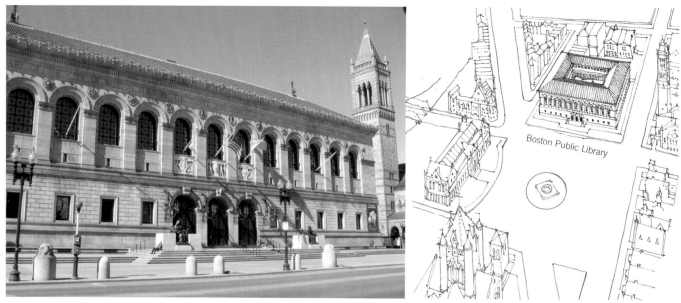

17.73 Boston Public Library

17.74 Aerial view: Copley Square, Boston

Boston Public Library

City Beautiful Movement

The economic depression of the mid-1890s forced U.S. corporations to look abroad for markets, and this helped set the stage for a rapid expansion of the U.S. economy. The architectural mood changed accordingly—from darker, heavier, Romanesque-inspired motifs such as those used by Richardson to the lighter and more ambitious motifs of the French Beaux-Arts. The turn to classicism was energized by the World's Columbian Exposition of 1893 in Chicago, which was staged to celebrate the four hundredth anniversary of Christopher Columbus's arrival in America. It championed a brand of Neoclassicism that was monumental and civic in scale. Most of the exposition buildings were of stucco and painted white—thus the nickname "the White City." Its integrated plan of buildings, parks, and walks became both a model and a corrective for the haphazard urbanism of the age. In the United States, only Washington, DC, was a properly and successfully planned city with a street and boulevard system allowing for future growth and the smooth flow of traffic.

Inspired by the exhibition, city fathers around the country began to draw up plans following some of its principles in a movement known as the City Beautiful. These cities included Cleveland, San Francisco, Chicago, Detroit, Baltimore, and St. Louis. Few plans were actually implemented in their totality, and of those, most were only partially completed. Nonetheless, at the turn of the 20th century, almost every major city in the United States had its share of City Beautiful buildings—train stations, banks, markets, town halls, and the like. Pennsylvania Station in New York City (1904–10), featured a block-long Doric columnar screen, a drive-in unloading street, a central waiting room modeled on Baths of Diocletian in Rome, and a steel-and-glass hall and circulation platform leading down to the various levels. The building was designed by McKim, Mead & White, one of the leading champions of the Beaux-Arts. Another example of their work is the Boston Public Library (1888–95), which faces Richardson's Trinity Church across Copley Square. Drawing on Henri Labrouste's Bibliothèque St.-Geneviève in Paris, its arcade, set up on a high base, has the names of famous authors etched into the spandrels. With its use of exquisite marbles and mosaics, it was one of the finest U.S. public buildings at that time. Its monumental entrance leads up to an expansive coffered, barrel-vaulted reading room, which spans the entire length of the building; its central courtyard is surrounded by an arcaded gallery in the manner of a Renaissance cloister. The library also features the thin tile vaults by the Catalan master builder Rafael Guastavino, and was thus an engineering as well as a design marvel.

17.75 Pennsylvania Station, New York City

Rise of Professionalism

Medicine and law were among the first fields to be professionalized; architecture lagged behind. Its first champions were the French. Jean-Nicolas-Louis Durand had argued that architecture should be regularized and rationalized. Benjamin Latrobe (1760–1820), a contemporary of Durand's who trained in England before going to the United States to practice took up Durand's argument, going so far as to predict that the age of the amateur gentleman architect was about to end. Latrobe wrote a letter to one of his former pupils, Robert Mills, the first professionally educated architect born in the United States, admonishing him to insist on his professional rights. The architect, like a lawyer or doctor, Latrobe wrote, works by means of a contract and has to make his objectives as clear as possible. Above all, he should do nothing gratuitously when designing for the government; he should also make sure that the drawings are clearly understood by the client. Latrobe also advised Mills to make sure his suppliers understood that only he was authorized to make payments, so that the client could not interfere by ordering arbitrary changes.

By the middle of the 19th century, the professionalization of the field was gradually winning converts, especially since the Beaux-Arts system was so successful. Unlike Neoclassicism, which was associated with colonialism, the late 19th-century Beaux-Arts style, though a European commodity, was imbued not only with the sophisticated taste of the French but also with the new principles of professionalism and modernization. It therefore became international and can be found in such diverse places as Argentina, Egypt, Mexico, and Japan. In England, the Royal Institute of British Architects (RIBA) was founded in 1834, and with it came increased attention to the architect's education, with RIBA sponsoring lectures and publications on a variety of subjects. Professionalism discouraged ad hoc, on-the-spot solutions in favor of precise architectural drawings. William Butterfield (1814–1900), who is often associated with the aesthetics of John Ruskin, is a clear demonstration of this shift. The first church he built required only nine drawings, but for the chancel of St. Mark's Dundela in Belfast (completed 1891), the contract was accompanied by about

17.76 View of an architect's office

forty drawings, including working details and fittings down to the boot scrapers. The new prerequisite for explicitness such as detailed specifications and drawings had its effect on the contractual relationship between client, architect, and craftsmen. By the middle of the 20th century, a building of any magnitude would require potentially one thousand drawings, accompanied by a detailed book of specifications.

In the United States, the American Institute of Architects (AIA) had been formed in 1836. But interrupted by the Civil War and handicapped by the immensity of the far-flung continent and the commensurate communications difficulties, architectural professionalism in the United States did not really blossom until after the World's Columbian Exposition of 1893 (also known as the Chicago World's Fair). The exposition buildings, designed on a monumental scale and integrated into a master plan, served to demonstrate what professional architects could accomplish. The architects displaying their skills at the exposition included Daniel Burnham, Richard M. Hunt, Henry van Brunt, and Charles Follen McKim—all AIA

leaders. The Tarsney Act passed by Congress that year established the requirement for limited competitions for federal commissions, with institute members advising the treasury secretary, the federal official responsible for governmental building appropriations. Though the Tarsney Act was never fully implemented, the status of the professional—as opposed to an architect working as an employee of the government—became increasingly secure. By 1895, the AIA had more than seven hundred members. In the first decade of the 20th century, Daniel Burnham's architectural firm was the world's largest and had become the model for countless later firms that utilized global business techniques. This new professional class had little patience with the midcentury battle between classical and medieval revival styles. That does not mean that Hunt, for example, who was schooled at the École des Beaux-Arts in Paris and who was a major advocate of architecture as a profession, was indifferent to style; rather, he had left the sectarian debates for a more fluid and individualist appropriation of the architectural vocabulary of the time.

European Ports

By the 1880s, we see the first globalization of the Industrial Revolution. Among the cities at the forefront of this development were Amsterdam, Hamburg, Barcelona, and Marseilles; all had become important international ports with thriving economies experiencing a vast influx of people who worked in the factories and the associated industries. In response to the need for housing their residents, these cities were also the first to benefit from new methods of urban planning. Unlike the residential districts of the 18th and early 19th centuries, the city districts arising now had to consider a more vast and complex network of railroad connections and tramlines, all of which had to be integrated with the docks and factories.

Barcelona's well thought out and detailed plan by Ildefons Cerdà i Sunyer (1859) was particularly innovative. It consisted in a grid with open spaces left for squares. Nor did he forget to accommodate pedestrians, trams, railways, gas conduits and sewers, or green spaces and gardens. (The latter were eventually removed by his peers, who accused him of being a Communist who pampered the underprivileged.) In New York City, the docks extended directly from the streets creating a unique and strong connection among city, commerce, and industry. One of the largest dock-warehouse constructions of the time, however, was in Hamburg (1885–1927), where the Baroque-era fortifications were torn down to make room for new development at the southern perimeter of the urban core. Although designed in a Gothic/Romanesque manner on the outside, the buildings, stretching over a kilometer along the Alster River, were steel structures with all the latest in hydraulic lifts and electrical illumination. It was a vast urban machine.

17.77 Leading port cities, ca. 1880

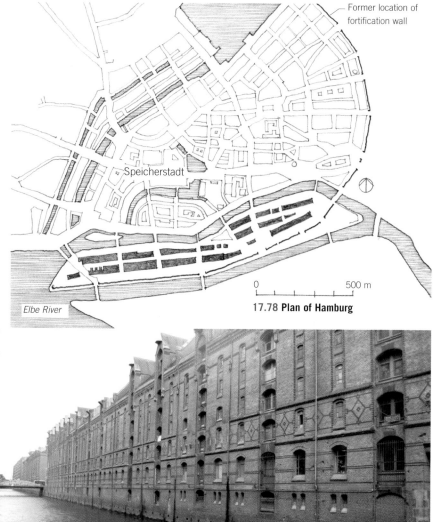

Former location of fortification wall

Speicherstadt

Elbe River

0   500 m

17.78 Plan of Hamburg

17.79 Hamburg warehouses

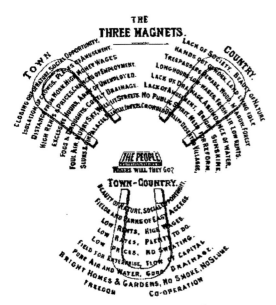

17.80 Ebenezer Howard's "Three Magnets" diagram

17.81 Ebenezer Howard's diagram of the garden city concept

Garden City Movement

Despite the recognition that planning tools had to curb and direct urban growth, the Victorian city became an increasingly complex and sociopolitical battleground, with many in the middle and upper classes preferring to turn their back on cities for the comfort and security of the suburbs, with their socially and economically stratified neighborhoods. The results shaped the debate about the nature of a city. There was, without a doubt, the uncomfortable density of life, the cagey interaction between the classes, and the persistence of poverty and crime. But side by side with these negatives were the benefits of urbanity: the centers of learning, the theaters, the libraries, and the concert halls. For every theory that decried the city as an uncontrollable behemoth, there were those who were deplored the blandness and false security of the suburbs.

It was in an attempt to resolve this dichotomy that Ebenezer Howard wrote his book, *Tomorrow: A Peaceful Path to Real Reform* (1892) and republished as *Garden Cities of To-morrow* (1902). The city suggested therein was to have the virtues of both the city and the suburbs, but in a highly controlled way that regulated or abolished the contested extremes and made for pleasant surroundings. Howards' garden city was not a suburb but a type of mini-city with a core and a perimeter. It was not meant to be fully dependent on a nearby great metropolis as a suburb would be, but it was no mere village

either. The size was set at a comfortable 6,000 acres, which were not owned by individual citizens but held in a trust. The town was to consume only a 1,000 acres at the center. In the center of the town was a park with public buildings, surrounded by shops. Running all around this central park would be a wide glass arcade, or "crystal palace," where purchases could be made. The population of the town was to be kept to thirty thousand. Factories, warehouses, and the like, fronting on a circular railway, were on the outer ring of the town. Beyond that were the farms. Since there was no land ownership, the town was run as a corporation. Rents would provide income for the company, which would then be invested back into the community.

Howard's vision did not arise in a vacuum. There had already been several attempts to create somewhat similar towns, but most of these were factory towns built by factory owners who wanted convenient access to the workforce. Port Sunlight (1888), not far from Liverpool, was an enlightened version of this. Founded by the owners of a soap manufacturing business, the town had schools, churches, and training centers. Most of the stores and businesses were, however, run by the factory owners.

Letchworth (1903), north of London, was the first garden city to actually be built on Howard's model. Though it did not develop completely as planned, it was not a failure,

as many had predicted it would be; it began to attract factories like the Spirella Company (1912), which manufactured corsets. Ultimately, the Garden City movement produced more than thirty communities in England. Howard's book also shaped the development in England of the so-called New Towns built after World War I. Canberra, the Australian capital, was also influenced by Howard's design concepts.

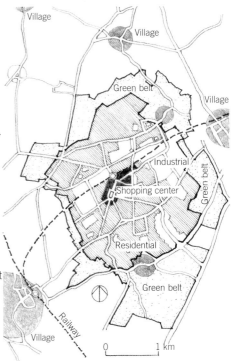

17.82 Plan of Letchworth, England

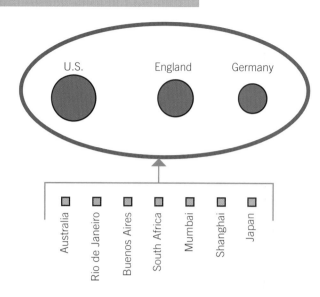

17.83 Global trade diagram, ca. 1900

Changing Global Economy

Between 1870 and 1910 the global economic situation changed considerably. England's economy was at such a height that its slide was not immediately noticeable, but by 1900, England had to share its economic power with the United States and, increasingly, with the economic might of Germany. The rise of Germany was not accidental. Its educational system was first-rate: by the end of the century, Germany possessed a literacy rate of 99.9 percent, an educational level that provided Germany with engineers, chemists, opticians, skilled workers for its factories, skilled managers, knowledgeable farmers, and skilled military personnel. In comparison, literacy in Britain, France, Norway, Sweden, and Australia was 30 to 50 percent. France was certainly the cultural world leader, but by 1880, it produced only 7.8 percent of world manufacturing output. By 1900, this had dropped to 6.8 percent; that year, Italy had only a 2.5 percent share of the global market. Meanwhile, Germany's output had risen to 13.2 percent due to its greatly expanded heavy industry. (This, ominously, gave it military capabilities that in time led to World War I.)

The most important rising economy of the time, however, belonged to the United States', which grew considerably beginning in the last decade of the 19th century. The United States had already begun to industrialize on a massive scale just after the Civil War. Raw materials were plentiful. Coal was found in abundance in the Appalachian Mountains. Large iron mines opened in the Lake Superior region of the upper Midwest. Steel mills thrived in places where these two important raw materials occurred together or in proximity. Large copper and silver mines opened, followed by lead mines and cement factories. The largest salt reserves in the world were found in New York and Pennsylvania. Mass-production methods developed at a fast pace. The result was the so-called Gilded Age.

Skyscrapers

If there is one building type that represents the confluence of new materials, new strategies of construction, and new attitudes toward capital and representation, it is the skyscraper. It did not appear suddenly, for it took considerable time for its function, production, design, and even its purpose to be synthesized. The most significant contributing factor was the improved quality of steel, which allowed prefabricated elements to be brought to the construction site and erected with relative rapidity. The technology of steel framing was well established by 1890; in fact, during construction, many buildings of that time would look as modern as buildings of today.

Questions about how to design the steel frame were, however, the least problematic part of the building. Elevators needed to be improved and their operation guaranteed. The same was true of the plumbing, electrical, and heating systems, and the integration of all these systems with one another. At the 1900 Paris Exposition, the designers of the U.S. exhibition chose to emphasize just this, using as an example the recently erected eighteen-story Broadway Chambers Building in New York City. The exhibition presented a 4-meter-high model of the building with an exterior skin in plaster that could be removed to show the underlying steel frame, complete with mechanical systems, boilers, pipes, and furnaces. It was an eye-opening lesson in an emerging architectural ideal.

17.84 Modern steel construction, the Woolworth Building

17.85 Reliance Building, Chicago

From a financial point of view, the idea was relatively straightforward. An investor, typically a bank, insurance agency, or newspaper, would finance the building and use it as a home office, occupying the lower, walk-in floor while renting out the rest of the building to business tenants. Besides having a stately home office, the owner could make a good investment in a booming rental market hungry for representative office space. The owner company's logo would be affixed to the top of the building and beam forth its message.

The Woolworth Building (1911–13) in New York City, designed by Cass Gilbert in a Gothic style, was at the time of its construction the world's tallest building. It was built for Frank W. Woolworth, owner of the famous five-and-dime chain. The whole was sheathed in elaborate terra-cotta tiles with equally elaborate Gothic-inspired detailing. The interior lobby had mosaic-covered vaults.

This commercialization of styles resulted in an increased need to outdo competitors. Many early designers assumed that a classical or Gothic front was still the appropriate response, but in Chicago,

which in the 1890s had more tall buildings than any other city in the world, a group of designers were beginning to challenge that notion. Among the most innovative was the firm of Daniel Burnham & Company, which designed the fifteen-story steel-and-glass Reliance Building in 1890, with the principal design credits going to John Root and Charles B. Atwood. Instead of the heavy cornice that is still seen in buildings like Dankmar Adler and Louis Sullivan's Wainwright Building in St. Louis, Missouri (1890), the Reliance

Building is topped with a thin square lid, and the top floor, which houses machinery for heating and other utilities, converts into a type of frieze. Bay windows reach out into space, giving the building an inner dynamic. The insistent verticality of the Wainwright Building has been replaced by a layered look, but instead of appearing heavy, one floor almost seems to float over the next thanks to the building's spandrels, which are lined with delicately ornamented, white terra-cotta tiles, giving the building an ethereal presence.

17.86 Woolworth Building, New York City

17.87 Wrigley Building, Chicago

Wrigley Building

The Reliance Building was more the exception than the rule. A look of modern engineering in tall buildings was not insisted upon and, in fact, ran counter to the idea that these buildings were meant to advertise old wealth and culture. For that very reason, most tall buildings after the World's Columbian Exposition were clad in historical styles. A typical example is the headquarters building of AT&T in New York (1912), which was then the largest and most innovative corporation in the United States. It was designed by the Beaux-Arts-trained architect William Welles Bosworth, an American who had studied at MIT, one of the first institutions in the United States to model itself on the Beaux-Arts system of education. Corporate representation at the turn of the 20th century was a form of modernity in its own right. In that sense, the skyscraper was similar to the train stations of

the 1860s, and much like the train stations of that period, skyscrapers competed against each other in size and lavishness.

It is often argued that Beaux-Arts modernism survived so long in the United States because of the hold that the system had on academe—but that is not the only reason. Beaux-Arts modernism had become the language par excellence of corporations eager to promote themselves. Historical awareness and reference to great architectural accomplishments of the past were an integral part of this ambition. That is the reason Bosworth chose to model his columns in the lobby of the AT&T Building on those of the Parthenon and also why, at the top of the Wrigley Building (1920–24) in Chicago, which was designed for the well-known manufacturer of chewing gum, the architects placed a reconstruction of

the Monument of Lysicrates in Athens (334 BCE). Would Lysicrates turn over in his grave or smile indulgently? It was not only the monument as a token of Athenian sophistication at stake here but also the fact that the French government had just completed its restoration in 1887. The clock tower presented the image that capitalism wanted to make history whole again by brazenly co-opting ancient history as a consumer brand. The building was designed by Charles Beersman, chief designer for the firm, Graham, Anderson, Probst & White, which was soon to become the largest architectural firm in the United States.

Casa Batlló

Antoni Gaudí (1852–1926), despite his artistic talent, was not a particularly good student at the school of architecture at Barcelona. The academic styles and the rationalization of construction did not appeal to him: he preferred history and economy. After a period during which he apprenticed with various local architects, he set out on his own. One of the characteristics of his work was his use of color. His architecture, more than any produced in the 20th century, must be experienced in person in order to be fully understood. Le Corbusier and Frank Lloyd Wright were consummate colorists, but for Wright, color was a question of patina, whereas for Le Corbusier, color served spatial articulation. For Gaudí, color was a tactile experience and sprang from Spanish folk sensibilities as well as from his fascination with the Mediterranean mosaic tradition and Spain's Islamic past. Gaudí experimented with colored stone and glass, polychrome glazes, and broken tiles and plates, and exploited the shadings of stone and brick.

Despite the seemingly impromptu character of his buildings, Gaudí was very much a perfectionist, working out every project in great detail. The facade of Palau Güell (1886–90) was completely redrawn twenty-eight times, and some of its details changed completely. This explains why it took him four years to perfect the columns for the nave of Sagrada Familia (1882–1926). The richness of Gaudí's forms might make his work seem preeminently sculptural, but according to him, his priorities were situation, measure, and material—and only then form. Already in his first works, he was creating

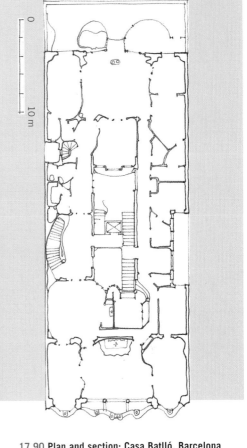

17.88 Roofscape: Casa Batlló

17.89 Casa Batlló

17.90 Plan and section: Casa Batlló, Barcelona

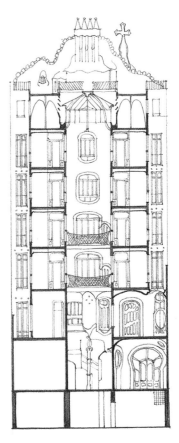

hyperbolic and trumpet-shaped helical forms, but always in combination with his refined sense of construction. As a young architect, he could imagine structural possibilities that seemed to defy conventional wisdom. One worker once waited hours after a particularly precarious-appearing corbel had been constructed to see if it would fall. It still stands today.

In the late 19th century, Barcelona had become one of the leading Mediterranean ports, specializing in the trade of cotton and metal. The wealth of the local bourgeoisie resulted in commissions such as the one for the Casa Batlló (1904–6) for Josep Batlló, a textile manufacturer, which involved renovating an existing building. Gaudí

modified the inner court, introducing a staircase with a tautly undulating outline. The facade shows wavy forms surfaced with ceramics in shades of blue. The enigmatic, masklike balconies and the stained-glass windows evoke floral, animal, and geological motifs. The roof of glazed brick looks like the scales of a dragon pierced by the tower, which has at its top a head of garlic that morphs into a three-dimensional cross— perhaps an allusion to St. George and the killing of the dragon, a story with much local resonance to Barcelona. At the level of the *piano nobile*, the malleable forms that seem to be made more of mud than of stone are held up by thin, bony colonnettes "deformed" in the middle and ornamented by vines.

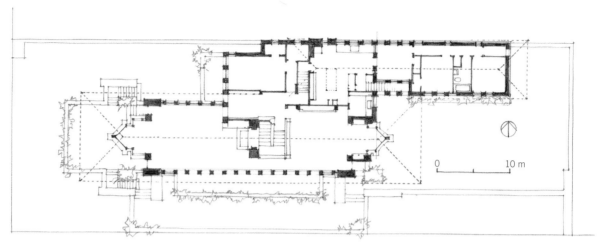

17.91 First-floor plan: Robie House, Chicago

Frank Lloyd Wright

The long and complex career of Frank Lloyd Wright (1867–1959) can be divided into several phases: from the time he opened his office in 1893 to the Robie House (1908–10); the Taliesin phase (1911–14); the period from the design of the Imperial Hotel to Fallingwater (1934) and Taliesin West (1938); and the period from the Johnson Wax Administration Building (1936) to the Marin County Civic Center (1957) and the end of his life in 1959. His production was vast and includes about four hundred houses and a dozen or so other major buildings. By the time Wright designed the Robie House in Chicago, his style had become quite distinct from the Victorian mansions that were then in vogue. Furthermore, unlike other architects who changed style slowly or at the behest of a client, Wright's break with tradition was driven by a personal stylistic development in search for ever greater abstraction. At the Robie House, its Shingle Style origins can still be seen in the service rooms, which are packed into a massive block against which the building rests. The hip roofs have been flattened so that they practically disappear. The fireplace has now become the spatial and visual hub of the building, freed from encroaching walls and linked only to a staircase.

The house is screened against the street, and no staircase is visible; it seems almost defensive while, at the same time, the design emphasizes the linearity of the street. The bands of white stone parapets form a series of striations that rise to meet the dark-edged roof lines, with the bands of windows recessive in the shadows. The main floor opens onto a balcony that runs along the entire southern exposure. And in good Arts and Crafts fashion, every aspect of the house was designed by Wright himself, from the carpets to the light fixtures.

A comparison of the Robie House with the Steiner House by Adolf Loos yields more similarities than are obvious at first glance. Both give the client an interior environment that is intimate, richly detailed, and crafted down to the last detail. Both are also abstract and mute to the outside world. The principal difference, and one that was to remain a difference between European- and American-style modernism, is their relationship to the outside. The American tradition was not adverse to incorporating porches and platforms into the living space of the building, an idea relatively rare in European domestic design until after World War II. (The way had been paved by the Shingle and Bungalow styles, as well as by the philosophy of Andrew Jackson Downing.)

Taliesin East

After a trip to Italy in 1909, Wright began to build at first a retreat and then a home in Spring Green, in southern Wisconsin, that came to be called Taliesin (1911–14). The name refers to the *Book of Taliesin*, a collection of poems and prophecies attributed to a 6th-century Welsh court poet. The building marked a significant departure from Wright's earlier homes, which

17.92 Robie House, Chicago

were constrained by their suburban lots and tended to be designed to move from formal to informal spaces. Taliesin, which sat on the top of a broad hill with views in three directions and had ample space to expand, was designed without this polarity. It was a highly personal expression, but it was also infused with what Wright thought was a uniquely American receptivity to the landscape. It was not "on" the hill, he claimed, but "of" the hill, for it was not easy "to tell where pavement and walls left off and ground began," surrounded as it was by low-walled garden courts reached by stone steps. The house reflects Wright's experiences in Italy, where he saw for the first time the great Renaissance and Baroque villas and gardens. It was, therefore, not just a house but a country estate, house, farm, studio, workshop, and family seat all in one.

The house, low and horizontal, with ungabled hip roofs, seems to respond rhythmically to the surrounding hills. The walls were of roughly dressed stone laid in textured horizontal courses, as if partially natural and partially manufactured. The house, with its broad, hooded roofs, gave the occupants a sense of being embedded in the landscape. It was, Wright explained, a "natural house," by which he meant not that it was like a cave or log cabin but that it was "native in spirit." Taliesin's plan organization is a geometric ordering of the landscape, with

17.93 Taliesin East, Spring Green, Wisconsin

17.94 Plan: Taliesin East

Pond

0   100 m

17.95 Site plan: Taliesin East

each part joined to the next in a meandering pattern of solids and voids that winds its way down the hill. The principal living block is a rectangle that has been eaten into by voids or expanded outward by terraces and rooflines. Subtle shifts of alignments create a dynamic within the house that is enhanced by placing the access points to the rooms into the corners.

In the 1930s, Wright built another home and office for himself in the Arizona desert called Taliesin West. He lived and taught there from 1937 until his death in 1959.

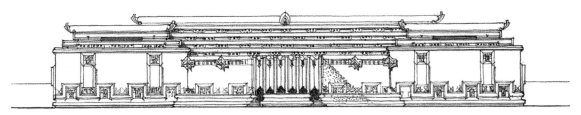

17.96 Lucknow University Library, India

Walter Burley Griffin

Newly united in 1901, Australians, under Prime Minister Edmund Barton, were looking for a style suitable to express their national aspirations. Some attempts at transforming an Arts and Crafts and Art Nouveau–derived interpretation of Australian flora and a Richardsonian-derived idea of civic buildings (such as Edward Raht's Equitable Life Assurance Society Building in Sydney, 1895) were finally rejected in favor of a more progressive modernism, as can be seen in the design of Canberra's new national capital. The winning entry of the 1912 competition was by a young, little-known architect from Chicago, Walter Burley Griffin. Strongly influenced by Frank Lloyd Wright's houses and Daniel Burnham's master plans, Griffin called himself a landscape architect to emphasize what he claimed was the organic derivation of his design. His proposal also drew on the City Beautiful movement in so far as it featured a picturesque ordering of the landscape with intersecting axial geometries. He proposed to use the irregular basin from the site to create a series of interconnected water tanks and even a lake, showcasing the main government center and capitol. The rest of the city was spread out axially, with star-shaped intersections forming the highly visible civic centers and nodes of residential suburbs.

Although Canberra was not developed until after World War II, Griffin created a successful practice in Australia, designing several houses and institutional buildings. His architecture derived largely from Wrightian sources, most particularly the latter's California houses. Griffin's Creswick Residence in Castlecrag (1926), the ten-story office building in Melbourne, and the Keith Arcade (1927) also drew on the decorative motifs of local flora. In 1935, Griffin had the opportunity to design a library in India and left Australia. His last set of buildings, therefore, are in Lucknow, India, where he unexpectedly died in 1937. As in Australia, Griffin tried to invent a new architectural vocabulary—this time suitable for modern India. He did not try to copy Wright but rather to translate Wright into a new national style and an alternative to both Beaux-Arts and European modernism.

Colonial Africa

The African slave trade was declared illegal in England in 1807, in 1808 in the United States, and in 1814 in Holland. In those areas of Africa under European control, the Europeans now transitioned their mission to transforming the population into industrious peasants working on cash-crop plantations, much as had been done in India and South America. Driving the change was the introduction of Belgium and Germany into African colonial politics. There was initially little to be gained financially; these colonial incursions were driven by the exigencies of

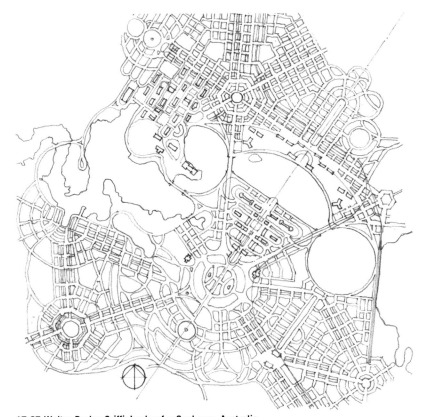

17.97 Walter Burley Griffin's plan for Canberra, Australia

17.98 Union Buildings: Pretoria, South Africa

17.99 Pretoria City Hall

political leverage in a global chess game—the English against the French, the French against the English, the Portuguese against the French and the English, and so forth, in a cruel afterglow of colonial power. Africa was rapidly partitioned, often in the name of the "sacred trust of civilization." Christianization, at first pursued haphazardly, became an increasingly important part of the European language of civilization. This was particularly true for the areas held by the British, which witnessed the development of religious and educational systems. The colonial rulers

did not hesitate to use missionaries, both Catholic and Protestant, to pursue their ends, but apart from churches, roads, mines, railroads, and houses for colonial masters, the Europeans did little to improve the lot of the Africans.

The discovery of gold in South Africa in 1876, at a time when gold prices had risen, was a boon for that country's colonial Dutch population, but it also attracted the British, who were eager to control the world gold market. In a bitter conflict, the

Second Boer War (1899–1902), the British took possession of Cape Colony, Natal, and Transvaal. In 1910, they officially created the Union of South Africa. The English architect Sir Herbert Baker (1862–1946) designed numerous buildings in the new dominion, including cathedrals, churches, schools, universities, and the Union Buildings in Pretoria (1910–13). That structure, in the English monumental style, was planned as the government center of the South African nation and as a gesture of reconciliation with the Boers after the terrors and disasters of the war. It is convex, with the main program, such as the committee chambers, in the middle. The two side wings represented the Boer and the English parts of the population; Africans were not represented. (After the first free elections in 1994, it became the residence of the president.) Baker took the lessons he learned in South Africa to New Delhi, where he partnered with Sir Edwin Lutyens in the design of British-ruled India's new capital.

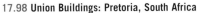

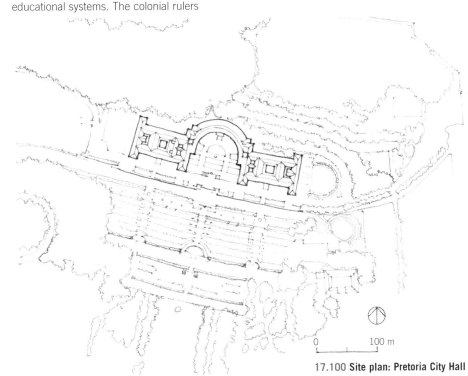

0   100 m

17.100 Site plan: Pretoria City Hall

17.101 **Municipal Theater, Rio de Janeiro**

17.102 **Presidential Palace, Havanna**

International Beaux-Arts

Late in the 19th century, one determinant in international trade was the U.S. depression of 1893, which affected the economy worldwide. With a pronounced (although momentary) drop in the purchasing power of U.S. companies, American entrepreneurs went abroad in search of markets. The expansion of the United States' global political reach—the result of the annexation of Hawaii in 1898 and its military victories in the Philippines and Cuba over the Spanish—helped U.S. firms focus on international possibilities for the first time. During the 19th century, England, and then increasingly Germany, had, for example, been the world's leading exporters of iron and steel. But since World War I, it was the United States that assumed that role. And it was not just building materials being exported, but entire building systems—and the engineers to go with them. American-engineered tall buildings, complete with Beaux-Arts cladding, went up from Buenos Aires to Shanghai. American-designed bridges were soon appearing in New Zealand, Taiwan, Manchuria, Japan, Mexico, and South America, and by 1910, skyscraper components produced in the United States were shipped to East Asia, South Africa, and Central America. Milliken Brothers, a leading American steel firm, established branch offices in London, Mexico City, Havana, Cape Town, and Sydney, erecting office buildings, mills, and factories with steel framing.

With the global economy centered on England and the United States, former peripheral countries underwent an economic upturn of their own, as materials and products could now be advantageously exported. This modernization at the global periphery, however, went hand in hand with the increasing disempowerment of the underclasses. In South America, the new upper class may have had factories built with U.S. steel, but on matters of the material culture, they more often than not flaunted the latest of French fashions; French urban design was also imported as a visible substantiation of their policies. One of the consequences was that Beaux-Arts eclecticism, with its associations with the professional class, developed into an international movement. There were few major metropolises that were not touched by this phenomenon.

These global realities left their most dramatic imprint in Argentina and Brazil, with most of its exports of beef, wool, and wheat supported by heavy investments from England. Rio de Janeiro, during its Republican phase from the 1880s to 1910s, was significantly rebuilt under its mayor, Pereira Passos, who came to be regarded as the "Haussmann of the Tropics." He relied on architects such as Ricardo Severo (1869–1940), who was greatly influenced by Beaux-Arts academicism. The Municipal Theater (1905) by the Brazilian architect Oliveira

Passos was designed to be reminiscent of the Paris Opera House.

The building of these structures coincided with the development of pubic hygiene and the introduction of electrical and gas services. As in Egypt, where debate still rages today as to the Egyptian authenticity of the neo-Mamluk style, in Rio de Janeiro, a camp developed in 1910 that argued that the Brazil's true national style was the early 19th-century Portuguese colonial architecture. The argument was that those structures were designed and built by local craftsmen, whereas the late 19th-century buildings belonged to a more alienated age. Today some ascribe Rio's urban difficulties to the aggressive modernization of the city under Passos. Others praise him for his foresight.

The former Presidential Palace in Havana, Cuba, was designed by the Cuban architect Carlos Maruri and the Belgian architect Paul Belau. It was inaugurated in 1920. Modeled loosely on the Palazzo Madama (1718–21) in Turin, Italy, by Filippo Juvarra, it sports an eclectic addition.

Kyoto National Museum

The first Asian country to modernize was Japan, but this happened only after 1854 when an American naval mission led by Commodore Matthew Perry, taking a page from the English, forced Japan to open its ports to American trade, a move that

17.103 **Hong Kong & Shanghai Banking Company Building**

17.104 **Kyoto National Museum, Japan**

hastened the demise of the Tokugawa dynasty (1603–1867), the last shogunate. The subsequent Meiji Restoration (1868) was a period of aggressive Westernization, with the goal of transforming Japan into a modern industrial and military power. Delegations from Japan were sent to European world exhibitions to learn the latest technological developments. The Japanese also studied the Egyptian modernization program under Isma'il Pasha. In 1895 Japan invaded China and Taiwan, then parts of Russia, and annexed Korea in 1910. The 1897 erection of the Kyoto National Museum, built in a French Baroque style, was meant to mark the emergence of Japan onto the world stage. This rapid introduction of Western styles—even though it was made as a way to compete in the rapidly expanding global economy, engendered a backlash from traditionalists. Nationalists denounced Western customs and by World War II had forced the government to return to a more traditional modality, at least in outer appearance, for underneath the call for tradition was a policy that continued the modernization of Japan's military machine.

Myongdong Cathedral

As with Japan, European culture arrived in Korea largely through the opening of its ports, in this case in 1876, leading to the building of Myongdong Cathedral (1898) in the Gothic style and the Toksugung Palace

(1909) in the Renaissance style. During the 1910 Japanese annexation of Korea, Japan continued this Westernization, using Western styles as a symbol of their own colonial footprint. The Bank of Korea Headquarters (1912) was built in a Renaissance style, and the Seoul Anglican Church (1916) in the Romanesque. Formal education in Western architectural concepts and engineering was first introduced in Korea in 1916.

17.105 **Myongdong Cathedral, Seoul, Korea**

Hong Kong & Shanghai Banking Company Building

Shanghai came into existence in the late Song dynasty as a small town of merchants and fishermen, but with the Treaty of Nanjing in 1842, which followed China's defeat in the Opium War of 1841 by British forces in Canton, its character changed radically. The Chinese were forced to open their ports—along with other cities—to British, French, American, and other foreign occupants, who brought along with each of the city's expansions new buildings, roads, and management practices. By the 1920s, Shanghai was called the Paris of the East. The earliest buildings erected by Westerners in Shanghai were a hybrid of Western and Chinese motifs, of which the Francisco Xavier Church in Dongjiadu (1853) is one of the few remaining examples. Others, like the Hong Kong & Shanghai Banking Company Building (1923–25), with its broad colonnaded neo-Grecian front, were more properly Western. Built for the second-largest banking house in the world in 1925, the building represents the apex of Shanghai's commercial prosperity. Upon its completion it was advertised as the "most beautiful building from the Suez Canal to the Bering Sea." Divided vertically into three portions in classical proportions of 2:3:1, the base of the first story centers on three arches that carry above it three stories of six colonnades topped by the pediment.

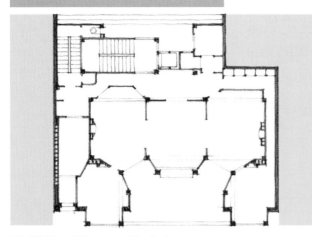

17.106 **Plan: 25b, rue Franklin, Paris**

25b, rue Franklin

In Spain, the young Antoni Gaudí was experimenting with concrete, producing forms that are still staggeringly fresh today, as in the strange vase- and bottle-shaped skylights of the Casa Mila (1905–10) in Barcelona. But the architect who most wanted to integrate the use of concrete into the worldview of the architect was Auguste Perret (1874–1954). Though by no means seeking as expressionistic a form as Gaudí, he argued that the visual properties of concrete's load-bearing capacity were just as important as its structural properties. Working in the spirit of Eugène-Emmanuel Viollet-le-Duc, Perret aimed to integrate architecture and civil engineering. Perret was thus the most "theoretical" and yet the most practice-oriented of architects working in concrete. His 25b, rue Franklin, in Paris (1902–4), an apartment building in a fashionable quarter of the city, aimed to demonstrate that concrete could be adapted to domestic architecture in an age when most thought it suitable only for factories and warehouses. Due to concerns about its weather-worthiness, the concrete was, however, not visible on the outside. Smooth, colored bricks covered the concrete elements, while tiles depicting chestnut leaves were applied to the thin brick walls that filled the spaces between the columns. Each floor consisted of a six-room apartment with a bathroom, staircase, and elevator at the rear. The five principal rooms were arranged symmetrically around a central salon. The plan was conventional; the design's novelty lay in the use of thin, lightweight walls and the allocation of all internal load bearing to slender columns.

17.107 **25b, rue Franklin**

As a civil engineer, Peret had a deep distrust of architectural freedoms. When asked to engineer a theater in Paris that was designed by Henry van de Velde, he complained that the building was structurally inconsistent and forced van de Velde to resign. Van de Velde had originally been a painter, and in teaching himself to design buildings had come to see architecture as creatively autonomous from engineering. It was Le Corbusier more than anyone else who understood and theorized the need to integrate the innovations of structure with those of living. That tension, between the requirements of engineering and those of design remains a point of theoretical contention to this day.

17.108 **Detail: 25b, rue Franklin**

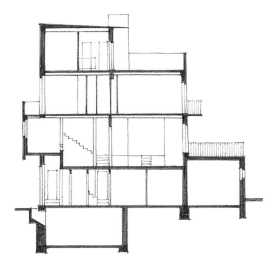

17.109 **Section and plan: Moller House, Vienna**

17.110 **Looshaus on Michaelerplatz, Vienna**

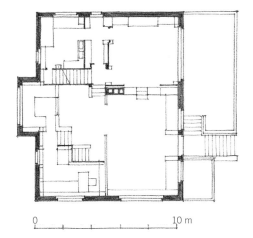

0   10 m

17.111 **Moller House, Vienna**

Adolf Loos

Adolf Loos (1870–1933) was born in Moravia (now part of the Czech Republic) and studied architecture at the Dresden Polytechnic, after which he spent three years in the United States. He eventually settled in Vienna in 1896 and worked for a local firm before establishing his own company. He soon began writing essays on a variety of subjects having to do with Viennese art and society. Most were critical of Art Nouveau, which at that time was all the rage in the great cities of Europe, including Vienna. In 1908 Loos wrote a now-famous article entitled "Architecture and Ornament" in which, relying on Jean-Jacques Rousseau's critique of civilization, he railed against the use of ornament by advanced European cultures. For Loos, ornament was appropriate in tribal societies, where it played an important part in social interaction, but for an advanced civilization, ornament was no longer a relevant form of communication. Loos was not opposed to using the color and texture of natural materials for their ornamental quality, however. His opinions put a damper on his career, but he did secure a number of jobs leading up to the design for a commercial building in Vienna in a style now called the Wiener Moderne; popularly, the building is called the Loos Haus, or Looshaus in German (1909–10).

By the time Loos designed the Steiner House (1910), even the residual classical motifs of his earlier work were gone, leaving only a pure white exterior. The building certainly anticipates—and indeed was highly influential in—the modernist aesthetic that would become the norm from the 1930s onward, although it differed markedly from later functionalist buildings. Here the stark exterior was meant to contrast with the interior. "On the outside, the building must remain dumb and reveal all its richness only on the inside," Loos wrote in 1914.

The Moller House (1926) is paradigmatic of Loos's approach. Its facade is simple and forbidding, with the entrance, balcony, and windows bound together into a tight compositional unit. Since the windows on the top floor face the rear, the number of windows on the facade is limited. Despite the external symmetry, the interior is labyrinthine. The living and family rooms on the second floor are separated by steps and framed openings to create a range of areas, some more private than others. The interiors of the principal rooms are richly outfitted with light-colored wood veneers on the walls and oriental carpets on the floors, creating a sense of sumptuous elegance. In this respect, though Loos is seen as the harbinger of the modern movement, his work maintained a strong allegiance to the Arts and Crafts ideal of interiority and intimacy.

The Factory Aesthetic

By the early 20th century, factory design had evolved considerably. The introduction of electricity in the 1880s freed the factory floor from the cumbersome system of pipes, gears, and belts that had driven machines during most of the 19th century. Advances in steel engineering allowed factory buildings to become larger and internal spaces wider. Glass was used extensively to permit illumination. Skylights were common, sometimes in sawtooth form or as part of a Pratt truss. Flat roofs were also adopted, since it was easy for fires to break out in the old gable roof system, with its complex wood supports. The development of concrete provided a fireproof—although expensive—alternative to buildings that were of brick, stone or terra-cotta. Standardized building types became widely available in the form of iron- and steel-frame structures.

The late 19th century also saw the emergence of a search for a factory aesthetic once it became clear that the building was—or could be—used for advertising. Some factories had main buildings that were in a type of Gothic or Romanesque—and occasionally classical—style. The Yenidze Tabakfabrik (1907–9) in Dresden, Germany, bloomed forth in an Oriental style, even using simulated minarets and a glazed dome to conform to the branding of its cigarettes. Usually, such buildings were designed without an architect. But even when an architect was involved, there was a noticeable difference between the image of the building that the architect designed and the factory itself, designed by engineers. The latter was seen—at least until the advent of modernism—as not really part of the architect's concern. The freedom engineers had resulted in a type of building that was designed around the concepts of function and utility. Decoration was eschewed, but there was a desire to express strength and stability. There was also a contradictory desire for light, and the creation of long steel and glass walls paved the way for what later came to be known as the curtain wall, used extensively in skyscrapers in the 1950s.

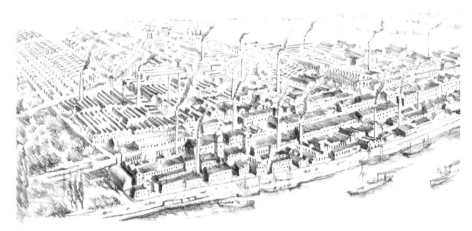

17.112 **View of Ludwigshafen, Germany**

17.113 **Yenidze Tabakfrabik, Dresden, Germany**

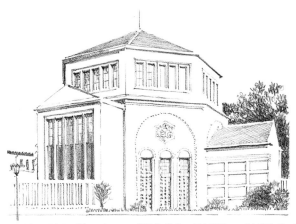

17.114 **AEG Pavilion, German Shipbuilding Exhibition of 1908, Berlin**

17.115 **Tea kettle by Peter Behrens, 1909**

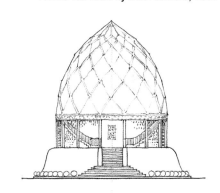

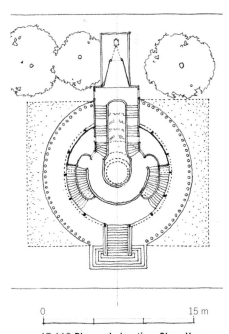

Deutsche Werkbund

The transformation of Germany from an agricultural society into an industrial one and from a country with limited national and military goals to a world power on par with England occurred at an astonishing pace. Between 1894 and 1904, the value of Germany's foreign trade doubled, and by 1913 Germany overtook Great Britain in percentage of world production. Large companies like Friedrich Krupp Werke (munitions, cannons, steel, and ships), the Allgemeine Elektrikitäts-Gesellschaft, or AEG (turbines, electric railroads, and equipment for the new German navy), and Siemens-Schuckert Werke (railroad and electrical equipment) were supported by the government through lucrative military contracts and protected from international competition by tariffs. Beginning in the mid-1890s and continuing until the outbreak of World War I, urban officials, functioning under the tight control of the imperial government and learning, belatedly, the lessons of England and France, organized special exhibitions to promote and glorify German production.

Though the architecture and architectural quality of these exhibitions varied, they were, for those who noticed, a bold showcase for innovation. German architects were not hampered by the Beaux-Arts system, which was never implemented in Germany. For the Nordwestdeutsche Kunstausstellung in Oldenburg in 1905, Peter Behrens's designed a highly abstracted and formal exhibition layout with square structures, their surfaces incised with simple geometrical forms; an octagonal, domed garden pavilion; and a rigorously symmetrical exhibition hall with a central cubical space to which were attached four smaller skylight boxes at the corners. At the German Shipbuilding Exhibition of 1908, Behrens built an octagonal, baptistery-like structure for AEG. The high altar was actually a ship's deck, on which stood a great searchlight, the most advanced of its kind in the world and the pride and joy of the German navy. At another exhibition from 1910, visitors saw Behrens's all-concrete pavilion for Zementwahrenfabrikanten Deutschlands (German Concrete Manufacturing Association).

At the 1914 Werkbund Exhibition in Cologne, a dramatic Glass House by Bruno Taut was on display. It consisted of two spaces: a type of crypt below, set within a cylindrical concrete plinth, and a domed space above. The crypt contained a pool at its center, with water cascading down small terraces decorated with pale yellow glass. Access to the dome above was by means of curving stairs at the top of the plinth, on which rested a fourteen-sided structure of concrete beams. On top of that structure, Taut set the prismatic dome with a double skin of glass—an outer, protective layer of reflective glass, and an inner layer of colored glass—creating a three-dimensional explosion of light, color, and geometry. Apart from the structure itself, all its surfaces were made of glass, in keeping with the pavilion's purpose: an advertisement for the glass industry. The walls were made of shiny glass tiles, transparent glass bricks, and translucent colored glass. Even the steps were made of glass.

17.116 **Plan and elevation: Glass House, Werkbund Exhibtion, Cologne, Germany**

17.117 **United Shoe Machinery Company, Beverly, Massachusetts**

Concrete

Portland cement was named after the tiny island of Portland in Dorset, England, where a desirable limestone used in its manufacture was found. But by 1900, U.S. manufacturers were outproducing the English, as well as perfecting new ways to integrate concrete with steel. By the end of the second decade of the 20th century, the demand for cement was staggering, as manufacturers competed with each other for ever stronger materials.

Initially, the use of concrete was thought to be advantageous because it was believed that it did not require skilled labor, and thus not a few early concrete buildings are in the English colonies, such as the Secretariat and Army Headquarters at Shimla, India (1886). As it turned out, while pouring concrete did not require great skill, the production and quality control of the material itself required highly developed technical competencies. What eventually spurred the broad acceptance of concrete was not its cost (for it turned out to be more expensive than originally thought) but its fire resistance. Since a steel frame could easily buckle when heated, it had to be protected by brick, tile, or cement. Concrete, by way of contrast, was inherently fireproof. Concrete construction was also fast, easy to maintain, and seismically stable.

Concrete construction did not require large heavy beams; a weaving of relatively thin steel bars could instead be embedded inside it. The problem of how to attach the bars to each other was solved in 1884 by Ernest Leslie Ransome, superintendent of the Pacific Stone Company of San Francisco, who patented a special machine that could twist iron bars into the necessary shapes and armatures. The United Shoe Machinery Company (1903–6), designed by Ransome set the tone for this technique in a design that allowed for a continuous band of windows from floor to ceiling.

The Kahn System of reinforced concrete developed by Albert Kahn had, by 1907, already been used in 1,500 U.S. buildings and 90 English ones, and in dozens of others around the globe. Kahn developed these ideas for new large-scale manufacturing enterprises, such as the Packard Motor Car Company manufacturing plant in Detroit, the Dodge Brothers Motor Car Company plant in Hamtramck, Michigan, and the Pierce Arrow plant in Buffalo, New York. He went on to build more than 1,000 buildings for Ford Motor Company and hundreds for General Motors. In 1923, he built a fifteen-story building in Detroit for Ford Motor Company, which was at the time the largest manufacturing corporation in the world.

Garnisonskirche

Ford's factories brought to the fore the radical modernity of reinforced concrete from the point of view of civil engineering, but the architectural question still remained open. The potential for concrete to take any form had already been noted in the mid-19th century and was, in fact, one of the

17.118 **Dodge Brothers Motor Car Company, Hamtramck, Michigan**

was made for a military base. It was designed by Theodor Fischer (1862–1938), a prolific architect and noted educator, and one of the founders of the Deutsche Werkbund. He argued for a contextual modernity and his work therefore seems more neo-medieval than modern today. Nonetheless, the building is now a landmark in the history of modern architecture. The body of the church consists of a reinforced-concrete skeleton with brick infill. The towers are huge empty silos 55 meters high, with a bell chamber suspended between them.

A second important building was the Breslau Jahrhunderthalle (1913), which showed off the virtuosity and elegance of concrete. Built to commemorate the centennial anniversary of the defeat of Napoleon's army in 1813 by the Prussian army near Breslau, Germany, the building was part of a campaign by the city to define itself as the " Metropolis of the East." It was designed by Max Berg, Frankfurt am Main's buildings department director, to serve as both an exhibition and assembly hall.

The Jahrhunderthalle was an enormous building, with an enclosed floor space of over 5,600 square meters that could hold ten thousand people. Due to the fires that had broken out at a building of the 1910 World's Fair in Brussels, the builders decided to use concrete—the first ever attempt to use the material for a building on that scale. The structure consisted of four large, curved arches that supported a continuous ring on which rested the dome. To provide a more secure environment against weather, the glazing was not laid in the interstices of the ribs. Instead, Berg designed a system of stepped glazing applied to the outside of the dome in the form of vertical windows and horizontal roofs. From the inside, the small horizontal roof planes disappear in the light that streams through the vertical apertures of glass.

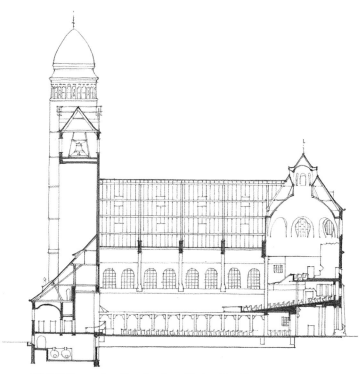

17.119 Plan and section: Garnisonskirche, Ulm, Germany

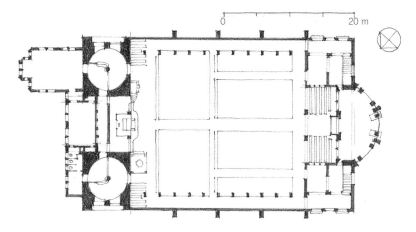

0   20 m

reasons that many designers—especially those working in accordance with the theories of John Ruskin—saw it as debasing architecture. For this reason, and because of the difficulty of working against the grain of antiquated building codes, the architectural advancement of reinforced concrete was thwarted in England; it was France and Germany that took the lead.

If the French contribution consisted of attempting to integrate concrete into the conventions of architectural practices, the Germans contributed toward its engineering. One of the earliest uses of concrete in a major public building in Germany was the Garnisonskirche ("Garrison church") in Ulm (1906–8), a Protestant church that, as its name implies,

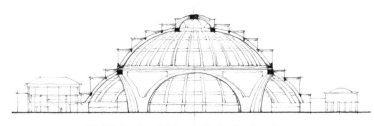

17.120 Section: Jahrhunderthalle, Breslau, Germany

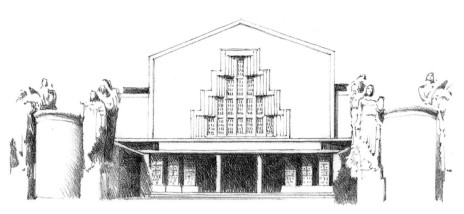

17.121 Pavilion of Commerce, 1908 Jubilee Exhibition, Prague

17.122 Pavel Janák's study for a facade

Expressionism

That modern architecture before and just after World War I was so imaginative and experimental might come as a surprise given its common association these days with functionalism. Expressionism, as it soon came to be known, had, however, begun to develop before World War I in the work of Bruno Taut and a few others. Particularly influential were the writings of Paul Scheerbart, who in 1914 published *Glass Architecture*, a book describing a utopian architecture of colored glass in combination with sparkling jewels and enamel. The Expressionists, as they are sometimes collectively called, despite their differences, all envisioned an architecture as far removed from classicism as could be imagined at that time. The old notion that architecture reembodied the power of the past gave way to a desire to create an architecture that spoke to the immediacy of perception and the psychology of the beholder. As one commentator, Heinrich de Fries, explained, "Buildings are in the highest degree alive…. We can only guess at the extent to which the art of spatial articulation will one day transcend the art of pictorial creation." Expressionism rejected the duality of interior and exterior, of building and landscape. It also opened architecture to influences from the other arts—in opposition to the Arts and Crafts movement, which had hoped to integrate the artistic conception within the framework of craft-making.

Czech Cubists

The Expressionist movement was particularly strong in Prague between 1910 and 1914. In the 1880s, Czech artists, dissatisfied with the poor standards of the Prague Academy of Painting, departed en masse for Munich, a leading center for the German Arts and Crafts movement. Many others went to Paris, where they encountered the work of Auguste Rodin, whom many Czechs admired for the spontaneity and expressiveness of his work. Other sources of inspiration were found in French Cubism, which began to be exhibited in 1908. But despite the pictorial innovations of Pablo Picasso and Georges Braque, the possibility of a Cubist architecture was not pursued in France—and certainly not in Germany, where French developments were generally viewed with suspicion. The introduction of Cubism into architecture in Prague was, therefore, a novelty, spurred on by sources such as the magazine *Der Sturm* ("The Storm"). Published in Berlin beginning in 1910, its contributors included Max Brod, Richard Dehmel, Karl Kraus, Adolf Loos, Heinrich Mann, and Paul Scheerbart. Czech Cubism was thus a synthesis of various European influences, including its own regional Baroque. The result was a distinct style, emerging already by 1905.

One of the leading architects among the Czech Cubists was Jan Kotera (1871–1923), a professor at the Prague School of Decorative Arts since 1898 and the chair of the department of architecture at the Prague Academy of Fine Arts from 1910. He saw prismatic shapes as appropriate to the intellectual vitality of the modern age. For him, structure had to give way to the

logic of visual dynamics. Modernity for him lay not in the expression of function, but in the expression of an object's inner dynamic. This was also true for Pavel Janák (1882–1956), whose idiosyncratic interpretation of Cubism led him to shift toward tapered, slanted, and triangular forms. He argued that the orthogonal architecture reflected its dependency on matter and weight, whereas the new Cubist style, with its angles, expressed the active nature of the human spirit and its ability to prevail over matter.

After World War I, with the downfall of the aristocratic regime in Germany, Expressionist architecture found one of its more realistic voices in Hans Poelzig (1869–1936), whose first major commission, the Grosse Schauspielhaus (1918–19) in Berlin, had a plaster ceiling hung from the rafters that looked like stalactites. Thousands of light bulbs, variously colored in shades of yellow, green, and red, were embedded in the vault so that the whole thing resembled both a cave and, when the lights were dimmed, a starry night sky. The foyer was supported by a single column that, like a fusion between a fountain and a plant, spread successive rings of colored petals—also illuminated by recessed colored light bulbs—until it reached the vault above.

17.123 Interior: Grosse Schauspielhaus, Berlin

17.124 A drawing for a futurist Città Nuova ("New City") by Antonio Sant'Elia

Another important figure in the expressionist camp was Hans Bernhard Scharoun (1893–1972), who rejected the crystalline shapes of some of the other Expressionists in favor of soft, rubbery forms. In his design for a stock exchange building (1922), he warped and bent space around the central lobby, giving the building the appearance that it had ingested the various aspects of the program.

In Italy, Expressionism took an even stronger form under the name of Futurists, initially a literary movement created by Filippo Tommaso Marinetti in 1909. (It was from his manifesto, *Le futurisme*, published in Paris, that the name of the movement was taken.) Marinetti was a keen follower of the cubist movement and even took a group of Italian painters to Paris to show them the recent work. Soon, however, the Italians developed their own distinctive style, significantly more aggressive in tone than the quiet utopianism of Scheerbart. The Futurists were particularly enamored of technology, speed, and machinery and expressed this in their painting and poetry. They saw the outbreak of World War I as a positive development for Italians and hoped it would propel the young country into the modern age. "Art," so Marinetti stated, "can be nothing but violence, cruelty, and injustice." The movement eventually came to include architecture, and in a 1914 manifesto, Umberto Boccioni proclaimed the Futurists' antipathy to the classical styles. Boccioni argued instead for an architecture of

"dynamic awareness." The leading architect among the group was Antonio Sant'Elia (1888–1916), who built little but who made influential visionary drawings of massive buildings with soaring heights.

In Germany, the Expressionists formed several groups, such as the Arbeitsrat für Kunst ("Worker's Council for Art") and the Novembergruppe ("November Group," named after the 1917 Russian Revolution). In 1918, the Novembergruppe, in its first manifesto, called upon Cubists, Futurists, and Expressionists to join together in the regeneration of Germany.

There was something unmistakably Romantic about Expressionism's rejection of rationalism and pragmatism. But it also created an architecture designed without the requirements of historical precedents. Up until then, visionary architecture had been only at the margins of architectural practice. The English Arts and Crafts, for example, had certain visionary ambitions, but it never produced a successful conception of the monumental or the urban. The Art Nouveau was similarly limited. Expressionism was the first the architectural movement that was both architectural and urban and that had no attachment to historical models. By the late 1920s, as the European building economies began to return to normal, the Expressionists were critiqued for their excesses and strangeness, but in truth they had shown that a nonhistorical modern architectural style was possible.

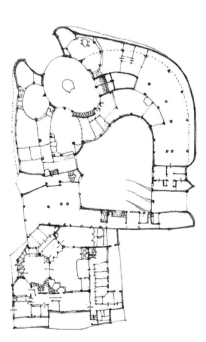

17.125 Han Bernard Scharoun's project for a stock exchange

17.126 Einstein Tower, Potsdam, Germany

17.127 Interior: Einstein Tower

The architect most associated with expressionism was Erich Mendelsohn (1887–1953), who was as famous for his drawings as he was for his buildings. His sketches, many unrelated to any commission, emphasized the building's flowing silhouette. There are no pictorial enhancements, no landscape features—just the building without context, drawn in dark lines on a white sheet of paper. Despite his seemingly impossible and grandiose ambitions for the field of architecture, Mendelsohn was an extremely successful architect, even during the 1920s, and one of the first professionally successful modernist architects, employing as many as forty people in his office.

Mendelsohn was naturally drawn to concrete, but the technology at that time was still rather limited, and even though he first conceived of the Einstein Tower in Potsdam, Germany (1917–21), as a concrete building, it was in actuality a brick structure with a concrete-stucco exterior. The tower, his first major commission, was built for the Astrophysical Institute in Potsdam and is still in use today. The form of the building's exterior seems in some places seems to have been carved out; in other places, it seems to have been molded. In the vicinity of the windows, it seems to be a soft encasement of

a mysterious, angular metallic structure within. In the approach to the building, a set of steps leads to an elevated deck that opens to the entrance lobby, with one stair leading down and another leading up the tower. The telescope at the top of the tower transmits light to instruments in the basement laboratory. Between the shaft and the base, to the rear of the building, there are study and sleeping quarters for the scientists.

17.128 Section: Einstein Tower

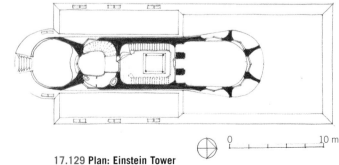

17.129 Plan: Einstein Tower

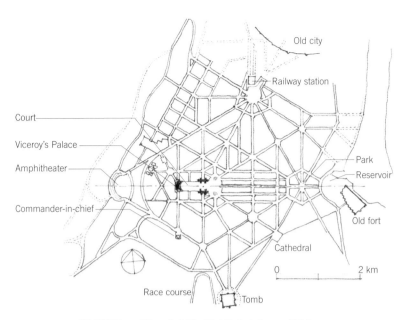

17.130 Plan of New Delhi by Sir Edwin Lutyens, 1911

Labels on plan: Old city · Railway station · Court · Viceroy's Palace · Amphitheater · Commander-in-chief · Park · Reservoir · Old fort · Cathedral · 0 — 2 km · Race course · Tomb

New Delhi

In 1911, at a coronation *darbar* in Delhi, India, George V announced his decision to build a new capital for imperial India, one that could unfalteringly display the English determination to maintain British rule in India in perpetuity. Calcutta had always been the seat of the colonial government, but this was an accident of history. The English chose Delhi to insure the identification of the new capital with the onetime Mughal seat of power. A debate immediately raged over whether the architecture should acknowledge an indigenous idiom or reflect the conventions of colonial Neoclassicism. After intense lobbying by advocates of both sides, Viceroy Lord Charles Hardinge decided that a design that was "plain classic" with a "touch of Orientalism" would be best. His argument was not that different from that of a century earlier, when a classical revival had been advocated based on the eternal principles of classical architecture. With that, the colonial ideologues were back to where they had started—except for the "touch of Orientalism."

New Delhi's master plan and the design of its principal building, the Viceroy's Palace (1921–27), was executed by Sir Edwin Lutyens. The secretariat buildings were designed by Herbert Baker, who had just completed the Union Buildings in Pretoria to great success. The master plan reflected Beaux-Arts academicism; a series of radial spokes were elegantly stitched together over 85 square kilometers to create an expansive vision of a capital city. Different classes of bungalows appropriate for various levels of officers were distributed around its expanse. At its center was the grand east-west path, King's Way, with the Viceroy's Palace and Secretariat raised on a hill as its western terminus. The other end of King's Way was marked by a diminutive memorial to the unknown soldier, designed by Lutyens.

Although they had a personal falling out, Lutyens's and Baker's designs harmonized well. Finished in red and yellow Rajasthan sandstone, both sets of designs stress the horizontal, utilizing the Indian *chajja*, or overhang, to cast long, continuous shadows that contrast sharply with the bright Indian sunshine. Small *chattris*, campaniles, and the domes provide the vertical counterpoint. Baker, ever more the imperialist than Lutyens, did not hesitate to incorporate some elephants and sandstone screens to make his designs more "Oriental" in tone. But the general impression of the entire viceroyal complex displays the restrained and accomplished use of a stripped-down neoclassical vocabulary and represents some of Lutyens's and Baker's best work. Indeed, the greatest impact is from the distance at the terminus of King's Way (now called Raj Path), where the broad horizontal sweeps off the complex effectively emphasize the three domes and two campaniles.

17.131 Viceroy's Palace, New Delhi

17.132 Lister County Courthouse, Sölvesburg, Sweden

17.133 Plan and section: Woodland Cemetery Chapel, Stockholm

Gunnar Asplund

Sweden had been fortunate to escape the ravages of World War I, and the comparative postwar prosperity left the young Gunnar Asplund (1885–1940) in an excellent position to make a name for himself with his design of the Woodland Cemetery (1917–20) in Stockholm (codesigned with Sigurd Lewerentz) and the Lister County Courthouse (1917–21) in Sölvesborg. The latter building is a simple rectangle with a circular courtroom embedded in the plan to the rear. From 1913 to 1914, Asplund had taken a trip to Rome, Ravenna, and Sicily that brought him into contact with the great architectural works of the past. He was drawn less to the most famous monuments than to simple medieval churches, nestled against other buildings or silhouetted against the open sky. Though he can be considered a modernist, his interest in nonmachine aesthetic monumentality has led many to view him as a classicist, but such distinctions are not clear-cut; Asplund's work is, in fact, a continuation of late 19th-century Romanticism.

Under Asplund, Swedish national Romanticism shed its overt allegiance to the Middle Ages and sought out an abstract formalism, as seen, for example, in the Stockholm Public Library (1920–28), a building of absolute functional clarity. It is composed of a cylindrical reading room within a U-shaped, coral colored building that contains other parts of the program. From afar, the impression is of a tower rising from the center of a square building. From the entrance, a visitor is conducted upward by a dramatic but simply designed staircase framed by an Egyptian-style portal to evoke a transition between outside and inside and between the known and the unknown. Within the reading room, above the three open tiers of books, rise the rough whitish surfaces of the cylindrical walls, ending in a row of windows and a flat ceiling. On the exterior, the facade is divided in two, with the base almost as tall as the upper part. Dividing the sections is an Egyptian-style frieze filled with mysterious symbols that refer to learning and the arts.

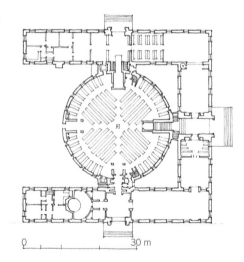

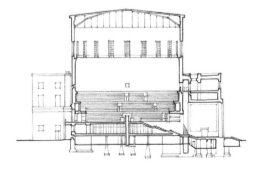

0   30 m

17.134 Plan and section: Stockholm Public Library

17.135 Hollyhock House, Los Angeles

17.136 Interior fireplace, Hollyhock House

Hollyhock House

Following the murder of his wife and six others by a deranged servant at Taliesin, Frank Lloyd Wright began to distance himself from the Arts and Crafts ideology in which he was then working. Both the Imperial Hotel (1923) in Tokyo and the Hollyhock House (1921) in Los Angeles are more monumental and scenic in compositional strategy than his earlier work. Both also drew more consciously from the local cultural references. In the case of the Hollyhock House, these derived from Mayan architecture that—though a thousand miles from the Mayan heartland in Guatemala—had come to be seen in the western United States as a type of regional exotic. The blatant use of pre-Columbian forms stemmed from Wright's belief that pre-Columbian architecture was a repository of strength and power. This was far different from the rustic but refined sensibility of Taliesin. The house is named after a flower from which its decorative motifs were generated.

The house, located in the Hollywood section of Los Angeles and built at the peak of excitement over that city's role in the fast-growing motion picture industry, was built for Aline Barnsdall, a wealthy oil heiress and a supporter of left-wing causes. She had planned for a design that included secondary residences, a theater, a director's house, and studios for artists. Because of financial and artistic differences, only the Hollyhock House and two secondary residences were

ever built. The site is on the top of an isolated hill in an otherwise flat city landscape. The basic diagram of the house is relatively simple, laid out as a U opening to the east, with the garden moving down the slope. At the head of the U is the living room, with the bedroom area to the south and the more public rooms to the north, close to the garage. The whole creates a complex set of closed and open spaces operating on different levels, with some of the roofs accessible as terraces. The building was built of stuccoed hollow tile and wood.

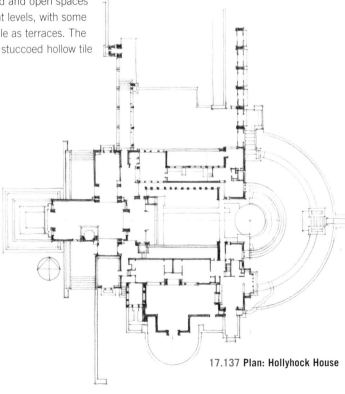

17.137 Plan: Hollyhock House

17.138 Bandung Institute of Technology, Bandung, Indonesia

17.139 Site plan: Bandung Institute of Technology

0   100 m

Dutch Kampung

While the English controlled India and most of the Chinese trade, the Dutch continued their hold on Indonesia, in spite of several English and French attempts to dislodge them. However, late 19th-century wars with France, the Acehnese, and the Javanese landed the Dutch colonial government deeply into debt. In response, the Dutch set production quotas, fixed prices, restricted travel, and raised taxes under a policy called the Cultivation System (1830–70). It was a disaster and led to massive starvation in the midst of bumper crops of export commodities. A disgruntled young Dutch colonial officer, Eduard Douwes Dekker, captured the hardships of these years for the Dutch public in the 1859 novel *Max Havalaar*. The ensuing outrage back in the Netherlands forced the hand of the colonial authorities, and in a series of legislative changes starting in 1870 the so-called Ethical Policy dismantled the forced cultivation of export commodities and opened the colonial economy to Dutch private enterprise. The policy sparked a large migration of Dutch to the East Indies, leading to a forceful spatial assertion of European identity against native and immigrant Asian societies. Using the Garden City model, the Dutch carved their colonial space out of the congestion and filth of the native neighborhoods in the colonial towns across Java and Sumatra, building Indian-style bungalows set in spacious gardens with outbuildings for kitchens and servants.

In 1901, the Dutch queen, Wilhelmina, announced that the Netherlands would from then on accept an ethical responsibility for the welfare of their Indonesian subjects. This announcement was a sharp contrast to the former doctrine of profit-making. The result, architecturally, was the search for hybrid styles. In fact, the Indonesian-born, ethnically Dutch architect Henri Maclaine Pont was one of the progenitors of the Indische style, an architecture dedicated to the fusion of Dutch and indigenous approaches. Hendrik Petrus Berlage, the noted Dutch architect, characterized the challenge as one of pulling together the universal qualities of Western modernism with "the local spiritual aesthetic elements of the [E]ast."

An exemplar of this approach was Pont's design for the Bandoeng Technische Hoogeschool ("Bandung Institute of Technology," 1920). The twenty buildings were laid out crossways to the site's principal axis in a Beaux-Arts manner. The wood trusses of the buildings were left exposed on the interiors of the halls in keeping with the strictures of the Arts and Crafts movement, while the roof form is a free interpretation of the traditional Sumatran *minangkabau* roof system found in many regions of Southeast Asia.

Politically, even though the Ethical Policy was the first serious effort to create programs for economic development in the tropics, it was ultimately insufficient to redress the social issues created by centuries of colonial control.

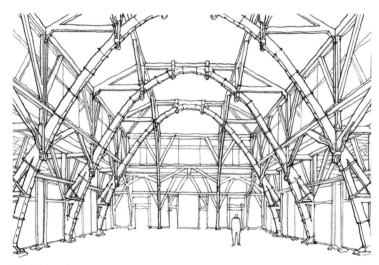

17.140 Interior: Bandung Institute of Technology

17.141 **Theo van Doesburg's color design for Amsterdam University Hall**

De Stijl Movement

After World War I, Expressionism in Holland gave way to a vibrant avant-garde culture that focused on issues of abstraction and color; at the center of it were Piet Mondrian and Theo van Doesburg. The latter still had ties to the expressionist cause in so far as he advocated a form of the three-dimensional color environment. It was a position that Walter Gropius rejected outright; eventually, so did van Doesburg's countryman, the architect Jacobus Johannes Pieter Oud (1890–1963). They argued that architecture needed to focus on social and economic realities and that it could not give itself over to abstract spiritual speculations. Initially, however, the artists of the de Stijl movement—a name that derived from the journal of the Dutch modernist movement—tried to rid architecture not only of historicism but also of conventional subject matter in favor of abstract vertical and horizontal elements. Function played a secondary role to form. Though the movement remained strong until the late 1920s, the differences between artists like van Doesburg and architects eager to work within the realistic needs of their clients had by then become unbridgeable.

Van Doesburg was certainly influenced by the work of painter Piet Mondrian. His designs for a cinema/dance hall, the Café Aubette in Strasbourg (1926–28), involved broad compositions of colored rectangles in relief, oriented at 45-degree angles. Mirrors were placed between the windows to reflect the ceiling and the three other walls, all treated in a manner that turned the architectural surface into a kind of plastic relief sculpture. As van Doesburg explained in several essays published in de Stijl between 1926 and 1928, the essence of the countercomposition was its opposition to the orthogonal character of architecture and nature. Art, he argued, in aspiring to the spiritual, must provide for architecture an additional dimension—the oblique—that architecture by itself was not capable of creating, given that it was shackled to weight and gravity. In that sense, art, for him, was opposed to functionality as well as to construction.

One of the few examples of de Stijl architecture is the Schröder House (1924), designed by Dutch architect Gerrit Thomas Rietveld, who lived and worked in Utrecht. The client, Truus Schröder-Schräder, the wife of a noted lawyer, wanted a house with as few walls as possible. It is built at the end of a block of conventional 19th-century attached rowhouses, giving it views in three directions. Rietveld exploited this to create a house in which the volumes seem to be composed of plains, some hanging free from the facade. The principal colors were white and gray, with red, yellow, and blue serving as accents. The ground floor was relatively conventional, but the upper floor had numerous movable walls that allowed for spaces to be opened or closed as desired.

17.142 **Schröder House, Utrecht, Netherlands**

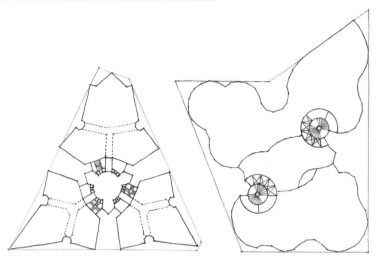

17.143 Plans for Friedrichstrasse Office Building and glass skyscraper projects

17.144 Friedrichstrasse Office Building project

Friedrichstrasse Office Building

In 1921 a competition was held for a tall office building along the Friedrichstrasse in Berlin, and though Ludwig Mies van der Rohe (1886–1969) did not win, largely because he flouted all the rules of the prospectus, his design has entered the lore of skyscraper history for its radical innovation. Mies began his training with his father as a stonemason, but his talent led him to Berlin, where he worked for a while for Bruno Paul, one of Germany's most influential art nouveau architects, and then for the more modernist-oriented Peter Behrens. The houses that Mies built during the 1920s were certainly competent, but hardly imaginative. They stood in sharp contrast with his unbuilt work, which was highly imaginative and a logical extension of the developing modernist aesthetic. His submission for the office tower competition, for example, shows a building composed of three angular prismatic towers linked in the middle by a circulation core, with an open cylindrical space left free all the way from bottom to top. The steel skeleton with cantilevered floor slabs is sheathed completely in glass. The design reduced the building to its fundamental elements: the circulation core and the office pods. Mies did not, as was conventional, envision each floor filling the site to maximum capacity. Instead, the building breaks apart the block into three separate thirty-story towers that only at the buildings' tangents touch the perimeter of the site. The core that contains the stairways, elevators, and lavatories constitutes a type of trunk clearly visible in the plans. Mies

showed the buildings rising high above the haphazard townhouse/apartment blocks.

This project, along with his contemporaneous design for a country house in brick, placed Mies firmly within an emerging modernist movement that was aiming beyond Expressionism, which was still the principal post–World War I aesthetic. Mies was no true Expressionist, but he nonetheless joined the Novembergruppe in 1922. The original political motivation of the group by that time had been lost, but the organization remained important because of its exhibitions, and Mies, in fact, soon became the director in charge of the Novembergruppe's architectural shows. In a series of blunt and terse texts, Mies laid out his ambitions: "We refuse to recognize the problem of form, but only the problems

of building," to which he added, "Essentially, the task is to free the practice of building from the control of aesthetic speculators and restore it to what it should exclusively be: building." This declaration of purpose was published in a journal called *G*, which appeared in July 1923 under the editorship of Hans Richter, El Lissitzky, and Werner Graeff and which announced its hostility toward romance and subjectivity in art. Though these skyscrapers, and the Brick Country House, had a minimal investment in their structural logic, Mies, by the mid-1920s, was moving toward a position that placed structure—stripped of allusions and illusions and the raw realities of building—into the center of architectural production.

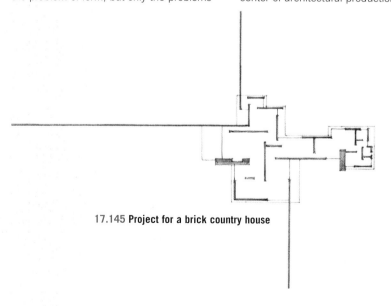

17.145 Project for a brick country house

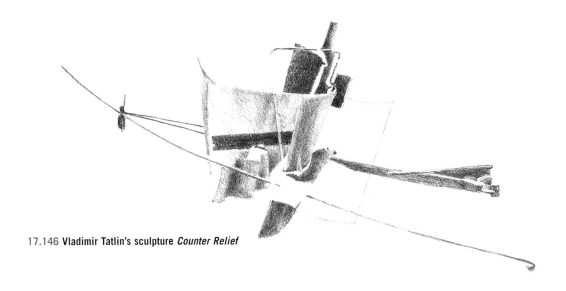

17.146 Vladimir Tatlin's sculpture *Counter Relief*

Russian Constructivism

When, in the 1860s, Karl Marx critiqued capitalist society and proposed an alternative world controlled by the proletariat, he assumed that change would take place in industrialized Europe. But when the revolution did come in 1917, it was in the underdeveloped country of Russia. It was, nonetheless, a moment of optimism and a vindication for all those who were hoping to see a better life for the repressed social classes. The Russian avant-garde wanted a clean slate, unencumbered by a largely feudal past, seeing in the new situation a singular opportunity for translating the arts into a politically purposeful reality. As a result, though the art and architecture of the Soviet Republic (and after 1922, the USSR) was related to a certain degree to European modernist ideas, it quickly developed it own aesthetic and theoretical platform.

Though most of the Russian architects differentiated themselves from some of the European functionalists, arguing that architects must work on a higher plane than that of pure function, there was a good deal of debate about the exact nature and value of aesthetic theory and its relationship to technology, politics, and function. Constructivism, the best-known movement outside of Russia, is often, but mistakenly, associated with the entirety of Russian Revolutionary art, but not all Russian art of the time was Constructivist: there were also the rationalists and suprematists.

The term *Constructivism* emerged at the beginning of the 1920s and was closely associated with the Society of Contemporary Architects (OSA). This movement was, among the various tendencies, the closest to the tenets of the European New Architecture, and to the work of Le Corbusier in particular. It was led by Moisei Ginzburg (1892–1946), whose structures aimed to embody the ideals of the new socialist order. For Ginzburg, art for art's sake was dead: art now had to reflect the newly established truth of the world. To sever art and by extension architecture from its subservience to the bourgeois class, architects had to draw their aesthetic from factory production, given that industrialization, now controlled by the Communists, would, so it was presumed, become the springboard for a truly universal human culture. Constructivism, though it was grounded in an image of industrial labor, was not a one-to-one translation of industry into aesthetics, but it was the first modernist aesthetic that admitted, and in fact glorified, the mass-produced object. Constructivists used the term *laboratory work* to describe their formal investigations and to emphasize their solidarity with both science and labor. Laboratory work was, however, not to be equated with the pragmatism of problem solving, for the Constructivists, though they admired utilitarianism, also spoke of the need for a formal language that was imbued with an aura of heroism.

That theme of heroism was tackled even more directly in the work of a competing group, headed by a charismatic figure, Nikolai Ladovsky. ASNOVA (a Russian acronym for the Association for the New Architecture), the group he founded in 1923, attributed to the new forms of architecture the power of affecting, in revolutionary ways, the psyche of the masses. Known also as the Rationalists, they differentiated themselves from the Constructivists; despite certain similarities, they intended to develop a more purely scientific foundation for the aesthetics of modern architecture.

The third major group, the Suprematists, focused on fundamental geometric forms such as squares and circles. In art, their best known representative was Kazimir Malevich, who painted simple geometric shapes on his canvases; in architecture, it was El Lissitzky (1890–1941). Lissitzky, who designed exhibition displays and propaganda works, was also greatly influenced by the aesthetics of the Bauhaus and de Stijl. Projects like his Wolkenbügel, however, which had towers supporting vast cantilevered buildings in the sky, show his daring formal vision.

Tatlin's Tower

Besides the Vesnin brothers and Moisei Ginzburg, Vladimir Tatlin (1885–1953) occupies a central position in early Constructivism and became, along with Malevich and Lissitzky, an important catalyst in the modernist movement of the 1920s. Tatlin studied art in Moscow and after a long journey working on ships as a sailor, he went to Paris, where he met Picasso and other cubists. During this period, he moved away from painting and began three-dimensional explorations into material and gravity. Some of his more interesting works were installed in the corners of a room as a type of dialogue with the walls and a diagonally redirected space—an experiment with the formalist concept of defamiliarization. Later in the decade, Tatlin defined his efforts as aiming at synthesizing the various branches of art with technology.

His artistic explorations and utopian theory coalesced in his project for a huge 400-meter-high tower (designed 1919) that was meant to straddle the Neva River in the center of Petrograd (St. Petersburg) in celebration of the newly founded Third (Communist) International. The monument, of which a 5-meter-high model was built, consisted of three volumes of glass suspended in a vast double spiral structure stiffened along its slope by a leaning truss. The lower space, a cube, was to complete one rotation on its axis once per year to correspond to the frequency of the meetings of the Communist International General Assembly. The second space, a pyramid, was to rotate on its axis once per month to corresponding to the meeting frequency of the meetings of the officers of the Secretariat.

The third and smallest room, a cylinder, was to rotate once per day to match the daily operations of the International. It contained, among other spaces, offices for a newspaper that issued pamphlets and manifestos. Radio masts rose from the peak of the monument, not unlike those at the Eiffel Tower, which Tatlin's edifice emulated implicitly. But here, the radio masts were meant to advertise the modernity of the radio as an instrument of social change.

The tower became a symbol of the young Soviet Republic, and smaller versions of it were carried in processions through Moscow like religious objects and presented at various exhibitions abroad. El Lissitzky was moved to write that the tower was the modern equivalent to Sargon's ziggurat but created in a new material for a new context. The iron, he added, represented the will of the proletariat, whereas the glass was a sign of a clear conscience. Another commentator saw the spiral as the symbol par excellence of modern times, whereas Viktor Shklovsky called it, in semiological terms, a monument "made of steel, glass and revolution."

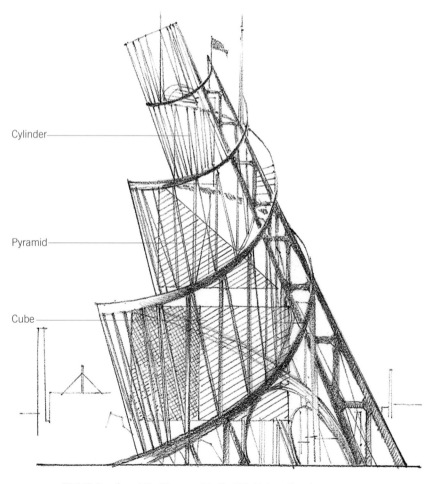

Cylinder

Pyramid

Cube

17.147 Drawing of the Monument to the Third International

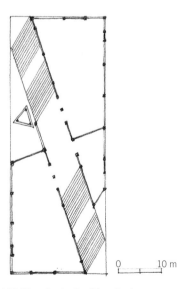

0   10 m

17.148 Plan: Soviet Pavilion, Paris

17.149 Rusakov Factory Club, Moscow

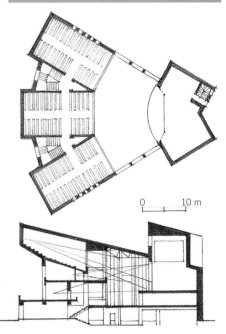

0   10 m

17.150 Plan and section: Rusakov Factory Club

Soviet Pavilion

Konstantin Stepanovich Melnikov (1890–1974), one of the most productive of the Russian modernist architects, has been hailed as one of the twelve greatest architects of the contemporary world. He adamantly refused, however, to be associated with any ism, and his highly idiosyncratic oeuvre featured works that differed radically from each other. He built about twenty structures, of which only a few survive. Like Tatlin, he began his career studying painting but widened his scope to include architecture, graduating from the Moscow School of Painting and Sculpture in 1917. He was trained in a neoclassical style, as was typical prior to the revolution.

One of his first major works was the Soviet Pavilion in Paris, which was built for the 1925 International Exposition of Modern Industrial and Decorative Arts; it had a startling angular composition with a staircase running diagonally up and then down the entire building. Though a relatively small building, the staircase gave it a monumental cast. The structure was built not of steel but of wood, fitted in Moscow by peasants wielding traditional Russian axes and shipped to Paris for assembly by French carpenters. The flying roof panels were painted red, the walls gray, and the window mullions white.

There was a debate in the USSR at the time about whether the new Soviet

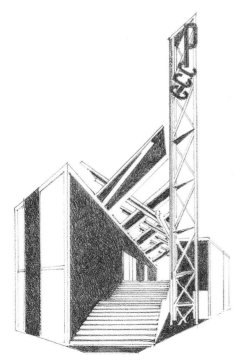

17.151 Soviet Pavilion, Paris

architecture should aspire to be technologically advanced or reflect local craft traditions. Melnikov favored the latter, but he was more than flexible when it came to larger commissions, such as the Rusakov Factory Club (1927). Workers' clubs had been created after the revolution to elevate the workers' culture and literacy while providing leisure places after their daily toils, but by 1924 most workers had shown themselves to be less than zealous for such uplift. A new generation of workers' clubs came into being that focused more on club activities than ideology.

At a time when living space in Moscow averaged 5 square meters per capita, the clubs were one of the few places outside of the factory where workers could meet and congregate. Melnikov went even further and interpreted them as an expression of a group individuality against the backdrop of urban anonymity. Melnikov's design is highly expressive, despite its symmetry and the simplicity of its plan. The lecture hall that was its main programmatic element was divided into three subunits that seemed to break through the building's exterior and to hover dangerously above the entrance. Each auditorium box seated 190 people, and each faced a large common stage. Three rooms for club functions were located in a mezzanine just below the seating.

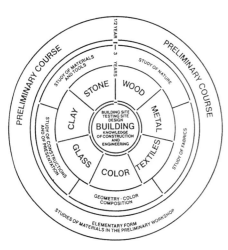

17.152 Diagram of the Bauhaus curriculum

17.153 The Bauhaus, Dessau, Germany

The Bauhaus

Before World War I, Walter Gropius (1883–1969), who had been a member of the Werkbund and had worked in Peter Behrens's office from 1908 to 1910, had every ambition of succeeding Hermann Muthesius as leader of the Werkbund. But after the war, it was clear to Gropius that the Werkbund was too conservative in its attitude toward industry. So, in 1919, he founded the Bauhaus in Weimar, one of the prestigious cultural centers of Germany. The school aimed to reach out to industry (although this outreach turned out to be mainly theoretical). The school was also significantly less pragmatically oriented than the Werkbund had been, and its relationship with the local government was never particularly warm. In 1924, a reduction of funding from the city forced it to move to from Weimar to Dessau; the move breathed new life into the institution, and indeed the time in Dessau was to be its most productive. The city even helped finance the campus, which was designed by Gropius and opened in 1926. Though it lasted only fourteen years, until it was forced to close by the Nazis, the Bauhaus became a lightning rod for debates, furthering modern architecture in the brief time between the early 1920s and the return of neoclassicism and nationalism in the 1930s.

Initially the Bauhaus's purpose was to produce a new "guild of craftsmen," but that does not mean it was reactionary, for Gropius also wanted a school that could unify the arts and close the gap between industry and craft. In that sense, unlike William Morris, who saw craft as a bulwark against industry, or the Werkbund, which was seeking an industrialized craft, Gropius wanted to uncover the internal ethos of industrial production itself. The question was not just how to make things, but how to perceive and experience things as well. For that reason, Gropius brought in painters, including Lyonel Feininger, Paul Klee, and Johannes Itten. The celebration of painters as form-makers reflected a not-so-subtle shift away from the social (and thus from the contentious political issues of the time) toward the language of abstraction and design. Itten was placed in charge of the basic course required of all incoming students. Its purpose was to free the students' creative powers and guide them in a suitable direction in their later studies. Personality conflicts led Itten to leave, and he was replaced by the Russian painter Wassily

17.154 Joost Schmidt's poster for the 1923 Bauhaus exhibition in Weimar

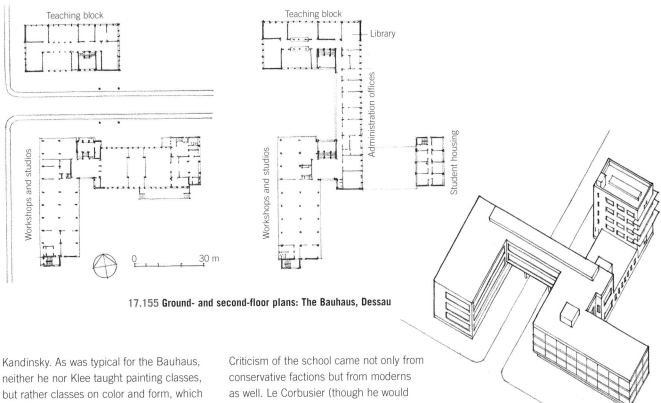

Teaching block

Teaching block — Library

Administration offices

Workshops and studios

Student housing

Workshops and studios

0   30 m

17.155 Ground- and second-floor plans: The Bauhaus, Dessau

17.156 Pictorial view: The Bauhaus, Dessau

Kandinsky. As was typical for the Bauhaus, neither he nor Klee taught painting classes, but rather classes on color and form, which had to be examined objectively, their use and application related to the contexts in which they were applied.

The program of the Dessau building (1924–26) included workshops, administrative offices, a lecture hall, and stage, as well as workrooms, a canteen, and student accommodations. Gropius divided the program into two major elements separated by a road and connected by a bridge. The bridge, fittingly, was where Gropius had his office: to go from the classrooms to the studio spaces, one had to pass by Gropius's office. The building was not particularly unified in the classical sense, for each element had its own programmatic logic. The dormitory at the east end stood awkwardly connected to the long, one-story space that contained the lecture hall and canteen, which in turn was linked to the main building whose two stories of studio spaces were transformed into a glazed box. The L-shaped area containing offices and classrooms, on the other hand, was designed with horizontal banding of white stucco that contrasted with the windows. The only two colors in the whole composition were white and black.

Criticism of the school came not only from conservative factions but from moderns as well. Le Corbusier (though he would change his mind later) argued that modern architecture could not be taught aesthetically, as it was allied primarily with industry. For him, architecture should not emerge out of decorative design. Similarly, Theo van Doesburg, the Dutch artist, argued that the Bauhaus, in emphasizing individual creativity, had abandoned the all-important search for a relationship between the artist and society. Despite these difficulties, the Bauhaus remained the leading school of modernist design in Europe.

In 1928, Gropius stepped down as head of the Bauhaus and appointed Hannes Meyer (1889–1954), a Swiss architect, to take over. Meyer's socialist political allegiances led to conflict with the government, and he was forced to resign in 1930. The position then went to Mies van der Rohe, who held the school afloat until it was officially closed by the Nazis in 1933.

17.157 Corner of the Bauhaus

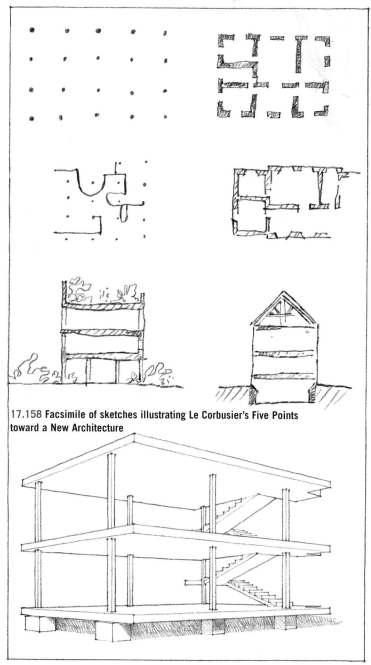

17.158 Facsimile of sketches illustrating Le Corbusier's Five Points toward a New Architecture

17.159 Column-and-slab structure for Dom-ino houses

Le Corbusier

Due to the dominance of the Beaux-Arts system, the design innovations taking place in other parts of Europe and in the United States had only minimal resonance in France. For modernism to develop it needed someone who could break through France's cultural isolation and provide a suitable alternative. That person was Charles-Édouard Jeanneret-Gris, who later changed his name to Le Corbusier (1887–1965), a Swiss-born architect who worked briefly in the offices of Auguste Perret and Peter Behrens and then moved permanently to Paris at the age of twenty-nine, in 1916. Le Corbusier's articles in *L'Esprit nouveau* as well as his epochal book, *Vers une architecture* (*Towards a New Architecture*, 1923), became the most significant summary statements of the ideals of the modernist movement to appear since World War I.

Jeanneret began his career designing houses in the Art and Crafts style in his native city of La Chaux-de-Fonds in Switzerland. But once in Paris, and after a travel tour to Turkey, Greece, Italy, and other parts of Europe and the Mediterranean in 1911, Jeanneret allowed his unique style to develop rapidly. He was strongly influenced by the modern painters and by the cubists in particular. In 1920, he took on the name Le Corbusier. *Vers une architecture* outlined Five Points toward a New Architecture: the *pilotis* (stilts) that support the building, the free plan with the only structural support coming in the form of columns, the free facade, the strip window, and the roof terrace. These features, he argued, were based on the structural properties of reinforced concrete as well as the increasing availability of mass-produced architectural elements. They also allowed the architect to work with pragmatic forms. The idea of the *pilotis* was to remain with Le Corbusier throughout his career. Inspired by Rousseauesque thinking that invested undisturbed nature with an ideal of plenitude, Le Corbusier's *pilotis* were meant to liberate the land from the oppression of a building that interrupted its flow and rhythm.

Villa Savoye

In the 1920s, Le Corbusier designed a series of houses in Paris and its suburbs that explored and demonstrated the possibilities of his Five Points. The Maisons La Roche-Jeanneret (1923), which now houses the Fondation Le Corbusier, was a combined set of houses for two different clients. Le Corbusier responded to the spatial demands of the different households by designing interweaving layers of spaces connected by a central court. The house was painted white, but on the inside, walls were painted in a variety of soft hues of red, yellow, and blue, as well as white.

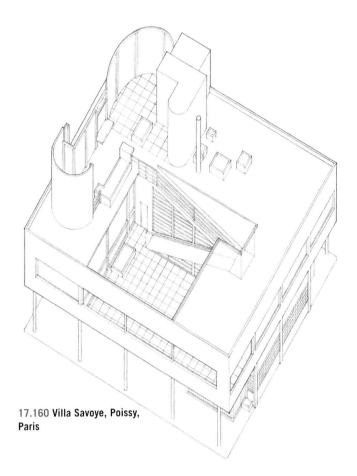

17.160 Villa Savoye, Poissy, Paris

His most influential work from this time was the Villa Savoye (1928–31) at Poissy, a suburb of Paris, where the client owned a large parcel of land that swelled up to a gentle hill. At its apex, Le Corbusier placed a cubic volume, lifted on *pilotis*, a column-and-slab construction in reinforced concrete. The walls were built of brick and stuccoed over. The plans on every floor were customized to their functional requirements, and a simple strip window was the centerpiece of the elevation.

The ground-floor plan was designed around the turning radius of the client's automobile, which, after dropping off his employer at the entry on axis with the center, was to be parked by the chauffeur in parking slots located around the curve. (In *Vers une architecture*, Le Corbusier had praised the design of the modern French automobile as an aesthetic achievement as great as the Parthenon.) Inside the front door and past the chauffeur's quarters, a carefully designed ramp rises up the middle of the villa. Living spaces were arranged around the ramp on three sides on the first floor. A terrace fills up the rest. The ramp reverses direction and ends on the roof, where a freestanding wall with a single window self-consciously frames the landscape. Although Le Corbusier celebrated the automobile, he also designed the building as a promenade with experiences unfolding at every turn. Once again, though the exterior was white (apart from the red entrance door), some of the interior walls were painted in pastel hues of beige, rose, and blue.

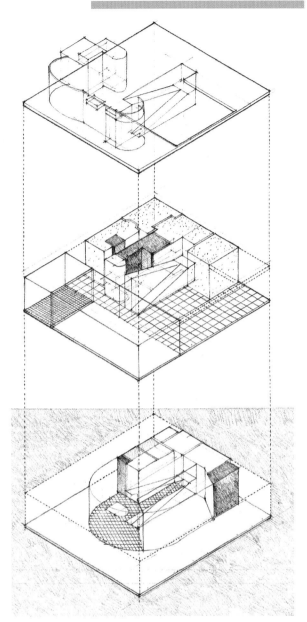

17.161 Expanded view of spaces: Villa Savoye

17.162 Villa Savoye

17.163 Lovell House, Hollywood Hills, Los Angeles

17.164 Lovell Beach House, Newport Beach, California

Lovell House

Modernist architecture did not produce any major inroads in the United States until the 1940s, with the arrival of Walter Gropius and Mies van der Rohe. There are two principal reasons for American resistance to modernism: Beaux-Arts architecture was still strong and taught in architecture schools, and Frank Lloyd Wright, the dominant U.S. architect, was a critic of the Europeans' boxy aesthetic. The earliest examples of European modernism are thus quite few and center on the efforts of two architects: Rudolf Michael Schindler (1887–1953) and Richard Neutra (1892–1970). Schindler, whose work was very much underappreciated at the time, was born in Austria but moved to the United States in 1914. He found employment in the office of Wright until branching out on his own, setting the tone for an architecture that had never been seen in the United States with his Lovell Beach House (1922–26). It was not a house in any traditional sense; nor was it a house in the Corbusian sense, with floor slabs and columns. Instead, a series of five concrete wall elements elevated the living quarters high over the ground to catch the sea breezes. The house appeared from below like the underside of a bridge. The floors, roofs, and walls were built of wood.

The same clients commissioned Neutra to design their principal residence (1927–29) in the Hollywood Hills in Los Angeles. It was built against a steep hill with views of the city to the south. The entrance was at the top level, where the family bedrooms and sleeping porches were also located. A staircase, enclosed on two sides by glass and with spectacular views, led down to the main floor and the living room, which faces south. The guest room and kitchen were to the north. It was the first completely steel-framed residence in the United States, the prefabricated elements bolted together in less than forty hours. The house was not a box, however, but rather a complex structure with extended balconies and sleeping porches on the upper floor suspended from powerful roof beams above. The dominant interior colors were blue, gray, white, and black. Carpets and draperies were in shades of gray. The metal trim was gray and the woodwork black. Potted plants softened the hard lines. The surface of the building was defined by glass and white steel panels.

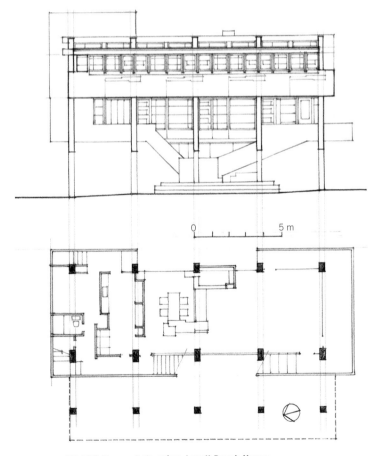

17.165 Plan and elevation: Lovell Beach House

1950 CE

The landmarks in the formation of the early modern movement include Walter Gropius's new school of design, the Bauhaus (founded 1919); Le Corbusier's book *Vers une architecture* (*Towards a New Architecture*), first published in 1923; and Ludwig Mies van de Rohe's Weissenhof Siedlung Exhibition in 1927. CIAM (Le Congrès Internationaux d'Architecture Moderne, or the International Congresses of Modern Architecture), founded in 1928, also played an important role as it quickly grew into an organization with dozens of members from around the world, all committed to the ideals of bringing functionalism and rationalism to building and urban planning. Modernism's appeal was, however, not universal. Germany under Adolf Hitler and the USSR under Joseph Stalin rejected the modernist aesthetic in favor of monumental neoclassical styles, opening up deep rifts between modernists and traditionalists. The Fascists in Italy were unusual in that they more readily adopted modern architecture—though often in a classicizing form—to express their nationalist ideals. Even in France, despite the work and efforts of Le Corbusier, only a handful of modernist buildings were built before World War II. And while modernism in Europe was highly contested, it was embraced in Ankara and Tel Aviv—places where more modernist architecture could be found during this period than anywhere else in the world.

It was really only after World War II that modern architecture came into its own and began to make significant and sustained contributions to urban space, such as at the Säynätsalo Town Hall in Finland and the Prager Strasse in Dresden, Germany.

Then there were two new modernist capitals: Chandigarh in India and Brasília in Brazil. The United States had only hesitatingly embraced modernism. But that changed when Mies van der Rohe arrived to teach at the Illinois Institute of Technology in Chicago, and Walter Gropius joined the faculty at Harvard University. Corporations were particularly eager to adopt the new style's sleek, anonymous surfaces, with the Lever House (1950–52), designed by the firm of Skidmore Owings & Merrill (SOM), and the Seagram Building (1958) by Mies van der Rohe, both in New York City, setting the tone. SOM soon specialized in designing corporate headquarters in the United States and abroad and became one of the largest architectural firms of the time. The relative coherency and anonymity of post–World War II architecture was offset by prestige commissions that introduced bold and exciting forms into the urban context, including the Guggenheim Museum (Frank Lloyd Wright, 1956–59), the Berlin Philharmonic Hall (Hans Bernhard Scharoun, 1956–63), the Sydney Opera House (Jørn Utzon, 1957–73).

By the 1960s, the conventions of modernism were breaking down, and architects began experimenting with large scales and simple forms in a style that came to be known as Brutalism, as exemplified by the Yamanashi Press and Broadcasting Center (Kenzo Tange, 1964–67) in Kofu, Japan, and the Royal National Theatre (Denys Lasdun, 1976) in London, buildings with exaggerated forms and large-scale massing. At that time, architecture's claims to universality, its anticontextual aesthetic, and the drabness of housing projects started to come under heavy criticism. A group from England, which came to be known under the banner of the journal it founded, *Archigram*, promoted an architecture influenced by Pop Art that was mobile, flexible, transitory, and youth-oriented. Counter-culture architecture, opposing the corporate and the drab, began to assert its presence in the discussions.

These and other critiques developed into a larger movement that in the 1970s came to be known as Postmodernism. Some architects, like Aldo Rossi in Italy, hoped for a return to history. Others, like Robert Venturi and Denise Scott Brown, sought out parody and irony. Still others, like Peter Eisenman in the United States and Oswald Mathias Ungers in Germany, aimed for a formalism more rigorous than even that of the modernists. The most enduring aspect of Postmodernism was its call for a heightened awareness of a building's context, but how context should be defined was much debated and varied from Daniel Libeskind's highly abstract Jewish Museum in Berlin (2001) to the efforts of Prince Charles of England to reawaken an interest in traditional styles. In the 1990s, in opposition to the conservative tenor of much architectural production, a group of avant-garde architects, among them Rem Koolhaas from Holland, called for a revival of modernist forms and abstractions. Advances in technology and computers also enabled architects to build structures that just the decade before would have been unthinkable. Frank Gehry's Guggenheim Museum (1997) in Bilbao, Spain, with its curved titanium skin, and Peter Cook and Colin Fournier's blue, bubble-shaped Kunsthaus (2003) in Graz, Austria, are notable examples.

▲ **Rockefeller Center**
1929–34

▲ **Barcelona Pavilion**
1928–29

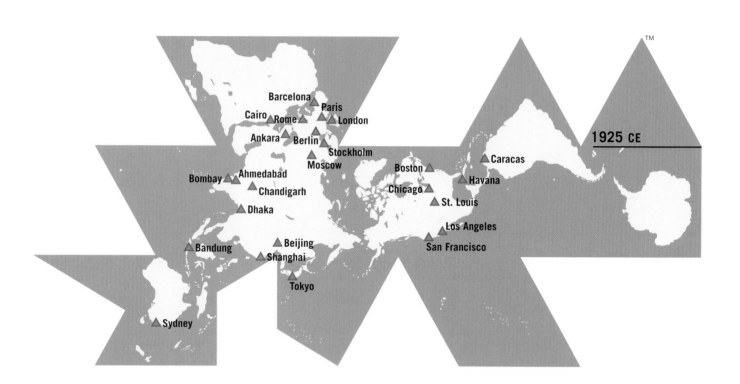

1925 CE

▲ **Lovell House**
1927–29

▲ **4D Dymaxion House**
1927

▲ **Weissenhof Siedlung**
1927

▲ Palace of the Soviets
1933

▲ Casa del Fascio
1936

▲ Brasília
1956–60

▲ Sher-e-Banglanagar
1961–82

▲ Esposizione Universale di Roma (EUR)
1937–42

▲ Zeppelinfeld
1937

▲ Säynätsalo Town Hall
1949–52

▲ National Schools of Art, Havana
1961–65

▲ Bata Shoe Factory
1937

▲ Health and Education Ministry
1936–46

▲ Olympic Stadium
1961–64

1950 CE

▲ Japanese Pavilion, Paris Expo
1937

▲ TWA Terminal
1956–62

▲ Sydney Opera House
1957–73

▲ Church of Christ the Worker
1958–60

▲ AT&T Building
1980–84

▲ Illinois Institute of Technology Library Building
1944–45

▲ School of Architecture, Ahmedabad
1965

▲ Mill Owners' Association Building
1954

▲ Guggenheim Museum
1956–59

▲ Piazza d'Italia
1975–78

▲ Yale University Art Gallery
1951–53

▲ Centre Georges Pompidou
1971–77

▲ Pyramide du Louvre
1989

▲ Salk Institute
1959–66

▲ Farnsworth House
1946–51

▲ Heidi Weber House
1965

▲ Magney House
1982–84

▲ Eames House
1945–49

▲ House for Dr. Bartholomew
1961–63

▲ Berlin Social Science Research Center
1981

▲ Fallingwater
1936–37

▲ Villa Mairea
1938–41

▲ Ronchamp
1955

▲ Chapel of Light
1989

18.1 Modern steel construction

Modernism

An inescapable problem in discussing 20th-century architecture is the definition of such terms as *modernity*, *modernization*, and *modernism*. For example, different artistic fields—and even different practitioners—tend to have contradictory understandings of the meaning of the word *modernism*. In the collages of Kurt Schwitters, modernism might be used to indicate fragmentation; in James Joyce's *Finnegan's Wake*, a heightened sense of subjectivity is implied; and to understand the music of Arnold Schoenberg, objectivity is the precondition. In architecture, modernism is associated with a radical break with past forms: the ballast of literal historical allusions is thrown overboard. In the late 1920s, buildings by Le Corbusier or Mies van der Rohe had white walls and simple forms, with the emphasis on function and structure. Pointing the way was Philip Johnson's and Henry-Russell Hitchcock's book, *The International Style*, which followed on the heels of an exhibition in the New York Museum of Modern Art (1932). In the Weimar Republic between 1923 and 1933, there arose the term *Neue Sachlichkeit* ("New Objectivity"); a critique of the overemotional aspects of some forms of Expressionism, it advocated clean lines and matter-of-fact design. The word *functionalism* also came into play, though this term also had several connotations. For Mies van der Rohe, the emphasis was on the clarity of a building's form and detailing; for Walter Gropius, it was on the building's massing and organization. For Le Corbusier, it meant the use of concrete and of the free plan, as defined by his Five Points. Although the early modernists usually preferred white walls, it was not an absolute. But where color was deployed, it often passed unnoticed in the black-and-white photographs of the time. The work of Frank Lloyd Wright and Alvar Aalto have a somewhat unusual position in the discussions about modernism; both are integral to its history and yet both were critics of its emphasis on functionalism, and both held that architecture should not promote a radical rupture with the past. What they also shared was a strong respect for the natural landscape—more so than most modernists of the time.

Despite these nuances and the debates that they engendered, the early 1930s was a moment of optimism for those who spearheaded the new movement. Significant works included: Gerrit Rietveld's Schröder House (Utrecht, Netherlands, 1924); Alvar Aalto's Viipuri Library (1927–35); Richard Neutra's Lovell House (Hollywood, California, 1927–29); Karl Ehn's Karl-Marx-Hof (Vienna, 1927–30); Clemenz Holzmeister's Grand National Assembly Hall (Ankara, 1928); Le Corbusier's Villa Savoye (Poissy, France, 1929–31); Mies van der Rohe's German National Pavilion (Barcelona, 1928–29); Johannes Duiker's Open Air School (Amsterdam, 1930; and Lúcio Costa and Oscar Niemeyer's Ministry of Health and Education (Rio de Janeiro, 1936–46).

The Arts and Crafts had helped to pave the way, especially in its attempts to raise the standards of bourgeois taste through education. The Bauhaus, founded by Walter Gropius in 1919, was, however, the first school to teach modernist design outright and attempt to bring the Arts and Crafts ethos up to date with modern industry. Everyday objects such as door handles, chairs, and dishes were designed with a view toward simplicity and practicality so that function itself equaled style. Though the Garden City movement, which began in the late 19th century, was an extension of Arts and Crafts ideals into the realm of the city, it was not until Le Corbusier wrote the book *Urbanism* (1924) that urban design was given a purely modern cast.

Modernism is also linked to the emergence of new materials like steel, concrete, and glass, which enabled, by the second half of the 19th century, the production of the skyscrapers, bridges, and train sheds that changed the image of the city in both plan and silhouette. Important in this respect was the work of Peter Behrens for the corporate giant Allgemeine Elektrizitäts-Gesellschaft (AEG). Gropius and others were particularly enamored of industrial buildings and their formal possibilities, and began to see them as potential models for design even before World War I. Mies van der Rohe, in particular, brought the aesthetics of steel and glass into the modern era with his skyscraper designs.

Though modernism and modernization are often linked, modernization actually predates modernism: it is a result of the 19th century's Industrial Revolution, with its shift from an agricultural to a factory-based economy. The consequences included the secularization of society, the emergence of a professional class, and the rationalization of the building industries. Though England and then Germany paved the way, modernization was not a purely European phenomenon; it was eagerly taken up in Turkey, Israel, Brazil, the United States, and elsewhere.

The politics associated with modernization have varied from totalitarianism and dictatorship to republicanism and democracy. An example of modernization impacting aesthetics is the Tennessee Valley Authority, which in the 1930s redesigned a huge area along the Tennessee River to create a series of strikingly modern dams for electricity generation. The tightest relationship between modernism and modernization was to be found in the days of the newly forming Soviet Union, when there was, for a few years, a sense of excitement about the new social promise of communism. El Lissitzky, Vladimir

18.15 **Barcelona Pavilion**

building framed by the roof and the top of the Tinian marble wall and then descending through various layers to the floor of the building. The floor, surfaced in white travertine and matching, to some degree, the whiteness of the roof, created for visitors a floating sensation interrupted only in the central room, where the space in front of the great onyx slab was covered by a thin black carpet. On the opposite wall, the glass was covered by drapery of scarlet silk. The central space was thus a type of stage set, its primary purpose being a reception area for visiting dignitaries.

18.16 **Barcelona Pavilion**

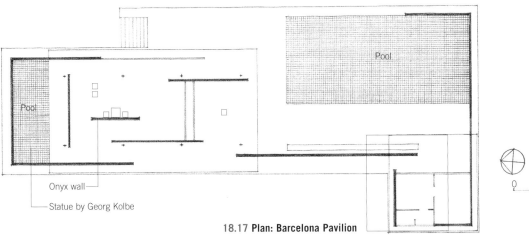

Pool

Pool

Onyx wall

Statue by Georg Kolbe

18.17 **Plan: Barcelona Pavilion**

0   10 m

Buckminster Fuller

Among the modernists, the person who most radically rethought the question of technology was Buckminster Fuller (1895–1983). In 1929, at the age of thirty-two, he decided to study what he called the ecological principles of life. His goal was to analyze nature's resources and think of ways to make them available to all of humanity through an informed, efficient, flexible, and responsible attitude toward design. His key concept was synergetics, which is what he called the underlying coordinate system of both physical and metaphysical nature. Using this theoretical platform, he hoped to coordinate the laws of nature with the processes of industrialization in the hope for improved social conditions.

What resulted in 1928, after a series of experiments with large-scale towers and multiple-family housing systems, was the project for the prefabricated, mass-produced 4D Dymaxion House in which plumbing and electrical networks, as well as appliances, were all contained in the central mast. The house could therefore operate independently of any utility network, which made it flexible enough to be located anywhere in the world. It was enclosed by transparent shuttering walls made of vacuum-pane glass, which eliminated the need for windows. A specially designed ventilation system made dusting unnecessary, and air drawn through vents was filtered and then heated or cooled as desired. An in-home laundry facility was designed to wash, dry, fold, and place clean laundry in appropriate compartments. The entire structure was to be mass-produced and flown to its site by blimps, with installation requiring only a single day. All of this, Fuller estimated, would cost only slightly more than a 1928 Ford or Chevrolet automobile. The 4D Dymaxion House, however, was never realized.

18.18 Model of a 4D Dymaxion House

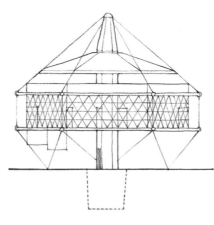

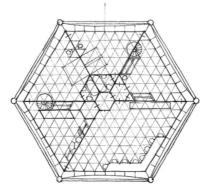

18.19 Plan and elevation: 4D Dymaxion House

18.20 Exterior view and plan: The Wichita House that Buckminster Fuller developed with the Beech Aircraft Company of Wichita, Kansas

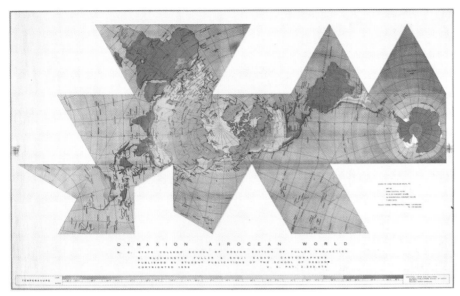

18.21 Buckminster Fuller's Dymaxion map

Fuller also had a great interest in geography and produced the Dymaxion map (1941), as an icosahedron that could be unfolded in different ways. (The term *Dymaxion* was derived from a combination of the words *dynamism*, *maximum*, and *ions*.) From the advent of the Dymaxion map to the geometries that led Richard Smalley and others to the Nobel Prize–winning discovery of carbon buckyballs (named for Fuller—who was affectionately known as "Bucky"—they are the most symmetrical large molecules known), Buckminster Fuller influenced a whole generation of architects, scientists, and visionary thinkers. He was one of the earliest advocates of renewable energy sources— solar, wind, and waves—and coined the term *Spaceship Earth* to emphasize the fact that we live on an ecologically interconnected planet.

Fuller's breakthrough discovery—and this one was fully practical—was the geodesic dome, which was designed to have the best possible ratio of volume to weight. Fuller determined that a network of triangular struts arranged on great circles (or geodesics) would create local triangular rigidity and distribute stress in a manner that would result in the most efficient structure ever designed. Geodesic domes, in fact, become stronger as they increase in size. Industry and the U.S. military immediately saw the potential of geodesic domes, and they were built by the hundreds around the world. The U.S. Pavilion at the Expo '67 (the popular name for the world's fair in Montreal in 1967) was, for example, a giant geodesic dome.

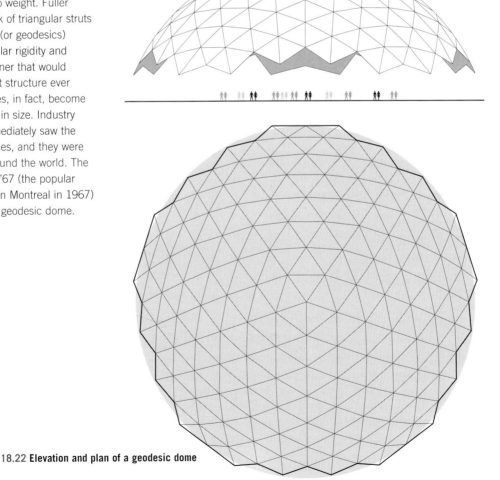

18.22 Elevation and plan of a geodesic dome

Palace of the Soviets

To celebrate the new Soviet state, Joseph Stalin planned to build a huge Palace of the Soviets in Moscow. A competition was held in 1931 under the hopeful auspices of the architectural community. It was believed that Russia, as an emerging world power, would continue the trend set by constructivists. Over 160 Soviet architects and firms and 24 foreigners volunteered designs; among the latter were Le Corbusier, Walter Gropius, Hannes Meyer, Erich Mendelsohn, and August Perret.

The competition was carried out in four phases. The first, open only to the Soviet architects, assisted in the formulation of the exact functions of the palace and only required that the building be conceived as a "people's forum" for mass demonstrations and rallies. The results of this phase, published and exhibited in Moscow, established the guidelines for the second stage of the competition, such as a large auditorium to accommodate 15,000 people and a series of spaces to serve as a theater and cinema.

The stipulations for the third stage of the competition stressed "monumental quality, simplicity, integrity and elegance" and the use "both of new methods and the best employed in classical architecture." Le Corbusier's design was conceived to optimize the functional requirements of the complex, but in a manner that created a striking visual image, especially from above. Unlike most of the competition entries, which tried to squeeze all the functions into a single mass, Le Corbusier distributed the functions into two main volumes. The foci of these volumes were the two wedge-shaped auditoriums, neatly fitted into the irregular site on the banks of the Moscow River. The plans of two auditoriums (designed with Gustave Lyon), were optimized not only for sightlines and acoustics but also for ease of access and egress. The sculptural drama of the design was provided by the auditoriums' roofs, which were suspended from splayed girders. The girders of the larger auditorium were suspended by cables from a soaring parabolic arch. This arch, much like Eero Saarinen's post–World War II arch in St. Louis still to come, would have towered above

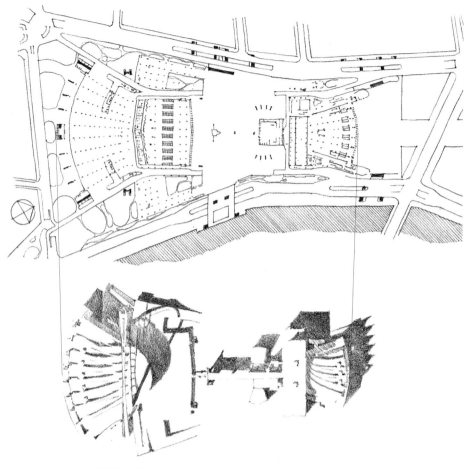

18.23 Le Corbusier's design for the Palace of the Soviets

the Moscow skyline and would have, from certain vistas, framed the bulbous domes of the Kremlin within its curve. The arch was intended as an inscription of modernity onto the skyline. It would have been the first modern building with such an ambition, apart perhaps from the Eiffel Tower, which had no particular program and was conceived as part of the preparations for the Paris World's Fair of 1889.

The modernists, however, were to be sorely disappointed. The award went to Boris Iofan and Vladimir Shchuko for a design that called for a towering wedding cake concoction of enormous massing and height. It was to be topped by a huge apotheosis of Vladimir Lenin. Despite being an expression of Soviet might, the edifice was

close in design to contemporaneous icons of capitalism, like the Wrigley Building (1920) in Chicago. In preparation for the construction of Iofan's building, the Cathedral of Christ the Savior was demolished in 1931. However, water from the adjoining Moscow River began to flood the site, delaying construction. By the outbreak of World War II, the steel skeleton was almost complete, but during the course of the war, much of that steel was melted down to make tanks to fight the Nazis. Nikita Khrushchev abandoned the project after Stalin's death in 1953 and had the already existing structure converted into a Moscow metro station and a giant public swimming pool. Recently, the Cathedral of Christ the Savior has been rebuilt at the site; it was consecrated in August 2000.

Mombasa

With the exception of a few countries, such as Ethiopia, most of Africa prior to World War I was still under colonial rule, with the occupying powers primarily interested in the extraction of goods. As a result, the principal building projects throughout the continent were train stations, port facilities, and urban layouts that separated whites from blacks. Mombasa, in Kenya, is an excellent example. It had long been a busy port with a complex multiethnic character. Its harbor, on the eastern side of the island, had a narrow entrance and afforded good protection. In the 16th century, the Portuguese hoped to control the city but were never able to assert their dominance over the sultan of Mombasa, who reigned over the relatively independent city until the middle of the 19th century, when it became a British protectorate. In 1887, the city's administration was relinquished to the British East Africa Association, which envisioned it as the sea terminal of the Uganda Railway (begun 1896). The aim was to connect the city with Buganda (part of present-day Uganda), a wealthy kingdom on the north shore of the Lake Victoria that the colonial powers were eager to exploit for coffee and tea; white settlers also hoped to set up cotton farms.

Construction of the line started at Mombasa and reached Lake Victoria in 1901. Indian traders set up corporations alongside the British, dealing in rice and coffee in particular. In the 1920s, Mombasa became Africa's leading harbor for kerosene and gasoline. Because the old city was compact and not very large, it left the rest of the island free for development. The English built a new harbor, Kilindini Harbor, on the island's west side, which could accommodate berths for large ships. In 1926, Walton Jameson, a town planning expert, laid out the new colonial city. Predictably, the train station was the conceptual apex of the design. A tripronged set of streets formed a business center running eastward, connecting to the old town. To the north and south of the business center, the city was divided according to race and class, with separate African and Swahili quarters; the more elite section was to the south, with its oceanfront, was separated from the business center by a zone of schools, a golf course, parks, and sports areas.

18.24 Old town, Mombasa, Kenya

Rail line

Residential area for Africans

Railway station

Docks

Commercial district

Old town

Warehouse district

Park area for whites

Mombasa Harbor

Kilindini Harbor

Residential area for whites

0   1 km

18.25 Plan of Mombasa, Kenya

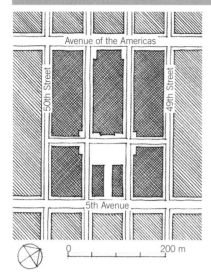

18.26 Plan diagram: Rockefeller Center

Rockefeller Center

By the late 1920s, New York had risen to the level of a world metropolis. Dozens of tall buildings had been constructed, including new civic and institutional buildings. Skyscraper architects had moved away from overt historicism and toward the elegant lines of art deco, as with the Chrysler Building (1928–30). The Chanin Building (1927–29) went even further, with a neutral, gridlike facade. Rockefeller Center, designed by Raymond Hood and Wallace Harrison, was nothing less than a city within a city, composed of fourteen buildings between Forty-eighth and Fifty-first streets in New York City. At the core of the composition was the seventy-one-story RCA Building (1931–32), which faced onto a sunken plaza defined on its flanks by low-rise buildings—the British Empire Building and the Maison Française. The RCA Building was sheathed in a yellowish limestone with aluminum trim; its windows arranged vertically in slightly recessed strips to emphasize its soaring qualities. In its complete avoidance of references to a classical past, as well as the thinness of its central tower, this building paved the way for the skyscraper aesthetic developed later by the modernists. Radio City Music Hall, containing the nation's largest indoor theater, was on the next block. Innovative was the introduction of a cross-street, Rockefeller Plaza, that divided up the central parcel.

Though rarely emulated, the center was much admired for its urban design implications. The setbacks, which were required by zoning regulations, were woven fluidly into the design that they seemed to be an organic part of the building—a quality different from that found at the RCA Building, the Chanin Building, or even the Empire State Building, with its stockier base. To emphasize the building's towering quality, the lower buildings were designed to look more substantial—almost like stone volumes that also help frame the views of the tower. Artists were brought in to create sculptures and murals—themselves excellent examples of Art Deco—for placement over the entrance doors and in the lobby. These included Paul Manship, who designed a gilded statue of a recumbent Prometheus. The Mexican socialist artist Diego Rivera was commissioned to create a mural for the lobby, but when it was discovered that it contained a portrait of Vladimir Lenin and other anticapitalist imagery, it was removed.

18.27 Rockefeller Center

Tall buildings constructed in New York City from 1920 to 1930 include:
Standard Oil Building (1920–28)
Bowery Savings Bank (1921–23)
Barclay-Vesey Building (1923–27)
Ritz Tower (1925–27)
Paramount Building (1926–27)
Chanin Building (1927–29)
Chrysler Building (1928–30)
RCA Building (1929–31)
McGraw-Hill Building (1930–31)
Empire State Building (1930–31)

18.28 Lower plaza, Rockefeller Center, New York City

18.29 **Bata Shoe Factory, Zlín, Czech Republic**

18.30 **Bata Shoe Factory**

Czechoslovakia

In many places in Europe, national Romanticism hindered the advancement of modernist architecture since many nationalists saw modernism—and its associations with industrialism and socially progressive politics—as antithetical to the idyllic past central to Romantic ideology. (To some extent, this why the first true example of modernism as a state-sponsored aesthetic flourished in Turkey and other non-European countries, where Romanticism had never become as firmly developed.) Nonetheless, nationalism, even in Europe, began to turn to modernism as an expression of a country's search for autonomy and capitalist strength. One of the first places where this was manifest was Czechoslovakia, which in 1918 emerged an independent state from the dismembered Austro-Hungarian Empire. The small Central European country inherited both a large portion of the former empire's ethnic diversity and its economic strength. In fact, Czechoslovakia became one of Europe's most politically stable and democratic systems during the restless interwar years. This stability is generally attributed to Tomá s Garrigue Masaryk (1850–1937), the first president of the republic and an internationally respected scholar-statesman. Though Czechoslovakian government officials never gave state sponsorship to modernism, this did not hamper the younger generation and the educated and prosperous middle-class from seeing modernism as

an articulation of Czechoslovakia's political emancipation from the old Austro-Hungarian Empire.

By 1937, the Bata Shoe Company had become the world market-leader in shoe production and the first manufacturer in Europe to mass-produce good-quality shoes at an affordable price. The company's founder, Tomás Bata invested in an extensive building program, first in his hometown of Zlín, where he located the company headquarters, and later in factory towns that he and his successor, Jan Bata, established on three continents. Bata had factories and sales organizations in thirty-three countries and was at the time one of the most international companies in the world. Bata systematically hired young Czech architects and engineers with international experience. One of these young professionals was Vladimir Karfik, who had worked for Le Corbusier and Frank Lloyd Wright.

The Bata headquarters (1937), a seventeen-story building designed by Karfik, was one of the first high-rise buildings in Europe. It was built with a structural frame of reinforced concrete on a module of 6.15 by 6.15 meters. This so-called Bata standard was the basis for all Bata buildings, ranging from factories and retail stores to various public buildings. Contrary to traditional dispositions in skyscraper design, three service pods were located on the perimeter of the building. This created

an unobstructed rectangle measuring 80 by 20 meters organized as an open-plan office in which reconfigurable office modules were the only spatial dividers. Electricity and telephone networks with plugs laid in the floor on a 3-by-3-meter grid facilitated flexibility in space organization. The most striking feature of the building was Jan Bata's office in the form of an elevator. As a vertically mobile unit, Bata could dock on every floor—thereby going wherever he was needed. Bata was also able to communicate with his employees throughout the building by means of an intercom. The interior of the office elevator, designed with wood paneling and double windows, was well lit by natural light. Among the most difficult tasks Karfik faced was how to make a sink with running cold and hot water possible in such a mobile environment, and how to adapt the cabin to quick temperature changes when moving in the shaft.

By the end of the 1930s, European modernism had stalled. Gropius and Mies had all but disappeared from the scene, and Le Corbusier received few commissions, prompting him to seek work outside of Europe. The reception outside of Europe was often more positive. Turkey and Israel and later Brazil and India were particularly important in this respect since there modern buildings were part of a highly visible nation-building effort.

Ankara

The impact of modernist architecture was first felt not in Europe, as might have been expected, but in Turkey. When the Turkish Republic was founded by Mustafa Kemal (also known as Atatürk) in 1923, modern architecture became part of the official state program. Atatürk's vision was a secular, industrialized nation based on technical and scientific progress, with institutions modeled after those in Europe. Ankara, at that time a small town in central Anatolia, was chosen as the new capital since it was more or less in the center of the nation. Its design (1927) by the German planner Hermann Jansen, can be considered, along with Canberra, Australia, among the first in a long string of modernist capitals that would include Brasília, Brazil; Chandigarh, India; and Islamabad, Pakistan. In contrast to other localities, where modernism was imposed by colonial masters, in Ankara, it was a triumphant statement that announced Turkey's independence. Bandung, Indonesia, was built by the Dutch; Beirut and Casablanca by the French; and Taipei (then part of China, now the capital of Taiwan) was largely planned by the Japanese. Ankara, by contrast, was an expression of a new politico-aesthetic phenomenon: national modernism.

18.31 Exhibition Hall for the Izmir International Fair, Ankara, Turkey

Most of the buildings were designed by architects and planners from Germany and Central Europe. The Austrian architect Clemenz Holzmeister (1886–1983), for example, designed the government district, including several ministries, the presidential palace, and the Grand National Assembly Hall. Despite the plain cubic facades, the overall organization was often indebted to classical principles and vocabulary. Nonetheless, the purpose was to visibly and progressively champion the ideals of the new Republic of Turkey. New schools, especially for girls; houses; centers of popular education; and places for physical education, recreation, leisure, and entertainment were among the typologies that became emblematic for the republic's stated aims. The Ismet Pasa Girls' Institute in Ankara, a vocational school, was designed by the Swiss Ernst Egli in 1930. Modern architecture and planning was also employed for model villages, factories, and large infrastructural projects such as the Cubuk Dam outside Ankara (1936). The exhibition hall, which also served as an opera house in Ankara, was designed by Turkish architect Sevki Balmumcu, who won the commission in a competition. It was erected to showcase the technological accomplishments of the Turkish Republic, as were the structures built for the Izmir International Fair.

18.32 Exhibition Hall for the Izmir International Fair

18.33 **Hadassah University Medical Center, Mount Scopus, Jerusalem**

Israeli Modernism

During the British mandate over Palestine (1920–48), modern architecture became the dominant style among Jews, who had begun to settle there in the name of Zionism in the search for a homeland. For them, modernism was a tabula rasa free from the memories of the Jewish diaspora. The argument focused on natural parameters such as heat, wind, light, topography, and materials, along with a streamlined practicality that accommodated the faster-spaced rhythm of modern life. There was no shortage of architects, since many were fleeing European fascism. Erich Mendelsohn, Alexander Klein, and Adolf Rading were particularly instrumental in consolidating Zionist and modernist design concepts. Mendelsohn's architecture—for instance, his Hadassah University Medical Center on Mt. Scopus in Jerusalem (1936–39)—consists of plain volumes, courtyards, and carefully punched blank walls. It was invested with abstracted, quasi-Oriental imagery, in contrast to the whitewashed international modernist architecture of Zeev Rechter's Engel House in Tel Aviv (1933), the city that came to embody Israel's modernism.

When founded in 1909, Tel Aviv was a small suburb to the north of the Arab city of Jaffa. Unlike Jaffa, with its mixed population, Tel Aviv was designed by Jews for Jews. Its city fathers welcomed the ethos of modernism, and by the late 1930s the city had become one of the few all-modern cities in the world. With the transition to Israeli statehood in 1948, Tel Aviv became the model for future development—especially since it was allied with Israel's massive modernization project, the blueprint for which was prepared by the state planning division headed by Arieh Sharon, a Bauhaus disciple of Hannes Meyer. Sharon's designs were of strict rational modernism cleansed of all Oriental symbolism.

In the 1960s, a new generation of Israeli-born architects began to critique the allegiance to modernism, seeking instead ways to establish communal identity using visceral ties with the past. Aligning themselves with post–World War II criticism—and particularly with the teaching of Team X and Louis Kahn—their architecture sought local expression in shaded communal spaces, hierarchical layouts, broken volumes, and local building materials, as was evident in the early example of Ram Karmi's Negev Center (1960).

18.34 **Engel House, Tel Aviv**

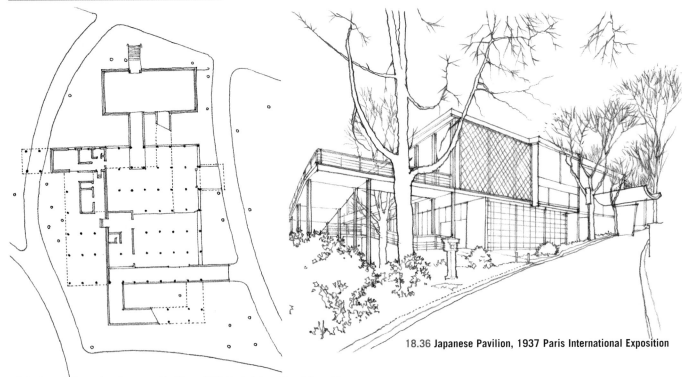

18.35 Ground-floor plan: Japanese Pavilion, 1937 Paris International Exposition

18.36 Japanese Pavilion, 1937 Paris International Exposition

Japanese Pavilion

The Japanese investment in industrialization began during the years of the Meiji period (1869–1912), after the United States' warships steamed into Japanese ports and forced the country to open its economy to international trade. In 1869, a new constitution pledged Japan to maintain this policy. The years of the Meiji period were thus characterized by rapid industrialization and mechanization accompanied by the adoption of Western clothes, habits, and manners. In the years leading up to World War II, European modernism began to establish a foothold among the country's avant-garde. Young Japanese architects traveled to Europe or took up apprenticeships with European architects; among them was Mamoru Yamada. He spent a considerable amount of time in Germany after completing the Electrical Laboratory for the Ministry of Public Works (1929), the only Japanese work to be included in Hitchcock and Johnson's famous International Style Exhibition of 1932 at the Museum of Modern Art in New York. His later work, Tokyo Teishin Hospital (1938), with its white tiled exterior finish, large standardized windows, and minimal ornamentation, is representative of Japanese

rationalist architecture of the prewar period. By the mid-1930s, the Japanese government began to repress the development of the modernist style and called for a return to more traditional looks. This coincided with the invasion in 1931 of Chinese Manchuria, which Japan wanted as a source of raw materials such as coal, oil, and bauxite.

A successful example of a modernist Japanese design in Europe is the Japanese Pavilion designed for the 1937 Paris International Exposition by Junzo Sakakura, who had trained under Le Corbusier in Paris from 1931 to 1936. Initially, he had been commissioned to oversee the construction of a traditional-style pavilion, but he surreptitiously modified that design to create a delicate structure of steel, glass, and concrete that was well integrated into its sloped and wooded site. The building was distinctly modern, yet clearly Japanese. Rather than the literal use of a traditional Japanese architectural vocabulary, Sakakura incorporated a steel frame reminiscent of wooden structures typical of Japanese residential architecture along with subtle ornaments that evoked design features from traditional architecture.

Villa Mairea

Alvar Aalto (1898–1976), a Finnish architect, came to modernism more cautiously than did the architects in Turkey and Brazil, where national interests propelled modernism forward aggressively. In Finland, a vibrant national Romantic tradition was popular at the time; it idealized village life, which Alto linked, somewhat incongruously, with his unbounded enthusiasm for Italy, and in particular for its rural towns. Aalto synthesized this ideal with his admiration of Frank Lloyd Wright and with the clean aesthetics of the modernists in the Villa Mairea (Noormarkku, Finland, 1938–41).

The overall planning is certainly Wrightian, and early sketches show a relationship in particular to Fallingwater. In terms of composition, however, Aalto's understanding of space is more Cubist—not in an obvious sense, as in Pavel Janák's work in Czechoslovakia, but in the asymmetrical tensions that exist in the plan between solid and void and between the implied square of the garden and the house, which is clamped against one corner. But what could be seen as Cubism can also be read as the introduction of a temporal coefficient into the design: the house appears to be growing

18.37 Living room: Villa Mairea, Noormarkku, Finland

18.38 Villa Mairea

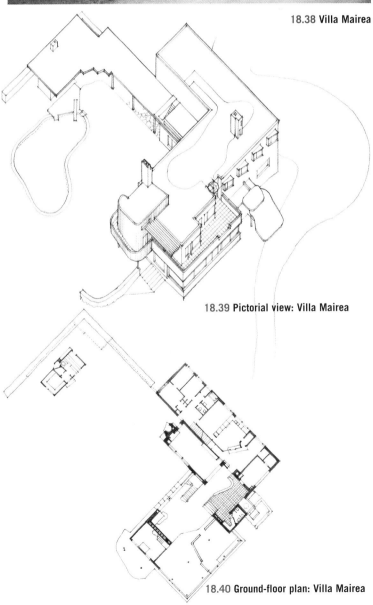

18.39 Pictorial view: Villa Mairea

18.40 Ground-floor plan: Villa Mairea

and expanding over time. Aalto also allowed for an overt regional gloss in his choice of the wood for the exterior and the use of rustic wooden rails for the balconies. These are, however, offset by steel railings that look like they've been borrowed from a ship and contrast with the smooth bamboo railings used for the interior staircase.

Because of its almost eclectic fusion of different motifs, Villa Mairea could be seen as breaking the mold of modernist reserve. But it could also be perceived as an extension of the late 19th-century approaches of Greene & Greene, Antonio Gaudí, Victor Horta, and Adolf Loos. Though all the modernists had unique styles, Aalto was consistently viewed as less beholden to rationalism and functionalism because of his use of curved lines, contrasting materials, and a penchant for picturesque massing. Aalto worked closely with his wife Aino (1894–1949), who was also Finnish, and much of the interior of the Villa Mairea was, in fact, was designed by her. They collaborated on the design of chairs made with bent plywood, a new technology at the time and far different from the heavy steel-frame chairs of most modernists. Aalto was a CIAM member, attending the second congress in Frankfurt in 1929 and the fourth congress in Athens in 1933. His reputation grew as a consequence of the Finnish Pavilion at the 1939 New York World's Fair and the Baker House Dormitory (1947) for the Massachusetts Institute of Technology in Cambridge.

18.41 Hanna House, Palo Alto, California

Usonian Houses

Throughout the 1930s, Frank Lloyd Wright continued to critique both the Beaux-Arts and modernists styles. Somewhat like Aalto, he tried to infuse modernism with a national Romantic sentiment—in his case holding out the ideal of democracy rooted in a simple life closely connected with the land. The traditional city, which derived from Europe, he argued, would eventually be replaced by a dispersed network of habitation. Anticipating this, he designed a futuristic Broadacre City (1932) that was to cover 10 square kilometers. Though Broadacre remained a utopian project, Wright was able to realize certain aspects of it with his Usonian houses. The origin of the name *Usonian* is not known, but it is likely derived from *U.S.-onia*, the name for a reformed American society that Wright tried to bring about for twenty-five years. The United States had a long tradition of pattern-book houses that could be constructed by local builders, without an architect. Wright's Usonian houses extended that tradition, except that what was to be imitated was not so much the individual plans as the general idea. The houses, built between 1936 and 1943, have characteristic features that would be incorporated into the American housing stock after World War II and that would remain characteristic of U.S. suburbs to some extent until the 1980s.

The Great Depression had left thousands homeless, and Wright was eager to show that contemporary architecture could accommodate the changed economic conditions without a loss of integrity. Wright proposed a single-story house that did not require expensive excavations for basements or upper-floor framing. Steel, which was expensive, was not used; instead, the houses were to be made of wood, brick, local stone, and prefabricated blocks. The bricks were not covered with stucco, and the wood was left plain, thus reducing finishing costs. The houses were sited not only to make optimal use of the lot but also to include as much openness as possible from the living room to the backyard. Heating was incorporated into the concrete floor in the form of looped water pipes buried under the slab. The elaborate and expensive millwork needed for door frames, for example, was eliminated. Wright fused the dining and living rooms and in some cases combined them into a single space. This was a radical departure from his earlier houses, and indeed from centuries of tradition: because of noise, smells, and the activities of servants, the kitchen was always set apart from the dining room. But the owners of these houses were not expected to be wealthy enough to be able to afford a maid. Wright also wanted to create spaces that were conducive to family conversation. The kitchen was also placed close to the carport, reducing the distance between the car and the kitchen to facilitate the transportation of groceries.

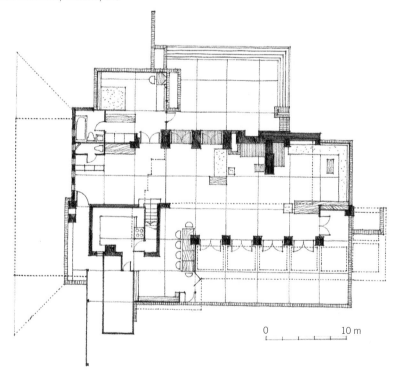

0   10 m

18.42 Plan: Bernard Schwartz House, Two Rivers, Wisconsin

18.43 Fallingwater, Bear Run, Pennsylvania

Fallingwater

Edgar J. Kaufmann had made a fortune made on his department stores. On the advice of his son, who was a student at the Taliesin School of Architecture, he engaged Wright in 1935 to design a family weekend and summer retreat on their woodland property at Bear Run in western Pennsylvania. (Their permanent residence was in Pittsburgh.) Unlike the bread-and-butter Usonian houses, Fallingwater (1936–37) is a dramatic statement on the possibilities of reinforced concrete expressed most memorably by a triple set of deeply overhanging cantilevered terraces that appear to float over a dramatic waterfall. The Kaufmanns had asked for a house from which they could look at the waterfall, but Wright built them one that was literally over the waterfall instead. A stair in the living room leads down to the top of the waterfall and to a small platform where people can sit and dangle their feet in the water.

Wright's justifications for his design lay in his conception of "organic architecture," a decidedly subjective term that for him indicated a building integrated into its site and context in the form of a sympathetic counterstatement. The diagonal plan and stepped section, for example, is a response to the contours of the site, a point particularly important to Wright and anticipated in part in earlier projects like the Freeman House

(1924–25). Here the ornamenting of the building's surface has given way to rustic, horizontally coursed yellowish stones that contrast with the smooth, stuccoed surfaces of the balconies and rooflines. Windows are hidden in recesses, with thinly mullioned glazing capturing some of the spaces in between the floor and roof to create indoor-outdoor rooms. When viewed from below the waterfall, the house seems to hover provocatively over the site, its straight lines contrasting with the huge boulders, and the white balconies contrasting with the forest's rich foliage. The stone walls that anchor the cantilevers mimic the stratified pattern of the rock ledges and rise up into the house in the form of towers that anchor the composition and seem almost like ancient ruins. Since the site is quite remote, Wright built a separate servants' quarter and garage just up the hill from the house. Today the site today is much more forested than it was originally, concealing the building more than Wright probably would have liked.

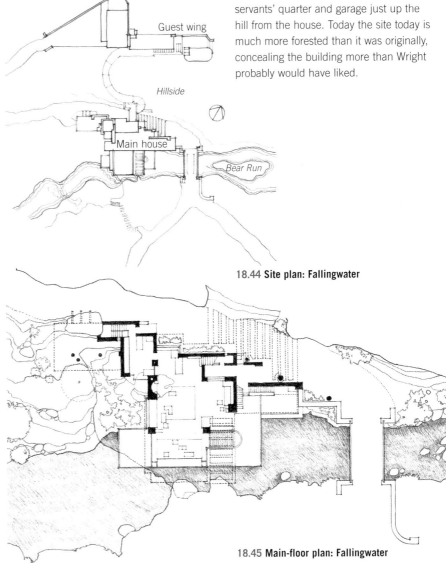

18.44 Site plan: Fallingwater

18.45 Main-floor plan: Fallingwater

18.46 **House by Lúcio Costa**

18.47 **Ministry of Health and Education, Rio de Janeiro**

Brazilian Modernism

The economic crash of 1929 shattered Brazil's export-oriented economy, giving rise to a powerful military that supported President Getulio Vargas (1883–1954) who, as a virtual dictator (r. 1930–45), created a tightly controlled state-sponsored program of modernization. Much as in Kemal Atatürk's Turkey, modern architecture was to be the visible imprint of his nationalist project. In 1930, the young architect Lúcio Costa was appointed director of the Escola Nacional de Belas Artes. Though Costa initially knew little about modern architecture, he soon became its leading advocate, bringing in a Russian émigré Gregori Warchavchik (1896–1972), who presented his "modernist house" at an exhibition that was opened to the public in 1930. It had a white, cubic volume (though a parapet concealed a pitched, tiled roof) that earned the architect a place in the 1930 CIAM congress.

Early in his own career, Costa had had little work and had spent his time studying books on the architecture of Walter Gropius, Ludwig Mies van de Rohe and, most of all, Le Corbusier. Le Corbusier himself had built little other than his "white" houses, but his books *Towards a New Architecture*, *The Contemporary City*, and *Precisions* were widely influential. In 1936, Gustavo Capanema, the thirty-three-year-old minister of education and health, took the bold step of commissioning Costa to build the ministry's official headquarters. Costa's initial design was a merger of the two halves of Le Corbusier's competition entry for the League of Nations project (1927). His final design, prepared in collaboration with Oscar Niemeyer (in consultation with Le Corbusier), was a fourteen-story tower located in the middle of a rectangular site. Ten-meter-high *pilotis*—much higher than what Le Corbusier had proposed—lift the structure off the ground. On the cross-axis, along one length of the site is the double-height block of the auditorium and the public spaces. Its most dramatic statement was the use of a curtain wall on the south side and a system of *brise-soleils*, or sunshades, on the other. Two towering curved shapes, covered with blue tiles, functioned as vents and storage for mechanical services. There was a restaurant on the roof terrace as well.

Costa and Niemeyer also collaborated on the design of the Brazilian Pavilion for the 1939 New York World's Fair, which carried the slogan "The World of Tomorrow." Costa wanted a building that would stand out not for its scale (the site was not big), nor for its luxury (Brazil was still poor), but for its inherent formal qualities. Simplicity and the suggestion of direct functionalism was its message. The two-story design lifted the main volume of the pavilion above the ground and made a statement out of its access ramp, whose large sweeping curve seemed to wedge itself forcefully into the upper floor. The ground floor was partially enclosed and had freestanding displays for national beverages like coffee, *maté*, and guarana. The garden to the rear showed off Brazilian flora. The upper floor, where the main auditorium was located, had an exhibition space with double-height steel columns that partially supported a free-plan mezzanine. Its facade had a *brise-soleil*, whereas the rear was glazed from top to bottom. The building became the icon for Brazilian modernism.

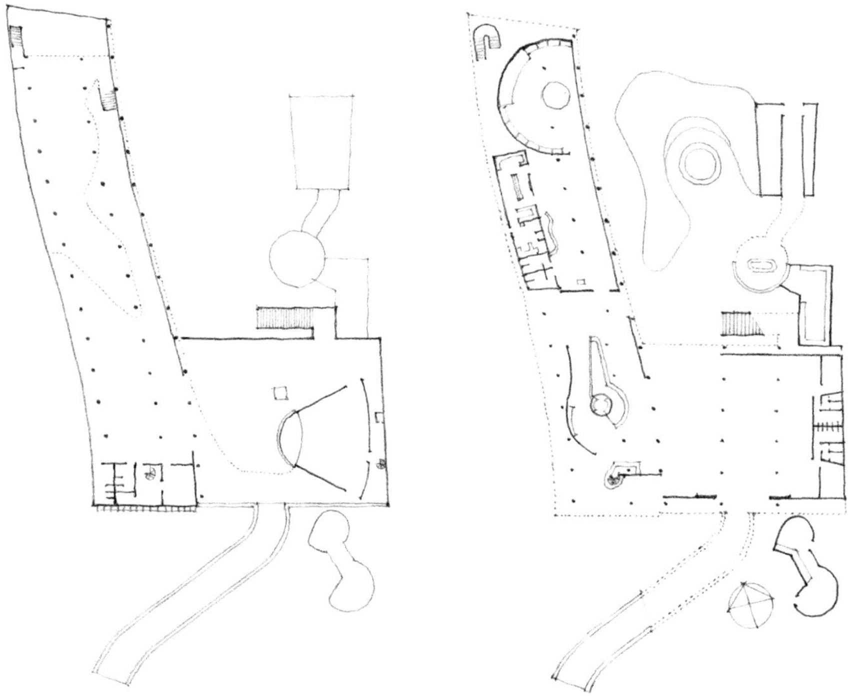

18.48 **Plans: Brazilian Pavilion, 1939 New York World's Fair**

Not everything in Brazil was European modernism and structural expression, however. Lina Bo Bardi (1914–92), for instance, designed a house made of adobe and straw, and Bernard Rudofsky, who lived in Brazil for three years (1938–41) and later wrote *Architecture Without Architects*, built a house for Joan Arnstein organized around five internal garden courtyards that extended the spaces of the living room, dining room, master bedroom, and children's bedrooms. Bo Bardi was one of the few independently practicing women architects among the early modernists. She was born in Italy. After graduating in Rome, she opened her own office, was involved in the Italian Communist Party, and after World War I created an influential journal, *A Cultura della Vita*, with Bruno Zevi. In 1946, she moved with her husband to Brazil and became a citizen in 1951. Her most important commission was for the São Paulo Museum of Art (1947). Sited at the top edge of a slope, she suspended the entire building in the form of a box from enormous concrete beams in order to open vistas to the horizon.

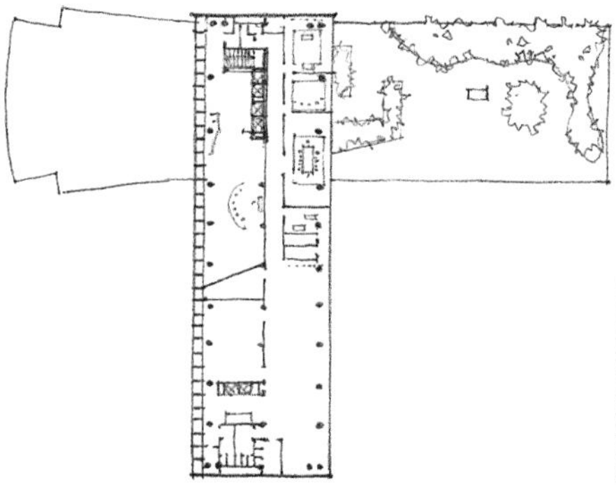

Third-floor plan

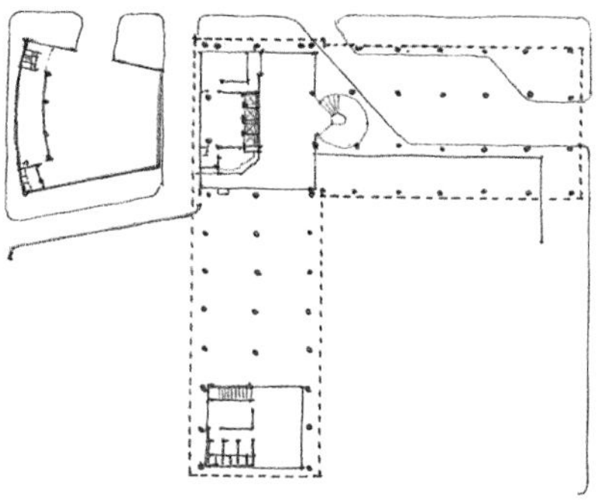

Ground-floor plan

18.49 **Plans: Ministry of Health and Education Building**

18.50 **São Paulo Museum of Art, Brazil**

18.51 **Palace of Italian Civilization, Esposizione Universale di Roma (EUR)**

parallels between Mussolini and the great patrons of the Renaissance, and beyond that to the Roman Empire. Members of the Italian Movement for Rational Architecture (MIAR), founded in 1928, looked for inspiration in Greco-Roman classicism as well as in the vernacular traditions of the Mediterranean region.

Some of the most significant examples of large-scale urban renewal requiring demolition in Rome, Milan, Turin, Bergamo, and Genoa were overseen by Mussolini's architect, Marcello Piacentini. He was also responsible for two significant new urban schemes: Città Universitaria (1932–35) and the Esposizione Universale di Roma (EUR, 1937–42), originally intended as the site of the 1942 Universal Exposition in Rome. The onset of World War II eclipsed plans for the exposition, but several pavilions were realized, including Ernesto La Padula's metaphysical and iconic Palace of Italian Civilization (1937–40). It was a glass box protected from the outside by a facade that consisted of six horizontal registers of identical arched loggias clad in travertine.

Italian Fascist Architecture

With the end of World War I, Italian architecture entered a new phase of self-awareness, spurred on by the rise of Fascism following Benito Mussolini's coup in 1922. Due to the strong nationalistic impulse at the core of Fascist ideology, Italian architects found themselves reflecting upon the role of tradition in their architecture. But this return to tradition, with its links to national Romanticism, had a very different character in Italy than it did in Germany. Italy's implementation of a vast state-sponsored building program that included the construction of post offices, train stations, civic buildings, and even small towns placed the country closer in spirit to Turkey than to Germany. For many architects, the Fascist critique of passivity seemed to legitimate modernism. Italian Fascist architecture, therefore, did not see itself as antithetical to clean geometries and white surfaces. There was, however, a fierce debate over the precise style that was to best represent the Fascist ethos. As a result, the avant-garde ideal of merging life and art fused in Italy with the sinister ambitions of totalitarianism, with artists and architects drawing numerous

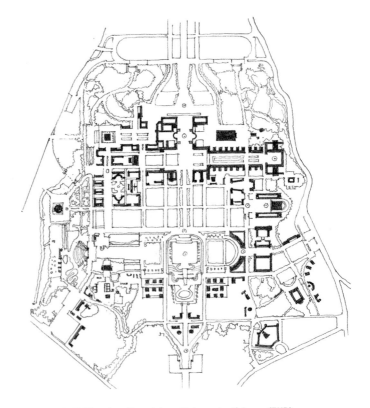

18.52 **Site plan: Esposizione Universale di Roma (EUR)**

18.53 Casa del Fascio, Como, Italy

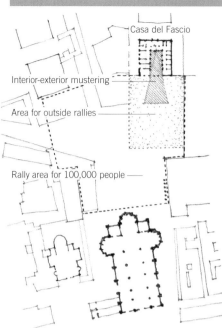

Casa del Fascio

Interior-exterior mustering

Area for outside rallies

Rally area for 100,000 people

18.54 Site plan: Casa del Fascio

Casa del Fascio

Among the many representatives of the modernist movement in Italy, Giuseppe Terragni (1904–43) was certainly the most prominent. He studied architecture at the Milan Polytechnic and became a member of Gruppo 7 (founded 1926), which consisted of seven architects unified in their advocacy of rationalism and Fascism. Giuseppe Terragni's Casa del Fascio (1933–36) in Como, designed as the regional headquarters of the Fascist Party, is not, despite its white boxy form, as ahistorical as it appears, for it fuses the model of the socialist meeting hall with the principle of an Italian palazzo by adhering to the traditional courtyard plan. The building was designed as a "house of glass," a descriptive term more apparent from the inside than the outside. Some 20 percent of its surface is glass, with large windows framing the city; the array of glass doors between the piazza and the atrium could all be swung open on demand. The meeting room of the *direttorio federale* ("provincial directorate") also overlooks the central atrium through a glass wall. This transparency symbolized the Fascist government's desire to be viewed as accessible and forthright, and that its leader and the people be seen as a continuum.

Unlike Le Corbusier's idea of architecture, which favored column grids, thin walls, and horizontal windows, Terragni created a complex, layered geometric architecture that allowed the building to be axial in approach and entry and yet have an interior of interpenetrating asymmetries that fit together almost like a puzzle. The plan is organized with offices along the eastern facade and meeting rooms along the opposite facade, separated by an atrium. On the front there is a balcony that faces onto the large piazza, but that allows speakers to address the crowds inside the building as well. The spiritual core of the building is the *sacrario*, or chapel, which is dedicated to the fallen heroes of the "Fascist Revolution." It is located to the left of the entrance foyer. To heighten the impression of entering a sacred precinct, Terragni made the floor level of the *sacrario* slightly lower than that of the atrium. The ceiling of the foyer is covered with black marble, whereas the walls are covered in red granite. The main hall is defined by an open structural system, with columns holding up large concrete beams on which are placed horizontal louvers that filter the light while a gap in the center allows for a controlled beam of direct light.

Meeting room of the *direttorio federale*

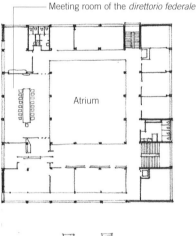

Atrium

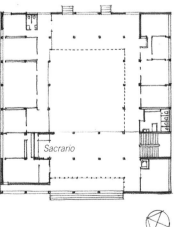

Sacrario

18.55 Ground- and first-floor plans: Casa del Fascio

18.56 **House of German Art in Munich, Germany**

18.57 **Zeppelinfeld, Nuremberg, Germany**

German Fascist Architecture

By the mid-1930s, modernist architecture began to develop along different tracks. In Europe, private-sector modernism takes shape in villas and houses. There are also examples from the public sector in the form of social housing, but mainly in places controlled by left-leaning governments, such as Vienna (during the period from 1919 to 1934) and the USSR. As previously discussed, Turkey and Brazil were the first to adopt modernism as an extension of nationalist politics. Though the fascist regimes in Germany and Italy were outspoken in their condemnation of Communism, their take on modern architecture was neither uniform nor totally negative. Italy attempted to link modernism with nationalist politics, while in Germany it came under attack by the National Socialists (Nazis) who came to power in 1933. Though no modernist architects were imprisoned, none received any commissions after 1933.

Adolf Hitler, who had once nursed ambitions of becoming a painter, took a great interest in architecture and set out guidelines on the matter, such as the need for German art to be clear and heroic and for buildings to be made for eternity. Modernism was generally disparaged and associated with corrupting, non-Germanic influences. One of Hitler's favorite architects was Paul Ludwig Troost (1879–1934), who designed the House of German Art in Munich (begun 1933); its blocklike mass and ornament-free white surface espoused a kind of stripped-down modernist classicism. The building was fronted by a long porch of columns standing in snappy military order. The enormous Zeppelinfeld by Albert Speer (1905–81), designed as part of a vast party headquarters complex, carries out the same ideas. Speer became Hitler's personal architect and not only designed the New Chancellery Wing but also made plans for a redesign of Berlin that would reflect the ambitions of the *Tausendjaehrige Reich* (the "Thousand-Year Empire"). The plan featured a wide and long boulevard cutting through the city, with an enormous vaulted hall at the apex of the composition. The hall had a vast loggia in front that led into an equally vast interior with rows of seating along the perimeter. Its purpose was to stage the great spectacles of political allegiance that were part of Nazi culture.

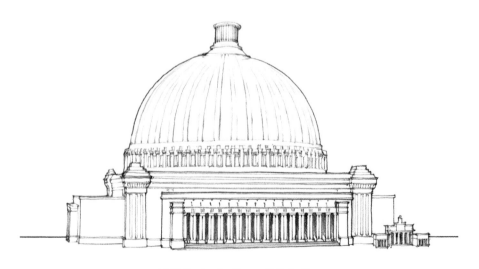

18.58 **Design for Victory Hall, Berlin**

18.59 Exterior view: Säynätsalo Town Hall, Finland

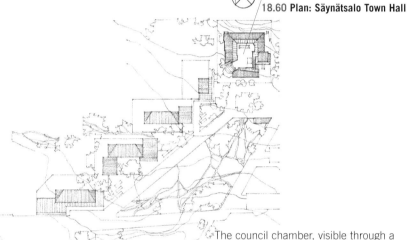

0 ⎯⎯⎯⎯ 10 m

18.60 Plan: Säynätsalo Town Hall

Säynätsalo Town Hall

By the time Alvar Aalto designed the Säynätsalo Town Hall (1949–52), his reputation was secure, largely due to the acclaimed Finnish Pavilion at the 1937 Paris International Exposition. In this town hall he began to move away from the modernist-cubist complexity of his early work toward the imagery of ancient Crete and medieval Italy that had fascinated him as a youth. The space, for that reason, is less a courtyard than a civic enclave raised above the lower slope. One enters it at a corner by means of a staircase molded into the landscape.

18.61 Site plan: Säynätsalo Town Hall

The council chamber, visible through a gap, is housed in a building that is square in plan and surmounted by a pitched roof that is, apart from a razor-thin line of dark flashing, not visible from the ground, making the volumes appear as abstract shapes. The external surfaces are all in textured brick in Flemish bond. The picturesque qualities of the composition are obvious. The staggers, angles, and shifts enhance the three-dimensional quality of the building, as do the windows of different sizes and proportions. In some places, the brick, where it touches the ground, rests on black tiles that cover the foundation; in other places, the brick appears to float effortlessly over the windows.

More modernist in flavor is the Seinäjoki Town Hall (1958), where Aalto returns to the cubist format, with its play of volume and solid, and of frame and opening. The site consists of two parcels straddling a busy road. Aalto created an esplanade through the site, with the buildings defining and expanding its spatial elements.

18.62 Town Hall, Säynätsalo

18.63 IIT Library Building, Chicago

Illinois Institute of Technology Library Building

International modernism in the United States—and even globally—would have developed far differently had some of its leading proponents not emigrated to the States during the Hitler regime. Mies van der Rohe came in 1937 to head the Chicago's Armour Institute of Technology (later renamed the Illinois Institute of Technology). The same year also saw the arrival of Walter Gropius, who taught at the Harvard Graduate School of Design. Marcel Breuer came to the United States as well and began a collaboration with Gropius before launching his own office in 1941. The publication in 1941 of the seminal *Space, Time and Architecture: The Growth of a New Tradition* by the Swiss historian and critic Sigfried Giedion was hugely influential: his book gave intellectual and historical depth to the modern movement. Giedion argued that modernism was the only style in sync with the times, as it could translate concrete, steel, and glass into an aesthetic of clean surfaces and visual transparency.

Mies was not only appointed head of the architecture department of the Illinois Institute of Technology (IIT) but was given the commission to lay out the campus. It became the first truly modern campus in history, with all buildings made of steel, brick, and glass. The site was laid out on a 24-foot grid, that being the dimension of the standard

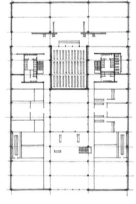

18.64 Main-floor plan: IIT Library Building, Chicago

U.S. classroom. The grid system also guaranteed that if only a part of the campus were constructed, future architectural unity could be preserved. The buildings were all rectangular and more or less of the same height, but varied in shape, according to program.

In designing the buildings, a new type of space became central to Mies's aesthetics. Whereas in earlier decades, his spaces flowed along walls and columns, here he became interested in large, vacuous spaces defined by a simple symmetry of form and bounded at the perimeter by columns conceived in rigorous geometrical order. Mies realized the potential of these ideas in the plans for his unbuilt library building (1942–43), where, however, he did not abandon his notion of a conceptual core, formed here by the book stacks placed in a square toward one end of the building and flanked by bathrooms and stairs. This conceptual mass was contrasted with an open courtyard that was to be fronted by an interior waiting room. The plan was flexible but not "free," as Le Corbusier would define it. It was layered, thickened, and thinned. Since this was to be a one-story building, the fire code permitted the use of unencased steel, allowing Mies to reveal the structural elements inside and out with maximum clarity. Mies elaborated on the theme again in the Crown Hall at IIT (1950–56) and later in his career at the National Gallery in Berlin (1962–67).

18.65 Crown Hall, IIT, Chicago

Farnsworth House

Of Mies van der Rohe's few commissions for private residences, the best known is the Farnsworth House (1946–51) in Illinois. Because the site, not far from a river, was prone to flooding, Mies elevated the house 2.2 meters above ground level. Entrance was gained by a broad flight of steps interrupted by a large, open podium without railings. Two sets of four columns support a roof cantilevered at both ends. There are no walls, but rather sheets of glass between the columns that span from floor to ceiling. The kitchen and bathrooms were unified into a single core element set to one side of the space to define two separate zones. The floors of white travertine, and the white painted steel frame, created a sense of grace and refinement. The curtains were of natural shantung silk and the woodwork of teak wood, Mies being very luxury-conscious when it came to the sparse, interior furnishings. There were difficulties, however, in actually living in the house (Mrs. Farnsworth complained of feeling like she was in a fishbowl). The house nonetheless became the model for several other experiments, the most notable being the private residence designed by Philip Johnson on his estate in New Canaan, Connecticut (1949). The Johnson house used steel for the posts but the roof was of wood, which was significantly easier to construct and repair. Johnson separated the bathroom core from the kitchen, which he reduced to the level of furniture.

18.66 Farnsworth House, Plano, Illinois

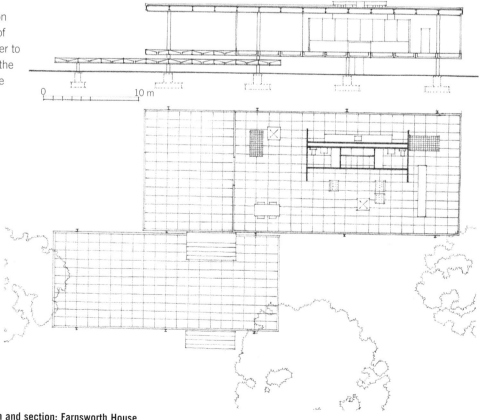

18.67 **Plan and section: Farnsworth House**

18.68 **Eames House, Pacific Palisades, California**

18.69 **Eames House**

Eames House

In the United States, John Entenza (1905–84), editor of the influential Los Angeles–based *Arts and Architecture* magazine, was an important but much-overlooked sponsor of modern architecture in America, bringing the works of many artists and architects to the public's attention. To combat the housing shortage after World War II, he started a drive to assemble well-designed houses rapidly and inexpensively using wartime technologies and materials. In January 1945, to speed his project along, he invited architects to construct prototype houses in Los Angeles to explore the feasibility of his idea. Of the twenty-four houses completed by 1966, one of the most innovative was a project by Charles and Ray Eames, a husband-and-wife team who designed a residence for themselves.

Born in St. Louis and trained in architecture at Washington University, Charles had taught in Michigan, where, at the Cranbrook Academy of Art, he met Eero Saarinen, with whom he entered into a competition project—Organic Design

in Home Furnishings—sponsored by the Museum of Modern Art in New York City. The Eameses had initially conceived of a pristine, Mies-like cube standing on two slender steel columns, cantilevered out from the slope of a hillside lot. However, in 1947, they designed it to enclose more space (without using any additional steel) and put it at the perimeter of the site, rather in its center. The house, anchored by a retaining wall, nestles against the hillside, parallel to its contours, making it a statement as much about the site, the location, and the inhabitants as about the deployment of prefabricated industrial materials. Their house featured extremely thin steel framing with exposed corrugated metal roofing and consisted of eighteen bays, 2.3 meters wide, 6 meters long, and 5 meters high, which determined the rhythm of the structure. Glazed panels—transparent, opaque, or translucent, as the situation demanded, and occasionally interrupted by painted panels in bright primary colors—gave the house a vibrant and playful character very different from the austerity of Mies's Farnsworth House.

The Eameses filled the house with a collection of items they had accumulated from around the world. They made a film called *House after Five Years of Living*, implying that their house was not so much a designer display but an organic organism with the patina of lived-in existence that reflected the character and preferences of its inhabitants. Other than designing plans for houses, the Eameses designed exhibitions, made films, and built toys and furniture. One of their earliest successes was a technique for bending plywood, which was used in World War II field hospitals for making leg splints and, later, for chair seats. They even designed a chaise longue and ottoman manufactured by the Herman Miller Company, whose headquarters they also designed. Their films were experimental and conceptual; the best-known, *Powers of Ten*, attempted to depict a post-Einsteinian universe.

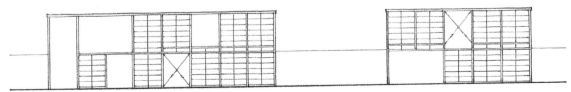

18.70 **Elevation: Eames House**

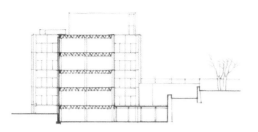

18.71 Section and first-floor plan: Yale University Art Gallery, New Haven, Connecticut

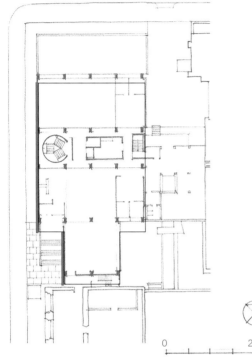

18.72 Yale University Art Gallery

Yale University Art Gallery

Louis Kahn (1901–74), like Wright before him, developed an aesthetic outside of the developing norms of international modernism. But that does not mean that his work was not influenced by modernism and its drive to master abstraction. The Yale University Art Gallery in New Haven, Connecticut (1951–53) is remarkably unrhetorical, with horizontally marked brick walls defining one direction and the aluminum glazing of the windows defining the other. He placed the building's programmatic needs within this simple framework by organizing them into cylinders and rectangles. The idea is not unlike the way Mies attempted to unify secondary program elements into a vertical spine, except that here they become almost sculptural. Kahn was intrigued by the interaction between humans and the technical systems that service them—

and that are therefore an integral part of the architectural world. So he chose to make a virtue out of electrical wiring, outlets, lighting fixtures, and ductwork, all of which are allowed to remain visible. The entrance, however, is almost invisible from the street, as it is on a higher level and separated by a wall and a set of stairs. Mies, more likely than not, would have placed the entrance at street level with lots of glass; Gropius might have built a thin canopy. But Kahn's entrance is something one finds somewhat unexpectedly—perhaps like in a medieval European town. Even the steps seem to indicate a change in the urban elevation. It is a subtle homage to the power of a type of space that is both intimate and urban. Kahn continually downplayed entrances in his architecture, de-emphasizing the ceremonial

aspect of approach. The uncompromising bluntness of the building foreshadows an aesthetic that came to be known as Brutalism, which was to take root in the late 1960s.

Kahn studied at the American Academy in Rome in 1950, followed by travels in Italy, Egypt, and Greece in 1951. Unlike most modernists who rejected the architecture of antiquity, he saw in it a struggle to make the building hold its own against the overwhelming grandeur of the landscape. For this reason, he preferred the archaic Temple of Paestum to the refined proportions of the Parthenon. His study of Greek and Roman architecture led Kahn to use simple but arresting forms—and even symmetries—at a time when these would have been frowned upon by functionalists.

18.73 Brasília

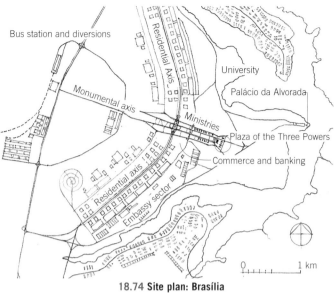

Bus station and diversions

Monumental axis

Residential Axis

University

Palácio da Alvorada

Ministries

Plaza of the Three Powers

Commerce and banking

Residential axis

Embassy sector

0   1 km

18.74 Site plan: Brasília

Brasília

In Brazil, modern architecture served as an expression of national identity and reached its zenith with the creation of Brasília in 1956 (inaugurated 1960). A hinterland capital had been proposed for Brazil since the late 19th century as a way to shift focus from the coastal towns and create a geographically accessible capital for the whole country. President Juscelino Kubitschek, who advocated rapid industrialization and who made the decision to go forward with the new capital, invited Oscar Niemeyer (1907–), the Brazilian-born and trained architect, to design the main buildings and, after a competition, Lúcio Costa to prepare the master plan. It was to be accessible mainly by airplane and thus meant to be the supreme manifestation in the processes of modernization. Costa's plan, which looked itself like a plane, was based on the CIAM principles separating habitation, recreation, work, and circulation. Designed around two axes intersecting to form a cross, Brasília was an automobile city. Long, high-speed roads—three multilane systems on each axis—with overpasses and underpasses at intersections were designed to enable rapid transportation. A dam built across the river Paranoa created long finger lakes around the southern, eastern, and northern edges of a U-shaped plateau on which the city was located. The main monumental axis of the city ran east-west, bisecting the plateau. On the north-south cross-axis, arranged in a gentle curve, were the main residential

units—the "superblocks"—organized in three layers, with parking at the eastern edge. Each superblock, 240 by 240 meters, was conceived as a grouping of six-story apartment units, raised on *piloti*, with play space for children within inner courts. Private dwellings were nestled between the fingers of the lakes in the north and south, and farther inland to the west were the airport and train station.

The functional, ceremonial, and visual focus of the city is the so-called Plaza of the Three Powers, at the eastern edge of the plateau. Approaching from the west, the eleven towers of the ministries start a grand procession culminating in the rectangular

blocks of the Foreign Ministry and the Treasury, beyond which, at the center of the axis, is the National Congress. This building is singular in the history of modern architecture. It houses two major chambers, the larger one for the Chamber of Deputies and the smaller one for the Senate. The raked visitors' seating of the round Chamber of Deputies is expressed in the roofline in the form of an upward turned bowl. The senate chamber has a traditional dome over it. Together, the saucer and dome, lifted clear above the ground on a giant platform, make for a memorable skyline, self-consciously designed as the icon of Brasília. Below, in two stories, accessed by a ramp, are all the offices.

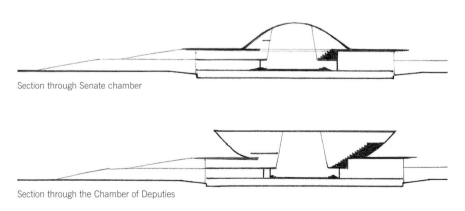

Section through Senate chamber

Section through the Chamber of Deputies

18.75 National Congress, Brasília

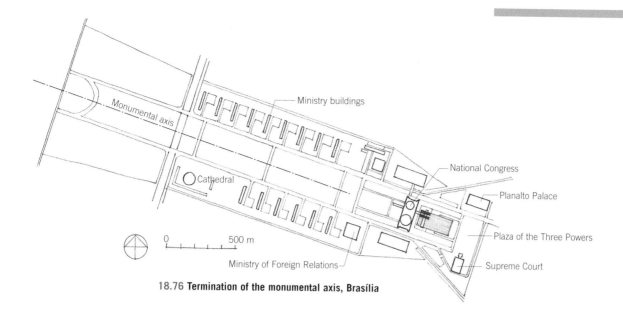

18.76 **Termination of the monumental axis, Brasília**

Farther east, in line with the ramp, rise twin towers, linked by the walkway of the Secretariat. They sit in the middle of a rectangular reflecting pool at the eastern edge of which is the climax of the whole complex, a gigantic plaza with the executive office of the president (the Planalto Palace) and the Supreme Court at either end. One of the multilane highways cuts through the plaza, next to the Planalto Palace, connecting to the peripheral roads and the residence of the president, the Palácio da Alvorada, at the water's edge.

These three buildings, all designed by Niemeyer, represent a monumentalization of the Brazilian national modern style. All are concrete slab structures, glazed all around and sandwiched between deep overhanging roofs and floor slabs. In the Planalto Palace, a whole story lies below the ground slab, and in the other two buildings the ground slab lifts the main floor above the ground. Within, the plans are more reminiscent of Mies's precise geometries than Le Corbusier's sensuous curves. The colonnades lining the expressive edges of the buildings (always only on two opposite sides, except in the later Foreign Ministry, where they line all four sides) were designed as delicately wrought curvilinear forms, expressive less of their character as load-bearing members and more as tie beams stretched thin by tension, almost to the point of disappearing at their edges. (Joaquim Cardoso did the structural

calculations.) In the Planalto Palace the colonnades face the plaza; in the Supreme Court, they are located toward the side; and in the Palácio da Alvorada they are turned laterally, forming a string of inverted arches across the facade.

After World War II, modern Brazilian architecture became widely influential in the development of modern architecture around the world (though it had actually begun as a derivative of European modernism). Brasília's Foreign Ministry was the model for New York City's Lincoln Center. Oscar Niemeyer effectively became the chief architect of the United Nations Headquarters (1947), also in New York City, after Le Corbusier was removed from the project and Wallace Harrison was appointed head of the United Nations Board of Design. Harrison's design of the Albany Civic Center (1962–68), one of the largest modernist-style civic centers in the United States, was inspired by Costa's and Niemeyer's Plaza of the Three Powers in Brasília.

18.77 **Ministry of External Relations, Brasília**

Chandigarh

After India attained independence in 1947 it was divided into two countries along religious lines, resulting in the creation of the new Islamic nation of Pakistan. In that division, the Indian state of Punjab lost its capital, Lahore, to Pakistan, so Jawaharlal Nehru, the first prime minister of independent India, decided to construct a new state capital at Chandigarh. Like Brazil's Getulio Vargas and Juscelino Kubitschek, Nehru modeled his development plans on Franklin Delano Roosevelt's New Deal and initiated a series of state-sponsored industrialization projects. His sentiment was expressly antinostalgic. He wanted Chandigarh to be a city, unfettered by the traditions of the past, and a symbol of the nation's faith in the future.

When Le Corbusier joined the project in 1952, the urban plan had already been prepared by Albert Mayer, an American town planner, on the principles of the City Beautiful movement, with superblocks accessed by gently curving roads. Le Corbusier shrunk the superblocks into 800-by-1,200-meter rectangular neighborhood units or sectors serviced by a diminishing hierarchy of roads and bicycle paths, according to CIAM principles. Within these sectors, Le Corbusier wanted to design multistory residential units (perhaps like those in Brasília or in his Unités d'Habitations, the first of which had just been constructed in Marseilles), but that idea was immediately dismissed by the officers in charge of the project, who were committed to a low-rise suburban image, inspired in part by the sprawling cantonments the British had built for their officers in colonial India. The state housing was therefore designed not by Le Corbusier, but by his cousin, Pierre Jeanneret (who was the project architect), and the English husband-and-wife team of Maxwell Fry and Jane Drew (who had been working in Africa), assisted by a team of nine Indian architects and planners. Most of the construction was made of load-bearing exposed brick walls, accented by random rubble-stone porticoes and concrete window protectors, plastered and painted white.

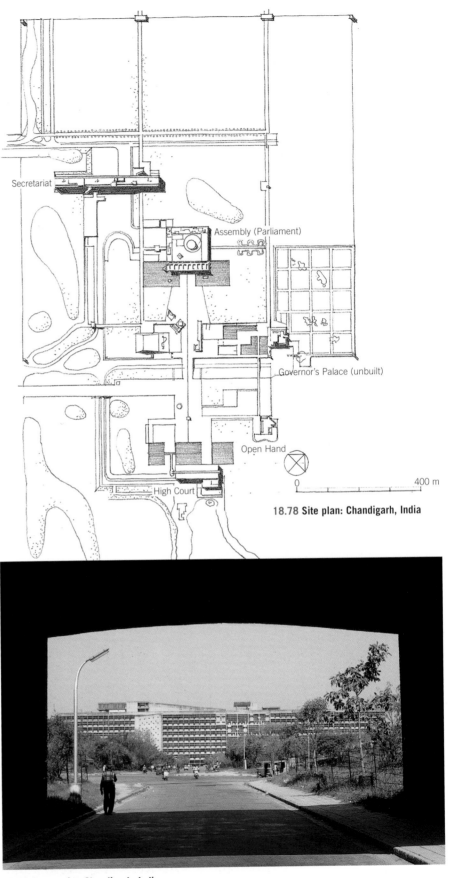

18.78 Site plan: Chandigarh, India

18.79 Secretariat, Chandigarh, India

Secretariat and High Court

Le Corbusier's Capitol Complex for Chandigarh (1951–62)—containing the High Court, Assembly, and Secretariat for the states of Punjab and Haryana—was located at the northern end of the city in a vast open plain, bound visually only by the distant Himalayan foothills. The boundaries are loosely defined by two adjoining 800-meter squares that contain two 400-meter squares. The vehicular roads are located somewhat below grade; the excavated earth was used to create the artificial hills that screen the Capitol from the rest of the city. An irregularly shaped pedestrian plaza, linking the Assembly and the High Court, studded with a set of symbolic follies, forms the conceptual center of the Capitol. The High Court, the first building to be constructed, is contained within a tight frame and endowed with a second roof (with suspended arches) built above the first one to provide shade. Three huge pylons create a monumental gateway fronted by two reflecting pools. The building's elevation has a rhythm determined by the divisions of the nine courts. The elevation, in fact, is almost the same as its plan. Although made of cast-in-place rough concrete, the High Court, with the pylons painted in soft pastels, appears lightweight and airy, particularly when reflected in the pools.

The Secretariat has a very different character. It takes the form of a long slab, with a dramatic roofline and a facade completely composed of *brise-soleils*. Staircases appear as attached towers with small windows. In the context of the larger composition, it functions as a backdrop to the Assembly. With its long double-loaded corridor, the building was a restatement of Le Corbusier's idea of a collective living solution, the Unité d'Habitation. But while the Unité was raised on robust concrete *pilotis*, the Secretariat sits directly on the ground.

18.80 **High Court, Chandigarh, India**

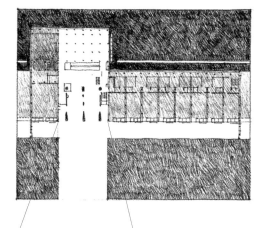

18.81 **Plan diagram and elevation: High Court, Chandigarh**

While the aesthetic origins of the sculpture are diverse, Le Corbusier's most ambitious hope for the Open Hand was articulated by him in a 1955 letter to Nehru, in which he proposed it as a symbol of the Non-Aligned Movement (NAM). Nehru's brainchild, NAM was an attempt to create an alternative to the divisive two-world (Communist versus capitalist) hegemony of the Cold War. Although not adopted for NAM, the Open Hand did become the symbol of Chandigarh as a city embodying Nehru's hopes for a modern India.

18.82 Assembly Building, Chandigarh, India

Assembly Building

Le Corbusier's Assembly Building (1953–63) is a masterpiece in organization and monumentality. On a trip to Ahmedabad in western India, Le Corbusier saw the form of a hyperbolic paraboloid arch under construction for a thermal power station and, mesmerized, immediately decided to use it as a motif in the Assembly Building. At this time he was also working, in conjunction with the mathematician and musician Iannis Xenaxis, on several projects in France, all of which explored the sculptural possibilities of ruled surfaces. For the design of the Assembly Building, Le Corbusier seems to have literally dropped the hyperbolic paraboloid arch into a box. Around the hall, a forest of columns, rising high into a black ceiling, created the foyer. The three edges of the box were given over to offices. *Brise-soleils* functioned as the skin. On the fourth edge of the box (the side facing the plaza), Le Corbusier built a monumental portal, opposite from and facing the portal of the High Court across the vast plaza. A row of thin pylons holds up a free-form roof that looks like the horns of a bull in outline, giving the Assembly Building the appearance of a majestic bull standing firm on the vast Indian plain—quite in contrast to Niemeyer's palaces in Brasília, which barely touch the ground and seem to fly above it in defiance of gravity.

Le Corbusier also gifted to Chandigarh the Open Hand Monument, which he devised as the city's symbol. It stands in the Capitol, a 23-meter-high sculpture of burnished steel.

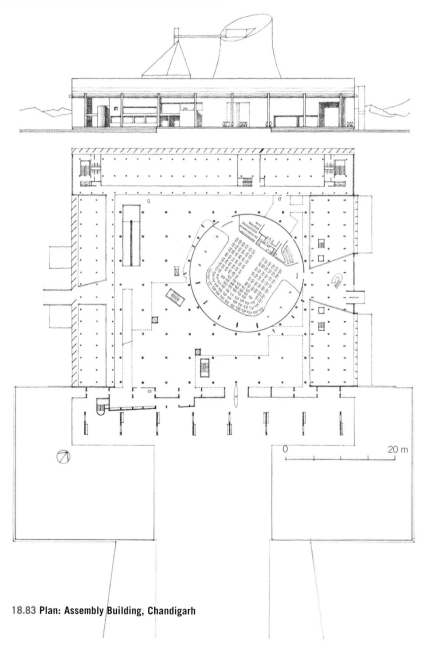

18.83 Plan: Assembly Building, Chandigarh

Ahmedabad

One of the Indian architects who admired Le Corbusier and had apprenticed in his atelier, Balkrishna V. Doshi, was at this time practicing in Ahmedabad, the textile capital of India. At Doshi's invitation, Le Corbusier designed the Shodhan and Sarabhai houses, a public museum, and the Mill Owners' Association Building in Ahmedabad. Constructed at the same time, in 1956, toward the end of Le Corbusier's life, the Shodhan and Sarabhai houses, along with the Mill Owners' Association Building, are skillful variations on Le Corbusier's older typologies and a succinct summary of some of his lifelong formal preoccupations. The Shodhan was a reinterpretation of the Villa Savoye: it has a central ramp around which the volumes are distributed, in this case with an open terrace on the second floor. The Shodhan, however, transforms the Villa Savoye's strip windows into a muscular *brise-soleil* and has a parasol roof, both of which have more in common with his project in Argentina, the Maison Currutchet (1949). Le Corbusier's Mill Owners' Association Building (1954) was his quintessential institutional statement, with a central ramp piercing midheight into the cubic volume of the main space. The north-south orientation made for the usual contrast between the airy *brise-soleil* on the two sides, but within Le Corbusier unleashed a carefully orchestrated but exuberant interplay of free forms and multiple heights that produce a palpable feeling of an inhabited sculptural volume. Years later Le Corbusier redid the Mill Owners' Association Building for his solitary commission in the United States, the Carpenter Center for the Visual Arts in Cambridge, Massachusetts, skillfully squeezing it into an uncomfortable site and finishing it with much greater restraint.

18.84 Three-dimensional view: Plans and site of the Mill Owners' Association Building, Ahmedabad, India

18.85 Mill Owners' Association Building

18.86 Notre Dame de Haut, Ronchamp, France

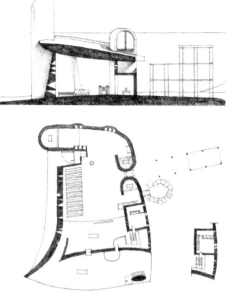

18.87 Section and plan: Notre Dame de Haut

Chapel at Ronchamp

Le Corbusier accepted two commissions from religious institutions. One was for a chapel, Notre Dame de Haut (1955) at Ronchamp, in the Jura Mountains of eastern France. The other was for a monastery at La Tourette (1957–60), near Lyon, France. Both commissions were made by a reformist wing of the Catholic Church trying to reestablish the relevance of their institution in the wake of faltering attendance. Appealing to the younger generation by adopting modern architecture was part of this effort. It was not only a bold experiment but also demonstrated that modernism could indeed create the kind of inward-oriented atmosphere conducive to contemplation. Although Le Corbusier was not a church-going Catholic, he welcomed the commissions because they allowed him to experiment with symbolic forms, which he had never done before in a European context.

The chapel is a singular and memorable edifice and stands today, along with the Rosaire Chapel (1949–51) by Henri Matisse, as one of the most outstanding modern religious expressions of the 20th century. Fundamentally, the building is a sculpture and thus challenged the conventions of functionalist restraint. Its principal design element is the curve deployed repeatedly to form a dramatic set of intersections and trapped, cavelike spaces. Three continuous walls, changing direction, thickness, and height, create a volume that defies the expectations of facade and interior. Two convex curves bulge out on the north and west, creating its back side, while two concave indents to the south and east represent the front. On top of the walls, on columns hidden in the walls, floats a thick, organic-appearing roof that comes to a sharp point at one end. It has been compared by some to a cushion, and by others to a hat.

Three towers, clustered together and with hooded tops, rise above the roof, forming vertical counterpoints to the building's general horizontality and earthbound appearance. Light washes down into the inner space of these towers and spills into the inner sanctum. Each tower has a specific function, serving as chapel, sacristy, and baptistery, respectively. The west wall is punctured by a series of irregularly placed, punched-out windows of various sizes and depths that bring spots of intense light to the interior. Inside, the roof hangs like a heavy cloth over the nave while sloping gently to the south toward the altar. A statue of the Virgin Mary stands in an alcove in the eastern wall and was designed so that it can be rotated to face both inside and outside, for those occasions when church services are held outdoors. Using stones from the site, Le Corbusier constructed a small, stepped pyramid near the church. The church bells are placed in a steel-framed structure to one side. Sited on the flat top of a hill in a forested area of the Jura Mountains, the building is reached by a gently curving road that leads up the hill and passes a low meeting and service building. From the top, serene views range in all directions, imparting to the church the aspect of a pilgrimage site. (Indeed, on the site there once stood a pilgrimage chapel, destroyed in World War II, which was dedicated to the Virgin Mary.)

18.88 Interior: Notre Dame de Haut

Guggenheim Museum

After World War II, modern architecture's insistence on a rationalized functional aesthetic ran up against the need to express monumentality, particularly in large civic structures. Frank Lloyd Wright's design for the Guggenheim Museum (1956–59) in Manhattan was particularly innovative in this respect, with a dramatic exterior form and a large interior space at its center formed by a curving ramp. The sides of the building are fully occupied by this gently spiraling ramp, designed to allow visitors to view art continuously, without interruption. It also enables everyone viewing the art to be seen—an idea close to the sensibility of Charles Garnier's Paris Opera House. The ramp, expanding in diameter as it ascends (or shrinking as it descends, as the case may be) generates an external profile that contrasts sharply with the rectilinear geometry of the surrounding Manhattan blocks. Wright defended the spiral by arguing that abstract art no longer needed to be seen in the traditional framework of rooms and walls. But as innovative and controversial as Wright's exhibition ideas were, there is no debate about the building's impressive central space. Accessed virtually directly from the street, it was conceived as an extension of the urban site. In that respect it constituted an important breakthrough in the relationship of modernism to civic space. Though the Museum of Modern Art (1938–39) by Philip Goodwin and Edward Durell Stone was technically the first modern building in New York City, the Guggenheim was the city's first truly modernist civic structure.

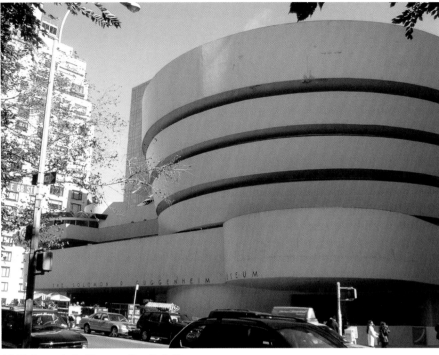

18.89 Guggenheim Museum, New York City

The project went through several permutations. At first the building was to be a type of private gallery, showing the works of Solomon R. Guggenheim, but in 1952 the museum expanded its definition to become something much broader, rivaling the Museum of Modern Art as an institution of experimentation and taste-making across the whole range of modern art. The expanded program forced Wright to make amendments and concessions, but he did not change his stance that flat paintings would be well served by hanging against curving walls, and the public's positive reception to the building offset complaints by curators and painters. The building was based on an innovative structural system of radially splayed concrete ribs that held the floor plates and came together at the top to form the dome. While the building soon became a Manhattan landmark, its success of its functional purpose—the display of paintings—remains questionable and was never imitated.

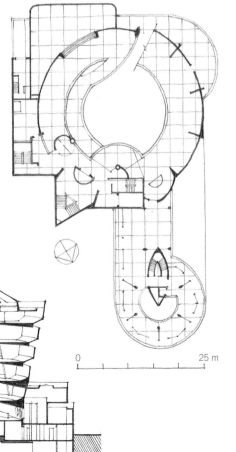

0   25 m

18.90 Plan and section: Guggenheim Museum

Touba

In 1887, Sheikh Amadou Bamba (1853–1927), a Muslim mystic, founded a homestead later called Touba in an isolated place outside of the town of Mbacké in what is now Senegal. He acquired a reputation as a holy man, and soon followers began to seek him out. He developed a form of Sufism, known as Mouridism, according to which the material world is not complete in and of itself: matter, it teaches, is relevant to life only insofar as it is infused by the divine. Bamba perceived also his mission as a social one; he wanted his adherents to return to the "straight path" of Islam. So Touba became a holy city in which everything frivolous— laughing, dancing, drinking alcohol—was forbidden.

At first the French colonial authorities viewed Bamba's growing popularity as a threat to their authority and sent him into exile, but since his position was one of nonviolence, they released him and eventually gave him their nominal support. In the 1920s, Bamba launched the construction of a large mosque; he was assisted by thousands of faithful volunteers in its construction. The reinforced concrete structure, which has been continuously enlarged, has three domes and five minarets, the central one being quite tall and visible for miles in the flat Senegalese landscape. The roofs of the domes are green and blue, and the walls are clad in a rose-tinted stone; the interior is richly decorated. Bamba died in 1927; his successors finished the building in 1963. It was only then that a city was laid out on a grid plan, with broad radiating streets emanating from the central square where the mosque is located.

The cemetery is located opposite the mosque and thus at the city center, which for Islam is unusual, since cemeteries are usually placed outside of a city. Here the cemetery functions as the gate to the hereafter and is an important part of the Sufi mystical experience. It was designed symbolically around an ancient sacred baobab tree (which died in 2003). On the *qibla* side of the mosque there is another tree, a palm tree, which marks the spot where the first birth in Touba took place. These trees are called palaver trees by the locals. (*Palaver* derives

18.91 Touba Mosque, Senegal

from the Portuguese *palavra*, which means speech or discussion.) Since ancient times, palaver trees have served as the heart of community meetings and been at the center of civic and religious functions; because of their longevity, the trees are considered the spiritual guarantors of a community's life. The tradition of the palaver tree can be found across central Africa. In Islamic areas, it is the mosque that serves as the political and social center of the Islamic community, which can bring the mosque into competition with this older tradition. Here, however, the old and new were fused, with the ancient tradition of the baobab tree blending the Sufi concept of a tree of paradise. Furthermore, the tall minaret is itself meant to be seen as treelike. Touba was recognized as model "peace city" by the United Nations Human Settlement Division in 1996.

18.92 Plan of Touba, Senegal

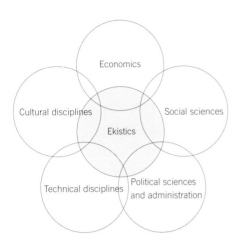

18.93 Diagram of ekistics and the sciences contributing to it

Ekistics

Constantinos Doxiadis (1913–75), the former chief town planning officer of Athens, started his own firm in 1951, and after that built in dozens of countries, including India, Bangladesh, Ethiopia, France, Ghana, Iran, Iraq, Italy, Jordan, Pakistan, and Syria. His was one of the largest international practices at the time. Doxiadis introduced issues like regional climate and geography into the discussion of modernism at a time when such considerations were still rare. He coined the term *ekistics*, derived from the Greek *oikos*, meaning "house," to refer to the science of human settlements. Doxiadis aspired to expand the scientific basis of architecture, urban design, and planning in order to reject arbitrary self-expression and monotonic versions of rationalism and also to embrace extratechnological and nonfunctionalist concerns. He soon surrounded himself with an international and interdisciplinary group that included global visionaries (like Buckminster Fuller and Margaret Mead), architects, planners, and United Nations consultants (such as Jaqueline Tyrwhitt and Charles Abrams), economists and environmental thinkers (including Barbara Ward and René Dubos), all of whom, to some degree, supported Doxiadis's vision.

His planning model was called Dynapolis, a term signifying a dynamic city that would change over time and allow its urban core to expand continually in a unidirectional manner in order to avert congestion and do away with the permanence and monumentality of stationary city centers. The business district and residential areas would also grow along this axis, and industrial areas would be pushed to the edges. This logic of functional separation extended to the system of social ordering, so that each residential sector was broken down into smaller communities arranged hierarchically.

The model of Dynapolis informed many plans for urban restructuring, from Baghdad (1958) to Athens (1960) to Washington, DC, and it became the basis for the creation of Islamabad, the new capital of Pakistan (1960). Doxiadis designed Islamabad's master plan and the prototypes of the major housing types, but the design of the individual buildings was assigned to local and foreign architects. The master plan was based on his concept of a moving core—the idea that the commercial hub of the city would continue to move and grow as necessary, creating a linear city in its wake.

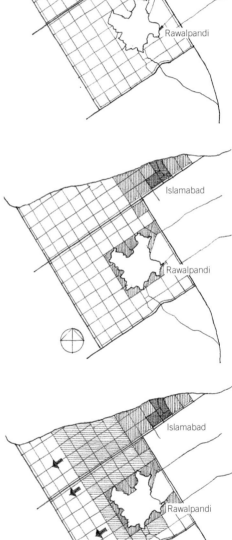

18.94 Islamabad, Pakistan: A growing dynametropolis

18.95 Berlin Philharmonic Hall

Architecture of Prestige

After World War II, in the face of massive housing shortages in bombed-out towns and cities, most municipalities quickly adopted regulations that allowed for modernist housing blocks to be built, which fundamentally changed the urban landscape of Europe. Against this backdrop, a few big cities were able to create high-end commissions that allowed architects more freedom to experiment. This engendered the prestige commission, an important driver of advanced architectural thinking. One of the first examples was the Berlin Philharmonic Hall (1956–63) designed by Hans Bernhard Scharoun, a German architect known prior to the war for his expressionistic designs. At the time, Scharoun had built little apart from a few villas. Berlin's city fathers were hoping he would design a building that would stand out against the miles of drab buildings that had shot up after the war.

The Philharmonic Hall's exterior has the appearance of several buildings compressed into each other. The front, which looks like the prow of a ship sharply diving into the landscape, is clad in a golden-hued metal skin that appears to be a shed or tent. The overall impression is liquid and muscular. The parterre on the interior is organized symmetrically around the orchestra, but the seating arrangement differs from established standards: balconies face in all directions, and even surround the musicians' platform.

They appear both compressed forward from within and inward from without. This vast interior was treated conceptually like a large boat elevated from below on columns: visitors enter not through a conventional lobby, which would then distribute people to the appropriate corridor, but from an area underneath the "hull" and then up through staircases to the different seating locations. The plan has had many imitators, the most recent being the projected design for the Elbe Philharmonic Hall in Hamburg, Germany, by the firm, Herzog & de Meuron.

18.96 Site plan: Berlin Philharmonic Hall

18.97 Plan: Berlin Philharmonic Hall

Sydney Opera House

Jørn Utzon's Sydney Opera House (1957–73) was another early prestige commission. Located right on the water's edge, with the graceful curve of the Sydney Harbor Bridge as a backdrop, Utzon's prizewinning contest entry imagined a series of successive interlocking shells of different heights hovering above a vast stepped platform, conjuring an image of ships' sails through outright technological virtuosity. Supported on 580 concrete piers sunk up to 25 meters below sea level, the shells are sheathed in white ceramic tile and contain five performance spaces. Although Utzon never completed the project himself, it quickly became the signature project of Australia and a national icon.

18.98 Sydney Opera House, Australia

First generation of post–World War II prestige buildings:

- Berlin Philharmonic Hall
  1956–63, Hans Bernhard Scharoun
- Sydney Opera House
  1957–73, Jørn Utzon
- Lincoln Center for the Performing Arts, New York City
  1962–65, Max Abramovitz, Pietro Belluschi, Philip Johnson, Eero Saarinen, and others
- John F. Kennedy Center for the Performing Arts, Washington, DC
  1964–71, Edward Durrell Stone
- Tokyo Olympic Stadium
  1964, Kenzo Tange
- Kimbell Art Museum, Fort Worth, Texas
  1967–1972, Louis Kahn
- New National Gallery, Berlin
  1972–78, Mies van der Rohe
- Palast der Republik, East Berlin
  1973–76, Heinz Graffunder and Karl-Ernst Swora
- East Wing, National Gallery, Washington DC
  1974–78, I. M. Pei

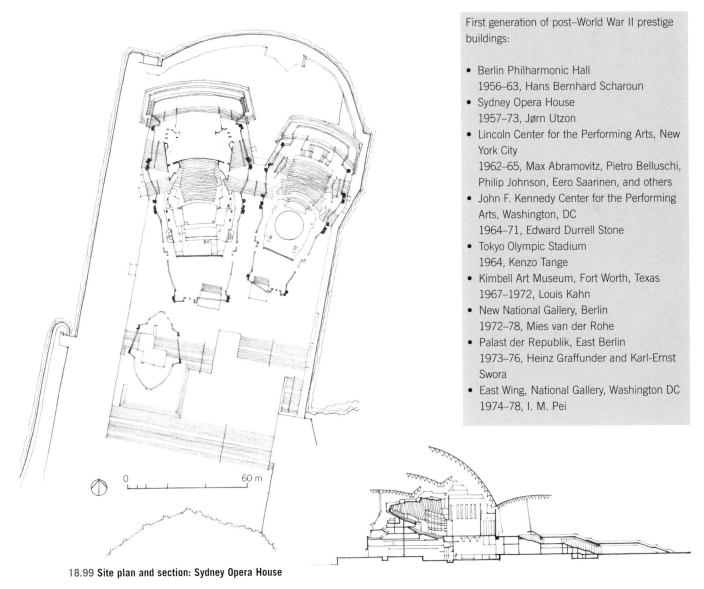

0   60 m

18.99 Site plan and section: Sydney Opera House

18.100 **TWA Terminal, John F. Kennedy International Airport, Queens, New York**

18.101 **TWA Terminal, John F. Kennedy International Airport**

Eero Saarinen

Born in 1910 in Finland, Eero Saarinen, Eliel Saarinen's son, injected poetry into the structural possibilities of reinforced concrete. Though Erich Mendelsohn had attempted this in the 1930s, he had built relatively little during a time when concrete was still rather experimental. Eero Saarinen's career ended prematurely with his death in 1961, but in the short space of eleven years, he had already worked on nearly thirty projects in Europe and the United States, some of which became international icons and symbols of the United States' postwar identity as a technological superpower. Among his works are the St. Louis Gateway Arch (1948–64), the General Motors Technical Center (1948–56) in Detroit, and the TWA Terminal (1956–62) at New York's John F. Kennedy International Airport.

Saarinen's 1947 competition-winning entry for the Gateway Arch at St. Louis, Missouri (1961–66), was conceived as a huge structure located on the banks of the Mississippi River. It was a monument meant to match—if not exceed—in scale, technological prowess, and symbolic stature, Paris's Eiffel Tower. Because it represented the gateway to the West it was seen as a dramatic reference to America's origins and a way of putting St. Louis on the international map. A catenary curve, the arch's span and rise are both 192 meters. It consists of a double skin of steel—stainless steel without and carbon steel within—reinforced where required by concrete. The two legs in section are equilateral triangles, 16.5 meters to a side at the ground tapering off to 5 meters at the summit. The Museum of Westward Expansion is located at the ground level, and a viewing deck at the top can be accessed by elevator. Saarinen's TWA Terminal (1956–62) at New York's John F. Kennedy International Airport was conceived as a bird with its wings spread and poised to take off. He designed the terminal largely by using models rather than drawings. It has no facade or right angles. Instead, its captivating forms and undulating interiors—along with its dramatic TWA-red carpeted floors—were meant to evoke a vision of grace and lightness.

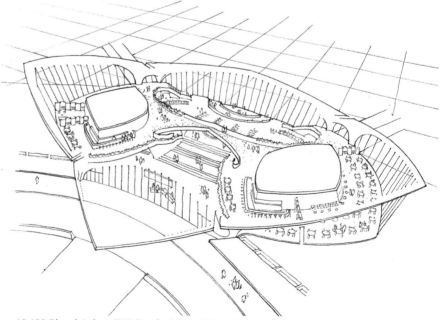

18.102 **Pictorial view: TWA Terminal, John F. Kennedy International Airport**

18.103 Aula Magna, La Ciudad Universitaria de Caracas, Venezuela

18.104 Diego Rivera House, Mexico City

Caribbean Modernism

In the Caribbean, modernism, as an expression of nationalist sentiments, was first propounded not by architects, but by poets and writers, including Rubén Dario (Panama), José Asunción Silva (Colombia), Manuel Gutiérrez Nájera (Mexico), José Enrique Rodó (Uruguay), José Martí (Cuba), Bienvenido Nouel (Dominican Republic), and Luis Lloréns Torres (Puerto Rico). It was not until the 1940s and 1950s that what is now called tropical modernism emerged as the language of autonomy and independence. Though strongly influenced by Le Corbusier, tropical modernism developed along its own regional lines, emphasizing not only clean lines but the need for shaded surfaces, wide windows, surrounding gardens, and lightweight construction. Among its proponents were Guillermo González-Sánchez in the Dominican Republic; Antonin Nechodoma and Henry Klumb in Puerto Rico; and Juan O'Gorman and Felix Candela, among others, in Mexico.

La Ciudad Universitaria de Caracas (1944–70) by the Venezuelan architect Carlos Raúl Villanueva, represents one of the highest expressions of modern architecture in Latin America. Built as an autonomous urban assemblage next to Plaza Venezuela, this compendium of more than forty buildings was developed during a period of radical economic, social, and political changes. At the center of the campus was a succession of spaces where inside and outside merge seamlessly into one another. Villanueva visualized a system of flows and paths, or "movements," as a fundamental design criterion; it was realized in his conception of the university's covered plaza, with its large canopy of irregular shape and varying height, protecting the shaded space within. Here Villanueva incorporated the work of several avant-garde artists of the time, including Fernand Léger, Antoine Pevsner, Victor Vasarely, Jean Arp, and Henri Laurens, as well as a group of Venezuelan geometric abstract artists such as Mateo Manaure, Pascual Navarro, Oswaldo Vigas, and Armando Barrios.

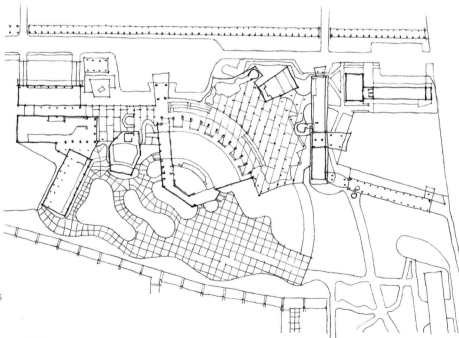

18.105 Plan: La Ciudad Universitaria de Caracas

Seagram Building

Skyscrapers had long been the primary symbol of the U.S. metropolis. In their early days, architects sought out a great deal of differentiation, but by the late 1920s, the look of tall buildings became more standardized, with the exception perhaps of a crowning element, like the Chrysler Building's (1928). Skyscraper design took its most dramatic change with Mies van der Rohe's Seagram Building (1958) in Midtown Manhattan, designed in collaboration with Philip Johnson and built as the headquarters for the Canadian distillers Joseph E. Seagram & Sons. The thirty-eight-story building is a vertical box with clean and sharp edges. Unlike early skyscrapers, whose bodies were punctuated by windows, here glass reaches from floor to ceiling and serves as the skin of the building. The visible edge of the floor plate is covered by bronze spandrels that create a light horizontal zippering effect to the floors during the day, when light reflects off the glass, and that is even more pronounced at night, when they contrast with the interior illumination.

Although the building is constructed entirely of structural steel, the fire code prohibited exposed steel, meaning that the steel supports had to be covered in fireproof concrete. Since this was not how Mies wanted the building to read from the outside, he used nonstructural, bronze-toned I-beams running vertically, like mullions, down the facades. These vertical mullions are equally spaced across the entire facade. Together with the horizontal spandrels, they create a pronounced grid pattern. This surfacing does not extend to the ground, however, allowing the building's real structure—the concrete-encased beams—to be visible in the lobby. The glass is not purely transparent, but tinted bronze, so that in certain lighting conditions, the whole building—its structure and its glass—seem to have a golden hue, perhaps, it has been argued, subtly suggesting the color of whiskey, one of the building owner's products.

In the 1960s, Chicago's skyline began to change, a consequence of the relaxation of height limits previously imposed by the city. Many towers were built, including several by Mies in his usual boxy style, such as the Lake Shore Drive Apartments (1948–51) and the Chicago Federal Center (1959–74). These building stimulated a vibrant (and still ongoing) discussion about the surface treatment of a tall building. Some architects developed the grid pattern by emphasizing different aspects of its composition; others worked with the reflective conditions of glass. Perhaps the culmination of the Miesian interrogation of the surface was the John Hancock Tower (1976) in Boston by I. M. Pei and Henry N. Cobb.

18.106 Seagram Building, New York City

18.107 Lobby, Seagram Building

18.108 Alcoa Building, San Francisco

Skidmore, Owings & Merrill

By the 1970s, Skidmore, Owings & Merrill (SOM), founded in 1936, employed about a thousand architects, engineers, and technicians who provided complete planning, design, engineering, and construction services. It was one of the world's first multitasking architectural corporations. The firm had seven principal offices located in New York City; Chicago; San Francisco; Portland, Oregon; Washington, DC; Paris; and Los Angeles. Commissions ranged from presidential libraries to routine industrial buildings. Though there was diversity in aesthetic production, perfecting the Miesian paradigm and making modernism the language par excellence for corporations was an important concept behind the firm's reputation. This can be seen in the headquarters of the Business Men's Assurance Company of America in Kansas City, Missouri (1963), situated outside of the city on the edge of a park. Unlike the Miesian preference for steel and glass, here the steel frame is clad in white Georgian marble. The windows are set back to create a stark, minimalist effect. The Alcoa Building in San Francisco (1964) took this design idea one step further: its exoskeletal cross-bracing serves both a structural purpose and provides a symbolic message. Although their unrelenting and uncompromising abstraction seems to make them mute and faceless, the absence of any rhetorical messages is belied by the idea that the form is not the expression of technological efficiency but technological elegance.

18.109 Business Men's Assurance Company of America, Kansas City, Missouri

18.110 Site plan and elevation: Business Men's Assurance Company of America

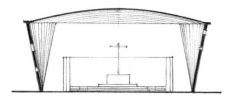

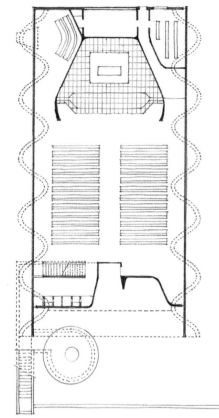

18.111 Section and plan: Church of Christ the Worker, Atlántida, Uruguay

18.112 Church of Christ the Worker

Uruguayan Modernism

The high-tech structural achievements of architects such as Eero Saarinen and Jørn Utzon can be contrasted with the work of the Uruguayan architect Eladio Dieste, who had been practicing since the early 1960s. Uruguayan president Jorge Batlle, and then the Batllistas, as his followers were known, undertook a series of socialist-oriented reforms that led to an economic expansion that was especially strong in the 1950s. An engineer by training, Dieste made his reputation building a whole range of structures, from grain silos, factory sheds, markets, maintenance hangars, fruit packing plants, warehouses, and bus terminals to a handful of churches of exceptional spans

and beauty. In most of his buildings he used Gaussian vaults, which are self-supporting shells that stand up not only because they are light but also because they are bent or folded in such a way that they are subject to limited lateral thrusts. Dieste also perfected techniques for reinforced masonry with the objective of minimizing the use of materials and maximizing the size of openings.

Dieste's Church of Christ the Worker (1958–60) in Atlántida, Uruguay, is a simple rectangle, with sidewalls rising up in undulating curves to the maximum amplitude of their arcs. The undulation enables the thin walls to be self-stabilizing, much as a bent sheet of paper has greater strength than a flat one. At the top, the geometry of the wall is merged with the continuous double curvature of the ceiling (reinforced with tie-rods concealed in troughs). The forms' beauty is augmented by the subtle interplay of light: while small, punched rectangular openings diffuse light through the interior, a triple row of baffles above the entrance, opening in opposite

directions, flood the space with indirect light. Dieste's warehouse for the fruit-packing plant in Salto (1971–72) consists of a series of large, discontinuous double-curvature vaults spanning approximately 150 feet. Not only do the vaults make the span seem effortless, but the glazed slits light up the vaults to create a space of rare sensuality.

18.113 Interior view: Church of Christ the Worker

18.114 School of Music, National Schools of Art, Havana

18.115 School of Ballet, National Schools of Art, Havana

National Schools of Art, Havana

In 1961, two years after the Cuban Revolution, Fidel Castro and Ernesto Che Guevara decided to transform the golf course of the Havana Country Club into an experimental project that would make art available to all. The master plan for the National Schools of Art (1961–65) was given to the young Cuban architect Ricardo Porro, who had just returned from exile. Porro invited his Italian colleagues Vittorio Garatti and Roberto Gottardi, who were living in Caracas, Venezuela, to collaborate. The three architects initiated a unique process: the design and construction of the schools occurred simultaneously with the beginning of the schools' academic activities. Porro designed the School of Plastic Arts and the School of Modern Dance; Gottardi, the School of Dramatic Arts; and Garatti, the School of Music and the School of Ballet. Even though each has its particularities, the five schools followed three common guiding principles: first, a response to the tropical landscape that allowed for an intimate relationship between nature and architecture; second, the use of earthen materials produced on the island instead of steel and cement; and third, the use of the *bóveda catalana*, or Catalan vault, as the primary structural system.

Though this ancient and versatile technique required very little by way of resources and materials and was chosen partially in response to Cuba's economically austere circumstances—made especially acute after the blockade imposed by the United States in October 1960—it conferred on the architecture the sensuality and eroticism that Porro claimed was prototypically Cuban. But by 1965 the schools, still unfinished, began to generate controversy. They were accused of being examples of an individualism that contradicted the increasingly influential standardized models of the Soviet-functionalist style. This eventually led to the project's abandonment. Castro's government, however, has since initiated a process of restoration, with Gottardi, the only one of the three architects still in Cuba, as its director.

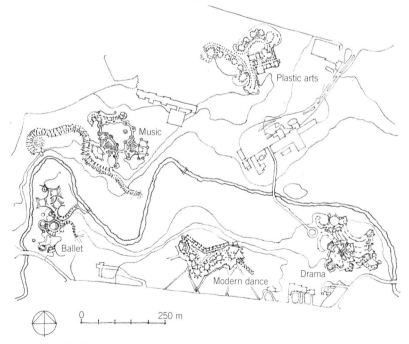

18.116 Site plan: National Schools of Art, Havana

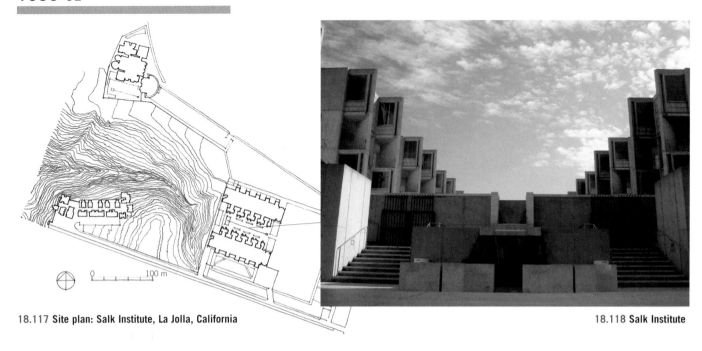

18.117 Site plan: Salk Institute, La Jolla, California

18.118 Salk Institute

Salk Institute

For Dr. Jonas Salk, the discoverer of the polio vaccine, medical research was not entirely the domain of scientists and administrators; it belonged to the public, and in the person of Louis Kahn, Salk found the architect who could transform that ideal into architectural form. The Salk Institute Building (1959–66) in La Jolla, near San Diego, California, is close to a bluff overlooking the Pacific Ocean. Three floors of laboratories, completely open in all directions, are separated by half-floors dedicated to mechanical ducts. As was typical of Kahn, the building went through several design permutations before its final form was agreed upon. In its final configurations it consisted of two rectangular laboratory blocks separated by a courtyard, with towers housing the scientists' study rooms projecting from the laboratories but sitting in the courtyard space. Circulation towers were located on the other side of the laboratories, aligned to the study towers that were separated from the laboratories by bridges in order to declare a physical and psychological differentiation. Whereas from the outside the building is austere and windowless, the courtyard, elevated one floor above the level of the site, captures the dramatic views toward the ocean. The diagonal walls of the towers allow each office to have an ocean view.

Originally, Kahn had envisioned the court as a lush garden, but in 1966, after seeing the work of Luis Barragán, Kahn invited him to see the designs, and it was Barragán who came up with the idea of an empty plaza. The plaza is entered from the east, through a quiet garden. A narrow waterway slices through the courtyard on its axis and ends in the quiet waterfall of a sunken viewing terrace—an area of repose. The building has no columns, but it is held up by concrete wall elements, with a reddish pozzolana additive placed in the concrete. The space between the elements on the piazza is left open to form a colonnade. Otherwise, Kahn used wooden infills. The concrete is meticulously poured, and Kahn emphasized the joints by means of V-shaped grooves. The holes left by the formwork were not patched but left visible across the surface of the material. These carefully crafted surfaces contrast with the textured whiteness of the courtyard's travertine pavement.

All of Kahn's work, but especially the Salk Institute Building, aims to restore the sense of monumentality and gravitas that he felt had been lost in modern architecture. In 1938, an architecture critic had written that "if it is a monument, it is not modern; if it is modern, it cannot be a monument." But by the late 1950s and 1960s, architects had begun to return to monumentality (as at Utzon's Sydney Opera House). Kahn, however, avoided the gesturalism of Utzon while trying to fuse architectural space with structure with architecture and yet not become subservient to the fallacy of rationalism. In this, his approach is somewhat akin to that of Mies van der Rohe, except that Kahn, in his admiration for Roman architecture, Scottish castles, and Greek temples wanted to emphasize the solidity and tactility of his buildings—unlike the buildings of Mies, which tend, despite his attention to detail and materials, to be cold and impersonal.

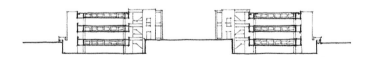

18.119 Section through laboratory buildings, Salk Institute

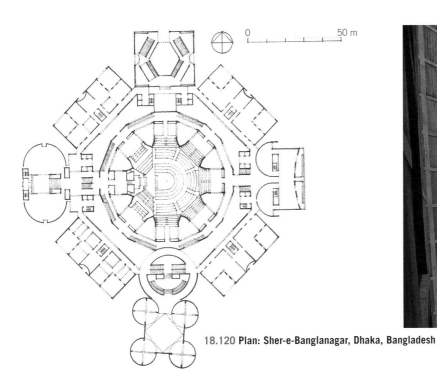

18.120 Plan: Sher-e-Banglanagar, Dhaka, Bangladesh

18.121 Interior: Sher-e-Banglanagar

Sher-e-Banglanagar

Louis Kahn spent more than a decade working on Sher-e-Banglanagar (1961–82) in Dhaka (as it came to be called after Bangladesh became independent in 1971)—and almost went bankrupt in the process. It was completed well after Kahn's death in 1974, but when it was finished in 1982, it instantly arrested the attention of the Bangladeshi populace and was celebrated as a triumphant display of their independence. What the Bangladeshi citizens see is a closely clustered assembly of monolithic concrete towers, slashed with huge triangular, rectangular, and semicircular openings. Together they form the outer envelope—the serving zone—to the central chamber of the parliament, with the trusses of the gigantic roof structure just visible from a distance.

The entrance to the building is from the north, through a large square building with grand staircases. The four buildings for offices are packaged between this building and the other axially placed elements, which are the minister's offices to the west, lunchrooms to the east, and a mosque to the south. The mosque, preceded by a circular ablution space, is formed by four round towers clamped against a rotated square; it is tilted a few degrees from the axis in order to orient it toward Mecca. Within, Sher-e-Banglanagar, much as the Pantheon's oculus,

is a studied essay in the use of natural light to illuminate monumental spaces—split, spliced, and reimagined through a series of cubist transformations. From the outside, however, Sher-e-Banglanagar sits in silent dignity, with a vast swath of land cleared all around it, first to make a reflecting pool and then a giant plaza. Unlike the great plazas of Brasília and Chandigarh, Dhaka's plaza became an instant success. Every day, thousands of people throng its vast expanse, playing, picnicking, protesting, or otherwise participating in the public affairs of civic life. Kahn's Sher-e-Banglanagar (like Le Corbusier's Chandigarh) was his largest, and final project, and along with the Kimbell Art Museum in Fort Worth, Texas, and the Salk Institute in La Jolla, California, certainly the finest of his later work. Where the Kimbell Art Museum is about the invention of the section and the very precise and subtle measurement of light in its galleries, and the Salk Institute is a singular and profound meditation on the framing of a view, Sher-e-Banglanagar, though of much cruder workmanship, is Kahn's most complex essay on the interplay of light and mass in a tightly controlled formal order.

18.122 Sher-e-Banglanagar

18.123 **Totsuka Country Club, Yokohama, Japan**

18.124 **Nichinan Cultural Center, Nichinan, Japan**

Metabolism

On the basis of the design for his internationally acclaimed Hiroshima memorial, Kenzo Tange (1913–2005) was invited to attend the eighth CIAM meeting, held in England in 1951, where he met Le Corbusier, Siegfried Giedion, Walter Gropius, and Jose Luis Sert, among others. It was at this congress that the question of the "urban core" was raised, rekindling Tange's interests in urban planning. Tange became a member of Team X after the dissolution of CIAM in 1956 and presented his design for the Tokyo City Hall (1957) at their Otterlo, Netherlands, meeting in 1959. To this meeting he brought Kiyonori Kikutake's drawings for the reorganization of Tokyo, which envisioned tall, circular residential towers on land and factories on giant cylinders in the bay. This was the beginning of his interest in urbanization as an organic system and led to the development of Metabolism. Tange presented his metabolist concepts at the World Design Conference held in Tokyo in 1958. This conference was conceived as an alternative to Team X and was attended by, among others, Kikutake, Kisho Kurokawa, Noboru Kawazoe, Fumihiko Maki, Peter and Alison Smithson, Jacob Bakema, Paul Rudolph, Ralph Erskine, Louis Kahn, Jean Prouve, Minoru Yamasaki, Balkrishna V. Doshi, and Raphael Soriano.

Unlike Team X, which approached urban design and planning by trying to solve problems at the human scale, the Metabolists worked at the largest scale conceivable, seeing their structures through a biological metaphor as an expression of the city's new life force. Despite this large scale, Metabolism was a philosophical proposition about inhabiting the earth in harmony with the forces of nature. Although Tange's urban plans bore little fruit, his architectural practice, patronized by Japan's elite, flourished. With an uncanny aesthetic sense rivaled by few who worked with exposed concrete at such large scales,

Tange built a celebrated body of work in the 1960s and 1970s. The Totsuka Country Club (1960–61) acquired its upward-turning profile from Chandigarh's Assembly; the Nichinan Cultural Center (1960–62), with its forceful fins, was a beast unto itself; and finally, the Olympic Stadium in Tokyo was a stellar display not only of the structural possibilities of concrete and tensile cable but of the ability of structure to generate poetic forms such as had been rivaled only by Santiago Calatrava in the recent past.

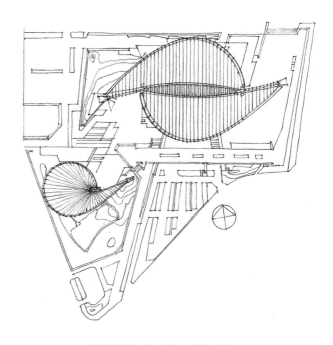

18.125 **Site plan: Olympic Stadium, Tokyo**

18.126 Herbert F. Johnson Museum of Art, Cornell University, Ithaca, New York

18.127 Foundling Estate, London

Brutalism

In the mid-1960s, numerous architects, led by Kenzo Tange, became interested in megastructures that consisted of simple, large-scale repetitive units packed with program. Cultural contexts were meant to play only a limited role in these buildings. Instead, the buildings emphasized material simplicity and secular anonymity. They spoke of the ethos of managerial grandness and implied a transnational utopianism. The Foundling Estate in London (1973) has long lines of housing stacked on massive piers. Though structures like these were soon maligned, they brought modernism to a new pitch in their fearless acceptance of large-scale realities.

Brutalism was particularly popular among university administrators, and many campuses in the United States have at least one example of late 1960s Brutalism, such as Kane Hall at the University of Washington, Seattle, designed by Walker & McGough (1969) and the Stratton Student Center at the Massachusetts Institute of Technology in Cambridge by Eduardo F. Catalano. Similar, but much larger, is the Rand Afrikaans University in Johannesburg, South Africa (1975), designed by William Meyer, which fused the latest trends in megastructure with ideas that were seen as specifically African. Trellick Tower (1967–73) by Ernö Goldfinger in London is similarly vast and imposing. The word *brutalism* derives from the French word for exposed concrete, *béton brut*, which was used by its defenders in an attempt to be "honest" with the material. Brutalism soon came to have connotations that were significantly less positive.

Chinese-born I. M. Pei (1917–) refined the Brutalist aesthetic by developing a distinctive style that appealed to many city leaders during the days in which museums and cultural buildings were coming into their own as an established aspect of a city's profile. His Herbert F. Johnson Museum of Art on the campus of Cornell University (1970–73) in Ithaca, New York, consists of a set of distinct vertical concrete masses holding the main mass of the gallery high in the air; huge panes of glass fill in the open volumes, making the whole structure unexpectedly transparent. Pei's East Building, National Gallery (1974–78) in Washington, DC, has numerous Brutalist motifs, such as the stark masses, deep recesses, sharp edges, and wide openings, but it was clad in a white sandstone that foreshadowed a new generation of elegant, modernist civic structures.

18.128 Terllick Tower, London

18.129 East Building, National Gallery, Washington, DC

18.130 A portion of Ron Herron's Walking City

Archigram

Archigram was a publication, begun in 1961, that quickly became known for its alternative ideas. Short for *Architectural Telegram*, *Archigram* was produced by the young English architects Peter Cook, David Greene, Michael Webb, Ron Herron, Warren Chalk, and Dennis Crompton. The full *Archigram* group later included Colin Fournier, Ken Allison, and Tony Rickaby. Though the actual collaborations between these architects were often sporadic and difficult, the magazine's agenda called for a holistic vision of the city and its parts as a living, flowing, pulsing, flexible organism. Challenging the grid established by Le Corbusier, *Archigram's* texts, collages, and comic book–style designs emphasized the use of anything but 90-degree angles and thematized the curving and twisting of Le Corbusier's straight lines. Using bright colors, a nonstandard format, and an explicitly cut-and-paste style of assembly, *Archigram* delivered visions of technologically advanced cities that walked on four legs, so-called Plug-In Cities that could be stacked and changed like cords in an outlet, and even Instant Cities that could be flown in and made to sprout like spring flowers in the hands of any eager architect, critic, or admirer. Though many of *Archigram's* structures were unbuildable, Peter Cook's recently built Kunsthaus in Graz, Austria, with its amorphous blue shape that

contrasts with the traditional architecture around it, gives some indication of the *Archigram* aesthetic and the excitement that it can generate.

The work of one member of the *Archigram* group, Mark Fisher, a student of Peter Cook at the Architectural Association in London, embraced the language and images of the youth culture that was then blooming in England and elsewhere. His investigations into inflatable technology led to the Automat in 1968. It was a user-responsive pneumatic structure supported by internal bracing cables that, attached to high-pressure jacks, allowed the structure to expand and contract in response to a user's weight requirements. Fisher improved the Automat in his design of the Dynomat, the surface of which was controlled by a series of valves, again responding to user interactions. The structure could be deflated and folded to fit in the back of a car.

In 1977, Mark Fisher was asked to design inflatable stage props for the Animals tour of the rock group Pink Floyd. During the design process Fisher created the theme of two towering pneumatic icons. For the first show, Fisher also designed a bloated, inflatable "nuclear family"—including 2.5 children. The most memorable of the Animals tour inflatables were the series of pigs, which flew over the audience's heads, snorting

and ultimately exploding above and behind Pink Floyd's stage. From his success with Pink Floyd's Animals tour, Mark Fisher went on to develop many of rock and roll's most memorable sets, including Pink Floyd's Wall and Division Bell sets and Lisbon's Expo '98.

Alternative Architecture

Beginning in the early 1960s and continuing through the end of the decade, numerous young architects, builders, and artists—mainly in the United States—began to seek out alternatives to professional architecture, building with sod or discarded building elements and studying vernacular practices around the world. They were part of a broader criticism of the social norms of the age, including the suburban lifestyle and the exploitation of natural resources. Though many of these people's names remain obscure, their efforts were sometimes spectacular, such as the house built by Bob de Buck and Jerry Thorman in New Mexico, a freeform maze of spaces gathered around the central shafts of concrete columns that

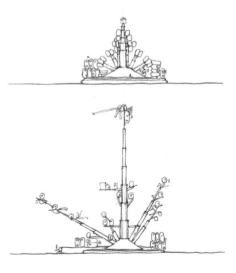

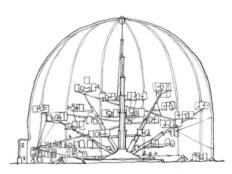

18.131 Peter Cook's Blow-Out Village

18.132 **A homemade dome**

are actually the chimney flues. The structure was decorated with hubcaps and built with wood scavenged from construction sites. The framing was plastered, giving it an organic feeling. In an interview, de Buck made the statement, "Tools not to have: straightedge, square, level, plumb."

In 1965, an artist community called Drop City was founded in southern Colorado. It attempted to combine innovative architectural form with social utopianism. The original founders were Gene Bernofsky, JoAnn Bernofsky, Richard Kallweit, and Clark Richert, art students and filmmakers from the University of Kansas and the University of Colorado. Their intention was to create a live-in work inspired by the "happenings" of painter and performance artist Allan Kaprow and the impromptu performances of John Cage, Robert Rauschenberg, and Buckminster Fuller. Residents constructed domes and zonohedra, using geometric panels made from the metal of automobile roofs and other inexpensive materials. The property deed stipulated that the land on which the commune was built was "forever free and open to all people." Eventually, tensions and personality conflicts developed, leading many of the occupants to leave. Nonetheless, there were several attempts to repeat the experiment, such as the Criss-Cross artists' colony in Colorado. Though dispersed and fragmented, this movement played an important part in demanding that architects developed greater ecological awareness. It also exposed the growing disenchantment with professional architecture and the modern movement in general.

One example of the tradition of alternative architecture is a building that, once the scourge of the neighborhood, is now a tourist attraction; it was made by Art Beal, a garbage collector for the town of Cambria, California. Known also known as Captain Nitt Witt or Dr. Tinkerpaw, he spent his life constructing a residence on from salvaged materials using only hand tools. The structure is made from car parts, cans, shells, TV antennas, driftwood, and local rocks.

18.133 **House by Art Beal, Cambria, California**

18.134 School of Architecture, Ahmedabad, India

18.135 Gandhi Ashram Museum, Ahmedabad, India

Post-Corbusier India

The Brazilian government was toppled by a military coup in 1965, arresting the development of Brazilian modernism. However, in South Asia, as in other parts of the postcolonial world, a more regional modern architecture continued to flourish. The Indian team of architects that had worked with Le Corbusier in Chandigarh continued to build throughout north India. Aditya Prakash, for instance, was responsible for designing many new campuses and universities, such as those in Ludhiana and Hissar, in the 1960s. In New Delhi, Shiv Nath Prasad developed Le Corbusier's brutalist

vocabulary at the Akbar Hotel (1965–69) and at the Sri Ram Center for Performing Arts (1966–72). In Bangladesh, Mazharul Islam used brick and concrete at his dormitory at Jahangir University (1969). In general, building was done with load-bearing brick walls. Concrete lintels and slabs and deep overhangs were used for protection from the sun. In Brazil, structural innovation became an integral part of the national modern style, but in India, architects readily experimented with low-tech solutions for their modernist buildings, using exposed brick and concrete constructed with simple technical skill and inexpensive finishes.

Balkrishna V. Doshi (1927–) and Charles Correa (1930–) were among the most prominent Indian architects. One of Doshi's successful early projects was the School of Architecture in Ahmedabad (1965), a reworking of Le Corbusier's design for the College of Art in Chandigarh. Unlike Le Corbusier's design, which was closed off and regulated by a very strict circulation system, Doshi's school maintained the principle of north light, but he opened the building up so

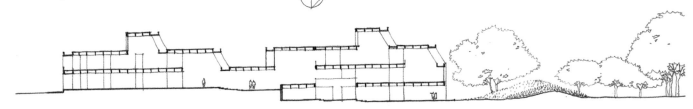

18.136 Plan and section: School of Architecture, Ahmedabad, India

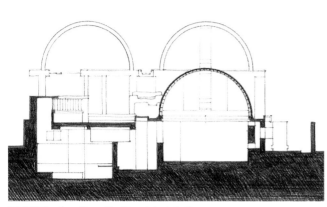

18.137 **Section: Sangath, Ahmedabad, India**

18.138 **Sangath, Ahmedabad, India**

that it operated as a multifunctional space. Later in life, Doshi moved in the direction of Louis Kahn, asking more fundamental questions of materials and assembly. The design of Sangath (1979), his own office, took on the task of rethinking a climatic response. The consequence was a structure that was just as much below ground as above, with a series of vaulted roofs (covered with broken china) derived from the original shed that stood on the site.

Correa extended Le Corbusier's fascination with sunlight to create a series of houses made of brick and concrete that used the concept of sections as well as a pergola roof to create microclimatic conditions. His Parekh House (1967–68) in Ahmedabad, for instance, had two sections: one for the summer and the other for the winter. The distant influence of Kahn's Trenton Bath House can be seen in Correa's design for the Gandhi Ashram Museum (1958–63), intended to house artifacts and an exhibition of the life of Mahatma Gandhi. Here Correa used a 6-meter grid composed of I-shaped brick piers to set up a network of spaces that were open to the sky, covered but open, and fully enclosed that showed an early skill in developing courtyardlike spaces to advantage. Correa used a mud-tile roof, held up on concrete beams, that drained rain water into channels in the concrete slabs. The water is then collected in a central pond through huge concrete gargoyles. Operable wooden louvers enabled air circulation in the enclosed spaces.

Correa's later work developed his climatic solutions for different sites and programs. For his residential tower in Bombay, the Kanchenjunga Apartments (1970–83), for instance, he punched out double-height spaces in the corners to create an open feel and to set up air circulation through each apartment. His Kovalam Beach Resort (1969–74) utilized the natural slope of an ocean-facing hill to create a rhythm of rooms and terraces open to the sky.

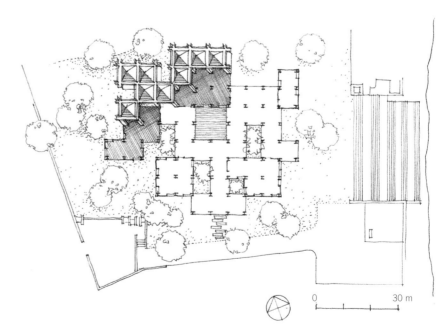

18.139 **Plan: Gandhi Ashram Museum, Ahmedabad, India**

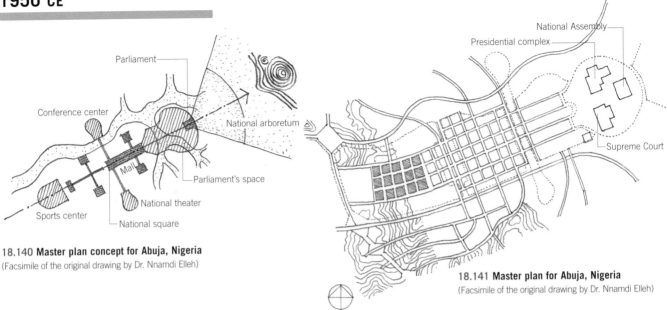

18.140 Master plan concept for Abuja, Nigeria
(Facsimile of the original drawing by Dr. Nnamdi Elleh)

18.141 Master plan for Abuja, Nigeria
(Facsimile of the original drawing by Dr. Nnamdi Elleh)

University of Ibadan

World War II left England and France considerably weakened. By the mid-1960s, almost all of the English colonies in Africa had achieved independence, including Uganda in 1962 and Zanzibar and Kenya in 1963. Most immediately embarked on an aggressive campaign of modernization. New capitals, schools, and hospitals had to be built, but since traditional architecture had been neglected, skilled builders and craftspeople were rare. In 1945, in all of Africa, including Egypt, there were only 26 cities with a population over one hundred thousand. By the 1970s, there were 120 such cities, but architectural development remained spotty.

After Nigeria's independence in 1960, several modernists arrived in Lagos, its capital, including the husband-and-wife team of Maxwell Fry and Jane Drew; they designed the city's University of Ibadan in the early 1960s, after having worked in Chandigarh, India. The university's nucleus is a series of connected buildings consisting of a ring of residential colleges arranged around a core of buildings devoted to teaching and administration. Open balconies, screens, and covered passageways make use of prevailing winds. The plan can be described as loosely hierarchical, with sports and residential complexes at one end and the classroom and administration buildings at the other.

By 1991, new oil revenues created wealth and stability, and Nigeria's capital was moved to a new city, Abuja, located on the Gwanga Plains in the middle of the country. Abuja's master plan (1976) was designed by Kenzo Tange, blending Lúcio Costa's airplane plan for Brasília with the circulation pattern of Tokyo. Anthropomorphically conceived, it had the shape of a body with a head, torso, arms, and tail. The head contained the three principal government buildings, the torso the main body of the city, and the arms the conference center and theater. Though it was designed as a site for a democratic government, the head can be easily barricaded in times of civil disturbances. Abuja is currently far from complete.

18.142 University of Ibadan, Nigeria

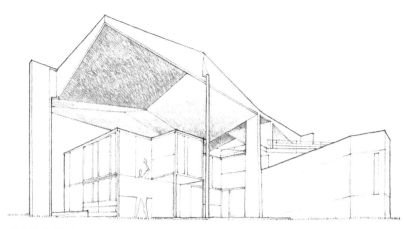

18.143 Heidi Weber House (Centre Le Corbusier), Zurich

Postmodernism

The word *postmodernism* does not refer to a particular definable style and so it is very different from other designations, like Georgian or Shingle Style or even the International style, which, despite its multiple meanings and origins in architecture, by the 1950s described a set of practices loosely defined around the ideals of CIAM. But what had seemed so promising in 1950 was by 1970 seen not only as constricting but also as failing to live up to its promises. More and more, critics began to associate modernism with capitalism, bureaucracy, and especially, with totalitarianism. And for Europeans, modernism after World War II meant endless rows of hastily built, drab-looking housing blocks. There were in Europe no Brasílias, Chandigarhs, or Dhakas, and few examples of successful civic modernism. In the United States, modernism was more successful. It had made significant inroads in domestic architecture, had thoroughly transformed the corporate landscape, and even had a few successful civic projects to show for itself, such as Lincoln Center (1956) in New York City and Civic Center Plaza (1965–66) in Chicago.

But even in the United States, vast housing blocks shot up that exacerbated post–World War II social and racial tensions. This led to the announcement of the "death of modernism" at the destruction in 1972 of the Pruitt-Igoe Housing Project (1952–5) in St. Louis, Missouri, which opened to a great deal of optimism but, because of mismanagement and changing attitudes,

became the very symbol of urban blight and racial imbalance. Beginning in the late 1960s, architects began to return to the question of context, history, traditions, and form as a way to revitalize the purpose and meaning of their profession. The protest against modernism began in the United States and developed in Europe into a global movement. Dreary housing projects for the lower classes continue, of course, to be built around the world. But they were

no longer associated with social progress. Postmodernism was, however, by no means a single or unified field of production, nor did it always mean a rejection of modernism. In fact, Le Corbusier's Heidi Weber House (1965), one of his last designs, shows that even he was able to rethink modernism's aesthetic once again. Two floating steel canopies, painted gray and held up on thin supports, shelter the house below, which is designed out of modular steel elements variously open to the interior with big sheets of glass or closed off by brightly colored panels.

The challenge to break the hold of functionalism was taken up by Philip Johnson (1906–2005), who was attracted to Russian Constructivism for purely aesthetic reasons when planning an office building in St. Louis. Michael Graves (1934–) was fascinated with the paintings of Le Corbusier and the architecture of the Dutch modernist Gerrit Rietveld. His buildings used color and applied the methodology of the collage. Other architects moved in the direction of social realism, such as Robert Venturi (1925–) and Denise Scott Brown (1931–), who were influenced by Pop Art and who turned their gaze at highway architecture and, most specifically, to Las Vegas, Nevada.

18.144 Piazza d'Italia, New Orleans

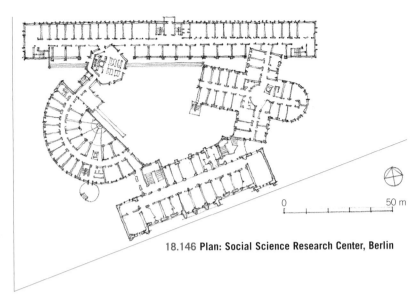

18.146 Plan: Social Science Research Center, Berlin

18.145 AT&T Building, New York City

Charles Moore (1925–93), by way of contrast, sought a deeper personal commitment to architecture than that which could be provided by a standard professional practice. In his writings are the beginnings of an interest in phenomenology, a movement that was to grow steadily in the United States and abroad and that was linked to a trend toward political conservatism in architecture.

Moving from Philip Johnson to Charles Moore, one can begin to recognize the inherent and unresolved complexity of Postmodernism, for though it heralded a release from the strictures of modernism it also had conservative leanings, as was brought to the fore by the phenomenologists, who, in the United States and elsewhere, began to replace the socially oriented architects in academia. Those who wanted to take up the issue of community-oriented architecture often left the field of architecture for the rapidly expanding discipline of urban planning. Among the very early phenomenologists, Christian Norberg-Schulz (1926–2000) was strongly influenced by the German philosopher Martin Heidegger and argued for a regionally based aesthetic, whereas Moore believed that architecture needed to integrate a sensitivity to landscape with an aesthetic determined by psychology and memory. At the opposite extreme from phenomenology was psychoanalysis, which among architects, unlike artists at the time, received very little interest.

Certainly one of the most intriguing aspects of Postmodernism was its interest in irony. No architecture before or after has allowed the designer to experiment with cultural and historical images with as free a hand as Postmodernism. Examples include New Orleans's Piazza d'Italia (1975–78) by Charles Moore; New York City's AT&T Building (1984) by Philip Johnson; the National Collegiate Football Hall of Fame (unbuilt, 1967) by Venturi, Scott Brown & Associates; and Chicago's Animal Crackers House (1976–78) by Stanley Tigerman. Tigerman, influenced by inflated pop art forms, built an addition to a house that looks like a series of rollers that can be turned by using the ventilators on the sides as knobs. It is half industrial and half cartoonish in character. Even more provocative were the designs of the New York–based firm known as SITE (Sculpture in the Environment), which received commissions from Best, a forward-looking supermarket chain. In one project, the firm peeled the brick facade from the box, and in another, it designed the facade to look as if it were in a state of decay and ruin. The irony was aimed at the strangeness of suburban architecture. It was the first firm to engage the question of the shopping mall through criticism and humor simultaneously.

Robert Stern (1939–) also interrogated the image of the American suburb in his Point West Place office building in Framingham, Massachusetts (1983–84),

which in essence placed an Egyptianesque facade onto an otherwise generic office building. James Stirling's project for the Berlin Social Science Research Center (1981) begins with an existing building; appended behind it, in the form of a collage, are buildings in the form of an amphitheater, a castle, an octagonal baptistery, and even a church. Through this historicism, which relies on precedents from the classical to the Renaissance, Stirling poked fun at a city whose history, unlike other European capitals, only began in the late 18th century. This instant Europeanization of Berlin was also meant to thumb its nose at Europe's fascination with its own past.

Buildings like the Berlin Social Science Research Center led many to criticize Postmodernism as a style without rules. But there were many Postmodernists who rejected irony and the open-endedness of the design process in favor of authenticity and seriousness. This movement was particularly strong in Europe. The German architect and theorist Leon Krier (1946–), a particularly strident critic of modernism, argued for a new Hellenism. In England, Prince Charles called for a return to pre-modern, home-grown English styles. In Italy, Aldo Rossi (1937–97) argued for a typological coherence to architecture and challenged both modernists and postmodernists by staying within the Brutalist aesthetic. At the Gallaratese (1969–73), a large apartment building project

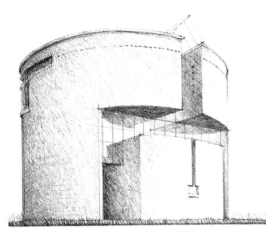

18.147 **House at Stabio, Switzerland**

18.148 **Centre Georges Pompidou, Paris, France**

on the outskirts of Milan, for example, Rossi designed one of the blocks with a rhetoric of extreme formalist stoicism. The result was the emergence of an ethos of regionalism that had many defenders, since it allowed for a criticism of modernism on the one hand, and of Postmodernism's penchant for irony and arbitrariness on the other. Regionalism was particularly strong outside of the West, where it tapped into nationalist and anticolonialist sentiments. But there were also a hand full of European regionalists, such as the Swiss architect Mario Botta (1943–) whose work drew somewhat vaguely on local, historical forms. Nonetheless, his buildings' plans remained in some sense modern, as did their massing.

Whereas many of the more conservative Postmodernists attempted to orient architecture back to its temporal, contextual, and historical roots, Peter Eisenman (1932–), along with John Hejduk (1929–2000) and a few others, rejected any softening of architecture in response to cultural pressures. Architecture, to maintain itself as a discipline, had to remain aloof from cultural traditions and bourgeois demands. Eisenman thus created for his buildings a set of formal constraints that had nothing to do with function or program. His radical formalism lies at the opposite end of the spectrum from Robert Venturi's pop contextualism. Nonetheless, both celebrated the disjuncture of expectations in the understanding of what

architecture is. Eisenman's architecture, however, maintained a focus on the design process by seeking out a self-referential language that excluded the traditional priority of client needs. For the design of a house he created a type of game in which a cube was cut, rotated, sliced, and otherwise manipulated. Whatever was left over was the "house": function, siting, weather, and use were given no consideration at all. He wanted to demonstrate that function is just as flexible as form and that a "house" is a semantic indicator of an architectural object, not its typology. This is different from the views of Rossi, who wanted functionalism to bend to the primacy of type.

Postmodernism, through the influences of Pop Art, also began to accommodate itself to the new medium of signage and advertising. The Centre Georges Pompidou (1971–77) in Paris, designed by the firm Piano & Rogers, was about "legibility." It was originally to have large billboards suspended from its metal structure. The service conduits, too, had to be legible. Air-conditioning ducts are blue, electricity conduits are yellow, elevator cables are red, staircases are gray, and the structure itself is white. Putting so much emphasis on visual impact, Postmodern architects had little to contribute to the topic of technology, but in his State of Illinois Building in Chicago (1979), Helmut Jahn left elements of the structure exposed especially on the interior to better reveal the workings of the building.

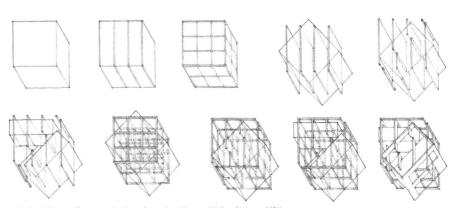

18.149 **Peter Eisenman's drawings for House III for Robert Miller**

18.150 Guggenheim Museum, Bilbao, Spain

Postmodern Museums

Throughout the 19th century and well into the 20th, the museum carried with it the imprint of the Enlightenment. The ordering of space, the systematization of knowledge, and the owning of precious objects went hand in hand with the conception of history, the advances of archaeology, and the understanding of art. Museums also become symbols of national pride, like the National Gallery in London (1861) and the Kyoto National Museum (1898). The imprint of Neoclassicism was so strong that the modern movement could do little to challenge it. In the United States, the National Gallery of Art (1941) in Washington, DC, is resolutely Neoclassical.

Apart from the Museum of Modern Art (1931) in New York, Frank Lloyd Wright's Guggenheim Museum (1951), and the National Museum of Western Art (1959) in Tokyo by Le Corbusier (designed with Kunio Maekawa, Junzo Sakakura, and Takamasa Yoshizaka), there are few well-known examples of museums in the modern style. It was only in the 1970s that the modern museum emerged as a force within design culture. The Centre Georges Pompidou in Paris defied all the predictions to become one of the city's most visited sites, but it was still more the exception than the rule.

By the 1990s, however, with the boom in the global economy and a heightened competition for tourist dollars, museums

became more than just signs of a city's cultural strength; they became instrumental to the economies of entire regions. A blockbuster exhibition could bring in millions of dollars in secondary revenue and taxes. If there is one building type that piqued the interest of architects, planners, politicians, and the public alike, it was the museum. What the civic center or philharmonic hall had been to the 1960s and the pedestrian zone to the 1980s, the museum had become in the 1990s. The transition began with the Neue Staatsgalerie (1977–83) by James Stirling and was in full swing by the opening of the Pyramide du Louvre by I. M. Pei in 1989.

Given the economic power of the museum, the architect was no longer expected to be responsible for preserving conservative traditions dating back to the ancient Romans; the architect was not even responsible for representing high culture, as Mies van der Rohe and Louis Kahn had thought so many decades ago. Rather, the architect was responsible for representing the irrefutable modernity of contemporary culture itself. The Guggenheim Museum in Bilbao, Spain, for example, not only revived an entire neighborhood—indeed, an entire city—but revived the museum industry itself. It is the only museum—and for that matter, the only piece of architecture—in history to have an economic principle named after it: the Bilbao effect. Soon cities around the world were vying for the top architects to design museums, from the Jewish Museum in Berlin (1998) by Daniel Libeskind to the Leeum, Samsung Museum of Art in Seoul, South Korea (2004), which has not one building but three: one by Mario Botta, one by Rem Koolhaas, and a third by Jean Nouvel.

18.151 Pyramide du Louvre, Paris

The Preservation Movement

For millennia, buildings followed the life cycles of use and abuse. In the early 19th century, largely as a consequence of national Romanticism and the Gothic Revival, the medieval churches of Europe began to be studied and repaired in a systematic way. This created an awareness of the vulnerability of architecture to the forces of time and changing tastes and also of the value of historical buildings to society. In the 20th century, modernism, with its progressive and antihistorical ambitions, did not see the restoration of ancient buildings as a key element of its mandate, but after World War II, with the destruction of historical buildings on the increase, preservation became less a field of local antiquarians and increasingly a discipline of its own. In 1949, the U.S. Congress created the National Trust for Historic Preservation to support the preservation of historic buildings and neighborhoods. Twenty-nine sites are currently designated as National Trust Historic Sites in the United States, including the Touro Synagogue in Newport, Rhode Island, and the Farnsworth House in Plano, Illinois. In addition, outdoor museum towns, made up of buildings moved from their original locations, were created; Williamsburg, Virginia, is one such example. Many of the missing colonial structures were reconstructed on their original sites during the 1930s with the financial support of John D. Rockefeller Jr. Since the emphasis was on U.S. colonial history, however, 720 Williamsburg buildings that postdated 1790 were demolished.

The destruction of Pennsylvania Station in New York City in 1964 was a watershed moment for the preservation movements. The majestic Neoclassical gateway to the city was replaced by the squat, drab Madison Square Garden complex. In 1965, the city passed the Landmarks Law, which created the New York City Landmarks Preservation Committee; this led to similar committees in other cities. By the 1970s, preservation had strong advocates and gained an increasingly vigorous political and academic profile in the United States and Europe. In 1972, an international treaty called the Convention Concerning the Protection of the World Cultural and Natural Heritage was adopted by UNESCO. Its first great success was moving

18.152 Abu Simbel, near Aswan, Egypt

Abu Simbel, the Egyptian temple on the Nile that had become endangered because of the construction of the Aswan Dam. Water would have filled up behind the dam, flooding the building, which was taken apart stone by stone and reassembled on higher ground against an artificial hillside. It is now, of course, a major tourist attraction, as are most of the UNESCO's protected properties. UNESCO has more recently moved to protect not only important monuments but also natural habitats, like the rainforests of the Atsinanana in Madagascar, as well as cultural zones like that of the Dogon in Mali. Currently, there are close to nine hundred "properties" protected worldwide, including modern buildings like the 1973 Sidney Opera House. The United States has only four sites on this list: the Statue of Liberty in New York Harbor; Monticello, the house Thomas Jefferson designed for himself in Virginia; Independence Hall in Philadelphia; and Cahokia, near Collinsville, Illinois.

There are few who doubt the importance of maintaining the artifacts of our past from willful or even benign destruction, but the debate as to what to preserve and how to preserve it is a heated one. Should buildings be rebuilt exactly as they were designed, or should new materials be used? Should buildings have the same program today as they had when they were designed? Should a building's context and environment be preserved? If a building was constructed in 1710 and had subsequent additions, should those be kept or removed? Is it appropriate to save only the facade of a building and put a modern building behind it, as is done quite frequently in Europe? Should buildings be preserved not for their architectural value, but for their cultural resonances? A case of the latter is the first McDonald's hamburger stand, which is now a museum 20 miles north of Chicago in Des Plaines, Illinois.

18.153 Chapel of Light, Ibaraki Kasugaoka Kyokai Church, Osaka, Japan

Japanese Postmodernism could be seen as a highly refined form of modernism and not really as Postmodernism at all, since it is stripped of all except the most basic of cultural references. But the rise of Postmodernism in other places was significantly messier and was often accompanied by the erosion of the secular nation-state as the common reference point for diverse communities. Since Postmodernism allowed alternative claims to the conventions of nationalism, irony almost never came into play: on the contrary, the search was usually for some form of regional authenticity based on traditions. Just what constituted "tradition" then became highly contested, particularly in places like South Asia, where different claims, due to India's complex past, could be made upon history and its associated aesthetics. For example, right-wing Hindu nationalists demolished a mosque in northern India in the early 1990s

The Postmodern, Non-Western World

Postmodernism originated in the West, where it was nurtured in the various architectural schools of the United States and Europe. The result was that even though postmodernism eventually became a global phenomenon, its non-Western version was somewhat less experimental. Just as modernism was, in one way or another, tied up with nationalism and national identity, Postmodernism, too, became enmeshed in those issues, part of a search for local identity that tended to narrow its focus. Nonetheless, Postmodernism had a profound impact on the non-Western world, primarily because it enforced, by implication, a negative view of modernism whether it was true or not. Postmodernism at any rate was associated less with irony than with an attempt to reclaim historical and cultural identities. Arata Isozaki (1931–), for example, became more literal in his references to Japanese forms, whereas younger, self-trained architects like Tadao Ando (1941–) gravitated toward elemental forms that stressed the interplay of light and materials in the experience of minimalist, poetic creations. His work became the hallmark of a new and very successful Japanese aesthetic that was highly modern and abstract and that also found common cause with traditional Japanese forms. His work in concrete, the predominant material of his expression, was immaculately poured. The Shingonshu Honpukuji ("Water Temple,"

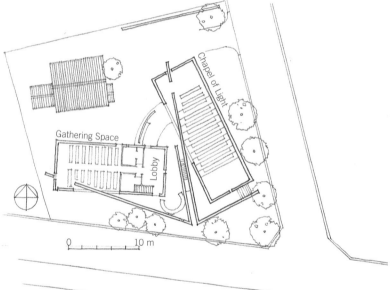

18.154 Site plan: Ibaraki Kasugaoka Kyokai Church

1991), for instance, focused on a singular moment in which a stair descended through a round pond with a smattering of water lilies. At his Chapel of Light, the main chapel at the Ibaraki Kasugaoka Kyokai Church (1989), the altar wall is composed of four pieces of concrete that hover weightlessly next to each other to create a luminous cross; at the rear, in another tour de force, the slight gap between the walls allows a blinding sliver of light to penetrate the dark stillness.

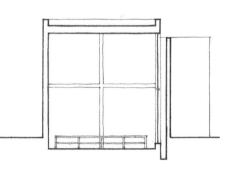

18.155 Section: Chapel of Light

18.156 Plan and section: House for Dr. Bartholomew, Colombo, Sri Lanka

0   15 m

on the grounds that it had been built on the foundations of a Hindu temple a millennium ago; the incident sparked religious riots. Similarly, the Islamic world saw a resurgence of orthodox claims to Islamic identity in cultural expression, forcing the rollback of national modernism in places such as Turkey and Egypt. Often, however, the tendency to see everything before modernism as traditional—that is, as firmly established and permanent—has left a gap in how to engage earlier aesthetic modalities in the modern world.

A long list could be made of architects of the postcolonial and non-Western world who are searching for a way to resolve this issue without resorting to, or endorsing, regressive, nationalist politics. For the most part, such architects, deeply steeped in the sensibilities of modern architecture, have attempted to reimagine their practices by referencing easily accessible and often somewhat stereotypical claims to mandalas and other traditional or iconesque construction systems. Others talk of urban morphologies, place-making, and even *genius loci*, a term that has its origins in European Romantic philosophy of the early 19th century. More realistic was the work of Hassan Fathy (1899–1989) in Egypt. He utilized ancient design methods and materials to create low-cost architecture; he also trained locals to make their own materials and build their own buildings. Climatic conditions, public health considerations, and ancient craft skills also affected his design decisions.

Geoffrey Bawa (1919–2003), an architect from Sri Lanka trained at the Architectural Association in London, engaged problems of managing large land and water systems while building with masons who know nothing of modern building techniques. He drew, nonetheless, on local solutions and developed an aesthetic that is freely eclectic in its expression. His house for Dr. Bartholomew (1961–63) utilized a mixture of locally available materials, including coconut trunks, granite, and fired-earth tiles, as well as concrete for the foundation. He also introduced water pools, not only for cooling but also to serve as visual beacons along a circulation path.

In Mexico, Luis Barragán (1902–88), who had collaborated with Louis Kahn on the design for the plaza at the Salk Institute Building, developed a design vocabulary of simple forms, their elegance heightened by the use of color. Somewhat like Tadao Ando, he maintained a minimalist aesthetic, insisting on stark plains in studied juxtapositions. As a consequence, his work has a strong poetic appeal. In his own house, he differentiated windows that were meant for framing a view and those whose function was merely to admit light. Barragán was little known in the world until a retrospective at the Museum of Modern Art in New York in 1975 made him famous.

18.157 San Cristobal Stables, Los Clubes, Mexico City

18.158 **Simpson-Lee House, Mt. Wilson, Australia**

18.1598 **Marie Short House, Kempsey, Australia**

Magney House

One of the most consistent explorations of a localized modernism was undertaken by Australia's Glenn Murcutt. Beginning with a sensibility strongly impressed by Mies van der Rohe's minimalist architecture, Murcutt's one-man practice has taken up small projects in the manner of California's Case Study Houses. His designs minimize the use of material while maximizing their effectiveness in controlling climate. His buildings disturb the land as little as possible and are constructed as efficiently as possible. A deep-seated knowledge of the site and of local conditions is cardinal to Murcutt's ethic; by choice, he has never practiced outside of Australia, although he teaches worldwide.

Murcutt's Magney House (1982–84), located 500 meters from the southern Pacific coast of Australia, has a masonry wall 2.1 meters high to the south to buffer the building against cold ocean winds. In contrast, the northern facade is completely glazed, though protected by retractable louvers, to take in the light and views. A continuous band of glazing about 2 meters off the ground encircles the house to admit ambient light and to make the sky visible from inside. Above this, two asymmetrical curves built with corrugated metal sheets not only protect the glazing and collect water that is stored in subterranean tanks but also give the house its signature roof profile as a "machine for living." Two vents from the kitchens hover above the roof like periscopes. Taut, V-shaped steel struts hold the roof overhang, calculated to keep the summer sun out and to admit the sun in winter. The plan is simple: a thin band of serving spaces to the south are separated from the northern bank of living spaces by a corridor, located exactly where the gully collecting water from the two roofs runs. Murcutt's Simpson-Lee House (1989–94) is built on the same principles but with a very different expression.

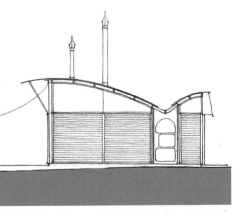

18.160 **Section: Magney House, Bingie Bingie, Australia**

Globalization Takes Command

The awareness that we live in a world of global relationships is now itself global. There is, however, no one equation that can describe this phenomenon—not even one containing a distinction between those ubiquitous variables, the global and the local, so intertwined have the two become. Instead of equating the global only with globalization and the rise of the multinational corporations, we would like to suggest—in the field of architecture—an overlay of seven different global trends, each coming to terms with contemporary reality in a different way. And even though there are overlaps, each is governed by a set of circumstances, ideologies, and politics that differentiates it from the others.

1

In 2008, construction activity around the globe was worth over $3.5 trillion, constituting about 10 percent of the world's economy. These numbers will only increase, despite the economic downturn of 2009, thanks to the economic developments taking place in Asia, Latin America, and eastern Europe. Though a vast proportion of these construction dollars are filtered through large, anonymous real-estate and engineering firms, whether owned privately or by the state, there are a host of large firms that provide architectural services at this level. One of these, Kohn Pedersen Fox Associates (KPF), founded in 1976 and originally working mainly in the United States and Europe, has recently designed the Tigamas master plan (1990), the Kuwait International Hotel (1991), the Singapore Arts Center (1992), the Tel Aviv Peninsula master plan (1996), as well as the De Hoftoren/ Ministry Headquarters of Education, Culture, and Science for the Hague (2003), to list only a small fraction of their work. Seattle-based Callison Architecture, with five hundred people under a single roof, is the retail expert of the world, having designed in the Philippines (Ayala Center Greenbelt), China (Bank of China, Shangdi Center), Japan (Seibu Department Stores), India (Gardens Galleria), Qatar (Pearl of the Gulf), Dubai (Diera City Centre), and Russia (Ikea stores). The St. Louis–based firm Hellmuth, Obata & Kassabaum (HOK) is another megafirm, with 2,500 employees worldwide. Its general style is a clean, professionalized version of Postmodernism, with a flair for color and design. The Japanese megafirm Nikken Sekkei, like New Delhi's Morphogenesis, is more straightforwardly modernist: many of its buildings are infused with a clean, rectilinear sensibility; its presentation and designs predicated on new computing possibilities. Gensler, NBBJ, RTKL, and Ellerbe Beckett, now part of AECOM, are some of the other large firms practicing worldwide.

GLOBALIZATION

19.1 Skyline of modern Shanghai

China has been a big draw since it opened to foreign investment in a massive industrialization and capitalization program the likes of which had never been seen before. By 2020, fifteen of the world's largest twenty cities are going to be in China. (India is not far behind.) During the first decade of the 21st century, the worldwide price of steel doubled because of the demand from China, raising the cost of tall buildings in the rest of the world has appreciably. While the material effects of this transformation were felt worldwide, another kind of competition for supremacy is being waged in Asia in the race to claim the world's tallest building. In less than ten years, this title has shifted from Kuala Lumpur to Shanghai to Taipei and then back to Shanghai. The power of tall buildings as a global icon was verified by the destruction of Minoru Yamasaki's twin towers at the World Trade Center by terrorists on September 11, 2001. That a handful of fanatical religious zealots planning vengeance in a remote field in the middle of Afghanistan could focus so precisely on these skyscrapers as the embodiment of the United States testifies to the continuing hold of architecture as an icon—as well as its perishability—in the global imagination.

2

A second way to map architecture at the global level is to follow the careers of those who self-consciously infiltrate the global economy with the principles of high design. Frank Gehry is the leader in this respect, designing opera houses, museums, and institutional headquarters the world over. These buildings are meant to be high profile and are readily used in tourist brochures. They are prestige commissions. This tendency began after World War II with such commissions as Jørn Utzon's Sydney Opera House (1957–73), Hans Bernhard Scharoun's Berlin Philharmonic Hall (1956–63), and Philip Johnson's and John Burgee's AT&T Building (1978) in New York City. The most recent examples include the construction in Seoul of the Leeum Samsung Museum of Art with buildings by Rem Koolhaas, Mario Botta, and Jean Nouvel. Qatar is being transformed into a world-class cultural center with the completion of five new museums, including the Islamic Museum by I. M. Pei and another one by Santiago Calatrava, the renowned Spanish architect-engineer.

The global commodification of prestige buildings should not lead us to dismiss the potential importance of these buildings in the history of architecture, for they are places where architects can experiment not only with new technologies but also with new ideas about program and function. For the public, these buildings are also the most accessible and visible examples of avant-garde architectural production. Nonetheless, these projects are not unambiguous. The Guggenheim Museum in Bilbao, Spain, has brought in millions in tourist dollars, and the advantages and disadvantages need to be continually kept in mind. But even this is not a new phenomenon. The "Bilbao effect" is today what the great international exhibitions were to the 19th century—economic engines that both promise an enhancement of awareness and knowledge but also extend the flattening process of capital. The Qatar museums are specifically aimed at tourists, whom officials hope will be lured to beach resorts and expansive desert landscapes— "all in a very safe environment." According to one official, "We expect tourism growth to more than double in the next six years, from the four hundred thousand visitors that presently visit Qatar to more than one million tourists in 2010."

19.2 Interior view: Santiago Calatrava's Quadracci Pavilion, Milwaukee Art Museum, Wisconsin

19.3 Quadracci Pavilion, Milwaukee Art Museum

Among the elite designers who work at the global scale of prestige commissions, only Rem Koolhaas, a Dutch architect, has a well-articulated theory about the status and future of a globalized architecture. His 1,376-page book, *S,M,L,XL*, written together with Bruce Mau, Jennifer Sigler, and Hans Werlemann (1995), combines essays, manifestos, diaries, fiction, travelogues, and meditations on the contemporary city. The book's large color graphics transformed architectural publishing. One of its themes was "bigness," part of an attempt to address the concerns of scale in the modern, global world. An essay in the book, "The Generic City," declares that the usual differences between architecture, the street, and the city are things of the past. Instead, architecture has to embrace and combine all of these. Furthermore, the anonymity of the city and its architectural components is an inevitable consequence of modern life—and perhaps an ideal to strive for.

19.4 The Office for Metropolitan Architecture's Central Public Library, Seattle, Washington

19.5 Sardarnagar, a new township near Bhuj, India, established by Hunnarshala (Sandeep Virmani, director) after the devastating earthquake of 2001

19.6 A courtyard of Sardarnagar

Despite this position, Koolhaas, like others, has become the favored architect of the governmental and capitalist elite, or at least those who want to think fast and preferably big, whether it be the Dutch for their embassy in Berlin; the Chinese and their CCTV tower in Beijing; the European Union and its headquarters in Brussels; Samsung, with its Leeum Museum in Seoul; or Prada, with its elegant store in New York City. The difference between KPF and Rem Koolhaas is thus blurry, for both operate at the intersection of high capital and high design. Koolhaas, however, has a practice that seeks to articulate much more strongly than KPF the autonomy of the architect and the symbolic celebration of the architect's name. To this effect, Koolhaas founded the Office for Metropolitan Architecture (OMA) in 1975, a pure design corporation that in his own words blends "contemporary architecture, urbanism, and cultural analysis" and tries to address the problems associated with contemporary globalization with truly innovative and radical solutions. Besides institutional buildings in Europe, the United States, and Asia, OMA has designed urban plans for large cities, proposed a new logo for the European Union, and even prepared the digital identity for a global high-fashion retail giant.

3

In contradistinction to the approach just outlined are the architectural practices that come from the direction of nongovernmental organizations (NGOs) that aim to solve pressing social and economic problems. Globally, one in seven people lives in slum settlements. By 2020, that number will increase to one in three. NGOs are an important part of the solution to this pending crisis since they are more flexible than government bureaucracies and thus often more capable of identifying problems and suggesting solutions that are acceptable to local communities.

Though the idea of the NGO dates to the early 20th century, the phrase *nongovernmental organization* only came into broader use with the establishment of the United Nations in 1945, when provisions were made for the creation of such organizations. Today, the amount of unacknowledged work done by NGOs around the world is staggering. An example is the building effort undertaken by Kutch Nav Nirman Abhiyan, a collection of forty NGOs in Kutch, in western India, which came together after the devastating earthquake of January 26, 2000, to undertake a range of development initiatives in the area of social work, primary education, and disaster management. It has also helped construct

more than twenty thousand dwellings built by the local communities themselves. The new structures used reinforcement techniques that make the buildings would be more earthquake resistant. Such work by "barefoot architects," as they have sometimes been called, is the other side of the world of global capital. Another organization, Architecture for Humanity, a San Francisco–based NGO, provides volunteered professional design services to community groups, social entrepreneurs, and other not-for-profit organizations the world over. It helps underprivileged communities plan and develop schools, clinics, and sport fields, among other things.

4

A fourth type of architecture operating at the global level is produced by local architects with small firms who, despite varying design methodologies, advocate a carefully crafted and well thought out relationship between program and the constraints formed by climate, site conditions, and materials. Though explicitly local by orientation, these architects constitute a global movement due to their shared ethic of design, which can be described broadly as one derived from modern architecture. At Atelier Feichang Jianzhu's Split House near Beijing, for example, the architect uses rammed earth not only for its natural thermal insulating properties but also because rammed earth has been a part of Chinese architecture since time immemorial. When framed against the backdrop of the nearby cliffs, it can even be seen through a Ruskinian ethos about the nature of material and geology. In Adirá & Broid & Rojkind's F-2 House, volcanic basalt, a common local material in Mexico City, is used as a visual and tactile contrast to the cast-in-place concrete. The aesthetic is close to that of Marcel Breuer, who helped create a form of modernism compatible with the open landscape and the need to capture the breeze. Both these houses are therefore high modernist in style—but that should not be any reason to condemn them. Designing within the context of "the local" does not require using or replicating ancient techniques or falsely aestheticize local customs, as is so often done by those, for example, who reduce the Chinese tradition of screening to working with metal screens.

The architecture of small firms is important to the development of architectural thinking since small firms can be often be more experimental and open-ended in their approach. Atelier Bow Wow in Tokyo, established by Yoshiharu Tsukamoto and Momoyo Kaijima, made a name for itself designing unusual structures like the Mado Building in Tokyo (2006) in the tight urban environments of Japanese cities. In Barcelona, the mid-19th century Santa Caterina Market was remodeled (1997–2005) by architects Enric Miralles and Benedetta Tagliabue of EMTB Associates. They added a wavy wooden roof over the whole building, practically filling the piazza. The colorful roof tiles are decorated to emulate the vibrant colors of the vegetables and fruits in the market stalls. The structure has brought new life to the economically depressed area of Barcelona's Gothic Quarter. Another architect, Teddy Cruz, works with the migrant communities of Los Angeles and also with the communities of Mexico just across the border, to learn and develop innovative housing solutions.

5

Irony is particularly remote in today's aesthetic and will, sadly, remain so, given the penchant to appear respectful to the ideologies of tradition and inheritance. For that reason, we would like to point to a fifth global phenomenon: architecture produced locally but by amateurs and architects with an open sensibility to the potential in ready-mades—a house in Massachusetts made completely out of newspaper (including the furniture), a house in Nevada using automobile tires, complete buildings made out cardboard tubes, squatter settlements in Mexico that make use of discarded building materials, architects who use off-the-shelf technologies to subvert expectations, and those who build houses with shipping containers. This type of architecture burst onto the scene in the late 1960s with Drop City in Colorado, which was a center of the counterculture movement. Since then, it has expanded into an informal movement all its own. Sean Godsell's Future Shack, for instance, combines a sun-shading device with a shipping container to design a mass-produced, relocatable house. The Rural Studio, developed by the late Samuel Mockbee at Auburn University in Alabama, is particularly exemplary. Working with the basic principle that even the poorest deserve the dignity of good architecture, Mockbee and his students designed and built a host of innovative and imaginative structures. Sidings made from salvaged automobile windscreens and license plates are only some of the ways in which he has advanced the frontier of architectural practice.

19.7 Antioch Baptist Church, Perry County, Alabama, a project of Auburn University's Rural Studio

6

A sixth category of global production revolves around the question of environment. It was only recently that mainstream architectural professionals began to acknowledge the impact buildings have on the environment. The production of materials like rubber, steel, and glass is highly polluting. And there are also issues of how much energy a building requires for heating and cooling, and the the question of a building's life span. The U.S. Environmental Protection Agency estimates that architectural debris comprises 25 percent of the nation's overall waste stream. This waste often contains materials such as lead paint, asbestos, fluorescent lightbulbs, light ballasts, treated lumber, and other items that pollute the environment.

The impact that industrialism has on the environment and society began to be critiqued in the late 19th century. Frederick Law Olmsted designed parks that were oasis of nature in the urban context, and Frank Lloyd Wright and others attempted to integrate the mechanical and the natural. But it was only with the ecology movement of the 1960s that environmentalism became a political issue. The slow success of that movement led to the emergence of the field of environmental management in the 1980s. Most of the issues involved law, government, and industry, and architecture has only recently begun to find a role within the debates. Today, some architects specialize in low-budget, design-build projects; others, in green housing projects, self-sufficient houses, solar houses, eco-villages, and now, so-called health houses.

The central term in this movement is the word *sustainability*, which, however, can mean different things to different groups. In the context of environmental management, the issues revolve around questions of politics, government, law, planning, and banking. Architectural design, as such, is often left to the end of the process. But this has begun to change, and most large firms now offer a specialization in green architecture. To establish a common standard of measurement, U.S. architects now use the Leadership in Energy and Environmental Design (LEED) Green Building Rating System.

19.8 Commerzbank, Frankfurt, Germany

The LEED system evaluates buildings along a wide spectrum of criteria but usually favors more technologically advanced solutions. Among architects who work with low budgets is Thomas Herzog in Germany, who combines conventional methods of environmental design—high spaces to reduce air-conditioning costs, for example—with high-end technology such as specially designed types of glass and cooling systems. William McDonough has championed the ideological imperative that sustainability should have for the leading corporations of the world. His headquarters for Volkswagen and his projected 65,000-square-meter plant, built on 320 acres of former rain forest in Brazil, are just two of his larger commissions. At the high end of green architecture is Foster & Partners' design for the Commerzbank in Frankfurt, Germany, now the tallest building in Europe. Interspersed in the tower are sky gardens. There are now firms that specialize in the greening of architectural projects just as there are firms that specialize in developing green master plans that look to future needs.

7

A final but increasingly important global formation centers on the World Heritage List to preserve buildings and building environments, created under the auspices of the United Nations Educational, Scientific and Cultural Organization (UNESCO) in 1972. Only thirty years old, the list now consists of more than eight hundred properties in 134 countries. The list is continually expanded, and some are hoping that even places like Chandigarh, India, will be placed on it. The square meters of space worldwide that is now curated, or under some form of protection, has increased over one hundred-thousand-fold, if not more—entire valleys, villages, and landscapes are now under protection.

As valuable as this is, it is just as much the lure of tourist dollars that drives the search for heritage as it is a need to preserve identity. The Dogon cities of Djenné were inscribed onto the UNESCO Heritage List in 1988, and now a road is being planned to reach the remote location. Being "protected" will certainly be a mixed blessing, given that this is a living community and not a set of fossilized ruins. More conventional is the protection of archaeological sites. More than four hundred thousand people visit the remote site of Machu Picchu in Peru every year. A road has now been built to carry tourists practically to the top of this remote mountain. In 1994, a new category was created by UNESCO: "cultural landscapes" were introduced to broaden the representation of what UNESCO calls human heritage, but what its delimitations are will become increasingly complex given that such cultural landscapes will become increasingly entangled with politics.

Global heritage is most certainly a form of global intermixing. Whether that intermixing is to be understood as a form of cultural liberation from the hegemony of the local or as cultural contamination by the hegemony of the global is a question that can only be resolved in each particular situation.

In the last decade, architectural educators have been asking for a textbook that looks beyond the Eurocentric approaches of the past. Ironically, recent decades have also seen the rising specter of nationalism, which has become a global phenomenon in its own right, as countries seek to establish their credentials in global historical narratives. This new nationalism, though it has played some role in awakening an awareness about local realities, has had, and continues to have, a dampening effect on learning about what lies over the horizon. The tension between the global and the national is the fundamental paradox of our age.

Today we live in a world that is significantly more static than centuries before—boundaries are controlled by international law and political alliances, UNESCO protects architectural and urban marvels of the past, and local and national regulations govern what can and cannot be built. We control our actions for the sake of global tranquility. But inequities and injustices about the location of boundaries persist, and so, too, do the tensions that result from inward-looking ideologies. In this environment, the maxim "know your neighbor" is all the more important, but at the same time all the more elusive, since we can all, no matter what country we are from, easily revel in our singularity—in the presumed uniqueness of our history.

This is something we need to guard against. A global history is not the history of all the modern nations added up like beads on an abacus. But neither is it a history that assumes a universal aspect to mankind and its productions. For a global history to be more than just dates and facts, it has to be rooted in the principle that each of us learns how he or she is indeed different in the eyes of others.

Glossary

abacus The rectangular stone slab forming the top of a column capital, plain in the Doric style but molded or otherwise enriched in other styles.

abbey 1. A monastery under the supervision of an abbot, or a convent under the supervision of an abbess. 2. The church of an abbey.

acanthus A Mediterranean plant whose large, toothed leaves became a common motif in the ornamental program of Corinthian and composite capitals and friezes.

accouplement The placement of two columns or pilasters very close together.

acropolis The fortified high area or citadel of an ancient Greek city, typically marked by an important temple.

Acropolis The citadel of Athens and site of the Parthenon.

adobe Sun-dried brick made of clay and straw, commonly used in countries with little rainfall.

adyton A restricted area within the *cella* of a Greek or Roman temple.

aedicule (pl: *aediculae*) A small construction designed in the form of a building—like a canopied niche flanked by colonnettes or a door or window opening—framed by columns or pilasters and crowned with a pediment.

ageya A Japanese pleasure house.

aggregate From the Latin *aggregare*, to add together. Any of various hard, inert mineral materials, as sand and gravel, added to a cement paste to make concrete or mortar.

agora A marketplace or public square in an ancient Greek city, usually surrounded by public buildings and porticoes and commonly used as a place for popular or political assembly.

alameda 1. A public promenade lined with shade trees. 2. In Latin America, a boulevard, park, or public garden with such a promenade.

Alcazar A castle or fortress of the Spanish Moors, specifically, the palace of the Moorish kings in Seville, Spain, which was later used by Spanish kings.

altar 1. An elevated place or structure upon which sacrifices are offered or incense burned in worship or before which religious rites are performed. 2. The table in a Christian church upon which the Sacrament of the Eucharist is celebrated.

amalaka The bulbous, ribbed stone finial of a *shikhara* in Indian architecture.

ambo Either of two raised stands from which the Gospels or Epistles were read or chanted in an early Christian church.

ambulatory 1. The covered walk of an atrium or cloister. 2. An aisle encircling the end of the choir or chancel of a church, originally used for processions.

amphitheater 1. An oval or round building with tiers of seats around a central arena, like those used in ancient Rome for gladiatorial contests and spectacles.

ang A lever arm in traditional Chinese construction, placed parallel to the rafters and raked at an angle to counterbalance the forces applied by the inner and outer purlins. The *ang* supports the outermost purlin by means of a bracket or crossbeam and is pinned at the inner end against a purlin. The ang first appeared in the 3rd century CE, but served purely as a decorative element after the Song dynasty.

annular Having the shape of a ring.

anta In Greek temples, a rectangular pier or pilaster formed by thickening the end of a projecting wall.

apadana The grand columnar audience hall in a Persian palace.

apse A semicircular or polygonal projection of a building, usually vaulted and used especially at the sanctuary or the east end of a church to define the space for an altar. Also called an exedra.

apteral 1. Without a colonnade along the sides. 2. Having no aisles, as a church. 3. Revealing no aisles, as a church facade.

aqueduct A conduit or artificial channel for conducting water from a remote source, usually by gravity, especially an elevated structure constructed by the Romans to carry a water channel across a valley or over a river.

arabesque A complex and ornate design that employs flowers, foliage, and sometimes geometric figures and the figures of animals to produce an intricate pattern of interlaced lines.

arcade 1. A range of arches supported on piers or columns, this composition dates back to Hellenistic times and was used mainly in Islamic and Christian architecture. 2. An arched, roofed gallery or passageway with shops on one or both sides.

arch A curved structure for spanning an opening and designed to support a vertical load primarily by axial compression.

architecture parlante "Speaking architecture," a term used in 18th-century France to describe the architecture of buildings that, in their plans or elevations, create an image that suggests their functions.

architrave 1. The lowermost division of a classical entablature, resting directly on the column capitals and supporting the frieze. 2. A molded or decorative band framing a rectangular door or window opening.

arcuate Curved or arched like a bow: a term used in describing the arched or vaulted structure of a Romanesque church or Gothic cathedral, as distinguished from the trabeated architecture of an Egyptian hypostyle hall or Greek Doric temple.

arris A sharp edge or ridge formed by two surfaces meeting at an exterior angle, like that formed by the adjoining flutes of a classical column.

ashlar A squared building stone finely dressed on all faces adjacent to those of other stones so as to permit very thin mortar joints.

ashram A house for resting in Indian architecture.

atrio In Mexican architecture, a large open court that is walled along the edges.

atrium 1. The main or central inner hall of an ancient Roman house, open to the sky at the center and usually having a pool for the collection of rainwater. Also called a *cavaedium*. 2. The forecourt of an early Christian church, flanked or surrounded by porticoes. 3. An open, skylit court around which a house or building is built. 4. A skylit, central court in a building, especially a large interior one having a glass roof and surrounded by several stories of galleries.

attic 1. A low story or decorative wall above an entablature or the main cornice of a classical facade. 2. A room or space directly under the roof of a building, especially a house; a garret.

axis 1. The line about which a rotating body turns. 2. A line about which a three-dimensional body or figure is symmetrical. 3. Any line used as a fixed reference in conjunction with one or more other references for determining the position of a point or of a series of points forming a curve or a surface. 4. A straight line to which elements in a composition are referred for measurement or symmetry.

bagh A garden in Indian architecture.

baldachino 1. A canopy of fabric carried in religious processions or placed over an altar or throne. 2. An ornamental canopy of stone or marble permanently placed over the high altar in a church.

balustrade A series of balusters used to support a rail in a stair or balcony. Also called a banister.

bangla In Bengal, a hut with a curved thatched roof, the form of which was emulated in brick temples.

GLOSSARY

banister See balustrade.

baptistery A part of a church or a separate building in which the rite of baptism is administered.

baradari A Mughal pavilion with triple arcades on each of its four sides, hence the translation of the word as "twelve-doored"; a summer house.

baray A large, shallow water tank in Southeast Asia.

barrel vault A vault having a semicircular cross-section.

base The lowermost portion of a wall, column, pier, or other structure, usually distinctively treated and considered as a separate architectural unit.

basilica 1. A large oblong building used as a hall of justice and public meeting place in ancient Rome, typically having a high central space lit by a clerestory and covered by timber trusses, as well as a raised dais in a semicircular apse for the tribunal. The Roman basilica served as a model for early Christian basilicas. 2. An early Christian church, characterized by a long, rectangular plan, a high colonnaded nave lit by a clerestory and covered by a timbered gable roof, two or four lower side aisles, a semicircular apse at the end, a narthex, and often other features, as an atrium, a bema, and small semicircular apses terminating the aisles.

bastion The projecting part of a rampart or other fortification, typically forming an irregular pentagon attached at the base to the main work.

batter A backward slope of the face of a wall as it rises.

bay 1. A major spatial division—usually one in a series—marked or partitioned off by the principal vertical supports of the structure. 2. Any of a number of principal compartments or divisions of a wall, roof, or other part of a building part marked off by vertical or transverse supports.

bazaar A marketplace or shopping quarter, especially in the Middle East, where goods are set out for sale. A bazaar is often comprised of rows of small shops or stalls in a narrow street, or of a certain section of town divided into narrow passageways.

beacon tower Any of the high towers built along a great wall at regular intervals from which warning signals or alarms could be sent back and forth by means of fire and smoke.

bekhnet The Egyptian word for "pylon" meaning "to be vigilant."

belvedere A building or architectural feature of a building designed and situated to look out upon a pleasing scene.

bema 1. The sanctuary space surrounding the altar of an Eastern church. 2. A transverse open space separating the nave and the apse of an early Christian church, developing into the transept of later cruciform churches.

bhumi 1. Earth in Indian architecture. 2. The horizontal relief of a *shikhara* or temple tower.

biyong Literally, "jade ring moat," a ritual structure in Chinese architecture enclosing a space in the shape of the *bi*, a flat jade ceremonial disk. Originally a separate structure, the *biyong* later became part of a single ritual complex with the *mingtang*.

blind arcade A series of arches simulating the pattern of the arcade on a wall surface.

bouleuterion A place of assembly in ancient Greece, especially for a public body.

boulevard Originally, the flat summit of a rampart; later, any major tree-lined thoroughfare which was often laid out over an old fortification.

bracket A support projecting horizontally from a wall to bear the weight of a cantilever or to strengthen an angle, as along an eave or under a bay window.

Brahmin Any of the priests belonging to the Indian upper class.

brise-soleil A screen, usually of louvers, placed on the outside of a building to shield the windows from direct sunlight.

broken pediment A pediment with its raking cornices interrupted at the crown or apex; the gap is often filled with an urn, a cartouche, or other ornament.

bungalow 1. In India, a one-story thatched or tiled house, usually surrounded by a veranda. The word derives from the Bengali word *bangla*, and was first used by the English colonists in India as a type of garden and plantation house. 2. In the United States, a derivative of the Indian bungalow, popular especially in the first quarter of the 20th century, usually having one or one-and-a-half stories, a widely bracketed gable roof, and a large porch, and often built of rustic materials.

buttress An external support built to stabilize a structure by opposing its outward thrusts, especially a projecting support built into or against the outside of a masonry wall.

cai One of eight grades of modular timber sections in traditional Chinese construction, based on the size and span of a building.

caitya A Buddhist shrine in India, usually carved out of solid rock on a hillside, having the form of an aisled basilica with a stupa at one end.

caldarium The room in an ancient Roman bath containing hot water.

camber A slight convex curvature intentionally built into a beam, girder, or truss to compensate for an anticipated deflection.

campanile The Italian word for a tower, usually a bell tower near but not attached to the body of a church.

candi A temple in Southeast Asian architecture.

cantilever A beam or other rigid structural member extending beyond a fulcrum and supported by a balancing member or a downward force behind the fulcrum.

cao A space in Chinese architecture.

capital The distinctively treated upper end of a column, pillar, or pier that crowns the shaft and takes the weight of the entablature or architrave.

cardo The main north-south route in an ancient Roman town.

caryatid A sculptured female figure used as a column, especially in ancient Greece.

castellated Having turrets and battlements, like a castle.

castrum An ancient Roman military camp having streets laid out in a grid pattern.

catacomb 1. An underground cemetery consisting of linked galleries and chambers with recesses for coffins and tombs. 2. The subterranean complex of layered corridors with burial vaults, chambers, and niches, covered with inscribed tablets and often decorated with frescoes, built by the early Christians in and near Rome.

cathedral The principal church of a diocese, containing the bishop's throne, called the cathedra.

causeway 1. A road or path raised above surrounding low or wet ground. 2. A raised passageway ceremonially connecting the valley temple with an ancient Egyptian pyramid.

cella Latin for the Greek word *naos*: the principal chamber or enclosed part of a classical temple where the cult image was kept.

cement A calcined mixture of clay and limestone, finely pulverized and used in concrete and mortar.

cenotaph A monument erected in memory of a deceased person whose remains are buried elsewhere, often having the form of a domed pavilion or temple replica.

cenoté The Mayan word for the deep water-filled sinkholes that the Itzá associated with the underworld.

centering A temporary structure or framework for supporting a masonry arch or vault during construction until the work can support itself.

central plan The plan for a building organized around a large or dominant space, usually characterized by two axes crossing each other at right angles.

chamfer A beveled surface, usually formed or cut at a 45-degree angle to the adjacent principal faces.

chan Meditation in Chinese (based on the sanskrit word *dhyan*); *zen* in Japanese.

chancel The space about the altar of a church for the clergy and choir, often elevated above the nave and separated from it by a railing or screen.

chapel A separately dedicated part of a church for private prayer, meditation, or small religious services.

char bagh The quadrangular design of Islamic gardens.

chattri In Indian architecture, a rooftop kiosk or pavilion having a dome, usually supported on four columns.

cheng The walling of a Chinese city.

chih In Chinese architecture, the bronze or stone disk between a column's base and its foot.

choir That part of a church, usually part of the chancel, set apart for clergy and singers.

chorten A memorial mound of earth in a Tibetan Buddhist religious center.

choros A group of minor actors offering commentary in classical Greek plays.

chu A column in Chinese architecture.

ci A Chinese shrine.

citadel A fortress in a commanding position in or near a city, used in the control of the inhabitants and in defense during attack or siege.

classical Of or pertaining to the art or architecture of ancient Greece and Rome, on which the Italian Renaissance as well as other styles, such as the Baroque, were based.

clerestory The uppermost section of a Gothic nave characterized by a series of large windows rising above adjacent rooftops to admit daylight to the interior.

cloister A covered walk having an arcade or colonnade on one side that opens onto a courtyard.

cloister vault A compound vault formed by four coves meeting along diagonal vertical planes.

coffer Any of a number of recessed, usually square or octagonal panels in a ceiling, soffit, or vault.

colonnade A row of regularly spaced columns carrying an entablature and usually one side of a roof structure.

colonnette A small, slender column used more often for visual effect than structural support.

colossal order An order of columns more than one story in height. Also called giant order.

column 1. A rigid, relatively slender structural member designed primarily to support compressive loads applied at the member ends. 2. A cylindrical support in classical architecture consisting of a capital, shaft, and usually a base, either monolithic or built up of drums the full diameter of the shaft.

composite order One of the five classical orders, popular especially since the beginning of the Renaissance but invented by the ancient Romans, in which the Corinthian order is modified by superimposing four diagonally set Ionic volutes on a bell of acanthus leaves.

compression A force that acts to press and squeeze together, resulting in a reduction in size or volume of an elastic body; many materials (e.g., masonry) are stronger in compression than in tension.

concrete An artificial, stonelike building material made by mixing cement and various mineral aggregates with sufficient water to cause the cement to set and bind the entire mass. Concrete is weak in tension, but the insertion of steel bars helps reinforce concrete to withstand tensile forces.

corbel A brick or stone projecting from within a wall, usually to support a weight.

Corinthian order The most ornate and least used of the five classical orders, developed by the Greeks in the 4th century BCE but used more extensively in Roman architecture; similar in most respects to the Ionic but usually of slenderer proportions and characterized especially by a deep bell-shaped capital decorated with acanthus leaves and an abacus with concave sides.

cornice 1. The uppermost member of a classical entablature, consisting typically of a *cymatium*, corona, and bed molding. 2. A continuous, molded projection that crowns a wall or other construction, divides it horizontally for compositional purposes, or conceals lighting fixtures, curtain rods, and the like.

corps de logis In French architecture, a term describing the central element of a building as opposed to its subsidiary wings and pavilions.

crenel Any of the open spaces alternating with the merlons of a battlement.

crennelation The regular alternation of merlons and crenels, originally for defense but later used as a decorative motif.

cromlech A circular arrangement of megaliths enclosing a dolmen or burial mound.

crossing The intersection of the nave and transept in a Latin cross-plan church, over which a tower or dome was often built.

cross-in-square A typical Byzantine church plan having nine bays. The center bay is a large square surmounted by a dome. The smaller square corner bays are domed or vaulted, and the rectangular side bays barrel vaulted.

crypt An underground chamber or vault used as a burial place, especially one beneath the main floor of a church.

cupola A light structure on a dome or roof, usually crowned with a dome and serving as a belfry, lantern, or belvedere.

curtain wall An exterior wall supported wholly by the structural frame of a building and carrying no loads other than its own weight and wind loads. Often consisting of glass panels, this modern innovation made possible other inventions like the *plan libre*, or free plan.

cyclopean wall A wall formed with enormous, irregular blocks of stones fitted closely together without the use of mortar. The methods of its construction were so hard to fathom that it was thought to have been erected by a race of giants—the Cyclops.

cyma recta A projecting molding having the profile of a double curve with the concave part projecting beyond the convex part.

cymatium 1. The crowning member of a classical cornice, usually a *cyma recta*. 2. See echinus.

dado 1. The part of a pedestal between the base and the cornice or cap. 3. The lower portion of an interior wall when faced or treated differently from the upper section, as with paneling or wallpaper.

darwaza An entrance gate in Indian architecture.

Decorated style The second of the three phases of English Gothic architecture from the late 13th through the late 14th centuries, characterized by rich tracery, elaborate ornamental vaulting, and refinement of stonecutting techniques.

dentil Any of a series of small, closely spaced, rectangular blocks forming a molding or projecting beneath the coronas of Ionic, Corinthian, and composite cornices.

deul A shrine in Orissan architecture.

diwan-i am In architecture of the Indian subcontinent, a hall for public meetings.

diwan-i khas In architecture of the Indian subcontinent, a hall for private meetings.

dolmen A prehistoric monument consisting of two or more large upright stones supporting a horizontal stone slab, found especially in Britain and France and usually regarded as a tomb.

dome A vaulted structure having a circular or polygonal plan and usually the form of a portion of a sphere, so constructed as to exert an equal thrust in all directions.

Doric order The oldest and simplest of the five classical orders, developed in Greece in the 7th century BCE and later imitated by the Romans. It is characterized by a fluted column having no base, a plain cushion-shaped capital supporting a square abacus, and an entablature consisting of a plain architrave, a frieze of triglyphs and metopes, and a cornice, the corona of which has *mutules* on its soffit. In the Roman Doric order, the columns are slenderer and usually have bases, the channeling is sometimes altered or omitted, and the capital consists of a bandlike necking, an echinus, and a molded abacus.

dormer A projecting structure built out from a sloping roof, usually housing a vertical window or ventilating louver.

dou-gong A bracket system used in traditional Chinese construction to support roof beams, project the eaves outward, and support the interior ceiling. The absence of a triangular tied frame in Chinese architecture made it necessary to multiply the number of supports under the rafters. To reduce the number of pillars would normally require the area of support afforded by each pillar to be increased by the *dou-gong*. The main beams support the roof through intermediary queen posts and shorter upper beams, enabling the roof to have a concave curve. This distinctive curve is believed to have developed at the beginning of the Tang period, presumably to lighten the visual weight of the roof and allow more daylight into the interior.

dromos A corridor in Mycenean architecture.

drum 1. Any of several cylindrical stones laid one above the other to form a column or pier. 2. A cylindrical or faceted construction, often pierced with windows, supporting a dome.

du Chinese for "capital"; hence, a city in Chinese architecture.

duomo The Italian designation for a true cathedral.

durbar 1. The court of a native prince in India. 2. The audience hall in which an Indian prince or British governor gave a state reception in India.

durga An Indian term for fort.

echinus 1. The prominent circular molding supporting the abacus of a Doric or Tuscan capital. 2. The circular molding under the cushion of an Ionic capital, between the volutes, usually carved with an egg-and-dart pattern.

eclecticism A tendency in architecture and the decorative arts (particularly during the second half of the 19th century in Europe and the United States) to freely mix various historical styles with the aim of combining the virtues of diverse sources or of increasing allusive content.

elevation An orthographic projection of an object or structure on a vertical picture plane parallel to one of its sides, usually drawn to scale.

enfilade An axial arrangement of doorways connecting a series of rooms so as to provide a vista down the entire length of the suite.

engaged column A column built to be truly or seemingly bonded to the wall before which it stands.

entablature The horizontal section of a classical order that rests on the columns, usually composed of a cornice, frieze, and architrave.

entasis A slight convexity given to a column to correct an optical illusion of concavity that would occur if the sides were straight.

exedra See apse.

facade The front of a building or any of its sides facing a public way or space, especially one distinguished by its architectural treatment.

fang 1. A tie beam in the *dou-gong* system of traditional Chinese construction. 2. A ward or district of a Chinese city.

fascia 1. One of the three horizontal bands making up the architrave in the Ionic order. 2. Any broad, flat, horizontal surface, as the outer edge of a cornice or roof.

fazenda "Hacienda" in Portuguese.

fen A modular unit in traditional Chinese construction, equal to one-fifteenth of the height and one-tenth of the width of a *cai*.

finial A relatively small, usually foliated ornament terminating the peak of a spire or pinnacle.

Flamboyant style The final phase of French Gothic architecture from the late 14th through the middle of the 16th centuries, characterized by flamelike tracery, intricate detailing, and frequent complication of interior space.

fluting A decorative motif consisting of a series of long, rounded, parallel grooves, like those on the shaft of a classical column.

flying buttress An inclined bar of masonry carried on a segmental arch and transmitting an outward and downward thrust from a roof or vault to a solid buttress that, through its mass, transforms the thrust into a vertical one; a characteristic feature of Gothic construction.

folly A whimsical or extravagant structure built to serve as a conversation piece, lend interest to a view, or commemorate a person or event, found especially in 18th-century England.

forum The public square or marketplace of an ancient Roman city, the center of judicial and business affairs, and a place of assembly for the people; it usually included a basilica and a temple.

frieze 1. The horizontal part of a classical entablature between the cornice and architrave, often decorated with sculpture in low relief. 2. A decorative band, as one along the top of an interior wall immediately below the cornice, or a sculptured one in a stringcourse on an outside wall.

frigidarium The room in an ancient Roman bath containing unheated water.

fu-chiao lu-tou In traditional Chinese construction, the system for supporting a corner condition with bracket supports.

gable The triangular portion of wall enclosing the end of a pitched roof from cornice or eaves to ridge.

gable roof A roof sloping downward in two parts from a central ridge so as to form a gable at each end.

gallery 1. A long, relatively narrow room or hall, especially one for public use and having architectural importance due to its scale or decorative treatment. 2. An upper-level passage in a medieval church above the side aisle and below the clerestory window used for circulation, seating, and even for the display of art.

garbha-griha A "womb chamber," the dark, innermost sanctuary of a Hindu temple where the statue of the deity is placed.

ghana-dwaras Literally "blind doors," they are implied doors in Hindu architecture.

ghat A broad flight of steps descending to a river in India, especially a river used as a sacred bathing site.

giant order See colossal order.

golden section A proportion between the two dimensions of a plane figure or the two divisions of a line in which the ratio of the smaller to the larger is the same as the ratio of the larger to the whole: a ratio of approximately 0.618 to 1.000

gompa A Tibetan Buddhist monastery.

gong 1. A cantilevered bracket in traditional Chinese construction. 2. A Chinese palace.

gopuram A monumental, usually ornate gateway tower to a Hindu temple enclosure, especially in southern India.

Greek cross A centralized church plan having the form of a cross whose arms are identical and symmetrical about the central space.

groin vault A compound vault formed by the perpendicular intersection of two vaults, forming arched diagonal arrises called groins.

guan A Chinese monastery.

hacienda 1. A large, landed estate for farming and ranching in North and South American areas once under Spanish influence. 2. The main house on such an estate.

haniwa A terra-cotta statue made for ritual use and buried with the dead as a funerary object during the Kofun period of Japan.

hashira 1. A sacred post in Shinto architecture, shaped by human hands. 2. A column, post, or pillar serving as the basic vertical member of a traditional Japanese wooden structure.

henge A circular arrangement of vertically oriented wooden posts or stones.

hipped roof A roof having sloping ends and sides meeting at an inclined projecting angle called a hip.

hippodrome An open-air stadium with an oval track for horse and chariot races in ancient Greece and Rome.

historicism 1. The reference to a historical moment or style. 2. In architecture, a building whose form adheres to the stylistic principles of an earlier period.

hôtel An 18th-century French townhouse having one or two stories oriented horizontally in a large suburban estate setting.

hypocaust A system of flues in the floor or walls of ancient Roman buildings, especially baths, that provided central heating by receiving and distributing the heat from a furnace.

hypostyle Of or pertaining to a hall having many rows of columns carrying the roof or ceiling.

icon A representation of a sacred Christian personage, as Christ or a saint or angel, typically painted on a wood surface and itself venerated as sacred, especially in the tradition of the Eastern Church.

imam A mosque's leader of group prayer.

insula A block of buildings or space surrounded by four streets in an ancient Roman town.

intihuatana The "hitching post of the sun" in Incan settlements.

Ionic order A classical order that developed in the Greek colonies of Asia Minor in the 6th century BCE, characterized especially by the spiral volutes of its capital. The fluted columns typically had molded bases and supported an entablature consisting of an architrave of three fascias, a richly ornamented frieze, and a cornice corbeled out on egg-and-dart and dentil moldings. Roman and Renaissance examples are often more elaborate and usually set the volutes of the capitals 45 degrees to the architrave.

iwan A large vaulted hall serving as an entrance portal and opening onto a courtyard: prevalent in Parthian, Sassanian, and later in Islamic architecture.

jami masjid "Friday mosque": a congregational mosque for public prayer, especially on Fridays.

jian 1. A standard unit of space in Chinese architecture, marked by adjacent frame supports. The nature and appropriate scale of a building determine the number of *jian* to be allotted; the resulting width, depth, and height of the building then determine the number of *fen* required for the cross section of each structural member. 2. The spatial unit that serves as the basis for the modular structure of a Chinese city: a number of *jian* connected become a building; several buildings arranged along the sides of a lot frame a courtyard; a number of courtyard units side by side become an alley; several alleys line up to create a small street district; a number of such districts form a rectangular ward; wards surround the palace-city and create a grid of streets.

jiangren A master craftsman in Chinese architecture.

jikido A dining hall in Japanese architecture.

jing In Chinese architecture, a room for private prayer.

Ka'aba A small, cubical stone building in the courtyard of the Great Mosque at Mecca containing a sacred black stone and regarded by Muslims as the house of God. It is the objective of Muslims' pilgrimages and the point toward which they turn in prayer.

kairo A roofed, semienclosed corridor in Japanese architecture.

kalan A shrine in Southeast Asian architecture.

kalyan mandapa In India, a hall with columns in which the marriage of the temple deity and his consort is ritually performed.

kami Sacred spirits related to Japanese architecture.

ke A Chinese pavilion of many stories.

ken A linear unit for regulating column spacing in traditional Japanese construction, equal to 6 *shaku* (5.97 feet or 1.818 meters) in the *inaka-ma* method, and in the *kyo-ma* method, initially set at 6.5 *shaku* (6.5 feet or 1.97 meters), but later varying according to room width as determined by tatami units.

keystone A voussoir at the crown of an arch serving to lock the other voussoirs in place. Until the keystone is in place, no true arch action is incurred.

kgotla The public meeting or traditional law court of a Botswana village.

kiva A square-walled and underground chamber used by Native Americans for spiritual ceremonies.

kodo A lecture hall in Japanese architecture.

kondo The "golden hall": the sanctuary where the main image of worship is kept in a Japanese Buddhist temple. The Jodo,

Shinshu, and Nicheiren sects of Buddhism use the term *hondo* for this sanctuary, the Shingon and Tendai sects use *chudo*, and the Zen sect uses *butsuden.*

kovil A Tamil temple.

kyozo The sutra repository in Japanese architecture.

Lanzón A column of rock portraying a Chavín mythical being who provided the god's oracular declamations.

lathe-turned Of or pertaining to a column whose cylindrical shaft is ornamented with incisions revealing its construction, during which it was laid on a lathe and then carved.

Latin cross A dominant church plan type in Western medieval architecture. Such a church is in the shape of a cross with a nave longer than the intersecting transept.

ling A purlin in traditional Chinese construction.

lingam A phallus; the symbol of the god Shiva in Hindu architecture.

lintel A beam supporting the weight above a door or window opening.

loggia A colonnaded or arcaded space within the body of a building that is open to the air on one side, with views into a public square or garden. Loggias can be built on either the ground floor or the upper floors of a building.

lotus A representation of various aquatic plants in the water lily family, used as a decorative motif in ancient Egyptian and Hindu art and architecture.

lou A Chinese multistoried pavilion or tower.

lu-tou In traditional Chinese construction, the base or lowest member in a set of brackets.

madrasa A Muslim theological school arranged around a courtyard and usually attached to a mosque, found from the 11th century on in Egypt, Anatolia, and Persia.

maharaja A great Indian king.

mahajanapadas Kingdoms of the Aryans.

mahastupa "Great stupa."

maidan The large open square of a city used as a marketplace or parade ground, especially in the Indian subcontinent.

mandala A Hindu or Buddhist diagram of the cosmos, often used to guide the design of Indian temple plans.

mandapa A large, porchlike hall leading to the sanctuary of a Hindu or Jain temple and used for religious dancing and music.

mandir A temple or palace in Indian architecture.

mani A Tibetan Buddhist wall of inscribed stones.

martyrium 1. A site that bore witness to important events in the life of Christ or one of his apostles. 2. A place where the relics of a martyr are kept. 3. A church erected over the tomb of a martyr or in honor of a martyr.

masjid A mosque.

masseria A system of plantation estates in Italy.

mastaba An ancient Egyptian tomb made of mud brick, rectangular in plan with a flat roof and sloping sides, from which a shaft leads to underground burial and offering chambers.

megalith A very large stone used as found or roughly dressed, especially in ancient construction work.

megaron A building or semi-independent unit of a building typically having a rectangular principal chamber with a center hearth and a porch, often of columns in antis. *Megarons* were traditional in Greece since Mycenaean times and believed to be the ancestor of the Doric temple.

men A gate in Chinese architecture.

menhir A prehistoric monument consisting of an upright megalith, usually standing alone but sometimes aligned with others in parallel rows.

merlon One of the solid parts between the crenels of a battlement.

metope Any of the panels, either plain or decorated, between triglyphs in the Doric frieze.

miao A Chinese temple. Also called a *shi*.

mihrab A niche or decorative panel in a mosque designating the *qibla*.

minaret A lofty, slender tower attached to a mosque with stairs leading up to one or more projecting balconies from which the muezzin calls the faithful to prayer.

minbar A pulpit in a mosque, recalling the three steps from which Muhammad addressed his followers.

mingtang "Bright hall": a ritual structure in Chinese architecture that serves as the symbolic center of imperial power. The first is presumed to have been built under the Zhou dynasty in the first millennium BCE.

minster Originally, a monastery church; later, any large or important church, as a cathedral or the principal church of a town.

miyan Eaves in Chinese architecture.

module A unit of measurement used for standardizing the dimensions of building materials or regulating the proportions of an architectural composition.

mortar A plastic mixture of lime or cement (or both) with sand and water, used as a bonding agent in masonry construction.

mortuary temple An ancient Egyptian temple for offerings and worship of a deceased person, usually a deified king. In the New Kingdom, cult and funerary temples had many features in common: an avenue of sphinxes leading to a tall portal guarded by a towering pylon; an axial plan with a colonnaded forecourt

and a hypostyle hall set before a dark, narrow sanctuary in which stood a statue of the deity; and walls lavishly decorated with pictographic carvings in low or sunken relief.

mosaic A decorative pattern or figural image or narrative made of small, usually colored pieces of tile, enamel, or glass set in mortar.

mosque A Muslim building or place of public worship.

mudra A stylized hand gesture intended as symbol in Buddhist and Hindu sculpture.

mullion 1. A vertical member between the lights of a window or the panels in wainscoting. 2. One of the radiating bars of a rose window.

muqarna A system of decoration in Islamic architecture created by the intricate corbeling of brackets, squinches, and inverted pyramids. Sometimes wrought in stone, it is more often found in plaster.

musalla A temporary place in which worshippers congregate to perform their prayers in Islamic architecture.

nandaimon The principal south gateway to a Japanese temple or shrine.

naos See *cella*.

narthex 1. The portico before the nave of an early Christian or Byzantine church, appropriate for penitents. 2. An entrance hall or vestibule leading to the nave of a church.

nave The principal or central part of a church extending from the narthex to the choir or chancel and usually flanked by aisles.

necropolis A historic burial ground, especially a large, elaborate one of an ancient city.

neoclassicism The classicism prevailing in the architecture of Europe, America, and various European colonies during the late 18th and early 19th centuries, characterized by the introduction and widespread use of Greek and Roman orders and decorative motifs, the subordination of detail to simple, strongly geometric compositions, and the frequent shallowness of relief in ornamental treatment of facades.

niche An ornamental recess in a wall, often semicircular in plan and surmounted by a half-dome and used for a statue or other decorative object.

nuraghe Any of the large, round or triangular stone towers found in Sardinia and dating from the second millennium BCE to the Roman conquest.

obelisk A tall, four-sided shaft of stone that tapers as it rises to a pyramidal point. Obelisks originated in ancient Egypt as a sacred symbol of the sun god Ra and usually stood in pairs astride temple entrances.

oculus A circular opening, especially one at the crown of a dome.

ogee A molding having a profile of a double curve in the shape of an elongated S.

ogive A rib crossing a compartment of a rib vault on a diagonal.

open plan A floor plan having no fully enclosed spaces or distinct rooms.

opet A secret chamber in Egyptian architecture.

opus incertum Ancient Roman masonry formed of small rough stones set irregularly in mortar, sometimes traversed by bands of bricks or tiles.

opus reticulatum An ancient Roman masonry wall faced with small pyramidal stones set diagonally with their square bases forming a netlike pattern.

oriel A bay window supported from below by corbels or brackets.

pagoda A Buddhist temple in the form of a square or polygonal tower with roofs projecting from each of its many stories, erected as a memorial or to hold relics. From the stupa, the Indian prototype, the pagoda gradually changed in form to resemble a traditional multistoried watch tower as it spread with Buddhism to China and Japan. Pagodas were initially made of timber but from the 6th century on were more frequently of brick or stone, possibly due to Indian influence.

pai lou A monumental gateway in Chinese architecture, having a trabeated form of stone or wood construction with one, three, or five openings and often boldly projecting roofs. *Pai lou* were erected as memorials at the entrances to palaces, tombs, or sacred places; related to the Indian *toranas* and the Japanese torii.

Palladian motif A window or doorway in the form of a roundheaded archway flanked on either side by narrower compartments. The side compartments are capped with entablatures on which the arch of the central compartment rests.

palmette A stylized palm leaf shape used as a decorative element in classical art and architecture.

panopticon A building such as a prison, hospital, or library arranged so that all parts of the interior are visible from a single point.

pantheon 1. A temple dedicated to all the gods of a people. 2. A public building serving as the burial place of or containing the memorials to the famous dead of a nation.

parapet A low protective wall at the edge of a terrace, balcony, or roof, especially that part of an exterior wall, fire wall, party wall that rises above the roof.

parti Used by the French at the École des Beaux-Arts in the 19th century, the design

idea or sketch from which an architectural project will be developed.

passage grave A megalithic tomb of the Neolithic and early Bronze Ages found in the British Isles and Europe consisting of a roofed burial chamber and narrow entrance passage covered by a tumulus. They are believed to have been used for successive family or clan burials spanning a number of generations.

pavilion A central or flanking projecting subdivision of a facade, usually accented by more elaborate decoration or greater height and distinction of skyline; used frequently in French Renaissance and Baroque architecture.

pediment 1. The low-pitched gable enclosed by the horizontal and raking cornices of a Greek or Roman temple. 2. A similar or derivative element used to surmount the major division of a facade or crown an opening.

pendentive A spherical triangle forming the transition from the circular plan of a dome to the polygonal plan of its supporting structure.

pergola A structure of parallel colonnades supporting an open roof of beams and crossing rafters or trelliswork, over which climbing plants are trained to grow.

peripteral Having a single row of columns on all sides.

peristyle 1. A colonnade surrounding a building or a courtyard. 2. The courtyard so enclosed.

Perpendicular style The final phase of English Gothic architecture, prevailing from the late 14th through the early 16th centuries, characterized by perpendicular tracery, fine intricate stonework, and elaborate fan vaults. Also called rectilinear style.

piano nobile The principal story of a large building, such as a palace or villa, usually one flight above the ground floor, with formal reception and dining rooms.

piazza An open square or public place in a city or town, especially in Italy.

Picturesque The late 18th-century term describing irregular and uncultivated landscapes and designs.

pilaster A shallow rectangular feature projecting from a wall having a capital and a base and treated architecturally as a column.

piloti A column of steel or reinforced concrete supporting a building above an open-ground level, thereby leaving the space available for other uses.

piye A Mexican ritual calendar composed of 20 hieroglyphs or "day signs," which combined with 13 numbers to produce a cycle of 260 days.

plinth 1. The usually square slab beneath the base of a column, pier, or pedestal. 2. A

continuous, usually projecting, course of stones forming the base or foundation of a wall.

podium 1. A low wall serving as the base for a colonnade or dome. 2. A raised platform encircling the arena of an ancient Roman amphitheater, where the seats for the privileged spectators were located.

pol A gateway in Indian architecture.

polis A Greek city-state.

portcullis A strong grating of iron or timber hung over the gateway of a fortified place in such a way that it could be lowered quickly to prevent passage.

porte cochere 1. A porch roof projecting over a driveway at the entrance to a building and sheltering those getting in or out of vehicles. 2. A vehicular passageway leading through a building or screen wall into an interior courtyard.

portico A porch or walkway with a roof supported by columns, often leading to the entrance of a building.

propylaeum A vestibule or gateway of architectural importance before a Greek temple precinct or other enclosure.

propylon A freestanding gateway in the form of a pylon that precedes the main gateway to an ancient Egyptian temple or sacred enclosure.

proscenium The front part of the stage of an ancient Greek or Roman theater upon which the actors performed.

pteron Greek word for "wing," but also "oar" and "sail": an early form of a peristyle raised on a lofty podium.

pu The distance between purlins in traditional Chinese construction.

puan A roof purlin in Chinese architecture.

pueblo A communal dwelling and defensive structure of the Native Americans of the southwestern United States. Built of adobe or stone and typically many-storied and terraced, pueblos were entered through the chambers' flat roofs by ladder. Pueblo structures were built on the desert floor, in valleys, or in the more easily defended cliff walls of mesas.

purlin A longitudinal member of a roof frame for supporting common rafters between the ridge and eaves.

pylon A monumental gateway to an ancient Egyptian temple, consisting either of a pair of tall truncated pyramids and a doorway between them or of one such masonry mass pierced with a doorway, often decorated with painted reliefs.

qibla 1. The direction toward which Muslims face to pray, especially the Ka'aba at Mecca in Saudi Arabia. 2. The wall in a mosque in which the mihrab is set, oriented to Mecca.

qin Sleeping chambers in Chinese architecture.

que A Chinese watchtower, also called a *hua biao*.

quoin One of the stones forming the external angle of a wall, usually differentiated from the adjoining surfaces by material, texture, color, size, or projection.

rammed earth A stiff mixture of clay, sand, or other aggregate and water compressed and dried within forms as a wall construction.

ratha A Hindu temple cut out of solid rock to resemble a chariot.

Rayonnant style The middle phase of French Gothic architecture from the end of the 13th through the late 14th centuries, characterized by circular windows with radiating lines of tracery.

rectilinear style See Perpendicular style.

rekha deul The sanctuary and convexly tapered tower of an Orissian temple.

rib Any of several archlike members supporting a vault at the groins and defining its distinct surfaces or dividing these surfaces into panels.

ribat An Islamic fortified monastery-like building providing soldiers with an opportunity to exercise their religion.

rose window A large, circular window, usually of stained glass and decorated with tracery, symmetrical about the center.

rotunda A round, domed building, or a large and high circular space in a building, especially one surmounted by a dome.

rustication Ashlar masonry having the visible faces of the dressed stones raised or otherwise contrasted with the horizontal and usually the vertical joints, which may be rabbeted, chamfered, or beveled.

sacristy A room in a church where the sacred vessels and vestments are kept.

sanctuary 1. A sacred or holy place. 2. The most sacred part of a church, in which the principal altar is placed. 3. An especially holy place in a temple. 4. A church or other sacred place where fugitives are immune from arrest.

sangha A Buddhist community.

scaenae frons The highly decorative wall or backdrop at the rear of the stage of a Roman theater.

schist A crystalline metamorphic rock found in northwest Pakistan that has a parallel or foliated arrangement of mineral grains.

section An orthographic projection of an object or structure as it would appear if cut through by an intersecting plane to show its internal configuration, usually drawn to scale.

sha In Chinese architecture, the finial atop a pagoda.

shaft 1. The central part of a column or pier between the capital and the base. 2. A distinct, slender vertical masonry feature engaged in a wall or pier and supporting or feigning to support an arch or a ribbed vault.

shi See *miao*.

Shi'ite A Muslim sect that believes Ali to be the successor to Muhammad.

shikhara The tower of a Hindu temple, usually tapered convexly and capped by an *amalaka*.

shinbashira The heart pilar, or central pillar of Japanese castles.

shiva lingam Another term for lingam.

shoro One of a pair of small, identical, symmetrically placed pavilions in a Japanese Buddhist temple structure from which the temple bell is hung.

sobo The priests' quarters in a Japanese Buddhist temple.

spandrel 1. The triangular-shaped, sometimes ornamented area between two adjoining arches or between an arch and the rectangular framework surrounding it. 2. A panel-like area in a multistory frame building, between the sill of a window on one level and the head of a window immediately below.

sphinx A figure of an imaginary creature having the body of a lion and the head of a man, ram, or hawk, commonly placed along avenues leading to ancient Egyptian temples or tombs.

spire A tall, acutely tapering pyramidal structure surmounting a steeple or tower.

splay A surface that makes an oblique angle with another, such as where a window or door opening widens from the frame toward the face of the wall.

squinch An arch or corbelling built across the upper inside corner of a square tower to support the side of a superimposed octagonal structure.

stambha In Indian architecture, a freestanding memorial pillar bearing carved inscriptions, religious emblems, or a statue.

stele An upright stone slab or pillar with a carved or inscribed surface, used as a monument, a marker, or a commemorative tablet in the face of a building.

stoa An ancient Greek portico, usually detached and of considerable length, used as a promenade or meeting place around public places.

stucco A coarse plaster composed of portland or masonry cement, sand, and hydrated lime mixed with water and applied in a plastic state to form a hard covering for exterior walls.

stupa A Buddhist memorial mound erected to enshrine a relic of the Buddha and to commemorate some event or mark a sacred spot. Modeled on a funerary tumulus, it consists of an artificial dome-shaped mound raised on a platform, surrounded by an outer ambulatory, with a stone *vedika* and four *toranas*, and crowned by a *chattri*. In Sri Lanka, the name for *stupa* is *dagoba*, and in Tibet and Nepal, it is *chorten*.

stylobate A course of masonry forming the foundation for a row of columns, especially the outermost colonnade of a classical temple.

suarloka A decorated frieze in Southeast Asian architecture.

Sufi A Muslim mystic.

sultan The ruler of a Muslim country.

Sunni A Muslim sect that considers Abu Bakr to be the successor to Muhammad.

synagogue A building or place of assembly for Jewish worship and religious instruction.

ta A Chinese pagoda in which a deceased high priest is buried.

tablero The rectangular panel sitting atop a sloping panel or *talud* in Mexican architecture.

takht The throne or elevated platform used by royalty in a mosque.

talud The sloping panel beneath the rectangular panel or *tablero* in Mexican architecture.

taypi In South America, the zone of convergence between the principles of *urco* (the west, high, dry, pastoral, celestial, male) and *uma* (the east, low, agricultural, underworld, female).

temenos In ancient Greece, a piece of ground specially reserved and enclosed as a sacred place.

tension A structural force that acts to stretch or pull apart a material, resulting in the elongation of an elastic body. Ductile materials like steel effectively resist tension.

tepidarium A room of moderately warm temperature in an ancient Roman bath, between the *frigidarium* and the *caldarium*.

thalassocracy A maritime trading economy initially defined by Aristotle.

thermae An elaborate public bathing establishment of the ancient Greeks and Romans, consisting of hot, warm, and cool plunges, sweat rooms, and athletic and other facilities.

thrust The outward force or pressure exerted by one part of a structure against another.

tianming The "mandate of heaven" as described by members of the Zhou dynasty.

Rites of worship, an ideology of "harmony," and sacrifices to ancestral deities all served to link political and religious authority under *tianming*.

ting A courtyard in Chinese architecture: the site of large, often ceremonial gatherings.

tirtha A place or site considered holy in Indian architecture.

tokonoma Picture recess: a shallow, slightly raised alcove for the display of a kakemono or flower arrangement. One side of the recess borders the outside wall of the room through which light enters, while the interior side adjoins the tana. As the spiritual center of a traditional Japanese house, the tokonoma is located in its most formal room.

torana An elaborately carved, ceremonial gateway in Indian Buddhist and Hindu architecture, having two or three lintels between two posts.

torii Derived from *torana*, a torii is a gateway in Japanese architecture.

torsion The twisting of an elastic body about its longitudinal axis caused by two equal and opposite torques, producing shearing stresses in the body.

trabeated Of or pertaining to a system of construction employing beams or lintels.

transept 1. The major transverse part of a cruciform church, crossing the main axis at a right angle between the nave and choir. 2. Either of the projecting arms of this part, on either side of the central aisle of a church.

triforium An arcaded wall corresponding to the space between the vaulting and the roof of an aisle, usually opening onto the nave between the nave arches and the clerestory.

triglyph One of the vertical blocks separating the metopes in a Doric frieze, typically having two vertical grooves or glyphs on its face, and two chamfers or half channels at the sides.

tumulus An artificial mound of earth or stone, especially over an ancient grave.

turret A small tower forming part of a larger structure, frequently beginning some distance above the ground.

tympanum 1. The recessed triangular space enclosed by the horizontal and raking cornices of a triangular pediment, often decorated with sculpture. 2. A similar space between an arch and the horizontal head of a door or window below.

tzompantli A skull rack in Central American architecture.

ulu Jami A Friday mosque having a large *sahn* for large congregations, dating from the 7th to the 11th centuries.

vahana Literally, "vehicle" of Hindu gods, usually in the form of an animal.

vault An arched structure of stone, brick, or reinforced concrete forming a ceiling or roof over a hall, room, or other wholly or partially enclosed space. Because it behaves as an arch extended in a third dimension, the longitudinal supporting walls must be buttressed to counteract the thrusts of the arching action.

vav An Indian step well.

Vedas The oldest sacred writings of Hinduism, composed between 1500 and 800 BCE, incorporating four collections of hymns, prayers, and liturgical formulas: Rig-Veda, Yajur-Veda, Sama-Veda, and Atharva-Veda.

vedika 1. A hall for reading the Vedas. 2. A railing enclosing a sacred area, as a stupa.

vihara A Buddhist monastery in Indian architecture, often excavated from solid rock, consisting of a central pillared chamber surrounded by a veranda onto which open small sleeping cells. Adjacent to this cloister was a courtyard containing the main stupa.

volute A spiral, scroll-like ornament, as on the capitals of the Ionic, Corinthian, and composite orders.

voussoir Any of the wedge-shaped units in a masonry arch or vault that has side cuts that converge at one of the arch centers.

wainscot A lining of wood, usually in the form of paneling, covering the lower portion of a wall.

wat A Buddhist monastery or temple in Thailand or Cambodia.

westwork The monumental western front of a Romanesque church, treated as a tower or towers containing a low entrance hall below and a chapel open to the nave above.

wetu Hut-shaped Native American houses.

xanadu A place of idyllic beauty and contentment; S. T. Coleridge's modification of Xandu, modern Shangtu and the site of Kublai Khan's summer residence in southeastern Mongolia.

xieshan The simple hip-and-gable style roof in Chinese architecture.

yingbi A screen wall in Chinese architecture that protects the main gate to a monastery or house against evil spirits, which were believed to only move in a straight line.

yin and yang In Chinese philosophy and religion, the interaction of two opposing and complementary principles—one that is feminine, dark, and negative (yin) and the other that is masculine, bright, and positive (yang)—that influences the destinies of creatures and things.

Yingzao Fashi A compendium of Chinese architectural tradition and building methods, compiled by Li Jie and printed in 1103 CE. It has thirty-four chapters devoted to technical terms, construction methods, measurements and proportions of architectural elements, labor management, building materials, and decoration.

zhi During the Han and Jin dynasties, a Taoist cave dwelling for the practice of asceticism and sacrificial offerings to the gods.

ziggurat A temple tower in Sumerian and Assyrian architecture, built in diminishing stages of mud brick with buttressed walls faced with burnt brick, culminating in a summit shrine or temple reached by a series of ramps: thought to be of Sumerian origin, dating from the end of the 3rd millennium BCE.

Bibliography

General Sources

Alfieri, Bianca Maria. *Islamic Architecture of the Indian Subcontinent.* London: Laurence King Publishers, 2000.

Barraclough, Geoffrey. *Hammond Atlas of World History.* Maplewood, NJ: Hammond, 1999.

Chihara, Daigoro. *Hindu-Buddhist Architecture in Southeast Asia.* New York: E. J. Brill, 1996.

Chinese Academy of Architecture. Beijing: China Building Industry Press; Hongkong: Joint Publishing Co., 1982.

Coaldrake, William Howard. *Architecture and Authority in Japan.* London, New York: Routledge, 1996.

Coe, Michael D., and Rex Koontz. *Mexico: From the Olmecs to the Aztecs.* London: Thames & Hudson, 2002.

Crouch, Dora P., and June G. Johnson. *Traditions in Architecture: Africa, America, Asia, and Oceania.* New York: Oxford University Press, 2001.

Evans, Susan Toby, and David L. Webster, eds. *Archaeology of Ancient Mexico and Central America: An Encyclopedia.* New York: Garland, 2001.

Ferguson, William M., and Richard E. W. Adams. *Mesoamerica's Ancient Cities: Aerial Views of Pre-Columbian Ruins in Mexico, Guatemala, Belize, and Honduras.* Albuquerque: University of New Mexico Press, 2001.

Grube, Nikolai. *Maya: Divine Kings of the Rain Forest.* Assisted by Eva Eggebrecht and Matthias Seidel. Cologne, Germany: Könemann, 2001.

Huntington, Susan L. *The Art of Ancient India: Buddhist, Hindu, Jain.* With contributions by John C. Huntington. New York: Weatherhill, 1985.

The Kodansha Bilingual Encyclopedia of Japan. Tokyo: Kodansha International; New York: Kodansha America, 1998.

Kostof, Spiro. *A History of Architecture: Settings and Rituals.* Revisions by Greg Castillo. New York: Oxford University Press, 1995.

Kowalski, Jeff Karl, ed. *Mesoamerican Architecture as a Cultural Symbol.* New York: Oxford University Press, 1999.

Kubler, George. *The Art and Architecture of Ancient America: The Mexican, Maya, and Andean Peoples.* New Haven, CT: Yale University Press, 1990.

Lang, Jon T., Madhavi Desai, and Miki Desai. *Architecture and Independence: The Search for Identity—India 1880 to 1980.* Delhi: Oxford University Press, 1997.

Loewe, Michael, and Edward L. Shaughnessy, eds. *The Cambridge History of Ancient China: From the Origins of Civilization to 221 BC.* Cambridge, UK, and New York: Cambridge University Press, 1999.

Meister, Michael W., ed. *Encyclopedia of Indian Temple Architecture, vols. 1 and 2.* Coordinated by M. A. Dhaky. New Delhi: American Institute of Indian Studies; Philadelphia: University of Pennsylvania Press, 1983.

Michell, George. *Architecture of the Islamic World: Its History and Social Meaning.* New York: Thames and Hudson, 1984.

Nishi, Kazuo, and Kazuo Hozumi. *What is Japanese Architecture?* Translated, adapted, and with an introduction by H. Mack Horton. Tokyo, New York: Kodansha International, 1985.

Schmidt, Karl J. *Atlas and Survey of South Asian History: India, Pakistan, Bangladesh, Sri Lanka, Nepal, Bhutan.* New Delhi, India: Vision, 1999.

Sickman, Laurence, and Alexander Soper. *The Art and Architecture of China.* Harmondsworth, UK: Penguin, 1971.

Steinhardt, Nancy Shatzman. *Chinese Architecture.* New Haven, CT: Yale University Press: Beijing: New World Press, 2002.

———. *Chinese Imperial City Planning.* Honolulu: University of Hawaii Press, 1990.

Tadgell, Christopher. *The History of Architecture in India: From the Dawn of Civilization to the End of the Raj.* London: Architecture Design and Technology Press, 1990.

———. *Antiquity: Origins, Classicism and the New Rome.* Abingdon, UK: Routledge, 2007.

———. *Islam: From Medina to the Magreb and from the Indies to Istanbul.* Abingdon, UK: Routledge, 2008.

———. *The East: Buddhists, Hindus and the Sons of Heaven.* Abingdon, UK: Routledge, 2008.

Thapar, Romila. *Early India: From the Origins to AD 1300.* Berkeley: University of California Press, 2002.

Tignor, Robert L., Jeremy Adelman, Stephen Aron, Stephen Kotkin, Suzanne Marchand, Gyan Prakash, and Michael Tsin. *Worlds Together, Worlds Apart: A History of the Modern World from the Mongol Empire to the Present.* New York: W.W. Norton, 2002.

Trachtenberg, Marvin, and Isabelle Hyman. *Architecture, from Prehistory to Postmodernity.* New York: Harry N. Abrams, 2002.

Online Resources

Great Buildings Online: www.greatbuildings.com/

Grove Art Online: www.oxfordartonline.com. Web access to the entire text of *The Dictionary of Art*, edited by Jane Turner (34 vols., 1996), and *The Oxford Companion to Western Art*, Hugh Brigstocke, ed. (2001).

Metropolitan Museum of Art Timeline of Art History: www.metmuseum.org/toah/

Taj Mahal: http://www.tajmahalindia.net/taj-mahal-monument.html

Wikipedia: The Free Encyclopedia: wikipedia.org/

3500 BCE

Arnold, Dieter. *The Encyclopedia of Ancient Egyptian Architecture.* Edited by Nigel and Helen Strudwick. Translated by Sabine H. Gardiner and Helen Strudwick. Princeton, NJ: Princeton University Press, 2003.

Burl, Aubrey. *The Stone Circles of the British Isles.* New Haven, CT: Yale University Press, 1976.

Clark, Grahame. *The Earlier Stone Age Settlement of Scandinavia.* London: Cambridge University Press, 1975.

Hawkins, Gerald S., and John B. White. *Stonehenge Decoded.* New York: Dorsett, 1965.

Jia, Lanpo. *Early Man in China.* Beijing: Foreign Languages Press, 1980.

McBurney, Charles, and Brian Montagu. *The Stone Age of Northern Africa.* Harmondsworth, UK: Penguin Books, 1960.

Mysliwiec, Karol. *The Twilight of Ancient Egypt, First Millennium BCE.* Ithaca, NY: Cornell University Press, 2000.

Nicholson, Paul T., and Ian Shaw, eds. *Ancient Egyptian Materials and Technology.* Cambridge, UK: Cambridge University Press, 2000.

Phylactopoulos, George A., ed. *History of the Hellenic World.* University Park, PA: Pennsylvania State University Press, 1974.

Possehl, Gregory L. *Harappan Civilization: A Recent Perspective.* New Delhi: American Institute of Indian Studies; Columbia, MO: Oxford and IBH, 1993.

Shafer, Byron E., ed. *Religion in Ancient Egypt: Gods, Myths and Personal Practice.* Ithaca, NY: Cornell University Press, 1991.

Wilson, Peter J. *The Domestication of the Human Species.* New Haven: Yale University Press, 1988.

BIBLIOGRAPHY

2500 BCE

Crawford, Harriet E. W. *The Architecture of Iraq in the Third Millennium B.C.* Copenhagen: Akademisk Forlag, 1977.

Downey, Susan B. *Mesopotamian Religious Architecture: Alexander through the Parthians.* Princeton, NJ: Princeton University Press, 1988.

Kemp, Barry J. *Ancient Egypt: Anatomy of a Civilization.* London, New York: Routledge, 1991.

Kenoyer, Jonathan M. *Ancient Cities of the Indus Valley Civilization.* Karachi: Oxford University Press; Islamabad: American Institute of Pakistan Studies, 1998.

Kubba, Shamil A. A. *Mesopotamian Architecture and Town Planning: From the Mesolithic to the End of the Proto-Historic Period, ca. 10,000–3,500 BC.* Oxford, UK: B.A.R., 1987.

Oppenheim, A. Leo. *Ancient Mesopotamia: Portrait of a Dead Civilization.* Chicago: University of Chicago Press, 1977.

Rossi, Corinna. *Architecture and Mathematics in Ancient Egypt.* Cambridge, UK, and New York: Cambridge University Press, 2004.

Sarianidi, Victor. *Necropolis of Gonur.* Translated by Inna Sarianidi. Athens: Kapon, 2007.

Shady, Ruth, and Carlos Leyva, eds. *La Ciudad Sagrada de Caral-Supe: Los Orígenes de la Civilización Andina y la Formación del Estado Prístino en el Antiguo Perú.* Lima: Instituto Nacional de Cultura: Proyecto Especial Arqueológico Caral-Supe, 2003.

1500 BCE

Byrd, Kathleen M. *The Poverty Point Culture: Local Manifestations, Subsistence Practices, and Trade Networks.* Baton Rouge, LA: Geoscience Publications, Department of Geography and Anthropology, Louisiana State University, 1991.

Chang, Kwang-chih. *Shang Civilization.* New Haven, CT: Yale University Press, 1980.

Clarke, Somers, and R. Engelbach. *Ancient Egyptian Construction and Architecture.* New York: Dover Publications, 1990.

Gibson, Jon L. *The Ancient Mounds of Poverty Point: Place of Rings.* Gainesville: University Press of Florida, 2000.

Moore, Jerry D. *Architecture and Power in the Ancient Andes: The Archaeology of Public Buildings.* Cambridge, UK, and New York: Cambridge University Press, 1996.

Oates, Joan. *Babylon: Ancient Peoples and Places.* London: Thames & Hudson, 1979.

800 BCE

Bell, Edward. *Prehellenic Architecture in the Aegean.* London: G. Bell & Sons, 1926.

Burger, Richard L. *The Prehistoric Occupation of Chavín de Huántar, Peru.* Berkeley and Los Angeles: University of California Press, 1984.

Castleden, Rodney. *The Knossos Labyrinth: A View of the Palace of Minos at Knossos.* London: Routledge, 1990.

Coe, Michael D. *The Olmec World: Ritual and Rulership.* Princeton, NJ: Art Museum, Princeton University, and New York: In association with Harry N. Abrams, 1996.

Damluji, Salma Samar. *The Architecture of Yemen: From Yafi to Hadramut.* London: Laurence King, 2007.

Diehl, Richard A. *The Olmecs: America's First Civilization.* London: Thames & Hudson, 2004.

Eck, Diana L. *Banaras, City of Light.* New York: Columbia University Press, 1999.

El-Hakim, Omar M. *Nubian Architecture: The Egyptian Vernacular Experience.* Cairo: Palm, 1993.

Jastrow, Morris. *The Civilization of Babylonia and Assyria: Its Remains, Language, History, Religion, Commerce, Law, Art, and Literature.* Philadelphia and London: J. B. Lippincott, 1915.

Li, Hsüeh-ch'in. *Eastern Zhou and Qin Civilizations.* Translated by K. C. Chang. New Haven: Yale University Press, 1985.

Pfeiffer, John E. *The Emergence of Society: A Pre-history of the Establishment.* New York: McGraw-Hill, 1977.

Ricke, Herbert, George R. Hughes, and Edward F. Wente. *The Beit el-Wali Temple of Ramesses II.* Chicago: University of Chicago Press, 1967.

Scoufopoulos, Niki C. *Mycenaean Citadels.* Gothenburg, Sweden: P. Åström, 1971.

Willetts, Ronald F. *The Civilization of Ancient Crete.* Berkeley and Los Angeles: University of California Press, 1976.

400 BCE

Ball, Larry F. *The Domus Aurea and the Roman Architectural Revolution.* Cambridge, UK: Cambridge University Press, 2003.

Barletta, Barbara A. *Ionic Influence in Archaic Sicily: The Monumental Art.* Gothenburg, Sweden: Åström, 1983.

———. *The Origins of the Greek Architectural Orders.* Cambridge, UK: Cambridge University Press, 2001.

Berve, Helmut. *Greek Temples, Theatres, and Shrines.* London: Thames & Hudson, 1963.

Camp, John M. *The Archaeology of Athens.* New Haven, CT: Yale University Press, 2001.

Clark, John E., and Mary E. Pye, eds. *Olmec Art and Archaeology in Mesoamerica.* Washington, DC: National Gallery of Art; New Haven: distributed by Yale University Press, 2000.

Coulton, John James. *Ancient Greek Architects at Work: Problems of Structure and Design.* Ithaca, NY: Cornell University Press, 1977.

Detienne, Marcel. *The Cuisine of Sacrifice Among the Greeks.* With essays by Jean-Louis Durand, Stella Georgoudi, Françoise Hartog, and Jesper Svenbro. Chicago: University of Chicago Press, 1989.

Dinsmoor, William Bell. *The Architecture of Ancient Greece: An Account of Its Historic Development.* New York: Norton, 1975.

Frye, Richard Nelson. *The Heritage of Persia.* Cleveland, OH: World Publishing, 1963.

Fyfe, Theodore. *Hellenistic Architecture: An Introductory Study.* Cambridge UK: Cambridge University Press, 1936; Oakville, CT: Aarhus University Press, 1999.

Grant, Michael. *The Etruscans.* New York: Charles Scribner's, 1980.

Hurwit, Jeffrey M. *The Art and Culture of Early Greece, 1100–480 BC.* Ithaca, NY: Cornell University Press, 1985.

Martienssen, Rex Distin. *The Idea of Space in Greek Architecture, with Special Reference to the Doric Temple and Its Setting.* Johannesburg: Witwatersrand University Press, 1956.

Scully, Vincent Joseph. *The Earth, the Temple, and the Gods: Greek Sacred Architecture.* New Haven: Yale University Press, 1962.

Taylour, William Lord. *The Mycenaeans.* London: Thames & Hudson, 1964.

Thapar, Romila. *Aśoka and the Decline of the Mauryas.* New Delhi and New York: Oxford University Press, 1997.

Warren, John. *Greek Mathematics and the Architects to Justinian.* London: Coach, 1976.

Winter, Frederick E. *Greek Fortifications.* Toronto: University of Toronto Press, 1971.

0

Ball, Larry F. *The Domus Aurea and the Roman Architectural Revolution.* Cambridge, UK, and New York: Cambridge University Press, 2003.

Boatwright, Mary Taliaferro. *Hadrian and the City of Rome.* Princeton, NJ: Princeton University Press, 1987.

Chase, Raymond G. *Ancient Hellenistic and Roman Amphitheatres, Stadiums, and Theatres: The Way they Look Now.* Portsmouth, NH: P. E. Randall, 2002.

Dallapiccola, Anna Libera, with Stephanie Zingel-Avé Lallemant, eds. *The Stúpa: Its Religious, Historical and Architectural Significance.* Wiesbaden, Germany: Steiner, 1979.

Hansen, Richard D. *Excavations in the Tigre Complex, El Mirador, Petén, Guatemala.* Provo, Utah: New World Archaeological Foundation, Brigham Young University, 1990.

Lawton, Thomas. *Chinese Art of the Warring States Period: Change and Continuity, 480–222 BC.* Washington, DC: Published for the Freer Gallery of Art by the Smithsonian Institution Press, 1983.

MacDonald, William Lloyd. *The Architecture of the Roman Empire.* New Haven: Yale University Press, 1982.

Rykwert, Joseph. *The Idea of a Town: The Anthropology of Urban Form in Rome, Italy and the Ancient World.* Princeton, NJ: Princeton University Press, 1976.

Sarkar, H. *Studies in Early Buddhist Architecture of India.* Delhi: Munshiram Manoharlal, 1966.

Schopen, Gregory. *Bones, Stones, and Buddhist Monks: Collected Papers on the Archaeology, Epigraphy, and Texts of Monastic Buddhism in India.* Honolulu: University of Hawaii Press, 1997.

Snodgrass, Adrian. *The Symbolism of the Stupa.* Ithaca, NY: Cornell University, 1985.

Stamper, John W. *The Architecture of Roman Temples: The Republic to the Middle Empire.* Cambridge, UK: Cambridge University Press, 2005.

Townsend, Richard F., ed. *Ancient West Mexico: Art and Archaeology of the Unknown Past.* New York: Thames & Hudson; Chicago: Art Institute of Chicago, 1998.

Ward-Perkins, John Bryan. *Roman Architecture.* Milan, Italy and London: Electa Architecture, 2003.

200 CE

Aveni, Anthony F. *Between the Lines: The Mystery of the Giant Ground Drawings of Ancient Nasca, Peru.* Austin: University of Texas Press, 2000.

Behrendt, Kurt A. *The Buddhist Architecture of Gandhara.* Leiden, Netherlands, and Boston: E. J. Brill, 2004.

Berrin, Kathleen, and Esther Pasztory. *Teotihuacán: Art from the City of the Gods.* New York: Thames & Hudson and the Fine Arts Museums of San Francisco, 1993.

Litvinsky, B. A., ed. *History of Civilizations of Central Asia, vol.3: The Crossroads of Civilizations, AD 250 to 750.* Paris: UNESCO, 1992.

MacDonald, William Lloyd. *The Pantheon: Design, Meaning, and Progeny.* Cambridge, MA: Harvard University Press, 1976.

MacDonald, William Lloyd, and John A. Pinto. *Hadrian's Villa and Its Legacy.* New Haven: Yale University Press, 1995.

Munro-Hay, Stuart. *Aksum: A Civilization of Late Antiquity.* Edinburgh, UK: University Press. 1991.

Phillipson, David W. *Ancient Ethiopia: Aksum: Its Antecedents and Successors.* London: The British Museum, 1998.

Romain, William F. *Mysteries of the Hopewell: Astronomers, Geometers, and Magicians of the Eastern Woodlands.* Akron, OH: University of Akron Press, 2000.

Sanders, William T., and Joseph W. Michels, eds. *Teotihuacán and Kaminaljuyu: A Study in Prehistoric Culture Contact.* University Park, PA: Penn State University Press, 1977.

Sharma, G. R., ed. *Kusana Studies: Papers Presented to the International Conference on the Archaeology, History and Arts of the People of Central Asia in the Kusāna Period, Dushambe (Tadjikistan) U.S.S.R., September 25–October 4, 1968.* Allahabad, India: Department of Ancient History, Culture and Archaeology, University of Allahabad, 1998.

Silverman, Helaine, and Donald Proulx. *The Nasca.* Oxford, UK: Blackwell, 2002.

Taylor, Rabun M. *Roman Builders: A Study in Architectural Process.* Cambridge, UK, and New York: Cambridge University Press, 2003.

Woodward, Susan L., and Jerry N. McDonald. *Indian Mounds of the Middle Ohio Valley: A Guide to Mounds and Earthworks of the Adena, Hopewell, Cole, and Fort Ancient People.* Blacksburg, VA: McDonald & Woodward, 2002.

Wang, Zhongshu. *Han Civilization.* Translated by K. C. Chang and collaborators, New Haven: Yale University Press, 1982.

400 CE

Aikens, C. Melvin, and Takayasu Higuchi. *Prehistory of Japan.* New York: Academic Press, 1982.

Asher, Frederick M. *The Art of Eastern India, 300–800.* Minneapolis: University of Minnesota Press, 1980.

Bandmann, Günter. *Early Medieval Architecture as Bearer of Meaning.* Translated by Kendall Wallis. New York: Columbia University Press, 2005.

Barnes, Gina Lee. *Protohistoric Yamato: Archaeology of the First Japanese State.* Ann Arbor: University of Michigan Center for Japanese Studies, Museum of Anthropology, University of Michigan, 1988.

Beal, Samuel. *The Life of Hiuen-Tsiang by Hwui Li.* New Delhi: Asian Educational Services, 1998.

Blanton, Richard E. et al. *Ancient Oaxaca: The Monte Albán.* New York: Cambridge University Press, 1999.

Cunningham, Alexander. *Mahâbodhi, or the Great Buddhist Temple Under the Bodhi Tree at Buddha-Gaya.* London: W. H. Allen, 1892.

Freely, John. *Byzantine Monuments of Istanbul.* Cambridge, UK: Cambridge University Press, 2004.

Harischandra, B. W. *The Sacred City of Anuradhapura.* New Delhi: Asian Educational Services, 1998.

Holloway, R. Ross. *Constantine and Rome.* New Haven: Yale University Press, 2004.

Imamura, Keiji. *Prehistoric Japan: New Perspectives on Insular East Asia.* London: UCL Press, 1996.

Khandalavala, Karl, ed. *The Golden Age of Gupta Art: Empire, Province, and Influence.* Bombay: Marg, 1991.

Krautheimer, Richard. *Early Christian and Byzantine Architecture.* New York: Penguin, 1986.

Mitra, Debala. *Ajanta.* New Delhi: Archaeological Survey of India, 1980.

Mizoguchi, Koji. *An Archaeological History of Japan: 30,000 BC to AD 700.* Philadelphia: University of Pennsylvania Press, 2002.

Ray, Himanshu P. *The Winds of Change: Buddhism and the Maritime Links of Early South Asia.* New Delhi: Oxford University Press, 1994.

Spink, Walter M. *Ajanta to Ellora.* Ann Arbor: Marg Publications for the Center for South and Southeast Asian Studies, University of Michigan, 1967.

Weiner, Sheila L. *Ajanta: Its Place in Buddhist Art.* Berkeley and Los Angeles: University of California Press, 1977.

Williams, Joanna Gottfried. *The Art of Gupta India: Empire and Province.* Princeton, NJ: Princeton University Press, 1982.

BIBLIOGRAPHY

600 CE

Adams, Cassandra. "Japan's Ise Shrine and Its Thirteen-Hundred-Year-Old Reconstruction Tradition." *Journal of Architectural Education* 52, no. 1 (1988).

Berkson, Carmel, Wendy Doniger O'Flaherty, and George Michell. *Elephanta, The Cave of Shiva*. Princeton, NJ: Princeton University Press, 1983.

Bock, Felicia G. "The Rites of Renewal at Ise." *Monumenta Nipponica* 29, no. 1 (1974).

Davies, John Gordon. *Medieval Armenian Art and Architecture: The Church of the Holy Cross, Aght'amar*. London: Pindar, 1991.

Freely, John. *Byzantine Monuments of Istanbul*. Cambridge, UK: Cambridge University Press, 2004.

Goldstein, Paul S. *Andean Diaspora: The Tiwanaku Colonies and the Origins of South American Empire*. Gainesville: University Press of Florida, 2005.

Hardy, Andrew, Mauro Cucarzi, and Patrizia Zolese, eds. *Champa and the Archaeology of My S'on (Vietnam)*. Singapore: NUS Press, 2009.

Harrison, Peter D. *The Lords of Tikal: Rulers of an Ancient Maya City*. New York: Thames & Hudson, 1999.

Janusek, John Wayne. *Identity and Power in the Ancient Andes: Tiwanaku: Cities Through Time*. New York: Routledge, 2004.

Kidder, J. Edward. *The Lucky Seventh: Early Horyu-ji and its Time*. Tokyo: International Christian University and Hachiro Yuasa Memorial Museum, 1999.

Kolata, Alan L. *The Tiwanaku: Portrait of an Andean Civilization*. Cambridge, MA: Blackwell, 1993.

Kramrisch, Stella. *The Presence of S'iva*. Princeton, NJ: Princeton University Press, 1992.

Krautheimer, Richard. *Rome: Profile of a City, 312–1308*. Princeton, NJ: Princeton University Press, 2000.

Malmstrom, Vincent H. *Cycles of the Sun, Mysteries of the Moon: The Calendar in Mesoamerican Civilization*. Austin: University of Texas Press, 1997.

Mathews, T. F. *Early Churches of Constantinople, Architecture and Liturgy*. University Park: Pennsylvania State University Press, 1971.

Mizuno, Seiichi. *Asuka Buddhist Art: Horyu-ji*. New York: Weatherhill, 1974.

Ngô Văn Doanh. *My Son Relics*. Hanoi: Gioi, 2005.

Robert, Mark, and Ahmet Çakmak, eds. *Hagia Sophia from the Age of Justinian to the Present*. Cambridge, UK: Cambridge University Press, 1992.

Schele, Linda, and Peter Mathews. *The Code of Kings: The Language of Seven Sacred Maya Temples and Tombs*. New York: Scribner, 1998.

Suzuki, Kakichi. *Early Buddhist Architecture in Japan*. Tokyo: Kodansha International, 1980.

Tartakov, Gary M. "The Beginnings of Dravidian Temple Architecture in Stone." *Artibus Asiae* 42 (1980).

Utudjian, Edouard. *Armenian Architecture, 4th to 17th Century*. Translated by Geoffrey Capner. Paris: Éditions A. Morancé, 1968.

Warren, John. *Greek Mathematics and the Architects to Justinian*. London: Coach, 1976.

Watanabe, Yasutada. *Shinto Art: Ise and Izumo Shrines*. New York: Weatherhill / Heibonsha, 1974.

Wharton, Annabel Jane. *Refiguring the Post-Classical City: Dura Europos, Jerash, Jerusalem, and Ravenna*. Cambridge, UK, and New York: Cambridge University Press, 1995.

800 CE

Atroshenko, V. I., and Judith Collins. *The Origins of the Romanesque: Near Eastern Influences on European Art, 4th–12th Centuries*. London: Lund Humphries, 1985.

Chandler, David P. *A History of Cambodia*. Boulder, CO: Westview, 2000.

Coe, Michael D. *The Maya*. London and New York: Thames & Hudson, 1999.

Ettinghausen, Richard. *Islamic Art and Architecture 650–1250*. New Haven: Yale University Press, 2001.

Flood, Finbarr Barry. *The Great Mosque of Damascus: Studies on the Makings of an Ummayyad Visual Culture*. Leiden, Netherlands and Boston: E. J. Brill, 2001.

Frederic, Louis. *Borobodur*. New York: Abeville, 1996.

Hattstein, Markus, and Peter Delius, eds. *Islam: Art and Architecture*. Translated by George Ansell German. Cologne, Germany: Könemann, 2000.

Horn, Walter, and Ernest Born. *The Plan of St. Gall*. Berkeley and Los Angeles: University of California Press, 1972.

Jackson, John G. *Introduction to African Civilization*. Secaucus, NJ: Citadel, 1970.

Joe, Wanne J. *Traditional Korea, A Cultural History*. Edited by Hongkyu A. Choe. Elizabeth, NJ: Hollym International, 1997.

Kelly, Joyce. *An Archaeological Guide to Northern Central America: Belize, Guatemala, Honduras, and El Salvador*. Norman: University of Oklahoma Press, 1996.

Lassner, Jacob. *The Shaping of Abbasid Rule*. Princeton, NJ: Princeton University Press, 1980.

Michell, George. *Pattadakal*. New Delhi and Oxford, UK: Oxford University Press, 2002.

Milburn, Robert. *Early Christian Art and Architecture*. Berkeley and Los Angeles: University of California Press, 1988.

Stuart, David and George Stuart. *Palenque: Eternal City of the Maya*. London: Thames & Hudson, 2008.

Tartakov, Gary Michael. *The Durga Temple at Aihole: A Historiographical Study*. New Delhi and New York: Oxford University Press, 1997.

Xiong, Victor Cunrui. *Sui T'ang Ch'ang-an: A Study in the Urban History of Medieval China*. Ann Arbor: Center for Chinese Studies, University of Michigan, 2000.

1000

Asopa, Jai Narayan. *Origin of the Rajputs*. Delhi: Bharatiya, 1976.

Conant, Kenneth John. *Carolingian and Romanesque Architecture, 800 to 1200*. Baltimore: Penguin, 1959.

Dehejia, Vidya. *The Sensuous and the Sacred: Chola Bronzes from South India*. New York: American Federation of Arts; Seattle: University of Washington Press, 2002.

———. *Yogini, Cult and Temples: A Tantric Tradition*. New Delhi: National Museum, 1986.

Desai, Devangana. *Khajuraho*. New Delhi and New York: Oxford University Press, 2000.

Dodds, Jerrilynn D. *Architecture and Ideology in Early Medieval Spain*. University Park: Penn State University Press, 1990.

Grossmann, Peter. *Christliche Architektur in Ägypten*. Leiden, Netherlands, and Boston: E. J. Brill, 2002.

Handa, Devendra. *Osian: History, Archaeology, Art and Architecture*. Delhi: Sundeep Prakashan, 1984.

Kowalski, Jeff Karl. *The House of the Governor: A Maya Palace at Uxmal, Yucatán, Mexico*. Norman: University of Oklahoma Press, 1987.

Michell, George. *Early Western Calukyan Temples*. London: AARP, 1975.

Miller, Barbara Stoler. *The Powers of Art: Patronage in Indian Culture*. New Delhi and New York: Oxford University Press, 1992.

Necipoglu, Gülru. *The Topkapı Scroll: Geometry and Ornament in Islamic Architecture*. Santa Monica, CA: Getty Center for the History of Arts and the Humanities, 1995.

Rivoira, Giovanni Teresio. *Lombardic Architecture: Its Origin, Development, and Derivatives.* New York: Hacker Art Books, 1975.

Spink, Walter M. *Ajanta to Ellora Bombay.* Ann Arbor: Marg Publications for the Center for South and Southeast Asian Studies, University of Michigan, 1967.

Steinhardt, Nancy Shatzman. *Liao Architecture.* Honolulu: University of Hawaii Press, 1997.

Tartakov, Gary M. "The Beginning of Dravidian Temple Architecture in Stone." *Artibus Asiae* 42 (1980).

Young, Biloine W., and Melvin L. Fowler. *Cahokia, the Great Native American Metropolis.* Urbana: University of Illinois Press, 2000.

1200

Bernier, Ronald M. *Temple Arts of Kerala: A South Indian Tradition.* New Delhi: S. Chand, 1982.

Bony, Jean. *French Gothic Architecture of the 12th and 13th Centuries.* Berkeley and Los Angeles: University of California Press, 1983.

Branner, Robert. *Burgundian Gothic Architecture.* London: A. Zwemmer, 1960.

Braunfels, Wolfgang. *Monasteries of Western Europe: The Architecture of the Orders.* Translated by Alastair Laing. London: Thames & Hudson, 1972.

Brumfield, William Craft. *A History of Russian Architecture.* Cambridge, UK: Cambridge University Press, 1993.

Buchwald, Hans Herbert. *Form, Style, and Meaning in Byzantine Church Architecture.* Brookfield, VT: Ashgate, 1999.

Cassidy-Welch, Megan. *Monastic Spaces and Their Meanings: Thirteenth-Century English Cistercian Monasteries.* Turnhout, Belgium: Brepols, 2001.

Chandler, David P. *A History of Cambodia.* Boulder, CO: Westview, 2000.

Coe, Michael D. *Angkor and the Khmer Civilization.* New York: Thames & Hudson, 2003.

Dehejia, Vidya, ed. *Royal Patrons and Great Temple Art.* Bombay: Marg, 1988.

Diehl, Richard A. *Tula: The Toltec Capital of Ancient Mexico.* London: Thames & Hudson, 1983.

Dodds, Jerrilynn D., ed. *Al-Andalus: The Art of Islamic Spain.* New York: Metropolitan Museum of Art and Harry N. Abrams, 1992.

Duby, Georges. *The Age of the Cathedrals: Art and Society, 980–1420.* Translated by Eleanor Levieux and Barbara Thompson. Chicago: University of Chicago Press, 1981.

Enzo, Carli, ed. *Il Duomo di Pisa: Il Battistero, il Campanile.* Florence: Nardini, 1989.

Erdmann, Kurt. *Das Anatolische Kervansaray des 13. Jahrhunderts.* Berlin: Verlag Gebr. Mann, 1976.

Findlay, Louis. *The Monolithic Churches of Lalibela in Ethiopia.* Le Caire, Egypt: Publications de la Société d'Archéologie Copte, 1944.

Fukuyama, Toshio. *Heian Temples: Byodo-in and Chuson-ji.* Translated by Ronald K. Jones. New York: Weatherhill, 1976.

Grabar, Oleg. *The Alhambra.* Cambridge, MA: Harvard University Press, 1978.

Guo, Qinghua. *The Structure of Chinese Timber Architecture: Twelfth Century Design Standards and Construction Principles.* Gothenburg, Sweden: Chalmers University of Technology, School of Architecture, Department of Building Design, 1995.

Kinder, Terryl Nancy. *Cistercian Europe: Architecture of Contemplation.* Grand Rapids, MI: W. B. Eerdmans Publishing and Cistercian Publications, 2002.

Kostof, Spiro. *Caves of God: The Monastic Environment of Byzantine Cappadocia.* Cambridge, MA: MIT Press, 1972.

Kraus, Henry. *Gold Was the Mortar: The Economics of Cathedral Building.* London and Boston: Routledge & Kegan Paul, 1979.

Krautheimer, Richard. *Early Christian and Byzantine Architecture.* Harmondsworth, UK, and New York: Penguin, 1986.

Liu, Dunzhen. *Chinese Classical Gardens of Suzhou.* Translated by Chen Lixian. Edited by Joseph C. Wang. New York: McGraw-Hill, 1993.

MacDonald, William Lloyd. *Early Christian and Byzantine Architecture: Great Ages of World Architecture.* New York: G. Braziller, 1962.

Mannikka, Eleanor. *Angkor Wat: Time, Space, and Kingship.* Honolulu: University of Hawaii Press, 1996.

Moynihan, Elizabeth B. *Paradise as a Garden: In Persia and Mughal India.* New York: G. Braziller, 1979.

Nath, R. *History of Sultanate Architecture.* New Delhi: Abhinav Publications, 1978.

Noma, Seiroku. *The Arts of Japan.* Translated and adapted by John Rosenfield. Tokyo and New York: Kodansha International; New York: Harper & Row, 1978.

Ousterhout, Robert G. *Master Builders of Byzantium.* Princeton, NJ: Princeton University Press, 1999.

Panofsky, Erwin, ed. *Abbot Suger on the Abbey Church of St.-Denis and Its Art Treasures.* Princeton, NJ: Princeton University Press, 1979.

Peroni, Adriano, ed. *Il Duomo di Pisa.* Modena, Italy: F. C. Panini, 1995.

Petruccioli, Attilio, ed. *Bukhara: The Myth and the Architecture.* Cambridge, MA: Aga Khan Program for Islamic Architecture, 1999.

Rabbat, Nasser. "Al-Azhar Mosque: An Architectural Chronicle of Cairo's History." *Muqarnas 13* (1996): 45–67.

Rowley, Trevor. *The Norman Heritage, 1055–1200.* London and Boston, MA: Routledge & Kegan Paul, 1983.

Settar, S. *The Hoysala Temples.* Bangalore, India: Kala Yatra, 1991–1992.

Starza, O. M. *The Jagannatha Temple at Puri: Its Architecture, Art, and Culture.* Leiden, Netherlands, and New York: E. J. Brill, 1993.

Strachan, Paul. *Imperial Pagan: Art and Architecture of Burma.* Honolulu: University of Hawaii Press, 1990.

Tobin, Stephen. *The Cistercians: Monks and Monasteries of Europe.* Woodstock, NY: Overlook, 1996.

Tozzer, Alfred M. *Chichen Itza and Its Cenote of Sacrifice: A Comparative Study of Contemporaneous Maya and Toltec.* Cambridge, MA: Peabody Museum, 1957.

Von Simson, Otto Georg. *The Gothic Cathedral: Origins of Gothic Architecture and the Medieval Concept of Order.* Princeton, NJ: Princeton University Press, 1988.

Wang, Eugene Yuejin. *Shaping the Lotus Sutra: Buddhist Visual Culture in Medieval China.* Seattle: University of Washington Press, 2005.

1400

Ackerman, James S. *Palladio.* Harmondsworth, UK: Penguin, 1966.

Ballon, Hilary. *The Paris of Henri IV: Architecture and Urbanism.* Cambridge, MA: MIT Press, 1991.

Battisti, Eugenio. *Brunelleschi.* Translated by Robert Erich Wolf. Milan: Electa Architecture; London: Phaidon, 2002.

Blair, Sheila S., and Jonathan M. Bloom. *The Art and Architecture of Islam, 1250–1800.* New Haven: Yale University Press, 1994.

Borsi, Franco. *Leon Battista Alberti: The Complete Works.* London: Faber, 1989.

Bruschi, Arnaldo. *Bramante.* London: Thames & Hudson, 1977.

Burger, Richard L., and Lucy C. Salazar, eds. *Machu Picchu: Unveiling the Mystery of the Incas.* New Haven: Yale University Press, 2004.

Chappell, Sally Anderson. *Cahokia: Mirror of the Cosmos.* Chicago: University of Chicago Press, 2002.

BIBLIOGRAPHY

1400 (continued)

Clarke, Georgia Roman House. *Renaissance Palaces: Inventing Antiquity in Fifteenth-Century Italy.* Cambridge, UK, and New York: Cambridge University Press, 2003.

Evans, Joan. *Monastic Architecture in France, from the Renaissance to the Revolution.* Cambridge, UK: Cambridge University Press, 1964.

Fedorov, Boris Nikolaevich. *Architecture of the Russian North, 12th–19th Centuries.* Translated by N. Johnstone. Leningrad: Aurora Art Publishers, 1976.

Goodwin, Godfrey. *A History of Ottoman Architecture.* London: Thames & Hudson, 1971.

Günay, Reha. *Sinan: The Architect and His Works.* Translated by Ali Ottoman. Istanbul: Yapı-Endüstri Merkezi Yayınları, 1998.

Hall, John W., ed. *Japan in the Muromachi Age.* Ithaca, New York: East Asia Program, Cornell University, 2001.

Hitchcock, Henry Russell. *German Renaissance Architecture.* Princeton, NJ: Princeton University Press, 1981.

Howard, Deborah. *Jacopo Sansovino: Architecture and Patronage in Renaissance Venice.* New Haven: Yale University Press, 1975.

Jarzombek, Mark. *On Leon Baptista Alberti: His Literary and Aesthetic Theories.* Cambridge, MA: MIT Press, 1989.

Kuran, Aptullah. *The Mosque in Early Ottoman Architecture.* Chicago: University of Chicago Press, 1968.

Lieberman, Ralph. *The Church of Santa Maria dei Miracoli in Venice.* New York: Garland, 1986.

López Luján, Leonardo. *The Offerings of the Templo Mayor of Tenochtitlán.* Translated by Bernard R. Ortiz de Montellano and Thelma Ortiz de Montellano. Albuquerque: University of New Mexico Press, 2005.

Millard, James, ed. *New Qing Imperial History: The Making of Inner Asian Empire at Qing Chengde.* London and New York: Routledge, 2004.

Murray, Peter. *Renaissance Architecture.* Milan: Electa; New York: Rizzoli, 1985, 1978.

Pandya, Yatin. *Architectural Legacies of Ahmedabad.* Ahmedabad, India: Vastu-Shilpa Foundation for Studies and Research in Environmental Design, 2002.

Prinz, Wolfram Schloss. *Chambord und die Villa Rotonda in Vicenza.* Berlin: Mann, 1980.

Rabbat, Nasser O. *The Citadel of Cairo: A New Interpretation of Royal Mamluk Architecture.* Leiden, Netherlands, and New York: E. J. Brill, 1995.

Ryu, Je-Hun. *Reading the Korean Landscape.* Elizabeth, NJ: Hollym International, 2000.

Smith, Christine Hunnikin. *Architecture in the Culture of Early Humanism: Ethics, Aesthetics, and Eloquence, 1400–1470.* New York: Oxford University Press, 1992.

Sumner-Boyd, Hilary, and John Freely. *Strolling Through Istanbul: A Guide to the City.* New York: Kegan Paul, 2001; New York: Columbia University Press, 2003.

Tafuri, Manfredo. *Venice and the Renaissance.* Translated by Jessica Levine. Cambridge, MA: MIT Press, 1989.

Talayesva, Don C. *Sun Chief: The Autobiography of a Hopi Indian.* New Haven: Yale University Press, 1942.

Treib, Marc, and Ron Herman. *A Guide to the Gardens of Kyoto.* Tokyo: Shufunotomo, 1980.

Van der Ree, Paul, Gerrit Smienk, and Clemens Steenbergen. *Italian Villas and Gardens: A Corso di Disegno.* Munich: Prestel, 1992.

Vogt-Göknil, Ulya. *Living Architecture: Ottoman.* New York: Grosset & Dunlap, 1966.

Von Hagen, Victor Wolfgang. *The Desert Kingdoms of Peru.* New York: New American Library, 1968.

Waldman, Carl. *Atlas of the North American Indian.* New York: Checkmark, 2000.

Wright, Kenneth R. *Machu Picchu: A Civil Engineering Marvel.* Reston, VA: American Society of Civil Engineers, 2000.

Zhu, Jianfei. *Chinese Spatial Strategies: Imperial Beijing, 1420–1911.* London and New York: Routledge Curzon, 2004.

1600

Argan, Giulio Carlo. *Michelangelo Architect.* Translated by Marion L. Grayson. London: Thames & Hudson, 1993.

Balas, Edith. *Michelangelo's Medici Chapel: A New Interpretation.* Philadelphia: American Philosophical Society, 1995.

Begley, W. E., and Z. A. Desai. *Taj Mahal: The Illumined Tomb: An Anthology of Seventeenth-Century Mughal and European Documentary Sources.* Cambridge, MA: Aga Khan Program for Islamic Architecture; Seattle: University of Washington Press, 1989.

Blake, Stephen P. *Half the World: The Social Architecture of Safavid Isfahan, 1590–1722.* Costa Mesa, CA: Mazda, 1999.

Blunt, Anthony. *Guide to Baroque Rome.* New York: Harper & Row, 1982.

Borsi, Francio. *Bernini.* Translated by Robert Erich Wolf. New York: Rizzoli, 1984.

Coaldrake, William Howard. *Gateways of Power: Edo Architecture and Tokugawa Authority, 1603–1951.* Ph.D. diss., Harvard University, 1983.

Coffin, David R. *The Villa in the Life of Renaissance Rome.* Princeton, NJ: Princeton University Press, 1979.

D'Amico, John F. *Renaissance Humanism in Papal Rome: Humanists and Churchmen on the Eve of the Reformation.* Baltimore: Johns Hopkins University Press, 1983.

De Tolnay, Charles. *Michelangelo: Sculptor, Painter, Architect.* Princeton, NJ: Princeton University Press, 1974.

Dussel, Enrique D. *The Invention of the Americas: Eclipse of "the Other" and the Myth of Modernity.* Translated by Michael D. Barber. New York: Continuum, 1995.

Evans, Susan, and Joanne Pillsbury, eds. *Palaces of the Ancient New World: A Symposium at Dumbarton Oaks, 10th and 11th October 1998.* Washington, DC: Dumbarton Oaks Research Library and Collection, 2004.

Gotch, John. *Alfred Inigo Jones.* New York: B. Blom, 1968.

Guise, Anthony, ed. *The Potala of Tibet.* London and Atlantic Highlands, NJ: Stacey International, 1988.

Günay, Reha. *Sinan: The Architect and His Works.* Translated by Ali Ottoman. Istanbul: Yapı-Endüstri Merkezi Yayınları, 1998.

Hersey, George L. *High Renaissance Art in St. Peter's and the Vatican: An Interpretive Guide.* Chicago: University of Chicago Press, 1993.

Hughes, Quentin. *Malta: A Guide to the Fortifications.* Valletta, Malta: Said International, 1993.

Inaji, Toshirō. *The Garden as Architecture: Form and Spirit in the Gardens of Japan, China, and Korea.* Translated and adapted by Pamela Virgilio. Tokyo and New York: Kodansha International, 1998.

Ishimoto, Yasuhiro. *Katsura: Tradition and Creation in Japanese Architecture.* Text by Kenzo Tange. Photos by Yasuhiro Ishimoto. New Haven: Yale University Press, 1972.

Krautheimer, Richard. *Roma Alessandrina: The Remapping of Rome under Alexander VII, 1655–1667.* Poughkeepsie, NY: Vassar College, 1982.

Lazzaro, Claudia. *The Italian Renaissance Garden: From the Conventions of Planting, Design, and Ornament to the Grand Gardens of 16th-Century Central Italy.* New Haven: Yale University Press, 1990.

Lees-Milne, James. *Saint Peter's: The Story of Saint Peter's Basilica in Rome.* Boston: Little, Brown, 1967; Chicago: University of Chicago Press, 1986.

Lev, Evonne. *Propaganda and the Jesuit Baroque.* Berkeley and Los Angeles: University of California Press, 2004.

Mann, Charles C. *1491: New Revelations of the Americas Before Columbus.* New York: Knopf, 2005.

Meek, Harold Alan. *Guarino Guarini and His Architecture.* New Haven: Yale University Press, 1988.

Michell, George. *The Vijayanagara Courtly Style: Incorporation and Synthesis in the Royal Architecture of Southern India, 15th–17th Centuries.* New Delhi and Manohar, India: American Institute of Indian Studies, 1992.

Millon, Henry A., ed. *Triumph of the Baroque: Architecture in Europe, 1600–1750.* New York: Rizzoli, 1999.

Nath, R. *Architecture of Fatehpur Sikri: Forms, Techniques & Concepts.* Jaipur, India: Historical Research Documentation Programme, 1988.

———. *History of Mughal Architecture.* New Delhi: Abhinav, 1982.

Necipoğlu, Gülru. *The Age of Sinan: Architectural Culture in the Ottoman Empire.* London: Reaktion, 2005.

Paludan, Ann. *The Imperial Ming Tombs.* New Haven: Yale University Press, 1981.

Partner, Peter. *Renaissance Rome, 1500–1559: A Portrait of a Society.* Berkeley and Los Angeles: University of California Press, 1976.

Rizvi, Kishwar. *Transformations in Early Safavid Architecture: The Shrine of Shaykh Safi al-din Ishaq Ardabili in Iran (1501–1629).* Ph.D. diss., Massachusetts Institute of Technology, 2000.

Sinding-Larsen, Amund. *The Lhasa Atlas: Traditional Tibetan Architecture and Townscape.* Boston: Shambhala; New York: Random House, 2001.

Studio, Fianico. *The Medici Villas.* Florence: Libreria Editrice Fiorentina, 1980.

Summerson, John Newenham. *Architecture in Britain, 1530 to 1830.* Harmondsworth, UK, and New York: Penguin, 1991.

———. *Inigo Jones.* New Haven: Published for the Paul Mellon Centre for Studies in British Art by Yale University Press, 2000.

Thompson, Jon, and Sheila R. Canby, eds. *Hunt for Paradise: Court Arts of Safavid Iran, 1501–1576.* Milan: Skira; London: Thames & Hudson, 2003.

Walton, Guy. *Louis XIV's Versailles.* London: Viking, 1986.

Zhao, Lingyang. *Zheng He, Navigator, Discoverer and Diplomat.* Singapore: Unipress, 2001.

1700

Arciszewska, Barbara, and Elizabeth McKellar, eds. *Articulating British Classicism: New Approaches to Eighteenth-Century Architecture.* Hants, UK: Aldershot, 2004.

Arshi, Pardeep Singh. *The Golden Temple: History, Art, and Architecture.* New Delhi: Harman, 1989.

Banerjea, Dhrubajyoti. *European Calcutta: Images and Recollections of a Bygone Era.* New Delhi: UBS, 2004.

Berger, Patricia Ann. *Empire of Emptiness: Buddhist Art and Political Authority in Qing China.* Honolulu: University of Hawaii Press, 2003.

Blunt, Anthony, ed. *Baroque and Rococo: Architecture and Decoration.* London: Elek, 1978.

Bourke, John. *Baroque Churches of Central Europe.* London: Faber & Faber, 1962.

Erlanger, Philippe. *The Age of Courts and Kings: Manners and Morals, 1558–1715.* New York: Harper & Row, 1967.

Gollings, John. *City of Victory: Vijayanagara, the Medieval Hindu Capital of Southern India.* New York: Aperture, 1991.

Gutschow, Niels, and Erich Theophile, eds. *Patan: Architecture of a Historic Nepalese City: Excerpts from a Proposed Research and Publication Project (1998–2000) of the Kathmandu Valley Preservation Trust.* Kathmandu, Nepal: Kathmandu Valley Preservation Trust, 1998.

Harman, William. *The Sacred Marriage of a Hindu Goddess.* Bloomington: Indiana University Press, 1989.

Herrmann, Wolfgang. *Laugier and Eighteenth-Century French Theory.* London: A. Zwemmer, 1962.

———. *The Theory of Claude Perrault.* London: A. Zwemmer, 1973.

Metcalf, Thomas R. *Ideologies of the Raj.* Cambridge, UK, and New York: Cambridge University Press, 1994.

Otto, Christian F. *Space into Light: The Church Architecture of Balthasar Neumann.* New York: Architectural History Foundation, 1979.

Pierson, William H., Jr. *The Colonial and Neocolassical Styles.* Oxford, UK: Oxford University Press, 1970.

Roy, Ashim K. *History of the Jaipur City.* New Delhi: Manohar, 1978.

Sachdev, Vibhuti, and Giles Tillotson. *Building Jaipur: The Making of an Indian City.* London: Reaktion Books, 2002.

Sarkar, Jadunath. *A History of Jaipur, c. 1503–1938.* Hyderabad, India: Orient Longman, 1984.

Singh, Khushwant. *A History of the Sikhs.* New Delhi and Oxford, UK: Oxford University Press, 2004.

Sitwell, Sacheverell. *Baroque and Rococo.* London: Weidenfeld & Nicolson, 1967.

Smith, Bardwell, and Holly Baker Reynolds, eds. *The City as a Sacred Center: Essays on Six Asian Contexts.* Leiden, Netherlands, and New York: E. J. Brill, 1987.

Smith, Charles Saumarez. *The Building of Castle Howard.* London: Faber & Faber, 1990.

Smith, Woodruff D. *Consumption and the Making of Respectability, 1600–1800.* New York: Routledge, 2002.

Wittkower, Rudolf. *Palladio and Palladianism.* New York: G. Braziller, 1974.

1800

Aasen, Clarence T. *Architecture of Siam: A Cultural History Interpretation.* Kuala Lumpur, Malaysia, and New York: Oxford University Press, 1998.

Atterbury, Paul, ed. *A. W. N. Pugin: Master of Gothic Revival.* New Haven: Published for the Bard Graduate Center for Studies in the Decorative Arts, New York, by Yale University Press, 1995.

Ayres, James. *Building the Georgian City.* New Haven, CT: Yale University Press, 1998.

Bastéa, Eleni. *The Creation of Modern Athens: Planning the Myth.* Cambridge, UK, and New York: Cambridge University Press, 2000.

Bergdoll, Barry. *Karl Friedrich Schinkel: An Architecture for Prussia.* New York: Rizzoli, 1994.

Brandon, James R., William P. Malm, and Donald H. Shively. *Studies in Kabuki: Its Acting, Music, and Historical Context.* Honolulu: University Press of Hawaii, 1978.

Brooks, Michael W. *John Ruskin and Victorian Architecture.* New Brunswick, NJ: Rutgers University Press, 1987.

Charlesworth, Michael, ed. *The Gothic Revival, 1720–1870: Literary Sources and Documents.* The Banks, Mountfield, UK: Helm Information, 2002.

Chattopadhyay, Swati. *Representing Calcutta: Modernity, Nationalism, and the Colonial Uncanny.* London: New York: Routledge, 2005.

Conner, Patrick. *Oriental Architecture in the West.* London: James & Hudson, 1979.

Crook, Joseph Mordaunt. *The Dilemma of Style: Architectural Ideas from the Picturesque to the Post-Modern.* London: Murray, 1987.

Drexler, Arthur, ed. *The Architecture of the École des Beaux-Arts.* New York: Museum of Modern Art; Cambridge, MA: MIT Press, 1977.

BIBLIOGRAPHY

1800 (continued)

Du Prey, Pierre de la Ruffinière. *John Soane, The Making of an Architect.* Chicago: University of Chicago Press, 1982.

Forêt, Philippe. *Mapping Chengde: The Qing Landscape Enterprise.* Honolulu: University of Hawaii Press, 2000.

Gosner, Pamela W. *Caribbean Georgian: The Great and Small Houses of the West Indies.* Washington, DC: Three Continents, 1982.

Herrmann, Wolfgang. *Gottfried Semper: In Search of Architecture.* Cambridge, MA: MIT Press, 1984.

Hitchcock, Henry Russell. *Early Victorian Architecture in Britain.* New Haven: Yale University Press, 1954.

Kaufmann, Emil. *Architecture in the Age of Reason: Baroque and Post-Baroque in England, Italy, and France.* New York: Dover Publications, 1968.

Leiter, Samuel L. *Kabuki Encyclopedia: An English-Language Adaptation of Kabuki Jiten.* Westport, CT: Greenwood, 1979.

Leiter, Samuel L., ed. *A Kabuki Reader: History and Performance.* Armonk, NY: M. E. Sharpe, 2002.

McCormick, Thomas. *Charles-Louis Clérisseau and the Genesis of Neo-Classicism.* New York: Architectural History Foundation; Cambridge, MA: MIT Press, 1990.

Metcalf, Thomas R. *An Imperial Vision: Indian Architecture and Britain's Raj.* Berkeley and Los Angeles: University of California Press, 1989.

Mitter, Partha. *Much Maligned Monsters: History of European Reactions to Indian Art.* Oxford, UK: Clarendon, 1977.

Moore, Elizabeth H., Philip Stott, and Suriyavudh Sukhasvasti. *Ancient Capitals of Thailand.* London: Thames & Hudson, 1996.

Port, Michael Harry. *Imperial London: Civil Government Building in London 1850–1915.* New Haven: Published for the Paul Mellon Centre for Studies in British Art by Yale University Press, 1995.

Pundt, Hermann G. *Schinkel's Berlin: A Study in Environmental Planning.* Cambridge, MA: Harvard University Press, 1972.

Schumann-Bacia, Eva. *John Soane and the Bank of England.* London and New York: Longman, 1991.

Stewart, David B. *The Making of a Modern Japanese Architecture: 1868 to the Present.* Tokyo and New York: Kodansha International, 1987.

Summerson, John Newenham. *Georgian London.* New York: C. Scribner's Sons, 1946.

Unrau, John. *Ruskin and St. Mark's.* London: Thames & Hudson, 1984.

Upton, Dell. *Architecture in the United States.* Oxford, UK, and New York: Oxford University Press, 1998.

Vernoit, Stephen. *Occidentalism: Islamic Art in the 19th Century.* New York: Nour Foundation, in association with Azimuth Editions and Oxford University Press, 1997.

Vidler, Anthony. *The Writing of the Walls: Architectural Theory in the Late Enlightenment.* New York: Princeton Architectural Press, 1987.

Watkin, David. *German Architecture and the Classical Ideal.* Cambridge, MA: MIT Press, 1987.

Whittaker, Cynthia Hyla, ed. *Russia Engages the World, 1453–1825.* Cambridge, MA: Harvard University Press, 2003.

1900

Baker, Geoffrey H. *Le Corbusier: An Analysis of Form.* New York: Van Nostrand Reinhold; London: E & FN Spon, 1996.

Blau, Eve. *The Architecture of Red Vienna, 1919–1934.* Cambridge, MA: MIT Press, 1999.

Borsi, Franco. *The Monumental Era: European Architecture and Design, 1929–1939.* Translated by Pamela Marwood. New York: Rizzoli, 1987.

Bozdoğan, Sibel. *Modernism and Nation Building: Turkish Architectural Culture in the Early Republic.* Seattle: University of Washington Press, 2001.

Cody, Jeffrey W. *Exporting American Architecture, 1870–2000.* London and New York: Routledge, 2003.

Collins, Peter. *Changing Ideals in Modern Architecture, 1750–1950.* Montreal and Ithaca, NY: McGill-Queens University Press, 1998.

Colomina, Beatriz, ed. *Privacy and Publicity: Modern Architecture as Mass Media.* Cambridge, MA: MIT Press, 1996.

Condit, Carl W. *The Chicago School of Architecture: A History of Commercial and Public Building in the Chicago Area, 1875–1925.* Chicago: University of Chicago Press, 1964.

Cunningham, Colin. *Victorian and Edwardian Town Halls.* London: Routledge & Kegan Paul, 1981.

Curtis, William J. R. *Modern Architecture Since 1900.* Oxford, UK: Phaidon, 1982.

Dernie, David. *Victor Horta.* London: Academy Editions, 1995.

Dutta, Arindam. *The Bureaucracy of Beauty: Design in the Age of Its Global Reproducibility.* New York: Routledge, 2007.

Dwivedi, Sharada and Rahul Mehrotra. *Bombay: The Cities Within.* Bombay: Eminence Designs, 2001.

Egbert, Donald Drew, and David Van Zanten, ed. *The Beaux-Arts Tradition in French Architecture.* Princeton, NJ: Princeton University Press, 1980.

Elleh, Nnambi. *African Architecture, Evolution and Transformation.* New York: McGraw-Hill, 1977.

———. *Architecture and Power in Africa.* Westport, CT: Praeger, 2002.

Evenson, Norma. *The Indian Metropolis: A View Toward the West.* New Haven: Yale University Press, 1989.

Friedman, Mildred, ed. *De Stijl, 1917–1931: Visions of Utopia.* Minneapolis: Walker Art Center; New York: Abbeville Press, 1982.

Golan, Romy. *Modernity and Nostalgia: Art and Politics in France between the Wars.* New Haven: Yale University Press, 1995.

Guha-Thakorte, Tapati. *The Making of a New "Indian" Art: Artists, Aesthetics and Nationalism in Bengal, c. 1850–1920.* Cambridge, UK: Cambridge University Press, 1992.

Hildebrand, Grant. *The Wright Space: Pattern and Meaning in Frank Lloyd Wright's Houses.* Seattle: University of Washington Press, 1991.

Hosagrahar, Jyoti. *Indigenous Modernities: Negotiating Architecture and Urbanism.* London and New York: Routledge, 2006

Irving, Robert Grant. *Indian Summer: Lutyens, Baker, and Imperial Delhi.* New Haven: Yale University Press, 1981.

Jarzombek, Mark. *Designing MIT: Bosworth's New Tech.* Boston: Northeastern University Press, 2004.

Kopp, Anatole. *Constructivist Architecture in the USSR.* Translated by Sheila de Vallée. London: Academy Editions; New York: St. Martins Press, 1985.

Kruty, Paul, and Paul Sprague. *Two American Architects in India: Walter B. Griffin and Marion M. Griffin, 1935–1937.* Champaign-Urbana: School of Architecture, University of Illinois, 1997.

Kultermann, Udo., ed. *Kenzo Tange, 1946–1969: Architecture and Urban Design.* Zürich: Verlag für Architektur Artemis, 1970.

Kultermann, Udo. *New Directions in African Architecture.* Translated by John Maass. London: Studio Vista, 1969.

Lahuerta, Juan José. *Antoni Gaudí, 1852–1926: Architecture, Ideology, and Politics.* Edited by Giovanna Crespi. Translated by Graham Thompson. Milan: Electa Architecture; London: Phaidon, 2003.

Levine, Neil. *The Architecture of Frank Lloyd Wright.* Princeton, NJ: Princeton University Press, 1996.

Lizon, Peter. *The Palace of the Soviets: The Paradigm of Architecture in the USSR.* Colorado Springs, CO: Three Continents, 1995.

Loyer, François. *Victor Horta: Hotel Tassel 1893–1895.* Translated by Susan Day. Brussels: Archives d'Architecture Moderne, 1986.

Maciuika, John V. *Before the Bauhaus: Architecture, Politics, and the German State, 1890–1920.* New York: Cambridge University Press, 2005.

Markus, Thomas A., ed. *Order in Space and Society: Architectural Form and Its Context in the Scottish Enlightenment.* Edinburgh, UK: Mainstream, 1982.

Martinell, César. *Gaudí: His Life, His Theories, His Work.* Translated by Judith Rohrer. Cambridge, MA: MIT Press, 1975.

Middleton, Robin, ed. *The Beaux-Arts and Nineteenth-Century French Architecture.* Cambridge, MA: MIT Press, 1982.

Moravánszky, Ákos. *Competing Visions: Aesthetic Invention and Social Imagination in Central European Architecture, 1867–1918.* Cambridge, MA: MIT Press, 1998.

Nitzan-Shiftan, Alona. *Isrealizing Jerusalem: The Encounter between Architectural and National Ideologies 1967–1977.* Ph.D. diss., MIT, 2002.

Oechslin, Werner. *Otto Wagner, Adolf Loos, and the Road to Modern Architecture.* Translated by Lynette Widder. Cambridge, UK, and New York: Cambridge University Press, 2002.

Okoye, Ikemefuna. *"Hideous" Architecture: Feint and Resistance in Turn of the Century South-Eastern Nigerian Building.* Ph.D. diss., Massachusetts Institute of Technology, 1995.

Oldenburg, Veena Talwar. *The Making of Colonial Lucknow, 1856–1877.* Princeton, NJ: Princeton University Press, 1984.

Pawley, Martin. *Buckminster Fuller.* London: Trefoil, 1990.

Pyla, Panayiota. *Ekistics, Architecture and Environmental Politics 1945–76: A Prehistory of Sustainable Development.* Ph.D. diss., Massachusetts Institute of Technology, 2002.

Rabbat, Nasser. "The Formation of the Neo-Mamluk Style in Modern Egypt" in *The Education of the Architect: Historiography, Urbanism and the Growth of Architectural Knowledge.* Edited by Martha Pollak. Cambridge, MA: MIT Press, 1997.

Rowland, Anna. *Bauhaus Source Book.* Oxford, UK: Phaidon, 1990.

Sarnitz, August. *Adolf Loos, 1870–1933: Architect, Cultural Critic, Dandy.* Cologne, Germany, and Los Angeles: Taschen, 2003.

Scriver, Peter. *Rationalization, Standardization, and Control in Design: A Cognitive Historical Study of Architectural Design and Planning in the Public Works Department of British India, 1855–1901.* Delft, Netherlands: Publikatieburo Bouwkunde, Technische Universiteit Delft, 1994.

Scully, Vincent Joseph. *The Shingle Style Today, or, the Historian's Revenge.* New York: G. Braziller, 1974.

Sheaffer, M. P. A. *Otto Wagner and the New Face of Vienna.* Vienna: Compress, 1997.

Siry, Joseph. *Carson Pirie Scott: Louis Sullivan and the Chicago Department Store Chicago Architecture and Urbanism.* Chicago: University of Chicago Press, 1988.

———. *Unity Temple: Frank Lloyd Wright and Architecture for Liberal Religion.* Cambridge, UK: Cambridge University Press, 1996.

Starr, S. *Frederick Melnikov: Solo Architect in a Mass Society.* Princeton, NJ: Princeton University Press, 1978.

Steele, James. *Charles Rennie Mackintosh: Synthesis in Form.* London: Academy Editions, 1995.

Steiner, Hadas. *Bathrooms, Bubbles, and Systems: Archigram and the Landscapes of Transience.* Ph.D. diss., Massachusetts Institute of Technology, 2001.

Stern, Robert A. M. *New York 1930: Architecture and Urbanism between Two World Wars.* New York: Rizzoli, 1987.

Stern, Robert A. M., Gregory Gilmartin, and John Montague Massengale. *New York 1900: Metropolitan Architecture and Urbanism, 1890–1915.* New York: Rizzoli, 1983.

Stewart, Janet. *Fashioning Vienna: Adolf Loos's Cultural Criticism.* London and New York: Routledge, 2000.

Summerson, John Newenham. *The Turn of the Century: Architecture in Britain around 1900.* Glasgow, Scotland: University of Glasgow Press, 1976.

Toman, Rolf. *Vienna: Art and Architecture.* Cologne, Germany: Könemann, 1999.

Turnbull, Jeff, and Peter Y. Navaretti, eds. *The Griffins in Australia and India: The Complete Works and Projects of Walter Burley Griffin and Marion Mahony Griffin.* Melbourne, Australia: Miegunyah, 1998.

Turner, Paul Venable. *Campus: An American Planning Tradition.* New York: Architectural History Foundation; Cambridge, MA: MIT Press, 1984.

———. *The Education of Le Corbusier.* New York: Garland, 1977.

Van Zanten, David. *Designing Paris: The Architecture of Duban, Labrouste, Duc, and Vaudoyer.* Cambridge, MA: MIT Press, 1987.

Woods, Mary N. *From Craft to Profession: The Practice of Architecture in Nineteenth-Century America.* Berkeley and Los Angeles: University of California Press, 1999.

Yaha, Maha. *Unnamed Modernisms: National Ideologies and Historical Imaginaries in Beirut's Urban Architecture.* Ph.D. diss., Massachusetts Institute of Technology, 2004.

Zabel, Craig and Munshower, Susan Scott, eds. *American Public Architecture: European Roots and Native Expressions.* University Park, PA: Penn State University Press, 1989.

1950

Baljeu, Joost. *Theo van Doesburg.* London: Studio Vista, 1974.

Bettinotti, Massimo, ed. *Kenzo Tange, 1946–1996: Architecture and Urban Design.* Milan: Electa, 1996.

Cannell, Michael T. *I. M. Pei: Mandarin of Modernism.* New York: Carol Southern Books, 1995.

Cavalcanti, Lauro. *When Brazil Was Modern: Guide to Architecture, 1928–1960.* Translated by Jon Tolman. New York: Princeton Architectural Press, 2003.

Cohen, Jean-Louis. *Le Corbusier and the Mystique of the USSR: Theories and Projects for Moscow, 1928–1936.* Translated by Kenneth Hylton. Princeton, NJ: Princeton University Press, 1992.

Cohen, Jean-Louis, and Monique Eleb. *Casablanca: Colonial Myths and Architectural Ventures.* New York: Monacelli, 2002.

Colquhoun, Alan. *Modernity and the Classical Tradition: Architectural Essays, 1980–1987.* Cambridge, MA: MIT Press, 1989.

Curtis, William J. R. *Balkrishna Doshi: An Architecture for India.* New York: Rizzoli, 1988.

———. *Le Corbusier: Ideas and Forms.* New York: Rizzoli, 1986.

Doxiades, Konstantinos Apostolouv. *Ecology and Ekistics.* Edited by Gerald Dix. Boulder, CO: Westview, 1977.

BIBLIOGRAPHY

1950 (continued)

Ellin, Nan. *Postmodern Urbanism*. New York: Princeton Architectural Press, 1999.

Fromonot, Francoise. *Glenn Murcutt: Buildings & Projects 1969–2003*. London: Thames & Hudson, 2003.

Ghirardo, Diane Yvonne. *Architecture after Modernism*. New York: Thames & Hudson, 1996.

———. *Building New Communities: New Deal America and Fascist Italy*. Princeton, NJ: Princeton University Press, 1989.

Grigor, Talinn. *Cultivat(ing) Modernities: The Society for National Heritage, Political Propaganda, and Public Architecture in Twentieth-Century Iran*. Ph.D. diss., Massachusetts Institute of Technology, 2005.

Ibelings, Hans. *Supermodernism: Architecture in the Age of Globalization*. Translated by Robyn de Jong-Dalziel. Rotterdam, Netherlands: NAi, 2002.

Jencks, Charles. *Kings of Infinite Space: Frank Lloyd Wright & Michael Graves*. New York: St. Martin's Press, 1985.

Jencks, Charles. *The Architecture of the Jumping Universe: A Polemic: How Complexity Science is Changing Architecture and Culture*. London: Academy Editions, 1997.

———. *The Language of Post-Modern Architecture*. New York: Rizzoli, 1991.

Kamp-Bandau, Irmel. *Tel Aviv, Neues Bauen, 1930–1939*. Tübingen, Germany: Wasmuth, 1994.

Khan, Hasan-Uddin. *Charles Correa*. Singapore: Concept Media; New York: Aperture, 1987.

Kirkham, Pat. *Charles and Ray Eames: Designers of the Twentieth Century*. Cambridge, MA: MIT Press, 1995.

Klotz, Heinrich. *The History of Postmodern Architecture*. Translated by Radka Donnell. Cambridge, MA: MIT Press, 1988.

Lodder, Christina. *Russian Constructivism*. New Haven: Yale University Press, 1983.

Loomis, John A. *Revolution of Forms: Cuba's Forgotten Art Schools*. New York: Princeton Architectural Press, 1999.

Makiya, Kanan. *The Monument: Art, Vulgarity, and Responsibility in Iraq*. London: Andre Deutsch, 1991.

McCoy, Esther. *Case Study Houses, 1945–1962*. Los Angeles: Hennessey & Ingalls, 1977.

Merkel, Jayne. *Eero Saarinen*. London and New York: Phaidon, 2005.

Mumford, Eric, ed. *Modern Architecture in St. Louis: Washington University and Postwar American Architecture, 1948–1973*. St. Louis, MO: School of Architecture, Washington University; Chicago: University of Chicago Press, 2004.

Murray, Peter. *The Saga of the Sydney Opera House: The Dramatic Story of the Design and Construction of the Icon of Modern Australia*. New York: Spon Press, 2003.

Neuhart, John. *Eames Design: The Work of the Office of Charles and Ray Eames*. New York: Harry N. Abrams, 1989.

Nilsson, Sten. *The New Capitals of India, Pakistan and Bangladesh*. Lund, Sweden: Studentlitteratur, 1973.

Pommer, Richard and Christian F. Otto. *Weissenhof 1927 and the Modern Movement in Architecture*. Chicago: University of Chicago Press, 1991.

Portoghesi, Paolo. *Postmodern, the Architecture of the Postindustrial Society*. New York: Rizzoli, 1983.

Prakash, Aditya. *Reflections on Chandigarh*. New Delhi: B. N. Prakash, 1983.

———. *Chandigarh: A Presentation in Free Verse*. Chandigarh, India: Marg, 1980.

Prakash, Vikramaditya. *Chandigarh's Le Corbusier: The Struggle for Modernity in Postcolonial India*. Seattle: University of Washington Press, 2002.

Robson, David. *Geoffrey Bawa: The Complete Works*. London: Thames & Hudson, 2002.

Skidmore, Owings & Merrill. *The Architecture of Skidmore, Owings & Merrill, 1950–1962*. New York: Praeger, 1962.

Smith, Elizabeth A. T. and Michael Darling. *The Architecture of R. M. Schindler*. New York: Harry N. Abrams, 2001.

Stanford Anderson, ed. *Eladio Dieste: Innovation in Structural Art*. New York: Princeton Architectural Press, 2004.

Stäubli, Willy. *Brasília*. London: Leonard Hill Books, 1966.

Steele, James. *An Architecture for People: The Complete Works of Hassan Fathy*. New York: Whitney Library of Design, 1997.

———. *Architecture for Islamic Societies Today*. London: Academy Editions; Berlin: Ernst & Sohn; New York: St. Martin's Press, 1994.

Stewart, David B. *The Making of a Modern Japanese Architecture: 1868 to the Present*. Tokyo and New York: Kodansha International, 1987.

Svácha, Rostislav. *The Architecture of New Prague, 1895–1945*. Translated by Alexandra Büchler. Cambridge, MA: MIT Press, 1995.

Taylor, Jennifer. *Australian Architecture Since 1960*. Sydney, Australia: Law Book Co., 1986.

Underwood, David Kendrick. *Oscar Niemeyer and the Architecture of Brazil*. New York: Rizzoli, 1994.

Von Vegesack, Alexander, ed. *Czech Cubism: Architecture, Furniture, and Decorative Arts, 1910–1925*. New York: Princeton Architectural Press, 1992.

Weston, Richard. *Alvar Aalto*. London: Phaidon, 1995.

Zukowsky John, ed. *The Many Faces of Modern Architecture: Building in Germany between the World Wars*. Munich and New York: Prestel, 1994.

Photo Credits

The publishers wish to thank the institutions and individuals who have kindly provided photographic materials for use in this book. In all cases, every effort has been made to contact the copyright holders, but should there be any errors or omissions the publishers would be pleased to insert the appropriate acknowledgment in any subsequent edition of this book.

PHOTO CREDITS

PHOTO CREDITS

Index

INDEX

INDEX

INDEX